HISTORY OF
THE SECOND WORLD WAR
UNITED KINGDOM MILITARY SERIES
Edited by J. R. M. Butler

The authors of the Military Histories have been given full access to official documents. They and the editor are alone responsible for the statements made and the views expressed.

Admiral of the Fleet Sir A. Dudley P. R. Pound, First Sea Lord and Chief of Naval Staff, 12th June 1939–15th October 1943.

Frontispiece

THE WAR AT SEA
1939–1945

BY

CAPTAIN S. W. ROSKILL, D.S.C., R.N.

VOLUME I
THE DEFENSIVE

This edition of The War at Sea: Volume One
first published in 2004
by The Naval & Military Press Ltd

Published by
The Naval & Military Press Ltd
Unit 10 Ridgewood Industrial Park,
Uckfield, East Sussex,
TN22 5QE England
Tel: +44 (0) 1825 749494
Fax: +44 (0) 1825 765701
www.naval-military-press.com

The War at Sea: Volume One first published in 1954.
© Crown copyright. Reprinted with the permission of
the Controller of HMSO and Queen's Printer for Scotland.

In reprinting in facsimile from the original, any imperfections are inevitably reproduced and the quality may fall short of modern type and cartographic standards.

Printed and bound by Antony Rowe Ltd, Eastbourne

CONTENTS

		Page
Editor's Preface	. . . .	xiii
Author's Preface	. . . .	xix

Chapter

I.	Maritime War and Maritime Strategy . .	1
II.	Maritime War—The British Shore Organisation .	15
III.	The Development of Sea–Air Co-operation .	29
IV.	Allied and Enemy War Plans and Dispositions .	41
V.	Opening Moves in Home Waters 3rd September–31st December, 1939 . .	63
VI.	The Sea Approaches and Coastal Waters 3rd September–31st December, 1939 . .	91
VII.	Ocean Warfare 3rd September–31st December, 1939 . .	111
VIII.	The Sea Approaches and Coastal Waters 1st January–31st May, 1940 . . .	123
IX.	The Home Fleet 1st January–9th April, 1940 . . .	147
X.	The Norwegian Campaign 8th April–15th June, 1940 . . .	169
XI.	The Control of the Narrow Seas 10th May–4th June, 1940 . . .	205
XII.	The Withdrawal from Europe 5th–25th June, 1940	229
XIII.	The Control of Home Waters 30th May–31st December, 1940 . .	247
XIV.	Ocean Warfare 1st January–31st December, 1940 . .	269
XV.	The African Campaigns 1st May–31st December, 1940 . . .	293
XVI.	Coastal Warfare 1st June, 1940–31st March, 1941 . .	321
XVII.	The Campaign in the North-West Approaches 1st June, 1940–31st March, 1941 . .	343

CONTENTS

Chapter		Page
XVIII.	Ocean Warfare 1st January–31st May, 1941	367
XIX.	The Home Fleet 1st January–31st May, 1941	389
XX.	The African Campaigns 1st January–31st May, 1941	419
XXI.	The Battle of the Atlantic 1st April–31st December, 1941	451
XXII.	Home Waters and the Arctic 1st June–31st December, 1941	483
XXIII.	Coastal Warfare 1st April–31st December, 1941	497
XXIV.	The African Campaigns 1st June–31st December, 1941	515
XXV.	Ocean Warfare 1st June–31st December, 1941	541
XXVI.	Disaster in the Pacific December 1941	553

APPENDICES

APPENDIX A.	The Board of Admiralty, September 1939–December 1941	573
APPENDIX B.	Defensive Arming of Merchant Ships—the position on 1st March 1941	574
APPENDIX C.	The Royal Navy and Royal Marines, Active and Reserve Strength, 1939–45	575
APPENDIX D.	Particulars of principal British and Dominion warships in commission, preparing to commission or building in September 1939	577
APPENDIX E.	Distribution of British and Dominion Naval Strength, September 1939	583
APPENDIX F.	Summary of the principal warships built for the Royal Navy under the 1939, War Emergency, 1940 and 1941 Building Programmes	588
APPENDIX G.	The German Navy at the outbreak of war	590
APPENDIX H.	The Italian Navy, Strength and Disposition, June 1940	593

MAPS vii

Page

APPENDIX J. The Principal British Mercantile Convoy Routes, 1939–41 598
APPENDIX K. German and Italian U-boats sunk, 1939–41, and analysis of cause of sinking . . . 599
APPENDIX L. Operation 'Dynamo'. Summary of British and Allied ships employed, troops lifted and British ships lost or damaged 603
APPENDIX M. Enemy Surface Commerce Raiders, 1939–41. Performance data and particulars of losses caused 604
APPENDIX N. German Supply Ships working with Raiders and U-boats, 1939–41 606
APPENDIX O. The Battle of the Atlantic Directive by the Minister of Defence, 6th March 1941 . . 609
APPENDIX P. Chronological Summary of Moves by the United States Government affecting the War at Sea, 1939–41 612
APPENDIX Q. German U-boat strength, 1939–41 . . 614
APPENDIX R. British, Allied and Neutral Merchant Ship Losses by cause and by theatres, 1939–41 . 615

INDEX 621

MAPS AND DIAGRAMS

Number	Subject	Facing page
1.	Naval Command Areas at Home, 1939, and Associated Maritime R.A.F. Commands	37
2.	Naval Command Areas and Associated R.A.F. Commands September 1939	43
3.	The English Channel, Ushant to Texel . . .	63
4.	The Northern Passages to the Atlantic, North Norway to Greenland	65
5.	The North Sea, including the coasts of the Low Countries and North Germany	71
6.	Scapa Flow, showing defences as completed 1940–41 .	74
7.	The Sortie of the *Scharnhorst* and *Gneisenau*, 21st–27th November, 1939, and the sinking of the *Rawalpindi* . .	83
8.	The Western Approaches to the British Isles . . .	91
9.	The Principal Atlantic and Home Waters Mercantile Convoy Routes, September 1939–April 1941 . . .	93
10.	British and German Declared Mine Areas, 1939–40 .	97
11.	The Cruises of the *Admiral Graf Spee* and *Deutschland*, 1939	115

MAPS

Number	Subject	Facing page
12.	The Battle of the River Plate, 13th December 1939	118
13.	The East Coast of Britain, including the Thames Estuary	127
14.	The Norwegian Campaign, British and German Naval Movements, 7th–9th April, 1940	159
15.	The Norwegian Campaign, British and German Naval Movements, 9th–13th April, 1940	171
16.	The First Battle of Narvik, 10th April 1940	175
17.	The Second Battle of Narvik, 13th April 1940	177
18.	Norway, Vestfiord and Approaches	page 181
19.	Central Norway, the Approaches to Trondheim	page 182
20.	The Sortie of the *Scharnhorst*, *Gneisenau* and *Hipper*, 4th–13th June, 1940	195
21.	The Sea Routes used during the Evacuation from Dunkirk, 26th May to 4th June, 1940	page 220
22.	The Bay of Biscay and the Approaches to Western France	233
23.	The Central and South Atlantic Oceans	273
24.	The Operations of Disguised German Raiders, January–December 1940	279
25.	The Cruises of the *Admiral Scheer* and *Admiral Hipper*, January–December 1940	287
26.	The Mediterranean Theatre	293
26A.	Operation 'Menace'; British and French Movements, 7th–16th September, 1940	page 313
26B.	Operation 'Menace'; the Second Bombardment, noon to 3 p.m., 24th September 1940	page 318
27.	The Cruises of the *Admiral Scheer*, *Admiral Hipper*, *Scharnhorst* and *Gneisenau*, January–May 1941	369
28.	The Straits of Gibraltar and the Approaches to the Mediterranean from the West	381
29.	The Operations of Disguised German Raiders, January–May 1941	383
30.	The pursuit of the *Bismarck*; the first phase, 23rd–24th May, 1941	397
31.	H.M. Ships *Hood* and *Prince of Wales* in action with the *Bismarck* and *Prinz Eugen*, 24th May 1941	page 403
32.	The pursuit of the *Bismarck*; the second phase, 24th–26th May, 1941	409
33.	The pursuit of the *Bismarck*; the final phase and final action, 27th May 1941	415
34.	The Indian Ocean and Approaches to the Mediterranean from the East	426
35.	Movements of British and Italian Fleets, 28th–29th March, 1941, leading to the Battle of Cape Matapan	429
36.	The Eastern Mediterranean, showing the naval losses incurred in the Greece, Crete and Syrian Campaigns, 1941	436
37.	The Western Atlantic and the Approaches to Newfoundland, Canada and the East Coast of the U.S.A.	453

LIST OF TABLES

Number	Subject	Facing page
38.	The Principal Atlantic and Home Waters Convoy Routes, June 1940–December 1941	457
39.	Typical Atlantic Convoy and Anti-Submarine Escorts, 1940–41	page 465
40.	The Arctic Convoy Routes, 1941, and the Approaches to Murmansk and Archangel	485
41.	The Interception of German Raider and U-boat Supply Ships, June–December 1941	page 543
42.	The Operations of German Disguised Raiders, 1st June–31st December, 1941	545
43.	The sinking of H.M. Ships *Prince of Wales* and *Repulse*, 10th December 1941	565

LIST OF TABLES

		Page
TABLE 1	Royal Navy—Aircraft Carriers in Service, 1939	31
TABLE 2	British Empire—Effective Naval Strength, 1939	50
TABLE 3	French Fleet—General Disposition, 1939	51
TABLE 4	Northern Patrol—Ships Intercepted, September 1939–January 1940	67
TABLE 5	Allied Merchant Ship Losses, September–December 1939	106
TABLE 6	Raider Hunting Groups, October 1939	114
TABLE 7	Northern Patrol—Ships Intercepted, January–April 1940	149
TABLE 8	Italian Merchant Shipping Losses, June–December 1940	307
TABLE 9	German Air Attacks on Shipping and Losses within 40 miles of the coast or of an R.A.F. Airfield, November 1940–June 1941	332
TABLE 10	The R.A.F.'s Air Minelaying Campaign, June 1940–March 1941	336
TABLE 11	The Air Offensive against Enemy Shipping, April 1940–March 1941	339–340
TABLE 12	Italian and German (Mediterranean) Merchant Shipping Losses, January–May 1941	439
TABLE 13	Comparison of Losses to Independently-routed and Convoyed Ships, November 1940–May 1941	458
TABLE 14	Royal Navy—Escort Vessel Strength, June 1941	464
TABLE 15	The Air Offensive against Enemy Shipping, April–December 1941	507
TABLE 16	German Air Attacks on Shipping and Losses within 40 miles of the coast or of an R.A.F. Airfield, April–December 1941	508

LIST OF TABLES

		Page
TABLE 17	The R.A.F.'s Air Minelaying Campaign, April–December 1941	511
TABLE 18	Comparative results obtained by Air Minelaying and by Direct Attack on Shipping at Sea, April 1940–December 1941	512
TABLE 19	Stores and Men transported to and from Tobruk, April 1940–December 1941	520
TABLE 20	Italian and German (Mediterranean) Merchant Shipping Losses, June–September 1941	528
TABLE 21	Malta Convoys, 1941	531
TABLE 22	Italian and German (Mediterranean) Merchant Shipping Losses, October–December 1941	537
TABLE 23	Allied Shipping Sunk or Captured by Enemy Warships and Armed Merchant Raiders, 1940–41	541
TABLE 24	The Interception of German Supply Ships, June 1941	544
TABLE 25	German Warship and Armed Merchant Raiders, 1939–1941	550
TABLE 26	Allied and Enemy Naval Forces in the Pacific, December 1941	560

ILLUSTRATIONS

Admiral of the Fleet Sir A. Dudley P. R. Pound	*Frontispiece*
	Facing page
The Reserve Fleet in Weymouth Bay, August 1939	16
Part of the Home Fleet off Invergordon, August 1939	17
Admiral of the Fleet Sir Charles L. Forbes	32
Admiral Sir John C. Tovey	32
Air Chief Marshal Sir F. W. Bowhill	33
Air Chief Marshal Sir P. B. Joubert de la Ferté	33
H.M.S. *Ark Royal* off Rosyth, August 1939	72
'The Squadron Navigating Officer', by Sir Muirhead Bone \} *Following*	
Naval Swordfish Torpedo-Spotter-Reconnaissance Aircraft \} *page* 72	
H.M.S. *Nelson* in Loch Ewe, 1st October 1939	73
'Fleet Minesweepers at work in the Straits', by Leslie Cole	100
'A Minesweeper', by Charles Cundall	100
An East Coast Convoy, 1940	101
Typical British Escort Vessels in Service 1939–1941	128
'The Wardroom and Mess Deck of an S. Class Submarine', by Stephen Bone	129
'Eleven O'Clock in the Fo'c's'le', by Henry Lamb	129

ILLUSTRATIONS

Facing page

'The Atlantic', by R. V. Pitchforth	144
'Ship's Boat at Sea', by Richard Eurich	144
Escort vessels on patrol, 1940	145
A destroyer in heavy weather, H.M.S. *Kashmir*, 1940	145
'The withdrawal from Dunkirk', by Richard Eurich	224
'Portsmouth Harbour after an Air Raid', by Richard Eurich	225
Vice-Admiral Sir James F. Somerville	240
'Force H' off Gibraltar	241
The German Supply Ship *Altmark* in Jossing Fiord, February 1940	288
The German heavy cruiser *Hipper* in dock at Brest, January 1941	288
The pocket-battleship *Admiral Scheer* leaving an ocean rendezvous	289
The *Admiral Scheer* captures a tanker	289
Admiral of the Fleet Sir Andrew B. Cunningham	304
H.M.S. *Warspite*, Mediterranean Fleet Flagship	305
'Air Attack on a Channel Convoy', by Sir Norman Wilkinson	336
'Falmouth Harbour, 1940', by John Platt	337
Atlantic Convoy at Sea on 10th June 1941	360
The Battle of the Atlantic, The Toll	*Following page* 360
The Destruction of a Focke-Wulf Kondor, July 1941	361
The *Bismarck* in Grimstad Fiord, 21st May 1941	400
The *Bismarck*, before sailing for the Atlantic	400
H.M.S. *Norfolk* shadowing the *Bismarck*, 24th May 1941	401
H.M.S. *Suffolk* in the Denmark Strait	401
The German battleship *Bismarck*	416
Oil track left by the *Bismarck*, 24th May 1941	417
The *Bismarck* on fire and sinking, 27th May 1941	417
Air depth-charge attack on a U-boat, December 1941	466
The Surrender of U.570 to a Hudson Aircraft, 27th August, 1941	467
U.570 in British service as H.M.S. *Graph*	467
Admiral Sir Percy L. H. Noble and Air Vice-Marshal J. M. Robb	472
Atlantic Convoy O.B.331 at sea, 10th June 1941 . *Following page*	472
H.M.S. *Keppel* searching for a convoy south of Iceland, October 1941	473
The Operational Plot of the Western Approaches Command, 24th December 1941	480
H.M.S. *Audacity* (Auxiliary Aircraft Carrier) and H.M.S. *Ariguani* (Fighter Catapult Ship) at sea 1941	481
'Convoy to Russia', by Charles Pears	496
'Convoy entering Murmansk', by Sir Norman Wilkinson	496
H.M.S. *Prince of Wales* with the Prime Minister on board passing through an Atlantic Convoy, August 1941	497
H.M.S. *Ark Royal* under bombing attack, November 1940	528
The Sinking of H.M.S. *Ark Royal*, 14th November 1941	529

EDITOR'S PREFACE

THE military series of the United Kingdom History of the Second World War has been planned in accordance with a Government decision announced to the House of Commons on 25th November 1946. The purpose of the history, said the then Prime Minister, was 'to provide a broad survey of events from an inter-Service point of view rather than separate accounts of the parts played by each of the three Services'. The historians have thus felt themselves under no obligation to tell the story of operations in the same detail as was thought appropriate in the case of the war of 1914–18. For such detailed narratives the student must turn to the unit or formation histories, of which many have already appeared. We have set ourselves to present a single series of volumes in which the whole military story, and every part of it, is treated from an inter-Service aspect. Here and elsewhere throughout our work the word 'military' is used to cover the activities of all three fighting Services, as distinct from the other sides of the national war effort which are treated in the Civil Histories edited by Sir Keith Hancock.

Even on the military side, however, it seemed that a 'broad survey' which confined itself to a description of campaigns and operations would fail to give a satisfactory account of how the war of 1939–45 was waged. The vast area over which operations were progressively extended, the number and the variety of the campaigns being fought simultaneously, the constant need of co-ordinating policy and strategy with governments overseas, together with the centralisation of command rendered possible by modern systems of communication —all these increased the range and importance of the part played by the supreme authority at home and seemed to demand that a fuller treatment of the higher direction of the war should be attempted than has been usual in military histories. It was accordingly decided to allot several volumes to Grand Strategy as devised in Whitehall and at Washington, including one volume on developments prior to the actual outbreak of war in September 1939.

For the rest, the history has been planned to cover the following themes or theatres: the defence of the United Kingdom, the maritime war viewed as a whole, the two campaigns of the early period in Norway and in north-west Europe, the strategic air offensive, and the three epic series of military operations on the grand scale in the Mediterranean and Middle East, in the Far East, and again in the north-west of Europe in 1944 and 1945. Additional volumes have been allotted to the history of Civil Affairs or Military Government in view of the novelty and importance of the problems involved in this field of military responsibility.

No doubt the proposed dual treatment of strategic problems, at the Whitehall level and at the level of theatre headquarters, involves a risk, indeed a certainty, of some overlapping. This would be the case even if it were not our aim, as it is, to make each group of volumes intelligible by itself and to that extent self-contained. We cannot unfortunately assume that the general reader, for whom as much as for military students our history is intended, will be prepared to buy or read the whole of our twenty or thirty volumes. We think that a moderate amount of overlapping is excusable and may even be welcomed if it avoids the necessity of constant reference to other volumes.

The question as to the degree of overlapping properly admissible has raised particular difficulties in the case of the volumes on 'The War at Sea', by Captain S. W. Roskill, R.N., of which the first is now offered to the public. The standpoint from which these volumes are written is primarily that of those responsible for the central direction of the maritime war; but decisions taken in the Admiralty with regard to one part of the world were constantly and continuously affected by the detailed progress of events in other parts, and in order to make strategy intelligible it has proved necessary for Captain Roskill to tell the story of the war at sea as a whole. Overlapping could to some extent have been avoided had Captain Roskill merely referred in a cursory way to operations described more fully in other volumes. But such a disproportionate treatment would have spoilt the symmetry and balance of his book. It has seemed better to accept the necessity for a considerable amount of overlapping, subject to the general principles, first, that Captain Roskill is concerned with events as they influenced decisions at the Admiralty, whereas they are treated, in greater detail, in other volumes as they affected those of the local commanders; and, secondly, that where considerable operations, such as the expedition to Dakar in September 1940, do not fall within the scope of the 'theatre' volumes, a fuller treatment by Captain Roskill is desirable.

The description of a war waged by Allies, in which 'integration' was successfully carried to lengths unattempted in previous campaigns, raises further problems. Granted that our commission is to write the history not of the Second World War as a whole but of the military effort of the United Kingdom, on what principle ought we to handle campaigns or actions in which men from the United Kingdom and from other nations fought side by side? Where United Kingdom forces served under foreign or Dominion command, or vice versa, it seems clear that decisions or actions of our fellow combatants must be described with sufficient fullness to preserve a proper balance in the story. On the other hand it is not desirable to duplicate accounts given in the histories sponsored by our Allies and the other nations of the British Commonwealth, especially when the primary sources are under their control. Arrangements have indeed been made with them for mutual information on points of special interest and for an exchange of drafts; it is hoped that these arrangements will at least reduce the likelihood of controversy due to ignorance of another nation's point of view, though they will not, of course, eliminate differences of interpretation. It has not been possible to make such arrangements in the case of the U.S.S.R.

With regard to the German military records, however, the Allied historians are fortunate, to an unprecedented degree, in having access to a mass of original documents, some of them of the highest importance, which were captured during the occupation of Germany and are now held under joint Anglo-American control. In the case of the other enemy Powers both the volume and the value of the documents captured are considerably less and details of their military plans and operations have of necessity been obtained from more conventional sources of information.

To the official United Kingdom records we have been allowed full access, and we have done our best to supplement them by reference to unofficial accounts, published and unpublished, written and oral. We have felt bound, however, to respect the requirements of military 'security', and in some cases cypher telegrams have been paraphrased, though not in such a way as to affect the sense. In accordance with the recognised British constitutional principle we have not held ourselves free to reveal individual differences of opinion within the War Cabinet nor, as a rule, to lift the veil of Civil Service anonymity.

We have taken it as our prime duty to present an accurate narrative of events. But events, properly speaking, include plans and intentions as well as actions, and it is the duty of a historian, as opposed to a mere annalist, to say why, as well as how, things happened as they did. He must interpret, not merely narrate, and interpretation implies a personal judgement. In any case the need to select from the vast mass of material implies a personal judgement of what is most relevant and important.

We all share the contemporary outlook, and some of us are laymen in military matters; it would be unbecoming in us to attempt to pronounce what a commander should have done or should not have done in a particular situation. Our ideal would be to let the facts speak for themselves, to point out how such a decision led to such a result, and to leave speculation and moralising to the strategists; but the facts can only speak to our readers as we have selected and presented them, and we have not shrunk from stating what seemed to us the lessons that emerged from a particular course of events.

It is normally the duty and desire of a historian to support his assertions and arguments by detailed references to his authorities.

Such references serve partly as an indication of his sources, partly as a challenge to his readers to verify his statements. Where, however, the main authorities are official documents which are not at present, and for some time are not likely to be, open to public inspection, published references have comparatively little point, since the challenge cannot be taken up. The nature of the material used can, we think, in most cases be sufficiently indicated in the prefaces or bibliographical notes to the several volumes. Accordingly our usual practice has been explained by Sir Keith Hancock in his introduction of the Civil Histories.[1] 'It has been decided not to clutter the published pages with references to official files which are not yet generally available to students. In the published series, footnotes have been confined to material that is already accessible. The completed documentation has been given in confidential print. There it will be immediately available to critical readers within the Government service. No doubt it will become available in due time to the historians of a future generation. The official historians of this generation have consciously submitted their work to the professional verdict of the future'.

In the use of enemy documents the historians' labours have been immensely lightened by the help of their colleagues charged with the collection, collation and interpretation of this vast mass of material. Work on the German and Italian documents has been directed by Mr Brian Melland; Colonel G. T. Wards has advised with regard to the Japanese. Valuable assistance in this matter has also been rendered by Commander M. G. Saunders, R.N., of the Admiralty Historical Section, and by Squadron Leader L. A. Jackets, of the Air Historical Branch. The maps have been prepared under the experienced direction of Colonel T. M. M. Penney, of the Cabinet Office Historical Section.

The appointment of a civilian editor to be responsible for the production of the military histories made it desirable that on general questions as well as special points he should be able frequently to consult authorities whose opinions on Service matters would command respect; I am fortunate to have had so helpful a panel of advisers as Vice-Admiral Sir Geoffrey Blake, Lieutenant-General Sir Henry Pownall, Air Chief Marshals Sir Douglas Evill and Sir Guy Garrod, and Lieutenant-General Sir Ian Jacob. These distinguished officers not only have given me the benefit of their experience and judgement in the planning of the history and the selection of writers, but have read and commented on the volumes in draft; in all these matters, however, responsibility rests with the Editor alone.

The history could not have been written without the constant

---

[1] *History of the Second World War: British War Economy* (H.M. Stationery Office, 1949), p. xii.

EDITOR'S PREFACE

assistance of the Service Historical Sections, and the historians would express their gratitude to Rear-Admiral R. M. Bellairs, Brigadier H. B. Latham and Mr J. C. Nerney, and also to Lieutenant-General Sir Desmond Anderson, of the War Office, and their staffs. The monographs, narratives and summaries produced by the Service Departments have greatly reduced the labours, though not the responsibilities, of the historians, and the staffs concerned have been lavish of their help in supplying information and comment. Similar acknowledgements are due to the authors of the Civil Histories, and we are grateful to Mr Yates Smith, of the Imperial War Museum, and to other librarians for the loan of books.

Finally, the historians in general and the Editor in particular are deeply indebted to Mr A. B. Acheson, of the Cabinet Office. His advice and help have been of the greatest service to us in many ways; indeed, without the relief provided by Mr Acheson in administrative matters a part-time editor could hardly have performed his task.

J. R. M. B.

AUTHOR'S PREFACE

THE policy which has governed the preparation of the Military Histories of the Second World War, and the problems peculiar to the volumes which set out to tell the story of The War at Sea, are so fully stated in the Editor's Preface that I have little to add to what he has written. It is, perhaps, worth emphasising that my charter is to tell the story of the maritime war in all its aspects. I have therefore tried to give adequate weight and space to the contribution of the Royal Air Force, and also to refer to the land battles and campaigns which markedly influenced our maritime strategy and operations. In the official histories of other recent wars the maritime side has been told almost exclusively from the naval angle. It is believed that the volumes of which this is the first, mark the first attempt made in modern times to write the official account of a maritime war in terms of more than one service. If, in spite of that purpose and object, the reader finds that the outlook of the writer is predominantly naval it may be said that the responsibilities of the Admiralty render this inevitable. Moreover, from the appointment of a naval officer to write these volumes it may, perhaps justifiably, be assumed that when the appointment was made it was recognised that such would be the case.

It may be desirable to add a few words about the sources of information which I have used. The vast majority are contained in Admiralty and Air Ministry papers and other State archives which are certain not to be made public, at any rate in their complete form, for many years. The Service Departments have, however, all published a number of Commander-in-Chief's despatches dealing with particular operations and actions, and these can be obtained through H.M. Stationery Office. Also on sale to the public are certain statistical documents, notably the White Paper (Cmd. 6843) giving particulars of enemy U-boats sunk during the war, and the Admiralty's statements of British warships and merchant vessels lost or damaged. But these must be used with caution by the civilian as later information has shown that the particulars published soon after the war are by no means always correct. I have, of course, made use of the latest information available, but even this is no guarantee against further revision being necessary. With regard to enemy documents, the German archives held by the Admiralty are so complete, and their exploitation has been so thoroughly carried out, that little or no guesswork is attached to what I have written about German motives and actions. But these documents too are unlikely to be available for scrutiny by the public for many years. Extracts from the minutes of the Führer Naval Conferences (that is to say

Hitler's meetings with his chief subordinates which dealt with naval affairs) were, however, published in Brassey's *Naval Annual* for 1948.

I have given a good deal of thought to the question of what 'times' should be used in my narrative, and also on the maps, to describe events which must be followed in some detail. In world-wide maritime operations it inevitably happens that forces working in different longitudes are keeping different times, even though they are part of the same strategic movement. Confusion is avoided by a simple system of dividing the world's surface into twenty-four equal zones, each of fifteen degrees of longitude, measured from the Greenwich meridian. Each zone has a letter allocated to it and the letter indicates that the time being kept is so many hours ahead of, or behind, Greenwich Mean Time (G.M.T.). The practised eye can thus relate the time given in any message to the common basis of G.M.T. at a glance.

The historian (or at any rate the British historian) is, while carry-out out research and analysis, more or less compelled to follow the system of reducing all times to G.M.T. It is, indeed, the only safe system to adopt. Unfortunately if the same method is used when he comes to write his narrative it will produce abundant absurdities and confuse the reader beyond recovery. A night action fought in the Pacific might, for example, be found to have taken place at high noon (G.M.T.) or a dawn landing at sunset. Plainly, therefore, the method which was essential to research must be discarded when the story is told. Yet the need to establish a common basis, for the enemy's movements as well as those of all our own forces, remains.

I have therefore adopted the system which seemed least likely to confuse the reader. The basic time in the narrative of any event has been taken as that shown by the clocks of the principal British or Allied forces engaged, and the times used by enemy forces have been adjusted to the basic time thus established. It may therefore well happen that a German reader, who, for example, knows that his ship sank a British ship at 6 p.m. on a certain day, finds in this book that it is stated to have happened at 7 p.m. The answer is that the German ship's clocks were, on the day in question, one hour behind the clocks of her British adversary. When one moves into the Pacific, where an inconvenient obstacle called the Date Line exists, it is possible that differences of a day, rather than of an hour, will be found to exist. These difficulties have been accepted for the sake of simplicity and of intelligibility to the reader.

Another troublesome matter has been the spelling of place-names on the maps and in the text. The Admiralty uses the spelling given in the many volumes of the Sailing Directions, which cover the whole world, as their standard. Unfortunately this often differs from the spelling used on Admiralty charts, many of which were printed long

AUTHOR'S PREFACE

ago and will only have the spelling of place-names revised when they are reprinted. The charts and maps reproduced in these volumes are nearly all based on Admiralty charts. To check and, if need be, alter the spelling of all names to accord with the Sailing Directions would have involved immense, and largely unprofitable, labour. I have therefore retained the chart spelling in the majority of cases. I have, however, taken the liberty of 'anglicising' certain names because retention of the phonetic spelling, even though used on charts, struck me as pedantic. Why, for instance, should Seidisfiord in Iceland, which was well known to all sailors and airmen involved in the Atlantic Battle, be referred to by its Icelandic title of Seydisfjördur or Seydisfjardar (both of which appear on Admiralty Charts) in this narrative? My object has been to make all place-names referred to easily recognisable and identifiable on the maps and in the text, and if inconsistencies are detected I can only plead that the large number of variations in spelling offered to me has been the cause.

It is, perhaps, proper to mention that in my efforts to gain a clear idea of the problems which constantly faced each naval Commander-in-Chief I have, unfortunately, found the all-important Atlantic theatre by far the most difficult. One reason has been that, early in the war, the Admiralty, in an understandable desire to reduce paper work, informed Commanders-in-Chief that they need not render periodical despatches. Happily for the historian most Commanders-in-Chief continued none the less to do so. Their despatches have proved of the utmost value to me not only for their contemporary accounts of actions fought and operations undertaken, but also because they reflect the thoughts of the Commanders-in-Chief on the progress of the war in their theatres. Unfortunately the successive Commanders-in-Chief, Western Approaches, did not, as far as I know, ever render a despatch. Though the Command's War Diary records in great detail the day-to-day occurrences in the various sub-commands, it is in no way comparable to a Commander-in-Chief's despatch. The Admiralty kept detailed records of the progress of each convoy, Escort Group commanders rendered Reports of Proceedings regarding their own doings, and the Royal Air Force Groups concerned in the Atlantic Battle documented their operations fully. These latter records were used by Commanders-in-Chief, Coastal Command, to write a series of despatches dealing with the air side of the Atlantic Battle. These, and many other records, have helped me greatly. But the lack of any naval despatches from the Western Approaches Command, giving a chronological survey of the whole vast problem of Atlantic shipping and escort, has proved a severe handicap, particularly for the first two years of the war. I have gone to considerable lengths to try to fill the gap by consulting the surviving Commanders-in-Chief and also officers who served on their staffs; but memories are notoriously fallible and, for all their kindness and help, I am only too well aware that there are gaps in my knowledge and in the story of the five years' Atlantic Battle as I have told it.

The Editor has acknowledged the debt which I and all military historians owe to the Historical Sections in the Service Departments. I will only amplify his acknowledgements by saying that the help of the Admiralty's Record Office staff under Mr H. H. Ellmers and the constant advice given to me by the staff of Rear-Admiral Bellairs' Historical Section have gone far beyond what might reasonably be expected. For the work of the Royal Air Force in the maritime war I have depended greatly on the expert knowledge and research of Captain D. V. Peyton-Ward, R.N., and on the very full narratives which he has prepared for the Air Ministry's Historical Branch. Though responsibility for historical accuracy remains my own, and where matters of opinion are expressed they must be taken as mine alone, the preparation of this work would, without the help so freely given in the Admiralty and Air Ministry, have been far beyond the capacity of one writer. I must also acknowledge my debt to the many officers, senior and junior, who have read my drafts and given me the benefit of their knowledge of policy, of operations and of incidents in which they themselves were concerned. I would thank Mr F. G. G. Carr, Director of the National Maritime Museum, for his co-operation in selecting and reproducing certain of the works of the Admiralty Official War Artists, and Mr G. H. Hurford of the Admiralty's Historical Section for his expert and painstaking work on the Index. Finally, I owe more than I can express to the patient and repeated help which the Editor himself has given to me.

S. W. ROSKILL.

Cabinet Office,
    February 1954.

Now than for love of Christ, and of his ioy,
Bring it England out of trouble and noy:
Take heart and witte, and set a governance,
Set many wits withouten variance,
To one accord and unanimitee. . . .

    * * *

Kepe then the sea that is the wall of England:
And than is England kept by Goddes hande.

> *The Libel of English Policie* (c.1436), attributed to Bishop Adam de Moleyns, printed in *The Principal Navigations, Voyages, Traffiques and Discoveries of the English Nation* ('Hakluyt's Voyages'), 2nd Edition, 1599.

[noy = harm]

CHAPTER I

MARITIME WAR AND MARITIME STRATEGY

> We must not forget at this moment how much we owe to those who have gone before us and have created the Fleet as it now is; those who worked so arduously and so long, to be ready for such a moment as has now been forced upon us.
> *Vice-Admiral Sir David Beatty's message to the 1st Battle Cruiser Squadron, 4th August 1914.*

THE volumes of which this is the first set out to tell the story of the development of our maritime strategy from 1939 to 1945, and of its application to the unceasing struggle for the control of communications across the broad oceans and in the narrow coastal waters. During the three centuries or so of our history as a world power it has several times happened that a far stronger continental coalition has pitted its might against Britain and her allies, has won a series of resounding victories on land only to find itself brought up against a method of waging war with which its leaders could not grapple and of which they had no clear understanding. Yet, ultimately, our maritime strategy, founded on centuries of experience of the sea, brought our enemies to utter defeat.

When Britain and France took up the new German challenge in 1939 they took it up on the Continent. But when the enemy's land victories of 1939 and 1940 had deprived us of all our continental allies a change of emphasis in our strategy became inevitable—if for no other reason, because only two methods of continuing the war against Germany remained open to us. One was the offensive use of our initially small bomber force against German military and industrial targets; the other was to exploit to the utmost our traditional capacity to employ a maritime strategy as the means of bringing overwhelming forces to bear against the enemy in theatres of our own choice.

The experiences of the last war appear to reinforce those of earlier struggles which had shown that the prosecution of a maritime strategy passes through several phases. In the first it is probable that our strategy will be defensive, particularly if a new continental coalition has to be constructed. During this phase our maritime power is used to defend these islands from invasion, to cut the enemy off from the rest of the world and weaken his economy by enforcing a blockade, to hold and reinforce certain key points and areas overseas and to bring to this country the supplies which are essential to its survival. But while it may be necessary to accept that our strategy must, during this phase, remain defensive it is of cardinal importance that no opportunity should be lost to assume the tactical and local offensive against such enemy forces as may present themselves. If such opportunities are lost the period of the strategic defensive may bring about a decline of morale and of the will to fight. Assuming however that war remains such as it has been hitherto, and that our commanders seize every opportunity for local and tactical offensives, the period of the strategic defensive possesses certain inherent compensations. Chief among these is that, while our war economy develops, while our resources are mustered and our military strength expands, the enemy is forced, if he wishes to attack us, to do so across seas which he does not control. Such ventures, if made, expose his forces to drastic counter-measures and may result in expensive failures. The unwillingness of the Germans to accept such risks during the recent war is underlined by the immunity from attack of such key points as Iceland and the Azores. During the second phase our maritime forces continue to carry out the functions which occupied their whole capacity during the first, but in addition the nation's offensive power is being developed. Forces of all arms are being built up, assembled and trained; and plans for their offensive employment are being prepared. This phase, which ends with the first major offensive operation, may well be entitled 'The Period of Balance' since the success or failure of the first offensive has yet to be decided. In the third phase the full advantages of the patient pursuit of a maritime strategy are reaped and our forces are transported overseas to assume the offensive.

It is the writer's intention to devote one volume to each of the three phases, thus defined, through which our maritime strategy passed. But before that narrative is opened it may be useful to consider in further detail certain aspects of maritime strategy in its modern form and also the method whereby a maritime war is fought.

Maritime strategy has been defined as 'the principles which govern a war in which the sea is a substantial factor'—a definition which plainly applies to the whole course of the recent struggle.[1] But whereas in the many previous wars successfully conducted by Britain on the basis of a maritime strategy the forces employed to that end were mainly ships, in the recent war aircraft came to exercise a profound and increasing influence on the success or failure of the strategy.

---
[1] J. S. Corbett. *Some Principles of Maritime Strategy* (1918), p. 11.

It is therefore essential to place in proper perspective from the outset of our story the extent to which this new instrument of war conditioned and controlled the execution of our maritime strategy. Precisely how great that influence would be was, in 1939, largely conjectural, but it did not take many weeks of war to demonstrate that it was very great indeed. It is undeniable both that some naval thought had rated the influence too low and that a body of opinion on the air side had rated it too high. Some account of the pre-war investigations into this matter will be given later; the essential point to stress here is that, wherever in these volumes reference is made to the control of sea communications, the reader must assume this to mean the exercise of such control by forces of no matter what arm or service as will enable our trade convoys, our troopships, our cargo vessels and tankers, our coasters and fishing vessels and, indeed, all forms of traffic upon the surface of the sea to pass on its way unhindered. It is therefore axiomatic to the entire consideration of our subject that control of sea communications in the modern sense necessitates a large measure of control of the air over those communications as well as control of the waters beneath the keels of the passing convoys. If either control of the air over the sea or control of the water beneath the surface of the sea is inadequate, then we should not possess sufficient control of the communications which pass on its surface.

The aim of maritime strategy is therefore not so much to establish complete control of all sea communications, which would be an ideal hardly attainable until final victory was almost won, as to develop the ability to establish zones of maritime control wherever and whenever they may be necessary for the prosecution of the war in accordance with the directions of the Government. And a zone of maritime control means no more than an ability to pass ships safely across an area of water which may be quite small in extent or may cover many thousands of square miles of ocean. Thus the enemy, mainly by the use of aircraft, established for some time a zone of maritime control in the central Mediterranean which, while it lasted, virtually denied to us the use of the communications through that sea. And the crisis of the whole struggle in the west developed, after the Battle of Britain had been won, from our need to establish a zone of maritime control over the entire length of the Atlantic shipping lanes and the enemy's sustained attempts to defeat that control. It must, however, be emphasised that complete control of even a restricted zone is rarely established, and that it is far more common for control to be in dispute than undisputed. Moreover, if control over a particular zone is lost by one belligerent it is by no means certain that it will pass to the other. In this stage it is more likely that control will remain in dispute and such, for example, was the condition in the English Channel in the summer of 1940. Furthermore, throughout the period when control of sea communications is in dispute, and even after the establishment of a reasonably firm zone of maritime control, sporadic attacks will remain a possibility. Such attacks on our sea communications persisted almost to the end of the recent war.

Wherever, therefore, a zone of maritime control is established, our own commercial and military seaborne traffic will be able to pass in reasonable safety. But there is a further effect of the establishment of such a zone. It will automatically bring about the denial to the enemy of the use of the same sea communications. In other words, the creation of such a zone produces a positive result to ourselves and a negative result to the enemy; and the latter can be as important as the former. Thus by creating a zone of maritime control in the focal area for shipping off the River Plate we protected our own South American trade and prevented the enemy from using the same routes; and when the zone of maritime control essential for the North African landings of 1942–43 had been completely established, we denied the enemy the use of sea communications adequately to succour and support his own armies in that continent.

The denial to the enemy of the use of sea communications is accomplished by the application of all the various instruments comprising maritime power, but the sum total of their effects can be described as being the establishment of a blockade. This is one of the chief means whereby a nation which is stronger at sea may be able to impose its will on one which, though stronger on land, is not self-supporting in food and raw materials. In spite of German arguments to the contrary, which read strangely from a nation well versed in the exaction of all sorts of rights, penalties and requisitions from nations subjugated by continental campaigns, it is a relatively humane form of war. In common, however, with other aspects of the exercise of maritime power it is slow and cumulative in its effects; on the other hand, it starts to function from the day on which hostilities open.

If we turn now to the means whereby a maritime strategy can be implemented, it is necessary to emphasise that, although modern developments have greatly changed the instruments of war and the various duties performed by each of them, the old-established principles governing their use do not seem to require modification. Maritime power is still 'the expression in material of the strategical and tactical ideas that prevail at any time'; but the material has changed out of all recognition, and within a space of about half a century.[1] From the days when British sea power first began to make

---

[1] J. S. Corbett, op. cit., p. 93.

itself felt throughout the length and breadth of the globe right down to comparatively recent times it was accepted that the fleet which controlled the sea routes and fought off all challengers must comprise three classes of warship. They were called the ships of the line or battleships, the cruisers and the flotilla vessels. The cruisers actually exercised control of our sea communications—supported by the battle fleets to prevent interference with our cruisers by more powerful enemy units—and the flotilla vessels acted as scouts for the battle fleet and carried out multifarious functions as escorts and in local defence.

There were, prior to the outbreak of war in 1939, plain indications that the old conception of the means whereby maritime power was wielded and a maritime strategy implemented was no longer valid. But the extent of the changes was, perhaps, not fully realised until some months after the outbreak of war. It seems, therefore, justifiable to attempt a redefinition of the elements comprising maritime power, and the chief reason why this has become necessary is that shore-based and carrier-borne aircraft have shown themselves to be capable of carrying out a part, and in some circumstances the whole, of the duties borne for so long by one or other class of fighting ship. In the recent war they acted repeatedly in the traditional function of the battle fleet to seek and destroy the enemy's principal naval units. The attack by naval aircraft on the Italian battleships in Taranto harbour in November 1940 was the first example of their successful use in this manner, and it is probable that this brilliantly conceived and executed operation influenced Japanese thought, and was a factor in the decision to employ similar methods against the American fleet in Pearl Harbour in December 1941. The United States Navy, when its turn came, also repeatedly demonstrated the capacity of carrier-borne aircraft to perform this function, and in the final phase of the Pacific war the two greatest Japanese battleships succumbed to the sustained attacks of naval aircraft alone. The heavy shore-based bombers of the Royal Air Force, after an inauspicious start, became an increasingly important factor in operations planned to the same purpose, and it was they who finally sank the German battleship *Tirpitz* after she had been disabled by various other forms of attack. So much for the capacity of shore-based and carrier-borne aircraft to execute a part of the traditional function of the battle fleet. In fleet reconnaissance work and shadowing an enemy, which were formerly the functions of ships classified as cruisers, the influence of aircraft became, as the recent struggle progressed, scarcely less profound. From small and uncertain beginnings and many failures in the difficult weather conditions of the North Sea, the reconnaissance aircraft of the Navy and Coastal Command played an increasing part, especially when the introduction of airborne radar enabled them to overcome the handicap of night or of low visibility.[1] In anti-submarine operations and convoy escort duties the aircraft of both Services first supplemented the arduous work of the flotilla vessels and then, in the crisis of the war, became a decisive factor in the struggle to defeat the U-boat. Lastly, the fighter aircraft of both services constantly acted as an integral part of the defences of the fleet, of mercantile convoys and amphibious expeditions and of naval bases or commercial ports, thus performing a part of the function of the third traditional class of fighting ship—the flotilla vessels.

Not only, therefore, have aircraft developed the capacity to carry out a part of the functions of all three traditional classes of fighting ship, but the conditions of modern warfare, and in particular the rapidity with which the enemy can develop a large variety of attacks, have altered the traditional conception of the functional employment of the ships themselves. For example, the enemy used his battleships and heavy cruisers as commerce raiders, and this forced us to use ships of equivalent strength as ocean convoy escorts; the Americans and we ourselves used battleships to escort and cover aircraft-carrier squadrons; specially equipped cruisers were used for anti-aircraft protection of convoys; and small aircraft carriers worked as flotilla vessels in anti-submarine operations and in the protection of shipping.

Only in the use of flotilla vessels does it seem that the older functions still hold good to any appreciable extent, and that, perhaps, because their duties were always the most varied. In fact it is plain that the traditional conception of the classification of fighting ships and their rôles in the exercise of maritime power requires radical reconsideration. The old names remain, but the functions have changed out of all recognition. Perhaps the truth of this argument is best demonstrated by the manner in which all the maritime powers involved in the late war used mixed forces comprising most, if not all, classes of ship and aircraft to carry out particular operations. The Americans called these Task Forces.

Study of recent trends and developments leads therefore to the suggestion that maritime power to-day rests on the possession of three essential elements. The first comprises all the varied instruments of war which work on or beneath the surface of the sea or in the air above it. It can be called the Strength Element, for it is on their strength and numbers that maritime control greatly depends. Second comes the possession and safety of the bases from which all the instruments of maritime power must work. If bases are lacking, or are inadequately defended, the ships and aircraft cannot fulfil their

---

[1] Radar was the American name for this device. It was first known in this country as R.D.F., which letters stood for Radio Direction Finding. As with many other developments of importance the title adopted had, in order to assist security, little relation to its true function. In these volumes the term radar, though not officially adopted by the British Services until much later, will always be used.

functions. This can be called the Security Element. The third element of maritime power comprises the Merchant Navy, which must be adequate to feed our home population, to bring in the raw materials needed by our industries, to carry our exports overseas and to transport our armies and their multifarious supplies to the theatres where they are required to fight. Nor is the Merchant Navy by itself enough. It must be supported by an adequate shipbuilding and ship-repairing industry to enable losses to be replaced and damaged ships to be returned rapidly to service. This can, perhaps, best be called the Transport Element. If it is inevitable that, in maritime war, the actions fought by the warships and aircraft gain most attention, it must never be forgotten that the purpose of those actions is, nearly always, the protection of the merchantmen; and without the steady devotion of the men who man those ships the whole structure of maritime power must crumble.

Such, then, appear to be the elements comprising maritime power in a modern context; and each of them must be present in adequate form if the nation's maritime strategy is to be fulfilled. But to leave the matter there is, perhaps, to oversimplify the issue and some expansion may be necessary.

Strength by itself cannot ensure success; it must be applied at the time and in the place where it is needed, in adequate and balanced form and for the whole of the required period. This plainly demands flexibility in the application of maritime power and concentration of its instruments. Concentration has been called 'the assembling of the utmost force at the right time and place', but it must not by any means be taken to necessitate the massing together of ships and aircraft.[1] A true maritime concentration is a far more subtle conception. It is well expressed by Mahan's definition of warships working in close co-ordination 'not huddled together . . . but distributed with a regard to a common purpose, and linked together by the effectual energy of a single will'.[2] If aircraft be included with the ships of which he was speaking, this is as true to-day as when it was written. A maritime concentration must, therefore, maintain its flexibility and cohesion whilst covering as wide an area as is necessary. Many examples in which a concentration of this nature was brought about on the Admiralty's orders will appear in our narrative, and it will be seen how they were often the antithesis of the massing of warships.

In operations for the defence of merchant shipping we have always to deal with a large variety of possible enemy objectives and combinations, and this will produce a tendency to disperse our forces. The proper answer is to keep our concentrations as open as possible

---

[1] J. S. Corbett, op. cit., p. 114.
[2] A. T. Mahan. *Sea Power in its Relations to the War of 1812* (Little, Brown, Boston, 1905), p. 316.

whilst maintaining their fundamental cohesion. But in applying this principle to the conduct of maritime war it is well to recognise that there will always be a conflict between maintaining cohesion and the requirement for our forces to reach out as far as possible and to cover the widest possible area. The point at which the extension of operations will destroy cohesion is indeed difficult to estimate, but that it exists is beyond doubt, as several examples from the late war will show. Perhaps the clearest indication of the point beyond which flexibility cannot be stretched without loss of cohesion lies in the existence or lack of a well-placed and powerfully held strategic centre on to which our forces could fall back in case of necessity. In all our operations against powerful German raiders in the Atlantic such centres existed at Scapa Flow, at Halifax and in the Straits of Gibraltar; and the knowledge that our widely separated groups and ships could, in case of necessity, fall back on those centres for support rendered the measures ordered by the Admiralty perfectly sound examples of maritime concentration.

There are certain other aspects of maritime concentration which merit some consideration. The first is that the degree of division of our maritime forces which we must accept is directly related to the number of ports and the length of coastline held by the enemy and from which he can attack our trade. Thus the enemy's control, after the summer of 1940, of the whole Norwegian, Danish, Dutch, Belgian and French coasts, and particularly of the first and last, greatly complicated the problem of watching the ports from which our sea communications could be attacked, and imposed the necessity for greater division of our strength. The immediate despatch to Gibraltar, in June 1940, of a British force to replace the lost French maritime power in the western Mediterranean, is an example of such division, and a wholly correct division of our forces. It was, however, fortunate that our naval superiority was such as to permit such a division being made without unduly weakening the Home Fleet which, as Lord Barham (First Lord of the Admiralty during the Trafalgar campaign) remarked, 'is the mainspring from which all offensive operations must proceed'. The division of our forces in this manner is dictated by the necessity to leave unwatched no port from which forays against our merchant shipping can be launched. But this requirement is modified by two factors, one of ancient establishment and the other of modern impact. The first is the extent to which the enemy's lines of operations cross our own home waters. If they do so entirely, as from the Danish, Dutch, Belgian, southern Norwegian and north-western French coasts, then the necessity to watch the ports on those coasts is much simplified. The second is that air reconnaissance has greatly eased the difficulties of simultaneously watching a large number of ports. Without this modern development the division of forces necessitated by watching so long a coastline and so large a number of ports would have been beyond our powers; for the requirement undoubtedly is to leave no port unwatched, since failure to do so will enable the enemy to adopt sporadic action from the unwatched ports. If all his ports are watched and we are thus able to deny to him the possibility of sporadic action, he must either remain inactive or concentrate his forces. This is exactly what occurred in the case of the stationing of the German battle cruisers at Brest from March 1941 until February 1942. They were watched, chiefly by air reconnaissance, blockaded and forced into inactivity. The sporadic action for which purpose they had been stationed there was denied to the enemy, and he was finally forced to concentrate by passing them to his home ports by the easiest route.

Maritime strategy in face of a threat to invade our shores also requires some special consideration. There is a tendency, in such circumstances, for the public to demand the massing of our forces around our coasts. Such a policy, if adopted, would be a false concentration; the attitude adopted would be wholly defensive, and the initiative would rest with the enemy who might thereby be given the very opportunity he seeks. The traditional British policy, and it has been successfully applied many times in our history, is quite different. In the first place the enemy transports which are assembling to carry, or are actually carrying his army, displace his warships as the primary object of our maritime forces. A firm grip over the assembly of the transports is established by blockade. To-day this includes bombing, bombardment and minelaying as well as constant watch and patrol off his assembly ports. The blockade is enforced by flotilla vessels and aircraft, but they must be supported by greater strength and covered by the battle force in the background.[1] The threat of invasion is clearly visible to the layman; the countermeasures are probably concealed from him. But they are none the less effective for their invisibility from the land, and there should be no uneasiness in British homes as long as the old methods are applied and the strength and vigour of our maritime forces remain unimpaired.

Assuming, however, that the old policy is adopted, the enemy must try either to force his invasion army through in one large mass, or to slip through whilst evading our blockading forces. The second choice can hardly be applicable to a modern expedition attempting to cross narrow seas. The first choice is extremely favourable to the defence; it produces exactly the conditions for which we have always

---

[1] The term 'battle force' is defined by the Admiralty as an 'expression used to denote the main naval concentration of force in an area'. In a modern context it will plainly include maritime air strength.

hoped and has, again and again in our history, led to decisive sea battles. It appears that Hitler intended to adopt this course in 1940, thereby following in the path of many earlier continental strategists, and that the British policy which frustrated and defeated the intentions of his forerunners also destroyed his plans. Indeed, study of contemporary German documents leaves little doubt that the quarrelsome vacillations of the German leaders were chiefly caused by the uneasiness which always seems to be produced among our enemies when it becomes apparent that an invasion is to be launched across seas which they do not adequately control. The lessons of 1940 appear to reinforce our knowledge that, although continental enemies have repeatedly tried to find a way to invade these islands without first defeating our maritime forces, no such short cut exists.

There remain for consideration before leaving this discussion on maritime warfare two further points of some importance. The first is the tradition of seeking decision with the enemy by battle at sea. This has long been a fundamental precept in our maritime services, and it is a tradition of immense power and value. None the less it is a precept which can be carried too far, and our history contains examples where it has only led to indecisive battles. It must, in truth, be constantly tempered by the judgment and experience of those responsible for the conduct of operations, since it is well established that, if enthusiasm for battle outruns judgment, the blow will fall upon air; whereas by waiting with forces correctly disposed we shall compel the enemy ultimately to offer an opportunity for action. It happened many times in the war that commanders of our maritime forces assumed the tactical offensive, often against superior strength, with great gallantry and most favourable results; and it now seems that our adversaries sometimes sacrificed a potential advantage through reluctance (often imposed on them by higher direction) to do likewise. None the less the well-known capacity of a defensive strategy in certain conditions to inflict grievous injury on the enemy and to stultify his purpose still holds good. Perhaps the outstanding example from the last war relates to the defeat of the enemy's attack on our merchant shipping. Though it was not at once accepted there now seems no doubt at all that it was the defensive strategy of sailing ships in convoy and of providing the convoys with powerful surface and air escorts which did most to accomplish that decisive victory. Yet it was the desire at once to assume the offensive against the U-boats which led to the persistent employment, during the first year and more of the war, of flotilla vessels to hunt enemy submarines in the vast ocean spaces instead of using them to escort our convoys. Not only did the early hunting groups achieve negligible success, but the dispersal of our slender resources in that manner led to our convoys being inadequately escorted, and so suffering heavy losses, and to many good opportunities to destroy the submarines which attacked them being missed. Equally the view that bomber aircraft could contribute most to the defeat of the U-boat by taking the offensive against the enemy's bases and his building and repair yards rather than by escorting and protecting the convoys far out at sea, is not substantiated by post-war analysis of their achievements. It is to-day impossible to avoid the conclusion that the most effective way of defeating the U-boat was by waiting for it in the vicinity of the prey which it was seeking.

The chief difficulty in implementing this policy of waiting is the reluctance of public opinion to believe that it can be a deliberate strategical move and not an example of timidity or pusillanimity on the part of our commanders. Yet the truth is that nearly all the really effective blows struck at our enemies' maritime power have come about through a deliberate tempering of the desire to seek and destroy the enemy by judgment and experience, which had taught that the object would be more assuredly achieved by offering the enemy a bait and then waiting for him to present himself. The sinking of the *Bismarck* and of the *Scharnhorst* provide examples of this, though in the case of the latter ship it was necessary to wait many months before she came to her destruction. All the major warships of the Japanese Navy which could be made fit for sea also came, ultimately, of their own accord to meet their end.

Finally—and this point is placed last in this discussion because it is not reached until the application of our maritime strategy has begun to bear fruit and the early strategic defensive can be exchanged for the offensive—we must consider the employment of maritime power to transport our armies overseas, to place them on shore in the chosen theatres, to support and supply them as may be necessary and to shift their bases forward as their land campaigns advance. It is plain that the establishment of an adequate and effective zone of maritime control in the approaches to, and the coastal waters off the disembarkation area is an absolute prerequisite for success in this type of operation. The functions of our maritime forces in an amphibious expedition of this nature differ considerably from those of the forces employed on mercantile convoy work. In the latter case their duties end with the safe arrival of the convoy in port; but in the former case they must continue to support and assist the army after it has landed, and continue to maintain the maritime control on which success on land hinges. Their function, in fact, ceases to be purely maritime; they become a part of one vast and integrated organisation comprising all arms of all services, and all working towards the common end of defeating the enemy's land forces.

The great merits of amphibious expeditions of this nature are their mobility and secrecy. By making good use of strategic and tactical feints and defeating the enemy's reconnaissance it is possible to achieve surprise in both spheres, as, contrary to all expectations, occurred in the case of all three major enterprises (North Africa, Sicily and Normandy) launched by us and our Allies against our European enemies during the late war.

Provided that the planning and organisation of the whole vast and complex undertaking are meticulously based on inter-service understanding and co-operation, fortunate is the nation to whom the ability to undertake such expeditions falls. Though the exercise of maritime power in defence of trade is essential to the nation's war economy, and it alone can produce the conditions from which the final decisive offensive will be launched, it is by exercising this same heritage in the despatch of great military expeditions overseas that a maritime strategy can be crowned by final victory.

Outline of the Admiralty's Organisation in 1941

NOTES: *All within the broken line formed the Naval Staff.*
Members of the Board of Admiralty are shown in capital letters.
For clarity certain Divisions and Departments have been omitted from this diagram.

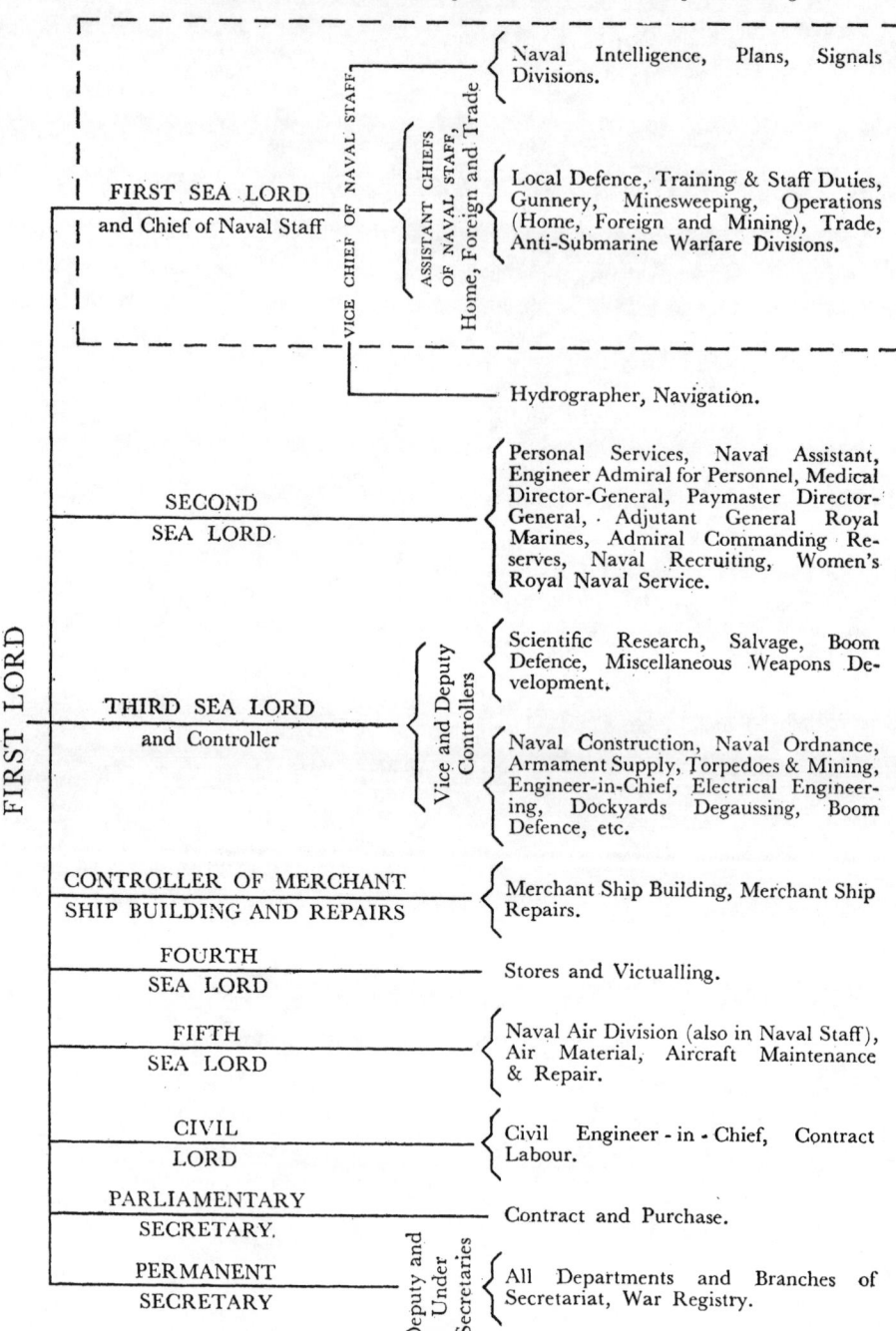

FIRST LORD

- FIRST SEA LORD and Chief of Naval Staff — VICE CHIEF OF NAVAL STAFF — ASSISTANT CHIEFS OF NAVAL STAFF, Home, Foreign and Trade
  - Naval Intelligence, Plans, Signals Divisions.
  - Local Defence, Training & Staff Duties, Gunnery, Minesweeping, Operations (Home, Foreign and Mining), Trade, Anti-Submarine Warfare Divisions.
  - Hydrographer, Navigation.

- SECOND SEA LORD
  - Personal Services, Naval Assistant, Engineer Admiral for Personnel, Medical Director-General, Paymaster Director-General, Adjutant General Royal Marines, Admiral Commanding Reserves, Naval Recruiting, Women's Royal Naval Service.

- THIRD SEA LORD and Controller — Vice and Deputy Controllers
  - Scientific Research, Salvage, Boom Defence, Miscellaneous Weapons Development.
  - Naval Construction, Naval Ordnance, Armament Supply, Torpedoes & Mining, Engineer-in-Chief, Electrical Engineering, Dockyards Degaussing, Boom Defence, etc.

- CONTROLLER OF MERCHANT SHIP BUILDING AND REPAIRS
  - Merchant Ship Building, Merchant Ship Repairs.

- FOURTH SEA LORD
  - Stores and Victualling.

- FIFTH SEA LORD
  - Naval Air Division (also in Naval Staff), Air Material, Aircraft Maintenance & Repair.

- CIVIL LORD
  - Civil Engineer-in-Chief, Contract Labour.

- PARLIAMENTARY SECRETARY — Deputy and Under Secretaries
  - Contract and Purchase.

- PERMANENT SECRETARY
  - All Departments and Branches of Secretariat, War Registry.

CHAPTER II

MARITIME WAR—THE BRITISH SHORE ORGANISATION

> It is good for us to studie in the time of peace how to defend ourselves in the time of warres and troubles; as generally we provide in harvest for to live in winter.
>
> William Bourne. *The Arte of Shooteing in Great Ordnance.* 1578.

Now that we have considered the meaning and purpose of maritime strategy, it may be helpful to the reader's understanding of what follows to describe briefly those aspects of the Admiralty's shore organisation which we shall meet in later chapters. It would be outside the scope of these volumes to attempt a full description of the whole vast and complex organisation which the Board of Admiralty controls from Whitehall. But the functions and work of certain divisions of the Naval Staff will be touched on; mention will be made of how ships, aircraft and weapons were designed and built for the Royal Navy; some account given of how the fleet was manned and, finally, the control of the fleet's movements and actions will be discussed.

Mr Churchill has told how, on the day that war was declared, he was offered the Admiralty, with a seat in the War Cabinet, how he returned to the First Lord's room that same evening after an interval of twenty-four years and was there joined almost immediately by his principal naval colleague.[1] The First Sea Lord was, in his capacity of Chief of Naval Staff, 'responsible to the First Lord for the issue of orders to the Fleet affecting war operations and the movements of ships'. He was also 'the responsible adviser to the Board [of Admiralty] on all questions of naval policy and maritime warfare'. In June 1939 Admiral Sir Dudley Pound was recalled from the Mediterranean Fleet, of which he had been Commander-in-Chief for the preceding three and a half years, to take over the office of First Sea Lord from Admiral of the Fleet Sir Roger Backhouse, who had been seriously ill for some months past. Admiral Pound brought to Whitehall a very long experience not only of high naval command at sea in home waters and the Mediterranean, but also of the working of every side of the Admiralty. As a captain he had been Director of the Plans

---

[1] W. S. Churchill. *The Second World War*, Vol. I (2nd Edition), p. 365.

Division of the Naval Staff. After serving as a young Rear-Admiral under Sir Roger Keyes, as Chief of Staff in the Mediterranean Fleet, he became Assistant Chief of Naval Staff from 1927 to 1929. He next commanded the battle cruiser squadron in the Atlantic Fleet as a Vice-Admiral. In August 1932 he returned to the Admiralty as Second Sea Lord and served in that capacity for three years. In September 1935 he went back to the Mediterranean Fleet as Commander-in-Chief.

The illness of Sir Roger Backhouse and his death just after Admiral Pound had taken office were a great loss to the Service and to the country, especially as they occurred at a most unfortunate moment, when the Navy was in the throes of preparing for a second war with Germany. But there was certainly no officer better equipped than Admiral Pound to succeed him. He was to carry a very heavy burden through no less than four years of war, the first three of which imposed a greater strain on the Navy and its whole organisation than any previous struggle. It was, perhaps, Admiral Pound's imperturbability which enabled him to lead his service through that period of great trial. No matter what disasters befell, or appeared to be pending, he never lost his outward calm. Only rarely did he show emotion; yet those who knew him well felt that strong emotions, most powerfully controlled, lay not far beneath the surface of his character. His capacity for work was enormous, his patience unlimited. His loyalty to his superiors was such that, if a decision was taken against his advice and things went wrong, he never let it be known that he had tried to prevent the steps which ended in misfortune.

The First Sea Lord's special responsibility was for maritime operations all over the world and Admiral Pound always had to master the details of their many intricacies. The continuous pressure of this work, which might demand that a difficult decision be made at any time of the day or night, was additional to his responsibility as adviser, with the Chief of the Imperial General Staff and the Chief of the Air Staff, to 'His Majesty's Government on defence policy as a whole'. His dual responsibilities—for it must not be forgotten that the Admiralty, unlike the War Office and the Air Ministry, was an operational centre—left Admiral Pound little time to keep his colleagues on the Board of Admiralty informed about current or projected operations. As it was, he generally worked until the small hours of the morning, and the short hours of sleep which he allowed himself were often broken into by the arrival of urgent messages. It is certainly the case that he constantly overworked himself, but how far this was inevitable where one man had to carry such great responsibilities it is hard to say.

If Admiral Pound carried centralisation of authority inside the

The Reserve Fleet drawn up for inspection by H.M. King George VI in Weymouth Bay, August 1939. H.M.S. *Effingham*, flagship of Vice-Admiral Sir Max Horton, in the foreground.

Part of the Home Fleet lying off Invergordon, August 1939. The ships shown are: (left-hand line) *Repulse, Royal Sovereign, Royal Oak, Resolution, Rodney*; (central line) 2nd Cruiser Squadron; (right-hand line) destroyers.

Admiralty too far, he was certainly right over the principles which he laid down, and himself scrupulously followed, regarding dealings with the other Services. Though some sections of the Naval Staff were, at times, impatient of his refusal to insist on what they regarded as essential, it seems to-day that Admiral Pound was right to maintain that reasonable compromises must be found. All the Services were beset by great difficulties, and serious inter-Service differences might well have brought irretrievable disaster during the years when we suffered a succession of grave defeats.

Though we, with all the necessary information from both sides available to us, may feel that Admiral Pound made occasional mistakes in the direction of maritime operations, the true measure of his accomplishment lies in the turn of the tide at sea in 1943. Happily he lived long enough to realise that the ultimate victory, to which he contributed so much, had become a certainty.

The composition of the Board of Admiralty changed considerably as the war progressed and new requirements arose; and in the Naval Staff new divisions were formed to meet new responsibilities.[1] Those with which we are principally concerned are the Plans, Operations, Intelligence and Trade Divisions, because their work constantly appears in the foreground of our story. But all the staff divisions advised the Board, with whom the ultimate responsibility lay, on matters of policy affecting the particular aspect of the war with which they were concerned. The welding of all the divisions of the Naval Staff into one integrated team rested with the Vice-Chief and Assistant Chiefs of the Naval Staff, under whom they worked. Throughout the war the Naval Staff met daily to review the previous twenty-four hours' actions, to consider the signalled reports which arrived in an unending stream from the naval authorities all over the world and to decide matters on which immediate action was necessary.

The Admiralty's War Plans for a conflict with Germany alone or with Germany and Italy combined were approved in January 1939; they will be described in some detail in a later chapter. Once war had broken out the planning of future operations replaced the preparation of war plans as the chief responsibility of the Plans Division. It became, in fact, a continuing function which lasted throughout the war. Not only did the Plans Division prepare all naval plans but its Director joined with his colleagues from the Army and Air Force to form the Joint Planning Committee, which advised the Chiefs of Staff on all inter-Service planning problems. Only a small proportion of the plans made received, for one reason or another, the approval of the Board of Admiralty or Chiefs of Staff; but planning for almost

---

[1] The composition of the Board of Admiralty throughout the period covered by this volume is given in Appendix A.

every conceivable eventuality had, none the less, to be carried out, because a sudden requirement for an emergency plan might arise. This was particularly the case during the period of the war when the initiative rested with the enemy.

The staff of Plans Division had to cover a far wider field than the making of operational plans. Long-term policy regarding the composition of all our fleets and squadrons came within its responsibility, as did the planning, for several years ahead, of the naval construction programmes. These were, moreover, subject to constant modification as the emphasis shifted from one aspect of the war at sea to another.

The work of Plans Division was closely linked and co-ordinated with that of the Intelligence Division, because information about enemy actions or intentions must greatly influence the preparation and execution of our own plans. As the approach of a second conflict with Germany became more and more clear, the Intelligence Division was able gradually to direct its work towards meeting the requirements which would certainly arise if war broke out. In particular, preparations had to be made to collect and distribute what is called 'Operational Intelligence'. This consisted of the day-to-day, even hour-to-hour, reports and deductions regarding the actions and movements of every one of the enemy's varied instruments of war. This work, the complexity and scale of which will be easily realised from the fact that it had to cover all the seas and oceans of the world, and that it might affect every British and Allied warship and any of our merchantmen at sea, was done in a series of rooms known as the Operational Intelligence Centre (O.I.C.). In February 1939 a Captain was specially appointed to the Intelligence Division to create and organise this centre. One section of the O.I.C. was wholly devoted to enemy submarines; for the German intention again to use them against our shipping was plain. In the Submarine Tracking Room a highly skilled and specialised staff made it their duty to collect, study and follow every sign of enemy submarine activity. They developed an uncanny skill in placing themselves in the enemy's position and so deducing his probable actions. Every piece of evidence, from reports of the torpedoing of merchantmen, which gave firm evidence that U-boats were present, to the crop of doubtful sightings and unreliable rumours which every day produced, was carefully sifted. The results were then used as the basis for routing our shipping clear of danger, and for counter-action by our own forces. There is no doubt at all that the skill of this room's staff, and the vigilance which they never relaxed for over five years, contributed greatly to the defeat of the U-boat. Another section of the O.I.C. dealt in similar manner with the activities of enemy surface ships.

In its final form the O.I.C. was linked by direct telephone and teleprinter lines to the operational headquarters of all the naval Commanders-in-Chief at home, to the headquarters of the Coastal and Fighter Commands of the Royal Air Force and to all the Area Combined Headquarters, the functions of which will be described in the next chapter. Liaison officers from Coastal and Fighter Commands were continuously on duty within the O.I.C. and themselves communicated instantly with their own people as soon as any matter which affected them arose. It was the intimate collaboration thus developed between the naval and air forces concerned with the same object which ultimately became the key to our success.

Before leaving the O.I.C. it must be made clear that, although the rooms beneath the Admiralty were the nerve centre, it was the operational staffs of the naval commands ashore and afloat, and of their colleagues in the headquarters of the associated R.A.F. Groups, who acted on the intelligence deduced in London. Though the Admiralty was always responsible for the broad disposition of our forces and occasionally assumed direct operational control in particular cases, it was, in general, the commands which planned and executed the movements based on the daily, even hourly, reports from the O.I.C.

There has been a good deal of criticism of the intelligence provided from London, particularly during the difficult days of 1940. Some of this criticism is well-founded and some incompletely informed. It must be remembered that it takes many years and much money to build up an efficient intelligence organisation, and further that, when not only the strategic initiative but also numerical and material superiority rested with the enemy, even good intelligence was unlikely to affect the outcome of a particular campaign. None the less it must be admitted that, during the early months of the war, the procurement by the enemy of intelligence regarding our warship dispositions and movements was superior to our own. It is now plain that the enemy's advantage in this respect was achieved, firstly, through regular air reconnaissance of our bases and, secondly, through the study he had made of our wireless traffic, which could and did reveal to him a great deal. It was many months before we were able to overtake the enemy in both these important sources of intelligence.

Nor was it only in the procurement of intelligence that we were, in the early days, at a disadvantage. Sometimes correct intelligence was available, but either it was ignored or its value and reliability were not realised. The correct assessment of intelligence will, however, always be difficult as long as the strategic initiative rests with the enemy, since he is able to strike in so many different directions. It is noteworthy that, after the initiative had passed into our hands in the autumn of 1942, the enemy, though doubtless possessed of much information regarding our invasion preparations, completely failed to anticipate our intentions. The situation in 1940 was, in fact, then reproduced in reverse.

Just as much of the work of the Director of Plans was done with his colleagues from the other services on the Joint Planning Committee, so did the Director of Naval Intelligence work with the heads of the War Office and Air Ministry's Intelligence departments on the Joint Intelligence Committee. Their object was to produce for the Chiefs of Staff intelligence 'appreciations' based on the knowledge, experience and requirements of all three services. It was, possibly, through the organisation and success of these inter-service bodies that our capacity to wage war successfully showed the greatest superiority over that of the enemy. The German records are full of instances of bitter disputes, disagreements and jealousies between the different arms and services, many of which were never resolved because Hitler's organisation was incapable of finding the reasoned solution to them. On our side disagreements were, inevitably, fairly frequent, but if they were not resolved by the appropriate inter-service body they could be referred to a higher authority and finally, if need be, to the War Cabinet. Once the decision was made all services then loyally abided by it.

The fleet expanded rapidly from the day of mobilisation until it reached its peak strength in about the middle of 1944, and this, together with the ever-widening area over which our control of sea communications was disputed, greatly increased the responsibilities of the Operations Division. It was soon divided into two divisions to deal with the Home and Foreign theatres; and separate sections were formed and made responsible for certain special types of operations such as minelaying, coastal force operations, irregular warfare and combined operations.

The Operations Divisions (Home and Foreign) were responsible for the distribution of the fleet all over the world and for the day-to-day, even hour-to-hour, movements of each of its units. Though each Commander-in-Chief regulated the movements of the ships and squadrons allocated to him, the responsibility for the distribution of our maritime strength rested, under the Board of Admiralty, with the Operations Divisions. It was, in fact, their organisation which exploited the flexibility of maritime power mentioned in our first chapter. To do so with speed and sureness, accurate information had constantly to be available regarding the position and condition of all our more important warships. This necessitated keeping operational plots showing their movements and, to some extent, their future intentions; comprehensive records of all damage received, all refits in progress and the current state of all important ships in regard to supplies of fuel, ammunition and stores also had to be kept.

The operational plots referred to above were, of course, intimately linked with the Intelligence Centre already described. The Operations Divisions received the incoming intelligence and took, or, on major issues, recommended to the Board, the necessary action. The orders finally approved as a result of this procedure were then sent by wireless, by cable or by other means, in the name of the Admiralty, to the fleets, squadrons, ships and authorities who would execute them.

The need for intimate collaboration between Plans, Intelligence and Operations will be evident even from the brief description given. It is no exaggeration to say that together they formed the trinity on which the execution of our maritime strategy chiefly rested.

The Trade Division developed rapidly from very small beginnings to one of the largest organisations within the Naval Staff under its own Assistant Chief of Naval Staff. The Admiralty assumed control of all British merchant shipping on the evening of the 26th August 1939, and this control was chiefly exercised through the Director of the Trade Division and his Naval Control Service staffs stationed in all ports used by British shipping all over the world. The procurement of merchant shipping tonnage by purchase, charter or other means remained the responsibility of the Ministry of Shipping (later amalgamated with the Ministry of Transport to become the Ministry of War Transport) as did the manning of the Merchant Navy.[1] The Admiralty's responsibility began shortly before a ship sailed on an outward voyage and ended with her safe arrival after completing the journey. The organisation of convoy escorts and the conduct of convoys at sea, the routes used by all shipping and the instruction of masters in the execution of the Admiralty's policy and orders all rested with the Trade Division.

In June 1939 a special section of Trade Division was formed to plan and organise the defensive arming of the whole British Merchant Navy. In co-operation with the Ministry of Shipping and the shipowners, anti-submarine and anti-aircraft guns were collected and distributed, the ships were made ready to receive them, and naval reservists and Merchant Navy crews were trained in their use. Officers were sent to the more important ports abroad to help the ships with the installation and use of the weapons; and reserves, not only of guns and ammunition but of equipment such as paravanes and smoke floats, were accumulated at the ports. The guns allocated to the merchantmen were, for the most part, naval weapons which had been removed from scrapped warships; but they were the best

---

[1] The Ministry of Shipping was formed in October 1939, but it was not until 9th May 1941 that the Ministry of Transport was amalgamated with that of Shipping under the combined title of Ministry of War Transport. The first head of the combined Ministry was Mr F. J. Leathers.

that could be provided. The chief difficulty was to find anti-aircraft weapons. The need for them had long been realised, but the shortage was so acute, even in the fighting services, that nothing like the required number of suitable weapons could be supplied to the Merchant Navy for several years.

The size and complexity of the problem of defensively arming the Merchant Navy is best indicated by giving a few figures. The number of ships requiring equipment was about 5,500 of which 3,000 were ocean-going vessels, 1,500 were coasters and the rest were small craft and fishing vessels. To give as many of them as possible anti-submarine protection, low-angle guns were, in general, the first to be mounted; by the end of 1940 some 3,400 ships had been so fitted. As the war progressed the need to equip many Allied vessels arose, and this remained an Admiralty responsibility until the United States took over the arming of the ships which they controlled. By May 1945 Britain and the Dominions had armed 9,500 ships, of which 5,600 were ocean-going vessels. No less than 50,000 anti-aircraft machine guns had also been supplied to merchantmen by the end of the war.[1]

The great scale on which weapons were provided led naturally to heavy demands for men to fight them, and to the need to train large numbers in their use. The nucleus of the guns' crews supplied to the Merchant Navy was formed of naval and Royal Marine reservists, but as the war progressed great expansion became necessary. Some 24,000 naval men were actually trained to fight the defensive armaments of merchantmen, and the Merchant Navy crews themselves supplied large numbers to help man their own ships' guns. Over 150,000 merchant seamen were trained in such duties.

The fitting of weapons in the ships presented peculiar problems, because no delays in harbour from that cause could be accepted. The work had therefore to be carried out piecemeal, and a ship might be stiffened to take a gun in one port but not receive the weapon until she called at another. Arming was carried out in all the major ports of the world, but the lion's share fell, as was natural, on the British shipyards. So much for the responsibilities and accomplishments of the Defensively Equipped Merchant Ship section of Trade Division.

To enable a continuous survey to be made of the success of the enemy's various methods of attack and of our own counter-measures, statistical analysis of all casualties to merchant ships was kept in Trade Division, and reports of their experiences were collected from the survivors of sunk or damaged ships. Yet another responsibility was to keep constantly up to date the Trade Plots which were maintained in rooms adjacent to the O.I.C., on which the positions of all our convoys and independently-routed merchantmen were shown.

To turn now to minesweeping, a separate Staff Division to carry

---

[1] Appendix B gives statistics of the Defensive Arming of Merchant Ships.

the responsibility for this type of warfare was not actually formed until the 2nd of October 1939, by which time the enemy's attempts to disrupt our coastal communications by minelaying had assumed menacing proportions. To deal with this threat a great number of small ships had to be requisitioned, purchased or built by the Admiralty and a wide variety of counter-measures developed. The minesweeping forces comprised, possibly, a greater variety of ships than any other branch of the naval service, ranging from fleet minesweepers of considerable size and speed and manned by Royal Navy crews, down to converted drifters and trawlers manned largely by fishermen who had joined the R.N. Patrol Service. These small ships were stationed at all ports in these islands and also abroad, wherever enemy mines might be laid.

The Anti-Submarine Warfare Division was to a great extent the twin brother of the Minesweeping Division since it dealt with the other under-water threat to our sea communications, namely the U-boat war in all its aspects. This required a large number of small anti-submarine vessels similar in some aspects to those employed on minesweeping. In fact many small vessels came to be equipped for both types of duty. From the earliest days of the war a large number of our best fishing trawlers was requisitioned by the Admiralty for conversion to anti-submarine duties; and each base and port had to have its quota of such vessels for local defence against the coastal type of submarine. Numerous small vessels, such as the 'Fairmile' types of motor launch, were also built for this purpose in the small boat-yards of the country—one of the earliest examples of the prefabrication and mass production of ships.

Whenever a serious attack on a U-boat was reported the results were carefully studied by an assessment committee, under the Director of Anti-Submarine Warfare, in order that the conclusions drawn might be as accurate as possible and the naturally optimistic hopes of the attacker verified. Since any assessment of the trend of the submarine war must depend greatly on the success of our counter-measures in achieving the actual destruction of U-boats, the monthly reports of the Anti-Submarine Warfare Division became documents of importance. It is worth noting that, in spite of the care with which all claims to have sunk U-boats were checked, the number actually sunk during the greater period of the war was somewhat less even than the relatively cautious assessments of this committee.

The importance to maritime strategy of the possession and security of the bases from which our forces must work has already been mentioned; the consequences of the insecurity of certain bases will appear later in our story. Here it must be mentioned that even before the outbreak of war a large number of pressing problems and unfulfilled requirements for the defence of naval bases and commercial ports were arising, and the Local Defence Division of the Naval Staff was formed in May 1939 to carry the responsibility for assessing their priority and for meeting them.

It must be mentioned that none of the work of the Naval Staff could have been effective without efficient communications in the fleets and squadrons and between them and Whitehall. The Admiralty controlled not only the central wireless stations in Britain, from which messages were passed to and from the fleet, but a network of stations all over the world—generally situated at or near our overseas bases, and it was on this network that rapid communication greatly depended. The responsibility for the whole naval communications organisation rested on the Signal Division of the Naval Staff, and the traffic which had to be handled grew rapidly to enormous proportions. The same division was responsible for the issue of all codes and cyphers to the fleet and, jointly with the Director of Naval Intelligence, for their security. Inside the Admiralty the coding or cyphering of outgoing messages, the decoding of the incoming traffic and the rapid distribution of all messages to those who might have to take action on them was the responsibility of an organisation called War Registry. It was manned by civilians and was under the Permanent Secretary.[1]

The responsibility for the manning of the fleet and for the training of all officers and men, rested with the Personnel Departments of the Second Sea Lord. On the 1st of January 1939 the strength of the Navy on the active list was under 10,000 officers, the greatest proportion of whom were, of course, in the lower ranks, and 109,000 ratings. To expand rapidly from this small nucleus to a strength which at its peak in mid-1944 reached 863,500 officers and men, plainly demanded the existence in peace-time of large reserves, of an organisation for rapidly recalling the reserves to the fleet, and also the training of large numbers of men called to the Colours under the National Service Act.

Rapid and smooth mobilisation is a long-standing tradition of the Navy. The reason is not far to seek, since an intending enemy can easily despatch raiders into the wastes of the oceans to wait upon events long before war is declared, and thus be ready to start attacks on our trade from the very opening of hostilities. In fact, Germany, by the preparations made long before the outbreak of war, showed herself to be well versed in such practices, and fully justified every measure of readiness which the Admiralty and the naval Commanders-in-Chief desired to take during the summer of 1939. In spite of the growing menace of the international outlook in the spring and early summer of that year, the Government of the day continued up to the eleventh hour to pursue a policy of doing nothing upon

---
[1] See diagram on p. 14.

which Hitler might place an unfriendly construction, or which might (so it was suggested) alarm the British populace. These volumes are not the place to discuss the cause and effects of such a policy, but the impact on naval preparedness was, of course, serious. As early as May the Commanders-in-Chief of the home ports, who were responsible for the smooth conduct of naval mobilisation and for the bringing forward to service of the ships of the Reserve Fleet, were expressing serious concern to the Admiralty over the need to press ahead with measures of naval readiness, and to obtain a change in the policy which was making it impossible to implement such steps effectively.

On the 1st of January 1939 the strength of the naval reserves totalled some 80,000 officers and men of several different categories, and instructions were issued on the 26th of May 1939 for 15,000 of these men to be called up to man the Reserve Fleet, which was brought forward to readiness for service on the 15th of June.[1] This fleet, consisting, in general, of the older ships of the Royal Navy which were maintained in serviceable condition but were not fully manned, could only be prepared for service by calling up a proportion of the reserves. It formed, in fact, the first and most rapidly attainable increase of naval strength. When all the peace-time reserves had been called back further expansion depended on the flow of National Servicemen, on the transfer of men from the Merchant Navy under special agreements and on other new measures. The calling-up of the last peace-time reserves was therefore far from being the final limit to the Navy's strength in war; but these reservists were, none the less, of great importance because they had all served periods in the Navy and did not need to undergo immediate further training. In fact the retired and emergency list officers, the pensioners and Royal Fleet Reserve ratings, the peace-time Royal Naval Volunteer Reserve and Royal Naval Reserve formed the first line of the Navy's reserve strength.

In addition to the Second Sea Lord's responsibilities for naval officers and men outlined above, the department of the Adjutant General, Royal Marines, also came within his sphere. The Royal Marines not only supplied a detachment to every major warship but fulfilled a long tradition of instant readiness to fight on land. They also manned an organisation called the Mobile Naval Base Defence Unit which, with its complete equipment, was held ready to proceed overseas to set up a temporary base wherever it might be required. The regiment's far-flung activities will constantly appear in our story. On the outbreak of war its strength, including reservists, was 16,146 officers and men. By the end of 1944 it had reached a total of over 36,000.

---

[1] Details of the composition of the naval reserves on 1st January 1939 are given in Appendix C.

Before leaving the Second Sea Lord's departments mention must be made of the Women's Royal Naval Service. It had been disbanded after the 1914–18 war, but was restarted in 1939. Then the W.R.N.S. quickly showed that they could carry out a large number of the duties formerly carried out by men in the naval shore establishments. The men were thus released for service at sea. By the autumn of 1944, when their strength reached its peak of 74,620 officers and ratings, no naval establishment at home or abroad was without its complement of 'Wrens' and their conduct, courage and capacity had won the affection and admiration of the whole service.

Lastly we must turn to the material and supply departments under the Third and Fourth Sea Lords. The responsibility of the former included the design and construction of all warships and of all their machinery, weapons and equipment. When naval aircraft began to occupy an ever-increasing importance in maritime war an additional member was added to the Board with responsibility for all air material. We cannot here describe in any detail the technical departments of the Third Sea Lord. It must suffice to say that every aspect of ship and weapon design and production, of scientific research and development, of naval construction, of marine and electrical engineering, of wireless and radar design and production was covered by one or other department of his vast organisation. The Fourth Sea Lord's departments dealt with the procurement and distribution all over the world of the stores and supplies, including fuel, on which the mobility of our maritime forces greatly depended.[1]

The responsibilities of the Fifth Sea Lord originally included the staff side as well as the material side of naval air warfare, but in January 1943 the two were separated and an Assistant Chief of Naval Staff (Air) was appointed to the Board. On the outbreak of war the Naval Air Division was responsible for the whole staff work of that aspect of maritime war, but as it rapidly gained in importance the work was split up between several new divisions. On the material side the fulfilment of the Admiralty's requirements for naval aircraft, their weapons and stores was the responsibility of the Air Ministry until July 1937, when control of the Fleet Air Arm was returned to the Admiralty. Departments to handle air material and personnel matters were then formed. The reasons for the backwardness of the Navy in design and production of aircraft will be discussed in the next chapter.

Treatment of the subject of Admiralty organisation should include some mention of the methods whereby the movements and operations of our fleets and squadrons were controlled. The Admiralty, as has been said, was an operational centre and could at any time exercise its

---

[1] See diagram on p. 14.

right to issue orders direct to the senior officers of fleets and squadrons. This long-standing right would, however, if not exercised with caution and restraint, plainly cut across the functions of the naval Commanders-in-Chief who, not unnaturally, were sensitive regarding interference in matters for which they carried the responsibility. While, therefore, the Admiralty's right to intervene in the conduct of operations cannot be disputed, the manner and the frequency of such interventions must naturally be regarded by the Commanders-in-Chief as important.

Soon after Admiral Pound became First Sea Lord in June 1939 he gave his views on this question to the Commander-in-Chief Home Fleet, Admiral Forbes. Admiral Pound proposed that the normal procedure should be for the Admiralty to give the Commander-in-Chief all the information and leave him to make the necessary dispositions but that, on certain occasions—notably when the fleet was at sea and keeping wireless silence—it might be necessary to alter his dispositions. He suggested 'that it be recognised that at times it will be necessary for the Admiralty to alter dispositions but that Admiralty control will cease as soon as possible'. Admiral Forbes, in his reply, agreed that the necessity to alter his dispositions might occasionally arise, but he claimed that discretion should be left to him whether or not to carry out the Admiralty's orders, because the Admiralty could not possibly be kept aware of the constantly changing conditions and circumstances which might prevail many hundreds of miles away at sea. He asked that 'if at all possible information rather than an order should be passed' to him by the Admiralty.

Though no reply appears to have been sent to Admiral Forbes, and this important issue cannot therefore be said to have been resolved before the outbreak of war, in October 1939 the First Sea Lord, apparently in reply to verbal representations from Flag Officers against Admiralty intervention in the conduct of their operations, expanded his views and the policy he proposed to adopt in a letter to a colleague. He stressed that orders would only be issued from Whitehall in certain special circumstances, and that Admiralty control would cease as soon as possible. He ended by saying, 'Why have Commanders-in-Chief and do their work for them? If they are not capable of doing it they must make room for someone who can'.

This correspondence has been quoted because it makes clear the personal views and outlook of the Chief of Naval Staff regarding the control of the fleet. The wide difference between those intentions and the policy sometimes followed will become apparent when the story of the early operations at sea is told.

CHAPTER III

THE DEVELOPMENT OF SEA-AIR CO-OPERATION

> 'Wide eyes that weary never
> And wings that search the sea'
> Swinburne. *To a Seamew. 1866.*

THE year 1937 saw two important decisions governing sea-air warfare. Between them they resolved the disagreements which had continued ever since the transfer of some 2,500 aircraft and 55,000 men from the Navy to the newly-formed Royal Air Force in 1918. They also formed the basis from which sea-air co-operation developed from small beginnings to great dimensions during the Second World War.

The first of those two decisions ended the compromise which had governed the control, administration and operation of the Fleet Air Arm since 1924 and which, though acceptable to the Air Ministry, had been a constant source of dissatisfaction and anxiety to the Admiralty. Under the 1924 agreement the Air Ministry remained responsible for the provision of naval aircraft, though the Admiralty specified the types and numbers required and provided funds to cover the cost of the Fleet Air Arm; the Admiralty provided the ships in which they were embarked and their specialised equipment; the Fleet Air Arm pilots (of whom more than half were naval officers) held Air Force rank, but the rest of the aircrews were all naval; the Air Force provided the skilled maintenance staff of the aircraft carriers; and when disembarked the Fleet Air Arm crews came under Air Force jurisdiction, whereas when embarked they were subject to naval discipline. These and other provisions of a complicated arrangement were greatly altered in 1937 when the naval air branch was reborn, though in a different form to that which it had possessed during the 1914–18 war. With the termination of the Air Force partnership in the Fleet Air Arm and the return to the Admiralty of responsibility for the Navy's shipborne aircraft and their crews the title of the Fleet Air Arm, which had been used to describe the Air Force units which worked with the Navy, became obsolete. Thenceforth naval aircraft became as much a part of the Navy as its destroyers, submarines and torpedo-boats. In these volumes, therefore, the Navy's aircraft and crews are, except when dealing with the period prior to 1937, referred to only as such.[1]

The second of the two decisions taken in 1937 was contained in a directive issued by the Air Ministry on the 1st of December stating that the primary rôle of the Coastal Command of the R.A.F. in war would be trade protection, reconnaissance and co-operation with the Royal Navy. It guaranteed that the aircraft belonging to Coastal Command would only be employed on other duties when the threat to our sea communications was insignificant, and thus not only met the Admiralty's views regarding the function of aircraft allocated to naval co-operation but eliminated its apprehensions regarding the diversion of Coastal Command aircraft.

The first of these two decisions put a term to the controversy which had marred relationships between the two services; and the second assisted the development of the intimate co-operation between the Navy and Coastal Command which was to contribute so greatly to the success of the nation's maritime strategy. Only one change was made to the 1937 arrangements during the last war, and that was the transfer to the Admiralty of the operational control of Coastal Command aircraft in April 1941. This, however, did not alter the status of Coastal Command as an integral part of the R.A.F.

It is outside the scope of the present volume to trace the various, and often painful steps along the road which led to the 1937 agreements. But the late hour at which those decisions were taken and the controversies which had prevailed during the previous two decades contributed so greatly to the weakness of the Navy's air strength and of the R.A.F.'s Coastal Command when war broke out that some knowledge of the background must be given.

In the Navy itself a division of opinion regarding the functions and importance of shipborne aircraft existed well into the nineteen-thirties. The conventional view then was that aircraft would, in a future war, prove valuable in assisting to bring about a decision by gun power with the enemy's fleet, but that they were not, of themselves, likely to strike decisive blows, or to act as substitutes for the big guns of the heavy ships, or to defend the fleets against air attack as the flotilla vessels defended them against shipborne torpedo attack. The conventional view prevailed, though with gradually lessened assurance, until late in 1931 when the appointment of Rear-Admiral R. G. Henderson as the first Rear-Admiral, Aircraft Carriers, led to the principles involved in the use of the new weapon being radically reconsidered, and to a more just position being allotted to the aircraft in the tactics and employment of the fleets. But throughout the

---

[1] Though strictly speaking incorrect, the title of Fleet Air Arm was none the less commonly used during the war. In 1953 it was decided to reintroduce it as the proper title of the Navy's air branch.

nineteen-twenties, when all the service departments were labouring under the acute difficulties caused by the Cabinet ruling that no war was to be expected for ten years—which date was constantly being moved forward—the section of the R.A.F. to which the Fleet Air Arm belonged, then known as Coastal Area, was the least-favoured part of that service. And from the beginning of 1929 until the end of 1932 the funds provided by the Admiralty were so small that only eighteen aircraft were added to the Fleet Air Arm. Not until 1936, by which time the R.A.F.'s two first expansion schemes had been approved, was Coastal Area placed under its own Commander-in-Chief with the title of Coastal Command.

But during the years when responsibility for the Fleet Air Arm was divided between the Admiralty and the Air Ministry there was one branch of naval aviation in which steady progress was made —and that was in the design and construction of aircraft carriers. Here there was no division of responsibility, the experiences of the 1914–18 war could be carried on into the ensuing period of peace and continued experiment and development were possible. The table below gives particulars of the ships of that class which were in service on, or shortly after, the outbreak of war and of the aircraft embarked in them at that time.

Table 1. Royal Navy—Aircraft Carriers in Service, 1939

Entered Service	Name	Aircraft Complement	Remarks
1920	Eagle	18 Swordfish	Converted ex-Chilean battleship
1923	Hermes	9 Swordfish	First ship to be designed and built as an aircraft carrier
1925 (reconstructed)	Furious	18 Swordfish 8 Skuas 4 Rocs	Converted from mammoth cruiser of the 1914–18 war
1928 (reconstructed)	Courageous	24 Swordfish	Ditto
1930 (reconstructed)	Glorious	36 Swordfish 12 Sea Gladiators	Ditto
1938	Ark Royal	42 Swordfish 18 Skuas	The first new Fleet aircraft carrier
[1917	Argus	Non-operational	Converted merchant ship]

[Notes on Aircraft Types
  Swordfish   Torpedo-bomber/spotter/reconnaissance
  Skua   Two-seater fighter/dive bomber
  Roc   Two-seater fighter
  Sea Gladiator Single-seater fighter]

In addition to the completed ships tabulated above six new fleet carriers of the *Illustrious* and *Implacable* classes were authorised in the naval programmes for 1936 to 1939. That such a substantial proportion of the available funds was devoted to building new aircraft carriers should dispel any idea that, after 1935, the Navy was any longer in doubt regarding the contribution of shipborne aircraft to maritime control.

In the equipment of the carriers with aircraft and trained crews our position, compared with the United States and Japan, was not so favourable. In September 1939 the Navy's strength was 232 first-line aircraft, over half of which were Swordfish, while 191 more were employed on training work. During the war it increased to 1,336 first-line aircraft organised in twenty-three 'Strike' and fifty fighter squadrons, and the number of naval air stations grew from four to forty-five. But we could not replace the obsolescent types of aircraft during the first two years of the war and even after that time we had to rely to a considerable extent on American production.

The doctrine current in 1939, based on peace-time training and development, summarised the duties of naval aircraft under the following headings:

1. Reconnaissance for the fleet to extend the vision of the surface ships and so enable the enemy to be first sighted by us and, after first sighting, to shadow and keep touch with the enemy.

2. Attack by striking forces on a faster enemy attempting to escape battle, thus reducing his speed to enable our surface ships to come into action.

3. To assist in protecting the fleet against submarine and air attacks and, in particular, to defend the carriers themselves.

4. Spotting for the fleet's gunfire in surface actions or shore bombardments.

Though the use of aircraft for protecting merchant shipping was reviewed before the war, and the value of the small aircraft carrier to work on the trade routes had been stressed in authoritative naval circles, little progress in that important development was accomplished until after war had broken out.

Once the decision that the Navy was to resume responsibility for the Fleet Air Arm had been taken in 1937, the Admiralty strenuously set about building the necessary organisation. A 'Fifth Sea Lord and Chief of the Naval Air Services' was added to the Board of Admiralty, and the departments necessary to handle naval air material and personnel were created. The entry of short-service officers and the training of ratings as pilots, which measures the Admiralty had previously opposed, were started early in 1938 and the Royal Naval Volunteer Reserve Air Branch, which was to supply a great proportion of the naval pilots and observers who fought at sea from 1939 to 1945, was formed in the autumn of the same year. But these measures had not borne fruit before war broke out.

Admiral of the Fleet Sir Charles L. Forbes, Commander-in-Chief Home Fleet 12th April 1938–18th December 1940.

Admiral Sir John C. Tovey, Commander-in-Chief Home Fleet 2nd December 1940–14th April 1943.

Air Chief Marshal Sir F. W. Bowhill, Commander-in-Chief Coastal Command 16th August 1937–14th June 1941.

Air Chief Marshal Sir P. B. Joubert de la Ferté, Commander-in-Chief Coastal Command 14th June 1941–5th February 1943.

ASSISTANCE FROM THE R.A.F. COMMANDS

During the period of transition the assistance of the Royal Air Force was indispensable and was freely given. As late as December 1940 some 2,000 R.A.F. officers and men were still serving in the Navy. The Air Ministry also undertook the training of naval maintenance crews, and allowed some of its own men to transfer to the sister service. In fact once the decision, which the Air Ministry had strenuously resisted, had been taken by the Government everything possible was done to ensure its loyal fulfilment.

From 1939 to 1945 much assistance was afforded to the Navy by the R.A.F. Commands at home. Fighter Command protected naval bases and installations against air attack, escorted coastal convoys, carried out tactical reconnaissance work and made attacks on enemy shipping in the narrow seas. Bomber Command provided striking forces against enemy warships and submarines, made many attacks on building yards or on factories engaged in producing submarine parts and deployed a considerable proportion of its effort against targets affecting the maritime war. But it was Coastal Command which, after the issue of the directive quoted at the beginning of this chapter, was charged with the specialised duty of co-operating with the Navy. This command had grown out of the old Coastal Area organisation already mentioned, and the first Air Officer Commander-in-Chief (Air Marshal Sir Arthur Longmore) was appointed in July 1936 at the time when the long-awaited expansion of the R.A.F. was at last beginning.

Concurrently with these administrative changes the Chiefs of Staff had ordered an investigation into the protection of seaborne trade, and as it was in this field that Coastal Command finally achieved its full stature, the progress of the investigation will be followed in some detail. The questions asked by the Chiefs of Staff of their Planning Sub-Committee were as follows:

1. How far they regarded air attack as a menace to our supplies of food and raw materials in time of war?
2. How such attack should be countered?
3. What part the Royal Air Force should play in the protection of trade?

It was from the extensive deliberations which followed on the asking of these questions, and from the determination of the Chiefs of Staff that an agreed solution should be achieved, that the duties allocated to Coastal Command before the outbreak of war, and so the disposition of its strength, stemmed. Nor was agreement easily reached. The Naval Staff considered that the early establishment of the convoy system would reduce the air threat to merchant shipping to 'manageable proportions' and that surface escorts, suitably armed, would 'prove the answer' to air attacks as well as to the submarine menace. But they qualified their advocacy of convoy by agreeing that if, in the light of experience, the system proved expensive in shipping losses from air attack, the matter would have to be reconsidered. Because the enemy, remembering the lessons of 1917, would not again risk alienating neutral opinion the Naval Staff considered that unrestricted air or submarine attacks were unlikely. The Air Staff, on the other hand, considered that our dependence on seaborne trade positively invited unrestricted attacks, and that to mass ships in convoy would result in heavier losses from air attack because it would bring large numbers of vulnerable targets close together. This was actually one of the arguments which had been used against introducing convoy to counter the U-boat menace in the 1914–18 war.[1]

The Naval Staff was confident of the great value of the new 'Asdic' anti-submarine detecting device.[2] In 1937 they reported to the Shipping Defence Advisory Committee that 'the submarine should never again be able to present us with the problem we were faced with in 1917'. There were, indeed, good grounds for confidence in the asdic, provided that the operators were thoroughly trained and the submarine target remained submerged. In such circumstances it could and did produce excellent results. But it was difficult to provide skilled asdic operators quickly to all the ships which needed them in war and, as will be told later, the asdic was almost useless against a surfaced submarine.[3] The Naval Staff also considered that anti-aircraft gunfire from the escort vessels would adequately protect the convoys against air attack. On both issues the Air Staff was sceptical. Another stumbling block on the road to agreement was the desire of the Air Ministry to use Coastal Command aircraft as part of its offensive striking force—a diversion from their proper function which the Admiralty could not accept.

In the agreement finally reached between the Joint Staffs the probability of unrestricted submarine and air attacks was accepted by the Navy, the introduction of convoy was accepted by the R.A.F.,

---

[1] See Fayle, *Seaborne Trade*, Vol. III (1924): 'The Submarine Campaign' (1924), p. 99.

[2] The name 'ASDIC' is derived from the initial letters of the Allied Submarine Detection Investigation Committee (of 1917) which was responsible for the development of an entirely new technique to detect a submerged submarine. Briefly stated, the principle of the asdic is that if an alternating electric current is applied to a quartz crystal suspended beneath a ship the crystal expands and contracts and its vibrations cause a pulse of sound waves to be sent through the water. If these waves strike an obstacle they are reflected, and the reflections are received in the crystal which sent them out. The application of this principle to anti-submarine warfare was greatly advanced from 1927 onwards by the staff of the Admiralty's anti-submarine experimental establishment at Portland. It must be understood, however, that although the asdic gave the direction of the submerged target and its distance it did *not* give its depth. The depth at which to explode the depth charges dropped or thrown by the attacking ship could therefore only be guessed. Hence the need to drop or fire a large 'pattern' of depth charges, set to explode at varying depth.

[3] See p. 355.

and the Air Ministry abandoned the proposal to divert Coastal Command aircraft at will to other duties. Concessions were thus made by both sides and the agreement which, as the Secretary of State for Air remarked, constituted 'an admirable piece of combined staff work' was approved by the Committee of Imperial Defence on the 2nd of December 1937.

The next, and most important, stage—that of defining the duties which Coastal Command aircraft should carry out—had now been reached. Until this issue had been clarified plans and dispositions could not be made, nor specialised training started, nor the most suitable types of aircraft ordered.

The Admiralty was, at this time, chiefly anxious about the powerful German surface warships which might be sent out to attack our sea communications. As the First Sea Lord put it to his colleagues on the Chiefs of Staff Committee, 'nothing would paralyse our supply system and seaborne trade so certainly and immediately as successful attack by surface [i.e. warship] raiders'. The submarine menace, on the other hand, was considered unlikely to prove serious, at any rate during the opening phase of a war with Germany. In consequence the Admiralty felt that the chief contribution which Coastal Command could make to the maritime war was constantly to watch the exits from the North Sea, and this became its primary responsibility. Anti-submarine co-operation, the precise form of which would have to be decided when it was known whether the enemy would or would not wage unrestricted warfare, was placed next, and co-operation with the Northern Patrol, which the Navy intended to establish on the outbreak of war to watch the passages to the Atlantic between the north of Scotland and Greenland, came third in order of priority.

The number of aircraft to be provided in the event of war with Germany, and their allocation were as follows:

(1) Home Waters:	For convoy escort duties	165
	For the North Sea reconnaissance	84
	In the northern area of the North Sea	24
	For the Northern Patrol	18
(2) Abroad:	At Atlantic Convoy assembly ports	48
	TOTAL	339

The above total was provided for in the current R.A.F. expansion scheme, but it was made clear that, by the 1st of April 1939, only 194 (or under two-thirds of the required total) would actually be available. This number was so disposed as to give priority to the North Sea reconnaissance. Unhappily not only were the necessary numbers of aircraft not available before the outbreak of war, but the performance of the aircraft with which the General Reconnaissance squadrons were then equipped—the Anson—was inadequate to the efficient execution of its function. More will be said on that score shortly.

The Munich crisis found Coastal Command far from fully prepared for war. The organisation into three groups (Nos. 15, 16 and 18) to cover all the waters surrounding these islands was incomplete and only No. 16 Group had been formed.[1] Of the fifteen squadrons comprising the Command only twelve could, because of shortage of men, be mobilised; and of those twelve squadrons eight had to move from their peace to their war stations. Less than a year of peace remained to improve matters.

Not the least important deficiency was the lack of an organisation for combined operational control of Coastal Command aircraft. This problem was tackled energetically and was solved by establishing an Area Combined Headquarters (A.C.H.Q.) to control the operations of each group. Within these A.C.H.Q.'s each service had its representative, who enjoyed full executive authority to act for it. At the end of 1938 sites were chosen at Plymouth (for No. 15 Group), Chatham (for No. 16 Group) and Rosyth (for No. 18 Group), and the all-important communications requirements were agreed. But only the Rosyth A.C.H.Q. was properly installed by the time war broke out. In the summer of 1939 the headquarters of the Commander-in-Chief, Coastal Command (Air Marshal Sir F. W. Bowhill), moved from Lee-on-Solent, where it was unsuitably sited, to Eastbury Park, Northwood, where the Commander-in-Chief was in close touch with the Admiralty and whence his own forces could be efficiently controlled.[1]

The duties allocated to the various squadrons of Coastal Command were promulgated on the last day of March 1939 and were little altered between that date and the outbreak of war. The majority of the squadrons was based in the north-east of these islands to carry out the North Sea reconnaissance work required by the Admiralty. No. 233 General Reconnaissance (G.R.) squadron was to carry out an 'endless chain patrol' during daylight between Montrose and the nearest point on the Norwegian coast (Obrestadt).[2] To guard against the possibility of raiders passing through this patrol line unobserved at night the three flying boat squadrons (Nos. 201, 209 and 228) were to search from Invergordon to the north of No. 233 Squadron's patrol as far as a line drawn from the Shetland Islands to the Norwegian coast near Stadtlandet, while two other G.R. squadrons (Nos. 224 and 269) were to search to the south of the Montrose-Obrestadt line from Flamborough Head. A gap which this left off

---
[1] See Map 1.
[2] See Map 5 (*facing p. 71*).

Map 1

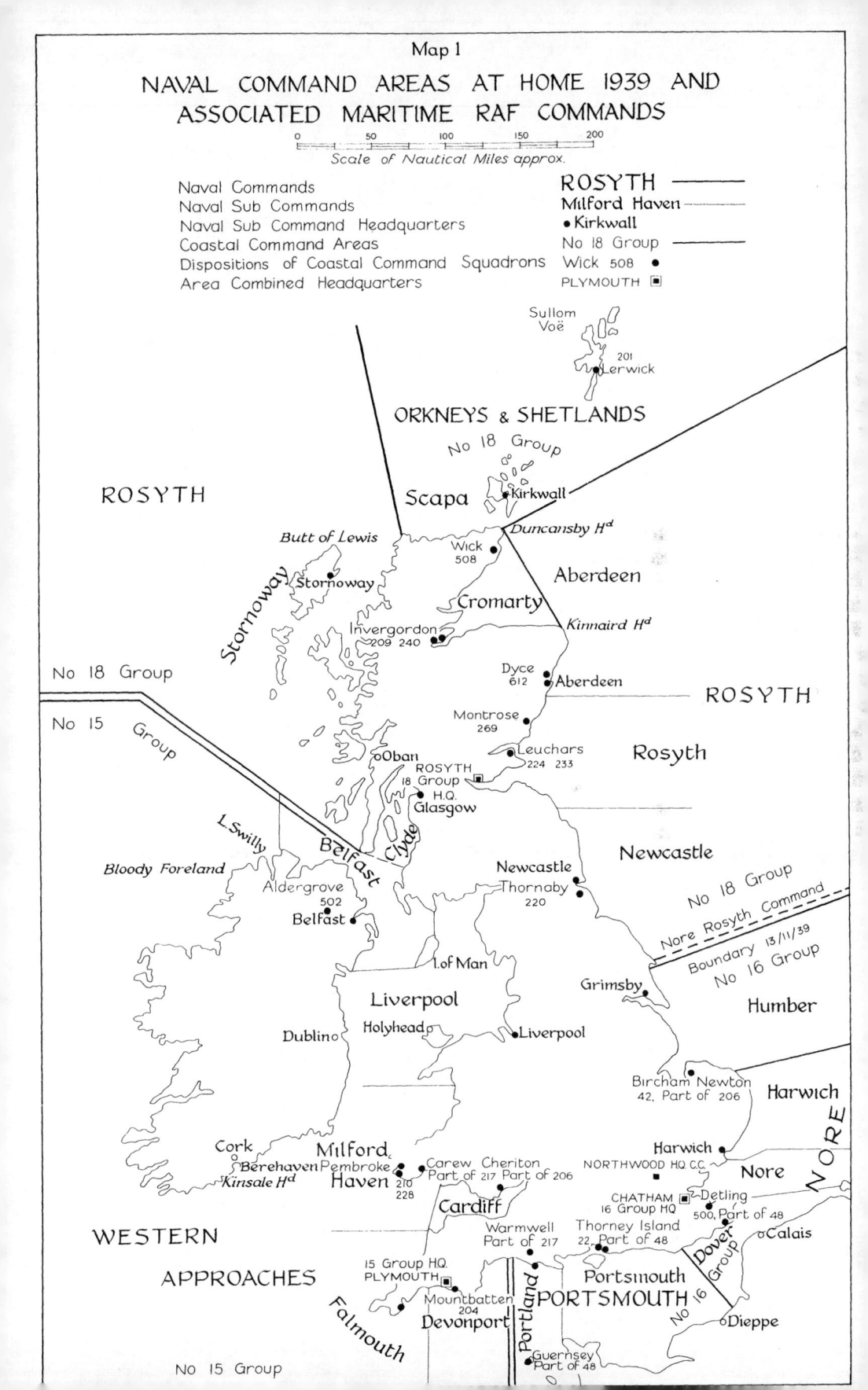

NAVAL COMMAND AREAS AT HOME 1939 AND ASSOCIATED MARITIME RAF COMMANDS

Scale of Nautical Miles approx. 0 – 50 – 100 – 150 – 200

Naval Commands — ROSYTH ———
Naval Sub Commands — Milford Haven ———
Naval Sub Command Headquarters — ● Kirkwall
Coastal Command Areas — No 18 Group ———
Dispositions of Coastal Command Squadrons — Wick 508 ●
Area Combined Headquarters — PLYMOUTH ▣

Sullom Voë
201 ● Lerwick

ORKNEYS & SHETLANDS
No 18 Group

ROSYTH

Scapa
● Kirkwall
Duncansby H^d
Butt of Lewis
Wick 508
Aberdeen
Stornoway ● Stornoway
Cromarty
Invergordon 209 240
Kinnaird H^d
Dyce 612 ● Aberdeen
ROSYTH

No 18 Group
No 15 Group

Montrose 269
Oban
ROSYTH 18 Group H.Q.
Leuchars 224 233
Glasgow
Rosyth

Belfast
Clyde
Newcastle
Thornaby 220
Newcastle

L. Swilly
No 18 Group
Nore Rosyth Command
Boundary 13/11/39
No 16 Group

Bloody Foreland
Aldergrove 502
● Belfast
I. of Man
Liverpool
Grimsby
Humber

Dublin ○
Holyhead ●
● Liverpool

Bircham Newton 42, Part of 206
Harwich

Cork ○
Berehaven
Milford
Pembroke
Carew Cheriton
Part of 217 Part of 206
● Harwich
NORTHWOOD HQ C.C.
Nore

Kinsale H^d
Haven 210 228
Cardiff
CHATHAM 16 Group HQ ▣
● Detling 500, Part of 48
○ Calais

Warmwell Part of 217
Thorney Island 22, Part of 48
Dover Group

WESTERN APPROACHES
15 Group HQ PLYMOUTH ▣
Portsmouth
PORTSMOUTH
No 16

Mountbatten 204
Devonport
Portland
○ Dieppe

Falmouth
Guernsey Part of 48

No 15 Group

the Danish coast was to be covered by north-south searches by the flying boats of No. 210 Squadron.[1] It was calculated that a ship which entered the area covered by the southern patrols at dusk would not steam far enough during darkness to escape the northern patrol at dawn next day. If bad weather dislocated the routine patrols and a raider might have escaped through all their lines, then the flying boats would search, as soon as weather conditions permitted, to the north-west of the Orkneys in the hope of locating the enemy ship after it had left the North Sea.

Though these patrols and searches appeared, on paper, to meet the Admiralty's requirements as far as was possible at the time, there were two factors which substantially reduced their effectiveness. The first was the bad weather which, for prolonged periods—especially in winter—prevails in the North Sea. That the Navy, with its long experience of the vagaries of the North Sea weather, doubted the reliability of the air patrols is shown by a letter written by the First Sea Lord (Admiral Sir Roger Backhouse) to the Commander-in-Chief, Home Fleet, in October 1938, when the plans referred to above were being framed. Admiral Backhouse wrote:

> 'In particular I am not at all sure that the arrangement for a continuous air patrol across the North Sea is workable all the year round. You know as well as I do what the North Sea is like in the winter months. I cannot believe that aircraft could maintain a daily reconnaissance under bad weather conditions. As ships are not stopped by bad weather or long nights to anything like the extent that aircraft are [stopped] we could never be sure that some would not get through unsighted.'

War experience was to show at an early stage that the First Sea Lord's doubts were well founded. Unfortunately time did not permit the effectiveness of the reconnaissance patrols during the winter months to be tested by exercises before war broke out.

The second factor limiting the effectiveness of the patrols was the low performance of the Anson, which had a range of only 510 miles and a speed of 144 knots. It could not even reach to the Norwegian coast at Obrestadt. The last sixty miles of the patrol line from Montrose had therefore to be covered by five or six of the Home Fleet's submarines, stationed at twelve-mile intervals, and carrying out diving patrols. This was rapidly proved to be an unsatisfactory arrangement.

As early as 1937 the Air Ministry had desired to replace the Ansons, but neither of the new types intended for that purpose could be available until later in 1938. As an emergency measure the purchase of Lockheed Hudsons from America was investigated, and orders for

---

[1] See Maps 4 and 5 (*facing pp. 65 and 71*).

250 aircraft of this type were placed. The Hudson possessed double the range and could carry five times the bomb load of the Anson, and the intention was to equip five reconnaissance squadrons with them. Only No. 224 Squadron had, however, received its Hudsons when war broke out.

Our weakness in flying boats was even greater, since only two squadrons had received the modern Sunderland, and the Lerwick, which was intended as the replacement aircraft for the other three squadrons, had proved a complete failure. As with the Hudsons, an endeavour was made, later, to obtain more modern types from America.

So far only the steps taken to meet the Admiralty's first requirement have been considered. For the second priority, that of anti-submarine duty, three G.R. squadrons (Nos. 224, 217 and 204) were allocated to the Thames estuary, the Channel and the Lizard areas respectively until such time as the convoy system was introduced. If and when that occurred, escorts for the convoys were to be provided by six squadrons. The Coastal Command aircraft thus allocated to anti-submarine duties were, from the beginning, given freedom to carry out attacks in all areas except those in which our own submarines were patrolling; but Bomber Command aircraft were forbidden to attack submarines during the first weeks of the war because it was considered that bomb loads might thus be wasted on targets of secondary importance, the bombs carried would probably be unsuitable for such attacks and the bombers' navigation might be insufficiently accurate to determine the limits of our own submarines' patrol areas. This order was, however, modified after three U-boats had been sighted in the Heligoland Bight but not attacked.

Yet another deficiency in the strength and equipment of Coastal Command remains to be recounted. It possessed very little striking power of its own wherewith to attack such enemy warships as might be sighted. Only one torpedo-bomber squadron (No. 42) was available for that duty, though another was held in reserve. And No. 42 Squadron was equipped with the obsolete Vildebeeste. This lack of striking power made Coastal Command largely dependent on Bomber Command to inflict damage on enemy warships; and the latter had received no training in attacking such targets.

The final version of Coastal Command's war plans was issued at the end of June 1939. Between the 15th and 21st of August the arrangements were tested in an exercise designed to deal with surface raiders breaking out from the North Sea. On conclusion of this rehearsal most of the squadrons moved to their war stations, and the war-time reconnaissance patrols were started almost immediately.

The reader will have remarked that the plans discussed above made no special provision for the protection of the great flow of shipping which must, in war as in peace, flow along the route off the east coast of these islands and which, in the event of war with Germany, was plainly very exposed to air attack. Not until early in 1939, and then only through the agency of a committee appointed to investigate other subjects, was this important matter forced into the foreground. To divert all the shipping from the east to the west coast ports was not practicable, because the handling facilities at the latter were inadequate and the strain on the inland transport system would have been intolerable. The Air Defence of Great Britain (A.D.G.B.) organisation was responsible for the defence of our cities and industries, and also for the defence of the ports themselves; but the ships which entered and left the ports would, if in convoy, be protected only by the escort vessels' guns and, if sailing independently, be quite unprotected. The short-range single-seater aircraft of Fighter Command included in the A.D.G.B. organisation were operated on the principle of control from the ground. Such control could not be extended more than a few miles from our shores and, moreover, the pilots were untrained in sea-air co-operation, which was not within the responsibilities of Fighter Command. But the need to introduce some measure of air protection for the east coast shipping could not be ignored and, in consequence, it was decided in the summer of 1939 to form four Trade Protection Squadrons of Blenheim fighters. They were allocated to Fighter Command. None was, however, brought into being until after the outbreak of war, when the start of enemy air attacks had rendered it imperative. Though the need for special protection for the east coast shipping was now recognised many months were to elapse, and serious losses were to be suffered from air attack, before it was properly organised.

Looking back to-day over the period prior to the outbreak of war, it cannot but be concluded that the slow progress made in the development of sea-air co-operation until 1937, when it was almost too late, was brought about, firstly, by the Cabinet's 'ten-year rule' regarding the possibility of war breaking out and, secondly, by the inter-service controversies which bedevilled all impartial discussion of the fundamental issues involved. Though it may be considered that this contributed to bringing us, for the second time in the present century, to the very edge of the abyss of defeat at sea, it must be recognised that, in the enemy's camp, the same problems were never satisfactorily resolved. Controversy and jealousy between the German Navy and the Luftwaffe continued throughout the war. They prevented the former from developing the use of air power at sea and greatly restricted the effectiveness of the latter when operating in a maritime rôle. It was, indeed, fortunate that the British Navy and Air Force abandoned such controversies and joined hands in a spirit which, as the war progressed, grew more and more comradely—and that they did so just in time. Nor should it be forgotten that if the Germans had, some years prior to 1939, found a solution to the problems outlined in this chapter and then concentrated even a reasonable proportion of their great energies on the maritime use of air power—as did the Japanese and the Americans—then the survival of Britain would indeed have been problematical.

CHAPTER IV

ALLIED AND ENEMY WAR PLANS AND DISPOSITIONS

> You cannot build ships in a hurry with a Supplementary Estimate.
> *Admiral Sir J. A. Fisher to Lord Charles Beresford. 27th February 1902.*

IN the last chapter we traced the development of Coastal Command's war plans up to the movement of all its squadrons to their war stations. We will now turn to the corresponding British naval war plans and, since the majority of the important German naval archives came into the Admiralty's hands at the end of the war, it will be possible to look over the shoulder of our principal enemy to see how he was, at the same time, planning his assault on our seaborne trade.

The Admiralty's war plans were formally approved by the Board on the 30th of January 1939 and were promptly issued to the naval authorities at home and abroad who, in the event of war, would be responsible for executing them. They were framed to deal with a war against Germany and Italy together; but account had also to be taken of the attitude of Japan, which, since 1936, had been acting towards Britain with increasing unfriendliness. Though it was not expected that Japan would join the Axis powers at an early stage in a war precipitated by the latter, 'nevertheless', the plans stated, 'we must be prepared for the active intervention of Japan against ourselves and France'.

After estimating which countries were likely to attack Britain and her ally and which to remain in a state of unfriendly neutrality, the broad strategy to be followed at sea was outlined. As must always be the case in a war with a European enemy, paramount importance was given to the home theatre, because any serious or prolonged loss of control of our coastal waters, or of the ocean trade routes which converge on these islands, would bring rapid and final disaster. Second only to the home theatre in importance came the Mediterranean, through which sea, in time of peace, pass the very important oil-tanker traffic from the Persian Gulf and the greater part of our trade with India and the Far East. Though it was hoped that, in the event of war, the passage of warships through the Mediterranean 'could occasionally be undertaken', it was considered that Italy's geographical position and her considerable naval and air power would prevent the use of that route by our merchant ships. It was accordingly accepted that our mercantile traffic would be diverted to the long route by the Cape of Good Hope. In spite of the closure of the Mediterranean it would be of cardinal importance to maintain a firm hold on the approaches to it from the east by the Red Sea and from the west by the Straits of Gibraltar; the supply of our land forces in the whole Middle East theatre would depend on the former, while the efficiency of our blockade of Italy and the safety of the north-south Atlantic trade routes would hinge largely on the latter. The forces stationed in the Red Sea were accordingly to be strengthened by detachments from the Mediterranean Fleet and the recall of certain warships from the Far East.

Our control of the western basin of the Mediterranean was greatly simplified by the presence of the greater part of the French Fleet in those waters, and by its well-placed bases in southern France and on the North African shore. Accordingly, it was agreed with our ally that the western basin should be a French responsibility. This enabled greater British strength to be allocated to the eastern Mediterranean without unduly weakening the Home Fleet.

Third in importance came the Far East, over which the attitude of Japan hung like a storm cloud. British interests in the China Sea and in the waters washing the islands of the Eastern Archipelago were great; and from that area came imports of food and certain essential raw materials. The sea routes to the east must, if possible, be kept open. But we were not strong enough to guard our home waters properly, to maintain a major fleet in the Mediterranean and to send a third fleet to the Far East. Since an attempt to station a strong fleet simultaneously in each of the three primary theatres would lead only to dangerous weakness in all of them, it was accepted that a fleet capable of fighting the Japanese Navy on anything like equal terms could only be provided by withdrawing nearly all British forces from the Mediterranean and by leaving the control of the whole of that sea to the French Navy.

Apart from disposing its principal strength in the two most important strategic areas the Admiralty also had to provide against sporadic attacks at any point along the thousands of miles of our highly vulnerable ocean trade routes which in the words of the war plans, are 'vital to the life of the Empire'. In 1939 some 3,000 deep-sea dry cargo ships and tankers and about 1,000 coasting vessels, totalling 21 million tons, were registered in Britain and the average number at sea on any one day was 2,500.[1] The need for large

---

[1] In this book the tonnage of merchant ships is always referred to in terms of Gross Registered Tons. This tonnage is calculated by measuring all the enclosed spaces of the ship and allowing 1 ton for every 100 cubic feet. Gross tonnage must be distinguished from net tonnage (the gross tonnage after deduction of all spaces devoted to the running of the ship and therefore without revenue-earning capacity) and deadweight tonnage —roughly the amount the ship can carry, including bunkers, when down to her marks. Throughout the war many of the official shipping statistics were compiled in terms of deadweight tons. Over an average block of cargo tonnage the ratio allowed was 5 gross tons to 8 deadweight. This ratio is inapplicable in the case of passenger or passenger-cargo liners.

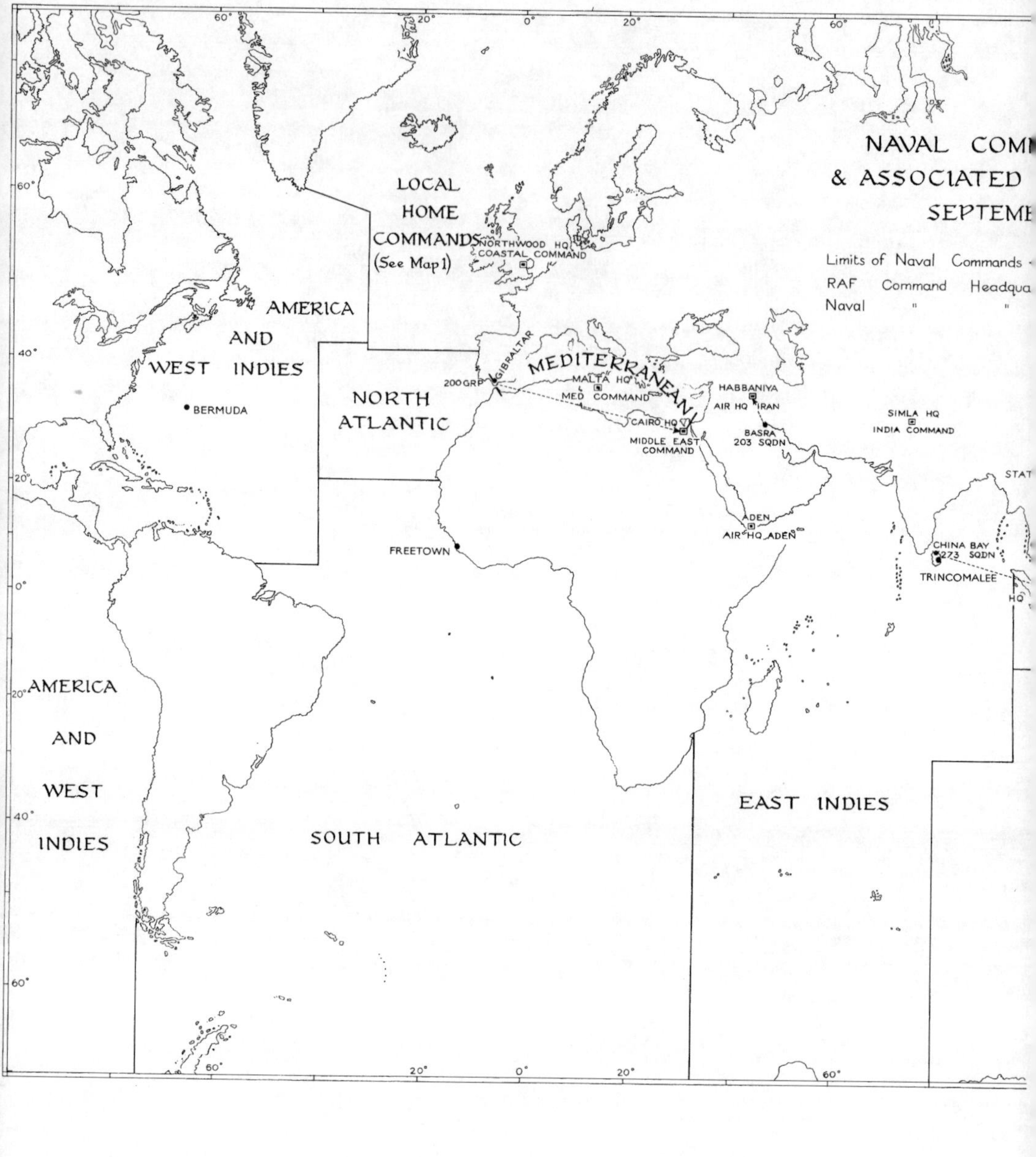

NAVAL COM
& ASSOCIATED
SEPTEM
Limits of Naval Commands
RAF Command Headqua
Naval " "
LOCAL
HOME
COMMANDS
(See Map 1)
NORTHWOOD HQ
COASTAL COMMAND
AMERICA
AND
WEST INDIES
BERMUDA
NORTH
ATLANTIC
GIBRALTAR
200 GRP
MEDITERRANEAN
MALTA HQ
MED COMMAND
CAIRO HQ
MIDDLE EAST
COMMAND
HABBANIYA
AIR HQ IRAN
BASRA
203 SQDN
SIMLA HQ
INDIA COMMAND
ADEN
AIR HQ ADEN
FREETOWN
CHINA BAY
273 SQDN
TRINCOMALEE
HQ
STAT
AMERICA
AND
WEST
INDIES
SOUTH ATLANTIC
EAST INDIES
60°
20°
0°
20°
60°
60°
40°
20°
0°
20°
40°
60°
60°
20°
0°
20°
60°

Map 2

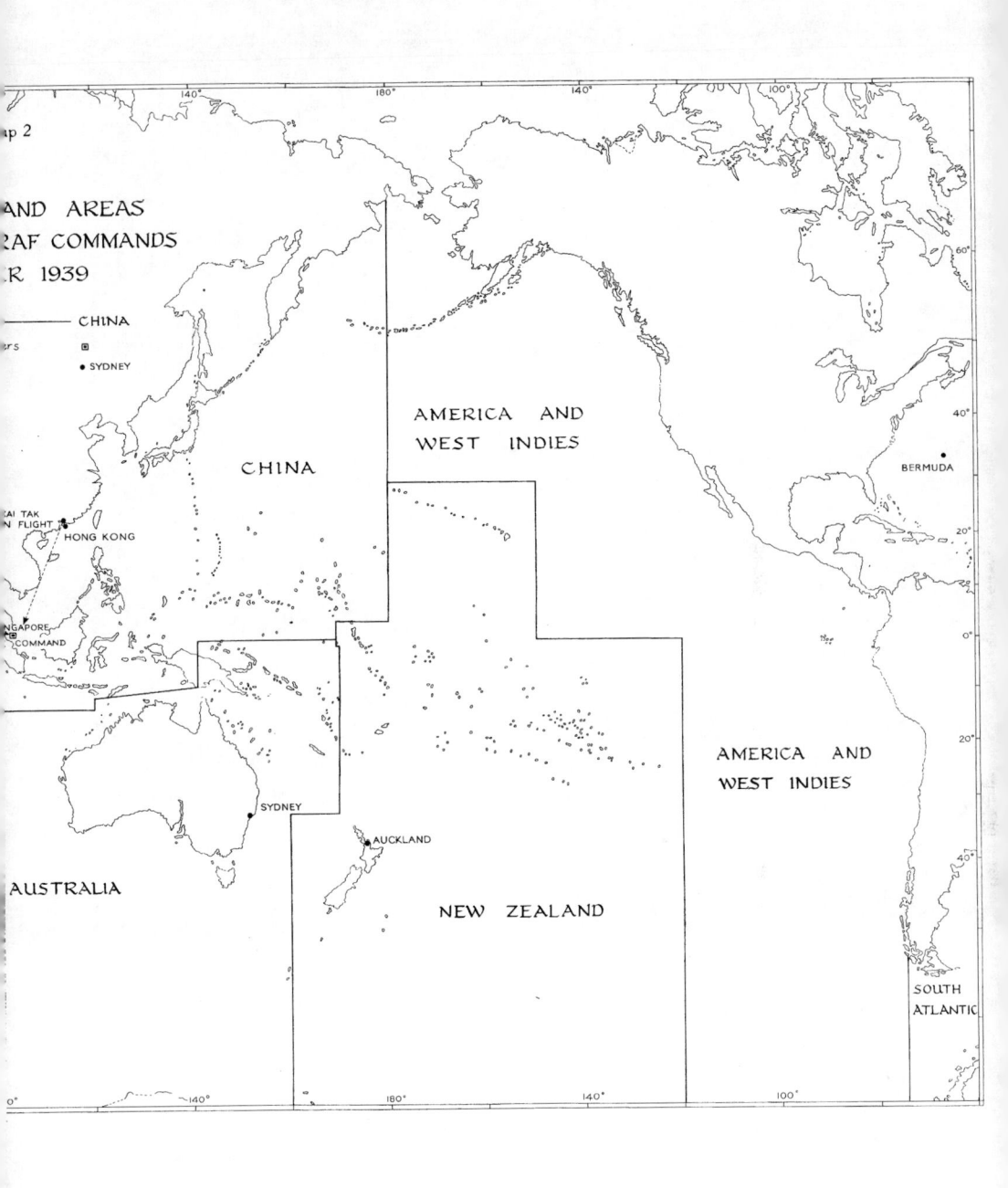

AND AREAS
RAF COMMANDS
R 1939

CHINA
SYDNEY

CHINA

AMERICA AND
WEST INDIES

BERMUDA

KAI TAK
N FLIGHT
HONG KONG

NGAPORE
COMMAND

AMERICA AND
WEST INDIES

AUSTRALIA

SYDNEY

AUCKLAND

NEW ZEALAND

SOUTH
ATLANTIC

numbers of cruisers to defend this great total of widely-dispersed merchant ships requires no emphasis. For many years after the First World War the Admiralty had insisted that seventy cruisers was the smallest number with which we could meet our responsibilities. Yet, from one cause or another, this minimum was gradually whittled down until, in 1939, our effective strength—including the Dominion Navies—was only fifty-eight. Though our cruiser strength was clearly quite inadequate, the attempt to hunt down and destroy the expected surface raiders and to patrol the focal areas of shipping where they were likely to work had, none the less, to be made. This would be the responsibility of the foreign naval commands—the North Atlantic Station (headquarters at Gibraltar), the South Atlantic (Freetown, Sierra Leone), the America and West Indies (Bermuda), the East Indies (Ceylon) and the China Station (Singapore and Hong Kong).[1] In addition to these British overseas commands the Dominions each accepted a measure of responsibility, dependent on the strength which they possessed, for control of the waters adjacent to their territories. This brought some relief to the Admiralty, whose overseas responsibilities were thereby reduced. In addition to protecting our own shipping and searching for enemy raiders, all the foreign commands, as well as the Home and Mediterranean Fleets, would be responsible for the enforcement of the blockade, which the Government intended to declare on the outbreak of war, by intercepting enemy merchant ships and by controlling the carriage of contraband of war to enemy (or possible enemy) destinations in neutral bottoms. The Admiralty was responsible only for intercepting ships at sea and for sending them into the control bases. Subsequent action regarding the cargoes rested with the Ministry of Economic Warfare and the Prize Courts.

The blockade was to be enforced by patrolling the entrances to the North Sea and Mediterranean. At home 'contraband control' bases were to be established in the Orkneys and the Downs (the anchorage in the English Channel off Deal); similar bases were to be set up at Gibraltar, Haifa, Malta and Aden.[2] There the ships' cargoes would be examined and any items which came within the definition of contraband removed, for subsequent condemnation in prize, before the ships were allowed to continue their journeys.

The establishment of a blockade has long been recognised as the right of a belligerent, provided that it can be made effective; but the delays to neutral shipping incident to recent developments in methods of blockade always lead to difficulties with the countries whose ships are involved. A balance has, therefore, to be struck by the Government between insisting on its full rights despite the

---
[1] See Map 2.
[2] See Maps 26 and 34 (*facing pp. 293 and 426*).

irritation caused to the neutrals and relaxing its measures to appease neutral sentiments, with the probability of contraband cargoes thereby reaching the enemy. It was not many weeks before the war produced difficulties of this nature, as, for example, when the United States Government protested against American ships being sent to the control base in the Orkneys, which lay inside the zone declared by the President as closed to American shipping.[1] The British Government several times relaxed the full stringency of its blockade measures in deference to neutral opinion.

It will be remarked that these measures only applied to control of enemy imports. Export control was not enforced till later—in retaliation for the Germans' illegal minelaying.

Though the blockade was certainly not complete during the early months of the war and substantial leaks were known to exist (for example in traffic from Black Sea ports to Italy), no less than 338,000 tons of contraband were seized during the first six weeks. Thus, from the earliest days of the war, did we enforce the slow stranglehold of the economic blockade.

Though our opening strategy was except for the blockade defensive, the importance of seizing every opportunity to prosecute a tactical offensive was not ignored. Thus the Commander-in-Chief, Home Fleet, was instructed 'to bring the enemy to action wherever and whenever his forces can be met' and the Commander-in-Chief, Mediterranean, was given a similar directive. In addition to this long-standing and traditional function the Home Fleet was required 'to close the North Sea to all movements of enemy shipping and to exercise contraband control of neutral shipping'; and the Mediterranean Fleet was 'to ensure the isolation of Italy from all sea communication with the countries outside the Mediterranean'.

Apart from the Home Fleet four naval shore commands were established in these islands—Portsmouth, the Nore (Chatham), the Western Approaches (Plymouth) and Rosyth—with responsibility for controlling our coastal waters and for defending the shipping which was funnelled into those waters from all the corners of the world.[2] In addition, in the case of the southern home commands and in particular of Portsmouth, the safe transport of the British Expeditionary Force to France would be a primary responsibility.

Since 'the traditional and well-proved methods' of convoy would provide the best protection against enemy submarine and air attacks, preparations for its introduction were forwarded and the Commanders-in-Chief abroad were given powers to order into convoy ships passing through their commands. Our cruiser strength

---

[1] See Map 10 (*facing p. 97*).
[2] See Map 1 (*facing p. 37*).

was, however, inadequate to enable ocean convoys to be formed at once; the Admiralty therefore intended to patrol the focal areas through which most shipping had to pass and to rely on 'evasive routing' to enable ships to sail independently and in safety from one focal area to the next. The control of all merchant shipping would be assumed by the Admiralty as soon as war seemed probable. It would be exercised through the Naval Control Service Staffs, who would be trained at home and then sent to their stations all over the world. The necessary instructions to the masters of all merchant ships had also been prepared and would be issued as soon as the emergency arose.

It was expected that the enemy would dispute our maritime control, firstly with his surface warships—and in particular the 10,000-ton 'pocket-battleships' of the *Deutschland* class which had been specially designed for that purpose—and by disguised armed merchant raiders; secondly, by U-boat warfare, though it was left for experience to show whether it would be of the 'unrestricted' type which the Germans waged in the First World War after 1917, or whether it would initially endeavour to conform to international law; thirdly, by air attacks, though here it was considered that the threat to our mercantile ports and to the great tonnage of shipping berthed in them on any day was greater than the threat to the ships while at sea; and, lastly, by minelaying in our shallow coastal waters, our river estuaries and in the approaches to our naval and mercantile ports. It was plain that the impact of German submarine warfare, air attacks and minelaying would first be felt in our home waters and in the sea approaches to these islands, and plans were therefore made to combat these threats. To protect the very important flow of shipping which must proceed up and down the length of our east coast, convoys were to be run between the Tyne and Thames from the outset. The Straits of Dover were to be closed and the passage of U-boats by the shortest route to the Atlantic blocked by the laying of a mine barrage across the narrows. To protect the east coast convoys from incursions by U-boats or surface ships another minefield was to be laid, in several stages, along the greater part of the length of that convoy route. To guard the approaches to the English Channel and the Irish Sea from the west and to cover the flow of military transports and store ships proceeding to and from French ports, a powerful squadron, called the Channel Force, was to be based at Portland. To deal with any attempt by the Germans to operate light forces in the southern part of the North Sea, certain cruisers and destroyers were detached from the Home Fleet to be based on the Humber. The Admiralty assumed direct operational control of this force. The northern exits to the Atlantic between the Faeröe Islands and Iceland and by the Denmark Strait were to be watched by a patrol of cruisers and, for the inshore sections, of trawlers.[1] This Northern Patrol would be responsible for enforcing our blockade in those waters; it was to be carried out initially by the older cruisers which had been brought forward for service from the Reserve Fleet. But they were to be replaced in due course by liners converted to armed merchant cruisers, and half of the total of fifty such ships was allocated to this duty.

All merchant ships approaching these islands from the west would, until in convoy, be given positions through which they were to pass and routes by which they would continue their approach; and those routes would be patrolled by ships and aircraft. It was in the organisation of the defence of this great flow of shipping inwards from and outwards into the Atlantic, and in extending our defence measures as far west as possible, that the Admiralty and Coastal Command were handicapped by the lack of naval and air bases in Eire. During the first war Bearhaven[2] in the south and Lough Swilly in the north had been of inestimable value for this purpose, and the Admiralty was not slow in pointing out to the Cabinet the probable consequences of the lack of their use in a second struggle with Germany. The First Lord took the matter up strenuously and repeatedly with his colleagues, and an approach was made to the Eire Government. But the desired result was not accomplished. Happily the bases in Northern Ireland at Londonderry and Belfast remained available to our use and when, in mid-1940, all our shipping had to be diverted round the north of Ireland the importance of bases in the south was reduced. But the handicap imposed by having to use Plymouth and Milford Haven, instead of Bearhaven, as the bases for the escorts working in the south-western approaches was serious.

To deal with the U-boats themselves it was considered that the surface vessels and aircraft 'allocated to trade protection could best be divided into anti-submarine hunting units and disposed at strategic points round the British Isles'. Finally plans were made to arm all merchant ships with anti-submarine and anti-aircraft guns and to instruct their crews in their use. It has already been told how this was organised.[3]

Having outlined the objects of our world-wide maritime strategy and the particular problems with which each theatre was concerned we shall now consider the forces assigned to execute that strategy.

By the 31st of August all ships of the Home Fleet, commanded by Admiral Sir Charles Forbes, had taken up or were proceeding to

---

[1] See Map 4 (*facing p. 65*).

[2] Also commonly spelt Berehaven. See Map 8 (*facing p. 91*).

[3] See pp. 21–22.

COMPOSITION OF THE HOME FLEET

their war stations. The organisation and disposition of the fleet was as follows:—[1]

At Scapa Flow in the Orkneys:
2nd Battle Squadron	*Nelson, Rodney, Royal Oak, Royal Sovereign, Ramillies.*
Battle Cruiser Squadron	*Hood* and *Repulse.*
Aircraft Carrier	*Ark Royal.*
18th Cruiser Squadron	*Aurora, Sheffield, Edinburgh, Belfast.*
12th Cruiser Squadron	*Effingham, Emerald, Cardiff, Dunedin.*
7th Cruiser Squadron	*Diomede, Dragon, Calypso, Caledon.*
6th and 8th Destroyer Flotillas	Seventeen destroyers.
1st Minesweeping Flotilla	Seven fleet minesweepers.

At Rosyth:
Aircraft Carrier	*Furious*

At Dundee:
2nd Submarine Flotilla	Depot ship *Forth* and ten boats.

At Blyth:
6th Submarine Flotilla	Depot ship *Titania* and six boats.

In addition to the foregoing ships and units under Admiral Forbes' command the following forces were stationed in home waters:—

In the Humber:
2nd Cruiser Squadron	*Southampton* and *Glasgow.*
7th Destroyer Flotilla	Nine destroyers.

At Portland:
Battleships	*Resolution* and *Revenge.*
Aircraft Carriers	*Courageous* and *Hermes.*
Cruisers	*Ceres, Caradoc, Cairo* (A.A. cruiser.)
18th Destroyer Flotilla	Nine destroyers.

To each of the four home naval commands certain light forces were allocated for local defence, anti-submarine and minesweeping duties; they were distributed by the Commanders-in-Chief to the various sub-commands organised in the smaller ports within their areas as might be necessary.[2] Thus Portsmouth (Commander-in-Chief, Admiral Sir William James) had the 12th and 16th Destroyer Flotillas (twelve destroyers), five anti-submarine vessels and eight minesweepers; the Nore (Admiral Sir H. Brownrigg) had the 19th Destroyer Flotilla (nine destroyers) and a few minesweepers at Dover and other small forces at Harwich and in the Thames estuary; to the Western Approaches command (Admiral Sir M. Dunbar-Nasmith, V.C.), where the emphasis was on convoy protection, were

[1] Particulars of British warships mentioned in these paragraphs are given in Appendix D.
[2] See Map 1 (*facing p.* 37).

assigned the 3rd, 11th, 12th and 17th Destroyer Flotillas (thirty-two destroyers in all), while Rosyth (Vice-Admiral C. G. Ramsey), which was responsible for the northern part of the east coast convoy route, had the 15th Destroyer Flotilla (eight destroyers) and eight escort vessels, all of which had good anti-aircraft armaments. It should be mentioned, before leaving the home shore commands, that towards the end of October Dover was made an independent command under Vice-Admiral B. H. Ramsay and that an Orkneys and Shetland command (Admiral Sir W. French) was established and placed under the Commander-in-Chief, Home Fleet, shortly before war broke out.

Turning now to the foreign commands, the Flag Officer North Atlantic (Rear-Admiral N. A. Wodehouse, who was relieved in November by Admiral Sir Dudley North) was ashore at Gibraltar and had under his orders the two old cruisers *Capetown* and *Colombo*, the 13th Destroyer Flotilla (nine destroyers) and a few minesweepers.[1] Ashore at Freetown, Sierra Leone, was the Commander-in-Chief, South Atlantic (Vice-Admiral G. H. d'Oyly Lyon), under whose orders was a comparatively strong force of cruisers comprising the *Neptune*, the 9th Cruiser Squadron (*Despatch, Dauntless, Danae* and *Durban*) and the South American Division (*Exeter, Ajax* and *Cumberland*) for guarding the important trade routes across that ocean, the seaplane carrier *Albatross*, one division of the 2nd Destroyer Flotilla (four destroyers), four escort vessels, two submarines and the usual small force of minesweepers. The Commander-in-Chief, America and West Indies Station (Vice-Admiral Sir Sidney Meyrick), had under his orders the 8th Cruiser Squadron (*Berwick, Orion, York*, and the Royal Australian Navy's *Perth*) and two escort vessels. In the Mediterranean was stationed, under Admiral Sir Andrew Cunningham, by far the greatest naval strength outside home waters. The principal units of the Mediterranean Fleet, based on Alexandria, by virtue of the Anglo-Egyptian treaty of 1936, were the First Battle Squadron (*Warspite, Barham* and *Malaya*), the aircraft carrier *Glorious*, the First Cruiser Squadron (*Devonshire, Sussex* and *Shropshire*), the Third Cruiser Squadron (*Arethusa, Penelope*), the *Galatea* and the anti-aircraft cruiser *Coventry*. Of flotilla vessels there was with this fleet a total of twenty-six destroyers of the 1st, 2nd, 4th and 21st Flotillas, four escort vessels, ten submarines and four minesweepers. The fleet was made to some extent self-reliant by the presence of the repair ship *Resource* and the depot ships *Woolwich* and *Maidstone*, which served the destroyers and submarines respectively, besides auxiliary vessels for the carriage of stores, fuel and ammunition. The insecurity of the peace-time base at Malta and the lack of

---

[1] See Map 2 (*facing p. 43*).

MEDITERRANEAN AND CHINA STATIONS

adequate base facilities at Alexandria made it essential for the Mediterranean Fleet to be as self-supporting as possible. The Admiralty had been forced reluctantly to accept that, in the event of war with Italy, the Mediterranean Fleet would not be able to use Malta as a main base. They had pressed for it to be defended as strongly as possible; but the Army and Air Force held that, with Sicily only sixty miles away, it was impossible to defend it effectively, and to try to do so might mean wasting some of our already inadequate air defences. In July 1939, however, authority was given to increase the gun defences; but very little had been done by the time Italy came into the war. In September the only ships which stayed on at Malta were seven submarines, twelve motor torpedo-boats, together with their depot ships, and a small minelayer. Their purpose was to harry the Italian communications to Libya. Small numbers of minesweepers were stationed at Alexandria, Haifa, Port Said and Malta, and three destroyers of the 21st flotilla had been passed into the Red Sea to strengthen the protection of the route past the Italian East African bases.[1] As soon, however, as Italy's intentions to remain neutral were clear, the greater part of Admiral Cunningham's forces was transferred to other theatres, and his fleet was not reinforced to a strength approaching that of September 1939 until a few weeks before Italy entered the war.

On the China Station (Commander-in-Chief, Admiral Sir Percy Noble) were four cruisers of the 5th Cruiser Squadron (*Kent, Cornwall, Birmingham* and *Dorsetshire*) and one division of the 21st Destroyer Flotilla, the remainder of which had been transferred to the Red Sea, the submarine depot ship *Medway* and the 4th Submarine Flotilla (fifteen boats). In the East Indies (Commander-in-Chief, Rear-Admiral R. Leatham) were three cruisers of the 4th Cruiser Squadron (*Gloucester, Liverpool* and *Manchester*) and seven escort vessels, of which five were manned by the Royal Indian Navy.

The Dominion navies were, on the outbreak of war, chiefly in their home waters, though the loan of their ships to the various theatres where active operations were in progress was to start almost immediately. The Royal Australian Navy consisted at this time of the cruisers *Canberra* (flagship of Rear-Admiral W. N. Custance), *Australia, Sydney, Hobart* and the much older *Adelaide*, all of whom were in or near their home waters, and the *Perth* which, as has been mentioned, had joined the 8th Cruiser Squadron in the West Indies. There were also five destroyers, which were later to join the Mediterranean Fleet, and two escort vessels. The two cruisers *Leander* and *Achilles* of the New Zealand Division of the Royal Navy were working on the South Pacific trade routes and the six destroyers of

---

[1] See Maps 26 and 34 (*facing pp. 293 and 426*).

the Royal Canadian Navy were divided between the east and west coasts of that Dominion.

The effective strength of the naval forces available to the British Empire on the outbreak of war was as follows:—

Table 2. British Empire—Effective Naval Strength, 1939

Battleships and battle cruisers	12
Aircraft carriers	6
Seaplane carriers	2
Fleet cruisers	35
Trade route or convoy cruisers	23
Fleet destroyers	100
Escort destroyers and sloops	101
Submarines	38

Though the greater part of this strength was concentrated in the two primary strategic areas already mentioned, a considerable proportion —especially of cruisers and escort vessels—was divided among the foreign commands.[1] In addition to the numbers given above, certain reinforcements were expected to arise from refits being finished and from the current naval building programmes; but the former was unlikely to bring any real gain in strength, because other ships would almost certainly have to take their place in the refitting yards. However, the battleship *Valiant* and the heavy cruiser *Suffolk* were expected to return to the fleet before the end of 1939.

Turning now to new construction, the first of the five battleships of the *King George V* class was not expected to be ready until the end of 1940, and only two of the six fleet carriers of the *Illustrious* class would be completed during that year. New cruisers were expected in better numbers since, of the twenty-one building, about half were due to complete in 1940. Thirty fleet destroyers and twenty of the smaller 'Hunt' class were on order, but few deliveries of these sorely-needed ships were expected for another year. Substantial additional orders for cruisers, destroyers, submarines and smaller vessels were placed on the outbreak of war, but no results could be expected from this emergency programme for many months to come.[2]

The arrangement whereby responsibility for the western Mediterranean was accepted by our French allies has already been mentioned. In addition to this the French Admiralty agreed to form and maintain a 'Force de Raid', consisting of its two newest battle cruisers, the *Dunkerque* and *Strasbourg*, one aircraft carrier, three

---

[1] Appendix E gives the distribution of the British Empire's naval strength in September 1939.

[2] Particulars of the First War Emergency Building Programme are given in Appendix F.

cruisers and ten destroyers, to work from Brest against enemy warship raiders in the eastern Atlantic. The general disposition of the principal units of the French Fleet at this time was as follows:—

Table 3. *French Fleet—General Disposition, 1939*

Station	Battleships and battle cruisers	Aircraft carriers	Cruisers	Large destroyers	Destroyers	Submarines
English Channel	—	—	—	—	7	—
Bay of Biscay	—	—	—	3	—	—
North Atlantic ('Force de Raid')	2	1	3	1	9	—
Mediterranean	3	1 (Seaplane carrier)	10	28	20	53
South Atlantic (Morocco)	—	—	—	—	2	4
Far East	—	—	2	—	5 or 6	2

It will make the enemy's naval plans and intentions clearer if the story of the rebirth and growth of the German Navy after its surrender in 1918 is first briefly traced. By the Treaty of Versailles its strength was limited to 15,000 men, but attempts to circumvent the terms of that treaty appeared very rapidly. For example, naval organisations were incorporated under cover in civil ministries, orders to destroy coastal fortifications were never carried out and the efforts of the Allied Control Commission to enforce the treaty were repeatedly frustrated.

Between 1920 and 1921 the transitional German Navy became the permanent service once again and regular exercises and visits abroad were arranged. Though new construction was limited by the virulent inflation of the currency then in progress, treaty evasion continued; orders were even placed for submarines to be built in Spain and Finland. The years from 1920 to 1924 marked the rebirth of the German Navy, but it was in the next period, from 1925 to 1932, that serious reconstruction was started. Admiral Zenker was in command for the first part of this phase, but before it ended he was succeeded by Admiral Raeder, whose part in Germany's second assault on our seaborne trade was to be very great. In 1925 the new cruiser *Emden* was launched and a large building programme was started. The first of the pocket-battleships, which were later to cause us much anxiety, was laid down in 1928. The building of U-boats abroad continued and crews for them were trained under the guise of receiving anti-submarine instruction. Preparations were even made to build up a naval air arm. The years 1933 to 1939, still under Admiral Raeder's supreme command, marked the period of rapid expansion. Although a pretence of limiting armaments was kept up until 1935, Admiral Raeder was in fact given a free hand to press on with reconstruction as soon as Hitler and the National Socialist Party had seized power. On the 16th of March 1935 the Treaty of Versailles was publicly repudiated, and on the following 18th of June the Anglo-German naval agreement was signed. By this treaty the Germans agreed to limit their naval construction to thirty-five per cent. of British strength except in submarines. They were accorded the right to build up to parity in submarine tonnage, but agreed not to exceed forty-five per cent. unless 'a situation arose which in their opinion made it necessary'.[1] Towards the end of 1936 Germany joined with other Powers in denouncing submarine war on merchant shipping in accordance with the London Protocol, which had been signed in November of that year.[2] But the sincerity of this declaration by Hitler did not exceed that of any other of his avowals, and the entire Anglo-German agreement was finally abrogated by him on the 26th of April 1939.

The first fruits of the 1935 naval negotiations were a large increase in German naval personnel. Covert organisations were openly revealed and the merchant navy was also prepared for war. Admiral Raeder and his staff now had to choose between two alternative policies. Either they could build up to the agreed proportions of British strength on the assumption that war would break out in about 1940, and aim to reach their full permitted strength by that date; or they could assume that war would be deferred for some years and embark on a longer-term programme whilst accepting a weaker fleet during the intervening years. As Hitler assured his naval advisers that no war would take place before 1944 or 1945 the second alternative was adopted in general. A short-term plan was, however, made to provide against the possibility of war with France only. The battle cruisers *Scharnhorst* and *Gneisenau* were thus built as answers to the new French ships *Dunkerque* and *Strasbourg* of the same class.[3] Raeder's choice of the long-term plan, combined with Hitler's miscalculation of the date when war would break out, was to have very lucky consequences for ourselves. It caused Germany to lose much of the advantage gained by the Anglo-German naval agreement and had the result that, in 1939, the German Navy was actually below its permitted strength. The German Naval Staff intended to allocate the agreed tonnage of capital ships to the three pocket-battleships, the two battle cruisers already mentioned and three new battleships. As

---

[1] Cmd. 4953. Treaty Series No. 22 (H.M.S.O., 1935). *State Papers*, Vol. XXIV.

[2] Oppenheim. *International Law*, 7th ed., ed. H. Lauterpacht, Vol. II (1952) p. 491.

[3] The German Navy always referred to the *Scharnhorst* and *Gneisenau* as battleships. As, however, they resembled our own and the French battle cruisers in speed, were much faster than our battleships and were regarded as battle cruisers by the Admiralty that classification has been retained throughout these volumes.

soon as Hitler abrogated the Anglo-German agreement four more battleships were ordered. Thus it was not until 1939 that full-scale naval preparations for war with Britain were started; and the resulting new construction could not be completed before 1942 at the earliest. A second and almost equally serious failure in German naval planning was that a destroyer force adequate to serve and protect the new heavy ships was not built; but this was caused more by constant changes in design and by technical difficulties with new equipment than by deliberate policy. It thus happened that when war actually broke out the German Navy was far less well prepared for it than the German Air Force.

It is important to realise that had the outbreak of war been deferred in accordance with Hitler's promise, and the long-term building plan thus been completed, the German fleet would indeed have been of formidable strength. It would have possessed no less than thirteen battleships, thirty-three cruisers, four aircraft carriers, some 250 U-boats and a large number of destroyers, almost all of which would have been of modern design. The threat to Britain which such a fleet would have constituted is not pleasant to contemplate, particularly when the age of the majority of our own warships is remembered. Hitler's wrong estimate of the date when war would break out may therefore be considered one of his more important mistakes, since it forced Admiral Raeder to abandon the long-term programme of building a balanced fleet and obliged him to build what he could use quickly to strike against our shipping. The German programme also included the conversion of a number of merchant ships into fast, heavily armed raiders. These were to cause us trouble enough and it was fortunate that these conversions, although a small threat compared with what the long-term German fleet would have become, did not start until after the outbreak of war.

The miscalculation by Hitler already referred to must have become clear to his advisers when, on the 3rd of April 1939, he ordered his armed forces to make ready for an attack on Poland in the following autumn. On the 10th of May the Navy and Air Force were told to prepare for the immediate opening of war on British shipping. The plans of the German Naval Staff will therefore now be studied.

The Battle Instructions for the German Navy, issued in May 1939, started with the premise that the war would be fought against Britain and France in the west and against one opponent, who might be Russia or Poland, in the east. Russia was, of course, temporarily eliminated as a possible enemy by the Russo-German pact signed in the following August. This released certain German naval forces from the Baltic.

The tasks of the German Navy were summarised as being the protection of their coasts, the defence of their own and attack on the enemy's sea communications, the support of land and air operations along the coast and service as a 'politico-strategic instrument of war to ensure, for example, the neutrality of the Scandinavian countries'. No mention was made of the possibility of waging war on the basis of a maritime strategy. In fact, because of the change of Hitler's intentions, the Germans did not possess the necessary strength; and the inadequacy of the navy to perform even the restricted duties allocated to it was admitted in the phrase 'the Navy is faced with a task for which its present development does not correspond'. The original organisation which the German Navy proposed to adopt in war was to establish, under the Supreme Commander (Admiral Raeder), two principal naval commands. They were to be known as the Naval Group Commanders, East and West, and their flags would be flown ashore at Swinemünde in the Baltic (later changed to Kiel) and at Wilhelmshaven respectively. There were also to be two Commanders-in-Chief for the same two theatres in command of the sea-going forces; their flags would be flown afloat but, after the pact with Russia had been signed, the post of Commander-in-Chief, East, was left unfilled.

The German U-boat fleet was commanded by Commodore Dönitz, who was stationed at first in the Baltic but moved back to Wilhelmshaven at the end of August, when it became clear that the war with Poland would spread westwards.

Since Russian neutrality greatly simplified the problems of the German eastern commands, it is not necessary to deal with their responsibilities beyond saying that they were to control the entrances to the Baltic and to secure the communications within that sea. The problems facing the western commands were, however, acute. To protect German shipping in the North Sea was admitted to be impossible 'because England . . . can and will strangle [these communications] . . . in the shortest possible time'. The attempt to do so was therefore abandoned in favour of making 'forces available . . . for offensive action against the enemy's supply lines' which 'can be successfully attacked only on the oceans'.

It can thus be seen that the German intentions corresponded closely to the appreciation made in the Admiralty's war plans. The German Naval Staff also anticipated correctly that 'England will choose . . . an open blockade' and that close blockade of the German coast was not practicable. Neither side seems to have realised at this time that air power had restored much of the old possibilities of close blockade. The German plans accepted that their forces would 'be excluded from the Channel in a very short time', which made the northern area of the North Sea the 'decisive point of the war at sea'. Their aims in this area were to be, firstly, 'constant disturbance of English operations in building up their blockade'; secondly, to afford 'assistance to the conduct of war in the Atlantic by keeping as many enemy forces as possible tied up' and, thirdly, to achieve 'occasional brief opening of the blockade for passage by Atlantic combat forces'. Permanent maritime supremacy could not be obtained in the northern North Sea, but they would try to compensate for this by 'intensive small-scale warfare, surprise attacks on weaker units' and to accumulate minor successes by 'constant harassing action'.

After outlining their objects in the North Sea the German plans turned to ocean warfare where, it was stated, 'the task . . . is war on merchant shipping'. The instructions then lay down that 'combat action even against inferior enemy naval forces is not an aim in itself and is therefore not to be sought. Even slight damage can decrease the effectiveness and the cruising endurance of our merchant raiders'. German surface forces were, therefore, to operate on the oceans. War on shipping in coastal waters was stated to be 'the prerogative of U-boats', and attacks on ports and bases were left to the German Air Force.

To help the surface vessels' work, supply ships were to be sent out before the outbreak of war, and efforts would be made 'to establish the necessary fuel and arms supplies by means of a secret organisation which was to be built up by German agents 'with the help of benevolent neutrals'. The ocean raiders were recommended to make sudden appearances in widely separated areas, followed by 'withdrawal into the ocean wastes'. Such conduct was considered to be particularly necessary in the Atlantic where the British reaction was expected to be 'especially lively'.

Minefields were to be declared in the Baltic and in the approaches to the Heligoland Bight, but shortages of mines necessitated strict economy in their use.[1] It is interesting to find that the German Naval Staff expected us to strengthen our control of the northern exit by again laying a barrage of mines right across the North Sea. Their view of the effect of this measure was indicated by the statement that 'this . . . would make the northern sortie practically impassable for us'. They do not seem to have remembered that the completion of the barrage towards the end of the previous war had only been made possible by the enormous number of mines produced in America, and that such a requirement for mines could not possibly have been met by ourselves for many months after war had been declared. Furthermore, the German Staff appears to have overlooked the fact that the barrage had actually caused them insignificant losses in the 1914–18 war.

The Germans anticipated that British maritime power would interrupt their communications across the Atlantic very quickly; that our open blockade would be maintained from a 'cutting off

---
[1] See Map 10 (*facing p. 97*).

position' between the Shetland Islands and Norway; that we should successfully close the Channel and carry out air attacks on their naval bases and minelaying operations in the Heligoland Bight. All these operations did, in fact, have their place in the British war plans. The Commander-in-Chief, West, was therefore instructed to take energetic action against the 'cutting off position' and to consider investing the approaches to our bases with mines laid by U-boats.

The submarine war on trade was, initially, to be carried out in areas where surface raiders could not work. Though the Germans do not seem to have obtained any knowledge of the performance of our asdic, respect was shown for 'the increased effectiveness of anti-submarine defences'. Operations in widely separated focal areas such as off the North American coast, in the West Indies, off the Cape Verde Islands and in the Bay of Biscay were therefore deemed to offer the best prospects of success. For various reasons, among which the desire to avoid friction with the United States played a part, German U-boats did not in fact work in the western Atlantic until many months later. Finally the plans expressed the intention to send U-boats to their operational areas before war had been declared, and this was actually done towards the end of August 1939.

Some mention must be made of the attitude of the German Naval Staff towards International Law as set out in the various Hague Conventions governing war at sea. Although all naval vessels and aircraft were required 'for the present' to wage war in accordance with these rules, the fundamental cynicism of the German attitude was expressed in the sentence: 'it therefore goes without saying that effective ... fighting methods will never fail to be employed merely because some international regulations ... are opposed to them'. The rapid changes in the German adherence to the rules of International Law and, in particular, their progress towards unrestricted U-boat warfare will be told as they took place. Here it is only necessary to state that German records leave no doubt that it was Admiral Raeder's steady pressure to obtain removal of the initial restrictions which led to the opening of virtually unrestricted war on merchant shipping very much earlier than had occurred in the war of 1914–18.

The allocation of German naval forces to accomplish the plans and objects outlined above must now be considered. Under the Commander-in-Chief, West, were placed the two battle cruisers *Scharnhorst* and *Gneisenau*, the pocket-battleship *Admiral Scheer*, the cruisers *Admiral Hipper* and *Leipzig*, three divisions of destroyers, the 1st U-boat flotilla (nine boats) and minor vessels for patrol purposes, local defence and minesweeping.[1] Nine naval air squadrons (about 100 aircraft) were also placed under his command. To the Eastern

---

[1] Particulars of all major German warships are given in Appendix G.

ALLOCATION OF GERMAN NAVAL FORCES, 1939

Command were assigned the cruisers *Nürnberg* (flagship) and *Köln*, four divisions of destroyers, two torpedo-boat flotillas and some minor war vessels. Certain other ships, including the cruiser *Königsberg*, were to be added after they had completed other initial duties. The Naval Staff retained direct operational control of two of the three pocket-battleships—the *Deutschland* (renamed *Lützow* in November 1939) and the *Admiral Graf Spee*—and also of three flotillas, totalling about twenty-two U-boats.

As regards ships under construction or projected for the German Navy, mention has already been made of Admiral Raeder's long-term intentions—the Z Plan—and it has been told how they came to be abandoned. On the outbreak of war there were, however, certain major warships being built for the German Navy which had been ordered before the birth of the Z Plan. The chief of these were the two very formidable battleships *Bismarck* and *Tirpitz*, whose construction had been started in 1936; these ships, though supposed to conform to the limiting displacement of 35,000 tons agreed by treaty between the major naval powers, actually displaced about 42,500 tons—some twenty per cent. larger than their announced size.[1]

As they mounted eight 15-inch guns in their main armaments, had a maximum speed of some twenty-eight knots and were very heavily protected, they outclassed even the new 14-inch gun battleships of the *King George V* class then building in this country, which conformed strictly to treaty limitations. In July 1939 the German Admiralty expected both ships to be completed before the end of 1940. The new aircraft carrier *Graf Zeppelin* was expected to commission for service in the middle of the same year.

The 8-inch cruisers *Blücher* and *Prinz Eugen*, which were sister ships of the *Hipper*, were also expected to be ready in the middle of 1940, and two more ships of the same class were also on the stocks. These were the *Seydlitz*, due to complete in the autumn of 1940, and the *Lützow* which was not expected to be ready before the end of 1941, and which was finally transferred to Russia in an uncompleted state in February 1940.[2] These cruisers, though their main armaments were the same in calibre and number as the British 'Washington

---

[1] As some confusion exists over the methods of computing the displacement of warships, it should be mentioned that displacements agreed in the Washington and other treaties were interpreted as standard displacements, which are the deep load displacements less the weight of fuel and reserve feed-water. The actual displacement of a ship of normal endurance on putting to sea is, therefore, some 20 to 30 per cent greater than the standard displacement. In these volumes all displacements given are standard unless specifically stated to the contrary.

[2] This ship must not be confused with the pocket-battleship *Lützow* which was the renamed *Deutschland* (see this page, above). The cruiser *Lützow* was, as agreed in the Moscow Pact discussions of August 1939, transferred to Russia and actually sailed from Bremen on 15th April 1940. The sale to Russia of the cruisers *Seydlitz* and *Prinz Eugen* and of the turrets of two battleships of the Z Plan was also discussed but finally refused by Hitler at his conference on 8th December 1939.

Treaty' 8-inch cruisers of 10,000 tons displacement, actually outclassed them in size, speed and protection. Though supposed to conform to treaty limitations they were, in fact, of 14,475 tons standard displacement and 18,500 tons at deep load—nearly half as big again as our own ships of the same class.

Whilst dealing with the deception practised by the Germans over the size of their new warships it is relevant to mention that the two battle cruisers *Scharnhorst* and *Gneisenau*, which were already in service, and which purported to be smaller than our own battle cruisers, and had a relatively light armament of nine 11-inch guns as against the 15-inch weapons in the British ships, actually exceeded their published displacement (26,000 tons) by about 6,000 tons. This enabled them to be heavily protected and reduced their inequality compared with the *Hood*, *Repulse* and *Renown*. Moreover, they were actually capable of a speed of thirty-one knots at deep load in smooth water, whereas the Admiralty believed their maximum speed to be only twenty-seven and a half knots. They could, therefore, outrun our battle cruisers if the need arose.

From the foregoing summary of Germany's naval strength on the outbreak of war it will be seen that, although greatly inferior to the British fleet in numbers, the German Navy consisted almost entirely of modern warships. The Royal Navy, on the other hand, was still equipped with a large number of ships whose design dated back to the 1914–18 war. Some had been modernised, others had not. But the age of the British ships and of their weapons, taken with the Navy's world-wide responsibility for the defence of our shipping, went a long way towards counteracting our superiority in numbers.

We may complete the story of the German naval plans and preparations by mentioning the dispositions taken up as tension mounted during the latter part of August 1939. The majority of naval vessels was concentrated in defence of their own coasts and in support of the invasion of Poland. On the 21st of August the *Graf Spee* sailed to her waiting position in the Atlantic, and three days later she was followed by the *Deutschland*. Their attendant supply ships *Altmark* and *Westerwald* were also despatched into the Atlantic. Complete secrecy regarding these movements was successfully maintained and they were not, in fact, known to the Admiralty until much later. By an unlucky chance the North Sea air reconnaissance patrols, which had been operating during the final peace-time exercises between the 15th and 21st of August, had stopped during these few days; but the use of darkness by the enemy and the limitations of these patrols made sighting unlikely even had they been flying.[1]

At the end of August the total German strength in U-boats was

---
[1] See pp. 37–38.

fifty-six, but ten of them were, for various reasons, not fully operational. Of the total of completed boats eight were of about 700 tons displacement and capable of operating as far as Gibraltar or the Azores; eighteen were smaller ocean-going boats of 500 tons which could reach out into the Atlantic as far as 15° West or work off the coasts of Spain or Portugal, and thirty were small 250-ton boats which could only be used in the North Sea and in British coastal waters. A very high proportion of the total strength was thus operational at the outbreak of war; but the U-boat Command expected that it would be impossible to maintain this high ratio for long.

It is interesting to compare the size of the pre-war German U-boat fleet as now known to us with the contemporary Admiralty assessment of its strength. Two days after war broke out the Director of Naval Intelligence informed the First Sea Lord that they had completed thirty coastal and twenty-nine ocean-going boats—three more than the correct total.

Between the 19th and 29th of August seventeen ocean-going U-boats sailed to their war stations in the Atlantic. On the 21st seven coastal-type boats took up stations in the southern North Sea ready to lay mines off the British and French Channel ports. They were joined by another on the 29th. On the 25th six more coastal boats sailed to patrol in the central North Sea. By the last day of August 1939 no less than thirty-nine U-boats were disposed to strike at our shipping and ports as soon as war broke out.

It will be seen from the foregoing figures that on the outbreak of war the German U-boat strength was only one less than the British total of fifty-seven operational submarines. The rapidity with which the Germans had increased their strength from the forty-five per cent. agreed in 1935 leaves no doubt regarding the advanced state of their plans and preparations for large-scale U-boat construction even before their intention to invoke the parity clause of the 1935 agreement was announced in 1938.

Though the Z Plan had been abandoned, the provision for U-boat construction which it had contained (162 boats by 1943 and 247 by 1948) formed the basis of the proposals now put forward to expand that arm. Dönitz realised that the strength possessed in 1939 was inadequate for his purposes, and that the numbers then building lent no hope of his being able to launch a decisive assault on our trade in the foreseeable future. For that purpose he assessed the need at 300 ocean-going boats. Admiral Raeder gave his support to these proposals with the result that, shortly after the declaration of war, Hitler approved a substantial increase in the number of boats to be completed in 1940 and a higher target for 1941. The Navy, however, considered the increases inadequate and, in October 1939, prepared plans to build up to U.850 and to achieve a monthly production of nearly thirty boats. Hitler approved, but refused to give absolute priority for materials to the programme. The result was that little progress was made.

In December 1939 Raeder produced modified proposals which aimed at a total of 372 boats by the beginning of 1942, but no decision had been taken six months later to implement even this less ambitious programme. The reason probably was that Hitler still hoped that Britain would make peace when she saw that Germany had conquered most of western Europe. Not until July 1940 did Hitler lift all restrictions on U-boat construction and so enable the Navy to place orders for about twenty-five boats to be completed monthly in 1941; and it was August of that year before U-boat building really got into its stride. The slowness with which the Germans expanded their U-boat construction was to have most fortunate consequences for Britain.

Before leaving the subject of the German Navy's strength and dispositions on the outbreak of war, it is perhaps desirable to add a few words about our principal enemy's position as regards maritime aircraft. In January 1939 the German Navy and Air Force agreed that the former should eventually have forty-one *Staffeln*, each of twelve aircraft, under its control. Nine *Staffeln* were to be equipped with flying boats for long-range reconnaissance, eighteen were to be of general-purpose types like the Heinkel 115, two were of shipborne catapult aircraft and the remaining twelve comprised the aircraft complement of the *Graf Zeppelin*; but this strength, 492 aircraft in all, had not nearly been reached when war broke out. The German Navy then actually possessed 120 aircraft at North Sea bases and 108 more in the Baltic—a total almost exactly equal to the Royal Navy's first-line air strength.[1] There were also six *Gruppen* (Wings) of Heinkel 111 bombers belonging to the German Air Force, which were earmarked for maritime operations against Britain such as minelaying and attacks on shipping. The first of the new Junkers 88 bombers had also been allocated to those purposes, but only a few had entered service by September 1939.

The Admiralty's war plans were, as has been mentioned, based on the assumption that Italy would join in the war at an early date, but as this did not happen until nearly a year later a description of the Italian Navy's intentions in the event of war with Britain and France will be deferred for the present. As, however, uncertainty regarding Italian intentions influenced Allied dispositions and strategy from the beginning of the war, it will be appropriate to summarise now the composition of their Navy and to compare it with the British

---

[1] See p. 32.

and French forces initially available to contest command of the Mediterranean.

Only the two old, though modernised, battleships of the *Cavour* class were in service in September 1939, but it was expected that the modernisation of the other two ships of the same class would be completed in 1940 and that the two new 35,000-ton battleships *Littorio* and *Vittorio Veneto* would enter service in the same year. Meanwhile the Italians were outnumbered by the three British and five French battleships in the Mediterranean, but as two of the latter were too old to be counted as effective capital ships the real Allied superiority was less than appears at first sight and would disappear altogether when the Italians had completed their 1940 programme. In 8-inch cruisers seven Italian ships were outnumbered by the three British and six French ships of the same class, but in 6-inch cruisers the Italians were superior, having eleven ships against three British and four French. Turning to flotilla vessels, sixty-one Italian destroyers and sixty-six torpedo boats could reasonably be balanced against a combined British and French strength of fifty-seven fleet destroyers and two dozen of smaller types. In submarines, however, of which the Italians had 105 compared with ten British and fifty-five French, they possessed a marked superiority inside the Mediterranean. It will thus be seen that, as long as a powerful proportion of the French fleet continued in the western basin, some grounds existed for the Italians to regard themselves as outnumbered at sea; but the excellent central position which their fleet occupied might justly have been considered as counter-balancing whatever may be regarded as the true numerical inferiority from which they suffered.[1]

---

[1] For full details of the Italian Navy see Appendix H.

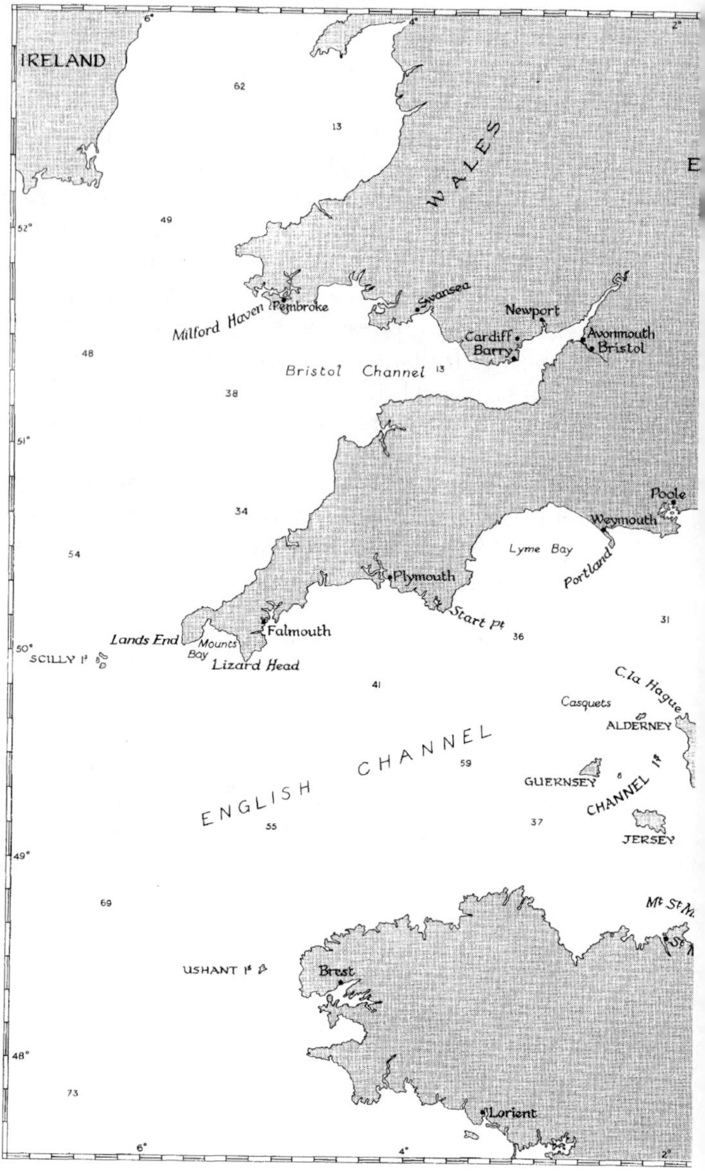

IRELAND
WALES
E
Milford Haven
Pembroke
Swansea
Newport
Cardiff
Barry
Avonmouth
Bristol
Bristol Channel
Poole
Weymouth
Lyme Bay
Portland
Plymouth
Start Pt
Falmouth
Lands End
Mounts Bay
Lizard Head
SCILLY Is
C. la Hague
Casquets
ALDERNEY
GUERNSEY
CHANNEL Is
JERSEY
ENGLISH CHANNEL
USHANT Is
Brest
Lorient

Map 3
THE ENGLISH CHANNEL
USHANT to TEXEL

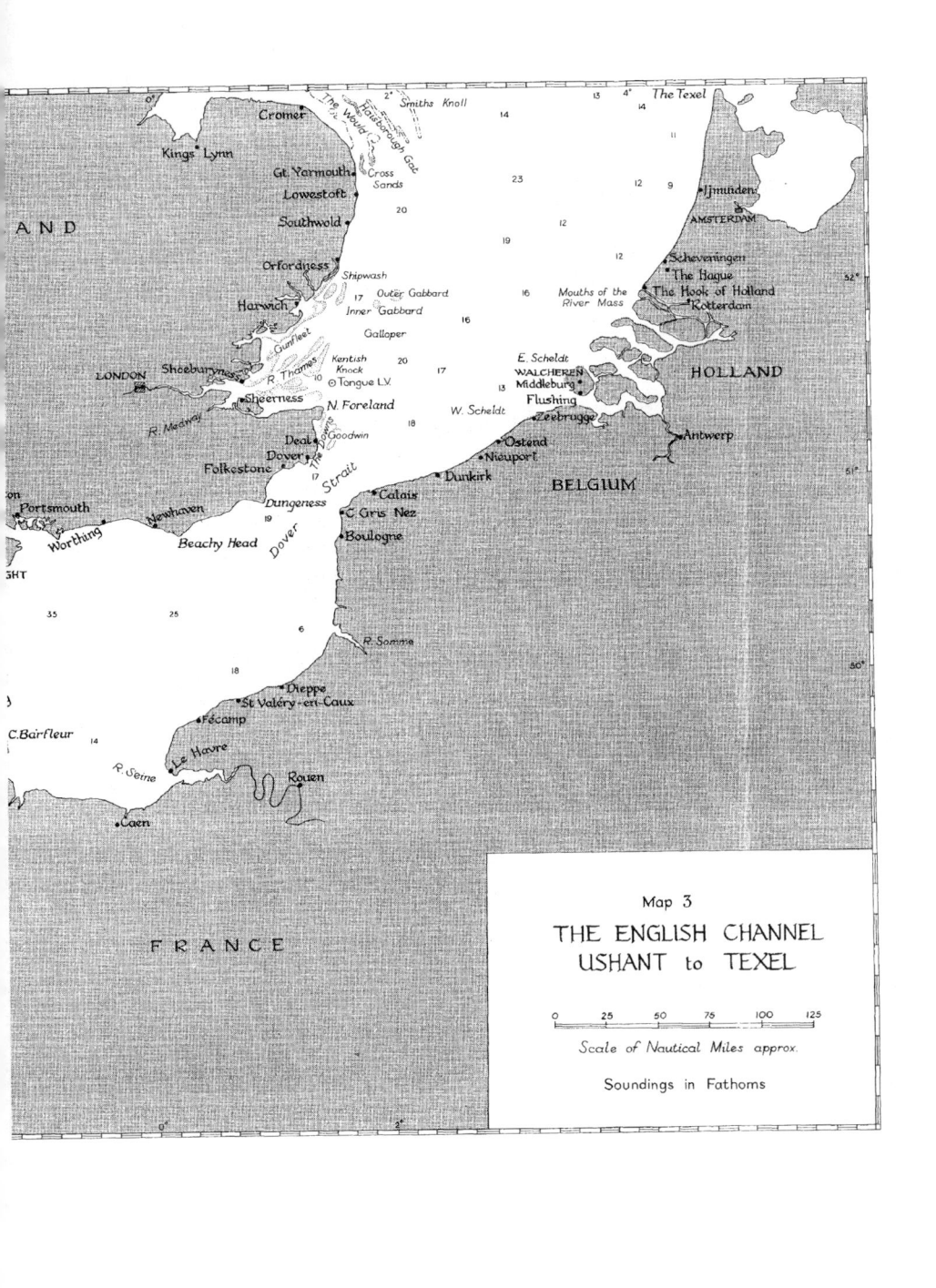

Scale of Nautical Miles approx.

Soundings in Fathoms

CHAPTER V

OPENING MOVES IN HOME WATERS

3rd September–31st December, 1939

> Of late years the world has become so deeply impressed with the efficacy of sea power that we are inclined to forget how impotent it is of itself to decide a war against great continental states, how tedious is the pressure of naval action unless it be nicely co-ordinated with military and diplomatic pressure.
>
> J. S. Corbett. *England and the Seven Years' War* (1907).

SINCE one of the first charges placed on the Royal Navy was the safe transport of the British Expeditionary Force and the Advanced Air Striking Force to the Continent we will first view that operation as complete in itself. The advanced parties sailed to Cherbourg from Portsmouth in destroyers of that command on the 4th of September. Owing to the likelihood of the enemy making air attacks on the ports of disembarkation the plans provided that no French ports east of Le Havre would be used except by hospital ships, which would use Dieppe, and by train ferries which would run to Dunkirk and Calais. On the 9th of September the first convoy of troopships sailed from Southampton and the Bristol Channel ports, and thereafter troopships and store convoys sailed regularly from Southampton, Avonmouth, Swansea, Barry and Newport. Escorts were provided by the local defence flotillas of the Portsmouth and Western Approaches commands and the whole operation was covered by the Channel Force, of which mention has already been made.[1] The first main landings took place at Cherbourg on the 10th of September and at Nantes and St. Nazaire two days later. Storeships were sent chiefly to Brest, Nantes and St Nazaire, and these ports as well as Cherbourg and Havre were used for vehicles as well.[2] By the 7th of October, 161,000 men, 24,000 vehicles and about 140,000 tons of stores had been transported without loss, and after the first few divisions had landed frequent maintenance and reinforcement convoys followed. There was virtually no enemy reaction

---

[1] See p. 45.
[2] See Maps 3 and 22 (*facing pp. 63 and 233*).

to this large movement. A few mines were laid off Dover and in Weymouth Bay, which were not among the ports of embarkation used for the British Expeditionary Force.

The movement of stores to the western ports of France placed a severe strain on shipping resources and on the escort forces. Moreover, it was desirable for military as well as for these naval reasons to make fuller use of the French Channel ports. The Admiralty repeatedly pressed this view, but the French, who were anxious not to invite air attacks on these ports, refused at first to agree. However, in October a start was made by sending cased petrol direct to Caen and in the following month a base was opened at Le Havre. Later still, stores were landed at Rouen, Fécamp, St Malo and Boulogne. Almost from the start of the movement rolling-stock and loaded wagons had been sent by train ferry to Calais and Dunkirk, but the conversion of two of the ferries to minelayers had slowed down this method of transport. In December leave traffic was started and the transport of 200,000 men each way during the next six months placed a new and heavy burden on the naval escort forces. By June 1940 about half a million men and 89,000 vehicles had been escorted across the narrow seas. The Portsmouth Command alone had sailed 731 transports and 304 laden convoys. Thus was complete control of the short sea communications to France planned and executed with entire success.

It has been told how, by the last day of August, all ships of the Home Fleet had moved or were moving to their war stations, while Coastal Command aircraft had started to fly the North Sea reconnaissance patrols. The fleet's watchful activity began that evening when Admiral Forbes went to sea from Scapa to patrol the waters between the Shetland Islands and Norway. The following day—the 1st of September—the Admiralty sent the first report of a possible movement by major enemy warships to Icelandic waters to await the outbreak of hostilities. Like so much of the early intelligence it was incorrect, although two pocket-battleships were, in fact, already waiting in the Atlantic.

When war was declared on the 3rd of September a blockade of Germany was immediately proclaimed, and the planned measures for the enforcement of contraband control by the fleet came into force. Submarine patrols off Horn Reef, in the approaches to the Kiel Canal and to Wilhelmshaven, off Terschelling and on the extension of the Montrose–Obrestadt air patrol line were fully manned from the flotillas based on Dundee and Blyth; the Humber force, consisting of the 6-inch cruisers *Southampton* and *Glasgow* and eight destroyers, was cruising off the Norwegian coast and the main body of the Home Fleet was at sea some 400 miles to the west of the Hebrides.[1]

On the 3rd of September Admiral Forbes carried out a sweep to

---
[1] See Maps 4 and 5 (*facing pp. 65 and 71*).

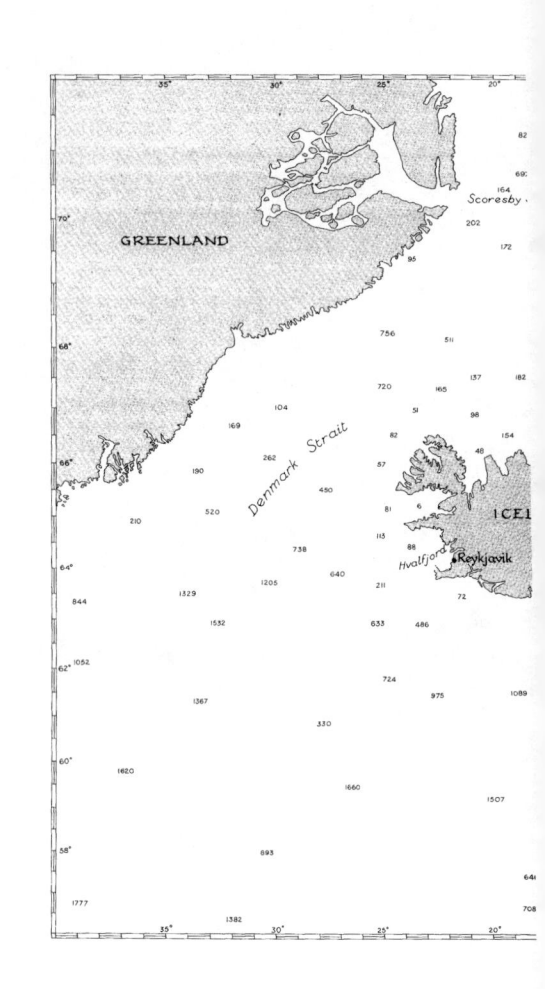

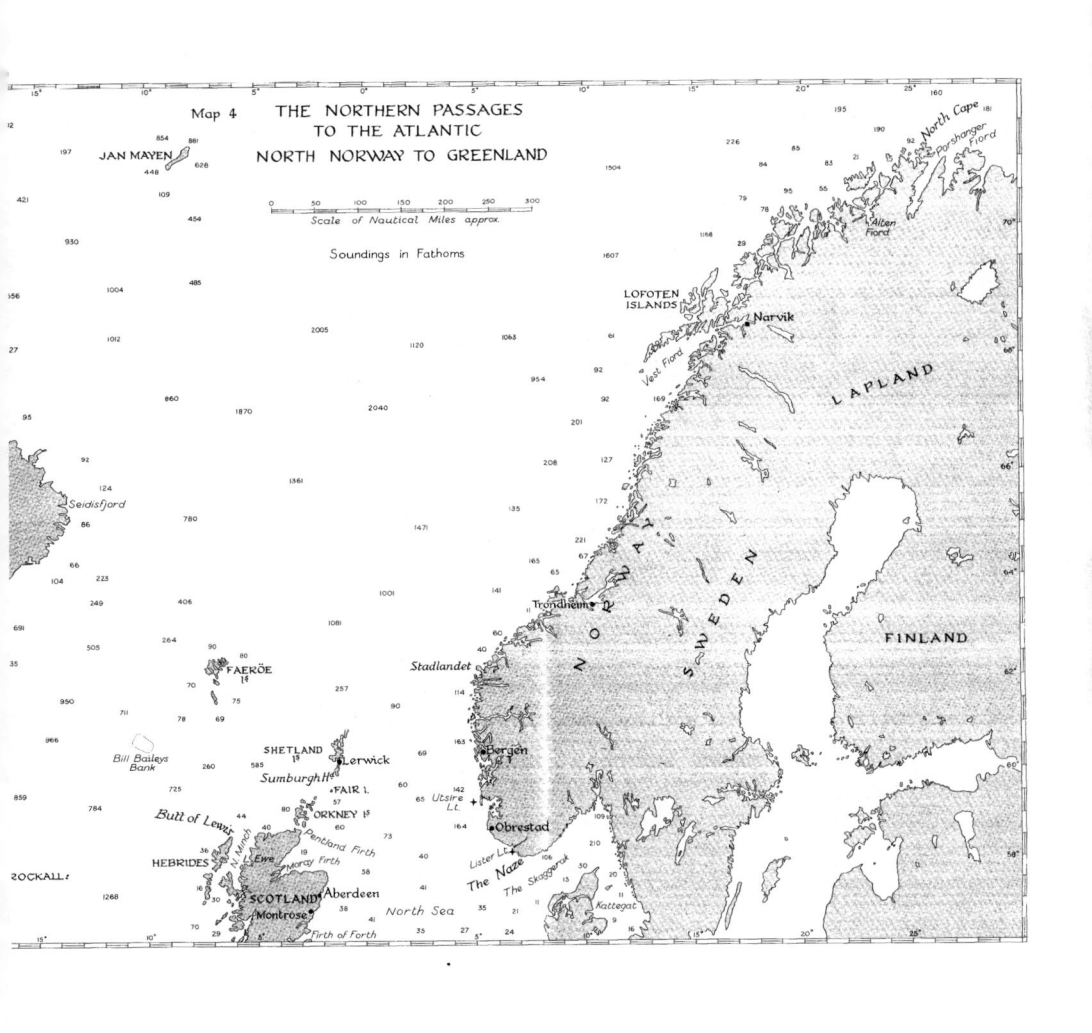

Map 4 THE NORTHERN PASSAGES TO THE ATLANTIC
NORTH NORWAY TO GREENLAND

the north in search of the liner *Bremen* which was known to be on passage home from New York. But, in fact, she had kept far to the north and had already reached Murmansk. On the evening of that day the Admiralty passed to the Commander-in-Chief a report that the German fleet was leaving Schillig Roads, and he therefore returned to the east through the Fair Isle Channel to the 'cutting off position' already described.[1] The fleet cruised to the east of the Orkneys, in thick fog, until the morning of the 6th of September when it returned to Scapa. On the next day Admiral Forbes sailed again with his main strength (the *Nelson, Rodney, Repulse,* the aircraft carrier *Ark Royal,* the cruisers *Aurora* and *Sheffield* and ten destroyers) for the Norwegian coast and patrolled as far north as 63° to intercept enemy merchant shipping. The battle cruisers *Hood* and *Renown,* two cruisers and four destroyers left Scapa a day later to patrol between Iceland and the Faeröe Islands, also with the object of enforcing our blockade measures. Partly on account of the bad visibility neither force accomplished anything, and they returned to Scapa on the 10th and 12th of September respectively. It should, however, be noted that these early operations of the Home Fleet in full strength were typical of the exercise of maritime power in both its positive and negative forms.[2] There was no period of 'twilight-war' for the fleet.

While the Home Fleet had thus been exercising its normal function of commanding the northern exits from the North Sea and covering the lighter forces on patrol, the first bomber attacks on the major units of the enemy fleet had taken place in the south.

At this time the policy of the Air Ministry, which the Cabinet had approved, was to build up and conserve the main strength of its bomber force for the onslaught on German industry. Apart from the few squadrons specially trained for pre-war bombing trials against a naval wireless-controlled target ship, no training in the search for warship targets, in their recognition or in the methods of attacking them had been carried out by Bomber Command. Though unwilling to dissipate its strength by small-scale attacks on what it believed to be secondary objectives—with which our naval forces were in any case prepared to deal—the Air Ministry was prepared to see what could be done against naval targets with a limited force. Moreover the policy regarding air bombardment, which had been agreed with the French Government before the war, was designed to avoid incurring the responsibility for initiating air attacks on the civil population. The most important shore targets could not, for this reason, be attacked.

Bombing the German fleet while at sea or in the open roadsteads of its bases—but not while in the dockyards—was, however, permitted. No time was lost in preparing for such an attack and, on the

---
[1] See pp. 55–56.
[2] See p. 4.

day war was declared, a Blenheim bomber, navigated by a naval observer, reconnoitred the Heligoland Bight and sighted warships apparently leaving harbour. A striking force of fifty-four bombers was despatched but failed to find the ships. Next day the same aircraft carried out a second reconnaissance and reported the presence of major warships in Schillig Roads, off Wilhelmshaven, and at Brunsbüttel at the western end of the Kiel Canal. Fourteen Wellington bombers formed the first wave of the striking force which was immediately sent out and fifteen Blenheims formed the second wave. The Wellingtons achieved no success and, although one aircraft attacked the *Scharnhorst* and *Gneisenau* at Brunsbüttel, neither ship was damaged. The cruiser *Emden*, lying off Wilhelmshaven, was attacked by Blenheims. She received some splinter damage from two bombs which exploded close to her and superficial damage from an aircraft which crashed into her, but the damage had been repaired and the ship was again fully operational twelve days later. The pocket-battleship *Scheer*, lying in Schillig Roads, was also attacked by Blenheims from low heights and was hit by three or four 250-pound bombs. Unfortunately none of these exploded—probably because the height from which the bombs were dropped was insufficient to work off the safety device of the bomb fuses. The ship was out of action only until the 10th of October. The Blenheims, of which five were shot down by anti-aircraft fire, had pressed home their attacks most gallantly, but the results achieved were not commensurate with the losses suffered. Fortunately the enemy bombers, as will be seen shortly, did no better in their early attacks on our own warships.

Meanwhile the Admiralty's plans to control the sea communications to these islands and to deny the seas to the enemy were taking effect in the north, though not entirely without difficulties and mishaps. The most serious of the latter occurred on the 10th of September when the submarine *Triton*, on patrol on the extension of the Montrose–Obrestadt air patrol line, torpedoed and sank the submarine *Oxley* which was similarly employed. To maintain correct position while on a diving patrol is a difficult task for submarines and both the boats involved in this tragic accident were, in fact, out of position. A repetition was narrowly averted on the 14th of September when the *Sturgeon* fired at the *Swordfish* but, happily, missed. As a precaution against further mishaps of this nature the distance between the submarines so employed was increased from twelve to sixteen miles. By the 20th of September replacement of the Ansons by Hudson aircraft enabled Coastal Command to cover the whole of this patrol line. The submarines were then withdrawn and employed on patrols in the Heligoland Bight, off Jutland, in the Skagerrak, off the Norwegian coast and to the west of the German declared minefield.[1]

---

[1] See Map 10 (*facing p. 97*).

The Northern Patrol, the principal weapon for the enforcement by the Home Fleet of our contraband control, started work on the 6th of September, but the shortage of cruisers and the age of the ships comprising the 7th and 12th Cruiser Squadrons kept the number of ships on patrol to an average of only two to the south of the Faeröes and three between the Faeröes and Iceland.[1] This was well below the strength considered necessary by Admiral Forbes. By the middle of October the conversion of liners to armed merchant cruisers had progressed, and as the first of the twenty-five allocated to the Northern Patrol began to arrive the density, and so the effectiveness, of those patrols was increased. It will be convenient to carry the story of the Northern Patrol on to the end of the year. In spite of the age and condition of the ships so employed and the extremely arduous conditions of service in those waters, many eastbound neutral ships whose destination might have been enemy ports, or whose cargoes might have contained contraband goods, were intercepted. The great majority of them was sent to the contraband control base at Kirkwall for examination. A steady toll was also taken of German merchant ships attempting to run the blockade. Most of these scuttled themselves to avoid capture, but in October the liner *Cap Norte* (13,000 tons), which was carrying reservists from South America to Germany, was successfully seized. The strength of the Northern Patrol—and so the degree of success achieved in enforcing the blockade—fluctuated considerably during this period. None the less, and in spite of the inevitable difficulties of enforcing a blockade with old or converted ships of indifferent sea-keeping quality in waters where bad weather or low visibility are normal rather than exceptional, the results achieved during this first phase of the war were substantial, as the following table shows.

Table 4. Northern Patrol—Ships Intercepted, September 1939–January 1940

Two-week period covered	Total number of ships sighted	Number of eastbound ships sighted	Number of ships sent in for examination (including prizes)	Number of ships entering voluntarily for examination	Number of German ships intercepted
7th–28th Sept.	108	62	28	No record available	1
29th Sept.–12th Oct.	64	26	20	,,	1
13th–26th Oct.	112	56	53	,,	6
27th Oct.–9th Nov.	79	26	20	,,	—
10th–23rd Nov.	93	57	50	,,	9
24th Nov.–7th Dec.	56	34	23	40	—
8th–21st Dec.	69	38	24	36	—
22nd Dec.–4th Jan.	95	43	35	21	—

[1] See Map 4 (*facing p. 65*).

On the 20th of December Vice-Admiral Sir Max Horton was relieved in command of the Northern Patrol by Vice-Admiral R. H. T. Raikes to become Vice-Admiral (Submarines), and during the same month the old cruisers of the C and D classes were transferred to theatres where the weather was less inclement.

Reverting now to the main strength of the fleet: on the 7th of September the Admiralty gave Admiral Forbes a greatly exaggerated estimate of the bomber strength available in north-west Germany for an attack on Scapa, and ordered a temporary base to be prepared on the west coast of Scotland. The Commander-in-Chief selected Loch Ewe and sent the *Guardian* there to lay anti-submarine nets. Between the 9th and 12th of the month the fleet flagship and other major warships arrived there, and prolonged discussions on the future of the fleet's bases began. Meanwhile the enemy's U-boat campaign had started and the Home Fleet was soon involved in attacks and counter-attacks. The sinking of U.39 by the *Ark Royal's* escorting destroyers on the 14th of September, after she had unsuccessfully attacked the aircraft carrier, was the first success in the latter category. On the same day aircraft from the same ship attacked U.30 with anti-submarine bombs. Not only were the bombs ineffective but two of the attacking aircraft were lost through dropping their bombs at such a low height that the explosions brought them down into the sea. The pilots were picked up and taken prisoner by their intended victim. On the 19th of September a report was received by Admiral Forbes that a U-boat was stopping and sinking fishing trawlers off the Butt of Lewis.[1] He at once sent ten destroyers and naval aircraft to hunt for her and the result was the sinking, next day, of U.27 and the capture of her crew. There was no doubt that, once asdic-fitted vessels knew where to seek their quarry and enough of them could be spared to do the job properly, a promptly executed hunt could achieve success—especially if aircraft were there to help.

The next important operation carried out by the Home Fleet was to cover an intended raid into the Skagerrak by the 2nd Cruiser Squadron (the *Southampton*, *Glasgow*, *Sheffield* and *Aurora*) and eight destroyers. Admiral Forbes sailed from Scapa on the 22nd of September, but a collision between two of the Humber Force destroyers caused the abandonment of the plan and the main fleet returned to its base on the 23rd. Two days later news was received that the submarine *Spearfish* had been badly damaged off Horn Reef and was unable to dive. Clearly she was in a position of grave danger. Admiral Forbes ordered the 2nd Cruiser Squadron and six destroyers to proceed at once to extricate her. The battle cruisers and the 18th Cruiser Squadron were ordered to act as cover and the heavy ships sailed at once in support. On the 26th the damaged submarine

---
[1] See Map 4 (*facing p. 65*).

FIRST AIR ATTACKS ON THE HOME FLEET

was met by the cruisers and destroyers and safely escorted to Rosyth. Meanwhile enemy flying-boats had started, at 11 a.m. on the 26th, to shadow the battleships and the *Ark Royal*; one of them was shot down by her Skuas. That afternoon a single enemy bomber attacked the *Ark Royal* and narrowly missed her with a dive-bombing attack from 6,000 feet. This led to the first of the many false enemy claims to have sunk this famous ship. Other dive attacks followed shortly, and the *Hood* received a glancing blow on the quarter from a heavy bomb which, however, caused no damage. The cruisers were subjected, shortly afterwards, to high-level attacks from 12,000 feet, but no hits were obtained. The attacks were quite unco-ordinated and no attempt was made to concentrate on the most important target present. The anti-aircraft gunfire of the fleet was, on this occasion, as ineffective as the bombing, and Admiral Forbes states in his despatch that 'the control personnel were obviously unprepared for such high performance dive-bombing'.

As ships completed refits or became available through re-dispositions ordered by the Admiralty, reinforcements were added to the Home Fleet during this period. Thus the cruisers *Norfolk* and *Newcastle* joined the 18th Cruiser Squadron on the 6th and 15th of September and the *Suffolk* joined the same squadron on the 1st of October to relieve the *Edinburgh*, which was transferred to the Humber Force. During the latter part of October the 3rd Destroyer Flotilla (nine of the I Class) and the 5th (eight of the K Class) were allocated to Admiral Forbes and at the end of that month the 3rd Submarine Flotilla (depot ship *Cyclops* and nine boats of the S Class) were attached to the Home Fleet. On the 7th of November the 4th Destroyer Flotilla from the Mediterranean joined, but four days later the Humber Force, consisting of four cruisers of the 2nd Cruiser Squadron, the 7th Destroyer Flotilla and four Tribal-class destroyers, were detached from Admiral Forbes to operate under Admiralty control in order to deal with a reported intention of the enemy to invade Holland by sea. Though this redisposition did not at the time seriously vitiate the Home Fleet's ability to control the northern exits, it was the first of many detachments of cruisers and flotilla vessels to the southern ports to deal with threats of invasion. The consequences of this policy will be discussed later.

An unexpected reinforcement of the Home Fleet submarines occurred on the 14th of October when the Polish boat *Orzel*, after making a most gallant escape from the Esthonian port in which she had been interned, evaded all the German forces searching for her and finally reached Rosyth. As her sister ship the *Wilk* and the destroyers *Blyskawica*, *Grom* and *Burza* had escaped to England at the time of the German invasion of Poland, most of the modern units of the Polish Navy escaped the enemy's clutches to join with the Royal Navy in continuing the fight. Their skill and gallantry were soon to earn them a great reputation. The final reinforcements of the year arrived early in December when the cruiser *Devonshire* (flying the flag of Vice-Admiral J. H. D. Cunningham) came back from the Mediterranean and her sister ship the *Berwick* from the West Indies. These two ships then formed, with the *Norfolk* and *Suffolk*, a homogeneous 1st Cruiser Squadron of four 8-inch gun cruisers.

But Admiral Forbes did not for long enjoy any real increase of strength: early in October the Admiralty received firm intelligence that a powerful enemy raider was at large in the South Atlantic and rapidly took steps to form a number of hunting groups, the details of which will be given in a later chapter, to seek out and destroy the raider and to afford additional protection to shipping in the focal areas where she was likely to work. Thus the *Ark Royal* and *Renown*, the heavy cruisers *Norfolk* and *Suffolk*, and also the *Effingham*, *Emerald* and *Enterprise*—the only Northern Patrol cruisers with satisfactory endurance—were all ordered abroad. The *Furious* at the same time replaced the *Ark Royal* as the fleet's only aircraft carrier. The presence of a second raiding pocket-battleship on our ocean trade routes was not known until the arrival at Kirkwall on the 21st of October of the crew of the Norwegian s.s. *Lorentz W. Hansen* which had been sunk by the *Deutschland* on the 14th. The day after this news was received the American s.s. *City of Flint* reached Murmansk with a prize crew from the same raider on board. The *City of Flint*, after leaving Murmansk, endeavoured to reach Germany through the inshore route (or 'Indreled') by which she could keep almost entirely inside Norwegian territorial waters, and an attempt to intercept her with the cruiser *Glasgow* and destroyers was unsuccessful. As the Norwegians interned the prize crew and the ship was turned over to their own flag the enemy gained no advantage from this attempted violation of Norwegian waters. But the Germans continued to use the 'Indreled' to their advantage; early in November the liner *New York* passed from Murmansk home to Germany by that route. As she was a merchant ship proceeding on a lawful voyage the Norwegians allowed her to pass.

The battle cruiser *Gneisenau*, the cruiser *Köln* and nine destroyers made a brief sortie from the 8th to the 10th of October. Their orders were to operate off the south coast of Norway, to attack any light forces met but to avoid contact with superior forces, to destroy British shipping and to try to entice the Home Fleet towards the Skagerrak where attacks by U-boats and aircraft could be made.

Admiral Forbes first heard of this sortie during the night of the 7th–8th of October and immediately brought the battle cruisers and light forces to short notice. At 1.20 p.m. on the 8th a reconnaissance aircraft of Coastal Command reported the force off Lister Light,

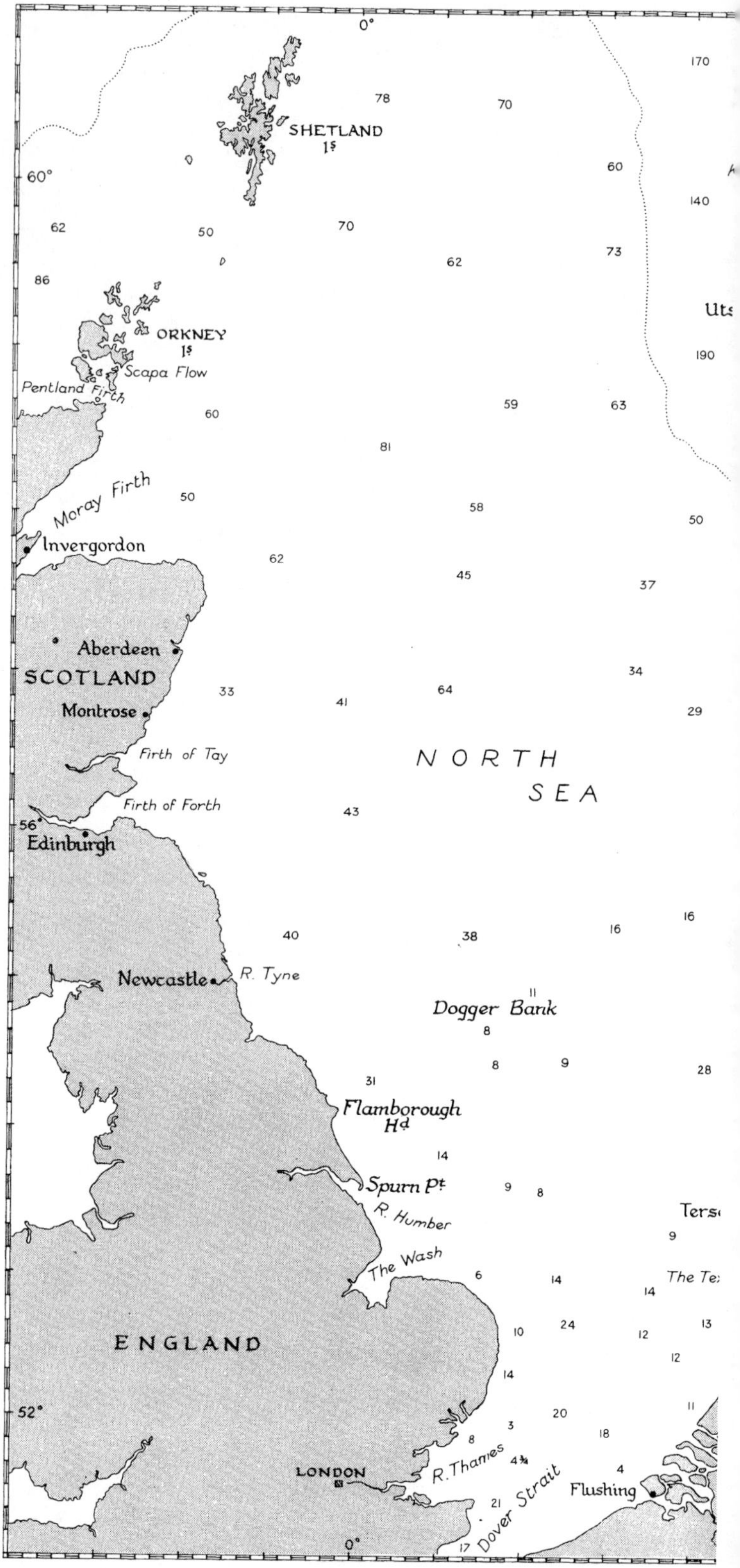

SHETLAND Is
ORKNEY Is
Scapa Flow
Pentland Firth
Moray Firth
Invergordon
Aberdeen
SCOTLAND
Montrose
Firth of Tay
Firth of Forth
Edinburgh
NORTH SEA
Newcastle
R. Tyne
Dogger Bank
Flamborough Hd
Spurn Pt
R. Humber
The Wash
ENGLAND
LONDON
R. Thames
Dover Strait
Flushing
60°
56°
52°
0°

Map 5
THE NORTH SEA

Scale in Nautical Miles approx.
0   25   50   75   100   125

Soundings in Fathoms   64

100 Fathom Line   ....

GERMAN SORTIE 8TH-10TH OCTOBER 1939

steering north, and all ships of the Home Fleet raised steam.[1] The enemy's course appeared to be set for a break out into the Atlantic, and it seemed possible that the Home Fleet might intercept him. Accordingly the battle cruisers *Hood* and *Repulse* with the cruisers *Aurora* and *Sheffield* and four destroyers sailed from Scapa and set course at high speed for a position fifty miles north-west of Stadtlandet, the headland 100 miles north of Bergen where the Norwegian coast trends away to the east. About an hour later the Humber Force left the Firth of Forth for the mouth of the Skagerrak whence they would sweep north to catch the enemy if he was headed back. At 6.40 p.m. on the 8th Admiral Forbes left Scapa with the main body of the fleet (the *Nelson, Rodney, Furious, Newcastle* and eight destroyers) for a position north-east of the Shetlands, while the *Royal Oak* and two destroyers patrolled to the west of the Fair Isle Channel. The battleships and battle cruisers were to reach their positions at dawn on the 9th and would then steer towards each other.

Throughout the afternoon of the 8th, Coastal Command aircraft continued to shadow the enemy. Twelve Wellington bombers were sent to attack, but failed to find him. At 5.30 p.m. the shadowing Hudson left the enemy in a position thirty miles west of Stavanger still steering north at almost twenty knots.

Next day, the 9th of October, Admiral Forbes' forces scoured the waters to the north, but without result. The Humber Force was bombed intermittently throughout the day. Although some hundred bombs were dropped no ship was damaged. From the intercepting position between the Shetlands and the Norwegian coast Admiral Forbes steered to the waters between the Faeröes and Iceland, where a last chance of catching the enemy might be obtained if he really was bent on breaking out into the Atlantic.[2] During the afternoon of the 10th the Admiralty told Admiral Forbes that an enemy force corresponding to that which he was seeking had passed south through the Great Belt early that morning. The enemy had actually reversed his course after dark on the 8th, re-entered the Kattegat at about midnight and was back in Kiel by 1 a.m. on the 10th of October. On receiving the Admiralty's report Admiral Forbes went to Loch Ewe and his other forces to Scapa.

This operation, typical of the many abortive sorties and sweeps made by the Home Fleet during this phase, gave few grounds for satisfaction. Our intelligence had been shown to be slow and inaccurate and our air reconnaissance, though successful in sighting and, for a time, in shadowing the enemy, had been favoured by the weather and by the enemy's choice of time. For it must be remembered that the Germans were, on this occasion, trailing their coat

---

[1] See Map 5.
[2] See Map 4 (*facing p. 65*).

and wished to be sighted and reported on a northerly course. The successful shadowing had not enabled our bombers to strike, but the German feint had drawn some ships of the fleet within range of air attack. The Luftwaffe had failed, however, to turn this to advantage. We now know that the enemy had hoped that this sortie might dissuade the Admiralty from making further detachments from the Home Fleet to search for the two pocket-battleships then at large in the Atlantic. This hope at any rate was not realised.

Naturally the weaknesses revealed led to discussion between the naval and air force commands concerned and between the Admiralty and Air Ministry regarding the steps to be taken to remedy them. Not only were serious doubts felt regarding the effectiveness of the North Sea air reconnaissances, but it had been shown that even when sightings took place bomber striking forces generally failed to find the enemy. In an endeavour to correct this state of affairs a system of reconnaissance in force by bomber aircraft, with freedom to attack any major warship within a certain area, had been authorised as early as the 28th of September. But this could not be considered a satisfactory solution, for it left too much to the weather and to chance sightings. The striking force's failure on the 8th of October led therefore to the matter being further considered at a meeting held the following day between the Ministers and service heads of the two arms. At this meeting the question of the conservation of the bomber force for strategic use, which was the official policy of the Cabinet, proved the predominant factor and all that was achieved to meet the Admiralty's requirement for prompt and effective attack against any suitable naval target sighted was to place three Bomber Command squadrons, who were, of course, not trained for maritime warfare, temporarily under the operational control of Coastal Command. They were, however, not to be sent into enemy bases and were to be returned to their original command immediately bombing of shore targets was authorised. A proper balance between the offensive use of air power against maritime targets and its strategic use on land was not to be easily or quickly achieved. In spite of the issue of orders on the foregoing lines and of the concern expressed by the War Cabinet over the need to inflict damage on enemy major warships, no bomber striking force or bomber-reconnaissance force succeeded, during the next six weeks, in finding and attacking such a target. Though it runs ahead of our narrative it is, perhaps, desirable to continue now to the next step: on the 7th of December a meeting was held in the Air Ministry to review the effects of the growing enemy attacks on our shipping and the failure to deal with them effectively from the air. As a result of this meeting a joint Admiralty-Air Ministry staff came into being on the 12th of December with Air Marshal Sir Philip Joubert de la Ferté as the Air

H.M.S. *Ark Royal* lying off Rosyth, August 1939. The ships in the background include the Submarine Depot Ship H.M.S. *Forth* with a cruiser behind her and, on the left, destroyers of the 'Tribal' Class.

'The Squadron Navigating Officer' (1st Minelaying Squadron, 1940). By Sir Muirhead Bone.

(*On loan from the Admiralty to the National Maritime Museum*)

Naval 'Swordfish' Torpedo-Spotter-Reconnaissance aircraft in flight, armed with torpedoes.

The Times

H.M.S. *Nelson*, flagship of Admiral Sir Charles Forbes, at anchor in Loch Ewe on 1st October 1939.

Force head and Vice-Admiral L. E. Holland as the naval head. This arrangement, however, contributed little to solving the pressing problems with which it was intended to deal, since the Joint Staff had no executive authority but could only advise the Naval and Air Staffs on the measures considered necessary.

The resistance of Bomber Command to the transfer to Coastal Command of a proportion of its meagre striking force for use against naval targets, in accordance with the powerful wishes of both the Admiralty and Coastal Command, continued right up to the middle of 1940, by which time we were fighting for our continued existence. Until a torpedo-bomber striking force, trained, organised and controlled by Coastal Command could be provided we continued to be severely handicapped by the fact that the command which carried out the reconnaissance work possessed no striking power, and the command which possessed the striking power lacked the equipment and specialised training necessary to find the targets or, if the target was located, to strike with weight and accuracy.

We must now return to the endeavours of the Admiralty, of Coastal Command and of the Commander-in-Chief Home Fleet to make effective use of sea and air power to defend our shipping when all the time the training, organisation and control of a vital factor in the latter element, namely the shore-based air striking force squadrons, were ill-adapted to such work.

After the last fleet operations (8th to 11th of October) the battleship *Royal Oak* had returned to Scapa. There in the early hours of the morning of the 14th she was torpedoed and sunk by U.47 (Lieutenant Prien) which had made a daring entrance to the Flow through Kirk Sound, the northernmost of the eastern passages, encumbered though it was by sunken ships.[1] At about midnight on a clear moonless night, while the northern lights flickered overhead, Lieutenant Prien, who remained throughout on the surface and had chosen a time near the top of high water, passed between the blockships and the northern shore. Though she touched bottom and also fouled the blockship's cable with her stem the U-boat got clear without damage and, at twenty-seven minutes past midnight, entered the Flow.

To the south-west the big ship anchorage was seen to be empty, but when Prien turned back again to the north he sighted what he believed to be two battleships close to the north-east shore. In fact these were the *Royal Oak* and the old seaplane carrier *Pegasus*, then used for transporting aircraft. At 12.58 a.m. Prien closed to 4,000 yards and fired three torpedoes (the fourth tube missed fire), and one of these hit the *Royal Oak* right up in her bows or possibly on the anchor cable. The explosion was so slight and the damage so small that on board the battleship the Captain and other officers who went

---

[1] See Map 6 (*facing p. 74*).

forward to investigate believed the explosion to have been internal. Meanwhile Prien turned to the south, fired his stern tube at the same target without effect, and then withdrew to reload his bow tubes. At 1.16 a.m. he returned and fired three more torpedoes at the *Royal Oak*, this time with immediate effect. Two of the salvo hit and, thirteen minutes later, the battleship rolled over on her side and capsized. Twenty-four officers and 809 men of her complement perished. U.47 now withdrew at high speed and retraced her passage through Kirk Sound, passing this time between the southern blockship and Lamb Holm. With the tide falling and a strong current flowing this was the most hazardous part of the whole operation, but she passed through safely, and by 2.15 a.m. was out in the open sea again. Meanwhile inside the Flow it was realised that a U-boat had probably penetrated the defences, but a search by every available vessel revealed no trace of her. Such doubts as might still remain were dispelled a few days later when the enemy announced Prien's success; but Admiral Forbes had not waited for this to take such remedial steps as lay within his power. The few fleet cruisers at Scapa were sent to Loch Ewe, while the Northern Patrol cruisers were ordered to use Sullom Voe, in the Shetlands, as their base temporarily—in spite of that harbour being protected only by nets.

It is now known that this operation was planned with great care by Admiral Dönitz, who was correctly informed of the weak state of the defences of the eastern entrances. Full credit must also be given to Lieutenant Prien for the nerve and determination with which he put Dönitz's plan into execution. Though all the battleships of the *Royal Oak* class were too slow, too old and too ill protected to take their place in the line, and Commanders-in-Chief who had to use them in that manner often found them to be more of an incubus than a strength, they did valuable work escorting convoys and covering landing operations later. But whether the ship herself be regarded as having great military value or not, the loss of so many valuable lives in such a manner was tragic. Prien's success did at least have the effect of hastening progress with the defence works at Scapa. Doubts naturally continued regarding the route by which he had actually entered. It might have been round one of the passages at the ends of the booms, to guard which the few available patrol vessels had been stationed, or it might have been through one of the imperfectly blocked eastern entrances. One thing only was certain—that all the entrances must be made as secure as was humanly possible with the least delay. But this would take time and, meanwhile, the Home Fleet was unable to use its chosen base. Ironically enough, one blockship destined to be sunk in the entrance actually used by U.47 arrived at Scapa on the day after the *Royal Oak* was sunk.

Submarine attack was, not unnaturally, followed by air attacks,

20' 10'

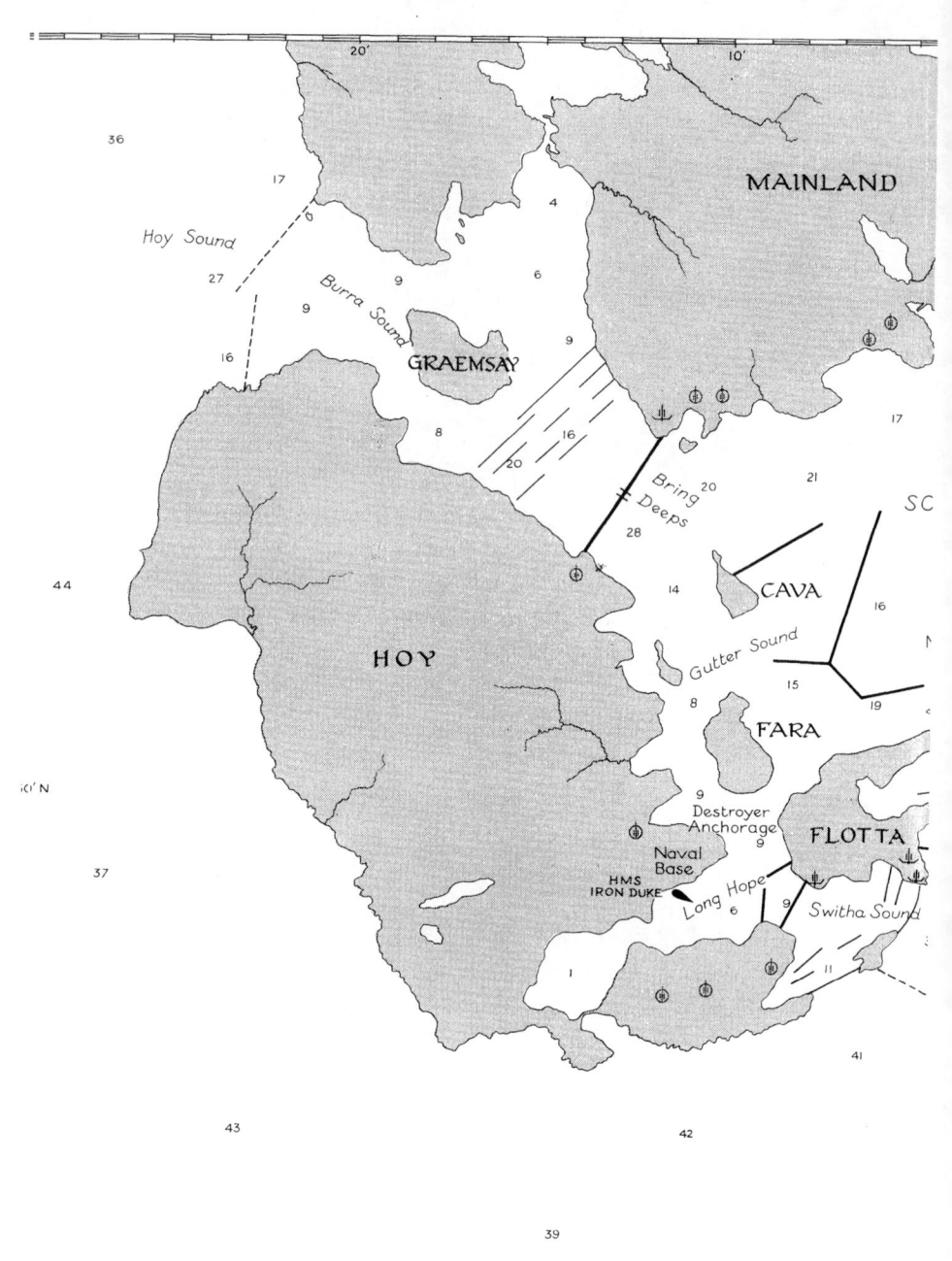

MAINLAND

36

17

Hoy Sound

27   4

Burra Sound   6

9

9   GRAEMSAY   17

16   9

8   16   21

20   Bring   20   SC
           Deeps

28   CAVA   16

44   14

HOY   Gutter Sound

8   15   19

FARA

9 Destroyer
   Anchorage   FLOTTA
37   9
           Naval
           Base   9
        HMS Long Hope   Switha Sound
        IRON DUKE 6   9

                    11
                              41

43   42

39

Pentland   Firth
                    41

46
        33
                24   STR
     20'   10'

SCAPA FLOW

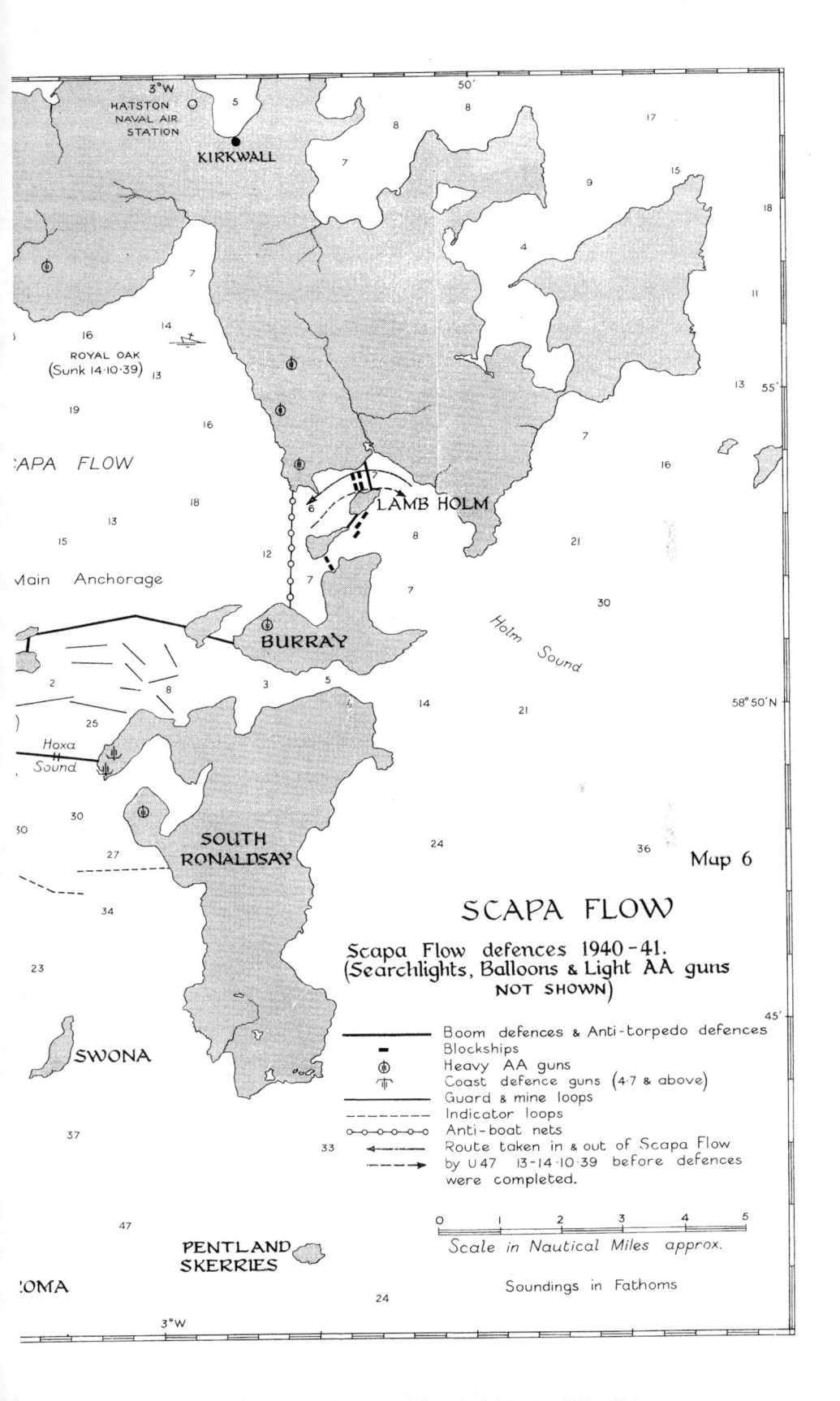

Scapa Flow defences 1940-41.
(Searchlights, Balloons & Light AA guns NOT SHOWN)

Map 6

Symbol	Meaning
▬▬▬	Boom defences & Anti-torpedo defences
●	Blockships
⊕	Heavy AA guns
⊥	Coast defence guns (4·7 & above)
───	Guard & mine loops
─ ─ ─	Indicator loops
○─○─○	Anti-boat nets
←──	Route taken in & out of Scapa Flow by U 47 13-14·10·39 before defences were completed.

Scale in Nautical Miles approx. 0 1 2 3 4 5

Soundings in Fathoms

Labels visible on map:
- HATSTON NAVAL AIR STATION
- KIRKWALL
- ROYAL OAK (Sunk 14·10·39)
- SCAPA FLOW
- Main Anchorage
- LAMB HOLM
- Holm Sound
- BURRAY
- Hoxa Sound
- SOUTH RONALDSAY
- SWONA
- PENTLAND SKERRIES
- 58°50'N
- 3°W

but on a far lighter scale than the intelligence authorities had, on the outbreak of war, indicated as likely. On the 16th of October two squadrons of Junkers 88 bombers attacked the ships lying in the Firth of Forth, where the air defences were at this time far stronger than at Scapa. They were met by Royal Air Force fighters and two were destroyed. One bomb hit the cruiser *Southampton* but passed through her side without exploding, and a destroyer was slightly damaged. But that was all.

The next day, the 17th of October, while the main body of the fleet was at sea, a raid in similar strength took place at Scapa. The absence of the fleet and the dispersal of all possible targets after the sinking of the *Royal Oak* left the attackers small choice of objectives since the Germans, like ourselves, were at this time anxious to avoid incurring the odium of starting air warfare against civil populations, and had therefore issued orders to confine attacks to warships. The old and partially demilitarised battleship *Iron Duke*, then in use as a base ship and floating coast defence battery, received underwater damage from a near miss and had to be towed into shallow water and beached, but that was the only result accomplished for the loss of one bomber brought down by the gun defences. Only naval fighters, of relatively low performance, were available on this occasion and they failed to intercept the attackers. A squadron of Royal Air Force Spitfires was sent north two days later in the hope of catching the enemy should he repeat the attempt, but proper control arrangements were still lacking and, when no further attacks occurred, it was withdrawn.

The lack of success of these early air attacks on our bases and the equal failure of our own corresponding attacks lent support to the view, which Admiral Forbes had always held, that the air threat to naval bases had been exaggerated and was, in fact, quite acceptable once the defences had been reasonably strengthened and were properly organised and controlled. The sense of security in the Fleet while in its bases was certainly improved by these experiences, and it was probably the enemy's lack of success on the 16th and 17th of October which gave the Home Fleet a brief and undisturbed interlude in the Firth of Forth between the 9th and 12th of November. But for the greater part of this period the fleet was far out of range of enemy aircraft. Admiral Forbes left Loch Ewe on the 15th of October and cruised for the next week well to the north to cover the Northern Patrol cruisers. He then returned to the temporary base and there, on the 21st, he received the intelligence already mentioned which made it almost certain that two enemy pocket-battleships were at large on our ocean trade routes.[1] The *Furious* and *Repulse* were sent to cover a Halifax convoy already at sea and thereafter to operate to

---
[1] See p. 70.

the south and east of Newfoundland, and Admiral Forbes was thus deprived of his only aircraft carrier. Furthermore the cruisers *Glasgow* and *Newcastle* were sent to meet a valuable convoy from the West Indies, which included nineteen oil tankers, and to cover it until it arrived off Land's End on the 25th of October.

The sinking of the *Royal Oak* and the weakness of the defences of Scapa against air attack provide a suitable opportunity to review the whole question of the choice of the fleet's main bases and their protection.

What the security of this island base is to our grand strategy the security of the fleet's main bases is to our maritime strategy. Unless their bases are reasonably secure against all probable forms of attack the main fleets cannot perform their functions, since they cannot remain at sea indefinitely. Replenishment of fuel and stores becomes necessary and, without returning periodically to a protected harbour, neither the machinery of the ships nor the bodies and minds of their crews can stand the strain of continuous cruising in waters where a constant and high degree of alertness is essential. Though the standard of self-maintenance in British warships is high, assistance from depot or repair ships, if not from fully equipped dockyards, ultimately becomes essential. The strain of operations involving constant watchfulness, particularly in the small ships and in northern waters, where for many months of the year the weather can provide a succession of storms of great severity, renders it just as necessary to arrange periods of rest for the ships' companies as to allow periods for carrying out maintenance work to the machinery and equipment of the ships themselves. Neither of these needs can be satisfied if a high degree of readiness has to be maintained while at anchor in the main base.

This requirement for the security of the fleet's main bases is so well known that it is almost a platitude to restate it here. But it is all too often forgotten in times of peace when it is hard enough to obtain money for the warships necessary to maintain 'the essentials of sea defence' and harder still to obtain it for land defences and harbour works at their bases. It is ironical, even tragic, to remember that the only fleet base on which substantial sums of money were spent during the years between the two world wars was Singapore, and that when the conditions against which it had been constructed finally arose we were as unable to base a properly balanced fleet on it as we were to defend it against the enemy's land and air assaults. Neither in home waters nor in the Mediterranean—the two theatres where our main naval strength was deployed for war against Germany and Italy—was there a properly defended base from which the fleets could work confidently and to which they could return in the knowledge of finding reasonable security. In the Mediterranean Gibraltar was poorly protected, while Malta was considered indefensible against Italian air power and no serious attempt was made to defend it until it was almost too late. At Alexandria the Mediterranean fleet was in foreign territorial waters, surrounded by foreign land, and almost all the essential installations of a main base were initially lacking. The effect on our strategy of the inadequacy and insecurity of our Mediterranean bases will be considered later when the tide of war swept over the Middle East. It was in home waters that the consequences of parallel weaknesses first became apparent and where the inevitable price in ships and lives was first exacted. The policy and events which led to such conditions will therefore be considered in some detail.

Until 1938 the three fighting services had been agreed that, in the event of war with Germany, the main units of the Home Fleet would be based on Rosyth, in the Firth of Forth, as had been the case during the final phases of the First World War. Strong arguments in favour of again using the same base appeared at that time to exist. It was well placed for the interception of German warships returning from a short foray northward, its air defence could be combined with the defence of the cities of Edinburgh and Glasgow, and radar stations, fighter defences and an Area Combined Headquarters to control all defending forces were already being provided in that area. To press the Royal Air Force to extend its meagre resources to a different base some 200 miles farther north was a serious matter which could only have been accomplished by weakening the air defences in the south.

In 1938 the problem was re-examined by the First Sea Lord (Admiral Sir Roger Backhouse) and the Commander-in-Chief, Home Fleet. They decided that Rosyth would not meet the changed requirements of a new war with Germany. It was badly placed for intercepting enemy warships attempting to break out into the Atlantic, to prevent which was to be one of the chief objectives of the Home Fleet, and its long approaches were vulnerable to mining, whereas the fierce tidal streams of the Pentland Firth afforded some protection to the main entrances to Scapa Flow. Moreover, Scapa was 150 miles nearer to the 'cutting off position' between the Shetland Islands and southern Norway, and from it the Home Fleet could more easily carry out the tasks of protecting the lightly armed ships of the Northern Patrol and of enforcing our contraband control measures in northern waters. Accordingly it was decided that the Home Fleet would, in the event of a new war with Germany, be based on Scapa Flow, and it was there that it concentrated at the time of the Munich crisis and again in the last days of August 1939. But Admiral Forbes only used it for the first few weeks of the war and, after the 1st of October, a period of wandering between Loch Ewe, the Clyde and Rosyth began for the Home Fleet and continued until March 1940 when, at last, it was able to return to its chosen base. After the sinking of the *Royal Oak* the First Lord told the Cabinet, on the 18th of October, that he thought Scapa was at present quite unfit as a base for the fleet. After much discussion it was decided to continue to use Loch Ewe as a temporary base while the defences of Scapa were being improved. But the enemy guessed correctly that we might make this move and, as Loch Ewe was even less well defended than Scapa, it was hardly surprising that Admiral Forbes' flagship, the *Nelson*, was seriously damaged on the 4th of December by one of a number of mines which had been laid in the entrance five weeks earlier by a U-boat. On the 21st of November the new cruiser *Belfast* was mined in the Firth of Forth and her back broken, which event showed that Admiral Forbes' fears regarding the vulnerability of the long approach to Rosyth to mining had been well founded.

It is plainly desirable to make some study of the reasons why this state of affairs came to pass. One factor undoubtedly was the late date (April 1938) at which the decision to shift the fleet's main base from Rosyth to Scapa was taken by the Admiralty. The change affected the other services' allocations and dispositions, and involved increased demands for equipment of which we were already woefully short. In the War Office it certainly caused some dismay. Not until early in 1939 did the Cabinet even consider the Chiefs of Staffs' proposals to increase the defences of Scapa; and the proposals were not approved until the following September—after war had broken out. A second factor was the refusal of the Government of the day to order, even as late as the spring of 1939, any measures of preparedness which might 'alarm the British populace' or might antagonise Hitler. On two occasions—at meetings held in the Admiralty on the 21st of March and the 14th of April 1939—Admiral Forbes was told that the Government had decided only to make such preparations as would not attract public attention and that he must be careful 'to do nothing to upset the populace'. Admiral Sir Andrew Cunningham, the Deputy Chief of Naval Staff, who was acting for Admiral Backhouse during the latter's illness, told Admiral Forbes that the Government was very nervous 'of bringing on an attack by publicly making preparations for such a thing'. Such a policy in Whitehall could only have the effect of stultifying the efforts of the men on the spot. But that they made and, after the outbreak of war, were still making constant efforts to improve the defences within the totally inadequate means available to them is beyond argument.

A third important factor was the acute shortage of labour in the Orkneys. Miners from the Midlands were sent up to work on the defences after the outbreak of war and, although paid double wages, rarely stayed for more than six weeks. Admiral Forbes several times pressed for a labour battalion to be sent north, but his appeals were not successful. Scapa had been well defended during the 1914-18 war but the greater part of the floating defences—booms and nets—had been removed and the shore defences dismantled during the years of peace. Moreover a Local Defence Division of the Naval Staff, specifically responsible for formulating and forwarding the defensive requirements of the fleet's bases, was not formed until May 1939.

During the interval between the decision to use Scapa and the outbreak of war no very great impetus appears to have been applied by the Admiralty to strengthen the defences; and when the senior naval officer on the spot reported in April 1939 that the defences were inadequate the Admiralty replied to the general effect that they were satisfied. In the following July Admiral Forbes drew attention to the state of the defences, but still no energetic response was obtained from Whitehall. Doubtless the governmental policy already mentioned made it difficult for the Admiralty to press defence preparations on an unwilling Cabinet. Moreover a dual misfortune occurred to the Board of Admiralty through the deaths in May 1939 of the Controller (Vice-Admiral Sir R. G. H. Henderson) and of the First Sea Lord in the following July; the changes in the membership of the Board may have contributed to the delay in meeting the requirements of the Commander-in-Chief, Home Fleet.

On the outbreak of war the Admiralty did, however, give orders to strengthen the defences of Scapa Flow. But the remoteness of the base from industrial centres, the shortage of labour in the Orkneys and of military material everywhere made the process of carrying out these somewhat tardy instructions inevitably slow. By the 31st of October 1939, there were still only eight heavy A.A. guns at Scapa, and they were placed to defend shore oil tanks rather than the fleet. There were no close-range A.A. weapons and only one squadron of naval fighters was stationed in the area. No Royal Air Force fighters were expected until early in 1940. Of anti-submarine defences there was still only a single line of nets across the three main entrances of Hoxa, Switha and Hoy, and the eastern entrances were imperfectly closed by the remains of the blockships of the 1914–18 war to which a few hulks had recently been added.[1] The first blockship sent to close the eastern entrances was sunk on her passage north; another arrived on the day after the *Royal Oak* was sunk.

The sinking of the *Royal Oak* naturally called for a stringent enquiry into the causes of the disaster and the First Lord finally reported to his colleagues that the senior officers on the spot had not taken

---

[1] See Map 6 (*facing p. 74*).

adequate measures to improve the defences of the base. The just allocation of responsibility must always, in such a case, be difficult, but it does now seem that the true causes went deeper than the conclusion quoted above and that the loss of the *Royal Oak* was the result not so much of a failure by the officers on the spot, who had in fact several times represented the weaknesses for which they were censured and had done their best to remedy them, as of the policy of the Government of the day and the failure of the Admiralty to obtain proper priority in time of peace for the defences of the fleet's chosen base. However this may be, the fact remains that the failure to defend Scapa Flow adequately against either air or submarine attack not only caused the loss of one battleship, damage to another and to a valuable new cruiser but vitiated the ability of the fleet to perform its proper functions.

The evacuation of the Home Fleet from its main base within a few weeks of the outbreak of war was actually caused by the unduly pessimistic estimate of the air threat which the Admiralty sent to the Commander-in-Chief on the 7th of September. It warned him that the enemy might attack his fleet, while in its base, with a force of 800 heavy bombers. In fact the total operational strength then possessed by the enemy was under 400 heavy bombers, and an attack on anything like the scale predicted was out of the question. Then, when the fleet moved to Loch Ewe, the *Royal Oak* was left behind at Scapa and the consequence of its insecurity against submarine attack was immediately reaped. As the First Lord, with understandable bitterness, expressed it to the First Sea Lord, 'We were driven out of Scapa through pre-war neglect of its defences against air and U-boat attack'.

There was now no disguising the peril in which the fleet lay at its temporary base. The Admiralty even considered that it was greater than at Scapa, but agreed to give Loch Ewe priority for certain additional anti-submarine defences. The abandonment of Loch Ewe and a move to the Clyde were considered at a meeting in the Admiralty on the 24th of October, but with this proposal the Commander-in-Chief 'totally disagreed', for it would mean the expenditure of an additional day in reaching the 'cutting off position' in the northern part of the North Sea. His urgent desire was to get the defences of Scapa so far improved that he could take the fleet back there at the earliest possible moment; but, if a choice of temporary bases had to be made, he preferred Rosyth to the Clyde, chiefly because the anti-submarine defences were at that time the stronger. In order to resolve these differences the First Lord, accompanied by the First Sea Lord and the Deputy Chief of the Air Staff (Air Vice-Marshal R. E. C. Peirse), visited Admiral Forbes on board his flagship in the Clyde on the 31st of October. The Commander-in-Chief rapidly convinced the First Lord that the proper base for the fleet was Scapa, and that improvement of the defences must therefore be pressed ahead as fast as possible. The slight effects of the enemy's air attacks on Rosyth had lent support to Admiral Forbes' view that the air threat could also be dealt with at Scapa, once the anti-aircraft and fighter defences of the latter base had reached the strength and efficiency of those defending the former.

It was accordingly decided that the anti-aircraft gun density at Scapa should be greatly increased, that heavy nets should be placed around the fleet anchorage to force torpedo-carrying aircraft to close to point-blank range before they could drop their weapons effectively, that two squadrons of Royal Air Force fighters of high performance should be stationed in the north of Scotland, that reinforcement by a further four squadrons would be made if the situation appeared threatening and that proper arrangements for the control of these fighters and an additional radar station would be established. All unused entrances to the Flow were to be totally and permanently blocked and the anti-submarine defences of the main entrance through Hoxa Sound strengthened; booms were to be extended to the shore and controlled minefields and indicator loops laid.[1] But all this could not be completed in a few weeks and for the next four or five winter months, during which prolonged spells of bad weather were certain, the fleet would have to continue to use temporary bases each of which possessed grave disadvantages. The Clyde, undoubtedly the most secure, was nearly 200 miles farther than Loch Ewe from the waters where the fleet might at any moment be required. But Loch Ewe was poorly defended. Rosyth was better placed geographically than the Clyde, but harder to defend against air attack. It was this factor which finally led to the decision to use the Clyde until the Scapa defences were adequate. The geographical disadvantage of the Clyde might be lessened by the arrival of reinforcements from the Mediterranean giving Admiral Forbes so great a superiority that the fleet could work in two squadrons keeping the sea alternately; but the number of destroyers available to screen the heavy ships would be the deciding factor and, in fact, shortage of destroyers and new demands on the fleet prevented this mitigation from ever being realised.

These differences of opinion and discussions have been dealt with at some length because they were endemic to the insecurity in which the fleet was placed. Had the enemy realised the weakness of its

---

[1] An indicator loop consists of a loop of cable laid on the sea bed. The passage of a steel ship over the loop will induce in it a small electric current which is recorded at a shore station. A controlled minefield operates on the same principle, but in this case a row of mines is laid down the centre of the loop and can be fired simultaneously from the shore station when the passage of a ship is detected. The defences of the entrances to important harbours generally included several controlled minefields, with indicator loops further to seaward to give warning of a ship's approach.

condition and exploited fully the possibilities of submarine attack and the use of the magnetic mine, or had he been sufficiently well informed to send his battle cruisers out into the Atlantic while the effective strength of the Home Fleet was at its lowest ebb, the results might well have been serious.

While the discussions on bases were in progress, and in spite of the grievous handicap from which the Home Fleet at this time suffered, it had to continue to exercise its functions.

On the 22nd of October, the Admiralty ordered Admiral Forbes to cover a convoy of iron ore ships then assembling at Narvik. As the enemy was bound to know about the sailing of this convoy the Commander-in-Chief sailed from Loch Ewe on the 23rd. The *Aurora* and four destroyers were to act as close escort for the convoy while the *Nelson*, *Rodney*, *Hood* and six destroyers formed the covering force. Admiral Forbes remained at sea until the last day of October and cruised to the north as far as the Lofoten Islands; but the whole area remained completely quiet. The convoy was brought in safely to the Firth of Forth and the heavy ships returned to the Clyde where, on the 31st of October, the visit of the First Lord, the First Sea Lord and Deputy Chief of the Air Staff took place.

The next operation was to cover the second Norwegian convoy between the 12th and 17th of November. This was successfully accomplished and, on the 20th, Admiral Forbes was back in the Clyde where, at 3.51 p.m. on the 23rd he received an enemy report from the armed merchant cruiser *Rawalpindi* (Captain E. C. Kennedy) on the Northern Patrol stating that an enemy battle cruiser was in sight four miles to the west of her position between the Faeröes and Iceland which was given as 63° 40′ North 11° 29′ West. A few minutes later a second report was received which identified the enemy, wrongly, as the *Deutschland*. Admiral Forbes ordered all ships to raise steam with all despatch.

Before describing the operations which followed it may be as well to remark on the reasons for the incorrect identification of the enemy by the *Rawalpindi*; for she had, in fact, sighted the battle cruiser *Scharnhorst* and her first enemy report had therefore been correct. To identify a strange ship sighted towards dusk in far northern waters is likely, in any case, to be difficult; but with the German major warships it was rendered more so by the similarity in silhouette of the pocket-battleships, of the battle cruisers and also (though they were not yet in service) of the new battleships *Bismarck* and *Tirpitz*. This was particularly the case when no means of comparing their relative sizes was available, or at distances where even fairly pronounced detail, such as the placing of turrets, could not be distinguished. It

MAP 7

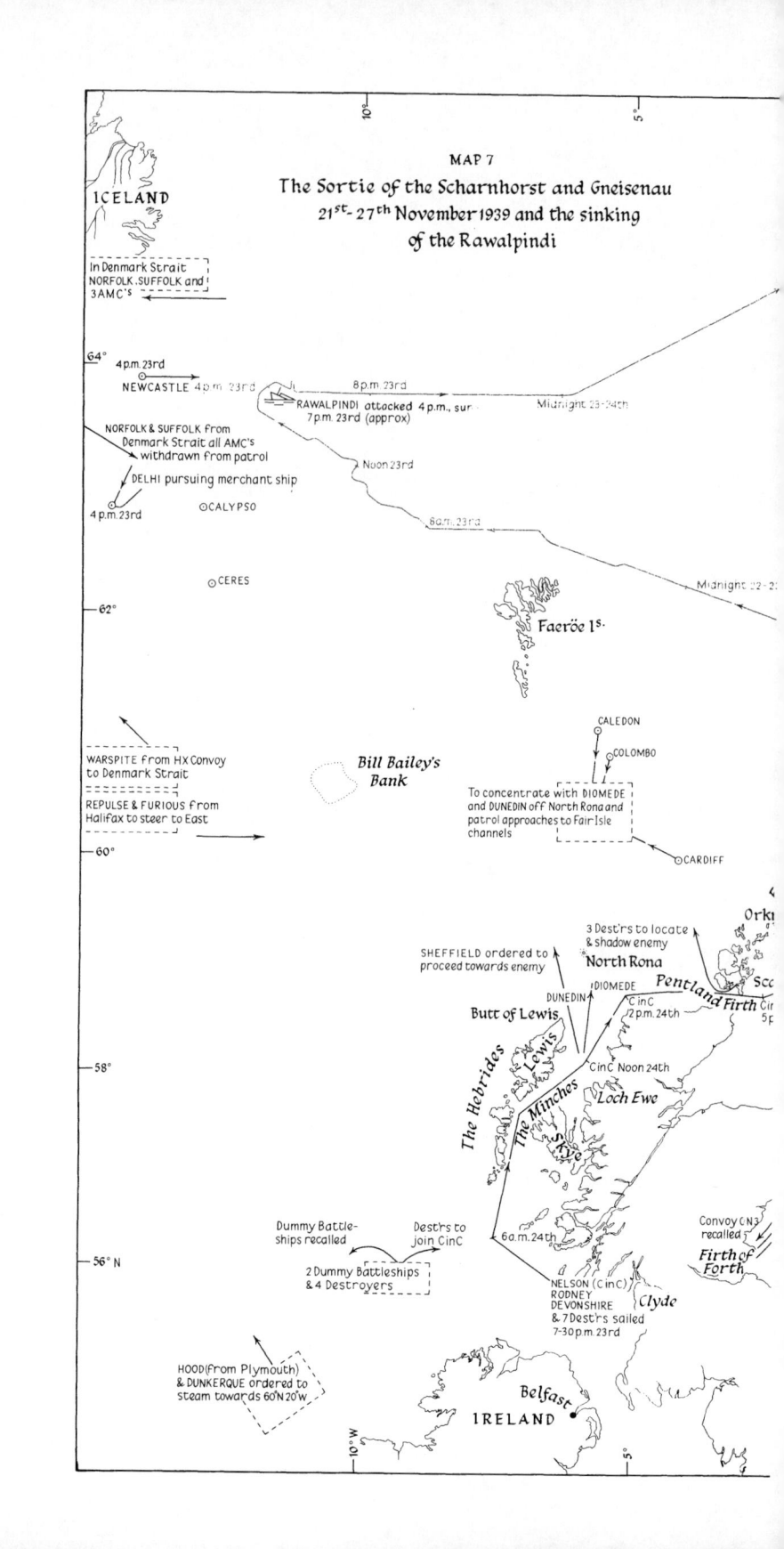

The Sortie of the Scharnhorst and Gneisenau
21st - 27th November 1939 and the sinking
of the Rawalpindi

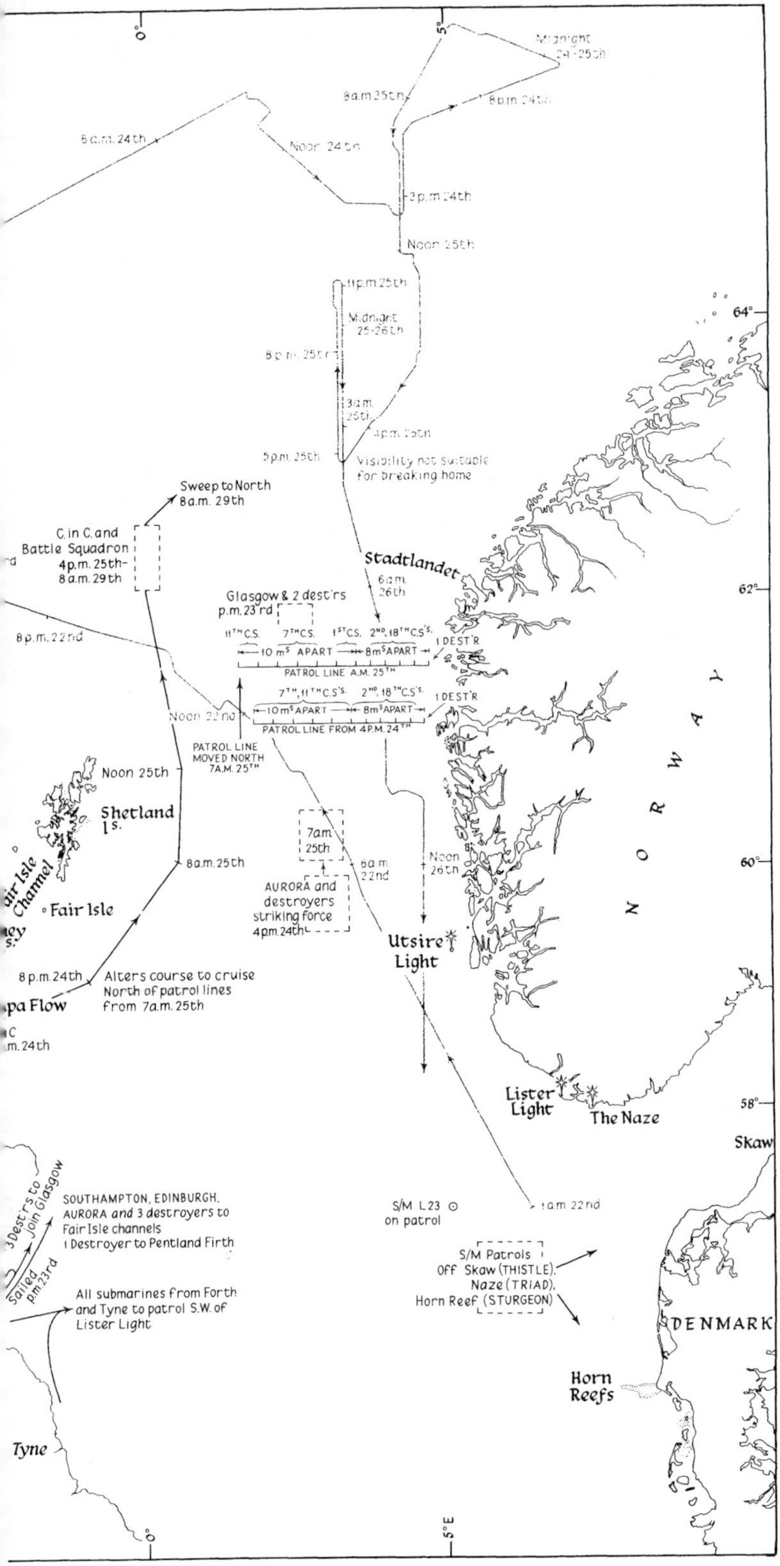

0°
5°
Midnight 24-25th
8a.m.25th
8p.m.24th
6a.m.24th
Noon 24th
3p.m.24th
Noon 25th
11p.m.25th
Midnight 25-26th
8p.m.25th
3a.m. 25th
4p.m.25th
5p.m.25th
Visibility not suitable for breaking home
64°
Sweep to North 8a.m. 29th
C.in C. and Battle Squadron 4p.m.25th- 8a.m.29th
Stadtlandet
6a.m. 26th
62°
Glasgow & 2 dest'rs p.m.23rd
11TH C.S.
7TH C.S.
1ST C.S.
2ND, 18TH C.S'S.
10 mS APART
8mS APART
1 DEST'R
PATROL LINE A.M. 25TH
8p.m.22nd
7TH, 11TH C.S'S.
2ND, 18TH C.S'S.
10mS APART
8mS APART
1 DEST'R
PATROL LINE FROM 4P.M. 24TH
Noon 22nd
PATROL LINE MOVED NORTH 7A.M. 25TH
Noon 25th
Shetland Is.
7am. 25th
8a.m. 22nd
Noon 26th
8a.m.25th
60°
Fair Isle Channel
Fair Isle
AURORA and destroyers striking force 4p.m.24th
NORWAY
Utsire Light
8p.m.24th
Alters course to cruise North of patrol lines from 7a.m.25th
pa Flow
m.24th
Lister Light
The Naze
58°
Skaw
3 Dest'rs to join Glasgow
Sailed p.m.23rd
SOUTHAMPTON, EDINBURGH, AURORA and 3 destroyers to Fair Isle channels
1 Destroyer to Pentland Firth
S/M L23 on patrol
1a.m. 22nd
S/M Patrols
Off Skaw (THISTLE).
Naze (TRIAD).
Horn Reef (STURGEON)
All submarines from Forth and Tyne to patrol S.W. of Lister Light
DENMARK
Horn Reefs
Tyne
0°
5°E

THE GERMAN BATTLE CRUISERS' SORTIE

is now known that, although without any intention to confuse identification, the Chief Constructor of the German Navy adhered deliberately to certain broad features in all the heavy ships designed by his department, and this produced a strong similarity in their silhouettes. In the case of the *Rawalpindi*'s sighting the second report was perfectly possible since the Admiralty and Admiral Forbes' ships all knew, from the adventures of the *City of Flint* and *Lorentz W. Hansen*, that the *Deutschland* had been at large in the Atlantic.[1] An attempt by her to break back through one of the northern passages during November was likely. In fact we now know that she left Wilhelmshaven on the 24th of August, passed through the Denmark Strait into the Atlantic and had returned by the same route on the 8th of November. By the 15th of that month she was back in Kiel again, but no intelligence to that effect had been received by the Admiralty at the time of the *Rawalpindi*'s sighting. She was not actually located in her home waters until four weeks after her return. Not until the middle of December was the Admiralty of the opinion that the *Gneisenau* also took part in the operations now to be described. The mistake made on the *Rawalpindi*'s bridge thus helped to confuse the Admiralty's intelligence regarding the movements and dispositions of the enemy's main units for some time.

The German battle cruisers, commanded by Vice-Admiral Marschall with his flag in the *Gneisenau*, had actually sailed from Wilhelmshaven at 2 p.m. on the 21st of November and they remained in company throughout the operation.[2] The intention of the German Admiral was to break through to the Iceland–Faeröes area, then move to the waters where our patrol lines were thought to be established and make a feint out into the north Atlantic, in order to draw off our patrols and dislocate our shipping movements. Finally he intended to sheer off into the mists of the far north whence, making use of the long nights, he would choose an opportunity to slip home at high speed. This does not appear a very aggressive plan for two of the most powerful warships afloat to execute, since nothing more than a brush with patrols, followed perhaps by a chase, was likely to result. But it seems probable that Admiral Raeder, on whose directions the orders were framed, felt that only small risks should be taken in this first venture by his largest and newest ships, and was prepared to be satisfied with slight results—or even with none.

The German battle cruisers passed north of the Shetland and Faeröe Islands and patrolled in the Iceland–Faeröe channel throughout the 23rd of November. Towards dusk the *Rawalpindi* was sighted by the *Scharnhorst*, which chased and engaged at 8,000 yards range, and destroyed the armed merchant cruiser after a one-sided action

---
[1] See p. 70.
[2] See Map 7.

which lasted only fourteen minutes.[1] The *Rawalpindi* fought to the end and obtained one hit on her powerful adversary.

Admiral Forbes had with him in the Clyde on the afternoon of the 23rd November the *Nelson* and *Rodney*, the cruiser *Devonshire* and seven destroyers of the 8th Flotilla. Three six-inch cruisers (the *Southampton*, *Edinburgh* and *Aurora*) and two more destroyers were at Rosyth. The forces on patrol consisted of three of the old C Class cruisers to the south of the Faeröe Islands, the *Newcastle*, *Rawalpindi*, two C Class and one D Class cruiser between the Faeröe Islands and Iceland, and the eight-inch cruisers *Norfolk*, *Suffolk* and three armed merchant cruisers in the Denmark Strait. The six-inch cruiser *Sheffield* and three of the D Class were at Loch Ewe or on passage from the Northern Patrol, while the *Glasgow* and two destroyers were at sea to the north-east of the Shetlands trying to intercept the German liner *Bremen*. An outward-bound Norwegian convoy was just leaving the Firth of Forth with three destroyers as escort; four more destroyers had recently sailed from Belfast to escort two dummy battleships, which were intended to attract the attentions of the Luftwaffe to Rosyth. Lastly there were five submarines on patrol.

The Commander-in-Chief recalled the Norwegian convoy and ordered its escort to join the *Glasgow* off the Shetland Islands, whence they were to search to the north. The dummy battleships were sent back to Belfast and their escort ordered to join his main body. The *Newcastle* and *Delhi*, the nearest ships to the *Rawalpindi's* position, were ordered to close and shadow the enemy and three destroyers were sailed from Scapa with orders also to locate and shadow. The Rosyth force, under the Vice-Admiral Commanding the 2nd Cruiser Squadron in the *Southampton*, was ordered to the Fair Isle Channel and there to spread and search. One destroyer from Scapa was placed in the Pentland Firth to guard that possible, though unlikely, route of return. The C and D Class cruisers on patrol were ordered to concentrate off North Rona and thence cover the approaches to the Fair Isle Channel. The *Sheffield*, from Loch Ewe, was sent to the enemy's last reported position and the *Norfolk* and *Suffolk* were ordered to proceed towards Bill Bailey's Bank (60° 30' North, 10° 00' West). The submarines from the Forth and Tyne were ordered to patrol on a westward line from the Lister Light and other submarines were stationed off Horn Reef, the Skaw and the Naze. Having thus redisposed his forces to maintain contact with the enemy and to cover all his likely return routes, Admiral Forbes hurried north by the Minches and the Pentland Firth towards a central position some 60 miles off the Norwegian coast (in 58° 36' North, 03° 00' East)—a position he could have reached far more

---

[1] On that date, in 62° North, 10° West, sunset is at 3.30 p.m. and sunrise at 9.20 a.m. approximately.

HOME FLEET'S ENDEAVOURS TO INTERCEPT

quickly had he been based at Scapa. All possible air searches had been requested, and the armed merchant cruisers were temporarily withdrawn from the patrol lines.

The Admiralty had, meanwhile, ordered certain other changes of disposition for the greater safety of shipping already at sea and to strengthen the searching forces. The *Warspite* was ordered to leave the Halifax convoy she was escorting and to steer towards the Denmark Strait. The *Repulse* and *Furious* were sailed from Halifax to the east, but the former was damaged by heavy seas and both had to return. The *Hood* sailed from Plymouth on the 25th of November and proceeded with the French battle cruiser *Dunkerque* towards a position (60° 00′ North, 20° 00′ West) from which the North Atlantic routes could be covered.

It now only remained to keep in touch with the enemy until such time as the heavy ships could bring him to action. The cruiser *Newcastle*, which was next in the patrol line to the *Rawalpindi*, had received her enemy reports and altered course to the east to close her position at full speed. Two hours later she sighted, first, a searchlight on the horizon and then gunflashes. Visibility was about eight miles, but there were several rain squalls in the vicinity which might at any time greatly reduce the visibility. At 6.15 the *Newcastle* sighted a darkened ship six and a half miles away and, two minutes later, a second ship to the right of the first who signalled with a bright lamp to her consort. By 6.22 the range was closing rapidly and the *Newcastle* reduced speed and altered course away. She had, in fact, been sighted by the German ships at this time. Quite apart from the orders received from Admiral Forbes, to her had fallen the traditional rôle of the cruiser in contact with heavy enemy units, namely to shadow and keep in touch with them. She had learnt that there were two enemy ships in company and that one of them was certainly heavily armed and armoured. For her to have engaged such a ship with her 6-inch guns would have courted disaster, but why the Germans, who knew that their presence had already been reported and that they had no friendly ships in the neighbourhood, did not attack the *Newcastle* immediately on sighting her is less easily explained.

Unfortunately for the successful performance of the *Newcastle's* object a rain cloud now drifted between the shadowing cruiser and the enemy and visibility was greatly reduced. We now know that the *Scharnhorst* was stopped and picking up survivors when first sighted by the *Newcastle*: and that, in response to the *Gneisenau's* signal made at 6.14 she got under way again after recovering one boat with twenty-one survivors and followed her senior officer in an easterly direction at high speed. The *Newcastle* emerged from the area of bad visibility at about 6.30 to find nothing in sight, and although she and the *Delhi* searched to the north-west and north-east until dawn next day they never regained contact. The *Newcastle*, like most British ships at that time, had no radar. Had she been so fitted she could hardly have failed to maintain contact—at any rate for some time. The German ships equally had no search radar sets, but were fitted with a set whose purpose it was to obtain ranges for their main armaments.

After the action the German Admiral decided to abandon the feint to the west owing to 'the rapid approach of darkness and time lost in picking up survivors', thus further reducing the already limited scope of his operation orders. Neither of the foregoing arguments appear to afford valid reasons for a rapid withdrawal since darkness would have covered the start of the feint movement, and the time lost in sinking the *Rawalpindi* and recovering one boat-load of survivors had only been about two and a half hours. The more probable reason, though not admitted in any German account, was that Admiral Marschall knew that his position had been reported and that other ships were already searching for him. He had to anticipate intensive air patrolling next day, and heavy naval forces were certain to be moved in his direction with the utmost rapidity. Discretion therefore appeared to indicate an immediate withdrawal although, in fact, no British ship capable of engaging his force on anything approaching equal terms was, at the time, within many hundreds of miles of his position.

After shaking off the *Newcastle* by steering to the east at high speed the German Admiral acted with great circumspection. He altered course to the north-east at about midnight on the 23rd–24th November and reached the vicinity of 65° 40′ North, 6° 00′ East the following evening.[1] He remained in this general area until 11 a.m. on the 25th of November when he shaped course to the south to re-enter the North Sea. On reaching 62° 55′ North, 3° 10′ East that evening Admiral Marschall found the visibility to be too good for his liking, and turned north again until midnight. Next morning in the bad weather and low visibility for which he had been waiting, he resumed his southerly course and, by daylight on the 26th of November, had reached the latitude of Stadtlandet at a distance of 20 miles from the coast. Apart from sighting, but not being sighted by, a ship which was probably one of the cruisers or destroyers of a patrol line established by Admiral Forbes between the Shetlands and the Norwegian coast, the German Admiral's anxieties were now almost over because the weather remained uniformly bad until he reached Wilhelmshaven Roads at 1 p.m. on the 27th of November.

Meanwhile Admiral Forbes with the *Nelson* and *Rodney* had taken up his intercepting position about 60 miles off the Norwegian coast, and had redisposed his cruisers from the evening of the 24th of November to improve the chances of catching the enemy if he broke for home.

---

[1] See Map 7 (*facing p. 83*).

During the forenoon of the 25th enemy flying-boats sighted a number of our searching forces and reported their positions to Admiral Marschall. These air reports played a part in causing the German Admiral to postpone his break-back till next day. The lack of an aircraft carrier to work with the fleet deprived the Commander-in-Chief of the possibility of conducting his own air searches, and the best efforts of Coastal Command failed to accomplish for him what the German flying-boats did for Admiral Marschall. Admiral Forbes waited in vain for a sighting report from his patrolling cruisers or aircraft off the Norwegian coast from the 25th to the 28th of November. He swept to the north on the 29th—on which day the *Rodney*, which had developed serious rudder defects, had to be sent back to the Clyde—and turned south again on the 30th. But during all this period of waiting not one sighting report reached him. In fact the enemy had already slipped back home through his cruiser line only some 100 miles inside his waiting position. The weather, or rather the clever use of periods of bad weather, had, of course, favoured the enemy's escape. But it was not only good luck and favourable weather which enabled him to complete his sortie unsighted and unidentified. Firstly there was the *Newcastle's* failure to maintain contact. Had she shadowed successfully even until dawn on 24th of November the chances of successful interception would have been greatly improved. And, more serious still, grave weaknesses in our intelligence regarding the movements of the major enemy warships and deficiencies in the capabilities of our patrolling aircraft were exposed by these operations. Lack of regular visual and photographic reconnaissance of the enemy's main bases handicapped our forces from the start, too sanguine pre-war estimates of the effectiveness of our North Sea air patrols greatly extended this handicap and, finally, the use by the Home Fleet of temporary bases several hundred additional miles from the 'cutting off position' in the North Sea all helped towards successful evasion by the enemy.

German intelligence, on the other hand, seems at this period to have worked fast and accurately; not only was the closely guarded secret of the use of Loch Ewe as a temporary base by the Home Fleet known to the enemy but each of the redispositions ordered by the Admiralty after the sinking of the *Rawalpindi* is correctly stated in Admiral Raeder's report to Hitler on the operation.

After his fruitless sweeps to the north on the 29th of November and in the reverse direction the following day Admiral Forbes ordered normal movements of shipping to be restarted on the 1st of December and, two days later, decided to call at Loch Ewe to fuel his destroyers on his way to the Clyde. It was while entering that temporary base early on the morning of the 4th of December that his flagship, the *Nelson*, was, as told earlier, damaged by a magnetic mine.[1] Not until the 4th of January, by which time five more of the eighteen mines laid in the channel had been exploded, was it considered safe to send her to Portsmouth for repairs. The event was skilfully kept secret from the enemy, but the implications were serious in the extreme since it was made clear that, until the magnetic mine had been mastered, any of our main ports and bases might be closed for weeks on end.

In the German Admiralty there was considerable jubilation over the success of Admiral Marschall's foray—jubilation which hardly seems to have been justified by the limited scope of Admiral Raeder's orders and the incomplete fulfilment even of those objects. The whole operation was, in fact, exactly of the type which the Admiralty had long expected and with which the Commander-in-Chief's plans and dispositions were intended to deal. From the enemy's point of view this sortie by his heavy ships had no effect on our control of sea communications, and the sinking of one armed merchant cruiser cannot be considered good grounds for Admiral Raeder's conclusion that 'for Germany the results of our first battleship operation may be rated very highly'.

But although the enemy's intelligence had been good it had not been good enough to enable him to take any advantage of an opportunity which occurred at this time to use his battle cruisers really effectively. The detachments made from the Home Fleet to hunt for the raiding pocket-battleships, the mining of the *Nelson* and the development of defects in the *Rodney* had temporarily reduced Admiral Forbes' strength to one capital ship—the *Hood*—and she could only steam 25 knots and was in urgent need of refitting. The arrival of the *Warspite* from the Mediterranean soon eased the situation, and by the end of the year the *Rodney*, *Repulse* and *Furious* had all rejoined, and Admiral Forbes again commanded a balanced fleet. But had Admiral Raeder used his battle cruisers more frequently and more determinedly during November and the early days of December he might have accomplished big results.

Two days after the *Nelson* was damaged Admiral Forbes transferred his flag to the *Warspite* at Greenock and there, on the 7th of December, he was visited again by the First Lord and First Sea Lord to review once more the future of the fleet's bases, the problems posed by the enemy's use of the magnetic mine and the disposition of certain major warships. Regarding the first matter it was readily agreed that there was no alternative but to continue to use the Clyde until such time as effective magnetic sweeps had been produced and the defences of Scapa improved sufficiently to permit the return of the fleet to the northern base.

It was decided that until the heavy ships could enter and leave

---
[1] See p. 78.

harbour in safety the Northern Patrol could not be properly covered and that it should therefore be reduced. The lack of effective countermeasures to the magnetic mine thus had a direct effect on the efficiency of our blockade measures. As reinforcements the battleship *Barham* was to join the Home Fleet, and the *Repulse* and *Furious* would rejoin Admiral Forbes' flag after bringing in the first Canadian troop convoy.

On the 12th of December Admiral Forbes sailed twelve of his destroyers to meet and bring in the first Canadian troop convoy. It consisted of five large liners, carrying 7,450 men of the First Canadian Division. That same morning Coastal Command aircraft, and also the submarine *Salmon*, sighted enemy surface forces in the central North Sea, steering west. We shall return to the adventures of this German squadron, which was actually on a minelaying sortie, in the next chapter. To Admiral Forbes the sighting reports presented a possible threat to the approaching Canadian troop convoy since, if the enemy ships were trying to break out into the Atlantic, they could reach the Fair Isle Channels late on the 13th. Accordingly he sailed from the Clyde with the *Warspite*, *Hood* and *Barham* screened by six destroyers. The enemy's intentions had, however, nothing to do with the convoy which, escorted by the *Repulse*, *Resolution* and *Furious* and covered by the heavy ships of the Home Fleet, arrived safely in the Clyde on the appointed day. The only untoward incident was a collision between the outward-bound liner *Samaria* and the *Aquitania*, one of the troop convoy, and also the *Furious*. It was fortunate that none of these three valuable ships received more than superficial damage. Enquiry revealed that the collision had been caused by the *Samaria* being given a route close to the inward-bound convoy's track. This happened because the routing authority in Liverpool had not been informed of the troop convoy's movements. Excessive security precautions are liable to produce unforeseen and unfortunate consequences.

The second Canadian troop convoy, of seven large liners escorted by the *Revenge*, was also met by a strong force of ten destroyers of the Home Fleet which sailed for that purpose on Christmas Day. The third similar convoy did not arrive until the 7th of February 1940 and once again the ocean escort was reinforced by the Home Fleet.

The approach of the Christmas period brought an increase rather than a relaxation of the Home Fleet's duties, for the Admiralty warned Admiral Forbes on the 17th of December of a possible attempt by a number of enemy merchant ships to reach home. The armed merchant cruisers, which had been withdrawn since the 9th, were therefore sent out on the Northern Patrol again and Admiral Forbes took his heavy ships to sea to cover them against an attempt by the enemy to repeat the foray in which the *Rawalpindi* had been sunk. The Admiralty also considered that the enemy might attack the homeward-bound Norwegian convoy (H.N.5), and this possibility meant that the fleet had to cover it as well as the Northern Patrol. In the event, however, the enemy did nothing. On Christmas Eve the Admiralty notified a minefield off the east coast from 58° 20' North to 51° 36' North and instructed all traffic to keep either to the north or to the south of the barrier.[1] The effects of this new declared area will be discussed in the next chapter.

On the 28th of December the battleship *Barham*, which with the *Repulse* and five destroyers had been ordered to remain in northern waters on covering duties, was torpedoed by U.30 in 58° 34' North, 6° 30' West. She reached Liverpool next day to dock but was out of action for three months. An error in the torpedoed ship's signal prevented an effective hunt being organised at once by her escorting destroyers, and the U-boat escaped unscathed.

On New Year's Eve the *Rodney* rejoined Admiral Forbes in the Clyde after being refitted at Liverpool and the Commander-in-Chief hoisted his flag in her the next day.

Thus ended the first phase of the Home Fleet's operations. The period discussed so far had been one of much arduous steaming, often in adverse weather conditions, and the accomplishments had been chiefly of a negative and unspectacular nature. The flow of shipping across the oceans had been well maintained and serious difficulties had not arisen until coastal waters were reached. Action with surface forces had so far been denied to the fleet, and the few U-boats sunk and the captures by the Northern Patrol were the only losses so far inflicted on the enemy. Disappointments had been many and handicaps, the chief of which had been the inability of the fleet to use its chosen base, not a few. But much valuable experience had been gained. It was known that our intelligence was slow and often inaccurate, and that the North Sea air patrols could not be relied on to sight and shadow enemy warships, nor bomber striking forces to find and attack them; it had been shown that, given the necessary gun and fighter defences, the fleet could be assured adequate security from air attack in its bases; that neither anti-aircraft gunnery nor bombing attacks on warships were at present able to achieve their predicted results appeared clear; and that properly organised and promptly executed asdic search could sink enemy U-boats had been demonstrated. The need to remedy weaknesses and deficiencies had been recognised, and the necessary measures to provide the remedies were in hand and were slowly beginning to take effect. But above all Admiral Forbes had shown, by his constant keeping of the seas, without regard to the weather or any of the difficulties which beset him, that the spirit of the fleet and its capacity to control the sea communications to these islands remained unimpaired.

[1] See Map 10 (*facing p. 97*).

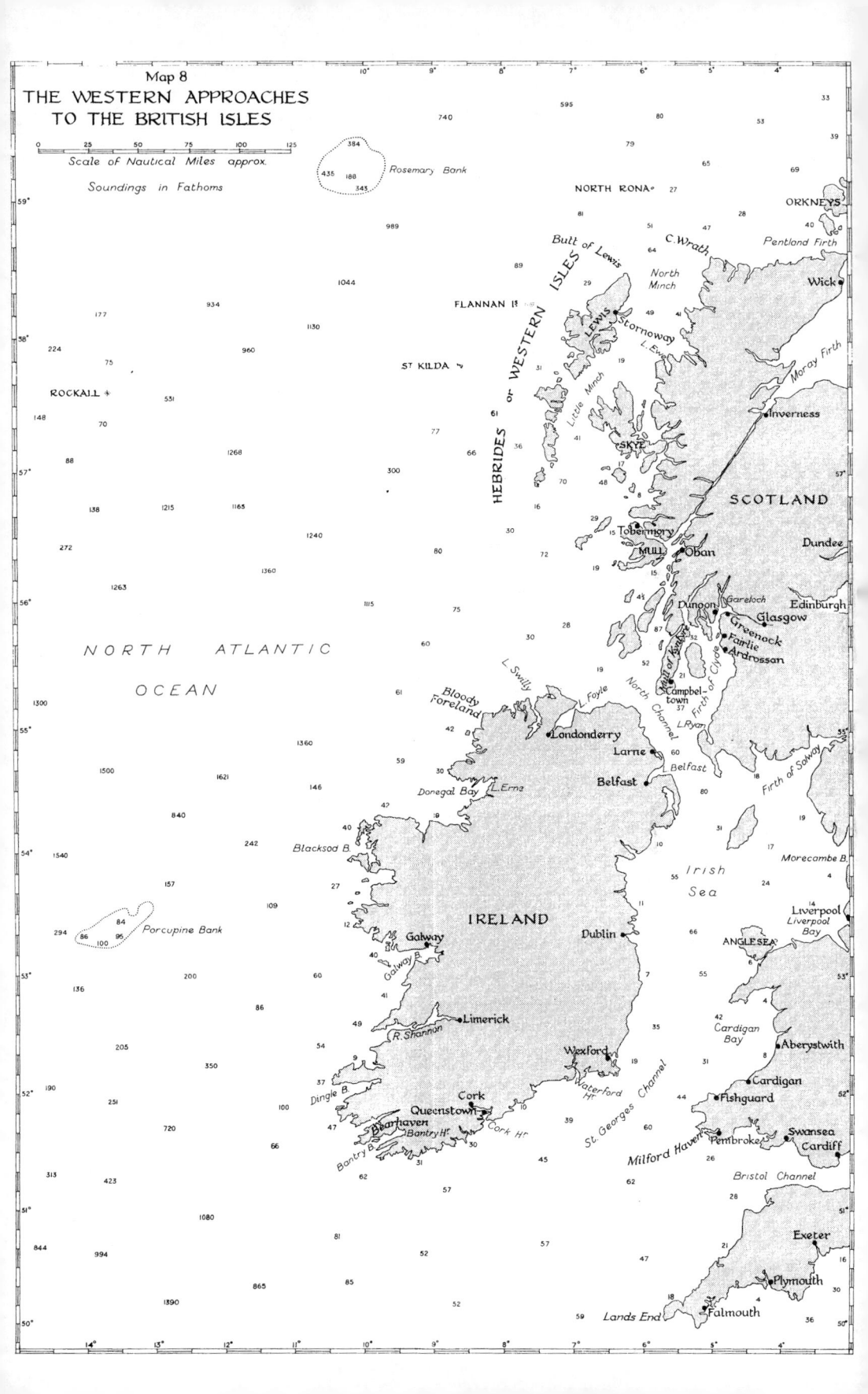

Map 8
THE WESTERN APPROACHES TO THE BRITISH ISLES

Scale of Nautical Miles approx.
Soundings in Fathoms

CHAPTER VI

THE SEA APPROACHES AND COASTAL WATERS

3rd September–31st December, 1939

> The necessity for consistent experiments to determine some satisfactory method of destroying magnetic and acoustic mines cannot be too strongly emphasised.
>
> Extract from the Final Report on Mine Clearance in Home Waters. 15th September 1919.

THE sea approaches to these islands with which, in these volumes, we are principally concerned comprise the waters to the west of our own and Eire's western shores; for it is to and from that direction that the greatest proportion of our shipping passes on its journeys between Britain and ports all over the world. Because so many ships come through these focal waters it was natural that the enemy should concentrate his onslaught there and that the continuous struggle, later called the Battle of the Atlantic, should largely have been waged in these *Western Approaches* from the Atlantic.[1] During the period with which we are now concerned shipping could approach this country from the west by either of two general routes. The first passed north of Ireland and led to the North Channel and into the Irish Sea from the north; these waters were called the *North-West Approaches*. The second passed south of Ireland and led to the English Channel, the St George's Channel and into the Irish Sea from the south; these were known as the *South-West Approaches*.

It will be convenient, however, in the pages which follow to consider the defence of shipping in the sea approaches and in our coastal waters together, since to separate the two, when no clearly defined boundary existed between them, would be artificial. It is also proposed to deal in turn with each of the three main weapons used by the enemy to attack our shipping. These were the mine, the submarine and aircraft.

Before we consider the enemy's offensive against our shipping the counter-measures taken by the Admiralty must be told. The chief of these was, of course, the convoying of merchant ships, and it has

---
[1] See Map 8.

been seen that arrangements for its introduction had been carried to an advanced stage well before the outbreak of war.[1] The Admiralty has, at different times, given various definitions to the expression 'convoy', but modern naval opinion has gained acceptance for the view that it should be defined as 'one or more merchant ships sailing under the protection of one or more warships'. In other words two requirements must be fulfilled before ships can be said to be sailing in convoy—they must be operated in an organised group and they must be provided with an escort. It is in this sense that the term is used throughout these volumes. It is unfortunate that the description 'unescorted convoy' was used during the early months of the war; it is now held that such an expression is a contradiction in terms and that, if no escort is present, the ships, though sailing in an organised group, cannot be called a convoy. To arrive at a fair and proper assessment of the results achieved by the convoy system the losses inflicted on such groups of ships must be excluded from every analysis of shipping sunk while in convoy, and this has been done throughout these pages.

The practice of escorting unarmed or lightly armed merchant ships by warships is of very ancient standing. In particular it was widely practised by this country and its enemies during the European wars of the seventeenth and eighteenth centuries. After the Napoleonic Wars convoy seems to have fallen into disfavour. The introduction of steam and the vast expansion in the amount of commerce carried and the number of ships employed to that end were certainly important factors in bringing about this change of opinion. In retrospect it does, however, seem curious that the principle of providing safe passage against all forms of sporadic war on trade by close escort, on the soundness of which history can provide innumerable examples, should have been lost to sight equally with the practice of making the close escort really effective by assembling and sailing merchant ships in convoy. The immediate success of the measure from 1917 until the end of the First World War proved that modern developments had not made the centuries-old practice obsolete.

The first convoy, consisting of eight important ships sailing from Gibraltar to Capetown, actually left on the 2nd of September before war had been declared. Three days later a troop convoy consisting of eleven transports with reinforcements for numerous bases and overseas garrisons left the Clyde for Gibraltar escorted by the battleship *Ramillies* and eight destroyers. These were, however, not mercantile convoys in the strict sense. A mercantile convoy system runs at regular intervals from the same port of assembly, and the number of days between successive convoys is called the 'convoy cycle'. The

---

[1] See pp. 44–45.

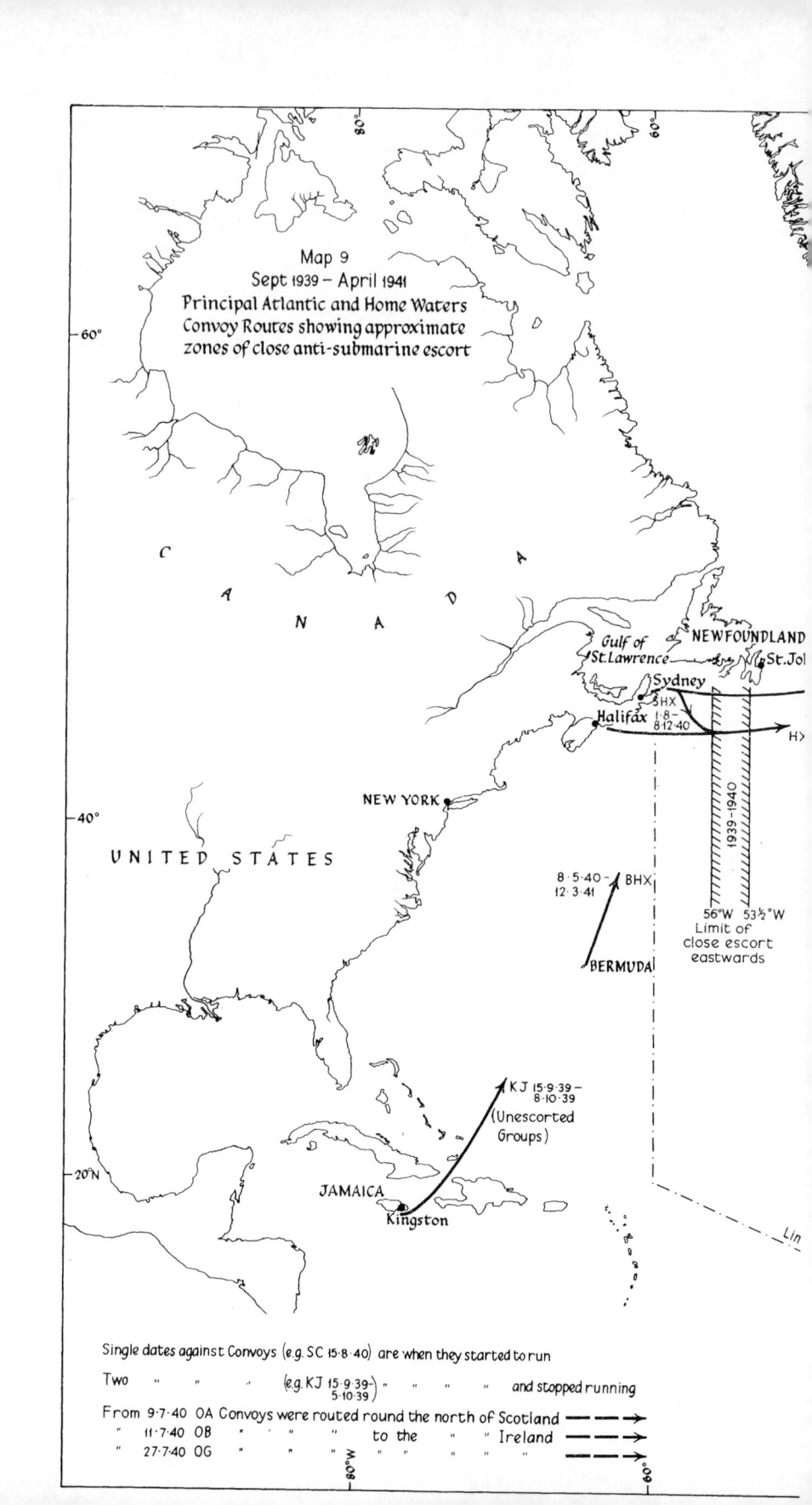

Map 9
Sept 1939 – April 1941
Principal Atlantic and Home Waters
Convoy Routes showing approximate
zones of close anti-submarine escort

CANADA

Gulf of St. Lawrence
NEWFOUNDLAND
St. Joh
Sydney
HX
Halifax 1.8-
         8.12.40

1939–1940
56°W 53½°W
Limit of
close escort
eastwards

NEW YORK

UNITED STATES

8.5.40 – BHX
12.3.41
BERMUDA

KJ 15.9.39 –
   8.10.39
(Unescorted
Groups)

JAMAICA
Kingston

Lin

Single dates against Convoys (e.g. SC 15.8.40) are when they started to run
Two   "   "   "   (e.g. KJ 15.9.39–) "   "   "   and stopped running
                              5.10.39
From 9.7.40 OA Convoys were routed round the north of Scotland ----→
  " 11.7.40 OB   "   "   "   "   "   "   " Ireland   ----→
  " 27.7.40 OG   "   "   "   "   to the "   " "   ----→

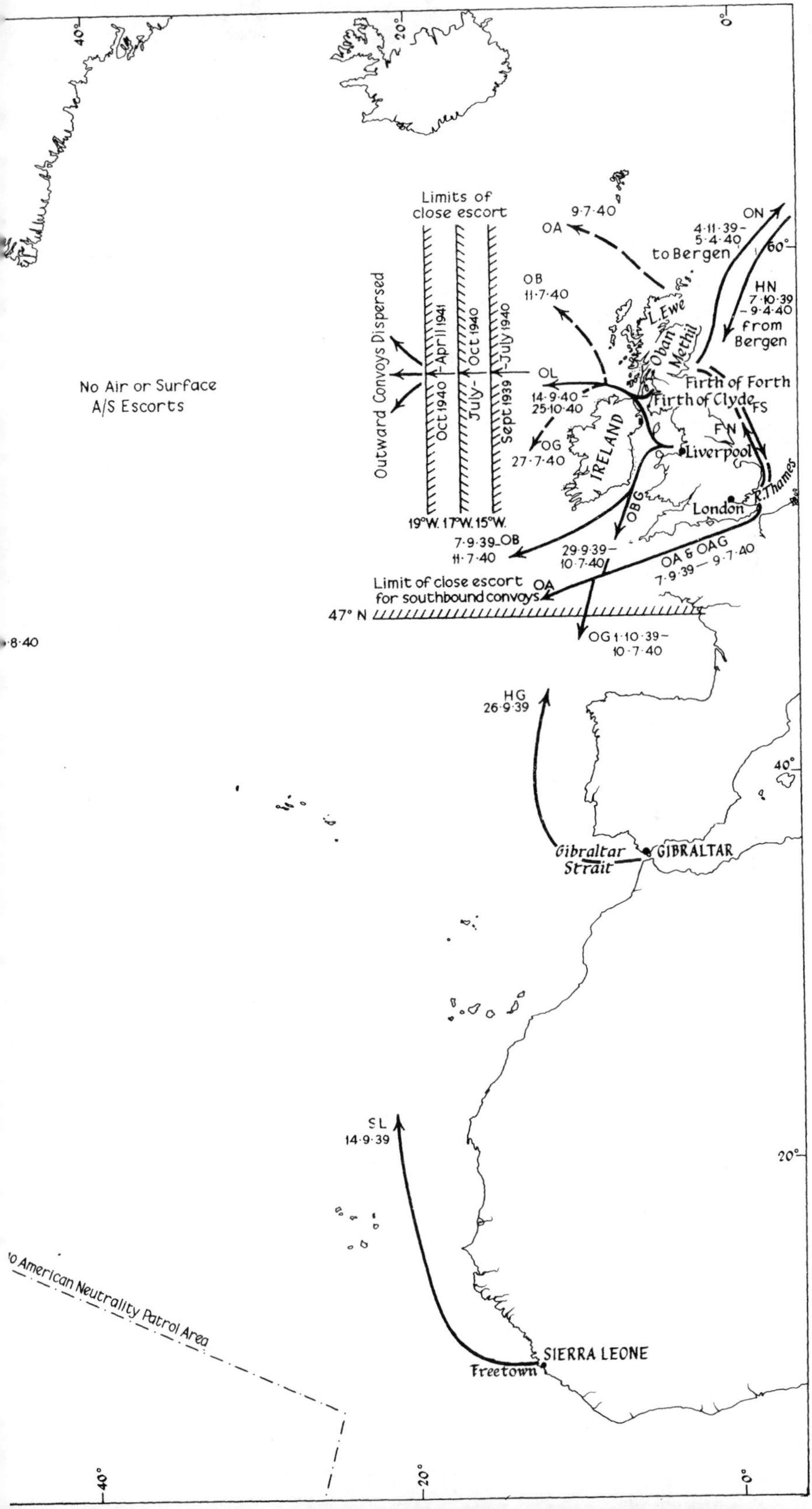

40°
20°
0°
Limits of close escort
9·7·40
OA
ON
4·11·39 – 5·4·40
to Bergen
60°
OB 11·7·40
HN 7·10·39 – 9·4·40 from Bergen
L. Ewe
Oban
Methil
Outward Convoys Dispersed
Oct 1940 – April 1941
July – Oct 1940
Sept 1939 – July 1940
OL
14·9·40 – 25·10·40
Firth of Forth
Firth of Clyde
FS
No Air or Surface A/S Escorts
OG 27·7·40
IRELAND
FN
Liverpool
R. Thames
London
OBG
19°W. 17°W. 15°W.
7·9·39 – OB 11·7·40
29·9·39 – 10·7·40
OA & OAG 7·9·39 – 9·7·40
Limit of close escort for southbound convoys
OA
47° N
·8·40
OG 1·10·39 – 10·7·40
HG 26·9·39
40°
Gibraltar Strait
GIBRALTAR
SL 14·9·39
20°
American Neutrality Patrol Area
SIERRA LEONE
Freetown

earliest mercantile convoys of the war were the east coast convoys between the Thames and the Firth of Forth (F.N.) or vice versa (F.S.). They started on the 6th of September and were initially sailed in each direction every second day.[1] These convoys were the special responsibility of the Rosyth Escort Force—composed of ships with good anti-aircraft as well as anti-submarine armaments. On the 7th of September outward-bound ocean convoys were started. One series (O.A.) sailed every alternate day down-Channel from Southend and another (O.B.) left Liverpool, generally on the same day, and steamed south through the Irish Sea. During the first phase of the war these outward ocean convoys were only given close escort as far as Longitude $12\frac{1}{2}°$ West; west-bound ships dispersed two days after the escorts had left and continued to their destinations independently. The destroyers generally waited at the rendezvous to bring back the next inward convoy. South-bound ships from the O.A. and O.B. convoys were formed into Gibraltar (O.G.) convoys when they reached a position off the Scilly Islands and proceeded with an ocean escort only, until they were met by anti-submarine vessels from Gibraltar to the west of the Straits.

The first homeward-bound convoy sailed from Freetown, Sierra Leone (S.L.), on the 14th of September and the next day a fast convoy (K.J.F. 1) left Kingston, Jamaica, for home. These convoys from Jamaica were not continued for long but were absorbed into the Halifax convoys. The first of the famous series of Halifax convoys (H.X. 1), around whose passages the Battle of the Atlantic was largely to revolve, sailed under Canadian local escort on the 16th of September, followed on the 19th by the first of the fast convoys from the same port (H.X.F. 1), while the first homeward convoy left Gibraltar (H.G. 1) on the 26th of September.

The Norwegian convoys from Bergen to Methil in the Firth of Forth (H.N.) and vice versa (O.N.) were not started until the first week of November, and their escort and safe passage was made the responsibility of the Commander-in-Chief, Home Fleet.

Map 9 shows the more important convoy routes operated during the first eighteen months of the war. In spite of the rapid organisation of a large number of convoys on the outbreak of war many ships already at sea could not be included in convoys during their current voyages. Moreover it had always been intended that ships able to steam over a certain speed (fifteen knots in the North Atlantic), and

---

[1] See Map 9. Each convoy route was allocated a pair of code letters generally, but not always, having a 'self-evident' signification. Thus F.N. 6 would be the sixth northward-bound east coast convoy. H.N. stood for 'Homeward Norwegian', O.G. for 'Outward Gibraltar', etc. The addition of a third letter F or S signified Fast and Slow sections of the same convoy. For simplicity convoy numbers were not generally continued above 99 but were then restarted at 1. Thus it is possible to find two convoys with the same numbers whose sailings were separated by many months. The code letters of the principal convoy routes are given in Appendix J.

also those unable to reach a speed of nine knots, should not be ordered into convoy. They would, instead, merely be given a route to follow and would sail independently. It was among the ships still sailing unconvoyed and the groups of ships sailing in company but for whom no escorts could be found that the U-boats found easy targets during this phase. For example, a group of unescorted ships from Jamaica was attacked in the Western Approaches on the 13th of October and lost two ships; four days later a similar group, homeward-bound from Gibraltar, was attacked off Cape Finisterre and three of their number were sunk. Losses among properly convoyed ships were very few. By the end of the year 5,756 ships had been sailed in them and only four had been sunk by submarines.[1] In spite of the chronic shortage of escort vessels the success of the system was immediately proved; it paid tribute not only to the careful planning by the Admiralty but to the work of the Naval Control Service staffs at home and abroad and to the willing co-operation of the owners and masters of the merchant ships themselves.

The organisation of convoys abroad was made the responsibility of the naval Commander-in-Chief of the theatre, and he was given the necessary powers to enforce Admiralty decisions in this respect. Thus it was on Admiralty instructions to the Commander-in-Chief, America and West Indies, and North and South Atlantic stations respectively, that the Kingston, Gibraltar and Freetown homeward convoys were started in September.

Experience of the system was bound to show where improvements could be made; and the possibility of making such improvements was kept constantly in the minds of the officers of the Trade Division of the Naval Staff. Thus the assembly port of the southward-bound east coast convoys was, at the end of November, altered from the Forth to the Tyne with the object of speeding the flow of shipping on the east coast, and ships proceeded to the Tyne independently. But losses among these independents became heavy and, in February 1940, the convoy system had to be extended to the Forth again.

It has often been said that the convoy system is bound to delay shipping. Superficially this is true, because the speed of a convoy must be the speed of the slowest ship, and loaded ships may have to wait before their convoy is ready to sail. Moreover, when a large number of ships arrives at the same port together the unloading arrangements may be unable to cope with them all. But there are certain other aspects of the problem which tend to show that delays caused by the convoy system have, in the past, been exaggerated and that, when the degree of danger is considerable, it is more economical in terms of tonnage saved to convoy the ships. In the Atlantic it was

---

[1] Appendix R gives monthly losses suffered by Allied merchant shipping and their causes.

REDUCTION OF DELAYS TO SHIPPING

certainly the case that losses among independently-routed ships were so much higher than among those convoyed that the wider use of convoy would, in terms of tonnage saved, have been more economical throughout the recent war. Examples also exist where independently-routed ships steamed much faster than the convoys, but made slower passages because they were so widely diverted from dangers. In fact it now seems that, except in waters where the danger to shipping is slight, it is better to convoy than not to do so. While a war is actually in progress it is bound to be difficult to reach a correct decision on this matter. But it seems clear that failure to convoy when one should have done so is likely to produce worse effects than convoying ships when one need not have done so.

To eliminate all possible causes of delays to our shipping was, of course, a continuous aim of the Admiralty and Ministry of Shipping. During the early days the Cabinet considered the same matter several times. Thus on the 10th of November the First Lord reported to the Cabinet his proposals for a number of measures to reduce delays. Such measures generally involved some reduction in the protection afforded to the ships, and to balance protection against speed of turning ships round became an important issue of policy. By the 17th of November the Ministry of Shipping considered that the initial difficulties were being satisfactorily overcome, but the position remained difficult because, even if imports were reduced from the normal peace-time figure of 60 million tons annually to a total of 47 million tons by rationing and other emergency steps, some 11 million tons of this figure would have to be imported in neutral ships, the chartering of which in time of war is never easy and always expensive.

Troop convoys were always given very strong escorts, drawn generally from the Home Fleet, and the main units of that fleet always covered their progress. Mention of such operations was made when we considered the operations of the Home Fleet during this initial phase.[1]

One of the difficulties encountered in these early days was to persuade neutral shipping to sail in our convoys. This problem also came before the Cabinet, and in November the First Lord suggested that we might get control of all free neutral shipping by charter or other means, and so extend the advantages of convoy to such shipping. At the end of November the First Lord pointed out that, whereas our own losses were steadily decreasing, those suffered by neutrals were rising. But this problem was not finally solved until virtually all European neutral shipping was eliminated by Hitler's 1940 land campaigns. Thereafter arrangements were made to con-

---

[1] See p. 89.

trol much of the shipping of occupied countries and so include it in our convoys.

The closing of the English Channel by a mine barrage across the Straits of Dover formed, as has been seen, part of the naval war plans and aimed both at securing the transports carrying the British Expeditionary Force to France from attack by enemy submarines or flotilla vessels, and at preventing the use by enemy submarines of the shortest route from their bases to the focal areas of our trade in the Western Approaches. The operation was carried out under the orders of the Vice-Admiral, Dover, by the minelayers *Adventure* and *Plover* augmented by the train ferries which were requisitioned and converted for the purpose.

The first of the three stages into which the completion of the barrage was divided was the laying of three lines of shallow and two of deep mines to the east from the Goodwins towards the Belgian coast. A secret channel was left off the Goodwins for use by our own ships.[1] This was started on the 11th of September and the minelayers laid about 3,000 mines during the six following days. They were escorted by the anti-aircraft cruiser *Cairo* and the 19th Destroyer Flotilla, which had been lent from the Channel Force and the Nore Command respectively, and were covered by the Humber Force.

The second stage was the laying of a deep minefield between Folkestone and Cape Gris Nez which, since it was less urgent than the first, was not started until the 25th of September. By the 23rd of October 3,636 mines had been laid and it was completed. The third and final stage consisted of the placing of a double system of indicator loops between the two minefields to detect any U-boats which might attempt the passage of the Straits.[2]

The Dover barrage undoubtedly accomplished its purpose. Only one U-boat is known to have passed through the Straits successfully, and that was on the night of the 11th–12th of September before even the first stage of the barrage had been completed. In October two enemy submarines were blown up and destroyed in the minefields and a third ran aground on the Goodwin Sands. She, too, had almost certainly been mined in the barrage. Thereafter the enemy abandoned the attempt to send his coastal submarines by the shortest route to the focal areas of the central and western Channel —the waters through which all shipping approaching or leaving the southern ports of Britain must pass.

The laying of the Dover barrage was the only defensive minelaying operation carried out in the first weeks of the war, though a declared area between the Humber and the Tyne, about twenty miles wide and a like distance offshore, was proclaimed on the 23rd of Septem-

---

[1] See Maps 3 and 10 (*facing pp. 63 and 97*).
[2] See footnote, p. 81.

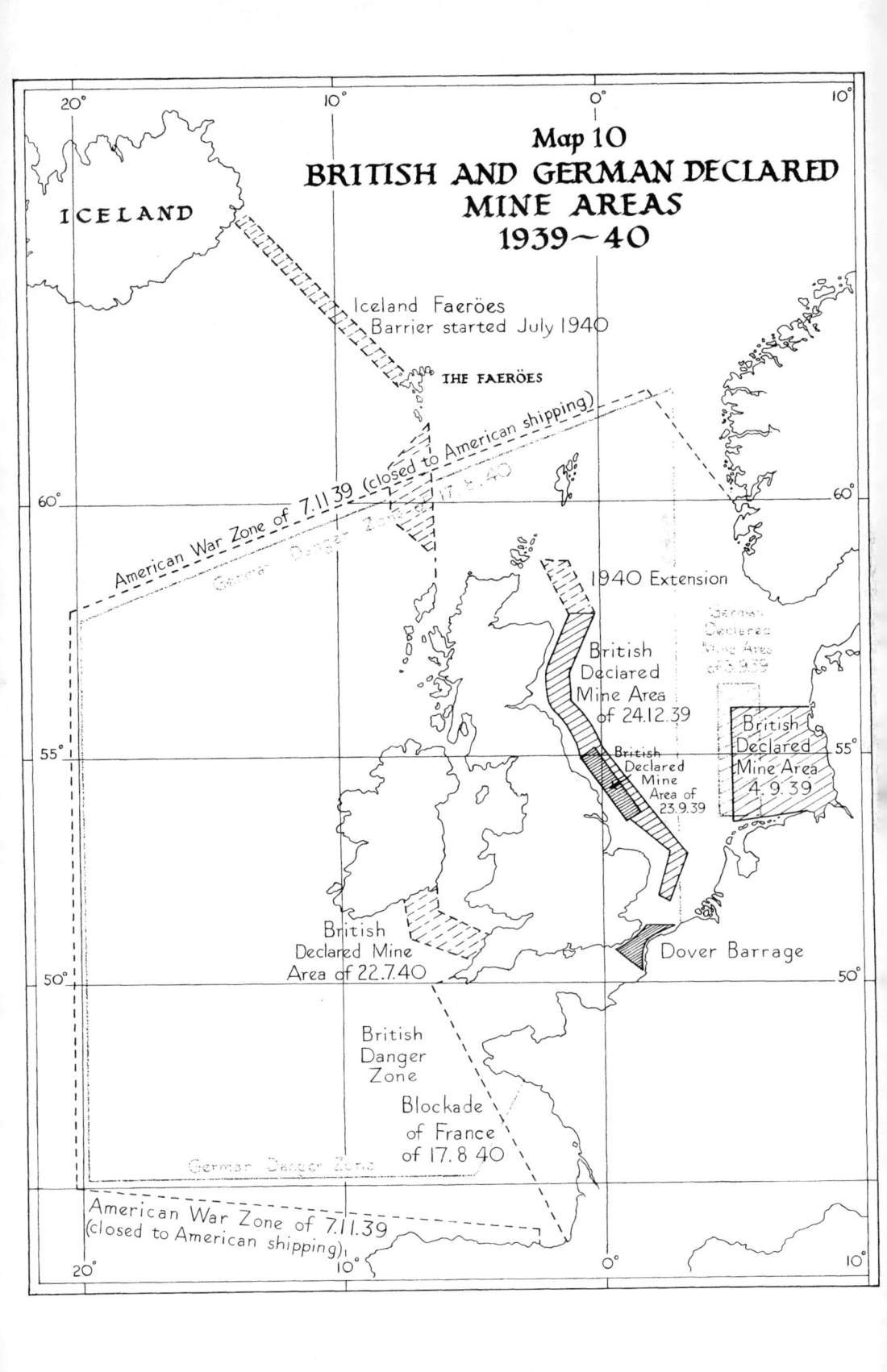

Map 10
BRITISH AND GERMAN DECLARED MINE AREAS 1939–40

ber.[1] This was, in fact, the genesis of the east coast mine barrier, whose purpose was to protect our coastal shipping against incursions by enemy surface vessels or submarines. No mines were, however, actually laid in these waters until the end of the year.

On the 19th November the First Lord placed before the Cabinet the Admiralty's proposal to lay a defensive mine barrage right across the North Sea, extended if possible to the Norwegian coast, with the object of completely closing the exits from that sea to enemy surface vessels and submarines. This proposal was, in fact, a repetition of the Northern Barrage of the closing months of the First World War. It required the laying of 181,000 mines at a cost of nearly £20 millions, and it was estimated that it would take two years to complete. Though the First Lord felt some misgivings regarding the expenditure of so prodigious an effort on a purely defensive measure, he finally commended the scheme and, on the 30th November, the Cabinet approved the start of the necessary preparations.[2] The Foreign Office meanwhile pointed out that the Norwegian Government was most unlikely to agree to the closure of the eastern end of the barrier—which had not been accomplished until two months before the end of the 1914–18 war—and that its effectiveness was therefore likely to be vitiated by the enemy's ability to continue to use Norwegian territorial waters. The Northern barrage proposal was thus intimately connected with stopping the enemy's use of the inshore route along the Norwegian coast, by his iron ore ships from Narvik in particular. This enemy traffic was, in fact, perfectly legitimate; but other uses to which he placed this geographical peculiarity of the Norwegian coastline were certainly less so. The legality of the iron ore traffic passing to Germany by this route did not, however, remove the natural desire of the Admiralty to bring it within our blockade. The First Lord repeatedly pressed on his colleagues the view that it should be stopped by mining the inshore route as a reprisal for German infringements of Norwegian neutrality. The Cabinet, however, refused to sanction the Admiralty proposals. Thus did the question of the control of the coastal communications off Norway begin to play a big part in the political and strategic thoughts and plans of both sides from the earliest days of the war.

Our offensive minelaying campaign, which was to last throughout the whole war and take on many and varied forms, started very soon after war was declared. To augment the forces available for this purpose two destroyers, the *Esk* and *Express*, were converted to minelayers in August 1939, and placed under the orders of the Commander-in-Chief, Home Fleet. A mined area in the Heligoland

---

[1] See Map 10.
[2] W. S. Churchill: *The Second World War* (Cassell & Co.), Vol. I, 2nd edition (1948), p. 453.

Bight was notified by the Admiralty on the outbreak of war, and mines were laid inside its limits by the destroyers on the night of the 9th–10th of September in positions which were believed to lie on the routes used by the German major warships when proceeding to and from their North Sea bases. However, after a second lay had been carried out, doubts arose regarding both the accuracy of the lays and the adequacy of our intelligence on enemy movements; the programme was therefore suspended until both had been improved. The minelaying flotilla was not again employed in an offensive rôle until the middle of December. By that time it had been reinforced by the destroyers *Ivanhoe* and *Intrepid*. The flotilla laid 240 mines in the mouth of the River Ems on the night of the 17th–18th of December without meeting any enemy opposition, and that was the last offensive minelaying operation of 1939.

The enemy meanwhile had not neglected either defensive or offensive minelaying. Like ourselves he notified a declared area in the North Sea. Its limits enclosed a rectangle, stretching north from Dutch waters for about 180 miles, and 60 miles wide. It overlapped with the British declared area.[1] His object was to bar the approaches from the west to his ports and bases on the North Sea coast.

By the end of the year, the Admiralty considered that the swept channels and the areas actually mined by the enemy were known accurately enough. It was accordingly decided to use the minelaying flotilla to place some small fields within the enemy declared area in what were believed to be his swept channels. A number of operations to this end were carried out early in the new year, and it is now known that an enemy torpedo-boat was blown up on one of these fields. This, however, was the only success achieved.

Turning now to the enemy's offensive minelaying, we come to the first important tactical success which must be credited to him. All the mines laid by our own forces in the operations already described were of the contact type and conformed to the requirements of International Law. The enemy had, however, developed and put into production the first of a long series of mines which can be broadly described as being of the influence type, whose explosion was caused not by actual contact with a passing ship but by the influence of a ship's magnetic field on the mechanism of the mine.

The Hague Conventions only refer to contact mines; but it could reasonably have been claimed by the Germans that the magnetic and other influence-type mines conformed to International Law—if they had laid them only in declared areas. But, from the start of their offensive mining campaign, they actually sowed all types of mines wherever they were considered likely to achieve results. It was in the

---

[1] See Map 10 (*facing p. 97*).

manner in which they were used rather than in the use of mines of the influence type that the illegality of the enemy's methods lay. The magnetic mine was, however, by no means a new weapon of war. Such mines had been made by ourselves during the First World War, and we actually laid some in the mouth of the River Scheldt and off Zeebrugge in 1918. That type of magnetic mine was not, however, successful and development was therefore pursued along different lines until, by 1939, the British standard magnetic mine was ready for production. Meanwhile counter-measures were being studied, and an Admiralty committee had been charged with investigating the protection of ships against such weapons. In July 1939 the first trials were done in the Solent with a magnetic sweep. It was a somewhat clumsy affair, but was reasonably successful against our own mines. It was difficult, if not impossible, to design in advance a sweep capable of exploding mines fired by all the numerous variations in magnetic influence which an enemy might employ. We had first to discover the 'firing rule' of the mines used against us. 'Mine destructor ships', which would carry a large magnet in their bows and explode mines ahead of themselves, were also considered by the Admiralty; but the construction of one was struck out of the 1939 Navy Estimates as 'unwarranted expenditure'. They were used later, as will be told shortly, but neither we nor the enemy found them to be successful.

The position on the outbreak of war was, therefore, that the entire British minesweeping force then in service, and the whole of the equipment planned and ordered for the large numbers of auxiliary minesweepers to be requisitioned and converted, were designed only to deal with moored contact mines; but research and development work had been carried to a point where production of a sweep could be started as soon as we became possessed of the necessary information regarding the type of magnetic influence required to fire the enemy's mines. It was in the first week of war that sinkings off the east coast raised the suspicion that the Germans were using ground mines of the influence type, as well as contact mines. This was confirmed when, on the 16th of September, the s.s. *City of Paris* was damaged by an under-water explosion but her hull was not penetrated.

The enemy was, perhaps, justified in claiming that we had been 'tactically and technically surprised'; but he was soon to discover that, thanks to the research work carried out before the war, the measure of surprise which he had achieved was not as great as he believed. And, happily for ourselves, he was not in a position to exploit his success to the uttermost, because on the outbreak of war his stock of magnetic mines was small. Meanwhile in the Admiralty a special staff had been placed under Rear-Admiral W. F. Wake-Walker to hasten the production of counter-measures in collaboration with the mining department of H.M.S. *Vernon*, the torpedo school at Portsmouth, and commercial firms whose work lay in that field.

On the 23rd of November the period of groping for knowledge in the dark ended with the recovery of a complete mine off the mudflats of Shoeburyness, where it had been dropped by an aircraft. It was dissected at great personal risk by Lieutenant-Commander J. G. D. Ouvry. We then discovered that the German mine was fired by a change of magnetism (as opposed to rate of change in the British mine) in the vertical (as opposed to the horizontal) field; and that it required the passage of a ship built in the northern hemisphere, which would therefore have its north magnetic pole downwards.[1]

The enemy realised that we were at first unable to sweep his mines and immediately planned a great increase in production. But it was too late, since before that could be achieved we were possessed of knowledge on which the design of the 'LL Sweep' could be firmly based, and, although a great production effort still had to be made, defeat of the magnetic mine was then in sight.

On the 20th of October the first success in exploding a magnetic mine harmlessly was obtained with an extemporised sweep. But by the end of that month we had lost nineteen ships of 59,027 tons by mines;[2] and many of them had been sunk on the five magnetic fields laid off the east coast and in the Thames estuary.

In November matters got worse and the Nore Command had great difficulty in finding and marking safe channels in the Thames estuary. At one time, in the middle of the month, only one of the three deep-water channels into the river was open, and it seemed that the enemy might succeed in completely stopping the flow of traffic in and out of the Port of London. Fortunately this did not occur, but twenty-seven merchant ships of 120,958 tons and the destroyer *Blanche* were sunk by mines during the month and many more damaged—including the cruiser *Belfast* and the minelayer *Adventure*. Diverting ships from ports off which mines were known to have been laid was not very successful and many ships were sunk in waters known to have been mined.

In the middle of November enemy aircraft started to drop mines, but they lacked the means of fixing their positions accurately and so contributed less than might be expected to augmenting our difficulties. Accurate minelaying by enemy submarines and surface

---

[1] In later mines the polarity was sometimes reversed. These would not only be actuated by a ship built in the southern hemisphere but also by ships built north of the equator whose magnetism had been reversed by excessive 'de-gaussing'. Moreover the inclusion in a minefield of a proportion of mines of both polarities would double the work of sweeping since it would have to be swept for 'South Pole down' as well as for 'North Pole down' mines.

[2] Unless specifically stated otherwise, the figures for merchant ship losses quoted throughout these volumes include Allied ships and neutral ships under British control as well as ships of British registry. They thus represent the best available estimate of the total damage done by the enemy's various weapons to the Allied cause.

'Fleet Minesweepers at work in the Straits.' By Leslie Cole.

(*National Maritime Museum*)

'A Minesweeper.' By Charles Cundall.

(*National Maritime Museum*)

An East Coast convoy, 1940, with an Anson aircraft of Coastal Command in the foreground.

vessels, with contact as well as magnetic mines, had been greatly assisted by the fact that coastal lights were kept burning for the benefit of our own vessels; on the 21st of November lights in the Thames estuary were therefore extinguished, and all traffic west of a line between the Downs and Orfordness was stopped during the hours of darkness. This measure brought immediate relief to the Thames approaches.

Meanwhile, the extemporised measures, which included sweeps, skids, mine destructor ships and specially converted Wellington aircraft, continued their endeavours, though only with occasional successes. The mine destructor ships, of which the *Borde* was the first, proved very vulnerable to damage by the mines they exploded. The minesweeping aircraft scored some successes, but suffered from the weakness that they could only sweep a narrow path which could not be marked. Both were abandoned as soon as better means became available, though the aircraft later proved valuable in assisting to keep the Suez Canal clear of magnetic mines.

Energetic measures were taken by the Admiralty to reduce the magnetism of the ships themselves. Though this could not make them immune from magnetic mines and did not in any way reduce the need to sweep the mines themselves, it did increase the confidence with which the crews of merchant vessels sailed through waters known to be mined. A special department was formed to deal with 'de-gaussing' all our warships and merchantmen. This involved not only an enormous and immediate demand on manufacturers of electric cable, but placed an additional strain on our overburdened shipyards. The effort involved in carrying out the programme was comparable in size and scope to fitting all our Merchant Navy with defensive armaments.[1] But whereas the latter had been provided for, and the necessary measures put in hand well before the outbreak of war, a similar organisation for 'de-gaussing' or 'wiping' the ships, and for keeping that part of their war-time equipment efficient, had to be built up from nothing. It was gradually extended to all the major ports of the world.

In December the enemy switched his chief minelaying activities from the Thames estuary to the narrow channels off the Norfolk coast through which the east coast convoys had to pass. Pressure on the Nore Command minesweepers and on the organisation for the control of shipping continued severe, though the general outlook was less critical than in the preceding month. Thirty-three merchant ships of 82,712 tons were sunk by mines and eight others damaged, but there was a decline in the number of magnetic mines laid, owing, we now know, to the enemy's stocks having run low. It was indeed

---

[1] See pp. 21-22.

fortunate that the enemy had only manufactured some 1,500 by the time war broke out, and was able to produce very few more during the first months of the war. On the other hand, his stores had held over 20,000 contact mines when war broke out and it was, therefore, on the laying of that type of mine that his campaign chiefly depended during the early months. The losses and dislocation caused by magnetic mines were, in fact, out of all proportion to the 470 mines actually laid during the first three months of the war.

On the night of the 12th–13th of December five enemy destroyers, covered by the light cruisers *Leipzig*, *Nürnberg* and *Köln* laid a large contact field off the Tyne. A Bomber Command striking force searched for the enemy without success but, at dawn on the 13th of December, the submarine *Salmon* (Lieutenant-Commander E. O. B. Bickford), on patrol in the Heligoland Bight, sighted the force. Nine days earlier she had sunk U.36 with torpedoes. Now she added to the success of a remarkable patrol by hitting both the *Leipzig* and *Nürnberg*. Unfortunately heavy counter-attacks prevented her making an enemy report until five hours later, which delay improved the chances of the damaged ships making good their escape. Two days later the submarine *Ursula* sighted the damaged *Leipzig* limping south along the Danish coast and attacked unsuccessfully, though her torpedoes sank one of the escorting flotilla vessels. The *Nürnberg* was out of action until May 1940 and the *Leipzig* until the following December, and even after that date could not be restored to full operational use, but was only employed on training duties. This bold minelaying operation by the enemy therefore ended with a substantial success to our submarines and a serious loss to his own cruiser strength—regrettable though it was that neither of the ships attacked was actually sunk.

To summarise this first phase of the minelaying campaign, the enemy had caused us substantial losses in the first four months of war, totalling seventy-nine merchant ships of 262,697 tons, and had dislocated the flow of our coastal shipping very seriously. One countermeasure which was denied to us, on account of the restrictive rules on air bombardment then in force, was to bomb the seaplane bases from which his minelaying aircraft were known to work, or the naval bases used by his submarine and surface minelayers. On the 12th of December the Air Ministry proposed to maintain bomber patrols over these bases; but the Cabinet would not permit bombs to be dropped. Yet the whole enemy campaign had been contrary to International Law and the Cabinet had only very recently introduced control of enemy exports in retaliation for these illegal methods of waging war.

To turn now from the enemy's minelaying campaign to the first phase of the U-boat war on our merchant shipping, it has been seen that his full available strength of ocean-going U-boats had sailed for the Atlantic before the outbreak of war, and that his coastal boats had been sent to patrol for short periods of about fourteen days in the North Sea and at the eastern end of the Channel.[1] On the 7th of September there were twenty-one ocean-going boats disposed from the northern entrance to the Irish Sea as far south as the Straits of Gibraltar. Such an effort could not, however, be sustained for long, and by the middle of the month some boats had returned to their home bases. On the 18th only eleven remained on patrol in the Atlantic.

But it was to be expected that such a large initial effort should cause appreciable losses in the first weeks of the war, because the Admiralty's control of merchant shipping had not yet had time to take full effect, and the organisation of convoys and other protective measures were still in their infancy. The first casualty occurred on the day war was declared, when the Donaldson liner *Athenia* was sunk without warning by U.30 in flagrant disobedience to Hitler's orders to wage submarine war only in accordance with the Hague Conventions. The Germans investigated the *Athenia* incident fully and decided to keep the truth secret. No disciplinary action was taken against the culprit, who was held to have 'acted in good faith' in the belief that the ship was an armed merchant cruiser. They never admitted responsibility for the sinking.

Hitler's original orders to the German Navy, including the U-boats, to wage war only in accordance with the Prize Regulations, were not issued in any altruistic spirit but in the hope that, after Poland had been crushed, Britain and France—and especially the latter—would make peace. As soon as it was realised that this hope was vain, removal of the restrictions on the methods of waging war at sea started. It will be appropriate to review now the various stages through which this process passed.

On the 23rd of September, Hitler, on the recommendation of Admiral Raeder, approved that 'all merchant ships making use of their wireless on being stopped by U-boats should be sunk or taken in prize'. As the immediate despatch of a wireless signal in such circumstances was included in the Admiralty's instructions to merchant ships and was essential—if for no other reason—to the rescue of their crews, this German order marked a considerable step towards unrestricted warfare. Next day, again as a result of representations by Raeder, the order forbidding attacks on French warships was cancelled. On the 30th of September observance of the Prize Regulations in the North Sea was withdrawn; and on the 2nd of October complete freedom was given to attack darkened ships encountered off the British and French coasts. Two days later the Prize Regulations were cancelled in waters extending as far as 15° West, and on

---
[1] See p. 59.

the 17th of October the German Naval Staff gave U-boats permission 'to attack without warning all ships identified as hostile'. The zone where darkened ships could be attacked with complete freedom was extended to 20° West on the 19th of October. Practically the only restrictions now placed on U-boats concerned attacks on liners and, on the 17th of November, they too were allowed to be attacked without warning if 'clearly identifiable as hostile'. Although the enemy this time carefully avoided the expression 'unrestricted U-boat warfare', it can therefore be said that, against British and French shipping, it was, in fact, adopted by the middle of November 1939. Neutral shipping was also warned by the Germans against entering the zone which, by American neutrality legislation, was forbidden to American shipping, and against steaming without lights, zig-zagging or taking any defensive precautions[1]; it was not until the following year that more drastic action was threatened.

Though the change from full observance of the Prize Regulations to virtually unrestricted U-boat warfare was made cautiously in order to avoid trouble with the United States or offending the 'friendly neutrals'—Russia, Japan, Italy and Spain—it is to be remarked that, in the First World War, it was not until the 31st January 1917—after nearly two and a half years of war—that the Germans reached a stage which, in the second war, took them only a few months to travel. It is impossible to avoid the conclusion that Admirals Raeder and Dönitz and the German Naval Staff had always wished and intended to introduce unrestricted warfare as rapidly as the political leaders could be persuaded to accept the possible consequences.

To return to the operations by the U-boats, in spite of the advantage gained by the dispositions taken up before war broke out, all did not go well with Dönitz's plans. In October the first attempt at co-ordinated attacks by several boats against the Gibraltar convoys failed completely; an intended thrust into the Mediterranean also came to nothing. In the following month a second attempt at co-ordinated attacks fared little better than the first. Mines laid by the smaller boats in the approaches to our ports on the west as well as on the east coast sometimes achieved important results; but these boats accomplished little in direct attacks on shipping.

The use by the U-boats of the northern route to the Atlantic, as the necessary consequence of our closure of the Dover Straits by the mine barrage already described, led to frequent sightings by aircraft of Coastal Command flying the normal North Sea reconnaissance patrols. The naval and air staffs at the Command's headquarters had been developing a system of special air patrols based on careful study of the probable times of arrival of U-boats in certain fairly well

---
[1] See Map 10 (*facing p. 97*).

defined areas. They were designed to harry the U-boats while on passage. This led, before the end of the year, to a full realisation of the great contribution which aircraft could make to the defence of merchant shipping against submarine attack—once an effective anti-submarine weapon had been provided. On the 13th of November a directive was issued to Coastal Command that action against U-boats was to be regarded as of equal importance to reconnaissance duties. This directive forms something of a landmark in the development of the great structure of sea-air co-operation. But progress in the employment of aircraft against U-boats was bound to be slow, since not only had Bomber and Coastal Command aircrews received practically no pre-war training in this highly specialised form of warfare, but a suitable weapon was still lacking. We shall return to that subject later. For the present it is only necessary to remark the complete lack of success obtained by air attacks on U-boats during these early months, and to record that conclusive evidence of the ineffectiveness of the weapons then used was soon received through mis-identification of our own submarines by friendly aircraft which, on two occasions, bombed them without inflicting any damage.

Before leaving the first phase of the U-boat war, it will be appropriate to consider two attacks which took place in September on our aircraft carriers. The first was against the *Ark Royal* which on the 14th of September was temporarily detached from the Home Fleet and operating to the west of the Hebrides as part of a hunting group against U-boats. The torpedoes missed astern of the aircraft carrier, whose escorting destroyers promptly counter-attacked, sank U.39 and captured her crew. But the escape of this important ship had been narrow, and such good fortune was not to be repeated when next a U-boat encountered a fleet carrier in search of the same quarry. On the 12th of September the enemy's wireless intelligence service estimated correctly that the *Courageous* was working in the Western Approaches, but no accurate knowledge regarding her movements was deduced. The War Diary of U.29 leaves no doubt that the sighting of the aircraft carrier at 6 p.m. on the 17th of September was entirely unexpected. The U-boat was, in fact, almost at the end of her patrol and was proceeding, as a final operation, to try to intercept a convoy reported by another U-boat, when she sighted the *Courageous* through her periscope. It was not until nearly two hours later that an attack could be made, and then only because the carrier suddenly altered course to 'fly on' her aircraft and so placed the U-boat in a favourable attacking position. Moreover, the *Courageous* was at the time screened by only two destroyers, since the other two comprising her escort had been detached to the assistance of a merchant ship which had been attacked. An unlucky chain of circumstances thus placed this valuable ship in a position of great danger, which Lieutenant Schuhart of U.29 exploited to the full. At 7.50 he fired three torpedoes at a range of less than 3,000 yards and two of them hit. The *Courageous* sank in fifteen minutes with the loss of her Commanding Officer (Captain W. T. Makeig-Jones) and 518 of her complement. U.29, though heavily counter-attacked until midnight, successfully returned to her base.

As a result of these attacks the Cabinet advised the withdrawal of fleet aircraft carriers from submarine hunting work. Our weakness in that class of ship, of which only the *Ark Royal* was of modern design, and the obvious danger to which submarine hunting would expose them, now makes it seem surprising that they should have been risked on that type of duty. It is possible that the understandable desire at once to take the offensive against the U-boats, and confidence in the protection which asdic-fitted destroyers would provide to heavy ships, both contributed to acceptance of the risks involved.

To summarise the results achieved in this first phase of the U-boat war, our merchant ship losses were as follows:—

Table 5. Allied Merchant Ship Losses, September–December 1939

September 1939	41 ships	153,879 tons
October 1939	27 ships	134,807 tons
November 1939	21 ships	51,589 tons
December 1939	25 ships	80,881 tons
TOTAL	114 ships	421,156 tons

Of the 114 ships sunk only twelve were in convoy; five more were stragglers from convoys when they were sunk. In accomplishing these results the enemy had, however, lost nine U-boats—about one-sixth of his total strength.[1] From the Admiralty's point of view the results achieved were by no means discouraging. But it was realised that, as the enemy's war construction programme gathered way, the campaign was bound to be intensified and that this first phase was little more than a preliminary skirmish between the opposing forces. During the last two months of the year the mine had actually surpassed the U-boat as the principal cause of our shipping losses.

Now that we have reviewed the first phase of the enemy's assault on our seaborne trade by mine and submarine, it remains to consider the start of his use of the air weapon for similar purposes. It will be remembered that the Naval Staff had, before the war, held the view that such attacks would be countered by the normal and proved methods of defending merchant shipping, such as the use of convoy, and had considered that the weapons mounted in the escort vessels

---

[1] Details of U-boats sunk are given in Appendix K.

would provide adequate defence.[1] The Air Staff had been sceptical on this matter, but the result had been that provision for the air defence of shipping had not been given high priority. Offensive action against enemy forces of all types which might attack our shipping was placed third and last in priority for the allocation of Coastal Command's exiguous forces. Thus not only were no aircraft available for that purpose on the outbreak of war, but no training in protecting shipping against air attack had been carried out between the two services concerned. Nor had the responsibility for counter-measures to air attacks on our shipping been clearly defined or firmly placed. That the chief reason for this state of affairs was the too-sanguine outlook of the Naval Staff towards the air defence of both warships and merchant shipping now seems clear. The pre-war statement of one of the Committee of Imperial Defence's sub-committees that 'the problem of the protection of merchant shipping from air attack is at present unsolved' was rapidly substantiated.

It was not until the 1st of August 1939 that the Committee of Imperial Defence finally sanctioned the formation of four Trade Defence squadrons to act as close escorts to merchant ships sailing between Southampton and the Firth of Forth when more than five miles from the coast—the limit of radio-telephone communications between Fighter Command Sector Headquarters and the single-seater fighters of that command—and on the outbreak of war there was little likelihood of these squadrons being ready before the following year.[2] However, when the enemy began to attack east coast shipping from the air in October, the formation of the four squadrons —Nos. 235, 236, 248 and 254—all of which were equipped with the fighter version of the Blenheim bomber, was hastened and all were formed on the 17th of that month.

The allocation of the responsibility for controlling these four squadrons proved difficult. Though the Admiralty and Air Ministry had agreed before the war that protection of shipping was among the responsibilities of Coastal Command, it was now realised that the coastal convoys constituted a special case. Fighter Command was already responsible for the defence of our ports and bases, and so of any shipping which might be within their limits, and its aircraft could be expected to afford some security to ships sailing within a few miles of the coast. It was accordingly decided that air protection of the coastal routes was, in principle, an extension of the existing zone of cover provided by Fighter Command, and it was to that command that the four Trade Protection squadrons were therefore initially assigned.

This arrangement was, however, of short duration, partly because

---

[1] See pp. 33–34.
[2] See p. 39.

the Blenheim fighter was not well suited to the work and partly because aircraft of that type were constantly in demand for other maritime duties, such as armed long-range reconnaissance or protection of the fleet at sea. Neither of these requirements were responsibilities of Fighter Command, and both were new commitments for Coastal Command. The only way of meeting them was to divert the Blenheim squadrons to these duties, which soon came to absorb virtually the whole of their capacity. It was, therefore, only logical that they should be controlled by the command within whose sphere lay the greater part of their work. In December they were temporarily transferred to Coastal Command and in February 1940 the transfer became permanent. This, however, left the responsibility of protecting coastal shipping with Fighter Command, but using the short-range aircraft of the Air Defence of Great Britain (A.D.G.B.) organisation instead of the longer-range Blenheim fighters.

It was on the east coast that these problems first had to be faced. Though the enemy's air attacks on shipping were initially inaccurate and caused little damage, it was plain that the moral effect on the crews of slow and defenceless coasting steamers, fishing trawlers and even light vessels—all at that time practically unarmed—might soon become serious. Moreover these early attacks could but be regarded as harbingers of a more intensive assault of this nature on our coastal shipping. By the last month of the year they had, in fact, become more frequent and effective and ten small ships totalling 2,949 tons were lost from this cause in December.

As these arrangements were gradually evolved, Fighter Command's aircraft began to work from coastal stations between Norfolk and the Moray Firth and, in order to be able rapidly to send out aircraft in response to calls for help, each station kept watch on the wireless frequency used by any convoy which might be passing through its sector. In the spring of 1940 Fighter Command's organisation was extended to the east and north to improve the protection afforded. Calls from shipping more than twenty miles from the coast were at first answered by any Coastal Command aircraft which might be available, but in May 1940 Fighter Command's responsibility was extended to forty miles offshore. All calls from shipping closer in were answered by Fighter Command aircraft from the nearest station.

It was not to be expected that this newly-evolved system would always be effective, and the frequent arrival of the fighters after the bombs had been dropped resulted in demands for constant cover to be provided over the convoys. This requirement could not easily be met from the forces then available to Fighter Command; and such a system ran counter to the principle of control of fighter interception from Group and Sector Headquarters, on which the whole A.D.G.B.

organisation was founded. Not until February 1940 was a daily routine of fighter cover over the east coast convoy route agreed to by Fighter Command.

The difficulties encountered over protecting coastal shipping from air attack have been told in some detail, because they were brought about through failure to foresee such a necessity in time of peace and to make proper provision for it in the war plans. Though it is unlikely that, even had the requirement been foreseen, more, and more suitable, aircraft and more weapons could have been allocated to that purpose before the outbreak of war, the various spheres of responsibility could have been defined, the necessary organisation set up and a certain amount of tactical training carried out. As it was, all of this had to be learned from experience gradually and often painfully accumulated after the outbreak of war.

But the arrangements described above, though largely extemporised and, at this time, often unsuccessful, have considerable historical interest because they were the genesis of a world-wide system of protecting ocean as well as coastal shipping from air attack. The final answer lay in the control of the fighter aircraft from the ships which they were protecting—for it was the ships which generally obtained the first visual or radar warning of impending attack. A long road was, however, to be travelled from the early arrangements described in the preceding paragraphs to the institution of a co-ordinated system of 'Fighter Direction' from warships —as it was called later. It was this method which finally proved the answer to the protection of ships from air attack. The whole art of fighter direction depended on efficient radar warning sets in the ships and efficient radio-telephone communications from the ships to the aircraft, neither of which existed in the early days. The need was recognised in naval circles first, for it was the ships which were attacked and could not defend themselves; but the principle of the control of its aircraft by ships was at first unacceptable to Fighter Command.

By the end of this first phase of the war the essential contribution of aircraft to the defence of trade, and the extent to which they would condition all maritime operations was widely realised in the Home Fleet and in the squadrons and flotillas responsible for protecting our coastal shipping. Opinion had, indeed, moved a long way from the pre-war contention, which had been reflected in the Admiralty's war plans, that, when at sea, the fleet would, by virtue of its anti-aircraft armaments and its carrier-borne fighters, be able to look after itself, and that the normal system of convoy and escort would afford adequate protection to our shipping against air attack.

While the staffs of the two services were working out the system of protecting coastal shipping, the Admiralty was doing all it could to equip the coastal convoys and fishing trawlers with some form of anti-aircraft armament. Early experience had shown that not only was a gun—even of obsolete type and probably ineffective—of great moral value to the crews, but that the effect of its fire on aircraft making low attacks was out of all proportion to the probability of the aircraft receiving lethal damage. Unfortunately the armament stores were nearly bare even of the light machine guns preserved after the 1914-18 war, and urgent steps, such as calling in weapons from ship and shore bases which stood in less immediate need of them, could not meet the whole of this new requirement for light anti-aircraft weapons. The Admiralty, therefore, instituted a search for substitutes and many and various were the devices of that nature sent to sea. We shall meet them again in later chapters.

It was not only the shortage of anti-aircraft weapons which handicapped the defence of merchant ships against air attack. The Navy did not possess anything like the number of trained gunners needed to fight the weapons; nor could the reservists who manned the merchant ships' defensive armaments entirely fill the gap. Though the shortage of anti-aircraft gunners did not come to a head until the following year there were, by the end of 1939, clear signs that many thousands of such men would be needed for the Merchant Navy.

CHAPTER VII

OCEAN WARFARE

3rd September–31st December, 1939

> I consider the protection of our trade the most essential service that can be performed.
> *Nelson to Captain Benjamin Hallowell.*
> 20th March 1804.

DURING the first phase of the war the enemy used his submarines, aircraft and minelayers to dispute our control of the sea communications in the approaches to these islands and in our coastal waters. The days when U-boats would range far out into the ocean spaces, would supplement and to some extent replace the surface raiders, still lay far ahead. During this period the enemy's threat to our merchantmen in the distant oceans came only from his powerfully armed pocket-battleships. The fast merchant ship specially armed for this purpose had not yet entered on the stage, because the German policy had been to avoid arousing suspicions by starting such measures in times of peace; but the enemy's war plans included converting no less than twenty-six ships into armed merchant raiders and this work was very soon started. One ship was fitted out at Murmansk, near to which the Russians had given their temporary friends the use of a base. The first armed merchant raider was to be ready to start work in February 1940, and Admiral Raeder intended to use them chiefly in the Indian Ocean. In November 1939 a proposal to ask Japan to allow the use of bases by merchant raiders and submarines operating in the Far East was approved by Hitler. The extent of the assistance to German raiding operations given by Russia and Japan before either was at war will become apparent later.

The effectiveness of surface raiders depends not only on the actual sinkings and captures which they accomplish but on the disorganisation to the flow of shipping which their presence, or even the suspicion of their presence, generates. Furthermore they are certain to necessitate redisposition and dispersal of the defending side's naval forces. This may weaken its maritime control in other theatres and thus improve the prospects of operations by other enemies in those theatres. Minelaying in remote waters is another potent weapon which the surface raider can employ, and Admiral Raeder always intended to equip his armed merchant raiders with mines. The impact of the enemy operations now to be discussed must not therefore be judged solely by the losses inflicted, which, in fact, were not serious during this early phase.

Admiral Raeder's policy was to use his pocket-battleships from the outset of the war for the purpose for which they had been designed. Accordingly, as already mentioned, the *Admiral Graf Spee* left Germany on the 21st of August and passed through the Faeröes–Iceland channel to her waiting position in mid-Atlantic. She was followed three days later by her sister ship the *Deutschland*, which took up a similar position in the North Atlantic. Each was attended by a supply ship. Their object was defined as being 'the disruption and destruction of enemy merchant shipping by all possible means'; enemy naval forces, even if inferior, were only to be engaged if such action would further the chief task. There is little doubt that this cautious policy was required by the enemy's knowledge that, since he lacked any overseas bases, serious damage received in action could only be repaired by bringing the damaged ship home. But it seems likely that it led not only to irresolution in action on the part of German senior officers but to the engagement of the enemy—even if superior in strength—with enhanced confidence by our own ships. The enemy's campaign against our Atlantic shipping was, from the beginning, affected by President Roosevelt's order of the 5th of September to the United States Navy to establish a Neutrality Patrol in the Atlantic, in order to discourage the belligerents from conducting warlike operations in the waters adjacent to the coastline of the countries of the Western Hemisphere. The Neutrality Patrol area ran initially from a point to the east of Halifax in longitude 60° West, south to latitude 20° North and thence to a point some 600 miles south of the Cape Verde Islands. From there it ran roughly parallel to the coast of South America.[1] Hitler was, from the outset, anxious to avoid any action which might alienate the United States, and he instructed German captains to avoid incidents which might have that effect. But German warships soon entered the Neutrality Patrol area in the south and no limit on its right to pursue and engage such enemies was ever admitted by the British Government. Apart from placing a by no means firm limit to the Atlantic waters within which the enemy was likely to attack our merchant ships, the American President's order brought little advantage to our cause.

The departure of the two pocket-battleships from their home waters was followed by a period of inactivity for them both, because of Hitler's hope that, with the successful conclusion of the Polish campaign, Britain and France would be prepared to make peace. Not until the 26th of September were they permitted to start attacks on British shipping, and, in the vain hope that it would contribute to

---

[1] See Map 11 (*facing p. 115*).

ADMIRALTY LEARNS THAT THEY ARE AT SEA

dividing the Allied countries, the ban on attacking French ships was maintained until the middle of the following month. When the raiding warships were finally allowed to start work their orders were to obey Prize Law. By doing so the Germans hoped to avoid trouble with neutral countries, and in particular with the United States. But this restriction did not last long.

The plans made and dispositions ordered by the Admiralty to deal with the expected threat from powerful surface raiders have already been outlined. The general policy was to patrol the focal areas with cruisers, to form ocean convoys in particularly dangerous waters or for the most valuable ships, but, in general, to rely on 'evasive routing' of shipping from one focal area to the next, at any rate until such time as escorts for ocean convoys were available. When the presence of a raider was known or strongly suspected hunting groups were immediately to be formed.

We now know that the *Graf Spee* narrowly escaped detection very early in her cruise, and before she had been allowed to start attacks on shipping. On the 11th of September, while in company with the *Altmark* in mid-Atlantic south of the equator, the pocket-battleship's reconnaissance aircraft sighted a British cruiser only about thirty miles away and on an approaching course. There is no doubt that this must have been the *Cumberland*, which was then on passage from Freetown to Rio de Janeiro. The aircraft was not sighted by the cruiser but was able to warn her parent ship, which immediately slipped away to the eastward. It was not the last time that a raider's reconnaissance aircraft gave timely warning of the approach of one of our cruisers.

The Admiralty had reason to suspect that one pocket-battleship was at large during the first weeks of the war and it was on the 1st of October, only a week after Hitler had allowed his raiders to start work, that the presence of such a warship in the South Atlantic was definitely confirmed. On that day the crew of the *Graf Spee's* first victim, the British s.s. *Clement*, which had been sunk off the coast of Brazil on the 30th of September and been picked up by another ship, reached the coast of South America. They reported, however, that the raider was the *Admiral Scheer*. The presence of a second raiding warship was not known until the 21st of October when the crew of the Norwegian s.s. *Lorentz W. Hansen* reached the Orkneys in another ship and reported that their ship had been sunk on the 14th by the *Deutschland* 400 miles to the east of Newfoundland.[1] On the day following receipt of this intelligence further confirmation was obtained from the arrival of the American s.s. *City of Flint* at Murmansk with a prize crew from the same pocket-battleship aboard.

---

[1] See p. 70.

I

RAIDER HUNTING GROUPS FORMED

The Admiralty acted promptly when the presence of each of these raiding warships was confirmed. On the 5th of October, as a result of the report of the crew of the *Clement* and after consulting the French Ministry of Marine, no less than eight powerful hunting groups were ordered to be formed. The world-wide nature of these redispositions and their effect on other theatres of war are best indicated by showing them in tabular form:—

Table 6. Raider Hunting Groups, October 1939

Name of Force	Composition of hunting group	Area of operations	Diverted from
F	*Berwick* and *York*	North America and West Indies	Halifax
G	*Exeter, Cumberland.* (*Ajax* and *Achilles* later)	South-east coast of America	South Atlantic
H	*Sussex* and *Shropshire*	Cape of Good Hope	Mediterranean
I	*Cornwall, Dorsetshire, Eagle*	Ceylon	China
K	*Ark Royal, Renown*	Pernambuco	Home Fleet
L	*Dunkerque, Béarn,* and three French 6-inch cruisers	Brest	—
M	Two French 8-inch cruisers	Dakar	—
N	*Strasbourg* and *Hermes*	West Indies	*Hermes* from Plymouth

In addition to forming these hunting groups the Admiralty allowed the Commander-in-Chief, South Atlantic, to retain four destroyers previously ordered home; the *Resolution, Revenge, Enterprise* and *Emerald* were sent to Halifax to escort homeward-bound Atlantic convoys and were followed later by the *Repulse, Furious* and *Warspite*, while the *Malaya* and *Glorious* were passed through the Suez Canal into the Indian Ocean. Force F never worked as a hunting group because, when the *Deutschland's* presence in the North Atlantic was confirmed, its cruisers were ordered to cover Halifax convoys. Forces G, H and K were placed under the operational control of the Commander-in-Chief, South Atlantic (Admiral G. H. d'Oyly Lyon), and the long and anxious searches in the wastes of the South Atlantic for the *Graf Spee* fell chiefly on these three groups.

The Admiralty's measures to hunt down surface raiders greatly depended on the ability of an attacked merchant ship to make a report by wireless immediately an enemy was identified, and instructions to that end had been issued to all masters. The enemy raiders soon became aware of this system and then took steps, such as the threat of immediate sinking, to prevent the transmission of these reports. But, as will be seen, the attacked merchant ships did in many cases manage to send these important messages in time and at grave risk to themselves.

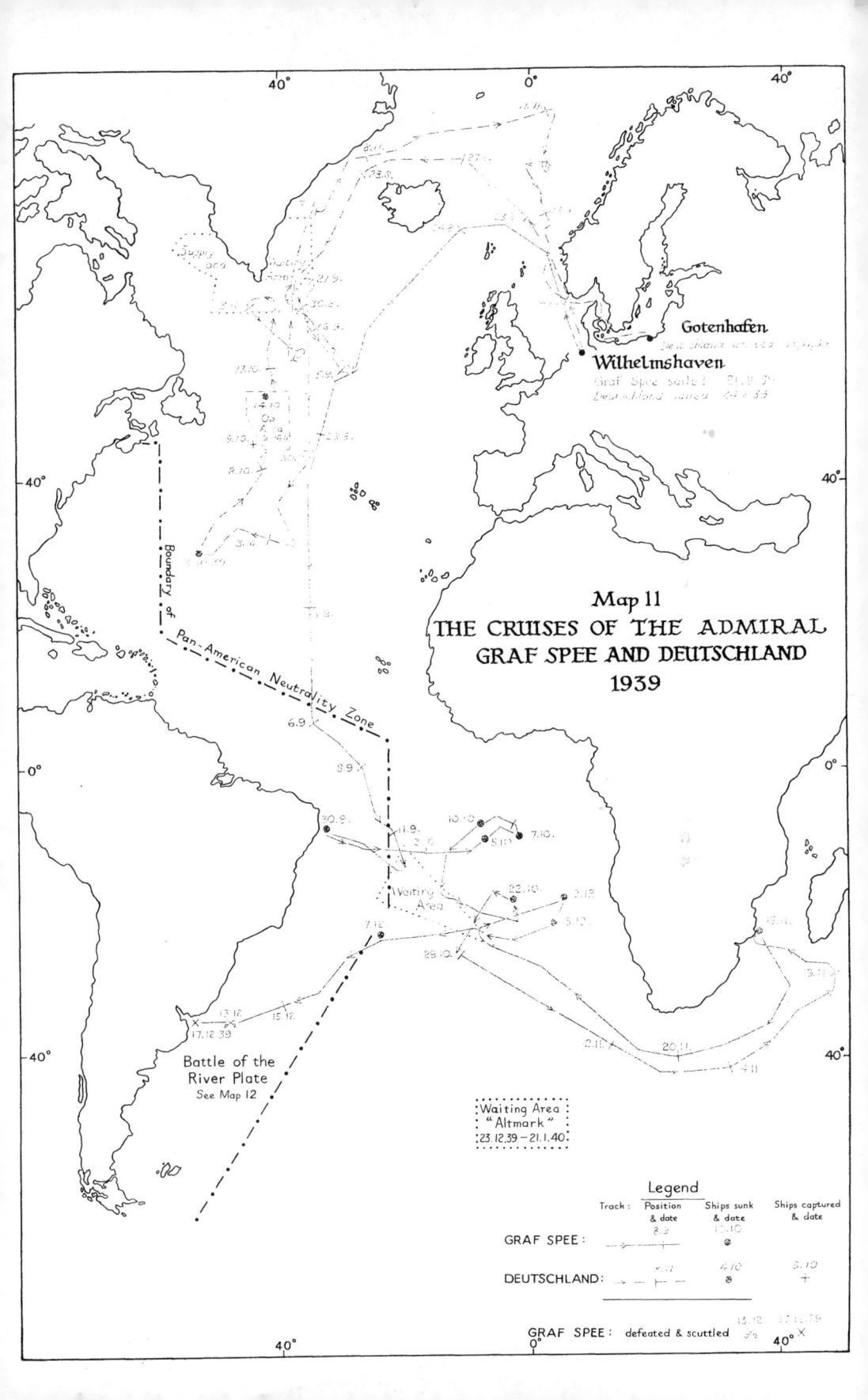

Map 11
THE CRUISES OF THE ADMIRAL
GRAF SPEE AND DEUTSCHLAND
1939

Battle of the River Plate
See Map 12

Waiting Area
"Altmark"
23.12.39 – 21.1.40

Legend

Track:	Position & date	Ships sunk & date	Ships captured & date
GRAF SPEE:			
DEUTSCHLAND:			

GRAF SPEE: defeated & scuttled

After sinking the *Clement* off Pernambuco on the 30th of September the *Graf Spee* crossed the South Atlantic and on the 5th of October found her second victim, the s.s. *Newton Beech*, who managed to send a distress message before she was captured.[1] The message was picked up by another merchant ship and passed to the cruiser *Cumberland* whom she met later the same day. The cruiser was, of course, keeping wireless silence and, assuming that the Commander-in-Chief at Freetown had received the message, did not pass it to him. It had, in fact, not been received at Freetown and Admiral Lyon therefore remained in ignorance of the raider's action for some weeks. Had this message been passed immediately, the raider and her supply ship might have been caught within the next few days. A chance to destroy the supply ship was also missed when, on the 9th of October, aircraft from the *Ark Royal*, which was on passage to Freetown, sighted a stopped ship to the west of the Cape Verde Islands. She claimed to be the American s.s. *Delmar*, and, having no destroyers with him, Vice-Admiral Wells (Vice-Admiral, Aircraft Carriers) decided not to close and investigate. It was later ascertained that the *Delmar* was in New Orleans on that date. But the *Altmark* had a narrow escape.

The *Graf Spee* sank or captured three more ships on the trade routes from the Cape of Good Hope between the 5th and 10th of October and then returned to her cruising ground in the centre of the South Atlantic, where, on the 15th, she fuelled again from the *Altmark* and transferred to her the crews of her victims. Then she steered to the east once more and sank the s.s. *Trevanion* on the 22nd of October. This ship made a distress message which was picked up by the *Llanstephan Castle* and passed to Freetown. The Commander-in-Chief organised extensive searches by all his forces, but without result.

There now followed a period of silence from the South Atlantic and of doubt in the Admiralty as to whether a pocket-battleship was still at large in that area. It must be remembered that the making of distress messages could at any time be simulated by the enemy to deceive us and disorganise our hunting operations, and that only two ships, the *Clement* and the *Stonegate*, which latter had been sunk on the 5th of October 600 miles east of Bermuda by the *Deutschland*, were at this time definitely known to have been victims of pocket-battleships. The *Trevanion*'s distress message, if genuine, might be attributable to an armed merchant raider, and the pocket-battleship which had sunk the *Clement* and *Stonegate* might meanwhile have returned to her home waters. The sinking of the *Rawalpindi* in the Faeröes–Iceland Channel on the 23rd of November was for some

---

[1] See Map 11.

116 PROBLEMS OF THE SOUTH AMERICAN DIVISION

time, it will be remembered, attributed to the *Deutschland*.[1] The weakness of our intelligence regarding the movements of major enemy vessels to and from home waters thus reflected itself in distant operations.

These deductions were, however, partially dispelled on the 8th of November when the masters of the *Clement* and *Stonegate* were released. Their reports left no doubt that two pocket-battleships had been involved and that one of them, believed by the Admiralty to be the *Admiral Scheer*, was probably still at sea. The *Graf Spee*, knowing that she was hunted, had actually steamed south-west after sinking the *Trevanion* on the 22nd of October, fuelled again from the *Altmark* far to the west of the Cape of Good Hope on the 28th and then, adopting a suggestion signalled out to her by Admiral Raeder, steered east around the Cape into the Indian Ocean, where her presence was confirmed on the 15th of November by the sinking of a small tanker in the Mozambique Channel. The next day she stopped a Dutch ship in the same area, after which she doubled back around the Cape again.[2]

Meanwhile the patrolling by British warships had not been entirely in vain, since three enemy merchant ships were intercepted —the *Uhenfels* on the 5th of November by the *Ark Royal* and destroyers, the *Adolph Woermann* by the *Neptune* off Ascension Island on the 22nd and the *Emmy Friederich* by the *Caradoc* in the Gulf of Mexico.

It is now time to turn to the movements of the three hunting groups principally concerned—Forces G, H and K. The first, the South American Division, was commanded by Commodore H. Harwood whose broad pennant was flown in the *Exeter* (Captain F. S. Bell) until the 27th of October, when she had to go to Port Stanley in the Falkland Islands for repairs; he thereupon transferred to the *Ajax* (Captain C. H. L. Woodhouse). The New Zealand cruiser *Achilles* (Captain W. E. Parry) had meanwhile rounded Cape Horn and replaced the *Exeter*, and Commodore Harwood continued to cover the Rio de Janeiro–River Plate areas with the *Achilles* and *Ajax*. Not least of the Commodore's anxieties was the fuelling of his ships, since he was operating off neutral coasts with the nearest British base 1,000 miles away. By the Hague Convention rules belligerent warships could only fuel once every three months in a port of any one neutral country, which meant that he could only use an Argentine, Uruguayan or Brazilian port once at that interval. Within these rules the governments of the countries concerned made no difficulties; but the fuelling restrictions produced many problems for Commodore Harwood. As long as a pocket-battleship was at large he could not afford to disperse his slender strength in cruisers.

---
[1] See pp. 82–83.
[2] See Map 11 (*facing p. 115*).

Yet he was required not only to keep his squadron at sufficient strength to deal with such a powerful enemy, but to patrol the focal areas on his station and to keep an eye on enemy merchant ships in many ports whence they might at any time make a dash for home.

At the beginning of December the *Exeter* and *Cumberland* were both at Port Stanley in case the enemy should conceive the idea of attacking it on the anniversary of the Falkland Islands battle of the 8th of December 1914; the *Achilles* was off Rio de Janeiro and the *Ajax* had recently sailed from Port Stanley for the River Plate. In the eastern Atlantic Forces H and K were patrolling in their respective areas. The *Neptune*, the submarine *Clyde* and four destroyers covered Freetown to Natal (Brazil) while, further north, the French cruisers *Dupleix* and *Foch*, assisted by the small aircraft carrier *Hermes* (a combination of Forces M and N) patrolled from Dakar.[1]

Between the 28th of November and 2nd of December Forces H and K patrolled south of the Cape of Good Hope to intercept the raider if she broke back into the Atlantic; but she had, in fact, already done so and had fuelled from the *Altmark* north-east of Tristan da Cunha on the 27th of November. On the 2nd of December the *Renown* sank the German merchantman *Watussi* after she had been sighted by a South African Air Force reconnaissance plane and, on the same day, a distress message was received from the British s.s. *Doric Star* far to the north and in the raider's former hunting ground.

Admiral Lyon at once altered his dispositions. Force H was ordered to cover the trade route from the Cape to the latitude of St. Helena; Force K was ordered to sweep north-west from the Cape to 28° South 15° West and thence proceed to Freetown. These sweeps did not succeed in catching the raider, but they did yield a useful secondary result, for the enemy merchantman *Adolf Leonhardt* was caught by the *Shropshire* on the 9th of December. On the other side of the ocean the *Ajax* and *Cumberland* had intercepted the *Ussukuma* on the 5th of the same month. Both ships scuttled themselves in spite of strenuous attempts to effect their capture. The *Doric Star* was sunk some 3,000 miles away from the South American focal areas guarded by Commodore Harwood, but he had always considered that, sooner or later, a raider would be tempted by the rich traffic off Rio de Janeiro and the River Plate. He calculated that the *Doric Star's* assailant could reach the former by the 12th of December and the latter one day later. He therefore decided to concentrate his forces. The *Exeter* was ordered to leave Port Stanley on the 9th and the *Achilles* to join him the following day. By 6 a.m. on the 12th the three ships were concentrated 150 miles off the entrance to the River Plate.

The *Graf Spee* found another victim, the s.s. *Tairoa*, on the day

---

[1] See Map 23 (*facing p. 272*).

after she sank the *Doric Star*, and then steered due west. In mid-ocean on the 7th of December she sank her last ship, the s.s. *Streonshalh*. She then steered direct to the estuary where Commodore Harwood's cruisers were waiting. Twenty-four hours after he had made his concentration, at 6.8 a.m. on the 13th of December, the *Ajax* reported smoke to the north-west and the *Exeter* was sent to investigate. Eight minutes later she signalled 'I think it is a pocket-battleship'. The long hunt was over.

A detailed description of the battle which now took place will be of less interest to posterity than the ocean-wide strategy which led to it, and it is therefore right, without in any way belittling the gallantry and tenacity with which Commodore Harwood's lightly armed cruisers tackled their formidable adversary, that it should occupy a smaller space in these pages. What matters is that the far-flung dispositions ordered by the Admiralty and the hunting operations conducted by the responsible Flag Officers finally yielded the desired result to one of the groups so employed and thus eliminated a serious threat to our shipping.

Commodore Harwood had long considered the tactics which he would use by day or by night on just such an occasion and he now put them into effect. In either case he intended to attack at once, but by day he would attack in two divisions to give his ships the benefit of being able to report each other's fall of shot. The first phase of the battle lasted from 6.14 a.m. to 7.40 a.m. The *Ajax* and *Achilles* engaged the enemy from the east, opening fire at about 19,000 yards range, while the *Exeter* left the line and turned west to engage her from the south, thus presenting the *Graf Spee* with the problem of either leaving one adversary unengaged or of dividing her main armament to engage both divisions at once.[1] She first chose the second alternative, but soon shifted the fire of all her six 11-inch guns to the *Exeter*, whose 8-inch salvos probably appeared the more dangerous. Moreover, her Captain had at first thought that his adversaries consisted of one cruiser and two destroyers—an error of identification which can easily be understood—and to engage the heaviest adversary with his main armament would be his obvious tactic.

The German gunnery was accurate during this phase and, indeed, remained formidably so throughout the day. Unlike her adversaries the *Graf Spee* had a radar set which, though not specially designed for gunnery purposes, could pass its ranges to the armaments. The *Exeter* was soon heavily hit, lost one turret and had her steering gear put out of action temporarily, though Captain Bell quickly regained control from the after steering position. She then resumed the action

---

[1] See Map 12.

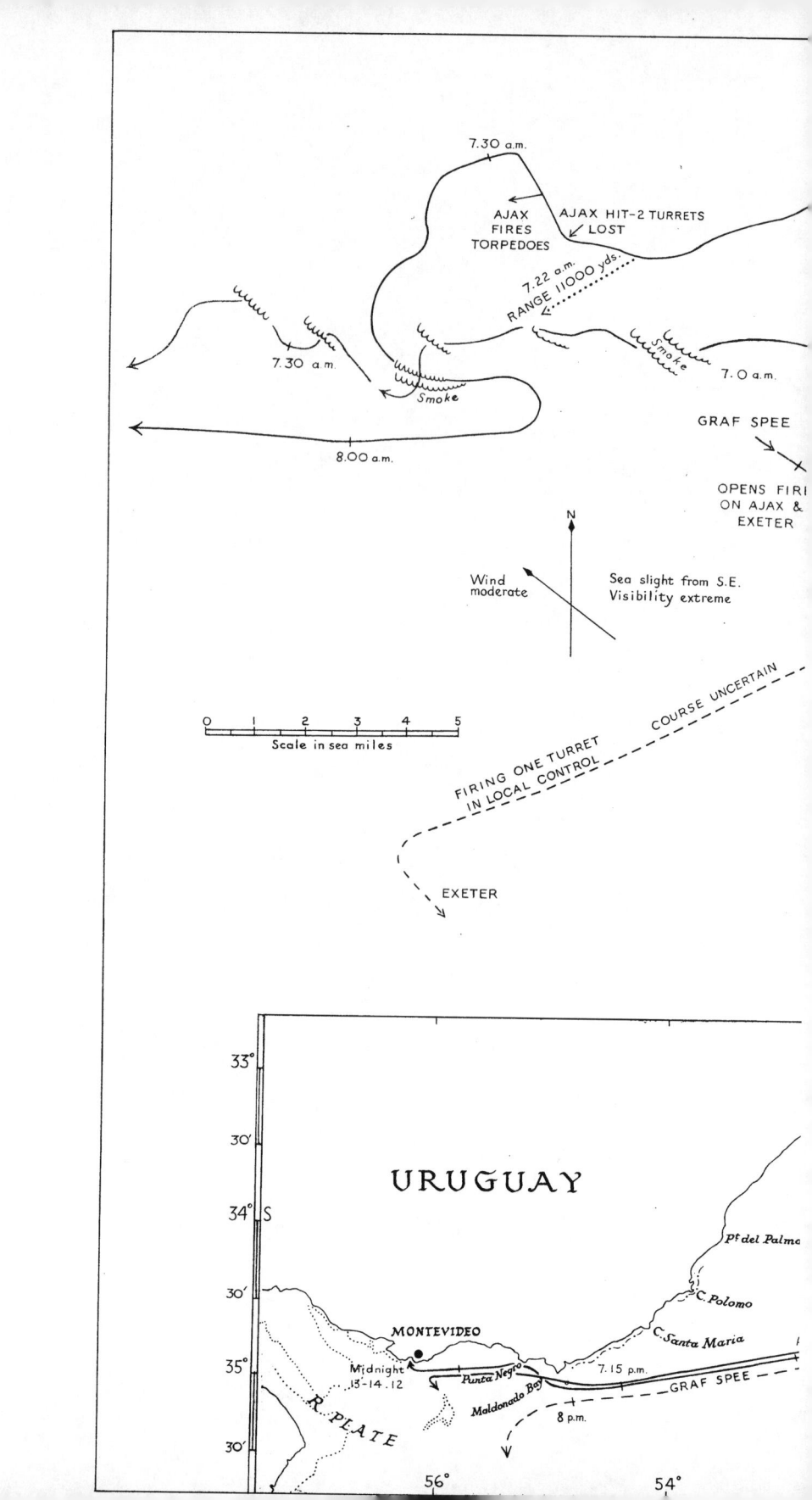

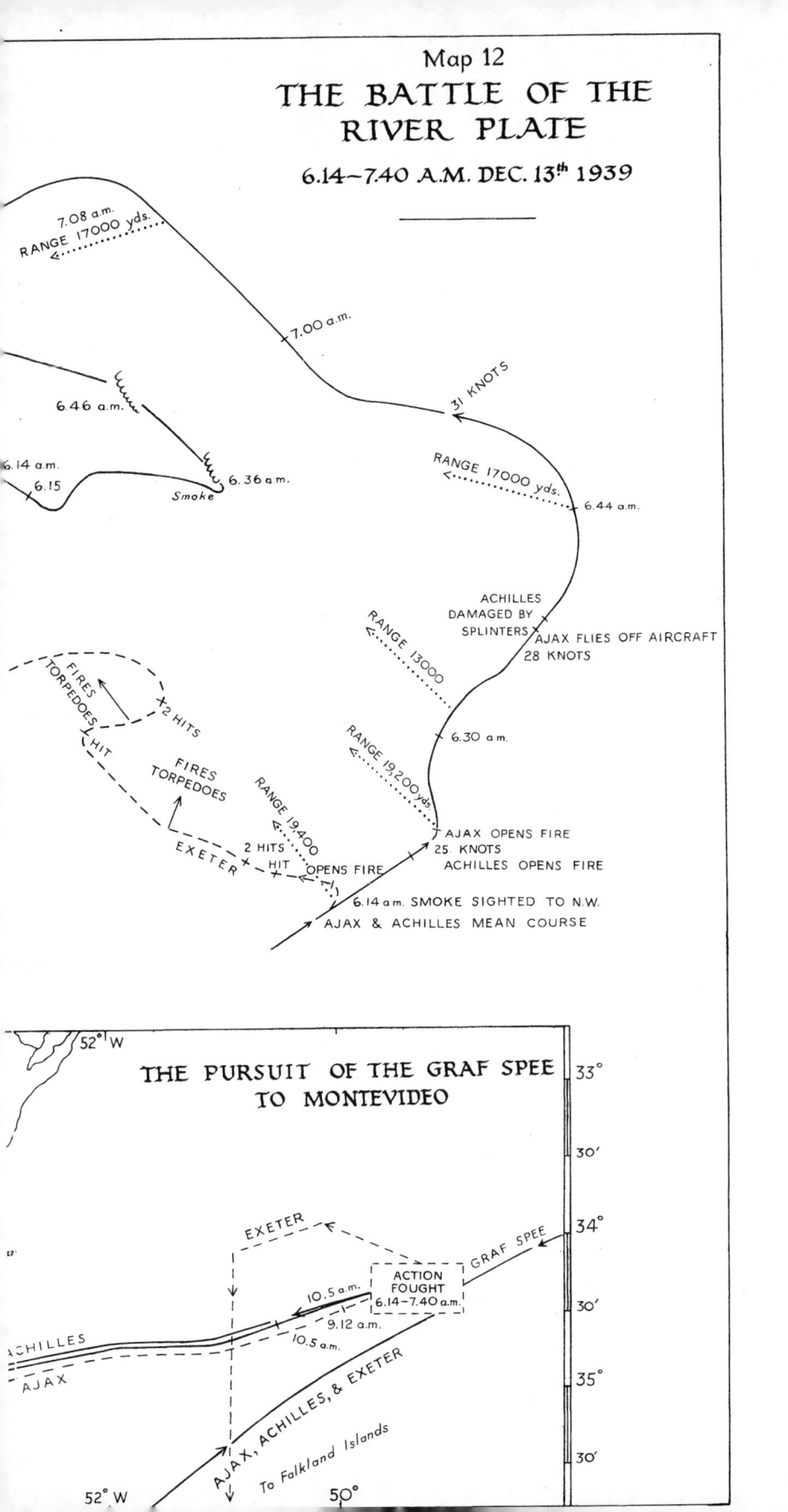

Map 12
THE BATTLE OF THE RIVER PLATE
6.14–7.40 A.M. DEC. 13th 1939

7.08 a.m.
RANGE 17000 yds.

7.00 a.m.

6.46 a.m.

31 KNOTS

6.14 a.m.
6.15
6.36 a.m.
Smoke

RANGE 17000 yds.
6.44 a.m.

ACHILLES DAMAGED BY SPLINTERS
AJAX FLIES OFF AIRCRAFT
28 KNOTS

RANGE 13000

6.30 a.m.

FIRES TORPEDOES
2 HITS
HIT
FIRES TORPEDOES

RANGE 19200 yds.

RANGE 19400
2 HITS
EXETER
HIT
OPENS FIRE

AJAX OPENS FIRE
25 KNOTS
ACHILLES OPENS FIRE

6.14 a.m. SMOKE SIGHTED TO N.W.
AJAX & ACHILLES MEAN COURSE

52° W

THE PURSUIT OF THE GRAF SPEE TO MONTEVIDEO

33°

30'

EXETER
GRAF SPEE
ACTION FOUGHT
6.14–7.40 a.m.
10.5 a.m.
9.12 a.m.

34°

30'

ACHILLES
AJAX
10.5 a.m.

35°

AJAX, ACHILLES, & EXETER
To Falkland Islands

30'

52° W   50°

and fired her torpedoes, only to receive further hits from 11-inch shells which left her with only a single turret in action. By 6.50 she was steering west with a heavy list to starboard but was still engaging the enemy with her solitary turret; by 7.30 she could keep up no longer and turned to the south-east to effect repairs.

Meanwhile the *Ajax* and *Achilles* had been engaged alternately by the enemy's secondary armament of eight 5·9-inch guns, but had not been hit. They were themselves firing in concentration, with the *Ajax* controlling, and were rapidly closing the range. Their fire was effective, and at 6.30 the enemy shifted one 11-inch turret on to the *Ajax* which was quickly straddled but not hit. At 6.40 the *Achilles* was damaged, but not seriously, by a heavy shell which burst on the water line. Some confusion to the two ships' gunnery now occurred through failure of the *Achilles*' gunnery wireless set, and both ships lost accuracy until 7.08 when the range was found again—still at about 16,000 yards. A smoke screen made by the enemy added at this time to the difficulty of spotting accurately the fall of shot. At 7.16 the *Graf Spee* made a large turn to port (to the south) apparently with the intention of finishing off the crippled *Exeter*. Both the smaller cruisers at once turned to her assistance and fired so effectively that the enemy abandoned his attempt and turned again to the north-west to re-engage the *Ajax*. She received her first 11-inch hit at 7.25 and lost both her after turrets. The range was about 11,000 yards but by 7.38 had closed to 8,000, and the *Ajax* now suffered another hit which brought down her topmast. The battle appeared to have taken a dangerous turn as the enemy was still firing accurately and had apparently suffered little damage; and the total armament remaining to the two British cruisers was little superior to the enemy's secondary weapons. Commodore Harwood therefore turned to the east under cover of smoke at 7.40, and thus ended the first phase of the action.

The *Graf Spee*, however, did not press her weakened adversaries but continued on westerly courses so that, after six minutes, the British cruisers turned back to the west and followed her. The second phase of the action consisted of shadowing the enemy on her course towards the River Plate while she turned periodically and fired a few salvos, some of which fell dangerously close, if ever the cruisers closed the range sufficiently. By 11.17 p.m., when Commodore Harwood finally recalled the *Achilles* from shadowing the enemy, it was quite clear that she intended to enter Montevideo. The Commodore now had to face a difficult problem: he must prevent the enemy from escaping once more into the oceans after he had fuelled or accomplished whatever purpose lay behind his entrance into neutral waters. And, for the time being, he had only two small cruisers, one with half her armament out of action, wherewith to accomplish it. At 9.46 the previous morning, when it had become clear that the *Exeter* must seek port, the Commodore had ordered the *Cumberland* to sail immediately from Port Stanley; but she could not join until the evening of the 14th. Until this much needed reinforcement, which would restore the squadron to its original strength, had arrived, the two smaller cruisers could only patrol the wide mouth of the river and hope to keep the enemy inside it. All other reinforcements were several thousand miles away. But the enemy made no attempt to escape.

Meanwhile, on the 13th, the Commander-in-Chief, South Atlantic, had sailed the *Dorsetshire* from the Cape of Good Hope for the Plate and the Admiralty ordered the *Shropshire* to follow on the 15th. Both ships were diverted to Port Stanley on the 18th but placed under the orders of Rear-Admiral Harwood.[1] Other reinforcements were also hastening to the scene. The *Ark Royal* and *Renown* were ordered to fuel at Rio de Janeiro and thence proceed to the Plate at full speed. The *Neptune* was also ordered there, and the 3rd Destroyer Division arrived at Pernambuco on the 15th and sailed for Rio within an hour. The *Ark Royal*, *Renown* and *Neptune* all reached Rio de Janeiro on the 17th, fuelled and hurried south. Thus was overwhelming strength directed towards the danger point. But it could not be concentrated there before noon on the 19th of December.

It is not necessary to follow in detail the diplomatic negotiations which were meanwhile proceeding in Montevideo. Captain Langsdorff obtained for the *Graf Spee* a seventy-two-hour extension of the permissible twenty-four hours stay in port in order to repair damage. The British Government's objections to this were more technical than real; for they had no desire to force the *Graf Spee* to sea before the reinforcements had arrived. British merchant ships were sailed from Montevideo at intervals and the Uruguayan Government was requested to allow them a day's clear start ahead of the enemy. The seventy-two-hour extension expired at 8.0 p.m. on the 17th of December. Captain Langsdorff believed that the *Ark Royal*, *Renown* and destroyers were already waiting for him outside, and as early as the 15th his gunnery officer had told him that he could see the *Renown* from the control tower. The spreading of false intelligence regarding the British reinforcements was therefore, at least in part, done by the enemy. On the 16th of December Captain Langsdorff reported to Berlin the strength of the concentration which he presumed, incorrectly, to be waiting for him outside the estuary and proposed to try to fight his way through to Buenos Aires. He added a request for a decision whether, if the attempt to make such a breakthrough would result in certain destruction of his ship without

---

[1] Commodore Harwood had been specially promoted to date the 13th of December

causing his adversaries appreciable damage, it was preferred for him to scuttle his ship or allow her to be interned. Admiral Raeder and Hitler, who discussed the matter the same day, were both agreed that the attempted break-through was the proper course but that scuttling was preferable to internment, and a reply in that sense was sent from Berlin at 5.17 that evening.

At 6.15 p.m. on the 17th of December Captain Langsdorff sailed down river with the German s.s. *Tacoma* following in his wake. At 7.56 the *Graf Spee* blew herself up. Shortly afterwards the British blockading squadron, which still consisted only of the *Cumberland*, *Ajax* and *Achilles*, steamed into the estuary and on towards Montevideo—passing the blazing wreck of the German pocket-battleship on the way. Three days later Captain Langsdorff shot himself, leaving behind a letter addressed to the German Ambassador in Montevideo but intended for Hitler, in which he explained the reasons which led him to commit his ship to her ignominious end. The action was considered at Hitler's conference with his war leaders on the 30th of December and, not without reason, Hitler then reiterated his previously expressed view that the *Exeter* should have been destroyed.

Thus ended the first challenge to our control of the ocean communications: far away in the North Atlantic, the *Graf Spee's* sister ship, the *Deutschland*, had been recalled on the 1st of November after sinking only two ships. She had reached Kiel on the 15th of the same month. The *Graf Spee*, though the more successful of the two, had, during a cruise lasting from the 26th of September until the 13th of December, sunk only nine ships totalling some 50,000 tons. It must stand to the credit of Captain Langsdorff that not one British life was lost through his ship's action against defenceless merchantmen.

This chapter has dealt primarily with the positive use of British maritime power. In our first chapter it was mentioned that such operations, if successful, always produced the secondary result of denying the use of the same communications to the enemy.[1] The truth of this is well demonstrated by the interceptions of German merchantmen by British warships which have appeared incidentally in these pages. But the effectiveness of this denial of the sea routes to the enemy went much deeper. On the outbreak of war Germany ordered all her merchant ships to seek the shelter of the nearest neutral port. Some were captured on the way, but by the 24th of September no less than 206 German ships were immobilised in Atlantic ports alone. Attempts were made at various times to get some of these ships home, but the successful blockade runners were few.

---

[1] See p. 4.

CHAPTER VIII

THE SEA APPROACHES AND COASTAL WATERS

1st January–31st May, 1940

> The suitability of the entire coast of the British Isles for minelaying ... imposes a gigantic task upon the minesweeping organisation and ... there are never enough minesweepers to meet the various commitments.
> *The Naval War Manual* (1948).

WITH the start of the new year offensive operations by our minelaying destroyer flotilla were continued with the object of laying small fields of contact mines in the channels through the German mined area in the North Sea. Two such lays were carried out during the first half of January, but the destroyers were then required for other purposes and did not return to minelaying until the 3rd of March, when the *Express*, *Esk*, *Icarus* and *Impulsive* laid 240 mines in the enemy channel. The flotilla was then diverted to anti-submarine duties and its only employment on minelaying during the period now under discussion was the laying of mines in Norwegian territorial waters early in April.[1] This formed part of the long conceived and frequently postponed plan to disrupt the enemy's flow of iron ore from northern Norway. It will be considered later when the events which led to the Norwegian campaign are reviewed. The period with which we are now dealing saw the start of a new form of offensive minelaying, that of mining the enemy's channels and estuaries from the air, in which Coastal Command, Bomber Command and naval aircraft all took part; this developed rapidly into an important factor in disputing the control of the enemy's coastal routes. It will be convenient at this stage to trace the growth of this campaign from its origins.

As far back as May 1936 the Admiralty had authorised the development of the Standard Magnetic Mine, and a trial order for a small number was placed in July 1939. A proportion of these was allocated to the Air Ministry for trials, and shortly after the outbreak of war the Admiralty announced that mines would be ready for use by the following summer. This estimate was, in fact, considerably

---

[1] See pp. 156–157.

improved on. It appeared that the mines would be available before there were suitable aircraft to lay them, since only the torpedo-bombers of Coastal Command (Bothas and Beauforts) were then intended for minelaying. The Botha was an unsuccessful aircraft, and neither it nor the Beaufort could reach the waters to the east of the Kiel Canal. However, the Air Ministry hoped to have forty-two aircraft continuously available for minelaying by the time the mines were ready. Unfortunately the failure of the Botha necessitated a search for another type which could be adapted to minelaying, and experiments in the use of Hampdens of Bomber Command were therefore started. They had a longer range than the Beaufort and would be ready in some numbers from February 1940 onwards.

Operational factors were meanwhile being studied by the Naval and Air Staffs and by Coastal Command. The ideal conditions for minelaying, which demanded a high degree of navigational accuracy, were found only on moonlight nights; but this restricted possible operations to about seven nights in each month. The most promising area was in the Elbe estuary since traffic there was dense, but in Kiel the depth of water came closer to the optimum of thirty feet. The Ems and Jade-Weser estuaries were also good, though they carried less traffic than the Elbe or Kiel Canal.[1]

In February the Foreign Office agreed that forty-eight hours' notice should be given of our intention to mine certain areas, including some which, in fact, would not at first be mined. It will be remarked that, unlike the Germans, we intended only to lay the mines in Declared Areas.[2]

Meanwhile difficulties in finding enough aircraft for the concentrated effort required to obtain good results continued, since the Beauforts were only coming slowly into use in Coastal Command and the Bomber Command Hampdens needed further training in this new duty. By recalling Nos. 49 and 63 Hampden Squadrons, which had been on loan to Coastal Command as a striking force, the strength assigned to minelaying was increased, and on the 1st of April it was decided that six Hampden squadrons and one of Beauforts should lay the 200 mines available for that month. Intensive training and reconnaissance flights by these squadrons continued, and on the 8th of April, coincident with the start of the Norwegian campaign, Bomber Command was authorised to lay thirty-eight mines in each of the Elbe, Lübeck and Kiel areas, while Coastal Command laid lesser numbers in the Jade-Weser and Ems estuaries. The first lay was carried out by Bomber Command on the night of the 13th–14th of April. Two nights later Coastal Command Beauforts followed suit, and very soon No. 815 naval air squadron, which was armed with

---

[1] See Map 5 (*facing p. 71*).
[2] See p. 98.

Swordfish aircraft and was then working under Coastal Command, joined the minelayers.

Heavy fog suspended air minelaying after the 25th of the month, but about 160 of the 200 mines allotted had been laid by that date—the majority by Bomber Command in the Elbe, Kattegat, Kiel Canal, the Belts and in the western Baltic. Early in May the Admiralty pressed for a greater number of aircraft to be turned over to minelaying; there were indications that it was producing good results, and the production of mines had been increased so rapidly that it was likely to outstrip the capacity of the aircraft so far made available to lay them. However, the start of the campaign in the Low Countries produced so many new problems for the Air Ministry and Bomber Command that it was some months before a greater effort could be devoted to minelaying.

It will be useful to summarise the results so far achieved. In April and May 263 mines were laid in 385 aircraft sorties. Ten aircraft were lost on these operations, but twenty-four enemy ships totalling some 33,635 tons were sunk by magnetic mines laid by aircraft and a further two ships of 4,114 tons were damaged. It will be seen that a considerable proportion of the aircraft sent out on minelaying sorties returned without laying their mines, but that the losses of aircraft so employed could be accepted. The ability of aircraft to carry offensive minelaying on to the enemy's short sea routes had been clearly demonstrated and as training improved and more aircraft became available more substantial results were plainly to be expected.

The defensive minelaying campaign continued during the phase now being considered. In January a start was made with the east coast mine barrier. Its purpose was to help protect the heavy flow of shipping passing up and down the length of our east coast. The Admiralty was particularly apprehensive about disguised merchant ships being used by the enemy to sow mines in those shallow waters; but raids by surface warships and submarine attacks were also possible. The mine barrier would give close control over our own shipping and make it easier to detect and deal with any enemy who might try to interfere with our traffic.[1] The minelayer *Princess Victoria* laid the first 240 mines about fifty miles north-east of Spurn Point on the 24th of January; but thereafter progress was slow. Apart from placing dummy mines along the greater part of the length of the barrier between the 6th and 13th of February only one more lay was carried out in that month.

One reason for the slow progress made with the east coast mine barrier was that in January it was decided to lay deep minefields

---

[1] See Map 10 (*facing p. 97*).

off the Moray Firth to try to catch the U-boats which had been causing trouble there. One of our minelayers was diverted to this new duty. The deep minefields might have accomplished their purpose if we could have spared surface vessels to patrol them continuously, and so force the U-boats to dive. As it was the minefields were not patrolled and the U-boats, which had all along been working on the surface in those waters, continued to do so with impunity. It was also found that defensive minefields such as the east coast barrier produced another effect. They marked for the enemy the positions where our own shipping had to enter and leave the swept channels; nor was he slow to take advantage of the chances which these new focal points offered for attacks on our shipping.

In March progress with the east coast barrier was as slow as in the preceding month and only one line of mines was laid. It was not until the first week of May, by which time the enemy was possessed of most of the Norwegian coast and was about to launch his campaign in the west, so securing greatly increased opportunities to interfere with our east coast traffic from his newly acquired bases, that substantial progress was made towards the completion of the barrier. Extensions were then laid by the minelayers *Princess Victoria*, *Teviot Bank* and *Hampton*.

Meanwhile the enemy, whose offensive mining had, as has been seen, achieved considerable initial success, continued to lay both magnetic and contact mines, using surface vessels, submarines and aircraft.

In January his destroyers laid large minefields, mostly of contact mines, off Blyth and Cromer Knoll, and magnetic mines in the Thames approaches. His U-boats continued to lay magnetic mines in the approaches to our more important bases and ports such as Liverpool, Loch Ewe, Cromarty Firth and Falmouth. In all, the enemy laid 174 magnetic and 345 contact mines during the first month of the year. His surface minelayers showed enterprise and boldness; and they met no opposition because at this time we expected that he would use only U-boats or aircraft for minelaying. We had not yet introduced precautions against the use of surface minelayers. Our coastal traffic was greatly dislocated by this means and losses from mining during the month amounted to twenty-one ships of 77,116 tons. In February the enemy continued to exploit his success. On the night of the 9th–10th his destroyers laid 157 mines, mostly of contact type, off Cromer Knoll and 110 magnetic mines in the Orfordness–Shipwash area.[1] This was carried out without interference though the enemy states that his ships sighted, but were not sighted by, our patrols while on passage. They were able accurately

---

[1] See Map 13 (*facing p. 127*).

Map 13

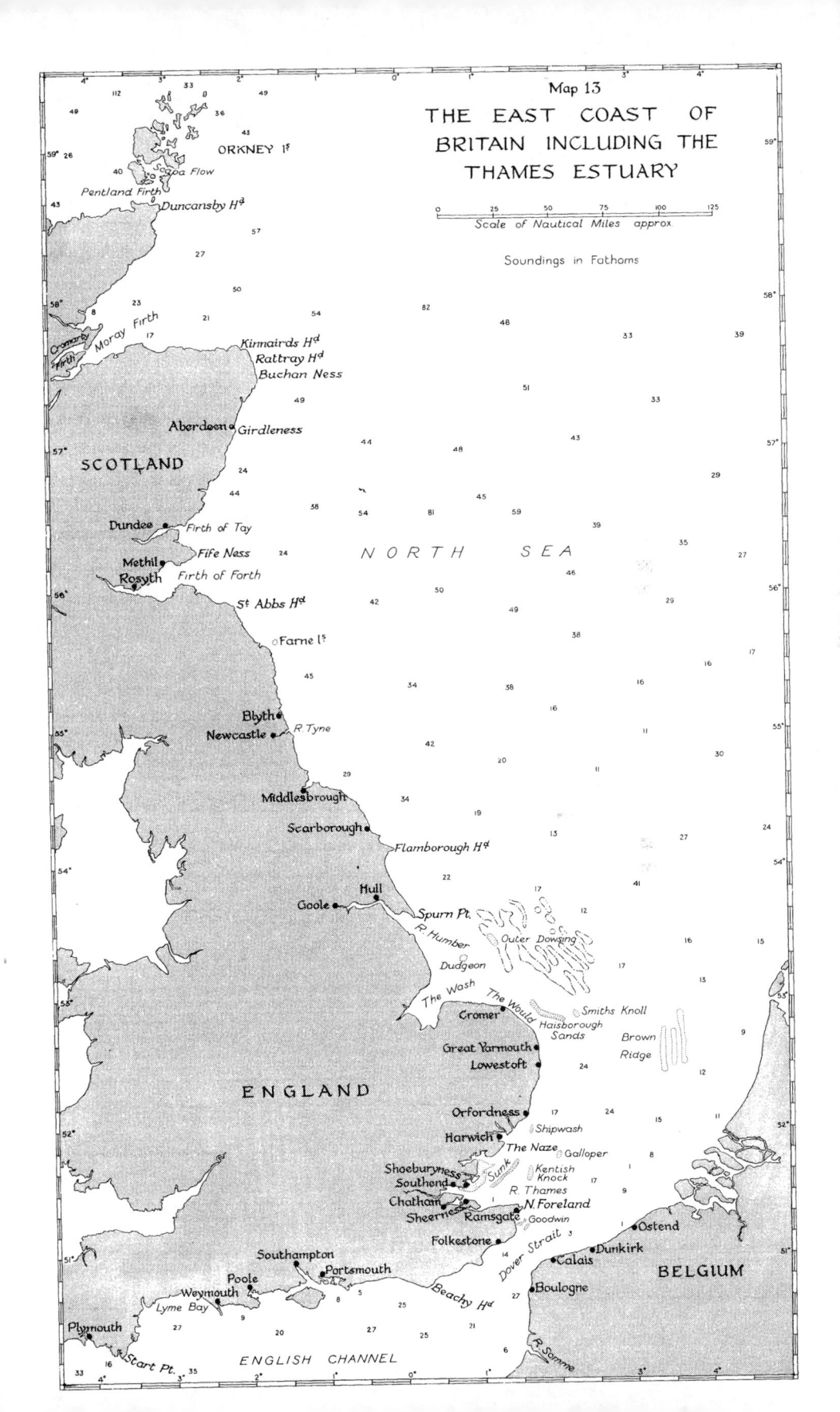

THE EAST COAST OF
BRITAIN INCLUDING THE
THAMES ESTUARY

Scale of Nautical Miles approx. 0 25 50 75 100 125

Soundings in Fathoms

to fix the position of the minefields by the light vessels which were then still in position and showing their normal lights. The new field off Cromer caused the loss of six vessels, and a further six were lost during the same month on older minefields. U-boats also laid nearly a score of magnetic mines in February, but these were not discovered till later. Our losses for the month were fifteen ships of 54,740 tons. Clearance of the magnetic fields proceeded only very slowly for lack of effective sweeping devices. The mine destructor ships ('*Bordes*') and also the minesweeping aircraft achieved some successes, but neither constituted a reliable and rapid antidote.

In March we lost fourteen ships of 35,501 tons to mines. No less than five of these were blown up on a new field laid to the east of the North Foreland by a small enemy merchant ship disguised as a neutral. She left Wilhelmshaven on the 7th of March and laid her mines two nights later without interference, because the gap between the Dover and east coast mine barrages was not patrolled effectively owing to the shortage of destroyers in the Nore and Dover Commands. This field was quickly discovered but proved of greater extent than was at first realised, and casualties continued. Moreover clearance was hampered by the enemy's use of explosive sweep destructors placed among the mines; not until the end of March was a channel cleared for large ships. The war of device and counter-device in minelaying and minesweeping had started in earnest. Meanwhile U-boats laid three small magnetic fields in the approaches to Liverpool, the Bristol Channel ports and Portsmouth.

Little progress was made with magnetic minesweeping until the end of March, and the losses and dislocation of shipping continued to cause serious anxiety. On the 28th of March, however, the first four of the 'LL Trawlers', whose sweeping device has already been mentioned, started work.[1] They rapidly exploded four mines in the Thames estuary. The damage received by the minesweepers themselves from these explosions was, however, serious and orders had to be given to strengthen all the seventy trawlers then fitting out for this duty. On the 31st the *Borde*, which had also been damaged, returned to duty and exploded two mines in the Sunk Channel. Eight more mine destructor ships were fitting out but were not yet ready. The minesweeping aircraft, which were now employed in threes flying in line abreast, contributed their quota by exploding nine mines in the Thames approaches. These successes, taken together, showed that the period of palliatives and of hasty improvisations was passing, and that the conquest of the magnetic mine was now in sight. But it was fortunate that the enemy possessed so few mines of this type during the early months of 1940, or our difficulties

---

[1] See p. 100.

might well have become critical. No magnetic mines were laid in the first half of April, but after the 17th of that month enemy aircraft carried out widely dispersed minelaying in the Downs, the Thames estuary and off the coast of Norfolk and Suffolk. These small fields caused us considerable embarrassment and the loss of seven ships, most of which were small coasting vessels.

A small German motor vessel, the *Ulm*, laid a contact field off Smith's Knoll on the 2nd of April. The mines were actually laid some distance outside the channel used by our shipping; but they caught and damaged one ship which had straggled from her convoy, and also sank a minesweeper. There is little doubt that the *Ulm* was sighted and chased by the submarine *Sealion* while on passage. But the latter never reported the incident until she reached her patrol area off the Skagerrak. Our total losses to mines in April were eleven ships of 19,799 tons sunk and two more damaged.

The pause in magnetic minelaying gave to the Nore Command, on whom the onus of dealing with the enemy's campaign and of keeping the east coast convoy routes and the Thames approaches open had chiefly fallen, a short breathing space in which to overtake the heavy accumulated arrears of magnetic minesweeping. When, however, we started to clear certain new fields the sweeps proved ineffective until it was realised that the enemy had now reversed the polarity of some of his mines, and had inserted delay-action devices in the mechanism of others.

There was little minelaying in our coastal waters during the month of May because the enemy was fully occupied with the campaign in Western Europe. Only three ships were sunk by mines off our own coasts. But losses off Norway, Holland, Belgium and France swelled the total of victims to twenty ships of 47,716 tons. Thus ended the second phase of the enemy's attempt to disrupt our coastal traffic by mine warfare. Although substantial losses had continued, there had been a steady decline from January onwards, and there were good grounds for believing that the critical period in November 1939, when all but one of the channels into the Port of London were closed, would never be repeated. Effective antidotes were now being supplied and experience in their use was being gained. Knowledge of the enemy's many ingenious devices was also improving.

The enemy's policy moved rapidly towards unrestricted submarine warfare during the last months of 1939, as has already been mentioned.[1] The process was continued during the present phase by extending the areas within which any ship might be attacked without warning. American ships and those of the 'friendly neutral' countries were excluded from these orders, but, as the former were still prohibited from entering the war zone and the latter were unlikely to

---
[1] See pp. 103–104.

Typical British Escort Vessels

Escort Destroyer, 'Hunt' Class, Type 1. H.M.S. *wilderness*. Completed Aug. 1940. Displacement 900 tons Armament 4 4-inch high Angle. Maximum speed 32 knots.

Sloop, 'Black Swan' Class. H.M.S. *Black Swan*. Commenced Jan. 1940. Displacement 1,250 tons. Armament 4-inch high angle. Maximum speed 19 knots.

Corvette, 'Flower' Class. H.M.S. *Alisma*. Completed Jan 1941. Displacement 865 Tons. Armament 1 4-inch. Maximum speed 16 knots.

Facing page 128

'The Wardroom and Mess Deck of an S-Class Submarine.' By Stephen Bone.

(*National Maritime Museum*)

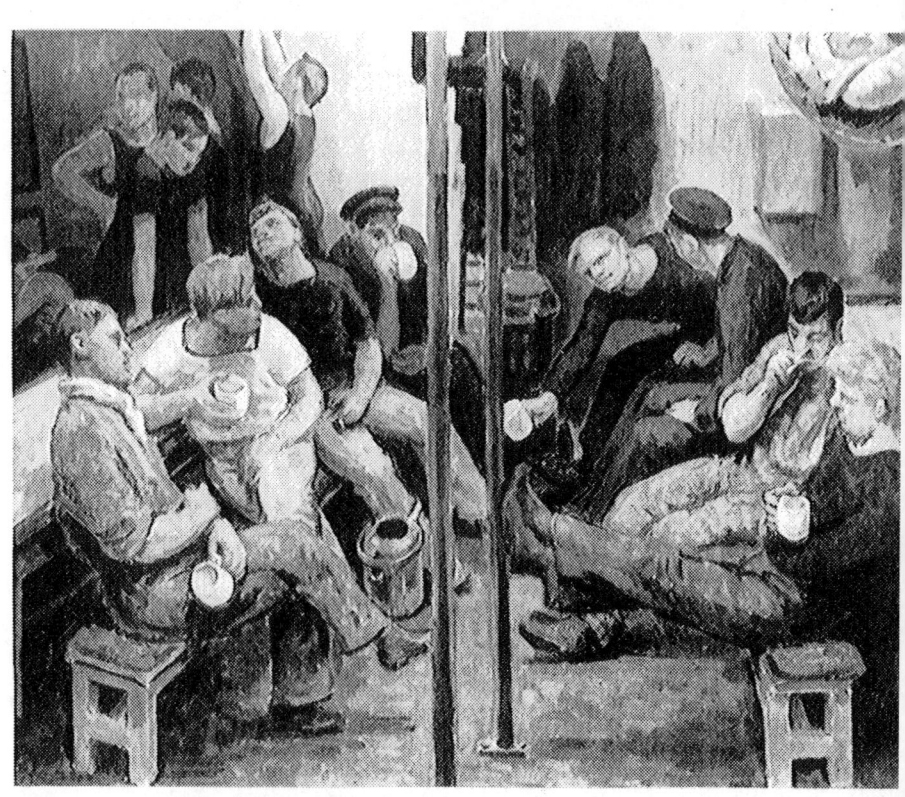

'Eleven o'clock in the Fo'c's'le.' By Henry Lamb.

be met on the British trade routes, this made little difference to the execution of German policy. In January and February the enemy widened the zones of unrestricted attack several times. Although the British Isles were not yet encircled by these zones, by the end of February they covered the whole of our east coast routes, the south-west approaches as far as 10° 30′ West, and the whole of the Irish Sea —including the approaches to the Clyde and Mersey. The ring through which every ocean convoy and every independently-routed ship had to break in order to reach its destination had become wider and more closely watched.

It will be remembered that the frequent sightings of U-boats by aircraft flying the standard North Sea reconnaissance patrols had, before the end of 1939, enabled the Air Force and Naval Staff Officers at Coastal Command Headquarters to calculate where they were most likely to be found. A system of harrying them from the air while on passage was then developed.[1] It was now realised that, whatever might be the failings of these reconnaissance patrols in accomplishing their primary purpose of locating and shadowing enemy warships attempting to break out of the North Sea, a valuable secondary accomplishment had been discovered. Increased emphasis was being placed on this aspect of Coastal Command's duties, and, as more aircraft became available, a greater number was allocated to this purpose. By the beginning of the year No. 18 Group had worked out the tactical problem of where best to seek the U-boats on their north-about passage, while No. 15 Group was employed chiefly on ocean convoy escort duties. Unhappily an effective anti-submarine weapon was still lacking, and the purpose of all this careful planning and arduous flying was largely frustrated by the absence of the means to put it to good effect. More will be said on that score shortly.

The year opened quietly with no U-boats in the Western Approaches for the first half of January; but six arrived in that focal area during the last half of the month. One of these sank three neutral ships off Ushant while on passage south, and on the 30th of January another attacked the Thames section of Convoy O.A. 80 which had been thrown into some disorder by bad weather. Only one escort, the sloop *Fowey*, was with the convoy, but the sinking of two ships led to the hasty despatch to its assistance of two destroyers and a Sunderland of No. 228 Squadron. Together they scored the first joint air-sea success in the U-boat war. After being attacked by the surface escorts the U-boat would probably have got away but for the presence of the Sunderland. As it was, the pursuit was maintained and U.55 finally scuttled and surrendered.

[1] See p. 104.

Mention has already been made of the doubtful merits of defensive minefields in that they tend to create artificial focal areas at their ends. Such was the case with the east coast barrier, which caused concentrations of shipping off the Thames and between the Orkneys and Kinnaird Head. No less than ten coastal U-boats operated against these concentrations during the month of January. Although this had been expected we were slow in taking counter-measures; and when groups of anti-submarine trawlers were stationed at Scapa and Aberdeen they were employed to hunt and not to escort and achieved no success. The U-boats generally attacked by night and on the surface, in which circumstances the asdic was practically useless. They caused us many casualties. No less than fourteen unescorted ships, all neutrals, and also the destroyer-leader *Exmouth*, were sunk during January. The losses were at first attributed to mines and much fruitless sweeping was ordered until the sighting by aircraft of U-boats on the surface dispelled this illusion. Even then the application of the remedy of convoy and escort was slow. Instead the laying of the deep minefield off the Moray Firth, already mentioned, was started; but it was no hindrance to the U-boats because they continued to attack while on the surface. It is worth remarking that the escorted Norwegian convoys passed safely through this danger area during this period of heavy sinkings among unescorted ships.

One of the steps taken to reduce shipping delays had been to shift the northern terminal of the east coast convoy system south from Methil, in the Firth of Forth, to the Tyne. This meant that ships had to sail independently between those two ports, thus presenting easy targets to the enemy. Towards the end of January a U-boat sank two ships off Farne Island. Once again mines were suspected, traffic was stopped and the area vainly swept. When traffic was restarted two days later the same U-boat sank two more ships. A hunt was then organised, but the U-boat commander was wary and had withdrawn. One consequence of these sinkings was that the gap in the east coast convoy system was closed by the starting of convoys between Methil and the Tyne. It was, after all, anomalous that ships in Norwegian convoys should be escorted between Bergen and the Forth and between the Tyne and Thames, but should sail independently between the Forth and Tyne.

At the other end of the mine barrier, in the southern North Sea, three 250-ton U-boats sank three ships in January, but these losses were, at the time, also attributed to mines. There were no attacks on U-boats in these waters during the same period; and sweeps by destroyers of the Nore Command were ineffective. No U-boats worked in the Channel during this month and none attempted to pass through the Dover barrage. Experience had shown this route to be too dangerous.

The Atlantic was clear of U-boats for the first ten days of January, but on the 18th a Danish ship was sunk off Cape Finisterre and two days later a Greek ship suffered a similar fate off the coast of Portugal. The U-boat was damaged by the destroyer *Douglas* which was searching ahead of a Gibraltar-bound convoy, but she was able to remain at sea and attacked a French convoy a short time later. This incident is of interest because, when the French convoy was reported, Admiral Dönitz made an attempt to reinforce the attacking U-boat by sending two more to join her. Though the distance was too great for this concentration to be effected, it was a harbinger of the 'wolf-pack' tactics which were to cause us great trouble later.

The total losses attributed to U-boats in January were forty ships of 111,263 tons, but in the following month they rose sharply to forty-five ships of 169,566 tons—the greatest success so far achieved by that arm. In both these months, however, only a very small proportion of the ships sunk—four in January and three in February—were actually in convoy at the time. The U-boats' victims were nearly all independently-routed ships or stragglers from convoys; but the number of ships sunk by each U-boat at sea reached a very high figure.

At the beginning of February there was only one U-boat in the South-Western Approaches. She attacked convoy O.B. 84 on the 5th and sank one ship, but the destroyer *Antelope*, although the sole escort of the convoy, brought swift retribution and sank U.41. By the 10th of February three more U-boats had arrived in these waters and they sank nine independently-routed ships in the following week. Their primary object was to intercept the *Ark Royal* and *Renown* which were then returning from Freetown after the raider-hunting operations in the South Atlantic already described; but in this they failed.[1] In the North-West Approaches to these islands U.53 sank four ships before being sunk herself by the destroyer *Gurkha* on the 23rd of February; and the minesweeper *Gleaner* sank U.33 while she was attempting to lay mines in the Clyde on the 12th of February. Admiral Raeder reported to Hitler, with regard to the latter loss, that so dangerous an attempt would not be repeated. The first U-boat attack on a Norwegian convoy took place on the 18th of February and, although the convoy escaped, the destroyer *Daring*, one of its escorts, was sunk. She was not long unavenged, however, since, when convoy H.N. 14 was attacked on the 25th, the submarine *Narwhal*, which formed part of its escort, sighted a U-boat on the surface; a hunt was promptly organised and U.63 finally surfaced and scuttled herself. The next attack on this shipping route was on the 1st of April, when one straggler was sunk; but the small results achieved by the enemy lent strong support to the belief that convoy

---
[1] See pp. 114, 115 and 120.

and escort still afforded the best protection against submarines. In the North Sea U-boats sank no less than twenty-two ships during February. All were sailing independently and twelve of them were lost in the focal area at the north end of the east coast mine barrier. As counter-measure the Commander-in-Chief, Rosyth, was given a new hunting group formed of destroyers removed from other commands; but once again no success was achieved by this means. In the southern part of the North Sea there was less activity, but three coasters were sunk off Yarmouth.

To return to the Atlantic: U.25, after fuelling from a tanker in Cadiz Bay, achieved some success. On the 3rd of February she sank the *Armanistan* to the west of the mouth of the Tagus. Her convoy was at the time unescorted because the escort had been detached, while in the Channel, to hunt for an imaginary U-boat, and the North Atlantic Command at Gibraltar did not send destroyers to meet this convoy until after it had been attacked. The enemy next gained intelligence of the sailing of convoy O.G. 18 and concentrated three U-boats off Cape Finisterre to lie in wait for it. On the 17th they attacked. Although only one ship of the convoy was sunk, the U-boats found several independently-routed targets in the same area.

March saw a substantial decline in sinkings by U-boats to twenty-three ships of 62,781 tons. Though the increase in convoys and reduction of independent sailings probably contributed to this, the primary cause undoubtedly was the withdrawal by the enemy of most of his submarines to prepare for the Norwegian campaign. In the South-Western Approaches three U-boats sank four ships and laid three minefields. The Western Approaches Command organised frequent hunts, but in every case the enemy had already left the area being searched and, by the 13th, all three were on passage to their home waters.

During March the enemy stationed a number of U-boats in the north with the object of intercepting major units of the Home Fleet. Although they failed in this object they sank four ships, all neutral, to the west of the Shetlands and one to the east of the same islands. But the destroyer *Fortune*, while acting as part of the Home Fleet's screen, sank one enemy (U.44) on the 20th.

In the southern North Sea three U-boats sank seven ships during the first ten days of the month and six of these were making the dangerously open passage to Dutch ports for which convoys could not be organised. The 11th of March saw the first success in the U-boat war obtained by Bomber Command aircraft, which sank U.31 in Schillig Roads. But she was soon raised and put into service again, only to be sunk a second time eight months later.

During March there was a decrease in activity off the Moray Firth, but on the 19th and 20th four Danish ships were sunk there. Most ships were now convoyed through this focus, but the Danes, in order to preserve an appearance of strict neutrality, had declined to allow their ships to join our convoys, with unhappy results to themselves. The next month, April, saw the smallest losses of the whole campaign to date. Only seven ships of 32,467 tons were sunk by U-boats, but this was chiefly because almost all Admiral Dönitz's forces were then employed off the Norwegian coast. U.22 was lost, probably by mining, during the month and four other boats were sunk in the North Sea and off the Norwegian coast by various ships and aircraft supporting our forces in Norway. Further reference will be made to these sinkings when the operations of the Home Fleet are considered shortly. The enemy's losses in this month were the heaviest since October 1939.

In May there was little activity for the first ten days. Although two U-boats were working in the northern North Sea, our trade with Scandinavia had entirely stopped and this deprived them of merchant ship targets. U.13 was, however, sunk by the sloop *Weston* off Lowestoft on the last day of the month. About the middle of the month four U-boats sailed for the Western Approaches. On the 30th U.101 sank one ship and next day she obtained another success in an attack on an H.G. convoy. A counter-attack by the *Arabis*, one of the new corvettes, only caused slight damage. These little ships were now beginning to enter service in increasing numbers and were a very welcome addition to the strength of our convoy escorts. Their chief merit was that they could be built quickly. Their weakness lay in having insufficient speed to overtake a U-boat retiring on the surface and in the obsolescent type of asdic with which they were at this time fitted. Their small size (900 tons) and lively movements made them extremely uncomfortable and exhausting to their crews in the stormy Atlantic. Yet they crossed and recrossed that ocean escorting the slow convoys in all weathers and it is hard to see how Britain could have survived without them.

During March and April there had been no U-boats off the coasts of Spain and Portugal. One arrived off Cape Finisterre towards the end of May and promptly sank five ships in a like number of days. One of these was a well-armed British tanker which, although attacked from the surface and on a favourable bearing, failed to open fire until too late because the master believed that he had to hoist his colours before doing so. Actually quite a number of merchant ships had, by this time, used their defensive anti-submarine guns to good purpose. But the incident of the tanker showed the need to instruct masters carefully not only in the technical use of their armaments but in the legal aspects of the defensive arming of merchant ships. The sinkings achieved by U-boats in May were only thirteen ships of 55,580 tons.

The Admiralty's assessments of the losses inflicted on the enemy and also of his total submarine strength were, in fact, nearly correct throughout this period. For example, by the end of April 1940 the Assessment Committee considered that nineteen U-boats had been destroyed and that forty-three were in service. The actual figures, we now know, were twenty-two and fifty-two. The enemy's operational strength had steadily declined since the beginning of the war and did not start to increase again until many months later. Yet the favourable trend of our shipping losses was suddenly reversed in February.[1] The explanation is not far to seek. Too many ships were at this time still sailing independently and too many escort vessels were being used to hunt for U-boats instead of escorting the convoys. While most convoys in the Western Approaches were being escorted by only one destroyer or sloop, numbers of asdic-fitted vessels were fruitlessly scouring the waters for enemies. In some cases convoy escorts were even diverted to join hunting groups when passing through the danger areas, thus reducing the escort of the convoys to vanishing point. The persistence of the belief that to send out flotilla vessels and aircraft to hunt for the U-boats was to take the offensive against them, whereas to use them to escort the convoys was to act wholly defensively, is, indeed, a marked feature of our anti-submarine policy during the first year of the war. It has been seen that the intention, in certain circumstances, to use destroyers on hunting operations had a place in the Admiralty's War Plans.[2] But the circumstances stated in the plans—namely the conduct of submarine warfare by the enemy in accordance with international law—can hardly be said to have prevailed after the first few weeks of war. That the First Lord himself was insistent that the U-boat should be searched for by hunting groups is shown by his minute to the First Sea Lord stating that 'nothing can be more important in the anti-submarine war than to try to obtain an independent flotilla which could work like a cavalry division on the approaches, without worrying about the traffic or the U-boat sinkings, but could search large areas over a wide front. In this way these areas would become untenable to U-boats. . . .'[3] It is also clear that a similar conception of anti-submarine warfare prevailed in some sections of the Naval Staff and in the Western Approaches Command at this time.

In September 1939 the whole problem had been reviewed by a committee appointed to report to the Admiralty on various aspects of the maritime war; its Chairman, Vice-Admiral Sir T. H. Binney, expressed the view that 'the best position for anti-submarine vessels is in company with a convoy' and recommended 'that, for the present,

---

[1] See p. 131 and Appendix R.
[2] See p. 46.
[3] W. S. Churchill. *The Second World War*, Vol. I (2nd Edition), p. 669.

every anti-submarine vessel with sufficiently good sea-keeping qualities should be employed with convoys rather than dispersed in hunting units'. This report was endorsed by the Vice-Chief of Naval Staff, not only expressing his complete agreement but also stating that 'this is the principle adopted'. Yet a study of the anti-submarine operations by the flotillas of the Western Approaches Command in particular shows that at this time many flotilla vessels were employed on hunting for U-boats instead of escorting the convoys.

That there should have been so wide a difference of opinion on so fundamental a matter is surprising, as is the fact that no clear direction regarding the policy to be followed was issued by the Admiralty to the commands chiefly concerned. Not the least important lesson to be learnt from a study of the early months of the U-boat war is that the enemy would be most easily found in the vicinity of the quarry which he was seeking, that his purpose could best be frustrated by protecting the quarry as strongly as possible and that escorting convoys would therefore produce abundant opportunities for a vigorous tactical offensive against the enemy—once he had shown himself.

It has been told how the aircraft of Coastal Command were by this time playing an increasing part in protecting shipping and harrying the U-boats, especially while on passage around the north of Scotland. The naval and air authorities concerned were now fully alive to the possibilities of sea-air co-operation in this form of warfare and, had the most energetic steps been taken to replace the ineffective anti-submarine bomb by depth charges suitably adapted to use from the air, important results could undoubtedly have been achieved by this means far earlier. Proposals to use depth charges for this purpose had reached the Admiralty from commanding officers of aircraft carriers many months before the war; but no scientific investigation of the arguments for and against the bomb was ever undertaken and the proposals were shelved. Similar suggestions were also received in the Air Ministry, but they were as reluctant as the Admiralty to make the change. As late as the 17th of April 1940, by which time ample evidence of the ineffectiveness of the anti-submarine bomb was available, the Air Ministry decided not to pursue the development of the depth charge further—and that in spite of favourable reports on trials carried out in the preceding months. Fortunately the Commander-in-Chief, Coastal Command (Air Marshal Sir F. W. Bowhill) got this ruling relaxed far enough to permit the trials to continue. It was chiefly by his personal efforts that the use of depth charges was introduced in Coastal Command during the summer of 1940, though at first on a trivially small scale. Not until the spring of 1941 was a satisfactorily modified depth charge brought into general use. This was to prove by far the most effective anti-submarine weapon placed in the hands of both naval and R.A.F. aircrews during the entire course of the war.

It would be tedious to try to follow this story through the labyrinth of arguments and counter-arguments with which it is entangled, but certain conclusions may be usefully remembered. The first of these is that the anti-submarine bomb was the first weapon designed specifically to deal from the air with what had been convincingly shown to be the most deadly method of attacking our merchant shipping. Yet no trials were ever carried out to test the bomb's behaviour beneath the surface of the element in which it was designed to work, or its effect on a submarine's structure. Moreover the rate of progress from its inception in 1925 until it came into service in 1931 was leisurely in the extreme; and even thereafter nothing was done to test its performance. The result was that the Navy and R.A.F. both entered a war in which the struggle at sea was certain to be a preponderant factor equipped only with anti-submarine bombs of doubtful quality, untried under action conditions but known to be unreliable in certain aspects and, furthermore, supplied with no suitable sight with which to aim them from low heights. That the small results achieved by our aircraft against U-boats during the early phases of the struggle stemmed largely from these causes is beyond dispute.

Before leaving the U-boat war, mention must be made of the attempt by the Admiralty to reintroduce decoy ships. They had achieved some spectacular successes in the first war, but the wisdom of expending a substantial effort on endeavouring to repeat a particular tactic—about which the enemy was certainly fully informed—appears open to question. However, plans had been prepared before the war, and between October 1939 and March 1940 eight decoy ships, which had been fitted out in the utmost secrecy, were commissioned. They were certainly a technical advance on the 'Q ships' of the first war, since they all had torpedo tubes and depth charges and some mounted as many as nine 4-inch guns.[1] It was hoped that if they fell in with an armed merchant raider they might engage her with success. The first sailed in December 1939 and the remainder early in 1940. One cruised between these islands and Gibraltar and thence into the South Atlantic, two worked between Sierra Leone, Gibraltar and Bermuda, two more were in the North Atlantic, one generally in the Western Approaches and two small ones were em-

---

[1] Decoy ships were, in fact, never called 'Q Ships' during the 1939–45 war. They were described by the code-word 'Freighters'. But the older title is so well established and widely recognised that it has been thought best to continue to use it in these volumes.

ployed in home waters. None of them ever sighted a U-boat or accomplished any useful purpose at all; two of them were torpedoed and sunk in the Western Approaches in June. The enemy was far too wary to be caught by a ruse which had been so well advertised between the wars and, moreover, secrecy had been so great that the ships were often in considerable danger of being sunk by our own forces. The extreme security precautions enforced with regard to these ships made it difficult for the Flag Officers chiefly responsible for the actual conduct of the anti-submarine war to criticise the project effectively. It was for this reason that it was not until December 1940 that a thorough enquiry was ordered. Once all the facts were known, their operations were immediately stopped.

The depredations of Admiral Dönitz's U-boats and our counter-measures thereto have now been considered up to the end of May 1940. But, in the meanwhile, the enemy had started unrestricted air warfare on shipping. It will be remembered that in the pre-war staff discussions the naval view had been that such a campaign was unlikely because of its effect on neutrals; but that if it was launched the normal defensive measures of convoy and escort would prove adequate. The Air Staff, on the other hand, expected such attacks to start at an early stage and was sceptical about the possibility of providing adequate defence by mounting guns in the merchant ships and providing anti-aircraft escort vessels to the convoys.[1] Experience was now to show that, although convoy formed a valuable, even essential, defence against air attack, and effective weapons mounted in either the merchantmen or their escorts could contribute substantially by keeping the enemy to a distance at which the likelihood of his hitting with bombs or torpedoes was reduced, only by fighter aircraft could complete command of the air over the convoys be assured. There was, in fact, some truth in the pre-war arguments presented by both the Naval and Air Staffs, and it was by putting the two—convoy and fighter protection—together that the air offensive against our shipping was finally defeated.

Though air attacks on merchant shipping, and particularly against our east coast convoys, had been expected since the start of the war, few had actually taken place during 1939, partly because of the restrictions on bombing imposed by Hitler and partly because of the unwillingness of the Luftwaffe to meet the German Navy's requests.

The Commander-in-Chief, Nore, had for some months been particularly anxious regarding the exposed state of the great mass of shipping, often totalling 100,000 tons, assembled off Southend to await convoy up the east coast, and the equally large mass, chiefly

---

[1] See p. 34.

of neutral shipping, assembled in the examination anchorage in the Downs. However, in spite of being offered these valuable and ill-defended targets, the enemy chose the entirely different, though scarcely less embarrassing, strategy of carrying out isolated but widespread attacks along the whole length of the east coast convoy route.

The new year was little more than a week old when these attacks started and between the 9th and 15th of January three ships were sunk and others damaged. A fortnight's lull followed, but on the 29th and 30th attacks were renewed on a much wider scale. Four ships were sunk and many others damaged. Light vessels were also repeatedly attacked. Not only had the Admiralty forborne to arm these, but Trinity House, which was responsible for their administration, had, in order to preserve their international and humanitarian character, declined to allow their use for any belligerent purpose, such as reporting enemy movements. But this altruism made no difference to the savagery of the Luftwaffe's onslaughts. Yet the German Navy, to whose minelaying operations they had been of some value, may well have been displeased by the extinction of their lights or the removal of the vessels, which were the natural consequences of the action by their comrades in the air.

By the end of January it was plain that these unrestricted air attacks might soon surpass the U-boat or the mines as the principal threat to our coastal shipping. Losses due to air attack had amounted to eleven ships of 23,693 tons during the month.

The counter-measures needed were obvious. Firstly came the protection of shipping by fighter aircraft, a duty for which Coastal Command had inadequate strength, nor had it suitable aircraft to deal with the Junkers 87 and Messerschmitt 109 types chiefly used by the enemy.[1] In consequence it was on Fighter Command that the requirement largely fell.

The extension of the protecting shield of Fighter Command's nation-wide organisation to the coastal convoys was, however, of slow growth, and many difficulties had to be surmounted and many concessions made by both services before it became effective. In the early months of 1940 Nos. 11 and 12 Fighter Groups, which covered the Nore Command's area, and also the other groups stationed along the east coast, usually only sent out fighters in answer to a 'help' call from a convoy—which meant that an attack had already started and that they would almost certainly arrive too late. Moreover, Fighter Group Headquarters did not always know the exact whereabouts of the convoys. When the fighters did arrive they often approached too close to the ships, which sometimes opened fire on them. Complaints of inadequate naval training in aircraft recognition

---

[1] See p. 107.

were countered by reports of failure by aircraft to make the proper recognition signals and of many cases of unnecessarily low flying above the convoys. These problems were, indeed, inevitable and endemic to the whole problem of fighter protection of shipping. They could only be solved gradually as each service gained experience of the difficulties and problems of the other.

To meet the demand for constant fighter protection over the convoys it was arranged at the end of February that patrols should be maintained over the four convoys generally at sea at any one time, and a fifth over the Dogger Bank fishing fleet, which had also been subjected to air attacks. Fighter Command had been reluctant to institute such patrols chiefly because they entailed a great amount of —possibly abortive—flying, thus aggravating problems of maintenance, and because they contravened the principle of controlling all aircraft from their Group or Sector Headquarters. But the seriousness of the threat demanded that exceptions should be made and experiments tried.

Second among defensive measures came the convoying of all shipping. This presented peculiar problems on the east coast, since the narrowness of the swept channels inside the mine barrier compelled convoys to steam in double, or even single line and so to string themselves out over a long distance. Moreover ships which did not officially belong to a convoy often joined up with one because they felt safer that way. These 'camp followers', as the escort commanders called them, complicated matters still more. Sometimes they brought a convoy up to a total of about sixty ships, strung out along about twenty miles of channel. Convoy control and discipline became very difficult since the senior officer of the escort at the head of the convoy might be far out of sight of the rear ships. From the earliest days the Rosyth Escort Force had been charged with this responsibility and its little ships had done, and were still doing, splendid work. But they could not possibly protect the entire length of a one- or two-column convoy of such size.

Arming the merchant ships themselves against air attack presented many difficulties, the greatest of which was the acute shortage of every type of automatic weapon suitable to such use. The Admiralty scoured its stores and depots for weapons, removed them from ships which were immobilised or stood in lesser need, tried to borrow from the Army but found that service even more destitute, and adopted many temporary and substitute devices. The need for a big increase in close-range anti-aircraft weapons for precisely this purpose had been foreseen well before the war, and after fairly prolonged trials and investigations the Naval Staff had decided, firstly, that it must go to a foreign country if supplies were to be augmented rapidly and, secondly, that the Swiss-made 20-mm. Oerlikon gun was the most promising weapon then on the market. An initial order for 1,500 guns for our merchant ships was therefore authorised shortly before the outbreak of war. The first Swiss-made guns were actually received just before the start of the Norwegian campaign. But there were so many claims for these excellent little weapons that it was a very long time before any merchant ship received one. Only a trickle of them had flowed to us by the time that the fall of France and the entry of Italy into the war cut us off from the source of supply. Meanwhile steps were being taken to start manufacture in England and, at the same time, prolonged negotiations were entered upon with the company's representatives for manufacture in the United States. The first British-made guns were produced by the end of 1940 and thereafter an increasing flow gradually developed to a flood as the result of vast American production. But the relatively lavish armament which merchant ships received during the last two years of the war was very remote from the present period when search was being made for any weapon or, if none could be found, for temporary substitutes. In order to hasten the design and supply of such devices the Admiralty formed, early in 1940, a department for Anti-Aircraft Weapons and Devices. Many and varied were the improvisations which it produced. In April 1941, chiefly to improve the training of the Merchant Navy in the use of its ever-increasing defences, the Admiralty appointed Admiral Sir Frederick Dreyer, a very senior officer of long experience with weapons, with the title of 'Inspector of Merchant Navy Gunnery'.

Much ingenuity was shown in producing substitutes for weapons and equipment which we now had no time to make. Plastic armour was developed to protect ships' bridges; rockets were designed to carry a wire up into the path of an attacking aircraft; a compressed-air thrower lobbed hand grenades at the Luftwaffe; kites and balloons were flown by ships, and even totally innocuous fireworks were supplied in the hope that they would deter the aircraft from making a close approach.[1] These, and many other similar experiments, served a purpose; but the crews of the merchant ships and fishing vessels knew that a light automatic gun like the Oerlikon, which fired an explosive shell, was the weapon they wanted and they felt that it was a long time coming into their hands.

A natural corollary of the immense demands for anti-aircraft weapons now coming from the Merchant Navy was that the Admiralty had somehow to find and train the men to fight them. The pre-war strength of the guns' crews trained under the Defensively Equipped Merchant Ship (D.E.M.S.) Organisation was completely inadequate to meet these new demands. The Admiralty appealed to

---

[1] See Appendix B.

the War Office for help and very soon Army machine-gunners began to sail in the east coast convoys. Thus was born an organisation which finally gained the dignified title of the Maritime Regiment of Royal Artillery. It reached a strength of 14,000 men in 1944. The Admiralty's D.E.M.S. crews were also expanded as fast as possible and finally reached a total of 24,000. Sailors and soldiers charged with the same duties interchanged freely; as many as sixty were ultimately sent to large liners, a cargo ship would be given between seven and twelve, while a tug would have one solitary anti-aircraft gunner. The Army gunners would board an inward-bound ship, possibly bringing their weapons with them, before she entered the danger zone and would leave her after she had reached her destination. They would then go to an outward-bound ship to see her safely through the first stage of her journey. The organisation was gradually extended to cover most of the world. In its final form a valuable refrigerator ship bound, for example, to New Zealand might have two 40-mm. Boförs guns and numerous light weapons, with the key members of their crews, placed on board in Liverpool, and be ordered to call at Kingston, Jamaica, on the outward voyage for their removal and transfer to an inbound ship. The organisation of this welcome and original addition to the anti-aircraft defence of shipping was worked out between the Admiralty's Trade Division and the Army's Anti-Aircraft Command. But the development of co-ordinated fighter and anti-aircraft defences for merchant shipping along our coastal routes was slow, and we must return to the early days of 1940, when all such measures were in their infancy and experience of the requirements was being gradually gained by all three services by a process of improvisation and of trial and error.

The acute difficulties of the months of January and February 1940 were aggravated by exceptionally severe weather. Conditions more normal to polar regions prevailed over the whole east coast during those months. For almost three weeks traffic in the Humber was suspended by ice. A ship specially strengthened for ice-breaking failed to force a passage out of Goole, and an attempt to break the ice with an empty collier of 1,500 tons resulted only in her riding up on the ice and remaining there. Floating pack ice reached a depth of 12 feet in the estuaries and swept away navigational marks. Fighter aircraft were sometimes immobilised for days on end on snow-bound and fog-bound airfields; and the guns and superstructures of merchant ships and escort vessels were permanently coated in ice and frozen spray. The same weather immobilised the German surface ships in their bases, but their aircraft appeared to be less affected than our own and attacks continued.

The difficulties of convoy organisation grew with the danger. The convoys became so large that they tended to become unmanageable and, for a time, a complete breakdown of the system threatened. At the end of January the Admiralty decided to increase the number of convoys and prohibited independent sailing during daylight along the most dangerous stretch of coast, that between the Thames and Cromer Knoll. By February nearly all shipping sailed in groups which, even if unescorted, made fighter protection far easier. Our counter-measures now appeared to be beginning to produce results. On the 3rd of February attacks took place between Rattray Head and Cromer.[1] The minesweeper *Sphinx* was sunk and six ships were damaged, but R.A.F. fighters destroyed three of the attackers.

On the 9th there were more attacks, stretching as far north as Aberdeen, where minesweeping trawlers were the target, and nine merchant ships were damaged. It was at this point that arrangements were agreed between the Admiralty and Air Ministry for standing patrols to fly over the convoys; on the 27th this step first proved its value when, off St Abb's Head, R.A.F. Spitfires drove off an attack and destroyed two enemy aircraft. Communications between ships and aircraft were, at this stage, very rudimentary and targets were often missed for lack of a ship-to-air fighter-direction system. But such difficulties were not confined to ourselves for, on the 22nd of this month, bombers of the Luftwaffe attacked and sank two of their own destroyers about 30 miles north of Terschelling. Owing to inadequate recognition signals they were mistaken for British destroyers from the Nore Command which, at this time, carried out numerous sweeps to seize enemy shipping creeping along the Dutch coast and to send neutral shipping into the contraband control station in the Downs.

Our losses to air attack fell to only two ships of 853 tons in February. In March enemy air activity increased but there were fewer independent sailings and fighter protection had improved. On the 2nd took place the first attack on shipping in the Channel, when the liner *Domala* was bombed off the Isle of Wight by one aircraft, set on fire and seriously damaged with heavy loss of life. On the 20th more attacks took place off Havre and Beachy Head. Appropriate steps were taken by the Admiralty to reduce independent sailings in the eastern Channel; and ships from the Low Country ports were ordered to the Downs, to join outward-bound (O.A.) convoys there instead of at St Helen's (Isle of Wight). But the enemy's attention was still directed chiefly to the heavy, and for us vital, flow of shipping along the east coast. On the first day of the month convoys F.S. 9 and F.S. 10 were attacked off Flamborough Head and the Tyne respectively, and next day a Methil–Tyne convoy (M.T. 20) was bombed. Some ships were damaged but none lost in these attacks on convoys.

---

[1] See Map 13 (*facing p. 127*).

But ships sailing independently on the same routes suffered more seriously.

The month of March also saw the first extension of the enemy's air attacks to our Norwegian convoys. This had, however, been anticipated, and the Admiralty had already transferred the anti-aircraft cruisers *Cairo* and *Calcutta* to Admiral Forbes for the specific purpose of defending them. This action was soon justified, for, on the 20th of March, the enemy made air attacks on convoy H.N. 20, sinking one ship and damaging three others. Similar attacks were repeated during the next fortnight on almost every outward and homeward Norwegian convoy. However, the Hurricanes newly stationed in the north of Scotland, and sometimes naval fighters from the Orkneys as well, combined with the gunfire of the escorting anti-aircraft cruisers, drove off every one of these attacks. No more ships were lost or damaged in Norwegian convoys. The most interesting lesson derived from the successful defence of these convoys was that a combination of shore-based fighter aircraft and powerful anti-aircraft escort could provide a high degree of immunity for shipping. In fact the long-established practice of protecting shipping by convoy and escort, adapted and modified to meet modern conditions, was once again proved to be the best answer. During the whole of March losses from air attack amounted to only seven ships of 8,694 tons. The Admiralty and Air Ministry could therefore justifiably feel that the defensive measures taken were proving themselves effective. But it was none the less realised that optimism must be tempered with caution, since it was plain that the enemy had so far employed only a fraction of his bomber force for this purpose, and that should he choose to direct his full strength to it an acute crisis might yet arise. We now know that Admiral Raeder repeatedly pressed for this to be done but that Marshal Göring was reserving his bomber strength for more dramatic purposes in Norway, the Low Countries and France. Nevertheless, the menace could not be ignored and the possibility of diverting the main flow of shipping to west coast ports was again reviewed by the Admiralty. This had been considered by the Chiefs of Staff and the Cabinet before the war and again in the closing months of 1939. The difficulty of making any large-scale diversion was, however, acute because of the congestion and delays it would cause on the west coast. The policy decided on was, therefore, only to order such diversions when they were forced on us and, meanwhile, to press ahead with the improvement of discharge and loading facilities in the western ports, which might at any time be required to deal with a greatly increased quantity of shipping.

In April and May there was little enemy air activity against our coastal traffic because the main strength of the Luftwaffe was, as in the case of the U-boats, deployed against Norway. Only minelaying operations were carried out against shipping by enemy aircraft during these months. The transfer of many flotilla vessels to the Norwegian operations left our coastal shipping almost unescorted at this time, and it was fortunate that the enemy was unable to take advantage of this. In April seven ships of 13,409 tons were lost by air attacks, but the following month, when the land campaign in the Low Countries started, saw a great increase to no less than forty-eight ships of 158,348 tons. For the first time the enemy's air attacks had overtaken the U-boat and the mine as the principal cause of our losses.

It has already been told how, during the present phase, the Royal Air Force began its offensive minelaying campaign in enemy-controlled waters.[1] But it was now realised that air power afforded other means whereby the control of such waters could be disputed. Moreover, the great changes which took place on land between April and June brought into prominence the value to the enemy of the coastal shipping routes along much of the long North European seaboard. The iron ore traffic from Narvik to the south was still of great importance during the months when the Baltic ports were frozen and, to keep German industry supplied with fuel and raw materials the traffic between the north German ports and Rotterdam or Antwerp was scarcely less important. But throughout the greater part of this phase our air operations against enemy merchant shipping were severely restricted by the British Government's policy on air bombardment in general. By this policy only warships, troopships or 'auxiliaries in direct attendance on the enemy fleet' could be attacked, and they only if identified beyond doubt. Even if an enemy merchant ship opened fire with her defensive armament our aircraft were forbidden to retaliate. They had at all times to conform to rules similar to those which, under international law, governed the use of force by warships intercepting a merchantman. This was in accordance with the 'Draft Hague Rules of Air Warfare' of 1923, which the British Government took as the basis for its policy, even though they had never been formally adopted by any country and had not acquired the status of international law. It will readily be understood how far this policy made air action ineffective against all types of enemy merchant ships, including, for example, disguised merchant raiders. During the whole of 1940 only sixteen enemy merchant ships, totalling 22,472 tons, were sunk by air attack and seventeen were damaged.

Though the need to relax these severe restrictions had been discussed throughout the preceding winter, it was the end of March 1940 before revised instructions were issued. Even then the new rules did not give our aircraft much greater freedom. But they did at least

---

[1] See pp. 124–125.

'The Atlantic.' By R. V. Pitchforth.

(*National Maritime Museum*)

'Ship's Boat at Sea.' By Richard Eurich.

(*National Maritime Museum*)

Escort Vessels on patrol, 1940. Left to right: H.M.S.'s *Holderness, Vivacious, Guillemot* and *Puffin*.

A destroyer in heavy weather. H.M.S. *Kashmir*, 1st September 1940.

enable them to deal with the anti-aircraft ships which had been particularly troublesome in the Heligoland Bight. Nor did the enemy's violent bombing attacks on our own east coast traffic lead to any retaliatory steps. It was the German attack on Norway which decided the British Government to relax the restrictions and, two days after that campaign started, unrestricted attacks were permitted off the south coast of Norway and in the Skagerrak. Shortly after this a free zone for attacks was established within ten miles of the whole Norwegian coast. The removal of the early restrictions did not, however, bring about any appreciable success in stopping the enemy's coastal traffic by air attack. In the first place such a requirement had not figured among the duties required of Coastal Command when they were formulated in 1937, nor in that Command's war plans.[1] In consequence no special organisation existed for starting such an offensive; nor had Coastal Command's aircrews been trained to that end. Secondly the severe shortage of aircraft of all types and the policy of conserving our meagre bomber strength to attack land targets in Germany had left Coastal Command with virtually no striking power. It is, therefore, hardly surprising that only small results were achieved at this time against the enemy's coastal traffic. But the month of April 1940 is, none the less, important since it marks the beginning of the offensive. As the land campaign moved westward in May, the focus of air operations moved with it and we find a start being made to interfere with shipping moving along the north German and Dutch coasts and to deal with his minor war vessels, such as E-boats (motor torpedo-boats), which were operating in those waters. But in this case also successful attacks were extremely rare. It was not until after the close of the present phase that the air bombardment rules issued in March were amended and the Royal Air Force given greater freedom to attack enemy shipping.

Before leaving the story of the second phase of the enemy's attempt to dispute control of our short sea routes it must be mentioned that the early days of May saw the arrival of a new threat when, on the 9th, E-boats attacked a force of cruisers and destroyers from the Home Fleet which was searching for an enemy minelaying force. The destroyer *Kelly* was badly damaged but, after a tow lasting 91 hours, was got into the Tyne safely. That, however, was the only appearance on the east coast of these fast, well-armed enemy craft up to the end of May 1940. They had so far only sunk two small merchant ships totalling 845 tons. Although the losses which they caused were always small when compared with those inflicted by the U-boats, mines and the bombers, they were to cause us some trouble in the next phase of the offensive against our coastal shipping routes.

---

[1] See p. 35.

CHAPTER IX

THE HOME FLEET
1st January–9th April, 1940

> '... your gallant Fleet, upon whom measureless causes depend.'
> *Mr Churchill to Admiral Forbes.* 17th April 1940.

WHEREAS the old year ended with a succession of storms of unusual persistence and severity even for the waters in which the Home Fleet must chiefly operate, the new year was but a few days old when a prolonged spell of very severe cold set in. It lasted for nearly two months and added no little burden to the cares of the Commander-in-Chief regarding the maintenance of his ships and the strain on their crews, to whom the arctic conditions brought much discomfort. None the less the fleet continued, through storm and ice, to carry out its functions and in February all classes of ship actually kept the seas for more days 'than ever before since the advent of steam'. The average time spent at sea by all ships of the fleet totalled twenty-three days during the month. Such a figure was, later in the war, easily surpassed by both American and British warships fighting on the other side of the world, but it must be remembered that no true comparison can be made between conditions in the calmer waters and generally fairer weather of the central Pacific and those in the habitually stormy reaches of the northern North Sea and the approaches to the Arctic Ocean. It was to be expected that such weather would quickly find any weak places in the design and construction of the ships, but by the end of February Admiral Forbes reported that, in general, his small as well as his larger ships had stood the strain very well.

Admiral Forbes' responsibility for the Norwegian convoys continued during the first months of the year, but some reorganisation was made necessary by the increasing number of neutral ships now joining them. After one convoy had reached a total of fifty-four ships it was decided that, after the 3rd of February, they would be run on a four-day instead of on a six- or eight-day cycle.

The story of these convoys can at this stage be conveniently continued up to their ending, which was brought about by the enemy's invasion of Norway. The submarine and air attacks made on them in the early months of 1940 were mentioned in the last chapter and it was then remarked how rare were the enemy's successes. The whole story of these convoys is, in fact, one of considerable success to our organisation and escort arrangements. Up to the end of March, 1,337 ships, mostly of neutral registration, had been convoyed in them. Only two ships, and they both stragglers, were sunk by torpedo and one was lost by air attack. One escorting destroyer was lost but one U-boat was sunk by the escorts, all of whom had been provided by the Home Fleet at no small strain on Admiral Forbes' destroyer resources.

The end of these convoys lacked nothing of the dramatic. On the 7th of April convoy H.N. 25 was preparing to leave Bergen and O.N. 25 was at sea bound to the same port. The latter was recalled at once and the Admiralty, rather surprisingly, ordered the former not to sail. The homeward-bound convoy had, however, already put to sea, but returned to the coast on the evening of the 8th. At dawn on the 9th the convoy was ready to sail again, but no escorts had arrived. The merchant ship *Fylingdale* (Captain J. S. Pinkney), which had been appointed 'guide of the convoy', met the German tanker *Skagerrak* in a fiord north of Bergen at about noon that day. Though Captain Pinkney could hardly have guessed the truth, that she was on her way to fuel German warships in Trondheim, her presence and conduct aroused his suspicions. He next heard, from an adjacent Swedish ship, that German troops had reached Bergen and he thereupon ordered the convoy to sail—which it did at 2 p.m. At 4.30 warships were sighted and the convoy scattered; but they turned out to be the belated destroyers of the escort. The whole convoy of thirty-seven ships reached home waters safely from under the very noses of the enemy. But O.N. 25, which had been in much less peril at the start, was less lucky for, when it was recalled on the evening of the 7th, twenty-four ships lost touch and continued on their voyage. Thirteen of these were sunk or captured by the enemy.

The turn of the year brought a series of successes to the enemy's anti-submarine measures in the Heligoland Bight. The submarines *Seahorse*, *Undine* and *Starfish* had all sailed at the end of December or beginning of January to patrol off Horn Reef and all three became overdue between the 9th and 16th of January. The *Seahorse* was sunk by enemy minesweepers off Heligoland on the 7th of January and was lost with all hands; but the crews of the other two boats were saved. These losses caused us to abandon submarine patrols in the Bight, and orders were given that no submarine should proceed east of the German declared mine area without special reasons. Furthermore no submarine was to enter another's patrol area until the boat to be relieved had reported herself. In place of the previous patrols those off the Skagerrak, the Dutch coast and to the west of the enemy's declared area were strengthened.

Submarine patrols off Heligoland were restarted on the 18th of February, when a sortie by the enemy's main units was expected. The *Salmon, Sunfish* and L.23 all sighted warships during these patrols; but in no case was the submarine in a position from which she could make an attack. Submarines also operated at this time against the iron ore traffic from Narvik, but the enemy's use of the inshore route through Norwegian territorial waters made opportunities to attack rare. Nevertheless, towards the end of March, the *Ursula* and *Truant* each sank a German ship just outside neutral waters. But by the end of that month it had become clear that, with the lengthening days and the enemy's increased use of air searches and patrols, our submarines would be faced with serious difficulties off the coast of Norway. In fact the full potentialities of aircraft for anti-submarine co-operation seem to have been realised by both belligerents at about the same time. On the 23rd of March the 10th French submarine flotilla, of twelve boats, joined the British submarines working in the North Sea. These substantial and welcome reinforcements worked from Harwich under the Nore Command.

Meanwhile the Northern Patrol, whose cruisers of the C and D classes were now being steadily replaced by armed merchant cruisers, continued to enforce the blockade by patrolling the exits to the Atlantic. The measure of success achieved is shown by the following figures:—

Table 7. Northern Patrol—Ships Intercepted, January–April 1940

Two-week period	Total number of ships sighted	Number of eastbound ships sighted	Number of ships sent in for examination	Number of ships entering voluntarily for examination	Number of German ships intercepted
5th Jan.–18th Jan.	127	48	30	19	—
19th Jan.–31st Jan.	123	56	28	7	—
1st Feb.–14th Feb.	92	49	21	21	—
15th Feb.–29th Feb.	92	61	24	13	1
1st March–14th March.	98	52	12	13	4
15th March–31st March	138	69	13	17	—
1st April–9th April*	54	26	12	8	—

* The start of the Norwegian campaign.

A steady toll, too, was taken of enemy merchant ships which attempted to break for home from the neutral ports which had sheltered them since the outbreak of war. On the 10th of January the German ship *Bahia Blanca*, while trying to evade our patrols by hugging the ice edge in the Denmark Strait, ran into the ice and sank. The following month a considerable operation was planned and executed by the Commander-in-Chief, Western Approaches, to intercept six German merchantmen which were expected to sail from Vigo. The Home Fleet lent the *Renown, Ark Royal, Galatea* and some destroyers; French warships and Coastal Command aircraft also co-operated. The results were very successful. The French ships working with the Western Approaches Command captured the *Rostock* just outside Spanish waters on the 11th of February; next day the destroyer *Hasty* captured the *Morea* off the Portuguese coast. On the 21st the cruiser *Manchester* and destroyer *Kimberley*, on the Northern Patrol, captured the *Wahehe*. The *Orizaba* was wrecked in the north of Norway, the *Arucas* scuttled when intercepted by the *York* on the 3rd of March and the last of the six, the *Wangoni*, was intercepted off Kristiansand (South) by the submarine *Triton* on the 28th of February but escaped in the dark.[1] She was the only one to reach her home waters. While this was happening in the east, far away in the west on the other side of the Atlantic other cruisers intercepted four more enemy merchantmen, all but one of which scuttled themselves.

The policy that merchant ships should destroy themselves to avoid capture had been adopted by the enemy before the outbreak of war and our Merchant Navy was thereby denied many valuable prizes. The Cabinet had considered measures to prevent scuttling as soon as the enemy's practice had become clear and on the 23rd of November 1939 approved the proposal that the intercepting warship could order the enemy to lower her boats and cast them adrift, and should send a warning signal that, if the ship was scuttled, her crew would be left to their fate. If the signal was disregarded the crew were, however, to be picked up. The first success for these measures was achieved by the *Manchester* in her interception of the *Wahehe* referred to above, but they were not generally successful in preventing self-destruction—partly because the scuttling charges had usually been fired before the warship's orders had been received and understood. In March four more homeward-bound enemy merchant ships were caught by the Northern Patrol, the *Wolfsburg* on the 2nd and *Uruguay* on the 6th by the cruiser *Berwick*, the *La Coruña* on the 13th by the armed merchant cruiser *Maloja* and the *Mimi Horn* on the 28th by the *Transylvania*. All of these scuttled and set themselves on fire to avoid capture. But this series of failures to run the gauntlet of our blockade, if it brought us few actual prizes, showed the enemy that such attempts were becoming increasingly costly; he did not renew his endeavour to get his isolated merchant

---

[1] The port of Kristiansand in the extreme south of Norway (58° 08′ North, 8° 00′ East) is referred to as Kristiansand (South) in these pages to distinguish it from Kristiansund which is situated at the entrance to the southern approach to Trondheim Fjord in 63° 08′ North, 7° 43′ East. (See Maps 4 and 19.) The same distinction is made in official documents relating to this period.

THE SEARCH FOR THE 'ALTMARK'

ships home until his position had been greatly improved by the land campaigns of the following summer, which gave him the use of the French west coast ports. Up to the 5th of April 1940 the enemy had lost by capture or scuttling fifty-eight merchant ships of approximately 300,000 tons, and a considerable proportion of these had been intercepted by the Northern Patrol. Eighty-two ships (480,000 tons) had successfully evaded our patrols and reached home; 246 more (about one million tons) still remained in ports abroad. In reviewing these results it must, however, be remembered that our patrols were far from complete in the early months of the war and that winter conditions had favoured evasion. By the end of the period with which we are now dealing the chances of an enemy blockade runner getting home had been greatly reduced.

The month of February also saw the safe arrival, on the 2nd, of the third Canadian troop convoy (T.C. 3) of five large liners escorted by the battleships *Valiant* and *Malaya* and met by a strong force of destroyers from the Home Fleet.

Though the chronic shortage of destroyers continued to cramp Admiral Forbes' operations he received cruiser reinforcements from the Mediterranean at this time. With the arrival of the *Arethusa* and *Penelope* early in the new year he was able to reorganise his cruisers into more homogeneous squadrons. Thus the 1st Cruiser Squadron comprised all the 8-inch-gun cruisers, the 2nd the four *Auroras* and the 18th the 6-inch-gun 'Town' class cruisers. The advantages of an organisation of this type are substantial, but the stress of operations for which ships had to be found regardless of type or class was soon to be felt, and the homogeneity was in fact to be lost almost as soon as it was achieved.

While these activities were in progress in home waters the oceans were being intensively searched for the 12,000-ton supply ship *Altmark* which had disappeared after the sinking of her parent ship, the *Graf Spee*, and was believed still to have some 300 British Merchant Navy prisoners aboard. These searches failed, for the reason that the *Altmark* stayed some time in the South Atlantic instead of breaking at once for home as had been thought likely. She actually started her homeward journey on the 22nd of January, passed between the Faeröe Islands and Iceland undetected at the height of the severe weather, and arrived off Trondheim on the 14th of February. On the evening of the 15th Admiral Forbes heard that she had passed Bergen at noon that day.

A force consisting of the destroyer *Cossack* (Captain P. L. Vian, commanding the 4th Flotilla), the cruiser *Arethusa* and four other destroyers had left Rosyth on the 14th with orders to sweep up the Norwegian coast from Kristiansand (South) on the night of the 15th/16th with the object of catching enemy ships returning to

Narvik. At ten minutes past midnight on the 16th Admiral Forbes told Captain Vian that his primary object now was to intercept the *Altmark*. But it was not until the following afternoon that firm news of her whereabouts was received. Just before 1 p.m. two separate Hudson aircraft of Coastal Command, which had organised intensive air searches, reported sighting her. The positions given by them were, however, some miles apart. In consequence of this Captain Vian divided his force to make two separate sweeps and, one hour after the aircraft had made their reports, the *Altmark* was sighted by the *Arethusa* four miles off Egerö Light, escorted by two Norwegian destroyers.[1] The destroyers *Ivanhoe* and *Intrepid* were told to board, but the *Altmark* refused to stop and their efforts to stop her were frustrated by the Norwegian escort. She then entered Jossing Fiord, an inlet one and a half miles long with very high cliffs, and anchored. At 4.10 p.m. Captain Vian followed her in and demanded from the Norwegian torpedo-boat *Kjell* that the British prisoners be handed over to him. The Norwegian replied that the *Altmark* had been examined at Bergen the previous day, was unarmed and had been given permission to use territorial waters. It was therefore clear to Captain Vian that measures to secure the release of the prisoners would require authority from the Admiralty, to whom he now signalled what had passed. He withdrew outside territorial waters whilst awaiting a reply. Plainly Captain Vian's report placed the Admiralty in a difficult position. If there were in fact no British prisoners on board, to make an international incident by authorising the use of force would be a serious matter. But to let the ship go if, as was firmly believed, the prisoners were still on board was unthinkable. At this juncture the First Lord himself took charge and, after communicating with the Foreign Secretary, told Captain Vian to offer the Norwegians joint escort of the *Altmark* back to Bergen.[2] If this was refused he was to board her, and, if the prisoners were found, she was to be seized in prize. It may be remarked that this decision could only be taken from London, but the Admiralty did not confine its signals and instructions to the decision of policy: it also sent operational messages to Captain Vian over the Commander-in-Chief's head. Though no untoward results occurred on this occasion, Admiral Forbes later pointed out to the First Sea Lord that as Captain Vian was operating under him the Admiralty's messages might have caused a conflict of orders.

At 10 p.m. Captain Vian re-entered the fiord. The Norwegians refused to co-operate but remained passive. He laid the *Cossack* alongside the *Altmark* and boarded her in old style. Some resistance was offered, but quickly collapsed, and the capture was easily

---

[1] See Map 5 (*facing p. 71*).
[2] W. S. Churchill. *The Second World War*, Vol. I (2nd Edition), pp. 506–507.

effected. It was found that the ship was in fact armed with heavy and light machine guns which, taken together with the presence of 299 British prisoners in her holds, showed that the inspection of the ship at Bergen had, to say the least, been perfunctory. By midnight the merchant seamen were all on board the *Cossack*, which left the fiord and reached Rosyth on the 17th. Admiral Forbes sailed his heavy ships to cover the *Cossack's* return until such time as it was plain that no enemy reaction—beyond the transmission of vitriolic broadcasts—was to be expected.

Though the rescue of the merchant seamen from the *Altmark* was no more than a successful minor operation and was soon to be submerged by a flood of major catastrophes, there is no doubt that, of all the events which took place during the first eight months of the war, it was the River Plate battle and the *Cossack's* rescue which caught the imagination of the British people the most strongly. Both showed that, once again, the Germans could not challenge us on the seas with impunity, and the cry of the *Cossack's* boarding party to the prisoners confined in the ship's holds, 'The Navy is here', rang throughout the length and breadth of the nation.

It was on the day following the return of the *Cossack* with the released prisoners—the 18th of February—that Admiral Forbes received a report from Bomber Command aircraft that major enemy warships appeared to be held in the ice off the entrances to their North Sea bases. As this indicated the possibility of a foray being made against our shipping—and the Norwegian convoys were particularly exposed to such attack—the submarines on patrol were redisposed, an outward-bound Norwegian convoy was sent into Scapa Flow and the main units of the Home Fleet sailed from the Clyde. The Commander-in-Chief's expectations were perfectly correct for, on the day when the bomber aircraft made their report, Admiral Marschall had sailed with the *Gneisenau*, *Scharnhorst*, *Hipper* and two destroyers with the object of attacking our shipping between the Shetlands and Norway.

Admiral Marschall's purpose was, however, frustrated, partly because Admiral Forbes had guessed his intentions and partly because the exceptional cold immobilised his reconnaissance seaplanes. He found the seas empty of traffic. Meanwhile when Admiral Forbes had, on the 20th, reached a position from which he could cover the Norwegian convoy—and the time taken to reach that position from the Clyde is to be noted—it was allowed to proceed on its way. The enemy squadron, whose intended blow thus fell on air, returned to Wilhelmshaven on the 20th and encountered difficulties in reaching the shelter of its base through the ice which had formed in the mouths of the Rivers Jade, Weser and Elbe. Progress was only possible with the help of ice-breakers, and the possibility of exploiting such an opportunity by heavy attacks from the air was not lost on the Admiralty and Air Ministry. Bomber Command had actually organised several attempts to do so after the first sighting report had been received on the 18th of February, but all except one were frustrated by the ice and snow on the airfields and by the frequent fogs; the one operation actually carried out accomplished nothing.

The failure to take advantage of this opportunity and the lack of success achieved by previous bomber attacks on naval targets underlined the lessons learnt during the first six months of the war about the conduct of such operations and the need for careful training. In the first place the restrictive rules regarding targets which might be attacked from the air had placed an unfair burden on the bomber aircrews and had greatly handicapped their efforts. These rules culminated in disciplinary action being taken against an officer who had, on his own initiative, attacked an enemy warship on Christmas Eve 1939. This incident led to revision of the rules on the 30th of December, and the new rules included permission to attack enemy warships at sight. Not until the following 11th of February was permission given to attack the enemy's anti-aircraft (or 'flak') ships from which our air patrols and striking forces had often suffered.

But the end of the restrictive rules did not of itself solve the difficulties of Bomber Command during these early months. Aircrews could not be trained in a few weeks to locate, keep touch with, identify and attack such fleeting targets as warships, which usually only left harbour when weather conditions handicapped all air operations. Moreover, the organisation for the control of Bomber Command aircraft militated against rapid and decisive planning and execution. Another lesson learnt was that the heavy bombers of these early days could not attack naval targets by day without suffering heavy losses. Up to the start of the land campaigns of 1940 Bomber Command carried out 861 sorties in which sixty-one tons of bombs were dropped on naval targets; but the results accomplished were insignificant and the losses of heavy bombers in daylight attacks had amounted to the substantial aggregate of $6\frac{1}{2}$ per cent. Though the abandonment of such attacks was not at once accepted and they were in fact repeated on several later occasions, these only served to confirm the lessons of the first six months.

However, the abandonment of daylight heavy-bomber attacks on enemy warships did not mean that Bomber Command ceased to contribute to the maritime war. The patrols established over the bases from which the enemy's minelaying seaplanes worked helped to curtail his activities of that nature and, on the 19th of March, the Command carried out the heaviest raid made by either side up to that date. The enemy seaplane base on the island of Sylt was the target, and the raid was in direct retaliation for the enemy's attack on Scapa Flow on the 16th of that month. Fifty heavy bombers were despatched and satisfactory results claimed, but photographic reconnaissance did not confirm them and we now know that, in fact, practically no damage was done. But the description of these air operations has taken us ahead of the current activities of the Home Fleet to which we must now return.

The serious handicap which the lack of a properly defended base imposed on all Admiral Forbes' plans has already been commented on, but these days were now nearly ended and the beginning of March saw the preliminary moves for the return of the fleet to its chosen base.[1] The defences against air attack were first tested by the arrival of the two dummy battleships which were last encountered on their way from Belfast to the Firth of Forth.[2] They were soon followed by the *Hood* and *Valiant* which arrived at Scapa on the 7th. Two days later Admiral Forbes in the *Rodney*, accompanied by the *Repulse* and *Renown*, entered the Flow; that same afternoon the First Lord, who had gone ahead from the *Rodney* by destroyer, presided at a meeting in the flagship at which the state of the defences of the base was reviewed. Though the approved scale had not been fully reached, much had been accomplished during the period of the Home Fleet's wanderings. Thirty-nine heavy A.A. guns were now in position, compared with eight five months earlier, and sixteen more would be ready very shortly. Three squadrons of Hurricanes were stationed at Wick, but the laying of nets and complete closing of the unused entrances was not yet finished.

The air defences were soon tested by a raid by fifteen German bombers on the 16th of March which caused the first civilian casualties in the British Isles and led to the retaliatory Bomber Command raid on Sylt three days later. The cruiser *Norfolk* was damaged, and so sensitive was the Admiralty to the air threat that Admiral Forbes was told to take the fleet to sea during the next moonlight period between the 19th and 26th of March. This same week saw the increased activity by enemy submarines at the northern end of the east coast mine barrier and, as told earlier, nine ships were sunk there while the fleet was far away to the north. A moonlight period offered as favourable opportunities to submarines working by night on the surface as to enemy aircraft sent to attack the fleet base.

While the heavy ships of the Home Fleet were at sea they covered two sweeps made on successive nights by the 2nd Cruiser Squadron and eight destroyers into the Skagerrak. It was while the destroyer *Fortune* was acting as part of the screen of the battle cruisers that she sank U.44 on the 20th of March, as was mentioned in the last

---

[1] See pp. 80–81.
[2] See p. 84.

chapter.[1] On the last day of March the cruiser *Birmingham* and two destroyers were sent from Scapa to capture enemy fishing vessels off the Norwegian coast and to cover part of the forces which had, after prolonged discussions in high places and many postponements, been ordered to lay mines in Norwegian territorial waters. This operation was called 'Wilfred', and since its execution coincided almost exactly with the enemy's invasion of Norway it will be appropriate to deal now with the background of the campaign in which the whole Home Fleet, and ships from the other Home Commands as well, were to be deeply involved during the following months.

The key to the story of the Norwegian campaign lies in the importance of the traffic in Swedish iron ore to Germany. Her total imports were estimated to have been twenty-two million tons in 1938, and over nine millions had already been cut off by our blockade. Another nine million tons came from Sweden. In the summer it was shipped chiefly from the port of Luleå in the Gulf of Bothnia, but in the winter, when this port was closed by ice, a proportion had to be railed to the Norwegian coast and shipped from Narvik. But almost the whole of the journey from Narvik to the Skagerrak could be made by the route through Norwegian territorial waters called the Indreled, or Inner Leads, which Mr Churchill has aptly described as 'the covered way'.[2] This made it impossible for us to apply our contraband control to this traffic. Nor were the iron ore ships the only ones to use this route. Blockade runners from the outer oceans normally entered the Leads in the far north and made for home along this thousand-mile protected channel. It was as natural that the Admiralty should seek a means to stop this traffic as it was for the enemy to be particularly sensitive towards any such measures being taken. Indeed the First Lord of the Admiralty was repeatedly representing to the War Cabinet that a situation of intolerable advantage to the enemy should be ended. His first attempt was made as early as the 19th of September 1939 and he recurred to the subject at frequent intervals during the succeeding months. His proposal was quite simple—that the Leads should be mined to force enemy traffic outside neutral waters. In January 1940 the reputed sinking by the enemy of three ships inside Norwegian waters provided a reasonable pretext for doing so. On the 6th of that month the Foreign Secretary actually told the Norwegian Minister in London that we intended to stop the iron ore traffic in this manner; but the reaction in Oslo and Stockholm was so unfavourable that the matter was shelved again. Throughout this period of inaction the Foreign Office remained in steady opposition to the First Lord's proposals. However, by the end of March the First Lord's persistence bore fruit in a decision to carry

---
[1] See p. 132.
[2] W. S. Churchill. *The Second World War*, Vol. I (2nd Edition), p. 478.

OPERATION 'WILFRED' AND 'PLAN R4'

out, on the 5th of April, the precise operation which the Admiralty had so long desired and for which so many good pretexts, including latterly the *Altmark* incident, had been provided. Thus was born Operation 'Wilfred'.

The minelaying involved action in three places by three separate forces. 'Force WB' of two destroyers was to simulate the laying of mines off Bud (62° 54' North 6° 55' East); 'Force WS' consisting of the *Teviot Bank* and four destroyers was to lay mines off Stadtlandet (62° North 5° East) and 'Force WV' composed of four minelaying destroyers with four destroyers as escort was to lay mines off Hovden in Vestfiord (67° 24' North 14° 36' East).[1] When a report reached Admiral Forbes on the 5th of April that all four Norwegian coast defence ships were believed to be at Narvik, he sent Vice-Admiral W. J. Whitworth, commanding the Battle Cruiser Squadron, with the *Renown* (Captain C. E. B. Simeon) and her screening destroyers to protect our own minelayers from interference by them. But a strong enemy reaction to these measures was to be expected and a plan, called 'R4', had been prepared to deal with any German attempt to seize Norwegian ports in retaliation. Stavanger, Bergen, Trondheim and Narvik were all to be occupied as soon as any such intention became clear. Troops for the first two places were embarked in the cruisers *Devonshire, Berwick, York* and *Glasgow* at Rosyth on the 7th of April. The transports to carry the troops to Trondheim and Narvik were assembled in the Clyde with the cruiser *Aurora*, in which Admiral Sir E. R. G. R. Evans had hoisted his flag, and six destroyers as escort. None of these forces was, however, to sail until we had received clear evidence that the enemy intended to violate Norwegian territory. The initiative was thus left with the enemy but, in order to obtain early information of any movement by his major warships, an increased number of submarines, sixteen in all, was sent to patrol all his probable approach routes. In view of the preparations thus made to deal with a strong enemy reaction to the minelaying operation it may seem surprising that the Admiralty did not order the Home Fleet to sea to take up a central position in the North Sea from which the minelayers could be covered.

The date for Operation 'Wilfred' was postponed by the Cabinet from the 5th to the 8th of April, and on the former date the *Teviot Bank* of 'Force WS' sailed from Scapa as did Admiral Whitworth in the *Renown*, screened by the destroyers *Greyhound, Glowworm, Hyperion* and *Hero*.

Next morning Admiral Whitworth was joined by the four minelayers of the 20th Destroyer Flotilla (Captain J. G. Bickford) and by the destroyers *Hardy, Hotspur, Havock* and *Hunter* of the 2nd Flotilla (Captain B. A. W. Warburton-Lee).

---
[1] See Maps 18 and 19 (*pp. 181–182*).

158 FIRST CONTACTS. THE 'GLOWWORM' SUNK

The *Glowworm* (Lieutenant-Commander G. B. Roope) of the *Renown's* screen soon parted company to search for a man fallen overboard and, in the thick and heavy weather prevailing, failed to rejoin her force. Two days later she met the *Hipper* and her escort and was overwhelmed but, in a truly heroic end, rammed and seriously damaged her largest adversary. Later, when the story of her last fight became known, her Captain was awarded a posthumous Victoria Cross.

Admiral Whitworth reached the approaches to Vestfiord on the evening of the 7th; the minelayers were detached and completed their lay in the early hours of the following morning.

Before the minelayers and Admiral Whitworth's force had sailed intelligence had begun to reach the Admiralty that some major enemy movement might be in train. As early as the 4th of April warning of an impending attack on Norway had come from Copenhagen; next day it was reported that the Great and Little Belts were clear of ice, which meant that shipping from the German Baltic ports could now move north through those passages. On the 6th indications of unusual enemy activity and signs of a threat to Norway increased. By that evening it was known that large-scale shipping movements were taking place in the Baltic and the Heligoland Bight. A special air search was sent to watch the latter. Admiral Forbes was informed of all this, but no action was taken to anticipate the enemy by sending the fleet to sea, nor was the squadron covering the minelayers, which must be imperilled if the enemy moved north in any strength, reinforced.

On Sunday the 7th of April the First Sea Lord was away from the Admiralty but his deputy (Rear-Admiral T. S. V. Phillips) and the First Lord were both on hand. But Admiral Pound's absence probably made no difference to the slowness with which the Admiralty reacted; that his views corresponded with those of the other senior members of the Board is borne out by his actions on returning to Whitehall that evening.

The truth appears to be that the attention of the Admiralty was concentrated exclusively on the possibility of a breakout by the German battle cruisers through one of the northern exits to the Atlantic. Any suggestion to dispose the fleet in the central North Sea, as would be necessary to dispute control of the routes from Germany to Norway, was regarded as a diversion from the primary object of protecting our Atlantic shipping. Such views were, as is natural, reflected in the Commander-in-Chief's actions.

At Scapa, on Sunday the 7th of April, Admiral Forbes had with him the *Rodney* (flagship), *Valiant*, *Repulse*, *Sheffield*, *Penelope* and ten destroyers. The French cruiser *Emile Bertin* and two French destroyers arrived as reinforcements that evening. At Rosyth were the *Galatea*

Map 14

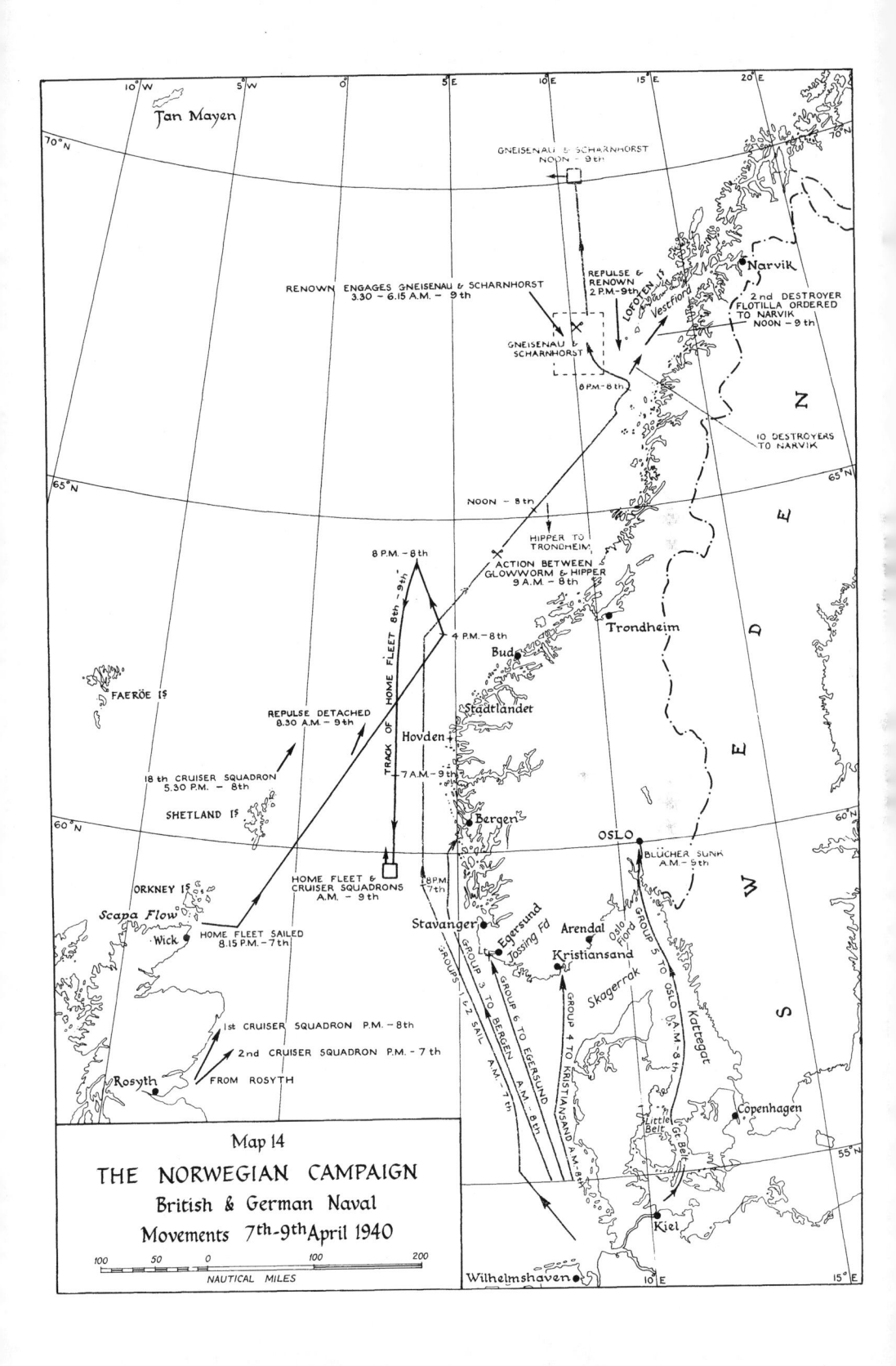

THE NORWEGIAN CAMPAIGN
British & German Naval Movements 7th-9th April 1940

(Vice-Admiral Sir G. F. Edward-Collins, commanding the 2nd Cruiser Squadron), *Arethusa* and four destroyers. Four more destroyers were at sea near Rosyth escorting convoy H.N. 24; the *Renown* and fourteen destroyers were at sea covering or escorting the minelayers, and the *Birmingham* had orders to join this force. Lastly the *Manchester* (Vice-Admiral G. Layton, commanding the 18th Cruiser Squadron), *Southampton* and five destroyers were at sea covering convoy O.N. 25.

At 11.20 that morning a report signalled two and a half hours earlier by the Coastal Command Hudson sent out to watch the activity in the Heligoland Bight reached Admiral Forbes. It stated that a cruiser and six destroyers had been sighted off Horn Reef steering north. Soon afterwards the Commander-in-Chief learnt that thirty-five heavy bombers had left to attack them. Next a report came in that three enemy destroyers had been sighted at 1.15 p.m. in 56° 06′ North 6° 08′ East steering south. They might, therefore, have been returning to base from some minor operation. This was followed twenty minutes later by an Admiralty message, which gave substantially correct intelligence regarding German intentions but ended with the unfortunate conclusion that 'all these reports are of doubtful value and may well be only a further move in the war of nerves'.

Meanwhile, at 1.25 p.m., part of the Bomber Command striking force found and attacked the enemy squadron, which they later reported as composed, possibly, of one battle cruiser, two cruisers and ten destroyers sighted off the entrance to the Skagerrak and steering north-west. No hits were obtained. Though the leader of the bomber striking force stated that he sent a wireless report soon after the attack, his message was unfortunately not received by any station. It thus happened that four hours elapsed before this important and reliable intelligence regarding the enemy's main forces reached Admiral Forbes. Not until 5.27 p.m. was the fleet ordered to raise steam and the outward-bound Norwegian convoy O.N. 25 recalled.

By 8.15 that evening the whole fleet had cleared harbour and set a north-easterly course at high speed.[1] This course would enable the fleet to intercept ships attempting to break out into the Atlantic but left the central North Sea uncovered. The Admiralty appears, at about this time, to have realised that the reports of an invasion of Norway might after all be correct. The wisdom of allowing the fleet to steer so far north was questioned, but it was decided not to interfere with Admiral Forbes' movement.

There was thus a complete failure to realise the significance of the available intelligence—let alone to translate it into vigorous and

---

[1] See Map 14.

early counter-action. Furthermore there had been a long delay before the first operational intelligence regarding the main enemy units had reached the Commander-in-Chief. Even if it be considered that the indications of enemy intentions received during the preceding days did not render it desirable to send the fleet to sea, yet, had it been at immediate notice for steam and had the bomber striking force's report reached the Commander-in-Chief with no delay, it would still have been possible for him to reach a favourable intercepting position in good time. As it was, the fleet was not brought to one hour's notice for steam until 2.20 p.m., when the Admiralty's warning of possible enemy intentions reached the Commander-in-Chief.

Early next morning, the 8th of April, Admiral Forbes intercepted the *Glowworm's* enemy reports, the last of which, timed 8.55 a.m. and received nine minutes later, faded out and indicated that she had probably been sunk.

Admiral Forbes ordered the *Repulse, Penelope* and four destroyers to go to the *Glowworm's* assistance while Admiral Whitworth, in the *Renown*, set course to cut off the enemy should he be bound for Vestfiord. The Admiralty now ordered all destroyers of 'Force WV' (the Vestfiord minelayers and escort) to join the *Renown*, an intervention which, as Admiral Forbes pointed out later, was to have unhappy results as it left Vestfiord totally unguarded at a critical time. Moreover, in the prevailing weather conditions, of which the Admiralty could not be fully aware, the *Renown* and destroyers might well have failed to meet each other.

The next message signalled by the Admiralty told Admiral Forbes that the intelligence sent him the previous day, originally classed as of doubtful value, might after all be true and that German forces might be on their way to Narvik. Admiral Forbes has stated that by this time he was convinced in his own mind that a German attack on Norway had started. None the less he continued to steam north-east. Numerous reports from our submarines in the Kattegat and other sources now told him that strong enemy forces were proceeding northwards.

At noon on the 8th Admiral Forbes arranged for a flying-boat to search ahead of him for the enemy, and at 2.30 p.m. she reported a battle cruiser, two cruisers and two destroyers in 64° 12′ North 06° 25′ East steering west. This was actually the enemy's Trondheim group, consisting of the *Hipper* and four destroyers, which was awaiting the time appointed for it to enter Trondheim. Its westerly course had no significance but was, of course, confusing to Admiral Forbes. To intercept these ships, which might well be the enemy's main force, the Commander-in-Chief altered course from north-east firstly to north and then, at 4.15 p.m., to north-west.

TROOPS FOR 'PLAN R4' DISEMBARKED

By this time a full gale was blowing from the N.N.W. and speed had to be eased for the sake of the destroyers. That evening Admiral Forbes judged that there was probably one battle cruiser to the north of him, which might be bound for Narvik, while other strong enemy forces were in the Kattegat or Skagerrak. He therefore sent the *Repulse, Penelope* and some destroyers to the north to reinforce Admiral Whitworth and turned south himself with the *Rodney, Valiant, Sheffield* and his screening destroyers.[1]

From the earliest hours of the 9th of April many reports came in of enemy ships proceeding west or north-west and of attacks by our submarines in the Skagerrak. Shortly before 5 a.m. the Admiralty signalled that enemy warships were said to be entering Oslo Fiord and approaching Bergen, while one was already reported to be at Stavanger and two more were approaching Trondheim. Under Plan R4 we had intended to occupy all these ports if clear evidence of the enemy's intention to violate Norwegian neutrality was received. But the four cruisers at Rosyth which actually had the troops for Stavanger and Bergen on board had been ordered by the Admiralty, on the forenoon of the 8th, to disembark them at once and to proceed to sea. Vice-Admiral J. H. D. Cunningham had accordingly sailed on the afternoon of the 8th. It may be considered strange that, at a time when events were clearly moving very rapidly in Norway, the troops which had already been embarked in readiness to proceed there should have been disembarked forthwith and without consultation with the Commander-in-Chief concerned. Mr Churchill states, with regard to this matter, that 'the 1st Cruiser Squadron which had been embarking troops at Rosyth for the possible occupation of Norwegian ports . . . was ordered to march her soldiers ashore, even without their equipment, and join the fleet at sea at the earliest moment. . . . All these decisive steps were concerted with the Commander-in-Chief. In short everything available was ordered out on the assumption—which we had by no means accepted—that a major emergency had come.'[2] But Admiral Forbes went to sea, as has been seen, on the evening of the 7th and kept wireless silence until the afternoon of the following day, by which time the troops had been disembarked and the 1st Cruiser Squadron was at sea. The first intimation he received regarding these events was contained in two Admiralty messages sent during the early afternoon of the 8th telling him that the cruisers had been ordered to disembark their troops and would leave Rosyth at 2 p.m. It is now known that the order to send the troops ashore and the 1st Cruiser Squadron to sea was given by the First Sea Lord after his return to the Admiralty late on the evening of the 7th. It was tele-

---
[1] See Map 14 (*facing p. 159*).
[2] W. S. Churchill. *The Second World War*, Vol. I (2nd Edition), p. 533.

phoned to Admiral Cunningham through the Commander-in-Chief Rosyth early next morning.

As the troops earmarked for Narvik and Trondheim, which had been embarked in transports in the Clyde, had not yet sailed, their escort, the cruiser *Aurora* and six destroyers, was ordered to Scapa to join the Home Fleet. The second half of Plan R4 was thus also jettisoned, and no military forces whatever were then available for immediate transport to the key positions on the Norwegian coast at the time when the enemy's forces were by no means established in those ports. It is arguable whether the rapid landing of four battalions at Stavanger and Bergen would have changed the outcome of the Norwegian campaign. It is, indeed, possible that, had we landed these troops, the full weight of the enemy's air power would at once have been brought to bear on the defenceless ports of disembarkation, thus rendering impossible their supply and reinforcement. But these very difficulties had to be faced later, and under even graver handicaps, and the earlier attempt, if made, might at least have given us the vital airfield at Stavanger, besides better port facilities than those which had to be made to serve the later expeditions. At the best it would, perhaps, have rallied Norwegian resistance and delayed the enemy's advance northwards. At the worst it could only have been as devoid of results as the later landings. In the light of subsequent events it does, therefore, seem that, if the precipitate abandonment of Plan R4 was in fact necessary, a new plan for the rapid landing of troops in Norway should at once have been substituted for it.

But it is time to leave Admiral Forbes searching for the enemy forces whose positions and intentions were far from reliably known to him and to turn to the enemy's plans and their execution.

The problem of Norway had been discussed between Hitler and his advisers nearly as often as it was discussed by the British War Cabinet during the first six months of the war. The enemy's view was that the neutrality of the Scandinavian countries was to his advantage, and should be respected so long as we allowed him to benefit from it; any attempt, however, on our part to limit the advantages which he derived from it would demand the most vigorous and rapid counter-measures. Since the enemy realised that we were unlikely to remain passive indefinitely, he proceeded to prepare plans to invade Denmark and Norway.

Early in October 1939 Admiral Raeder had drawn Hitler's attention to the advantages of possessing bases in Norway; and it was at his instance that definite plans to invade that country were first put forward some months later. It was also Raeder who, in December 1939, produced the Norwegian traitor Quisling in Berlin to reinforce his arguments. In mid-December Hitler ordered that the necessary planning should be carried out. The invasion of the Low Countries

THE GERMAN PLAN

and France was also being planned at the time, and the original intention was to invade Norway about a month before the offensive in the west was launched. The 20th of March 1940 was the date first chosen for the Norwegian operation, but it was soon postponed until early April. On the 1st of March Hitler signed a directive ordering the occupation of Denmark and Norway; at the conference held on the 26th he approved that it should be carried out on about the 7th of April, and on the 2nd he gave orders that the attack should start on the 9th.

The enemy's plan depended on the achievement of surprise, on the rapidity with which the opening moves, involving the seizure of the same key ports on which British eyes were focused, could be completed, and on the use of German shore-based aircraft to offset British naval supremacy. On the 9th of March Admiral Raeder warned Hitler that the operation was 'contrary to all principles in the theory of naval warfare' but stated his belief that 'provided surprise is complete our troops can and will be successfully transported to Norway'. Having thus soberly assessed the full risks involved he decided to accept them and to hazard the whole available German naval strength on the operation. Only the *Admiral Scheer*, the *Prinz Eugen*, and the light cruisers *Leipzig* and *Nürnberg*, all of which were refitting or repairing action damage, could not take part.

The plans involved the use of six army divisions, some 800 operational aircraft and about 200 transport planes to supplement the first sea-borne landings. The ports of Oslo, Kristiansand (South), Bergen, Trondheim and Narvik were to be occupied simultaneously. On the 6th of March Admiral Raeder issued his orders to the German Navy. These will now be studied in some detail.

The naval forces for Norway were divided into six groups of which the first and second were to operate in the north and the remaining four in the south. Group 1 consisted of the battle cruisers *Gneisenau* and *Scharnhorst* and ten destroyers under Vice-Admiral Lütjens. Its function was to cover the whole operation and, after crossing a line between the Shetlands and Bergen, to join with Group 2 to create a diversion by drawing off the main British strength from the Norwegian coast. It was then to patrol in the Arctic and finally cover the return of the other naval units to Germany, which Admiral Raeder had always assessed to be the most hazardous part of the whole operation. The destroyers of Group 1 were to carry 2,000 troops for the occupation of Narvik.

To Group 2, under the Captain of the *Hipper*, were allocated four destroyers, and the 1,700 troops embarked were to occupy Trondheim. Group 3 consisted of the light cruisers *Köln*, *Königsberg*, the old training cruiser *Bremse*, an E-boat (motor torpedo-boat) flotilla, two torpedo-boats and the depot ship *Karl Peters* and was to land 900 men at Bergen. Group 4, under the Captain of the light cruiser *Karlsruhe* was to land some 1,100 men at Kristiansand (South) and Arendal, for which purpose the depot ship *Tsingtau*, three torpedo-boats and an E-boat flotilla were also allocated to him. Group 5 consisted of the 8-inch cruiser *Blücher*, the pocket-battleship *Lützow* (formerly called *Deutschland*), the light cruiser *Emden*, three torpedo-boats and several smaller vessels. It was to land 2,000 men to occupy Oslo. The final Group, number 6, consisted only of minesweepers but was to occupy the cable station at Egersund in addition to carrying out minesweeping duties.

Twenty-eight U-boats were disposed from Narvik and the Shetlands in the north to the Skagerrak and eastern approaches to the English Channel in the south, but their dispositions soon became known through the capture of a chart on which they were marked. Partly in consequence of this and partly because of the defects from which German torpedoes at this time suffered—a matter on which Dönitz commented bitterly—the U-boats inflicted few losses during the operations now to be discussed. Throughout the month of April they only sank one store transport bound for Norway, five other merchant ships in the North Sea and the British submarine *Thistle*.

For the occupation of Denmark a separate group, which included the old battleship *Schleswig-Holstein*, was to land troops to seize the principal ports in the Great Belt; four groups of small craft were to occupy Copenhagen and other key points on the Danish coast.

To follow up the initial landings at Bergen and ports to the south of it some 3,700 troops with vehicles and stores were to be embarked in fifteen ships; but for Narvik and Trondheim the use of transports was considered too dangerous and six merchantmen were therefore disguised and loaded with the military stores destined for those two ports.

On the 6th of April, when the British Operation 'Wilfred' was in course of preparation, the enemy started embarking his troops, and the first groups—those bound for Narvik and Trondheim—sailed late that evening. By the early hours of the 9th the carefully laid German plan was in full motion. But at noon on the previous day there occurred an incident which caused the German Naval Staff acute anxiety and might have compromised their entire plan. The Polish submarine *Orzel* intercepted and sank the German s.s. *Rio de Janeiro* off Kristiansand (South) and German troops were picked up by a Norwegian destroyer and fishing craft. The rescued soldiers stated that they were on their way to Bergen 'to protect it against the Allies'. The report reached Oslo that evening but was not credited; the defences were not brought to immediate readiness and no precautionary steps, let alone mobilisation, were ordered. The Admiralty also received the report, but there too its significance does not appear to have received special recognition, since it was not even passed to Admiral Forbes until late that night (the 8th). The Admiralty's attention was still directed on the northern exits to the Atlantic and on bringing the enemy battle cruisers to action. Their diversionary movement to the north was to have its designed effect. It will be recalled that, in our first chapter, it was suggested that, once an invasion has started, the primary objective of the defending fleet changes from the enemy's main units to his transports.[1] If, as he has stated, Admiral Forbes had by this time recognised the enemy's real intention, then pursuit of his heavy ships had lost its purpose and in fact would aid the enemy's intention.

Meanwhile, this eleventh-hour warning having been neglected by the British, the enemy's assault proceeded along the lines set out in his plans. At Trondheim and Bergen the landings were practically unopposed, though shore batteries at Bergen damaged the *Bremse* and *Königsberg* and, by immobilising the latter, gave the Navy's aircraft the opportunity to attack and sink her next morning, the 10th. At Kristiansand (South) the shore defences resisted for a time, but that port and Arendal were both occupied by noon. Only at Oslo was there a serious check. The ships of Group 5 entered the fiord at midnight on the 8th–9th and passed the outer defences, but, at 4.20 a.m., at the narrowest part of the fiord, some eighteen miles from Oslo, the shore batteries opened fire on the *Blücher* at point-blank range and crippled her. Torpedoes fired from the land defences sealed her fate and at 6.23 she sank with heavy loss of life among her crew and the embarked troops.

The Captain of the *Lützow* now took command, withdrew the force and landed the troops ten miles down the fiord. Heavy air attacks eliminated Norwegian resistance in the fiord that afternoon and, meanwhile, the capital city had been occupied by airborne troops. But the check in the narrows of the fiord gave time for the escape of the Royal Family and of the Government and for the evacuation of the gold reserve.

At Narvik the landings went exactly according to plan. The ten German destroyers of Group 1 arrived off the entrance to Vestfiord on the evening of the 8th. As the British minefield patrol had ten hours earlier been ordered by the Admiralty to join Admiral Whitworth, the Germans encountered no opposition.[2] At dawn next morning they appeared off Narvik, overwhelmed the Norwegian coast defence ships *Eidsvold* and *Norge* and disembarked their troops.

While the enemy's occupation of Narvik was proceeding, Admiral Whitworth in the *Renown*, with nine destroyers in company, en-

---
[1] See p. 9.
[2] See p. 160.

countered the *Gneisenau* and *Scharnhorst* on their way to take up their patrolling position in the far north, about fifty miles from the entrance to Vestfiord. The first sighting took place at 3.37 a.m. on the 9th and two enemy ships were recognised, though one was misidentified and reported to be of the *Hipper* class.[1] The *Renown* opened fire at 4.5 a.m. in heavy seas and through intermittent snow squalls at a range of some nine miles; her adversaries did not respond until some minutes later. For about ten minutes both enemies then engaged the British battle cruiser, but it was she who scored the first effective hit, which, at 4.17, put the *Gneisenau*'s main armament control system out of action. The enemy now endeavoured to break off the action; but the *Renown* pursued in a rising wind and rough sea, and at 4.34 obtained a second hit, which crippled the *Gneisenau*'s forward turret, and a third hit further aft. She herself received two hits from heavy shell which fortunately did no damage at all.

By 5 a.m. the enemy had disappeared in a rain squall and, though the pursuit was continued and the enemy was briefly resighted, only a few more salvos were fired at them. Admiral Whitworth made every effort to overtake his adversaries. The destroyers could not, in the prevailing weather, keep up with the *Renown* and, early in the action, they were ordered to part company and proceed to patrol the entrance to Vestfiord. The battle cruiser went on alone and, for a time, steamed at twenty-nine knots. But her pursuit was unsuccessful and by 6.30 the enemy had passed out of sight to the north.

In considering this brief action, in which the honours must surely go to the single, slower and more lightly protected British ship, the historian is bound to ask himself why she alone was in a position where an encounter with heavy enemy forces was realised to be possible. The Commander-in-Chief showed his anxiety to protect the minelayers from interference by giving Admiral Whitworth that duty, and a strong enemy reaction to Operation 'Wilfred' had long been anticipated by the Admiralty. Admiral Forbes had available at Scapa on the 7th of April the *Repulse*, *Valiant* and *Rodney*. But the *Repulse* was unmodernised and had not got the *Renown*'s speed, while the two battleships were, of course, much slower still. Moreover he considered it necessary to hold back some heavy units to cover the cruisers with the troops for Plan R4 aboard. Thus the encounter actually took place between two modern German battle cruisers each mounting nine 11-inch guns and one much older, though modernised, British ship mounting six 15-inch guns; it would certainly seem therefore that the enemy lost a great opportunity to destroy his slower and less well protected adversary. And it now appears clear that his loss of the tactical initiative was due to

---

[1] See pp. 82–83.

Admiral Whitworth's immediate engagement and vigorous pursuit under most difficult conditions of sea and weather.

Shortly before 7 p.m. that evening Admiral Whitworth received an Admiralty message ordering him to concentrate on preventing any enemy force from reaching Narvik, and, in very heavy weather, he disposed his forces to patrol the entrance to Vestfiord. He learnt shortly afterwards that reinforcements, including the *Repulse*, had been detached by Admiral Forbes to his assistance.

CHAPTER X

THE NORWEGIAN CAMPAIGN
8th April–15th June, 1940

> As for honour, who know not (that knows anything) that in all records of late times of actions chronicled to the everlasting fame and renown of this Kingdom, still the naval part is the thread that runs through the whole wooft, the burden of the song, the scope of the text?
>
> Hollond. *First Discourse of the Navy.* 1638.

AT the end of the last chapter it was seen how the enemy, by careful planning, by daring acceptance of risks, by ruthlessly exploiting the desire of small neutral countries to keep out of the war and by the possession of the strategic initiative, successfully accomplished the overrunning of Denmark and the occupation of all the key ports on the Norwegian coast.

Once his true intentions were realised in London the issues became simplified, since the first requirement plainly was to prevent the enemy using the sea to build up his strength ashore in Norway. The second, and later, requirement would be to secure to ourselves the use of the same element to carry help to our new ally. These then became the tasks of the Royal Navy and Air Force and, in reading the story of the struggle which rose out of these requirements, the fact that it was maritime control of the approaches to Norway which was in dispute must be borne constantly in mind.

It was told in the last chapter how on the evening of the 8th of April the Commander-in-Chief ordered the *Repulse* and lighter forces to reinforce Admiral Whitworth's single battle cruiser while he himself, with the *Rodney, Valiant, Sheffield* and light forces turned south to meet the other powerful enemies which had been reported to be coming north from the Skagerrak; and how, in the very early hours of the following morning and before the reinforcements had joined him, Admiral Whitworth, with only the *Renown*, had met and engaged the *Gneisenau* and *Scharnhorst*.[1]

From the Commander-in-Chief's point of view the situation was on the evening of the 8th indeed confused, but an Admiralty message timed 6.42 p.m. made him decide to dispose his forces so as to intercept the northern enemy squadron when it tried to return, and

---
[1] See Map 14 (*facing p. 159*).

also to locate the forces which he believed to be still coming up from the south. Admiral J. H. D. Cunningham's cruisers (the 1st Cruiser Squadron) were therefore ordered to sweep north while Admiral Edward-Collins' squadron (the 2nd) was held in readiness to strike at the enemy should he be encountered during the night. Meanwhile reinforcements in the shape of the *Warspite* (Captain V. A. C. Crutchley, V.C.) and *Furious* (Captain T. Troubridge) were coming to Admiral Forbes up the west coast of Scotland from the Clyde. But, because of the pressure from London to get all our forces to sea as quickly as possible, the *Furious* had unhappily sailed without embarking her fighter squadron. She was therefore unable to give the fleet any fighter protection during the next two days, just when it first became really necessary.

During the night of the 8th-9th several messages reached the fleet flagship from the Admiralty. They maintained the objectives which had already been given to Admiral Forbes but did little to dispel the prevailing obscurity about what was actually happening in Norway. Numerous reports of the enemy's invasion were, however, now coming in. Throughout the night Admiral Forbes held on to the south and, early on the 9th, he was joined by Admiral Layton with the *Manchester* and *Southampton* of the 18th Cruiser Squadron and by the seven cruisers and thirteen destroyers under Admirals Cunningham, Edward-Collins and the French Admiral Derrien. At 6.20 a.m. Admiral Forbes asked for intelligence regarding the enemy's strength in Bergen, which he proposed to attack. The Admiralty had a similar thought at about the same time, but wished him also to prepare to attack Trondheim and to continue to watch Narvik as well. Accordingly at 11.30 Admiral Layton was detached to attack Bergen with four cruisers (the *Manchester, Southampton, Glasgow* and *Sheffield*) and seven destroyers. It was believed that at least one cruiser of the *Köln* class was in harbour there, and that the shore defences might now be in enemy hands. But the southward movement of the fleet on the 9th had taken this force some eighty miles away from its objective, and the heavy seas still running made the retracing of this distance slow. Early in the afternoon aircraft reported two enemy cruisers in harbour, but just afterwards came Admiralty orders cancelling the attack. We now know that, had the attack then been carried out, the *Köln, Königsberg, Bremse* and other units of the enemy's Group 3 would have been caught in harbour, and that the enemy had not yet got the shore batteries back into service. It seems therefore that the attack might well have achieved a valuable success against the warships and transports, though the subsequent extrication of our forces under air attack might well have been difficult. Admiral Forbes was, however, prepared to accept that risk in order to strike a blow at the enemy at his most vulnerable moment

Map 15

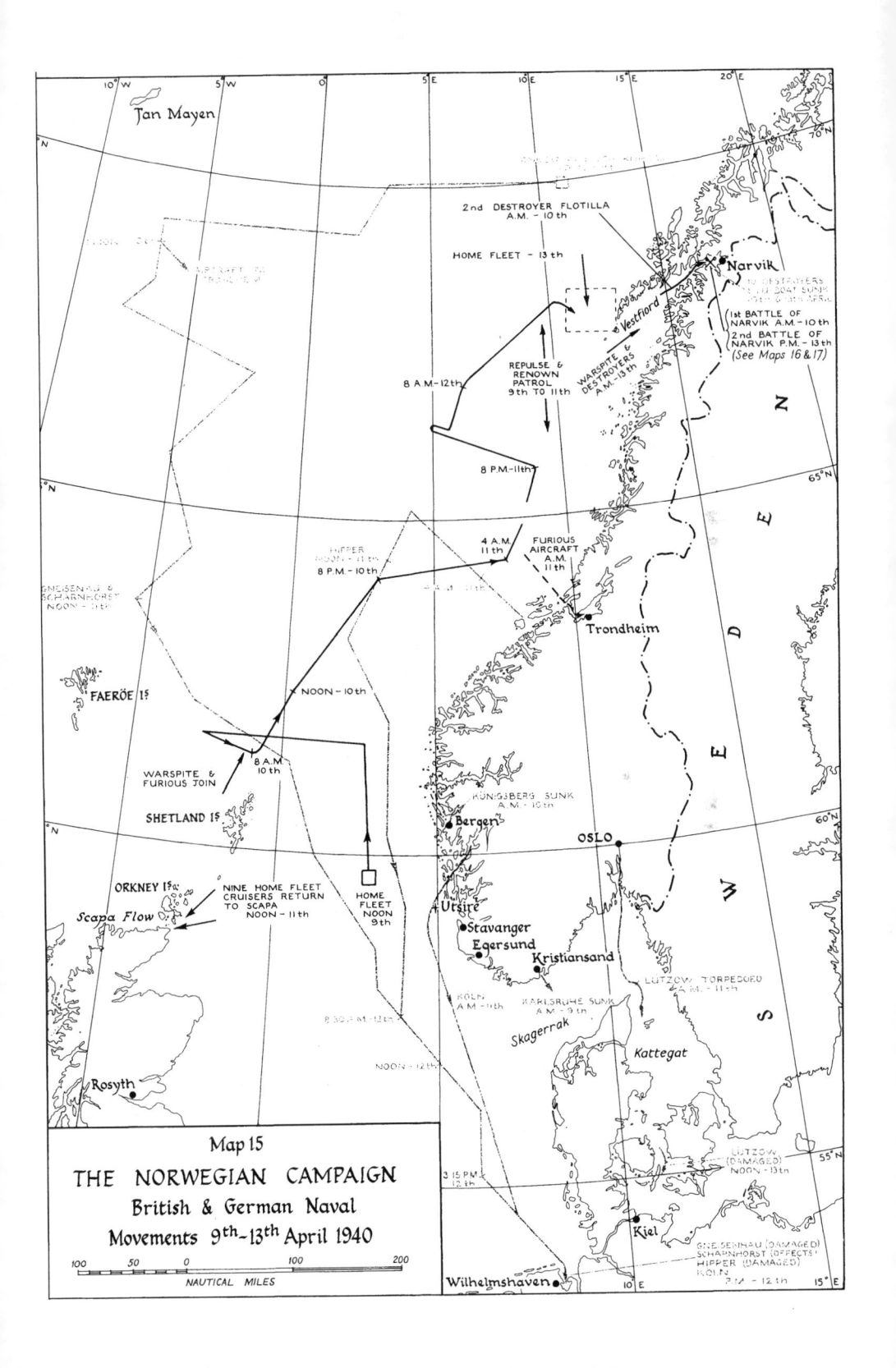

THE NORWEGIAN CAMPAIGN
British & German Naval
Movements 9th–13th April 1940

and at one of the two really important points of disembarkation in southern Norway which were accessible to attack from the sea. Various reasons appear to have prompted the Admiralty's action. It was believed, incorrectly, that the Norwegian shore defences were in enemy hands, and there appears to have been a feeling that the Commander-in-Chief intended to employ too few and too small ships. But whatever were the decisive causes the Admiralty's intervention now certainly seems to have been ill-judged. Another opportunity to strike rapidly at the enemy before he had consolidated his position, and one which, if taken, might well have eased the weight of his air power, was also lost. Coastal Command aircraft reported that Stavanger airfield, which had been practically empty on the 9th, had a heavy concentration of some forty aircraft on it next day. The Air Officer Commanding-in-Chief prepared to strike at this concentration at once and with his full strength, but the Air Ministry cancelled his proposal in deference to the policy still in force regarding the bombing of shore targets.[1]

At noon on the 9th of April Admiral Forbes reached his southernmost position (59° 44′ North, 2° 57′ East) and turned north again.[2] The weather had now cleared and enemy aircraft had been shadowing for some time. In the afternoon the expected bombing attacks started. Though the *Rodney* was hit neither she nor any other major unit received serious damage; but the destroyer *Gurkha* was sunk. The implications of such sustained attacks when no fighter protection was available were, however, clear. Anti-aircraft gunfire could not alone protect the fleet, some of whose ships expended forty per cent. of their ammunition. To operate under such conditions would plainly involve very serious hazards.

Meanwhile, as the *Furious* was on her way to join the fleet, the possibility of reviving the cancelled attack on Bergen in a different form by using her torpedo-bombers had occurred to Admiral Forbes. The Admiralty assented and proposed, in addition, an attack by R.A.F. bombers the same evening and one by naval aircraft from the Orkneys the following morning (the 10th). But the afternoon's bombing had convinced the Commander-in-Chief that the aircraft carrier could not be employed in the latitudes where the enemy's air power had so recently made itself felt, and he therefore proposed to use her aircraft against Trondheim and to leave Bergen to the Royal Air Force. Admiral Forbes' message of 10.30 p.m. that night makes clear the extent to which the enemy's air power was already conditioning maritime control. He proposed to leave the southern area mostly to submarines, owing to German air superiority; and submarines alone, or nearly alone, were unlikely effectively to dis-

---
[1] See pp. 144–145.
[2] See Maps 14 (*facing p. 159*) and 15.

pute, let alone to deny, the use of short sea routes such as those across the Skagerrak and Kattegat. It was, however, at this juncture that the Cabinet relaxed the restrictions so far placed on attacks by our submarines and aircraft on enemy merchant ships. Such attacks were now permitted in an area east of the German declared minefield, and also within ten miles of the south coast of Norway.

But to return to Bergen. At 6 p.m. on the 9th, while all important ships of the enemy's Group 3 were still in harbour there, twelve Wellingtons and twelve Hampdens of the Royal Air Force attacked them, but with little result. The *Köln* and two torpedo-boats put to sea at 8 p.m. that night for the return journey, but the activity of the Home Fleet caused the commander of the German group to postpone the break-back. The cruiser therefore lay low for the night in a fiord south of Bergen. She weighed again the following afternoon, the 10th, and arrived home safely. The *Königsberg* had been damaged by the Norwegian shore batteries and was unfit for sea. She fell a prey to dive-bombing attacks by fifteen naval Skuas of Nos. 800 and 803 Squadrons, led by Captain R. T. Partridge, R.M., and Lieutenant W. P. Lucy, R.N., operating from the Orkneys near to the limit of their endurance. They attacked early on the morning of the 10th, obtained three hits and sank the ship. It was the first occasion on which a major warship was sunk by air attack.

On the night of the 9th–10th of April the cruisers of Admirals Layton and Edward-Collins swept the coast of Norway as far south as Utsire to prevent reinforcements reaching Stavanger and Bergen. Though they met no enemy ships, the submarine *Truant* (Lieutenant-Commander C. H. Hutchinson) caught the cruiser *Karlsruhe* shortly after she had left Kristiansand (South) for home and damaged her so severely that she had to be sunk by her own escort. The Commander-in-Chief meanwhile sent back some of his cruisers and destroyers to fuel and, early in the morning of the 10th, received his first news of the attack by the 2nd Destroyer Flotilla on enemy ships at Narvik. Shortly afterwards the *Warspite* and *Furious* joined his flag and thus brought his strength up to three battleships (the *Rodney*, *Valiant* and *Warspite*), one aircraft carrier, three heavy cruisers (the *Devonshire*, *Berwick* and *York*) and eighteen destroyers. With this force Admiral Forbes steered north to a position from which he could launch the torpedo-bombers from the *Furious* against Trondheim, and also cover the convoy H.N. 25 which had so luckily escaped from Bergen.[1]

It is now time to take leave temporarily of the main body of the Home Fleet and to return to the far north to see how Admiral Whitworth's forces had fared since we left them patrolling off Vestfiord on the 9th of April in accordance with the objectives given by the Admiralty that morning. Shortly after these orders had been

---
[1] See p. 148.

received Admiral Forbes ordered Captain Warburton-Lee of the 2nd Destroyer Flotilla to 'send some destroyers up to Narvik to make certain that no enemy troops land'.

At 11.38 a.m. the Admiralty told Admiral Whitworth that enemy forces had arrived at Narvik and that he must prevent reinforcements reaching them; but he did not receive this message till next day. However, his object had already been stated to be to watch Narvik and to prevent the enemy landing there, so this delay probably had no effect on his dispositions, particularly as he knew that his Commander-in-Chief had already detached Captain Warburton-Lee to Narvik. At noon the Admiralty intervened directly in the conduct of these operations by telling Captain Warburton-Lee that there were indications that the enemy had actually landed at Narvik and ordering him to sink or capture their transports. He was also given discretion to follow this up by landing a party to recapture the place. This intervention, which appeared to Admiral Whitworth to indicate the strength with which the Admiralty desired the attack to be carried out, was to produce difficulties a short while later when, as must often happen in war, new intelligence revealed the enemy's strength more precisely.

Captain Warburton-Lee, however, had received clear orders from his Commander-in-Chief and decided to take the four available destroyers of his own flotilla up the fiord and to leave Captain Bickford, of the 20th Destroyer Flotilla, with a mixed force to patrol the minefield. He therefore proceeded in the *Hardy* with the *Hotspur* (Commander H. F. H. Layman), *Havock* (Lieutenant-Commander R. E. Courage) and *Hunter* (Lieutenant-Commander L. de Villiers) in company, but, happily, was joined by the *Hostile* (Commander J. P. Wright) after he had started. At 4 p.m. he stopped off the pilot station at Tranöy to try to glean more precise intelligence of the enemy's strength, and there he learnt that the opposition would be far stronger than had been expected.[1] The Norwegians thought he would need 'twice as many ships' to deal with the six large destroyers they had seen go up to Narvik, and even that was to prove a substantial underestimate of the enemy's true strength of ten large destroyers which had been detached from his Group 1 to capture the place. Captain Warburton-Lee sent this information to Admirals Forbes and Whitworth at 5.51 p.m. and added 'intend attacking at dawn high water'.[2]

It was natural that this news should cause Admiral Whitworth to

---

[1] See Map 18 (*p. 181*).

[2] It is a well-known naval convention that when a junior officer has decided on a certain course of action and wishes to inform his senior officer of his decision, but is not specifically seeking the approval of the latter, then the junior officer will preface his message with the word 'Intend'. A message so worded not only does not seek the senior officer's approval but makes clear that no reply is expected *unless the senior officer disapproves*.

consider reinforcing the 2nd Flotilla. The *Repulse* had joined him at 2 p.m. that afternoon, and he had the cruiser *Penelope* and four large destroyers also on patrol. But he could only do so by depriving his heavy ships of their screen and by delaying Captain Warburton-Lee's attack, and so possibly losing the advantage of surprise. And, moreover, the Admiralty, though not at the time possessed of this more accurate intelligence, had ordered the operation to be carried out by the 2nd Flotilla. Furthermore, delay and revision of the plan might, he considered, cause confusion. He therefore decided to leave matters alone. In the wisdom of later events it certainly appears that reinforcement would have been preferable, even at the cost of slight delay, and that, had Admiral Whitworth sent it, the second battle of Narvik would perhaps have been unnecessary and the place itself might have been more promptly recaptured. How much the Admiralty's intervention contributed to this it is difficult to say. At any rate it was continued in such a form as virtually to take the matter out of Admiral Whitworth's hands, since the Admiralty continued to communicate direct to Captain Warburton-Lee as he steamed towards his objective. At 8.59 that night they approved the gallant intention already reported by him, and finally, apparently realising the inequality of the odds, in the early hours of the 10th the First Sea Lord signalled: 'You alone can judge whether, in these circumstances, attack should be made. We shall support whatever decision you take'.

Captain Warburton-Lee, however, had already taken his decision, and after delaying his progress so as to arrive off Narvik at dawn he proceeded—through continuous snowstorms, in very low visibility and along strange channels beset with navigational hazards—to arrive at his destination shortly after 4 a.m. on the 10th. Complete tactical surprise was achieved. To follow the details of the attacks which now took place would go beyond the scope of this narrative.[1] It must suffice to say that at 4.30 a.m. the *Hardy*, *Hunter* and *Havock* went into the harbour and, by torpedoes and gunfire, sank the German Commodore's ship, the *Wilhelm Heidkamp*, and also the *Anton Schmidt* and damaged three more destroyers.[2] The *Hotspur* and *Hostile* had remained outside; they joined in a second attack in which some merchant ships were sunk. It had not been discovered that there were three more enemy destroyers in Herjangs Fiord.[3] Captain Warburton-Lee then drew off, having every reason to be well satisfied with the results so far achieved. He accordingly decided to make one more attack, after which he proceeded down Ofot Fiord on his return

---

[1] See T. K. Derry, *History of the Second World War: The Campaign in Norway* (H.M.S.O., 1952), pp. 44–46.
[2] Appendix G gives particulars of all German warships.
[3] See Map 16 (*facing p. 175*).

Map
NAR
First Battle –
British i
German i

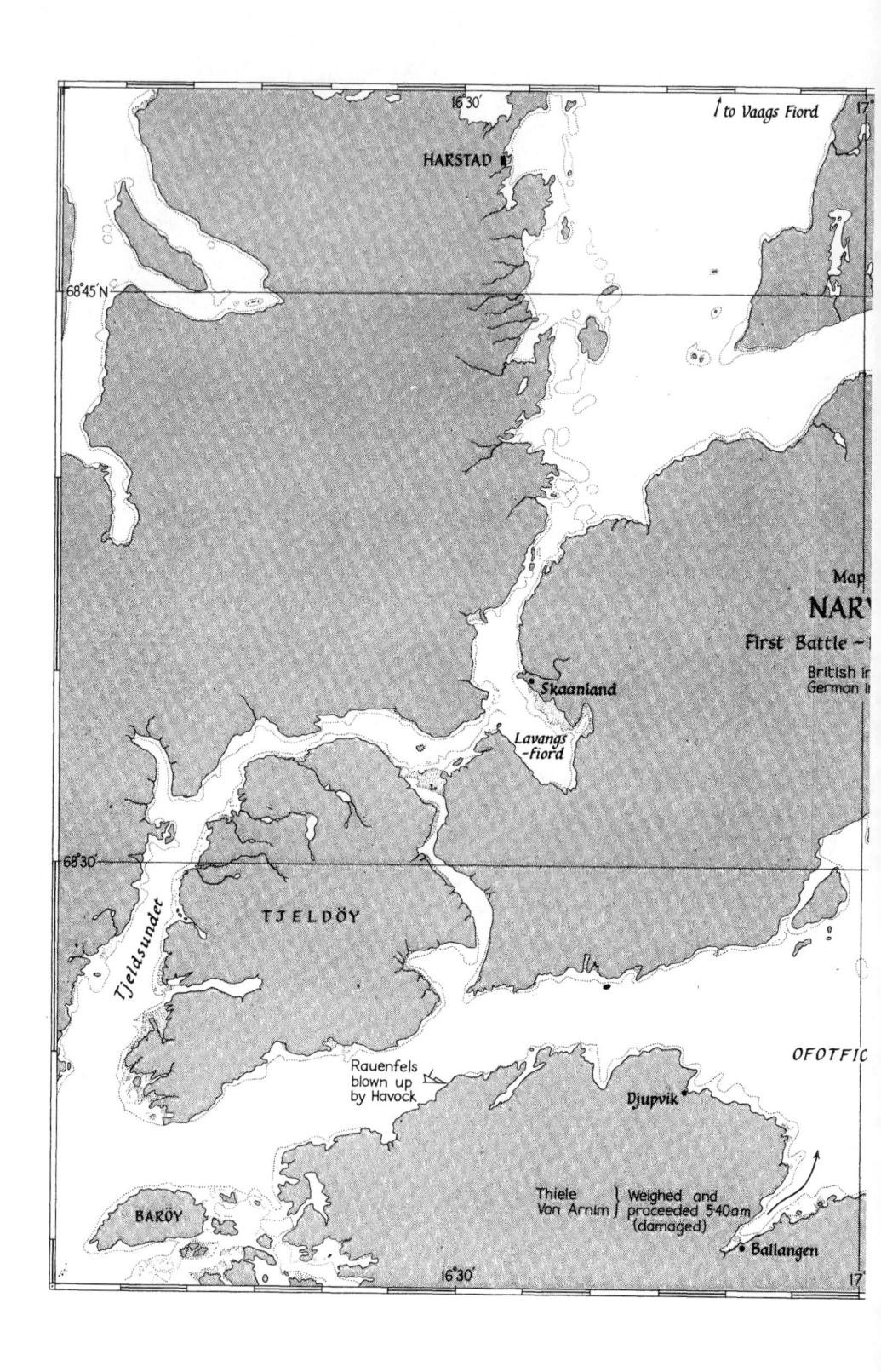

HARSTAD
to Vaags Fiord
68°45'N
Skaanland
Lavangs
-fiord
68°30'
TJELDÖY
Tjeldsundet
Rauenfels
blown up
by Havock
OFOTFI
Djupvik
BARÖY
Thiele | Weighed and
Von Arnim | proceeded 5·40am
(damaged)
Ballangen

16
...VIK
10th April 1940
...in Red
...in Blue

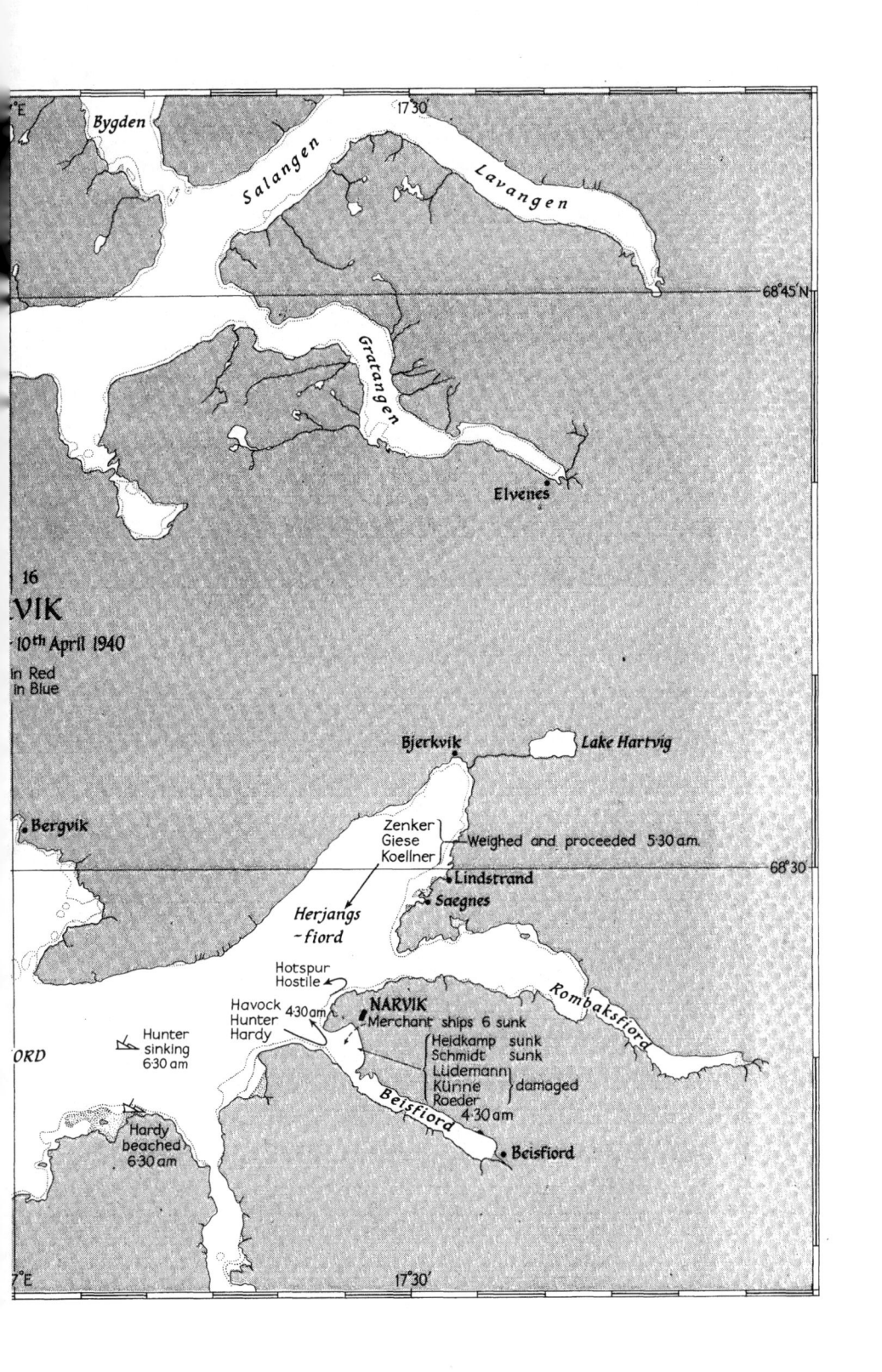

journey. But, just before 6 a.m., the good fortune which so often attends on the commander, who, when possessed of the advantage of surprise, will attack even heavy odds, deserted him. The three fresh destroyers appeared from Herjangs Fiord and a running fight ensued. But this was not all, since two more enemy destroyers, which had been in Ballangen Fiord, appeared ahead of him, and the British flotilla thus found itself between two fires from more heavily armed adversaries.

The *Hardy* was soon disabled and her commander killed. For his action on this day Captain Warburton-Lee was awarded a posthumous Victoria Cross. The *Hunter* was sunk and the *Hotspur* so severely damaged that she drifted on to the sinking *Hunter*. The *Hostile* and *Havock*, ahead of the remainder, were almost untouched and now turned back to their assistance. But the greatly superior enemy had not escaped damage and declined to press his advantage. He thus missed a good opportunity to destroy the entire British force, and allowed the damaged *Hotspur* to be extricated.

The action ended at 6.30 but, on the way out, the *Havock* sank the valuable German ammunition ship *Rauenfels*. The losses suffered by each side were two destroyers sunk; but five more German destroyers were damaged fairly severely as compared with the disabled *Hotspur* on our side. Some half-dozen enemy-controlled merchant ships were also destroyed.

Admiral Whitworth intercepted Captain Warburton-Lee's last signals at about 6 a.m. and at once sent the *Penelope* and all four destroyers of his screen to his assistance. But it was too late, and Admiral Forbes' new orders had already stated that his object was now to prevent the escape of the remaining enemy ships. That evening the Admiralty told the Commander-in-Chief that recapture of Narvik now took priority over attacking Bergen or Trondheim and that an expedition was being prepared for that purpose.

But the Admiralty naturally wished to finish off the remaining enemies in Narvik harbour and gave this duty directly to the light cruiser *Penelope* and certain destroyers. This renewed intervention from London caused Admiral Whitworth to protest that he had now been given three different objectives—to prevent the enemies' escape, to prevent their reinforcement and to attack them. The attack by the *Penelope*, originally timed for dawn on the 12th, was finally cancelled and, as, unhappily, she ran ashore on the afternoon of the 11th, she took no further part in the campaign. Next day the Admiralty, believing that two cruisers and about six destroyers were still at Narvik, decided to renew the attack on a far heavier scale.

Meanwhile Admiral Forbes and the main units of the Home Fleet were, as already mentioned, preparing to use the *Furious'* torpedo-bombers to attack Trondheim, where the original enemy forces had consisted of the heavy cruiser *Hipper* and four destroyers. But the *Hipper* and one destroyer sailed on their return journey on the evening of the 10th; they narrowly escaped running into Admiral Forbes' fleet during the night.[1] So when the eighteen torpedo-bombers left their carrier at 4 a.m. next morning there were only three destroyers in the harbour. Two of these were attacked but, because of the shallowness of the water, the torpedoes failed to find even these lesser targets and no results were achieved. This was indeed disappointing, but the truth was that the fleeting chance of catching the enemy during the vulnerable period of the initial disembarkations had already passed. Admiral Forbes now continued north towards Narvik, where he intended to launch another attack by his carrier aircraft.

While this shift of theatre was in progress, ships of the 1st and 18th Cruiser Squadrons searched the Inner Leads from Aalesund to Vestfiord for enemies, but none was found. The reason was that the short sea route to Oslo was all that the enemy at this time needed to build up his invasion forces, and he was not attempting to transport troops by sea to the north.

Air attacks on the fleet were renewed that afternoon, the 11th, and the destroyer *Eclipse* was seriously damaged; but a more significant event was the escape south, through our surface and air patrol lines, of the enemy's two battle cruisers which were reported on the morning of the 12th off the south-west corner of Norway. In fact, after breaking off the action with the *Renown* in the early hours of the 9th Admiral Lütjens had stood away to the north for about six hours until he had reached 69° North, where he altered to the west.[2] At 10 a.m. on the 10th, when far to the north of the Faeröes, he turned south and by the following evening was some 100 miles to the east of those islands. Admiral Lütjens realised from wireless interceptions that the main strength of the Home Fleet was off the Norwegian coast between Vestfiord and Trondheim. During the night of the 10th–11th he therefore passed to the east of the Shetlands—actually only forty miles offshore—and at 8.30 next morning effected a rendezvous with the *Hipper* from Trondheim. On this, the last stage of the hazardous homeward journey, they were sighted off Egersund by our reconnaissance aircraft and the largest striking force yet prepared for a naval target, consisting of 92 Coastal and Bomber Command aircraft, was sent out to attack. But none succeeded in finding them. Aided by low visibility, snow, sleet and rain, the ideal conditions for such an evasion, they reached the Jade without incident that evening, the 12th of April.

Only one of the major enemy warships concerned in these operations remains to be accounted for—the pocket-battleship *Lützow*

---
[1] See Map 15 (*facing p. 171*).
[2] See Map 15.

16°30'

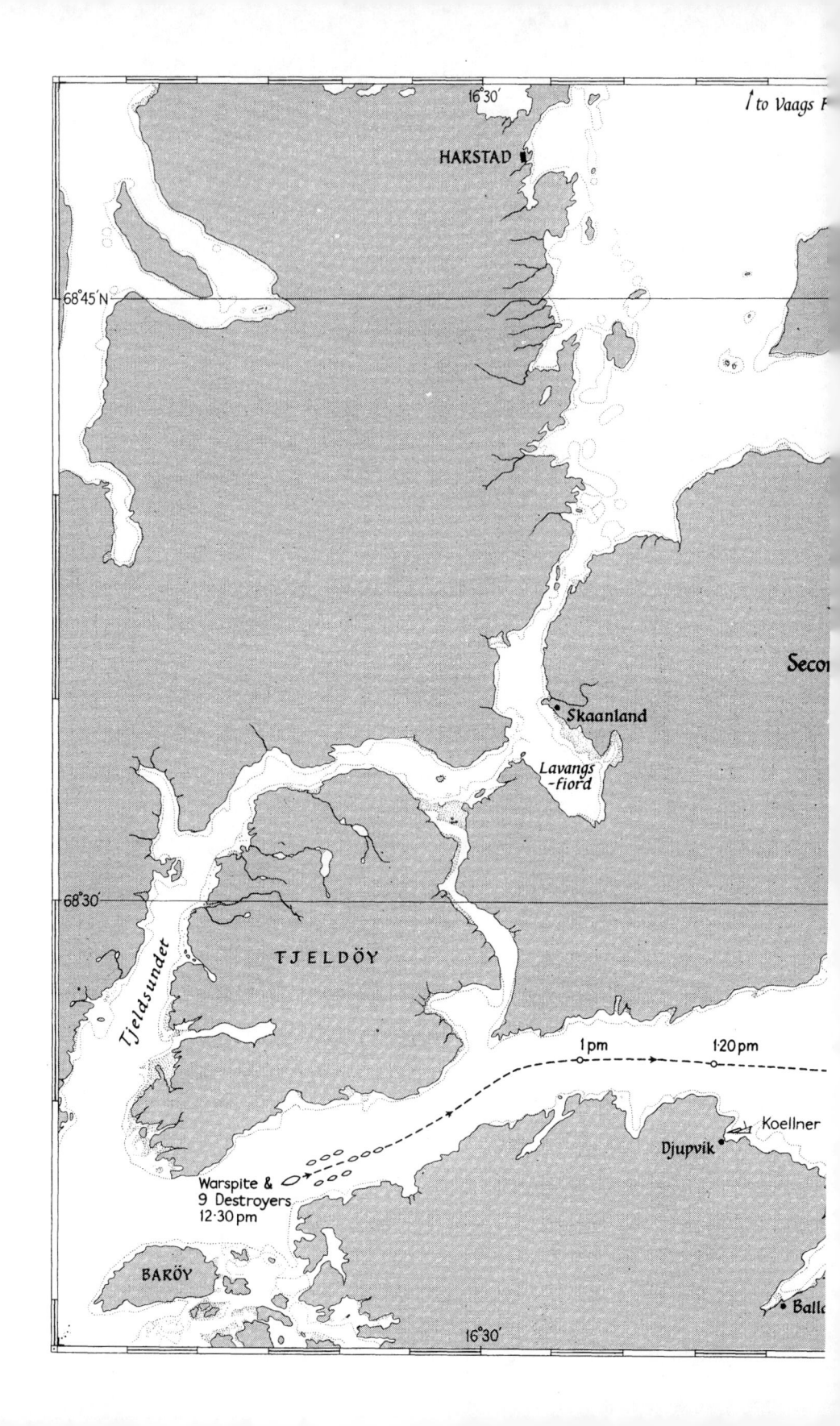

HARSTAD

↑ to Vaags F

68°45'N

Seco

Skaanland

Lavangs-fiord

68°30'

Tjeldsundet

TJELDÖY

1 pm   1·20 pm

Koellner
Djupvik

Warspite &
9 Destroyers
12·30 pm

BARÖY

Balla

16°30'

Map 17
...VIK
...–13th April 1940

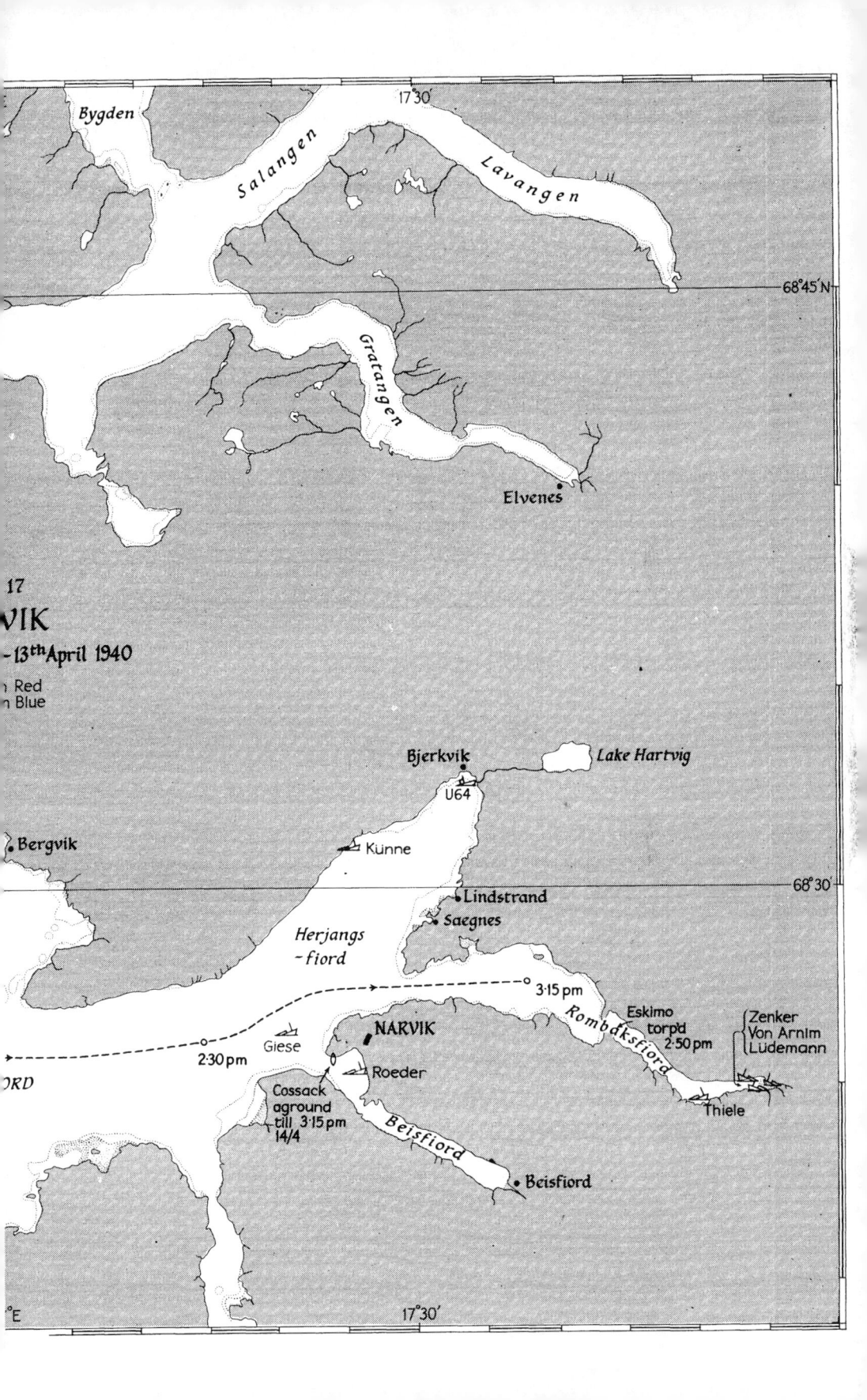

... Red
... Blue

Bygden

Salangen

Lavangen

17°30'

68°45'N

Gratangen

Elvenes

Bergvik

Bjerkvik
U64

Lake Hartvig

Künne

Lindstrand

68°30'

Saegnes

Herjangs-fiord

3·15 pm

Giese
2:30 pm

NARVIK

Roeder

Rombaksfiord

Eskimo torp'd 2·50 pm

Zenker
Von Arnim
Lüdemann

Cossack aground till 3·15 pm 14/4

Beisfiord

Beisfiord

Thiele

17°30'

which, as we saw earlier, took command in Oslo Fiord after the sinking of the *Blücher* on the 9th.[1] She left for Kiel on the afternoon of the 10th and, just after the following midnight, was torpedoed and seriously damaged by the submarine *Spearfish*. Most of her crew were removed, she was taken in tow and, heavily escorted, she finally reached Kiel on the evening of the 13th.[2] She was so badly damaged that she was out of action for twelve months.

During the afternoon of the 12th Admiral Forbes arrived off the Lofoten Islands to cover and support the attack on the ships in Narvik by the *Furious*' aircraft. No previous reconnaissance was carried out and the weather conditions remained most unfavourable to accurate bombing. One squadron got through the low clouds and snowstorms, but their bombs did no damage; the second had to turn back. Thus ended another gallant but abortive attempt to strike from the air at the bases which the enemy had seized. But hardly had this attack been organised when the Admiralty sent instructions that the final destruction of the enemies remaining at Narvik should be compassed from the sea, and Admiral Forbes accordingly decided to use the battleship *Warspite* and a strong force of nine destroyers, all placed under Admiral Whitworth's orders. Aircraft from the *Furious* would attack again in synchronisation with the surface ships, which assembled inside Vestfiord early on the morning of the 13th of April and moved up through the narrow waters shortly afterwards.

The first success was obtained by the *Warspite's* reconnaissance aircraft, which bombed and sank U.64 while scouting ahead of Admiral Whitworth's force. This aircraft also gave warning of the presence of one enemy destroyer in a small bay, in a position of torpedo advantage, thus enabling her to be promptly destroyed as the squadron passed up the fiord. Warning of Admiral Whitworth's approach had meanwhile reached the senior officer of the 4th German Destroyer Flotilla, and he ordered his six serviceable ships out to meet the enemy.[3] From 1 p.m. until 2 p.m. a hot destroyer action took place just outside Narvik harbour and the German ships then retired into Rombaks and Herjangs Fiords, up which they were relentlessly pursued to their utter destruction. Eight large German destroyers and one U-boat were lost to the enemy on that afternoon, at the cost of serious damage only to the *Eskimo* and *Cossack;* and the risks which had been accepted in sending a battleship into such confined waters were abundantly justified by the devastating effects of the *Warspite's* 15-inch gunfire.[4] By 6.30 p.m. Admiral Whitworth

---

[1] See p. 165 and Map 14 (*facing p. 159*).

[2] See Map 15 (*facing p. 171*).

[3] See Map 17.

[4] The destroyed enemy ships were the *Georg Thiele, Hans Lüdemann, Hermann Künne, Diether Von Röder, Wolfgang Zenker, Erich Giese, Erich Koellner* and *Bernd Von Arnim*, plus the submarine U.64. Details of the armaments of German ships are given in Appendix G.

was proceeding out to sea again, having left sufficient ships behind to look after the damaged ones. He had considered the possibility of landing a force to occupy the town at once, but had decided against it as he could not possibly raise a strong enough landing party to oppose the 2,000 highly-trained German soldiers known to be ashore. But the rapid occupation of Narvik itself was in the Admiralty's mind as well, and a signal came that evening urging that it should be accomplished 'to ensure [an] unopposed landing later'—just when Admiral Whitworth was recommending that this should be undertaken by forces from home without delay. Next morning he repeated his conviction 'that Narvik can be taken by direct assault without fear of meeting serious opposition on landing'. The enemy forces were, indeed, in a difficult condition ashore. They had lost their ammunition reserves in the *Rauenfels*, sunk on the 10th, and their motor transport had been captured in the *Alster* by the destroyer *Icarus* on the following day. But, unhappily, no military force was available to seize this chance to exploit a favourable tactical situation and, when the forces did arrive, they were not suitably embarked or properly equipped for a rapid or opposed landing. It was perhaps at this juncture that the troops embarked for 'Plan R4', but thrown ashore so hastily on the morning of the 8th, could best have been used.[1] But they were without most of their equipment, and the cruisers in which they were to have been transported to Norway were now hundreds of miles away. Not until the 28th of May—some six weeks later—was the capture of Narvik finally accomplished.

The story of the first phase in the Norwegian campaign can be conveniently broken here because new circumstances—namely the dispatch of the first, hastily organised military forces for Narvik from the Clyde on the 11th of April—now began to affect the whole of our maritime strategy in that theatre.

From the 8th of April, when Admiral Forbes had estimated, correctly, that a full-scale invasion was in progress, until the departure of the first troop convoy he had only one object—to dispute control of the sea routes on which the enemy had largely to depend to supply and reinforce his first spearheads. But a second was now added. He was required, whilst continuing his endeavours to deny the enemy the use of the sea, to control the waters between Britain and the bases which the War Cabinet intended to establish on Norwegian territory; and he had, in fact, already had to make substantial detachments from his strength to cover and escort the first convoy. It must have been clear to Admiral Forbes that, while the routes across the North Sea could, by judicious use of his powerful

---

[1] See p. 161.

fleet, probably be made reasonably secure, to control the necessary coastal waters in Norway under the weight of air attack which he had himself several times experienced would be hazardous and difficult in the extreme, unless fighter protection could be provided from adjacent shore airfields. But there were no operational airfields to the north of Stavanger, which itself was already in enemy hands. If the Commander-in-Chief had few illusions regarding the difficulties ahead he can have had none about what was required of him and his fleet, for the First Lord had, on the 17th of April, written to tell him that 'All that has happened makes me sure that Hitler has made a grave strategic blunder in giving us the right, as we have always had the power, to take what we like on the Norwegian coast'. The right we certainly now had, but a right sadly weakened by the lack of effective preparations for the type of operation thus forced on us. The power, which must be maritime power, we did not then possess in sufficient measure, for we lacked one of the instruments already seen to be essential to the successful prosecution of maritime war. In Admiral Forbes' words, 'the scale of air attack that would be developed against our military forces on shore and our naval forces off the Norwegian coast was grievously underestimated when the operations were undertaken'. But before starting to probe the causes of difficulties yet to come we must endeavour to summarise the result of the first five days of the campaign. That we had failed to deny the enemy the use of the sea was as clear by the 15th of April 1940 as it is today. But when the critical first days of the Norwegian campaign are reviewed it seems that the opportunity to inflict really serious injury on the enemy's expedition was, as is usual in such cases, a fleeting one and occurred during the night of the 7th–8th of April while the transports carrying his main forces were moving through the Skagerrak. Had the Home Fleet's flotillas, supported by cruisers, then been sent into those waters in strength the results might have been considerable. But the intelligence which indicated the need to adopt such bold and vigorous action was ignored or misinterpreted, and the opportunity was allowed to pass. Only submarines were present to dispute control of the passages to Norway, and they had to work under conditions of great danger and difficulty. Our submarines did splendid service and inflicted substantial losses, but they could not of themselves deny the enemy reasonable control of the short sea routes.[1] Aided by the clever, if unscrupulous, use of surprise the enemy's first landing parties had been able to seize all the key

---

[1] Apart from the attacks by submarines on enemy warships and the sinking of the transport *Rio de Janeiro* by the Polish submarine *Orzel* already mentioned, between 8th and 14th April the *Sunfish* sank four enemy merchant ships or transports, the *Triad*, *Sealion* and *Snapper* one each and the *Orzel* one tanker. Other ships were certainly damaged. But the submarine *Thistle* was sunk by U.4 on 10th April, the *Tarpon* by German anti-submarine craft on the 14th and the *Sterlet* on the 18th.

points on the Norwegian coast. But the arrangements to follow up these landings had gone badly awry in the case of the two northern ports, Narvik and Trondheim. At the former we had almost completely destroyed the ships which were to supply the initial landing parties, and none of the three disguised merchant ships reached their destination. At Trondheim one finally arrived, three days late. Of the three tankers allotted to the ports, one succeeded in reaching Narvik from Murmansk but the others were intercepted.

But with the ports of Oslo, Kristiansand (South) and Bergen and the airfield at Stavanger in his hands the enemy was none the less bound to be able to build up his armies for their northward march by using the short sea routes to Oslo, supplemented by his air transport service. He had risked almost his entire naval strength to accomplish his end, and the losses suffered, though considerable in the sum, he considered a reasonable price to pay. In spite of the difficult state in which his landing parties in the northern ports now found themselves, he had therefore set us a task which, under the conditions then prevailing, was impossible of fulfilment. But since the policy of the Allied Governments was 'to give Norway as much assistance as possible' the attempt had, none the less, to be made. The next sections will therefore tell the story of our endeavours to conduct an overseas land campaign without the degree of control of the coastal waters adjacent to the ports of disembarkation which is a cardinal necessity for success in such a venture.

The first expeditionary force for Norway left the Clyde in three liners on the 11th of April and was joined later by two more liners from Scapa. Admiral Layton met the convoy, which was known as N.P. 1, with the cruisers *Manchester* and *Birmingham* on the 13th. The troops embarked were originally all destined for Narvik, where the land forces were to be commanded by Major-General P. J. Mackesy. He sailed from Scapa in the *Southampton* on the 12th of April. Admiral of the Fleet Lord Cork and Orrery, who had been appointed Flag Officer, Narvik, on the 10th, and under whose orders certain naval forces had been placed when operating within 100 miles of Vaags Fiord, left Rosyth in the *Aurora* on the 12th and arrived at Skjel Fiord two days later.[1] Admiral Forbes detached strong forces of the Home Fleet to cover and escort convoy N.P. 1 but himself proceeded to Scapa, from the operations already described, with the *Rodney*, *Renown* and six destroyers on the evening of the 15th of April, while the *Warspite* and *Furious*, under Admiral Whitworth, were detached to work under Lord Cork in the Narvik area.

This, then, was the general position of our naval forces when, on

---
[1] See Map 18 opposite.

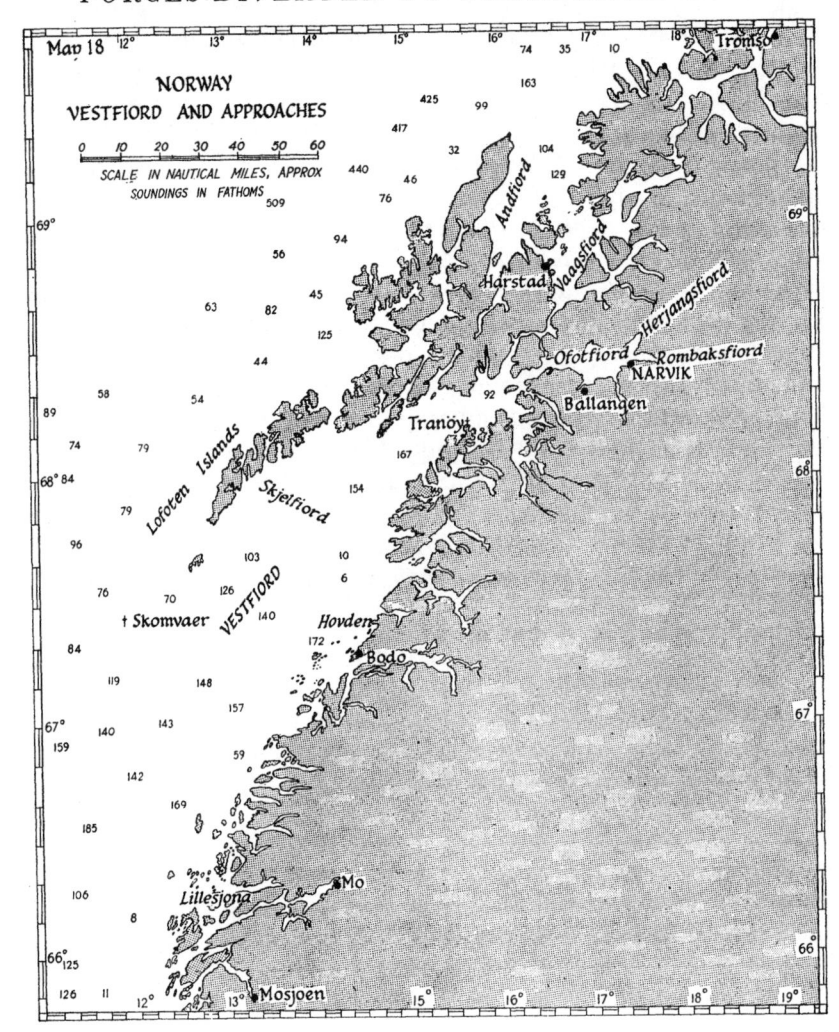

the 14th of April, Admiral Layton received orders to detach two troopships from his convoy with one brigade of troops to Namsos, about 100 miles north of Trondheim, against which operations were now being mounted.[1] It is, therefore, convenient to leave the northern expedition, now substantially reduced, proceeding towards Vestfiord and to turn to events in the Trondheim area.

Early on the 13th of April Captain Pegram of the *Glasgow* intercepted an Admiralty message to the Commander-in-Chief proposing that the two cruisers working in the Indreled should land some 350 seamen and Royal Marines at Namsos in order 'to forestall the Germans'. Later the same day he received orders to carry this out.

---

[1] See Map 19 (overleaf).

This was the first Allied landing on Norwegian soil, and the troops in the two ships detached from convoy N.P. 1 were to become the first flight of the main forces which were subsequently to relieve the seamen and marines and undertake the attack on Trondheim from the north (operation 'Maurice'). The advance party landed from the cruisers at dusk on the 14th, and next day Major-General A. Carton de Wiart, V.C., who had been appointed to command the 'Maurice' forces, arrived there by air. Meanwhile Admiral Layton, with the *Manchester*, *Birmingham*, *Cairo* and three destroyers, was steering towards Namsos with the two transports from convoy N.P. 1. However, the enemy's bombing had already produced difficult conditions at Namsos and this force was therefore ordered from London to proceed to Lillesjona, 100 miles to the north, instead of to Namsos, and there it anchored on the 16th. The first thousand troops were ferried from Lillesjona to Namsos that evening in destroyers, and next day the Polish transport *Chrobry* was taken into the latter place to disembark the rest of the troops and their stores. The naval parties temporarily landed then returned to their ships.

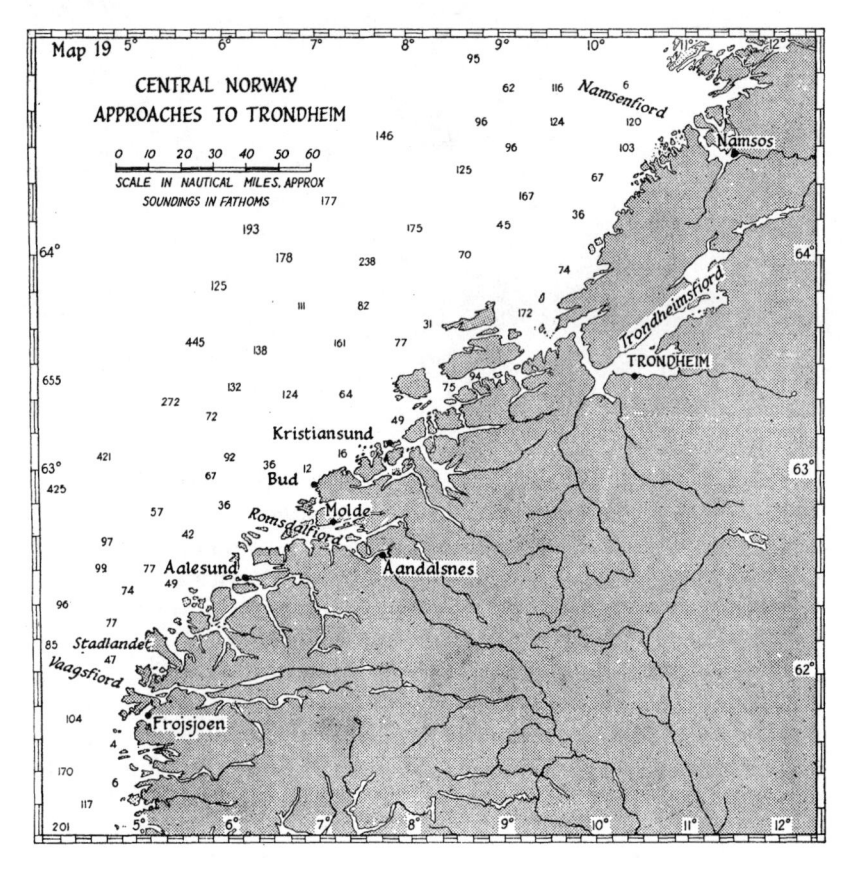

Map 19. CENTRAL NORWAY APPROACHES TO TRONDHEIM

The first reinforcements received by General Carton de Wiart were the Chasseurs Alpins who came over in four French troopships escorted by the French cruiser *Emile Bertin* and destroyers. They reached their destination on the 19th, and were led into the fiord by the A.A. cruiser *Cairo*. The enemy attacked this convoy from the air and hit the *Emile Bertin*, but the troopships were successfully cleared and sent home again on the 20th. Shortly afterwards the enemy bombers attacked the town of Namsos in strength. Further reinforcements, also French, arrived on the 22nd, but their storeships could not be unloaded. These were the last troops to arrive at Namsos. As early as the 21st the General had raised doubts regarding the feasibility of the whole undertaking because of the insecurity of his base and the enemy's complete ascendancy in the air. The next French troops were, in fact, diverted from Namsos to Narvik.

Stores and guns were landed at Namsos on the 27th and 28th, but meanwhile the troops had fared ill on shore and evacuation was looming prominently in the picture. There we will temporarily leave the Namsos forces; we will turn to the landings which had meanwhile taken place to the south of Trondheim as part of the pincer movement aimed at the recovery of that important place.

The minor operation now put in train with the object of occupying Aalesund was designed to neutralise the adjacent stretches of the Indreled and to create a diversion while the troops of Operation 'Maurice' were landing at Namsos. The four sloops *Auckland*, *Black Swan*, *Flamingo* and *Bittern* sailed from Rosyth on the 14th and 15th of April with 700 seamen and marines, hastily collected from ships which were refitting at the time. These little ships, overcrowded and heavily loaded, met very bad weather and had to put into Invergordon for shelter. While there, they received Admiralty instructions to divert the landing parties to Aandalsnes. They sailed again on the 16th and arrived at their destination late the following evening. By 7 a.m. next morning the landing parties had been disembarked and the ships sailed to take another naval party to the small port of Molde and some guns to be mounted at Aalesund. Up to this point the operation had fared fortunately, but after the 20th of April Aandalsnes was bombed almost daily and with ever-increasing weight and effect. The little seaport was soon almost completely destroyed. The naval landing parties remained ashore and became absorbed in the larger expedition called 'Sickle', whose brief career will now be traced.

Admiral Edward-Collins with the cruisers *Galatea*, *Arethusa*, the A.A. cruisers *Carlisle* and *Curacoa* and two destroyers sailed from Rosyth early on the 17th of April with 1,000 troops on board. These were landed without incident at Molde and Aandalsnes the next evening, the 18th, and the cruisers left again in the small hours of the following morning. On the 20th bombing started in earnest, and the *Carlisle* and *Curacoa* bore the chief brunt of almost continuous attacks until the latter was hit and badly damaged on the 24th. The experiences of these two specially equipped ships were repeated and confirmed by other A.A. ships stationed at Namsos and at Aandalsnes during these difficult days. Their radar sets were rendered almost useless by the high cliffs and surrounding land; the same cliffs prevented any appreciable warning being received visually; the narrow waters left little room for manœuvring, yet it was essential for the ships to remain under way; ammunition expenditure was extremely high and no stocks were available for replenishment locally. When a ship had fired the greater part of her ammunition she must return to a home base. Moreover the actual protection afforded to the bases by the gunfire of the guard ships was slight, and was chiefly due to the enemy concentrating his attacks on the ships. A like number of guns deployed ashore would have been far less vulnerable to the enemy's attacks and would have given the ports better protection; but there were no heavy anti-aircraft guns ashore. Moreover these anti-aircraft cruisers and sloops were costly and valuable ships which, used in the manner for which they had been designed, rendered excellent service, particularly on our coastal and short-sea convoy routes. To use them as floating substitutes for properly organised base defences was only justifiable because every other form of defence against air attack was lacking. From the point of view of economy of force it could, as Admiral Forbes was soon to point out, hardly be justified.

The work of the bases themselves could be done only under cover of darkness. Unloading could not start till 9 p.m. and must finish by 2 a.m. to enable transports and storeships to get clear of the fiords before daylight. And at that time of year, in those latitudes, the nights were rapidly shortening.

Such, in brief, were the problems which faced the base staffs at every point of landing in central Norway during April 1940. It was not the fault of the Army that properly organised anti-aircraft batteries could not be set up on shore, nor that of the Air Force that fighter protection could not be provided. The necessary equipment existed at home, though by no means in plentiful quantities, but it could not be embarked, transported by sea, disembarked and installed on shore in a strange land, much of which was still under deep snow, in a matter of days. Every effort was, in fact, made to get guns and fighter aircraft across to defend these bases, but the problem was too big and too difficult to yield to any amount of improvisation. And with the bases daily, even hourly, under the lash of the enemy's air power the military operations could not possibly prosper.

Reinforcements for 'Sickle', however, arrived in the midst of the bombing on the 21st of April and from that convoy the storeship

Cedarbank was torpedoed and sunk—the only success obtained by enemy submarines against all our troop and store convoys bound for Norway during these operations.[1] The following day the *Arethusa* brought stores, light anti-aircraft guns and the advance party of the R.A.F. for an extemporised fighter station which it was hoped to establish on a frozen lake nearby. She landed all these and left again within four hours. In London further reinforcement of the 'Sickle' force was still intended, and Admiral Edward-Collins therefore left Rosyth on the 22nd with the *Galatea, Sheffield, Glasgow* and six destroyers carrying 2,200 men, all of whom were successfully landed at Molde and Aandalsnes the next day. The final reinforcement of 1,600 men and 300 tons of stores was carried over by Admiral Layton in the *Manchester, Birmingham, York* and three destroyers from Rosyth on the 24th. They, too, were put ashore without loss. The Navy could do no more and, as Admiral Edward-Collins noted, 'it is remarkable that my ships have now carried out this operation three times without molestation'. The arrival of these reinforcements coincided with the utter failure of the hoped-for fighter protection from the frozen lake. The Gladiators were transported by the *Glorious* (Captain G. D'Oyly-Hughes), recently returned from the Mediterranean, and flown ashore, only to be overwhelmed by enemy bombers within a few hours. By this time the realities of the situation were plain. On the 27th the first definite proposals to evacuate 'Sickle' were sent home. Next day the Cabinet took the decision to abandon central Norway altogether. But before telling the story of the evacuation of all the 12,000 men so hopefully carried to central Norway it is necessary to revert for a time to the main body of the Home Fleet, and to view the operations described in the last pages through the eyes of Admiral Forbes.

It has been mentioned that the first phase of the campaign left the enemy's spearheads in Trondheim and Narvik in a critical condition through the almost complete destruction of their supply and store ships.[2] The Germans realised that their slender hold on Narvik depended on retaining their almost equally tenuous grip on Trondheim, which place they aptly described as 'the pivot of all operations'. The importance of Trondheim was certainly realised in London too and, as the enemy was not long in learning of our intention to land an expedition in that area, he adopted the policy of reinforcing it as rapidly as possible by land and air—since the direct sea route was still denied him—whilst using his air power and submarines to harass the ships on which our own expeditions depended.

In spite of the Cabinet's full realisation of the importance of Trondheim, no clear-cut decision, such as that issued by the enemy, was

---
[1] See p. 164.
[2] See p. 178.

taken regarding the relative priorities of that place and Narvik. On the 10th of April Narvik was, in fact, given first priority and it is noteworthy that our forces in that area finally reached a total of 30,000 men compared with the 12,000 taken to central Norway.

However by the 16th of April it was considered in London that the 'capture of Trondheim [was] . . . essential' and from this need developed the proposal to make a frontal attack on the place with the main units of the Home Fleet. The code name of the operation was 'Hammer'. Such a proposal had already been tentatively put to Admiral Forbes two days earlier and his reply showed his serious misgivings, for he remarked that 'bombing would start almost immediately' and that 'to carry out an opposed landing . . . under continuous air attack' was hardly feasible. But the weight of the enemy's air power had to be experienced to be appreciated and, on the 15th, the Admiralty pressed the Commander-in-Chief to 'consider this important project further'. The same message told Admiral Forbes that the attack 'could not take place for seven days devoted to careful preparation'; he thereupon asked for the plan to be brought to him at Scapa by a representative of the Admiralty for study and discussion. Accordingly Rear-Admiral L. E. Holland arrived on board the *Rodney* on the 18th of April with the plan and a personal letter from the First Lord to the Commander-in-Chief strongly urging the merits of the proposed attack. Admiral Forbes had already told the Admiralty that he would not take the troops to Trondheim in transports but was prepared to do so in warships, and to this the Admiralty had agreed and had altered the plan accordingly. What was surprising to the Commander-in-Chief was that, when the plan arrived, he found that the attack was to take place on the 22nd-23rd of April, which meant that the 'seven days devoted to careful preparation' had been more or less eliminated. This reinforced his misgivings, since an intricate operation of this nature, involving the synchronised use of all arms of all three services, plainly required the most detailed and careful preparation. On the 19th, the day after the plan had arrived in the *Rodney* at Scapa, the Chiefs of Staff changed their mind, and Operation 'Hammer' was cancelled.

The reasons for this sudden change of mind are not even now easy to assess, but there seems no doubt that the Naval Staff, with its large commitments, for cruisers and destroyers in particular, at Narvik, Namsos and Aandalsnes, must have wondered from what source the additional ships for Trondheim could possibly be found. Furthermore the Navy was running very short of anti-aircraft ammunition, and the Admiralty had already urged on Admiral Forbes the need for strict economy in its use. Finally the cruiser *Suffolk* had struggled back to Scapa on the 18th of April with her quarter-deck awash after bombarding Stavanger airfield the previous day and suffering nearly seven hours of continuous bombing during her withdrawal. It seems possible that each of these considerations —which, in the sum, supported Admiral Forbes' original contention that 'to carry out an opposed landing . . . under continuous air attack was hardly feasible'—contributed to the abrupt cancellation of the operation. The considered judgement of the Commander-in-Chief was that it would have been a 'gamble which might have succeeded but probably would not', and, although the abandonment of the attempt was the subject of much criticism at the time, it now seems that his judgement was correct. This much at least is certain, that the German view corresponded closely with that of Admiral Forbes in holding that 'a direct assault on Trondheim would only have been possible in the first days of the operations'; and it must be remembered that, when the Commander-in-Chief had wished to make an attack on the enemy ships in Bergen, it had been the Admiralty who had cancelled it.[1] To have hazarded a great proportion of our naval strength on an operation which could not have decisively affected the outcome of the war at a time when the threat in the west was becoming more and more plain would, it now seems, have been to court a more serious setback than the loss of central Norway.

The first troops which had been assembled for the attack on Trondheim were therefore diverted to Aandalsnes, and the Home Fleet settled down to the continuation of its arduous duties of convoying troops and supplies to Norway and providing cruisers for use as fast troop carriers. On the 17th of April, when Admiral Forbes returned to Scapa prior to the discussions on Operation 'Hammer', he gave the Admiralty his proposals for the future employment of the fleet. Since these give a clear picture of the strategy which the Commander-in-Chief desired to implement they will be considered in some detail.

Firstly the fleet was to enforce a close blockade of Narvik, and to support the military forces operating in that area. It would give similar support to the forces at Namsos and Aandalsnes, and would endeavour to prevent the use by the enemy of the inshore shipping lanes off the Norwegian coast. Submarines were to continue to dispute the short sea routes across the Skagerrak and Kattegat, while surface sweeps would be carried out in those waters to relieve the pressure of the enemy's anti-submarine measures. Finally the harassing of the enemy-controlled airfields was to be the responsibility of the Royal Air Force, except in the Narvik area where carrier-borne aircraft could be used to that end. It will be noted that frontal attacks, such as that proposed against Trondheim, had no place in Admiral Forbes' strategy.

But the execution of these plans was made far more difficult by

---

[1] See p. 170.

the Home Fleet's strength being steadily reduced in April and May, as Italy's attitude became increasingly hostile and the threat of the enemy's campaign in the west became clearer. The *Warspite* left Narvik on the 24th of April to return to the Mediterranean where, as flagship of Admiral Sir Andrew Cunningham's fleet, she was to perform outstanding service; on the 3rd of May Admiral Edward-Collins was ordered to Sheerness with the *Galatea* and *Arethusa*, and eight destroyers were sent to Harwich to be handy in case the invasion of the Low Countries should take place. Ten days later the Mediterranean Fleet was reinforced with the anti-aircraft cruiser *Carlisle*, eight destroyers and three sloops; and on the 18th of May three more destroyers were diverted to the Humber where, on the 27th, they were joined by the cruisers *Manchester*, *Birmingham* and *Sheffield* commanded by Admiral Layton. The need to hold such substantial forces on the south and east coasts to deal with an invasion threat will be discussed in a later chapter. It was soon to cramp the strategy and restrict the operations of Admiral Forbes' fleet, which was thereby deprived of sufficient destroyers even to screen his heavy ships.

But it is time to return to the expeditions to Namsos and Aandalsnes which we left in an increasingly critical state, owing to the destruction of their bases from the air and the impossibility of supplying their troops.

On the 28th of April the Admiralty told Admiral Forbes that it had been decided 'to re-embark the force landed at Namsos and Aandalsnes as soon as possible', and it was therefore planned to extricate the latter in two nights (30th April–1st May and 1st–2nd May) while the force from Namsos would be embarked one night later (2nd–3rd May). Late on the 29th of April the *Glasgow* and two destroyers arrived at Molde to receive the King and Crown Prince of Norway, the Government and the country's gold reserve. The scene lacked nothing of the dramatic, for the cruiser went alongside the small quay with fire hoses playing while 'the whole scene . . . [was] brilliantly lit by the flames of the burning town'. But the embarkation was carried out without a hitch, and the *Glasgow* proceeded north to Tromsö that same night.

It now became clear that not a day must be lost if the troops were to be rescued since, on the night of the King's escape from Molde, Aandalsnes was for the first time bombed continuously throughout the brief hours of darkness.

At 10.30 p.m. on the 30th Admiral Edward-Collins arrived at Aandalsnes with the *Galatea, Arethusa, Sheffield, Southampton*, six destroyers and one transport, while one destroyer and a transport were sent to Molde. By good luck the concrete quay at Aandalsnes had survived, which greatly expedited embarkation, since it enabled one cruiser to go alongside while the destroyers ferried the men off to the other ships in the stream. About 2,200 men were safely embarked and the whole force hurried out of the fiord before dawn. 'Once again', the Admiral reported, 'and contrary to all expectations Romsdal Fiord was entered, the operation completed and forces withdrawn without loss'. Next day the usual air attacks took place and that night Admiral Layton took in the *Manchester, Birmingham*, five destroyers and two anti-aircraft ships at 11 p.m. to fetch the last of the troops, believed to be about 2,900. The destroyers ferried all the first flight out to the cruisers, which sailed at once; the *Auckland* and *Calcutta* remained behind for the rearguard, which was supposed to consist of 200 men. Actually 700 more turned up. They were embarked by the *Calcutta* in fifteen minutes, while the *Auckland* took on board the rearguard proper in seven minutes. In all some 2,200 men were taken off that night, and again not a casualty was incurred.

It now remained to make one more venture—and that, perhaps, the most desperate since it was increasingly probable, as each day passed, that the enemy would realise what we were doing—to extricate the 5,400 troops at Namsos. Admiral J. H. D. Cunningham sailed from Scapa on the 29th with the *Devonshire, York*, the French cruiser *Montcalm* (Admiral Derrien), five destroyers and three French transports; four more destroyers had already gone ahead.

On the 1st of May fog prevented the larger ships from approaching the coast, but some destroyers groped their way in and found the air clear in the fiord. It was thus plain that Namsos itself was exposed to air attack, and Admiral Cunningham became anxious to complete the embarkation in one night—for which he had already prepared alternative plans. The General declared this to be impossible during the few hours of darkness available. None the less Admiral Cunningham considered that 'to attempt to spread [the] evacuation over two nights would be courting disaster' and, moreover, the transports were running short of fuel. He therefore decided to use some of his warships as additional transports and at least bring off every possible man in one night. Accordingly Captain Vian in the *Afridi* led in the transports, followed by the *York* and *Nubian*. He was joined inside the fiord by three more destroyers. Admiral Cunningham remained on patrol outside with the *Devonshire, Montcalm* and four destroyers. Two of the French transports went straight alongside, while destroyers and smaller craft ferried men off to the third transport and the *York*. The first group of ships got clear away and reached Scapa safely, but the offshore fog lifted in time to enable the enemy to bomb the later ships. His bombers extended their attacks some 200 miles to seaward, and attacked Admiral Cunningham's force persistently until late in the afternoon of the 3rd. Two ships, the *Afridi* and French destroyer *Bison*, were sunk and a small number of casualties among the rearguard from Namsos, which had been embarked in the latter ship, were the only Army losses suffered during all these hazardous evacuations.

The successful extrication of force 'Maurice' from so critical a situation was in no small measure accomplished by the determined and skilful handling of the three French transports under Rear-Admiral Cadart, to whom Admiral Cunningham paid a warm tribute in his report.

On the 4th and 5th of May the whole force, except the two lost destroyers, reached Scapa, and so ended the first of the many military withdrawals which characterised the early months of the war; their success depended entirely on the skilful use of maritime power to control the Army's line of retreat from its oversea bases. General Carton de Wiart has given the soldier's view of this accomplishment in his autobiography. He writes, 'In the course of that last, endless day I got a message from the Navy to say that they would evacuate the whole of my force that night. I thought it was impossible, but learned a few hours later that the Navy do not know the word.'[1]

We must now return to Convoy N.P. 1 which we left steaming towards Vestfiord after the detachment of two of the transports on the 14th of April to join the Namsos expedition. The remainder arrived at their destination, escorted by the *Valiant* and nine destroyers, next day. But before the convoy entered harbour a U-boat warning was received and the destroyers *Fearless* and *Brazen* went ahead to search for and attack her. They quickly found and sank U.49, and from her the disposition of all the U-boats stationed by Admiral Dönitz in the North Sea in support of the invasion of Norway was recovered.[2] After this fortunate start the convoy entered Andfiord and the troops were disembarked near the small port of Harstad, which was to be the main base of operations.[3] The naval and military commanders of the expedition now met for the first time, and the 'diametrically opposed views' with which they had left London became apparent. In consequence of this, of the deep snow which lay everywhere and of the fact that the transports had not been 'tactically loaded' Lord Cork's proposal to make an immediate attack on Narvik had to be abandoned.[4]

---

[1] A. Carton de Wiart. *Happy Odyssey* (Jonathan Cape, 1950), p. 174.
[2] See p. 164.
[3] See Map 18 (*p. 181*).
[4] 'Tactical loading' of ships means that stores and equipment are embarked and stowed in such an order that the items which will be needed first when the troops disembark are most easily accessible, and the last-needed items are at the bottom of the holds. Unfortunately the most efficient loading of a cargo from the point of view of economy of space generally conflicts with the requirements of tactical loading. It is therefore inevitable that tactical loading is wasteful of cargo-carrying capacity.

On the 20th Lord Cork was appointed in supreme command of the expedition, and four days later he carried out a bombardment of Narvik by which it was hoped, though vainly, that the garrison would be induced to surrender. Thereafter the majority of the larger ships returned to home waters but, by arrangement with Admiral Forbes, some ten destroyers were made available to carry out the multifarious duties which in a combined operation always fall to the lot of that class of ship.

It would be outside the scope of these volumes to deal in any detail with the operations which led, finally, to the capture of Narvik; it must suffice to say that three battalions of French Chasseurs Alpins arrived on the 27th of April, followed next day by General Béthouart who had been appointed to command all the French military forces in the area.[1] Early in May two battalions of the French Foreign Legion and four Polish battalions were safely transported and, with the arrival of a few motor and assault landing craft (M.L.C.s and A.L.C.s) and a battery of 25-pounder guns as well, Lord Cork proposed to attack Narvik on the 8th of May. But this also had to be postponed and a landing at Bjerkvik, at the top of Herjangs Fiord, was substituted. This operation was covered by all the warships available; they bombarded any targets sighted ashore and the *Ark Royal's* fighters kept watch overhead. It succeeded with very small losses. The *Ark Royal*, however, was sent home on the 21st to embark R.A.F. aircraft for the new airfields near Narvik, just when the enemy's air attacks began to increase in weight and frequency. On the 14th the Polish transport *Chrobry* was lost, and between that date and the 26th a dozen warships, transports or storeships were sunk or seriously damaged by air attacks, ending with the loss of the anti-aircraft cruiser *Curlew*. These events made it plain that, unless shore-based fighters could be provided in adequate strength in the very near future, the situation which had arisen around Trondheim would be reproduced at Narvik. During the whole of May the most strenuous efforts were made to overcome the severe weather conditions ashore and to complete improvised fighter airfields. On the 21st the first R.A.F. fighters were flown ashore from the *Furious*, and a second squadron was carried over in the *Glorious* a few days later.

Meanwhile the evacuations from central Norway had resulted in the acceleration of the enemy's northward advance. The War Cabinet felt great anxiety regarding the steady progress towards Narvik of his hardy and specially trained troops and, above all, of the rapid extension of his air power towards our improvised and vulnerable bases in that area. In consequence detachments were landed at Mo, Bodö and Mosjöen to undertake delaying operations; these were

---

[1] See T. K. Derry. *The Campaign in Norway* (H.M.S.O.), Chapter X.

put under Lord Cork's command on the 7th of May.[1] Their maintenance and safety thus became another commitment for his already fully extended flotilla vessels—and all to little purpose since, by the 9th, the enemy's heavy pressure northwards was clearly more than could be contained by those small detachments. On the 14th of May Lord Cork sent reinforcements to Bodö in the transport *Chrobry* and it was at the start of that trip that she was bombed and destroyed. The following day he reported that 'we must hold on and fight at Mo; if that goes the whole Narvik situation becomes precarious'. A second attempt to reinforce Bodö was made on the 17th by the *Effingham*, *Cairo* and destroyers and ended in the loss of the first-named ship through running ashore. Her troops were, however, carried to their destination in small craft. Meanwhile the authorities in London, who could hardly realise to the full the difficulties of conducting operations in country such as the approaches to Narvik where the deep snow was only now beginning to thaw, expressed 'increased disappointment at [the] stagnation around Narvik and [the] delay in occupying [the] town'; to which Lord Cork replied, with understandable acerbity, that air protection 'might be described as a necessary preliminary to a combined operation on whatever scale', and that the final assault must therefore await the completion of the shore airfields.

Meanwhile the enemy's long-expected campaign in the west had opened with the invasion of Holland and Belgium on the 10th of May. In consequence of its immediate success and of the imminent threat to the security of our island base it was decided, on the 24th, to withdraw entirely from Norway, but to capture Narvik first in order to destroy the railway and the iron ore loading plant. These orders were received by Lord Cork and General Auchinleck, who had succeeded General Mackesy in command of the military forces, on the 25th of May; it was decided forthwith to evacuate Bodö, which had been so recently reinforced but where the enemy's pressure was now severe. The retreat began on the 29th and all 4,000 troops were safely embarked by the ships which Lord Cork had on his station. So ended the subsidiary landings designed to delay the enemy's northward progress, and not only was the way to Narvik now wide open to him but, more ominously, Bodö airfield had just become ready for use. It was plain that, even had the Cabinet decision already mentioned not been dictated by the changes in the strategic situation then occurring in the west, we could not have held on in the Vestfiord area much longer.

The final assault on Narvik, for which much less naval support was now available, was fixed for the 27th–28th of May. The

---

[1] See Map 18 (*p. 181*).

NARVIK CAPTURED. EVACUATION ORDERED

hazardous nature of the enterprise was well demonstrated by the arrival of the enemy's bombers at about 4 a.m. on the 28th, while our fighter airfield was fogbound and no air opposition could be offered to them. Fortunately the troops had mostly been disembarked and only the A.A. cruiser *Cairo*, in which the naval and military commanders and their staffs were all embarked, was hit. By 10 p.m. that evening the town was in Allied hands and the advance was pressing eastward along the railway. Demolition work was at once carried out on the already damaged ore quays, the electric power supply and the railway. The Cabinet's final, and strictly limited, objective was thus accomplished.

It remains only to recount the story of the evacuation of the 24,500 Allied troops still present in the Narvik theatre. For the outward passages the North Sea had repeatedly been crossed and recrossed by highly vulnerable convoys, for which only light escorts could generally be provided. Yet there had been no reaction by the enemy's surface ships and little by his submarines; no troopships or storeships had been lost or damaged on the way to and from Vestfiord and only one on the way to central Norway. Control of the open sea appeared, therefore, to have been effectively secured, but, on the 30th May, Admiral Forbes asked the Admiralty to keep him informed, particularly about the sailing of the groups of troopships. Next day Lord Cork told him that he would appreciate the provision of covering forces from the Home Fleet. On the 2nd of June the aircraft carriers *Ark Royal* and *Glorious*, sent to provide fighter protection during the evacuation and later ordered to embark the shore-based R.A.F. fighters, arrived off the coast again; fifteen troop transports followed shortly afterwards. Lord Cork expected to have only two cruisers, the *Southampton* and *Vindictive*, one A.A. cruiser, the *Coventry*, and ten destroyers—very exiguous forces with which to safeguard the removal of so many men and so much valuable equipment. The storeships were sent to the base at Harstad to load, and sailed in a slow convoy on the 7th of June, having taken on board much more equipment than General Auchinleck had originally believed possible. Admiral Vivian in the *Coventry* was in charge of the embarkation arrangements and shepherded in the troopships. The men were ferried off to them chiefly by night, in every type of flotilla vessel and small craft, from numerous embarkation points in the fiords, while naval aircraft from the carriers and R.A.F. fighters kept watch overhead.

On the 4th, 5th and 6th of June 15,000 men sailed in six large troopships and the *Vindictive* to one of the two rendezvous appointed by Lord Cork about 180 miles to seaward.[1] Thence they were to sail

---

[1] See Map 20 (*facing p. 195*).

O

for home as an organised group covered and escorted by the *Vindictive* and by destroyers sent out for that purpose by Admiral Forbes. On the 7th and 8th 10,000 more men were embarked in seven more troopships and by the morning of the latter day the embarkation was finished. The first group was met by the *Valiant* and Home Fleet destroyers at 1 a.m. on the 8th and had an uneventful passage to the Clyde. On the following morning the second group left its rendezvous escorted by the *Southampton*, in which Lord Cork was flying his flag, the *Coventry* and his five remaining destroyers. The *Ark Royal* and the three destroyers of her screen joined this convoy and they too reached home waters without incident.

But an operation (called 'Juno'), which the Germans had planned about the middle of May with the object of diverting our warships from the inshore shipping routes and of threatening our ill-defended bases in the Vestfiord area, now exerted its influence. The sortie was originally timed for the 25th of May to relieve the pressure on the enemy's own forces at Narvik by attacking our ships and shore installations. It was a bold plan and, in view of the great reduction in Lord Cork's naval strength which had taken place at that time, might well have succeeded in causing us serious losses. The *Scharnhorst*, *Gneisenau*, *Hipper* and four destroyers were to carry out the operation under Admiral Marschall's orders. They actually left Kiel on the morning of the 4th of June with the intention of striking at Harstad on the night of the 8th–9th.[1] It is quite plain that the enemy had no prior knowledge of the evacuation, nor of the exceptional convoy movements then in progress across the northern part of the North Sea; but, on the 7th, air reports of two groups of ships were passed to Admiral Marschall, who thereupon decided to attack the southernmost of those groups. This led to the sinking, on the morning of the 8th, of the tanker *Oil Pioneer*, her escorting trawler, the *Juniper*, and of the troopship *Orama*, which was returning to England empty and independently. The immunity of the hospital ship *Atlantis*, which was with the *Orama*, was, however, respected. But this was small fry to engage the attention of the most powerful ships of the German Navy, and Group Command West now ordered Admiral Marschall to leave attacks on the convoys to the *Hipper* and destroyers, and to fulfil his proper objective of attacking our naval forces and shipping around Harstad. The Admiral, however, who had guessed, correctly, that evacuation was in progress did not carry out these orders. The *Hipper* and destroyers were detached to Trondheim on the 9th, because they could not be fuelled again at sea, and he himself continued with the two battle cruisers to search for other quarry in the open sea. By ill luck they encountered that

---

[1] See Map 20 (*facing p. 195*).

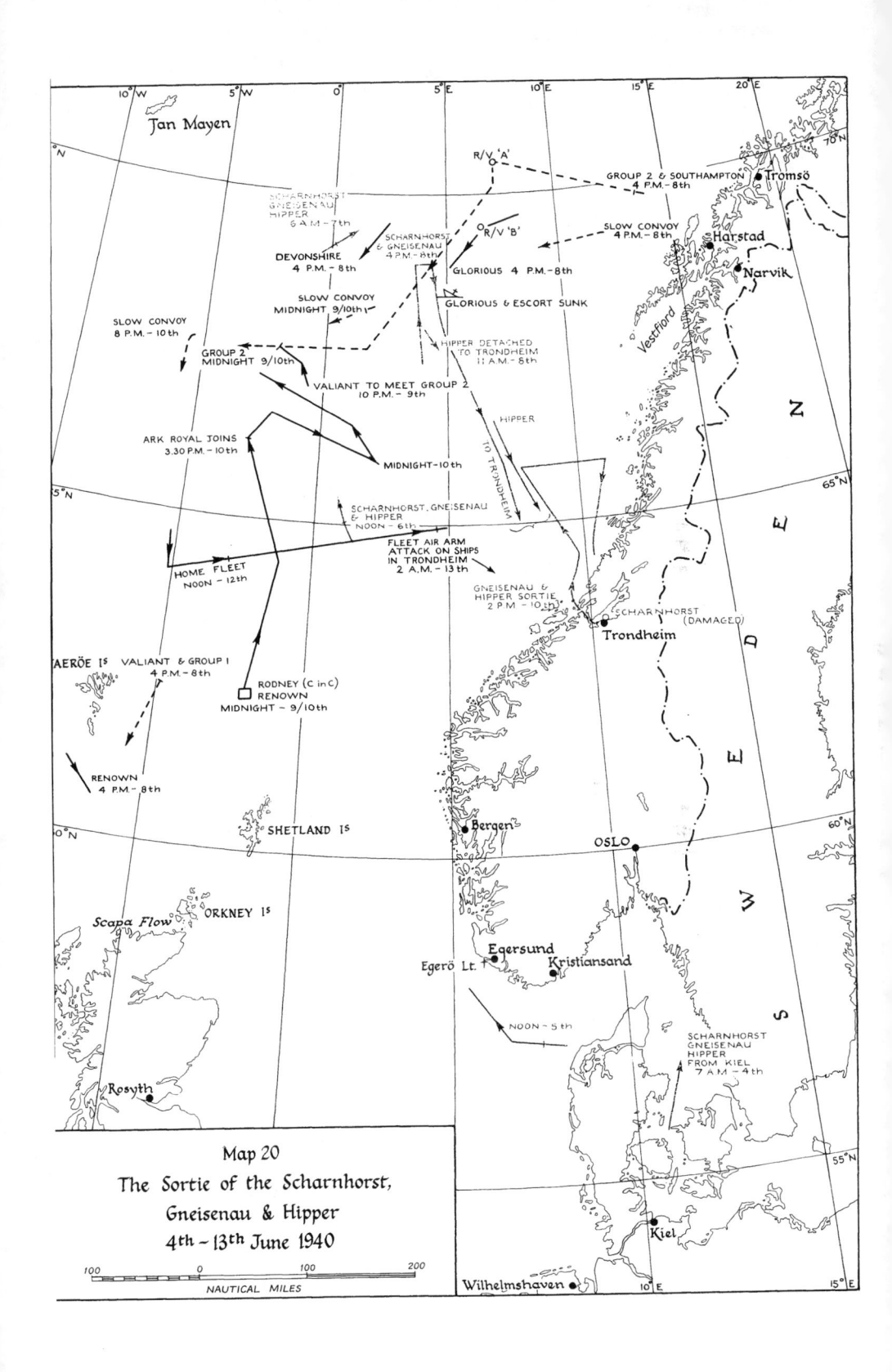

Map 20
The Sortie of the Scharnhorst,
Gneisenau & Hipper
4th - 13th June 1940

afternoon the *Glorious*, escorted only by her two attendant destroyers the *Acasta* (Commander C. E. Glasfurd) and the *Ardent* (Lieutenant-Commander J. F. Barker). She had, in the small hours of the previous morning, successfully completed the difficult task of flying on the last of the shore-based Royal Air Force Hurricanes and Gladiators—none of whose pilots had ever before made a deck landing—and had been ordered to proceed home independently because she was short of fuel. It is reasonable to suppose that such an unusual operation may have disorganised the normal arrangements in the aircraft carrier; but she had on board sufficient Swordfish aircraft wherewith to maintain reconnaissance flights and to form a small striking force should the need arise. While the truth regarding her condition is unlikely ever to be known, it seems strange that no patrols were flown at this time for her own protection, nor a striking force kept prepared. What is certain is that she was caught not only unawares but virtually defenceless when, at 4 p.m., the German battle cruisers sighted her smoke. The *Scharnhorst* opened fire half an hour later at a range of some 28,000 yards, at which the carrier's light armament was useless. The German gunnery was, as usual in the early stages of an action, accurate, and heavy shells soon caused damage to the hangars. This frustrated the strenuous but vain efforts being made to get the torpedo-bombers armed and away. The destroyers, in accordance with the heroic tradition of their class, made for their giant adversaries at high speed and laid a smoke screen which, for a time, shielded the *Glorious* from the plunging fire of the heavy shells. But it only postponed the inevitable, for at about 5.20 the *Glorious*, stopped and on fire, had given the order to abandon ship and, eight minutes later, the *Ardent*, having fired all her torpedoes, was overwhelmed by gunfire and sunk. At about 5.40 the aircraft carrier turned over to starboard and sank, leaving only the *Acasta* to carry on the hopeless fight. She steered again at the enemy with her guns blazing and fired a salvo of torpedoes, one of which hit the *Scharnhorst* abreast her after turret and damaged her severely. At eight minutes past six, the *Acasta* too was overwhelmed.

The loss of one of our few aircraft carriers was serious enough; but the loss of nearly all her ship's company, including the naval pilots and observers who, so recently, had fought with brilliant dash and determination over the mountains of Norway, and of nearly all the Royal Air Force crews who, because of their country's crying need for fighter aircraft, had, although ordered to destroy their aircraft, chosen instead to fly them on to the carrier's deck, was tragic in the extreme. The enemy made no attempt at rescue operations. On the 11th of June, two and a half days after the action, three officers and thirty-five men of the *Glorious*' company and one man from the *Acasta* were picked up by a small Norwegian fishing vessel and landed in the Faeröes. Another rescued five men from the *Glorious*, who with two from the *Ardent* picked up by a German seaplane were made prisoners-of-war. All the rest of that fine ship's company were lost. Something has already been said regarding the work of the Navy's airmen in the Norwegian campaign. It will always stand as a splendid chapter in the long naval tradition of sacrifice and gallantry. As Captain Troubridge of the *Furious* said in his report on their operations, 'their honour and courage remained throughout as dazzling as the snow-covered mountains over which they so triumphantly flew'.

The unswerving constancy of purpose of the young men who bore the brunt of the sea and air fighting during these unhappy weeks shines in strong contrast to the indecision and mismanagement at home which marred the whole campaign. The young Naval Air Service, so recently evolved and so few in numbers, showed not only its ability to carry the centuries of fighting tradition into the new element, but also its power to strike sudden and deadly blows at long range and to perform at call functions for which its men had never been trained. And their comrades of the Royal Air Force showed the qualities which, a few weeks later, saved their country and made the free world ring with their fame.

Of its small ships the Navy has always expected—and as regularly received—service given regardless of the sacrifice involved, but the example of the destroyers, sloops and trawlers in the Norwegian campaign has never been excelled. The names of Warburton-Lee of the *Hardy*, Roope of the *Glowworm*, Glasfurd and Barker of the *Acasta* and *Ardent*—all lost in unhesitatingly attacking heavy, even hopeless, odds—should be remembered for ever in the Navy's long story of unquestioning devotion to duty.

The last fight of the *Acasta* and *Ardent*, and the torpedo hit on the *Scharnhorst* obtained by the former while almost in her death throes, probably saved Lord Cork's lightly escorted convoy, which was coming down from the north and was routed through the same area; for the German battle cruisers abandoned the operation and returned to Trondheim, where they arrived on the afternoon of the 9th.

But the news of this desperate fighting was slow in reaching Admiral Forbes, because the *Glorious*' wireless had been wrecked early in the action and no intelligible enemy reports were received by him from the stricken ship. The hospital ship *Atlantis* gave the first news of the enemy's presence when she met the *Valiant* on the morning of the 9th, twenty-four hours after the sinking of the *Orama*. The battleship was hastening back from escorting the first group of troopships to join the second, now some 400 miles to the north of her, and she at once broadcast the news passed to her by the *Atlantis*. This broadcast produced a signal from Admiral Cunningham in the

Devonshire who, with the King of Norway on board, had left Tromsö on the evening of the 7th. For he, and he only, had picked up a cryptic whisper from the *Glorious* referring to an earlier message and reporting the presence of two pocket-battleships. Admiral Cunningham had, very naturally, refused to break wireless silence to pass this garbled message and thus reveal the position of his ship while on so important a mission. He was, in fact, only about 100 miles to the west of the *Glorious* when she was attacked, so Lord Cork's convoy was not alone in narrowly escaping disaster. Not until the Germans broadcast their claims on the afternoon of the 9th was the probable truth revealed to Admiral Forbes, who then left Scapa in the *Rodney* with the *Renown* and six destroyers and ordered other redispositions to protect the returning convoys.

It is natural that the reader should ask why, with such a large movement of troopships and storeships taking place, the whole Home Fleet was not already at sea to cover their progress, or at least a powerful proportion of its strength so disposed. Admiral Forbes had originally intended to send the *Repulse* and *Renown* to escort the Narvik troopships, but his intention had been changed by a message sent by one of our 'Q ships', which reached him on the 5th of June, reporting two unknown ships, possibly raiders, north-east of the Faeröes and perhaps making for Iceland, the safety of which was then seriously exercising the Admiralty.[1] In fact we now know that the 'Q ship' could not have sighted the German battle cruisers, but her report, combined with Admiral Forbes' constant anxiety regarding the defenceless state of the Northern Patrol cruisers, had important consequences. Admiral Whitworth with the *Repulse* and *Renown*, two cruisers and five destroyers was sent to intercept the possible raiders, to investigate a report of a landing in Iceland and to protect the Northern Patrol. The *Valiant* alone was ordered to join the troop convoys.

The detachments already mentioned, together with the heavy calls for destroyers to take part in the evacuation from Dunkirk, had reduced the Home Fleet to a total strength of four capital ships, two cruisers and thirteen destroyers, and the fact that the destroyer shortage would curtail his operations had been pointed out to the Admiralty by Admiral Forbes on the 3rd of June. Yet it is arguable that a stronger covering force could still have been provided, and the wisdom of deflecting the battle cruisers far to the west while the troop convoys to the east were so lightly defended must remain in doubt.

Though previous experience had shown all too plainly that reliance could not be placed on the North Sea air reconnaissance patrols to sight and report enemy warships breaking out to the north,

---

[1] See pp. 136–137 regarding operations by 'Q ships'.

these operations certainly underlined the weakness of our intelligence. As Admiral Forbes pointed out to the Admiralty on the 15th of June, 'the quite unexpected appearance of enemy forces ... in the far north on 8th June which led to the sinking of the *Glorious*, two destroyers and a liner ... shows that it is absolutely essential that our scheme of air reconnaissance should be overhauled. ... The enemy reconnoitre Scapa daily if they consider it necessary. Our reconnaissances of the enemy's main bases are few and far between. ... It is most galling that the enemy should know just where our ships ... always are, whereas we generally learn where his major forces are when they sink one or more of our ships.' But these weaknesses had been evident since the early days of the war, and knowledge of their existence might have seemed to render it more than ever advisable to provide strong forces to cover a great movement of defenceless troopships and store carriers against surprise attack. Moreover, whatever may have been the deficiencies in the North Sea air patrols, the safety of the returning ships and convoys could have been improved had air escorts been requested, or a special air search made of the waters through which they would pass. In fact the secrecy maintained with regard to the whole evacuation was so extreme that Coastal Command was never officially informed of the Government's intention. Though the Air Officer Commanding-in-Chief had been told unofficially, the command staff remained entirely in the dark. Whether a full measure of air co-operation would have saved the lost ships is now wholly speculative, but that it should have been requested and that, if requested, it would have been provided to the limit of the Command's resources is certain. Not for the first time does excessive secrecy appear to have hampered efficiency.

After these tragic events the *Repulse*, *Newcastle* and *Sussex* joined Admiral Vivian, who was escorting Group II of the troopships and the slow convoy of storeships from Harstad, on the 10th. Apart from air attacks on the *Valiant* and *Ark Royal* the rest of the passage to home bases was uneventful.

It is appropriate that the final blows in the campaign should have been struck by naval aircraft and by one of our submarines, both of which branches of the sea service had borne a heavy share of the fighting, and had suffered grievous losses. Early on the 13th of June fifteen Skuas from the *Ark Royal* attacked the enemy warships in Trondheim and hit the *Scharnhorst* with a 500-pound bomb which, unfortunately, failed to explode. Strong fighter opposition was encountered and eight of the attacking aircraft were lost. A week later the *Gneisenau* and *Hipper* sailed from Trondheim and set course in the direction of Iceland to divert attention from the damaged *Scharnhorst*, which was then attempting to reach her home base. During the night of the 20th of June the submarine *Clyde* attacked the *Gneisenau* and scored one torpedo hit which put her out of action for nearly six months. The enemy force thereupon returned to Trondheim, whence it ultimately reached its home base without receiving further damage. The Admiralty, however, who still knew nothing about the *Acasta's* torpedo hit on the *Scharnhorst* on the 9th of June, believed that she had been the *Clyde's* victim and that the *Gneisenau* was therefore still undamaged. Not until the latter ship docked in Germany in July was the fact that both battle cruisers had received serious damage surmised in London.

So ended a campaign which had been opened with high hopes in London, though with more realistic expectations in the fleet. It was marked throughout by failure and defeat on land and by heavy losses on the sea and in the air—losses which we could ill afford in view of the new commitments which were already arising. Though it would have been unthinkable to leave a new ally to her fate, the efforts made to save her were not, in general, happily conceived.

As regards the lessons learnt in Norway it must always be remembered that, because of our own lack of preparedness and the enemy's possession of the initiative, the Cabinet, the Service Departments and the Commanders of all our forces were at this time compelled to fight as best they could with what they had. Yet when every allowance has been made for these factors there remained certain lessons which could not be denied. The first concerned the effect of air power on the control of the sea. It could no longer be doubted that, if effective air cover was lacking, warships could not operate protractedly and the Army could not be maintained overseas. Secondly, there was the old lesson that if a secure base cannot be established in an overseas theatre of war the land campaign cannot prosper. Thirdly the need for the most careful planning and preparation before launching a combined operation was abundantly clear, as was the need to equip and train men of all services for such a purpose in time of peace. But perhaps the most fundamental lesson related to the command organisation which must be set up to plan and execute amphibious expeditions. If the command organisation is clear beyond doubt to all concerned and if every link in the chain of command is well and truly forged, and assembled in correct sequence, then great risks can be taken in the planning of the expedition and in the conduct of the operations. In Norway the acceptance of great risks was inevitable but, in the north, the divided command organisation reduced the possibility that they would be successfully accepted. The development of our inter-service command organisation to its final form in which Naval, Air and Army Commands, with closely integrated staffs, worked under the Supreme Commander of an overseas expedition will be told in other volumes of this series. Here it is only necessary to consider the consequences of a divided naval command.

Whereas in central Norway the conduct of maritime operations was in the hands of the Commander-in-Chief, Home Fleet, the Narvik campaign was placed in a different category from the start by the appointment of Admiral of the Fleet Lord Cork and Orrery—'an officer of the highest attainments and distinction',[1] but senior to Admiral Forbes and to the First Sea Lord himself—as Flag Officer, Narvik, and, finally, in supreme command of the campaign in that area. It was not the fact of his seniority nearly as much as the division of responsibility which produced difficulties. Lord Cork's command extended to 100 miles from Vaags Fiord, but he was always mainly dependent on Admiral Forbes for the provision of the necessary naval forces and support. Just as Admiral Forbes could not from day to day, even hour to hour, compute the needs of the Narvik area and assess their importance in relation to his numerous other commitments, so was it difficult for Lord Cork to know exactly what the Home Fleet could do or was actually doing for his assistance. In the final evacuation the returning ships and convoys narrowly escaped disaster on a large scale. It seems wrong to attribute this to Admiral Marschall's failure to carry out his orders, though the German Naval Staff criticised his action in attacking the southern shipping and ascribed the interception of the *Glorious* to 'an extraordinary stroke of luck'. Had he attacked Harstad as planned on the night of the 8th–9th of June he would, in fact, have found it empty, though a few days earlier a mass of shipping would have been at his mercy there. The German Naval Staff's criticism of a Commander-in-Chief who exercised his undoubted right to alter his intentions as the situation demanded appears therefore unjustifiable. None the less had better intelligence—or mere chance—guided Admiral Marschall's ships to the rendezvous or the routes of the main convoys, Lord Cork could have done little to avert disaster, for the heavy ships of the Home Fleet were then all far away to the west. Happily we were saved from this ultimate consequence of a divided command. But the escape was a narrow one.

In the planning and execution of the invasion of Denmark and Norway the German armed forces achieved a high degree of integration and co-ordination. It is interesting to remark that in this matter, so vital to success in combined operations, the German record thereafter deteriorated steadily. On the other hand the serious defects in our own planning and organisation revealed by the Nor-

---

[1] W. S. Churchill. *The Second World War*, Vol. I (2nd Edition), p. 415.

wegian campaign were gradually eliminated as experience was gained.

Taking the campaign as a whole, the enemy accomplished the safeguarding of his iron ore supplies, tightened his control of the short sea passages across the Baltic and obtained possession of very valuable and well-sited bases from which submarines, surface vessels and aircraft could be sent out on to our trade routes, and from which he could also intensify his operations against our coastal shipping. But his fleet had been severely handled and ended the campaign with no major warship fit for sea. This was to have important, even vital, results during Hitler's campaign in the west. Lastly, the prosecution of these arduous maritime operations had shown that, ship for ship, the new German Navy was no more a match for its British counterpart than its predecessor had been during the First World War. That Admiral Forbes' fleet had confirmed our ancient ascendancy at sea must always stand as one of the decisive accomplishments of the period.

It will be plain to the reader of this brief account of the maritime operations carried out as part of the Norwegian campaign that the Admiralty frequently intervened directly in the operations of the Home Fleet. The diversion of the destroyers of 'Force WV' from the entrance to Vestfiord, the orders sent directly to Captain Warburton-Lee on his passage up the fiord to Narvik and the cancellation of Admiral Forbes' intended attack on Bergen are but three examples of a policy which was, in fact, constantly applied. In view of the difficulties and uncertainties which this produced it will be appropriate to consider more fully a matter which was briefly touched on earlier, namely the relations between the Board of Admiralty and the various Naval Commanders-in-Chief.[1]

In theory the Admiralty, whilst having the right to issue orders directly to any ship or squadron, limits its instructions to the strategic movements and disposition of our forces, to supplying to the Commanders-in-Chief and Flag Officers the plans which the Board requires to be executed and the necessary intelligence regarding the enemy's intentions. The tactical conduct of operations is left to the Flag Officers concerned. In practice, however, conditions of modern warfare render difficult the constant and uniform adherence to these principles. Commanders-in-Chief have always been sensitive on this matter of Admiralty intervention, and it is natural that this should be so, for a fleet cannot serve two masters whose orders may at any time conflict. Moreover the immediate responsibility for the conduct of operations does not, except in particular cases, rest with the Admiralty.

---

[1] See pp. 26–27.

The personal views of the First Sea Lord on this question have been quoted, and it will be remembered that Admiral Forbes represented, in his reply, that even the limited degree of intervention proposed by Admiral Pound went too far.[1] No attempt was, however, made, then or later, by the First Sea Lord to reconcile his proposals with the views expressed by the Commander-in-Chief, but in November 1939 Admiral Pound reiterated, in a letter to another Flag Officer, his determination that Commanders-in-Chief should normally be left free to conduct their own operations without constant intervention from Whitehall.

The reader will therefore ask why it was that, throughout the campaign described in this chapter, the Admiralty's actions ran contrary to the First Sea Lord's expressed intentions. There can be no doubt that the powerful personality of the First Lord was a large factor in bringing this about. Mr. Churchill used, during critical periods of naval operations, to spend long hours in the Admiralty Operational Intelligence Centre and the tendency for him to assume direct control therefrom is easily to be understood. Many of the signals sent during such periods bear the unmistakable imprint of his language and personality and, admirable though their purpose and intention were, it now appears plain that they sometimes confused the conduct of operations and increased the difficulties of the Commander-in-Chief. Mr Churchill makes an interesting comment on this question. Dealing with the cancellation by the Admiralty of the intended attack on Bergen he says: 'Looking back on this affair I consider that the Admiralty kept too close a control upon the Commander-in-Chief, and, after learning his original intention to force the passage into Bergen, we should have confined ourselves to sending him information.'[2] It may, however, be considered that this comment does not go deep enough, since not only was the action taken by the Admiralty in respect of the Bergen attack by no means an isolated example of intervention from Whitehall at this period, but it fails to expose the inevitably difficult position in which a Naval Commander-in-Chief is placed if his plans and intentions are at any time to be altered or cancelled by his superiors ashore. The whole question is one which must be approached with caution. To suggest that the Admiralty should never intervene in the conduct of operations would, at any rate while the policy of collecting and disseminating all operational intelligence in London is maintained, go much too far in the opposite direction. That the centralised naval intelligence system has immense and proven merits is beyond dispute, but the price of this is an increased tendency to intervene in operations,

---

[1] See p. 27.
[2] W. S. Churchill. *The Second World War*, Vol. I (2nd Edition), pp. 536–537.

since, if the intelligence organisation is working in the designed manner, it is bound to be the best-informed agency and, if that is the case, then the right to make the best use of its information must be conceded. The truth appears, as is generally the case on such issues, to lie in the question of degree rather than of principle. Provided that the practice of passing information rather than orders is normally adhered to, and provided that due weight is always given in London to the infinite variability of the many factors such as the weather, the visibility and the remaining fuel endurance of the fleet—factors which still to-day, and in spite of all scientific advances, greatly condition the conduct of operations of war at sea—then the desirability of making a direct intervention when the need has plainly arisen will hardly be disputed.

CHAPTER XI

THE CONTROL OF THE NARROW SEAS
10th May–4th June, 1940

> It may be said to England, Martha, Martha thou art busy about many things, but one thing is necessary. To the question what shall we do to be saved in this world there is no answer but this, Look to your moat.
>
> Marquis of Halifax. *A Rough Draft of a New Model at Sea.* 1694.

IT was told in the last chapter how the opening of Hitler's campaign in the west in the early hours of the 10th of May caused the British War Cabinet to decide on the final evacuation of Norway. The state of unpreparedness of the invaded countries had reduced the possibility of their resistance being prolonged. It was, however, hoped and believed that the rapid advance of the British and French armies into Belgium would forestall the enemy's major blows, which were expected to be directed through Belgium towards the Channel ports. But whatever might be the outcome of the land campaign—and there was still a good deal of unrealistic thinking and under-estimation of the enemy's power and purpose in Paris and, to a lesser extent, in London—it was plain to the Cabinet that our naval and air strength were quite inadequate to support a costly overseas campaign in Norway when control of our own coastal waters might at any moment be seriously threatened. Even before our commitments in Norway had been finally liquidated, reinforcements were, therefore, sent to the Commander-in-Chief, the Nore, chiefly at the expense of the Home Fleet. Furthermore, the demolition of dock and harbour facilities in the ports of the Low Countries, the blocking of certain of those ports and the evacuation of all shipping therefrom—the planning of which had been completed as early as October 1939—would demand additional naval forces in the south. Accordingly on the 8th of May the Nore Command (Admiral Sir Reginald Plunkett-Ernle-Erle-Drax) was reinforced by the *Galatea* and *Arethusa* of the 2nd Cruiser Squadron, while the *Birmingham* and four destroyers of the 2nd and four of the 5th Flotilla were all ordered to Harwich.

The opening of the enemy's land campaign in the west differed in one important, even fundamental, respect from his invasion of Denmark and Norway. Though he still held the initiative and was thus able to strike when and where he chose, no degree of strategical surprise was this time achieved. In fact this very move had been one of the subjects most frequently considered by the War Cabinet ever since the beginning of the war. As far as the naval and air forces operating to control the narrow seas were concerned, the brief campaign in the Low Countries differed both from the Norwegian campaign which preceded it and from the invasion of France which followed. To Norway the Allies sent considerable military forces to dispute the enemy's overland advance; in France we were deeply committed to land operations by the presence of the British Expeditionary Force. But to Belgium no military forces were conveyed directly by sea and to Holland only an insignificant force. The commands concerned with the maritime aspects of the campaigns in these countries were, therefore, generally free from the anxiety and responsibility of ensuring the safe passage of troop and store convoys for the Army under the threat of attacks by enemy air, submarine and surface forces. They had two objectives: the first, a positive one, was to ensure the timely withdrawal of shipping, the removal of gold reserves and other valuables and the evacuation of important personages; the second was the negative purpose of preventing the enemy from capturing intact those war supplies, chiefly oil, which could not be removed and from gaining early use of the docks and harbours of which he would soon be possessed. The enemy's reaction to these plans was expected to include magnetic mining of the approaches to the ports, and LL. sweepers were therefore sent to keep the channels clear. Vigorous action by the enemy's surface vessels was not expected, because the heavy losses and damage inflicted by the Home Fleet during the Norwegian campaign were known to have left Admiral Raeder with few ships fit for service.

In Holland the enemy's initial onslaught was launched from the air against the chief cities and centres of communications. Although the Dutch army resisted these spearheads valiantly and with some initial success, the enemy's ground forces, covered by overwhelming air superiority, could not be stemmed. On the 15th of May Dutch resistance was broken and the enemy reached the outskirts of Rotterdam, where continued resistance led to savage dive-bombing of the defenceless city next day. On the 13th the Dutch army surrendered. Meanwhile the Franco-British armies had advanced into Belgium but, by the day of the Dutch surrender, it had become clear that the enemy's main offensive was directed near the hinge of the Allied swing into Belgium, between Sedan and Dinant on the Meuse. The collapse of the French 9th Army had left a wide breach through which poured the German armoured and motorised divisions to outflank completely all the Allied forces to the north. Then began the general retreat which was, for the British Expeditionary Force, to end on the beaches of Dunkirk. But before the story of that epic is told we must revert to the Dutch and Belgian coastal operations.

The Admiralty's plans for meeting the expected attack on the Low Countries were based on the assumption that Dutch resistance could not last for long. They decided, however, that a minefield should be laid off the coast to the north of Ijmuiden, to hamper coastal operations by enemy surface vessels, and that demolition parties should be sent to Ijmuiden, the Hook of Holland and Flushing to ensure that the enemy did not capture those valuable ports intact.[1] A similar party was organised to deal with Antwerp, but naval operations off the Belgian coast were made the responsibility of the French 'Amiral Nord' (Vice-Admiral Abrial) whose headquarters were at Dunkirk. Since, however, Admiral Abrial had no anti-aircraft ships, four British destroyers which had been converted to that function were lent to him.

In the British command organisation almost all the Dutch coast had, before the war, been made the responsibility of the Commander-in-Chief, the Nore, but the Flag Officer, Dover (Admiral Ramsay), was in charge of operations off the Belgian coast.[2] At the start of the campaign Admiral Drax was given command of all British ships working off the coasts of both the Low Countries, but demolition work in the ports was soon placed under Admiral Ramsay, while Admiral Drax remained responsible for blocking the Belgian ports and for all minelaying. This arrangement made it certain that each command would be conducting operations within the geographical command area of the other. Thanks, however, to the short distances involved, to the close proximity of the two headquarters concerned and to the intimate collaboration of the two staffs no untoward incidents occurred. Each command did everything within its power to meet the needs of the other, while Admiral Forbes in the Home Fleet and the Commanders-in-Chief, Rosyth, Portsmouth and Western Approaches all watched closely the progress of the fighting at the eastern end of the Channel and came to the assistance of the Nore and Dover commands as soon as any requirement was foreseen or formulated. Though the command arrangements worked smoothly it may be doubted whether the divisions of responsibility mentioned above were really necessary. But the rapid movement of forces from one command to another during this period provides an excellent example of flexibility in the exercise of maritime power. For instance, at 7.30 a.m. on the 10th of May the destroyer-leader *Codrington*, then in Scapa Flow, was ordered to raise steam, and at

---
[1] See Map 3 (*facing p. 63*).
[2] See Map 1 (*facing p. 37*).

8 a.m. the next day she was secured to an oiler in Dover Harbour, having steamed 530 miles in twenty-three hours; on the 12th Admiral Drax asked the Admiralty if cruiser reinforcements could be sent to him should enemy cruisers move towards the Dutch coast and, within an hour, Admiral Forbes, without waiting for the Admiralty's reaction, had placed the *Manchester*, **Sheffield** and *York,* which were then lying at Rosyth, at his disposal.

The demolitions at the four principal ports were, therefore, planned at Dover by Admiral Ramsay, and his orders were issued on the 7th of May. One destroyer was to take each demolition party to its destination, while military parties were also embarked for Ijmuiden, the Hook and Antwerp to ensure that the very large oil stocks in or near those ports were destroyed. The blocking of Ostend and Zeebrugge, the importance of which lay in the fact that they were the terminal points of canal systems running into the heart of industrial Germany, had already been planned in the Admiralty, and the orders had been issued early in October 1939.

On the day that the enemy's campaign opened, four destroyers left Dover with the demolition parties, the *Princess Victoria* and the 20th (minelaying) Flotilla sailed to lay the defensive minefield off the Dutch coast, Admiral Edward-Collins' cruisers (the 2nd Cruiser Squadron) went to Ijmuiden to bring back the Dutch gold reserves and to clear the port of merchant shipping, the blockships were brought to short notice and reinforcements of flotilla vessels were ordered to the Nore command and Dover by the Admiralty. Next day, the 11th, the *Arethusa* and two destroyers escorted back two merchantmen carrying the Dutch bullion and, on the 12th, the *Codrington* embarked the Crown Princess and her family at Ijmuiden and brought them to England. The demolition and blocking of that port were put in train on the 14th and, thanks in no small measure to the co-operation of the Dutch Fortress Commandant, were successfully completed.

The military party which had been sent to Amsterdam to destroy the large oil reserves at first encountered difficulties from the Dutch but, finally, fired all the stock. It was by no means only at Amsterdam that our parties had difficulties with the local authorities. It is indeed natural that the owners of valuable property should resent the desire of foreigners, even though allies in war and acting under the imminent pressure of a common enemy, to destroy their property. In the Low Countries such resentment certainly prevented the demolitions at Flushing, the Hook and Antwerp being completed; and in some French ports similar difficulties were encountered later.

The party sent to the Hook included a military section ordered to destroy the oil stocks at Rotterdam, but their purpose was obstructed at the first attempt even though a considerable part of the city was already in enemy hands. Not until the afternoon of the 13th were the tanks set on fire.

To secure the safety of our demolition parties a Royal Marine guard was hastily sent across in two destroyers on the night of the 11th–12th, and was followed by a composite battalion of Irish and Welsh Guards the next night. The destroyer-leader *Malcolm* (Captain T. E. Halsey, commanding the 16th Destroyer Flotilla) arrived at the Hook early on the 13th and took charge of the evacuations which were now in train. At noon Queen Wilhelmina arrived on the jetty and was taken on board the destroyer *Hereward*, which carried her and her suite to Harwich. That evening the Dutch Government and Allied legation staffs embarked for England in the destroyer *Windsor*. Next day it was clear that Dutch resistance was ending, so the Cabinet ordered the Guards and Marines to be brought back. The six destroyers sent from Dover to transport and protect the troops were to be joined by two more off the Hook, and on the afternoon of the 14th, after being delayed by fog, the evacuation was successfully accomplished. Even at this eleventh hour the Dutch obstructed the demolition work; it was therefore never carried out, nor was the harbour blocked. The last ships left at 8 p.m. just before the Germans entered the town. Offers to embark Dutch troops were refused and a plan to lift some of their army with destroyers from the Hook, Ijmuiden, Scheveningen and Texel was abandoned.

At Flushing better success attended the naval demolition party and sixteen merchantmen were cleared for England on the 11th, on which day French troops arrived by transport and also crossed the Scheldt by ferry. But enemy air pressure, by bombing and magnetic mining, was severe, our destroyers were continuously in action and damage began to mount. On the 12th some air cover was afforded by Blenheims and Hurricanes sent over from England, but the former were too slow to intercept the enemy dive-bombers and the latter's short endurance limited their patrols to periods of about half an hour.

On the 14th we received news of the impending surrender of the Dutch, but they expressed the intention to continue resistance on the island of Walcheren, aided by the French troops. Next day bombing was heavier, the destroyer *Winchester* was damaged and the *Valentine* was lost while endeavouring to protect one of the Scheldt ferries. On the 16th the enemy's steady advance forced back the French troops, and the passage of the retreating Allied soldiers through Flushing hampered the work of the demolition parties. Some damage was done, but German reports show that the harbour was again open to shipping by the 5th of June. Finally, on the evening of the 17th, three days after all the other Dutch ports had been evacuated, the British party crossed the Scheldt and continued to Dunkirk by road.

The demolition and blocking operations described in the preceding paragraphs were carried out under Admiral Ramsay's general direction, but Admiral Drax, from his headquarters at Chatham, was meanwhile directing the concurrent offshore operations. In fact, the offshore and inshore ships constantly interchanged duties and, in assisting each other, really acted as one force. Captain G. E. Creasy, commanding the 1st Destroyer Flotilla, was generally in charge of the offshore patrols in the *Codrington* and had under his orders a very mixed flotilla of from six to eight destroyers.

These eight days had imposed a heavy strain on the destroyers and minesweepers from Dover and the Nore. They had worked in mine-infested waters under almost continuous air attacks. Yet they had performed all the multifarious duties which commonly fall to ships of that class. Indeed, there seemed to be no limit to the variety of their tasks—embarking, transporting and disembarking troops, evacuating Allied Royalties, missions and legations, bombarding aerodromes and beaches, towing, screening, escorting, repelling air attacks and attacking submarine contacts. Yet nearly all the ships concerned were veterans of the V and W classes built for the 1914–18 war. Losses were not severe as long as the ships had enough sea-room to manœuvre but, in the cramped conditions of the ports and the narrow approaches thereto, their self-defence was severely handicapped. So far only the *Valentine* had been lost, but the *Winchester* and *Westminster* had both been seriously damaged. Though the demolitions had not always been completed and only Ijmuiden was blocked, nearly all shipping had been got away, the Royal Family and the Government had been brought to England to carry on the fight, and most of the gold reserve and stocks of diamonds had been removed. The Dutch Navy was mostly stationed in the East Indies, but the cruiser *Jacob van Heemskerck*, one destroyer and seven submarines, two of which were new and incomplete, left Dutch bases soon after the invasion had started and all reached British ports safely. Nevertheless the British flotillas could hardly be allowed a day of rest or recuperation, since the campaign now moved swiftly to the west.

The demolition party for Antwerp had sailed from Dover with those organised for the Dutch ports and reached its destination in the destroyer *Brilliant* on the evening of the 10th of May. Its most important duty was to get away the large amount of shipping present in the port. No less than twenty-six Allied ships and fifty tugs sailed on the 12th, and by noon on the 14th some 600 barges, dredgers and floating cranes had also left. On the evening of the 16th, in face of a plainly critical situation, demolition work was at last allowed to begin and, by the next afternoon, some 150,000 tons of oil had been made unusable and the entrances to the docks and basins blocked. But much that was desirable had to be left undone.

The operations off the Belgian coast were conducted by Admiral Abrial from Dunkirk, but six British destroyers worked at different times under his orders; of these the *Whitley* was sunk by bombing on the 19th. Large numbers of refugees were brought home from Ostend in Belgian, French and British transports and destroyers between the 15th and 18th while LL. trawlers kept the channels clear of mines, and suffered losses by air attacks while doing so. The demolitions at Zeebrugge were a responsibility of the French and they, too, met with opposition from the Belgian authorities. On the 25th the first attempt was made to block the port, for which purpose Captain G. A. Garnons-Williams had sailed from Sheerness in the destroyer *Vega* with two blockships for Zeebrugge and three for Ostend. The Admiralty, however, cancelled the blocking of Ostend shortly after the force had sailed, probably because it was expected that more evacuations would be made from that port. The force was heavily bombed while on passage, but suffered no serious damage. When, however, the ships entered Zeebrugge they came under fire from French soldiers who, apparently having no knowledge that we intended to block the port, somewhat hastily presumed that the ships were German. The first blockship got off her course and grounded, and the second scuttled herself ineffectively near the first. The operation having thus failed in its purpose the Admiralty at once decided to repeat it. On the 26th of May two of the blockships originally destined for Ostend, with the *Vega* again in command, sailed from Sheerness for Zeebrugge. While on passage the enemy attacked from the air and with E-boats (motor torpedo-boats) but caused no damage; this time the object was successfully accomplished. The Admiralty still desired to block Ostend, whence evacuations had now ended, and actually sailed three more blockships for that purpose on the 29th of May, but when the Air Ministry stated that air cover could not be provided the operation was cancelled. By this time the full efforts of the Navy and Air Force were concentrated on the rescue of the British Expeditionary Force from Dunkirk, and no forces could be spared to complete the obstruction of the Belgian ports.

While these events were in train off the Belgian coast the eyes of the British War Cabinet, the Service departments in London, the commanders of all our naval, military and air forces and, indeed, of the whole British people were becoming more and more focused on a small portion of French and Belgian soil inside which the British Expeditionary Force and part of the French northern armies were rapidly becoming constricted.[1] The progress of the land fighting which brought about this critical condition must therefore be briefly

---

[1] See L. F. Ellis. *History of the Second World War: The War in France and Flanders, 1939-1940* (H.M.S.O., 1953).

recounted before we turn again to the sea and to the tense drama of the rescue of virtually our entire fighting force.

Brief mention was made earlier of the main offensive launched by the enemy on the 13th of May against the French 9th Army, whose disintegration left a wide breach on the southern flank of the Allied left wing which had meanwhile advanced into Belgium. The enemy was quick to exploit the opportunity, the breach was rapidly widened and deepened and by the morning of the 17th it was clear that a serious situation had arisen in the south; for the German armour was now directing its thrust straight at the British base areas around Arras and the whole communications system on which our armies relied. On the 20th, by reaching Amiens and Abbeville, the enemy actually severed the main rail communications of our armies. By the 19th of May a crisis was plainly approaching, and the first suggestions of the possible need to withdraw the B.E.F. were received in London from Lord Gort's headquarters; a meeting was at once held in the Admiralty and it was decided that such an operation, though still considered unlikely, should be controlled by Admiral Ramsay from Dover.

On the 20th representatives from the War Office and Ministry of Shipping met Admiral Ramsay at Dover to come to grips with the many urgent problems which would certainly arise if a great evacuation had to be attempted. It was still expected that, if the need arose, we should be able to use several French ports; and the Navy at once stressed the importance of using all possible harbours rather than relying on lifting men from the beaches. Long experience had taught how hazardous the latter would be, how wholly dependent on wind and weather and how vulnerable to the enemy's counter measures, especially when few specially designed landing craft were available. Admiral Ramsay meanwhile took all possible advance steps to organise the necessary personnel ships—which undoubtedly could carry troops across the narrow seas fastest and in the greatest numbers—and small craft and boats for local transport and ferry duties. Such foresight was to be rapidly rewarded, since, after the 20th, the state of affairs in France grew still worse. The decision was taken this day to supply the armies, who needed some 2,000 tons of stores and ammunition daily, through a new base at Dunkirk. But the enemy now swung due north along the coastal roads towards Boulogne, which was soon isolated.[1] We will look briefly at the dramatic events of 22nd–24th May in that port and in the adjacent one of Calais.

On the 22nd of May, following the precedent established in the ports of the Low Countries, the Admiralty sent demolition parties to Boulogne, Calais and Dunkirk in the destroyers *Vimy*, *Venomous* and

---

[1] See Map 3 (*facing p. 63*).

Wild Swan, each of whom had already taken part in the arduous events of the preceding days. Early on the same day the 20th Guards Brigade (two battalions) was carried to Boulogne under the escort of the *Whitshed* and *Vimiera*. There they found a difficult state of affairs; for large numbers of miscellaneous troops, which had been employed on labour duties, had made their way to Boulogne in an unorganised state, and their discipline was not good. But the steadiness of the Guardsmen and the arrival of the naval parties soon restored a measure of order, and steps were taken to get the wounded and refugees on board the ships. But the enemy's tanks and artillery were very close and the Guards were soon under heavy pressure. To control the dock area and organise orderly embarkation 200 seamen and marines were hastily carried across in the destroyer *Vimy* on the 23rd. That afternoon Admiral Ramsay sent across two more destroyers, the *Keith* and *Whitshed*, in case complete evacuation should suddenly be required. The destroyers were actually under artillery, mortar and small arms fire whilst alongside disembarking troops and embarking wounded, and the situation in the port was tense in the extreme. The *Keith's* Commanding Officer (Captain D. J. R. Simson) was killed on his bridge and that of the *Vimy* mortally wounded. Meanwhile the demolition party went about its work as fast as possible.

During the afternoon of the same day, the 23rd, the need already anticipated by Admiral Ramsay arose; evacuation of Boulogne was ordered and he sent the *Vimiera*, *Venomous* and *Venetia* to carry it out. At 6.30 p.m. the enemy made a heavy air attack. The fresh destroyers met the *Whitshed* outside the port and her Commanding Officer (Commander E. R. Conder), the senior officer present, signalled Admiral Ramsay that he would not enter until air cover was provided. Fifty minutes later Royal Air Force fighters were overhead, the *Wild Swan* had joined the waiting flotilla and the entry now started. The *Whitshed* and *Vimiera* went in first, engaged the enemy batteries in a fierce gunfire duel, and berthed. The Welsh Guards were hailed and marched down to the jetty in perfect order followed by the equally steady Irish Guards and Royal Marines. Each ship embarked about 1,000 men and, at 8.20, they left harbour and were replaced by the *Wild Swan*, *Venomous* and *Venetia*. Again the enemy opened a murderous fire on the little ships; the *Venetia* was damaged, her Commanding Officer wounded and she backed out of the harbour. But all three ships fought a furious action of very unusual character, for the quick-firing naval weapons were aimed over open sights at enemy tanks, guns and machine-gun positions only a few hundred yards away. To add to a state of affairs which was already hazardous enough, the French coastal batteries, which had not been rendered unserviceable, were now turned on to the ships. But the *Wild Swan* and *Venomous* held the enemy troops at bay while our men embarked steadily. Shortly before 9.30 p.m., with about 900 soldiers between them, they slipped and left harbour, all the time under a heavy fire which they steadily returned. They arrived safely at Dover and with miraculously few casualties.

But Admiral Ramsay knew that many of our men must still be in the town and had already sent across the destroyer *Windsor*. At 10.30 p.m. she arrived and embarked some 600, including many wounded, and also the naval demolition party. Still the Navy would not abandon its comrades, and the Admiral ordered two more destroyers across. Only the *Vimiera* arrived. In the early hours of the 24th she entered the stricken port in an eerie silence and berthed. But the remnants of the Guards were some distance away and it took time to fetch them. By 2.45 a.m. this little ship had no less than 1,400 men on board. Though dangerously overloaded she arrived home safely. Thus were removed from out of the very jaws of the enemy 4,360 men. Some 300 of the Welsh Guards were left behind. Had the *Wessex* arrived with the *Vimiera*, as Admiral Ramsay had intended, they too could probably have been rescued.

The story of the two days' fighting in Boulogne has been told in some detail because important lessons may be derived therefrom. First is the fact that the inevitable hazards of an evacuation by sea under heavy enemy pressure will be greatly increased if discipline ashore is relaxed. The naval weapons which fought the German armoured vehicles and held off the enemy troops played a big part in making the rescue of our soldiers possible; the ships themselves were splendidly handled and the bearing of the Guards, Royal Marines and naval shore parties in most unusual and trying circumstances was magnificent. In the light of later knowledge and experience it may seem that, had we not attempted to rescue the soldiers in daylight but waited instead until the friendly shield of darkness had fallen on the scene to blunt the enemy's air weapon and the vision of his gunners, more men could have been brought home with less likelihood of damage to the ships. Lastly, and this had become almost a truism since Norway, the need for air cover if control of coastal communications was to be assured had again been demonstrated.

The Cabinet had decided to attempt to delay the enemy's advance towards the last life-line of the B.E.F. by holding Calais as well as Boulogne for as long as possible. From Calais, however, there was to be no general evacuation of the main body of the troops, so the function of the ships was to reinforce and supply the army and to bombard shore targets. The threat to Calais had become plain as early as the 21st of May and, at about noon on the 22nd, personnel ships escorted by the ever-present destroyers took across one battalion

THE SIEGE OF CALAIS, MAY 1940

of Queen Victoria's Rifles and some tanks. On the same day the remainder of the 30th Brigade (two more Rifle battalions) and the 3rd Royal Tank Regiment embarked at Southampton. They arrived at Dover early on the 23rd and left at once for Calais under destroyer escort. The troops were landed the same afternoon, as was the customary naval demolition party. Air raids were incessant and by the evening the harbour was under artillery fire as well. Next day, the 24th, Admiral Ramsay reinforced the destroyers present off the port with the *Grafton*, *Greyhound* and the Polish *Burza* and evacuation of non-fighting troops was begun.

The destroyers carried out supporting bombardments all day, but the enemy bombers took a heavy toll. The *Wessex* was sunk and the *Vimiera* and *Burza* were damaged. The *Wolfhound* and *Verity* next entered with ammunition for the troops and a Royal Marine guard for the port, and returned with wounded. At about midnight on the 24th–25th Brigadier Nicholson was told that the fighting troops would not be evacuated and that he must fight to the last. In spite of this order there remained a possibility that a last-minute evacuation might yet be called for and, in the very confused conditions then prevailing, which often made orders obsolete almost as soon as they were issued and caused frequent changes in both policy and plans, Admiral Ramsay felt that he should not abandon the hope of rescuing at any rate some of the garrison. He therefore organised and sent over, during the night of the 25th–26th, a force of yachts, trawlers and drifters, some with boats in tow. A number of these small vessels entered the port and brought men, many of them wounded, off to the larger ships waiting outside. Thus the launch *Samois* made four trips into the beleaguered port and each time rescued casualties, while the virtually unarmed trawler *Conidaw* berthed early in the morning of the 26th, grounded on a falling tide and remained there till the afternoon under ceaseless gunfire. She then got off and sailed with 165 men on board, including the remnants of the Royal Marine guard, all of whose officers had been killed or captured.

That day, the 26th, preparations for the evacuation of the main British Expeditionary Force from Dunkirk were in full swing at Dover; but bombardments in support of the Calais garrison were again carried out, this time by the *Arethusa* and *Galatea* of the 2nd Cruiser Squadron as well as by destroyers. Hospital carriers were also sent over, but the enemy fired heavily on them and prevented their entry into the port.

The end came during the afternoon, when the Riflemen could resist no more. The last ship to enter Calais was the yacht *Gulzar*, which left Dover on the evening of the 26th and berthed alongside just after midnight. Her crew searched for wounded men, but none could be found. However, fifty soldiers were embarked from the end of the breakwater at 1 a.m. on the 27th—some hours after the enemy had captured the whole town.

There is little doubt that the greater part of the garrison could have been rescued had higher policy permitted evacuation. The contrary decision was based on the need to delay by all possible means the advance of the enemy's armoured columns towards Dunkirk. Enemy records make it clear that the stand of the Guards at Boulogne and of the Royal Tank Regiment and Rifle Regiments at Calais undoubtedly contributed to that end.

In the Calais operations our ships suffered far less heavy damage than at Boulogne and the loss of the *Wessex* was the only serious casualty. But fewer troops were brought back and the harbour was used much less. The exact numbers brought home from Calais have never been accurately determined, but can hardly have exceeded 1,000 men.

From these brief but dramatic secondary operations we must now turn back to the main body of the British Expeditionary Force which we left on the 21st of May conducting a series of delaying actions as it retreated with all its normal supply lines cut and its tactical and logistic state becoming hourly more difficult.

In order to reduce the numbers to be fed and supplied Lord Gort had, on the 20th, ordered all unessential men to be sent home; 27,936 of these were brought across before the start of the main evacuation. The necessity for a great evacuation across the narrow seas now loomed large in Government and Service circles in London; during the next two days the Admiralty began to make definite preparations to carry it out. The need for large numbers of small ships was clear and, on the 22nd, the Commanders-in-Chief, Portsmouth and the Nore, were directed to take over and man the fifty 200-ton Dutch motor coasting vessels, known as 'Schuyts', which had been brought to England before the Dutch surrender. When ready, these little vessels were to be placed at Admiral Ramsay's disposal. That evening the Admiralty informed all authorities that the operation for which these and other ships were being prepared would be known as 'Dynamo'—the first use of that historic code word.

On the 26th of May the Cabinet authorised Lord Gort to put in hand his plan to withdraw to Dunkirk with a view to evacuation. The hopes of a Franco-British offensive to the south, which might release the northern armies from their trap, could not now materialise and, moreover, the complete collapse of the Belgian army on the left flank of the B.E.F. was plainly imminent. Lord Gort heard from London of the steps in hand to effect the evacuation of at any rate some of his troops and, at 6.57 that evening, the Admiralty gave the order to begin operation 'Dynamo'. The aim at this time was to try to lift 45,000 men in two days; it was believed that no more would be possible. Captain W. G. Tennant was appointed Senior Naval Officer, Dunkirk, to take charge of the naval shore embarkation parties which were to be sent over forthwith.

Thus the stage was set for an operation which has no parallel in the long history of warfare; one of incalculable difficulty and hazard with the scales of success greatly weighted in the enemy's favour, for he was certainly possessed of the land and air strength wherewith to destroy the very attempt. Yet its success far exceeded the hopes of even the most sanguine. The Germans had, in the preceding months, accomplished the rapid surrender of many armies and nations against whom their military might had been launched: Poland, Denmark, Norway, Holland and Belgium had all been laid prostrate under the swastika in a matter of a few days. It was not unreasonable for them to expect a similar surrender of the British and French armies encircled at Dunkirk.

To tell the story of Operation Dynamo in full would go beyond the scope of this volume. Nor is it possible to mention more than a few of the many hundreds of ships and boats, manned by men of all the services and by civilians from all walks of life as well, who made the rescue possible. Moreover even to-day, after much research has been devoted to the tracing of the stories of individual vessels, many points of detail remain in doubt, many reports were never written and many eye-witness accounts were lost with the gallant crews of the more than two hundred ships and boats which never returned.[1] For our story of the struggle to keep open the short sea routes on which everything depended, it must suffice to give a brief account of the chief events of each day and then to summarise the achievement. But before doing so it is necessary at once to place in proper perspective the contribution of the Royal Air Force to the success of the operation. Complaints of the inadequacy of the air cover afforded to the ships and men of the sister services had started with the Norwegian campaign and had recurred during the Dutch and Belgian coastal operations and the sieges of Boulogne and Calais. Now they rose in a crescendo of recrimination as our troops returned to these shores after enduring days and weeks of bombing by enemy aircraft which rarely seemed to meet any opposition. Our soldiers and sailors knew what they wanted—constantly to see British fighters above their heads and to feel the relief from bombing which they knew their presence would bring. Because they saw them but seldom, they presumed, understandably if hastily, that in their hour of trial and peril the Air Force

---

[1] Appendix L summarises the ships which took part in Operation Dynamo and those lost or damaged. Particulars of the troops brought home by them are also given.

was doing little or nothing to contest the enemy's command of the skies. Such sentiments were at the time very widely expressed and even found place in Admiral Ramsay's official despatch. It is possible now, with all the information and records available for study, to take a more balanced view.

In fact, although Fighter Command was by no means clear of other responsibilities and calls which had somehow to be met, nearly every operational squadron which it possessed took part in the fighting over the Continent which culminated at Dunkirk. And many of the squadrons thus employed were sent across again and again during the evacuation to try to keep the skies clear of enemies. Careful study of our own statistics and of the losses sustained by the enemy leaves no doubt that, in spite of the heavy casualties to our ships and the serious effects of the enemy bombing, Fighter Command's contribution to the success of the evacuation was substantial. Between the 26th of May and the 4th of June our fighter aircraft flew a total of 4,822 hours over Dunkirk and 106 of their number were lost on such sorties. Fifty-eight first-line enemy aircraft were destroyed by them in the neighbourhood of Dunkirk and seventy-five more in other areas where their destruction may have contributed to the success of Operation Dynamo. The Air Ministry's comment on Admiral Ramsay's despatch, that 'it was not to be expected that all air action would be visible from points on the coast', must, in sum, be accepted as a fair answer to all those who, at the time, felt that too little had been done to protect them from the German bombers.

But we must return to Sunday the 26th of May and the start of the evacuation. Personnel ships—mostly fast passenger vessels employed on the cross-channel and other similar services in peace-time and still manned almost wholly by Merchant Navy crews—had been sent across during the afternoon; they brought back the majority of the men evacuated on the first day. Hospital carriers, whose work was made especially hazardous by the enemy's total disregard of the Hague Conventions and by their conspicuous white hulls and blazing lights, brought back some casualties, but we soon had to discontinue their use. So far all the men had been embarked from the harbour. Evacuation from the beaches did not start for another twenty-four hours, and then only in a very small way to begin with. Very few inshore craft and boats had as yet arrived, but the Admiralty had already taken steps to collect all spare ships' boats from the home ports and to place them at Admiral Ramsay's disposal.

On the 26th the army started to organise the Dunkirk bridgehead and to withdraw the three British army corps within the perimeter. Next day it became known that the King of the Belgians had sought an armistice; it was plain that this surrender would leave a wide gap in the bridgehead, through which, unless it was quickly filled, the enemy could reach the vital beaches. Dunkirk was heavily bombed on this day and great damage inflicted. It was decided that evacuation from the harbour was, at any rate for the time, impossible and all troops were sent to the beaches. There the shortage of boats made embarkation very slow indeed. The personnel ships sent by the normal route to Dunkirk came under heavy fire and all suffered damage.

The attention of Admiral Ramsay's staff and of the officers sent across to organise the evacuation was at this time specially directed to the beaches east of Dunkirk; but they all still felt that large numbers of troops could only be embarked at a high rate from the harbour. Those beaches stretch continuously almost to the mouth of the Scheldt, but we are concerned only with the single stretch of ten miles of shelving sand, with the open dunes behind, nearest to Dunkirk. This stretch had been divided into three sectors, one of which was allocated to each British army corps. The three sectors were Malo beach, nearest to Dunkirk, then Bray beach, and lastly La Panne beach just over the Belgian frontier.[1] In the port itself, the enemy's bombing had already reduced the inner harbour of Dunkirk to a shambles and it was never used during the evacuation. The outer harbour was, however, protected by breakwaters on the east and west sides. They were not designed for the berthing of ships, but alongside them there was, fortunately, plenty of water. On the evening of this day, the 27th, Captain Tennant experimented with berthing ships alongside the east mole and found it perfectly practicable. This was to have important results.

The events of the early morning had shown that the normal, and shortest, route from Dover to Dunkirk—Route Z, of thirty-nine miles —which passed close off the enemy-held shore to the east of Calais was, for the last twenty miles of its length, too vulnerable. An alternative northerly route—Y, of eighty-seven miles—was therefore adopted, although this diversion doubled the length of each ship's passage. Later, in order to cut down the time spent on passage, a central route, X, of lesser length (fifty-five miles) was arranged. The northerly route had first to be swept for mines, but was brought into use on the 27th.[2]

That evening matters appeared very unpromising. Captain Tennant reported that only the beaches could be used, and asked for every available craft to be sent there immediately since he considered that 'evacuation tomorrow night is problematical'. Admiral Ramsay reacted with characteristic energy and determination. The A.A. cruiser *Calcutta*, personnel ships, many destroyers, minesweepers and

---

[1] See Map 21 (*p. 220*).
[2] See Map 21.

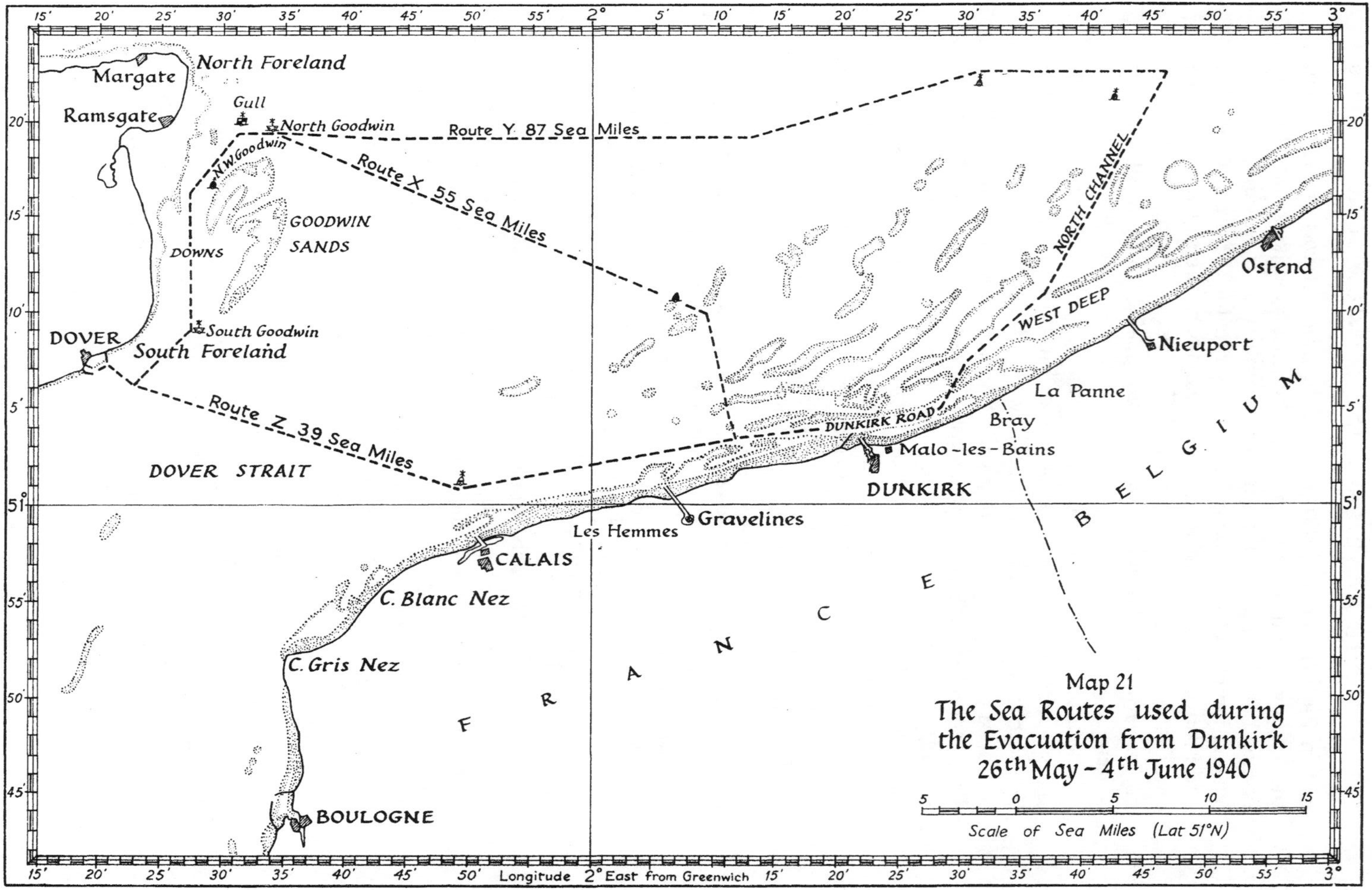

Map 21
The Sea Routes used during the Evacuation from Dunkirk 26th May – 4th June 1940

drifters were all ordered to the beaches, where they were to use their own boats to ferry men off to the ships. The temporary abandonment of the use of the port led to false rumours that the town was in enemy hands and so to orders not to approach, or else to return to England, being passed from ship to ship. Up to midnight on the 27th–28th 7,669 men were disembarked in England and it is noteworthy that nearly all had been lifted from the harbour.[1]

The next day, the 28th, was a day of great anxiety and tension, for, although the first and urgently needed supplies of food, water and ammunition arrived on the beaches, the enemy's advanced troops reached the outskirts of Nieuport. The danger that, in consequence of the Belgian surrender, he might prevent the completion of the defences of the perimeter was very present. But the emergency measures taken by Lord Gort to meet this serious threat were successful.

Early on the 28th conditions had improved inside the outer harbour and Captain Tennant asked for ships to be sent in. The destroyers *Mackay, Montrose, Vimy, Worcester, Sabre* and *Anthony* all entered and embarked large numbers of men, while other destroyers continued to lift men from the beaches. Substantial reinforcements were moved by the Admiralty from all the home ports to Dover, including seven more destroyers—the *Verity, Harvester, Esk, Malcolm, Express, Shikari* and *Scimitar*—and many minesweepers, some from as far north as Rosyth.

The vulnerability of the personnel ships, of which one—the *Queen of the Channel*—had already been sunk and several more damaged by bombs or gunfire, was also a matter for anxiety, since their large carrying capacity and comparatively high speed made them very valuable ships. Moreover, some of their civilian crews, many of whom had already taken part in the Boulogne and Calais operations, were feeling the strain. It was therefore this day decided that personnel ships should not be used during the hours of full daylight, and that evacuation from Dunkirk by day must thenceforth be done by warships and small vessels.

The Dutch schuyts started to reach the evacuation area this day, the 28th of May, when a continuous service running from Margate and Ramsgate was begun.[2] They proved excellent ships for the purpose. During the afternoon Admiral Ramsay signalled his plan for the following night. The various measures mentioned had placed at his disposal a greatly increased and still increasing fleet. He there-

---

[1] The daily totals of men evacuated from Dunkirk given in this chapter are the Admiralty's final figures. They cover each day's disembarkations in England from midnight to the following midnight. The War Office made separate calculations, but the total of men brought home, as computed by the War Office, only differs from the total assessed by the Admiralty by 397.

[2] See p. 216.

fore ordered seven personnel ships, three hospital carriers and two destroyers to embark men from the east mole of the outer harbour, while some twenty destroyers, nineteen minesweepers, seventeen drifters, from twenty to forty schuyts, five coasting steamers and many motor boats, tugs, lifeboats and ships' boats worked off the beaches. And far-reaching steps to collect still more small boats from all the rivers, ports and estuaries of the south were now in hand in England.

Dunkirk harbour was in continuous use all this day, the 28th, and, thanks to the increased effectiveness and strength of our fighter patrols and to the pall of smoke which hung over the stricken town, the enemy's air activity was much less dangerous. The total landed in England was 17,804, the majority of whom (11,874) had come from the harbour; but it now appeared certain that the swelling number of ships taking part would rapidly improve on these figures, provided that the perimeter could be held and the enemy's air power kept in check.

On Wednesday the 29th of May French troops poured into the perimeter and greatly increased the congestion within its boundaries; but by the evening the organisation of its defence had been completed and a breathing space, even if only a short one, appeared to have been gained. Yet the story of this day's work is chiefly one of losses suffered, for the toll was heavy. The destroyers *Montrose* and *Mackay* were damaged by collision and grounding; the *Wakeful* and *Grafton* were sunk by torpedoes from E-boats, which the enemy had sent to lie in wait by night on the routes used by the evacuation fleet, and whose small silhouette and deadly weapons constituted a most serious menace; the personnel ship *Mona's Queen* blew up on a magnetic mine, one of many which the enemy was laying on the shipping routes and off the coast. But it was the repeated and heavy bombing attacks which wreaked the heaviest damage. Among the warships the destroyer *Grenade* was sunk and the *Gallant, Jaguar, Greyhound, Intrepid, Saladin* and the sloop *Bideford* were all damaged by bombs, while the personnel vessels *Normannia, Lorina* and *Fenella* were sunk and the *Canterbury* damaged from the same cause. The merchant ship *Clan Macalister*, which had carried over eight assault landing craft (A.L.C.s), was also sunk, as were the boarding vessel *King Orry* and the special service vessel *Crested Eagle*. Many smaller craft were also lost or damaged but, none the less, 47,310 troops, including some 2,000 wounded, were landed in England; and of these 33,558 were lifted from the harbour and 13,752 from the beaches. Perhaps the most important development of the twenty-four hours was the great increase in the number of men taken off the beaches. As yet only a very small number of French troops had been brought across, and only one French torpedo-boat and a minesweeper had so far arrived at Dunkirk; but during the afternoon three more torpedo-boats and another minesweeper entered the harbour to embark troops.

In the evening persistent reports reached Dover to the effect that the harbour entrance was blocked, and that it was impossible to embark any more men from the moles. Communication with Captain Tennant was very difficult, and at Dover it was hard to gain a clear picture of what was happening. In consequence of these reports Admiral Ramsay ordered that all ships approaching Dunkirk should be diverted to the beaches. In fact the harbour was not blocked, and a good opportunity was thus missed to embark large numbers of men from the moles during the night of the 29th–30th. Only five small ships actually entered and they lifted only a few hundred men instead of the 10,000 or so who could have been rescued.

As a result of the heavy losses sustained by the destroyers, and particularly by those of the larger and more modern types, the Admiralty decided on the 29th to withdraw all those of the 'H', 'I' and 'J' classes. This left Admiral Ramsay with insufficient destroyers wherewith to carry on, and the withdrawn ships had to be sent back to him next day.

The naval organisation afloat was further strengthened on the afternoon of the 29th by the appointment of Rear-Admiral W. F. Wake-Walker as Rear-Admiral, Dover, 'for command of seagoing ships and vessels off the Belgian coast'. On his staff were Commodores G. O. Stephenson and T. J. Hallett (both of whom were retired Flag Officers serving again as Convoy Commodores), who were to take charge off La Panne and Bray respectively, while Captain Tennant continued responsible for the shore organisation on the other side. A strong party of naval officers also went across during the afternoon to take charge of the actual beach embarkations. It had been shown that naval knowledge of, and experience in, boats was essential on the beaches if the maximum rate of embarkation was to be accomplished and needless losses of boats avoided. The northern route (Y) had now come under enemy gunfire, and a change was therefore made to the central route (X) during the daylight hours.[1] This route was the better protected from submarine and torpedo-boat attack owing to the close proximity of sand-banks and of our own minefields. It took the enemy three days to discover the change and another respite was thus gained.

That the good results achieved on the next day, Thursday the 30th of May, were the fruits of the many and various measures taken during the preceding days is certain. There was still much confusion off the French coast; this was inevitable during an operation which was based on a long series of desperate improvisations rather than on

---

[1] See Map 21 (*p. 220*).

a carefully prepared and co-ordinated plan. But the beach at La Panne came under enemy shellfire—which seemed to indicate that the evacuation could not be prolonged much further.

The scene there, when Admiral Wake-Walker first viewed it at dawn on the 30th from the minesweeper *Hebe*, showed a line of men patiently waiting at the water's edge while thousands more were taking cover in the dunes. Small craft and boats were ferrying men off to the waiting ships; but many boats were lying broached to on shore, or were drifting empty out to sea after being cast adrift by the soldiers who had used them. Plainly the wastage of the boats which had been so laboriously collected and transported was enormous, and the need to provide naval crews for them urgent. A surf was running on the beach and made it difficult to embark the men; but the sky was overcast and a light mist enveloped the scene later. This and the strong patrols sent over by Fighter Command reduced the weight of the enemy's air attacks. The build-up of the fleet continued all day and the vast variety of small craft and boats—such as lifeboats, wherries, cockle-boats, eel-boats, speedboats and pinnaces—some manned by naval crews, some by civilians, others with mixed crews, all arrived steadily. From the harbour too the evacuation continued at a steady though reduced rate, mainly in personnel ships and French vessels, of which fifteen had now arrived. This day saw the peak of the beach embarkations when 29,512 men were lifted from them. The total number brought across was 53,823.

Meanwhile a conference took place at Dover at which it was decided to press on with the evacuation 'with the utmost vigour', with the object of reducing the British Expeditionary Force to a rearguard of some 4,000 men by the early hours of the 1st of June. At that time a special flotilla of boats and tugs would be sent over to bring back the rearguard and the naval beach parties. But this plan had, like so many others, to be changed, because it was found that the covering positions could not be held by so small a force. Withdrawal into the perimeter was however completed on the 30th, and next day Lord Gort and some of his staff were brought home in accordance with instructions from London. The same day, the 31st, saw a great and much needed improvement in communications, both between Dover and Dunkirk and between the headquarters in Dunkirk and the various parties stretched out along the shore to the east. The destroyer *Wolsey* arrived to act as wireless link with Dover, and the *Wolfhound* brought over a strong party of naval signalmen.

But the early hours of the 31st found conditions far from favourable on the beaches, where an unpleasant, if small, sea was breaking; and the on-shore wind continued to freshen during the forenoon. By 10.30 Admiral Wake-Walker reported that beach embarkation was practically impossible: at the same time Captain Tennant signalled

'The Withdrawal from Dunkirk.' By Richard Eurich.

(*National Maritime Museum*)

'Portsmouth Harbour after an Air Raid. H.M.S. *Revenge* leaving.' By Richard Eurich.
(*National Maritime Museum*)

that enemy artillery fire was making the port too hazardous to permit ships to remain there for any length of time. Admiral Ramsay accordingly suspended the despatch of additional personnel ships. But, as some compensation for these serious troubles, the small boats, whose great urge to contribute to the rescue of the army was to become one of the most famous features of the whole operation, were now arriving by hundreds. In spite of the heavy artillery fire and bombing, evacuation continued steadily from the port and few ships suffered damage there. Towards evening the weather moderated on the beaches and, although many boats were lost from one cause or another, embarkation continued at a good rate from Bray and Malo, but more slowly from La Panne. In spite of the unpropitious start to the day and the difficulties encountered as each hour passed, the evacuation reached its zenith with 22,942 men lifted from the beaches and 45,072 from the harbour—68,014 men in all.

Meanwhile the perimeter had again been contracted and, before midnight on the 31st May–1st June, La Panne was abandoned and the waiting troops sent from there to Bray; from that beach men were steadily embarked during the early hours of the 1st of June. And inside the harbour large numbers were being lifted, chiefly by personnel ships and destroyers, while under heavy gunfire and bombing attacks. As examples of the numbers crammed on board these ships it may be mentioned that the Solent steamer *Whippingham* took 2,700 men off, the *Maid of Orleans* 1,856 and the destroyers *Icarus*, *Vanquisher* and *Windsor* 3,000 between them. As soon as it was daylight the enemy intensified his air attacks and losses began to mount. The destroyer-leader *Keith*, flying Admiral Wake-Walker's flag, and the destroyer *Basilisk* were sunk, as was the minesweeper *Skipjack* with many troops on board. After a brief lull the attacks were renewed; the destroyer *Havant* and the French *Foudroyant* went down and the personnel vessel *Prague*, with 3,000 French troops on board, was seriously damaged. The *Brighton Queen* and the *Scotia*, both heavily loaded with French soldiers, were also sunk and many other ships were damaged. Mines and E-boats added to the heavy toll taken by the Luftwaffe.

There now remained only a part of the British 1st Corps, and the French troops who were to hold an inner perimeter behind our men and through whom ours were finally to withdraw. It was hoped to complete the evacuation, using both Malo beach and the harbour, during the darkest hours of the night of the 1st–2nd June. But it soon became known at Dover that this could not be accomplished. Though the last beach, that of Malo, and all three routes to Dover were now under artillery fire, damage from this cause had not, so far, been serious; it was therefore decided to extend the evacuation until 7 a.m. on the 2nd. From the one remaining beach work was slow and difficult, but the destroyers *Codrington*, *Sabre*, *Windsor*, *Whitshed* and *Winchelsea* lifted large numbers from the harbour. The total to reach England on the 1st June was 64,429—of whom 17,348 came off the beaches and 47,081 from the harbour.

There can have been few of the exhausted crews of the great fleet who did not think that the evacuation was now nearly over. Yet it was to continue for another two days and nights. By dawn on the 2nd it was believed at Dover that some 6,000 British troops remained, and Admiral Abrial estimated the French total to be about 65,000. Admiral Ramsay prohibited daylight evacuation on this day, for a repetition of the previous day's losses simply could not be afforded. Instead it was decided to lift the remaining British and 30,000 French troops during the following night—all from the harbour, since Malo beach too was now unusable—and, if possible, to repeat the same plan the next night. The night's work was carefully organised to save time by all possible means, and the movement across the Channel started at 5 p.m. Meanwhile the demolition party carried out its work in the port, and arrangements were put in hand finally to block the harbour entrance. The ships ordered across for the night's work included eleven destroyers, thirteen personnel ships, minesweepers, drifters, schuyts and a supporting host of small craft. The French and Belgians each supplied a contingent. Admiral Wake-Walker controlled the ships from a motor boat in the harbour, while Captain Tennant directed on shore. Previous experience had been turned to good account, for this was the smoothest and most rapid embarkation so far accomplished. The destroyers *Venomous*, *Windsor* and *Winchelsea*, the personnel ships *King George V*, *St. Helier*, *Royal Sovereign* and *Rouen*, all loaded quickly and left. But the troops, who had to be disengaged from the fighting line, did not arrive fast enough and many ships returned empty.

On the 2nd of June 6,695 men from Malo beach and 19,561 from the harbour landed in England. Next day, the 3rd, 26,746, three-quarters of whom were French, were brought across in the night operation just described. Many more could have been embarked had they arrived in time.

It was believed that there now remained some 40,000 French troops who were holding the shrunken perimeter and had made possible the previous night's withdrawal of their comrades. Their abandonment was not to be thought of, and the ships must therefore go across once more. This movement, which was to take place between 10.30 p.m. on the 3rd and 2.30 a.m. on the 4th of June, was, however, to be the last.

The previous night's successful plan was, in general, repeated. But only nine of the forty-one destroyers and a like number of the forty-five personnel ships originally allocated to the operation now remained. During the afternoon Admiral Ramsay learnt that the total number to be embarked was about 30,000 and this figure, fortunately, was just within the capacity of the ships still available. But it was plain that success would depend wholly on the speed with which the job was carried out.

Admiral Wake-Walker, who had gone to Dover for the final conferences, returned to Dunkirk at 10 p.m. Fog off the English coast delayed the ships' arrival, but on the other side it was, fortunately, clear. The *Whitshed* entered first, at 10.15 p.m., and was soon followed by other destroyers—the *Sabre, Venomous, Malcolm, Vanquisher* and *Express*—and by the personnel ships *Autocarrier, Canterbury Côte d'Argent, Princess Maud, Lady of Mann, Royal Sovereign* and *Tynwald*. Corvettes, minesweepers, schuyts, trawlers and small craft brought the total number of ships up to about fifty. The harbour was very congested when the first ships arrived, but some sort of order was restored and large numbers of troops embarked. The *Venomous* took 1,200, thus bringing her total for five trips in four days to no less than 4,410 men. The *Princess Maud* sailed with 1,270, the *Lady of Mann* with 1,244 and the *Royal Sovereign* 1,350. The last ship to leave the east mole was the *Tynwald* at five minutes past three on the 4th of June with 3,000 troops on board. Meanwhile at the west mole the smaller ships had done excellent work and had lifted some 10,000 troops. The total for the twenty-four hours was 26,175. But several thousand French troops had to be left behind when, at 3.30 a.m., heavy enemy shelling began again and the evacuation had to be stopped. The Germans were now only three miles from the harbour. The discipline and bearing of the men who could not be embarked left a deep impression on all who witnessed the final scene. Some at least escaped later and were picked up by our offshore patrols.

Meanwhile the three blockships, which had sailed from the Downs at 8.30 on the 3rd and had been led across by the destroyer *Shikari*, entered the port. One was mined outside, but the others sank themselves in the channel near their predecessors of the previous night's incomplete blocking operation. The *Shikari* embarked 383 troops and left at 3.40 a.m.—the last ship to leave the port.

The fleet of rescue ships was dispersed at 10.30 a.m. on the 4th, and Operation Dynamo was ended officially by an Admiralty message timed 2.23 p.m. on that day.

It had started with the modest hope of rescuing 45,000 men. Actually 308,888 men were brought across in British ships and 29,338 more in Allied ships, making a total for Operation Dynamo of 338,226 or, if the men brought back before the official start of the operation be included, a grand total of 366,162 men rescued between the 20th of May and the 4th of June. Except for the wounded, who because of the enemy's callous attacks on hospital ships had to be left behind, virtually all the surrounded troops of the British Expeditionary Force were saved and, although nearly all their equipment was lost, this great body of trained men was now available to defend our shores against the threatened invasion and to form the nucleus of the new armies which were soon to prosecute our offensive operations overseas.

Apart from the almost miraculously favourable weather, this 'great deliverance' was due to the maintenance of our control of the narrow seas, to the fighting qualities of the army which held the enemy at bay during the evacuation, to the fortitude and endurance of the crews of the ships, great and small, to the gallantry of our outnumbered airmen overhead and the patience of the troops waiting their turn on the beaches or in the harbour. It was a combined operation in the fullest sense, carried out under Admiral Ramsay's inspiring leadership.

Of the enormous number of ships and boats of all types employed it was the destroyers and personnel vessels which brought back by far the greatest proportion of men, and most of these were embarked from the moles of the outer harbour. But six British and three French destroyers were lost and nineteen other British destroyers were damaged. As it had been off the Low Countries, at Boulogne and again at Calais, so was it at Dunkirk: the destroyers led the operation with selfless gallantry and suffered most heavily. And those losses were to be felt grievously during the anxious months that followed, when every flotilla vessel was needed in the struggle for control of the ocean communications. Second only to the destroyers in the numbers of troops lifted came the personnel vessels, and they too suffered heavily. Of the forty-five ships of this type which took part, eight were sunk and nine were so seriously damaged that they had to be withdrawn.[1] But the smaller ships contributed a great quota and, if space prohibits mention of their individual stories here, they will surely be remembered collectively for their contribution to one of the greatest epics in their country's long history.

---

[1] See Appendix L.

CHAPTER XII

THE WITHDRAWAL FROM EUROPE
5th–25th June, 1940

> I very much believe that England . . . will finish by having nearly all Europe her enemies.
> *Nelson to Sir Gilbert Elliot.* 16th May 1796.

THE rescue of the original British Expeditionary Force was by no means the end of the evacuations from western Europe, and control of the narrow seas and of the approaches to these islands continued, during the remainder of June 1940, to be of paramount importance to the rescue of large numbers of British and Allied troops and civilians from the onrush of the enemy's land forces.

After the evacuation of the main British Expeditionary Force and the surrender of all the French forces north of the Somme the enemy was free to turn south and attack the defensive positions which the French had taken up on a line which broadly followed the courses of the rivers Somme and Aisne and continued to the Maginot Line forts in the east. The new German offensive started on the 5th of June. Using far greater forces than those which now remained to the French the enemy broke through in a number of places. The Maginot Line was outflanked and the French defence disintegrated. Paris fell on the 14th of June and the great ports of Cherbourg, Brest and Nantes were plainly threatened by the deep penetrations made by the German armoured divisions. On the 17th of June the French Government, in which Marshal Pétain had succeeded M. Reynaud, asked for an armistice. On the 22nd a surrender was signed, by whose terms the entire French coastline from the Belgian to the Spanish frontier passed into enemy hands, and the French fleet was to be 'collected in ports to be specified, demobilised and disarmed under German or Italian control'.

It had been the policy of the British War Cabinet to return the B.E.F. to France as soon as it could be reorganised and re-equipped. There were already two divisions in France. The 1st Armoured and the 51st (Highland) Divisions had been to the south of the Somme when the Germans broke through to the coast at Abbeville, and they had become separated from the rest of the British forces under Lord Gort. There were also about 150,000 men employed at bases or on the lines of communications, many of whom were now no longer required. It was decided firstly to evacuate all those who were no longer needed in France, and to remove as much of the surplus stores and equipment as possible. The fighting formations remained under French orders. The 52nd Division was sent to France as reinforcements, and the movement across of the 1st Canadian Division was started.

The French surrender, when it came, produced the need immediately to bring back the British fighting formations as well as all the base troops. The reconstituted forces of our Czech and Polish allies had also, if possible, to be rescued, and many thousands of British and Allied civilians saved from capture and internment.

An operation called 'Aerial' was therefore planned with the purpose of bringing home all the remainder of the British Expeditionary Force from the ports of north-western France. It quickly had to be extended to every important port as far south as the Spanish frontier. Coming so soon after the prodigious effort of Dunkirk and the serious losses suffered during those nine days of unremitting toil and hazard, these new evacuations placed a further strain on the already overtaxed forces of the southern naval commands. The flotilla vessels necessary to provide proper escorts for all the troopships simply did not exist. But control of the narrow seas and of the western and south-western approaches to these islands could still be exercised by virtue of the broad influence of our maritime power represented by the Home Fleet at Scapa Flow, by the local operations of the light forces stationed in the south and by our home-based air power. It has already been mentioned that the German fleet at this time possessed insufficient surface strength wherewith to dispute that control. In fact Admiral Raeder did not attempt to use his few surviving ships for that purpose. But it does seem remarkable that the seven U-boats which, it is now known, the enemy sent to work on the routes between the ports of western France and our home bases should have been totally unsuccessful in disputing our control of those routes. Such, however, was the case. It thus happened that we were able to bring back to these islands nearly 200,000 more British and Allied troops, besides many civilians, and to save as well a considerable quantity of military equipment and transport.

A minor operation which can conveniently be considered as part of the new series of evacuations was the blocking of the port of Dieppe, for which plans had to be made very hastily. Once more Captain G. A. Garnons-Williams was in command in the destroyer *Vega* and, on the 10th of June, two out of his three blockships were successfully sunk in the approach channel, though the mining of the third ship just outside prevented the blocking of the inner entrance to the port.

But before Dieppe had been blocked troops were being embarked at Havre. The plan for Operation 'Cycle', as it was called, followed the same general lines as its many similar predecessors, and a demolition party had accordingly been sent across before the end of May. The enemy started to bomb the port and town early in June and on the 7th did a great deal of damage. The order was given to start embarkation on the 9th, and Admiral Sir William James, the Commander-in-Chief, Portsmouth, on that day sent the destroyer-leader *Codrington*, six more British and two Canadian destroyers, and a number of smaller warships to meet off the coast in the very early hours of the 10th. Large numbers of schuyts and small craft were also sent across, beach parties were landed and senior naval officers appointed to take charge afloat and on shore in the port. After a twenty-four-hour postponement the work proceeded smoothly, except for the damage and dislocation caused by the enemy's bombing. On the 11th the personnel vessel *Bruges* was destroyed by air attack, but next day strong patrols of home-based fighters were sent across, and the enemy bombers then kept clear. The heaviest lift was made on the night of the 12th–13th, and by dawn on the latter day the evacuation was completed. Of 11,059 British troops embarked at Havre nearly 9,000 were taken direct to Cherbourg.

Meanwhile the French force of which the 51st Division formed a part had been separated from the main French armies by an enemy thrust which captured Rouen and the lower Seine. The 51st Division fell back with the French towards Havre, sending part of the division ahead to cover the port. These reached their destination and were later evacuated, but the remainder of the French and British forces were cut off by German armoured divisions which turned north from Rouen and reached the coast near St Valéry-en-Caux.[1]

Admiral James had arrived at Havre on the 10th of June and quickly realised that evacuations might be necessary from one or more of the small ports further east. He therefore sent destroyers along the coast to reconnoitre, and it was an ominous sign that they came under fire from enemy guns installed on the cliffs near St Valéry. The *Ambuscade* was damaged by them that evening. Admiral James signalled home that he expected that large numbers of men would have to be taken off from St Valéry, and he made his preparations accordingly. The 51st Division and the French were moving there at this time, but roads were congested and progress slow. As they took up defensive positions to cover evacuation enemy tanks broke through to the cliffs which commanded the little port and the beaches. The rescue plainly had to be done that night, if at all.

---

[1] See Map 3 (*facing p. 63*).

At 6 p.m. Admiral James accordingly told the *Codrington* that 'evacuation from St Valéry is to commence this evening'. Two hours later the commander of the 51st Division reported that this night would probably offer the last chance. All his men who could be extricated and spared from the perimeter moved to the beaches and the harbour, all of which were under enemy fire. There they waited throughout the night—but no ships came in. Towards dawn the General had to move them back into the town, and at 7.30 a.m. he signalled to Admiral James that there was still 'a faint possibility of withdrawal . . . being accomplished' the next night. The Admiral replied that fog had prevented the ships from getting in the night before and that every effort would be made next night. But it was too late. The French General had ordered a surrender, and although the 51st Division held on for some hours longer, and even started a last attempt to dislodge the enemy from the cliffs, there could now be only one end. Some 6,000 men of the Highland Division, including Divisional Headquarters, were forced to lay down their arms—the only instance during this campaign where a considerable body of British troops fell back to the sea but could not be rescued.

Though a great fleet of 67 merchant ships and 140 small craft had been assembled, most of them lacked wireless equipment, and the fog made it impossible to control them by visual signals. Only at Veules, at the eastern end of the perimeter, were any number of men taken off and that, too, was done under heavy fire. In all 2,137 British and 1,184 French troops were rescued. So ended a sad episode—sad because of the splendid quality of the troops involved and the narrow margin by which their rescue was frustrated.[1] Had they arrived twenty-four hours earlier all might have been well. Again the destroyers led the operation and again it was they who bore the chief brunt of the enemy air attacks. The *Bulldog*, *Boadicea* and *Ambuscade* were all damaged in Operation 'Cycle'.

The decision to bring home the remainder of the British Expeditionary Force (Operation 'Aerial') was taken on the 15th of June. The ports of Cherbourg, St Malo, Brest, St Nazaire and La Pallice were to be used; the evacuations from the first two were to be directed by Admiral James from Portsmouth while Admiral Dunbar-Nasmith, Commander-in-Chief, Western Approaches, directed the remainder from Plymouth. This time it was hoped to embark transport, guns and equipment as well as the men.

Admiral James considered that he had far too few flotilla vessels to organise a convoy system. He therefore arranged for a continuous

---

[1] See L. F. Ellis. *The War in France and Flanders, 1939–1940*, for a fuller account.

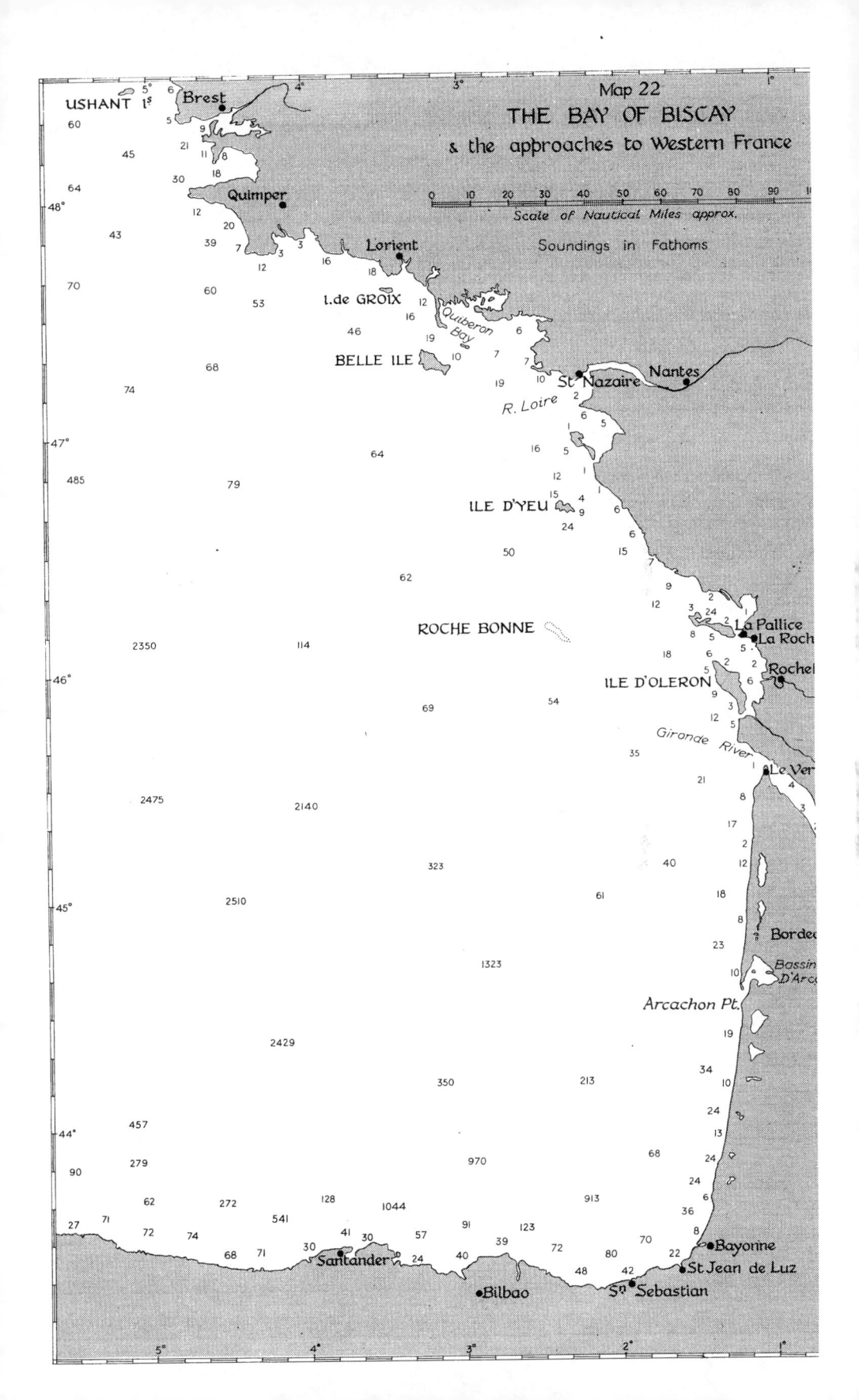

Map 22
THE BAY OF BISCAY
& the approaches to Western France

Scale of Nautical Miles approx.
Soundings in Fathoms

flow of independently-routed troopships, motor-transport and storeships to sail between Southampton and Cherbourg or St Malo, while coasters crossed from Poole and schuyts from Weymouth.[1] The few available warships patrolled the shipping routes. Between the 15th and 17th most of the 52nd Division embarked at Cherbourg, and on the 18th 'Norman Force', a composite force of various formations, arrived and followed suit. Meanwhile demolition of the fuel reserves at Caen and in the port was started, two destroyers covered the withdrawal of the rearguard and home-based fighters patrolled overhead. Late on the afternoon of the 18th the last bodies of men embarked and the last transport sailed. In all some 30,630 men were brought home, including the 9,000 already taken to Cherbourg from Havre. This time the enemy's air power was successfully kept in check and no ships were damaged. Meanwhile embarkation had also been proceeding at St Malo, whence the 1st Canadian Division sailed for home on the 16th. By the evening of the 17th 21,474 men had been embarked without loss and, early next day, the final search was made for stragglers. Demolitions were continued until the enemy's advanced troops were almost at the gates of St Malo.

While Admiral James was thus concluding the evacuations organised from Portsmouth, which had started so unhappily at St Valéry but ended more successfully, his colleague at Plymouth was organising the even larger rescues from the ports of the Biscay coast. On the 16th of June British naval officers arrived at Brest and St Nazaire to take charge of the embarkations.[2] The Admiralty attached particular importance to the departure from Brest of the new and nearly completed French battleship *Richelieu*.

Though neither the French authorities nor the headquarters of the British Expeditionary Force realised at first the need to get the troops embarked without delay—the latter was in fact planning to leave in ten to fourteen days' time—the Cabinet ordered the operation to start on the 16th of June.

Some personnel ships were already in the port and Admiral Dunbar-Nasmith was sending over more, including the large liners *Arandora Star*, *Strathaird* and *Otranto*. Numbers of small craft were also assembled in west country ports, though the need to use them did not this time arise.

Embarkation started as soon as the order was given from London, and proceeded rapidly. On the 17th the senior naval officer at Brest was told that the job must be finished that evening and, after a very busy and rather confused day, he succeeded in getting all the troops embarked and the shipping away within the prescribed time.

---

[1] See Map 3 (*facing p. 63*).
[2] See Map 22.

Some ships which were not completely filled were sent south to St Nazaire, while others returned home. The evacuation was actually ended prematurely. Had it continued for another twenty-four hours many more vehicles and a greater quantity of stores could have been loaded in the motor-transport and storeships. But our intelligence was at fault in believing the enemy to be much nearer than he actually was. As regards men, complete success was accomplished. The total of British fighting men embarked was 28,145, a large number of whom belonged to the Royal Air Force. In addition 4,439 Allied soldiers were rescued, making a total of 32,584 from Brest. The ships which carried these large numbers to safety suffered no losses at all. It is, however, to be remarked that the enemy's air activity over Brest during the evacuation was confined to occasional minelaying, which caused inconvenience and some delays while channels were swept by the trawlers sent over for that purpose but had little effect on the operation as a whole. Had the Luftwaffe's heavy bombers intervened the story might well have ended differently. All the troopships had to be routed home independently as no flotilla vessels were available to escort them, but the enemy's submarines took no greater part than his bombers in disputing control of the sea routes home from Brest.

On the 18th, the day following the end of the evacuation, demolitions were carried out in the port by the French in co-operation with a British party, and at 4 p.m. that afternoon the French fleet sailed. Unfortunately most of the ships steered south to Casablanca and Dakar; a few came to British ports to carry on the fight. By the 19th the great naval base was clear of shipping and the demolition party was withdrawn in the destroyer *Broke*.

Evacuations from St Nazaire proceeded concurrently with those from Brest, but presented peculiar difficulties owing to the strong tides and navigational hazards of the River Loire. Moreover the second new French battleship, the *Jean Bart*, was in the St Nazaire dockyard, and it was unthinkable that she should fall into the enemy's hands intact. It was believed that between 40,000 and 60,000 British and Allied troops were retreating towards Nantes, which lies some fifty miles up the river from St Nazaire. Since navigational and tidal difficulties were bound to render embarkation slow it was decided to make a start on the morning of the 16th of June. Three destroyers—the *Havelock* (Captain E. B. K. Stevens, commanding the 9th Destroyer Flotilla), *Wolverine* and *Beagle*—were then present and the liners *Georgic*, *Duchess of York*, *Batory* and *Sobieski* (both Polish) were already waiting in Quiberon Bay, some twenty miles north-west of the Loire estuary, where there was a good anchorage for large ships but anti-submarine defences were wholly lacking. On the 15th Admiral Nasmith ordered across the liner

Lancastria and a number of cargo ships. A large concentration of valuable shipping was thus assembled in or near Quiberon Bay, highly, if unavoidably, exposed to air or submarine attack. After a short delay, caused by enemy aircraft mining the channel, embarkation started on the afternoon of the 16th and, by the evening of that day, about 13,000 base troops with their stores and transport had been got on board four liners and certain cargo ships. The *Georgic*, *Duchess of York* and the two Polish liners then sailed for home.

That day the enemy's bombers attacked the shipping in Quiberon Bay, but only succeeded in damaging the liner *Franconia*. Loading of stores proceeded during the night, and more ships were sent across from England or down from Brest by Admiral Nasmith. The destroyers *Highlander* and *Vanoc* also joined the flotilla under Captain Stevens.

The next day, the 17th, revealed a scene of great activity with flotilla vessels and small craft, French as well as British, ferrying troops out to the big ships waiting in the roads, while still more ships were arriving to play their part, and our fighters patrolled in the sky. A successful morning's work produced high hopes of accomplishing yet another successful evacuation without loss. But this was not to be. At 3.35 p.m. there was a heavy air attack and the *Lancastria*, which had embarked 5,800 troops, was hit, caught fire and sank fifteen minutes later with great loss of life. About 3,000 men perished in the waters of the Loire—the most grievous single loss suffered during all these hazardous operations. It is not clear why so many lives were lost from a ship which sank fairly slowly in a crowded roadstead. True there were not enough lifebelts for the exceptional numbers embarked, and the waters were covered by a film of burning oil fuel, but the Master of the *Lancastria* has testified that no panic occurred, and small craft were certainly present in some numbers. An anti-submarine trawler, the *Cambridgeshire*, saw the ship struck and went at once to her assistance. She estimated that she rescued between 900 and 1,000 men. Why more of the small ships did not follow suit is obscure, but as enemy air raids were almost continuous between 3.45 and 4.30 p.m. they may have been so busy defending themselves and their consorts that they never realised what had happened to the *Lancastria*. But it is unlikely that the full reasons for the tragedy will ever be completely explained. Mr Churchill has told how it came about that the news of it was so long withheld.[1]

In spite of these losses the embarkation proceeded during the afternoon and evening and on into the night of the 17th. Soon after dawn on the 18th a convoy of ten ships with 23,000 men on board sailed for Plymouth. Only 4,000 men now remained ashore.

Reports of the speed of the enemy's advance were, as at Brest,

---
[1] See W. S. Churchill. *The Second World War (1949)*, Vol. II, 172.

greatly exaggerated and this led to a decision to hasten the end of the evacuation. At 11 a.m. on the 18th twelve ships sailed in convoy with the last troops and by early afternoon the operation was ended, except for the usual search for stragglers by small craft. Again the end was premature and again much more transport and equipment could have been saved had we possessed accurate intelligence of the enemy's movements.

At noon on the 18th the destroyer *Vanquisher* arrived with Vice-Admiral T. J. Hallett on board. He had been sent over to ensure that the *Jean Bart* sailed or, if necessary, was destroyed. The French base and dockyard staff worked hard to get the great ship undocked and away early on the 19th; they intended to destroy her themselves if that could not be accomplished. Admiral Hallett sent tugs ahead to help with the undocking and waited anxiously in Quiberon Bay. Though the battleship was late in reaching the rendezvous with the *Vanquisher* she finally turned up with a French destroyer escort. Admiral Hallett remained in company until she had turned south —for Casablanca.

Meanwhile, on the same afternoon, Admiral Nasmith heard that 8,000 Polish troops were waiting at St Nazaire. He at once sent seven transports and six destroyers for them. But only 2,000 men were, in fact, there and much of the shipping so urgently collected was therefore hazarded needlessly. Embarkation thus actually continued from St Nazaire for a full forty-eight hours after its official end. In all 57,235 troops, of whom 54,411 were British and 2,764 Allied, were brought home from St Nazaire and Nantes.

Well before the last man had been lifted from St Nazaire evacuations had started from La Pallice which, with the adjacent ports of Rochefort and La Rochelle, forms an important naval base. On the 16th the British senior naval officer for the port arrived by destroyer; but no personnel ships had entered by the next morning to embark the 10,000 troops whom Admiral Nasmith had been told to expect there. The ships had, in fact, been diverted to Brest or St Nazaire. Accordingly cargo ships were requisitioned and the waiting troops embarked at once in them; all their transport was abandoned. The convoy sailed very early on the 18th but, once again, the evacuation was ended too early. The Commander-in-Chief, hearing that more troops were expected, then sent ships south from Brest and embarkation was resumed on the evening of the 19th. In spite of air raids 4,000 Polish troops left that night. On the 20th it again appeared that the job had been completed; but again reports of further arrivals reached the Commander-in-Chief, who once more sent transports and destroyers to fetch them. Actually very few were found at this third attempt, and the shipping collected for them was finally diverted still further south to the ports of the River Gironde. It is easy to see how greatly the difficulties were increased by the faulty information on which Admiral Nasmith had to work. In all 2,303 British and a large number of Polish troops were brought back from La Pallice.

This evacuation actually completed the plan to withdraw the B.E.F. originally visualised in Operation 'Aerial'; but the collapse of French resistance and the request for an armistice made still more rescue work essential with the least possible delay if the last of the Allied troops, much valuable shipping and all British civilian refugees, embassy and legation staffs were not to fall into the enemy's hands. These last and hastily improvised operations began from the ports of the River Gironde and moved finally to Bayonne and St Jean-de-Luz near to the Spanish frontier.

To get some sort of organisation started in these ports the cruiser *Arethusa* arrived at Le Verdon from Gibraltar on the evening of the 16th of June while the destroyer *Berkeley*, which had brought over from England all the senior naval officers for the ports and distributed them down the coast, went up the river to Bordeaux to act as wireless link. All British and some Allied shipping was cleared from the port the next day and the embarkation of refugees commenced. Admiral Nasmith had meanwhile diverted to the Gironde sufficient shipping to lift the Allied troops (chiefly Polish and Czech), whose arrival on the coast had long been expected but whose movements were by no means clear to the Commander-in-Chief at Plymouth. Dramatic meetings were now taking place in Bordeaux, where the First Lord (Mr A. V. Alexander), the First Sea Lord and Lord Lloyd had arrived from England to endeavour to persuade Admiral Darlan to move the whole French fleet—including the ships still in the Mediterranean ports—out of the enemy's reach. Mr Churchill has told the story of this unsuccessful mission.[1]

During the 18th and 19th ships were sailed with some thousands of refugees and Allied troops, but the majority of the former had already been diverted to Bayonne. The British Embassy and consular staffs came down river from Bordeaux, many of them in the *Berkeley*, on the 19th and embarked in the *Arethusa*. The Ambassador himself, Sir Ronald Campbell, stayed at Bordeaux for a few more days, but on the 23rd he left for Arcachon. He eventually sailed for England from St Jean de Luz in the *Galatea* (flagship of Rear-Admiral A. T. B. Curteis, commanding the 2nd Cruiser Squadron). The *Arethusa* returned home on the 20th with the President of Poland and many of his Ministers on board.

Meanwhile embarkations continued at Le Verdon and, early on the 20th, Rear-Admiral F. Burges-Watson arrived in the destroyer *Beagle* with a demolition party for Bordeaux, and steamed at once up the river. His chief object was the destruction of the great oil

---

[1] See W. S. Churchill. *The Second World War*, Vol. II, p. 191.

stocks at the port, but difficulties arose at once with the French authorities and were accentuated when, on the 22nd, the armistice terms became known. They then firmly refused to allow any demolitions to be carried out. Admiral Burges-Watson was about to use surprise to fulfil his orders when the Admiralty cancelled them. Three days later the Admiralty ordered Admiral Nasmith to send a destroyer force to Bordeaux to destroy the oil stocks, but again it was cancelled, this time by decision of the Cabinet.

Meanwhile the embarkations at Le Verdon were not progressing entirely smoothly, since most of the Polish troops had arrived at this port instead of at Bayonne where the shipping was now awaiting them. Admiral Nasmith took rapid steps to bring the ships and the soldiers together and, by the morning of the 23rd, the last 6,000 Poles had been embarked and the personnel vessels sailed.

On the 19th of June Admiral Nasmith sent four large liners—the *Batory* and *Sobieski* (Polish), the *Ettrick* and *Arandora Star*—to Bayonne for the refugees known to be assembling there and for the Polish troops believed to be moving towards that port. During the next two days some 9,000 of the latter embarked and sailed in the two Polish transports, but it was then decided to shift the evacuation to St Jean-de-Luz where the port facilities were better. Meanwhile ample shipping to accommodate the remaining refugees and Polish troops had arrived from home, or from the Gironde ports. But bad weather delayed progress with the embarkation until the 24th, when the French authorities ordered that, on account of the armistice terms, all evacuations must cease by noon on the 25th. At 2.30 that afternoon the last troopship sailed for home. In all about 19,000 soldiers —almost all Polish—were brought home from Bayonne and St Jean-de-Luz.

That evening a sad accident occurred. While manœuvring, the anti-aircraft cruiser *Calcutta*, to which Admiral Curteis had transferred his flag, rammed and sank the Canadian destroyer *Fraser* with heavy loss of life. But all the other troopships and warships arrived home safely.

While these evacuations were in progress on the Biscay coast large numbers of refugees and some Czech and Polish troops had assembled at various places on the south coast of France. On the 23rd of June the Admiralty ordered that as many as possible should be embarked in whatever shipping could be collected for the purpose, and taken to Gibraltar. Two destroyers of the Mediterranean Fleet were sent to organise the work, which was finished by the following midnight. Some 10,000 Allied troops and civilians, mostly crammed in small cargo ships, were carried to Gibraltar between the 24th and 26th of June and thence, ultimately, to the United Kingdom.

It will be appropriate to conclude the story of the withdrawal from Europe by telling how, in accordance with a recent Cabinet decision to bring to England all men of military age, women, and children from the Channel Islands, embarkation was started there on the 19th of June and continued till the 22nd. All types of ships from large liners down to small craft were used, and the operation was conducted by Admiral James from Portsmouth in conjunction with the Home Office. By the 23rd of June it was known that all who wished to leave the islands had done so and the evacuation was ended. In all 22,656 persons were removed under the official scheme, but a good many more probably used private transport. The shipping sailed unescorted, but the enemy made no attempt to interfere. On the 30th the Germans landed in the Channel Islands and, for the first time for many centuries, a part of the British Isles passed temporarily under enemy rule. But this sad event was undoubtedly necessary: the Admiralty had insisted that the islands could not be supported while the enemy held the whole of the adjacent French coast.

Thus ended not only Operation 'Aerial' for the withdrawal of the remainder of the B.E.F. but a number of other hastily organised and extemporised evacuations of a like nature. In the main they were successfully carried out and the losses suffered were astonishingly small. The evacuation from Dunkirk so impressed the free world, and has remained so long and so justly in the thoughts and imagination of its people, that the scope and scale of the series of operations described in this chapter seems never to have been fully realised.

In Operations 'Cycle' and 'Aerial' 191,870 fighting men were brought to England, of whom 144,171 were British, 18,246 French, 24,352 Polish, 4,938 Czech and 163 Belgian. If to this figure is added the totals for the preliminary evacuations from Dunkirk (27,936) and that for Operation 'Dynamo' (337,829), a final figure of 558,032 men is reached. Of this total 368,491 were British and 189,541 Allied troops. Moreover a large number of civilians also safely reached home from many different starting points. Except for the Channel Islands (22,656) no accurate assessment of the civilian total can be given, but it is known that some 10,000 passed through Gibraltar from French Mediterranean ports. It therefore seems likely that between 30,000 and 40,000 British subjects also reached their homeland at this time. Furthermore, though much equipment was abandoned, and some of it needlessly, no less than 310 guns, 2,292 vehicles and 1,800 tons of stores were saved. The effects of this prodigious rescue on the course of the war are incalculable. The small scale on which the enemy reacted was, indeed, remarkable, but it must be remembered that many of the Luftwaffe's bombers had been withdrawn to prepare for the assault on Britain.

But it was not only for the rescue of the soldiers that these operations deserve to be remembered. The psychological impact upon the free peoples was immense, for it had been shown that Hitler's all-conquering armies could be denied the full fruits of their land victories by the skilful and determined application of maritime power. In the United States, whose President and people had been watching with breathless absorption the progress of the struggle in Europe, the effects were profound and undoubtedly contributed to the readiness with which great and generous help was soon to be given to a sorely pressed but wholly determined Britain.

Thus were the ports and estuaries of the French Biscay coast, through which the Navy had in 1814 supplied Wellington's Army advancing from Spain, used to embark the last British fighting men from Europe a century and a quarter later. And the foothills of the western Pyrenees which, after twenty years of war, had seen the long-awaited invasion of Napoleon's France by one British army, now saw the complete withdrawal of another.

Though the strategic situation had, in a few weeks, changed out of all recognition in the enemy's favour, and a new enemy had chosen this moment to make his ignoble intervention, we had at least succeeded in removing, or causing to be removed, out of the enemy's immediate reach a small but important part of the powerful French Navy, including its two newest battleships.

But our coastal waters were now open to far more concentrated attacks by all the enemy's varied weapons, and our ocean communications were much more severely threatened by his possession of so many new and well-placed bases. Plainly the new phase into which the war had passed was bound to be of exceptional anxiety to those responsible for the control of the sea routes; and the first great question was the effect of the French surrender on the disposal and subsequent actions of the large part of the French Navy which still lay within range of the enemy's grasp. It will be logical now to review the first steps taken by the Admiralty, with the approval of the Cabinet, to eliminate once and for all or, if that could not be done, at least to reduce, the serious threat which the possession by the enemy of those ships would constitute.

The most important French naval vessels to reach British ports at the time of the French surrender were the old battleships *Courbet* and *Paris*, the large destroyers *Léopard* and *Le Triomphant* and the smaller *Mistral* and *Ouragan*, seven submarines—including the big *Surcouf*—six torpedo-boats and a number of minesweepers. Apart from the *Jean Bart* and *Richelieu*, now at Casablanca and Dakar respectively, the modern battle cruisers *Dunkerque* and *Strasbourg*, the older battle-

Vice-Admiral Sir James F. Somerville, Flag Officer Commanding
Force H 28th June 1940–10th January 1942.

'Force H' off Gibraltar.
Left to right: H.M.S.'s *Ark Royal*, *Malaya* and *Renown*.

ships *Bretagne* and *Provence*, a seaplane carrier and six large destroyers were at the naval base of Mers-el-Kebir, near Oran. Nearby, in Oran, were seven more destroyers and four submarines. Six cruisers (Marseillaise class) were at Algiers and four eight-inch cruisers (Algérie class) were at Toulon, while the remaining three ships of the latter class were at Alexandria with the French Eastern Mediterranean squadron under Admiral Godfroy. Thus a relatively small proportion of the French Navy had, by the end of June, been definitely removed beyond the enemy's reach; and it was clear that should the ships in the North African ports alone move back to metropolitan France and fall to the disposal of Germany and Italy, our Mediterranean Fleet would be greatly outnumbered and our prospects of continuing to control the sea routes of the world would be most seriously threatened. Moreover the Franco-German armistice terms, which were known in London, stated that the 'French Fleet . . . shall be . . . demobilised and disarmed under German or Italian control'. In British eyes this might well mean that they would be handed over as fighting units. Although Marshal Pétain and Admiral Darlan had repeatedly declared that no warship would be allowed to fall into enemy hands, not only did such declarations appear to the British Cabinet to contradict the armistice terms, but it was considered unlikely that the new French Government would for long retain the power to enforce its will in this respect. In that case the only safeguard remaining to our country was the 'solemn declaration' of the Germans and Italians that the French fleet would not be used for their own purposes. The value of such declarations seemed, in the light of recent experience, somewhat questionable and, moreover, there were indications that the Germans were issuing instructions to the French fleet in Admiral Darlan's name.

Such, then, was the background to the difficult decisions which faced the British Cabinet and Admiralty as the month of June 1940 drew to a close. The first requirement plainly was to replace, as far as we could and as quickly as possible, the lost French maritime power in the western basin of the Mediterranean. Secondly, steps had to be taken to watch certain French warships stationed abroad, whose intentions were in doubt; thirdly, we had to prevent the enemy from possessing himself of the French warships and using them for his own purposes.

To meet the first requirement the Admiralty decided, towards the end of June, to base a powerful force at Gibraltar to work in the western basin and to cover our convoy routes from Sierra Leone and Gibraltar. In the eastern basin of the Mediterranean and in the approaches to it by the Red Sea Admiral Sir Andrew Cunningham's fleet and the forces of the East Indies Command had a firm grip, and no immediate anxiety was felt regarding the consequences of the strategic changes on land. In the west it was a very different matter, and it was for this reason that the famous 'Force H', which was to perform so many, varied and widely-ranging services, was quickly created. But it was fortunate that we possessed at that time a sufficient margin in surface ship strength to enable this new fleet—for such it became—to be brought into existence at once and without unduly weakening our control in other theatres. On the 23rd of June the *Ark Royal* (flag of Vice-Admiral L. V. Wells) and *Hood* arrived at Gibraltar. Five days later Force H was officially formed from these two ships, the battleships *Valiant* and *Resolution*, the light cruiser *Arethusa* and four destroyers. On the last day of the month Vice-Admiral Sir James Somerville hoisted his flag in the *Hood*. The Admiralty described Force H as a 'detached squadron' under Admiral Somerville's command. The ambiguity of this description was soon to produce difficulties, but the commander of the force was certainly never in any doubt that his was intended to be an independent command, that he was responsible direct to the Admiralty and was not under the orders of Admiral Sir Dudley North, the Flag Officer, North Atlantic, whose base at Gibraltar he was, however, to use.

In addition to the ships allocated to Admiral Somerville there were at Gibraltar at this time nine destroyers (mostly of 1914–18 war design), a few minesweepers and armed boarding vessels under the command of the Flag Officer, North Atlantic. Originally their functions had been to provide local escorts for convoys sailing to and from Gibraltar, to patrol the Straits and to enforce our contraband control in those waters. Now the Gibraltar local defence flotilla was, by arrangements made between the two Flag Officers concerned, frequently used as well to supplement Force H's meagre destroyer strength.

The Cabinet was determined that there should be no hesitancy or weakness in handling the difficult question of the future of the French warships. Accordingly, early in July, the French ships which had come to British ports were boarded and seized. At Alexandria Admiral Cunningham's patient perseverance finally bore fruit, and Admiral Godfroy was persuaded, after prolonged and difficult negotiations, to immobilise his ships. Unhappily no such bloodless solution was achieved with Admiral Gensoul at Oran. Admiral Somerville was ordered to carry out at this port on the 3rd of July an operation (called 'Catapult') designed either to place the French warships permanently beyond the enemy's reach or to achieve their destruction.

To accomplish the purpose of the War Cabinet Admiral Somerville had with him the *Hood, Valiant, Resolution, Ark Royal,* two small cruisers, the *Arethusa* and *Enterprise*, and eleven destroyers—a force which certainly appeared adequate to deal even with determined French resistance. His instructions were to offer Admiral Gensoul four alternative courses—namely to put to sea and join forces with our ships, to sail with reduced crews to any British port, to sail with reduced crews to a French West Indian port, or to scuttle his ships within six hours. Failing acceptance of any of these alternatives, the possibility of the ships being demilitarised in their present berths remained. The Admiralty told Somerville that should Gensoul suggest that he should put such measures in hand, and should he be prepared to carry them out to our satisfaction, such a solution could be accepted even if all the four alternative proposals previously made to the French Admiral had been rejected. Failing solution on any of these lines the ships in Mers-el-Kebir were, said the Admiralty, to be destroyed.

The restrictions with which the Admiralty hedged acceptance of demilitarisation at Oran were, however, severe; for Somerville was told that he must first be satisfied that the necessary measures could be carried out under his own supervision within six hours, and also that they would prevent the ships being brought into service for at least one year in a fully-equipped dockyard port. It may well be considered that these restrictions made the suggestion impossible of fulfilment, at any rate during the few hours allowed.

Captain C. S. Holland was sent ahead by destroyer early on the 3rd of July to negotiate on the basis of the first four British alternatives. He arrived at about 8 a.m., but Admiral Gensoul refused at first to meet him. The British emissary could therefore only ask for the written proposals to be given to the French Admiral and await a reply. At 10 a.m. Gensoul's answer was received. It was uncompromising; nor did a further exchange of written statements made during the forenoon achieve any progress towards a solution.

The possibility of avoiding a resort to force was, unhappily, greatly reduced by the wording of the message in which Gensoul communicated the British proposals to the French Admiralty. Ignoring altogether the first three alternatives offered, he reported that he had been presented with an ultimatum in the form of 'sink your ships within six hours or we will use force'. It is hardly surprising that when Admiral Darlan and the French Council of Ministers received the British proposals in that form, they should have supported Admiral Gensoul's expressed intention to resist.

Early in the afternoon mines were laid in the harbour entrance to prevent the French ships carrying out what appeared, from Admiral Gensoul's latest reply, to be their intention—to put to sea and fight. When, however, no signs of an attempt to leave harbour were apparent Admiral Somerville postponed the time at which he would resort to force from 1.30 to 3 p.m.

At 2.40 p.m. the French Admiral at last agreed to receive the British delegates, but it was 4.15 before Captain Holland arrived on board the *Dunkerque*. Time was now running out. While the discussions were in progress the Admiralty intercepted a French signal ordering all their forces to rally to Gensoul's assistance. They at once told Admiral Somerville that he must 'settle matters quickly' or he would have reinforcements to deal with. Admiral Somerville therefore signalled to Gensoul that, if one of the alternatives offered was not accepted by 5.30, the French ships would be sunk. Events were now moving rapidly to a climax.

Captain Holland passed a summary of Gensoul's final statement to Admiral Somerville at 5.20 p.m. and added that 'Gensoul says crews [are] being reduced and if threatened [he] would go to Martinique or U.S.A., but, this is not quite our proposition. Can get no nearer'. He left the *Dunkerque* at 5.25 and as he passed out of the harbour the French fleet was clearing for action.

At 5.54 p.m. Admiral Somerville opened fire, and after a short but violent engagement, the *Bretagne* was blown up and the *Dunkerque* and *Provence* and a number of lesser ships seriously damaged. The loss of life among the French seamen was tragically heavy. But the *Strasbourg* and five destroyers won clear of the harbour and back to Toulon, although the battle cruiser was attacked offshore by the *Ark Royal's* torpedo-bombers. The British Cabinet's object was, therefore, not fully accomplished. The antagonism which this action aroused in the French Navy was natural, and the possibility of obtaining that service's future co-operation in the war against Germany and Italy was largely eliminated. In the British Navy as well strong feelings were aroused, and all three Flag Officers concerned in carrying out the Cabinet's orders—Admirals Cunningham, Somerville and North—viewed them with horror and incredulity and did what they could, with so little time allowed, to postpone the issue.

It can be argued indefinitely that, had the British alternatives been presented before a display of force was made, or had more time been allowed for negotiation, or had Admiral Gensoul signalled a fair summary of the British terms, a peaceful solution might have been found. But the lack of contact between the British and French Governments prevented any negotiation on normal diplomatic lines; and the French officers still in London were not fully informed about the trend of affairs in their own stricken country, about the naval clauses of the armistice terms so recently accepted, nor about French intentions with regard to their fleet. On the British side the matter had been fully and repeatedly discussed in London before Admiral Somerville's instructions were despatched, and the Cabinet was determined that, if need be, the task should be carried through to the end.

In neutral countries the reaction was not unfavourable. It seemed to be widely realised that Britain, fighting alone to secure her sea life-lines, simply could not afford to allow her very existence to be jeopardised by any uncertainty or weakness in her handling of so dangerous a situation.[1]

A few days later force, though on a more moderate scale, was used against the *Richelieu* at Dakar. In the new circumstances produced by the French surrender the long sea route round the Cape of Good Hope had become the chief line whereby our armies in Egypt could be supplied and our trade from India and the East brought to this country. That the enemy should become possessed of the former French bases which flanked that route and be able to make use of the French warships which had reached them was intolerable. It was therefore decided to put the *Richelieu* out of action by carefully-planned attacks which would, it was hoped, cause little or no loss of life. On the 7th of July Captain R. F. J. Onslow in the small aircraft carrier *Hermes* was placed in command of a force which included the cruisers *Dorsetshire* and *Australia* and ordered to take the necessary steps. In the small hours of the morning of the 8th a motor-boat penetrated the defences and dropped depth charges under the battleship's stern to damage her rudders and propellers. Unfortunately, owing to the shallowness of the water, they failed to explode. Three hours later the aircraft carrier attacked with six torpedo-bombers and obtained one hit which distorted a propeller shaft and flooded three compartments. Though it took the French a year to repair her to a state of seaworthiness with the resources available at Dakar, the ship was not effectively immobilised by these attacks and, in emergency, could have put to sea at short notice. But she stayed in Dakar and played an important part in frustrating our next operation against the base, as will be recounted in a later chapter.

Meanwhile another British force had been ordered to watch the French warships in the West Indies and, if necessary, to prevent their return to France. But they never made the attempt. Accordingly on the 12th of July the patrol was withdrawn at the same time as the British Government announced that no further action would be taken against French warships in their North African or colonial ports. Thus ended the first and acutely difficult series of decisions and operations necessitated by the fall of France and by the possible consequences of that surrender on our control of the sea. Nevertheless, uncertainty regarding the disposal of the French warships continued for many months to cause serious anxiety to the British Cabinet and Admiralty; it was not finally removed until the landings of November 1942 had won for us the African bases at which lay many of the more important ships.

---

[1] For a fuller account of the action at Oran see I. S. O. Playfair, *History of the Second World War: The War in the Mediterranean and Middle East* (H.M.S.O.), Vol. I. (*In the press*)

CHAPTER XIII

THE CONTROL OF HOME WATERS
30th May–30th December, 1940

> Whatever plans may be adopted, the moment the enemy touch our coast, be it where it may, they are to be attacked by every man afloat and on shore: this must be perfectly understood. *Never fear the event.*
> Nelson. *Memorandum on the defence of the Thames.* 15th July 1801.

MANY times in this country's history have continental enemies intended to invade these islands across the narrow seas; and, to deal with such attempts, certain strategic and tactical principles have gradually been evolved. In these volumes we are not concerned with the history of past threats of invasion; but a brief glance at the manner in which the problems which arose again in 1940 were faced in the First World War may be justifiable because it is possible that, when the threat developed far more rapidly and to a far higher degree of likelihood in 1940, the Naval Staff looked back at the orders issued on the earlier occasion and wished to apply the same principles. Alternatively the senior officers serving in the Admiralty may have remembered the measures ordered in the 1914–18 war. There are, at any rate, many points of similarity in the two sets of plans to defeat invasion. But the circumstances which prevailed in 1940 certainly made the invasion threat of that year far more serious than at any period of the earlier war. In the first place most of the British Army was, after its return from Dunkirk, so deficient in equipment as to be almost unarmed. Secondly, whereas in the first war the German army had been fully engaged in heavy fighting on two enormous fronts, in 1940 it was, for the time being, free of all other major commitments and able to launch its full might against Britain. Thirdly, the factor of air power had recently been shown, in Norway and the Low Countries, to be of decisive importance to an invader; and, lastly, the enemy now stood on the Channel coast which he had tried so long and so vainly to reach in the war of 1914–18. It is important that these differences should be remembered when the policy adopted in 1940 is reviewed in the light of what we now know regarding the enemy's intentions and his failure.

In October 1914 the First Lord of the Admiralty, Mr Winston

Churchill, asked his department to answer a number of questions regarding the plans and functions of the Grand Fleet and of the detached squadrons and flotillas of the Navy to deal with an invading expeditionary force. To his first question, 'What is the function of the Grand Fleet?' the reply was that it should 'prevent the High Seas Fleet from obtaining command of the sea and forcing [Britain] to surrender by either starvation or invasion'. The answer went on to say that against starvation there was no second line of defence after the Grand Fleet and, if that were destroyed, 'starvation follows as a matter of course'. To defeat invasion, on the other hand, there were second lines of defence in the shape of the naval forces based in the south and the Army on land. The Admiralty ended by saying that 'the principal function of the Grand Fleet appears to be to ensure that the outer sea communications are unmolested to such a degree as to obviate any risk of starvation. . . . If this is so we have no right to risk the Grand Fleet in operations where there are two other lines of defence' (that is to say by bringing it south to defeat an invading force). After answering all the First Lord's questions the Admiralty stated that 'the whole question of resisting invasion rests with obtaining the earliest information of the actual embarkation of troops'. The First Lord did not, apparently, dissent from the principles then stated.

Towards the end of May 1940 it became plain that little time might be granted us to complete our preparations, and on the 28th of that month the Admiralty first signalled its opinions and intentions to all the naval Commanders-in-Chief and then followed up the signal next day with a full letter. The evacuation from Dunkirk was, of course, in full swing at the time.

As far as can be discovered the Admiralty did not in any way alter the opinions and orders issued in May 1940 until early in the following year, when a revised appreciation was made to bring the earlier one up to date, chiefly in the matter of the enemy's strength and dispositions. The same principles are stated in both sets of orders. They were, in fact, founded on the experience of centuries. Though the principles stated were old, their translation into a modern context is interesting. The Admiralty was considering only the defeat of seaborne invasion; the various forms of air action open to the enemy were dealt with in contemporary inter-service documents.

It was expected that the enemy's main attempt would be by the shortest route, so as to try to achieve surprise, but that they might carry out diversions or subsidiary landings at other points. They were expected to make the greatest possible effort and to be prepared to accept 'catastrophic losses' to achieve their object. To defeat the attempt the Admiralty stressed the importance of 'attack before departure'; to accomplish that, 'we must have early indication of assembly by means of our intelligence and reconnaissance'. Air attack, mining and bombardment were the three counter-measures to be employed. In case 'attack before departure' was impossible or unsuccessful it was essential to 'attack at the point of arrival'. As we could not tell exactly where that would be 'our forces must be disposed to cover the area Wash to Newhaven as a whole' and 'reconnaissance must be as complete as possible'. Next the Admiralty considered the 'happy possibility that our reconnaissance might enable us to intercept the expedition on passage'. They expected that the German battle cruisers would be used to create a diversion in the north; and, because of the commitment still present at Narvik and of the vulnerability of our Northern Patrol, that diversion 'must be countered'. In the southern North Sea the enemy was expected to employ about five cruisers and his two old battleships, which had to be opposed by a sufficient and properly balanced force of heavy and light units.

As for the enemy's naval strength, it was believed, we now know erroneously, that both the battle cruisers were in effective state. No pocket-battleships were available, but his two old battleships, two heavy and at least two—possibly four—light cruisers were thought to be fit for sea. Actually only two cruisers were ready for service. His destroyer strength was known to be weak after his losses in Narvik and was assessed at between seven and ten. Forty to fifty U-boats, a like number of motor torpedo-boats, eight escort vessels and sixteen torpedo-boats completed his naval strength; it was, indeed, slender support for a great overseas expedition, even had it been as great as the Admiralty supposed.

To deal with the enemy invasion fleet while on passage, the Admiralty decided that a striking force of four destroyer flotillas (at full strength thirty-six ships), with cruiser support, would be required. These forces were to be stationed so as to be able to strike at the expedition at its point of arrival as well as while it was on passage. The Humber, Harwich, Sheerness and Portsmouth or Dover were chosen as the striking-force bases.

The Admiralty also stated that 'the maximum number of . . . destroyers, escort vessels, corvettes, etc., as can be spared from escort duties should be allotted to the area'—presumably in addition to the four striking-force flotillas—and that small craft should 'be collected immediately for watching close inshore and hampering the enemy's operations'. The latter requirement was the genesis of the Auxiliary Patrol, of which more will be said shortly.

To say that flotilla vessels which 'can be spared from escort duties' should be sent south was perhaps easier than to find any such ships; for the Norwegian campaign and the recent losses in the narrow seas had seriously depleted our already inadequate strength. It is certain that, judged on an absolute standard, none at all could be spared from escort duties. It was, however, reasonable to accept that if the invasion danger was immediate the convoys must be stripped of their escorts. But the decision was bound to be difficult, because whether it was justifiable to hold a great proportion of our flotilla vessels in the south must, in large measure, depend on the amount of warning we might count on receiving from our air reconnaissance and intelligence service. Hence the importance attached to reconnaissance in 1940 as well as in 1914.

If even as little as twenty-four hours' warning of invasion could be guaranteed, then we could move forces from the northern bases such as Scapa, Forth and Clyde, to the threatened point in good time. It will be remembered how, during the evacuation from Dunkirk, Home Fleet destroyers reached Dover in a day and how some Home Fleet cruisers were held at Rosyth ready to support them if needed.[1] Moreover, escort vessels from the Western Approaches Command could also reach the narrow seas in one or two days, for they were only escorting convoys to 17° West—some 300 miles west of Ireland—at this time, and few of them would be at the furthest end of the zone of escort at any moment. But it was difficult for anyone to say how much warning of the invasion fleet's departure would be received, since it depended largely on the weather. It has been told how our air reconnaissance had failed to find enemy warships creeping up the Norwegian coast, generally in carefully chosen bad weather, and this may have reduced confidence in the ability of the Royal Air Force to give early warning of invasion. But an invasion fleet crossing narrow seas is a far easier target to find than a single warship at extreme reconnaissance range. In retrospect it does, therefore, seem that greater confidence might have been placed in the probability of obtaining sufficient warning, and the need to hold a large number of cruisers and destroyers away from their normal functions reconsidered. The issue is of importance because it led to a serious difference between Admiral Forbes and the Admiralty, which clouded the last months of his command of the Home Fleet.

While the Admiralty was thus assessing the invasion danger and considering the best means of countering it the Cabinet was reviewing the same problems. On the 26th of May the Chiefs of Staff reported that 'while our Air Force is in being our Navy and Air Force together should be able to prevent . . . a serious seaborne invasion of this country', but that if 'Germany gained complete air superiority . . . the Navy could hold up invasion for a time but not for an indefinite period'. 'The crux of the matter', they concluded, 'is air superiority.' Their view was accepted by the Cabinet.

---

[1] See pp. 207–208.

In this volume we are not concerned with the reasons why the struggle in the air foreseen by the Cabinet did not start immediately after our withdrawal from Europe. Nor can we follow the ebb and flow of the crucial air battles when they did start in earnest. Our concern lies only with the measures taken to deny the enemy sufficient control of the narrow seas to launch his invading armies.[1]

The Admiralty proceeded to take up many trawlers and drifters, small craft and boats to form the Auxiliary Patrol outlined in the plans. The purpose of the patrol, for which very little armament was available, was to keep watch close offshore in case enemy raiding or invasion forces slipped past the more powerful patrols stationed further to seaward. As the Nore Command recorded, 'trawlers and drifters were requisitioned at great speed from the fishing industry and given patrol positions as far north as Flamborough Head'. On the 10th of July the Prime Minister noted that 'the Admiralty have over a thousand armed patrolling vessels of which two or three hundred are always at sea' and gave it as his opinion that 'a surprise crossing should be impossible'.[2] By 'surprise crossing' Mr Churchill no doubt meant a crossing in strength; the Admiralty had made it plain that they could not guarantee the immunity of our shores from raids. In fact they later told the Cabinet, somewhat pessimistically, that 100,000 men might be landed without being intercepted at sea. To that estimate, which was rather greater than that given to the First Lord in 1914, the Prime Minister replied that he believed the Navy would be better than its word, and gave it as his view that raids by five or ten thousand men were probably the limit of the enemy's capabilities.

To turn now to the effect on the Home Fleet of the preparations to meet invasion, as early as the 17th of May the Admiralty suggested that the fleet's battleships should be stationed at Plymouth; Admiral Forbes' objections to this proposal started a long controversy on the whole question of the employment of the heavy ships of the Home Fleet in face of the invasion threat. The Commander-in-Chief considered that, whereas an invasion of Eire was quite possible, no such operation against Britain could be mounted unless and until the Luftwaffe had defeated the Royal Air Force and that, until there was some sign of the enemy gaining such a victory, the fleet should continue to carry out its functions undisturbed. The Cabinet had, in fact, recorded a similar opinion when they had accepted the view that 'the crux of the matter is air superiority'. To deal with invasion of Eire, Forbes considered that a strong Northern Patrol and a powerful covering force based on Scapa provided the best defence

---

[1] For a full account of the Battle of Britain see the forthcoming volume in this series by Basil Collier, *The Defence of the United Kingdom*.
[2] See W. S. Churchill. *The Second World War*, Vol. II, p. 253.

and would, moreover, enable us also to protect Iceland and the Faeröe Islands, which were of great importance to our control of the Atlantic routes. But if the enemy showed signs of trying to move an invasion fleet across the North Sea, the Commander-in-Chief agreed to move his main forces to Rosyth. This did not entirely satisfy the Admiralty who, on the last day of July, suggested that two battleships should be based at Liverpool. On the 20th of July policy regarding the heavy ships was finally stabilised by an Admiralty order that they should not move into the southern North Sea unless the enemy used his major warships to support an expedition. If, however, the enemy did so, 'our own heavy ships are to engage them at the earliest opportunity'. That decision met, in effect the views of the Commander-in-Chief. It is interesting to recall that a similar discussion arose in 1916 on the question of the employment of the Grand Fleet in the event of invasion. The Admiralty had issued detailed orders regarding the functions and movements of the Grand Fleet and Admiral Jellicoe replied that in his opinion the difficulties of a landing had been underestimated, and so its likelihood exaggerated; that the orders to himself should state no more than that the objective of the Grand Fleet was the enemy High Seas Fleet, and that such strength as he could spare from dealing with that primary objective should be used to attack the enemy transports and his covering fleet. The operations of the Grand Fleet must, he submitted, be left to its Commander-in-Chief. His views prevailed on that occasion.

In 1940 the disposition of the Home Fleet's cruisers and light forces provided a more serious disagreement between the Commander-in-Chief and Whitehall. It has been mentioned that the Admiralty had always intended that the light forces in the south should have cruiser support, and the need to provide such support is indisputable. But it may be felt that the measures taken went further than the need justified. Many cruisers had been detached to the Mediterranean and to Force H in recent weeks, and if the Home Fleet's cruiser strength fell below a certain point it certainly could not carry out its functions. But from the early days of July until the end of August most of the remaining Home Fleet cruisers were dispersed by the Admiralty around our coasts. Two of the 2nd Cruiser Squadron were brought to the Humber and Sheerness; two of the 18th Cruiser Squadron moved between the Humber, Sheerness, the Firth of Forth and Southend; one of the same squadron came to Portsmouth and another to Plymouth, while one ship of the 1st Cruiser Squadron was moved to the Clyde. These dispositions provoked, on the 4th of July, a request from Admiral Forbes that the Admiralty might inform him which cruisers of the Home Fleet could be considered as coming under his command. Simultaneously with the dispersal of the Home Fleet cruisers in this manner, the Prime Minister, on the 1st of July, minuted that 'the Admiralty should endeavour to raise the flotillas in the narrow seas to a strength of forty destroyers' and added, with grim realism, that the 'losses in the Western Approaches must be accepted meanwhile'.[1] The flotilla strength which the Prime Minister wanted in the south corresponded approximately with the four striking flotillas mentioned in the Admiralty's plans and, of course, the defeat of invasion had to take priority over the defence of shipping if, as was certainly believed to be the case, an invasion attempt was imminent. But the dispositions certainly showed little confidence in the capacity of the Royal Air Force and of the intelligence services to give even the small amount of warning which was required to defeat the expedition while on passage.

The Home Fleet and the Western Approaches Command were therefore called on to sacrifice flotilla vessels to the southern commands to an extent which greatly restricted the operational capacity of the former and reduced almost to vanishing point the escorts which the latter was able to provide for our Atlantic convoys. The Nore Command in particular was reinforced so substantially that, on the 29th of July, there were six destroyers of the 21st Flotilla at Sheerness, eighteen of the 16th, 18th and 20th Flotillas at Harwich, where six more large, modern fleet destroyers of the 5th Flotilla were also about to arrive; five corvettes were also operating from the same port. There was thus, at the end of July, a total of thirty-two destroyers of all types and five corvettes in the Nore Command alone.

The consequences in the Western Approaches were serious. In March, April and May 1940 our total losses of merchant shipping from all causes were 107,009 tons, 158,218 tons and 288,461 tons respectively. In the succeeding four months, although the total of operational U-boats was very small, they rose to 585,496 tons, 386,913 tons, 397,229 tons and 448,621 tons.[2] The enemy was not slow to understand the reason for his success. In the autumn Admiral Raeder reported to Hitler that 'the weakness of the British defence and escort forces . . . was a great advantage for our submarines'.

Admiral Forbes had no doubt of the seriousness of the situation. Early in August he urged the release of the anti-submarine trawlers which had been taken off escort duty and sent to join the Auxiliary Patrol; he also pleaded for more flotilla vessels to be released to the convoys, which now needed escort much further to the west. Almost at the same time the Prime Minister minuted to the First Lord and First Sea Lord that 'the repeated severe losses in the north-west approaches are most grievous. . . . There seems to have been a great falling off in the control of these approaches. No doubt this is largely due to the shortage of destroyers through invasion precautions. . . .

---

[1] W. S. Churchill. *The Second World War*, Vol. II, p. 207.
[2] See Appendix R for the causes of these losses.

Anyhow, we cannot go on like this'.[1] All of which was only too true and exposed the dilemma in which we were placed by the need to prepare against invasion whilst maintaining adequate control in the Atlantic. That dilemma was as difficult of solution as it was critical, because the correct choice depended not only on the result of the air battles which had only just begun, but also on estimating rightly the amount of warning which would be received if the invasion fleet sailed.

We will now temporarily take leave of these islands at a time when, under the inspired and inspiring leadership of the Prime Minister, the land forces were re-equipping themselves after Dunkirk and extemporising new strength, the Air Force was braced to meet the inevitable onslaught of the Luftwaffe, the Navy's ships and craft were patrolling and peering into the mists for the first sign of approaching enemies, and the civil population was preparing itself for the worst. For it is time to see what were the enemy's plans and intentions.

The Germans had not undertaken before the war any long-term planning for the invasion of these islands. The first mention of such a project appears to have been made by Admiral Raeder in discussion with Hitler on the 21st May 1940, but the suggestion was then firmly rejected by Hitler as impossible of achievement. At the end of June, however, the Führer completely changed his view. On the 2nd of July he ordered appreciations to be prepared and planning for Operation 'Sealion' to begin; a fortnight later he issued a directive stating that 'since England, in spite of her militarily hopeless situation, shows no sign of coming to terms, I have decided to prepare a landing operation ... and, if necessary, to carry it out'. The preparations were to be entirely completed by the middle of August—barely a month after the issue of the directive—which certainly appears to indicate a lack of understanding of the complexity of a modern, large-scale amphibious expedition; the preliminary air offensive was to start on the 5th of the same month. The enemy realised, correctly, that to neutralise the Royal Air Force was an essential preliminary, and that the success of the invasion would be dependent on this and on the ability of the Luftwaffe to prevent the Royal Navy pressing home its attacks on the invasion fleet. The German Navy was quite inadequate to accomplish the latter object and believed the Luftwaffe incapable of acting in effective substitution for naval strength. Marshal Göring, however, who knew nothing of maritime war, seems to have had complete confidence in the ability of the Luftwaffe to accomplish both tasks.

The plan envisaged landings over a wide area between Ramsgate and the Isle of Wight, and the German army command was entirely

---

[1] See W. S. Churchill. *The Second World War*, Vol. II, p. 531.

confident that it was feasible. When, however, the army proposed to make an initial landing with thirteen divisions and to follow these up with a further twenty-seven, the Navy realised the impossibility of the plan and tried to insist that landings should be made on a much narrower front between Deal and Beachy Head.[1] A compromise plan providing for four separate landings between Folkestone and Selsey Bill was finally reached, but as late as the end of August the two services had by no means agreed how to carry it out. Meanwhile the assembly of the necessary transports, barges, tugs and motor boats at ports between Delfzijl (in Holland) and Havre proceeded. Preparations were also made to lay protective minefields and to station U-boats to intercept our attacking forces.

The British reaction was to attack the concentrations from the air, to bombard the ports from the sea and to harry enemy traffic with light forces. On the 13th of September R.A.F. bombers sank a number of barges in Ostend, and our warships now carried out bombardments of the enemy-held ports as far west as Cherbourg. Next day Admiral Raeder told Hitler that 'the present air situation does not provide conditions for carrying out the operation'. Thus was the traditional British reaction to an invasion threat brought into play once more, though in modernised form. As one authority put it many years ago, 'we keep a hold on it [i.e. the invasion army], firstly, by flotilla blockade and defence stiffened as circumstances may dictate by higher units, and secondly by battle-fleet cover. It is on the flotilla hold that the whole system is built up'.[2] By the 15th the German Navy had completed most of its hasty preparations, but Raeder still held to his view that the operation was a gamble which should only be launched as a last resort.

Though the enemy's records make it clear that he realised the need to defeat the R.A.F. as a preliminary to launching his invasion army, the Luftwaffe now tried to put into action Marshal Göring's plan to subdue and conquer this country by the use of air power alone. The Luftwaffe then found the resistance of the Royal Air Force much stiffer than it had expected, and this led to a series of postponements. Moreover there had now set in the inevitable despondency caused by the knowledge that an operation which was absolutely dependent on maritime control was to be launched, in spite of the fact that such control was not possessed and could not be acquired. Unsuitable weather and the consequences of the bombing of the invasion ports by the Air Force were among the reasons given for postponement. It is not necessary to follow these vacillations in detail, but on the 17th of September the invasion was postponed indefinitely, and on the 12th of October it was formally deferred until the spring of 1941

---

[1] See Map 3 (*facing p. 63*).
[2] J. S. Corbett. *Some Principles of Maritime Strategy*, p. 219.

when the project would be reconsidered. Hitler insisted, however, that preparations for a landing should be continued 'purely as a means of [exerting] political and military pressure on the English'. Finally, on the 13th of February 1942, when the German campaign against Russia had been in progress for eight months without achieving the rapid victory which Hitler had anticipated, he decided that the men and ships earmarked for Operation 'Sealion' should be released for use elsewhere.

To return now to these threatened islands, strenuous steps were meanwhile being taken to repel the invader. The Admiralty rapidly mounted, and in some cases temporarily manned, guns and torpedo tubes to defend the harbours which the enemy might try to seize. Preparations to immobilise the ports by destroying the docks, wharves, cranes and other equipment were also put in hand. Since we had now lost control of the Straits of Dover and the enemy was known to be mounting big guns to try to command the narrows, a number of heavy naval weapons was also erected by the Admiralty near Dover. Both sides expended a big effort in providing and erecting this artillery. The first intention of the Germans was to use theirs to cover the invasion fleet from flank attacks, but as the opportunity for such employment never arose they were actually used to bombard our coastal towns, for counter-battery work and to shell our passing convoys and our minesweepers. Our own guns, of which the first was in action by the 15th of September, were used against the enemy batteries and his shipping. Many long-range duels were fought between the batteries which faced each other across the Straits. In England damage was caused in the towns, and the shelling which, in contrast to air attacks, started without warning had some moral effect among the bombarded populations and the crews of the slowly passing merchantmen. But in fact neither side did appreciable damage to the other's batteries or to his shipping. The command of the Straits now depended chiefly on air power.

The main offensive began on the 13th of August. From that date until the middle of September the enemy made a determined attempt to destroy the Royal Air Force and open the way to invasion. Those five weeks saw the victories by which Fighter Command frustrated the German hopes and intentions. Later the enemy greatly reduced the scale of his daylight attacks and turned most of his attention to night raids on London and other cities. If we now realise that by the end of September the Luftwaffe had, in Admiral Forbes' words, been 'soundly defeated' and so the possibility of invasion removed, it must be remembered that such an estimate could hardly have been reached at the time. What the British Government did know was that the losses and wastage of Fighter Command's aircraft were rising so steeply that by mid-September a state would soon be reached when our resistance was bound to diminish. Happily the losses inflicted on the enemy, or his lack of perseverance, saved the situation. But the margin of victory had been dangerously small.

We must now return to the Home Fleet where the rising shipping losses, the removal of so much of its strength to the south and the consequent impossibility of conducting offensive operations were causing its Commander-in-Chief grave misgivings. Admiral Forbes considered that offensive blows against the enemy-held coasts would force Hitler to disperse his forces and so assist to frustrate his invasion plans. In particular he wished to attack the Norwegian coast. But such blows were forbidden by London while 'the attempted invasion of the United Kingdom is so imminent'. The Commander-in-Chief was also warned that the enemy was expected to employ the new battleship *Bismarck* as well as his two battle cruisers and other forces to support 'attempted invasion on a large scale'. We now know that the *Bismarck* was not nearly ready for service (she did not complete trials until March 1941), that the battle cruisers had both been put out of action off Norway, and that the Germans were actually trying to get their more important naval units ready for sea to raid our Atlantic shipping routes or to create a diversion in the far north if the invasion fleet should sail. But none of this was, of course, known to the Admiralty and the Cabinet at the time. In consequence of these reports Admiral Forbes moved a large part of his fleet to Rosyth on the 13th of September. But he considered that the recent Royal Air Force victories had 'removed the threat of invasion completely' and continued to press for our maritime dispositions to be reconsidered.

On the 28th of September the Commander-in-Chief made his final appeal to the Admiralty on this subject. In this letter the functions of all three services were discussed and the Admiral urged that 'the Army, assisted by the Air Force, should carry out its immemorial rôle of holding up the first flight of an invading force and that the Navy should be freed to carry out its proper function— offensively against the enemy and in defence of our trade—and not be tied down to provide passive defence to our country, which had now become a fortress'.

On the last day of October the Prime Minister asked Admiral Forbes for his views on the possibility of the enemy attempting to launch his invasion fleet. He replied that 'while we are predominant at sea and until Germany has defeated our fighter force invasion by sea is not a practical operation of war'. With regard to the possibility of invasion during the forthcoming winter months Forbes made three points. Firstly, that it would have to be carried out within range of the enemy's shore-based fighters, which restricted the possible landing points to the coast between the Wash and Mount's Bay; but

S

the distances involved and the time which the enemy could afford to spend on passage actually narrowed the area still further to the coastline between the North Foreland, or possibly still further west, and Poole. Secondly, that merchant vessels and not barges would have to be used during the winter months, and all the ports which the enemy might attempt to seize were strongly defended. Thirdly, that a surprise invasion in fog or low visibility was improbable, because fog occurred only on about five days of each winter month and was difficult to forecast beyond a short time ahead, and also because such conditions would make the handling of an invasion fleet at sea extremely hazardous and the safe arrival of the assault forces at their correct landing places at the proper time almost an impossibility.

Admiral Forbes' views regarding the disposition of our forces and the value of the Auxiliary Patrol were not shared by the naval Commanders-in-Chief in the south, on whom, of course, the immediate problem of finding and defeating an invasion force would fall. Admiral Drax, at the Nore, strenuously insisted on the need to keep the large ships of the 18th Cruiser Squadron at Sheerness or Southend because 'to destroy an invading force we need gunfire and plenty of it'. He also considered that 'as long as the enemy maintains vast numbers of barges and small craft in the ports nearest to our coasts we should keep up our auxiliary patrols'. And the other Commanders-in-Chief agreed with him. On the 22nd of September Admiral Drax issued a call to his command to be ready 'to show the world how Britain at bay can deal with these enemies'. To the Nore Command the invasion menace was certainly very near at hand. To Admiral Forbes, on the other hand, it seemed not only that the function of the Army was being incorrectly interpreted, but that the Navy was being called on to carry out part of the Army's function of holding up the first flight of the invaders until the warships could get there to destroy the transports. And he considered that this was weakening the execution by the Navy of its proper rôle. 'In fact', he wrote, after the September air battles had been fought, 'as there appears to be no possible chance of the enemy gaining control of the air over our coasts, the defence has been immeasurably strengthened' by the new factor of air power.

We who lived through those anxious days are perhaps too near to the events to be justified in stating a conclusion on the issue discussed above. Moreover it would be unfair to disregard what Mr Churchill has called 'the pressures under which the men responsible lived' at that time.[1] For the purposes of contemporary history it is enough that the intention to invade was defeated; it may

---

[1] W. S. Churchill. *The World Crisis 1915* (Thornton, Butterworth, 1923), p. 11.

be left to posterity to decide whether or not the maritime dispositions ordered were the best to defeat invasion, if it had been launched. Two points must, however, be made clear. Firstly, the difference between Admiral Forbes on the one hand and the Admiralty and his brother Commanders-in-Chief in the south on the other hand lay only in the question whether the means employed to defeat invasion were the best, having regard to the country's one other vital requirement—to avoid starvation. Secondly, the orders and intentions issued by the Admiralty in May corresponded in many ways with the views which Admiral Forbes stated later; and many statements made by the Prime Minister, the Cabinet and the Chiefs-of-Staff—some of which have been quoted above—expressed similar views. It was in the translation of the accepted policy and views into executive action that the divergence seems to have occurred.

If Admiral Forbes' belief that the invasion attempt had been defeated by the end of September was ahead of the intelligence available in London, a similar realisation did gradually spread over the country as the autumn nights began to lengthen into winter with all its accompaniment of gales, cold and fog in the North Sea and English Channel. Thus, gradually, the disturbance to our maritime strategy was relaxed and the Home Fleet and all the varied instruments of our maritime power reverted to their normal functions of 'acting offensively against the enemy and in defence of our trade'.

It is now necessary to return to the beginning of this period and to review other events in home waters up to the end of the year. The first major operation of the fleet was an attempt to intercept the *Gneisenau*, which had been damaged by a torpedo from the submarine *Clyde* on the 20th of June, on her return journey from Trondheim to Germany.[1] On the 27th of July intelligence had indicated the possibility of such a movement being about to take place and Admiral Forbes therefore sent the *Renown*, *Repulse*, the 1st Cruiser Squadron and eight destroyers out on an intercepting course. But no enemy ships were sighted and no firm reports of the enemy's movements were received until two days after their successful completion. On the 28th of July our aircraft reported Trondheim to be clear of enemy warships, and on the 1st of August both battle cruisers were identified in Kiel.

Ever since the return to Trondheim of the *Scharnhorst*, which had been damaged by the *Acasta*'s torpedo on the 9th of June, and of the *Gneisenau* and the *Hipper* after their foray against our shipping returning from Narvik, major enemy warships had remained in or near Trondheim. The presence of these ships on the Norwegian coast

---

[1] See p. 199.

naturally led to a request by the Admiralty that every endeavour should be made to watch them from the air. No. 18 Group of Coastal Command flew many reconnaissances in June and July for that purpose and suffered heavy losses—no less than seventeen aircraft in June—in doing so. Now that we possess full details of the enemy ships present in Trondheim during this period, it is of interest to note that on no occasion was the presence of both battle cruisers correctly reported, and that the two cruisers—for the *Nürnberg* arrived there as well in the middle of June—were generally reported as destroyers. Just as the *Rawalpindi* and the *Glorious* reported their assailants to be pocket-battleships, so did our aircraft fail to distinguish between the different classes of ships present, and often reported wrongly the actual number of major warships present as well.[1] Clear weather made the reconnaissance aircraft very vulnerable to attack by the fighters stationed near Trondheim, and low visibility either prevented flying altogether or made careful reconnaissance of the fiords extremely difficult. To attack these important ships while in harbour, or soon after leaving port, was only possible for submarines or from the air; and for the latter purpose Coastal Command only possessed Hudson aircraft and the Beauforts of Nos. 22 and 42 squadrons—a quite inadequate force. Moreover Coastal Command had, at this period of the invasion threat, to meet many other requirements, and our submarines, as will be seen shortly, could not keep continuous patrols off the enemy base. It thus occurred that for some six weeks an unusual concentration of important enemy warships was continuously present in Trondheim and was never correctly reported, let alone successfully attacked. The *Gneisenau* sailed from Trondheim with the *Scharnhorst* on the 20th of June and, as already mentioned, was torpedoed by the *Clyde* soon after her departure and put back into port. The *Scharnhorst* steamed south and was heavily but ineffectively attacked by naval torpedo bombers from the Orkneys and by Coastal Command aircraft, but received no further damage before reaching Kiel on the 23rd. The *Hipper* left Trondheim on the 25th of July, and until the 9th of August scoured the area between Tromsö and Bear Island and to the west of Spitzbergen for British shipping believed to be sailing from Petsamo.[2] She was never reported while on this mission, but she accomplished practically nothing. Finally the *Gneisenau*, *Nürnberg* and four destroyers left Trondheim on the 25th of July and passed south to Kiel. All the enemy warships from Trondheim thus returned safely to their home bases, and both the German battle cruisers were thus in dock at Kiel for repairs by the end of July. While the success of the important warship movements just described underlined the con-

---

[1] See pp. 82–83 regarding the similarity of the silhouettes of major German warships.
[2] See Map 40 (*facing p. 485*).

tinued unreliability of our air reconnaissance, the simultaneous presence of the two ships in dock did, for the first time, indicate to the Admiralty the probability that both had received damage. But, in addition to the *Scharnhorst* and *Gneisenau*, the pocket-battleship *Lützow* was then also repairing torpedo damage at Kiel, and the 8-inch cruiser *Prinz Eugen*, sister ship to the *Hipper*, was completed and about to commission in the same port. Moreover, at Hamburg the construction of the *Bismarck* was progressing, though not so fast as the Admiralty at this time believed, while her sister-ship the *Tirpitz* was under active construction at Wilhelmshaven, where the pocket-battleship *Scheer* was also present. With the threat of invasion very much to the fore it was natural that the Admiralty should endeavour to delay by all possible means the entry or return of these important ships into service, Requests were therefore made that Bomber Command should attack them in their bases. Raids were started during the first days of July, and continued whenever conditions were favourable throughout the months of August, September and October, during which a total of 1,042 bomber sorties aimed 683 tons of bombs at these naval targets. But the weight of attack which Bomber Command could devote to this purpose on any one night was only some twenty-five to forty heavy bombers—Hampdens, Whitleys and Wellingtons—and this was insufficient to achieve any very favourable results. The *Prinz Eugen* was hit by two bombs on the 1st–2nd of July, the *Lützow* was hit a week later by one which failed to explode, and the persistence of the raids, though on a small scale, caused some damage in the dockyards, and so delayed somewhat the progress of construction and repair work. But no damage of an important nature was caused to the ships themselves.

These attacks on the German naval bases were not the only demand made on the Royal Air Force to assist the defeat of the enemy's invasion plans and his attacks on our ships and convoys, since aerial minelaying continued to figure prominently in the Admiralty's requests. But it will be convenient to defer consideration of that campaign for the present and to continue the narrative of the operations of the Home Fleet during the latter half of 1940.

Late in August the plans of the War Cabinet for the expedition against Dakar (Operation 'Menace'), which will be described in a later chapter, necessitated considerable detachments. The *Barham* and four destroyers sailed for Gibraltar on the 28th, and the cruisers *Devonshire* and *Fiji* were sent on the last day of the month to escort the troopships on their passage south. Next day the *Fiji* was torpedoed by a U-boat. She was later replaced by the *Australia*, which had been placed at the Admiralty's disposal by the Commonwealth Government and had recently joined the 1st Cruiser Squadron.

On the 6th of September Admiral Forbes took the *Furious* and other forces to sea to attack shipping off the Norwegian coast, where it was beyond the range of the naval dive-bombers stationed in the Orkneys. Only two ships were sighted. Though one was believed to have been sunk, post-war records do not confirm any such success. Other plans of a similar nature were, as already mentioned, cancelled by the Admiralty on account of the invasion threat, but No. 801 Squadron struck several times from the Orkneys at shore targets and shipping in southern Norway. On the 13th and 14th of October a destroyer raid was carried out by the *Cossack* and three other destroyers. An enemy convoy had been reported by air reconnaissance off Lister Light and was intercepted by the destroyers off Egersund at midnight.[1] Though it was believed at the time that the whole convoy was destroyed, it is now known that only two of the four ships were sunk; it was not a mercantile convoy which was attacked but ships carrying anti-submarine defence equipment to Trondheim.

On the 12th of the same month an attack was carried out against the shore installations and oil tanks at Tromsö by the *Furious'* aircraft. They achieved complete surprise and claimed good results, but German records show that the damage done was in fact negligible. Such operations were of value, however, in preventing the enemy from enjoying the undisturbed use of the Norwegian coastal waters. We now know that the Germans expected us to make a greater air and sea effort towards that end, and considered us unenterprising in attempting so little. The truth is that Admiral Forbes desired to do exactly what the Germans feared he would do—constantly to harry and destroy German shipping off Norway with his aircraft and light forces. It was the expectation of invasion and the diversion of so great a proportion of the Home Fleet to the south which prevented more being attempted.

Admiral Forbes received certain reinforcements of newly completed ships at this time—notably the cruisers *Kenya*, *Dido* and *Phoebe*—and on the 16th of October the new battleship *King George V* was safely escorted from the Tyne to Rosyth. But these reinforcements were offset by orders in November to detach other ships to the Mediterranean and to Force H; frequent calls were also made to provide powerful escorts to the troop convoys on the first stretch of their long passage to the Middle East round the Cape of Good Hope, and for the *Furious* to carry urgently needed aircraft for the same theatre to Takoradi on the Gold Coast. Moreover, many ships had developed serious defects or were long overdue for refit.

The *King George V* arrived at Scapa on the 2nd of December and the new aircraft carrier *Formidable* on the 12th, but the latter ship and the cruiser *Norfolk* were almost at once detached to Freetown to form

---

[1] See Map 5 (*facing p. 71*).

a new hunting group, known as Force K, which was to work from Freetown against the *Admiral Scheer*, at this time raiding commerce in the South Atlantic.

The last operation of the year was designed to cover the waters round Iceland and the Faeröes with the heavy ships of the fleet against any attempt by the enemy to send out warship raiders during the Christmas season. Though several incorrect reports of such moves were received, the area remained quiet but, in the south, the *Hipper* revealed her presence by an attack on a Middle East troop convoy.

In the early days of July all our Atlantic convoys had, in consequence of the enemy's newly-won possession of French bases and the denial to us of the use of naval and air bases in Eire, been diverted from the routes passing south of Ireland to the north-west approaches, and all shipping bound for our east coast ports now passed around the north of Scotland through the Pentland Firth or the Fair Isle Channels.[1]

Though Admiral Forbes was not responsible for these convoys he could not remain indifferent to the safety of the steady flow of merchant shipping. As was to be expected, the enemy's U-boats and aircraft soon began to pay attention to this route and in consequence Home Fleet destroyers, of which the Commander-in-Chief was woefully short, had frequently to be detached either to augment the convoys' escorts or to hunt the U-boats. The naval aircraft stationed in the Orkneys were similarly employed, and an anti-aircraft cruiser was often detached to afford additional protection against marauding bombers while the convoys passed around the Scottish coast. During the month of August such air attacks became frequent and several ships were sunk.

The Admiralty endeavoured to improve the protection of these routes by a defensive minefield laid between the Orkneys and Iceland, to be mentioned again shortly, and by the completion of the east coast mine barrier. But, as has been remarked earlier, these very measures produced focal points for shipping in the north-west approaches, the Minches, the area of North Rona and off the Moray Firth, and the U-boats were not slow to discover and exploit this result.[2] Another defensive minefield was laid in the last days of July and early August to the south of the St. George's Channel to close that approach to our shipping routes to Liverpool and the Clyde. In August the 1st Minelaying Squadron, consisting of four converted merchant ships commanded by Rear-Admiral W. F. Wake-Walker, completed the east coast barrier and the field in the St. George's Channel; they also laid a line of mines off North Rona. In all, 8,918 mines were laid during the month. In September the squadron con-

---
[1] See Maps 4 and 9 (*facing pp. 65 and 93*).
[2] See pp. 126 and 130, and Map 8 (*facing p. 91*).

centrated on laying the new northern barrier, but Admiral Forbes remained sceptical of its value, particularly when, owing to congestion of mines ashore, unstable ones had to be laid and this denied the use of certain waters to our own ships. In October minelaying was discontinued because Admiral Forbes was unable to supply escorts for the minelaying squadron, but in the following month a field was laid off the north of Iceland with the object of restricting the open waters of the Denmark Strait.[1] In December the first section of the Iceland–Faeröes minefield was laid. These last operations were powerfully covered by the Home Fleet.

Though large-scale defensive minelaying continued in 1941 it will be appropriate to summarise now the results achieved by this considerable effort. It will be recalled that great numbers of moored mines had originally been ordered for the Northern Barrage, which the Admiralty wished to lay between the Orkneys and Norway.[2] But the German occupation of Norway rendered this defensive measure obsolete, even if such operations could still have been carried out in face of the enemy's air attacks; for the barrage would now have been wrongly placed. It was accordingly decided instead to lay extensive minefields from the Orkneys and Faeröes to Iceland and Greenland, using deep-laid mines to catch U-boats and shallow mines to endanger surface vessels. Apart, possibly, from some slight deterrent effect on the freedom with which enemy ships passed through these waters the minefields seem to have accomplished virtually no results. During the entire war only one U-boat was destroyed by mines in this area, and no enemy surface vessel was ever damaged or sunk by them. Not only does the effort seem to have been unprofitable, but the minefields were a source of anxiety to our own ships which had to work in those waters. But the great quantities of moored mines now being produced could not be held in store on land and the Admiralty decided therefore that laying should be continued. Even accepting that the original proposal for the Northern Barrage was justifiable—and the misgivings of the First Lord on that score have already been commented on—it seems clear that in the changed circumstances of mid-1940 the production programme should have been stopped and unwanted mines jettisoned rather than valuable ships and many men employed on a project of such doubtful value.

Meanwhile the Northern Patrol continued its endeavours to watch the exits to the Atlantic, but with less success than during the early months of the war. Though the reduction in interceptions was partly caused by the decreased flow of neutral shipping, the efficiency of the patrol was vitiated by the removal of trawlers for anti-invasion duties

---

[1] See Map 4 (*facing p. 65*).
[2] See p. 97.

in the south. Moreover, since the enemy was now well informed regarding our patrol lines, he was able to inflict heavy losses with his U-boats on the unprotected armed merchant cruisers carrying out the patrols. Three of these ships—the *Carinthia*, *Scotstoun* and *Andania*—were torpedoed and sunk in June.

In July the better weather helped to produce better results in the number of ships intercepted. But on the 2nd of August the Admiralty decided to establish a new Western Patrol to watch the approaches to western Europe and North Africa, and this further depleted the meagre forces available to watch the northern exits. In August another A.M.C., the *Transylvania*, was sunk by a U-boat, there were many gales, and the detachment of trawlers to the south made the patrol largely ineffectual. In September and October respectively only eight and six ships were intercepted. On the 18th of November it was decided that the armed merchant cruisers would in future patrol the Denmark Strait, and that the passage between the Faeröe Islands and Iceland would be guarded only by trawlers and by the minefield already mentioned. Two more A.M.C.s—the *Laurentic* and *Patroclus*—had been sunk by U-boats off Bloody Foreland in November when returning from the Western Patrol. In December the patrols were very thinly disposed and the weather was extremely severe; yet fifteen merchant vessels were intercepted.

The employment of valuable liners, soon to be in great demand as troop carriers, on these patrol duties plainly required radical reconsideration, as they were always in danger from U-boats when proceeding from Liverpool or the Clyde to their patrol areas. Moreover not only had the original purpose of the Northern Patrol—the enforcement of our blockade of Germany—practically disappeared with the changed conditions of the war, but the ships were no match even for the armed merchant raiders which they might encounter breaking out from the North Sea, let alone for the enemy's warship raiders. After the heavy losses of November Admiral Forbes proposed that the armed merchant cruisers should be withdrawn until anti-submarine protection could be afforded them. But the Admiralty insisted that the patrols should be maintained. A modified policy was therefore introduced in December whereby ocean boarding vessels, which were a new type of auxiliary warship just beginning to enter service, replaced the armed merchant cruisers of the Western Patrol. The A.M.C.s of the Northern Patrol would now work from Halifax, escort a homeward-bound convoy to 25° West, and then carry out two patrols in the Denmark Strait with an interval for fuelling in the Icelandic base at Hvalfiord before returning to Halifax. But the truth is that our whole system of reconnaissance of these northern waters was, in Admiral Forbes' words, 'more illusory than real', as was shown by several undetected outward and homeward passages of German armed merchant raiders and warships made at this time. There were rarely more than two A.M.C.s to patrol the 300-mile wide Denmark Strait and four trawlers in the 240-mile Faeroes–Iceland passage; the minefields laid between Scotland and the Faeroes had little or no effect on enemy movements and the air patrols flown from this country and from Iceland were, as yet, far from regular. The real needs, as the Commander-in-Chief pointed out at the close of the year, were for more trawlers of long endurance, for more long-range reconnaissance aircraft, for good air bases in Iceland and for wireless direction-finding stations in Iceland, Greenland and the Faeroes. But none of this could be realised for a long time to come and meanwhile the situation remained full of danger. Our Atlantic convoys were being diverted ever further to the north in the endeavour to avoid the waters to the west of Rockall and off north-west Ireland, where the enemy's U-boats and long-range aircraft had been taking a heavy toll; they were thus more exposed to sporadic attacks by raiders breaking out through one of the northern passages.

During the height of the invasion threat our submarine patrols were, in accordance with the broad policy laid down by the Cabinet, generally diverted to intercept the expected invasion fleet. On the 6th of July the *Shark* was lost off southern Norway by depth charge attack from aircraft, and on the 9th the patrols which had been maintained off Trondheim to intercept the *Gneisenau* had to be withdrawn because of the shortness of the nights and the enemy's efficient counter-measures. Though some successes were obtained by the Home Fleet's submarines and three minelaying operations were carried out, conditions were now very difficult indeed. Not only did the perpetual daylight in the north prevent the charging of batteries on the surface, but the enemy's air and surface patrolling of the coastal waters was very intensive; and his aircraft were now using with good effect the airborne depth charge—a weapon which was still not available to our own anti-submarine air patrols. But perhaps the greatest factor in bringing success to the enemy's counter-measures was his ability at this time to locate our submarines by means of his wireless interception service. Possessed of this advantage and of a lethal weapon with which to attack the located submarines, it is not surprising that the enemy inflicted severe losses. In addition to the *Shark*, the Dutch submarine O.13, the *Salmon*, *Narwhal*, *Thames*, and *Spearfish* were all sunk between June and August.

In consequence of these losses the inshore patrols were abandoned and, instead, our submarines were disposed to intercept U-boats in the Bay of Biscay, in the North Sea and on the Atlantic shipping routes. While off Lorient on the 20th of August, the *Cachalot* torpedoed and sank U.51. In September several more attacks on U-boats were made by our submarines, but it is now known that none was successful. Several successes were, however, scored against the enemy's transports and mercantile traffic off the Skagerrak and in the Bay of Biscay, but in November the loss of the *Swordfish* and of the Dutch submarine O.22 swelled the total of casualties. By way of recompense the *Thunderbolt* sank the Italian U-boat *Tarantini* off the Gironde on the 15th December, and it is now known that our own and the German submarine losses during this period were, in fact, exactly equal.[1]

The enemy's superiority in intelligence at this time, exemplified by his successes against our submarines, whose dispositions were, we now know, disclosed to him, brought him also wider benefits. It was suggested earlier that his efficient and regular air reconnaissance of our main bases and the skilful work of his wireless interception service were the main factors in bringing this about.[2] The former was, taking account of our shortage of modern aircraft of all types, probably unavoidable, but that the latter should have continued so long may, perhaps, be attributed to misplaced confidence in the security of our cyphers. Not until mid-1940 does it seem to have been realised that the Germans were able to read our cyphered messages. The cyphers were changed in August of that year, and the enemy's post-war comment on the consequence to himself is worth quoting. 'A great set-back for German naval strategy at this time was the change by the Admiralty of naval codes and cyphers. The insight into British operations, which had lasted so long, thus came to an end. Knowledge of British movements had spared German vessels many a surprise encounter with superior forces and this had become an element in operational planning.'

The last month of the year saw the first change in the command of the Home Fleet, for on the 2nd of December Admiral Forbes hauled down his flag and came ashore after transferring his command to Admiral J. C. Tovey. Though the fifteen months of Admiral Forbes' war command brought no great sea victory in home waters such as might catch the public's imagination, they saw the steady application of the long-established principles for the maintenance of the sea communications to these islands. Moreover, in the Norwegian campaign the Home Fleet's surface ships, submarines and aircraft had inflicted such damage on the enemy as deprived him for many months of anything resembling a balanced maritime force. Though criticisms, some of them public, were levelled at the Commander-in-Chief at the time, this was probably inevitable in the early stages of a war for which the nation was ill-prepared and which, on land, was marked only by defeats. But even when viewed at this comparatively

---

[1] See Appendix K for details of enemy U-boat losses.
[2] See p. 19.

near distance it does seem that the policy and strategy which Admiral Forbes attempted to pursue—though often frustrated by causes outside his control—were generally justified by subsequent events, and that his steady hand on the reins controlling our vital maritime power contributed greatly to bringing the country through this anxious period with its maritime strength not only unimpaired but growing.

Admiral Tovey took over a Home Fleet which was stronger and better balanced than that commanded by Admiral Forbes during most of the period covered by this chapter. As regards capital ships the *King George V* was now in service, and the *Nelson, Rodney, Hood* and *Repulse* were all again based on Scapa instead of being divided between that base and Rosyth. True the only aircraft carrier which might have been working with the fleet—the *Furious*—was still employed carrying Royal Air Force aircraft to Takoradi for the Middle East theatre, but in cruisers there was a great improvement. There were eleven ships of this class available, belonging to the 2nd, 10th, 15th and 18th Cruiser Squadrons, and four more were expected shortly to return from refits. Only in destroyers was there still a great weakness, since of these but seventeen were available. It was fortunate that the Home Fleet's strength could be somewhat restored and concentrated at this time after the many months of weakness and dispersal, for the enemy's new *Bismarck* was approaching completion, the *Scharnhorst, Gneisenau* and *Lützow* were all expected to complete their repairs early in the new year and the powerful new cruiser *Prinz Eugen*, though not yet fully operational, was in service. A recrudescence of activity by his major surface vessels was therefore clearly to be expected.

As to the security of the main base at Scapa, though Admiral Tovey soon pressed for increased protection from air attack, its general condition had improved out of all recognition since the anxious early days when the fleet had been forced to wander from one ill-protected anchorage to another. The equipment of the main base to enable maintenance work and minor refits and repairs to be carried out at Scapa had also improved. This was of direct benefit to the day-to-day operational strength of the fleet, since it reduced the necessity to send ships into dockyard hands in the south. Thus the arrival, in the latter part of August, of a small floating dock capable of lifting destroyers was, in the opinion of the Commander-in-Chief, equivalent to an appreciable increase in the destroyer strength of the fleet. Indeed, the provision of such facilities must always be an essential part of the organisation of any fleet base, and their almost complete absence during the early months of the war had not been the least of the handicaps under which Admiral Forbes had laboured.

CHAPTER XIV

OCEAN WARFARE
1st January–31st December, 1940

> Commerce destroyers scatter, that they may see and seize more prey.
> A. T. Mahan. *The Influence of Sea Power on History* (1889).

In the last chapters the reader's attention has been chiefly directed to the maritime operations which took place between the early days of April and the beginning of June 1940 in the relatively confined waters off the shores of these islands and the European seaboard. Though a large proportion of Britain's naval strength was then deployed at home, the security of our ocean trade routes continued to demand constant vigilance and carefully planned dispositions against the renewal of the enemy's attempts to disrupt the flow of shipping along them. It is therefore necessary to retrace our steps to the beginning of the year, and to turn our attention from the intensive struggle in the narrow seas and coastal waters to the events which had meanwhile taken place on the broad oceans which, at the end of 1939, had been temporarily cleared of enemy surface warships. But a renewal by the enemy of sporadic warfare was to be expected, with surface ships as well as with his U-boats, and the relative quiet which prevailed as the New Year dawned could not be taken as anything more than a lull.

The depredations of the enemy's U-boats during the first half of this phase still generally took place in the western and south-western approaches to these islands and have therefore been considered, in an earlier chapter, with the measures taken to protect our coastal and short-sea routes.[1] But the foreign naval commands, though not yet fully involved in the U-boat war, were not without their difficulties during this period, by no means the least of which was caused by the chronic shortage of escort vessels and the resulting delays to shipping. It was, for instance, this ever-present trouble which led to the fast Halifax (H.X.F.) convoys being discontinued for a time after the middle of February. Furthermore the heavy demands of the Norwegian campaign drained away the strength of our ocean escort forces. For example the Halifax escort force, now com-

---
[1] See pp. 128–135.

manded by Rear-Admiral S. S. Bonham-Carter, had, at the start of the year, consisted of four battleships (*Royal Sovereign*, *Resolution*, *Revenge* and *Malaya*), two cruisers (*Emerald* and *Enterprise*) and four armed merchant cruisers; by the end of May it was reduced to one battleship, one cruiser and eleven armed merchant cruisers. At the same time our convoys were getting bigger and bigger, largely because more neutral ships were now joining them. Not only did the larger convoys need more escorts, but the assembly and arrival ports became more congested and this tended to delay the flow of shipping. In the endeavour to reduce these delays Bermuda was substituted for Halifax as the assembly point for ships starting their homeward journeys from ports south of the Chesapeake. The Bermuda convoys (B.H.X.) met and joined the appropriate Halifax convoys at sea in about 41° North 43° West.[1] This arrangement was first introduced for convoys which sailed from Bermuda and Halifax on the 7th and 8th of May respectively. But there was also a steady stream of independently-routed ships, most of which were considered too fast or too slow to join a convoy. Of independent sailings during this period the most interesting was, perhaps, that of the liner *Queen Elizabeth* on her maiden voyage to New York on the 2nd of March. There she was converted into a troopship and later joined the other giant liners *Queen Mary* and *Aquitania* as fast troop transports. They were first employed in that capacity to bring Australian and New Zealand troops from their home countries to the Middle East theatre or to Britain.

After the requirements of the main fleets had been met, few cruisers—and those generally the least modern ships—could be allocated to the foreign commands as ocean convoy escorts and to patrol the long sea routes. But the Admiralty's plans to supplement our meagre cruiser strength by converting some fifty liners to armed merchant cruisers were now beginning to yield results. By February 1940 forty-six such ships had been commissioned. As these conversions progressed, however, doubts began to arise whether it was justifiable or necessary to use large and valuable ships in this manner. Not only were the ships themselves already needed as troop transports—and it was realised that the requirement for ships capable of that rôle was bound to increase as the war continued—but they absorbed large numbers of officers and men in their crews, and were extravagant also in maintenance and upkeep as naval auxiliaries. Furthermore it was soon demonstrated that they were practically defenceless against U-boat attack, and many were lost to this cause while on patrol in the Atlantic;[2] and their obsolete armaments, composed of guns removed from scrapped warships, and extemporised

---

[1] See Map 9 (*facing p. 93*).
[2] See p. 265.

fire control arrangements made them incapable of engaging the well-equipped German disguised raiders on anything like equal terms. Early in January the First Lord, Mr Churchill, asked the First Sea Lord to consider whether the armed merchant cruisers, which he described as 'an immense expense and also a care and anxiety', were really essential. But the Naval Staff, under constant pressure to increase ocean escorts and to provide the foreign commands with ships capable of performing some of the functions of cruisers, replied that they were 'indispensable auxiliaries at the present time'. The programme for their conversion and employment therefore continued unchanged. By February ten were allocated to the Freetown Escort Force, four to the Halifax Escort Force, some twenty were employed on the Northern Patrol and the remaining dozen were divided between the Mediterranean, Pacific and Indian Oceans.

On the 27th of April all except the fastest shipping was diverted from the Mediterranean to the long haul round the Cape and, after a temporary relaxation of the order, it was reimposed on the 16th of May; thereafter it remained in force until the North African and Sicily landings enabled the short route to the East to be brought into use once more in 1943. The month of May 1940 therefore marks the important success to the enemy of denying to us the regular use of the Mediterranean routes. It will be appropriate to analyse the effect of this change on our maritime strategy. The distance round the Cape from the Clyde to Suez, assuming that no major diversions from the shortest route are ordered, is 12,860 miles. For a convoy to reach the Middle East theatre and return to Britain by this route therefore necessitated a journey some 20,000 miles longer than the round voyage using the Mediterranean. And ocean escorts had somehow to be found to accompany the convoy throughout the whole of the greatly lengthened journey. Nor were the time factor and the increased escort requirements the only unfavourable aspects of this problem. The supply and reinforcement of the Army of the Nile and of the forces now being built up in East Africa necessitated the use on the long route of fast liners to carry the troops and of fast cargo ships (such as refrigerator ships) to carry their equipment and stores. And such ships were far from plentiful. If one convoy of about twenty-five ships sailed each month, the new requirement meant that about 150 of our best merchant ships were kept permanently on this service. Plainly this was a very serious matter for the Ministry of Transport, which had to find the ships, as well as for the Admiralty which had to control and direct their movements and protect them on passage.

The story of the first, tragic duty which fell to Admiral Somerville's Force H has already been told.[1] We will now continue the story of

---

[1] See pp. 242–245.

Force H and of the North Atlantic Command from the return of the former to Gibraltar after the attack on Oran. During the weeks succeeding the fall of France the problem of controlling French traffic passing through the Straits was difficult, and a number of French warships and merchant ships passed in both directions. The Admiralty's first orders were that the warships were not to be hindered unless they were making for a Biscay port. They were therefore generally only shadowed by a destroyer or aircraft until such time as their destination appeared certain. Merchant ships, however, were to be intercepted if outside territorial waters and unescorted, and brought into Gibraltar. As, however, they kept in Spanish waters as far as possible and were nearly always escorted, no effective control over their movements or cargoes could be enforced. Not until November was a French merchantman intercepted. The difficulties produced on the station and the changes in policy ordered from London with regard to French traffic past Gibraltar will be considered more fully in a later chapter.

The homeward-bound Gibraltar convoys (H.G. convoys) continued to run smoothly at this time. In July ninety-six ships sailed north in six convoys, but thereafter no more than two convoys were sailed during each month. They comprised from twenty to fifty merchant ships.

On the 9th of July the Prime Minister suggested sending Force H to Casablanca to dispose of the *Jean Bart* and other French ships in that port, but his proposal was not put into effect, possibly because shortly after the Oran operation Admiral Somerville was ordered to take his ships north from Gibraltar to attack French shipping in the Biscay ports. He sailed for the latter purpose on the 22nd of July but, three days later, the orders were cancelled from London. Early in August the greater part of Force H returned home for a short time and, during the visit, Admiral Somerville transferred his flag from the *Hood* to the *Renown*. On the 20th of August he was back on his station again.

When the enemy gained possession of the ports and bases on the French Biscay coast it was expected that he would exploit his new advantage to station major warships there, to attack our Atlantic shipping. It was also considered that the enemy might now attempt to launch amphibious expeditions or raids against points of strategic importance such as the Azores or Canary Islands.[1] The Admiralty was fully alive to the danger of those islands falling into enemy hands and was determined to frustrate any attempt to gain possession of them.

The safety of the Atlantic islands therefore now played a large part

---

[1] See Map 23 (*facing p. 273*).

Map 23
The Central and South Atlantic Oceans

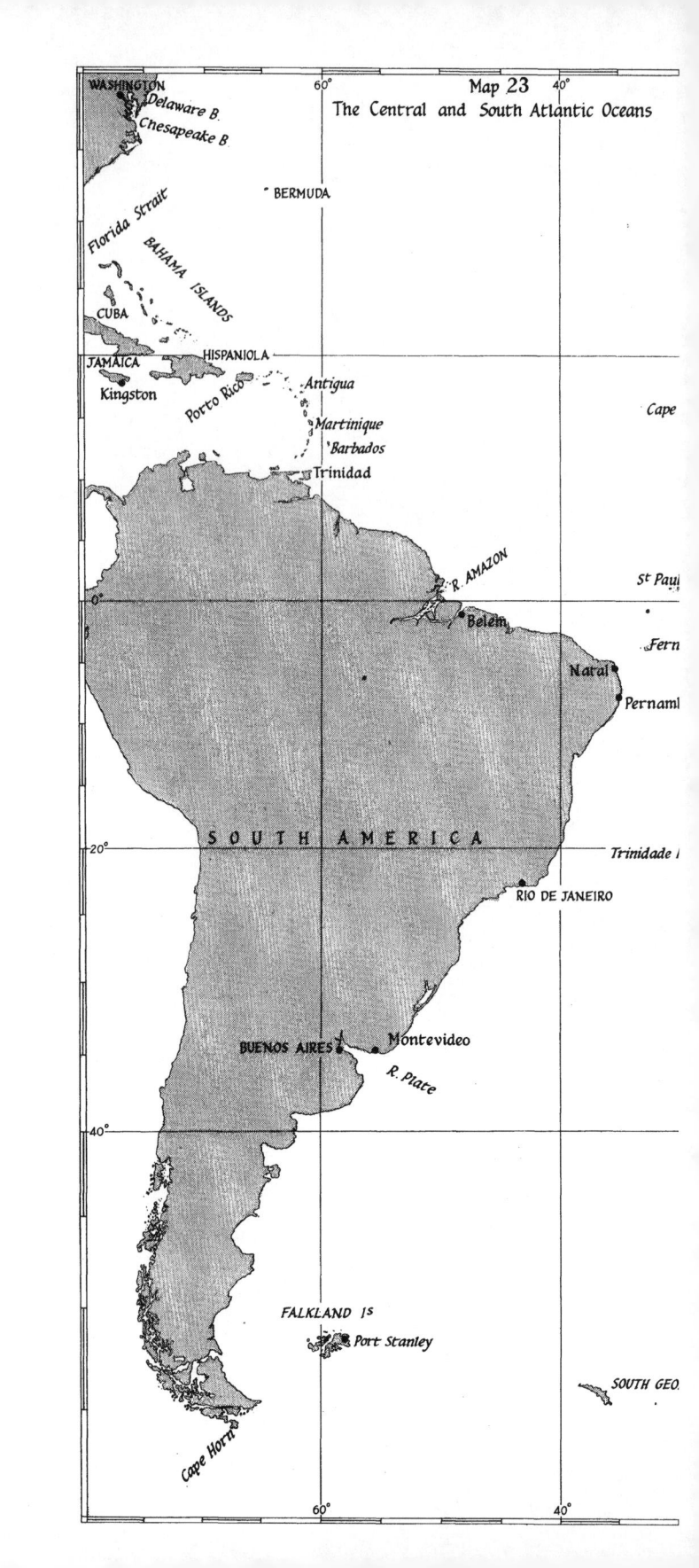

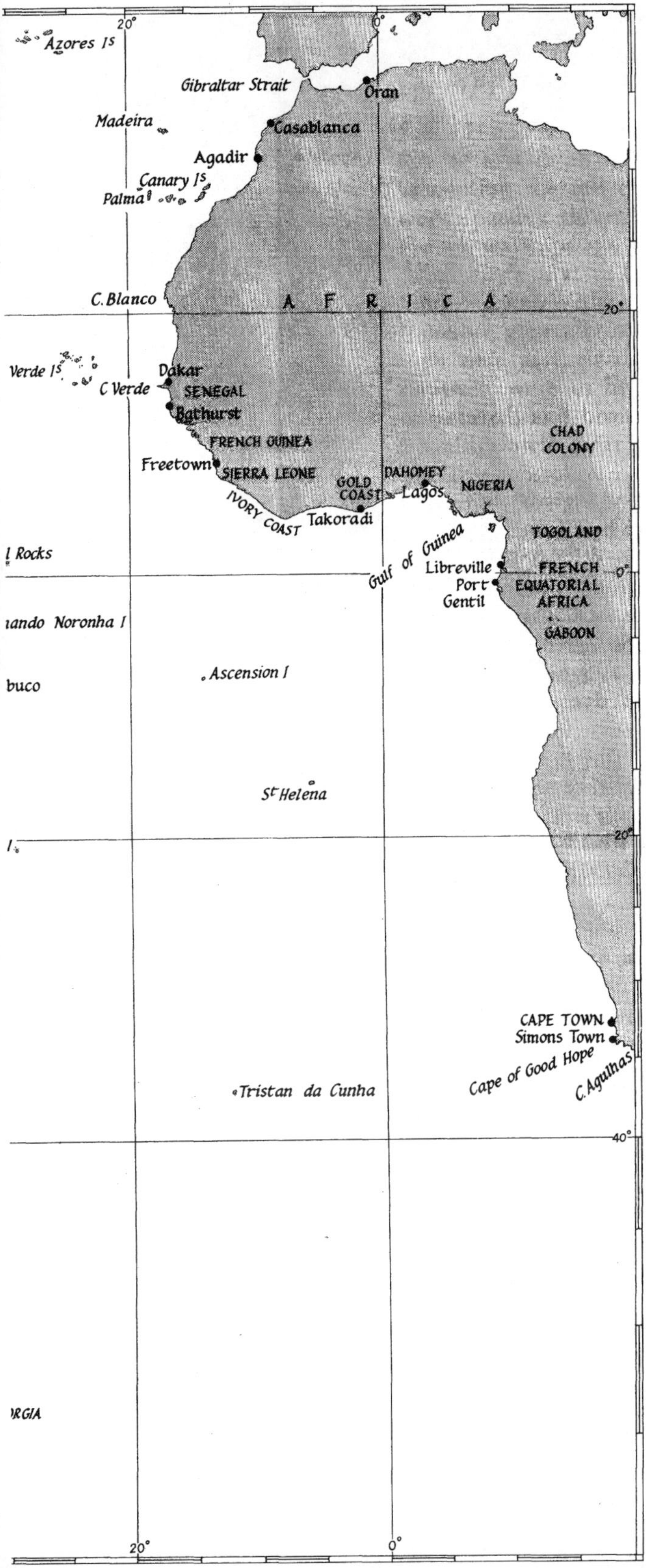
Azores Is
Gibraltar Strait
Oran
Madeira
Casablanca
Agadir
Canary Is
Palma
C. Blanco
A F R I C A
Verde Is
Dakar
C Verde
SENEGAL
Bathurst
FRENCH GUINEA
CHAD COLONY
Freetown
SIERRA LEONE
GOLD COAST
DAHOMEY
Lagos
NIGERIA
IVORY COAST
Takoradi
TOGOLAND
l Rocks
Gulf of Guinea
Libreville
Port Gentil
FRENCH EQUATORIAL AFRICA
GABOON
ıando Noronha I
Ascension I
buco
St Helena
CAPE TOWN
Simons Town
Cape of Good Hope
C. Agulhas
Tristan da Cunha
RGIA
20°
0°
40°

in the movements of Force H. On the 1st of October Admiral Somerville, who had sailed to intercept the French battleship *Richelieu*, which was expected to attempt to return from Dakar to a Biscay port, was diverted by the Admiralty to protect those islands from a possible German landing. Though he returned to Gibraltar on the 4th, he was told to continue the watch on the Atlantic islands, and two transports on their way home from the abortive Dakar expedition (of which more later) were diverted and held in readiness to land troops on the Azores. Similar alarms continued until the end of the year and a cruiser was generally kept on patrol in the neighbourhood of the islands. In mid-December Force H sailed there in strength on reports of an expedition being about to leave Bordeaux. In fact no such movement was ever attempted by the enemy, who considered the risk involved in sending an expedition overseas far from his home bases while our fleet was intact too great. But the British Government intended to occupy the Spanish or Portuguese Atlantic islands if Germany attacked Spain or Portugal, and an opinion to that effect which Hitler expressed at his conference on the 14th of November was perfectly correct. It is, however, interesting to note the views expressed by Admiral Raeder at the same meeting. He warned the Führer that an attempt to forestall us in seizing the islands 'would certainly be a very risky operation' and that even if, by good fortune, the occupation was successful the supply problem thereafter would be insuperable and that 'the possibility of holding the islands is unlikely'. The German Naval Staff certainly had no illusions about the risks involved in sending an expedition across seas which they did not control.

After the fall of France and the closure of the Mediterranean the importance of Freetown, Sierra Leone, and the problems which beset the Commander-in-Chief, South Atlantic, whose headquarters were at that base, were greatly increased. Well before the outbreak of war Admiral Lyon had told the First Sea Lord that, because of its undeveloped state, Freetown was not a satisfactory convoy assembly port or command headquarters. Yet in spite of all its inadequacies it had to be used for both purposes, for the sufficient reasons that it was well placed strategically and that no better British-controlled base existed between Gibraltar and Capetown. As long as we had been able to use the French base at Dakar, and the French ships stationed there and at Casablanca were working in close co-ordination with our own forces, the deficiencies of Freetown were mitigated. Once French assistance had not only disappeared but been replaced by what might at any moment become active hostility, the problem of protecting the merchantmen sailing on the very important South Atlantic shipping routes became acute. Moreover the closure of the Mediterranean meant that every supply ship and troop transport bound for the Middle East had to pass through the command; and most of them had to call at Freetown to replenish with fuel, water and stores. In May a convoy of five large liners, including the *Queen Mary*, with Australian and New Zealand troops aboard, passed through on its way to this country. At the end of June the first of the famous series of W.S. troop convoys left home for the Middle East escorted by the heavy cruiser *Cumberland*. The second W.S. convoy followed on the 4th of August in two sections—fast and slow—each escorted by a heavy cruiser, and thereafter they continued to sail at about monthly intervals. Cruiser escorts were provided from home and from the South Atlantic and East Indies commands to secure their safety during the whole long journey. Special convoys of fast motor-transport ships to carry urgently needed tanks and other fighting vehicles to the Army of the Nile had to be organised at the same time and the first two of these (Convoys A.P. 1 and 2), to whose rapid arrival the Cabinet attached great importance, reached Suez in less than five weeks. But British and Empire troops were now being moved over almost every ocean route. Australians and New Zealanders were being carried in fast liners to the Middle East; West African troops from Lagos and Takoradi to Mombasa to take part in the attack on the Italian East African Empire; British and Indian troops from Bombay to Suez, to the Persian Gulf and to Malaya; South Africans from Capetown to East Africa and Egypt, while the flow of Canadians across the North Atlantic to Britain continued steadily. The true significance of maritime power could not be better demonstrated than by the scope and scale of these movements involving the transport of thousands of men and many thousands of tons of stores, ammunition, tanks and vehicles across the great oceans. And the enemy, in spite of his utmost endeavours, did not seriously interfere with any of them.

The forces under the Commander-in-Chief, South Atlantic, comprised at this time a varying but considerable number of cruisers. Early in July he had the heavy cruisers *Cornwall*, *Cumberland* and *Dorsetshire*, the old light cruisers *Dragon* and *Delhi*, the small aircraft carrier *Hermes*, the seaplane carrier *Albatross*, three armed merchant cruisers and two sloops. In addition the Freetown Escort Force, of seven armed merchant cruisers, was controlled by him and provided ocean escorts for the S.L. convoys. On the other side of the Atlantic the cruiser *Hawkins* and the armed merchant cruiser *Alcantara* formed the South American Division under Rear-Admiral Harwood and watched over the traffic to and from Rio de Janeiro and the ports of the River Plate. In addition to these long-range trade protection forces a number of anti-submarine trawlers was based on Freetown for local defence duties; and small auxiliary war vessels carried out similar duties at Simonstown, Capetown and Port Stanley in the

Falkland Islands. These converted auxiliary war vessels were now reaching the foreign commands in some numbers, and their arrival did something to improve the local escort situation and ensure against the ports being closed by mines laid by raiders. The chief shortage was, of course, in cruisers of sufficient endurance to patrol the ocean routes extensively and of adequate gun power to engage any raider they might encounter.

With the heavy demands for convoy escorts brought about by the use of the Cape route—no less than eight S.L. convoys sailed in July —and the need to watch the French warships in Dakar, no ships could be provided to form raider hunting groups. Though the Admiralty and the South Atlantic Command had for some time suspected, from the unexplained disappearance of ships on passage, that a disguised raider was at work somewhere in those vast tracts of ocean, it was not until nearly the end of July that the presence of at least one such ship was definitely confirmed. Almost simultaneously with this intelligence the first U-boat arrived and, on the 3rd of August, sank a ship to the south-east of the Cape Verde Islands.

Meanwhile traffic through the South Atlantic Command continued heavy in both directions. In August three southward-bound troop convoys called at Freetown and were followed by three more in September, while from four to six S.L. convoys sailed homeward during each of these months. Early in September Vice-Admiral R. H. T. Raikes succeeded Admiral Lyon as Commander-in-Chief at Freetown.

In October the Admiralty issued new orders for dealing with Vichy French ships. Warships were not to be allowed to proceed to ports south of Dakar, and all submarines except those encountered on the surface and under escort were to be treated as hostile. Merchant ships were to be sent into Freetown for examination. As, however, escorted merchant ships were still allowed to proceed unmolested, this attempt to regain control of the contraband traffic carried by them was unsuccessful.

During the autumn months shipping traffic continued heavy in both directions and the ships available were still inadequate to provide proper escorts. For example, in November two troop convoys passed through Freetown southward bound and seven S.L. convoys sailed homeward. For three of the latter no ocean escort could be found. Such density of traffic and slender escorts invited further attention from the U-boats and, in the middle of the month, four ships were sunk by them off Freetown. Local escorts through the focus of traffic were essential; yet only one sloop and a few anti-submarine trawlers were available. The Admiralty promised six of the new corvettes to Admiral Raikes, but the first two did not arrive until nearly the end of the year. Air searches were flown by the few Royal Air Force aircraft on the station, but without result.

The America and West Indies Command, where Admiral Sir Charles Kennedy-Purvis relieved Admiral Meyrick as Commander-in-Chief in April 1940, shared with the North and South Atlantic Commands the responsibility for guarding the central and southern Atlantic shipping routes.[1] At the beginning of the year three or four of the old C and D class cruisers and a few sloops were allocated to the West Indies station. With these slender forces the watch on the large number of German merchant ships which had taken shelter in neutral American ports had to be maintained and, if they sailed in an attempt to run the blockade, steps had to be taken to intercept them. In February two such ships were caught off San Domingo. One of them, the *Hannover*, was successfully seized by the *Dunedin* and the Canadian destroyer *Assiniboine*, and was towed to Jamaica after a four-day struggle against the fires started by her own crew. She was a valuable prize and served her captors well. We shall meet her again later as the auxiliary aircraft carrier H.M.S. *Audacity*. Other German merchant ships were intercepted later in the year, but their self-destruction was so thoroughly carried out that no more prizes were secured. A few succeeded in reaching Japan from South American ports; they could not all be watched without far greater cruiser strength than we possessed at this time.

After the land campaigns of the summer the West Indies Station, like most foreign commands, was involved in the difficult problem of keeping a watch on French warships. The cruiser *Emile Bertin* was at Martinique with a large quantity of bullion on board, the aircraft carrier *Béarn* was in the same port loaded with American aircraft bought on joint Anglo-French account, and the cruiser *Jeanne d'Arc* was at Guadeloupe. Though the Cabinet and the Admiralty were anxious about the possibility of either of the first two ships returning to France with their valuable cargoes and though patrols were kept off the port for a time, the use of force inside the American Defence Zone was not a solution which could be countenanced. By withholding oil supplies and the application of American pressure the ships were finally kept satisfactorily immobilised.

Another urgent problem brought into prominence by the great changes which occurred in Europe during the summer months was the safeguarding of the Dutch islands of Curaçao and Aruba, with their very valuable but ill-defended oil installations, and of the tanker traffic which constantly flowed between them and the nearby oil ports of Venezuela. Troops were taken to the islands immediately after the invasion of Holland, and Dutch warships working under the

---

[1] See Map 2 (*facing p. 43*).

West Indies Command thereafter played a part in guarding these valuable possessions of their country.

On the 18th of July survivors from two British merchant ships sunk by a disguised raider reached a small West Indian island. It was the first firm intelligence that such a ship was at large in the central Atlantic. The Commander-in-Chief stopped all independent sailings, routed all convoys closer to the American coast and sent all his ships out to patrol the passages through the West Indian islands. Ten days later an action—about which more will be said shortly—was fought between the armed merchant cruiser *Alcantara* of the South American Division and a disguised raider, which might have been the ship responsible for the sinkings off the West Indies earlier in the month or a second raider. The cruiser *Dorsetshire* was sent from Freetown and the *Cumberland* from Simonstown to search the oceans, but the enemy was far too elusive to be trapped by so few ships.

Disguised raiders having thus made their first appearances in the West Indies and South Atlantic commands, it will be appropriate to review the enemy's plans to employ converted merchant ships on this type of sporadic warfare. The ships chosen were, in general, capable of only moderate speed, but possessed long endurance. Most of them were ships of seven or eight thousand tons, armed with six to eight modern 5·9-inch guns in addition to torpedo tubes and, in most cases, one or two aircraft.[1] They were fuelled and provisioned to enable them to make long cruises and were furnished with numerous and skilful aids to disguise. Their funnels and topmasts were telescopic, dummy funnels and derrick posts could be fitted; false bulwarks, false deck houses and dummy deck cargoes were other devices employed; and repainting was often carried out at sea to render valueless any reports of their colouring which the Admiralty might obtain and promulgate.

To extend their active life still further the enemy arranged for a succession of supply ships—tankers and dry cargo vessels—to break out from his home ports, or to leave the neutral harbours in which they had been sheltering since the outbreak of the war, and to meet the raiders. The rendezvous would be either in the unfrequented vastnesses of the oceans or in remote island anchorages where disturbance was unlikely, and there they would refuel the raiders and replenish their stores and ammunition. As examples of the enemy's supply organisation, the tanker *Winnetou* left Las Palmas in the Canary Islands in April 1940 to supply raiders working on the Atlantic and Pacific shipping routes, the *Weser* left Manzanillo in Mexico in September for the Pacific, but was promptly intercepted by the Canadian armed merchant cruiser *Prince Robert*; and the *Regensburg*, *Ermland* and *Winnetou* all worked at times between

---
[1] See Appendix M for details of German armed merchant raiders.

Japanese ports and various meeting places in the Pacific Ocean. But the raiders often kept captured prizes—particularly if they should happen to be loaded tankers—to supplement the services of the regular supply ships and to accommodate the crews of captured or sunken vessels until such time as they could be brought home to Europe or landed on some remote shore. The supply ships serviced the enemy's raiding warships as well as his merchant raiders and, when his U-boats started to extend their activities, they and the raiders themselves often met and replenished U-boats on the high seas as well.

In the Atlantic these secret meetings and replenishments were always made at sea but, in the Pacific, anchorages in the Japanese-mandated Marshall and Caroline Islands or in the Marianas Group were used, and one raider actually carried out a month's self-refit at Maug in the Marianas.[1] Japanese naval or government vessels sometimes visited and superficially inspected the ships while in these harbours, but their disguises were never penetrated nor their true function revealed. Though we have no direct evidence of deliberate Japanese assistance to the raiders before their country was at war, it is difficult not to conclude that they must have known and connived at the use to which their territory was being put. Another unfrequented island put to a similar use was the French possession of Kerguelen in the southern Indian Ocean.[2]

These carefully planned and co-ordinated supply arrangements enabled armed merchant raiders to make very long cruises. Thus the first and only cruise of the *Orion* (Raider A) lasted for 510 days, during which she steamed over 112,000 miles, and the *Komet* (Raider B) returned finally to Bordeaux after fifteen months at sea.[3]

The Admiralty's counter-measures naturally included strenuous efforts to locate and destroy the supply ships as well as the raiders themselves, and the best way to accomplish this was the discovery of the rendezvous used by them. It was not many months before these measures began to yield satisfactory results.[4]

---

[1] See Map 24 (*facing p. 279*).

[2] See Map 24.

[3] The Admiralty gave to each raider an alphabetical identity letter as soon as sufficient knowledge had been acquired, and these letters were continued in use right to the end of her career. The Germans gave to them warship names and also Ship Numbers and generally referred to them as 'Ship Number 16', etc. The new name superseded, of course, that which the ship had previously borne as a merchantman. Thus each raider had no less than four different identification names or numbers. For example, Raider C in the Admiralty's catalogue was the German 'Ship Number 16', whose warship name was the *Atlantis* but which, during her innocent lifetime, had been the motor ship *Goldenfels* of the Hansa Shipping Company of Bremen. For simplicity throughout these pages the Admiralty's identity letters and the German warship names only will be used, but full particulars of the identities of all the enemy's armed raiders, together with performance data and a summary of their careers, are given in Appendix M.

[4] Appendix N gives a complete list of all supply ships used by the Germans to service their warship and merchant raiders and their final fate.

Map 24

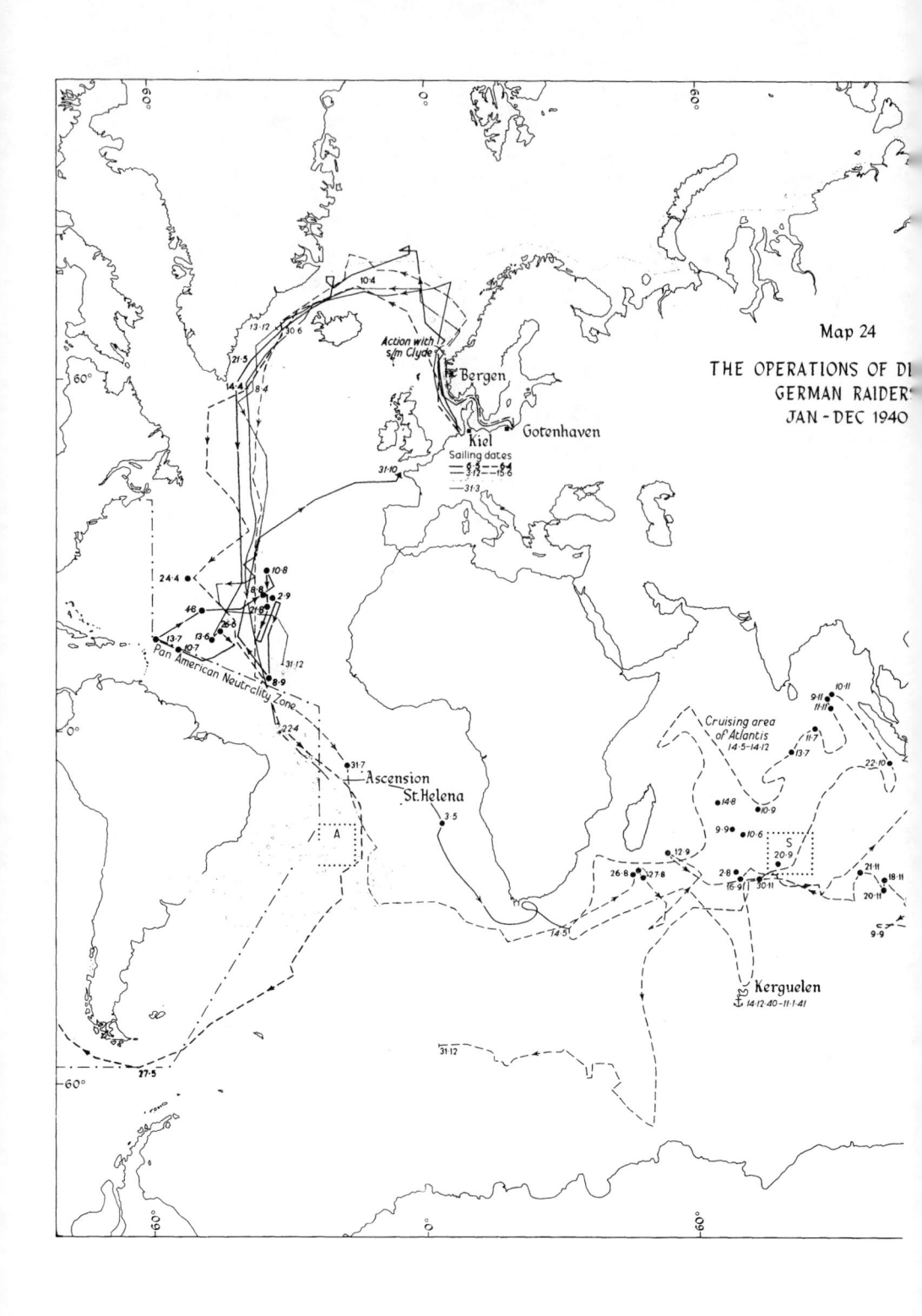

THE OPERATIONS OF DI
GERMAN RAIDER
JAN - DEC 1940

Map Legend

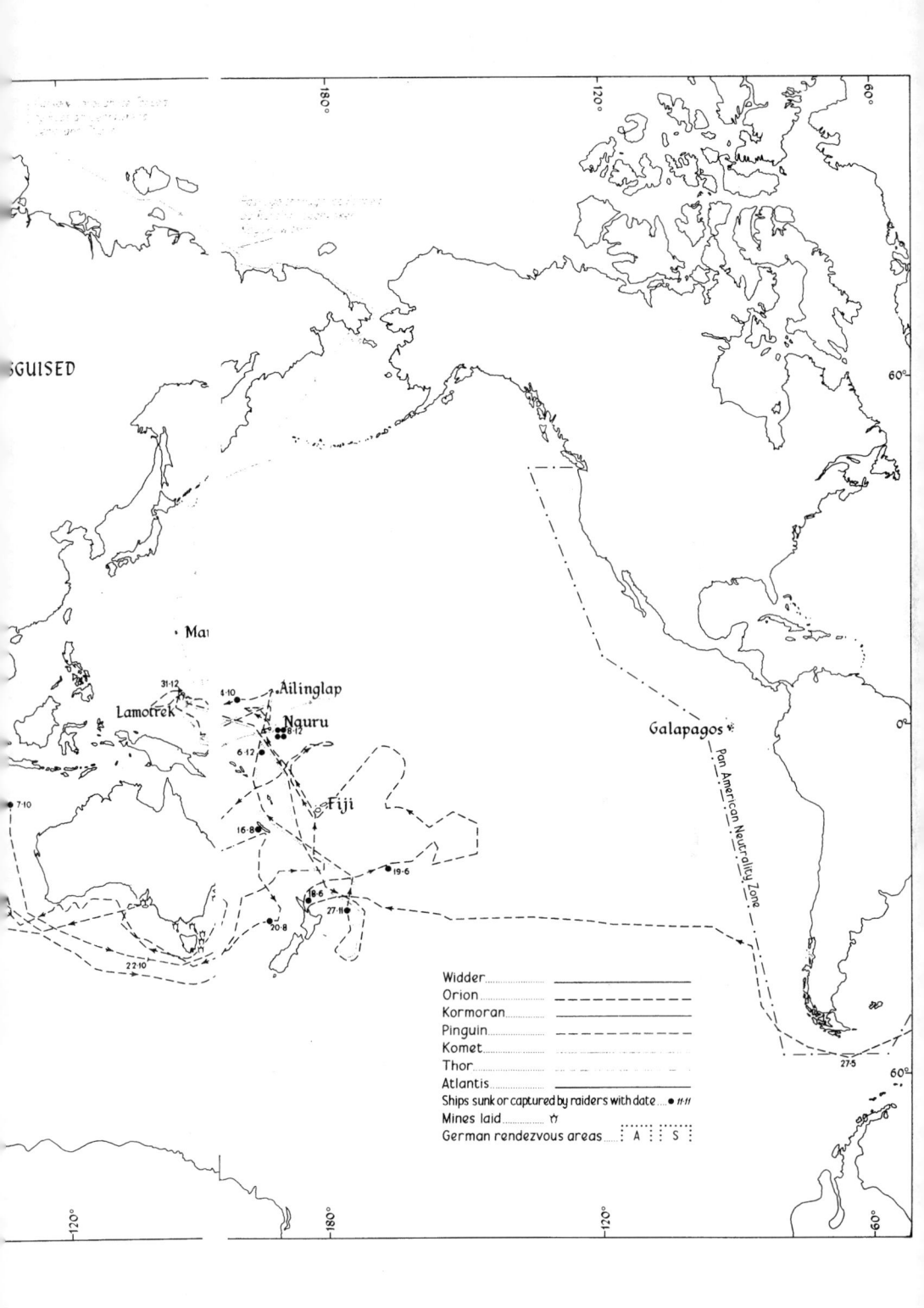

- Widder .... ———
- Orion .... – – –
- Kormoran .... — — —
- Pinguin .... — — —
- Komet .... — · —
- Thor ....
- Atlantis .... ———
- Ships sunk or captured by raiders with date ..... ● *11·11*
- Mines laid .... ☆
- German rendezvous areas ..... ┆A┆ ┆S┆

Map Labels

- Mai(?)
- Lamotrek
- Ailinglap
- Nguru
- Fiji
- Galapagos
- Pan American Neutrality Zone

Dates visible on map

31·12, 4·10, 8·12, 6·12, 7·10, 16·8, 19·6, 18·6, 27·11, 20·8, 22·10, 27·5

All the merchant raiders employed similar tactics to approach their intended victims or to lure the latter to approach close to themselves. They avoided long-range actions and relied on surprise to overwhelm the victim before his defensive armament could inflict damage on the raider. The first step after revealing his true identity was to try to prevent the victim sending a report by wireless. If the victim complied he was generally required only to abandon the ship, which was then sunk or captured, but if he used his wireless the raider at once opened a devastating fire and took all possible steps to jam the message. It is to the great credit of the Merchant Navy that many ships' masters chose the gallant alternative of reporting the raider's presence and position and accepting the consequences rather than submit to the enemy's orders. Several ships also fought their small defensive armaments right to the end.

It is only fair to mention that the captains of German armed merchant raiders generally behaved with reasonable humanity towards the crews of intercepted ships, tried to avoid causing unnecessary loss of life and treated their prisoners tolerably. The only exception was the captain of the *Widder* (Raider D) who also later commanded the *Michel* (Raider H). His conduct was so far contrary to the Hague Conventions that he was brought to trial and convicted as a War Criminal in 1947.

Three of these formidable ships were put into service by the end of 1939, and three more in the first half of 1940. The Germans called these six ships the 'first wave'. A 'second wave' of five more ships was also being fitted out as rapidly as possible, and the first ship of the second wave (the *Kormoran*, Raider G) actually went to sea before the end of 1940. A total of nine such ships reached the oceans, but another was seriously damaged while leaving on her first cruise (the *Togo*, Raider K) and two more were fitted out but never got to sea. Only one ship, the *Thor* (Raider E), made two successful cruises, but the *Komet* (Raider B) was sunk in the English Channel when leaving on her second cruise. The Italians sent out one merchant raider, the *Ramb I*, which accomplished nothing during her short career, and the Japanese later employed three such ships, but achieved only small successes. The casualties caused to our shipping by armed merchant raiders were therefore almost wholly accomplished by the Germans.

The first to leave Germany was the *Atlantis* (Raider C) on the last day of March 1940. She was followed by the *Orion* (Raider A) on the 6th of April and the *Widder* (Raider D) on the 5th of May.[1] Two more raiders, the *Thor* (Raider E) and *Pinguin* (Raider F), sailed from Germany in June; and the *Komet* (Raider B) left Bergen on the 9th of July to make, with Russian assistance, a remarkable passage, lasting two months, to the Bering Sea by the long and ice-

[1] See Map 24.

bound route to the north of Siberia and thence into the open waters of the Pacific. Thus by the middle of the year, when the first climax of the war had been reached, when demands for naval forces were at a peak and recent losses and heavy damage to ships off Norway and in the Channel had by no means been made good, the Admiralty was faced with the difficult problem of finding, identifying and bringing to action no less than six well-armed raiders all thoroughly trained in sporadic ocean warfare. Only one of these six was brought to action in 1940, and she escaped vital damage on two occasions.

By the end of the year these ships had caused us the loss of fifty-four merchantmen totalling 366,644 tons. Their clever use and frequent changes of disguise, their carefully thought out tactics in making the approach to their intended victims, and the measures taken to prevent the latter from sending raider reports by wireless sometimes succeeded, for a time, in keeping the Admiralty in ignorance of their presence; consequently the disappearance of ships which had become overdue was sometimes attributed to submarines or to the normal hazards of the sea. However, by the middle of May the Admiralty's suspicions that at least one armed merchant raider was at sea in the South Atlantic were confirmed by the discovery of mines off Cape Agulhas. They had been laid by the *Atlantis*.

But our strategic condition had changed greatly since the closing months of 1939 when a number of powerful hunting groups had been formed to search for the *Graf Spee*, and many new and pressing commitments made it impossible to reintroduce such far-reaching counter-measures.[1] All that the Admiralty could now do was to escort important ocean convoys, such as those carrying troops from the Dominions or India to this country or the Middle East, with powerful enough ocean escorts to deter any raider from attacking them, and to patrol the focal areas of shipping with armed merchant cruisers and such cruisers as could be spared from other duties.

Not until the end of November, when the pocket-battleship *Scheer* was also known to be at large, could the Admiralty attempt to form new hunting groups to search and cover the South Atlantic; and of the three groups organised for the purpose none reached its intended strength during the present phase.

The movements of the six merchant raiders and the losses caused by them will now be considered in turn.[2]

The *Atlantis* (Raider C) sailed from Kiel on the 11th of March and spent the remainder of that month completing preparations and training her crew for her first sortie. On the last day of March she left her home waters and steamed north along the Norwegian coast disguised as a Russian merchant ship bound for Murmansk. When

---
[1] See Table 6, p. 114.
[2] See Map 24 (*facing p.* 279).

far to the north she turned west and broke out through the Denmark Strait on the 7th of April without having sighted or been sighted by any patrol vessel. During the succeeding days in the North Atlantic she sighted several ships but molested none of them. Her orders declared her primary aim to be the disorganisation of our shipping by sudden appearances at widely separated points rather than the sinking of a large tonnage. On the 17th of April, having thus far accomplished nothing, she was ordered into the South Atlantic, where she was to appear on the Capetown to Freetown route and so try to force us to relax our naval pressure in the North Sea at the height of the Norwegian campaign. On her way south she disguised herself as a Japanese and in that rôle secured her first victim on the 3rd of May —the British ship *Scientist*—in 19° 53′ South, 3° 46′ East. The raider then steamed south at high speed to carry out the minelaying operation off Cape Agulhas already mentioned. She then moved into the Indian Ocean and changed her disguise again, this time assuming the appearance of a Dutch cargo steamer.

On the 10th of June, on the route from Australia to the west, she surprised and captured the Norwegian tanker *Tirrana*; she kept this ship in company with a prize crew on board until, in early August, she detached her, with all the prisoners captured from merchantmen up to that time, and ordered her to make a port in western France. The British submarine *Tuna*, however, sank the prize off the mouth of the Gironde when her homeward journey was nearly completed. Meanwhile the *Atlantis* shifted her activities further north to the traffic lanes approaching Ceylon, and there she captured and sank the British ship *City of Bagdad*—herself an ex-German prize—on the 11th of July. The raider again moved rapidly away from the scene of her last success, sank another British ship two days later, and then returned to the Australian routes further south. In August she secured two more victims, neither of which managed to send a wireless report, so effective were her tactics of surprising her victim, often at night. The *Atlantis* continued her depredations in September; on the 9th she encountered, in 22° 13′ South, 67° 20′ East, the valuable British ship *Athelking*, which managed to send a wireless signal and was heavily shelled in consequence. Next day another British victim, the *Benarty*, was secured and again the raider's presence was reported; but much valuable information, including secret mails, was captured. The raider's boarding-parties invariably made a prompt and thorough search of each of her captures for such information, and several times obtained Merchant Navy codes, Admiralty instructions to merchant ships and papers of value to the enemy's intelligence service. The raider used her aircraft to stop this last ship by bombing and machine-gun fire, but this new tactic was not very successful as it naturally led to the prompt sending of a raider report.

THE 'ORION' (RAIDER A)

A large French ship, the *Commissaire Ramel*, en route from Fremantle to Capetown and England, was next surprised, again at night, on the 20th of September, after which the *Atlantis* decided to leave the Australian routes. Her presence had several times been reported, and, moreover, another raider, the *Pinguin* (Raider F), of whom more later, was now working in those waters. The *Atlantis* had now been six months at sea, had steamed some 32,000 miles and had sunk or captured nine ships of about 66,000 tons. Her captain decided next to lie low for a period in a waiting position in 22° South, 84° East and then to attack shipping in the approaches to the Sunda Straits between Java and Sumatra. A Yugoslav ship was captured on the 22nd of October and sent in prize to Italian Somaliland, but the following month brought a bigger haul. Two loaded Norwegian tankers, the *Teddy* and *Ole Jacob*, were captured and kept by the raider for her own use, and in the same week the British ship *Automedon* was attacked and sunk, though not before she had sent a raider report and, in consequence, been savagely shelled. Again search of the captured ship yielded valuable intelligence to the enemy. The raider now made a rendezvous with her two Norwegian tanker prizes, took in fuel from both, then sank the *Teddy* and sent the *Ole Jacob* off to Japan in charge of a prize crew which was to send the secret material captured from various ships back to Germany. The raider meanwhile moved off to the south-west and, early in December, met the *Pinguin* and a supply ship in 34° 47′ South, 59° 55′ East. She transferred her prisoners to the latter and then sailed for the island of Kerguelen to refit. There she arrived on the 14th and received some hull damage through grounding. The end of the year found her still refitting in the shelter of the French island, and there we will leave her for the present. She had so far sunk or captured thirteen ships totalling nearly 94,000 tons and her cruise was to last many more months.

The second to sail was the *Orion* (Raider A) on the 6th of April. She was a steam-driven ship of some 7,000 tons, but her best speed of about 14 knots was less than that of the majority of ships which the enemy employed on this type of work. Her departure from Germany coincided with the minelaying operation 'Wilfred' which marked the start of the Norwegian campaign, and she was lucky not to be caught as she crept up the Norwegian coast on her way to the Denmark Strait.[1]

Her orders were to show herself in the North Atlantic and there, on the 24th of April, she found her first victim, the British ship *Haxby*. After fuelling from a supply tanker sent out from the Canary Islands she rounded Cape Horn and on the night of the 13th–14th of June

---

[1] See pp. 156–157 and Map 24 (*facing p. 279*).

laid 228 mines off the port of Auckland, New Zealand. These mines only secured one victim, the British ship *Niagara*, but by ill-luck she had just left Auckland with about £2½ millions of gold ingots on board. The subsequent recovery of the greater part of the ten tons of gold, from deep inside a big ship sunk in a depth of 438 feet in strong tidal currents where many mines were still present, was one of the most remarkable feats of salvage ever carried out. It was done chiefly by two divers working from a small, ancient and decrepit ship which was taken off the mud in Auckland harbour and made into an improvised salvage vessel.[1]

The *Orion* was now ordered to the Pacific and moved firstly on to the shipping route from Australia to Panama. There, on the 19th of June, she captured the Norwegian ship *Tropic Sea*, which she sent in prize to France, but the ship was intercepted by one of our submarines near the end of her journey. As the *Tropic Sea* had on board prisoners from the *Haxby*, the Admiralty now, four months after the start of the *Orion's* cruise, obtained its first firm and accurate intelligence regarding her operations. No wireless raider reports had so far been received from any of her victims. After a period in the Coral Sea the *Orion* moved to the Tasman Sea, and there on the 20th of August she attacked the British ship *Turakina*, which at once transmitted a report and fought her enemy most valiantly. A search by the New Zealand cruiser *Achilles* and by aircraft was at once organised, but the raider had moved to the south of Australia. While cruising off that coast she was sighted by R.A.A.F. aircraft, but her disguise was not penetrated.

In October the *Orion* moved north to the Marshall Islands where she met the *Komet* (Raider B), which had entered the Pacific by the Arctic route, and two supply ships. The two raiders now remained in company for a time. On the 27th of November they intercepted and sank the British liner *Rangitane* shortly after she had left Auckland, which led to another fruitless search by the *Achilles* and by shore-based aircraft. They then steamed north to carry out a long-cherished plan to attack the island of Nauru, whence valuable supplies of phosphate are obtained. The attack was carried out on the 7th–8th of December and led to the sinking of four phosphate ships of some 21,000 tons. The raiders then returned to the Japanese islands to replenish again. They landed over 500 of their prisoners on Emirau Island, whence they were soon rescued. By the new year the Admiralty became aware that these raiders' captures had given the enemy possession of our merchant ship signal codes and of our instructions to merchant shipping. The *Orion* returned to the Marshall Islands and again replenished from her supply vessels during the last days of

---

[1] See *Niagara Gold*, by R. J. Dunn (A. H. and A. W. Reed, Wellington, 1942) for a full account of this salvage feat.

the year. She had now been 268 days at sea and a refit was essential. To carry this out she shifted to the Mariana Islands on the 12th of January 1941 and remained there with two supply ships in attendance for the next four weeks. The second part of her cruise will be told later.

The *Komet* (Raider B) had parted from the *Orion* after the joint operations already described, including the first attack on Nauru. On the 27th of December she attacked the phosphate island again, this time alone, and destroyed the oil tanks and phosphate plant. Thence she passed far to the south of New Zealand into the Indian Ocean to meet the *Pinguin* (Raider F) and a supply ship at Kerguelen early in March 1941.

The *Komet* had accomplished nothing by herself before the end of the year, and although her cruise was to last until nearly the end of November 1941 she achieved little further success. Jointly with the *Orion* she had sunk seven ships of about 43,000 tons.

The third ship of the first wave of raiders was the *Widder* (Raider D) which broke out through the Denmark Strait on the 19th of May and worked continuously in the North Atlantic.[1] In June she sank a British tanker and captured a Norwegian vessel of the same type about midway between the Cape Verde Islands and the West Indies. Next month she secured two more victims further to the west. It was when survivors from these two ships, the *Davisian* and *King John*, reached the West Indies on the 18th of July that the presence of a raider within the limits of his station first became known to the Commander-in-Chief, West Indies, and led to the counter-measures already described.[2] From the 4th of August to the 2nd of September she cruised further north, between Bermuda and the Canary Islands, and sank five ships, two of which were tankers. It was in these waters that these valuable ships, independently routed, could often be found on passage from the oil ports in the Caribbean to West Africa or Gibraltar. After this successful period the *Widder* moved south again and sank a Greek ship in mid-Atlantic, to the north of St. Paul's Rocks, on the 8th of September. She then returned to Brest, where she arrived safely on the last day of October. Compared with the prolonged cruises made by other raiders hers had been short; but it was by no means unfruitful since she sank or captured ten ships of 58,645 tons. The ruthless methods employed by her captain have already been mentioned.

The fourth ship of the first wave, the *Thor* (Raider E), left by the same route as the *Widder* in the middle of June and she too worked continuously in the Atlantic. After finding six victims in the central and southern parts of that ocean she encountered the A.M.C.

---
[1] See Map 24 (*facing p. 279*).
[2] See p. 277.

Alcantara on the 28th of July in 24° 39′ South, 33° 07′ West near the island of Trinidade, which lies in the South Atlantic some 600 miles east of the Brazilian coast.[1] Rear-Admiral Harwood, commanding the South American Division with his flag in the cruiser *Hawkins*, had appreciated from reports received from the West Indies and from the fact that several ships were overdue at Freetown that at least one raider was at work in the Atlantic and that she might be moving south. He therefore sent the *Alcantara* to the vicinity of Trinidade Island while he himself patrolled the shipping routes between Rio and the Plate. His guess was correct but it brought no success, for, in the encounter which followed, the *Thor* easily outranged and outfought the *Alcantara* and damaged her seriously without herself sustaining sufficiently grave injury to end her cruise. She moved into the quiet waters of the South Atlantic and, in about 37° South, carried out her own repairs and replenished from a supply ship. Early in September she was again ready for work.

On receiving the reports of the *Alcantara's* action the Admiralty took energetic steps to increase the range of the A.M.C.s' guns and improve their fighting power; but no very early improvements were possible. The *Thor* was able to continue cruising in the central and southern Atlantic and secured two more victims in September and October. Then, on the 5th of December, she met another armed merchant cruiser, the *Carnarvon Castle*, off the east coast of South America in 30° 52′ South, 42° 53′ West. The action followed the same lines as that with the *Alcantara* four months earlier. Again the big, lightly-armed British ship was outranged and seriously damaged, and again the enemy escaped serious injury. Though the British ships had in both these actions done the best they could with the weapons provided to them, the results, after so many months of fruitless scouring of the oceans, were intensely disappointing. Immediately the news of the *Carnarvon Castle's* action was received Commodore Pegram, who had succeeded Admiral Harwood in command of the South American Division at the end of August, took the *Enterprise* north to search for the raider. On the 9th of December the heavy cruiser *Cumberland* joined him and a week later the *Newcastle* reached the station from home. A force capable of engaging a pocket-battleship was thus once more assembled in the focal area which had invited the *Graf Spee* to her destruction, and, as the *Scheer* was now known to be at large, Commodore Pegram kept his ships concentrated off Rio de Janeiro or the River Plate. But the *Scheer* remained in the north until the end of the year and the *Thor* steamed clear of the scene of her action to repair her injuries at sea.

---

[1] See Maps 23 and 24 (*facing pp. 273 and 279*). This small island must not be confused with the large island of Trinidad in the West Indies. The same spelling is sometimes used for both islands.

Though the *Thor* accomplished nothing more before the end of the year, she had taken the measure of our armed merchant cruisers and was to put her experiences to good account later when she encountered a third ship of that class. Furthermore the knowledge that they had little to fear from such encounters was quickly communicated to the other raiders who were thus able to work with greater confidence.

The outward passage of the Denmark Strait by the *Thor* was repeated very shortly afterwards, between the 24th and 30th of June, by the fifth ship of the first wave, the *Pinguin* (Raider F). She too worked initially in the Atlantic and obtained one victim there in July.[1] Next month she moved to the southern Indian Ocean and cruised slowly eastwards along the route from Australia to the Cape. Between the 26th of August and 7th of October she sank or captured six valuable ships, four of which were tankers. One of her prizes, the Norwegian tanker *Storstad*, was converted into an auxiliary minelayer and renamed *Passat*. She and her parent ship laid numbers of mines off Australian and Tasmanian ports and in the Bass Straits in late October and early November. Both then moved westwards again. The route where she had found the tankers on her eastward journey now yielded four more prizes, three of them British refrigerator ships. Towards the end of the year the *Pinguin* steamed far to the south to search the Antarctic for the Allied whaling fleets.

The sixth and last ship of the first wave of raiders was the *Komet* (Raider B), whose exploits after passing into the Pacific by the Arctic route have already been told up to the end of the year in conjunction with those of the *Orion* (Raider A). The first ship of the 'second wave', the *Kormoran* (Raider G), had meanwhile sailed from home. She broke out through the Denmark Strait undetected in the middle of December and moved south into the central Atlantic. She had found no victims by the end of the year.

The first nine months of the period of cruiser warfare inaugurated early in April by the departure of the *Orion* and *Atlantis* was therefore marked by considerable successes to the enemy and, except for the occasional interception of supply ships, total lack of success to our counter-measures. The reasons for this are not far to seek. Changes wrought by the enemy's land victories, the loss of our principal ally and the addition of the Italian fleet to our enemy's strength, had left us with quite inadequate forces to patrol in sufficient strength even the most important focal areas of our shipping, let alone the thousands of miles of open ocean between the focal areas. But there was one hopeful sign to be read even at this early stage. With one exception, to be told shortly, not a single convoy was, during this period, effectively attacked on the high seas by a surface raider. Every one of the

---
[1] See Map 24 (*facing p. 279*).

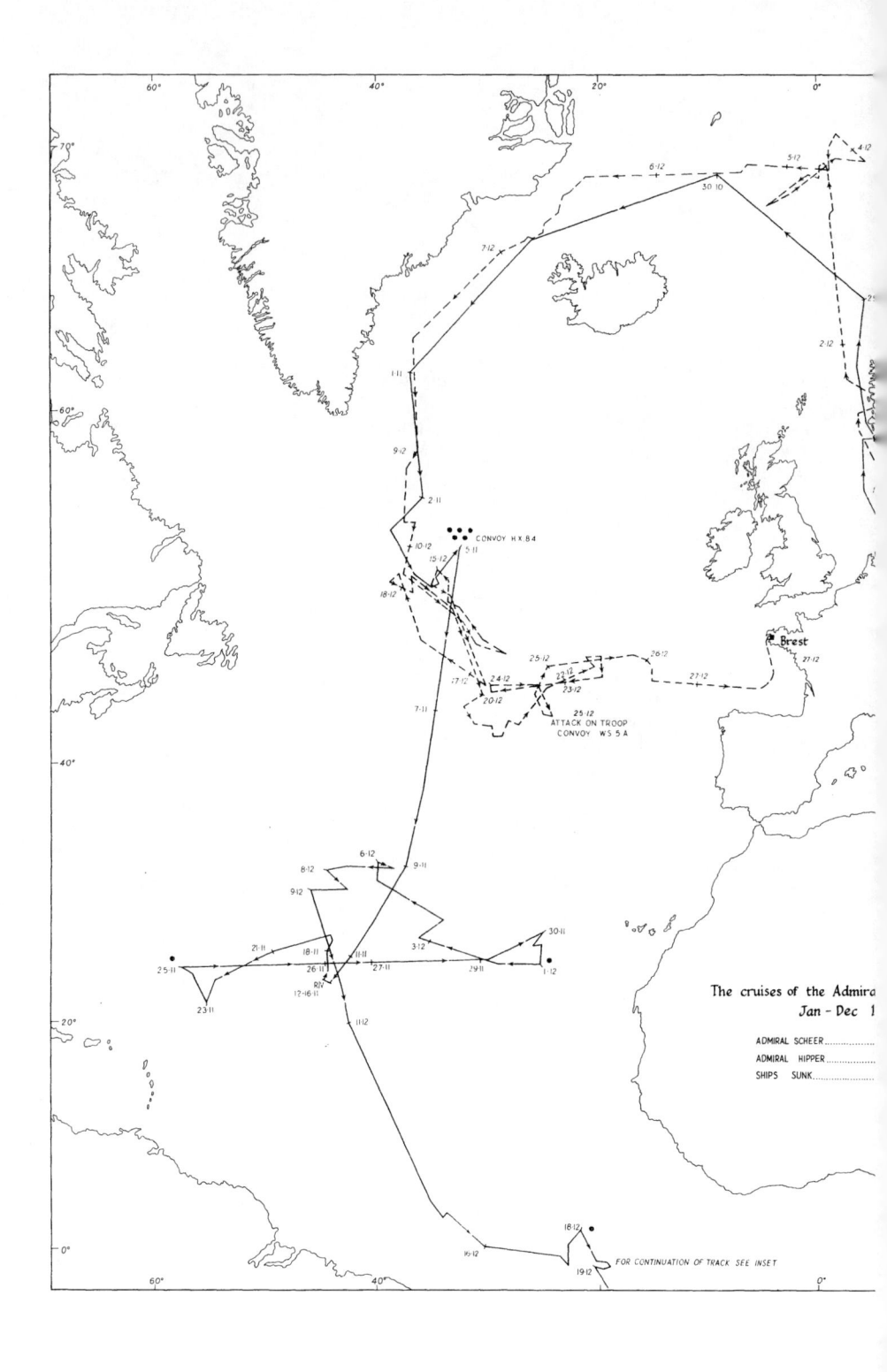

The cruises of the Admiral
Jan – Dec 1

ADMIRAL SCHEER
ADMIRAL HIPPER
SHIPS SUNK

CONVOY H.X.84

ATTACK ON TROOP
CONVOY W.S 5 A

Brest

FOR CONTINUATION OF TRACK SEE INSET

Map 25

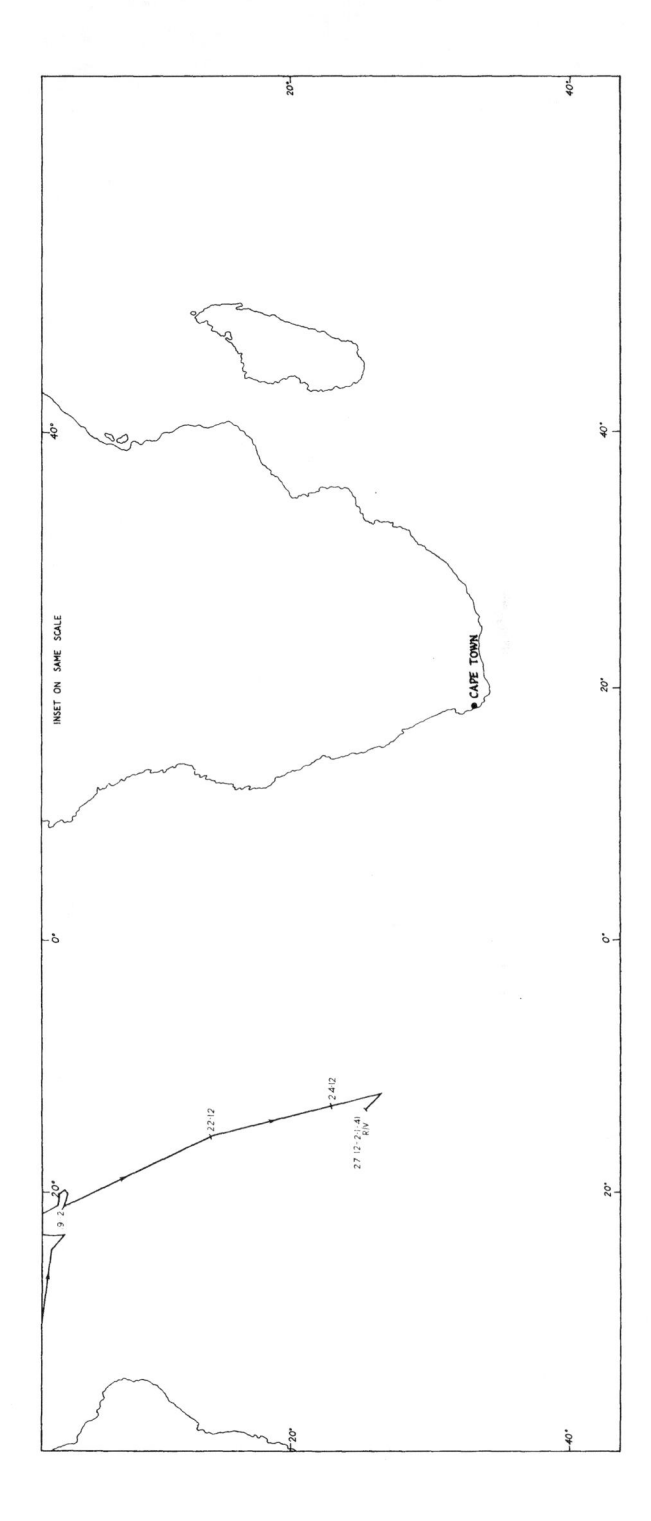

Scheer, and Admiral Hipper
940

ships captured or sunk had been sailing independently, whereas our homeward- and outward-bound Atlantic, Gibraltar, Middle East and many other convoys had been left untouched by the raiders, even though their escorts were often pitifully inadequate. It therefore seemed likely that if the convoy system could be extended and improved—and such was the Admiralty's firm intention—the depredations of the surface raiders would be increasingly restricted.

But while the enemy had six raiders at sea in October 1940 he was planning sorties on to the Atlantic routes by the cruiser *Admiral Hipper*, the pocket-battleship *Admiral Scheer* and, as soon as the damage received in the Norwegian campaign had been repaired, by his battle cruisers as well.

The *Hipper* was the first to leave German waters. She sailed in September for St Nazaire where the enemy intended to base her; but she developed engine defects while still off the Norwegian coast and had to return home. Indications from wireless traffic that the *Hipper* was at sea were received by the Admiralty on the 28th of September, and in consequence Admiral Forbes sailed powerful forces from Rosyth and Scapa to intercept her. But no enemy ship was sighted. On the 27th of October the *Scheer*, which had come through the Kiel Canal from the Baltic, sailed north from Brunsbüttel.[1] No intelligence was received in London regarding these preliminary movements, and her passage out of the North Sea and into the Atlantic by the Denmark Strait was undetected. The first news of the *Scheer's* presence on the shipping routes was received when she attacked a Halifax convoy on the 5th of November. As this was by no means the only instance of the undetected departure of enemy merchant raiders and warships at this time it will be appropriate to consider the reasons.

During the summer months of 1940 the threat of invasion by sea was considered by the Cabinet to be the greatest and most immediate danger to this country. In consequence all our resources, including sea and air patrols and reconnaissances, were primarily devoted to detecting the invading forces which the enemy might, it was considered, launch from any of the many bases now in his possession. It thus came about that, just as the cruisers needed to patrol the Denmark Strait and the Iceland–Faeröes Channel were mostly diverted to southern ports, the main object of the North Sea air reconnaissances was changed from finding and shadowing warships attempting to break out of the North Sea to the reporting of any mass of enemy shipping which might be assembled in Norwegian, Danish, Dutch or German ports and moved towards our eastern shores.[2] But as the period of favourable weather passed and the days

---

[1] See Map 25. [2] See pp. 252–253.

began to shorten, the invasion threat was considered in Whitehall to have receded somewhat, and the air reconnaissances gradually reverted to their original purpose. It was told earlier how, for a variety of reasons, the aircraft of Coastal Command had not been very successful in accomplishing their object. They were now, in the autumn of 1940, to find conditions even more difficult. Whether in the Bay of Biscay, where new reconnaissances had now been organised, or across the North Sea to the Norwegian and Danish coasts, it was essential for our patrol aircraft at times to approach closely to the enemy-held shores if their objects were to be fulfilled. But the enemy now maintained patrols of fighter aircraft off these shores, and this made close approach in clear weather by the slow and lightly-armed reconnaissance planes almost suicidal. Daily searches therefore became impracticable, cloud cover was regarded as essential and, once low cloud was present, visibility was probably reduced and the conditions approached those for which the enemy always waited before sending out or bringing home his raiders. Thus the effectiveness of Coastal Command's searches was further reduced just when the enemy was planning and putting into action a number of movements, early warning of which could best be derived from our air patrols. In the case of the *Scheer's* break-out certain patrols were flown across the North Sea at the critical time; but they were still primarily anti-invasion searches, and none of them sighted the pocket-battleship as she steamed north close inshore. Another chance of sighting her occurred when she turned south through the Denmark Strait; but no regular air patrols were, at this time, being flown from the newly-established bases in Iceland to watch those narrows, and the raider therefore passed through the second critical area undetected. After the *Scheer's* presence in the Atlantic had become known patrols were flown to cover the Denmark Strait, the Iceland–Faeröes Channel and the approaches to the Biscay ports against an attempt by the raider to break back to Germany, or to make a French port. But as she did none of these things all this patrolling was in vain. One result of the *Scheer's* break-out was that the use of No. 98 Squadron, which was based in Iceland, to obtain some air coverage of the Denmark Strait was authorised.

The *Scheer's* undetected passage of the Denmark Strait took place on the last day of October just as the *Widder* (Raider D) was entering Brest at the end of her first cruise. On the 5th of November the *Scheer* obtained her first victim, the independently-routed British *Mopan*, which unfortunately failed to send a raider report. Had she sent a report she might have saved the homeward-bound Halifax convoy H.X. 84, consisting of 37 ships escorted only by the armed merchant cruiser *Jervis Bay* (Captain E. S. F. Fegen), which the pocket-battleship encountered in 52° 45′ North, 32° 13′ West that

The German Supply Ship *Altmark* in Jossing Fiord, Norway, on 16th February 1940. (See pages 152–3.)

The German Heavy Cruiser *Admiral Hipper* in dock at Brest on 26th January 1941. (See pages 291–2 and 371–2.)

A German Pocket-Battleship at sea on raiding operations.
(1) The *Admiral Scheer* steaming away from a rendezvous with a U-boat.

(2) The *Admiral Scheer* captures a tanker. (Taken by one of the German prize-crew placed on board the captured ship.)

same evening.[1] The convoy at once scattered and made good use of its smoke-making apparatus to cover its dispersal, while the escorting warship unhesitatingly challenged her redoubtable adversary to a most unequal duel. The result was a foregone conclusion, but Captain Fegen's action gained enough time to save all the convoy except five ships. He was awarded a posthumous Victoria Cross for his gallantry and self-sacrifice. One of the ships attacked and set on fire was the British tanker *San Demetrio*. Her crew abandoned the ship, but later one of her boats resighted her and a handful of the crew, under the Second Officer, boarded and got the fire under control. The engines were restarted and, in spite of the lack of almost all navigational aids, the ship was brought safely to port with the greater part of her valuable cargo intact.

As soon as the *Jervis Bay*'s enemy reports were received by the Admiralty and the Commander-in-Chief, Home Fleet, steps were taken to search for the raider and to divert all shipping temporarily. Admiral Forbes considered that the enemy was either making a short raid on shipping with a view to an early return—either by the northern route or to a French port—or a more prolonged cruise, in which case she would probably move in a southerly direction. The Home Fleet could only intercept her if she was making a short foray, and the Commander-in-Chief therefore sent the battle cruisers *Hood* and *Repulse*, three ships of the 15th Cruiser Squadron and six destroyers from Scapa to cover the approaches to Brest and Lorient, while he himself with the *Nelson* and *Rodney* sailed to cover the Iceland–Faeröes passage. But the Admiralty diverted part of the battle cruiser force to the last-known position of the raider, and the *Rodney* to escort homeward-bound convoys. In fact all these dispositions and searches were made in vain, because the *Scheer* was making a prolonged cruise and steamed immediately south into the central Atlantic. Apart from sinking five of the convoyed ships her sudden appearance on the Halifax route seriously disorganised the entire flow of shipping across the Atlantic. The next two homeward-bound Halifax convoys and also a Bermuda–Halifax convoy were recalled. Many ships were thus delayed, and the assembly ports became seriously congested. The normal convoy cycle was not resumed in the North Atlantic until H.X. 89 sailed on the 17th of November. The loss of imports caused to this country by the pocket-battleship's sudden appearance on our principal convoy route was, therefore, far greater than the cargoes actually sunk by her.

After breaking off the action with the *Jervis Bay*'s convoy the pocket-battleship steamed south. Had Force H been available to make a search to the west from Gibraltar she might now have been inter-

---

[1] See Map 25 (*facing p. 287*).

cepted; but Admiral Somerville was about to carry out an operation inside the Mediterranean and could not hunt for the raider. Having replenished from a supply ship in 22° North, 46° 20′ West the *Scheer* next moved towards the West Indies and, on the 24th of November, sank the *Port Hobart* south-east of Bermuda. The British ship made a raider report, but did not say whether her assailant was a warship or a disguised raider. Though her message caused the *Scheer* to move east towards the Cape Verde Islands, it did not help to clarify matters in the Admiralty or in the headquarters of the Commanders-in-Chief abroad who were trying to catch the raider.

On the 24th of November the Admiralty gave orders for three groups of ships to be formed to search for the several disguised raiders and the pocket-battleship now known to be at large. 'Force K', consisting of the new aircraft carrier *Formidable* and the cruisers *Berwick* and *Norfolk*, was to be sent from home to the Freetown area. But the stresses of the maritime war in other theatres were such that this force did not arrive until early in 1941, and the *Berwick* never joined it. The small aircraft carrier *Hermes* and a D-class cruiser were allocated to the neighbourhood of St Helena, and the cruisers *Cumberland* and *Newcastle* were, as already mentioned, sent to reinforce the South American Division. Meanwhile, as a precautionary measure, Admiral Raikes routed all shipping passing to and from the South Atlantic to the east of the Cape Verde Islands where its progress could be more easily watched and protected.

The pocket-battleship which was causing the greater part of the trouble meanwhile sank another British ship, the *Tribesman*, about 900 miles west of Bathurst on the 1st of December and then moved to the Pernambuco–Azores route, which she searched without result. After meeting the tanker *Nordmark* at a rendezvous just north of the equator on the 14th, she steamed towards the route between Freetown and South American ports. There, on the 18th, she captured the British ship *Duquesa*, which was loaded with foodstuffs, in broad daylight and deliberately allowed her to make a raider report in order to divert attention from the *Hipper* which, far away to the north, had just started to make her first foray into the Atlantic. In this purpose she accomplished some success, since Admiral Raikes sent the *Neptune* and *Dorsetshire* westward from Freetown for 500 miles; the *Hermes*, *Dragon* and the A.M.C. *Pretoria Castle* met at St Helena and thence searched north-east; and the Admiralty ordered Force K, which was on passage to Freetown, to pass west of the Azores. But the meshes of the net which the Admiralty was trying to draw around the raider were far too big and she escaped from it without difficulty. Five or six groups were necessary to have a reasonable chance of catching her, and the forces wherewith to create them simply could not now be spared.

On Christmas Day, when the *Hipper*, as will be told shortly, attacked a Middle East troop convoy, the forces mentioned above were redisposed to meet that new threat and, far away to the south, the *Scheer*, with her prize the *Duquesa* in company, was meeting the raider *Thor* and two supply ships in 15° South, 18° West. The pocket-battleship's cruise was not by any means yet ended. And, to add to the anxieties of the South Atlantic command, the U-boats now renewed their attacks off Freetown and sank three ships during the last ten days of the year. The German Naval Staff had meanwhile decided to exploit the diversionary effect, which they expected the *Scheer's* appearance to have on the Admiralty's dispositions, by sending out the *Admiral Hipper*. The presence of this ship at Brunsbüttel was actually detected on the 29th of November by photographic reconnaissance, but its significance was apparently not realised, since no special measures were taken to strengthen the reconnaissance patrols. The German cruiser sailed next day, crept north up the Inner Leads and was not sighted by our air patrols. She then waited until bad weather had stopped all flying, and broke through the Denmark Strait on the night of the 6th–7th of December while it was unwatched.[1] Her escape into the Atlantic followed therefore the same general pattern as that of the *Admiral Scheer* and, furthermore, the *Kormoran* (Raider G) followed the warship only a few days later by the same route.

The *Hipper's* orders differed from those of the pocket-battleship, since she had been told to attack our convoys instead of our independently-routed shipping. She therefore twice probed the route believed to be used by our Halifax convoys but, since she was too far to the south, she failed to find any shipping. She then moved to the Sierra Leone route, but there, too, she was unsuccessful until, on Christmas Eve, she gained touch with the southbound troop convoy W.S. 5A, of twenty ships bound for the Middle East, some 700 miles to the west of Finisterre. In accordance with the Admiralty's normal policy this convoy was powerfully escorted by the cruisers *Berwick*, *Bonaventure* and *Dunedin* and the aircraft carrier *Furious*, which was also carrying cased aircraft to Takoradi, to be flown thence to Egypt. The *Hipper* shadowed the convoy by night and approached to attack in the first dawn of Christmas Day. The strength of the escort took her by surprise and the cruisers drove her off, but then lost touch in the prevailing low visibility. The *Hipper* received only slight damage, but this, combined with her machinery defects, made her return to port and she entered Brest on the 27th. She was the first major German warship to use a French port. The convoy, which had been ordered to scatter rather prematurely, had some difficulty in reforming, but only

---

[1] See Map 25 (*facing p. 287*).

two merchant ships and the *Berwick* received slight damage. From the enemy's point of view the encounter, and indeed the whole sortie of the *Hipper*, was not satisfactory. She had accomplished very little and it was plain that because of her low endurance and unreliable machinery she was unsuited to commerce raiding. As soon as the Admiralty heard of the *Hipper's* attack the cruiser *Naiad*, which had left the same convoy the previous day on relief by the *Berwick*, was ordered to rejoin it; the *Kenya* was sent from Plymouth to meet two other Sierra Leone convoys then approaching the scene of the action, and the *Repulse* and *Nigeria* were sent from Scapa to protect the two most westerly of the Atlantic convoys then at sea. The northern passages were also covered by ships of the Home Fleet in case the enemy broke back that way. It was, however, expected that the *Hipper* would make for a French port, and the approaches to Brest were therefore patrolled by Coastal Command aircraft during the succeeding days. But our aircraft were prevented by enemy fighters from approaching close inshore and, as the *Hipper* made Brest unexpectedly from the south, she entered the port undetected. She was, in fact, not sighted there until the 4th of January although shipping in Brest had been bombed two days earlier. Once she had been located in dock she was heavily attacked by both Coastal and Bomber Command aircraft. In spite of a total 175 sorties being flown for that purpose and 85 tons of bombs being aimed at her, she escaped damage at this time.

The enemy's last move of the year against our ocean trade routes was to send out the *Scharnhorst* and *Gneisenau* on the 27th of December. It had taken six months to repair the damage received in the Norwegian campaign, but even so the sortie was abortive. The *Gneisenau* received structural damage in moderate seas off the Norwegian coast and the squadron therefore returned to Kiel. But once again the move of the warships from their home ports was not detected by our patrols, which, in fact, were concentrated at the time on finding the *Hipper*. By the end of the year it was plain that only by greatly strengthening and extending our system of air patrols, particularly in the North Sea and the Denmark Strait, and by carrying out regular visual and photographic reconnaissance of his principal bases could the succession of undetected departures by the enemy's raiding warships be prevented. As Admiral Forbes had reported in the previous June, we were indeed at this time 'seriously handicapped vis-à-vis the enemy since . . . they always knew our dispositions and we rarely knew theirs'.

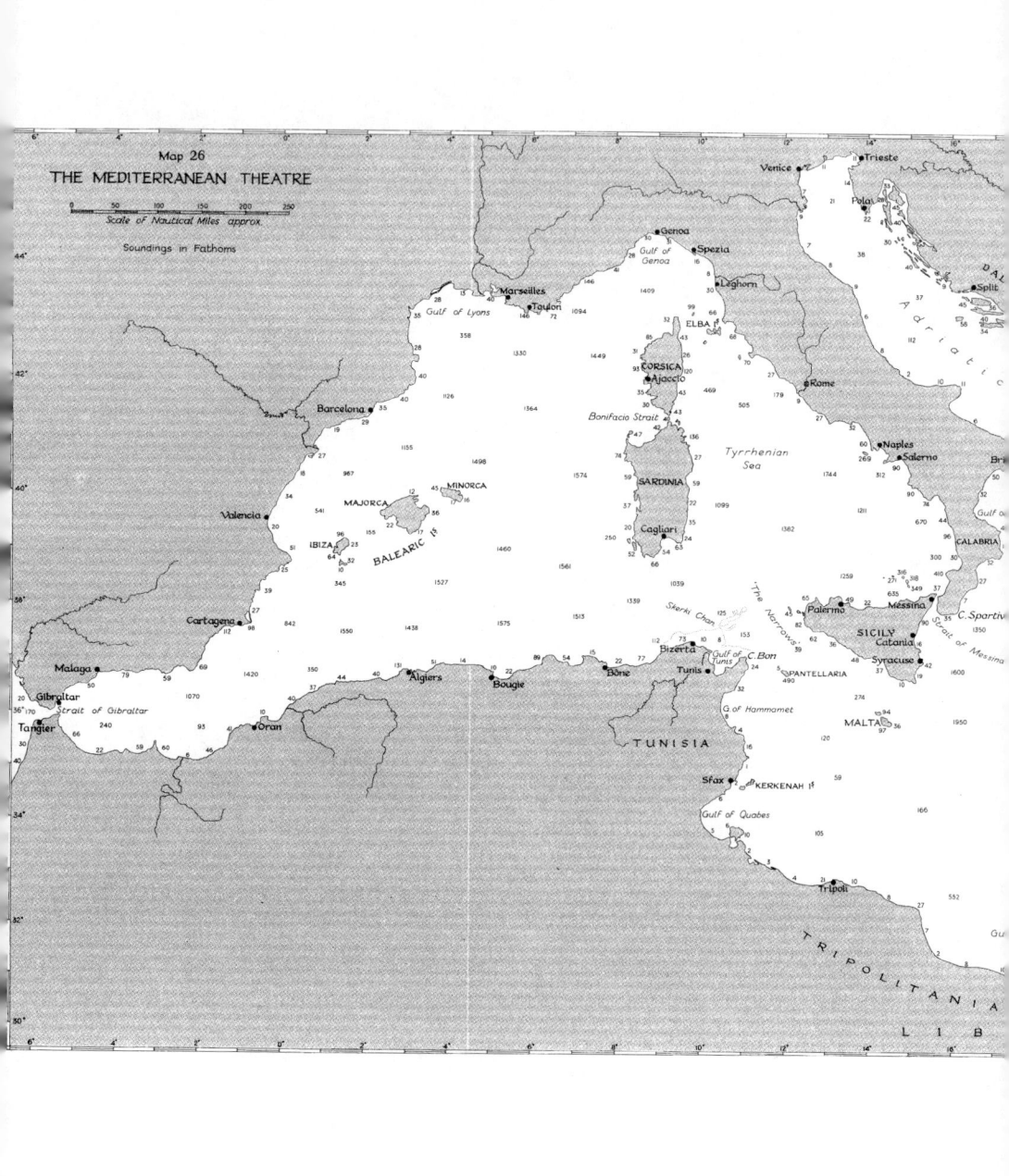

Map 26
THE MEDITERRANEAN THEATRE
Scale of Nautical Miles approx.
Soundings in Fathoms

ALBANIA
GREECE
IONIAN
CORFU
CEPHALONIA
ZANTE
Gulf of Patras
Corinth Canal
Dubrovnik
Kotor
Salonika
Athens
PIRAEUS
Nauplia
Kalamata
C. Matapan
KITHERA
ANTIKITHERA
THE DODECANESE
LEROS
KOS
RHODES
Dardanelles
Sea of Marmara
Bosporus
Istanbul
Varna
Smyrna
Suda Bay
Canea
CRETE
Famagusta
CYPRUS
Alexandretta
Tripoli
SYRIA
Haifa
Jaffa
P. Said
Suez Canal
Suez
Alexandria
Mersa Matruh
Gulf of Es Sollum
Tobruk
Gulf of Bomba
Derna
Benghazi
CYRENAICA
of Sidra

CHAPTER XV

THE AFRICAN CAMPAIGNS

1st May–31st December, 1940

> Laurels grow in the Bay of Biscay—I hope a bed of them may be found in the Mediterranean.
> *Nelson to Sir Gilbert Elliot*, 4th August 1794.

THOUGH a fuller account of the war in the Mediterranean will be found in the relevant volumes of this series, the ebb and flow of the campaigns in that theatre constantly and fundamentally affected our maritime strategy all over the world.[1] In order, therefore, to preserve the completeness of the narrative which these volumes endeavour to present, some account will now be given of the maritime operations connected with the campaigns in Africa from the entry of Italy into the war until the end of 1940.

At the beginning of the struggle in the Mediterranean it seemed possible, even likely, that the considerable Italian submarine strength would prove an important factor. No less than a hundred were in commission, and about four-fifths of that number were, initially, ready for service. We now know that sixteen were sent out at once to patrol between Gibraltar and Sicily, ten in the Gulf of Genoa and twenty between Greece and Alexandria—very large numbers when compared with the strength which the Germans were at this time able to dispose in the much greater expanses of the Atlantic. Yet the Italian U-boats accomplished very little during the present phase or thereafter; they suffered heavy losses and the numbers on patrol were soon reduced to ten at each end of the Mediterranean.[2]

It thus soon became apparent that the struggle for control of the Mediterranean routes would not, as in the Atlantic, be waged chiefly between the U-boats and the air and surface escorts, but would depend mainly on air power, and therefore on the possession by one side or the other of land bases from which to operate aircraft. Sicily therefore at once assumed a dominant position in the campaign; Sardinia also played a part, and the importance of Malta as an air base came fully to equal its importance as a naval base. Furthermore

---

[1] See I. S. O. Playfair, *The Mediterranean and Middle East*, Vol. I. (*In the press.*)

[2] In this book the war-time practice of referring to all enemy submarines as U-boats, regardless of nationality, is adhered to.

the defence of shipping would depend greatly on the land situation in Greece, Crete, Libya and north-west Africa, from all which territories aircraft could readily attack the convoys or could be used to defend them. Thus the maritime war soon came to be closely affected by the progress of the land campaigns.[1]

The Admiralty's plans and dispositions regarding control of the Mediterranean sea routes in the event of Italy joining her Axis partner have already been considered.[2] It will be appropriate now to review the Italian Navy's intentions. A directive was issued by the Chief of the Italian Armed Forces (Signor Mussolini) on the last day of March 1940 which laid down for the navy a policy of 'the offensive at all points in the Mediterranean and outside'. When commenting on Mussolini's directive, Admiral Cavagnari, the Chief of the Italian Naval Staff, pointed out that an offensive against the Anglo-French fleets would soon be exhausted through irreplaceable losses, whereas any losses inflicted on them could be replaced from the superiority which the Allies held at the outset. He also considered that weakness in the air seriously vitiated the Italian fleet's capacity for offensive action, and came to the conclusion that Italian naval strategy must therefore be defensive. The main defensive tasks of the Italian fleet were considered to be the closing of the Adriatic and Tyrrhenian Seas to our forces and the establishment of safe communications by sea with Libya and the Dodecanese. The offensive objects were to be the interruption of French communications to North Africa and to keep open certain sea routes for the eventual despatch of troops to enemy territory. Two raiding forces were to be formed with their fastest ships to work in the Gulf of Lyons and against the North African coast; various minefields were to be laid off Allied bases, and attacks by light torpedo craft on our warships when in harbour were mentioned. But an attack on Tunis, which seems to have been recognised as one of the keys to control of the central Mediterranean, was not considered possible in face of superior Allied naval strength. The forces available to the Italians with which to carry out their strategy and the relative strengths of the opposing fleets have already been given, and it has been pointed out that, even before the fall of France, any superiority which the Allies possessed was more theoretical than real.[3] After that event had taken place the Italians greatly outnumbered in all classes of warship the strength which the Admiralty could dispose at both ends of the Mediterranean.

In looking back to-day at Italian naval intentions in the light of our knowledge of their failure effectively to dispute control of the

---

[1] See Map 26 (*facing p. 293*).

[2] See pp. 41–42 and 48–49.

[3] See pp. 60–61. Appendix H gives full details of the strength and disposition of the Italian Navy in June 1940.

Mediterranean, it seems clear that their chief error lay in the belief that their own communications to North Africa, on which the fate of their armies must ultimately depend, could be secured by defensive measures alone. For the first year of the Mediterranean war they do not seem to have realised the importance of eliminating Malta, nor of accepting the challenge on any of the numerous occasions when British fleets and squadrons offered battle. The plans seem to have contained few indications of the methods whereby the 'offensive at all points' urged by Mussolini would be implemented. None the less the Italian navy exerted an important influence on British strategy and dispositions because, even after its handling had been shown to be ineffective and shortage of oil had restricted its movements, its existence could never be ignored; and British ships which were often urgently required elsewhere had to be used to contain that 'fleet in being'.

Before Italy's entry into the war arrangements had been agreed with the Germans that each navy would retain full liberty of action in its own theatre, but that intelligence and technical developments would be exchanged. The German navy would be responsible for submarine and surface vessel operations in the Atlantic, and would keep the two *Scharnhorsts* in the North Sea in order to force the French and ourselves to station the greatest possible number of capital ships outside the Mediterranean. The Italian navy would play a part in the submarine war in the Atlantic south of the latitude of Lisbon, and possibly send surface vessels and submarines into the Indian Ocean. In the Mediterranean it would 'seek to bring to action the greatest number of enemy forces'.

Mention has already been made of the reinforcements sent from the Home Fleet in May to Admiral Sir Andrew Cunningham at Alexandria as the Italian attitude became more threatening, but it may be useful briefly to recapitulate. Early in that month the battleships *Royal Sovereign* and *Malaya* arrived at Alexandria from the Atlantic, the cruiser *Orion* from the West Indies and her sister-ship, the *Neptune*, from the South Atlantic. The cruiser *Gloucester* came from the East Indies, the *Liverpool* from China and the *Sydney*, lent by the Commonwealth Government, from Australia. The anti-aircraft cruiser *Carlisle*, the netlayer *Protector*, sixteen destroyers and three sloops all came from the Home Fleet, a total of ten submarines from China and the East Indies and, finally, on the 14th May the famous *Warspite* returned to her original station and rehoisted Admiral Cunningham's flag. The aircraft carrier *Eagle* and the battleship *Ramillies* came through the Suez Canal from the east a short time later.

Of the French ships stationed in the eastern Mediterranean two battleships soon returned to the west, but the *Lorraine* remained and a cruiser squadron under Vice-Admiral Godfroy came to Alexandria to co-operate with our forces. Their service with Admiral Cunningham's fleet was all too brief. The bloodless solution ultimately found to the difficulties in which they were placed by the French surrender has already been mentioned.[1] Lastly it will be recalled that, at the end of June, Force H was formed under Admiral Somerville at Gibraltar with the primary purpose of replacing the lost French maritime power in the western basin.[2]

As soon as Mussolini's intention to join his Axis partner was clear beyond doubt, the Red Sea, then still a part of the command of Vice-Admiral R. Leatham, the Commander-in-Chief, East Indies, assumed great importance and the threat of the Italian destroyers and submarines, based at Massawa on the flank of our convoy route to Suez, demanded immediate counter-measures.[3] Accordingly on the 24th of May the Red Sea was closed to shipping until convoys had been formed, and the anti-aircraft cruiser *Carlisle*, three sloops and a division of destroyers passed southward through the Suez Canal to provide the necessary escorts. As it happened, the Italian threat to this route proved more theoretical than real; the submarines were easily dealt with—of the eight originally based east of Suez no less than three were destroyed and one was captured intact in June; the destroyers, of which there were initially nine, never interfered effectively with the steady progress of our convoys, and bombing by Italian aircraft was equally devoid of results. The Chiefs of Staff, who at the end of 1939 had stated that 'we might expect that, even in the early stages [of a war with Italy], it would be possible to pass occasional convoys through the Red Sea', were proved correct in their somewhat guarded forecast.

Hardly had Admiral Cunningham's fleet been strengthened sufficiently to meet his numerous commitments and to engage the Italian Navy on something like equal terms, when the French surrender brought to the front the whole question whether we could, in the new circumstances, afford to keep a major fleet in the eastern Mediterranean. On the 6th of June he had told the First Sea Lord that all his officers and men were 'imbued with a burning desire to get at the Italian Fleet'. Little more than a week later he received a message from Admiral Pound which was plainly fraught with the most serious implications.

Mr Churchill has written that 'so formidable did the situation appear at the end of June that Admiralty first thoughts contemplated the abandonment of the Eastern Mediterranean and concentration at Gibraltar', and has quoted his minute of the 15th of July in which

---

[1] See p. 242.
[2] See pp. 241–242
[3] See Map 34 (*facing p. 426*).

he says that he 'vetoed the proposal to evacuate the eastern Mediterranean and bring Admiral Cunningham's fleet to Gibraltar'.[1] That the fall of France and the loss of French maritime power in the western Mediterranean greatly increased the British Navy's responsibilities and underlined the many acute shortages from which, at this time, that service and the whole country suffered, requires no emphasis. It was perfectly natural therefore for the First Sea Lord to seek ways and means to mitigate the consequences of the blow, and he had good grounds for regarding the protection of the Atlantic routes as paramount. During the hectic days preceding and following the fall of France, when the future of that country's navy hung in the balance, it must have been difficult for him to see how the all-important safety of the Atlantic could be assured without disturbing our strength in the eastern basin of the Mediterranean. Actually, on the 17th of June, Admiral Pound signalled to the Commander-in-Chief a tentative proposal that part of the Mediterranean Fleet should come westward to Gibraltar and the rest be sent there round the Cape, and Admiral Cunningham replied at once to the effect that the suggested movements were practicable, but that the consequences would be the loss of Egypt and of Malta. On the same day the Prime Minister minuted to the First Lord that 'it is of the utmost importance that the fleet at Alexandria should remain to cover Egypt from an Italian invasion which would otherwise destroy prematurely all our position in the East. . . . Even if Spain declares war it does not follow that we should quit the eastern Mediterranean.'[2] Next day Admiral Cunningham sent another message lest his first should have been read, in London, as 'somewhat acquiescent', expressing his 'earnest hope that such a decision would never have to be taken' and deprecating the 'landslide in territory and prestige' which would result. So much for the views of the responsible Commander-in-Chief. How far these views influenced the final decision to drop the proposal is not clear even to this day. The Chiefs of Staff received the Admiralty's proposal on the 17th—the day that Admiral Cunningham's replies were received in London—and referred it to their Joint Planning Sub-Committee. The conclusion of the latter was that 'the . . . political, economic and military reasons for retaining the fleet in the Eastern Mediterranean outweigh the purely naval reasons for its withdrawal'. Possibly in consequence of this and of Admiral Cunningham's replies, the Chiefs of Staff never recommended withdrawal to the Defence Committee or Cabinet. On the 3rd of July the Chiefs of Staff told all Commanders-in-Chief that it was intended to keep the fleet in the eastern Mediterranean.

---

[1] See W. S. Churchill. *The Second World War*, Vol. II, pp. 390 and 392.
[2] Ibid., p. 563.

With the entry of Italy into the war the long-deferred reinforcement of the air defences and military garrison of Malta, regarding whose weakness and deficiencies Admiral Cunningham had often but vainly protested, could not be further delayed. The use of an aircraft carrier to ferry fighter aircraft to the island was discussed in London in mid-July; the First Sea Lord considered it 'quite practicable' and the Air Ministry was informed that the old training carrier *Argus* (Captain H. C. Bovell) would be made available. She was accordingly sent out early in August with twelve Hurricanes, which were successfully flown to Malta from a position south-west of Sardinia (Operation "Hurry"). Though the Chiefs of Staff had only two months earlier recorded as their opinion that 'there is nothing practicable we can do to increase the powers of resistance of Malta', that very process was thus embarked on not only at the eleventh hour but under far more hazardous conditions than had prevailed before Italy entered the war. Operation 'Hurry' was, in fact, the first of a long series of difficult and costly operations which might have been reduced or avoided had it been possible to strengthen the island's defences before its danger became acute. The price of the pre-war parsimony which was the basic cause of this neglect was first paid in the following November when, in a second operation by the *Argus*, eight out of the twelve Hurricanes ran out of fuel and were lost at sea. An enquiry established that the pilots had not been adequately trained regarding the range and endurance of their aircraft.

The *Argus* was also the first aircraft carrier to be used to carry fighter aircraft to Takoradi, on the Gold Coast, whence they were flown right across the African continent to Egypt. She arrived there for the first time on the 5th of September 1940.

The first brush between Admiral Cunningham's main fleet and the Italian Navy occurred on the 9th of July off the Calabrian coast, while the former was covering the passage of two convoys from Malta to Alexandria. The enemy was at sea with the similar purpose of covering a convoy to North Africa. In the action which followed, the British were, on paper, superior in capital ships, of which they had three against two Italians. But the *Royal Sovereign* was too slow to keep her position in the line and the *Malaya* also never got within range. In cruisers and destroyers the Italians were greatly superior.

The action consisted firstly of an unsuccessful attempt to slow down the enemy with torpedo-bombers from the aircraft carrier *Eagle*, then of a long-range gun duel. After the battleship *Cesare* had been hit the Italians turned away and retired under cover of a smoke screen, while skirmishes took place between the opposing destroyers. In the final phase there was heavy but ineffective bombing by Italian shore-based aircraft, much of which was aimed at their own ships. Admiral Cunningham pursued to the westward until evening when he was only twenty-five miles from the Calabrian coast; but the enemy made good his escape and the British fleet, still under bombing attack, steered firstly to the south of Malta and then, after the safe passage of the convoys had been assured, returned to its base at Alexandria. Though the failure to bring the enemy to battle was disappointing, the brief encounter was of interest because it indicated the unwillingness of the Italian fleet to stand and fight, and the probable tactics of its commanders after contact between surface forces had occurred. Admiral Cunningham's ships were, in general, slower than the enemy's, and the prospects of bringing them to action were therefore greatly dependent on the ability of his carrier-borne aircraft to strike effectively at long range and so allow the heavy ships to come up. And as yet the Commander-in-Chief had only the obsolescent *Eagle* and her small striking force wherewith to accomplish that purpose, while the Italian battleships could out-range all of ours except the *Warspite*. Admiral Cunningham accordingly told the First Sea Lord that he 'must have one more ship that can shoot at a good range'. But, if it caused the enemy little material damage, the action off Calabria probably helped to establish the ascendancy over the Italian surface forces which was to be so marked a feature of the naval campaign in the Mediterranean and was ultimately to reduce their theoretically powerful fleet to virtual impotence. As regards the air attacks, the Italian high-level bombing was courageously carried out and sometimes unpleasantly accurate in aim. Though the cruiser *Gloucester* was the only ship hit on this occasion the feeling in the fleet was that such attacks were by no means an insignificant danger.

The lessons which the Italian Navy may have derived from the action off Calabria were quickly emphasised by an encounter, on the 19th of July, between a small squadron consisting of the Australian cruiser *Sydney* (Captain J. A. Collins, R.A.N.), with five destroyers, and two Italian cruisers off the north coast of Crete. After a running fight the *Bartolomeo Colleoni* was sunk.

At the end of August additional reinforcements were sent to Admiral Cunningham from home and the battleship *Valiant*, the new aircraft carrier *Illustrious*, the anti-aircraft cruisers *Calcutta* and *Coventry*, and light forces reached Gibraltar on the 29th. An operation to pass this force through to the eastern basin started forthwith, under the cover of Admiral Somerville's Force H, and the opportunity was taken further to reinforce the land and air defences of Malta. The eastern and western forces met to the south of Sicily, and the whole movement was completed without serious interference by the Italians, although their main fleet was sighted at sea. After their return to Gibraltar Admiral Somerville's ships all became involved in the expedition against Dakar (Operation 'Menace'), which was already in train and of which further mention will be made later.

The safety and supply of Malta continued to cause anxiety at home and to Admiral Cunningham, but on three occasions in October and November reinforcements and stores were successfully carried there from Alexandria under cover of the Mediterranean Fleet. But on the 28th of October a new commitment arose from the unprovoked Italian invasion of Greece and, a fortnight later, the movement of British troops northwards from Egypt began, initially on quite a small scale. The enemy's action on land at once produced the necessity to occupy the island of Crete and the opportunity to establish an advanced base at Suda Bay on its northern shore. This was rapidly accomplished, but the material essential to its proper defence, particularly against air attack, was not available and in consequence the security of this valuable new base was seriously prejudiced from the start.

On the 7th of November more reinforcements for Admiral Cunningham—the battleship *Barham*, the cruisers *Berwick* and *Glasgow* and three destroyers from home—reached Gibraltar and at once sailed east in company with Force H. Malta was again reinforced on the way, with men and guns carried in the warships, and the additional strength reached Alexandria unmolested. The result of this operation and of its predecessor in August gave grounds for believing that the Italian attempts to dispute control of the east-west route were not as effective as the Admiralty had expected. This revived the question whether it might not be possible to pass urgently needed material, and in particular tanks, to Egypt through the Mediterranean instead of round the Cape—a risk which the Prime Minister had long desired to accept.[1] But before that could be tried Admiral Cunningham was at last able to carry out a long-cherished plan to use his torpedo-bombers to attack the Italian fleet in its base at Taranto.

It had been intended that the *Illustrious* (Captain D. W. Boyd) and *Eagle* (Captain A. R. M. Bridge) should both be used, but the latter ship was prevented from taking a direct part by defects caused by the many bombs which had narrowly missed her during the action off Calabria. Some of her aircraft and crews were therefore transferred to the *Illustrious*, on board which ship two striking forces of twelve and nine aircraft were formed from Nos. 813, 815, 819 and 824 squadrons, led by Lieutenant-Commanders K. Williamson and J. W. Hale. They flew off at 8.40 and 9.30 p.m. respectively on the 11th of November from a position some 180 miles south-east of the Italian base, achieved complete surprise and, in spite of its strong defences, quickly sank at their moorings the new *Littorio* and two of the older

---
[1] See W. S. Churchill. *The Second World War*, Vol. II, pp. 391 *et seq.*

Giulio Cesare class battleships. All but two of the aircraft returned safely to their parent ship. Although from the nature of this attack it was not to be expected that the ships would be permanently disabled, the results achieved by so few Swordfish were not only remarkable in themselves but were accomplished at a singularly fortunate period when, with grave uncertainty still surrounding the future of the French fleet, the balance of maritime power by no means rested firmly in our hands. In spite of the failure of the Italians ever to use their battleship strength effectively, account always had to be taken of its existence, and by this 'well conceived and brilliantly executed' attack one threat to our maritime control in that theatre was greatly reduced. This was, perhaps, the first occasion when, in any theatre, long-range air reconnaissance provided our forces with accurate and timely intelligence. A few Glenn Martins (later called Marylands) which had recently arrived at Malta took photographs of the enemy base, showing the ships present and their berthing, on the day before the attack and the photographs were flown from Malta to the *Illustrious*. Nor was the damage to the Italian battleships the end of our success. While the attack on Taranto was in progress our light forces, under Admiral Pridham-Wippell, were making a raid into the Straits of Otranto. In the early hours of the 12th of November they met a convoy bound for Brindisi and destroyed three of its four ships. Thus was British maritime power reasserted in the central basin of the Mediterranean in no uncertain fashion, and the reward for filling the long-felt need for long-range reconnaissance aircraft quickly and abundantly reaped.

A fortnight later the first attempt was made to pass a small convoy direct from Gibraltar to Alexandria. In addition to the fast merchantmen *Clan Forbes* and *Clan Fraser* (for Malta) and *New Zealand Star* (for Alexandria) some 1,400 soldiers and airmen were embarked in the cruisers *Manchester* (flag of Vice-Admiral L. E. Holland) and *Southampton* for the passage right through to Egypt; opportunity was also taken to pass four of the new corvettes to the eastern Mediterranean. The plan was for Force H, under Admiral Somerville in the *Renown*, with the *Ark Royal*, *Sheffield*, *Despatch* and nine destroyers, to accompany the convoy, while a powerful proportion of Admiral Cunningham's strength—the battleship *Ramillies*, the cruisers *Newcastle*, *Berwick*, *Coventry* (anti-aircraft) and five destroyers—would meet Admiral Somerville to the south of Sardinia. Force H, the convoy and its escort and the detached force from Alexandria would then keep company to a position between Sicily and Cape Bon, which would be reached at dusk so as to make the hazardous passage of 'The Narrows' in darkness.[1] Force H, with the *Ramillies*, *Newcastle*

---
[1] See Map 26 (*facing p. 293*).

and *Berwick* from the eastern Mediterranean, would then return to Gibraltar, while the convoy and its escort passed to the south of Malta to be met by the remainder of the Mediterranean Fleet next day.

The three merchant ships passed Gibraltar during the night of the 24th–25th of November and were met by Force H next morning. The operation proceeded according to plan until the morning of the 27th, by which time the *Ramillies* and her cruiser consorts had passed westward through the Narrows but had not yet met Force H. At 6.30 a.m. a Sunderland flying-boat from Malta reported strong enemy naval forces off Cape Spartivento, the southern tip of Sardinia, then some seventy miles to the north-east of Force H and the convoy. A short time later one of the *Ark Royal's* aircraft also sighted the enemy. In fact the Italians had sent out from Naples and Messina the battleships *Vittorio Veneto* and *Giulio Cesare*, seven 8-inch cruisers and sixteen destroyers as soon as they learnt of the start of a movement involving our forces from both the eastern and western ends of the Mediterranean. They were therefore greatly superior to Admiral Somerville's force before he had met the ships from Alexandria—which were at the time still some fifty miles to the east of him—and would still be considerably superior even after that junction had been made. But Admiral Somerville well knew that his object, the safe passage of the convoy, would best be achieved by a resolute tactical offensive, and at 11.30 a.m. he therefore spread Admiral Holland's cruisers in the van and turned towards the enemy at high speed. Soon afterwards the *Ramillies* and her consorts from Alexandria joined Force H but, as the battleship was much slower than the *Renown*, Somerville's striking power was not thereby appreciably strengthened. At 12.20 action was joined between the most westerly of the two groups of Italian cruisers and our own cruiser line, and the enemy at once retired towards his own heavy units under cover of smoke. The *Renown* joined in a few minutes after the cruisers had opened fire, and the action was continued at long ranges until about 12.30 while the enemy retired in a north-easterly direction. Of our ships only the *Berwick* was hit in this running fight. Meanwhile the Italian Commander-in-Chief, Admiral Campioni in the *Vittorio Veneto*, had come to the opinion that the British force was superior to his own and, more justifiably, that the danger of damage by air attack on his capital ships was serious. At 12.15 he therefore signalled to his cruisers not to become involved in a battle.

At one o'clock the enemy battle fleet was sighted ahead of our cruisers and opened fire on them. The cruisers retired towards the *Renown* but, when the enemy heavy ships were seen to have turned away to the north-east, Admiral Holland at once followed in the same direction. Meanwhile the *Ark Royal* had, at 11.30, launched her first torpedo-bomber striking force—eleven aircraft of No. 810 squadron—against the Italian battleships. At about 12.40 they attacked the enemy flagship. Though one hit was claimed in this attack, none was, in fact, obtained. By 1.15 the surface action had practically ended.

By this time our forces were rapidly approaching the enemy coast and Admiral Somerville had to consider whether further pursuit would assist towards his object of securing the safe passage of the convoy. He realised that he was unlikely to come up with the retreating enemy unless their speed could be reduced, and that a headlong pursuit might well endanger the convoy. At 1.12 he therefore abandoned the chase and ordered his forces to rejoin the convoy, the most hazardous part of whose passage was now approaching. Half an hour later a report of a damaged enemy cruiser ten miles off the Sardinian coast reached the Admiral, and he ordered the *Ark Royal's* aircraft to attack her. At 2.10 p.m. a second striking force was therefore flown off the carrier. Nine torpedo-bombers were given the enemy battleships as their target and seven dive-bombers were ordered to attack the damaged cruiser. The torpedo-bombers obtained no hits and, as the damaged cruiser could not be found, the bombers attacked others of the enemy's cruiser force then steering north along the coast of Sardinia. This too failed to achieve any result. Later in the afternoon enemy bombers attacked Admiral Somerville's force as it steamed south towards the convoy. Although the *Ark Royal* was surrounded by bomb splashes, she received no damage. By 5 p.m. the convoy was sighted and the operation thereafter proceeded according to plan.

Though this indecisive action was satisfactory to neither side the Italians certainly failed either to hinder the passage of the convoy or to inflict appreciable damage on our weaker surface forces. From our own point of view the failure of the air striking forces to slow up or damage the retreating enemy was certainly disappointing; but it was known that the *Ark Royal's* aircrews lacked the high degree of training and experience necessary to achieve good results. Admiral Somerville was criticised in London for abandoning the pursuit. This criticism, by itself, may not have been unreasonable. But, instead of awaiting his return to harbour and calling for a written report, the Admiralty at once sent out Lord Cork and Orrery to enquire into the circumstances; and the Board of Enquiry was set up even before the squadron had reached Gibraltar. Admiral Cunningham has told of his strong dislike of this action from London.[1] To Admiral Somerville the setting up of an enquiry implied a lack of confidence in his leader-

---

[1] See Viscount Cunningham of Hyndhope, *A Sailor's Odyssey* (Hutchinson, 1951), pp. 292-93.

ship which might produce serious consequences in his squadron. He wondered, with some reason, 'who is playing these sort of games with the Navy?' Though the right of the Admiralty to criticise and, if need be, to chastise its Flag Officers is indisputable, the handling of the whole matter was certainly unfortunate. The Board of Enquiry, once possessed of all the relevant facts, entirely upheld Somerville's action.

Admiral Cunningham revictualled Malta once more before the end of the year and himself visited the besieged island between the 20th and 22nd of December. He reported that 'the base was as effective as when war broke out and far better defended against air attack or invasion', but that serious deficiencies none the less still existed.

Towards the end of 1940 various proposals were raised at home to use the Commando troops of the Combined Operations Command, whose director was at this time Admiral of the Fleet Sir Roger Keyes, to capture enemy-held islands in the Mediterranean. Though none was actually carried out, the principles involved are of sufficient interest to justify a brief survey of their history and the reasons for their final demise. On the last day of October Admiral Keyes proposed to the Chiefs of Staff that a raid should be made on the small, rocky island of Pantellaria about 150 miles north-west of Malta. A plan was accordingly prepared and in the middle of November the Prime Minister expressed himself strongly in favour of it. He wanted to 'begin with Workshop' (the code name for Pantellaria) and then to attack the Dodecanese Islands, including Rhodes or Leros, as well. The Defence and Chiefs of Staffs' Committees went on discussing the plans and they and Admiral Keyes met the Prime Minister to exchange views. Meanwhile Admiral Cunningham, who had of course been informed of the intention, told London in no uncertain terms of his dislike of the proposal. To him it meant adding one more supply commitment to his overburdened fleet at a time when Malta was giving him difficulty enough and, moreover, for an unprofitable reason. The possession of Pantellaria would not, he considered, make any real difference to the command of the Narrows as long as the enemy held Sicily, with its numerous airfields and harbours, close by. His views carried weight in London and, early in December, the First Sea Lord pointed out that Pantellaria had 'so far caused us very little trouble'. The Chiefs of Staff now recommended dropping the proposal. The Prime Minister, whose eye was always focused on any opportunity to take the offensive, was dissatisfied at this and, early in 1941, asked the Chiefs of Staff to reconsider it. They, however, supported the First Sea Lord's opinion that 'even if it were possible to capture Pantellaria we should not be enabled by its use to control the passage through the Narrows'. The Prime Minister however, as

Admiral of the Fleet Sir Andrew B. Cunningham, Commander-in-Chief Mediterranean 1st June 1939–1st April 1942 and 20th February 1943–14th October 1943, First Sea Lord and Chief of Naval Staff 15th October 1943–10th June 1946.

H.M.S. *Warspite*, Mediterranean Fleet Flagship. (See page 295.)

he has said, remained unconvinced.[1] Not until the closing months of the year were similar suggestions raised again.

In reviewing the matter to-day it seems that, while the importance of losing no chance to strike an offensive blow is undeniable, to accept additional and probably unprofitable commitments at a time when our maritime forces were barely adequate to control the essential sea routes, to hold the key positions in which our armies were being built up and to secure the supply and safety of the British Isles, was to invite a weakening of the forces available to carry out those primary objects and so to jeopardise our whole maritime strategy.

It has been told how we were, at this time, deprived of the use of the direct sea route through the Mediterranean, except for the passage of occasional military convoys from Alexandria to Malta or from Gibraltar to Egypt under cover of our full available strength. Though this must be accounted an important strategic success to the enemy, it did not mean that the control of the seas, and in particular the use of the routes from Italy to North Africa, had passed to the Italians. The period provides an excellent example of control being in dispute.[2] In fact, from the first days of Italy's entry into the war, Admiral Cunningham had wished to prosecute a vigorous campaign against the enemy's supply routes. But to deprive the Italians of the use of the short sea passages to Africa plainly depended chiefly on the work of our light surface forces, submarines and aircraft; and all three arms could best fulfil that purpose if they could be based on Malta. Unhappily the insecurity of that island base prevented surface forces being stationed there regularly; and even the few submarines which had been left there soon had to be withdrawn. Although, on paper, Admiral Cunningham had initially possessed considerable submarine strength in the 1st Submarine Flotilla (by the end of August seventeen boats, including two minelayers, had arrived) they were of the older O, P and R classes which had been transferred to him from the East Indies and China Stations. Apart from their age and, in some cases, their defective state, they were rapidly shown to be too large to work safely and effectively in the central Mediterranean; and there were other serious handicaps as well. Firstly, Alexandria was too far from the operational areas, Malta could not be used and, until the Italians attacked Greece at the end of October, the Cabinet would not allow Cunningham to establish an advanced base at Suda Bay in Crete. Secondly, although restrictions on attacks on merchant shipping in home waters had been largely removed in April, they remained in force in the Mediterranean until mid-July; and submarines cannot deal effectively with supply traffic under the rules of 'visit and search' applicable to surface ships. Thirdly, the

---

[1] W. S. Churchill. *The Second World War*, Vol. II, pp. 552 and 618, and Vol. III, p. 52.
[2] See pp. 3-4.

remoteness of their base and the fact that the enemy routed his traffic down the west coast of Sicily to Tripoli and thence through the shallow coastal waters eastwards to Benghazi meant that the most profitable waters were out of reach of, or too dangerous for, our submarines. Nor were the Italian counter-measures to be despised. Mines were laid outside as well as inside declared areas and often in unexpectedly deep waters. These, along with the activities of aircraft and patrol boats, made the approaches to enemy coasts and ports highly dangerous, especially to the large boats then comprising the 1st Flotilla. Admiral Cunningham lost one-third of his strength in the first few days of the war and ten boats (one of them Greek) had failed to return from patrols by the end of the year. But the Italians also found the Mediterranean dangerous waters for submarines and they suffered even heavier losses (fourteen boats inside the Mediterranean and twenty in all) during the same period. Yet another difficulty was that our stocks of modern torpedoes on the station rapidly proved quite inadequate; obsolete weapons had to be used and emergency measures instituted, such as transport of torpedoes by submarine. Apart from these handicaps it was our policy during these early months to use our submarines against the enemy's warships rather than his supply traffic, and the change of emphasis, combined with the lifting of restrictions, did not become fully effective until some eight months after Italy's entry into the war.

A number of different factors thus combined to reduce the scale and effectiveness of the work of our submarines on the routes between Italy and Africa during these early months of the war. But a change began to be apparent before the end of the year. The use of Malta, to a limited extent, had again become possible; the first of the newer and smaller boats of the *Triton* and *Unity* classes had arrived and quickly proved their value; a new flotilla (the 8th) had been formed at Gibraltar, and experience had been gained of the type of attack likely to prove fruitful in the Mediterranean, and of counter-attack to be expected. It was clear that a new phase of submarine warfare was about to open.

While our submarines laboured under the difficulties described above, our air striking forces were in no better case. Though the Air Officer Commanding, Mediterranean, reported home in August that 'fifteen aircraft would produce results out of all proportion to [the] numbers involved', the only striking force available was a few naval Swordfish of No. 830 Squadron which had fortuitously reached Malta. These Swordfish, the carrier-borne aircraft of the Mediterranean Fleet when disembarked, and such few R.A.F. bombers as were available in Egypt, all did their best. But they were too few in numbers and of too unsuitable types to achieve substantial results against the enemy's supply traffic. None the less, occasional outstanding successes were obtained, as when three Swordfish from the *Eagle's* No. 824 Squadron sank a depot ship, a destroyer and a submarine in the Gulf of Bomba on the 22nd of August. But these only served to emphasise the results which even modest air striking power could have accomplished.

It thus came about that, for a variety of reasons, the denial to the enemy of the use of the trans-Mediterranean routes was not, during this period, effective enough to influence the campaign on land. We now know that the Italians succeeded in passing over 690,000 tons of shipping to Libya between June and December 1940, and that under two per cent. of the traffic on that route was intercepted and sunk.

The Italian Admiralty's statistics of their shipping losses during this phase, which do not distinguish the Mediterranean from other theatres, nor include German shipping or that formerly belonging to conquered countries, are given below.

Table 8. Italian Merchant Shipping Losses, June–December 1940
(Number of ships—Tonnage)

	By surface ships	By submarines	By air attack	By mine	By other causes	Total
June .	—	—	1— 440	8— 8,956	8—14,025	17— 23,421
July .	2— 520	—	3—11,459	1— 3,864	2— 486	8— 16,329
August	—	1— 1,968	2— 4,798	1— 2,298	2— 65	6— 10,129
Sept. .	—	3—10,706	4—10,431	1— 568	—	8— 21,705
Oct. .	—	2— 7,758	—	3—10,030	3— 2,380	8— 20,168
Nov. .	4—16,938	—	1— 57	—	1— 93	6— 17,088
Dec. .	4— 1,416	4—24,112	4— 8,854	2— 6,803	7—16,015	21— 57,200
Total .	10—18,874	10—44,544	15—36,039	16—33,519	23—33,064	74—166,040

While the events recounted above were taking place inside the Mediterranean, the Red Sea Force, which had been strengthened from the East Indies station, continued successfully to protect the troop and trade convoys on the last stretch of their long passage to Suez. In the middle of August British Somaliland was evacuated under overwhelming Italian pressure on land; but this made no appreciable difference to the progress of the war, or to the control of the sea routes off the East African coast. It was, in fact, the only retreat made in that theatre and, shortly after it had been carried out, we started to built up our land forces for the assault on the Italian possessions in Somaliland, Abyssinia and Eritrea. The naval forces on the station then acted constantly, and traditionally, in support of the army on land. Meanwhile the coast of Italian Somaliland was successfully blockaded and the remaining enemy naval forces based within the Red Sea lapsed into a state of complete ineffectiveness. By the end of the year our control of the East African coastal routes and of the southern approaches to Suez was assured, and from this time the conquest of the Italian colonies, to which no reinforcements or supplies could be carried beyond a trickle by air from North Africa, became certain. The stage was thus set for the slow but steady application of our maritime strategy to accomplish its first big success—the destruction of Italian imperial hopes and ambitions in East Africa.

But while the prospects of early success in East Africa were thus developing, the British Cabinet's desires and intentions had not prospered equally on the other side of the continent, where the possibility of the Germans filtering into the French West African colonies bordering our route to the Cape was alarming. Hence arose the attempt to install General de Gaulle's Free French movement in Senegal, a colony which, with its base at Dakar, would in wrong hands gravely threaten, and in the right hands help to protect, our convoys passing along that coast.[1] General de Gaulle himself first proposed that the attempt should be made, and the Prime Minister immediately accepted the idea. On the 8th of August Mr Churchill issued a directive stressing the importance of Dakar and stating that ample British supporting force was to be provided. On the 12th, Vice-Admiral J. H. D. Cunningham, who had been in command of the 1st Cruiser Squadron in the Home Fleet, and Major-General M. N. S. Irwin were appointed as naval and military commanders of the expedition, to which the code name 'Menace' had been given. There now followed a period of discussions, of planning and of postponement until, on the 27th of August, the War Cabinet gave its final approval. Unfortunately, reliable intelligence regarding the state of French feeling in Senegal and of the defences of Dakar did not reach London until the 28th. Though this indicated that de Gaulle would not be welcomed and that serious resistance to his movement would certainly be encountered, it arrived too late to influence the Cabinet decision. On the 29th Admiral Cunningham and General Irwin left London and, on the last day of the month, the expedition sailed for Freetown in three sections from Scapa, the Clyde and Liverpool. It was expected to reach Freetown, where it would be joined by substantial reinforcements from Gibraltar, on the 13th of September.

The Scapa group consisted of three transports escorted by the cruiser *Fiji* and three destroyers; the Clyde group, of the *Devonshire*, flying Admiral Cunningham's flag, one destroyer and three Free French sloops; and from Liverpool sailed three more transports escorted by three destroyers. In all some 4,200 British troops and 2,700 Free French troops were embarked in the transports. Certain other ships, including those with the expedition's mechanical trans-

---

[1] See Maps 23 and 26A (*facing p. 273 and on p. 313*).

port, sailed for Freetown, with a Sierra Leone mercantile convoy, on the 26th of August. The naval forces allocated to Admiral Cunningham, called Force M, comprised two battleships (the *Barham* and *Resolution*), the aircraft carrier *Ark Royal*, the cruisers *Devonshire*, *Fiji* and *Cumberland*, ten destroyers and certain minor vessels.

The only important incident on the outward journey was the torpedoing of the *Fiji* by a U-boat on the 1st of September, which necessitated her return to the Clyde. She was replaced by the *Australia* from the Home Fleet.[1] But southward progress was slower than had been expected, and it soon became clear that the attack on Dakar could not take place before the 19th.

When still some 300 miles north-west of Dakar, on the 11th of September, Admiral Cunningham received news from Gibraltar of the passage of a French force, consisting of the cruisers *Georges Leygues*, *Gloire* and *Montcalm* and three large destroyers, to the west through the Straits. This introduced an unforeseen and probably adverse factor into the operation.

It is inevitable that, in studying the expedition and the causes of its failure, the responsibilities and actions of the senior officers concerned should come under review. It is therefore necessary to give the reader a full account of the orders regarding the treatment of French warships which had been issued from London.

On the 4th of July the Admiralty told all Flag Officers that, as a result of the attack on Oran, 'we may be at war with France shortly', and that ships were to be prepared for attack but were not to fire the first shot. Various other statements of policy reached the Service authorities at Gibraltar at about the same time as the Admiralty message of the 4th of July. Admiral Sir Dudley North, the Flag Officer commanding the North Atlantic Station, was thereby left in some uncertainty regarding what action he should take if French warships attempted to pass through the Straits. On the 6th he therefore asked the Admiralty to clarify the matter. In their reply next day the Admiralty said that French warships should, in these circumstances, be dealt with in accordance with the message of the 4th—namely, that contact with equal or superior forces should be avoided, but that inferior forces were to be stopped and ordered into a British port. But, as so often happens during a period of difficult and strained relationships, these orders were soon modified by others. On the 12th the Admiralty took a more hopeful view and signalled that, as 'the *Richelieu* has now been dealt with and the *Jean Bart* could not complete for a considerable period', no further action was to be taken in regard to French ships in their colonial and North

---

[1] See p. 261.

African ports.[1] But the Government 'reserved the right' to deal with warships proceeding to enemy-controlled ports. This message was assumed by Admiral North—and with some reason—to supersede the orders given on the 7th about dealing with French warships attempting to pass through the Straits. The Admiralty did not, however, say that those orders were cancelled; but Admiral North was so sure of the correctness of his interpretation that he never asked whether this was so. He therefore considered that no further action would now be taken against French warships already present in, among other ports, Casablanca and Dakar and that, in the case of ships proceeding to those ports, action would only be taken by orders from and on the responsibility of the Government. Although the forces organised for Operation 'Menace' had been sent out with the purpose of overthrowing the Vichy element in Senegal and installing General de Gaulle's government in that colony, the directives issued to the commanding Admiral and General stated that the operation 'should, if at all possible, be carried out without bloodshed . . . '. In view of this, of the fact that we were not at war with the Vichy Government and that our enemies were certainly not in occupation of the French West African colonies, Casablanca and Dakar could hardly be considered as coming within the description of enemy-controlled ports in the sense of the Admiralty message of the 12th of July quoted above. Thus it appeared to Admiral North that, in the absence of orders from home, French warships were free to make the passage to Casablanca or Dakar, and that his duty was only to keep the Admiralty informed as early as possible of any such movements. He acted on that assumption throughout the tangled events which follows.

It was told earlier how, when Force H was formed at the end of June, the Admiralty described it as a 'detached squadron', and how Admiral Somerville was in no doubt that this meant that his was an independent command responsible direct to the Admiralty.[2] It is certain that, although Somerville was the junior of the two Flag Officers present at Gibraltar, he never regarded himself as being under Admiral North's orders and that the latter agreed with and accepted that interpretation of the Admiralty's definition. His view that he was correct in doing so gained some support when numerous operational signals were sent by the Admiralty direct to Somerville. Both the Flag Officers seem to have been satisfied that they could best discharge their responsibilities by working very closely together, and that their precise constitutional positions could well be left unclarified. It will be plain that, if Force H was an independent command, its Flag Officer must be responsible for all its actions. It

---

[1] See p. 245.
[2] See p. 242.

may therefore be considered illogical that North, and not Somerville, was held responsible by the Admiralty for the passage of the Straits by the French warships being made without an attempt by Force H to stop or divert them. The reason for the Admiralty's decision will be discussed later.

In the light of after events it may seem that Admiral North would have been wise to ask the Admiralty whether Somerville was or was not under his orders. But it is doubtful whether, even had he done so, the Admiralty would have given a clear answer quickly, because, when it was later admitted in London that the position of Force H was 'not left quite as clear as it might have been' and that 'it seems true to say that it was an independent force', the redefinition of its position to the satisfaction of the Admiralty proved difficult. The truth is that the chain of command was ill-defined and that such vagueness, besides being operationally dangerous, placed the responsible officers in an unfair position.

There is another aspect of the problem to be considered. The orders for Operation 'Menace' had not been issued to Admiral North, but he and his colleague did know that large forces were at sea within or near his command area and that their destination was Dakar. In the light of this knowledge, though incomplete, it might be argued that particular importance should have been attached to preventing any French forces moving towards the scene of an impending and delicate operation. The Admiralty certainly took that view later. But Admiral North considered that the Admiralty would, as they had done on many previous occasions, signal direct to Somerville if they required any action taken by Force H and that, for reasons already given, the policy was to allow French warships to proceed unmolested to ports not in the enemy's control.

Turning now to study the actual events of the 9th–12th of September, on the evening of the former day our Consul-General in Tangier reported to Admiral North that he had received reliable intelligence regarding the passage of the Straits within the next seventy-two hours by a French squadron bound for an unknown destination. Twenty-four hours later the British Naval Attaché in Madrid reported to Gibraltar and the Admiralty that the French Admiralty had informed him that a squadron of six ships had left Toulon the previous day; no destination was mentioned. We now know that the French Admiralty had asked the German and Italian Armistice Commission for permission to move certain warships from Toulon to West Africa at the end of August, because the Chad Territory had declared for de Gaulle and the Vichy Government desired to prevent the Free French movement spreading in the adjacent colonies. The movement was approved on the 1st of September.

The Admiralty received the Madrid report, which had an 'Immediate' priority, at 11.50 p.m. on the 10th; Admiral North received it at eight minutes past midnight. In the Admiralty no special significance was attached to the intelligence, and the First Sea Lord's attention was not drawn to it until the forenoon of the 11th. In the Foreign Office the report made by the Consul-General Tangier on the 9th was not even decyphered for several days.

At 4.45 a.m. on the 11th the destroyer *Hotspur*, on a submarine hunt in the Straits, reported that she had sighted this force and was shadowing, but, at 5.55, Admiral North directed her to cease doing so. At 6.17 North told the Admiralty about the *Hotspur's* sighting and that he had directed her to take no action. Half an hour later he sent a further message saying that he intended 'to keep in touch with this force by air' and would 'report its probable destination'.

On the morning of the 11th Admiral North assumed, with valid reason, that the Admiralty had received the previous day's report from the Naval Attaché Madrid. He also assumed that the Admiralty would order Admiral Somerville to take any action they desired when they learnt from his own recently despatched messages that the Madrid report had been proved correct. He therefore took no action himself beyond organising the air reconnaissance to watch the French ships' progress. But, at 5.30 a.m., Admiral Somerville brought the *Renown* to one hour's notice for steam.

At about noon on the 11th the Admiralty seems to have realised the full significance of these events in relation to Operation 'Menace', and ordered the *Renown* and all destroyers to raise steam for full speed. Two hours later Admiral Somerville was told that he must prevent the French ships from reaching Dakar or any Biscay port, but might allow them to proceed to Casablanca. The *Renown* put to sea at 4.30 p.m., but it was by then too late to intercept the French squadron, which arrived at Casablanca at about that time. At 3.42 p.m. Admiral Cunningham, in command of the naval forces for Operation 'Menace', received the report from Admiral North, already mentioned, telling him of the passage of the six French ships southward. At 8.6 p.m. on that evening, the 11th, the Admiralty ordered Admiral Somerville to establish a patrol to intercept the French forces if they sailed southwards from Casablanca, and this the Admiral carried out by patrolling with the *Renown* and six destroyers between Cape Blanco (N) and Agadir until early on the 14th, when he had to return to Gibraltar for fuel.[1] But Dakar is 1,319 miles to the south of Casablanca and the distance, combined with the slender forces comprising Admiral Somerville's patrol, made it easy for the French cruisers to evade him on their southward passage. By

---

[1] See Map 26A. Cape Blanco south of Casablanca is referred to as Cape Blanco (N) to distinguish it from the similarly-named promontory farther south.

3.30 p.m. on the 13th an aircraft reported that no French cruisers remained at Casablanca.

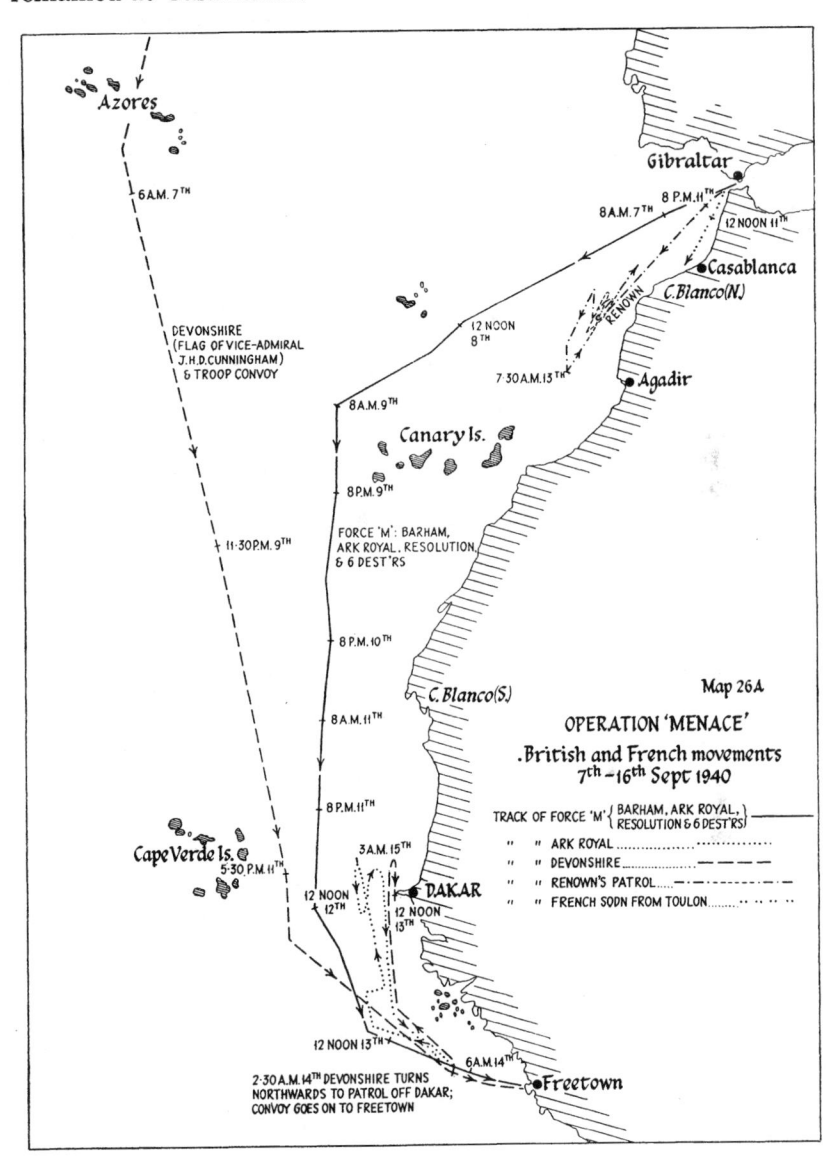

Map 26A

OPERATION 'MENACE'
British and French movements
7th–16th Sept 1940

It seems unlikely that Force H, which at the time had only the *Renown* and a few destroyers, could actually have stopped the French squadron in the Straits, at any rate without the use of force. And Admiral North believed that the policy stated on the 12th of July 'to avoid contact with equal or superior [French] forces' was still in effect. That a battle between Force H and the powerful French squadron may actually have been narrowly averted is indicated by our present knowledge, from German sources, that permission to move the ships to West Africa had been granted on the express condition that they resisted British attack.

It is, perhaps, possible to take the view that, as soon as he knew about the approach of the French squadron, Admiral North should have pressed the Admiralty for an immediate decision regarding any action which he might be required to take against it. But his assumption that the Admiralty had received the Madrid report was certainly justified. The consequence of the events described above was that the Admiralty felt that they no longer 'retained full confidence in an officer who fails in an emergency to take all prudent precautions without waiting for instructions' and, on the 15th of October, they told Admiral North that he 'would be relieved at the earliest opportunity'. In Admiral Somerville, however, the Admiralty still retained confidence, and he continued in command of Force H. The professional judgement of the First Sea Lord must, of course, be regarded as paramount on such a matter; but there is evidence that Ministers had lost confidence in the Admiralty's representative at Gibraltar after the attack on the French fleet in Oran in the previous July, and this may have affected the later decision to relieve him.[1] After he had returned to England Admiral North asked that he might be given 'an opportunity in due course to vindicate myself before whatever board or tribunal their Lordships may see fit to appoint'; but this and subsequent similar representations were consistently refused.

It is now time to turn to the progress of the main forces towards Dakar.[2] The *Barham* and four destroyers from the Home Fleet arrived from Scapa at Gibraltar on the 2nd of September and left four days later for Freetown. The greater part of Force H, namely the *Ark Royal, Resolution*, and six destroyers, accompanied them. It will be noted that this powerful force was far away to the south when the French squadron passed through the Straits, while Admiral Cunningham in the *Devonshire*, escorting the troop convoy, was still farther south. All these ships had met by the evening of the 13th, when the news that the French cruisers had left Casablanca for Dakar reached Admiral Cunningham. Shortly after midnight the Admiralty told him to employ all his available ships to patrol off Dakar to intercept the French cruisers. The convoy and its escort was therefore sent on to Freetown and, at 2.30 a.m. on the 14th, the Admiral turned north and set course for Dakar, then 400 miles away. Other ships comprising Force M, now reinforced by the cruisers *Cumberland* and *Cornwall* which had been diverted to Admiral

---

[1] See p. 244.
[2] See Map 26A (*p. 313*).

Cunningham by the Commander-in-Chief, South Atlantic, were hastening to join him in the execution of what had now become his primary object. By the evening of the 14th the patrol off Dakar had been established. But it was too late by a few hours. The same afternoon Vichy had broadcast the safe arrival of the cruisers at Dakar, and next morning this was confirmed from photographs taken by the *Ark Royal's* aircraft. The troop convoy reached Freetown that afternoon, the 14th of September, and by the following evening all Admiral Cunningham's forces were returning to the same base. The future of Operation 'Menace' now plainly had to be reconsidered in the light of the new circumstances which had arisen. On the 16th the Admiralty told Cunningham that the Government had decided that it was now impracticable. The Admiral and his military colleague were, however, of the opinion that, with the reinforcements now present from the South Atlantic command, they could deal with the French cruisers; and General de Gaulle was emphatic that the plan should not be cancelled. At about noon on the 18th they received authority to 'do what they thought best to give effect to the original purpose of the expedition' and it was therefore decided to carry out Operation 'Menace' on the 22nd.

Meanwhile, on the 19th, the French cruisers again appeared on the scene and were sighted by the *Australia* some 250 miles west of Freetown steering south-east. Chase was at once given by Admiral Cunningham's cruisers and destroyers, while the *Australia* and *Cumberland* shadowed the three Frenchmen who had now turned again to the north-west. One of them, the *Gloire*, broke down, was intercepted and finally agreed to go to Casablanca. The other two—the *Georges Leygues* and *Montcalm*—were followed by the *Cumberland* right up to Dakar but, although contact was established, attempts at parley failed and they could not be prevented from re-entering the port. Meanwhile another French cruiser, the *Primauguet*, which had been at Dakar before the beginning of these tangled events, was intercepted by the cruisers *Cornwall* and *Delhi* on the 18th and finally shepherded safely into Casablanca after five days of continuous shadowing and persuasive pressure. The Vichy French forces at Dakar thus lost the services of two cruisers but this, unfortunately, did not affect the outcome of Operation 'Menace'. The French squadron from Toulon had originally been destined for Libreville in Gaboon and it is certain that it carried no reinforcements for the Dakar garrison. None the less, it is reasonable to suppose that its safe arrival at Dakar stiffened the will of the local authorities to resist the British purpose with force.

It will be seen from the foregoing account that, quite apart from a failure of security in England which gave prior knowledge of our intentions, the Vichy Government and its representatives in the West African colonies must by now have known all about them.

What little chance of achieving any measure of surprise at Dakar may possibly have existed at the end of August, when the forces had sailed from England, had long since vanished as the result of all these contacts and negotiations between the warships involved. By the 20th of September all the forces were assembled at Freetown and the plan of attack was ready. They sailed from Freetown in three groups between the 19th and 21st and had an uneventful passage north. The intention was to arrive off Dakar at dawn on the 23rd; while the major warships and transports all lay off the port, the first contact would be established by Free French airmen landed for that purpose from the *Ark Royal*, and by General de Gaulle's emissaries to the Governor. Subsequent action would depend on how these envoys were received.

The inevitable handicaps under which our forces now laboured were increased by the mist which veiled the whole scene when the forces arrived off Dakar and which steadily worsened throughout the day. The poor visibility made aircraft reconnaissance and spotting for the ships' gunfire in any duel between ships and shore batteries more difficult, and enhanced the well-known handicap under which warships engage well-sited shore guns.

The attempt to win over the airfield at Dakar wholly failed and the sound of gunfire gave early warning to Admiral Cunningham that resistance was to be expected. The emissaries sent into the harbour were no more fortunate and had to make an early retirement under fire.

French naval forces now attempted to leave harbour. Two of the large destroyers were first forced to return, and, when two submarines were also reported by the *Ark Royal's* watchful aircraft to be leaving, Admiral Cunningham ordered these to be attacked and turned his main forces towards the harbour in support. The first shot of the surface action was fired by the French forts at our destroyers at 10.51 a.m. Ten minutes later the whole fleet was under fire from the shore batteries. Admiral Cunningham replied with a few salvoes directed at the forts but soon, in accordance with the policy to use no more force than was necessary, he ceased fire. Shortly afterwards the *Cumberland* was damaged by a heavy shell hit and had to withdraw. The destroyers *Foresight* and *Inglefield* had also been hit. At 11.54 a message was received from the Governor-General of French West Africa saying 'We confirm that we will oppose all landings'; but it was decided to postpone the use of further force until the attempt to make a peaceful landing some ten miles to the east of Dakar had been made in accordance with the operation plan. General de Gaulle agreed that this attempt should be made during the afternoon; but a baffling period of uncertainty now followed, chiefly because communications between Admiral Cunningham and

THE ULTIMATUM REJECTED

General de Gaulle had broken down, and the transports with the Free French troops could not be found in the now denser mist. By the late afternoon it was plain that the landing could not, after so many delays and misunderstandings, be carried out that day and Admiral Cunningham therefore cancelled it. But a minor landing was, none the less, attempted between 5 and 6 p.m. from the three Free French ships which formed part of the expedition. It was repulsed with a few casualties.

The day—a day only of failure and confusion—was now drawing to a close, with our forces in an unfavourable and dangerous state lying off a hostile coast in dense fog. After consulting with de Gaulle the agreed form of ultimatum was broadcast at 11.45 p.m. It told the Governor-General, the Admiral and the people of Dakar that the Allies must at all costs prevent the enemy becoming possessed of the base, and demanded acceptance of our terms by 6 a.m. Two hours before its expiry an unqualified refusal was received from the Governor and, at dawn on the 24th of September, Admiral Cunningham's heavy ships approached their bombarding stations off the coast, while the *Ark Royal's* aircraft took off to attack the *Richelieu* and other warships.[1] Though visibility was rather better than on the previous day, the projected long-range bombardment was still prevented by mist and the warships were therefore redisposed for action at closer ranges. While this was being done the destroyer *Fortune* attacked and sank the French submarine *Ajax* when about to attack our ships, on whom the shore batteries had opened fire. The *Barham*, *Resolution*, *Australia* and *Devonshire* replied by engaging the French warships in the harbour. The conditions for bombardment were made even more difficult by a smoke screen laid by a French destroyer to the east of the anchorage and the results achieved by the fleet's gunfire and air attacks were certainly not sufficient to cause the surrender of the port. By 10.10 all targets were totally obscured by smoke and the fleet withdrew to the south.

The bombardment was renewed by the *Barham* and *Resolution* in the afternoon, while the *Richelieu* and shore batteries replied once more. The *Resolution* suffered four hits, and the French again employed smoke to shield their ships. Again our gunfire achieved no important success and between 1.20 and 1.30 p.m. the duel petered out. The position was now discouraging. While neither the *Richelieu* nor the shore batteries had been put out of action our ships had been subjected to steady and accurate fire; nor had repeated attacks by the *Ark Royal's* aircraft accomplished greater success than the bombarding ships. At 2 p.m. Admiral Cunningham withdrew to the south to meet and consult with General de Gaulle. The conference that followed resulted in a decision to land British troops and to

---
[1] See Map 26B overleaf.

renew the bombardment next day with the object of finally compassing the destruction of the French warships.

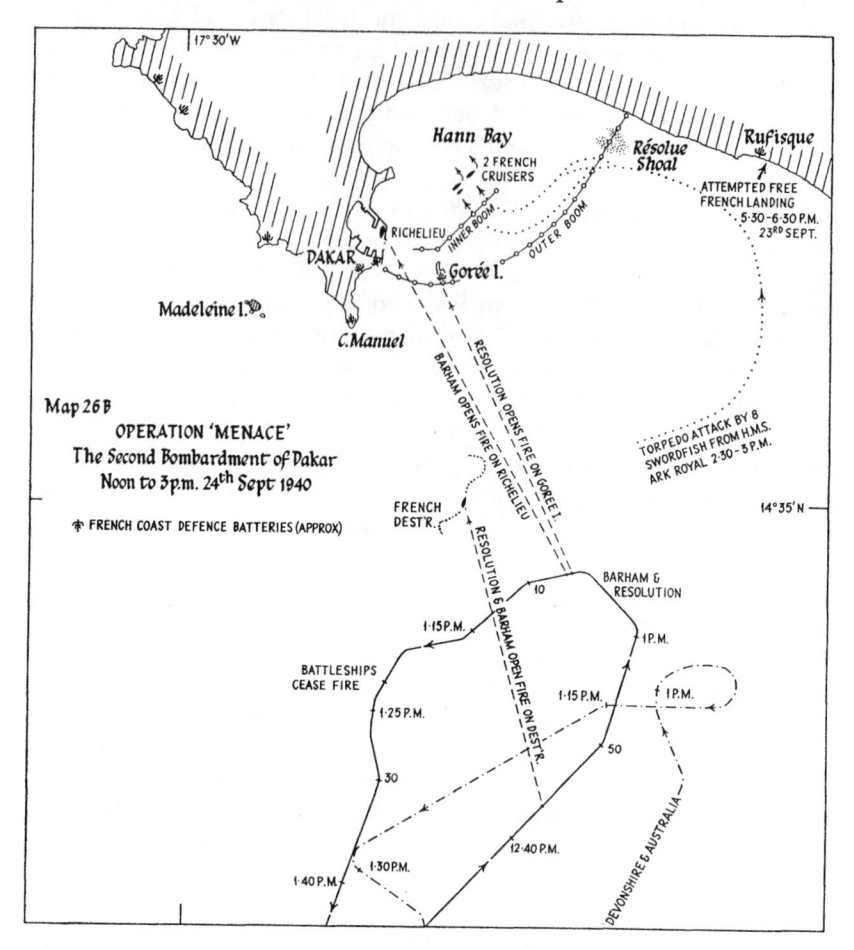

Map 26B
OPERATION 'MENACE'
The Second Bombardment of Dakar
Noon to 3 p.m. 24th Sept 1940

The 25th of September dawned fine and clear and the fleet again took up bombarding stations. Whilst doing so, just before 9 a.m., the *Resolution* was hit by one of several torpedoes fired by a French submarine and seriously damaged. The gunfire duel repeated the form taken the previous day; the fire of the *Richelieu* and of the shore batteries was again accurate, whilst our own had doubtful effect. It was plain that more damage would probably be incurred before the French ships were put out of action, and that the possibility of the surrender of Dakar was now remote. Moreover the ships of Admiral Cunningham's force were urgently required on other stations.

After considering all the factors involved and summarising the unhappy experiences of the last three days, the British Commanders decided, shortly before noon on the 25th, to withdraw all forces to Freetown. Their decision was quickly confirmed by the arrival of orders from the War Cabinet to the same effect early in the afternoon. On the 29th all ships, including the damaged *Resolution* and *Cumberland* were back in Freetown; so ended in total failure an amphibious expedition on which considerable hopes had been based. The importance of Dakar to our control of the Cape route was undeniable and the threat of its use by enemy warships and aircraft real. Yet no enemy surface raiders or submarines ever used it as a base of operations against our trade routes and, in the light of subsequent knowledge, the whole expedition might therefore be regarded as unnecessary. But the additional security to be derived from obtaining its use was well worth an effort to install General de Gaulle's forces there—provided that such a success could be achieved at reasonable cost. Where the plan came to grief was in the too sanguine estimates of the support available to the Free French cause in Senegal, and in the breaches of security which undoubtedly occurred before the military forces sailed from this country, thus causing the loss of all possibility of surprise. The inevitable difficulties of conducting a combined operation at a great distance from home bases were enhanced by the international character of the enterprise, with all the problems of personality and language which that involved; and the arrival of the squadron from Toulon perhaps further reduced the chances of success. The only consoling feature in an otherwise unhappy story was that the ability of the Navy safely to convey large expeditions overseas had again been demonstrated. Given adequate force, better security and planning and a fully integrated command system, success should fall to the side equipped with this capacity and able to exploit its use. The lessons learnt off Dakar in September 1940 were fully applied in later operations of a similar nature.

The failure of Operation 'Menace' did not mark the end of the service of Admiral J. H. D. Cunningham off the West African coast, and certain of the ships which had taken part in the attack on Dakar remained on the station for a time to take part in other moves in the French colonies. To understand these it is necessary to retrace our steps to the previous August when a *coup d'état* had established General de Gaulle's cause in the French Cameroons. The Chad Territory (inland in French Equatorial Africa) had also declared for the Free French, but as French Guinea, Gaboon, Dahomey, Togoland and Ivory Coast had, like Senegal, adhered to Vichy it will be realised that, in the French colonies which flanked the sea routes to the Cape, de Gaulle had so far found little support.[1]

On the 2nd and 3rd of October a joint British-Free French expedition, whose naval forces were commanded by Admiral

---
[1] See Map 23 (*facing p. 273*).

Cunningham in the *Devonshire*, left Freetown for Duala in the Cameroons, which the Free French intended to use as the base from which their cause would be extended in the West African colonies. De Gaulle's troops arrived there on the 7th. Disagreement between the British Government and the Free French leader soon arose once more. The General wished at once to attack Libreville and Port Gentil in Gaboon, but, as the British Government expected that a change of political tone in metropolitan France would take place shortly, they wished to avoid again antagonising the French and urged de Gaulle to hold his hand. The outcome was that, when de Gaulle insisted on proceeding with his intention, Admiral Cunningham was instructed to take no active part. In spite of this the Free French were, this time, successful and by the middle of November both their objects had been attained. Admiral Cunningham, whose flag had now been transferred to the *Neptune*, was then told to remain in the Cameroons to discourage any retaliatory expedition being sent from Dakar. It thus happened that, by the end of the year, the whole of French Equatorial Africa was under Free French control—a not insignificant accomplishment in view of the fact that the trans-African air route from Takoradi on the Gold Coast was now developing its great contribution to the reinforcement of our air power in the Middle East.

CHAPTER XVI

COASTAL WARFARE

1st June, 1940–31st March, 1941

"The true processe of English policie . . .
Is this, that who seeth South, North, East and West,
Cherish Merchandise, keepe the Admiraltie;
That we bee Masters of the narrowe see."

The Libel of English Policie, c. 1436
Attributed to Bishop Adam de Moleyns.

[Seeth = Saileth]

WE must now retrace our steps temporarily to the middle of 1940 and review the struggle for control of our coastal waters. It had continued unceasingly during the more distant events described in recent chapters, and constituted a heavy drain on our naval and air resources.

In the earlier chapters dealing with control of the coastal waters around these islands the war in the sea approaches has been considered concurrently. But after the fall of France the latter became merged with the campaign in the Atlantic, which, although closely linked to the coastal warfare, assumed a separate identity and is henceforth the subject of chapters devoted to the successive phases of the Battle of the Atlantic. On the other hand, just as the enemy's land victories of 1940 deprived us of the use of the coastal waters off the shores of the conquered territories of our Allies, so did they impose on the enemy the necessity to control those same waters for his own purposes. The need and the opportunity to prevent enemy shipping from using the coastal routes off the European seaboard were thus opened up to our sea and air forces. In consequence to carry the war into the waters off the shores of Norway, Denmark, the Low Countries and France—not to mention those of Italy and her overseas possessions—now gained a new importance and produced new possibilities for offensive action.

But during the period now reached, while our strategy perforce continued to be defensive, the struggle in the narrow seas was also defensive in the main. It centred upon the absolute necessity to maintain the flow of shipping up and down the east coast and, to a lesser extent, along the English Channel. Though the vulnerability of our ports on those coasts and of the traffic plying to and from them had long been recognised, and measures had been considered even before the outbreak of war for the diversion of as much of that traffic as possible to the west coast, the ports of the Clyde, Mersey and Bristol Channel were not only severely congested but were themselves exposed to heavy bombing raids from the enemy's newly-won bases in western Europe. Moreover the closure of the ports on the Channel coast to ocean-going traffic, and the diversion of all Atlantic shipping to the north of Ireland and of the east coast traffic round the north of Scotland, made it all the more important that the North Sea ports, and the Port of London in particular, should be kept working as near to full capacity as possible. This meant that the convoys had to be kept sailing regularly to and from Southend, and had to be strongly protected throughout the length of their hazardous journeys. Fully aware of the importance of this traffic the enemy now did his utmost to disrupt it by all the varied forms of attack at his disposal. For this purpose his light naval forces could use not only the French Channel ports but also the very favourably placed bases of Den Helder, the Hook and Ijmuiden in Holland;[1] his bomber and minelaying aircraft squadrons could also be moved so much closer to our coastal waters that the use of short-range dive-bombers against our east coast and Channel convoys became possible. In June the Grimsby fishing fleet was twice attacked; in July the bombing of shipping was intensified, and for the first time losses off the east coast to air attack exceeded those caused by mines. Nor were the merchant and fishing vessels the only targets for the bombers. Attacks on our minesweepers, on the convoy escorts and on the anti-invasion patrol vessels became very intense and widespread. The little ships sorely lacked effective light anti-aircraft guns; and it was difficult to arrange for their protection by the short-range aircraft of Fighter Command, because the whole Air Defence of Great Britain organisation was at this time concentrated on the defeat of the Luftwaffe's attempt to secure command of the air over southern England as a prelude to invasion of our shores. But strategic considerations were not alone in producing difficulties of this nature. The Admiralty held that ships must be allowed to open fire without hesitation on unidentified aircraft which approached them in an apparently hostile manner, because experience had proved that a heavy volume of prompt and well-directed fire from close-range weapons would often deter an attacking aircraft from his purpose and upset his aim, even if it did not frequently cause his destruction. But at this time the training of even regular naval crews, let alone of the reservists who manned most of the minesweepers and patrol vessels, in the visual recognition of aircraft was rudimentary. This led to many occasions when our own aircraft—even those sent specially

---

[1] See Maps 3 and 5 (*facing pp. 63 and 71*).

to protect a ship or convoy—were fired on by the men whom they were endeavouring to defend. The Navy constantly pressed for protection by short-range fighters but insisted that any unidentified aircraft which approached within 1,500 yards of a ship should be fired on; the Royal Air Force, not unnaturally, disliked what they regarded as irresponsible and dangerous action by the men of the sister service. For a time the difference of outlook produced serious difficulties, but the solution—that guns' crews should be more carefully trained in aircraft recognition and that aircraft should never avoidably make an apparently hostile approach to a ship—was plain at an early stage, and gradually protection by short-range fighters improved and errors in identification of aircraft decreased. But for a time severe shipping losses were suffered, and protection from the air was irregular and often ineffective. The naval view was that standing patrols should be flown over the convoys; but this would have been an extravagant use of our precious fighters. The Royal Air Force preferred therefore to extend 'cover' to the convoys from the various Sector Headquarters off whose area of responsibility a convoy might be passing, but not to send out the fighters until an attack developed. This, however, tended to result in the arrival of the fighters after the enemy bombers had done their worst and withdrawn.

In July the enemy's attacks on shipping were very widespread up and down the east coast and in the Channel, where through-convoys of coasting vessels (called C.W. and C.E. convoys) had now started to run between the Thames and the Bristol Channel. The passage was at this time hazardous in the extreme, for not only were the convoys fairly large, consisting generally of between twenty and thirty ships, but they were also very slow, and during most of their passage they were within easy range of the enemy's dive-bomber bases in France. But coal in particular could not be carried in adequate quantities to the south coast ports, which needed 40,000 tons a week, by any other means and the sailing of the convoys had therefore to continue. Few people in the south of England who at this time burnt a coal fire in their stoves can have realised the cost and sacrifice of carrying that coal to them. The hazards of the Channel route at this time can best be realised by describing the progress of one convoy. During the afternoon of the 25th of July convoy C.W.8, originally of twenty-one ships, was passing westwards through the Straits of Dover. A small escort of R.A.F. fighters was with it continuously, but the enemy had so filled the air with his own fighters that it was impossible for the ground control to tell which raids contained the dive-bombers. In consequence the air escort was never strong enough to defend the convoy, on which at least four separate dive-bombing attacks were made. On the 25th five merchant ships were sunk by bombs; later the two escorting destroyers and four more of the convoy were damaged. Enemy E-boats (motor torpedo-boats) next joined in the fray and on the 26th they sank three more ships. Only eleven of the convoy passed Dungeness. It was plain that the enemy had made a determined attempt to destroy the convoy, and that to defeat such a scale of attack ample fighter strength must be kept over the Straits for as long as the enemy bombers were about.

Losses such as those suffered by Convoy C.W. 8 were certainly serious and they caused the Admiralty temporarily to stop the Channel convoys while special measures were being devised. Yet, during this last week of July, which saw the heaviest attacks in the Channel, no less than 103 ships were convoyed through the Straits. The losses to air attack in the Channel between the 10th of July and the 7th of August were only 24,000 tons, which was considerably less than the losses suffered from mines during the same period. The chief danger of such intensive dive-bombing was, perhaps, to the morale of the crews of the coasting vessels. It was essential to keep these little ships sailing.

It was therefore decided that each convoy's passage should be made into a combined naval and air operation. From Fighter Command's point of view the chief difficulty was that the enemy held the initiative. He could assemble large numbers of bombers and fighters over the French coast and launch them at our convoys when he chose. The factor of surprise, the advantage of height and, generally, numerical superiority were thus all in the enemy's favour. Though we had learnt to our cost that to attack enemy bombers while so many of his fighters were about was highly dangerous, our pilots continued to tackle heavy odds unhesitatingly. To redress the balance of numbers the Air Ministry stressed to Fighter Command the need to use more powerful formations over the Straits. Though this did not always result in the convoys being well protected it did give our fighter pilots a better chance of taking on their enemies on something approaching level terms.

In addition to strengthening the fighter protection it was decided to provide the Channel convoys with balloons flown from small ships; they were quickly formed into a unit called the Mobile Balloon Barrage Flotilla. This extemporised and possibly unique force, among whose crews could be found men of at least a dozen different nationalities, sailed for the first time with Convoy C.W. 9 on the 4th of August. Later, kites were substituted for the balloons, which could too easily be destroyed by machine-gun fire.

To stiffen the anti-aircraft gun defences of the merchant ships a special organisation was created in July. Young seamen were formed into teams of light machine-gunners and trained in the gunnery school at Portsmouth. Two or three teams would be sent to each ship

THE SUCCESS OF THE NEW MEASURES

of a westbound convoy before it sailed from the Thames. At the end of that journey they would either make the next passage in an eastbound convoy, or, if none was sailing at once, they would return by train to Southend ready to take another west-bound convoy through. The discipline and high morale of these gunners, to whom the proud title of 'Channel Guard' was given, helped a great deal to keep the vital coastal traffic sailing at this difficult time.

To make it easier to defend these convoys their size was reduced from some twenty-five to about a dozen ships; and destroyers of the new *Hunt* class, which had better anti-aircraft armaments, replaced the older ships first employed as escorts. The surface and air escorts were also greatly strengthened, and it was soon a commonplace sight for Channel convoys to be preceded by minesweeping trawlers and closely escorted by perhaps two destroyers, three or four anti-submarine trawlers, half a dozen Motor Anti-Submarine Boats (M.A/S.B.s) or Motor Launches (M.L.s) and surrounded by six or eight balloon vessels. Overhead flew the Hurricanes and Spitfires of Fighter Command. The result of all these measures was that, although it was inevitable that some losses should be suffered on so dangerous a passage, they were never again serious. In particular the measures taken by Fighter Command curbed the savage onslaughts of the Junkers dive-bombers. British resolution in facing new perils and in improvising the means to overcome them thus defeated the enemy's attempt to close the English Channel to our coastal traffic.

On the 5th of August the Channel convoys were restarted with C.E. 8 which sailed from Falmouth and crept along the coast to the east, mostly by night. In daytime shelter was taken in various harbours. This convoy got through safely but the next westbound convoy (C.W. 9) was not so fortunate. It consisted of twenty-five ships and passed the Straits of Dover on the afternoon of the 7th of August. It was heavily attacked by E-boats that night, lost three ships and became badly disorganised. Next morning it was straggled out over a distance of about ten miles. Air attacks now began. But No. 145 Squadron of Hurricanes met the superior enemy far above the convoy's head, shot many of them down and, although the convoy was barely aware of what had happened, undoubtedly saved it from heavy losses. Not a ship was sunk by the bombers.

But the enemy used other weapons besides the bombers and the E-boats to dispute control of the Channel route. On the 12th of August he started to shell the convoys in the Straits of Dover from the long-range batteries which he had constructed near Cape Gris Nez.[1] This new trial was nerve-racking to the crews during a passage at, perhaps, only five or six knots. But it was remarkably ineffective

---

[1] See p. 256.

in causing casualties to the ships. It continued to be a regular feature in the passage of the Straits until early in 1943.

The failure of the air attacks on C.W. 9 marked the end of a phase, for the Luftwaffe next turned its chief attention to inland targets. Though the many and various hazards of the Channel route were to continue for a long time, it had been shown that, given adequate defences, we could keep the coastal traffic flowing. Before taking leave of the Channel convoys it is desirable to place these operations and the losses they caused us in fair perspective. The total loss inflicted by the Luftwaffe on our Channel convoys was only a tiny proportion of the four million tons of coastal shipping which entered or left our many harbours at this time. The seriousness of the enemy's effort lay in the fact that, at their peak, one ship in three in these convoys had been damaged or sunk. Such unattractive odds could, if continued, make it impossible to man the ships. Fighter Command certainly inflicted substantial losses on the enemy, but lost seventy-five of its aircraft in doing so. No clear-cut victory in the air was obtained, or claimed. What is certain is that, had not the fighters' effort been greatly increased during this period, our losses would have been far heavier and the convoys would probably have stopped sailing.

In August a new and potentially dangerous development was introduced by the enemy in his attacks on our east coast shipping. On the 23rd, aircraft of the German Navy's Air Arm attacked Convoy O.A. 203 in the Moray Firth with torpedoes, sank two ships and damaged a third. Fortunately, the number of torpedo-carrying aircraft then possessed by the enemy was so small—only about two dozen—that he could not persist with this type of attack. The starvation of the German Navy of aircraft was then, and later, chiefly caused by the jealousy of the Luftwaffe and its desire to retain all air operations in its own hands. In consequence this new threat was never fully developed but, at the time, it caused considerable anxiety.

Though minelaying still caused substantial losses and much inconvenience, the enemy's initial success with the magnetic mine had been overcome by the midsummer of 1940, and casualties from this cause had fallen appreciably. But new developments in the minelaying campaign were expected; the various possibilities were already exercising the minds of the Naval Staff and occupying some of the activities of the Admiralty technical and research establishments concerned with this type of warfare. In August and September unexplained explosions occurring near ships raised suspicions that a new type of mine was being used, detonated by the sound waves produced by the passage of a ship. On the 25th of August the Admiralty issued a warning to that effect. Suspicion changed to certainty in the following month when an acoustic mine was recovered and dissected, and the frequency of the sound waves to which it responded, discovered. The necessary counter-measure could now be developed with assurance. By November the first acoustic sweeps were in use, and on the 24th three mines were exploded by them in the Thames estuary. But the counter-measure was still far from perfected, and at this time the sweepers were very liable themselves to be damaged by the detonation of acoustic mines only a short distance ahead of them. But the acoustic mine was not the only new development in the unceasing war between mine and minesweeper, for the enemy had started to fit delay devices to his magnetic mines, and had also introduced an explosive sweep cutter, which could be laid in among his moored minefields. The former device made the repeated sweeping of every channel necessary before it could be declared clear of magnetic mines and the latter, by destroying our mine sweeps, delayed the clearance of the moored minefields.

The enemy continued to lay magnetic mines, with or without delay devices, and moored mines as well as the new acoustic mine; the strain on our minesweeping forces, and the difficulty of keeping the swept channels and river estuaries open, were thus greatly aggravated. It was fortunate, however, that the enemy repeated the mistakes made in the early days of the magnetic mine: he started to lay the new type before he had a large enough stock to achieve a really great success, and he allowed specimens to come into our hands by dropping them on land. Throughout the summer the minesweepers of the Nore Command toiled unceasingly to keep the Thames estuary and the swept channels off the east coast clear of mines and, in spite of repeated air attacks, gradually overtook arrears in clearing known moored and magnetic minefields. At the end of September the important Would Channel was reopened for the first time since the previous December; this enabled the convoys to be routed closer inshore, and so receive better air protection from short-range fighters.[1] In answer to the enemy's persistent bombing of the sweepers, the decision was taken in August to substitute night for day minesweeping. This, in the intricate waters of the Thames estuary, where most of the normal navigational marks had been removed or their lights extinguished, presented peculiar difficulties, since effective minesweeping depends greatly on navigational accuracy. The Commander-in-Chief, Nore, overcame the difficulty by using yachts and drifters as night navigation marks for the sweepers; later buoy lights were replaced, but shaded from overhead. The new technique was very successful and night minesweeping hereafter became a common practice which continued until the end of the war.

---

[1] See Map 13 (*facing p. 127*).

In spite of all that our minesweepers could do enemy aircraft and E-boats continued steadily to infest our coastal waters with mines of all types, and constant vigilance was necessary, especially in the Nore Command, to keep the channels open. The enemy's minelaying effort had now reached a high pitch of intensity and some eighty aircraft were employed on every suitable night. To give but one example of the scope of their activities, on the night of the 12th–13th of December at least fifty mines were dropped in the Thames estuary between Southend and the Isle of Sheppey. Sweeping was at once started and continued for four days without result. Then mines suddenly started to detonate all over the danger zone, seven ships were sunk in one day, and losses continued until the end of the month. The mines had been fitted with a four-and-a-half-day delay mechanism.

Though the enemy's main effort was directed to the east coast, other waters were by no means neglected. The E-boats frequently laid mines in the south coast swept channels as well and, in September, destroyers laid a big field, interspersed with explosive sweep-cutters, off Falmouth. In August and September we lost only twelve ships of some 20,000 tons on mines, but in the following months the new measures introduced by the enemy caused a big rise and October, November and December each saw the loss of twenty-four ships (133,641 tons in all) from this cause. During the whole of 1940 the enemy's minelaying campaign caused us the loss of 201 merchant ships totalling 509,889 tons, and more than half of that total (116 ships of 355,776) was lost within the Nore Command area—a convincing demonstration of the importance which the enemy attached to the disruption of our east coast traffic.

Losses declined to ten ships in January and February 1941, partly because the new acoustic sweeps were by now in wider use; but in March E-boats laid moored mines off the east coast again and aircraft dropped large numbers of magnetic and acoustic mines in the Mersey as well as in the Thames and Humber. In consequence losses rose to nineteen ships of 23,585 tons. At the end of the present phase it appeared that, even if the crisis produced by the first magnetic mines had been successfully overcome, and the defeat of its acoustic successor was well in hand, the limit of the enemy's ingenuity in mine design had not yet been reached.

Though the mines themselves could only be eliminated by the persistent efforts of the sweepers, there is no doubt that the increasing use of convoy was a big factor in reducing our losses from mines. It could not, by itself, prevent ships being mined; but the closer control which it produced made it easier to keep ships on safe courses or to divert them quickly from dangerous waters. Whereas for the first three months of the war, when our losses to mines had been very serious, only half our coastwise shipping sailed in convoy, the proportion had risen to ninety per cent. by April 1940. Of the eighty-nine ships sunk by mines in British coastal waters between the 1st of October 1940 and the end of March 1941 all but nineteen were sailing independently.

As regards our own minesweeping forces, at the beginning of this period it had been estimated that a total of 400 vessels fitted to deal with 'influence' type mines was required, and the Admiralty had taken strenuous steps to provide that number of ships. The number of trawlers to be equipped was increased to 124, and fourteen were bought from Portugal; thirty whale-catchers were requisitioned from the industry, more drifters were taken over and a new and simple design of 105-foot wooden minesweeper was produced to provide the balance. Between February and September 1940 the minesweeping force increased from 400 to 698 ships, of which more than half were fitted for 'influence' sweeping. But coastal minesweepers were not the only type needed; larger and faster ships were essential to work with the fleet and to accompany fast and important troop convoys into and out of port. Though the first of the fast minesweepers ordered on the outbreak of war were now ready for service, more were wanted and, as building capacity could not be found at home, the help of the Dominions was sought. By the end of the present phase fast minesweepers, minesweeping trawlers and motor minesweepers were being built on British account all over the world, while the Americans had begun work on wooden all-purpose minesweepers which were to prove invaluable later.

It will be remembered that at the time of Dunkirk E-boats were used as fast torpedo craft to lie in wait on the shipping routes, and that in July and August they several times attacked our Channel convoys.[1] The enemy was, however, slow to exploit the successes achieved by them and not until September did the E-boats start torpedo attacks on our east coast convoys in earnest. He now had between ten and fifteen such craft fit for operations, and this figure remained fairly constant throughout the current phase. They were difficult targets to deal with, for not only were they hard to sight while lying in wait on the convoy routes by night, but our escort vessels were too slow to catch and destroy them. Though the Nore Command used corvettes and trawlers to strengthen the convoy escorts, the lack of fast, powerfully armed motor gun-boats was felt acutely. Our Coastal Forces consisted at this time of a few motor torpedo-boats (M.T.B.s) designed for offensive use, of motor anti-submarine boats (M.A/S.B.s) for inshore work against U-boats and of motor launches (M.L.s) for local defence of ports and estuaries. Each of these lacked either the speed or the gunpower to deal with

---

[1] See pp. 222 and 324.

the E-boat; and a gun-boat with the speed of an M.T.B., a powerful but light armament and a radar set capable of detecting her adversary could not be developed overnight. In September several convoys were attacked and the destroyers and corvettes which bore the brunt of this new threat could not give effective protection. Attacks continued in October and November, but on the night of the 19th–20th of October the first success in destroying one of these elusive enemies was achieved by destroyers of the Nore Command. In March 1941 the first motor gun-boats (M.G.B.s), which were converted M.A/S.B.s and still possessed only a somewhat primitive armament, entered service and were sent to the east coast. The flotilla was soon to be commanded by Lieutenant-Commander R. P. Hichens, R.N.V.R., who, until he was killed in action in April 1943, made an outstanding contribution to the development of Coastal Force craft and to their tactical employment against the enemy. The boats were first used to patrol outside the mine barrier along the routes believed to be used by the enemy to and from his Dutch bases, and many fierce engagements took place near Brown Ridge and off the Hook of Holland or Ijmuiden.[1] Gradually, as the equipment and numbers of our boats improved and new tactics were developed, ascendancy was gained over the enemy. But at the time with which we are now concerned the E-boats were a source of constant anxiety and the losses which they caused—twenty-three ships of 47,985 tons in 1940—though much less than the mine or the bomber, were by no means negligible.

Important though the defence of our coastal traffic was, the Nore and Dover Commands did not at this time concentrate all their forces and attention on defensive precautions to the exclusion of the offensive. Our Coastal Force craft, though still few in numbers and generally ill-equipped, and the destroyers allocated to those two Commands made fairly frequent sweeps along the coast of the Low Countries and on the French side of the Channel to intercept enemy coastal shipping. But those routes were at this time sparsely used by mercantile traffic, and few targets were found. The actions fought by our light forces were generally against auxiliary war vessels employed on minesweeping and patrol duties; but the offensive sweeps at least showed the enemy that we did not intend to allow him to develop an unhindered flow of inshore traffic such as would ease his land transport problems and facilitate the supply of his forces in western France.

To turn now to the enemy's air offensive, the months of September, October and November 1940 saw widespread attacks on our mercantile docks and harbours all over the country; much damage was caused and many ships were destroyed alongside the quays to which they had been escorted through so many and diverse perils. But the

---

[1] See Maps 3 and 13 (*facing pp. 63 and 127*).

AIR ATTACKS ON SHIPPING CONTINUE

defence of shipping which has reached its destination forms no part of the story told in these volumes; and yet the losses suffered and the delays caused in the ports emphasised, if any emphasis were necessary, the need to bring the convoys home safely, to see them started safely on their outward journeys and to protect them wheresoever they might sail over the broad oceans of the world. The enemy did not, however, confine his attacks to the ports, and in November much bombing of shipping took place in the approaches to the Thames and along the east coast and Channel convoy routes. Eleven ships were sunk and seventeen more damaged during this month within forty miles of the coast—the range to which the protection of Fighter Command could at this time be extended. The shore-based fighters, however, soon caused heavy losses among the vulnerable Ju.87 dive-bombers, and after the middle of the month they were seldom used in such attacks. From December 1940 to February 1941 the protection of shipping was generally afforded by means of 'cover' from the fighter stations ashore, and few patrols were flown over the convoys. Priority for fighter protection was still at this time given to the aircraft industry. Fortunately these same months saw a lull in the attack on coastwise shipping from the air, and losses close off the coast fell sharply. The enemy was now using dive-bombers in small numbers instead of making the mass attacks which had caused the heavy losses of the previous autumn. But in late February and early March 1941 bombing increased once again and our losses rose correspondingly. Many ships were sunk in daylight, especially off the Naze, Orfordness and Ramsgate.[1] This period also saw a serious rise in losses in the Atlantic from causes which will be discussed in the next chapter, and on the 27th of February the Prime Minister gave 'absolute priority' to the defence of the north-west approaches. The defence of the Clyde, Mersey and Bristol Channel ports now became the chief responsibility of Fighter Command. This, however, was cold comfort to those responsible for the safety of the east coast convoys, losses among which close offshore rose steeply in March, when no less than twenty-one ships were sunk in daylight within forty miles of the coast and forty-four more damaged. In spite of the priority given to the north-west it was plain that fighter protection off the east coast had to be improved. But it was not until April 1941, which falls outside the phase with which we are now concerned, that the number of sorties flown by the shore-based fighters in defence of shipping off our coasts greatly increased. Sinkings by daylight then promptly dropped by half. The clear need was for radar-fitted escort vessels to call the fighters up and to direct them on to their

---

[1] See Map 13 (*facing p. 127*). The promontory called the Naze on the Essex coast should not be confused with that of the same name on the southern coast of Norway, also several times mentioned in these pages.

targets. But this had already been declared to be impracticable by Fighter Command. None the less trials in that direction had, by the end of 1940, been started by the Commander-in-Chief, Rosyth, and No. 14 Group of Fighter Command, though the ships were still only allowed to pass information to the aircraft and not, as was plainly essential, to 'control' them. Not until June 1941 was agreement on the principles involved in this long overdue co-ordination of the activities of the two services at last achieved. The enemy, however, did not confine himself to daylight attacks; in February he began to attack by night as well. As fighter protection by day improved, he concentrated increasingly on attacks in darkness, and these produced new problems for the escort vessels. The table below shows the trend of the enemy's air attacks on our coastal shipping at this time. It has been extended beyond the current phase to illustrate the effectiveness of Fighter Command's counter-measures when they came to be applied in earnest.

Table 9. German Air Attacks on Shipping and Losses within 40 miles of the coast or of an R.A.F. Airfield, November 1940–June 1941

	German Air Force sorties against shipping		No. of merchant ships sunk			No. of fishing vessels sunk	No. of naval craft sunk	British fighter sorties on trade defence	
	Day	Night	Day	Night	Not recorded which	Day and Night	Day and Night	Day	Night
Nov. 1940	1,280	530	7	4	Nil	Nil	4	402	Nil
Dec. 1940	1,010	355	Nil	1	Nil	1	Nil	504	Nil
Jan. 1941	950	330	2	Nil	Nil	1	Nil	350	Nil
Feb. 1941	985	595	2	1	2	3	5	443	Nil
Mar. 1941	1,610	615	12	8	2	9	3	2,103	Nil
April 1941	1,706	590	4	10	1	3	6	7,876	Nil
May 1941	1,223	570	1	9	Nil	4	7	8,287	Nil
June 1941	789	435	2	14	Nil	2	7	7,331	56

One corollary of the slowly improving fighter protection for coastal shipping was the need to set up a service for the rescue of pilots who, through enemy action or accident, might come down in the sea. Such an organisation had not been considered prior to the summer of 1940, but the losses of R.A.F. pilots at that time emphasised its importance and an improvised service, using small motor-boats and Lysander aircraft, was quickly introduced. But the equipment then available was unsuitable to the purpose, and the work of boats and aircraft quite unco-ordinated. In January 1941 a Directorate of Air-Sea Rescue was established in the Air Ministry with an R.A.F. officer as director and a naval officer as his deputy. But, as with so many other requirements which, owing to the changed nature of the war, had not been foreseen, the development of the service and the provision of good equipment were inevitably slow. It was not until 1942 that special Air-Sea Rescue squadrons were formed by the R.A.F. and boats suitable for work in the open sea could be provided.

The nine months period covered by this chapter was therefore one of acute difficulty for those responsible for defending our coastal shipping, and many new and unforeseen problems had to be dealt with, sometimes by hasty improvisations, as they arose. But the skill and fortitude of the minesweepers, the convoy escorts, the Coastal Force craft and the host of other small vessels working off our shores and of the fighter pilots overhead succeeded, none the less, in keeping the coastal shipping lanes open and in maintaining a steady flow of traffic along them. During the first six months of 1941 no less than $16\frac{1}{2}$ million tons of shipping passed up or down the main east coast channel between the Thames and Flamborough Head while another half million tons passed the North Foreland in Channel convoys. Losses to mines, E-boats and aircraft had certainly been appreciable, but with the extending use of convoy, improved minesweeping devices, the expansion of our Coastal Forces, more efficient anti-aircraft weapons for the little ships and, above all, better co-ordination of fighter protection there were good grounds for thinking that our control of these essential communications could and would be maintained.

It has been mentioned that the enemy found himself, after his land victories of 1940, in a position somewhat analogous to our own as regards the protection of coastwise traffic. The Germans could only supply their occupation forces, feed the civilian populations of conquered countries and bring home certain essential industrial raw materials by running convoys along the greater part of the long continental coastline now controlled by them. The traffic up and down the Norwegian coast, from the German North Sea ports to Holland, Belgium and northern France and along the Biscay coast thus came to offer valuable targets to our submarines, our minelayers, our Coastal Force craft and our bombers. They were all used to deny the enemy the free use of these waters.

The work of our submarines, which were under the control of the Commander-in-Chief, Home Fleet, off the Norwegian coast and in the North Sea during the latter half of 1940 has already been told.[1] It will be remembered that the great dangers attendant on their use in northern waters during the long summer days, and the losses suffered, had led to the inshore patrols off Norway being temporarily abandoned. Patrols in the Bay of Biscay and against U-boats passing from the North Sea into the Atlantic were then substituted. Though our submarines were still too few to achieve substantial results they

---
[1] See pp. 266–267.

certainly imposed on the enemy the need to devote considerable reserves to safeguarding the approaches to his newly-won bases. They made occasional attacks on important merchant ships but, by Admiralty decision, the primary objective of our submarines remained, and was to remain until late in 1943, the enemy's surface warships rather than his mercantile traffic.

Before the beginning of the new year the longer nights had enabled submarine patrols off Norway to be restarted, and the policy of employing our submarines in those waters and in the Bay of Biscay was continued until the end of the phase with which we are now concerned. The number of boats able to carry out these widely dispersed patrols was, however, small and their successes were, in consequence, few. The *Snapper* was lost, probably on a mine, while on a Biscay patrol in January and the *Sturgeon* sank an enemy tanker off Obrestadt in March. Towards the end of February our submarine strength for these offensive patrols was further reduced by the transfer of four boats of the T class with the depot ship *Forth* to Halifax. They were intended to provide additional protection to our Atlantic convoys against attacks by the enemy warships then at sea.

The strengthening of the extensive minefields from northern Scotland to the Faeröe Islands and Iceland by the four converted merchant vessels which comprised the 1st Minelaying Squadron was continued during the present phase.[1] It absorbed a large effort and a great number of mines and, although stocks were plentiful, was a less urgent matter than completion of the east coast barrier which, at the time of the fall of France, was still unfinished and formed, moreover, an important part of the Cabinet's plans to defeat the enemy's preparations for invasion. The latter duty was carried out by the 20th Destroyer Flotilla whose six minelaying destroyers worked under the Nore Command. Their activities were, however, by no means limited to the laying of defensive minefields, for at this time they were frequently employed to lay small minefields in enemy-controlled waters. It was while the 20th Flotilla was on one such mission on the last day of August that large enemy forces were reported by a reconnaissance aircraft off the Dutch coast steering west. It was considered that this force might be connected with the enemy's invasion plans and our destroyers were therefore ordered to intercept it. Actually the enemy ships comprised a small minelaying force on passage from Cuxhaven to Rotterdam. But the 20th Flotilla ran into an enemy minefield forty miles north-west of the Texel—the northern flank of the mined corridor laid to defend his invasion fleet. The *Esk* and *Ivanhoe* were sunk, the *Express* seriously damaged and the flotilla's commander fatally injured. The surviving ships continued to serve as minelayers

---

[1] See pp. 263–264.

for a short time, but the shortage of destroyers in the fleet for escort was so acute that they reverted to those duties in April 1941.

Our offensive minelaying thereafter devolved chiefly on our submarines and on the aircraft of Bomber and Coastal Command which had already shown their ability to sow mines in waters to which no surface ship could possibly penetrate; their operations, though still on a very small scale, were believed to be producing good results. From July to October 1940 our air minelaying was, in accordance with the Cabinet's directions, devoted chiefly to impeding the enemy's invasion plans. New laying areas were therefore established off the Dutch, Belgian and north-east French coasts and these were mined by naval aircraft working under Coastal Command early in July. In August, because of the increasing use made of the French Biscayan bases by enemy U-boats, mines were laid off Brest, St Nazaire, Lorient and La Rochelle. This policy was continued until the end of the year firstly by Bomber Command, and in December by naval Swordfish as well. Meanwhile the longer-range aircraft of Bomber Command, though still very few in numbers, were reaching out to the enemy's more distant bases—principally Kiel Bay and the Elbe estuary. At first only one squadron of Hampdens was so employed, but on the 4th of July two more squadrons were allocated to minelaying. The emphasis was, however, restored to bombing Germany for the last four months of the year, and the number of mines laid fell correspondingly.

But our own experiences with the enemy's magnetic mines had shown that air minelaying could help substantially in disputing the use of coastal and short-sea communications. By August, therefore, production of such mines—for which the Admiralty held responsibility—had been stepped up and was still increasing, and the training of aircraft crews in this specialised duty was improving.

At this time discussions took place between the Royal Air Force Commands concerned, the Admiralty and the Air Ministry regarding responsibility for producing and distributing the mines, and for controlling the aircraft ordered to lay them. With one Service Department (the Admiralty) acting as producer and distributor of mines and deciding the broad policy as to where they should be laid, and one command of the Royal Air Force (Coastal Command) exercising operational control of all aircraft employed on minelaying, while a different Command (Bomber) actually supplied the majority of aircraft and crews, there was plenty of room for confusion and misunderstanding. The growing complexity of the air minelaying campaign, with several different types of mine being used in different waters, indicated the need to reconsider responsibilities in the whole field of aerial mine warfare. After considerable inter-service discussion, however, it was decided that no fundamental changes could be made at this time.

In November the Admiralty reviewed the whole campaign, divided the minelaying areas into three different categories of importance and asked the Air Ministry to provide enough aircraft to lay mines once a week in, at any rate, the most important waters. Plenty of mines were now in store; the difficulty was to find the aircraft to lay them. Five squadrons employed solely on minelaying were needed. But the requirement could not, at this time, be met, partly because of the increasing need to allocate long-range aircraft to escort and anti-submarine duties in the north-west approaches. In consequence, for the last three months of 1940 the number of minelaying sorties and the total of mines laid fell to a small figure.

It was, of course, difficult to divide our still inadequate resources in the most effective manner. Bombing was then the only means of carrying the war into Germany and the Air Ministry certainly did not wish to see its small bombing effort further reduced. Moreover quite a large share of the bombing effort was devoted to maritime targets, and it was believed that good results were being obtained thereby. Only now, with all the enemy's naval records in our possession, are we able to see that, apart from its rôle in the struggle in the north-west approaches, it was by minelaying rather than by bombing naval targets on shore or in harbour that the Royal Air Force could at this time have contributed most to the maritime war. However an increase in minelaying was promised at the end of the year by the decision to allocate the first squadrons of Stirlings and Manchesters to this duty, because they were not yet fully equipped for bombing.

The table below summarises the results achieved by the air minelaying campaign during the nine-month period with which we are now concerned.

Table 10. The R.A.F.'s Air Minelaying Campaign, June 1940–March 1941

	Number of R.A.F. minelaying sorties	Aircraft losses on minelaying operations	Number of mines laid	Enemy ships sunk by air-laid mines	Enemy ships damaged by air-laid mines
June 1940	199	5	158	8— 3,292 tons	Nil
July 1940	273	4	245	13—12,962 tons	1— 50 tons
August 1940	229	2	188	11— 8,325 tons	3— 1,590 tons
Sept. 1940	109	3	80	16—14,448 tons (plus 7 barges)	1— 5,971 tons
Oct. 1940	138	3	106	4— 2,269 tons	1—1,668 tons
Nov. 1940	64	Nil	50	4— 710 tons	1— 1,432 tons
Dec. 1940	110	4	87	6— 7,342 tons	1— 2,245 tons
Jan. 1941	83	2	65	9—14,724 tons	1— 42 tons
Feb. 1941	109	4	91	4— 1,632 tons	Nil
March 1941	101	2	79	Nil	2— 2,327 tons
TOTAL	1,415	29	1,149	75—65,704 tons	11—13,325 tons

'Air Attack on a Channel Convoy off Beachy Head.' By Sir Norman Wilkinson.
(*National Maritime Museum*)

'Falmouth Harbour 1940.' By John Platt.

(*National Maritime Museum*)

The great majority of the enemy's losses was caused by mines laid by Bomber Command aircraft in the western Baltic and the waters off Denmark and southern Norway. In spite of the small strength devoted to air minelaying during the present phase, it thus played a substantial part in denying the enemy the free use of the coastal waters adjacent to the territories controlled by him. Though we did not, of course, possess this knowledge at the time, we had acquired much experience of the losses and disorganisation caused to ourselves by the enemy's air minelaying, and this alone might have led to an increased effort of the same type being made against the enemy. Such, however, was not the case, and in the early days of 1941 Bomber Command, which alone possessed suitable aircraft in sufficient numbers, actually excluded minelaying entirely from the tasks laid upon its Group Commanders. This decision was soon modified to allow a few aircraft to be so employed, if not available for bombing. But the result was that for the succeeding months the minelaying effort remained, as can be seen from the table above, very small and devolved chiefly on Coastal Command, whose aircraft could not reach the waters where minelaying would be most effective. Though the Commander-in-Chief, Coastal Command, continued to press either for a long-range squadron to be allocated to himself for minelaying, or for Bomber Command to reconsider the orders restricting the use of its own aircraft for that purpose, neither proposal was accepted. Thus for the last three months of this period air minelaying was confined to the approaches to north German, Low Country and French ports, and even there few aircraft were employed. The more distant, and more fruitful, waters were left alone.

It has already been told how, shortly before the start of the present phase, air attacks on enemy merchant ships in certain zones had at last been permitted by the British Government.[1] Early in June 1940 the restrictions on bombing merchant ships were further relaxed by allowing attacks on 'naval auxiliaries of whatever description . . .; on troop transports or military supply ships whether at sea or in port'; and, furthermore, in certain special areas all shipping was henceforth to be treated as naval auxiliaries. Thus, at last, the Royal Air Force was given reasonable freedom to extend the bombing offensive into the enemy's coastal waters. But the long maintenance of the restrictions inevitably meant that training in this new and specialised form of warfare had not been carried out, since to train crews in a function which they might never be allowed to perform would have been extremely wasteful. This, and the lack of adequate striking power in Coastal Command, made it impossible quickly to exploit the newly-gained freedom. But the attacks now launched against the enemy's coastal traffic, if they caused him few losses and

---

[1] See pp. 144–145.

Y

little damage, did have the effect of forcing him to increase his escort forces. In mid-July another relaxation of the restrictions on air action against shipping was introduced by the announcement of 'sink at sight' zones in the North Sea and off the Scandinavian coast; on the 20th September similar freedom was given in the Channel and Bay of Biscay. It is to be remarked that these zones were publicly announced by the British Government in exactly the same way as was done for minefields in accordance with international law. It was not until mid-March 1941—almost at the end of the period with which we are now concerned—that permission was given to attack enemy or enemy-controlled merchant shipping at any time, whether at anchor or under way, at sea or in port. It will therefore be seen how very slow and cautious was the British Government's approach to the acceptance of air warfare against enemy shipping.

Responsibility for the new offensive was divided between the three Coastal Command Groups concerned in the maritime war—No. 18 Group for the northern North Sea, No. 16 Group for the southern North Sea and English Channel and No. 15 Group for the Bay of Biscay. The commercial traffic in the areas for which Nos. 16 and 18 Groups were responsible was much the greatest, and emphasis was at once placed on the iron ore traffic from Narvik to the south, and the industrial traffic between north German and Dutch ports. Unhappily Coastal Command still lacked a torpedo striking force. The first Beaufort squadron had been diverted to minelaying, because Coastal Command possessed no other aircraft which could carry a mine, and technical and training difficulties delayed the active use of the second squadron. In these straits the Command had largely to rely on the three naval air squadrons lent by the Admiralty. These, at the end of June 1940, comprised one squadron of Swordfish torpedo-bombers, one of Skuas and one of Albacore dive-bombers. To them were added periodically certain of Coastal Command's Hudson, Blenheim and Anson squadrons; but the latter were often required to carry out other of the Command's manifold duties and were by no means constantly available for attacks on shipping. In the summer two Blenheim squadrons (Nos. 53 and 59) were lent from Bomber Command; but they were normally used on anti-invasion tasks. In September two Beaufort squadrons (Nos. 22 and 42) became operational, and Coastal Command was at last possessed of a small but modern torpedo-bomber striking force able to reach to the Norwegian coast. Though anti-shipping sorties in the North Sea now became frequent, the results achieved were, for reasons to be discussed shortly, not substantial.

On the 6th of February 1941 Hitler ordered that all German striking power should be directed against our overseas supply system, and with the failure to break the defensive power of the R.A.F.

German strategy entered a new phase. The heavy U-boat attacks in the north-west approaches and intensified bombing on the east coast which followed were the immediate causes of the issue of the Prime Minister's Battle of the Atlantic directive on the 6th of March, and led to the transfer of Coastal Command squadrons to the north-west. Though Bomber Command lent some more Blenheim squadrons to take over the North Sea anti-invasion patrols, it was inevitable that attacks on enemy coastal shipping should decline. In fact the results achieved by such attacks as were made continued slight, and lack of aircraft was not the only cause of this. As early as the middle of 1940 the Commander-in-Chief, Coastal Command, had realised that better results would not be produced until a leaf was taken out of the enemy's book, and our aircraft attacked from low heights, as did his Focke-Wulfs and dive-bombers. That heavier aircraft losses would thereby be incurred was accepted. The development of very low attacks, which were to produce important results later, can thus be dated to the present phase. The complete results now known to have been achieved by aircraft attacks on enemy shipping at sea throughout the present phase can best be given in tabular form.

Table 11. The Air Offensive against Enemy Shipping, April 1940–March 1941

I. *Attacks at Sea by R.A.F. Aircraft*

Month	Aircraft sorties against shipping	Number of ships sunk and tonnage	Number of ships damaged and tonnage	Aircraft losses
April 1940	616	3— 7,970	1— 1,939	21
May 1940	809	1— 750	Nil	18
June 1940	774	Nil	1— 1,293	14
July 1940	791	1— 29	2— 6,704	14
August 1940	393	Nil	Nil	7
Sept. 1940	623	1— 1,626	6—19,550	10
Oct. 1940	419	1— 763	2— 5,550	18
Nov. 1940	336	1— 1,234	1— 5,898	7
Dec. 1940	279	1— 1,159	1— 6,728	12
Jan. 1941	250	1— 1,326	Nil	7
Feb. 1941	269	Nil	Nil	13
March 1941	615	2— 8,581	2— 1,680	17
TOTAL	6,174	12—23,438	16—49,342	158

(*Continued overleaf*)

(*Table 11, continued*)

II. Attacks by Naval Aircraft

(The number of sorties made and the aircraft losses suffered are not known)

Month	Number of ships sunk and tonnage	Number of ships damaged and tonnage	Remarks
April 1940	2—13,569 (A)	1—1,999	(A) Includes the German cruiser *Königsberg* (6,000 tons)
May 1940	5— 1,091	Nil	
June 1940	1— 281	Nil	
July 1940	Nil	1— 255	
August 1940	Nil	Nil	
Sept. 1940	Nil	Nil	
Oct. 1940	Nil	Nil	
Nov. 1940	Nil	Nil	
Dec. 1940	Nil	1—1,501	
Jan. 1941	Nil	Nil	
Feb. 1941	Nil	Nil	
March 1941	Nil	1—1,376	
TOTAL	8—14,941	4—5,131	

It thus happened that, although the opportunity for offensive blows by all arms against the enemy's coastal traffic was fully realised, the serious losses in the North Atlantic and the many other calls on our maritime forces prevented a regular and heavy effort being applied to that object at the present time.

Although our strength was still too small to enable the new opportunities to be fully exploited, there remained one method of harassing the enemy forces in those theatres, of extending his garrisons and enhancing the anxieties which the attempt to command a great length of coastal waters without the necessary maritime strength must inevitably produce. In many of our previous wars with continental nations we had used our sea power to land small bodies of determined men on the enemy's coasts to accomplish limited objects, such as the destruction of small but important harbour works. Though the successes thereby achieved could not generally be claimed to be of first importance, the mere threat of such raids had the effect of locking up large enemy forces and disproportionate quantities of war material in purely defensive rôles. It prevented the enemy concentrating his land forces for profitable offensive operations; it interfered with their training; and the need to keep large numbers of men idle in garrison duties generally caused a lowering of morale. It was, therefore, to be expected that the British Cabinet and Chiefs of Staff would seize the opportunity to revert to this traditional use of maritime power. Accordingly orders were given to press ahead with forming and training special bodies of men, converting suitable ships and boats and making the necessary plans.

When the preparations were far enough advanced it was decided to carry out, early in March 1941, a raid in strength against the Lofoten Islands on the north side of the approaches to Vestfiord, with the object of destroying the Norwegian fish oil factories from which the enemy was known to be deriving substantial benefit.[1] The Norwegian Government in exile and the heads of the Norwegian Service missions in London helped in choosing the best objectives, in preparing the plans for the operation (whose code name was 'Claymore') and in providing detailed geographical and local intelligence. On the 22nd of February two cross-Channel steamers which had been converted to carry landing craft arrived at Scapa. They had on board some 500 men of Nos. 3 and 4 Commandos, fifty Royal Engineers especially trained in demolition work and a like number of Norwegian troops. The land forces were commanded by Brigadier J. C. Haydon and a naval raiding force, comprising five destroyers under Captain C. Caslon in the *Somali*, was organised to escort and support the troops. These forces sailed northwards very early on the 1st of March, fuelled in the Faeröes and thence steamed for the entrance to Vestfiord, where a submarine had been stationed as a navigation beacon. Admiral Tovey himself sailed a day later with the main body of the Home Fleet to provide cover from a position some 200 miles to seaward of the Lofoten Islands, and from that position he detached the cruisers *Edinburgh* and *Nigeria* to give close support to the raiding force. In the very small hours of the 4th of March, and in ideal weather conditions, the raiders passed the entrance to the fiord and then divided into two groups to attack the two principal objectives. By 5 a.m. the first landings had taken place. Surprise was complete, and there was virtually no opposition until after the Commandos were ashore. All the objectives on shore were found and destroyed, while the naval forces dealt easily with the enemy-controlled shipping present, the most important of which was the fish factory ship *Hamburg* of 9,780 tons. She and numerous smaller cargo vessels were sunk, while the landing parties were met with great local enthusiasm and captured over 200 German prisoners. By 1 p.m. all the landing craft had been hoisted, the light naval forces had concentrated again and met their supporting cruisers, and they all steamed down Vestfiord again to reach their home bases safely on the 6th of March, bringing with them not only their prisoners but over 300 Norwegian volunteers for service against the common enemy.

The raid was a complete success. The command organisation had proved sound and inter-service co-operation had been excellent. But, above all, this minor operation was important because it showed our capacity once again to exploit one of the greatest of the benefits conferred by maritime power—the capacity suddenly to land bodies

---
[1] See Map 18 (*p. 181*).

of troops on an enemy-held coast. Though the great amphibious landings of the later years of the war, in which this ability developed to its full stature, still lay in the comparatively remote future, the Lofoten raid showed how far we had progressed from the ill-planned and inadequately equipped attempts at amphibious operations made during the spring and summer months of 1940. Henceforth no enemy coastal garrison could feel secure from surprise, and no enemy coastwise shipping sail in certainty that our light forces and our maritime aircraft might not suddenly descend upon them in overwhelming strength.

CHAPTER XVII

THE CAMPAIGN IN THE NORTH-WEST APPROACHES

1st June, 1940–31st March, 1941

> The fast vessels needed for escort against submarine attack cannot be improvised.
> Lord Jellicoe. *The Submarine Peril*, 1934.

THE last three chapters have told the story of the defence of these islands against invasion, the defence of our ocean communications and the defence of the offshore sea routes up to the end of 1940. But the campaign in the Atlantic has not so far been considered separately from the continuous campaign to control all the sea approaches to these islands and the coastal waters around them, for the reason that it did not begin to assume a separate identity until the fall of France had opened our Atlantic convoy routes to greatly increased attacks by U-boats, surface raiders and aircraft. It then quickly surpassed in importance the enemy's attacks on our coastal shipping, and soon became merged into the greater struggle shortly to be called the Battle of the Atlantic. It is to the opening phases of that campaign that we must now turn.

At the end of May 1940 we were able to give our Atlantic convoys anti-submarine escort only as far as longitude 12–15° West—that is to say some 200 miles to the west of Ireland.[1] In July the dispersal point for outward-bound convoys was moved to 17° West and there it remained until October when it was found possible to extend close escort as far as 19° West. After the escort vessels had left their convoys the outward-bound merchant ships continued to steam in company for about another twenty-four hours, after which they dispersed to their various destinations. The escorts meanwhile moved to a new rendezvous to meet and bring in the next homeward convoy. The Halifax (H.X.) convoys were, at this time, running on a four-day cycle and a Bermuda–Halifax section was sailed one day before the H.X. convoy which it was to join. Canadian destroyers attached to the Halifax Escort Force provided local escort to the H.X. convoys for the first three or four hundred miles of the long eastward journey.

---

[1] See Map 9 (*facing p. 93*).

After their departure the ocean escort—generally an armed merchant cruiser—alone remained with the convoy until it reached the distant rendezvous with the waiting escort vessels from the Western Approaches.

Up to the middle of the year ships bound for Gibraltar and West Africa sailed as part of the normal outward-bound Atlantic (O.A. and O.B.) convoys, but in July a regular cycle of convoys direct to Gibraltar (O.G. convoys) was started.[1] They sailed from the Clyde or Mersey through the North Channel, and were accompanied for the first lap of the voyage by local anti-submarine escorts and thereafter by one or two sloops. The North Atlantic Command sent destroyers from Gibraltar to meet and bring in the section bound for that base, while the Sierra Leone section dispersed and proceeded independently to Freetown, to fuel and receive instructions for the next part of the ships' journeys. Meanwhile the sloops which had escorted out an O.G. convoy met the next Gibraltar-home (H.G.) convoy, taking over responsibility from the locally-based destroyers. The homeward convoys from Sierra Leone (S.L.) were escorted by an armed merchant cruiser from the time they left Freetown until they were met by destroyers of the Western Approaches Command; but when the U-boats began to appear off the West African coast anti-submarine vessels were sent to the South Atlantic Command to provide local escorts.

In August steps were taken to relieve the growing congestion in the port of Halifax, and at the same time to increase the flow of imports during the good weather of the summer months, by instituting a separate cycle of slow Atlantic convoys from Sydney, Cape Breton Island.[2] Ocean escorts were, at first, provided by long-endurance sloops withdrawn from the West Indies and Western Approaches Commands. The first of these slow convoys (S.C.1) sailed on the 15th of August escorted by the sloop *Penzance*. Nine days later she was sunk by a U-boat. The *Dundee*, while escorting S.C. 3, was also sunk, and these losses were evil portents of the long-drawn days and nights of ceaseless attack and counter-attack which were to mark the agonisingly slow eastward progress of the S.C. convoys. Though originally intended only to run during the summer they were, in fact, continued into the winter, even though an ocean escort could not always be provided, and the fierce North Atlantic gales sometimes scattered the labouring merchantmen far and wide on the waters.

The protracted nature of the Atlantic struggle, and the complexity of the escort problem so long as the endurance of all our escort vessels, except the sloops, was insufficient to enable them to

---

[1] See Map 9 (*facing p. 93*).
[2] See Map 9.

NEED FOR ADVANCED BASES IN ICELAND

accompany a convoy throughout its journey, are best illustrated by quoting the average time the principal convoys spent at sea. The figures, which cover the whole war and make allowance for diversions ordered while on passage, are as follows:

Convoy	Planned speed	Time on passage
H.X.	9–10 knots	15·2 days (from New York)
S.C.	7½–8 knots	15·4 days (from Sydney)
S.L.	7½ knots	19 days (from Freetown)

Outward-bound convoys, moreover, commonly made slower passages than those homeward bound, and winter passages were almost always slower than those made during the summer. If a convoy was delayed by diversions or by bad weather, the escort vessels waiting at the ocean rendezvous might run short of fuel and have to return. If a convoy got badly off its course or the weather was exceptionally tempestuous or foggy, difficulty might be experienced in bringing the convoy and the waiting escorts together at all.

The further extension westward of close escort for the Atlantic convoys depended mainly on the rapidity with which the naval and air bases in Iceland could be completed. The anxiety of the War Cabinet regarding the security both of that island and of the Danish Faeröes has already been mentioned.[1] The threat which the enemy could bring to bear on our Atlantic shipping routes should those outposts fall into his possession was, indeed, plain from the time when the success of his Norwegian venture was assured, and the Cabinet had acted promptly. On the 8th of May Royal Marine advance parties left Greenock in the cruisers *Berwick* and *Glasgow* for Iceland and arrived at Reykjavik two days later. The squadron searched the eastern fiords for signs of enemy activity and then returned to its base with all German nationals from Iceland on board. A week later two large transports carried an infantry brigade to Iceland, and on the 23rd of May the transport *Ulster Prince* brought an army detachment to Thorshavn in the Faeröes, where also the marines had first taken possession. In the middle of June the first of several reinforcements of Canadian troops were carried direct from Halifax to Iceland, and small garrisons were established in various fiords which the enemy might attempt to use. Early in July reinforcements of Canadian troops from Halifax and of British troops from the Clyde were taken to Reykjavik, and measures to defend possible landing-places against German assault were put in hand. An anti-submarine boom was started at Hvalfiord, a short distance to the north of Reykjavik, where the principal naval base was to be established.[2]

---

[1] See p. 197.
[2] See Map 4 (*facing p. 65*).

But the creation from nothing of all the necessary shore installations was bound to be slow. Parallel but subsidiary measures to those in hand in Iceland were begun at Thorshavn and at Stornoway in the Hebrides, where it was desired to develop air bases to improve the protection of the large amount of shipping now passing round the north of Scotland.

The need to defend the Atlantic convoys against U-boat attack much further to the west had been apparent even before the dramatic events of the summer months had altered the whole shape of the war. But the enemy's occupation of Norway and of the French Biscayan coast increased the urgency of such measures, because the passage of U-boats from the French bases to our shipping routes was some 450 miles shorter than from their home ports in Germany, and this gave them correspondingly greater reach out into the Atlantic ocean. Furthermore the small 250-ton coastal U-boats could now be used on the ocean routes and all types would, at any rate for some time, enjoy an easier and safer passage to their operational areas than through the more closely-watched northern exits from the North Sea.

An increase in the number of U-boats which the enemy was able to keep at sea was therefore to be expected. In fact we now know that, whereas in the previous phase some fourteen out of an operational total of thirty-three could be kept at sea simultaneously, he was now able to increase the number to about sixteen out of a smaller total strength. Thus, although the size of the effective U-boat fleet was still falling—the lowest total of the war (twenty-one) was actually reached in February 1941—this advantage to us was more than offset by the effects of the enemy's gains on land in 1940. In July, which saw the diversion of our shipping to the north-west approaches, the first Atlantic U-boat base was brought into service at Lorient. The Admiralty now assessed the total of completed U-boats at seventy-one and believed that twenty-four had been destroyed since the start of the war. Actually twenty-five had been destroyed and fifty-one boats (four more than the Admiralty estimate) remained to the enemy. Though the Prime Minister and his advisers considered the Admiralty estimate of successes far too conservative and asked for an independent enquiry into the matter, post-war information confirms its accuracy.

It has been told how our flotilla and escort strength had been seriously depleted by the losses incurred in the narrow seas during the preceding months, and how the precautions taken against invasion had further reduced the numbers available for escort duty. During June and July 1940 even comparatively large convoys could generally be given only one surface anti-submarine escort. Nor were air escorts and patrols more plentiful, for Coastal Command also had been ordered to give first priority to scouting the North Sea for the enemy's expected invasion fleet and now, moreover, had to undertake many other duties which had not been foreseen when the war plans were framed. Though the Air Officer Commanding-in-Chief constantly pressed the Air Ministry to increase his strength, priority for new long-range aircraft was still being given to Bomber Command for the air offensive against Germany, and little could be spared for the maritime war. Thus when, early in June, the Admiralty requested that reconnaissance aircraft should be based on Iceland—plainly one of the most important steps towards improving the protection of the Atlantic routes—the request had to be refused. There were at this time only a few Battles and some naval Walrus amphibians based there, and neither type was suitable for work with the Atlantic convoys, or intended for that purpose. Not until early in 1941 was approval given to the Air Ministry's proposal to form an Iceland Air Force composed of a flying-boat squadron, a Hudson squadron and one of long-range fighters, controlled by an Area Combined Headquarters at Reykjavik. These squadrons ultimately became part of No. 15 Group of Coastal Command but, as effective operations did not start until April 1941, this very desirable development had no influence on the campaign in the Atlantic during the present phase.

The inadequacy of Coastal Command's strength in the summer of 1940 was, in fact, a source of constant anxiety to its Commander-in-Chief and to the Admiralty, but as the matter did not come to a head until the autumn, by which time the serious trend of our shipping losses was all too plain, we will consider the measures taken to strengthen the command's resources later.

In August Italian U-boats started to work in the Atlantic, firstly in the waters between the Azores and Spain and subsequently against our shipping in the North Channel. By the end of November no less than twenty-six of them had joined their German allies in the Atlantic; but this great increase in the enemy's operational strength was nullified by the incapacity of the Italian crews. They accomplished virtually nothing and early in December Dönitz sarcastically remarked that he would in future 'dispose of the German U-boats . . . without considering the Italians'. By May 1941 their strength in the Atlantic was reduced to ten.

It was fortunate that at this time the Prime Minister's persistent efforts to gain to our use a number of the old and surplus destroyers then held in reserve by the United States Navy at last achieved success, through the arrangement whereby the lease of naval and air bases in Newfoundland and Bermuda was granted as a gift, while similar bases in British Guiana and five of our West Indian colonies were leased in exchange for fifty of the destroyers. Mr Churchill has himself given a full account of the negotiations which led to this agreement.[1] For the purposes of our story it is only necessary to remark that the agreement reduced our responsibility for the defence of our possessions and shipping in the western Atlantic and Caribbean. But Britain was not the only country to benefit. The United States was now able to begin preparing the naval and air bases which were essential to the protection of its own eastern seaboard and coastal shipping.

Our need for more escort vessels was so acute that any type of ship with a turn of speed, with even rudimentary anti-submarine equipment and obsolete guns, was most welcome. The American destroyers all belonged to the era of the 1914–18 war; they had not been properly modernised and only essential maintenance work had been done to them; none was asdic-fitted, and their guns and torpedoes were by no means fully efficient. Refits, conversion to our own methods of warfare and some essential modernisation had to be carried out in the overloaded dockyards of this country as soon as they arrived. Yet the gift was not only of immediate value but, regarded as a portent for the future, gave good grounds to our hard-pressed country for believing that increasing help would soon be forthcoming from across the Atlantic. The agreement between the two Governments was signed on the 5th of September and, as the Americans had already begun to bring the ships forward from reserve, the British crews were immediately shipped to Halifax, where we were to take them over. The American crews gave every help to our men in learning about the strange equipment; the Canadian Navy and Halifax dockyard did all that they could to speed the work of transfer, and as our own men had but one idea—to get the ships back to England and into service in the Western Approaches as quickly as possible—it was not long before the groups of these newly-renamed 'Town Class' destroyers began to cross the Atlantic eastbound.

Meanwhile on the Atlantic shipping routes the campaign was developing most unfavourably for Britain. The months of July to October 1940 were later called by German U-boat commanders 'the happy time'. They were only to enjoy one other such period, off the American east coast in 1942. It was the period when the U-boat aces—Prien, Kretschmer, Endras, Frauenheim and others—achieved their fame. Their attacks were generally made on ships sailing independently, on inadequately defended convoys or on stragglers from convoys. Plenty of these targets could then be found, since our outward-bound convoys dispersed between 15° and 17° West, nearly all were weakly escorted and many ships still had to be sailed independently. In these four months, so unhappy for ourselves, 144

---
[1] W. S. Churchill. *The Second World War*, Vol. II, pp. 353–368.

unescorted and 73 escorted ships were sunk by U-boats, and by way of return only six U-boats were accounted for. An even more serious portent was that only two of these six were destroyed in attacks on our convoys.[1]

It was inevitable that a lag should occur before all our shipping could be diverted to the north of Ireland. The enemy rapidly established bases for his bomber and long-range reconnaissance aircraft in Norway and western France and, by the beginning of July, was bombing and reporting as far west as the 9th meridian such shipping as was still passing south of Ireland. On the 15th of July therefore the southern route was completely abandoned, and for many months thereafter the English Channel was only used by local convoys of coasting vessels.[2]

In June sinkings by U-boats amounted to fifty-eight ships of 284,113 tons—by far the highest figure yet achieved. The enemy quickly discovered the new routes used by our shipping, and in July his U-boats sank thirty-eight ships of 195,825 tons. One of these was, unhappily, a troop transport, the *Mohammed Ali el Kebir*, which met her fate off the Irish coast with the loss of 120 lives while on passage to Gibraltar with one destroyer as escort. But, in spite of the severity of the enemy's campaign, the special protection always afforded to troopships succeeded in making such losses very rare, and many thousands of troops were safely escorted through the Atlantic danger zone at this time.

The battle between the enemy's U-boats and long-range bombers and our own escorts and patrols had now opened in earnest, and our naval and air forces were stretched as never before. On the 17th of August Hitler declared a total blockade of the British Isles and gave warning that neutral shipping would be sunk at sight. His U-boats, stimulated by the successes achieved in the two preceding months, now became bolder and carried out many attacks close off the north-west coast of Ireland. Brest, Lorient and La Pallice were now all in use as bases for the U-boats, which could, in consequence, cruise as far out as 25° West, far beyond the present range of our surface and air escorts. All his available submarine strength was now devoted to the Atlantic routes, and attacks on our east coast and Channel convoys were left entirely to aircraft and E-boats. But the U-boats were by no means the only menace in the Atlantic. The first squadron of Focke-Wulf 'Kondor' (F.W.200) four-engined long-range reconnaissance aircraft—which, let it be remembered, were an adaptation from a German civil air liner—appeared in August and worked initially from a base at Merignac, near Bordeaux, against shipping in the Irish Sea and off west and north-west Ireland. In the autumn

---

[1] See Appendix K for details of U-boats sunk during this period.
[2] See pp. 323–325.

the same squadron started to work from Stavanger in Norway as well. Besides reporting the position of our convoys they carried out many attacks on ships sailing independently or straggling from convoys; and against them we had, as yet, virtually no defence. In August the U-boats sank fifty-six ships of 267,618 tons, and aircraft a further fifteen ships of 53,283 tons. During the three months so far considered Coastal Command aircraft continued to intercept U-boats in the northern transit area off north-east Scotland fairly frequently, but no attack was successful until, on the 16th of August, U.51 was seriously damaged by the airborne depth charges which, at long last, were just beginning to enter service.

In this same month the first attempt was made to form a joint sea and air striking force in the north-west approaches. It was handicapped by shortage of escort vessels and of properly equipped aircraft, and was very short lived. None the less, valuable experience was gained, and the recommendations which its commander made when it was dissolved in September were put to good purpose later. In the Admiralty a Trade Plot had now been established alongside the Submarine Tracking Room. The position of all convoys was there plotted at four-hour intervals, and all evasive routing of shipping away from dangerous waters was conducted from that room.

In September the U-boats sank fifty-nine ships of 295,335 tons and the majority of the losses were inflicted close off the Irish coast. No less than 70 per cent of the sinkings were accomplished in night attacks by surfaced U-boats, and these tactics, to which further reference will be made shortly, combined with the use of several U-boats in 'pack-attacks', caught the defence at its weakest spot. The long-range bombers continued to aid the U-boats by reporting the position of convoys, and themselves attacked stragglers and ships sailing independently. Fifteen ships of 56,328 tons were sunk by aircraft in September. Our counter-measures to both forms of attack were ineffective, because surface escorts were still lamentably weak, no air escort could be provided by night and the type of radar then fitted in aircraft was of little use. October was still worse. Particularly heavy losses occurred between the 18th and 20th of the month in attacks on convoy S.C. 7 (17 ships sunk), H.X. 79 (14 ships sunk) and H.X. 79A (7 ships sunk). The Trade Protection meeting in the Admiralty, now held weekly, had just urged that an efficient radar set for anti-submarine surface and air escorts must be developed, that the use of airborne depth charges should be increased, that radio-telephony should be developed for rapid communication between escort vessels and aircraft, and that an experiment should be tried in routing convoys along a comparatively narrow avenue of ocean—or 'tram lines', as it was called. Close after these heavy attacks the Defence Committee met under the Prime Minister's chairmanship. The recommendations already mentioned were approved, and the decision was taken that more escort vessels must be sent to the north-west approaches at the expense of anti-invasion precautions on the east and south coasts. Thus, in the face of dire necessity, were the escort vessels returned to their proper function.[1] The urgent need for bases in Eire was also discussed, but the issue was not pressed; among other objections, the additional military commitment which such action would probably entail simply could not be accepted. The U-boat sinkings this month, October, were the highest so far accomplished—sixty-three ships of 352,407 tons—and nearly all occurred within 250 miles of the north-west corner of Ireland, aptly named Bloody Foreland. Again our counter-measures were ineffective, and for the same reasons as in the preceding month. Coastal Command was still desperately short of suitable aircraft and weapons, of trained crews and of bases in the north-west. The average daily strength of the command had, in fact, only increased from 170 aircraft at the start of the war to 226 over a year later.

On the 26th of October the Canadian Pacific liner *Empress of Britain* (42,348 tons), on passage home from the Middle East, was bombed and set on fire when she was seventy miles north-west of Donegal Bay. She was taken in tow and escorted towards home, but there were only two destroyers with her when, two days later, she was torpedoed and sunk by U.32. Though the assailant was herself sunk by other destroyers on the 30th, the loss of this splendid ship —the only one of our 'giant liners' to fall victim to the enemy—was a tragedy. It underlined the effect to Britain of the lack of air and naval bases in western Ireland, from which all shipping passing close off those shores could have been so much better and more easily protected.

In November the U-boats continued active for the first half of the month and worked between 8° and 23° West, but one from Lorient went south to the Freetown area and there sank four ships. The 'ace' commander Kretschmer sank the armed merchant cruisers *Laurentic* and *Patroclus*, which were returning from Atlantic patrols, on the 3rd. Moreover the sudden appearance of the *Admiral Scheer*, which attacked convoy H.X. 84 in mid-Atlantic on the 5th, brought a new and serious anxiety.[2] But from the 13th nearly to the end of the month a lull occurred and the U-boat sinkings for the month dropped to thirty-two ships of 146,613 tons. The long-range bombers, however, were more active. They made many attacks and sank eighteen ships of 66,438 tons. Our total losses for the month reached the high figure of ninety-seven ships of 385,715 tons. Though Coastal Command did its best to intercept the long-range bombers off south-west Ireland,

---

[1] See pp. 253–254.
[2] See pp. 288–289.

the Blenheim fighters, which were the only aircraft available for such a purpose, were too slow and too weakly armed to catch and destroy them.

The Admiralty and Coastal Command now urged that an endeavour should be made to reduce the scale of the enemy's attacks by bombing his U-boat and Focke-Wulf bases heavily. In November Coastal Command and, occasionally, Bomber Command had made light raids on these targets, but they had accomplished nothing. The attacks were stepped up in the following month when a total of 124 heavy bombers made three raids on Bordeaux and Lorient. It was believed at the time that good results were obtained, but it is now known that no significant damage was done to any U-boat or to the bases from which they and the long-range bombers worked.

The decrease in sinkings by U-boats in November did, however, give ground for hope that the tide had started to turn. More escort vessels were at last becoming available through the return of destroyers from anti-invasion duties and of ships damaged in the previous summer's fighting in the narrow seas; more of the new corvettes were entering service and the ex-American destroyers were also coming forward.

The result was that the number of convoy escorts rose gradually to an average of two per convoy, and even this meagre increase in their strength at once produced favourable results both in reducing the sinkings of merchantmen and in destroying U-boats. But the position was still far from satisfactory. The enforced use of the north-west approaches by all our shipping had, of course, not been foreseen or provided against, and in consequence properly equipped naval and air bases were lacking on the coastline bordering the focal waters. The effect of the denial to us of bases in Eire has already been mentioned, but even in Northern Ireland, whose loyal Government had long been willing and anxious to grant all possible facilities, and in western England and Scotland the naval and air bases had at first to be improvised. Furthermore none of our escort vessels had sufficient endurance to make the Atlantic passage without refuelling, and advanced fuelling bases, which could only be established in Iceland, were essential if the protection of our convoys was to be extended further west.

The two schools of thought regarding the protection of shipping from U-boat attack which existed early in the war have already been mentioned, and it has been told how that which favoured the pursuit of those elusive targets by hunting for them instead of escorting the convoys as strongly as possible came to be discredited.[1] But those who desired to use every available flotilla vessel and aircraft for escort

---

[1] See p. 10 and pp. 134-135.

purposes and to combine escorts with the evasive routing of convoys away from the most dangerous areas had not yet gained complete and final acceptance for their views. The alternative of establishing patrolled lanes along which all shipping should steam, and of directing a heavy bombing offensive on U-boat bases and building yards was still much discussed. The supporters of the patrolled shipping lanes could claim, with some justice, that greater economy in the use of surface vessels and aircraft was thereby achieved. But the length of the lanes which had to be patrolled was constantly increasing, and continuous patrols could hardly be maintained in all weathers throughout their whole length. Moreover this method had been tried and shown to be unsuccessful in the First World War prior to the general introduction of the convoy system in 1917.[1] Fortunately the protagonists of powerful convoy escorts and evasive routing—far to the north in the case of the Atlantic convoys—obtained their way in general, and a prompt dividend was secured in the destruction of three U-boats by convoy escorts. U.32, which had sunk the *Empress of Britain* on the 28th of October, was herself caught and sunk by the destroyers *Harvester* and *Highlander* two days later; U.31 was sunk by the *Antelope* in co-operation with shore-based aircraft on the 2nd of November and U.104 by the corvette *Rhododendron* on the 21st of November. But that the old heresy of the hunting group was not yet entirely dead was shown by a tendency at this time to order convoy escorts to leave their charges and search for U-boats reported in waters often quite remote from the convoys which they were supposed to be protecting. Such searches were as uniformly unsuccessful as the earlier hunting groups, and while they were in progress the convoys themselves were left in great peril.

During December the U-boats in the North Atlantic were hampered by bad weather, but were active chiefly between 15° and 20° West. Only one convoy, H.X. 90, was attacked but that was by four U-boats, two of which were commanded by Kretschmer and Schultz, working by night on the surface. They sank eleven ships, including the armed merchant cruiser *Forfar*, the convoy's ocean escort. To find better weather and to get clear of our slowly strengthening escorts, some U-boats now moved south. These sank five ships off Portugal and four off Freetown. Neither of these areas possessed as yet any properly co-ordinated air and surface anti-submarine organisation. At Gibraltar No. 200 Group of Coastal Command still consisted only of one squadron of the obsolete London flying-boats and a few naval Swordfish. These were controlled by the Air Officer Commanding, Mediterranean, to meet the needs of the

---

[1] See Fayle. *Seaborne Trade*, Vol. III: *The Submarine Campaign* (Murray, 1924), pp. 90–91. 'The areas of concentration [i.e. the patrolled routes] were, in the long view, little better than death traps.'

Flag Officer, North Atlantic. Reinforcements did not reach Gibraltar until after the end of the present phase; nor had an Area Combined Headquarters, which experience at home had shown to be essential to the proper co-ordination of air-sea operations, yet been organised there. The first Sunderland flying-boats did not reach Freetown until March 1941 and it was the following May before any Catalinas (P.B.Y. American flying-boats) could be spared for Gibraltar.

The southward movement of the U-boats was largely responsible for the increase in sinkings in December to thirty-seven ships of 212,590 tons.

Now that the account of this first phase of the Battle of the Atlantic has been carried to the end of the year, it is proposed to break the story in order to describe, firstly, the night surface attacks in strength introduced by Admiral Dönitz and, secondly, the change in the control of Coastal Command's aircraft which was at this time being considered in London.

It has been told how the months of June to October marked the great successes achieved by individual U-boat commanders. As long as the enemy's strength in submarines remained small he had no choice but to allow each boat to work by itself, to the best of its commander's ability. But as the numbers controlled by Admiral Dönitz increased he was able to introduce attacks by several U-boats working together. He had long been awaiting the opportunity to make this change in tactics, and the 'wolf-packs', as they came to be called, were gradually introduced between October 1940 and March 1941. The change caught us unawares and unprepared, for reasons which will be explained shortly.

The tactics of the 'wolf-pack' depended firstly on the position and route of a convoy being established in the headquarters of the U-boat Command, now situated at Lorient. Once this had been accomplished with reasonable certainty, the information was passed to the senior officer of one of the groups of U-boats organised for pack attacks. The group commander would generally order the boat nearest to the convoy to make contact with it, and to continue to shadow it while 'homing' the other boats of the group on to the convoy by wireless. When all or most of the group had gathered to the shadower, attacks on the surface would be started and, if possible, continued on several successive nights. During daylight all the attackers would withdraw clear of the convoy. Actually the first employment of U-boat groups on this principle was not entirely successful, partly because sufficient numbers were not yet available and partly because the U-boat Command tried to exercise too rigid a control over the attackers. But the development was, from the British viewpoint, full of the most serious implications, since the enemy had adopted a form of attack which we had not foreseen and against which neither tactical nor technical counter-measures had been prepared.

Mention was made earlier of the great confidence felt in naval circles before the war regarding the effectiveness of the asdic.[1] Certainly in skilled hands and used in the circumstances for which it had been designed—that of submerged attack—it was a great advance on any previous submarine-detecting device. But if the enemy adopted surface attacks the asdic, which had an effective range of some 1,500 yards and could not detect a surfaced U-boat, immediately lost much of its value. And this is precisely what now occurred. Instead of finding ourselves possessed of 'means of countering a submarine which are very effective', as the asdic was described in 1937, our flotilla vessels had to fall back on the hope of visual sighting and, as many of our escorts were too slow to catch a surfaced U-boat, even if they sighted one, they were unlikely to achieve her destruction.

The reader will naturally ask why the employment by the enemy of such tactics was not foreseen, and why we had concentrated our energies and attention on dealing with attacks by submerged U-boats only. When British naval training and thinking in the years between the wars are reviewed, it seems that both were concentrated on the conduct of surface ships in action with similar enemy units, and that the defence of trade was also considered chiefly from the point of view of attack by enemy surface units. The statement made by the First Sea Lord, in August 1939, to his colleagues on the Chiefs of Staff Committee, regarding the potential threat to our trade of the enemy's raiding warships indicates how far this aspect dominated naval thought before the war.[2] Our own submarines were trained towards the same end, and our naval aircraft practised reconnaissance work and attacks on surface ships more than anti-submarine work. Furthermore Coastal Command was told that reconnaissance of the exits from the North Sea with the object of sighting enemy surface ships was its principal duty. In our own Navy night attacks by surfaced submarines had certainly been carried out in pre-war exercises, sometimes with outstanding success. But submerged attacks were the more common practice, and we appear to have assumed that an enemy would conform to that method of warfare. Moreover we seem, in the period between the two world wars, to have lost sight of the fact that the Germans had developed the night attack on the surface in the 1914–18 war and, in its later phases, had achieved the great majority of their successes by that means. There was, in fact,

---

[1] See p. 34.
[2] See p. 35.

nothing new in night attacks by surfaced submarines.[1] The submarine on the surface becomes, in effect, a torpedo-boat, and it was certainly recognised that defence against attack by ships of that type was best afforded by flotilla vessels organised and working in integrated escort groups. But, apart from the acute shortage of all types of flotilla vessel at this period of the war, the severe losses suffered in the previous months and the manifold calls made on those which remained had resulted in the virtually complete destruction of the organisation of the flotillas, and their reduction to heterogeneous groups of ships of varying type, unfamiliar with their senior officer or with each other. The loss of tactical coherence, especially under the difficult conditions of a night attack on a convoy, was bound to have serious effects.

Such, briefly stated, appears to be the background to our lack of preparation to meet the change in U-boat tactics. But, fortunately for us, there were certain weaknesses inherent in the 'wolf-pack' attacks which could be, and finally were, exploited to the uttermost. Firstly its success depended chiefly on the shadowing U-boat remaining in contact with the quarry. If it could be driven off or sunk the rest of the group would lose their sense of direction, and would probably waste many days vainly scouring the seas. Secondly, the tactic depended for its success on frequent wireless signals being sent by the shadowing U-boat, and such signals enabled the position of the sender to be established approximately by direction-finding stations, or by ships fitted with appropriate receiving apparatus. Thirdly, if our evasive routing were successful, large numbers of U-boats might well spend long periods fruitlessly waiting for sighting reports. True, the enemy's long-range aircraft could to some extent nullify the effects of our evasive routing but, fortunately, he did not possess such aircraft in large numbers, nor always use them in close and efficient co-operation with his U-boats; and, furthermore, by routing our convoys further to the north we were able to keep them beyond the range of the Focke-Wulfs until near the end of their journey. Before the war Dönitz had estimated that, if we adopted a world-wide convoy system, 300 U-boats would be necessary to achieve decisive results. He, at least, had no illusions about the effectiveness of the convoy system. By the spring of 1941 we still had many ships sailing independently, but the convoy system was in wide and steadily increasing use. Yet the enemy then possessed an operational strength of only

---

[1] In a book by Captain Karl Dönitz, published in Berlin in 1939, the possibilities of night attacks by surfaced submarines were strongly presented. 'The U-boat which is surfaced at night has', states the author, 'the very great advantage over surface ships of a smaller silhouette. . . . The night attack delivered on the surface provides the U-boat with a particularly effective method. . . . At night the U-boat, once in the vicinity of the enemy, becomes an ideal torpedo-carrier . . . because she will be able to make a surface torpedo attack.' *Die U-bootswaffe* (E. S. Mittler, Berlin, 1939, p. 39). Trans. M. G. Saunders.

thirty U-boats. Plainly he could not expect decisive results when possessed of such small numbers.

The result, then, of all these factors and considerations was that, in spite of our unpreparedness, the new tactics, though full of menace, did not achieve outstanding success. The number of ships sunk by each U-boat at sea had averaged eight per month from July to October 1940; but it fell to two per month in February 1941 and continued to fall throughout that year until the vast mass of unprotected and unconvoyed shipping off the east coast of America provided the U-boat commanders with their second 'happy time' during the first seven months of 1942. We now know that the enemy was actually forced to change his tactics by the growing effectiveness of our defence measures, and particularly by the convoy system; which fact surely provides the final judgement on the doubts expressed before the war about the desirability of convoy. Though it may be correct to include convoy among the methods of exercising defensive control of the sea routes, it has great offensive tactical possibilities in that the would-be attacker must approach within range of the escorts' weapons. To regard it as a wholly defensive measure, compared in particular with the employment of hunting groups, is therefore fallacious. Furthermore the difficulty of creating the necessary world-wide organisation for the control of shipping, and the belief that the loss of carrying capacity inherent in working the convoy system could not be accepted, both now appear to have been exaggerated. An organisation for the control of shipping is essential in time of war, whether it sails in convoy or independently, and the loss of carrying capacity caused by heavy sinkings of independently-routed ships is likely in the end greatly to exceed the loss caused by sailing those same ships in convoy.

The location and, if possible, the destruction of the shadowing U-boat has already been mentioned as the first requirement for dealing with the 'wolf-pack'. Research work to produce a suitable direction-finding wireless set which could be fitted in anti-submarine vessels was therefore started forthwith; but the first set was not ready until July 1941. Eighteen months later it had become a normal weapon in the armoury of the anti-submarine vessel. Secondly, since the asdic was almost useless in the circumstances already described, it was essential to improve the means of visually sighting a submarine by night. Star shell were used to begin with but soon a more efficient illuminant, known as the 'snow flake', was devised with the object of turning night as far as possible into day. But it was plain to all who were engaged on solving the problem that an efficient radar set would contribute more to the defeat of the surfaced U-boat than any other single measure. Certain technical developments in the radar field had made this possible by March 1940, and by the following January sets which were capable of detecting the presence of a surfaced U-boat began to be fitted in aircraft of Coastal Command and also in escort vessels. Thus did radar come to fill the gap left by the inability of the asdic to detect a submarine once it had surfaced. But this was only the first step towards compassing its destruction. It still remained necessary for the escort vessel or aircraft to close to a range at which its guns, bombs or depth charges could be used to good effect; and in the last stages of this approach, during which the radar contact would fade away, visual sighting remained an absolute requirement.

The type of flare carried by aircraft before the war was found of little use, and a slow-dropping flare was not perfected for another two years. It was therefore decided to fit powerful searchlights in aircraft employed as convoy escorts or on anti-submarine patrols, and thus the Leigh Light, named after its inventor, Squadron Leader H. de V. Leigh, was developed. The use of airborne radar combined with this searchlight was to provide the needed solution, since the former enabled the first contact to be obtained at long range and a silent approach to be made, while the second enabled the U-boat to be suddenly illumined and so caught unawares just before the aircraft carried out its attack. The important factor of surprise was thus placed in the hands of the attacking aircraft. But the development of these counter-measures to their full, even decisive, stage was inevitably slow, and during the period with which we are now dealing Coastal Command was still grievously handicapped by shortage of suitable aircraft, by lack of a lethal weapon with which to attack a U-boat and by the need to achieve a high degree of training in this very specialised work.[1] Though the closest co-operation now existed between the Admiralty's Submarine Tracking Room and the Headquarters of Coastal Command, full integration of the work of the two services was by no means yet accomplished. But the tactical employment of air escorts was now being improved steadily, for example, by exploiting to the full the speed and mobility of aircraft to sweep ahead of and around the convoys instead of keeping them, like the surface escorts, in a fairly constant position close to the convoy. As regards surface escorts, not only were their numbers now at last beginning to increase but they were being formed into Escort Groups in the Western Approaches Command. This enabled the same ships to remain together, and to get thoroughly to know the Group Commander's methods. The tactical handling of the ships, which, in the inevitable confusion of a night attack by a group of U-boats on a convoy of perhaps forty ships, was an important matter, was thereby improved. It is, however, justifiable to record that the

---

[1] See pp. 135–136.

proposal to create these escort groups met with opposition from the personnel departments of the Admiralty.

It was, by this time, fully realised in the Admiralty and in the commands concerned with the prosecution of the Atlantic battle that success could only be built on a foundation of thorough training of officers and men, not only as individuals but as members of a group. The inevitable and continuous dilution of the crews of escort vessels with untrained men was a consequence of the rapid expansion of the Navy, and of the need to find crews for the new ships now completing in large numbers. But it lent further emphasis to the need to provide additional training facilities. The pre-war anti-submarine school at Portland could not by itself cope with the requirement, and, moreover, after the fall of France it was very unfavourably placed to continue its full activities, let alone to expand them greatly. It was accordingly decided to move all anti-submarine training to new bases in Scotland. The Portland establishment moved to Dunoon in Argyll, a second establishment was formed in July at Campbeltown, the experimental work was moved to Fairlie in Ayrshire and, perhaps most important of all, a sea training establishment known as H.M.S. *Western Isles* was opened at Tobermory in the Inner Hebrides. On the 12th of July Commodore (Vice-Admiral retired) G. O. Stephenson was appointed to command the *Western Isles*, and under his guiding genius every new escort vessel thereafter underwent a month's intensive training in anti-submarine warfare. After completing this period the ships would join their groups in the Clyde, Mersey or at Londonderry to undergo a further period of group training under the direction of the captain in command of all the escort groups based there. A complementary measure was the start of a tactical school at Liverpool to train the officers of the escort vessels in U-boat methods and in counter-attack procedure.

All this was not of course accomplished in a short time, but it started in a small way during the present phase and it finally created the escort groups whose skill and dash came to be greatly feared by the enemy. Moreover, once a group had been formed, every endeavour was made to prevent it being broken up. Only rarely could a group work at its full strength of about eight ships, because some were inevitably refitting or repairing damage. The normal operating strength of a group was, perhaps, two-thirds of its full numbers; but it was soon learnt that it was better to use a weak group than to break up a group to obtain a numerically stronger escort. In fact the early escort groups were far from homogeneous in class and type. They included not only a few destroyers but corvettes, ex-American destroyers and even trawlers, but they had been trained together, and tactical coherence was more important than homogeneity.

Not only did training thus gradually progress but the equipment of the escort vessels themselves was also improving steadily. Radio-telephony made rapid inter-communication of orders possible, and the number of depth charges which could be dropped or fired in each attack was increased from the pre-war five to double that number. Finally, on the 7th of February 1941 the headquarters of the Western Approaches Command were moved from Plymouth to Derby House, Liverpool, where the Commander-in-Chief and his staff were in much closer contact with the Atlantic shipping control organisation, with the commodores of convoys and masters of individual merchantmen, with the commanders of the escort groups and, perhaps most important of all, with No. 15 Group of Coastal Command (Air Vice-Marshal J. M. Robb). This formation had been made responsible for air operations in the north-west approaches when a new group, No. 19 (Air Vice-Marshal G. R. Bromet), had been formed at Plymouth to take over No. 15 Group's former responsibility for the south-west area. In the new command headquarters at Derby House an operations room was started, and there a plot was maintained which was a duplicate of the Trade Plot in the Admiralty, with which it was linked by direct telephone. There, under the direction of a highly skilled staff from both Services, the naval and air sides of the Atlantic battle were fully integrated, and a constant watch was maintained over the whole vast battlefield and over the hundreds of warships, merchantmen and aircraft involved in the unremitting prosecution of the campaign.

Ten days after the headquarters of the Western Approaches Command moved to Liverpool Admiral Sir Percy Noble succeeded Admiral Dunbar-Nasmith as Commander-in-Chief, Western Approaches, and the latter became Commander-in-Chief, Plymouth. The Admiralty's instructions to Admiral Noble were that he 'would be directly responsible for the protection of trade, the routing and control of the outward and homeward-bound ocean convoys and measures to combat any attacks on convoys by U-boats or hostile aircraft within his command'.

So much for the development of new tactics by the enemy and of our counter-measures. Before, however, we return to the story of the unceasing battle in the Atlantic, a second digression must be made. The acute difficulties of Coastal Command and the ineffectiveness of our counter-measures during the period already described led to constant pressure being applied by the Air Officer Commanding-in-Chief and the Admiralty to obtain more aircraft for the maritime war. Early in November 1940 a proposal was made to the Defence Committee that Coastal Command should be transferred bodily

Atlantic Convoy O.B. 331 in 58° 00′ North, 11° 40′ West on 10th June 1941.

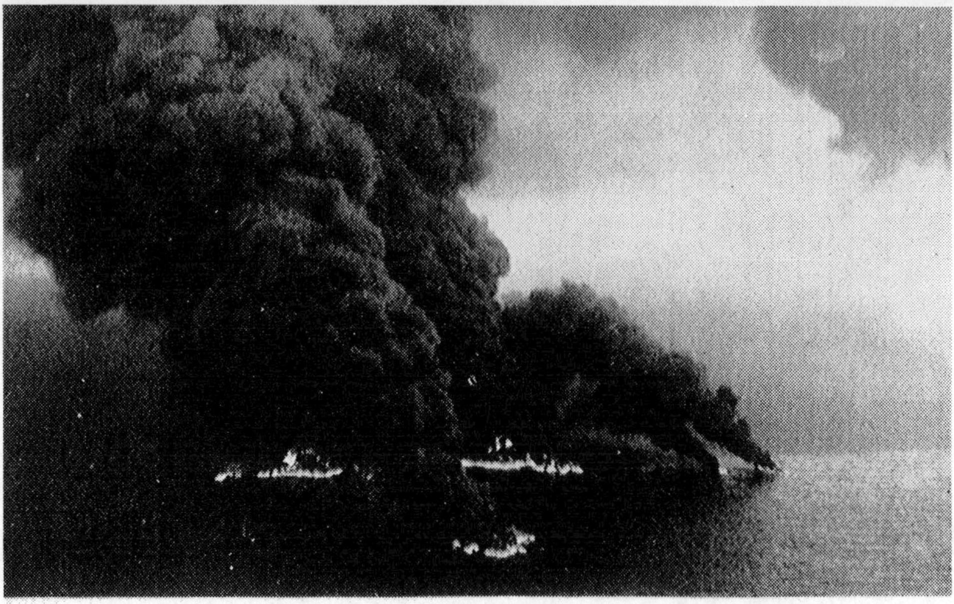

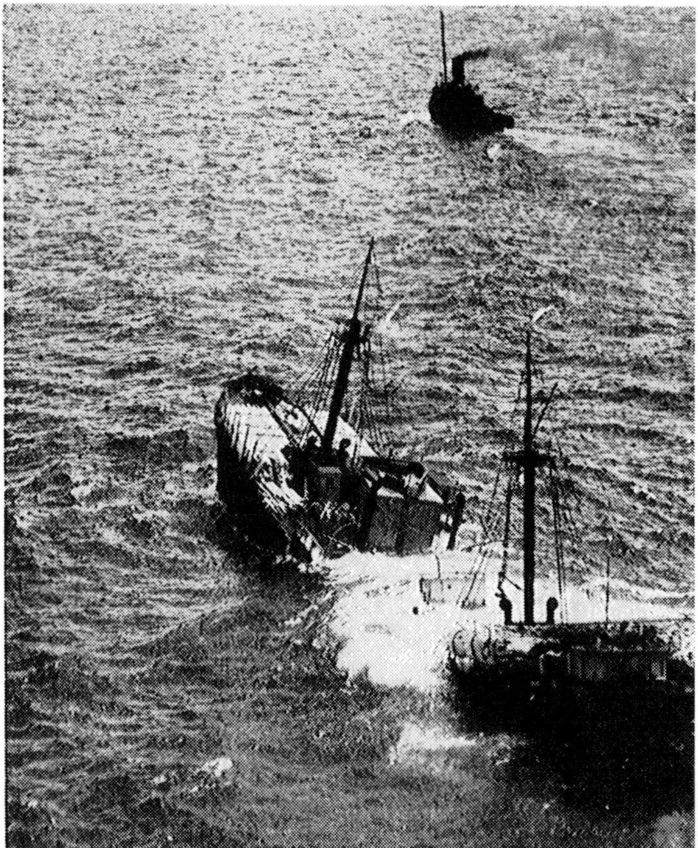

The Battle of the Atlantic.
The toll.

The destruction of a Focke-Wulf 'Kondor' in 54° 00′ North, 13° 35′ West on 23rd July
(Note convoy in background of lower photograph.)

from the Air Ministry to the Admiralty. This proposal, which had not emanated from the Admiralty, would have involved a 'surgical operation' on the Royal Air Force at the height of a crisis in the war. The first result was that the Prime Minister ordered a full enquiry to be made into all the implications. When this enquiry had been completed the Defence Committee considered the matter again; on the 4th of December they decided that Coastal Command should remain an integral part of the Royal Air Force, but that operational control should be taken over by the Admiralty. Though the transfer did not take effect until the 15th of April 1941 it will be convenient to consider now what this change meant and how the control was thenceforth exercised by the Admiralty. The change was not, in fact, as far-reaching as might at first sight appear. The Admiralty did not now issue orders to the Headquarters of Coastal Command, nor were the various Groups forming that command placed under the orders of the naval Commander-in-Chief responsible for naval operations in the same area. The working of the Area Combined Headquarters, in which the naval and air sides of every command were intimately integrated, remained unaffected. Under the new arrangement the naval Commander-in-Chief stated his requirements for protection, escorts or patrols and the Air Officer Commanding the Coastal Command Group then issued his orders to meet the naval requirements. If the Home Fleet were at sea a more direct measure of naval control was, however, exercised by the Admiralty through Coastal Command Headquarters. What the Defence Committee's decision undoubtedly did accomplish was not so much to effect a radical change in the administrative arrangements of the two Services, or the day-to-day conduct of maritime operations, as to emphasise the predominance of the naval requirements. Moreover the enquiries already mentioned did have the effect of bringing the really urgent needs of Coastal Command into the limelight. Thus the Admiralty and Air Ministry agreed on a programme for the expansion of the Command's reconnaissance and long-range fighter squadrons, and it was decided that all the Catalinas now on order from America should be allocated to Coastal Command.

This arrangement, even though reached very late and in a time of crisis, was certainly wise. The complete transfer of Coastal Command to the Admiralty could hardly have been successfully carried through at such a juncture and, in fact, went far beyond the proposals of the Navy, whose only object was to obtain proper priority for the allocation of aircraft and trained crews to the maritime war. It is interesting to compare the manner in which the difficult question of the control of maritime aircraft was answered at this time by the British Service Departments and Cabinet with the enemy's endeavours to solve the same problem. The matter actually came to a head in the German High Command a few months after the solution outlined above had been reached in London. But no such happy and workable compromise was reached by them. In August 1940 a new group of the German Air Force had been formed for reconnaissance purposes in the Atlantic and to strike against our shipping. It consisted mostly of Focke-Wulf long-range bombers. This group was instructed to co-operate with the U-boat command; but Admiral Dönitz could not control the aircraft to suit his real needs and the animosity between Marshal Göring and Admiral Raeder prevented any real inter-Service understanding being developed. Early in 1941 complaints by Raeder and Dönitz led to the Air Force group being transferred bodily by Hitler to the Navy—a 'surgical operation' similar to that which we were to avoid—and this aroused the strong resentment of the German Air Force. At the end of February Hitler issued a new directive whereby responsibility for air operations was allocated by areas to one or other of the two Services. The Atlantic was given to the Air Force, against the advice of Raeder who immediately protested. None the less the February directive continued in force for the remainder of the war, and although the commander of the Atlantic air group was personally co-operative with the German Navy the bad relations between the heads of the two Services frustrated the full, and possibly decisive, participation of the Luftwaffe in the Atlantic struggle.

It is now time to return to the story of the struggle with the enemy's U-boats and aircraft which we left at the turn of the year. In January 1941 sinkings by U-boats fell to twenty-one ships of 126,782 tons and these casualties mostly occurred among ships which had dispersed from convoys beyond 20° West, or among stragglers from convoys. Only two convoys were attacked during the month. The drop in sinkings was partly caused by the wintry weather; but our evasive routing was now producing good results by diverting our convoys from known dangers. In the Admiralty's Submarine Tracking Room good use was made of wireless reports sent by shadowing U-boats, to assess the threat to particular convoys and to divert them elsewhere. But the long-range bombers continued their depredations; twenty ships of 78,517 tons were sunk by aircraft in January, and many others were damaged. The need for special measures to counter these air attacks had long been recognised, but time was needed to bring them into full effect. Independently-sailed ships were now routed far to the north, out of range of the bombers working from Bordeaux or Stavanger, and convoys were brought in towards the coast along a fairly narrow lane patrolled or covered by our long-range fighters, more of which were now being sent from the

MEASURES TO DEAL WITH FOCKE-WULFS 363

east coast to Northern Ireland. On the east coast the convoys were routed closer inshore to enable protection to be afforded by Fighter Command aircraft. Anti-aircraft weapons, of which supplies were still woefully inadequate, were diverted from guarding shore establishments to the merchant ships. To man these guns more and better-trained seamen or marines from the Admiralty's Defensively Equipped Merchant Ship organisation, or soldiers of the Maritime A.A. Regiment, were now available. These guns' crews were of inestimable value not only because they understood the job of shooting at enemy aircraft, but because their presence helped to stiffen the resolution of the men of the Merchant Navy who, themselves generally unarmed, had to bring their ships through so many dangers. Yet another measure was to embark naval fighters in the old seaplane carrier *Pegasus* which would accompany convoys and catapult them when an enemy was sighted. An attempt was also made to surprise the enemy bombers by fitting up an anti-aircraft 'Q Ship' which, with its armament concealed, would straggle invitingly behind a convoy. The tactic was, however, worn threadbare and she achieved no more success than her anti-submarine counterparts.[1] But in spite of all that we could do the Focke-Wulfs' activities increased in February, when enemy aircraft sank twenty-seven ships of 89,305 tons; and U-boat sinkings for the month rose to thirty-nine ships of 196,783 tons. Our total losses exceeded 100 ships and 400,000 tons for the first time since the previous October.

One feature which was now causing much anxiety was the heavy losses sustained by ships which, sometimes deliberately and sometimes in spite of their masters' best endeavours, became detached from the convoy to which they belonged. These 'stragglers' or 'rompers' provided no less than half of the sinkings achieved by the U-boats and aircraft during the month. The Admiralty made every endeavour to eliminate these tendencies by, for example, slowing down convoys, finding better quality fuel for the ships and by educating the ships' officers to the dangers of such practices. Yet the very preference for finding such victims now exhibited by the enemy gave some grounds for optimism; it showed an increasing unwillingness to attack our convoys and, since more and more ships were now sailing in convoy and stronger escorts were being provided, it seemed that he must, sooner or later, choose between attacking the convoys at the price of the losses he would almost certainly suffer thereby and allowing greater immunity to our shipping. As we now know, he chose the former alternative, with consequences which brought our escorts their first substantial success in the struggle.

Meanwhile measures to meet the enemy's expected spring

---
[1] See pp. 136–137.

offensive in the Atlantic were being urged by the Prime Minister. On the 27th of February the Chiefs of Staff recommended that more escort vessels should be released from the east coast to the Western Approaches, that six squadrons of Hudsons should be transferred from work over the North Sea, that airfield construction in the northwest and the delivery of the long-awaited Catalinas from America should be hastened by all possible means and that more guns should be lent by Anti-Aircraft Command to merchant ships. These proposals were approved on the 1st of March and on the 6th the Prime Minister issued his famous Battle of the Atlantic directive ordering that 'we must take the offensive against the U-boat and Focke-Wulf wherever we can and whenever we can. The U-boat at sea must be hunted . . . the Focke-Wulf and other bombers . . . must be attacked in the air and in their nests'. He proceeded to indicate the various measures to be adopted by each Service and Department to accomplish those ends and the priorities to be observed in producing the necessary equipment.[1] On the 19th of March the first meeting of the newly-formed Battle of the Atlantic Committee took place. The Prime Minister took the chair and the committee's members consisted of the War Cabinet and other Ministers, the Chiefs of the Naval and Air Staffs and certain scientific advisers. It met initially once a week. But in the same month, as had been expected, the tempo of the enemy offensive with both U-boats and long-range bombers increased, and the difficulties of coping with this rising offensive were enhanced by the activities of the German raiding warships, which forced us to use reconnaissance aircraft to search for them while at sea and to watch them when in port. The *Hipper* made a brief sortie from Brest in February, and the *Scharnhorst* and *Gneisenau* were twice sighted at sea by our warship convoy escorts during the month. The full story of the cruises of these ships will be told in the next chapter, but here it must be noted that, in a month already dark with the menace of the U-boat and long-range bomber, the German warship raiders sank or captured seventeen ships of 89,838 tons and his armed merchant raiders four more ships of 28,707 tons. To this considerable total the U-boats added forty-one ships of 243,020 tons and the bombers a like number of ships of 113,314 tons to make our total losses for the month 139 ships and, for the first time since June 1940, over half a million tons of shipping. But this serious rise in losses was offset by a success which can now be appraised as having greater importance than could possibly have been realised at the time.

Two U-boats (U.70 and U.47) were sunk by the corvettes *Camellia* and *Arbutus* and the destroyer *Wolverine* in attacks on convoy

---

[1] Mr Churchill's directive is quoted in full in *The Second World War*, Vol. III, pp. 107–109. It is reproduced in Appendix O to this volume.

END OF U-BOAT 'ACES', MARCH 1941

O.B. 293 on the 7th and 8th of March and two more (U.99 and U.100) by the destroyers *Walker* and *Vanoc* in attacks on convoy H.X. 112 on the 17th. On the 23rd the trawler *Visenda* sank another (U.551). In one month the enemy not only thus lost one-fifth of his operational U-boat fleet, but three of the boats destroyed were commanded by celebrated 'aces'. The death of Prien in U.47, of Schepke in U.100 and the capture of Kretschmer from U.99 not only deprived the enemy of the services of three of his most successful U-boat commanders but marked the end of the period of ascendancy of the individual exponent of this type of warfare. Thereafter the lone operations of such men were increasingly replaced by the pack tactics already described. And the fact that all these successes were obtained by the anti-submarine escorts of convoys emphasised, if any emphasis were by this time necessary, that it was in the defence of convoys by powerful surface and air escorts that the greatest injury could be done to the enemy's striking power.

CHAPTER XVIII

OCEAN WARFARE

1st January–31st May, 1941

> The officer who shall have charge of a convoy entrusted to him is to consider the protecting of it as his most particular duty. . . . He is never to chase himself, nor to suffer any other ship which forms a part of a convoy to chase so far from the Fleet as to run any risk of being separated from it. . . .
> *Regulations and Instructions relating to His Majesty's Service at Sea.* 1806.

WHEN the New Year opened the pocket-battleship *Admiral Scheer*, with two armed merchant raiders—the *Thor* (Raider E) and *Pinguin* (Raider F)—temporarily in company, was refitting herself at a rendezvous in the South Atlantic, where two supply ships and two prizes had also assembled or were expected shortly. The *Scheer's* repairs were completed on the 5th of January and after refilling her fuel tanks she moved on to the Capetown–Freetown route on the 8th. The *Thor* was ordered to work on the same route but to the south of the 30th parallel of latitude, while the *Pinguin* steamed far to the south to strike against the Allied whaling fleets.

The *Kormoran* (Raider G), which was the first ship of the second wave of armed raiders and had broken out through the Denmark Strait in mid-December, was at this time moving south in the Atlantic.[1] The *Atlantis* (Raider C), which we left refitting at Kerguelen Island, was about to restart work in the northern waters of the Indian Ocean and, because of the concentration of raiders in the South Atlantic, the *Admiral Scheer* was transferred to the southern part of the Indian Ocean at the end of January.

The *Orion* (Raider A) had completed nine months' successful cruising and was about to begin a refit at Maug in the Japanese-mandated Mariana Islands. She had supply ships, which were working to and from Japan, in attendance, and would be ready for sea in February. The *Komet* (Raider B), which had entered the Pacific by the Bering Strait and taken part with the *Orion* in the first attack on the phosphate island of Nauru, had just attacked the same

---

[1] See p. 286.

island again by herself and was now moving into the southern Indian Ocean, passing far to the south of New Zealand and Australia.[1]

The remaining raider of the six which had comprised the first wave—the *Widder* (Raider D)—had returned to Brest on the last day of October 1940, but three similar ships—the *Michel* (H), *Stier* (J) and *Togo* (K)—were fitting out or were soon to be taken in hand for that purpose. Their active careers did not, however, start during the present phase.

As regards the other German major warships, the *Scharnhorst* and *Gneisenau* were both still at Kiel; but the long period spent in repairing the torpedo damage received in the Norwegian campaign was now nearly over, and they were expected to be ready for sea before the end of January. The *Hipper's* repairs were almost completed in Brest and the German Naval Staff was planning renewed attacks on the Halifax and Sierra Leone convoy routes by her and the battle cruisers. The *Hipper's* sister ship the *Prinz Eugen* was structurally complete and had run her trials, but was not yet ready for service, while the battleship *Bismarck* had also recently completed her first trials in the Baltic and the time was approaching when she would be ready. Work on the aircraft carrier *Graf Zeppelin* had been suspended, at Raeder's suggestion, in April 1940. When the Germans had gained possession of the bases on the French Atlantic coast the Naval Staff tried to get work on the ship resumed and Hitler approved that she should be finished; but difficulties over providing suitable types of aircraft at once arose with the Luftwaffe, and for this reason work did not, in fact, progress.

Thus, although the *Scheer* was the only enemy warship actually at work on the ocean trade routes at the turn of the year, no less than six merchant raiders were at large at the time. And an even greater threat was likely to arise in the very near future when the battle cruisers and the *Hipper* were ready. To the serious losses now being inflicted by U-boats and long-range aircraft in the Atlantic, and the likelihood that such attacks would be intensified as the short days and bad weather of the winter months receded, there had to be added the grave challenge of renewed forays by powerful warships against our convoys. Moreover the success with which the enemy had, during the preceding months, passed his warships and armed merchant raiders in and out by the northern passages to the Atlantic, and the knowledge that our resources in cruisers and reconnaissance aircraft were inadequate to watch those exits closely and so give timely warning to the Home Fleet, increased the heavy anxieties which marked the early months of 1941.

---

[1] See p. 284 and Map 24 (*facing p. 279*).

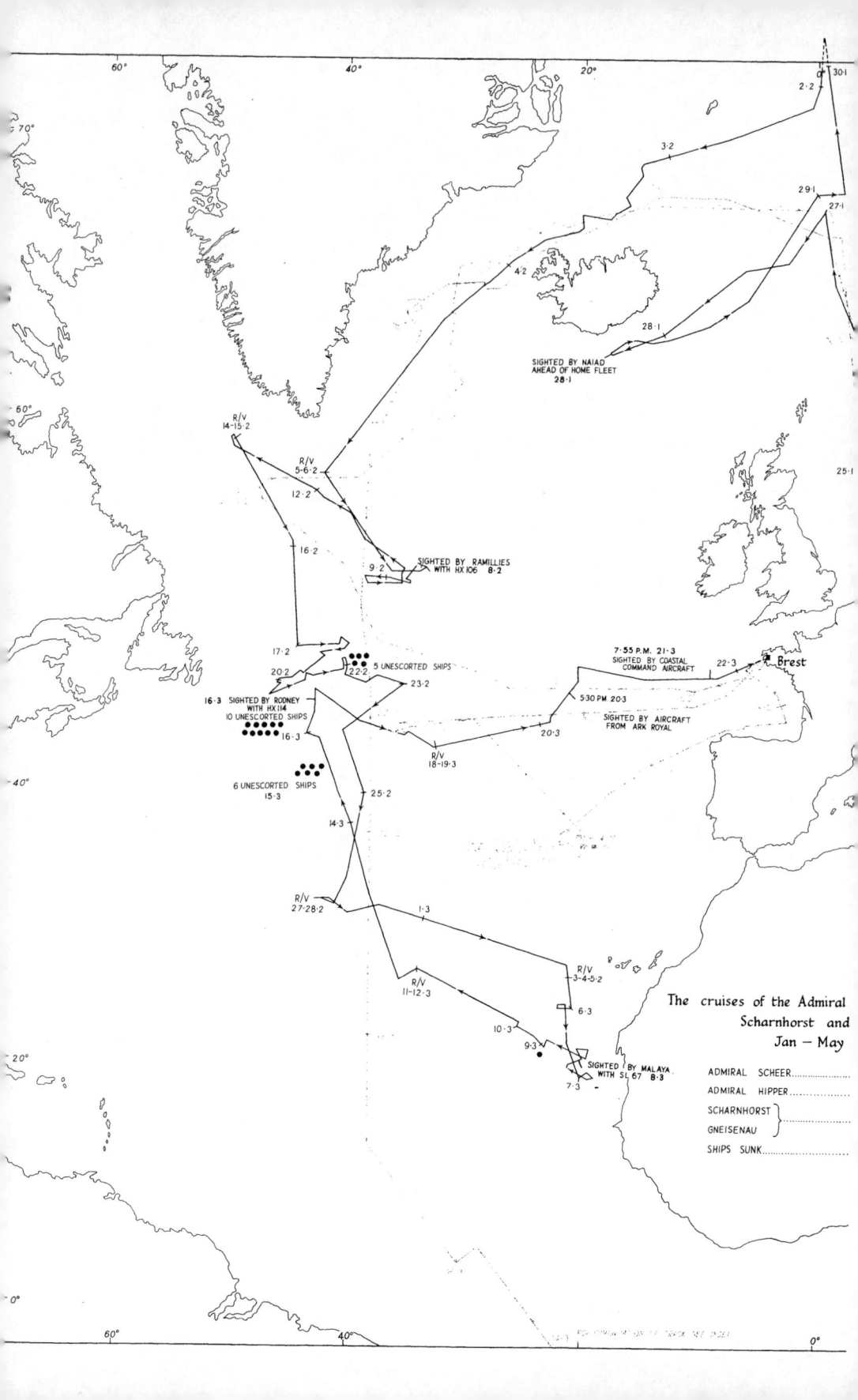

The cruises of the Admiral
Scharnhorst and
Jan – May

ADMIRAL SCHEER ....
ADMIRAL HIPPER ....
SCHARNHORST }
GNEISENAU   } ....
SHIPS SUNK ....

Map 27
Scheer, Admiral Hipper,
Gneisenau
1941

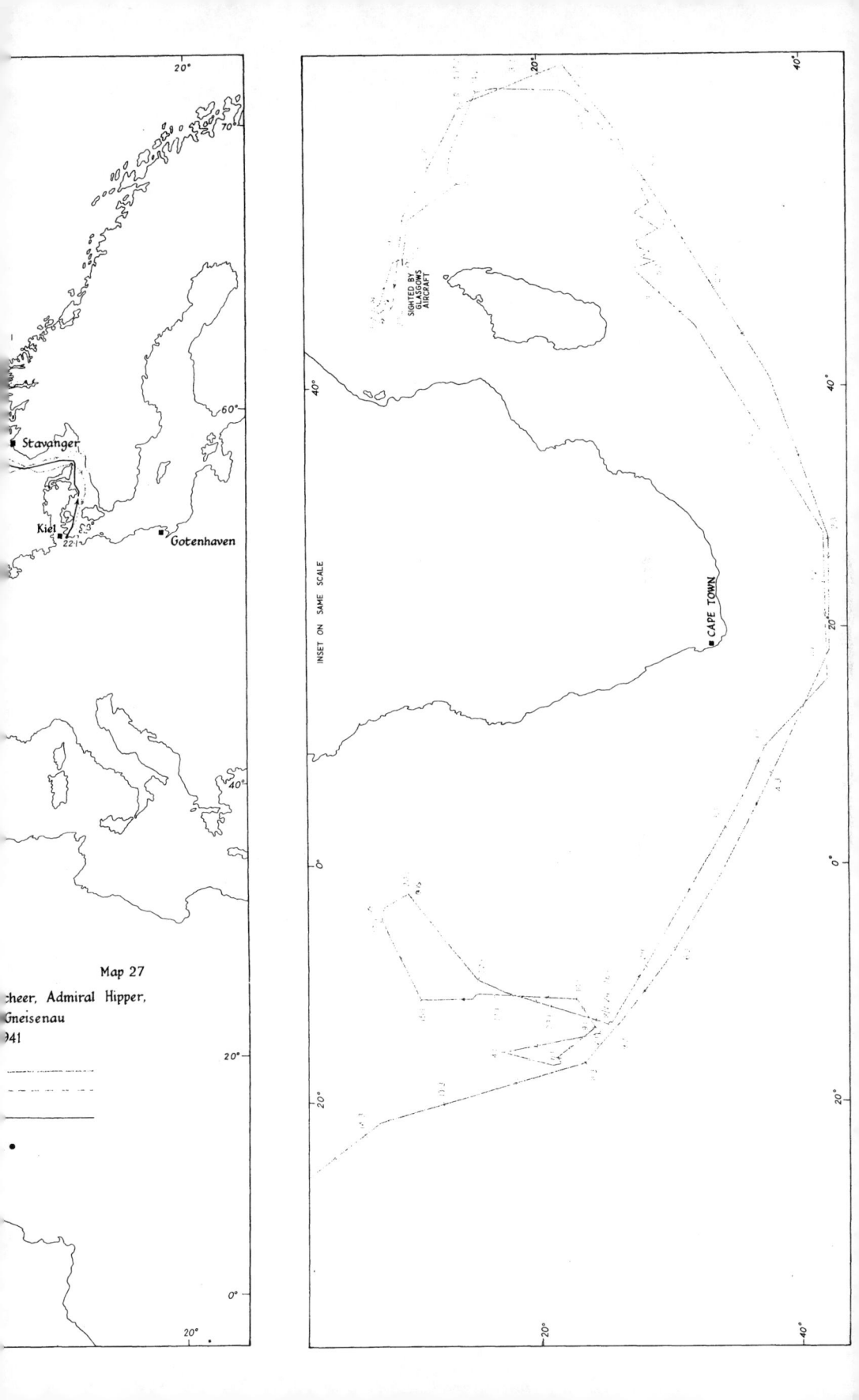

The operations of the enemy's warship raiders and the Admiralty's counter-measures will be considered before the pursuit of the far-flung and elusive armed merchant raiders.

On the 8th of January the *Scheer* moved from the rendezvous in the South Atlantic where she had fuelled and refitted and, acting on information from Germany, first of all searched for the troop convoy (W.S. 5A) which the *Hipper* had unsuccessfully attacked on Christmas Day.[1] She failed, however, to locate it. Nor did her captain desire to become engaged with so powerful an escort as was believed to accompany that convoy. On the 17th of January a loaded Norwegian tanker was captured on the Capetown–Freetown route and sent in prize to Bordeaux. The *Scheer's* captain now changed his tactics and, instead of generally approaching his intended victims by night, adopted the ruse of making the approach in broad daylight while simulating the signals of a British warship. The first success obtained by this means was the capture of the Dutch ship *Barneveld* on the Freetown to Capetown route on the 20th of January.[2] A British ship which happened to be passing through the same waters in the opposite direction was seized a few hours later. The *Scheer's* ruse was so successful that no distress messages were sent by either ship, and for many months the Admiralty remained unaware of the cause of their disappearance.

But the pocket-battleship considered it advisable to leave the neighbourhood of these successes quickly. She therefore steamed back to her mid-ocean rendezvous, where she met the tanker *Nordmark* and also the merchant raider *Thor*. After replenishing her fuel and supplies and transferring the recently captured prisoners, the *Scheer* steamed off south-east, passed far south of the Cape of Good Hope in the early days of February and entered the Indian Ocean. For nearly a week she searched the routes from Australia to the Cape but did not sight a single ship. She did, however, meet the *Atlantis* (Raider C), which had two prizes in company, and a supply ship in 13° South, 64° East, and again filled her tanks to capacity. At this time the enemy's supply and servicing organisation for his raiders was certainly working at a high pitch of efficiency. On the advice of the *Atlantis'* captain the *Scheer* now moved to the northern exit from the Mozambique Channel, used her aircraft for reconnaissance to good purpose and, on the 20th of February, promptly captured a British tanker by employing the ruse which she had used successfully in the South Atlantic. Another victim—a Greek ship—was found the same day and a third on the following day. But the last, the British ship *Canadian Cruiser*, made a raider report before

---

[1] See pp. 291–292.
[2] See Map 27.

she was finally brought to. Another report was sent by the next victim—a Dutch ship attacked on the 22nd—and it was therefore clear that a longer stay in this fruitful area might be dangerous. This and orders recalling her to Germany by the end of March made an early return to the South Atlantic necessary. But before the pocket-battleship had left the region of her recent successes the counter-measures taken by the Commander-in-Chief, East Indies (Vice-Admiral R. Leatham), on the raider reports already mentioned nearly succeeded in intercepting her. The British forces in the area consisted only of the cruisers *Hawkins* and *Australia*, which were escorting the important troop convoy W.S. 5B across the equator north-bound towards Aden; of the light cruiser *Emerald*, which had charge of another Middle East troop convoy further south; of her sister ship the *Enterprise* now steaming towards the reported position of the raider but still many miles to the north; and of the cruiser *Glasgow* which was some 140 miles north-west of the position of the last raider report. The *Glasgow* alone was in a position whence early interception might be possible, but the Commander-in-Chief none the less took steps to release some of the escorts from their convoys to form a hunting group.

Four and a half hours after the Dutch ship made her raider report on the morning of the 22nd of February the *Glasgow's* aircraft sighted the pocket-battleship in 8° 30′ South, 51° 35′ East. The cruiser at once signalled an enemy report. Her intention was 'to attack by night and shadow by day'. By the afternoon the small aircraft carrier *Hermes*, the heavy cruisers *Canberra*, *Australia* and *Shropshire* and the light cruisers *Capetown* and *Emerald* were all moving from various directions towards the *Glasgow*, and the Admiralty, as always on these occasions, had promptly released other ships from their duties to join the hunt. But it was clear that no concentration could be effected for many hours, so great were the distances involved, and that the only hope of catching the enemy lay in the *Glasgow* keeping in touch. That, unfortunately, she failed to do; her aircraft lost contact when visibility became reduced. The *Scheer*, which was not sighted again, actually steamed 100 miles to the east to shake off the pursuit and then resumed a south-westerly course. On the 24th the Commander-in-Chief dispersed the ships involved in the hunt to their normal duties. Meanwhile the pocket-battleship passed 400 miles to the east of Mauritius and then steamed well to the south of the Cape of Good Hope back into the Atlantic without further incident. There she met the tanker *Nordmark* at the previous rendez-vous. The *Pinguin* and *Kormoran* with their own supply ships were also present, and stores and prisoners were exchanged.

On the 11th of March, having completed refitting her engines and cleaning her water-line, the *Scheer* steamed away to the north on her homeward passage. She crossed the equator on the 15th and the Halifax convoy routes on the night of the 22nd–23rd. After waiting two days she found favourable weather for the break-back on the 27th and entered the Denmark Strait. The chief preoccupation of the Commander-in-Chief, Home Fleet, and of the Admiralty at the time of the *Scheer's* return was the search for the battle cruisers *Scharnhorst* and *Gneisenau*, which were at large in the North Atlantic, and the protection of our numerous convoys from their depredations. In consequence many of Admiral Tovey's battleships and cruisers were at the time detached as ocean escorts to the convoys or employed in searching for these powerful and dangerous raiders. The enemy battle cruisers therefore accomplished the subsidiary purpose, planned by the German Naval Staff, of diverting attention from the pocket-battleship's return. The two battle cruisers, however, succeeded in reaching Brest on the 22nd, and the greater part of the Home Fleet thereupon returned to its bases.

But Admiral Tovey was fully conscious of the need to watch the northern exits closely and continuously. He had, in fact, several times represented his anxiety regarding the inadequacy of our patrols in those waters. On the 26th of March he informed the Admiralty that he intended to keep two cruisers on patrol in the northern passages and the *Nigeria* and *Fiji* were sailed for that purpose next day. Unfortunately they were soon diverted elsewhere. On the 28th and 29th the Admiralty warned Admiral Tovey that wireless intelligence indicated a possible break-back by a warship from the south of Iceland on the latter date. The *King George V*, which had been escorting a Halifax convoy, was sent to intercept and four cruisers were ordered to the eastern end of the Iceland–Faeröes mine barrier. Air searches were requested, but bad weather prevented any being flown. But it was in any case too late by forty-eight hours, for the *Scheer* had already passed through those waters and was now off the Norwegian coast. Her anchor was dropped—for the first time in five months—at Bergen on the 30th, and on the 1st of April she reached Kiel. She had steamed 46,419 miles and had demonstrated the excellent qualities of her class for commerce raiding. She claimed to have sunk or captured 151,000 tons of shipping but her actual achievements were the sinking of the *Jervis Bay* and sixteen ships of 99,059 tons.

It will be convenient next to tell the story of the second sortie by the *Hipper*. This ship had reached Brest on the 27th of December 1940 after an unproductive cruise lasting for some three weeks.[1] Our reconnaissance aircraft reported her to be still in harbour on the 1st of February, but on the 4th they failed to locate her. She actually

---

[1] See p. 292.

sailed just after she had been reported still at her berth on the 1st, and steamed to a position some 1,000 miles to the west of Finisterre to fuel and await developments. In contrast to the orders given to her captain for his first cruise, he was this time allowed to attack lightly escorted convoys as well as single ships. But the low endurance of her class was a constant anxiety to the German Naval Staff, which kept the *Hipper* at the refuelling rendezvous until the 9th. When she was given permission to start work she steamed on to the Sierra Leone convoy route between the Azores and the coast of Portugal.[1] On the 11th of February she attacked a single merchant ship, but at dawn next day, in 37° 12′ North, 21° 20′ West, she encountered an unescorted group of nineteen ships (called convoy S.L.S. 64) which had left Freetown on the 30th of January. Among them she was able to play havoc without fear of retribution. She actually sank seven ships totalling 32,806 tons. But her presence had been reported and her fuel was again running low so her captain decided to return at once to Brest, which he approached from the south and so again made port undetected on the 14th. Next day Coastal Command's reconnaissance aircraft reported that the cruiser was back in harbour. Her brief foray southwards and her escape back to Brest were aided by the absence of Force H from Gibraltar at the time; for Admiral Somerville's ships had sailed a short while previously to operate in the central Mediterranean and to carry out a bombardment of Genoa, and the enemy was aware of his movement.[2]

But the German Naval Staff wanted to get the *Hipper* back to Germany to complete her refit and to remedy her constantly recurring defects. She had escaped damage in the numerous bombing attacks made during her previous five weeks' stay in Brest and she now came through more attacks unscathed, although in a heavy raid on the 24th of February fifteen bombs fell within 200 yards of her. The planning of her return was not an easy matter for the German Naval Staff owing to the almost simultaneous break-back of the *Scheer* and the operations of the battle cruisers in the Atlantic. To avoid interfering with the other warships the *Hipper* was ordered to pass through the Denmark Strait ahead of the pocket-battleship; she therefore sailed from Brest on the 15th of March to fuel at a rendezvous south of Greenland. She soon found weather which was sufficiently bad to hamper our patrols and, on the 23rd, she passed through the narrow ice-free passage in the Denmark Strait. Though she sighted that evening what she thought were two patrolling cruisers, she was not detected by them and her evasive action was successful. She fuelled again at Bergen and reached Kiel on the

---

[1] See Map 27 (*facing p. 369*).
[2] See p. 425.

28th of March. No prior intelligence regarding her movement was received by the Admiralty and the patrols of the Northern passages had therefore not been intensified. But the undetected passages home made by the *Scheer* and *Hipper*, when they became known in London, strongly emphasised the need to watch the northern passages more continuously and closely.

The two battle cruisers, now commanded by Admiral Lütjens, sailed from Kiel on the 23rd of January and passed north between the Shetland Islands and Norway. They then turned west with the intention of breaking into the Atlantic south of Iceland. No less than five supply ships had been previously despatched to various ocean meeting places to refuel them. On the 20th of January the Admiralty sent Admiral Tovey warning of the possibility that a raider might be attempting to break out and, in consequence, two cruisers were at once sailed from Scapa to patrol to the west of the Iceland–Faeröes passage. Nothing happened at first, but on the 23rd definite intelligence of the passage of the battle cruisers through the Great Belt on that day was received in London. At midnight on the 25th–26th Admiral Tovey in the *Nelson* with the *Rodney*, *Repulse*, eight cruisers of the 2nd, 15th and 18th Squadrons and eleven destroyers left Scapa for an intercepting position 120 miles south of Iceland, whence both the possible exits to the Atlantic could be covered. Air patrols were also organised to watch the waters between the Faeröe Islands and Iceland. On the 27th Admiral Tovey divided his forces to enable some ships to refuel at Scapa while the remainder continued to patrol in about 62° North, 21° 30′ West. Just before daylight next morning, the 28th, the cruiser *Naiad* sighted and reported two large vessels and turned to keep contact with them. Admiral Tovey at once moved his heavy ships to support the *Naiad* and ordered his other cruisers to spread and search at high speed. But the German ships' radar seems to have produced better results than the sets fitted in the Home Fleet cruisers, and the enemy, in fact, had detected the presence of two of Admiral Tovey's cruiser line some six minutes before the *Naiad* made her sighting. This enabled them to turn away at once and to increase speed, causing the *Naiad* to lose touch. Nor was it ever regained. Though the Commander-in-Chief afterwards concluded that the sighting had been false, we now know that it was the *Scharnhorst* and *Gneisenau* of which the *Naiad* obtained a brief glimpse in the dawn twilight, and that they therefore narrowly escaped running right into Admiral Tovey's force.

Although the German Admiral's orders stated that if he was sighted during the break-out he was to continue on his course and, presumably, accept battle, he turned away to the north and disengaged skilfully at high speed. The enemy ships fuelled again in the Arctic and then made a second attempt, this time by the Denmark

Strait, on the 3rd and 4th of February.[1] On this occasion they got through undetected, for Admiral Tovey, after contact had been lost on the 28th, had first steamed to the west to cover a Halifax convoy and then returned to Scapa on the 30th. The narrow escape of the enemy ships and their subsequent successful break-out were all the more disappointing because, for the first time, accurate intelligence had enabled the Home Fleet to take up a favourable position in good time. From the enemy's point of view there was good reason for satisfaction over the successful start of Admiral Lütjens' cruise and for Raeder's congratulatory signal on his accomplishment. On the 5th and 6th the German ships fuelled at a rendezvous off southern Greenland and then at once started to search the Halifax convoy route. At dawn on the 8th of February the masts of an eastbound convoy were sighted. This was convoy H.X. 106 which, in accordance with the Admiralty's new policy of providing battleship escort to as many ocean convoys as possible, was accompanied by the *Ramillies*. The German squadron divided in order to attack simultaneously from the north and south and it was the *Scharnhorst* which, at 9.47 a.m., sighted the fighting top of the escort. This at once altered matters; Lütjens broke away without engaging and the convoy proceeded on its journey unharmed. But the *Ramillies*, having sighted only one ship and that at long range, could not give the Admiralty exact intelligence of the enemies which had threatened her charges. She signalled that she had sighted what was possibly a *Hipper* class cruiser, which fitted in well with the expectation that the *Hipper* herself, or possibly the *Scheer*, might attempt a break-back by the northern passage at this time. Such, in fact, was Admiral Tovey's immediate appreciation of the situation, and he accordingly sailed all his available forces to the west to take up positions from which the return routes could best be watched and covered. Air searches were also arranged, and the Admiralty issued the customary orders diverting other ships to the waters where they might be needed. By the evening of the 9th these forces, organised in three powerful separate groups, were all favourably disposed to intercept the enemy, if he took the expected course.

But Admiral Lütjens, after breaking contact with convoy H.X. 106, remained quiet in or near his fuelling rendezvous until the 17th of February, when he resumed operations against the Halifax route. So far his squadron had accomplished nothing, but he now intended to try his luck further west, in 45–50° longitude, where he considered that our shipping would be less strongly protected. His hope was, to some extent, well founded. Though powerful escorts now accompanied many eastbound convoys throughout the length of their

---

[1] See Map 27 (*facing p. 369*).

journeys the westbound convoys had to be dispersed to their various destinations on the North American seaboard approximately in the longitude selected by Lütjens for his second attempt. Soon after sunrise on the 22nd the smoke of a number of ships was sighted about 500 miles east of Newfoundland. They had recently dispersed from an outward-bound convoy, and, as they were scattered over a considerable area of ocean, the raiders were able to attack them in succession. Five ships, totalling 25,784 tons, were sunk, but raider reports were made by several of them. Although the enemy used the usual jamming technique one message was picked up at Cape Race station, and within a few minutes the Admiralty knew that powerful surface raiders were for the first time working off the North American coast. Admiral Lütjens realised that an alarm would be raised and shipping diverted from these waters, so he now moved south, fuelled in mid-Atlantic between the 26th and 28th, and then shifted to the Sierra Leone route. His squadron will be left, temporarily, making its passage southwards.

It was mentioned earlier that, towards the end of February, four submarines of the T class and the depot ship *Forth* were transferred from the Home Fleet to Halifax.[1] The large Free French submarine *Surcouf* was also sent there at this time. The use of a submarine as additional escort to convoys had first been tried in 1939 when the *Graf Spee* had been at large and had since been continued on the Gibraltar route. It was hoped that the submarine might be able to use her torpedoes against a raider which approached the convoy, or, possibly, against an attacking U-boat. Her presence was also deemed to be of some moral value in showing the crews of the merchant ships that the ocean escort—possibly one slow and vulnerable armed merchant cruiser—was not their only defence from surface ship attack. But the chance of a powerful and fast warship raider approaching within striking distance of the submarine was, in reality, remote and, moreover, the friendly submarine was a source of anxiety to our own anti-submarine escort vessels when they were with the convoy. The revival of the practice in 1941 was therefore short-lived, but it was tried again later when our Russian convoys were threatened by enemy warships in the far north. It never achieved any success and seems, in retrospect, to have been an incorrect employment of our submarine strength, all of which would have been better used on offensive patrols off the enemy-held coastline.

Returning now to Admiral Lütjens' squadron, which we left southward-bound to the Sierra Leone convoy route, the next incident occurred on the 8th of March when the *Malaya's* patrolling aircraft sighted the enemy battle cruisers about 350 miles to the north of the

---

[1] See p. 334.

Cape Verde Islands.[1] They were also briefly sighted by the *Malaya* herself, which was escorting convoy S.L. 67, but again the German Admiral forbore to attack a convoy escorted by a single battleship. As Lütjens knew that he had been sighted and reported, he now left the Sierra Leone route and, after sinking one independently-routed ship on the 9th, fuelled again in mid-ocean. He was now ready to make another attack on the Halifax route.

Meanwhile the Admiralty and Admiral Tovey were doing all they could to cover the convoys and to catch the battle cruisers if they broke for home. The *Rodney* and *King George V* were sent from home to cover two convoys due to leave Halifax on the 17th and 21st and, when wireless intelligence indicated a possible break-back, the Commander-in-Chief in the *Nelson* with the *Nigeria* and two destroyers took up a position to the south of Iceland.

But Admiral Lütjens kept his two supply ships with him to extend his band of vision as he steamed north and, on the 15th and 16th of March, thus obtained his biggest success. No less than sixteen ships from recently dispersed convoys, totalling some 82,000 tons, were sunk or captured between 40° and 46° North and 43° to 46° West—some distance south of the position off Newfoundland where he had made his earlier attack.[2] The Admiralty received many raider reports from the attacked ships, and on the evening of the 16th the *Rodney* briefly sighted the enemy. The *King George V* was at once ordered to leave Halifax and cover the threatened area, while Admiral Tovey strengthened his cruiser patrols in the northern passages against a possible break-back and kept what remained to him of the Home Fleet in the covering position south of Iceland. But all was in vain, for Admiral Lütjens had been told to be clear of the North Atlantic by the 17th of March in order to facilitate the return of the *Scheer* and *Hipper* to Germany. Moreover the German Naval Staff had still larger ambitions and needed his ships to work with the *Bismarck* and *Prinz Eugen* in the following month. He therefore broke off his foray and made for Brest.

The wireless reports of the ships attacked on the 15th and 16th, the accounts of survivors rescued by the *Rodney* on the evening of the latter day and her own brief sighting of the enemy squadron, made it appear virtually certain to the Admiralty that it was the two battle cruisers which had again appeared in the western Atlantic. But identifying the enemy squadron did not make it any easier to arrive at a correct estimate of its probable future movements, and so to dispose our forces in the most favourable positions to intercept it. All recent experience suggested that the enemy raiders would, after completing their foray, attempt to return to Germany by one or

---
[1] See Map 27 (*facing p. 369*).
[2] See Map 27.

other of the northern passages, and it was upon those waters that attention was concentrated during the succeeding days. The Home Fleet's dispositions were based on this assumption, as were the Admiralty's requests to Coastal Command for air reconnaissance and patrols. From the 17th to the 20th intense patrolling was accordingly carried out over the Denmark Strait and the Iceland-Faeröes passage. But at 5.30 p.m. on the latter date a reconnaissance aircraft from the *Ark Royal* of Force H, which had been called north from Gibraltar by the Admiralty, sighted the two battle cruisers about 600 miles west-north-west of Finisterre. We now know that as soon as he was sighted Admiral Lütjens turned from his north-easterly course to due north with the deliberate object of misleading the pursuit; he returned to his first course as soon as the shadowing aircraft had disappeared. The ruse was successful, because a series of accidents combined to prevent knowledge of the enemy's course on first sighting reaching Admiral Somerville at once. The aircraft could not make an immediate report because her wireless had failed; she therefore returned to make a visual report. The latter was signalled as she passed the *Renown* on her way to the *Ark Royal* but, unhappily, gave the enemy's course as north and did not say that it had first been north-east. The enemy's course on first sighting was not mentioned until after the aircraft had landed on; nor did the carrier, which had become separated from the flagship by about twenty miles, immediately signal it to the Admiral, who was thus deprived for some hours of intelligence which might have given him the right clue to the enemy's destination.

Although Coastal Command's patrols were adjusted to cover the approaches to the Bay of Biscay as soon as it was known that the enemy had been sighted, it was not until the following day that his probable destination was correctly guessed in London. When the *Ark Royal's* aircraft made the first sighting at 5.30 p.m. on the 20th, Admiral Somerville was about 160 miles to the south-east, too far away to launch a striking force immediately. It was therefore urgently necessary to keep in touch while the carrier endeavoured to close. Unfortunately low visibility prevented night shadowing or attack by carrier-borne aircraft, and next morning conditions were little better. Contact was thus lost almost as soon as it had been made. Admiral Somerville's disappointment was intense. As he wrote to a brother Flag Officer 'it was extremely unlucky that we did not sight them earlier in the afternoon. Goodness knows how many thousands of miles the boys have flown looking for those two ships'.

The brief sighting did, of course, re-direct the Admiralty's attention from the northern passages to the Bay of Biscay, and our forces were redisposed accordingly on the 21st. The *Hood* and *Queen Elizabeth* had just joined Admiral Tovey's *Nelson* on patrol south of Iceland and the Admiralty ordered him to steer south at full speed with all three ships.[1] Coastal Command's air patrols over the waters of Biscay were intensified, and Bomber Command formed a striking force of twenty-five Wellingtons to attack as soon as contact was regained. Cruisers from the 10th and 18th Squadrons were also ordered to concentrate to the south. But unless the *Ark Royal's* torpedo-bombers could slow down the enemy—which possibility had been eliminated by ill luck and by the bad weather on the 20th and 21st—the chances of catching him were now slight, for Admiral Tovey's heavy ships were many hundreds of miles behind, and the German squadron was rapidly approaching waters where it would be protected by shore-based aircraft. The enemy's intentions had been recognised too late.

The German squadron was sighted once more at sea, by a Hudson of No. 220 Squadron of Coastal Command on the evening of the 21st, but by that time it was within 200 miles of the French coast and the last chance of intercepting it had faded away. The two battle cruisers entered Brest on the morning of the 22nd, but they were not definitely sighted there until six days later, after Coastal Command had scoured all the French ports between Cherbourg and Bordeaux for them. The weather was generally unfavourable to air reconnaissance and Admiral Lütjens had disguised his real destination with skill right up to the last hours of his approach to the French coast.

Once the enemy squadron was known to have reached port the normal movements of Atlantic shipping were restarted, and the Home Fleet returned for a short time to Scapa or the Clyde. Admiral Tovey was then immediately called on to provide powerful escorts for convoys proceeding overseas and, in particular, for the Middle East troop convoys. Force H returned to Gibraltar and then patrolled the north-south convoy route, to which the *Hood*, *Fiji* and *Nigeria* were also sent at the end of the month. All the available submarines were disposed off Brest and across the Bay of Biscay, and Coastal Command intensified its watch on the port. The heaviest possible scale of air attack on the two battle cruisers was asked for, and all preparations to deal with an attempt to break-back to Germany were put in hand. During the succeeding days the Admiralty maintained three or four separate forces, each comprising one or more capital ships with cruisers or destroyers in company, disposed so as to intercept the enemy should he come out. But a blockade of such nature imposes a tremendous strain on the forces involved and it

---

[1] Neither of the newly joined ships was in proper operational condition at the time. The *Hood* had recently completed a long-deferred refit and was running trials. The *Queen Elizabeth* had only arrived at Scapa to begin trials after a long refit and rearmament on the 21st of February. But the urgency was considered such as to justify the employment of ships which were unlikely to develop their full fighting capacity if an action were to take place.

cannot be sustained for long periods. On the 19th of April a new anxiety was added by a report that the *Bismarck* and light forces had passed the Skaw steering north-west the previous day. The patrols in the northern passages then had to be strengthened and the *Hood* was sent to support the cruisers there. Thus ended the first and only foray made by the German battle cruisers against our Atlantic shipping.

Before turning again to the outer oceans it will be appropriate to summarise the results achieved by the battle cruisers and the lessons learnt from our unsuccessful pursuit. In a cruise lasting from the 23rd of January to the 22nd of March they not only sank or captured twenty-two ships of 115,622 tons but also, for a time, completely dislocated our Atlantic convoy cycles, with serious consequences to our vital imports. Their depredations forced the wide dispersal of our already strained naval resources, and successfully diverted attention from the returning *Scheer* and *Hipper*; while, by their subsequent arrival in a Biscay port, they became an imminent threat to all our Atlantic shipping. Their foray had been skilfully planned, well co-ordinated with the movements of other raiders and successfully sustained by the supply ships sent out for the purpose. Their final withdrawal from the Atlantic to Brest had been cleverly carried out; and the measures of evasion and deception employed were to a large degree successful. Admiral Raeder's congratulatory message to Lütjens was certainly well merited and the jubilation of the German Naval Staff over the results accomplished appeared to be well founded. They were not to know for some months yet that this sortie would mark the peak of German surface ship activity and success.

From the British point of view our counter-measures had certainly been haunted by bad luck. From the *Naiad's* sighting on the 28th of January, which might have led to the early defeat of the enemy's plan, to the frustration of the *Ark Royal's* shadowers and striking force on the 20th and 21st of March the goddess of fortune had consistently favoured the enemy. Yet there were several not unimportant factors which could be counted as favourable to our cause. Our watch over the northern exits—for so long urged by Admirals Forbes and Tovey as paramount—was at last improving; our intelligence had, for the first time, given early and accurate warning of the enemy's probable intentions; the Admiralty's policy of giving as many convoys as possible close escort by battleships had certainly saved two of them from disaster; the increasing skill and intensity of Coastal Command's reconnaissance searches promised that any attempts to repeat the operation would be still more hazardous; and Bomber Command was beginning to bring a heavy weight of attack to bear on the bases in western France which the enemy desired to use for his surface ships. The operation taught many lessons, and they were put to good account a few weeks later when a similar but even more serious threat arose.

It was mentioned earlier how, after the enemy had gained possession of the French Atlantic bases, the safety of the Spanish and Portuguese Atlantic Islands (the Canaries, Azores and Cape Verde Islands) became a matter of great concern to the Admiralty.[1] Not only would an enemy landing on them threaten the whole safety of our Atlantic convoy routes but, if the Germans invaded Spain and captured Gibraltar, or deprived us of its use as a base, those islands were the only possible alternative from which we could command the western approaches to the Mediterranean and secure the all-important route to the Cape of Good Hope. As the Admiralty said in a review of our maritime strategy sent to all Commanders-in-Chief in mid-August, 'if the Germans decide to move into Spain we should almost certainly find ourselves unable to use Gibraltar . . . . Only in the Canaries is it possible to find a suitable alternative. We cannot therefore afford to be without either the one or the other, and the occupation of the Canaries is a commitment for which we have constantly to be prepared'. It has already been mentioned that Hitler's views about the Atlantic islands were the same as our own; he wanted to seize them, but Raeder warned him of the impossibility of holding them in the face of British maritime power. The British Government and Admiralty had, however, to be ready to forestall any such attempt.

Plans to occupy the Canaries were therefore prepared by the Director of Combined Operations and on the 9th of April 1941 they received Cabinet approval, though the Government reserved to itself the right to order the sailing of the expedition.

The forces and shipping were therefore assembled, naval and military commanders were appointed and rehearsals for the landings were carried out in Scotland. On the 15th of May it was decided to hold the forces at seven days' notice to sail.

As the expedition never actually left this country for the Atlantic islands, it is unnecessary to go into details, but a few figures will show how large a commitment it would have been and how such an enterprise tends to absorb more and more ships and men as its planning progresses. Originally 10,000 men were to be sent in five transports, but in July the number of troops was doubled to enable the other Atlantic islands to be dealt with after the Canaries. The naval forces were to consist of one battleship, three aircraft carriers, three cruisers and nineteen destroyers.

At the end of July the threat to Gibraltar seemed less imminent, so the Chiefs of Staff advised postponing the operation until Septem-

---

[1] See pp. 272–273 and Maps 23 (*facing p. 273*) and 28 (*facing p. 381*).

THE AZORES

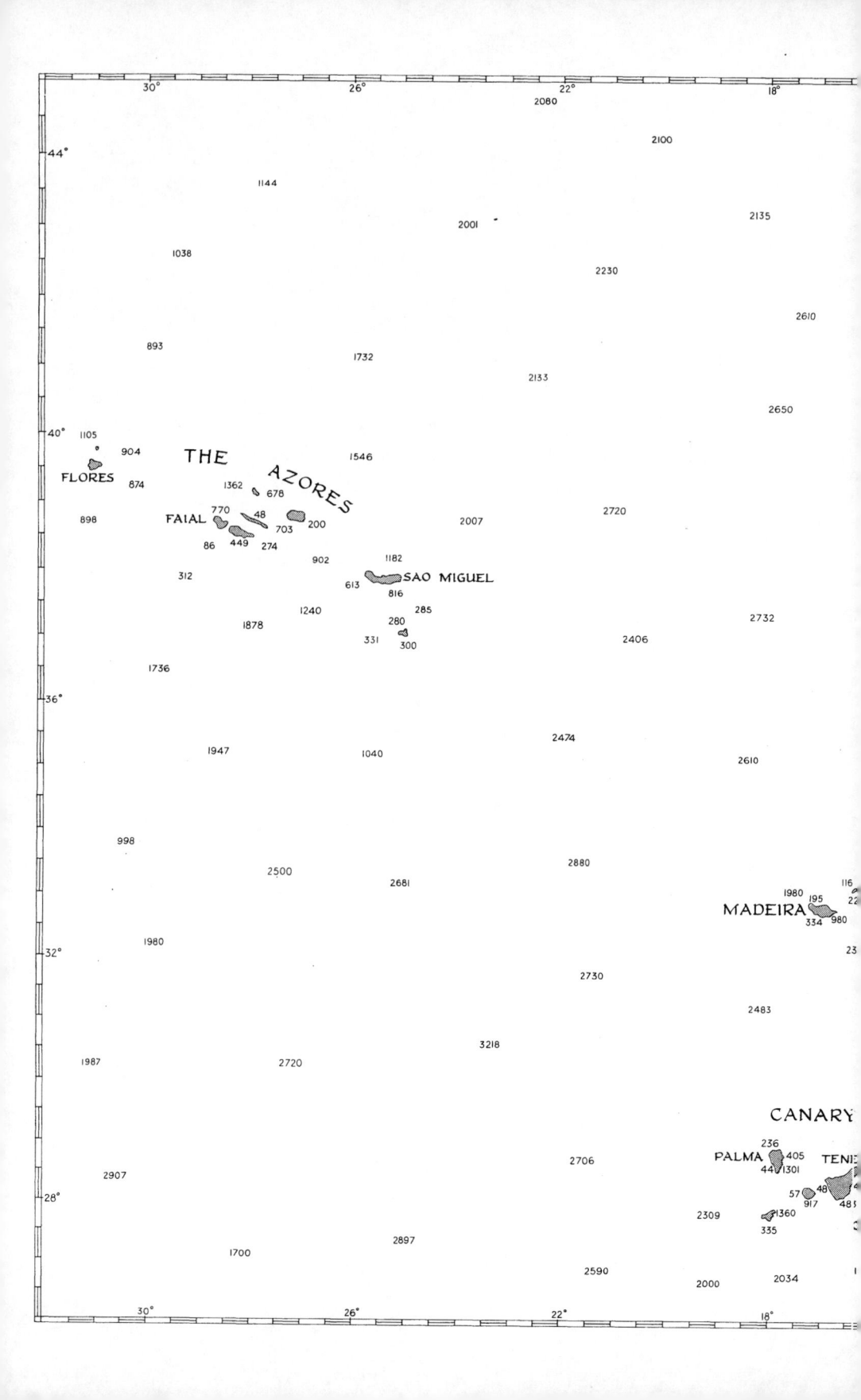

FLORES

FAIAL

SAO MIGUEL

MADEIRA

CANARY

PALMA **TENE**

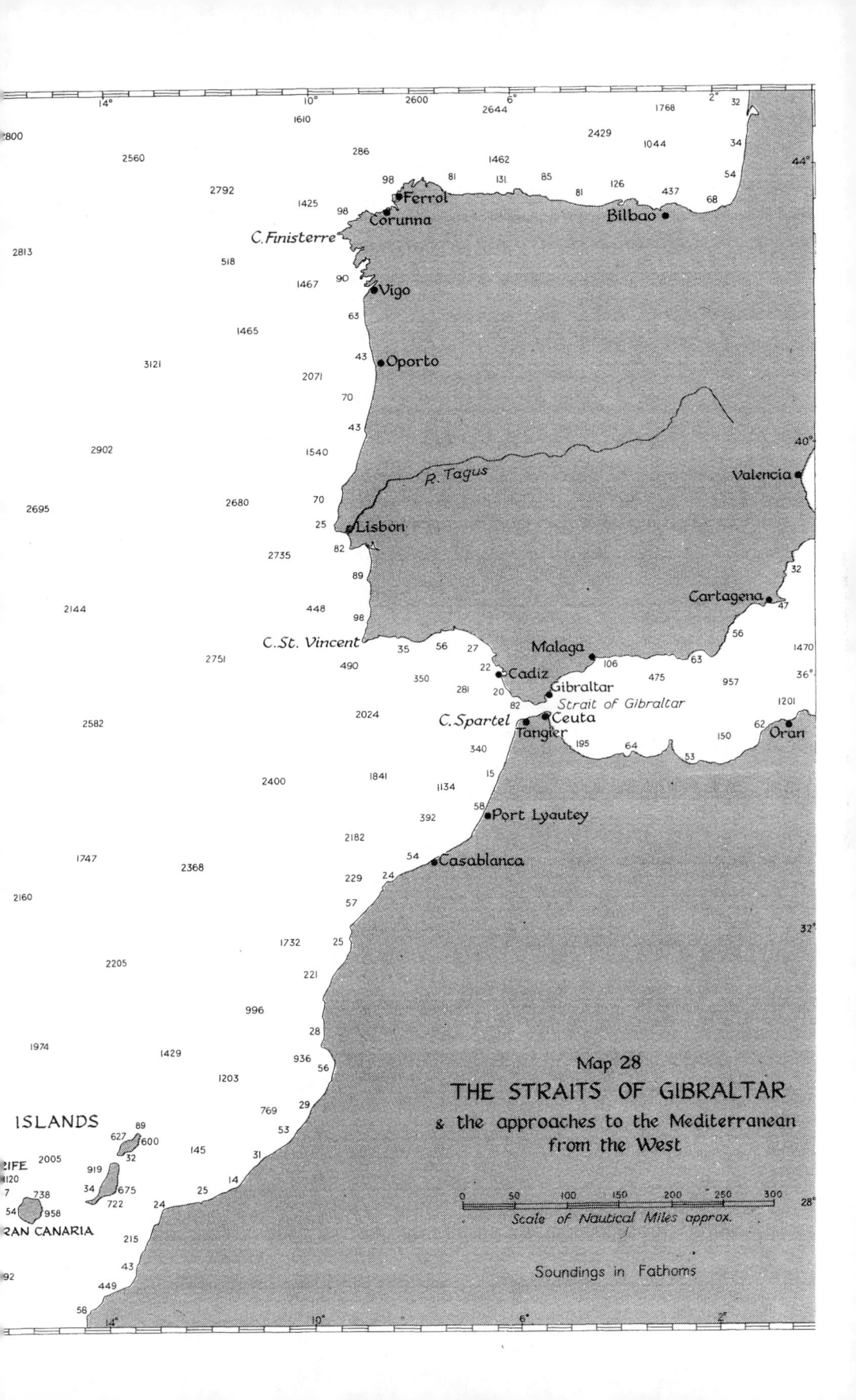

Map 28
THE STRAITS OF GIBRALTAR
& the approaches to the Mediterranean from the West

Scale of Nautical Miles approx.

Soundings in Fathoms

ber and the Cabinet accepted their view. The safety of the Atlantic islands, which figured prominently in the Admiralty's cares and responsibilities during the first six months of 1941, thus receded from the forefront of our strategic thoughts as it became clearer that General Franco intended to procrastinate about joining the Axis and would not allow German troops to pass through Spain to attack Gibraltar. But it was fortunate for us that we did not have to accept the heavy overseas commitment which 'Operation Puma' would certainly have constituted at a time when the threat to our vital trade routes was serious and our maritime forces stretched to the limit.

While the German warships were causing great anxiety and serious dislocation to the Atlantic routes, the armed merchant raiders were continuing their depredations in the outer oceans and it is to their activities that we must now return.

In mid-January the *Atlantis* (Raider C) was ready, after her refit at Kerguelen, to continue her cruise and she made, firstly, a short journey along the route between Australia and Capetown.[1] She had no success, so she soon moved to the north of Madagascar and from the 23rd of January to the 3rd of February worked there and in the vicinity of Seychelles. In those waters she first sank the British ship *Mandasor* after using her aircraft to bomb and machine-gun her victim, and then captured the *Speybank*, which she surprised in a night attack. The latter ship, with a prize crew on board, was kept as an additional supply ship; she was successfully brought back to Bordeaux, renamed *Doggerbank* and fitted out as an armed minelayer and U-boat supply ship. Her varied career lasted until March 1943 when she was sunk in error by a German U-boat in the Atlantic.

On the 27th of January, when the *Atlantis* was cruising some 600 miles to the north of Seychelles, she sighted a big ship on the horizon which she identified, we now know incorrectly, as the *Queen Mary*.[2] The raider guessed that she was carrying troops to Africa, but as the liner herself was probably heavily armed and likely to have cruiser escort the *Atlantis*' captain bore away at once. His log for that day contains the significant remark that 'in the course of conversation' the captain of one of the British ships previously sunk by the raider 'confirmed that the *Queen Mary* was continuously transporting troops in this area and was always accompanied by a small cruiser'. The pocket-battleship *Scheer* was, at this time, in the South Atlantic and

---

[1] See Map 29 (*facing p. 383*).

[2] The *Queen Mary* was at Sydney at the time of this incident. The liner sighted by the raider may have been the *Strathaird*, which left Bombay for Capetown on the 24th of January.

would soon enter the Indian Ocean. The intelligence thus gratuitously provided to the enemy might have given her the chance of attacking one of our great troop convoys.

The next ship sighted by the *Atlantis* was the British *Troilus*, which was keeping a very good look out and was wary of allowing any strange ship to approach her closely. Her alertness and the possession of a good turn of speed enabled her to escape from the raider, but next day, the 2nd of February, the Norwegian tanker *Ketty Brövig* was surprised by night, captured and retained by the raider for supply purposes. A month later, however, she and the supply ship *Coburg* were both intercepted by the cruisers *Leander* and *Canberra* in the Indian Ocean. This marked the end of the *Atlantis*' successes until April, though she continued to cruise in the Indian Ocean and met the *Scheer* in mid-February during the pocket-battleship's brief foray into the same waters.[1] On the last day of March she received congratulatory messages from Admiral Raeder on completing a year's raiding; and decorations were liberally distributed to the ship's entire crew. Early in April she shifted to the South Atlantic, where her first victim was the Egyptian liner *Zamzam*, en route from New York to Suez, which was sunk on the 17th. The 220 passengers, including 135 American citizens, were transferred to the supply ship *Dresden*.

The *Atlantis* continued to work in the South Atlantic in May and sank the British ship *Rabaul* on the England to Capetown route on the 14th; but three days later she had a narrow escape when, at night, she sighted two warships which she correctly identified as the *Nelson* and *Eagle* in 19° 07′ South, 4° 42′ East. The raider took clever evasive action and escaped undetected from what her captain described as 'a most unpleasant position'. Still on the Cape route, she surprised by night and sank, on the 24th of May, the British ship *Trafalgar* bound for Alexandria by the Cape, and on the 17th of June the *Tottenham* bound for the same destination. But the latter ship managed to get a raider report through to Ascension Island and other stations. On the 21st of June the raider learnt that her supply ship, the *Babitonga*, had been intercepted that day. This was, in fact, only one of many such successes achieved during this month in a series of farflung searches organised by the Admiralty to disrupt the enemy's system of supplying his surface raiders and U-boats at ocean rendezvous. They will be referred to in greater detail later.[2] One more victim—the British ship *Balzac*—was obtained in the South Atlantic during June, but she fought the raider and sent a wireless report before she was destroyed. This fact, and knowledge of our recent successes against supply ships, made the *Atlantis*' captain change his theatre of operations once more and he steamed away to the south,

---

[1] See p. 369.
[2] See pp. 542–544.

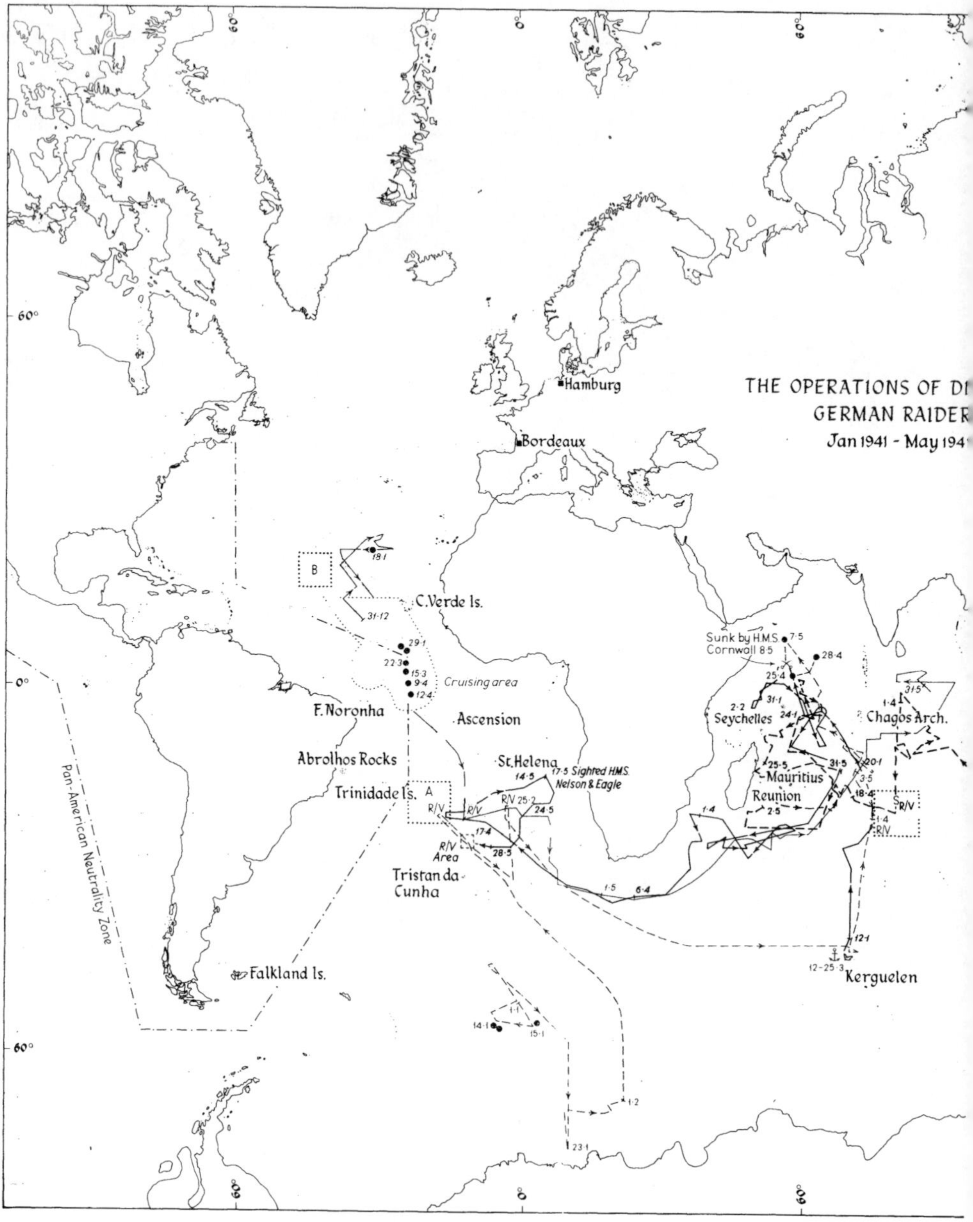
THE OPERATIONS OF
GERMAN
Jan 1941 - May
Hamburg
Bordeaux
C.Verde Is.
Cruising area
F. Noronha
Ascension
Abrolhos Rocks
Trinidade Is.
St.Helena
17·5 Sighted H.M.S. Nelson & Eagle
R/V Area
Tristan da Cunha
Falkland Is.
Pan-American Neutrality Zone
Sunk by H.M.S. Cornwall 8·5
Seychelles
Chagos Arch.
Mauritius
Reunion
Kerguelen

Map 29

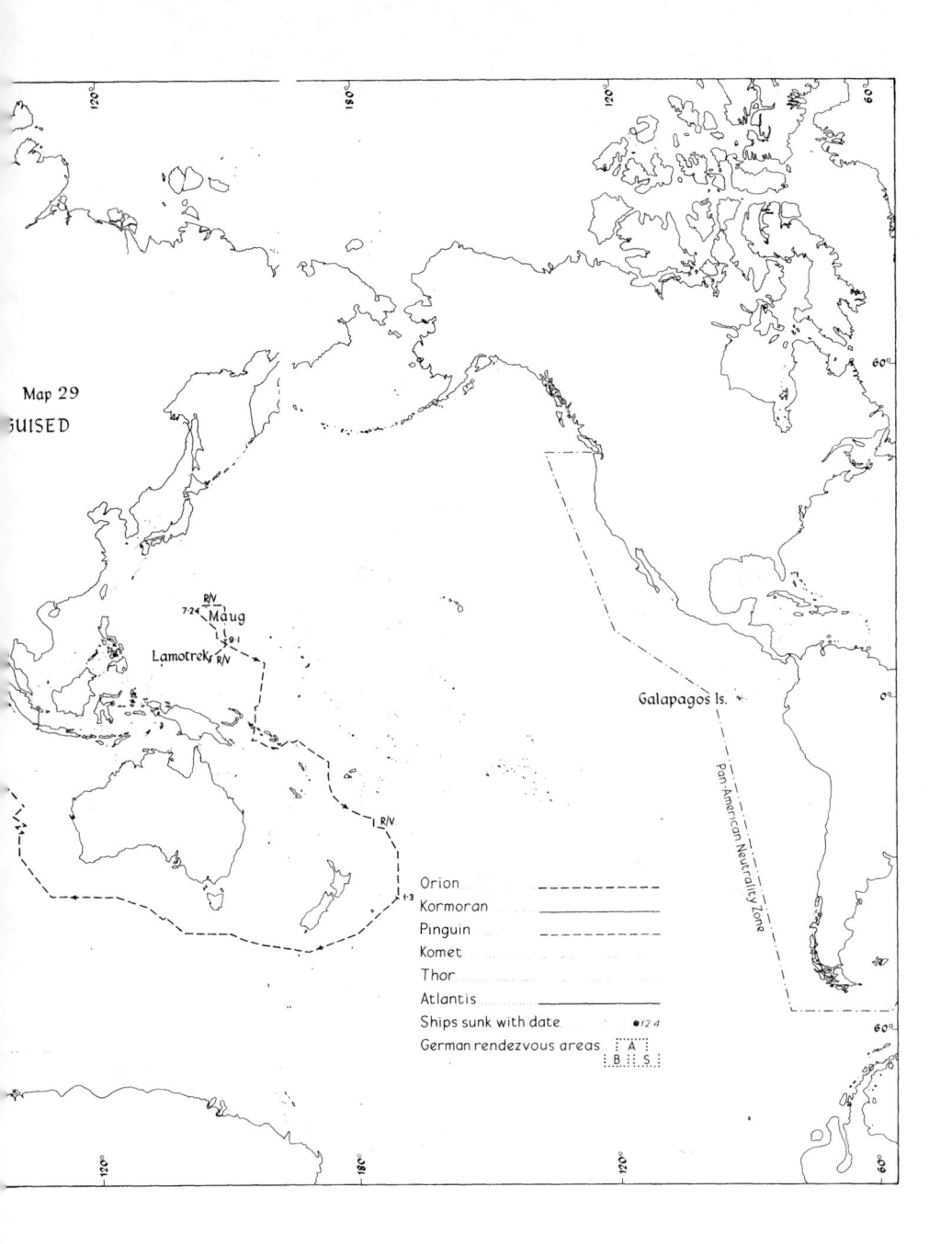

GUISED

Maug
Lamotrek

Galapagos Is.

Pan-American Neutrality Zone

Orion ----------
Kormoran ----------
Pinguin ----------
Komet
Thor
Atlantis
Ships sunk with date   ● 12.4
German rendezvous areas   A
                          B   S

firstly, to a rendezvous with the *Orion* (Raider A) and then to make for the Pacific via the Indian Ocean.

Though the *Atlantis* was not finally brought to book for nearly another six months her long career of useful service to the enemy was now nearly over, for she only sank one more ship. During the phase with which we are now concerned she sank or captured eight ships totalling 47,101 tons and her accomplishments since the beginning of her cruise in March 1940 were twenty-one ships of 140,904 tons.

The *Orion* (Raider A), the second ship to leave German waters, started to refit in the Mariana Islands on the 12th of January and was not ready to resume her cruise until the 6th of February. She then passed through the Solomon Islands and south of New Zealand and Australia into the Indian Ocean. But the *Scheer*, *Atlantis* and *Pinguin* had all been working recently in these waters, and in consequence of their depredations our shipping had been widely diverted from its normal routes. The *Orion* therefore achieved no successes, and we now know that she herself was nearly caught when, on the 18th of May, her aircraft sighted a British cruiser on a converging course only forty-five miles away. The raider at once made a big alteration of course and slipped away at high speed. The ship sighted by her aircraft must have been either the *Cornwall* or the *Glasgow*, both of which had recently sailed from Mauritius to search for raiders to the north-east. It was not the first time that a raider's aircraft saved her parent ship from detection.[1] In this case the escape was very narrow, for the *Orion* herself sighted smoke little more than twenty miles away that same afternoon. Moreover on the 10th of May she learnt that the *Pinguin* (Raider F) had been sunk by the cruiser *Cornwall* two days earlier midway between Seychelles and Socotra.[2] In mid-June she passed round the Cape of Good Hope into the Atlantic and, as already mentioned, met the *Atlantis* north of Tristan da Cunha on the 1st of July. She had now cruised for nearly six months without accomplishing anything.

The *Thor* (Raider E) was far more successful than the *Orion* during the present phase. She had already engaged and escaped from two of our armed merchant cruisers and was still at work in the South Atlantic at the beginning of 1941.[3] But it was not until March that she swelled the total of her victims. In that month she sank one British and one Swedish ship in the central Atlantic, north of the equator, and on the 4th of April she had a third engagement with a British armed merchant cruiser and sank the *Voltaire* (Captain J. A. P. Blackburn) which had left Trinidad for Freetown early in the month with orders to search two areas west of the Cape Verde Islands on the

---

[1] See p. 113.
[2] See Maps 29 and 34 (*facing p. 426*).
[3] See p. 285.

way. As soon as the Germans announced this success another ship, the Canadian armed merchant cruiser *Prince David*, was sent to search the *Voltaire's* route; the sighting of large quantities of wreckage in a position midway between Trinidad and the Cape Verde Islands seemed to confirm the German claim. But the truth was not learnt until much later, when survivors from the *Voltaire* were repatriated from Germany. It then became known that the much weaker and slower British ship had fought a gallant action against her adversary, one of whose first hits put her wireless out of action and prevented an enemy report being transmitted. The *Voltaire* was soon enveloped in flames but continued to fight back until, about two hours after the action started, she sank. The *Thor* herself received some, though not serious, damage. She rescued 197 survivors, including the *Voltaire's* captain. The policy of fitting slow and vulnerable liners with a few obsolete weapons and sending them out to act as trade route cruisers thus suffered the inevitable nemesis. But our shortage of cruisers had been so acute that the Admiralty could not find any more effective means of increasing their numbers, and the necessary modern guns and equipment to give the converted liners even a reasonable chance of engaging a German raider successfully simply did not exist in 1939.

The *Thor* secured one more victim—a Swedish ship—on the 16th of April, which brought her total sinkings to eleven merchantmen of 83,301 tons and the *Voltaire*. She reached the Bay of Biscay on the 23rd of April and passed undetected up-Channel to Hamburg where she arrived on the 30th. In 1942 she reappeared on a second cruise, but this and her ultimate destruction will be told in a later volume.

The *Pinguin* (Raider F) was last encountered at a mid-Atlantic rendezvous with the *Scheer* during the first days of January, and it has been mentioned that she then steamed far to the south to attack the Allied whaling fleets in the Antarctic.[1] In this she was very successful for, on the 14th and 15th, she captured three Norwegian whale-oil factory ships, each of some 12,000 tons, and eleven of their attendant whale-catchers—a substantial success for an armed merchant raider to achieve single handed. She reappeared in the Indian Ocean in April and sank three British ships just to the north of the equator. Her last victim, the tanker *British Emperor*, was sunk on the 7th of May in 8° 30′ North, 56° 25′ East, but managed to send a raider report. It was picked up by the cruiser *Cornwall* (Captain P. C. W. Manwaring), then 500 miles away to the south on passage from Mombasa towards Seychelles. For the first time one of the many raider reports wirelessed by attacked merchant vessels at imminent peril to themselves was to bring the retribution for which they called. The cruiser at once turned to the north to close the area in which the

---

[1] See p. 286.

raider had been reported and then, using both her aircraft, started a systematic search in the direction of the enemy's most probable movement.

By the small hours of the next day, the 8th, the *Cornwall* was very close to the raider, which actually sighted her—or detected her by radar—and immediately turned away. At dawn the cruiser's aircraft were again launched and at 7 a.m. one of them sighted a suspicious ship which identified herself as the Norwegian *Tamerlane*, which she closely resembled. The *Cornwall* turned on to a closing course and, using her aircraft to keep in touch, approached the suspicious ship at high speed. Just after 4 p.m. the cruiser herself sighted the *Pinguin*, which thereupon started to send raider reports purporting to come from the *Tamerlane*. The *Cornwall*, still uncertain as to whether the ship might not be a genuine Allied merchant ship trying to escape from what she believed to be an enemy warship, twice ordered her to heave to and twice fired warning rounds. At 5.15 p.m. when the *Cornwall* was uncomfortably close, the raider realised that the game was up, discarded her disguise and opened a rapid and accurate fire with her 5·9-inch guns, one round of which hit the cruiser and put her steering out of action temporarily. After a short delay the *Cornwall's* gunfire became accurate and at 5.26 the raider blew up. Twenty-two British or Indian prisoners and sixty German survivors were rescued. The methods employed by the *Cornwall* in shadowing, trying to identify and in closing the raider were the subject of some adverse Admiralty comment. The action certainly emphasised the skill with which such enemy ships disguised their identity, the serious dilemma in which the captain of a ship was placed while trying to pierce the disguise, and the danger of approaching such a ship—which must possess the tactical advantage of surprise—too closely and on bearings favourable to her gun and torpedo fire. These difficult questions were by no means easily solved. Ultimately all Allied ships were given secret call signs and, as a further insurance, a system was introduced whereby an intercepting warship at once called the Admiralty to verify whether a suspicious ship actually was what she claimed to be. These measures succeeded largely in solving the doubt regarding identity, but they were not introduced until many months ahead; meanwhile the uncertainties from which the *Cornwall's* captain suffered were reproduced in many other contacts between British warships and ships which sometimes turned out to be friendly merchant vessels and sometimes were discovered, much later, to have been raiders or enemy supply ships.

The *Pinguin's* active career had lasted for about ten months and she sank or captured twenty-eight ships of 136,551 tons.

The sixth and last ship of the first wave of raiders—the *Komet* (Raider B)—had, after the second attack on Nauru at the end of

December 1940, passed far to the south of New Zealand and Australia to Kerguelen Island in the southern Indian Ocean, where she met the *Pinguin* and a supply ship early in March 1941. In May she met one of the Norwegian whale-catchers captured by the *Pinguin* in the Antarctic in the previous January and fitted her out as a minelayer. This small auxiliary was used to mine the approaches to important ports in New Zealand in June. The *Komet* meanwhile cruised off the west coast of Australia until the end of May.[1] Since December 1940 she had steamed 36,000 miles and had accomplished virtually nothing. Her active career was to last for another five months and she succeeded in getting back to Germany in November 1941. The rest of her story must be deferred to a later chapter.

The *Kormoran* (Raider G), the first ship of the second wave of raiders, had only just started her cruise at the beginning of the year, after breaking out by the Denmark Strait in mid-December 1940. She secured her first victim—a Greek ship—in the central Atlantic on the 6th of January and twelve days later attacked by night and sank the tanker *British Union*, which, however, transmitted a raider report. The armed merchant cruiser *Arawa* was in the vicinity, saw the gun flashes and closed. But the raider made good her escape. On the 29th she sank the large British ship *Afric Star* and also the *Eurylochus* which was carrying aircraft to Takoradi, but again both ships sent raider reports. As there were military and mercantile convoys in the vicinity, the Commander-in-Chief at Freetown sent the *Norfolk* to cover the Sierra Leone route while the *Devonshire* searched the area where the raider was last reported. She, however, had moved away; she fuelled from the supply tanker *Nordmark* on the 7th of February and met the *Pinguin* on the 25th in the South Atlantic, after which she steamed north again to supply two U-boats with fuel and stores. In the middle of March she met the *Scheer*, then on her passage home, in the central Atlantic and the two ships exchanged stores and prisoners.[2] For seven weeks the *Kormoran* had achieved no successes, but she now cruised just outside the American defence zone and on the 22nd of March sank a small British tanker. She next captured, three days later, the large British tanker *Canadolite*, which she sent in prize to Bordeaux; then, early in April, she made a rendezvous with two supply ships in 50° North, 35° West, after which she returned to her former hunting ground. There, on the 9th and 12th of April, she secured two more victims. This marked the end of four and a half months' cruising in the North Atlantic where she had sunk or captured eight ships of 56,708 tons. She now moved south, met the *Atlantis* and fuelled in 28° South, 12° West prior to entering the Indian Ocean. Cape Agulhas was rounded on the 2nd of May and

---
[1] See Map 29 (*facing p. 383*).
[2] See p. 370.

she met two supply ships on the 14th. Six days later she reached her new operational area which lay north of 20° South and east of 80° East. The *Orion* and *Komet* were about to leave the Indian Ocean for the Atlantic and Pacific respectively and the *Kormoran* was to take over their former theatre. But for four weeks she sighted nothing. On the 24th of June she was 200 miles south-east of Madras, off which port her captain intended to lay mines. But a ship which the raider thought was an armed merchant cruiser hove in sight and caused her to cancel the minelaying. Two days later she scored a double success in sinking a Yugoslav and a British ship after which she moved off, early in July, to refit in 6° South, 86° East. There we will leave the *Kormoran* for the present. She had so far sunk or captured ten ships of 64,333 tons.

One more enemy raider made a brief appearance during the present phase, and that was the only ship which the Italians sent out for such a purpose. The *Ramb I* had sailed from Massawa on the 20th of February, but was intercepted and sunk by the New Zealand cruiser *Leander* (Captain R. H. Bevan) on the 27th to the north of the Maldive Islands. She had accomplished no results whatsoever and only put up a half-hearted resistance at the end. But the *Leander* experienced similar difficulties to the *Cornwall's* in establishing the suspicious ship's identity.

Though losses caused by armed merchant raiders had continued to be fairly high during the first half of 1941 they dropped heavily after the end of March and, except for one short period a year later, never rose again to comparable figures.[1] In spite of the many pressing and world-wide commitments and anxieties which at this time beset the Admiralty the counter-measures adopted were slowly beginning to take effect. The interception of the raiders themselves was bound to be a difficult and lengthy process until far more cruisers could be spared to scour the oceans, but by striking at their supply ships a term could be set to the raiders' careers and their continued activity made more difficult. To accomplish this it was essential to discover the rendezvous used by them and evidence to that end was slowly accumulated in London. When the evidence was sufficient to justify diverting part of our meagre strength in cruisers the Admiralty struck. But the account of those successes belongs to the next phase and, as another operation by the enemy's major warships had meanwhile taken place in the North Atlantic, it is to those waters that we must first return.

---

[1] See Appendix M.

CHAPTER XIX

THE HOME FLEET
1st January–31st May, 1941

> Now for the services of the Sea, they are innumerable . . . it is an open field for Merchandize in Peace, a pitched Field for the most dreadful fights of Warre. . . .
> *Purchas, His Pilgrimes.* 1625.

WITH the widening scope and intensity of the maritime war which marked the early months of 1941 the operations of the various naval commands ashore and afloat, and of the associated commands of the Royal Air Force, became increasingly interlocked and interdependent. Though each naval Commander-in-Chief was still responsible for the security of a designated area of ocean and for the movements of all naval forces and merchant shipping within that area, it became increasingly common for ships or squadrons either to be temporarily detached to another command or to pass through different commands for particular purposes. The squadrons of the Royal Air Force allocated to co-operate in the maritime war also began to be shifted more frequently, not only from one group or command to another which might temporarily have greater need of their services, but also from one theatre of war to another. In fact it was at this period that the flexibility of our maritime power, always one of its greatest merits, again came to be fully exploited.

But for the historian the increasing integration of all the instruments comprising our maritime power and the constant shift and re-shift of squadrons, ships and aircraft present peculiar difficulties. No longer can the story of each command's plans, efforts and operations be considered as a separate entity. They must be woven into the immense tapestry depicting the maritime war as a whole, in which each command and each unit is a thread of varying strength and importance but still only a thread in the whole tapestry.

Some of the operations of the Home Fleet during the early months of 1941 have already been described under other headings. Thus, for example, Admiral Tovey's endeavours to intercept the *Scharnhorst* and *Gneisenau* on both their outward and homeward passages in February and March 1941 were told in the story of the defence of our shipping on the broad oceans; and the work of the Home Fleet submarines has been treated as a part of the struggle for control of coastal waters. There remain, however, to be considered certain other operations which took place during the present phase in which the Home Fleet played the predominant though by no means the only part. The most important of these was the chase and ultimate destruction of the great new battleship *Bismarck*. It is therefore to the Home Fleet and to the beginning of the year that we must now revert.

Before the story of that climax of the surface ship operations is told it may be mentioned that the strengthening of the northern mine barrier by the ships of the 1st Minelaying Squadron was continued from the beginning of the year and, since the minelayers had to be escorted and provided with a covering force, their protection made heavy calls on the Home Fleet itself. In January over 2,000 mines were laid in two lines between Iceland and the Faeröe Islands, and in February an even greater number was laid. But premature explosions were observed in the minefields and these produced doubts regarding the stability of the mines used, and of the effectiveness of the barrier itself. However the Admiralty ordered that laying should continue, and in March the squadron sailed three times and laid, in all, 6,100 mines. In the following month a further section of the Iceland-Faeröes field was laid and, on the 26th, mines were laid in the Denmark Strait, off the north-west corner of Iceland, to restrict the waters through which enemy surface ships must pass to reach the Atlantic trade routes.[1] This minefield influenced the first phase of the pursuit of the *Bismarck*, as will be told later. Towards the end of April the Admiralty reviewed minelaying policy for the next three months, and decided that a double line of mines between the Faeröe Islands and Iceland should be the first priority and should be completed by the end of May. Thereafter the strengthening of the northern section of the east coast barrier would take precedence; but this could not be undertaken before midsummer. In actual fact the large-scale operations against the enemy surface ships in May prevented any considerable progress being made with any of our defensive minefields until later in the year.

The new year was but a few days old when the Admiralty issued warnings that enemy surface ships might be about to attempt to return to Germany by one of the northern passages, and twice the main body of the fleet sailed from Scapa to the west. But on neither occasion were the reports correct. The presence of the *Hipper* in Brest had been confirmed by air reconnaissance on the 4th of January, and thereafter a close watch was kept on her movements. She was attacked from the air on many occasions but received no serious damage, though the German Naval Staff considered her escape fortunate and were much concerned over the danger to which she was exposed from the air. The story of her second cruise in February and of

---

[1] See Map 30 (*facing p. 397*).

her final safe return to Germany in March has already been told.[1]

On the 15th of January the *King George V* sailed from Scapa to the Chesapeake with Lord Halifax, our new ambassador to the United States, on board. She arrived on the 24th and sailed again next day to escort an important homeward convoy, which included twenty-four tankers. By the 6th of February she was back at Scapa. During her absence an outward enemy movement was again suspected to be imminent and cruisers were sailed to patrol the northern passages. It was, we now know, on the 23rd of January that the enemy battle cruisers actually sailed from Kiel on their long-expected foray. The warning received and the consequential favourable disposition of the fleet, the narrow escape of the enemy squadron when south of Iceland on the 28th and their subsequent successful escape by the Denmark Strait have already been described.[2]

On the very day that these two formidable warships passed northwards through the Great Belt, a successful minor operation was carried out by the Home Fleet in the North Sea. It merits attention on account of the bold and careful planning which it involved and the courage and determination of the Norwegians to whom its success was due. Five Norwegian merchant ships—the *Elizabeth Bakke, John Bakke, Tai Shan, Taurus* and *Ranja*—sailed from Gothenburg that afternoon and passed through the Skagerrak to the west. Their intention was known in advance, and Admiral Tovey sailed two forces of cruisers and destroyers to meet them. The rendezvous was successfully made and all the ships reached Scapa safely in spite of enemy air attacks. But their escape from a chance encounter with the northward-bound enemy battle cruisers was certainly narrow.

It has been mentioned that, as a result of the attacks by the *Hipper, Scharnhorst* and *Gneisenau* on our Atlantic and Sierra Leone convoys, the Admiralty decided that battleship or cruiser ocean escorts were to be provided for the convoys whenever possible, and that detachments were to be made, generally from the Home Fleet, for this purpose. Fortunately Admiral Tovey's cruisers had recently been considerably reinforced and he was able to meet this new commitment without prejudice to the other responsibilities of his fleet. But the need to provide exceptionally powerful escorts to the important W.S. troop convoys now sailing every month to the Middle East continued, and this, added to the new requirements, kept the number of cruisers actually available to the Commander-in-Chief at little more than the minimum needed to work with his heavy ships and to patrol the northern passages. Thus, for example, convoy W.S. 5 B, consisting of twenty-one ships totalling 418,000 tons with 40,000

---

[1] See pp. 371–373.
[2] See pp. 373–374.

troops on board, sailed from home on the 12th of January escorted by the *Ramillies, Australia, Naiad, Phoebe* and an anti-submarine screen of twelve destroyers, while, on the 8th of February, the *Rodney*, three cruisers and three destroyers were sent with the first part of the next convoy, W.S. 6, until its escort was taken over by Force H from Gibraltar on the 17th. The *Rodney* then left to meet and bring in a Halifax convoy, the *Norfolk* escorted two other North Atlantic convoys, while the *Edinburgh* met and relieved the *Royal Sovereign* as ocean escort to the Canadian troop convoy T.C. 9. Concurrently the cruiser *Mauritius* escorted the second part of W.S. 6 to Gibraltar, and the *Arethusa* took the same route with an outward-bound Gibraltar convoy. All these escort requirements arose in the latter part of January or early days of February; they are mentioned in some detail since they show how wide a dispersal of our strength was forced on us by the threat of the raiding warships and how great a margin, of cruisers in particular, was necessary if the many convoys at sea on any one day were all to be safeguarded. It was indeed fortunate that we could count on a small margin at this time, but how slender it was became clear when a break-back by the enemy battle cruisers appeared virtually certain between the 16th and 22nd of March. Admiral Tovey had then to choose between stationing his forces to deal with an attempt to use those passages or disposing them to anticipate return to a French Biscay port. When, on the 28th and 29th, there were signs that the *Scheer* was about to attempt the homeward passage of the Denmark Strait, little strength remained to Admiral Tovey to meet this new requirement while maintaining his blockade of the battle cruisers, which had meanwhile succeeded in reaching Brest.[1]

On the 28th of March photographic reconnaissance confirmed the presence of the battle cruisers in the French base, and during the next three weeks the Admiralty disposed almost the whole strength of the Home Fleet and Force H in positions some 500 miles to the west, in case the enemy ships attempted to return home. The two or three squadrons thus employed, each of which comprised at least one capital ship, returned one at a time to Scapa or Gibraltar to fuel and then resumed their patrols, while Admirals Tovey and Somerville alternated in command of the blockading forces. It is, however, to be remarked that Admiral Tovey, even at this early date, considered that, if the enemy ships decided to break for home, their most probable route was up the English Channel.

On the 19th of April the situation was further complicated by a report that the *Bismarck* and light forces had passed the Skaw steering to the north-west the previous day. The cruiser patrols in the northern

---

[1] See p. 378.

passages were at once strengthened and the *Hood* diverted to their support. The report was, however, false. Yet another anxiety was introduced on the 22nd when air reconnaissance firmly identified one heavy and two light cruisers in Narvik. The Admiralty thought that these might well be the *Lützow*, *Emden* and *Köln*. This report was also incorrect, and we now know from the War Diary of the German Norway command, which intercepted the erroneous report of our reconnaissance aircraft, that 'transports and patrol vessels in the harbour [were identified] as a battleship, two cruisers and two destroyers'. These two misleading reports show how faulty intelligence or incorrect identification of enemy forces could increase the tension and difficulties of an already anxious period.

Meanwhile important successes had been achieved by the Royal Air Force in their heavy and persistent attacks on Brest. In spite of the escape of their major warships from damage in our early air attacks and the immunity of the *Hipper* while recently in Brest, the Germans were fully conscious of the dangers to which the battle cruisers were now exposed. Though the *Scharnhorst's* refit could not be completed before June, it was hoped to have her sister ship ready to sail again in time to join with the *Bismarck* and the heavy cruiser *Prinz Eugen* in May. Meanwhile the German Navy pressed for the air defences around Brest to be strengthened. Little, however, was done; and the failure adequately to defend the base contributed substantially to the utter defeat of the ambitious plans of the German Naval Staff to attack our Atlantic shipping simultaneously with at least three, and possibly four, powerful warships.

On the 6th of April the only one of four aircraft of No. 22 Squadron of Coastal Command which found the target hit the *Gneisenau* with a torpedo and damaged her severely. The aircraft, commanded by Flying Officer K. Campbell, did not return and the achievement of its crew therefore remained unknown in London.[1] Next day, however, it was observed that the *Gneisenau* had been moved into dry dock. Five days later, on the night of the 10th–11th of April, the same ship received four hits in a raid by Bomber Command which, ever since the ships had been located in Brest, had put a heavy weight of attack on the port. Nor were these bombing and torpedo attacks the only measures taken by the Royal Air Force against these two ships. Almost the whole of Coastal Command's minelaying effort, supplemented by a considerable parallel effort from Bomber Command, was, during the latter part of March and the whole of April, devoted to the approaches to Brest. And in two sorties at the end of March the new fast minelayer *Abdiel* laid nearly 300 mines in the approaches. In April 106 more mines were laid by aircraft. In addition to attack-

---

[1] Flying Officer Campbell was later awarded a posthumous Victoria Cross.

ing the ships themselves and assisting to block them in by mines, Coastal Command aircraft patrolled intensively to ensure that, if they broke out of the base, they should be sighted as early as possible.

While, therefore, the heavy ships waited hopefully far out to sea and our submarines patrolled off the entrance channels, the enemy ships were pounded from the air and 'sewn in by mines'. Here, in truth, was a combined air-sea operation conducted in complete harmony of purpose. And, to the chagrin of the German Naval Staff, it was successful in destroying their hopes for a surface-ship foray which would have constituted a most formidable menace to our Atlantic shipping.

The damage sustained inside Brest harbour, though still to a great extent shrouded from the eyes and ears of the British authorities, immediately forced the German higher command to reconsider their plans. Admiral Raeder and the Naval Staff strongly desired still to send out the *Bismarck* and *Prinz Eugen*, even if no diversionary sortie by the battle cruisers from Brest was possible. Admiral Lütjens demurred; but he was in the unenviable position of opposing a daring plan which he himself would have to carry out. This weakened his case and the contrary view therefore prevailed. The stage was thus set for what was to prove one of the most dramatic series of maritime operations of the whole war.

On the 1st of May the two battle cruisers were known to be still in Brest, and both were believed to have been damaged. The *Bismarck* and *Prinz Eugen* were known to be complete and ready for service, and the *Lützow*, *Emden* and *Köln* were also presumed to be ready. The possibility of a new break-out by surface forces was therefore abundantly clear. Admiral Tovey tightened his watch on the northern exits and kept at least one heavy and one armed merchant cruiser on patrol in the Denmark Strait. The *Hood* and four destroyers were based on Hvalfiord to cover the convoys passing to the south of Iceland, while at Scapa the Commander-in-Chief had the *King George V, Prince of Wales, Rodney*, and two or three 8-inch cruisers, about half a dozen 6-inch cruisers and some ten destroyers. The rest of his ships were absent on ocean escort duties. Throughout the month the smaller 6-inch cruisers (*Arethusa* class) took turns to patrol the Iceland-Faeröes gap, while the heavy 8-inch cruisers did the same in the Denmark Strait. In spite of the plain approach of a new and serious challenge in the Atlantic the blockade was, at this anxious time, never relaxed and an opportunity was found to intercept three eastbound Italian tankers, a German blockade-runner (the s.s. *Leche*) and a German trawler bound for Greenland with a weather-reporting party aboard. But these were trivial incidents compared to the major clash now pending.

Let us now look at the enemy's intentions after the immobilisation of the battle cruisers in Brest. They believed that the *Tirpitz* as well as the *Bismarck* would be necessary to accomplish the destruction of our battleship convoy escorts and their charges as well, and the proposal was, therefore, that the *Bismarck* should, by her presence in the Atlantic, tie down our battleship escorts while the *Prinz Eugen* was freed for commerce raiding. Originally the *Bismarck* was intended to return to Brest, but after the *Gneisenau* had been damaged there on the 6th of April this was changed, and the battleship was ordered to return either to Trondheim or to a home port after completing her foray. Only if she had received no damage, or if our dispositions forced it on her, was she to make for a French west coast port. The southern limit of her zone of operations was to be 10° North, but it was realised that the absence of the battle cruisers would enable the full British strength to be concentrated in the north—a distinctly adverse factor from the enemy's point of view. Five tankers and two supply ships were sent out to replenish the squadron; the fate which overtook most of them will be told later.[1] The German plan did not include direct co-operation between the U-boats and surface forces. Admirals Lütjens and Dönitz decided that the U-boats should continue their normal patrols and that, if an opportunity for co-operation should arise during the surface-ship foray, it should be exploited. The *Prinz Eugen* was damaged by a magnetic mine—doubtless one of those laid by our aircraft—on the 23rd of April, which caused a fourteen-day postponement of the squadron's departure, and it was not until the 18th of May that Admiral Lütjens sailed from Gdynia with his two ships for the Atlantic. In spite of all the care taken by the enemy to conceal or disguise the movement British intelligence worked as rapidly and accurately as in the case of the break-out by the battle cruisers in February.[2]

Early on the 21st, warning of the northward movement was received in London and intensive patrolling and search by Coastal Command aircraft was at once started. Later that same day they discovered the enemy ships in Korsfiord, a short distance south of Bergen, where they fuelled before sailing north the same evening.

To Admiral Tovey in his flagship at Scapa the intelligence of the German movement received on the 20th came as no surprise. For the previous ten days the enemy's air activity between Jan Mayen Island and Greenland and his frequent reconnaissance of Scapa Flow had directed the Commander-in-Chief's attention to the narrow passage of water between Iceland and the edge of the icefields off Greenland's eastern shore. On the 18th, he had warned the *Suffolk* (Captain R. M. Ellis) which was on patrol in the Strait to

---

[1] See pp. 542–544.
[2] See p. 373.

watch the passage carefully, in particular near to the edge of the ice. On the 19th the *Norfolk* (Captain A. J. L. Phillips), flagship of Rear-Admiral W. F. Wake-Walker, commanding the 18th Cruiser Squadron, had sailed from Hvalfiord to relieve the *Suffolk*, which returned to the same base to fuel. When the air reconnaissance of Bergen had identified the two ships for certain the Commander-in-Chief at once sailed the *Hood* (Captain R. Kerr), flying the flag of Vice-Admiral L. E. Holland, commanding the Battle Cruiser Squadron, with the *Prince of Wales* (Captain J. C. Leach) and six destroyers from Scapa to Hvalfiord.[1] The *Birmingham* and *Manchester*, which were patrolling the Iceland–Faeröes passage, were ordered to fuel in Iceland and then return to their patrol; and the *Suffolk* was sent at once to rejoin her sister ship, the *Norfolk*, in the Denmark Strait. The fleet flagship *King George V* (Captain W. R. Patterson) with the cruisers *Galatea, Aurora, Kenya, Neptune, Hermione* and five destroyers remained at Scapa at short notice. The Admiralty now made an important contribution to the strength of the Home Fleet by cancelling the departure of the new aircraft carrier *Victorious* (Captain H. C. Bovell) and the *Repulse* (Captain W. G. Tennant) with a W.S. convoy and placing them at Admiral Tovey's disposal. Having carried his preparations thus far the Commander-in-Chief could only await the receipt of further intelligence, but, because of bad visibility in the North Sea, this was not at once forthcoming. At length on the evening of the 22nd the uncertainty was dispelled by a naval aircraft despatched from Hatston air station in the Orkneys on the initiative of its commanding officer and carrying a very experienced naval observer—Commander G. A. Rotherham. Under most difficult flying conditions this aircraft penetrated to the fiord where the enemy ships had been sighted on the 21st. It was empty. The aircraft then searched Bergen harbour, also with negative results, and so was able to report that the enemy had sailed. This report reached Admiral Tovey at 8 p.m. on the 22nd and was at once accepted by him. Of all the possibilities open to the enemy, that of a break-out into the Atlantic not only constituted the greatest threat but was supported by the most recent Admiralty intelligence. The Commander-in-Chief decided to act on the assumption that this was the enemy's plan. He therefore ordered his cruisers to concentrate in the two possible passages which might be attempted, and, at 10.45 that night, the main fleet sailed from Scapa to the north-west to cover the cruisers and to take up a favourable position to intercept the enemy whichever passage he might try to force. Intense air patrols of all the passages were also requested from Coastal Command.

German air reconnaissance had meanwhile been defeated by the

---

[1] As the battleship *Prince of Wales* served as a battle cruiser on this occasion she is referred to as such in the narrative.

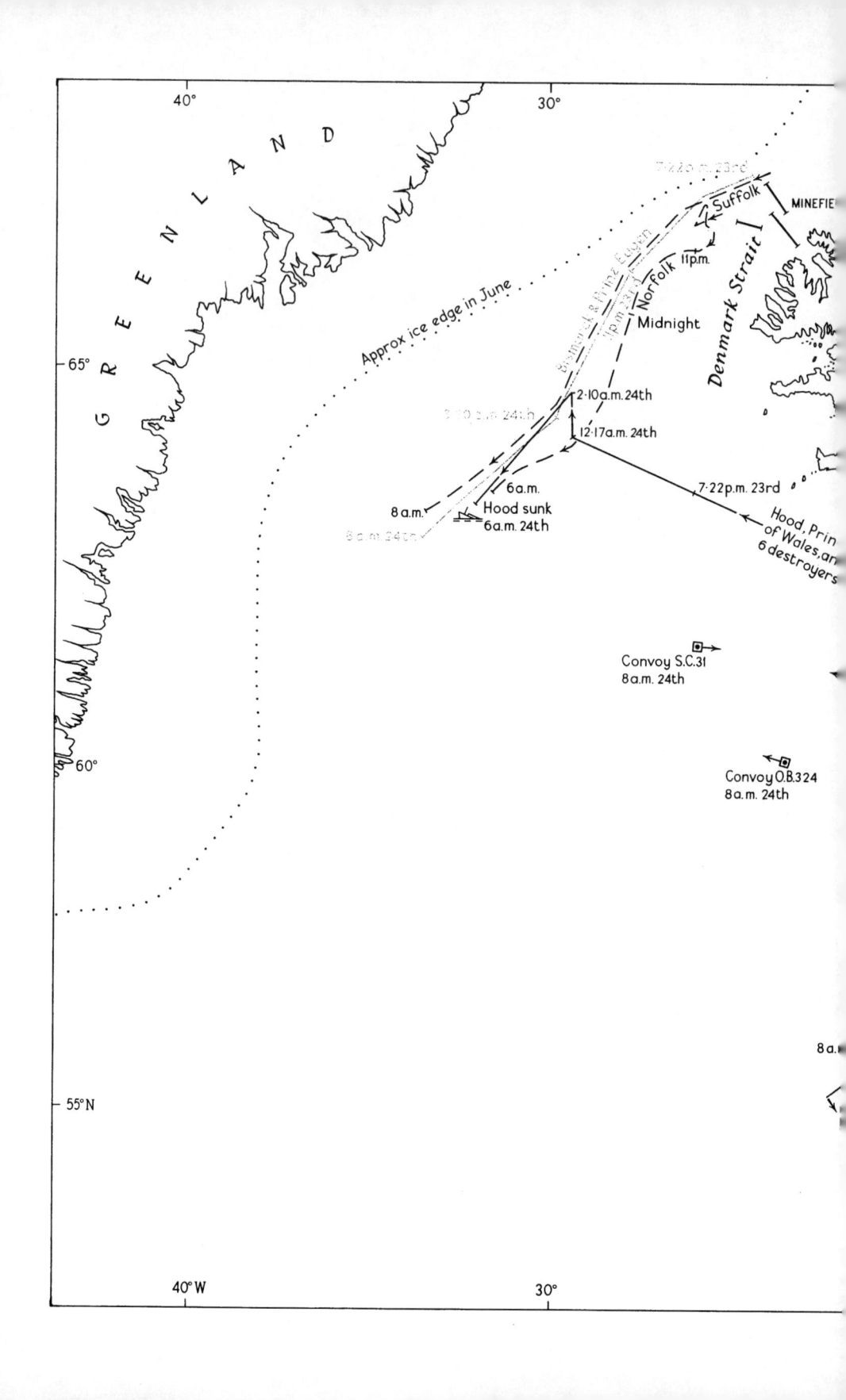

Map 30

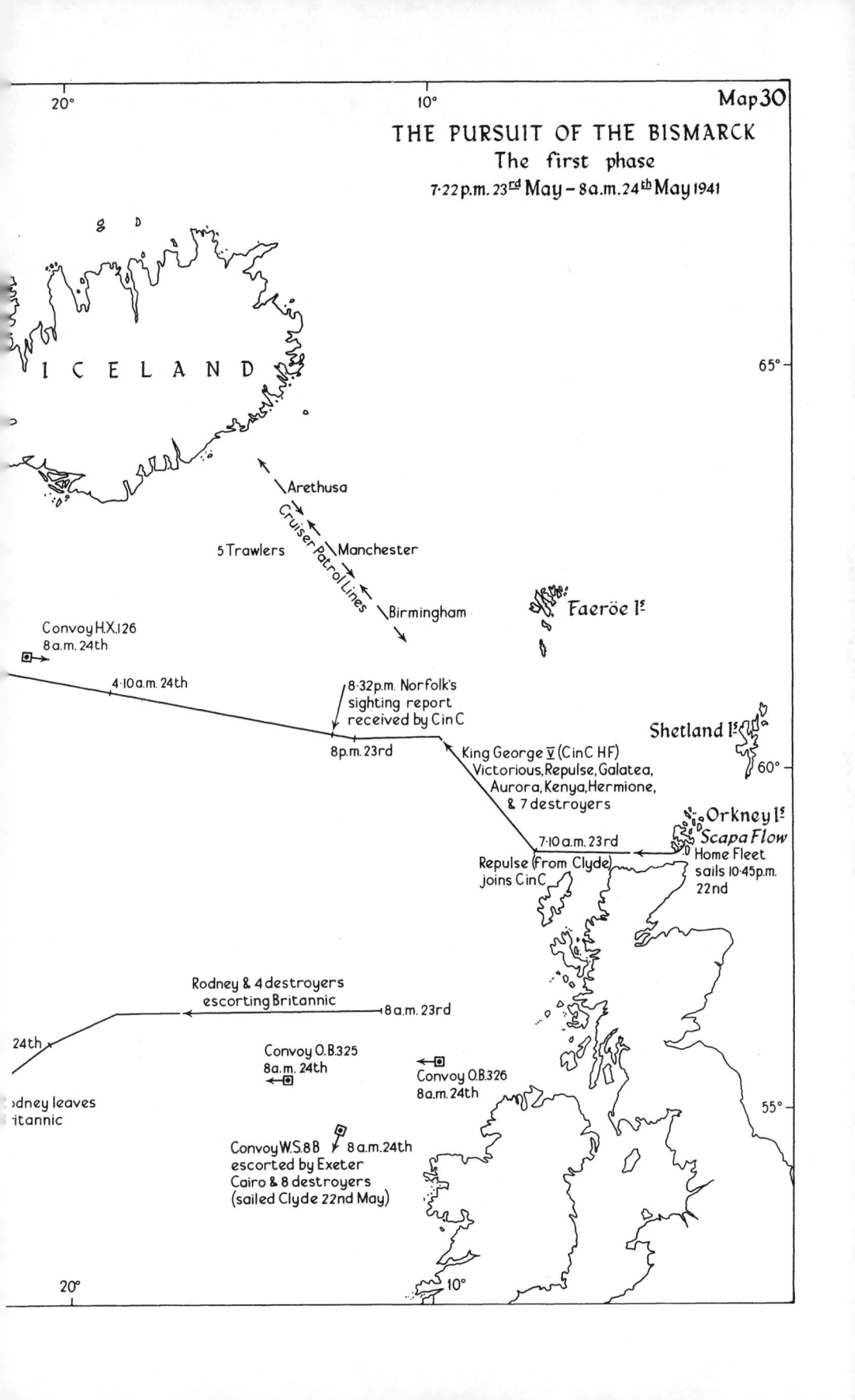

THE PURSUIT OF THE BISMARCK
The first phase
7·22 p.m. 23rd May – 8 a.m. 24th May 1941

bad weather, and the departure of the Home Fleet was not observed. Admiral Lütjens, therefore, though he knew he had been sighted near Bergen, did not know that the British fleet was moving towards the passage which he intended to use. To Admiral Tovey the most immediate problem was to ensure that all his ships took up their dispositions not only in comfortable time before the enemy could reach the passages but, since a long pursuit far from their bases was probable, with their tanks as nearly as possible full of fuel. This demanded nice judgment of the moment at which each force should be sailed. Thus fuel supply and the endurance of their ships at once became an overriding factor in the movements of the British and the German Commanders-in-Chief, and remained so throughout the operation.

On the 23rd the weather interfered very seriously with our air patrols, few of which could be flown. But Admiral Wake-Walker ordered his two cruisers to cover the gap between the ice edge and the minefield off the north-west corner of Iceland so as to use the modern radar set with which the *Suffolk* was fitted to the best advantage.[1] That afternoon the weather was clear over and close to the ice, but misty on the other side of the strait towards the land. At 7.22 p.m., shortly after she had completed her investigation of the ice edge, the *Suffolk* sighted the *Bismarck*, steaming with the *Prinz Eugen* astern of her, on a south-westerly course similar to her own and about seven miles away. The cruiser then slipped into the mist to take cover from so powerful an adversary, but maintained contact by means of her radar. She thus extricated herself from a position of considerable peril, while still keeping the enemy under constant observation, and was able to signal the first of her many accurate reports of the enemy's position and movements. An hour later she emerged again briefly from the mist, obtained another sighting, sent a further report and then took cover once more. At the same time the *Norfolk*, which had been closing the enemy since her sister ship's first sighting, also made visual contact, but at the dangerously short range of six miles. The *Bismarck* immediately fired at her the first shots of the series of actions which were to end three and a half days later. The *Norfolk* disengaged under cover of smoke without receiving damage, and signalled the first enemy report which was actually received in the battle fleet—then some 600 miles away to the south-east. The *Suffolk's* earlier reports had not got through to Admiral Tovey.

Admiral Wake-Walker's two cruisers now proceeded to carry out, with great skill and determination, the traditional rôle of ships of their class in touch with a superior enemy squadron. In spite of steaming at high speed through rain, snow, ice floes and mirage effects they

---

[1] See Map 30.

held on, the *Suffolk* on the enemy's starboard quarter and the *Norfolk* to port. Meanwhile Admiral Holland, with the battle cruiser force, was closing the enemy at high speed.

We will now turn to the bridge of the battle cruiser flagship to try to reconstruct the situation as it appeared to Admiral Holland from midnight on the 23rd–24th until action was joined. The only positive evidence which we possess lies in the messages sent by the Admiral to the *Prince of Wales* and the destroyers. Though conjecture must inevitably enter into an attempt to analyse the motive behind these signals, it is, perhaps, justifiable to try to interpret from them the thoughts which may have passed through the Admiral's mind as the two forces closed rapidly towards each other.

The Admiral's trained mind would first have considered the strengths of the two forces now converging. He knew that his main adversary was a ship of the latest design, and certainly one of the most powerful warships afloat. Her speed, moreover, was certainly not less than that of his own squadron, and perhaps greater by a knot or two. As regards fighting efficiency he had with him one ship which had been designed about a quarter of a century earlier and had never been thoroughly modernised, and one which was so new that her armaments had not yet been fully tested nor her ship's company adequately practised in their use. Moreover, the *Hood* was not in first-class fighting condition, because as soon as she had completed a long-overdue refit in the middle of March she had been sent out on Atlantic patrols without having a proper chance to regain full efficiency.[1]

Admiral Holland must also have considered whether it would be to his advantage to fight the enemy at long or short ranges. He had no information regarding the ranges at which the *Bismarck* would be most vulnerable to the gunfire of his own ships, but he did know that the *Prince of Wales* should be safe from vital hits by heavy shells from maximum gun range down to about 13,000 yards, and that the *Hood* should become progressively more immune from such hits as the range approached 12,000 yards and the enemy shell trajectories flattened. At long ranges the *Hood*, which lacked heavy horizontal armour, would be very vulnerable to plunging fire by heavy shells.[2] There were, therefore, strong arguments in favour of pressing in to fight the *Bismarck* at comparatively short ranges.

We cannot tell whether Admiral Holland ever balanced up the arguments in favour of the *Prince of Wales*, rather than the *Hood*,

---

[1] See pp. 377–378 and footnote (1), p. 378.

[2] In March 1939 the Board of Admiralty decided to carry out a major reconstruction of the *Hood* whose armour protection was known to be inadequate to withstand German 15-inch shells. She was to be fitted with more horizontal and vertical armour. Before work could be started war had broken out, and nothing could then be done to improve the ship's protection.

leading his squadron into battle. But, after it was all over, Admiral Tovey wrote to the First Sea Lord that he had 'very nearly made a signal . . . that the *Prince of Wales* should lead the line so that the better protected ship would draw the enemy's fire'. He had not done so because he did not consider 'such interference with so senior an officer justifiable'. After the loss of the *Hood* the Commander-in-Chief wished he had sent the signal. Equally we cannot guess whether Admiral Holland considered the arguments in favour of going into battle in open order (1,000 yards apart) rather than in the more conventional close formation at four cables distance (800 yards), and of giving his squadron freedom of manœuvre. With ships of different classes and performance the open formation might be considered advantageous; the difficulty of concentrating the gunfire of ships equipped with different calibres of gun would certainly be known to the Admiral.

Whereas the fighting efficiency of the two British ships was not entirely satisfactory and one of them was certainly ill-protected, the enemy ships had spent many months testing and perfecting their equipment in the Baltic. It was almost certain that a high pitch of efficiency had been reached by them both before they sailed from home waters.

To offset the serious handicaps from which the British squadron suffered there was the advantage of heavier broadsides; but it was true that this superiority might, for reasons already given, be proved by battle to be more theoretical than real. A more solid advantage lay in the possibility of achieving surprise, and this may well have been in the foreground of Admiral Holland's thoughts. For this purpose it was essential to conceal the approach of the British squadron, which requirement would forbid the use of wireless or radar until battle was about to be joined. Admiral Holland therefore had to rely chiefly on Admiral Wake-Walker's two shadowing cruisers to bring him to his quarry. But the four destroyers still with the battle cruiser squadron might be used for reconnaissance, and an opportunity might arise to use the *Prince of Wales*' aircraft for a similar purpose.

The enemy's intention to break out into the Atlantic and then attack our shipping must by this time have been clear. The dangers of such a threat would need no emphasis. The enemy must, if possible, be stopped. But recent sorties by German warships had shown that their strategy was to avoid engagement, even with inferior forces. It was reasonable to expect the *Bismarck* to take drastic evasive action, such as the *Scharnhorst* and *Gneisenau* had taken when they ran into the Home Fleet's cruisers south of Iceland in the previous January, as soon as she knew that a powerful British squadron was approaching.[1] This would make it important to force an action as quickly as

[1] See p. 373.

possible, since a second chance might never occur. Such, it is suggested, were the principal factors affecting Admiral Holland's preliminary orders and decisions.

The battle cruiser squadron prepared for action at fifteen minutes past midnight on the 24th of May and, at that time, it was expected to gain contact with the enemy at any time after 1.40 a.m. Evidently Admiral Holland intended to accept battle at the earliest possible moment, even during the darkest period of the brief Arctic night.[1]

Shortly after midnight a development occurred which, from Admiral Holland's point of view, was fraught with dangerous possibilities. The shadowing cruisers lost touch with the enemy in a snowstorm. This must have meant that the Admiral's plans and intentions had to be reconsidered. Whereas, up to that moment, concealment of the battle cruiser squadron's approach had been the cardinal requirement, it was now displaced by the need to regain touch with the enemy as quickly as possible. At seventeen minutes past midnight Admiral Holland altered from the westerly course which he had been steering to intercept the enemy to due north and reduced speed to 25 knots.[2] It seems certain that this change from a course which was bound to bring the British squadron into action if the enemy held on to the south-west was based on a guess that the enemy must have eluded the shadowing cruisers either by turning right round to hide in the Arctic mists or, possibly, by an alteration to the south-east. The ice would prevent the enemy making any considerable distance towards the west. If this is the case Admiral Holland's guess was wrong, for the enemy actually continued to steer south-west; and the British Admiral's action had the unhappy result of causing his squadron to 'lose bearing' on the enemy—or, less technically expressed, to drop behind.

At half-past twelve Admiral Holland told his squadron that if the enemy had not been sighted by 2.10 a.m. he would alter course to the south until the cruisers had regained contact. He also told his destroyers that when he altered to the south they were to continue to search to the north. This order and its consequences will be discussed more fully later. The difficulties facing the Admiral during this period of uncertainty were accentuated by the visibility becoming rapidly worse. The *Prince of Wales* had been given discretion to fly off her Walrus amphibian aircraft before action was joined, and at 1.40 a.m. she had made it ready. But because of the bad visibility her intention to use the aircraft was abandoned.

---

[1] In these latitudes, in the middle of May, twilight (taken to start and end when the sun is 12 degrees below the horizon) lasts all night. The night of 23rd–24th May was, however, unusually dark. Sunset and sunrise on 24th May were at 1.51 a.m. and 6.37 a.m. respectively by the British Fleet's clocks which were keeping Greenwich Time adjusted for Double Summer Time.

[2] See Map 30 (*facing p. 397*).

The German Battleship *Bismarck* in Grimstad Fiord, Norway, shortly after her arrival there, a.m. 21st May 1941. (The *Bismarck* is the right-hand ship. The other three ships had been ordered to go alongside her while at anchor to protect her from torpedo-bomber attacks.)

The *Bismarck* taken from the Cruiser *Prinz Eugen* shortly before they sailed from Norway for the Atlantic, 21st May 1941. (See page 395.)

H.M.S. *Norfolk* shadowing the *Bismarck* south of the Denmark Strait, 24th May 1941.

H.M.S. *Suffolk* recovering her seaplane in the Denmark Strait. Note the ice-edge in background.

At 1.47 a.m. Admiral Holland signalled his tactical intentions. He proposed to concentrate the fire of both his heavy ships on the *Bismarck* while leaving the *Prinz Eugen* to the care of Admiral Wake-Walker's cruisers. But the cruiser Admiral was not told of this, presumably because Holland still wished to preserve wireless silence, and, moreover, Admiral Wake-Walker was unaware of the battle cruiser squadron's rapid approach. As he was shadowing from a position some fifteen miles astern of the enemy when battle was joined, he was in no position to carry out his share of Admiral Holland's plan. Furthermore, the *Prinz Eugen* had by that time taken station ahead of her flagship and so was the more distant ship from the British cruisers.

At 2 a.m. Admiral Holland carried out his intention to turn to the south while awaiting full daylight, and the destroyers held on to the north. He also told the *Prince of Wales* to search an arc of the horizon with her gunnery radar set. When, however, Captain Leach reported that his gunnery radar would not cover the desired arc and suggested using his search set, permission was refused. The reason may have been that the Admiral feared that the transmissions of the more powerful search set would give away his position.

At 2.47 the period of uncertainty was ended by the *Suffolk* regaining contact. It must then have become clear to Admiral Holland that the enemy had made no alteration while the cruisers were out of touch. From this time onwards a steady flow of reports came in from the cruisers, while the *Prince of Wales* obtained the cruisers' position from their wireless transmissions. The results were passed to the *Hood*, which should thereby have been enabled to develop an accurate plot of the position, course and speed of the enemy as well as of our own forces. This matter is important because the success of the tactics of the approach to battle would depend greatly on the accuracy of the flagship's plot.

At 3.40 Admiral Holland increased speed to 28 knots and turned inwards to make contact. The visibility had started to improve from 2 a.m. onwards and by 4.30 was about twelve miles. Now was, perhaps, the time to fly off the *Prince of Wales'* aircraft and to use the squadron's radar sets. The *Prince of Wales* actually tried to prepare her aircraft for launching, but its fuel had become contaminated with salt water. It was finally jettisoned just after fire had been opened. The order not to use radar 'until action was imminent' remained in force.

We must now consider the tactics of the final stages of the approach to battle. It seems likely that Admiral Holland had originally intended to make a nearly end-on approach, from fairly fine on the enemy's bow, to a range at which the vulnerability of his flagship would be mitigated and his superior gun power might be decisive, and then to deploy parallel to the enemy's course. His first intercepting course would certainly have enabled this to be done and, moreover, it is known that the Commander-in-Chief himself favoured closing the range rapidly in such a manner. But Admiral Holland's turn to the north from seventeen minutes after midnight until 2.10 a.m. had caused the enemy to gain so much bearing that such an approach was now out of the question. The British squadron did not possess a sufficient margin of speed to win back the lost bearing. The result was that, when the battle cruiser squadron sighted the enemy at 5.35 a.m. and came into action eighteen minutes later, the course on which they closed placed the enemy too fine on the starboard bow of the British ships to enable their after turrets to open fire.[1] But, to the *Bismarck* and her consort, the *Hood* and *Prince of Wales* were only slightly before the beam, and all the guns of the German ships were therefore bearing. It thus came to pass that the most substantial advantage possessed by the British squadron—its eight 15-inch and ten 14-inch guns to the enemy's eight 15-inch and eight 8-inch—was lost. And, moreover, as one of the *Prince of Wales*' forward guns could, because of a defect, only take part in the first salvo the British squadron actually went into action with only four 15-inch and five 14-inch guns against the enemy's full broadsides. As the First Sea Lord commented shortly after the action, the British squadron had gone in 'fighting with one hand only when it had got two' which 'certainly wanted some very good reason'. The reasons why this unfavourable tactical development occurred have been suggested above. The result was that during the first, all-important minutes of the battle the relative weight of broadsides was substantially in the enemy's favour. The British squadron, moreover, went into battle in close order and was manœuvred throughout by the Admiral. Individual captains thus had no freedom to adjust their courses to the best advantage of their own ships.

All four ships opened fire at a range of about 25,000 yards between 5.52 and 5.53 a.m. and the two German ships concentrated their fire initially on the *Hood*.

At 5.49 Admiral Holland had made the signal to concentrate the squadron's gunfire on the left-hand ship, which was in fact the *Prinz Eugen*, and the order to shift target one ship to the right—on to the *Bismarck*—was only given a few seconds before opening fire. In the *Prince of Wales*' control position it was realised almost as soon as the two ships were sighted that the right-hand, or rear, ship was the *Bismarck*, and it was on her that the gunnery officer had trained the armament and on her that, in disregard of the Admiral's first signal, he opened fire. It will never be known for certain at which ship the

---

[1] See Map 31.

BATTLE IN DENMARK STRAIT, 24TH MAY 403

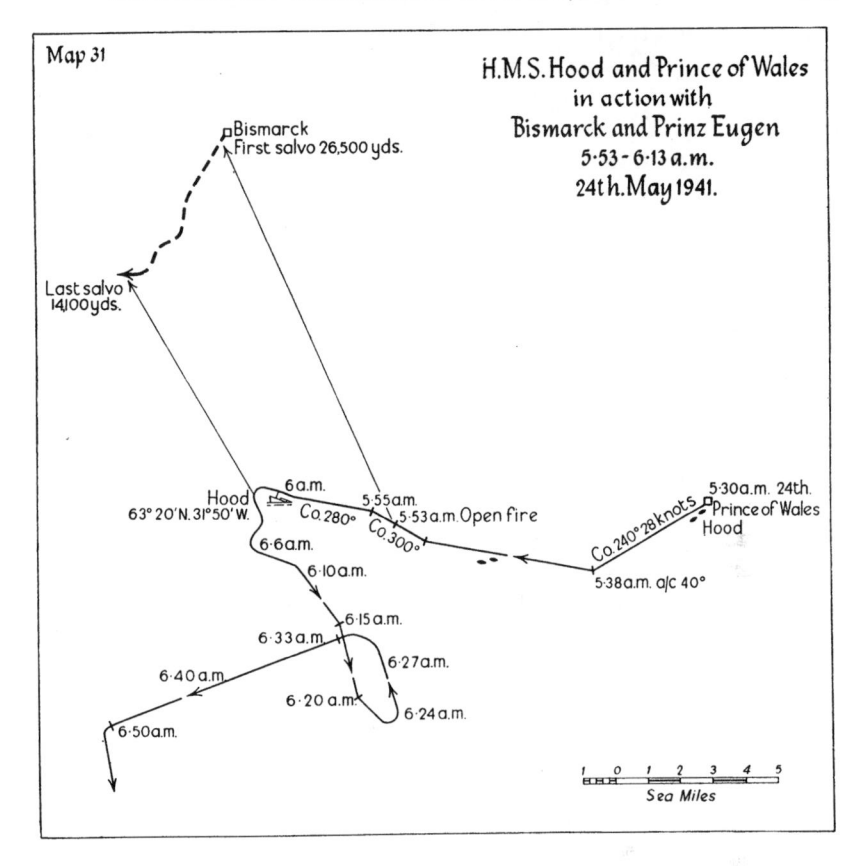

Map 31

H.M.S. Hood and Prince of Wales in action with Bismarck and Prinz Eugen
5·53 - 6·13 a.m.
24th. May 1941.

Hood fired her few salvos, but it seems probable that the error in identification which appears to have been made on her bridge was passed to her main armament control and was never corrected.[1] If this is the case—and the possibility is supported by the *Prinz Eugen's* report on the action and by the conviction of the *Prince of Wales'* control crew that no salvos except their own fell at this time around the *Bismarck*—then the tactical situation which had developed was overwhelmingly favourable to the enemy; for the *Prince of Wales* could only bring five of her guns to bear on the *Bismarck*, the *Hood* was firing at the enemy cruiser and the *Bismarck* and *Prinz Eugen* could and did bring the full weight of their eight-gun broadsides to bear on the unlucky *Hood*.

It is not known where, relative to her target, the *Hood's* first salvos fell, but if, as suggested above, they were aimed at the *Prinz Eugen* she was certainly not endangered by them. The *Prince of Wales'* first shots fell well beyond the *Bismarck* and it was not until her sixth salvo

---

[1] See pp. 82–83 regarding identification of German warships.

that she crossed the target. The *Bismarck*, on the other hand, opened fire on a range of almost exact accuracy, though whether this was obtained by radar or by her optical rangefinders cannot be stated with certainty. The Germans have always concentrated on producing very fine rangefinder instruments. Again and again have their ships, in both wars, opened fire with great accuracy. Bearing in mind the performance of the radar sets then fitted in British ships and knowing that the Germans were not ahead of us in radar design, it seems likely that the *Bismarck's* opening range was obtained optically. The British ships were handicapped in obtaining good rangefinder results by the fine angle and high speed of the approach. Not only would the rangefinders in the after turrets not bear on the target, but those in the forward turrets were incapacitated by the seas and spray which were sweeping over them. The *Prince of Wales* actually opened fire on a range obtained by her small control position rangefinder.

As regards radar, the British ships had both been recently fitted with new sets specially designed to obtain ranges for their main armaments and capable of producing results on a battleship target out to a range of ten or eleven miles. The *Prince of Wales'* modern search radar set could also transmit ranges to the main armament. It must, however, be remembered that radar was at this time still in its infancy and that many ships were experiencing difficulty in obtaining the designed performance from their sets, owing, in no small measure, to inexperience of the operators in their maintenance and use. The Admiralty, fully alive to the great potentialities of this new development, had sent an officer to check both ships' sets at Scapa[1]—by chance on the day before they sailed on this operation—and they had then produced the designed performance. Both ships twice exercised with their sets during the westward passage and reported them correct. The radar policy ordered by Admiral Holland during the approach had, probably for reasons already suggested, forbidden the use of any set unless and until action became imminent, and it seems certain that transmission was not started until very shortly before fire was opened. In the *Prince of Wales* no results were obtained from either of her sets throughout the action. Yet the *Suffolk*, using a set identical to that fitted to the battleship's main armament, was successful in holding the *Bismarck* out to ten miles range. Whether the failure to obtain good ranging results was avoidable or not must remain a matter for conjecture. What is clear is that the angle of the approach gave the enemy the better chance of obtaining accurate initial ranges as well as the advantage in effective weight of broadsides.

The handling of the four destroyers which remained to Admiral

---

[1] The officer in question was the author of this history.

Holland of the six originally allocated to him also demands further consideration. At about 9 p.m. on the 23rd, when the squadron increased speed to 27 knots, they were told to follow at their best speed. But they kept up well with the heavy ships, and the Admiral then considered spreading them ahead for reconnaissance purposes. He did not, however, actually order them to act in this manner, but at 11.18 p.m. stationed them as a close screen ahead of the battle cruisers. They maintained that station until shortly after 2 a.m., when the heavy ships altered course to the south. It was mentioned earlier that the Admiral had ordered that the destroyers should then continue on the former course and search to the north. This they did, and it thus happened that the heavy ships lost touch with the four destroyers, and that when battle was joined, these were some thirty miles away to the north in a position from which they could play no part whatever. They remained helpless and inactive beyond the northern horizon, and could only return to the scene of the battle in time to search for survivors from the *Hood*.

There can be little doubt that Admiral Holland detached the destroyers for reconnaissance purposes at 2 a.m. because the cruisers were then out of touch with the enemy, and he considered it vital to use all his resources to regain contact. But the result was that the possibility of using the destroyers as a torpedo striking force during the gun battle was lost. It must always be difficult to strike the correct balance between dispersal of ships for reconnaissance purposes and their concentration for battle. It must also be difficult to decide between maintaining wireless and radar silence for purposes of concealment and using the former to achieve tactical co-ordination and the latter to assist in the search. It may be considered that, in the present instance, the light forces were too readily detached, that wireless silence could with advantage have been broken to establish direct contact with the cruisers, and that the search radar in the *Prince of Wales* should have been used, at least intermittently, well before action was joined.

The *Bismarck's* second or third salvo, or possibly one from the *Prinz Eugen*, started a fire amidships in the *Hood*, probably among the anti-aircraft ammunition. At 6 a.m., just as the squadron was being turned to enable the after turrets to join in the engagement, the *Hood* was straddled again and blew up with a huge explosion between the after funnel and the mainmast. Three or four minutes later she had disappeared and the *Prince of Wales* had to alter course to avoid her wreckage. There were only three survivors—one midshipman and two ratings—from her company of 95 officers and 1,324 men, and the occurrence had been grimly reminiscent of the destruction of three

British battle cruisers by internal explosions following enemy shell hits in the Battle of Jutland twenty-five years earlier.

The exact cause of the loss of the *Hood* will never be established for certain. The Admiralty ordered searching enquiries to be made into the disaster and the final conclusions of the second enquiry were that the fire on the upper deck occurred among the 4-inch and U.P. rocket ammunition stowed in that vicinity, but was not the cause of the loss of the ship.[1] That was considered to have been caused by at least one of the main magazines being penetrated by one or more shells from the *Bismarck*. The design and protection of this twenty-five-year-old ship were such that penetration of the magazines by modern high-velocity armour-piercing shell was quite possible at those ranges. It would be outside the scope of these volumes to attempt detailed and technical discussion of the causes of the disaster.

The sudden destruction of the battle cruiser flagship enabled the enemy ships to bring the full weight of their combined fire to bear on the *Prince of Wales*. The range had now closed to about 18,000 yards, and the adversaries had their secondary as well as their main armaments in action. Almost at once (at 6.2 a.m.) the British ship sustained a heavy shell hit on the compass platform, which killed or wounded almost all the officers and men stationed there except the Captain, and within a very few minutes she had received four hits from 15-inch shells and three from the *Prinz Eugen's* 8-inch armament. At such comparatively short ranges the enemy's gunfire was plainly deadly. Moreover, the ship's fighting capacity had become drastically reduced. In addition to the defective gun in her forward turret another four-gun turret was now temporarily incapacitated by mechanical breakdowns. In these circumstances Captain Leach decided to break off the action and, at 6.13, turned away under cover of smoke. The range was then 14,600 yards.

The loss of Admiral Holland left Admiral Wake-Walker in command of the ships present and he, believing that the Commander-in-Chief would arrive with greatly superior force early next day, decided

---

[1] The U.P. (Unrotated Projectile) equipment, also called the Naval Wire Barrage, was a war-time development produced by the protagonists of the rocket for anti-aircraft defence purposes. The *Hood* had been fitted with five such equipments on her upper deck and no less than 9·4 tons of ammunition for them was carried in light steel lockers fitted in exposed positions. This was contrary to long-established Admiralty practice regarding the protection of ammunition. Moreover the weapons were, in fact, useless for anti-aircraft defence. Shortly after the loss of the *Hood* the Admiralty ordered their removal from all warships.

that the correct policy was to keep in touch, but not to attempt to re-engage the enemy with the damaged and defective *Prince of Wales* and his two cruisers. The difficult decisions taken at this time by Captain Leach and Admiral Wake-Walker were later fully supported by the Admiralty.

We now know that the *Prince of Wales* had in fact obtained two hits on the *Bismarck* with her 14-inch shells—no mean accomplishment by a newly commissioned ship whose armament was to some extent untried—and that it was one of these hits which caused a leak of fuel oil and contamination of the fuel in other tanks. This reduced the *Bismarck's* endurance sufficiently to cause Admiral Lütjens to abandon the Atlantic foray, and at 8 a.m., only two hours after the battle, he signalled his intention of making for St Nazaire. The damage inflicted by the *Prince of Wales* thus greatly improved the possibility of early interception by Admiral Tovey, provided always that the shadowing cruisers meanwhile maintained contact with the enemy.

The three British ships now concentrated and continued to shadow the enemy as he steered in a south-westerly direction throughout the forenoon, attempting in vain to shake off his pursuers. Meanwhile Admiral Tovey, in the *King George V*, with the *Repulse*, *Victorious*, four cruisers and nine destroyers in company was about 330 miles away to the south-east steering at high speed to join and support Admiral Wake-Walker.[1] The earliest time at which he could intercept the enemy was at about 7 a.m. next day, the 25th, but the Commander-in-Chief realised that, even assuming the cruisers did not lose touch, prospects of bringing the enemy to action were not good—unless his speed could be reduced. It was, therefore, with relief that, at 1.20 p.m., Admiral Tovey learned that the *Bismarck* had altered course to the south and had reduced speed to about 24 knots. In fact the visibility had fallen drastically towards noon and only the *Suffolk's* radar had enabled touch to be maintained. Interception by Admiral Tovey's force was now far more likely, and the possibility of the enemy attempting to break back to the north, though still by no means entirely eliminated, appeared to be diminished.

In London the hunt was meanwhile being watched with tense anxiety, and the Admiralty had already acted to bring every possible battleship, aircraft carrier and cruiser—some nineteen major warships in all—towards the area in which renewal of the action seemed likely to occur. Force H, under Admiral Somerville, had been called north from Gibraltar late on the evening of the 23rd; the *Rodney* and four destroyers were about 550 miles south-east of the enemy and were ordered to close; the *Ramillies* was ordered to leave her Halifax

---

[1] See Map 32 (*facing p. 409*).

convoy and place herself to the west of the enemy and the *Revenge* to leave Halifax and close towards the *Bismarck*, while the cruiser *Edinburgh* left her Atlantic patrol to join the shadowing force. Coastal Command aircraft now played a valuable part in helping the shadowers to keep touch with the enemy and with each other. Thus was the concentration of all the instruments of maritime power, some from thousands of miles away, co-ordinated as by a single directing mind. But escape was still quite possible, and the Commander-in-Chief decided that he must call on the aircrews of the *Victorious* to try still further to reduce the enemy's speed, since there was as yet no firm evidence that the *Bismarck* had received appreciable damage in the first action.

At 2.40 p.m. that afternoon, the 24th, Admiral Tovey therefore detached Rear-Admiral A. T. B. Curteis, commanding the 2nd Cruiser Squadron, with the *Galatea*, *Aurora*, *Kenya* and *Hermione* to proceed with the *Victorious* to a position within 100 miles of the enemy, from which the carrier's torpedo-bombers were to be launched. But the *Victorious*, the only ship available to carry out such an attack, was, like the *Prince of Wales*, newly commissioned and by no means fully efficient. She had been on the point of starting off for Gibraltar with a cargo of Hurricanes for Malta and only had No. 825 Squadron of nine Swordfish and No. 802 Squadron of six Fulmars to strike at and shadow the enemy; and even these were inexperienced and only partially trained. At 10 p.m. Admiral Curteis was within 120 miles of the enemy as indicated by the shadowing cruisers' reports, and he decided to wait no longer. In very bad weather the nine torpedo-bombers, led by Lieutenant-Commander E. Esmonde, followed shortly by Fulmars for shadowing, took off from the aircraft carrier's deck and flew through scudding rain clouds to the south-west over the darkening sea. At 11.27 p.m. a radar contact was obtained and the *Bismarck* was briefly sighted through a gap in the clouds, only to be lost to view almost at once. But the shadowing ships were successfully located, and they were able to redirect the aircraft towards their quarry. Just after midnight the attacks started and were pressed home most gallantly under conditions of the utmost disadvantage, since all possibility of surprise had been lost when the aircraft were sighted during the first approach. One torpedo hit was obtained amidships; but it caused no serious damage to the heavily-protected battleship. The Swordfish squadron then rounded off their remarkable exploit by all managing to re-locate their parent ship and landing in safety in the dark. Two of the shadowing Fulmars were, however, lost.

We will now retrace our steps for a few hours and view the situation through the enemy's eyes. Admiral Lütjens' first object was to rid himself of the persistent shadowers. All U-boat operations against

Map annotations

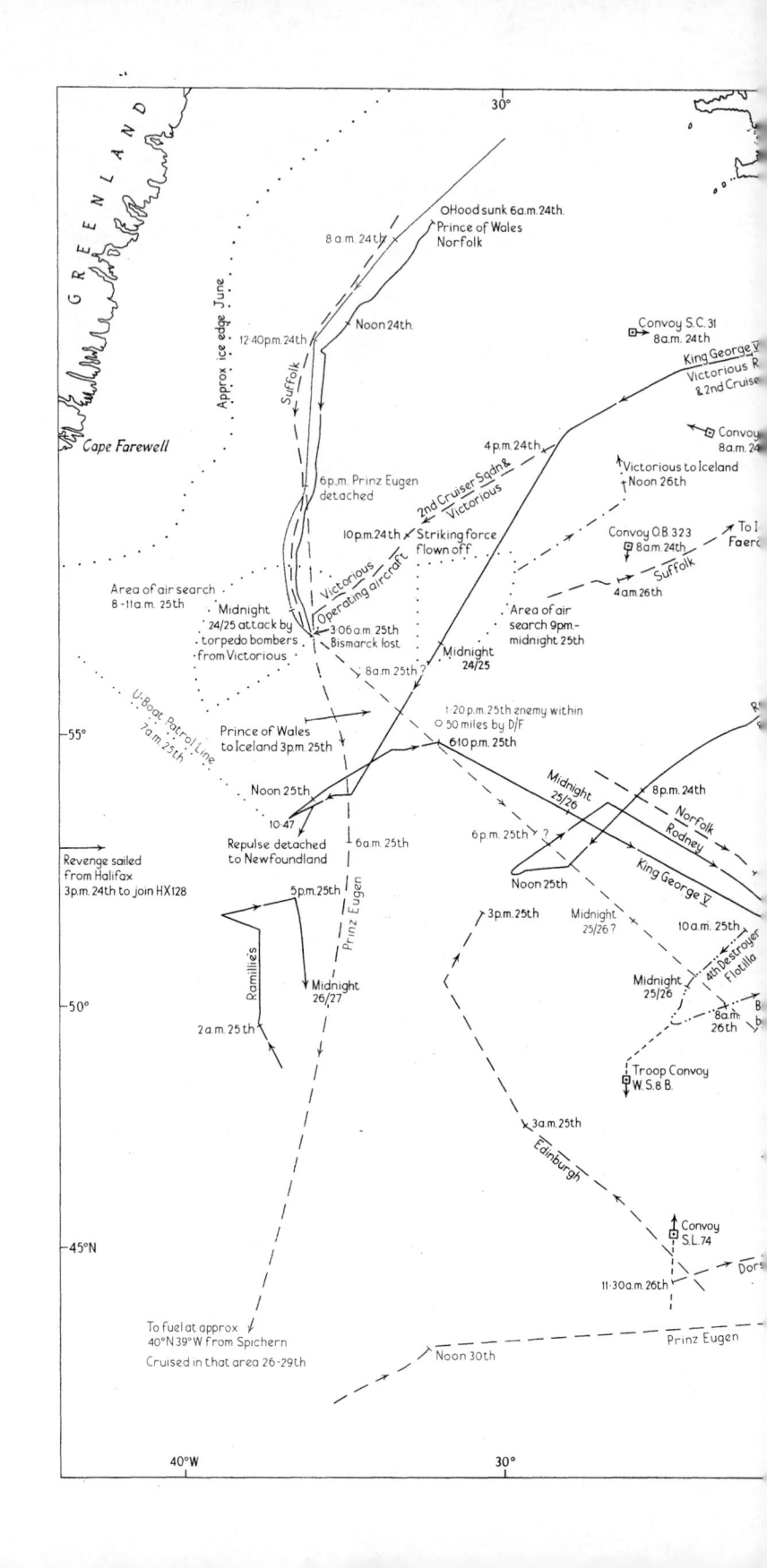

- GREENLAND
- Cape Farewell
- Approx. ice edge June
- 30°
- Hood sunk 6 a.m. 24th
- Prince of Wales
- Norfolk
- 8 a.m. 24th
- Noon 24th
- 12.40 p.m. 24th
- Suffolk
- 6 p.m. Prinz Eugen detached
- 2nd Cruiser Sqdn & Victorious
- 4 p.m. 24th
- 10 p.m. 24th Striking force flown off
- Victorious Operating aircraft
- Convoy S.C. 31 8 a.m. 24th
- King George V
- Victorious R & 2nd Cruiser
- Convoy 8 a.m. 24
- Victorious to Iceland Noon 26th
- Convoy O.B. 323 8 a.m. 24th
- To Faero
- Suffolk 4 a.m. 26th
- Area of air search 8-11 a.m. 25th
- Midnight 24/25 attack by torpedo bombers from Victorious
- 3.06 a.m. 25th Bismarck lost
- 8 a.m. 25th ?
- Midnight 24/25
- Area of air search 9 p.m.-midnight 25th
- U-Boat Patrol Line 7 a.m. 25th
- -55°
- Prince of Wales to Iceland 3 p.m. 25th
- Noon 25th
- 10.47
- 6 a.m. 25th
- 1.20 p.m. 25th enemy within 50 miles by D/F
- 6.10 p.m. 25th
- Midnight 25/26
- 6 p.m. 25th ?
- 8 p.m. 24th
- Norfolk
- Rodney
- King George V.
- Revenge sailed from Halifax 3 p.m. 24th to join HX 128
- Repulse detached to Newfoundland
- 5 p.m. 25th
- Prinz Eugen
- Noon 25th
- Midnight 25/26 ?
- 10 a.m. 25th
- 4th Destroyer Flotilla
- Midnight 25/26
- 8 a.m. 26th
- Ramillies
- Midnight 26/27
- -50°
- 2 a.m. 25th
- 3 a.m. 25th
- Troop Convoy W.S.8.B.
- Edinburgh
- -45°N
- Convoy S.L.74
- 11.30 a.m. 26th
- Dors
- To fuel at approx 40°N 39°W from Spichern Cruised in that area 26-29th
- Noon 30th
- Prinz Eugen
- 40°W
- 30°

Map 32

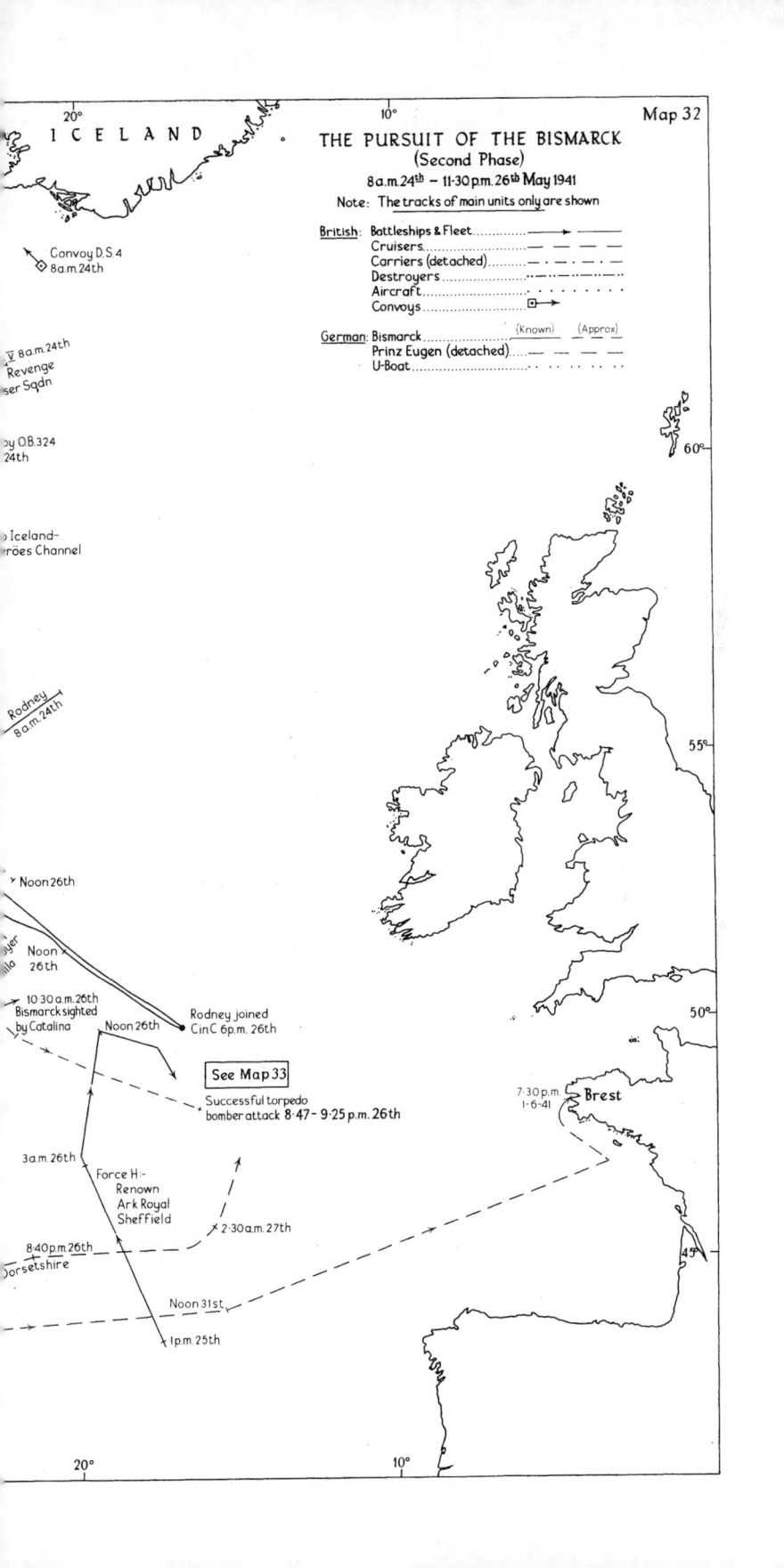

ICELAND

THE PURSUIT OF THE BISMARCK
(Second Phase)
8 a.m. 24th – 11.30 p.m. 26th May 1941
Note: The tracks of main units only are shown

British: Battleships & Fleet..............
Cruisers................................
Carriers (detached)...............
Destroyers..........................
Aircraft...............................
Convoys..............................

German: Bismarck................... (Known) (Approx)
Prinz Eugen (detached).....
U-Boat..............................

Convoy D.S.4
8 a.m. 24th

V. 8 a.m. 24th
Revenge
ser Sqdn

y O.B.324
24th

Iceland-
röes Channel

Rodney
8 a.m. 24th

Noon 26th

Noon
26th

10.30 a.m. 26th
Bismarck sighted
by Catalina

Rodney joined
CinC 6 p.m. 26th

Noon 26th

See Map 33

Successful torpedo
bomber attack 8.47 – 9.25 p.m. 26th

7.30 p.m.
1·6·41 Brest

3 a.m. 26th

Force H:-
Renown
Ark Royal
Sheffield

2·30 a.m. 27th

8.40 p.m. 26th
Dorsetshire

Noon 31st

1 p.m. 25th

shipping had been suspended by Dönitz in case they were needed to help the surface ships. Seven were on patrol not far off the *Bismarck's* course, and on the 24th Lütjens asked for these to be spread south of Cape Farewell.[1] He hoped to lure the shadowing cruisers into this trap. But by the evening he realised that he was unlikely to shake off the pursuit because the British ships' radar, of whose existence German intelligence had not warned him, was too effective. The damage received from the *Prince of Wales'* gunfire, and in particular the loss of fuel caused by one of her hits, had made the intended foray in the Atlantic impracticable. He therefore decided to detach the *Prinz Eugen* on to the trade routes and to make for a French port with the battleship. We do not know the reasons which governed his decision not to attempt the homeward passage to Germany by the northern route. In Germany it was expected that he would take that course.

Between 6 and 7 p.m. the *Bismarck* fell back towards her pursuers with the object of creating the diversion necessary to allow the *Prinz Eugen* to break away unobserved. A brief gun action with the shadowers followed, without damage to either side, and the German cruiser slipped away to the south-west undetected. The *Bismarck* then resumed her southerly course with the British cruisers still clinging tenaciously to her tail. Just after 1 a.m. on the 25th another brief skirmish, again without result, took place between pursuers and pursued, and then Admiral Lütjens secured the very success for which he had been vainly trying ever since he was first sighted on the evening of the 23rd. The shadowing cruisers lost touch with him. The *Suffolk* obtained her last contact at 3.6 a.m. as she was starting the outward leg of her anti-submarine zig-zag. On the return leg she failed to pick him up again.

Admiral Tovey attributed this misfortune to over-confidence bred of the successful use of her radar during the preceding thirty-six hours. In the wisdom of after events it certainly seems that to carry out a wide zig-zag at the extreme limit of her radar's performance was to invite exactly what happened. At 4 a.m. the *Suffolk* reported that she had lost touch, and she and her sister ship then searched in the direction in which they thought the enemy must have steered, towards the west. But this actually took them away from their quarry which, soon after the *Suffolk's* last contact, had altered course from south to south-east to head directly towards St Nazaire. The fleet flagship was then little more than a hundred miles away to the south-east and closing the enemy rapidly; but Admiral Tovey's hopes of bringing his ships into action within the next few hours immediately fell to the ground.[2] The margin whereby the *Bismarck* had escaped

---

[1] See Map 32.
[2] See Map 32.

him was narrow but, for the time being, enough. Thus ended 'in the treacherous twilight of a northern middle watch' the first phase of the pursuit.

There now followed a period of anxious searching. The *Suffolk* and *Norfolk* were already seeking the enemy to the west and south-west of his last known position; the *Victorious* was told to start air searches to the north-west at dawn, and the four ships of the 2nd Cruiser Squadron were ordered to supplement the work of the carrier's aircraft. Admiral Tovey had balanced the various alternatives open to the enemy. He considered that the most serious threat would arise from his meeting a supply tanker, probably south of Greenland or in the Davis Strait, and so being able to start his onslaught on our convoys with full tanks. He concluded that to make such a rendezvous would be the enemy's next intention. It was impossible to search simultaneously in all directions, and the sector between north and south-east was therefore left, for the time, unwatched. By ill chance it was through that sector that the enemy was now actually steaming.

But the unsearched sector was by no means entirely empty of British ships. The *Rodney* had placed herself across the track towards the Bay of Biscay, the cruiser *Edinburgh* was to the south of the *Rodney*, the *Dorsetshire* was approaching the same area with a convoy and the battleship *Ramillies* was patrolling to the south of the Commander-in-Chief. And, answering the Admiralty's farsighted beckon, Force H—the *Renown* (Captain R. R. McGrigor) and *Ark Royal* (Captain L. E. H. Maund), and the cruiser *Sheffield* (Captain C. A. A. Larcom)—though still 1,300 miles away to the south-east was hastening towards the waters through which, if the enemy was bound for France, he must certainly pass. The meshes of the net were still amply wide to enable a single enemy to slip through unobserved; but it was, none the less, drawing tighter. Though no one, at this time, knew whether the enemy was inside the great ocean area around which the net was being drawn, he did, in fact, pass less than 100 miles astern of Admiral Tovey at 8 a.m. on the 25th and, later that day, still closer to the *Rodney* and *Edinburgh*. But his progress towards the south-east remained undetected.

Admiral Tovey now gained the impression, from bearings of the enemy's wireless transmissions sent out to him by the Admiralty, that the *Bismarck* was breaking back to the north-east—towards the Iceland–Faeröes passage. The deduction was incorrect, and the mistake was partly caused by the Admiralty's method of signalling the bearings. It caused the Commander-in-Chief to reverse his course at 10.47 a.m. and to steer at high speed to cover that possible avenue

A CATALINA RE-SIGHTS THE ENEMY

of escape, while the movements of the searching forces were adjusted to conform. But the pursuit of this false scent caused the fleet flagship to drop still further behind the fleeing enemy.

As this day of uncertainty and anxiety advanced, the enemy's true destination was the subject of constant review both in London and in the fleet flagship. Though the general movement of the various squadrons and ships of the Home Fleet continued throughout the forenoon and afternoon to be north-easterly, the Admiralty did, at 11 a.m., tell Force H to act on the assumption that the enemy was making for Brest; and, as the day advanced, opinion in London hardened in favour of that port being his true destination. But it was not until the evening that the Commander-in-Chief, Home Fleet, and all other forces were told to act on that assumption. At 6.10 p.m. the fleet flagship accordingly altered course to the south-east. But she was, by that time, about 150 miles behind, and the prospects of catching the enemy were therefore anything but good.[1]

Throughout the 25th long-range Catalina aircraft of Coastal Command had been covering the enemy's most probable tracks both towards the Iceland–Faeröes passage and towards the west of France; but only our own forces were sighted by them. Next day an even wider scheme of searches was organised to watch the northern escape routes and the approaches to the Bay of Biscay. At 10.30 a.m. on the 26th a Catalina aircraft of No. 209 Squadron (Flying Officer D. A. Briggs), which was flying the southernmost of the Bay patrols, sighted the *Bismarck* and came under heavy and accurate fire from her. But she managed to send a report before losing contact. The turning point in the long and arduous chase had suddenly come; and the clouds of uncertainty which had descended at 4 a.m. on the 25th, when the *Suffolk* reported that she had lost touch, were at once dispelled. But knowledge of the enemy's position and of his true intention did not by any means make it certain that he would be caught. It will be appropriate to review the positions of the various forces at the moment when the enemy was resighted.[2]

The Catalina's report placed the enemy 690 miles slightly north of west from Brest, which port he could, at the speed at which he was then steaming, reach late on the evening of the 27th. The time available to intercept him before he came under the protecting wings of the Luftwaffe's heavy bombers was, therefore, plainly short, probably no more than twenty-four hours. The fleet flagship was about 130 miles away to the north, and Admiral Tovey's chances of catching the *Bismarck* were therefore slender, if her present speed was maintained. The *Prince of Wales* and the *Repulse*, both short of fuel, had

---

[1] See Map 32 (*facing p. 409*).
[2] See Map 32.

long since been detached to Iceland and Newfoundland respectively; but the *Rodney* (Captain F. H. G. Dalrymple-Hamilton) had joined the Commander-in-Chief at 6 p.m. the previous evening, so that the battle squadron again possessed the advantage of substantial gun superiority—if only an opportunity to use it could be created. But shortage of fuel in the *King George V* and *Rodney* was now causing Admiral Tovey serious anxiety: if the pursuit to the east were prolonged much further, his ships might be unable to return at reasonable speed to a home base, and so might be caught by the expected onslaught of the German heavy bombers, or fall victims to the U-boats which the enemy was certain to have directed towards the track of the *Bismarck's* pursuers. And the destroyers which had been screening the heavy ships had, by now, all had to return to replenish their fuel tanks. That the dangers—though not allowed to influence the pursuit—were real is shown by the knowledge gained much later that, at 8 p.m. on the 26th, the *Renown* and *Ark Royal* passed, while unescorted, quite close to U.556. She was one of half a dozen U-boats which had been on passage to or from the Atlantic, and had been ordered to concentrate and lie in wait for the *Bismarck's* pursuers some 450 miles from the French coast. Happily the U-boat had already expended all her torpedoes.

Such, then, was the position and state of the pursuing forces at the time of the resighting of the *Bismarck*. So far it gave little ground for expecting that they would catch the fleeing enemy. But a glance at the operational maps in the Admiralty showed that Admiral Somerville's northward progress from Gibraltar had now placed Force H in a most favourable, even ideal, position to bar the *Bismarck's* eastward progress. Having steamed hard through heavy seas and a rising gale of wind, it was now seventy miles to the *east* of the position where the enemy had been resighted and directly in the path to Brest. Though the *Renown* could not possibly engage the battleship in a gun duel there was at least a good chance that the *Ark Royal's* aircraft and the cruiser *Sheffield* could shadow her continuously, and that the carrier's torpedo-bombers would strike home a deadly enough blow to enable the battle squadron to catch up and kill the hunted enemy. As Admiral Tovey described it later he himself was, at this time, 'a terribly long way off, and again our only hope lay in the Fleet Air Arm'. Meanwhile coming in from the west were five destroyers of the 4th Flotilla (Captain P. Vian), which had been detached by the Admiralty at 2 a.m. that morning from a W.S. convoy to join Admiral Tovey and replace the latter's departed destroyer screen. Plainly the resighting of the *Bismarck* and the position reached by Force H had immediately transformed the outlook; hopes rose correspondingly in London and in every one of the ships involved in the long pursuit.

ATTACKS BY 'ARK ROYAL'S' SWORDFISH 413

The Catalina's report had placed the enemy some twenty-five miles too far to the west, but two of the *Ark Royal's* searching Swordfish soon found the *Bismarck*, and a succession of them now kept touch while the carrier prepared to launch her striking force. At 1.15 p.m. the *Sheffield* was detached to the west to find and shadow the enemy, but the signal reporting this had not been decoded in the *Ark Royal* by the time her striking force had left. This nearly had disastrous consequences. At 2.50 p.m. fourteen Swordfish armed with torpedoes had left the carrier's heaving, spray-swept flight deck and were flying towards the enemy through low, unbroken clouds and over a storm-wracked sea. The results of the attack were awaited with the utmost anxiety in the Admiralty and in the fleet flagship; for on its success all seemed to depend. At 3.50 the aircraft, which had approached by radar, attacked through the clouds. Not till after the torpedoes had been launched was it realised that they had been aimed—not at the *Bismarck* but at the *Sheffield*, which was then some twenty miles to the north of the enemy. Fortunately the cruiser at once realised what had happened, took drastic avoiding action and all the torpedoes missed or were exploded harmlessly by their magnetic pistols. The disappointment, even dismay, at the anti-climax which had occurred at the moment when it had seemed that, at long last, success lay within grasp was intense. Not a moment was lost in rectifying the mistake. Yet it may not have been altogether a misfortune, for the failure of the magnetic torpedo pistols caused them to be replaced by contact pistols for the second attack. And the next torpedoes were also set to run at a shallower depth.

The first striking force returned to the carrier, and by 7.10 p.m. a second force composed of fifteen Swordfish of Nos. 810, 818 and 820 Squadrons led by Lieutenant-Commander T. P. Coode was off again on the same errand. This time they were ordered first to find the *Sheffield*, which would direct them to the target.

At 8.47 p.m. the attacks started. In the prevailing conditions of low rain cloud, strong wind, stormy seas, fading daylight and intense and accurate enemy gunfire, it was natural that perfect timing and co-ordination of all the attacks was not achieved. They were actually spread over a period of thirty-eight minutes, but individual aircrews pressed in most gallantly and two of the thirteen torpedoes released found their mark. One hit was on the armour belt and, like the earlier one obtained by the *Victorious*' aircraft, had little effect. The other was right aft, damaged the *Bismarck's* propellers, wrecked her steering gear and jammed the rudders. It was this hit which sealed her fate.

Shortly after this happy turn of events Captain Vian's five destroyers, shepherded towards the quarry by the *Sheffield*, came upon the scene. The Catalina's sighting report had been intercepted while they were steering to join Admiral Tovey the previous morning, and Captain Vian had thereupon immediately altered course to the south-east, in disregard of his previous orders from the Admiralty. In doing so he undoubtedly interpreted correctly his Commander-in-Chief's unspoken wish, even though this left the battle squadron still without a destroyer screen. Not only did Captain Vian's initiative provide a final chance of slowing down the *Bismarck* by torpedo attack should the *Ark Royal's* Swordfish fail in that purpose but, throughout the night, while air shadowing was impossible, his reports were invaluable in keeping Admiral Tovey informed of the enemy's position and his state.

Soon after the destroyers gained touch Captain Vian realised that the enemy's speed had been drastically reduced. He defined his primary object as 'the delivery of the enemy to the Commander-in-Chief', but permitted attack by torpedoes to be made during the night, provided that they did not involve the destroyers in heavy losses. The Polish-manned *Piorun* tried to create a diversion to the west while the other destroyers got in their attacks from the south-east. She soon became involved in a gun action with the giant enemy at close range. Between 1.20 and 7 a.m. on the 27th the *Cossack*, *Zulu*, *Maori* and *Sikh* all fired torpedoes, and all in turn came under heavy fire.[1] It is likely that two hits were obtained. But the destroyers were, perhaps, fortunate to escape damage from an enemy which, though crippled, was still possessed of the full hitting power of all his armaments. The Commander-in-Chief fully approved the manner in which the 4th Flotilla conducted its night operations.

As soon as the news of the result of the torpedo-bomber attacks was confirmed by the reconnaissance aircraft's reports of the enemy's slow speed and erratic progress, Admiral Tovey turned his two battleships to the south in the hope of bringing the enemy finally to book that same evening against the after-glow of the sunset. But he was too far off and the light failed before he could find his quarry. There were so many friendly ships about, and the enemy's exact position was so uncertainly known that Admiral Tovey decided against seeking night action. He was confident that, with Captain Vian's destroyers in touch, the enemy would not slip through his fingers. During the night the enemy's exact position was established by plotting the destroyers' wireless transmissions in the flagship.

As dawn broke on the 27th the destroyers took up positions in four sectors from which the enemy could be continuously observed and awaited the arrival of the battle squadron. The *Ark Royal* had prepared yet another striking force, but visibility was now too bad to launch it. Admiral Tovey had already warned Force H, which had performed its crucial task so successfully, to keep clear during the

---

[1] See Map 33 (*facing p. 415*).

THE PURSUIT
23rd N
The Fi
Night Attacks by
10·30 pm – midni

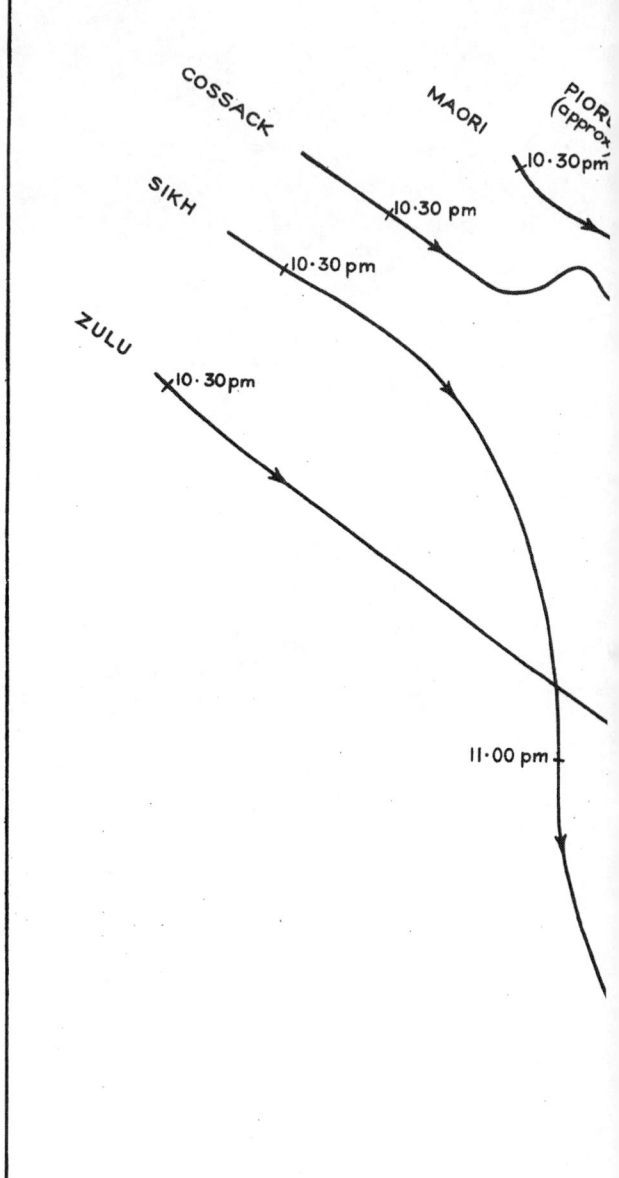

COSSACK

MAORI

PIOR
(approx
10·30 pm

SIKH
10·30 pm

10·30 pm

ZULU
10·30 pm

11·00 pm

0

Nautica

of the BISMARCK
May 1941
nal Phase
4th Destroyer Flotilla
ght 26th May 1941

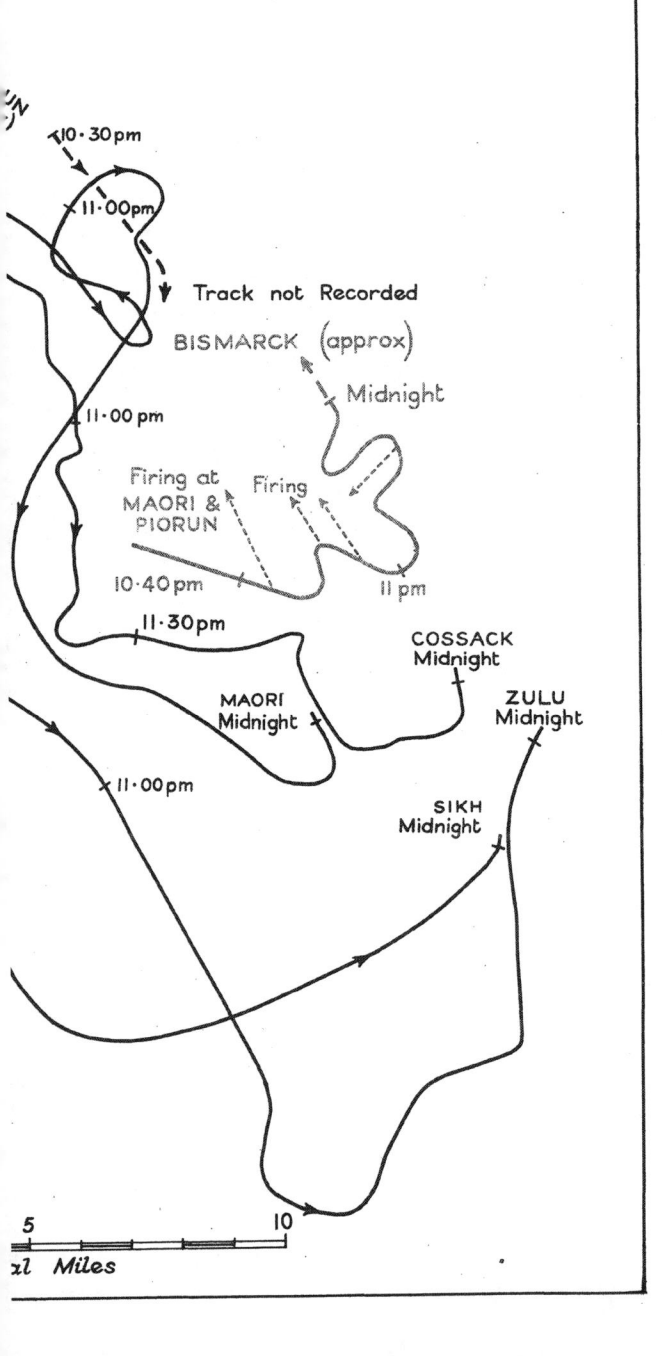

10.30 pm
11.00 pm

Track not Recorded
BISMARCK (approx)
Midnight
11.00 pm

Firing at MAORI & PIORUN
Firing
10.40 pm
11 pm
11.30 pm

COSSACK Midnight
MAORI Midnight
ZULU Midnight

11.00 pm

SIKH Midnight

5 10
Miles

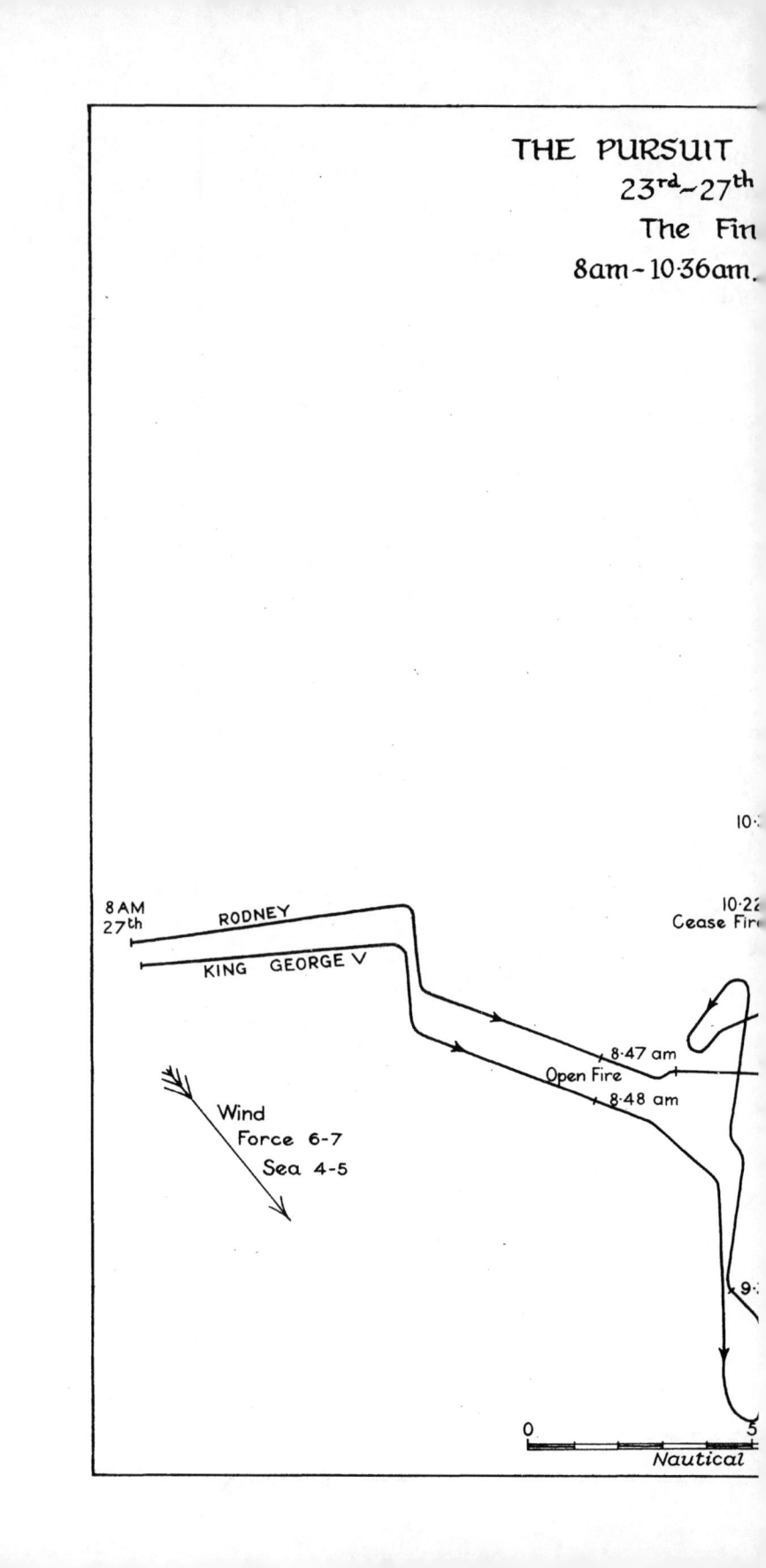

THE PURSUIT
23rd–27th
The Fin
8am–10.36am.

10·

8 AM
27th   RODNEY   10·2͏
                                                    Cease Fir͏

     KING GEORGE V

                                          8·47 am
                                       Open Fire
                                          8·48 am

   Wind
   Force 6-7
   Sea 4-5

                                                         9·

                                            0   5
                                              Nautical

of the BISMARCK
May 1941
nal Action
n. 27th May 1941

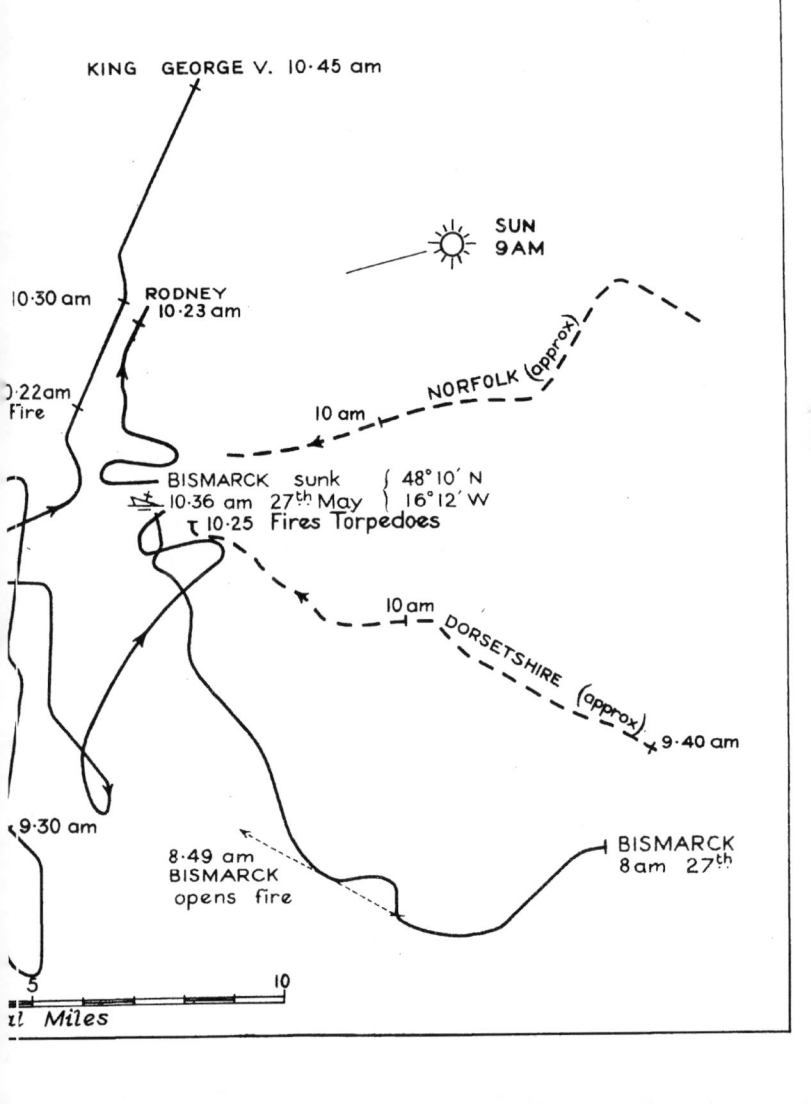

KING GEORGE V. 10·45 am

SUN 9AM

10·30 am

RODNEY 10·23 am

NORFOLK (approx)

10 am

):22 am Fire

BISMARCK sunk { 48° 10′ N
10·36 am 27th May { 16° 12′ W
10·25 Fires Torpedoes

10 am

DORSETSHIRE (approx)

9·40 am

9·30 am

8·49 am
BISMARCK
opens fire

BISMARCK
8 am 27th

5   10
Miles

THE 'BISMARCK' SUNK, 27TH MAY 1941

approach of the heavy ships. The *Dorsetshire* (Captain B. C. S. Martin), too, was closing in from the south. Of the ships which had seen the beginning of the long pursuit only the *Norfolk* was still in the hunt, and she was some ten miles from the Commander-in-Chief.

But the margin of success had been exceedingly narrow, for Admiral Tovey had decided that if the *Bismarck* had not been slowed down by midnight on the 26th–27th, he would have to break off the chase. Whether the other ships present could have finished off so redoubtable an enemy need not be argued, since the *Ark Royal's* Swordfish had eliminated the need to make the attempt. But they had done so by a margin of only some three hours in a pursuit which had lasted for as many days.

It is not intended to follow the final gun action between the *King George V*, *Rodney* and *Bismarck* in full detail. After first favouring the enemy the wheel of fortune had settled firmly in the British favour, and the result was a foregone conclusion. At dawn the light was very variable and Admiral Tovey decided to await full daylight and then to approach 'with the advantage of wind, sea and light'. The *Rodney* was ordered to assume open order from her flagship and manœuvre as she liked. The battle squadron approached from the north-west on a course nearly opposite to the general trend of the *Bismarck's* erratic and slow progress.[1] All three ships opened fire between 8.47 and 8.49 a.m. during the end-on approach, and the British ships deployed independently to the south a few minutes later at a range of about 16,000 yards. The enemy's first salvos nearly hit the *Rodney*, but thereafter the accuracy and volume of the *Bismarck's* fire fell away rapidly. Soon after 9 a.m. she started to sustain heavy damage from hits by armour-piercing shell. After running to the south for some twenty minutes both British ships turned north on to courses nearly parallel to the enemy's and the action was continued. Gradually the range was reduced to what can justly be described as point-blank target practice. By 10.15 the giant battleship had been reduced to a flaming shambles, and all her guns were silent. Admiral Tovey, conscious of his acute shortage of fuel, now broke off the gun action and ordered the cruisers to sink the enemy with torpedoes, while he hurried away to the north. But the *Dorsetshire* had anticipated this order and fired two torpedoes into the wallowing hulk's starboard side and one into her port side. At 10.36 the *Bismarck* had disappeared in 48° 10′ North, 16° 12′ West, with her flag still flying. She had fought gallantly to the finish, even after overwhelming strength had been concentrated against her. A total of 110 survivors was rescued

---

[1] See Map 33.

by the *Dorsetshire* and *Maori*. The threatened presence of enemy submarines curtailed the rescue work.

Admiral Tovey's rapid disengagement and return northwards achieved his object of avoiding the threat of heavy bombing attacks and U-boats. But two destroyers 100 miles to the south of him were not so fortunate and the *Mashona* was sunk off the coast of Galway on the 28th. All our other forces returned safely to their bases and had soon resumed their normal duties of escorting convoys and patrolling the seas.

In reviewing the wide scope of these operations which began so disastrously but ended in exacting triumphant vengeance for the loss of the *Hood*, we may note the many points of similarity between this successful pursuit and the vain search for the two battle cruisers in the previous January, February and March.[1] In both cases the first contact with the enemy was made by our cruisers in far northern waters; on both occasions the first contacts were lost, and there followed a period of uncertainty as to whether the enemy would return to Germany north-about or make for a French port; the need to guard against the first possibility both times resulted in the heavy ships of the Home Fleet resuming the pursuit, when contact had been regained, many miles behind the enemy; it was the *Ark Royal*, of Force H, coming north from Gibraltar, which on both occasions next reported the enemy's position accurately; and Coastal Command's Biscay patrols sighted both enemy forces as they approached the French coast. But there the analogy ends, for in the May pursuit the element of luck, which can never be wholly absent in war and which had certainly favoured the enemy in the March operations, deserted the German cause, and the tenacity of the ships and aircraft turned the initial disaster into an important—and, moreover, a very timely—success.

The strategic control exercised by the Admiralty followed the same lines on both occasions and the skill with which the many widely-separated but integrated moves were made is to be admired.[2] In Admiral Tovey's words 'the accuracy of the information supplied by the Admiralty and the speed with which it was passed were remarkable; and the balance struck between information and instructions passed to the forces out of visual touch with me was ideal'.

The material lessons derived from this action were many. Even

---

[1] See p. 373 *et seq.*
[2] See pp. 26–27.

The German Battleship *Bismarck*.

il track left by the *Bismarck* after her action with H.M.S.'s *Hood* and *Prince of Wales*, 24th May 194
south of the Denmark Strait. Taken by an aircraft of Coastal Command. (See page 407.)

he *Bismarck* on fire in the final action with H.M.S.'s *King George V* and *Rodney*, 27th May 194

taking account of her tremendous size (42,345 tons standard displacement and 52,700 tons at extreme deep load) the amount of punishment which the *Bismarck* withstood was remarkable. No less than seventy-one torpedoes were fired at her and at least eight of them—possibly as many as twelve—scored hits. The number of 16-inch and 14-inch shell hits which she sustained without sinking or blowing up cannot be assessed, but was certainly very large. The ability of the Germans to build tremendously stout ships had been demonstrated in the First World War. The art had certainly not been lost in the interval between the two wars.

On the British side the loss of the *Hood* had shown how necessary it was not only to keep the matrix of our Navy—the battle fleet—modern and up to date, but how easily the delusion could be fostered that old ships could be made to do the work of the new ships which we should have built but did not build. That delusion has, through the centuries, cost us many ships and many thousands of British sailors' lives. The failures among the new 14-inch armaments of the *King George V* and *Prince of Wales* were disturbing. They showed how long a period may elapse before a weapon of new design is past its 'teething troubles' and really fit for battle. The danger of allowing our margin of strength to sink so low that newly commissioned and recently refitted ships have to be sent into action before they can possibly have achieved full efficiency was also emphasised. On the credit side was the tenacity with which the cruisers shadowed the enemy for so many long and arduous hours, the far-ranging and finally successful searches of Coastal Command, and the dash and determination of the naval aircrews under conditions in which it had never been imagined that carrier aircraft could and would be operated. And the instinctive manner in which every commanding officer in every class of ship had guessed and correctly interpreted the wishes of the Commander-in-Chief proved the soundness of our basic naval training and traditions. Admiral Tovey must have felt justly proud of them when he wrote that 'the co-operation, skill and understanding displayed by all forces during this prolonged chase gave me the utmost satisfaction. Flag and Commanding Officers of detached units invariably took the action I would have wished, before and without receiving instructions from me'.

Nothing more was heard of the *Prinz Eugen* until she was located in Brest on the 4th of June. She had actually set a southerly course after parting company with the *Bismarck* on the 24th of May to refuel in mid-Atlantic. This she successfully accomplished. Two days later she developed engine defects, and her Captain decided to break off his foray and make for Brest. Her approach was detected on the 27th of

May, but she slipped through our submarine patrols and entered the port on the 1st of June. Her cruise was completely devoid of results.

    Thus were the ambitions of the German Naval Staff to strike simultaneously with all their most powerful surface ships at our Atlantic convoys utterly brought to nought. The two battle cruisers were now immobilised in Brest, and one of them was seriously damaged. The *Prinz Eugen's* brief excursion had confirmed what had been learned from the *Hipper's* experiences—that the 8-inch cruisers were unsuited for commerce raiding. And the Germans had lost the pride of their fleet. Though the truth was to remain concealed from the British Cabinet and the Admiralty for many months to come, it is now plain that the actions described in this chapter marked the final defeat of the enemy's attempts to disrupt the flow of our Atlantic shipping with his surface forces. Never again were the ambitions of the spring of 1941 resurrected, and such surface forces as remained to him were hereafter used only in the Baltic and against the ships carrying supplies to North Russia. But that runs ahead of the stage now reached in our story.

CHAPTER XX

THE AFRICAN CAMPAIGNS
1st January–31st May, 1941

> It takes the Navy three years to build a ship. It would take three hundred to rebuild a tradition.*
> *Admiral Sir Andrew Cunningham to his staff at Alexandria.* May 1941.

AT the end of 1940 the strategic situation in the Mediterranean and Middle East appeared to be by no means unfavourable to the British cause. In spite of the enemy's sweeping successes in Europe our control of the seas had been maintained and, although our mercantile shipping resources were severely strained, the reinforcement of the Middle East and the building up of the armies in East Africa had proceeded steadily by the use, in general, of the long Cape route. By the air attack on Taranto and by the two surface ship encounters with the Italian Fleet, Admirals Cunningham and Somerville had established a clear ascendancy within the Mediterranean; and the occasional use of the direct through-route by fast convoys bound for Egypt had been shown to be practicable. The Italian Navy's threat to the Red Sea shipping routes had proved illusory and the Regia Aeronautica, though its high-level bombing had sometimes been uncomfortably accurate, its torpedo attacks a considerable menace and its shadowing and reporting of our movements well executed, had not been able to drive our fleets and squadrons from the central basin. The air threat had not, in fact, developed to the serious proportions which had been anticipated. In the Western Desert General Wavell had recently struck the Italian Army hard, and it was in full retreat; we had occupied Crete and our hold on the island had greatly improved our control of the eastern basin, while long-neglected Malta had withstood Italian attacks and received modest reinforcements. Finally a new sea-air route for the more rapid reinforcement of our air strength in the Middle East had been opened and was being developed through Takoradi on the Gold Coast. There seemed, at the turn of the year, to be solid grounds for hoping that, in the next phase, we should be able to assume the offensive, bring the Italian East African Empire crashing to the

---

* There is no doubt that Admiral Cunningham expressed this thought to his staff several times during the evacuation from Crete. The exact words used varied on different occasions, but the purpose behind them remained the same.

ground and drive the Italian forces west from Libya. Yet during the next five months only one of these hopes—and that perhaps the least important—was brought to fruition, while in every other direction we suffered severe reverses. It was, of course, the intervention of German forces, and of the Luftwaffe in particular, which swung the pendulum again in the enemy's favour and caused the War Cabinet's principal hopes to be deferred for another two years and more. This chapter sets out, therefore, to tell the story of a phase of the war which saw the temporary extinction of the light which, at the end of 1940, had seemed to shine, as yet feebly, on the road towards victory.

It was early in the new year that the portents appeared in the sky, for Hitler had moved one 'Fliegerkorps' of the Luftwaffe to Sicilian airfields in January. In his directive to its commander he stated that 'the most important task is to attack the British Navy, particularly in . . . Alexandria but also in the Suez Canal . . . and in the straits between Sicily and the north coast of Africa'. To carry out this task 'Fliegerkorps X', which had taken part in the Norway campaign with success and had specialised in attacks on ships, had, by mid-January, a strength of 150 bombers and dive-bombers, about two dozen twin-engined fighters and a few reconnaissance aircraft based in Sicily. In the following month it was reinforced by single-engined fighters as well. The Italian Air Force had about forty-five bombers and dive-bombers and seventy-five fighters in Sicily; seventy bombers and twenty-five of its fighters were based in Sardinia, and they played a part in attacking Force H and the convoys it was escorting eastward from Gibraltar. The German air reinforcements were not, as the Italians had suggested, placed under their orders, but worked as an independent command.

To oppose this great concentration of the enemy's air power there were in Malta, on the 15th of January, fifteen Royal Air Force Hurricanes. Another eighteen arrived in the convoy operation shortly to be described or were flown from Egypt very soon, but the great disparity between the two sides' air forces continued throughout the first phase of the battle for Malta which was now about to open.

The Army of the Nile, whose offensive had started on the 9th of December, was still driving victoriously westward leaving hordes of Italian prisoners behind it. Tobruk was captured on the 22nd of January, Derna on the 30th, and on the 6th of February Benghazi was reached. Then the decision to reinforce the Greeks in face of the plainly growing German land threat from the north not only stopped the army's drive towards Tripoli, but led to the newly-won territory being weakly held.

Meanwhile the Mediterranean Fleet had had its first encounter with the Luftwaffe, and the pattern followed only too closely the

OPERATION 'EXCESS'

experiences of the Home Fleet off Norway and of our light forces in the narrow seas at home during the previous summer. A fast military convoy consisting of three ships for the Piræus, with stores for the Greek Army, and one for Malta left Gibraltar on the 6th of January and was followed next day by Force H—now consisting of the *Renown*, *Malaya*, *Ark Royal*, *Sheffield* and seven destroyers. The new cruiser *Bonaventure* and four more destroyers sailed with the convoy as its close escort for the first part of the passage.

As the entire naval strength from both ends of the Mediterranean was to be engaged in this operation, which had been called 'Excess', Admiral Cunningham took the opportunity simultaneously to pass two merchant ships from Alexandria to Malta and eight empty ones in the opposite direction, while the cruisers *Gloucester* and *Southampton*, with two destroyers, under Rear-Admiral E. de F. Renouf, sailed ahead of the main fleet to carry troops to the island. The movements were complex and demanded careful timing if all forces were to arrive at the appropriate moment in the Narrows between Sicily and the Tunisian coast and exchange guardianship of the main eastbound convoy.

By dawn on the 9th of January Admiral Somerville was ahead of the convoy and covering it from any surface ship interference from the north-east. The convoy was soon joined by the *Southampton* and *Gloucester*, which had landed their troops in Malta the previous day. An Italian air attack was beaten off by the carrier's fighters and by gunfire that afternoon and, at dusk, Admiral Somerville turned over the convoy to Admiral Renouf who, with three cruisers and five destroyers, escorted it through the Narrows. Force H, meanwhile, returned to Gibraltar. On the 10th there was a dawn encounter between the convoy escorts and two Italian torpedo-boats, one of which was sunk, and a short while later Admiral Cunningham joined with the main force from Alexandria, which included the *Warspite*, *Valiant* and the aircraft carrier *Illustrious* (Captain D. W. Boyd). So far all had gone well; the only mishap had been the mining of the destroyer *Gallant*.

But Admiral Cunningham had been shadowed continuously ever since he had sailed from Alexandria and, in the course of the afternoon of the 10th, heavy dive-bombing attacks were made by German Junkers 87s and Junkers 88s assisted by Italian torpedo and high-level bombers. It was only the Germans who were effective. They concentrated on the aircraft carrier, which quickly received six hits from heavy bombs and three very near misses. It is probable that only her armoured flight deck saved her from destruction; but she was severely damaged and only with difficulty limped into Malta after dark. There she was the principal target in more attacks and received further damage. But temporary repairs were carried out while she awaited a favourable opportunity to escape out of the trap which the Luftwaffe had closed on her. On the evening of the 23rd she slipped out of harbour to reach Alexandria safely two days later. Nor was this the end of the story for, on the afternoon of the 11th, the *Gloucester* and *Southampton* were subjected to similar attacks; both were hit and the second-named caught fire and had to be sunk.

Though the object of the operation had been accomplished the cost had been heavy, and the set-back to the fleet's control of the central Mediterranean was plain. Admiral Cunningham at once reported home that the essential purpose had now become the defeat of the Luftwaffe; more fighter aircraft and anti-aircraft guns were therefore needed in Malta and more radar-fitted ships in his fleet; heavy attacks on the Sicilian airfields were also essential. In Admiral Cunningham's words 'the disablement of the *Illustrious*, the loss of the *Southampton* and the heavy air attacks on Malta quickly made it clear that, until fighter protection was available, not only must the through-Mediterranean convoys be suspended but the fleet itself would operate by day within range of the dive-bombers only at considerable risk'. As regards Malta the first and immediate question was whether reinforcement of the island's defences had been left too late, since 'this strategic island' would, as Admiral Cunningham reported, now 'have to fight it out with Sicily'.

One consequence of the Luftwaffe's successes in the central basin in January was that in the following month Admiral Cunningham reopened the question of the strength, organisation and control of No. 201 Group of the R.A.F. on which he had to depend for all air co-operation. He proposed that it should be reorganised on the same lines as Coastal Command at home, to provide better protection for our own ships and a striking force to attack the enemy's. This did not appeal to the Air Officer Commanding-in-Chief, Sir Arthur Longmore, who considered that the way to meet the Navy's requirements, which he did not in any way challenge, was to strengthen the air forces allocated to the Middle East and not to divide up his command. To this the Admiral replied that he did not mind which Service controlled the maritime air forces and was quite content that they should remain under his air colleague; but more aircraft and of more suitable types for the war at sea, and better co-ordination between the naval and air forces concerned in that war, were essential. The matter was referred to London, but no changes were made until the following September.

While these events were happening at sea the westward advance of the Army of the Nile continued, and the Inshore Squadron of the Mediterranean Fleet, which had been formed early in January, strove hard to keep it supplied; for the Army had far outrun its land communications. The rapid clearance and reopening of Tobruk was the most important step, and this was accomplished in a matter of five days. When the Army reached Benghazi the Inshore Squadron followed. But that port presented a far more difficult problem than Tobruk, for not only was it severely damaged but it lay within easy range of the enemy's aircraft which, by intensive bombing and mine-laying, held up the clearance work and prevented the port being reopened. The monitor *Terror* was damaged there on the 22nd of February and sank two days later while trying to reach Alexandria, and numerous small vessels were also lost. By the 24th the impossibility of using the port while its anti-aircraft defences were so inadequate was realised, and all ships were withdrawn.

A period of comparative stability was now expected on the land front, and a rapid recovery of the initiative by the enemy was believed to be unlikely. It was soon to be shown how far this expectation was from the mark. But, quite apart from our under-estimate of the consequences to the land campaign of the arrival of the 'Afrika Korps' under General Rommel, serious problems and difficulties had arisen far in the rear and on the flanks of the Army of the Nile. The first of these was the priority given by the War Cabinet to the immediate despatch of reinforcements to Greece; and the second was the Luftwaffe's arrival in Sicily. Not only had the latter brought increased and imminent peril to Malta, but from their new bases in Rhodes and the Dodecanese the enemy's minelaying aircraft could now reach the Suez Canal. If the canal were blocked or closed for any length of time our whole position in the Middle East would be endangered.

The Luftwaffe's onslaught on Malta started, as has been seen, soon after the berthing of the damaged *Illustrious* there on the 10th of January; it was continued unremittingly during February and March. By the middle of March the condition of the island fortress was clearly becoming critical, seeing that no supplies had been carried to it since Operation 'Excess' early in the new year. On the 23rd of March, however, a small convoy was slipped in by Admiral Cunningham under cover of a fleet operation. Bad weather and the clever use of evasive routing this time defeated the enemy's watchful air patrols. But the relief was only temporary; attacks were renewed as soon as the convoy berthed and two of its ships were hit. There, for the moment, we will leave the beleaguered island.

The first magnetic mines were dropped in the Suez Canal on the 30th of January by aircraft working from an airfield near Benghazi, and several ships were mined in the passages. Minesweeping aircraft were at once sent out, but parts of the canal were several times closed in February and serious delays occurred in the flow of shipping carrying urgently needed supplies and reinforcements. The new aircraft carrier *Formidable*, sent out by the Cape to relieve the damaged *Illustrious*, was among the ships delayed.

In February the true nature of the enemy's threat to Greece also became clear. Bulgaria joined the Axis on the 1st of March, and the entry of German troops followed on a big scale. The transport of British reinforcements to Greece (Operation 'Lustre') started on the 5th, and thereafter the movement of the troops and equipment was carried out continuously in convoys sailing to the Piræus every three days. For the first three weeks the troop and supply convoys ran continuously between Egypt and Greece, in spite of a mounting scale of air attack from the enemy's bases in Rhodes and the islands of the Dodecanese. Only meagre and occasional fighter protection could be provided from our partially developed bases in Crete, and the only proper solution to the problem—to put the enemy airfields out of action—could not be undertaken for lack of the necessary long-range bombers. In all, twenty-five ships, totalling 115,026 tons, were lost in Operation 'Lustre'; but most of the losses occurred either after ships had reached their ports of destination or while they were returning unloaded. Only seven ships were sunk while in convoy at sea; 45,793 soldiers were safely carried to Greece in warships and personnel vessels, and a further 12,571 in mechanical-transport ships. In spite of all the manifold and increasing burdens now falling on the Mediterranean Fleet the purpose of the War Cabinet had been faithfully carried out.

This large movement by sea could not be concealed from the enemy, and it was natural that he should try to interrupt the flow of shipping, by surface vessels as well as aircraft. The Germans spurred their Italian allies to use their fleet to this purpose and it was this that led to the Battle of Cape Matapan, to be described shortly.

Meanwhile the development of a properly defended forward base at Suda Bay in Crete had been proceeding, though all too slowly, since the necessary materials were not available in adequate quantity in the Middle East. It had been intended to set up the Mobile Naval Base organisation there, and the Royal Marine units and equipment were sent out from England for that purpose.[1] But only a part reached the intended destination. The weakness of its defences meant that Suda Bay could never be used except as an advanced fuelling station and that throughout the reinforcement of, and evacuation from, Greece the fleet had to work from Alexandria, nearly 500 miles away from the scene of operations. The heavy cruiser *York* was torpedoed at Suda by an Italian 'one-man torpedo-boat' on the 26th of March and subsequently became a total loss. Once again the inevitable price for using an inadequately defended base was exacted.

It thus happened that while we were moving men and materials northward from Africa the enemy was doing his utmost to build up his military strength in the same continent by shipping the 'Afrika

---
[1] See p. 25.

Korps' southward from Italy. To interrupt the latter flow was a plain requirement, but to spare the forces necessary to accomplish it was a different matter, especially while Malta was under the scourge of the Luftwaffe. For the first three months of the year our submarines and aircraft offered the only means whereby the short sea route to Tripoli could be disputed. Of aircraft very few were available, and to use them effectively from Malta was virtually impossible in the conditions then prevailing. The submarines, on the other hand, did most gallant and effective work. They patrolled unremittingly off Sardinia, Tunisia and Tripoli; they laid mines in the approaches to the enemy's departure and arrival ports, and they attacked his convoys at every opportunity and with considerable success. Besides inflicting severe losses on troop and supply convoys, such as to cause the enemy grave anxiety, the *Upright* (Lieutenant E. D. Norman) sank the Italian cruiser *Armando Diaz* in a night attack on the 25th of February and the *Rorqual* torpedoed and sank an Italian U-boat on the last day of March. But where the sea route is short and fast ships are available for the transhipment of men and supplies, submarines alone cannot wholly deny the use of sea communications. The co-operation of surface forces and of air search and striking forces is essential if the price is to be made too heavy to the enemy. And at this time none of these could be provided in adequate strength. Thus the enemy's land forces were built up more rapidly than had been expected, he was able to counter-attack at the end of March, and, a fortnight later, had driven the Army of the Nile back to the Egyptian frontier.

While the Mediterranean Fleet was fully employed guarding and covering the 'Lustre' convoys to Greece, Force H, working from Gibraltar, was not idle. The part which it played in passing the 'Excess' convoy through to the east has already been told; and it will be remembered that, in the middle of March, Admiral Somerville came north to the Bay of Biscay to co-operate with the Home Fleet in the attempt to intercept the *Scharnhorst* and *Gneisenau* on their passage from the Atlantic to Brest.[1] In between these two operations time was found to make a cleverly disguised foray into the Gulf of Genoa and to carry out, at dawn on the 9th of February, heavy and undisputed sea and air bombardments of Genoa, Leghorn and Spezia with the *Renown, Malaya, Ark Royal, Sheffield* and ten destroyers. Complete surprise was achieved and the whole force returned to its base without suffering a single casualty, having inflicted much damage on enemy shore installations.

While the events in the narrows of the Mediterranean and in North Africa were disconcerting, the war in East Africa had during the same period taken a decisive turn in our favour. In January British Empire forces had started to advance simultaneously from the

---
[1] See pp. 377–378.

Sudan and Kenya into Italian Somaliland, Eritrea and Abyssinia and, by the beginning of the summer, the dream of Mussolini to found an East African Empire had been shattered. Our complete control of the sea routes along the East African coast and through the Red Sea made it a relatively easy matter to supply our own forces and to prevent supplies from reaching the enemy. The forces under the Commander-in-Chief, East Indies (Vice-Admiral R. Leatham), co-operated continuously with the armies inshore, and warships on passage to Suez joined from time to time in the offshore operations. Thus the *Formidable*, on her way to join Admiral Cunningham, used her aircraft to mine Mogadishu and to attack enemy warships in Massawa, while the small aircraft carrier *Hermes* and the cruisers *Shropshire*, *Capetown*, *Ceres* and a few destroyers bombed and bombarded coast defences, supply dumps and concentrations of enemy troops.[1] Kismayu was captured on the 14th of February, and, of the sixteen Axis merchantmen sheltering there, only one escaped. The northward advance now became very rapid and Mogadishu fell on the 25th. Many British Merchant Navy prisoners, landed there after capture by German armed raiders, were released. Berbera was recaptured on 16th of March and British Somaliland restored to the Empire; and, when the enemy ships in Massawa put to sea, most of them suffered the same fate as those which had tried to escape from Mogadishu. The campaign did not end until the Italians surrendered on the 19th of May, but by the end of March the collapse of their East African Empire was plainly imminent. Once again the ability conferred by maritime power rapidly to carry large bodies of fighting men to the theatre where they were needed and, thereafter, to keep them supplied from the sea had proved decisive. As General Cunningham stated in his special order at the end of the campaign, 'to [the Navy] also fell the task of opening successive ports and giving us our life-line'. Of the Italian naval forces which had been stationed in the Red Sea—originally nine destroyers, eight U-boats and certain lesser ships—by the 1st of April 1941 one destroyer, half the U-boat strength and the solitary auxiliary cruiser *Ramb I* had been accounted for.[2] During the next ten days eight destroyers were sunk or put out of action, largely by the *Eagle's* Swordfish which worked from the shore air station at Port Sudan. Before the Army had reached Eritrea all enemy naval opposition had been eliminated. Apart from its important local influence, this had the immediate effect of enabling President Roosevelt to announce, on the 11th of April, that the Red Sea was no longer a 'combat zone', and was therefore open to American shipping. Before leaving the East African campaign and the control of the shipping routes which made its success possible, the

---
[1] See Map 34.
[2] See p. 387.

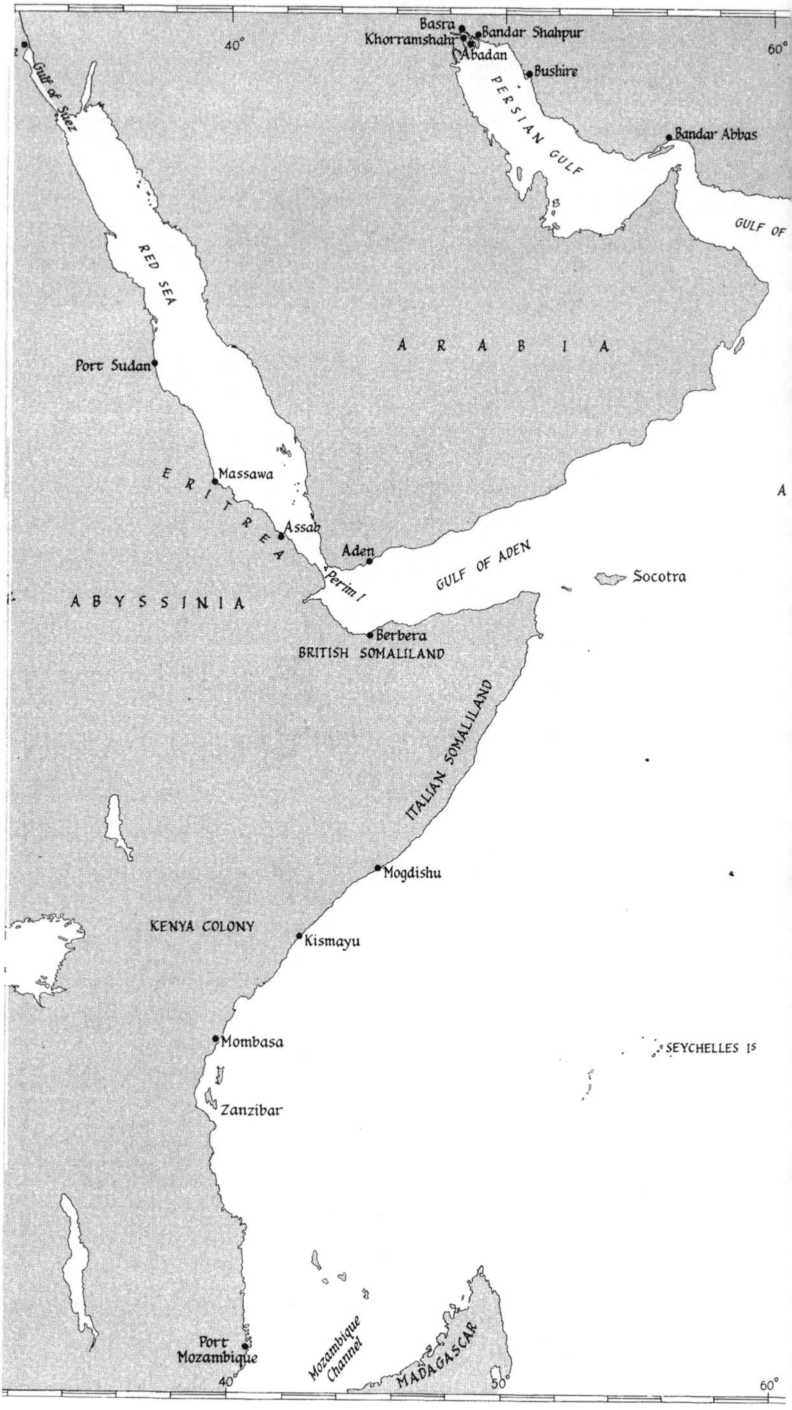

40°
60°
Gulf of Suez
Basra
Bandar Shahpur
Khorramshahr
Abadan
Bushire
PERSIAN GULF
Bandar Abbas
GULF OF
RED SEA
ARABIA
Port Sudan
Massawa
ERITREA
Assab
Aden
Perim I
GULF OF ADEN
Socotra
A
ABYSSINIA
Berbera
BRITISH SOMALILAND
ITALIAN SOMALILAND
Mogdishu
KENYA COLONY
Kismayu
Mombasa
SEYCHELLES IS
Zanzibar
Port Mozambique
Mozambique Channel
MADAGASCAR
40°
50°
60°

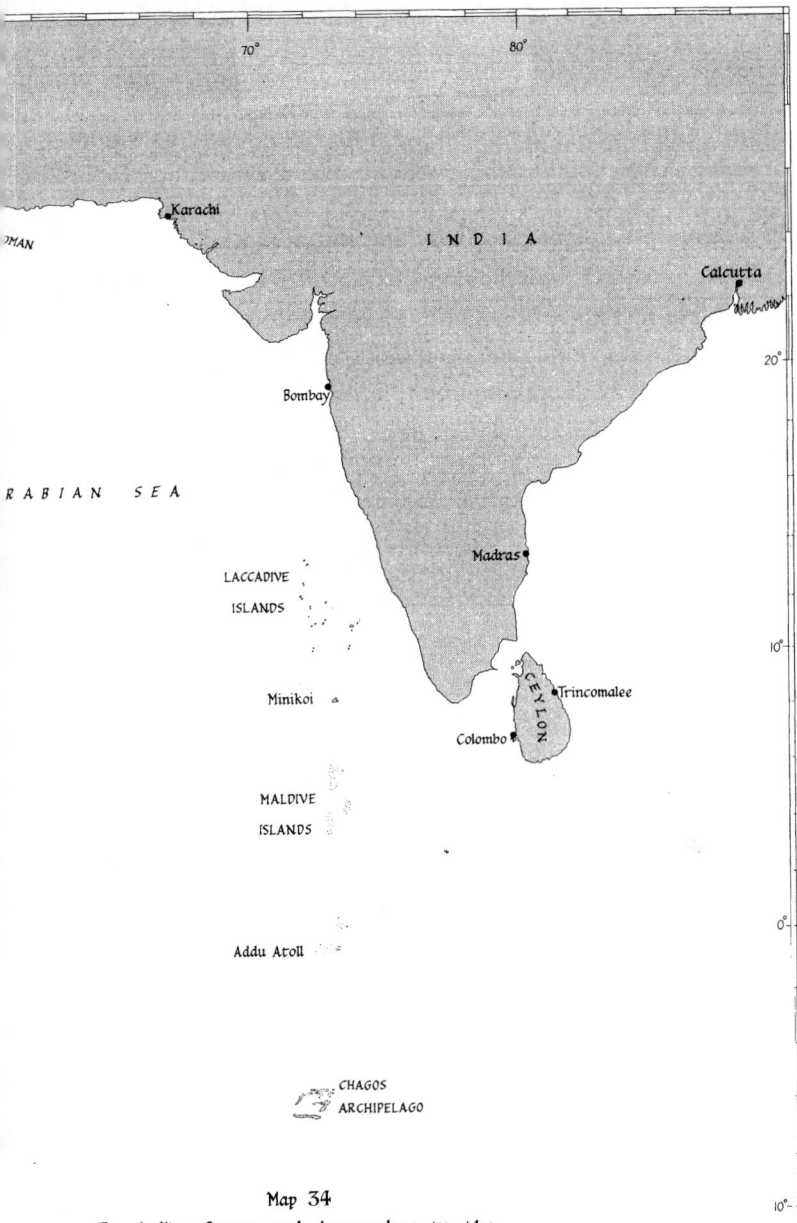

Map 34
The Indian Ocean and Approaches to the
Mediterranean from the East

size of the troop movements involved should, perhaps, be indicated. From the start of the war to the end of April 1941 no less than 643,198 men had passed through the East Indies Command in both directions to or from the various ports used to supply and reinforce our armies in Africa. The figure includes enemy prisoners of war removed from the theatres, but the great majority consisted of British Empire fighting men of one or other Service. The enemy completely failed to dislocate this great flow of troopships, and losses suffered while at sea were insignificant.

While the ships of the East Indies Command were mostly employed to support and supply our armies during their advance in East Africa and in protecting the ships passing up and down the Red Sea, a new demand arose within Admiral Leatham's command area. On the 4th of April a *coup d'état* was staged in Baghdad against the Regent of Iraq and his Government, with the object of admitting the forces of the Axis powers to the country. The Regent took refuge in a British warship then present at Basra. The Government of India at once agreed to a request for the use of Indian troops in a theatre where they had fought with distinction in the first World War and, on the 18th, the first convoy arrived at Basra, whither Admiral Leatham had hurried with two cruisers. A second convoy left India on the 22nd of April and, on the 2nd May, after revolting Iraqi forces had besieged the airfield at Habbaniya, the start of hostilities was ordered. Though the first few days were anxious, the successful defence of the airfield and the prompt despatch of military forces from India, supported by ample naval strength, led to the rapid collapse of the revolt. On the 1st of June the Regent re-entered his capital.[1]

It is now necessary to return to the more fiercely contested struggle for control of the Mediterranean waters.

Mention has been made of the enemy's knowledge of the movement of our troops from Egypt to Greece. The first sign that the Italian fleet might be contemplating a sortie against the convoys bound for the Piræus reached Admiral Cunningham on the 25th of March. He was anxious to take no action which might cause the enemy to postpone his intention, but at once cleared the area of convoys so that, if he struck, his blow should fall on air. At the same time, while preserving every possible appearance of unpreparedness, Cunningham made such dispositions as would enable him to bring the enemy surface forces to battle. The Vice-Admiral, Light Forces (Vice-Admiral H. D. Pridham-Wippell), with the cruisers *Orion*,

---

[1] See the forthcoming volume of this series by I. S. O. Playfair. *The Mediterranean and Middle East*, Vol. II for a full account of the campaign in Iraq.

Ajax, *Perth* and *Gloucester* and four destroyers was ordered to be south-west of Gavdo Island at daylight on the 28th of March, and there five more destroyers were ordered to join him.[1] Destroyers in the Piræus were brought to short notice, the naval torpedo-bomber squadrons in Crete and Cyrenaica were reinforced, submarines were sent out on patrol and the Royal Air Force was requested to reconnoitre the Aegean and the waters west of Crete as intensively as possible on the 28th, and to be ready to attack any targets found.

At noon on the 27th an R.A.F. flying boat sighted three enemy cruisers about 320 miles to the west of Crete steering south-east. Admiral Cunningham thereupon decided to wait no longer, but to take the battle fleet to sea and to call Admiral Pridham-Wippell's force to meet him. He sailed at dusk on the 27th with the *Warspite*, *Barham*, *Valiant* and *Formidable* in company, screened by nine destroyers of the 10th and 14th Flotillas.

At dawn next day air searches were started by the *Formidable*, and very soon a report was received of an enemy cruiser and destroyer force south of Gavdo Island, in the area where Admiral Pridham-Wippell was operating. It was soon confirmed by the sighting of these same ships by the Vice-Admiral, Light Forces, himself.[2] Admiral Cunningham turned to close and increased speed. Reports from aircraft continued to come in and indicated that there was another enemy force—possibly battleships—to the north of his cruisers; but the situation was far from clear. Shortly before 11 a.m., however, the light forces reported two battleships sixteen miles to the north of them and turned south-east under cover of smoke. Admiral Pridham-Wippell was now in a very uncomfortable position, with the enemy cruisers on his starboard quarter and the battleships to port. The *Formidable* was therefore ordered to strike at once at the battleships, while the Commander-in-Chief moved to the support of the threatened light forces. At noon the enemy battleship—and there now appeared to be only one, of the *Littorio* class, present—was estimated to be forty-five miles slightly north of west from Admiral Cunningham. Ten minutes later Admiral Pridham-Wippell lost touch with it, but the *Formidable's* striking force soon returned and reported, we now know erroneously, having obtained one torpedo hit on the battleship. At this stage matters were further complicated by a flying boat's report of a third enemy force of two *Cavour*-class battleships and three heavy cruisers to the north. In fact this force consisted only of 8-inch cruisers and destroyers.

At 12.30 Admiral Pridham-Wippell, with all his ships unscathed by the enemy battleship's long-range fire, made contact with his Commander-in-Chief, who now turned west in pursuit of the *Littorio*-

---
[1] See Map 35 (*facing p. 429*).
[2] See Map 35.

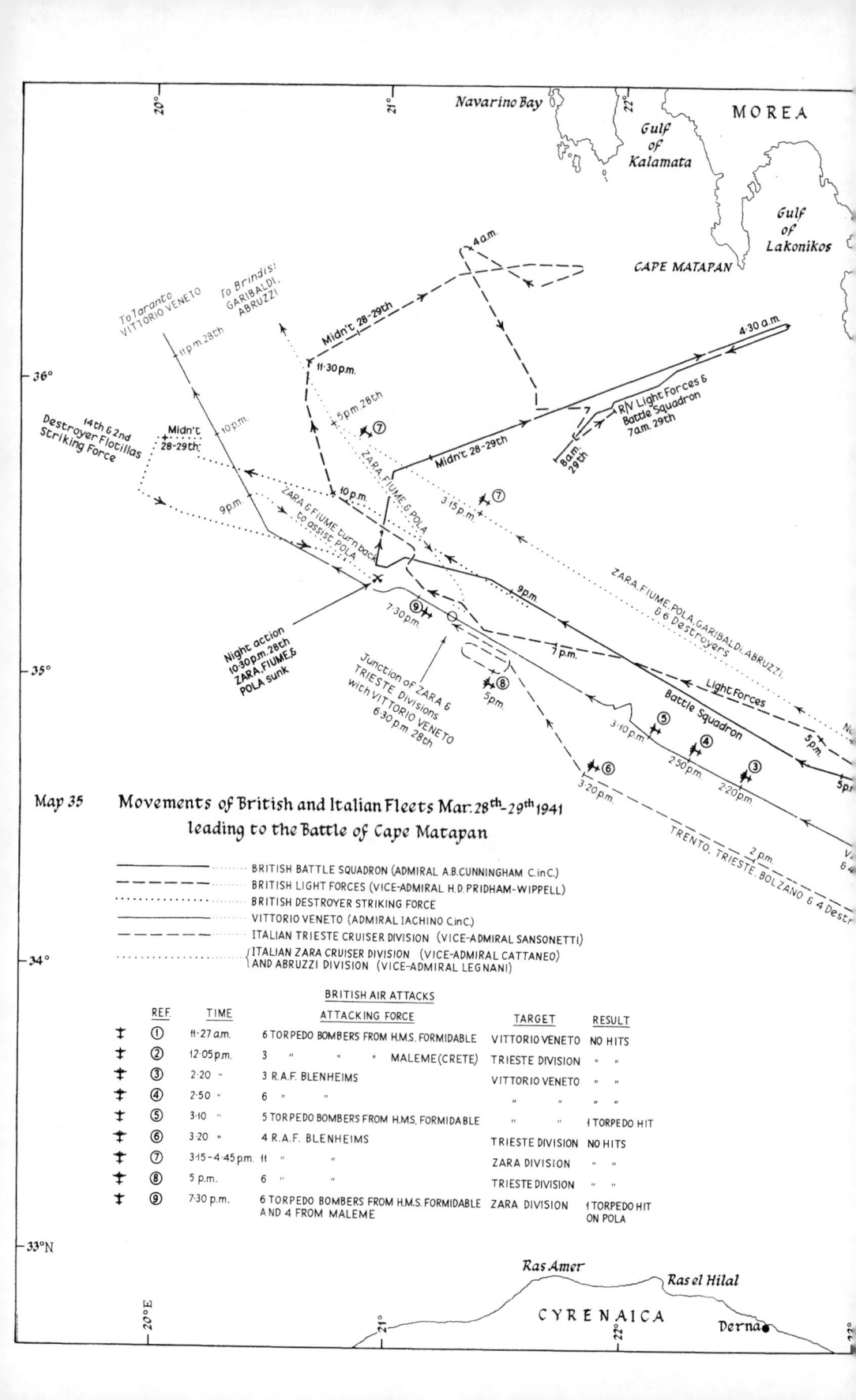

Map 35. **Movements of British and Italian Fleets Mar. 28th–29th 1941 leading to the Battle of Cape Matapan**

		BRITISH BATTLE SQUADRON (ADMIRAL A.B. CUNNINGHAM C. in C.)
		BRITISH LIGHT FORCES (VICE-ADMIRAL H.D. PRIDHAM-WIPPELL)
		BRITISH DESTROYER STRIKING FORCE
		VITTORIO VENETO (ADMIRAL IACHINO C. in C.)
		ITALIAN TRIESTE CRUISER DIVISION (VICE-ADMIRAL SANSONETTI)
		ITALIAN ZARA CRUISER DIVISION (VICE-ADMIRAL CATTANEO) AND ABRUZZI DIVISION (VICE-ADMIRAL LEGNANI)

BRITISH AIR ATTACKS

REF.	TIME	ATTACKING FORCE	TARGET	RESULT
①	11·27 a.m.	6 TORPEDO BOMBERS FROM H.M.S. FORMIDABLE	VITTORIO VENETO	NO HITS
②	12·05 p.m.	3 " " " MALEME (CRETE)	TRIESTE DIVISION	" "
③	2·20 "	3 R.A.F. BLENHEIMS	VITTORIO VENETO	" "
④	2·50 "	6 " "	" "	" "
⑤	3·10 "	5 TORPEDO BOMBERS FROM H.M.S. FORMIDABLE	" "	1 TORPEDO HIT
⑥	3·20 "	4 R.A.F. BLENHEIMS	TRIESTE DIVISION	NO HITS
⑦	3·15–4·45 p.m.	11 " "	ZARA DIVISION	" "
⑧	5 p.m.	6 " "	TRIESTE DIVISION	" "
⑨	7·30 p.m.	6 TORPEDO BOMBERS FROM H.M.S. FORMIDABLE AND 4 FROM MALEME	ZARA DIVISION	1 TORPEDO HIT ON POLA

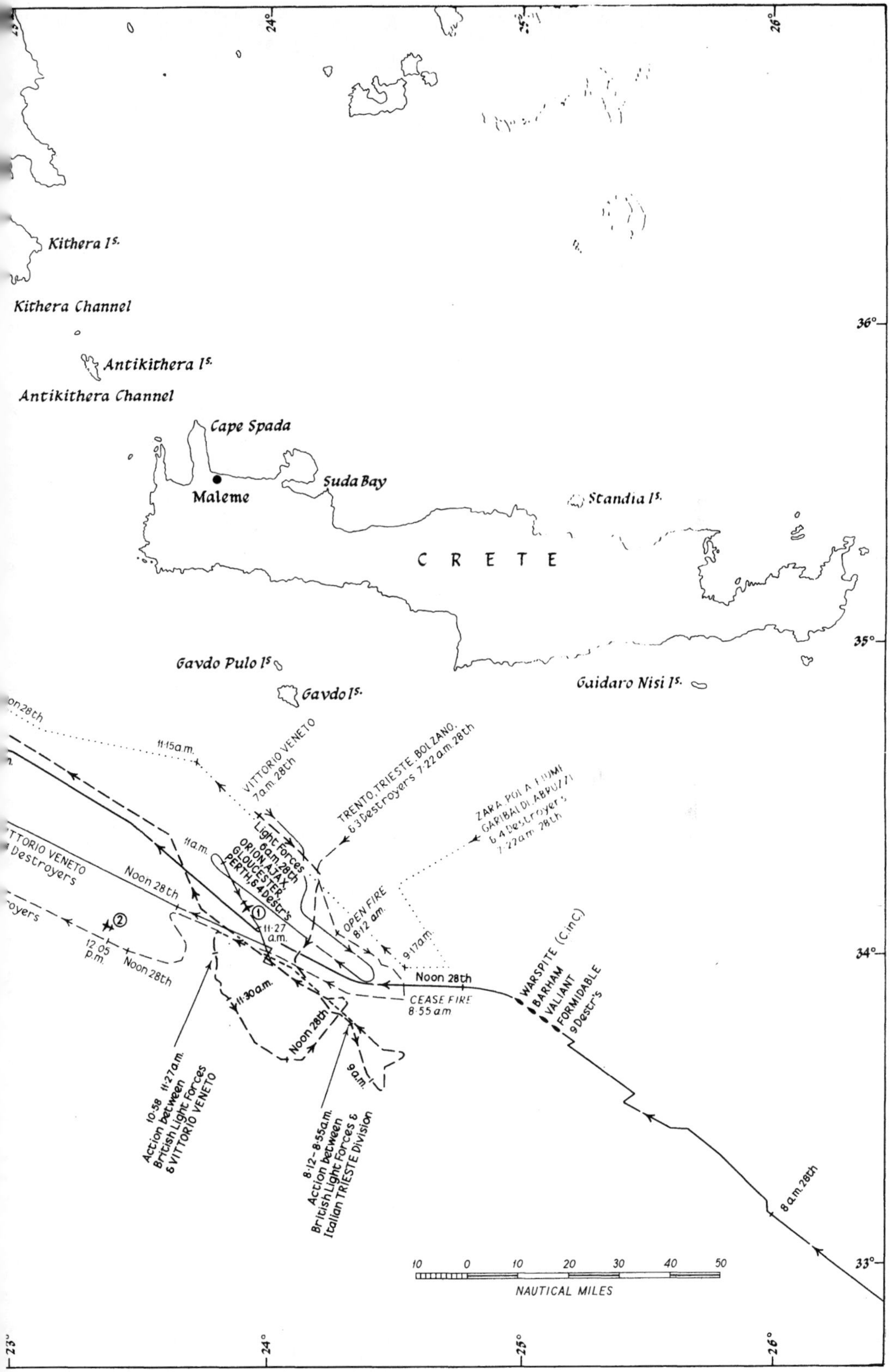

24°
25°
26°
36°
35°
34°
33°
23°
Kithera Is.
Kithera Channel
Antikithera Is.
Antikithera Channel
Cape Spada
Maleme
Suda Bay
Standia Is.
C R E T E
Gavdo Pulo Is.
Gavdo Is.
Gaidaro Nisi Is.
11·15 a.m.
VITTORIO VENETO 7 a.m. 28th
TRENTO, TRIESTE, BOLZANO. & 3 Destroyers 7·22 a.m. 28th
ZARA, POLA, FIUME GARIBALDI, ABRUZZI & 4 Destroyers 7·22 a.m. 28th
Light Forces 6 a.m. 28th ORION, AJAX, GLOUCESTER, PERTH, & 4 Destr's
11 a.m.
Noon 28th
12·05 p.m.
11·27 a.m.
OPEN FIRE 8·12 a.m.
9·17 a.m.
CEASE FIRE 8·55 a.m.
11·30 a.m.
9 a.m.
WARSPITE (C.in C.)
BARHAM
VALIANT
FORMIDABLE
9 Destr's
10·58 – 11·27 a.m. Action between British Light Forces & VITTORIO VENETO
8·12 – 8·55 a.m. Action between British Light Forces & Italian TRIESTE Division
8 a.m. 28th
10 0 10 20 30 40 50
NAUTICAL MILES

AIR ATTACKS ON THE ITALIAN FLEET 429

class battleship (actually the *Vittorio Veneto*), and ordered his aircraft carrier to fly off another striking force. But it soon became plain that all three enemy forces had turned westwards, and that prospects of catching them were not good, unless the battleship's speed could be reduced. Air searches were therefore resumed. The second air striking force of five torpedo-bombers attacked between 3.10 and 3.25 p.m. and claimed three hits on the *Vittorio Veneto*, reducing her speed to 8 knots. The actual result was one hit, on the battleship's port quarter, and her speed was restored to 19 knots by 7 p.m. Other naval Swordfish, flying from Maleme in Crete, and R.A.F. Blenheim bombers from shore bases in Greece had meanwhile attacked the enemy cruisers; but neither achieved any success.

By 4 p.m. it was clear that the injured *Vittorio Veneto* was making better progress to the west than was justified by the air report of her speed reduction, and that she would not be caught by the British fleet before dusk. Admiral Cunningham therefore sent his light forces ahead to regain contact and flew off a third air striking force against the same target.

The situation remained somewhat obscure until, at 6.30, the *Warspite's* reconnaissance aircraft sent a series of reports which placed the *Vittorio Veneto* fifty-five miles from Admiral Cunningham. The other enemy force of heavy cruisers, some of which had at first been mistakenly identified as battleships, was still to the north-west of his main concentration. By 7.30 the *Warspite's* aircraft had reported the enemy's cruising order and the composition of his forces with an accuracy which aroused the Italian Commander-in-Chief's admiration and envy. The *Vittorio Veneto* was steering north-west with two destroyers ahead and two astern of her; on each side of this centre column steamed three heavy cruisers, and outside them were columns of three or four destroyers. Their speed was given as 15 knots. It was through the concentrated gunfire of this massed array of warships that the *Formidable's* third striking force of eight torpedo-bombers, joined shortly by two more from Maleme, attacked at sunset. The enemy's barrage was so intense that the targets could not easily be identified, nor the results of the attacks observed. The *Vittorio Veneto* escaped further damage; but one torpedo struck the cruiser *Pola* amidships and brought her to a standstill. This was to have important consequences since, at 8.30 p.m., the Italian Commander-in-Chief ordered back the heavy cruisers *Zara* and *Fiume* and a division of destroyers to assist the damaged ship. He believed that the British battle squadron was still far to the east of him.

By 7.35 p.m. it was known that the third air striking force had achieved no decisive success, and Admiral Cunningham therefore resolved to accept night action, in spite of the enemy's superiority, in order to force a decision before the enemy could get under cover of the dive-bombers based on southern Italy and Sicily. He therefore ordered his destroyers to attack. Soon after 9 p.m. Admiral Pridham-Wippell reported passing close to an unknown ship which was stopped. The Commander-in-Chief decided to investigate. He turned to a westerly course and made for the position at 20 knots in single line ahead; two destroyers were stationed on either bow. The night was dark and cloudy, with no moon; visibility was about two and a half miles. An hour later the *Valiant's* radar detected a stopped ship to port about eight miles away. Admiral Cunningham now handled the battle squadron as though it had been a destroyer division. He turned first to the south-west, bringing his ships into quarter line. Radar reports were coming in steadily, and in tense readiness the great ships held on towards the enemy. At 10.20 p.m. the target was only four and a half miles away, and the destroyers on the port side were told to move over to starboard of the battleships. The destroyer *Stuart* gave the first alarm at 10.23, and almost at once darkened ships were sighted from the bridge of the fleet flagship. Cunningham turned his ships together to starboard, which brought them into line ahead again. Their turrets were already swinging round from the bearing of the stopped target on to these new enemies. The *Formidable* was told to haul out of the line of fire and, just before 10.30, the battleships opened fire with devastating effect at about 3,000 yards range. The unfortunate targets were the heavy cruisers *Zara* and *Fiume*. They were immediately crippled and set on fire, and at 10.38 the Commander-in-Chief told the destroyers to finish them off. The two Italian destroyers which had been with the heavy cruisers were sunk by the *Stuart* and *Havock* between 11 and 11.15 p.m. The stopped ship, which had originally drawn the battle squadron to the scene, was the heavy cruiser *Pola*. She was found by the destroyers *Jervis* and *Nubian* and sunk at 4 a.m., after many of her company had been taken off.

At midnight the Commander-in-Chief gave his scattered forces a rendezvous and, at daylight on the 29th, he resumed the search for the enemy battleship. But contact was never regained, for the main Italian force had made good progress to the west during the night and succeeded in shepherding the damaged *Vittorio Veneto* out of Admiral Cunningham's reach. The fleet was shadowed by aircraft and attacked by German bombers this day, but suffered no damage. Normal convoy movements to and from the Piræus were resumed and on the evening of the 30th Admiral Cunningham returned to Alexandria.

Though the escape of the enemy battleship prevented the Commander-in-Chief feeling entirely satisfied with the results of the battle, to the world as a whole the destruction of three of his 'fast, well-armed and armoured' cruisers and two large destroyers for the loss of only one aircraft appeared a substantial victory. It certainly eliminated the possibility of surface ship interference with the current troop movements to Greece. The success of the difficult evacuations, which were so soon to strain the Mediterranean Fleet to the limit, also owed much to the action fought off Cape Matapan on the night of the 28th of March. Moreover the victory came at a time when serious anxiety was felt regarding the threat to our maritime control outside the Mediterranean as well as in those more restricted waters, and when our land operations in North Africa, on which high hopes had been built, were faring ill. On the 3rd of April Benghazi was lost and three days later the Germans invaded Greece and Yugoslavia. It was clear that the full power of the German army, as well as that of the Luftwaffe, would soon be launched against our outnumbered land and air forces in Greece.

The flow of reinforcements and supplies which had, for all the efforts of our submarines and aircraft, been reaching General Rommel, chiefly through the port of Tripoli, was a source of great anxiety to the War Cabinet at this time. In London it seemed clear that, unless drastic action was taken to stop that flow, the strength of the Afrika Korps would soon imperil our whole position in North Africa. The Commanders-in-Chief of the theatre were, of course, alive to the danger and, on the 8th of April, Admiral Cunningham told the Admiralty that he was sending four destroyers of the 14th Flotilla (Captain P. J. Mack) to Malta to intensify the attack on the enemy's supply traffic to North Africa. The destroyers would arrive at Malta on the 10th or 11th.

In the early hours of the 15th of April the Admiralty, with the approval of the Cabinet, told Admiral Cunningham that it was 'evident that drastic measures were necessary to stabilise the position in the Middle East', and insisted that air action from Malta, submarine attacks and surface vessel sorties were not enough to interrupt the traffic to Tripoli decisively. Heavy and consistent mining might be effective, but 'we cannot wait until it is proved'. The alternatives were to bombard the port or to block it. The message ended by saying that 'the Admiralty had decided that [the] *Barham* and a C-class cruiser should be used to block the port'. The same evening the First Sea Lord told the Commander-in-Chief that 'His Majesty's Government had decided that the Navy must do everything possible to prevent supplies reaching Libya from Italy'. It will be seen that the Admiralty, acting as the mouthpiece of the War Cabinet, thus sent the Commander-in-Chief a clear-cut decision. They did not seek his views on how the Cabinet's purpose could best be put into effect, nor ask what he was already doing and what more he could do to further that purpose.

The Commander-in-Chief received the decision taken in London with serious misgivings. He answered that the price which the Government and the Admiralty were ready to pay could only be justified 'if the success of the operation is reasonably assured and if . . . the result will be efficacious'. He did not consider that either of those conditions would be fulfilled and, rather than sacrifice the *Barham* and many of her company, he would withdraw his previously expressed dislike of using his ships to attack a shore target far distant from their base and involving a long passage through extremely dangerous waters. If he must make the choice between 'sacrificing a first-class fighting unit' and exposing his fleet to risks which he considered unjustifiable he would choose the latter course and would 'attack with the whole battle fleet'.

On the 16th Admiral Cunningham told the First Sea Lord that 'he was not idle about the Libyan situation'. He was, presumably, referring to Captain Mack's destroyers, which had by now arrived at Malta. None the less, on the same day that this message was received in London pressure was intensified by the issue of a directive by the Prime Minister stating that the Navy would fail in its duty if it did not stop the traffic to Libya. The Admiralty passed on the directive verbatim to Admiral Cunningham.

Meanwhile Captain Mack had scored a substantial success. In a night raid on the supply route on the 16th he destroyed an entire convoy of five ships totalling some 14,000 tons for the loss of one of our own destroyers, the *Mohawk*. This news evidently reached London as a bolt from the blue, for the First Sea Lord at once signalled that he 'had no knowledge of the destroyer operations on the Libyan coast' when the earlier messages about stopping supplies to Tripoli had been sent. The same evening Cunningham told the Admiralty that he hoped to fit in the bombardment of Tripoli as part of a large fleet movement designed also to revictual Malta. But the successful raid by the destroyers had caused a change of front in London, since it was thought that the enemy would now stop trying to run convoys to Tripoli, at any rate for a time. 'Bombardment' they, said, 'is considered of greater importance than blocking', though the latter was not definitely abandoned.

Finally, on the afternoon of the 17th, Admiral Cunningham reported his 'intention to carry out a bombardment of Tripoli by night . . . at about 5 a.m. on the 21st'. This decision might, it now seems, have been reached more easily had the method of implementing the Cabinet's purpose been left to the Commander-in-Chief from the beginning.

Admiral Cunningham's plan included the subsidiary purposes of slipping the fast supply ship *Breconshire* into Malta and of releasing a convoy of empty ships from the island. Virtually the whole of his strength was to be thrown in. He sailed from Alexandria early on the

BOMBARDMENT OF TRIPOLI, 21ST APRIL 433

18th of April and steered first for the eastern end of Crete. The fleet fuelled in Suda Bay the next day and then sailed to the west. Early on the 20th the light forces, which had been employed on other missions, joined the main fleet, as did the *Breconshire*, and the westward progress continued. The Malta force was detached that evening, and in the early hours of the next morning, the 21st, the fleet passed the submarine which was marking the route to Tripoli. Meanwhile R.A.F. Wellingtons and naval Swordfish from Malta had attacked the port with bombs. It is uncertain how far these diversions enabled the fleet to approach undetected but, when the first rounds were fired into the port by the battleships, cruisers and destroyers at 5 a.m., the enemy was taken completely by surprise; for the next hour, a heavy rain of shells of large and small calibre was directed at the shipping in port and the oil tanks and installations on shore, while the *Formidable's* aircraft illuminated the scene with flares and spotted for the ships' gunfire. Only one ship was sunk in the harbour, but much damage was done on shore. By 6.30 the fleet was withdrawing again at high speed to the north-east and, by noon on the 23rd, had returned to Alexandria unscathed. The incursion in strength into enemy-controlled waters had been completely successful. But Admiral Cunningham considered that this should perhaps be regarded more as a measure of Italian incapacity than as grounds for believing that such risks could frequently be accepted with impunity. He told the Admiralty that he remained 'strongly opposed to this policy of the bombardment of Tripoli by the Mediterranean Fleet. We have got away with it once but only because the German Air Force was engaged elsewhere'. He considered the job could be done more economically and, in terms of sound strategy, should be done by heavy bomber squadrons from Egypt, and to support the argument he quoted some figures which, in a further exchange of messages, the Prime Minister was easily able to refute.

Meanwhile the Army of the Nile had fared ill in Cyrenaica. Tobruk was invested by the 11th of April, and a long period of hazardous work by the Inshore Squadron to run supplies through to its garrison now started. No fighter protection for the ships was possible, since all our bases were now too far to the east, and heavy losses from bombing were inevitable. None the less throughout April some 400 tons of stores were landed daily, and many troops were transported in both directions by night in small ships of many types.

Nor was Tobruk the only anxiety, the only besieged garrison to be fed, supplied and reinforced at this time; Malta, which was even more important, made yet heavier demands on the fleet and measures had to be found to continue the flow of fighter aircraft in particular to the island. This could only be done by using aircraft carriers to carry the fighters within range of Malta, and, in spite of the hazards, such operations now had to be repeated. On the 2nd of April the *Ark Royal* left Gibraltar with twelve Hurricanes, which the *Argus* had ferried out from home, and flew them off next day. They arrived safely. Three weeks later a similar, but bigger, reinforcement was carried out concurrently with passing naval reinforcements—the cruiser *Dido*, the new fast minelayer *Abdiel*, and six destroyers—to Malta. Twenty-three Hurricanes were flown off on the 27th, and they and the naval forces all arrived safely. The naval reinforcements were designed to increase the pressure on the enemy's supply routes to North Africa, and Admiral Cunningham had sent the cruiser *Gloucester* to Malta to support the light forces in that task. But the damage from enemy bombing was mounting, mining of the entrance channels was frequent and the minesweeping forces worked under great difficulties. It was becoming clear that surface forces could not easily work from a base exposed to air attack on such a scale. In May more air reinforcements were several times flown to Malta from the west; but a description of those operations must be deferred for the present as crucial events were now taking place in the eastern basin.

The German onslaught on Greece opened on the 6th of April, and very heavy air attacks were at once made on the Piræus.[1] That night the *Clan Fraser*, loaded with explosives, was hit, caught fire and blew up. The explosion destroyed ten other ships of over 41,000 tons and virtually put the port out of action; this, in Admiral Cunningham's words, was 'a shattering blow', for it deprived us at once of the only reasonably equipped base through which reinforcements and supplies could be passed to the Army. The Aegean convoys continued, but they now had to use small and poorly equipped ports for unloading. The Greek Navy was also deprived of its main base and, on the 24th, the surviving ships were placed under Admiral Cunningham's orders and arrived in Alexandria.[2]

By the 16th it had become plain that the Army's position on shore could not be maintained for long and that withdrawal would probably be necessary. The planning was at once completed and, on the 21st of April, withdrawal was approved by the Cabinet. It had originally been planned to take place on the 29th, but the date was advanced to the 24th by reason of the rapid collapse of the situation on land. The operation was given the code name 'Demon' and, from the start, it was realised that it would be a desperate enterprise; for

---

[1] See the forthcoming volume of this series by I. S. O. Playfair, *The War in the Mediterranean and Middle East*, Vol. II, for a full account of the Greek campaign.

[2] These included the old cruiser *Giorgios Averoff*, a repair ship, six large destroyers, two torpedo-boats and six submarines. A Yugoslav submarine and two motor torpedo-boats also reached Alexandria at this time, but none of that country's three large destroyers managed to get away.

the enemy's practically uncontested air power had produced chaotic conditions on land, communications were constantly breaking down and intelligence was vague and unreliable. No air protection could be provided over the ports of embarkation, and this meant that work could only be carried out during the short hours of darkness. Transports could not arrive until one hour after dark, and had to be clear of the coast by 3 a.m. And, as the Piræus could not be used, all embarkations would have to be made from minor ports or over the open beaches. About twenty of the former were selected but only eight were actually used.

All Admiral Cunningham's light forces, except those recently detached to work from Malta, were to take part. They comprised six cruisers, nineteen destroyers, three escort vessels or corvettes, six landing craft and the three fast 'Glen' transports—*Glengyle, Glenroy* and *Glenearn*—recently sent out for use as assault ships by the Commandos. Eight Merchant Navy transports were to be brought close inshore and the small ships and craft would ferry the soldiers out to them. To make such forces available Admiral Cunningham took away the ships allocated to the Desert Army's communications and left his own battle fleet without a destroyer screen. The evacuation was to be conducted by Admiral Pridham-Wippell (Vice-Admiral, Light Forces) flying his flag in the *Orion*.

It is natural that the story of Operation 'Demon' should recall to the reader the 'Dynamo' of the previous June. The difficulties surmounted and losses suffered in the latter were described earlier, and it will be remembered that they were not light.[1] Yet the Mediterranean Fleet, though required to rescue only about one-fifth of the number of soldiers brought back in 'Dynamo', had to face and overcome even more serious difficulties. Not only were the sea passages to and from the points of embarkation far longer, but there were no well-equipped bases near at hand to which damaged ships could easily return, where ready hands would supply the needs of the ships and where replacements for casualties would at once be forthcoming. Instead of having a united and grimly determined people and all the resources of a great industrial nation close behind its back the Mediterranean Fleet had to work from a base in a wavering and neutral country 400 miles away. Suda Bay and Alexandria could not possibly be regarded as adequate substitutes for Chatham, Dover and Portsmouth. And over and above all this loomed the knowledge that whereas the Spitfires and Hurricanes of Fighter Command had patrolled, fought in and sometimes cleared the skies over the Dunkirk

---

[1] See p. 216 *et seq.*, and Appendix L.

beaches, virtually no air protection could be expected off the Grecian shores. The fleet went to the Army's assistance well aware that the Luftwaffe would be in undisputed possession of the skies and would do its utmost to frustrate our purpose.

Evacuation started on the night of 24th–25th of April and continued for five nights on end without remission. Then for two more nights stragglers were fetched from the southern tip of the Morea. Moreover the sudden descent on the Corinth Canal bridge by paratroops on the 26th endangered the southern evacuation points far earlier than had been expected. A highly hazardous task thus became critical. Nearly 1,300 soldiers were embarked from the Piræus before the evacuation proper had started; on the first night 11,250 were embarked from Raphtis and Nauplia; the next night (26th–27th) 5,750, including 1,000 wounded, were taken off from Megara and about 19,500 in all from five different embarkation points.[1] On the 27th–28th the *Ajax* and three destroyers fetched another 4,750 from Raphtis and Nauplia and on the following night a further 4,320 from Monemvasia. The *Perth*, *Phoebe* and nine destroyers were sent to Kalamata on the 28th–29th hoping to bring off some 10,000 men. When the ships arrived they found that a small enemy column had penetrated to the harbour and captured the naval officer charged with organising the evacuation. Though control was, in fact, quickly regained in the town, the embarkation arrangements were not restored in the short time available, and the ships sailed prematurely after rescuing only 450 men from adjacent beaches. The final total of men brought away from Greece was 50,732—about 80 per cent of the number originally carried there in Operation 'Lustre'. Casualties, especially to the unarmed transports, were heavy. The *Pennland*, *Slamat* and *Costa Rica* were all sunk by bombs, and the *Ulster Prince* was lost in Nauplia harbour. From the *Slamat* 700 men were rescued by the destroyers *Diamond* and *Wryneck*. Both rescuing ships were bombed and sunk a short while later and from all three ships only one officer, forty-one ratings and eight soldiers survived.

By the 4th of May the fleet had reassembled at Alexandria for repairs and a brief period of rest but, an ill-omen for the future, the enemy had already stretched out his tentacles to all the principal Greek islands. Control of the Aegean and of the approaches to the Dardanelles had now passed into his hands, and the threat to Crete in particular and to Cyprus, Syria and all that lay to the east was

---

[1] See Map 36.

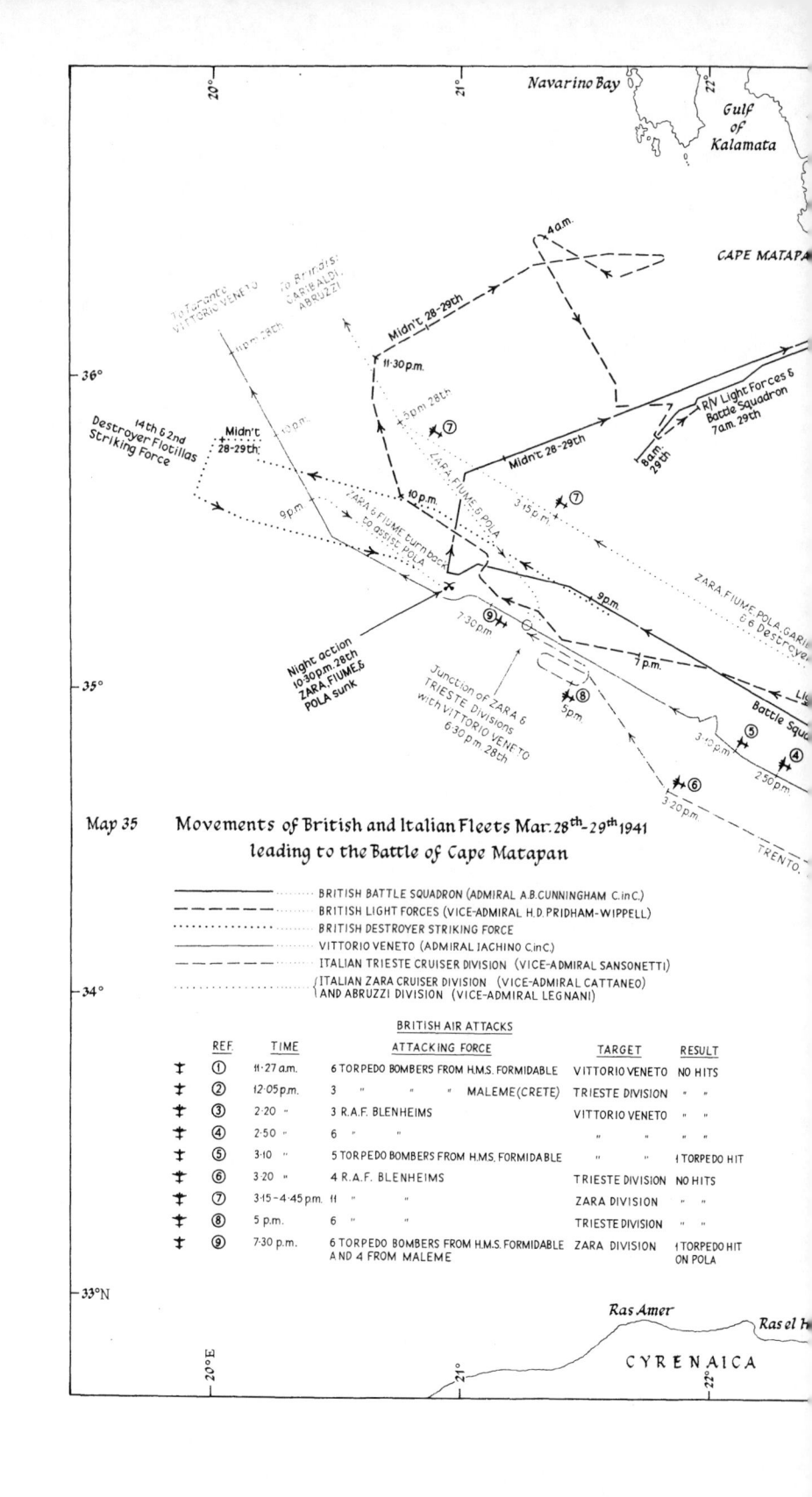

Map 35 **Movements of British and Italian Fleets Mar. 28th–29th 1941 leading to the Battle of Cape Matapan**

———————————— BRITISH BATTLE SQUADRON (ADMIRAL A.B.CUNNINGHAM C.inC.)
– – – – – – – – – – – BRITISH LIGHT FORCES (VICE-ADMIRAL H.D. PRIDHAM-WIPPELL)
·················· BRITISH DESTROYER STRIKING FORCE
———————————— VITTORIO VENETO (ADMIRAL IACHINO C.inC.)
– — – — – — – — ITALIAN TRIESTE CRUISER DIVISION (VICE-ADMIRAL SANSONETTI)
·················· { ITALIAN ZARA CRUISER DIVISION (VICE-ADMIRAL CATTANEO) AND ABRUZZI DIVISION (VICE-ADMIRAL LEGNANI) }

BRITISH AIR ATTACKS

REF.	TIME	ATTACKING FORCE	TARGET	RESULT
①	11·27 a.m.	6 TORPEDO BOMBERS FROM H.M.S. FORMIDABLE	VITTORIO VENETO	NO HITS
②	12·05 p.m.	3 " " " MALEME (CRETE)	TRIESTE DIVISION	" "
③	2·20 "	3 R.A.F. BLENHEIMS	VITTORIO VENETO	" "
④	2·50 "	6 " "	" "	" "
⑤	3·10 "	5 TORPEDO BOMBERS FROM H.M.S. FORMIDABLE	" "	1 TORPEDO HIT
⑥	3·20 "	4 R.A.F. BLENHEIMS	TRIESTE DIVISION	NO HITS
⑦	3·15–4·45 p.m.	11 " "	ZARA DIVISION	" "
⑧	5 p.m.	6 " "	TRIESTE DIVISION	" "
⑨	7·30 p.m.	6 TORPEDO BOMBERS FROM H.M.S. FORMIDABLE AND 4 FROM MALEME	ZARA DIVISION	1 TORPEDO HIT ON POLA

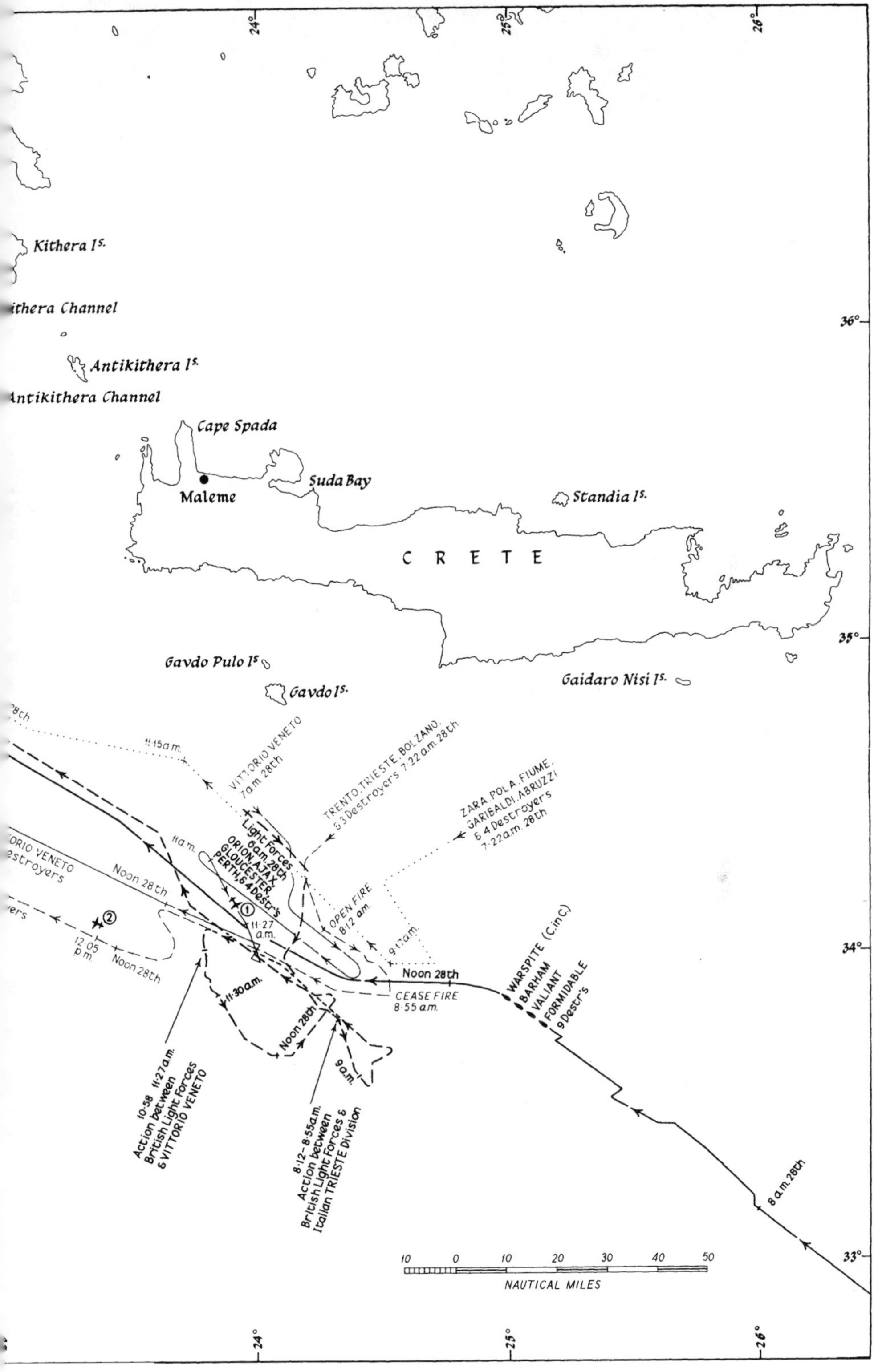

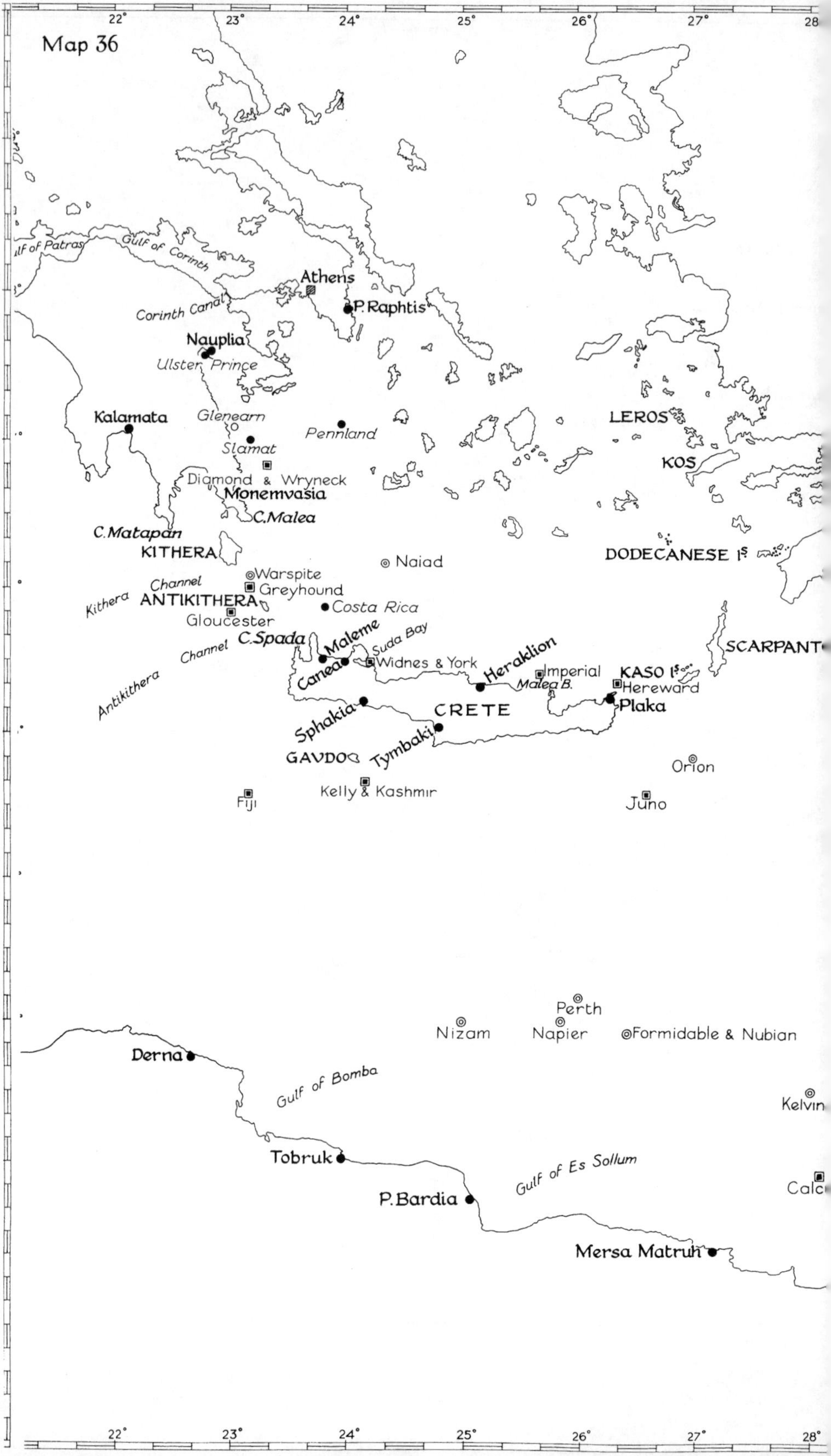
Map 36
22°
23°
24°
25°
26°
27°
28°
Gulf of Patras
Gulf of Corinth
Athens
Corinth Canal
P. Raphtis
Nauplia
Ulster Prince
Kalamata
Glenearn
Pennland
Slamat
Diamond & Wryneck
Monemvasia
C. Malea
C. Matapan
KITHERA
Naiad
Warspite
Greyhound
Kithera Channel
ANTIKITHERA
Costa Rica
Gloucester
C. Spada
Maleme
Suda Bay
Antikithera Channel
Canea
Widnes & York
Heraklion
Imperial
Malea B.
KASO Is
Hereward
Plaka
Sphakia
CRETE
Tymbaki
GAVDO
Orion
Kelly & Kashmir
Fiji
Juno
LEROS
KOS
DODECANESE Is
SCARPANT
Perth
Nizam
Napier
Formidable & Nubian
Derna
Gulf of Bomba
Kelvin
Tobruk
Gulf of Es Sollum
P. Bardia
Calc
Mersa Matruh

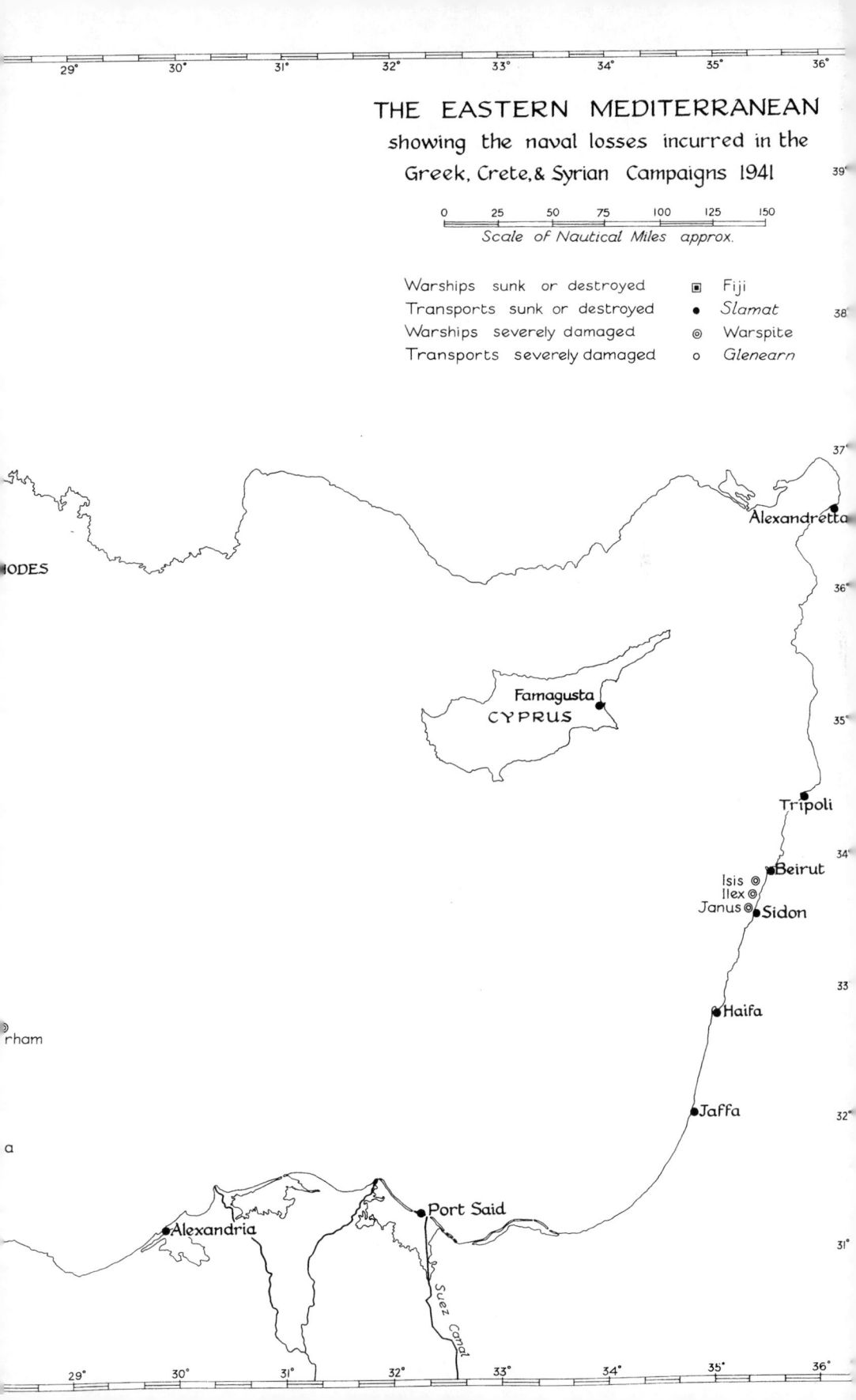

THE EASTERN MEDITERRANEAN
showing the naval losses incurred in the Greek, Crete, & Syrian Campaigns 1941

Scale of Nautical Miles approx.

Warships sunk or destroyed — Fiji
Transports sunk or destroyed — *Slamat*
Warships severely damaged — *Warspite*
Transports severely damaged — *Glenearn*

Alexandretta

Famagusta
CYPRUS

Tripoli
Beirut
Isis
Ilex
Janus — Sidon

Haifa

Jaffa

Port Said
Alexandria

Suez Canal

plain. But before we consider the enemy's attempts to exploit his new-won advantages we must turn briefly to the west again.

The reasons why the Defence Committee decided at this time to attempt to pass straight through the Mediterranean a convoy of fast motor-transport ships carrying tanks to the Army of the Nile have been set out in full by Mr Churchill and need not be repeated here.[1] The Admiralty expressed grave doubts regarding the success of the experiment now that the Luftwaffe was established in strength in Sicily, but, once the decision had been taken, provided maximum strength for the operation (called 'Tiger'), and used the opportunity to send substantial naval reinforcements to Admiral Cunningham and also to carry some additional relief to Malta. The convoy of five 15-knot merchant ships (*New Zealand Star, Clan Lamont, Clan Chattan, Clan Campbell* and *Empire Song*) loaded with tanks passed Gibraltar on the 6th of May and was accompanied on the first stretch of the eastward passage by Force H, strengthened by the battleship *Queen Elizabeth* and the cruisers *Naiad* and *Phoebe*, all of which were destined for Alexandria. Six of the destroyers with Force H went through to Malta. Meanwhile Admiral Cunningham had sailed westward to meet the convoy. He detached a light force to bombard Benghazi on the night of the 7th–8th of May and, on the afternoon of the 9th, met the convoy fifty miles south of Malta. Unfortunately two of the merchant ships had been mined the previous night and although one was able to continue the voyage the *Empire Song* blew up. The four surviving ships arrived safely with 238 tanks and forty-three Hurricanes. The Prime Minister's faith that such an operation could be successfully carried out was thus justified.

The next duty placed on Force H was to carry fighter reinforcements once more to Malta. The operation followed a now familiar pattern. The *Furious* arrived at Gibraltar on the 18th of May, and transferred some of her Hurricanes to the *Ark Royal*; both carriers then sailed to the east. Forty-eight fighters were flown off on the 21st and all but one arrived safely. Whereas in January there had only been fifteen Hurricanes in Malta the total had now increased fivefold. From the arrival there of the damaged *Illustrious* on the 10th of January to the middle of May, when the German bombers were transferred from Sicily to the east, sixty-two German and fifteen Italian aircraft had been destroyed over Malta. But the casualty rate among the Royal Air Force fighters carried there at the cost of so great an effort had been heavy; thirty-two had been lost in combat and nearly as many destroyed on the ground. Thus ended the first phase of the enemy's attempt to put the island and its installations

[1] See W. S. Churchill. *The Second World War*, Vol. III (1950), pp. 218–220.

out of action by air attack. Though his onslaught had not been decisively repulsed, and the island had suffered grievous injury, the enemy had not maintained his object sufficiently long to achieve the result he desired. Yet when one looks back to-day at the nakedness of Malta's defences at the start of the present phase, the closeness of the enemy's bases and the size of the forces which he deployed against the island, its survival appears remarkable. It seems safe to say that, but for the development of the new technique by which R.A.F. fighters were flown in from aircraft carriers, this 'linchpin of the campaign in the Mediterranean', as Admiral Cunningham called it, would have been totally incapacitated even if it had not fallen to the enemy. As it was, the heavy mining of the harbours had produced serious difficulties for the surface ships sent there to harass the enemy's African supply route. Before the end of May all light forces were needed for the evacuation of Crete, and the Malta-based destroyers were therefore taken away. Though two small convoys were slipped through in that month, it now became necessary to employ submarines to carry in the most urgently needed stores.

While Force H was thus employed, well inside the Mediterranean, in reinforcing the fighter defences of Malta, a chain of events had started in the far north in the later stage of which Admiral Somerville's ships were, as told in the last chapter, to play a principal part. The *Bismarck* was sighted in the Denmark Strait on the evening of the 23rd of May. Six hours later the Admiralty called Force H to the north and, at 2 a.m. on the 24th, Admiral Somerville had cleared Gibraltar and was heading out into the Atlantic.[1] The flexibility of maritime power and the invaluable part played by our few aircraft carriers was never better demonstrated than by the *Ark Royal's* performance in flying off two dozen Hurricanes to Malta well inside the Mediterranean on the 21st of May and in crippling the *Bismarck* with her Swordfish torpedo-bombers some 450 miles to the west of Brest six days later.

As we have seen, the attempt to station light forces at Malta to harry the enemy's supply routes to Africa had to be temporarily abandoned because of the insecurity of their base. The importance of interrupting the traffic by all possible means was, however, fully realised at home. In April the Chiefs of Staff had considered sending some R.A.F. Beauforts there, but the idea had to be abandoned. Only a few naval Swordfish remained to do what they could by way of air attacks. In these circumstances the prosecution of the campaign devolved mainly on the Mediterranean Fleet's submarines, and they made many daring and successful attacks on troop transports and supply ships. Admiral Cunningham had long pressed for the removal

---

[1] See p. 410 *et seq.*

of the restrictions on submarine warfare, which had been imposed at the beginning of the war and which had already been largely abolished in home waters. Restrictions were, however, continued in the Mediterranean until the 5th of February 1941, when the Cabinet, in order to prevent Italian convoys moving through Tunisian territorial waters, approved that all ships met to the south of latitude 35° 46′ North should be assumed to be enemy transports and could be sunk at sight.

One of the most successful of our submarines was the *Upholder* which made many profitable patrols and, on the 24th of May, sank the loaded liner *Conte Rosso* (18,000 tons) after a hazardous and difficult attack. Her captain, Lieutenant-Commander M. D. Wanklyn, was awarded the Victoria Cross. But our submarines now began to suffer heavy losses themselves and in May the *Usk* and *Undaunted* both failed to return from patrols. None the less the submarines continued their activities unremittingly and in June they found many valuable targets. Though they could not by themselves be decisive on so short a route, we now know that the combined effects of the attacks by aircraft, surface ships and submarines caused General Rommel serious and continuous anxiety and certainly prevented him from exploiting the favourable position reached through his recent success on land.

The Italian Admiralty's post-war assessments of the merchant ship losses incurred during the current phase are given below.

Table 12. Enemy Merchant Shipping Losses January–May 1941

(1) Italian (includes losses outside Mediterranean)

(Number of ships—Tonnage)

Month	By surface ships	By submarine	By aircraft	By mine	By other causes	Totals
Jan.	1— 62	5—15,202	1— 3,950	5— 4,755	19—16,190	31— 40,159
Feb.	Nil	1— 4,957	2— 113	Nil	15— 8,717	18— 13,787
Mar.	Nil	8—22,615	1— 7,289	Nil	4— 1,673	13— 31,577
April	9—22,135	3— 8,181	2— 4,557	1— 2,576	Nil	15— 37,449
May	3— 3,515	8—38,842	3— 9,704	8—22,610	5—12,071	27— 86,742
Totals	13—25,712	25—89,797	9—25,613	14—29,941	43—38,651	104—209,714

(i) The losses shown under 'Other causes' include ships scuttled to avoid capture. (ii) Of the twenty-five ships sunk by our submarines, all except three small vessels of less than 500 tons were sunk by submerged attack with torpedoes. (iii) Of the ships sunk by air attack five of 9,817 tons were sunk by bombs and four of 15,796 tons by torpedoes.

(2) German (Mediterranean only)

	By surface ships	By submarine	By aircraft	By mine	By other causes	Total
January to May 1941	4—14,008	1—1,927	1—3,950	5—22,319	Nil	11—42,204

We must now return to the eastern Mediterranean, where the stage was set for the battle which was to prove the supreme test for Admiral Cunningham's hard-run ships—the Battle for Crete. It forms no part of our story to tell of the military dispositions and preparations to hold the island, of the impossibility of re-equipping the soldiers carried there from Greece, of the total inadequacy of the air defences and of the early withdrawal of what little air strength had originally existed. All that part of the story belongs to the volumes of this series specifically concerned with the Mediterranean operations. We are concerned here only with two aspects of this desperate struggle. The first is the denial to the enemy of the use of the sea to make landings on the island, and the second is the need to keep open our own sea communications to enable our garrison to be supplied and reinforced and also, in the final issue, to evacuate the troops if their position on land became untenable.

To ensure that no seaborne landings took place Admiral Cunningham had, since the 14th of May, kept light forces in the waters across which they must pass. But these forces could not, because of the enemy's undisputed control of the air, make use of Suda Bay. They had instead to work from Alexandria, 420 miles away to the south. Admiral Cunningham's general plan was to employ three groups of light forces to sweep the most probable sea approaches from Greece to Crete by night; they would retire to the south of the island by day. Part of the battle fleet would support the light forces from a position to the west of Crete, while the rest, with the aircraft carrier *Formidable*, many of whose fighters had already been expended in Operation 'Tiger', would be held in reserve at Alexandria. Mines were laid off certain enemy departure ports, and motor torpedo-boats were stationed at Suda Bay for offensive operations close inshore.

The forces sailed from Alexandria on the 14th, and on the 16th and 17th all preparations for the prearranged night sweeps were put in hand. Intelligence did not indicate any probability of enemy activity, so the covering force was relieved by the reserve force from Alexandria on the 17th and returned to that base; it fuelled there and was off again northward on the 19th. During these final days of preparation reinforcements and a few tanks were carried in warships to the garrison.

Early on the 20th the enemy opened the attack with very heavy bombing followed by landings by parachute, glider and transport aircraft. The naval dispositions at the time the attack started were as follows: Rear-Admiral H. B. Rawlings was covering the light forces from a position 100 miles west of Crete with the battleships *Warspite* and *Valiant*, one cruiser and ten destroyers. Rear-Admiral E. L. S. King in the cruiser *Naiad* with the *Perth* and four destroyers was

THE ATTACK ON CRETE STARTS

withdrawing southward from the Kaso Strait.[1] Rear-Admiral Glennie in the *Dido* with the *Orion* was steering from the Antikithera Strait to join Admiral Rawlings, and the cruisers *Gloucester* (Captain H. A. Rowley) and *Fiji* were on the way from Alexandria to join the same force. As soon as Admiral Cunningham learnt that the enemy had launched his attack the various forces closed towards the threatened island, but kept out of sight of land. That night (the 20th–21st) the prearranged sweeps were carried out but, apart from a brush with Italian motor torpedo-boats, no engagements resulted. The sea passages were, in fact, then clear of invasion forces.

On the 21st the majority of the forces remained south-west of Kithera, and heavy air attacks were made on various squadrons and ships. The first casualty, the destroyer *Juno*, occurred in a bombing attack just after noon to the south-east of Crete. No seaborne forces had, as yet, been sighted, but that afternoon air reconnaissance reported groups of small craft moving south towards Crete. Admirals King and Glennie and Captain Rowley were therefore ordered to take their forces into the Aegean that night to find and engage them, while Admiral Rawlings moved with the heavy ships to support the light forces.

Shortly before midnight Admiral Glennie, who now had the *Dido*, *Orion*, *Ajax* and four destroyers under his command, met a convoy of light craft, crowded with German troops and escorted by Italian torpedo-boats, some twenty miles off Canea on the north coast of Crete. For two and a half hours the British squadron played havoc among the convoy, sank many ships and small craft and one of its escorts. The exact enemy losses in this action are not known but were certainly heavy. The intended landing from the sea was wholly frustrated. Admiral Glennie, now very short of anti-aircraft ammunition, then withdrew and was ordered back to Alexandria to replenish.

Captain Rowley, with the *Gloucester*, *Fiji* and two destroyers, also swept into the Aegean, but found no targets. The force was heavily bombed during the withdrawal, but suffered no damage.

At dawn on the 22nd, Admiral Glennie and Captain Rowley were about to join Admiral Rawlings' support force south-west of Kithera. A reinforcement of five destroyers of the 5th Flotilla from Malta under Captain Lord Louis Mountbatten was also about to join; other fresh destroyers were on the way north from Alexandria. Admiral King, with four cruisers and three destroyers, was off the north coast of Crete. He was about to sweep further north in search of convoys. Air attacks on this force started immediately and continued without a break. At 10 a.m., when about ninety miles from the Cretan coast and still under heavy air attack, our force met an enemy convoy and

---
[1] See Map 36 (*facing p. 436*).

forced it to turn back. Admiral King, however, was acutely conscious of the dangerous position of his force, which was now far to the north with the day not yet half spent and anti-aircraft ammunition running short. He therefore abandoned the pursuit and withdrew to the west, a course of action which did not appeal to the Commander-in-Chief, who considered that the whole convoy should have been destroyed, and that the price which would probably have been exacted for doing so would have been worth paying.

During the withdrawal the *Naiad* was hit by bombs and severely damaged. The *Carlisle* was also hit, and her captain killed. Admiral Rawlings had meanwhile learnt of Admiral King's withdrawal and predicament, and at once moved eastward to his support. The two forces met early in the afternoon in the Kithera Channel. Just as the junction was being made, the flagship *Warspite* was hit and seriously damaged by a bomb. Both forces now withdrew to the south-west, still under air attack. So far the situation at sea, though tense and anxious, was not wholly unfavourable, since all attempts to invade by water had been frustrated, and the losses suffered had not been disproportionate to the success achieved. But the next few hours were to bring a big change.

The first ship to be caught by the bombers, unsupported, and sunk was the destroyer *Greyhound*. The *Gloucester*, *Fiji* and two destroyers were ordered to her assistance, and were continuously attacked while rescuing survivors. Admiral King had not known that Captain Rowley's force was almost out of anti-aircraft ammunition when he sent him to support the *Greyhound*. But he himself was in like state, and therefore asked Admiral Rawlings for close support. The latter moved in again at the best speed of which the damaged *Warspite* was capable. At 3 p.m. the rescuing ships were given discretion to withdraw. But it was too late. While within sight of the supporting *Warspite*, the *Gloucester* received several hits and was brought to a standstill, badly on fire. The captain of the *Fiji* reluctantly decided that he must leave her and steamed southwards with two destroyers, still under heavy attack. At 6.45 p.m., having survived some twenty formation attacks and fired almost every round from her anti-aircraft guns, the *Fiji* fell a victim to a single aircraft's attack. At 8.15 she sank. The destroyers returned after dark and rescued over 500 of her crew.

The detachment of the *Gloucester* and *Fiji* was, in Admiral Cunningham's opinion, a mistake brought about by disregard of a lesson which had not then been fully realised in the Mediterranean, namely that a whole force should be moved to a danger point rather than a detachment made from that force. On this occasion a heavy price was exacted.

That night destroyers searched for survivors from the *Gloucester* and

Fiji and moved right into Canea Bay to seek enemy landing forces; but none was found. Further east other destroyers patrolled off Heraklion, also without result. In fact the enemy had abandoned the attempt to make landings from the sea until after his airborne forces had overwhelmed the island's defenders. It was this night that the unresting destroyers fetched off the King of Greece and the British Minister from the south coast of Crete.

In the early hours of the 23rd Admiral Cunningham gained the impression, from an error made in a signal, that the heavy ships had run out of ammunition and therefore ordered Admiral Rawlings back to Alexandria. This deprived Lord Louis Mountbatten's destroyers of support during their dawn withdrawal from the Aegean. At about 8 a.m. heavy air attacks started against his force, which was then only some forty miles to the south of Crete. The *Kelly* and *Kashmir* were quickly sunk but the *Kipling* had seen the attacks, closed and managed to pick up 279 survivors from the two ships, including the flotilla's commander. She was heavily bombed while doing so but, happily, escaped unscathed. Meanwhile the majority of the naval forces engaged, many of which were running very short of fuel as well as of ammunition, were returning to Alexandria where they arrived late that evening, the 23rd.

On land the garrison had fared ill on the 21st and 22nd, and Suda Bay had been so heavily bombed that its continued use as a base even for small craft, or as an entry for supplies and reinforcements for the Army, was practically impossible. Destroyers and the fast minelayer *Abdiel* were now the only ships able to get through with urgently needed stores, and they made a number of hazardous dashes in and out of Suda Bay on successive nights. The use of merchant ships for this purpose was several times attempted but was found to be suicidal. Even the fast 'Glens' could not do the round trip quickly enough to escape loss.

While Admiral Cunningham's fleet was thus straining every nerve to frustrate seaborne landings and to keep the Army supplied, and was suffering heavy losses in the process, signals were reaching the Commander-in-Chief from London, which not only seemed to instruct him in the objects already being pursued, but implied criticism of the periodical return of the surviving ships to Alexandria. On the 24th, since the Chiefs of Staff had asked for an 'appreciation', Cunningham gave it as his opinion that the scale of air attack now prevented his ships from working by day in the Aegean or off the coasts of Crete. The fleet could, therefore, no longer guarantee to prevent seaborne landings without incurring losses which might lead to sacrificing the command of the eastern basin. The Chiefs of Staff seem to have taken the view that the Admiral was unwilling to accept risks in order to accomplish their objectives. They replied that more drastic action was required, that risks must be accepted to prevent reinforcements reaching Crete in strength and that 'only experience would show how long the situation could be maintained'—a message which Cunningham has described as 'singularly unhelpful'.[1] He answered that he did not fear losses, but must avoid such losses as would cripple his fleet without securing any commensurate advantage; he pointed out that in three days he had lost two cruisers and four destroyers while a battleship, two more cruisers and four destroyers had been severely damaged. Indeed, while actually writing this reply, he received news of more damage to his fleet. This whole exchange of messages certainly seems to show how little it was realised in London that a tremendous effort was being made to meet the crisis, and how great was the handicap of having to work the ships over 400 miles from their base and almost entirely without air cover.

While these signals were being exchanged, operations to the north of Crete were continued by cruisers and destroyers which swept along the coast on the nights of the 24th–25th and 25th–26th, without finding any targets. Then, on the 25th, Admiral Pridham-Wippell sailed again from Alexandria with the *Queen Elizabeth*, *Barham*, *Formidable* and nine destroyers to attack the enemy's main air base on Scarpanto Island, fifty miles east of Crete, with naval bombers. The attack took place on the 26th and achieved surprise, but the bombers were too few to have much permanent effect on the enemy's air effort. That afternoon dive-bombers penetrated the screen of the remaining naval fighters, twice hit the aircraft carrier and damaged another destroyer. On the 27th the battleship *Barham* was also damaged, and the rest of the force then returned to its base.

By this time the state of affairs on shore had become critical and the decision was taken on the afternoon of the 27th to evacuate Crete. For the fleet this meant that, after the unremitting toil and strain of the previous weeks, all the hazards of an evacuation in the teeth of practically unopposed air power now had immediately to be faced. Though the limit of endurance seemed already to have been reached and passed, the call to rescue about 32,000 soldiers had to be met. The over-strained men rose at once to answer it with their battered ships. The Royal Air Force promised to give what protection it could, but warned that it would be meagre and spasmodic.

The intention was to evacuate the troops only between the hours of midnight and 3 a.m., and to use Heraklion on the north coast and three small ports, Sphakia, Plaka Bay and Tymbaki, on the south and east coasts.[2] Only at Heraklion were there any port facilities. All the others would involve lifting men from open beaches.

---
[1] Viscount Cunningham of Hyndhope, *A Sailor's Odyssey* (1951), p. 375.
[2] See Map 36 (*facing p. 436*).

At 6 a.m. on the 28th, the cruisers *Orion*, *Ajax* and *Dido* and six destroyers sailed for Heraklion under Admiral Rawlings. Two hours later four destroyers under Captain S. H. T. Arliss sailed for Sphakia. The latter force accomplished its object almost unmolested, and was back at Alexandria on the afternoon of the 29th. Admiral Rawlings' force had a very different experience. It was attacked during the approach and suffered damage to two ships. On entering the port the destroyers ferried men out to the cruisers and, at 3.20 a.m. on the 29th, they all sailed again with the entire Heraklion garrison of some 4,000 men aboard. Then occurred a most unlucky delay in the withdrawal. The destroyer *Imperial* had been 'near missed' by bombs on the outward journey but appeared to be undamaged. She had carried on to Heraklion and, with the *Kimberley*, had embarked the rearguard of the troops. At 3.45 a.m. the *Imperial's* steering gear jammed and she nearly collided with the cruisers. Admiral Rawlings had to decide whether to wait for her or to remove her troops and sink the ship. It was essential to put as many miles as possible between his force and the enemy's air bases before daylight. The *Hotspur* was accordingly sent back to take off the soldiers and sink the *Imperial*, which had reported that she was quite unable to steer. An hour later the *Hotspur*, which now had 900 men on board, rejoined Admiral Rawlings. But day was now breaking, and it was after sunrise when the force turned south for the Kaso Strait. Enemy aircraft were already on the look-out and the expected bombing attacks soon started. The *Hereward* was damaged, left behind and lost, and other damage further reduced the speed of the squadron. The promised fighter support had been sent, but the short endurance of the Blenheims and the lateness of the ships prevented it being there when required. The *Orion* and *Dido* were also hit and severely damaged, with high casualties among the soldiers crowded on board. But they managed to struggle on southwards. The force entered Alexandria on the evening of the 29th, practically out of both fuel and ammunition. The start of the evacuation had thus been little short of disastrous. But, after anxious consultation with London, it was decided none the less to persevere. The decision was amply justified, since the embarkations from Sphakia were completed without meeting heavy opposition and without loss to the ships employed.

On the night of the 29th–30th Admiral King with the *Phoebe*, *Perth*, *Calcutta*, three destroyers and the fast transport *Glengyle* lifted 6,000 men from the little port. During the withdrawal the *Perth* was hit and damaged, but the return voyage was successfully completed. Next night Captain Arliss made the trip with his four destroyers, two of which were damaged during the operation. Fifteen hundred soldiers were rescued. On the night of the 31st May–1st June Admiral King sailed for the last attempt, successfully embarked 4,000 men and returned to Egypt without loss, though the anti-aircraft cruiser *Calcutta*, which, with the *Coventry*, had been sent out to meet and support him, was attacked and sunk.

Admiral King's return to Alexandria on the afternoon of the 1st of June marked the end of the Battle of Crete. The Navy had fulfilled every one of the tasks given it. No seaborne landings were made by the enemy until his airborne forces had conquered the island. About 18,600 of the 32,000 men comprising the garrison were embarked and most of them reached Egypt safely. But the losses inflicted by the enemy bombers had been very severe. Two battleships and one aircraft carrier had been damaged, three cruisers and six destroyers sunk and six cruisers and seven destroyers damaged. But the effort made by the fleet had truly been magnificent. As Admiral Cunningham said in his despatch, his men had 'started the evacuation already overtired and . . . had to carry it through under savage air attack . . . it is perhaps even now not realised how nearly the breaking point was reached. But that these men struggled through is the measure of their achievement'. Nor was it only the Navy which paid a heavy price for the endeavour to save something of Greek liberty. In Operations 'Lustre' and 'Demon' thirty-two Allied transports, supply ships and fleet auxiliaries totalling 128,418 tons were destroyed, or had to be abandoned in the various Greek and Cretan harbours used, and twelve ships of 94,406 tons were lost at sea. Many of them were fast ships of good lifting and carrying capacity, which were particularly valuable for the rapid transport of tanks, vehicles and ammunition all over the world, and which could ill be spared.

Buried among the mass of official documents accumulated by Operations 'Lustre' and 'Demon'—the 'Reports of Proceedings' of the ships involved, tables of convoy sailings, copies of signals sent and received and statistics of many kinds—some more intimate and human papers are, rather surprisingly, to be found. It appears that some of the soldiers rescued, N.C.O.s and privates as well as officers, wrote down their personal experiences just after their escape and left them in the ships which took them off. Thence they ultimately reached the Admiralty and so came to be incorporated in the official records. To the historian these simply expressed personal stories have a particular appeal and interest, for they reveal what the soldiers felt at the time. In every one of these accounts appears the sustaining, almost blind, faith that, if they could only reach the sea coast somewhere, the Navy would rescue them. One young New Zealander calls it 'the ever-present hope of contacting the Navy' and another wrote that during all the long retreat in Greece 'our one thought and hope was the Navy'. What happened when they reached the sea is vividly recorded by a third. 'With a torch we flashed an S.O.S. and, to our tremendous relief, we received an answer. It was the Navy on the job—the Navy for which we had been hoping and praying all along the route.' It is perhaps in these records that the purpose and justification of all that was endured by the maritime services at this time is to be found. Admiral Cunningham well knew what was required when he gave his clarion call to the fleet that 'we must not let them (the Army) down'. That summons, and, perhaps, a deep, instinctive understanding of the issues involved and the tradition to be maintained, must surely have been the inspiration which brought the Mediterranean Fleet, scarred but triumphant, through its supreme ordeal.

The lessons of the battle were plain. Complete control of the air now enabled an invasion to be carried out across narrow seas without control of the surface waters by ships; and control of the surface waters by ships could not for long be maintained in the face of overwhelming air power. The answer to air power could only be air power, and the strengthening of the Royal Air Force in the Middle East was therefore the first requirement if our control of the Mediterranean routes was to be restored and extended.

In reviewing the events in the eastern Mediterranean during the spring of 1941, the similarity between the demands made on Admiral Cunningham's fleet, the trials and losses endured by his ships and men and their final triumph, though at great cost to themselves, and those made on Admiral Forbes' Home Fleet in the North Sea and Norwegian coastal waters in April and May 1940 may be remarked. In both cases the Navy was required, at short notice, to carry or escort a hastily prepared military force many hundreds of miles overseas, to a theatre far distant from any well-organised base of its own and, finally, to fetch back its survivors. The distance from Alexandria to the temporary bases used in Greece and Crete is comparable to the distance from Scapa to Namsos and Aandalsnes; and the strength of the Army sent to Norway was about the same as that sent to Greece. In both cases the cruisers and destroyers, working close inshore in support of the Army, bore the brunt of the enemy's air onslaught, while the battle squadrons supported them from covering positions to seaward. Off Norway, and off Greece and Crete, defence by our own shore-based fighter aircraft was too weak and intermittent to blunt the enemy's air weapon, and in both campaigns naval aircraft, working from their carriers, tried to remedy the lack of shore-based aircraft. When one looks at particular operations, such as the evacuations from Namsos and Aandalsnes by Admirals Edward-Collins', J. H. D. Cunningham's and Layton's cruisers and destroyers, and those from Greece and Crete carried out by Admirals Pridham-Wippell, Rawlings and King, the similarity becomes more striking.[1]

If it be accepted that many points of similarity exist between the Norway campaign of 1940 and the brief Greek and Crete campaigns of the following year, the historian must ask why the lessons learnt in the first were not applied in time to prevent a repetition of similar events in the second. The fighting men certainly asked such questions very pointedly at the time. Before Norway the ability of the bomber to dispute, if not to control, coastal waters overseas, to prevent the establishment of well-found advanced bases, and to dictate the amount of support which the Navy could give to the Army on shore could fairly have been regarded as one on which opinions might differ. But after that campaign no such differences could be, or were, held either in London or in the fleet. It was known that the Navy could not alone adequately and consistently control narrow waters over which the enemy held command of the air. It is natural to ask why, therefore, the fighter aircraft strength in the eastern Mediterranean had not been reinforced to such a degree as to make a repetition of the same failings impossible, and why the most energetic steps were not at once taken to prepare advanced airfields from which those fighters could operate. But it must be remembered that not only was the technique of rapidly constructing advanced airfields, which was to reach its zenith during the American thrusts across the Pacific in 1942 and 1943, then in its infancy, but that all the heavy equipment and stores necessary for that purpose had to be carried 12,000 miles to Egypt round the Cape. Yet, even after allowances have been made for all the difficulties, one cannot but feel that more could have been done to defend our bases in Crete and to prepare to meet an airborne invasion. We had, after all, occupied the island for six months before the German onslaught started.

The question of our numerical weakness in the air in the Middle East is more difficult. Though the urgent need for air reinforcements was overwhelmingly plain to the Commanders-in-Chief on the spot, the matter, as viewed from London, was not so simple. In the spring of 1941 the War Cabinet was not yet aware of Hitler's intention to attack Russia, and indications that such was his purpose did not become strong until May. Nor was it easy to assess the consequences of the defeat of the Luftwaffe over Britain in 1940. It would have been rash to assume that a second challenge in the air, as a preliminary to invasion, would not be offered in the following year. In consequence the policy was to use Bomber Command's main strength to strike at Germany and to assist in the Battle of the Atlantic, and to preserve for Fighter Command a sufficient margin to ensure that a second

---

[1] See pp. 188–190.

THE CAMPAIGN JUSTIFIED

challenge could be met as successfully as the first. The first priority for what fighter strength could be spared from home was given to Malta, and second priority to the Middle East theatre. Starvation of the latter was caused only by the impossibility of spreading our still slender resources to all the points where they were needed.

If this argument be accepted, it remains only to consider whether the decision to go to the aid of Greece, in full knowledge of our weakness, was strategically sound. We now know that the battle for Greece and Crete helped to upset the timetable for Hitler's attack on Russia. Moreover his victory in Crete cost him almost the whole of his 11th Fliegerkorps. We can, perhaps, justifiably criticise the failure to make the best use of what aircraft we had in the Middle East by developing more and better airfields in Greece and Crete, and by improving our aircraft repair and servicing organisation in Egypt. Had we done so the fleet could have been better protected and a heavier toll exacted from the enemy. But it is now plain that the decision to fight in Greece and Crete was as politically necessary as it was strategically justified by later events. The fighting man did not pass through these ordeals in vain.

CHAPTER XXI

THE BATTLE OF THE ATLANTIC
1st April–31st December, 1941

> ... Our trade must be exceedingly exposed for want of convoys and cruisers ... for want of frigates.
> *Lord Sandwich.* 1778.

BEFORE opening the story of the second phase of the struggle for control of the Atlantic shipping routes it may be useful to remind the reader that in July 1940 the escort forces of the Western Approaches command could only accompany convoys as far as about longitude 17° West—that is to say some 300 miles to the west of Ireland—and that in the following October it was possible, thanks to the establishment of advanced fuelling bases in Northern Ireland, to extend this distance some 100 miles further west. It was not until April of the following year, when the fuelling bases in Iceland were ready, that any further extension of the escort vessels' protecting shield became possible. Once this had been accomplished, anti-submarine escort became possible to a greatly increased distance from our shores—as far as some 35° West, which is more than half way across the North Atlantic.

Well before the start of the present phase the Admiralty, in consultation with the Canadian Navy, had been planning to provide convoys with anti-submarine escort right across the Atlantic. The controlling factors were, firstly, the number of escort vessels available; secondly, the training of their crews both as individual units and as members of a group accustomed to work together and, thirdly, the provision of the necessary base facilities in Iceland, Newfoundland and eastern Canada. Fortunately the escort vessels ordered under the Admiralty's war emergency programmes were now completing in considerable numbers.[1] New escort groups were being regularly formed and, after undergoing a period of intensive individual and group training, were being sent to their stations at the eastern or western ends of the convoy routes or to the half-way mark in Iceland. The Royal Canadian Navy played a great part in creating the necessary bases and in providing escort vessels to watch over the western portion of the north Atlantic routes. From very small

---
[1] See Appendix F.

beginnings—it comprised only about 3,600 officers and men and possessed only seven destroyers and five minesweepers on the outbreak of war—it was now expanding rapidly. Seven of the ex-American destroyers were now Canadian-manned, and many corvettes and minesweepers were building in Canadian yards.

Early in April the Admiralty decided that four escort groups of the Western Approaches command should work from Greenock and Londonderry, and be responsible for the northern convoy route from Britain to Iceland and from Iceland to 35° West. To strengthen this somewhat meagre force eleven ships of the 1st and 6th Minesweeping Flotillas, which were asdic-fitted and would be based at Scapa, were allocated to Admiral Noble, while Admiral Tovey provided additional support to the escort groups by detaching four Home Fleet destroyers to work with them from Iceland.

In addition to anti-submarine escorts, arrangements still had to be made to protect the H.X. and S.C. convoys against surface raiders; the general policy was to provide each convoy with a battleship, cruiser or submarine escort in addition to the normal armed merchant cruiser. But shortage of ships often reduced the strength of the ocean escorts below what was desired, and it was usual to eliminate the A.M.C. if a battleship was with a convoy. When, in mid-April, anti-submarine escort was extended to 35° West, the battleship generally returned to Halifax on reaching that longitude while the A.M.C., if present, would go to Iceland to refuel.

Air cover in mid-Atlantic was improved by the transfer of ten Hudsons of No. 269 Squadron and also a Sunderland flying-boat squadron to Iceland in April. The Hudsons worked from a shore airfield, while the flying boats had a depot ship—the *Manela*—moored in Reykjavik harbour. The control of all R.A.F. aircraft in Iceland was transferred to No. 15 Group of Coastal Command and an Area Combined Headquarters was established in Reykjavik.

It will thus be seen that it was at the start of the present phase that the full benefit of the far-sighted action taken nearly a year earlier in occupying Iceland was first fully reaped. The ships of the Home Fleet and Western Approaches command, the airmen of No. 15 Group, many Canadian and American escort vessels and innumerable Allied merchant ships now became all too familiar with its bleak and precipitous coastline, the deep inlets which formed its harbours, the poor holding ground which gave the ships constant anxiety and, in particular, with the violence of its sudden, blinding and shifting storms. The treachery of the Icelandic climate during the long winter months, the inhospitality of its harbours and the virtual certainty that little rest or relaxation would be possible in them soon aroused the British sailor's intense dislike of the place. To come in from fighting the enemy and the elements only to find that the fury

Map 37

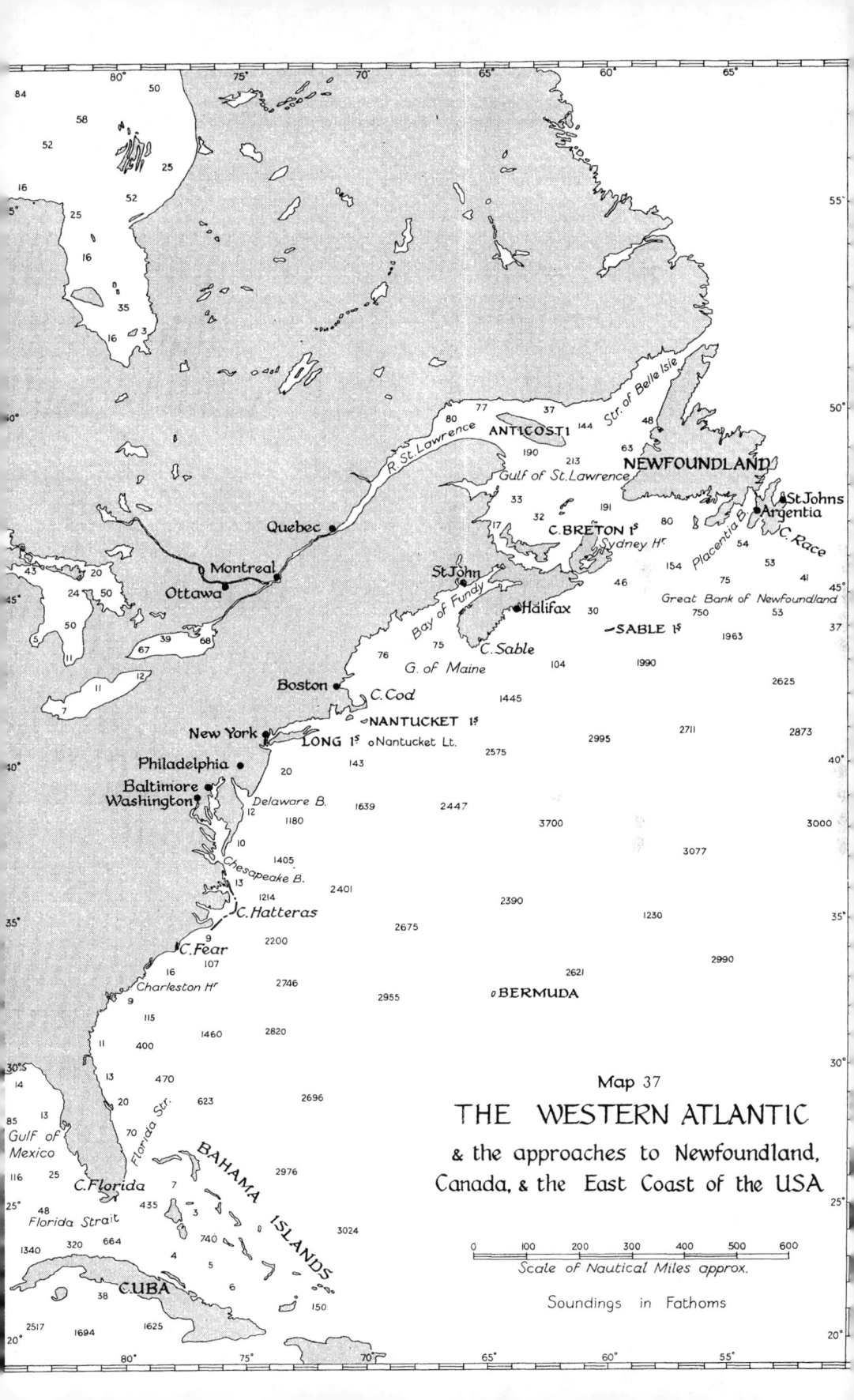

THE WESTERN ATLANTIC
& the approaches to Newfoundland,
Canada, & the East Coast of the USA

Scale of Nautical Miles approx.

Soundings in Fathoms

of the latter had followed him with intensified malevolence awoke all his wide capacity for sardonic humour. Yet however deeply and justly the sailor may have apostrophised the place everyone involved in the Battle of the Atlantic well knew that Iceland was now playing a vital part in the struggle.

On the 23rd of May the strength of the escort forces allocated to the eastern half of the northern route was increased to five groups while three groups and a sloop division, based on Liverpool, assumed responsibility for the southerly routes to Gibraltar and Sierra Leone. It was also decided, in consultation with the Canadian Navy, that an escort vessel base should immediately be opened at St. John's, Newfoundland.[1]

At the end of May the Canadian Navy reported that seven corvettes were immediately available for the newly constituted Newfoundland Escort Force and that fifteen more would be ready to join in June. The total strength of the force was, initially, thirty destroyers, nine sloops and twenty-four corvettes. On the 6th of that month a separate naval command, under a Canadian officer, Commodore L. W. Murray, was established at St. John's, and on the last day of the same month Iceland also was made an independent naval command under Rear-Admiral R. J. R. Scott.

By the middle of May eight Canadian destroyers and twenty corvettes were on escort duty, chiefly on the western section of the north Atlantic route, under the operational control of the Admiralty. Canadian Naval Headquarters had agreed without hesitation that control of Canadian ships should be freely exercised from London in exactly the same manner as was the case with British ships. The Canadian Navy thus accepted the chief responsibility, at this stage of the war, for providing not only local escort in the waters off Newfoundland but also ocean anti-submarine escort over the first section of the homeward convoy route from the north American seaboard to the rendezvous south of Iceland, where the mid-ocean escorts took over.[2] With the creation of the St. John's Escort Force and the establishment of bases there and in Iceland the Admiralty's plans for continuous escort across the Atlantic could at last be realised, and on the 27th of May Convoy H.X. 129 sailed from Halifax under this new measure of protection.[3]

On the southerly Atlantic route to Sierra Leone continuous escort was not established until mid-July. Convoy S.L. 81 sailed homeward on the 14th of that month and was the first to be escorted right

---

[1] See Map 37.

[2] See J. Schull. *The Far Distant Ships* (Department of National Defence, Ottawa, 1950) for a full account of the part played by the Royal Canadian Navy in the Battle of the Atlantic.

[3] See Map 38 (*facing p. 457*).

through. Sloops and ex-American coastguard cutters (of which more will be said shortly) were used on this route on account of their greater endurance; fifteen of the former class and ten of the latter were based on Londonderry for the purpose. Corvettes from Freetown escorted the convoys between that base and about latitude 19° North, where the long-range Londonderry groups took over. On the outward journey the reverse arrangement was made, and in 19° North the corvettes met the convoys, while the Londonderry group went on to fuel at Bathurst in Gambia. These outward convoys (O.S.) to Freetown were started in July.

On the 10th of July a change was also made on the Gibraltar route. Whereas it had been the custom for only one sloop to go right through with the convoys and for strengthened escorts to be provided at either end of the route, an escort group of about five corvettes and a sloop thereafter accompanied the convoys throughout their entire passage. An escort force of twenty-two corvettes was stationed at Liverpool for the purpose.

One interesting result of the changes made in the organisation of anti-submarine escorts in the Atlantic was that they enabled most of the armed merchant cruisers, which had acted as ocean escorts since the early days of the war and had suffered heavy losses in performing that duty, to be withdrawn. They ceased service with the Sierra Leone convoys in August, and in October they were also taken from the Halifax Escort Force. Though some continued for a time to serve in the same capacity on foreign stations, the majority of these large and valuable ships now reverted to the control of the Ministry of War Transport and were, for the most part, henceforth used as troopships.

It will be appropriate to consider next the increasing participation of the United States in the Battle of the Atlantic since it was during the present phase that the Neutrality Patrols of the early months of the war came to be replaced by more active measures.[1] The forces allocated to the Neutrality Patrol had been greatly increased in the previous February when the United States Atlantic Fleet was created and placed under the command of Admiral E. J. King. On the 11th of March the Lend-Lease Bill became law, and the President was now able to put into effect certain important measures which had been dependent on approval of that Bill. Among them was the transfer to the Royal Navy of the ten coastguard cutters already mentioned. The offer of these ships had been made to the Prime Minister in February, and gladly accepted. Now that transfer was possible, crews were at once collected from British warships refitting in America and by mid-June they had all been brought across the

---

[1] See p. 112.

Atlantic. They were re-named after British coastguard stations, and formed a very valuable reinforcement to the long-range escort groups working on the Sierra Leone route.[1]

In March the 'Atlantic Fleet Support Group' was formed. It consisted of three destroyer flotillas and five flying-boat squadrons. In the following month the 'Security Zone' patrolled by Admiral King's ships and aircraft was extended much further towards Britain—from 60° to 26° West.

Early in April the refitting of British ships in American yards was approved. The battleships *Malaya* and *Resolution*, both of which had recently been damaged in action, were among the first to benefit from a measure which relieved this country's overloaded dockyards of an important part of their immense burden. From this time onwards it was rare for any American Navy yard, and many private yards as well, not to have at least one British ship in its hands for refit or repair of action damage. The building of warships of many types and of merchant ships on British 'Lend-Lease' account also dates to this time.

In the same month of March that saw the approval of the Lend-Lease Bill American air bases were opened on the east coast of Greenland and naval and air installations formed at Bermuda. Meanwhile the staff discussions which had been in progress in Washington had achieved agreement regarding a combined strategy and the shape which American assistance in the Atlantic would take in the event of the United States declaring war. A mission had also arrived in England to choose the naval and air bases which American forces would use in such an eventuality. Two pairs of naval and air bases were selected as an insurance against one being put out of action by bombing. After trying unsuccessfully to persuade the Government of Eire to grant them the use of Lough Swilly, the mission's choice fell on Gare Loch in the Clyde for a destroyer base and Loch Ryan, at the entrance to the same estuary, as a base for naval aircraft.[2] The second pair of bases chosen were Londonderry and Lough Erne, which were already in use by British naval and air forces respectively.[3] The materials required to create these bases started to cross the Atlantic in June, in British ships.

On the 15th of May the United States Navy took over the leased base at Argentia in south-east Newfoundland, and on the 7th of July a United States marine brigade, supported by powerful naval forces, arrived at Reykjavik to relieve the British garrison and to carry out 'police observation' duties between America and Iceland. This move

---

[1] Appendix P gives the chronology of American assistance to Britain in 1941.
[2] See Map 8 (*facing p. 91*).
[3] See S. E. Morison. *The History of United States Naval Operations in World War II* (Little, Brown & Co., Boston, 1948), Vol. I, pp. 53–55.

meant that henceforth there would be a steady flow of American shipping to and from Iceland, and that naval forces would have to protect it. Such forces were not, however, at this time allowed to escort British convoys.

These developments in American Atlantic policy, though encouraging to our cause, did not greatly ease the strain on Britain and Canada, who continued to bear almost the whole burden of the Atlantic struggle. In fact, the adoption of end-to-end escorting had increased that strain, since not only were larger numbers of escort vessels more than ever necessary but new bases had to be rapidly created, and a most careful organisation started to dovetail all the complex movements of warship and air escorts with those of the convoys themselves.

The complexity of the escort problem had greatly increased since the early days of the war, and careful timing and co-ordination of all movements was essential if the new system was to work smoothly and efficiently. Between the American seaboard and the Port of London a convoy would now probably pass through the hands of four different escort groups.[1] The first would be a Canadian group from St. John's which would escort a Halifax convoy to the Mid-Ocean Meeting Point in about longitude 35° West. There a British group from Iceland might meet the convoy and take over its escort, while the St. John's group returned with an outward-bound convoy. In about 18° West, at the Eastern Ocean Meeting Point, a Western Approaches group would take over from the Iceland group and bring the convoy to the west coast of Scotland where ships bound for the east coast would be detached to join, at Loch Ewe, with a coastal (W.N.) convoy to pass round the north of Scotland under different escort and so reach London. The ships bound for west coast ports would meanwhile proceed towards their destinations under the Western Approaches escorts. It will easily be understood that, if any serious delays occurred in mid-ocean through bad weather or diversion of the convoy from U-boat danger zones, the escorts might run short of fuel and so fail to relieve each other on time, thus, perhaps, leaving a convoy unprotected. The responsibility for the working of the whole Atlantic convoy system rested, under the Admiralty, on the Commander-in-Chief, Western Approaches. To Admiral Noble and his staff in Derby House, Liverpool, the Admiralty supplied an unceasing flow of intelligence derived from the plots in the Submarine Tracking Room. This information formed the basis of the routes initially given to convoys and to ships proceeding independently. Once at sea, if danger arose, diversion from this route would be ordered by the Commander-in-Chief or, perhaps,

---

[1] See Map 38 (*facing p. 457*).

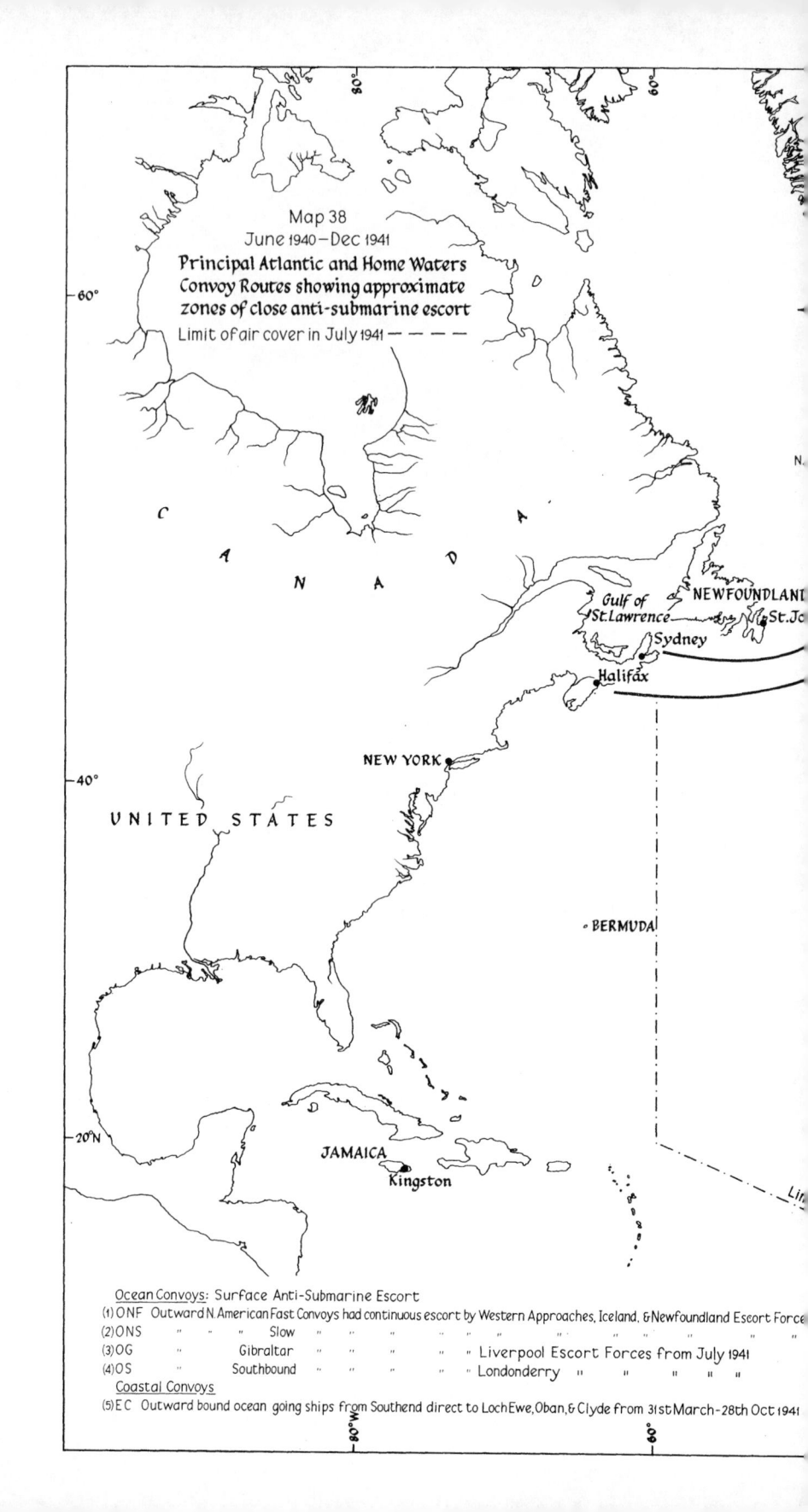

Map 38
June 1940 – Dec 1941
Principal Atlantic and Home Waters
Convoy Routes showing approximate
zones of close anti-submarine escort
Limit of air cover in July 1941 – – –

Ocean Convoys: Surface Anti-Submarine Escort
(1) ONF Outward N. American Fast Convoys had continuous escort by Western Approaches, Iceland, & Newfoundland Escort Force
(2) ONS   "   "   "   Slow   "   "   "   "   "   "   "   "   "   "
(3) OG   "   "   Gibraltar   "   "   "   " Liverpool Escort Forces from July 1941
(4) OS   "   "   Southbound   "   "   "   " Londonderry   "   "   "   "
Coastal Convoys
(5) EC Outward bound ocean going ships from Southend direct to Loch Ewe, Oban, & Clyde from 31st March – 28th Oct 1941

Map labels

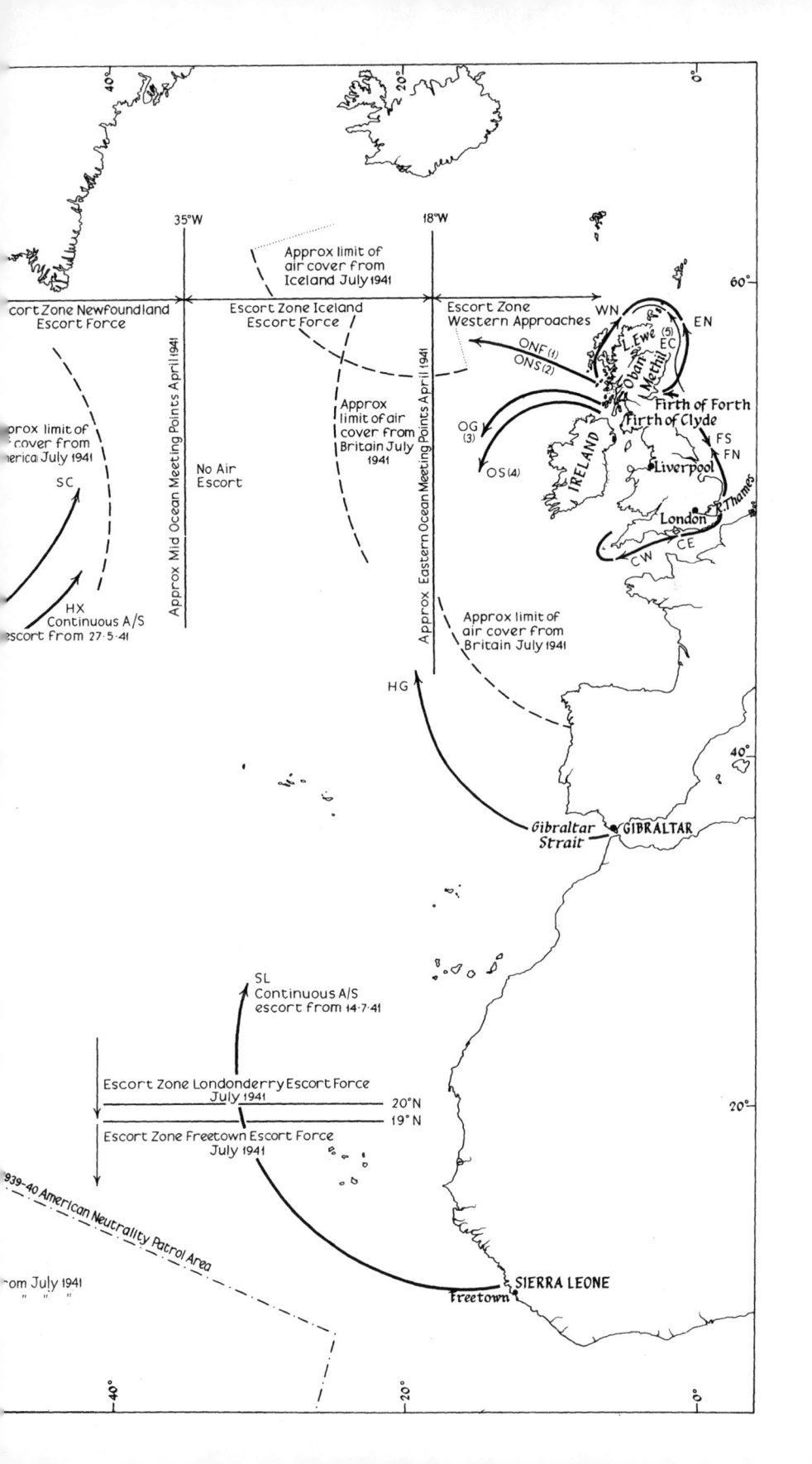

- 40° / 20° / 0°
- 35°W
- 18°W
- 60°
- Approx limit of air cover from Iceland July 1941
- Escort Zone Newfoundland Escort Force
- Escort Zone Iceland Escort Force
- Escort Zone Western Approaches
- Approx Mid Ocean Meeting Points April 1941
- Approx Eastern Ocean Meeting Points April 1941
- Approx limit of air cover from Britain July 1941
- No Air Escort
- Approx limit of air cover from America July 1941
- SC
- HX Continuous A/S escort from 27·5·41
- WN, EN, EC, Loch Ewe (5), Oban, Methil
- ONF (1), ONS (2)
- OG (3)
- OS (4)
- Firth of Forth, Firth of Clyde, FS, FN
- IRELAND, Liverpool
- London, R. Thames, CW, CE
- Approx limit of air cover from Britain July 1941
- HG
- Gibraltar Strait, GIBRALTAR
- 40°
- SL Continuous A/S escort from 14·7·41
- Escort Zone Londonderry Escort Force July 1941 — 20°N
- 19°N
- Escort Zone Freetown Escort Force July 1941
- 20°
- 1939–40 American Neutrality Patrol Area
- from July 1941
- SIERRA LEONE, Freetown
- 40° / 20° / 0°

by the Admiralty in exercise of its world-wide strategic control, and additional escorts might also be moved to the waters where danger threatened.

As regards outward-bound convoys it has been mentioned that losses were frequently suffered after they had parted in mid-ocean from their escorts.[1] The Admiralty had long wished to provide continuous escort for them as well as for the homeward convoys, but until July 1941 the chronic shortage of escort vessels had prevented this measure being introduced. In that month, however, it was found possible to abolish the outward (O.B.) convoys from Liverpool and to substitute fast and slow outward convoys to North America, called O.N.F. and O.N.S. respectively, and also the through convoys (O.S.) to Freetown already mentioned. Thus, after nearly two years of war, the homeward convoys from North America (H.X. and S.C.) at last had their outward counterparts.[2]

One other important change took place early in the current phase. In November 1940 the upper speed limit for inclusion in Atlantic convoys had, by Cabinet decision, been reduced from fifteen to thirteen knots in an endeavour to speed up the turn-round of shipping and to avoid delaying the faster ships. This led to heavy sinkings among independently-routed ships, and it did not take many months to confirm the view that more safety with less speed would, in the long run, accomplish a greater saving of tonnage than more speed with less safety. This had become clear to Admiral Noble by the new year, and in January he proposed that the fifteen-knot upper speed limit should be reinstituted. The Admiralty did not, however, concur at the time and it was not until five months later, and after more pressure from Admiral Noble, that the minimum speed for ships routed independently was restored to its former figure. The Admiralty's Trade Division kept a careful analysis of the consequences of the decision that thirteen-knot ships should be sailed independently. Early in May 1941 they reported that, in spite of every possible measure having been taken to ensure the safety of independently-routed ships with speeds between thirteen and fifteen knots, losses among them had greatly exceeded those suffered by ships in convoy. The comparative statistics set out below (Table 13 overleaf) were given to the Cabinet and were accepted.

The same report pointed out that losses among ships which were too slow to be included in convoys had been 'tragic'. On the homeward route no less than one-quarter of such ships had been sunk. Even among independently-routed ships capable of more than fifteen knots the loss rate had been as high as among convoyed ships.

---

[1] See p. 348.
[2] See Map 38 and Appendix J.

Table 13. *Comparison of Losses to Independently-routed and Convoyed Ships, November 1940–May 1941*

Independently-routed (13 to 15 knots)

	Freetown route	Halifax route
Homeward-bound	11·7%	10·1%
Outward-bound	3·7%	3·7%
Rate of loss on round voyage	15·4%	13·8%

Convoyed

	Freetown route	Halifax route
Homeward-bound	3·7%	4·0%
Outward-bound	1·8%	1·8%
Rate of loss on round voyage	5·5%	5·8%

The speed below which it is profitable to order ships into convoy will vary on different routes with the degree of danger and the length of the journey; and it will be influenced by the weapons and tactics used by the enemy.[1] Though the difficulty of reaching a correct decision at any period of a war may be admitted, the figures summarised above left no doubt that the reduction of the upper speed limit for inclusion in Atlantic convoys had been an expensive mistake.

At the time when the far-reaching changes in the Atlantic convoy system and in the organisation of the surface escort forces, already described, were taking place, parallel improvements were being made with regard to air escorts and patrols by Coastal Command and by the Royal Canadian Air Force. In April anti-submarine escort for westbound convoys had been extended to 35° West, and the U-boats suffered losses in attacking them. Early in May therefore they started to work still further to the west, in the attempt to find unescorted targets from recently dispersed convoys. This brought into prominence the need to organise air co-operation from the

---

[1] See pp. 94–95.

North American coast. On the 20th of May a heavy attack on convoy H.X. 126 in 41° West added impetus to this requirement, and early in the following month a conference took place between the British and Canadian air authorities at Coastal Command Headquarters. One result was the immediate transfer of nine Lend-Lease Catalinas to the Canadian Air Force. Air escort for convoys was then practicable to a maximum distance of some 700 miles from the British Isles, 600 miles from the coast of Canada and some 400 miles to the south of Iceland. But a gap about 300 miles wide remained in mid-Atlantic where no air escort could yet be provided.

The policy of the Admiralty and Air Ministry was at this time two-fold: to defend our convoys from the air by close escort and by distant support in waters where a U-boat threat might be developing and, secondly, to harass the U-boats by making offensive sweeps and patrols on their transit routes across the Bay of Biscay and off the north of Scotland. At the start of the present phase the shortage of aircraft, and the need to watch and attack the enemy battle cruisers in Brest harbour, restricted the attention which could be paid to the routes used by new U-boats outward-bound from Germany to the bases in western France, and by the operational U-boats on their way to and from the bases on the Biscay coast. It thus happened that the steady stream of new U-boats now being sent out from Germany was not seriously impeded. Nor was the bombing of the U-boat yards and bases, one of the objects to which the Prime Minister's Battle of the Atlantic directive of the 6th of March had given absolute priority for the next three months, effective in delaying the U-boat construction programme. Post-war records make it clear that, in fact, it had negligible effect on the large number of U-boats now building.[1]

Early in July Air Chief Marshal Sir Philip Joubert de la Ferté, who had succeeded Sir Frederick Bowhill as Commander-in-Chief, Coastal Command, in the preceding month, proposed that Bomber Command should attack each Biscay U-boat base in turn to the limit of its resources. The enemy was starting to build concrete shelters for his U-boats in western France and since the excavation work had to be carried out behind watertight caissons they were, at this stage, highly vulnerable to air attack. Once the tremendously thick concrete roofs were in place the shelters were, as we were to learn in due time, practically immune from bombing attack. But Bomber Command considered that better results would be achieved by attacks on industrial targets in Germany, and throughout 1941 little attempt was made to prevent the enemy completing the work on his U-boat shelters.

The strength available at this time to No. 15 Group, which was

---

[1] See p. 352 and Appendix K, Table III.

responsible for all air co-operation in the North Atlantic, consisted of three squadrons of Catalina flying-boats (Nos. 200, 210 and 240), one squadron of Whitley (No. 502) and part of a squadron (No. 221) of Wellington long-range bombers and two and a half squadrons of Hudsons (Nos. 224, 233 and part of 269). These all worked from bases in western Britain or Northern Ireland. In addition, in Iceland there was a squadron of Sunderland flying-boats (No. 204), a Norwegian-manned squadron of Northrops (No. 330) and part of No. 269 Hudson Squadron. On the Canadian seaboard and in Newfoundland were based R.C.A.F. squadrons which escorted all convoys passing through the Belle Isle Straits, between Newfoundland and Labrador, and the homeward-bound North American convoys as far as 55° West. American naval and army aircraft were also now flying 'Neutrality Patrols' from Argentia.

Though these dispositions were a big advance on the meagre air cover provided over the Atlantic convoys in 1940, the mid-Atlantic air gap was still unbridged. The only aircraft which could have accomplished this were American Liberators flying from Iceland and Newfoundland, but another eighteen months was to elapse before they became regularly available for this important task. Meanwhile many merchant vessels were lost in the ocean gap which our aircraft could not reach.

At Gibraltar the obsolete London flying-boats were replaced by Catalinas in May, but it was not until July that operational control of No. 200 Group was transferred to Coastal Command.[1] The first Hudsons did not arrive until December, and in that month No. 200 Group was disbanded. All R.A.F. work from Gibraltar was then placed under a newly appointed Air Officer Commanding, and an Area Combined Headquarters was set up inside the Rock. Thus, after more than two years of war, the North Atlantic Station at last became possessed of reasonably good air co-operation, controlled and organised on the same basis as had been found essential at home.

In the south Atlantic a squadron of Sunderlands (No. 95) had arrived at Freetown in March and started patrols and convoy escort work forthwith. In April they worked from Bathurst (Gambia) as well. But heavy sinkings took place in this area in May and in consequence the Sunderland squadron was reinforced; a Hudson squadron (No. 206) was sent out in June and more reinforcements followed in August. Control of these aircraft was at first exercised by the commander of the Sunderland squadron who worked in the Naval Headquarters at Freetown, but in October an independent Air Command was created for West Africa and an Area Combined Headquarters opened at the base. From June to the end of the year

---

[1] See pp. 353–354.

TACTICAL EMPLOYMENT OF AIR ESCORTS

sinkings off West Africa sharply declined, partly because shipping was routed far away from the dangerous waters and partly as a result of the improved surface and air escorts provided.

It will be appropriate to consider next the tactical employment of the aircraft engaged in the Atlantic Battle. At the start of this phase the number of U-boats which they sighted and attacked was increasing rapidly; but the number of successful attacks carried out remained very small, in spite of the long awaited airborne depth charge now being in general use.[1] Investigation into the causes revealed that speed in making an attack was the first essential, since any appreciable delay would enable the U-boat to get well below the surface before the depth charges arrived, and furthermore the point of aim could then only be guessed. Next came the need to release the charges at a low height, to detonate them at a much shallower depth than had been previously used, to space them close together and to release them all in one 'stick'. At the end of July Coastal Command issued revised attack instructions on these lines. Technical developments, such as a shallower depth charge pistol and a low-level sight were also to be pressed on; in August white camouflage was introduced to help aircraft to make an unseen approach. The importance of radar as an aid to detecting U-boats, especially at night and in low visibility, continued to be stressed, but delays had occurred in fitting efficient long-range sets and the results continued disappointing. Throughout this phase visual sightings of U-boats still greatly exceeded radar contacts. But successful attacks on U-boats by Coastal Command aircraft none the less continued to be comparatively rare. From the outbreak of war until September 1941 forty-nine German and thirty-five Italian U-boats were destroyed, but Coastal Command had only contributed the destruction of one and the surrender of a second, while three had been destroyed in joint operations with surface craft.[2]

Responsibility for air co-operation to the south-west of Britain had been placed on No. 19 Group in the previous February, and attacks on U-boats passing through the Bay of Biscay therefore fell within its sphere. But its strength was at first so small that it could do little more than provide convoy escorts in the Irish Sea and off our south-west coast, and also keep watch on the enemy surface ships in Brest. By July, however, patrols were being flown in the Bay, and sightings of U-boats led to regular flights being made with the object of attacking them while on passage through those waters. Night attacks were still impracticable since the Leigh Light was only in the experimental stage.[3] But the start of the Bay offensive, which was to yield

---
[1] See pp. 135–136.
[2] See Appendix K, Table III.
[3] See p. 358.

substantial successes in a later phase, can be dated to this time. In these waters, as on the convoy routes, air attacks produced, at first, few successes, but with the development of the new tactics already mentioned an improvement began to take place. The first success was the destruction of U.206, outward-bound, by a Whitley aircraft on the 30th of November, and Admiral Dönitz at this time noted in his War Diary the increasing danger from air attack to his U-boats while on passage across the Bay.

While No. 19 Group of Coastal Command was turning its attention to the Bay of Biscay, No. 18 Group was doing the same to the waters to the north of the Shetland Islands. But the precise routes used by new U-boats passing from Germany to the Atlantic could not at this time be located, and with the approach of winter the patrols were temporarily abandoned.

We will now turn from the evolution of our own sea and air organisation, strategy and tactics during the spring and summer of 1941 to the enemy. By April the number of U-boats in commission was rising fast and had for the first time passed the 100 mark. Of these roughly one-third was operational, one-third was working up efficiency in the Baltic and one-third was employed in the schools to train new crews for the additional 230 U-boats which were being built. Admiral Dönitz had resolutely resisted the temptation to sacrifice his long-term training programme by starting to increase his operational strength at too early a stage. Of the thirty operational boats about twenty were at sea in April, but in June their number had increased to an average of thirty-two. At the beginning of the period the great majority of the boats at sea were in the central North Atlantic, but the successes achieved by our convoy escorts in March had forced them to seek unescorted targets, and these could only be found further to the west, before the escort had joined a homeward convoy or after it had left an outward convoy.[1] A small number of U-boats was generally stationed off north-west Ireland to report outward-bound shipping—a duty on which the long-range Focke-Wulf bombers were also employed. The need to seek unprotected targets further west naturally reduced opportunities to attack, and the average sinkings accomplished by each boat at sea therefore started to decline—a fact of which the British Admiralty could not, of course, be aware. In an endeavour to restore the rate of sinking to the high figures achieved during the summer and autumn of 1940 the enemy sent U-boats to patrol off the Azores and the coast of West Africa, where anti-submarine escort was not yet provided to all convoys and many ships were still routed independently. Their exploits will be recounted shortly.

---

[1] See pp. 363–365.

In the North Atlantic the phase with which we are here concerned opened badly for ourselves with a heavy attack on convoy S.C. 26 by seven U-boats in longitude 28° West before the close escort had joined. Six ships were sunk, but when the escort arrived two days later U.76 was promptly sunk by the destroyer *Wolverine* and the sloop *Scarborough*. The attacks then ceased. The Admiralty's reaction to this attack was to hasten progress on the naval and air bases in Iceland, and by the middle of the month it was possible to escort convoys as far as 35° West. At the end of April H.X. 121 was attacked in 23° West in spite of the presence of an anti-submarine escort. Four ships were sunk but, again, they were not unavenged since U.65 was sunk by the corvette *Gladiolus*. The total sinkings by U-boats in April were 43 ships of 249,375 tons; but only ten ships were sunk while in convoy.

The days were now lengthening rapidly and our convoys were being routed ever further north to gain the fullest possible air and surface protection from the new bases in Iceland. These measures put a temporary stop to night attacks by U-boats, since our patrolling aircraft prevented them chasing and shadowing the convoys on the surface by day in order to close in and attack after dark. But none the less the month of May saw a sharp rise in sinkings to fifty-eight ships of 325,492 tons, more than half of which were sunk in the neighbourhood of Freetown by the group of six U-boats which Dönitz had sent there to find unescorted targets. The Admiralty diverted all possible shipping from the area and, as already told, strengthened the air and surface anti-submarine forces in West Africa. In the North Atlantic convoy O.B. 318 was intercepted early in May and lost five ships, but its escort retaliated by sinking U.110. A worse fate attended H.X. 126 a fortnight later when it was attacked as far west as 40° by a pack of nine U-boats while without anti-submarine escort. Five ships were sunk and the convoy was ordered to scatter. Four more were lost after the ships had dispersed. It was this attack that led to the immediate introduction of continuous anti-submarine escort right across the Atlantic.

Though the struggle was still fraught with difficulties and danger to ourselves, and though in the month of June sinkings by U-boats reached the high figure of sixty-one ships of 310,143 tons, there were signs that some easement, if only a temporary one, would shortly be felt. In the first place, Hitler's attack on Russia had started on the 22nd, and this brought relief through the diversion of the main strength of the Luftwaffe eastwards. Not only did air attacks on our ports of discharge, which had been very heavy in the two preceding months and had reached a climax in the raids on Liverpool in May, decline markedly, but the losses at sea caused by the enemy's long-range bombers, which had totalled 100,000 tons in April, May and

464 NUMBER OF ESCORT VESSELS INCREASING

June, also fell sharply. Though the start of the Russian campaign was without doubt the greatest factor in bringing about this favourable trend, our escort groups were now gaining strength from the transfer of the American coastguard cutters and the new construction now completing in our own shipyards and those of the Dominions.[1] In the middle of June the Admiralty reported to the Prime Minister's Battle of the Atlantic Committee that the number of escort vessels had reached the following totals:—

Table 14. Royal Navy—Escort Vessel Strength, June 1941

	In commission	Building
Destroyers and escort destroyers	248 (including 59 undergoing refits)	157
Corvettes	99	44 in Britain 52 in Canada (plus 3 of new design)
Trawlers and A/S yachts	300	47
Sloops and coastguard cutters	48	3

The corvettes were at this time completing at a rate of six to eight in each month, but the Admiralty still considered this inadequate. They pointed out that, though the position had certainly improved during the past year and it was now possible to provide convoys with an average strength of five anti-submarine escorts, we still had far to travel to achieve really adequate escort strength, let alone possess a sufficient surplus to enable concentrations of U-boats to be attacked wherever they were located, and reinforcements to be sent to threatened convoys.

The realism of the Admiralty view can perhaps best be understood by mentioning that a convoy of forty-five ships would cover about five square miles of sea. With one escort ahead of the convoy, one astern of it and one on each side there would still be wide gaps through which a U-boat could penetrate undetected, since each escort's asdic set would only sweep an arc of some 80° ahead of it to a distance of about a mile. Furthermore the escorts had many other duties besides searching, listening and watching continuously for U-boats. Stragglers had to be urged forward into their proper places, survivors from sunken ships had to be rescued, sometimes a damaged ship had to be towed, or one which had developed a defect and fallen out of convoy given protection. These, and the many other duties which always fell to the convoy escorts, would all tend to reduce the number of ships actually shielding a convoy at any time. Furthermore when a U-boat was located she had to be attacked,

---

[1] See p. 454.

Map 39
TYPICAL CONVOYS & ANTI-SUBMARINE ESCORTS 1940-41

(A) Large convoy (45 ships) with weak escort (1 Destroyer & 3 Corvettes)

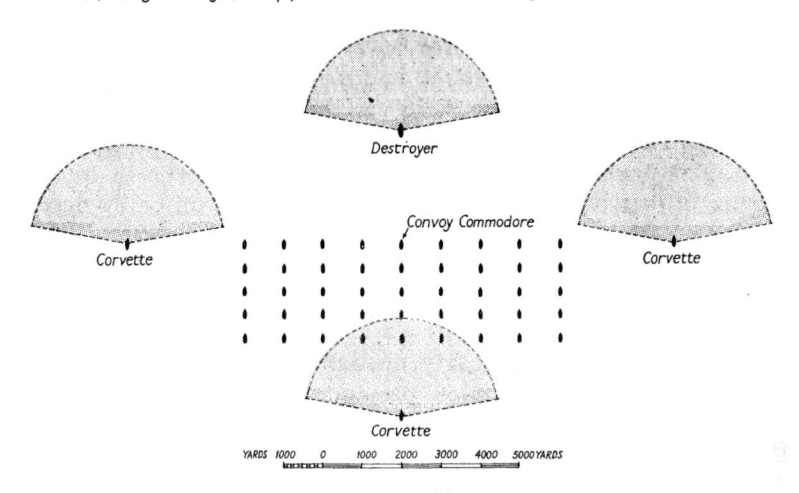

(B) Large convoy (55 ships) with strong escort (3 Destroyers & 7 Corvettes)
Formation in fine weather with no indication of direction of U Boat attack

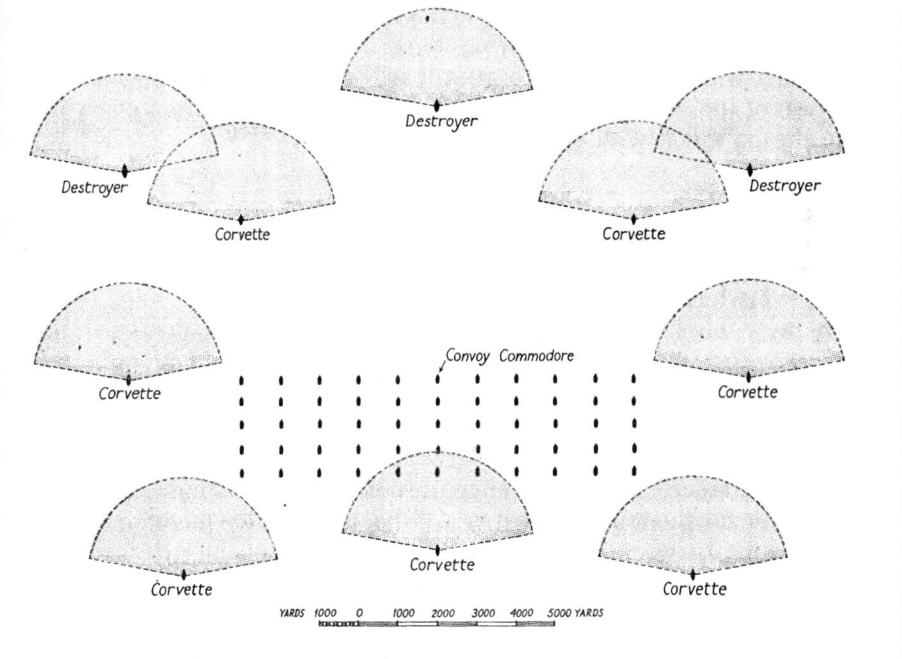

Note:- The shaded area ahead of each escort shows the area swept by its Asdic for speeds under 12 knots (160° arc out to 2500 yards)
Detection of a submerged submarine is, under average conditions, likely only within 1200-1500 yards

which meant detaching at least one escort. German U-boats were being constructed more and more strongly to resist depth charge explosions, the evasive tactics of their commanders had improved and deceptive tricks—such as the release of oil to try to persuade the attacking ship that the U-boat had been sunk—were commonly employed. To achieve success it was essential that escort vessels which found their quarry should maintain the attack relentlessly, and search persistently between attacks until such time as positive evidence of destruction was obtained. This would probably necessitate leaving the convoy and remaining in the vicinity of the U-boat for some hours, with the result that more ships might well be sunk by other U-boats. Only the provision of more escort vessels could resolve the dilemma. Until this was achieved the senior officers of Escort Groups could only carry on day after day and night after night throughout the long, slow passages, meeting each problem as it arose and all too often watching their helpless charges sink one by one, or blow up in the sheet of flame which became the well-known sign that a tanker or a ship loaded with explosives had been hit. Often contacts were gained with submerged U-boats, or a surfaced attacker was sighted and pursued, but success eluded the avenging escorts because of a call to another duty. Only the officers and men who manned the little ships during those months, and the merchant seamen whom they tried to guard, will remember the long-drawn strain of the Atlantic passages and the constant frustration of trying to do too much with too little.

On the 23rd of June the enemy located convoy H.X. 133 to the south of Greenland and a pack of ten U-boats closed in. Attacks started while the convoy was escorted by only four ships. The enemy's wireless traffic had, however, revealed his purpose and reinforcements from the escorts of two outward-bound convoys were diverted to the help of the threatened convoy by the Admiralty. There now followed one of the first examples of what can justly be described as a convoy battle between evenly matched contestants. Thirteen escorts had been concentrated—and it was indeed rare at this time for them to outnumber a U-boat pack. Five merchant ships were sunk between the 24th and 29th, and one of the stripped outward convoys lost two more. But the joint efforts of the escorts accounted for U.556 and U.651 and the attacks were finally beaten off. The battle had certainly not gone wholly in the enemy's favour.

The various factors which combined to produce an improvement in the Atlantic struggle in the middle of the year have already been mentioned. Sinkings by U-boats actually fell to twenty-two ships of 94,209 tons in July and twenty-three ships of 80,310 tons in August.

1

Air depth-charge attack by a Whitley aircraft of No. 502 Squadron on U.563 on 1st December 1941 in 47° 00′ North, 11° 35′ West. A 'stick' of six depth-charges, set to explode at 40 feet, was dropped on the surfaced U-boat. The aim was accurate but the explosions were too deep, and the U-boat, though damaged, survived.
(1) The splash of the depth-charges entering the water,
(2) The first part of the 'stick' exploding. Bullet splashes appear around the U-boat,
(3) The second part of the 'stick' explodes and the U-boat disappears in a smother of spray.

2   3

Facing page 466

The surrender of U.570 to a Hudson aircraft of Coastal Command in 62° 15′ North 18° 35′ West on 27th August 1941.

U.570 in British service as H.M.S. *Graph*.

No major attack on an Atlantic convoy took place until September.

In July the enemy realised that the accomplishments of the U-boats were not rising proportionately to their increase in numbers, or to the losses which they were incurring. He decided that he must try to improve their performance by attacking shipping nearer to our shores. His concentration was therefore moved to the waters between Ireland and Iceland. But the Admiralty had anticipated the move and organised intensive air and surface sweeps, patrols and searches in those waters. As it was well within the range of Coastal Command's Wellingtons, Whitleys and Hudsons they were able to make a big contribution to defeating the enemy's plan. In August they made eighteen attacks on U-boats. U.452 was sunk by a Catalina and the trawler *Vascama*, and U.570 surrendered to a Hudson of No. 269 Squadron (Squadron Leader J. H. Thompson) beneath which it had injudiciously broken surface. This valuable prize was successfully towed to Iceland and finally entered British service as H.M.S. *Graph*.

In certain quarters in London the reduction in losses in the summer months led to a surge of optimism and to some premature conclusions that the corner had been turned in the Battle of the Atlantic. One result was a proposal to divert Coastal Command's few long-range bombers to the offensive against German shore targets. It was successfully resisted. But the desire of the Cabinet to increase the weight of the bombing offensive against Germany was so strong that the matter was raised again by the Prime Minister in October, and only withdrawn when the First Lord and Chief of the Air Staff jointly represented the probable consequences in the Atlantic.

As the year advanced, the enemy's U-boat construction programme gained momentum, the total of operational U-boats increased steadily, from sixty-five in July to eighty in October, and the rate of commissioning new boats was also rising.[1] By the 1st of September the Admiralty assessed the enemy's total strength at 184 U-boats, and his losses up to that date at forty-four. The actual figures, we now know, were 198 and forty-seven respectively. By the end of the year it was estimated that this total would reach 229—which was, in fact, slightly below his actual accomplishment. It was clear to the Admiralty that new U-boats were entering service much faster than we were sinking them, and that a renewal of the assault on an even greater scale than in the previous spring must be expected. 'We require', reported one member of the Board of Admiralty when faced with the proposal to divert Coastal Command aircraft to Bomber Command, 'every single surface ship and every long-range aircraft we can possibly muster. Any suggestion that the corner has been turned is not supported by facts.'

---

[1] See Appendix Q.

The Admiralty's view was rapidly proved correct, and the hopes raised in midsummer were shortlived. In September the U-boats sank fifty-three ships of 202,820 tons—a very sharp increase on the previous months' figures. Instead of diverting some of Coastal Command's aircraft to bomb Germany, the need to allocate a proportion of Bomber Command's effort to the Biscay U-boat bases, which had been rejected in July, was now reconsidered. But the proposal was still viewed with disfavour and, by a decision taken in October, only one of the bases, Lorient, was made a target for Bomber Command.

The heavy sinkings in September were accomplished chiefly by attacks on four convoys. Two of them were slow homeward-bound convoys (S.C. 42 and 44) which the enemy located when they were to the south of Greenland. They lost twenty ships and one escort vessel, but two U-boats were destroyed by way of recompense. The other two attacked convoys were homeward-bound from Freetown and Gibraltar—convoys S.L. 87 and H.G. 73. The former consisted of only eleven ships and had four escorts; but seven of the merchantmen were sunk; the latter was reported off Cape St. Vincent by a long-range aircraft, and ran into a concentration of U-boats. In spite of a strong escort of ten ships the convoy lost nine of its twenty-five merchantmen. Such heavy losses to comparatively well-escorted convoys were disturbing but, fortunately, rare. In the case of H.G. 73 the breakdown of the escort vessels' radar sets contributed to the heavy losses, but the successful co-ordination of the enemy's air reconnaissance with his U-boats, and the lack of air escort for the convoys, were the main factors. The Gibraltar convoys were almost certain to be reported by aircraft because, for a great part of their journey, they had to steam within range of the Focke-Wulfs which the enemy kept stationed near Bordeaux for the purpose. We will return later to their depredations and then see how the Admiralty combated the menace.

As an example of the enemy's methods and of the trials and difficulties of the escorts, we will follow the progress of one of the two slow North Atlantic convoys which were attacked in September. Convoy S.C. 42 originally comprised sixty-four ships, carrying some half million tons of cargo, and was escorted by one Canadian destroyer and three corvettes. The convoy left Sydney (Cape Breton Island) on the 30th of August and was routed far to the north. On the seventh day Cape Farewell, the southern tip of Greenland, had been rounded; but the listeners at the Admiralty's direction-finding stations knew that a pack of U-boats was gathering around the convoy. It was therefore diverted still more to the north, hugging the unfriendly Greenland shore. The convoy's slow progress and the unmistakable signs of U-boat activity were being anxiously watched in the Admiralty. At first it seemed that it would be taken just clear of the U-boat concentration. But it was not to be. On the morning of the 9th, a ship which had dropped slightly astern reported sighting a periscope and being missed by torpedoes. Two escorts searched for the enemy, but without result. The merchantmen were making a lot of smoke which, so the Commodore noted, must have been visible for thirty miles. This may have helped to lead the U-boats to their quarry. At 7 p.m. the convoy altered from north to north-east as an evasive measure; but it was of no avail. Two and a half hours later the moon rose and, almost at once, the first ship was sunk. The attacks now started in earnest and four U-boats were sighted in rapid succession that evening, some of them inside the convoy columns. Between dusk and midnight seven more ships were sunk, including a tanker which exploded in the all too familiar sheet of flame. We now know that no less than seventeen U-boats had been called towards the convoy, though not all of them made contact. At least eight were involved in the attacks during the night of the 9th–10th, outnumbering the escorts by two to one. Soon after midnight the Canadian destroyer *Skeena* chased a surfaced U-boat up and down inside the convoy columns. After two more ships had been sunk contact was gained with a submerged U-boat; three of the escorts joined in, but there was no time for a protracted attack because survivors had to be rescued, and the convoy could not be left unprotected. Next evening, the 10th, the attacks started again, and there was now one less escort, since one of the corvettes was towing a damaged tanker towards Iceland. Two ships were sunk but two more corvettes (both Canadian), diverted to the convoy by the Admiralty, soon arrived and they at once sank U.501. In spite of this success five more ships went down that night. At noon on the 11th a fresh escort group of five ships from Iceland joined. Two of them, the destroyers *Veteran* and *Leamington*, sank U.207 that same afternoon. But German records show that only the fog which shrouded the convoy during the night prevented the attacks being continued.

It has been mentioned how the Admiralty's Submarine Tracking Room derived much benefit from the wireless signals passed between U-boat Headquarters and the boats at sea, and also from the homing signals which a shadowing U-boat would send to call her comrades towards a convoy.[1] We now know that we were not alone in employing such methods and that the Germans paid as much attention to the wireless messages sent by the Commander-in-Chief, Western Approaches, to divert convoys from danger zones, and used the

---

[1] See p. 356.

intelligence derived from them to deploy his U-boats to the best advantage. Like ourselves they found that the more signals were sent by wireless the easier it was to deduce the other side's intentions.

In order to retaliate against the escort vessels, which, when present in sufficient numbers, were now causing his U-boats considerable discomfiture, Dönitz had ordered, in the middle of August, that they rather than the merchant ships should henceforth be regarded as the primary targets. Though this change of policy caused the loss of a number of these hard-driven little ships and of their gallant crews, it did not materially affect the ebb and flow of the long-drawn battle, since others were now coming forward in increasing numbers to take their places. Probably it merely resulted in the safe arrival of a number of merchant ships which would otherwise have been sunk.

To turn now to the South Atlantic, the heavy losses of May, when no less than thirty ships of 176,168 tons were sunk within 600 miles of Freetown and Bathurst, were not repeated in the succeeding months. In June five ships were sunk, in July and August one, in September none, and in the last quarter of the year only six ships were sunk off the West African coast. In truth the offensive had been defeated by routing every possible ship away from the area, and by strengthening the air and surface escort and patrol forces. Until the following spring U-boats paid only occasional brief visits to those waters. A threatened offensive off the Cape of Good Hope in the last month of the year was defeated by the interception of the two ships, the *Python* and *Kota Penang*, which had been sent out from France to supply the U-boats, and also of the armed merchant raider *Atlantis*, which had been ordered to act as a U-boat supply ship.[1] The U-boats detailed for this distant lunge were thereupon recalled. The Admiralty's policy of striking at the supply ships thus proved as effective in countering the enemy's U-boat strategy in distant waters as it had been in curtailing the operations of his surface raiders.

In spite of the increased losses suffered in September 1941 that month produced an important change affecting the Battle of the Atlantic. A meeting between Mr. Churchill and President Roosevelt took place off Argentia on the 10th of August, and on the 4th of September the order was given for the American 'Western Hemisphere Defence Plan Number 4' to be implemented.[2] By this plan, not only were German surface raiders attacking the shipping route between the United States and Iceland to be destroyed but, more important still, the United States Navy was henceforth allowed to escort convoys comprising ships not of American registry, and Canadian warships were permitted to escort ships flying the American

---

[1] See p. 542 and pp. 544–545 and Map 41 (*p. 543*).
[2] See W. S. Churchill. *The Second World War*, Vol. III, pp. 385–400.

flag. Here, indeed, was a big step towards the safeguarding of the North Atlantic shipping. Starting with H.X. 150, which sailed on the 16th of September, the United States Navy provided escorts for certain Atlantic trade convoys eastwards as far as the Mid-Ocean Meeting Point. The responsibility for the organisation of the Atlantic convoy system and for routing all shipping, whether sailing independently or in convoy, continued however to rest with the British Admiralty. The effect of the new arrangement was, in sum, to bring a substantial accession of escort vessel strength to the Western Approaches command. But the burden of responsibility and the day-to-day exercise of operational control remained unchanged.

The British and American staffs now worked out the details of each individual convoy's surface and air escort, and agreed upon the rendezvous south of Iceland where the British escort from the Western Approaches would take over. The American escort then went to Iceland to fuel and came south again in time to meet an outward (O.N.) convoy at a similar rendezvous.

The Mid-Ocean Meeting Points (M.O.M.P.S.) were, by agreement with the Americans, shifted further to the east at this time— from about 26° West to 22° West and to the north of latitude 58°. This change enabled the Western Approaches escort groups to return eastwards without refuelling in Iceland, an economy of force which meant that three groups could be diverted from the North Atlantic to strengthen the Gibraltar and Sierra Leone convoy escorts. None the less the problem of endurance and fuel supply for the escorts remained a constant anxiety, since any considerable delay on the oceans, caused by diversions or bad weather, might still force them to return to harbour to replenish their tanks, and so wreck all the carefully dovetailed movements of merchant shipping and escorts. Fuelling the escorts at sea from a tanker accompanying the convoys was admittedly the best solution, but tankers could not yet be spared for such service, special equipment had to be supplied to them and to the escorts, and a whole new organisation fitted into the already complex pattern. Not until the middle of 1942 was the practice actually started in the Atlantic.

To summarise and recapitulate the arrangements introduced in September, the Canadian Navy continued to escort east-bound convoys from the departure ports to the Western Ocean Meeting Points south of Newfoundland. There H.X. convoys would be taken over by American escorts who would accompany them to the Mid-Ocean Meeting Points (in about 58° North, 22° West) and hand them over to a British group from the Western Approaches command. The slower S.C. convoys continued as before to have Canadian escorts, augmented if necessary by some British ships, for the first part of their journey, and were relieved in turn by British groups from

Iceland and from home waters as they progressed eastwards. The outward counterparts of the S.C. convoys (O.N.S.) were protected in the same way on their westward journeys.

In an endeavour to avoid still further compromising American neutrality, mixed British and American escorts were avoided. But as the American forces in Iceland had to be supplied by American ships and U-boats were now allowed by Hitler to work in the waters off Cape Race, off southern Greenland and in the Straits of Belle Isle, it was inevitable that incidents between them and American warships should occur. Nor were they long in starting. On the 4th of September, the date that the new arrangements were announced, the American destroyer *Greer*, on passage to Iceland, was attacked by U.652 and replied with depth charges. On the 17th of October the destroyer *Kearney* was torpedoed, and on the last day of the same month the *Reuben James* was sunk while escorting the British convoy H.X. 156—the first American loss in the Atlantic struggle.

United States Navy Catalinas and United States Army Flying Fortresses were now working from Argentia as air escorts in close co-ordination with the Canadian Air Force, and other American Catalinas were based on Iceland. It was not, however, until early in 1942 that operational control of the latter was finally merged in the British Area Combined Headquarters at Reykjavik. The careful planning which had preceded the introduction of these far-reaching steps enabled the change-over to be made smoothly, and such difficulties as the initial American reluctance to permit the ships and authorities of one nation to communicate with those of the other except through Washington and London were soon eliminated. From the British point of view the changes of September 1941 made American participation in the Battle of the Atlantic a reality, and what that reality meant to the Admiralty, to the Flag Officers, to the captains and crews of the ships and aircraft who had for so long fought this vital and unending struggle alone, may not easily be realised by posterity. At the time it brought an immediate sense of relief and a conviction that, though the road might yet be arduous and many setbacks suffered, the Battle of the Atlantic would finally be won. Thus, at long last, the period throughout which Britain and Canada, acting as one nation, had kept the Atlantic routes open passed into a new and more promising phase. The accomplishment of the little ships which bore the chief burden of the first phases cannot be better summarised than by quoting from the American history. 'Nevertheless', says Professor Morison, 'the story of this Anglo-Canadian period of trans-Atlantic convoys is a glorious one. Thousands of merchant vessels were taken safely across by a distressingly small number of armed escorts, losing less than two per cent. . . . For two years, summer and winter, blow high, blow low,

Admiral Sir Percy L. H. Noble, Commander-in-Chief Western Approaches 17th February 1941–19th November 1942. Air Vice-Marshal J. M. Robb, Air Officer Commanding No. 15 Group of Coastal Command 23rd February 1941–27th March 1942. (See page 360.)

(Overleaf) Atlantic Convoy O.B. 331 at sea in 58° 00′ North, 11° 40′ West on 10th June 1941.

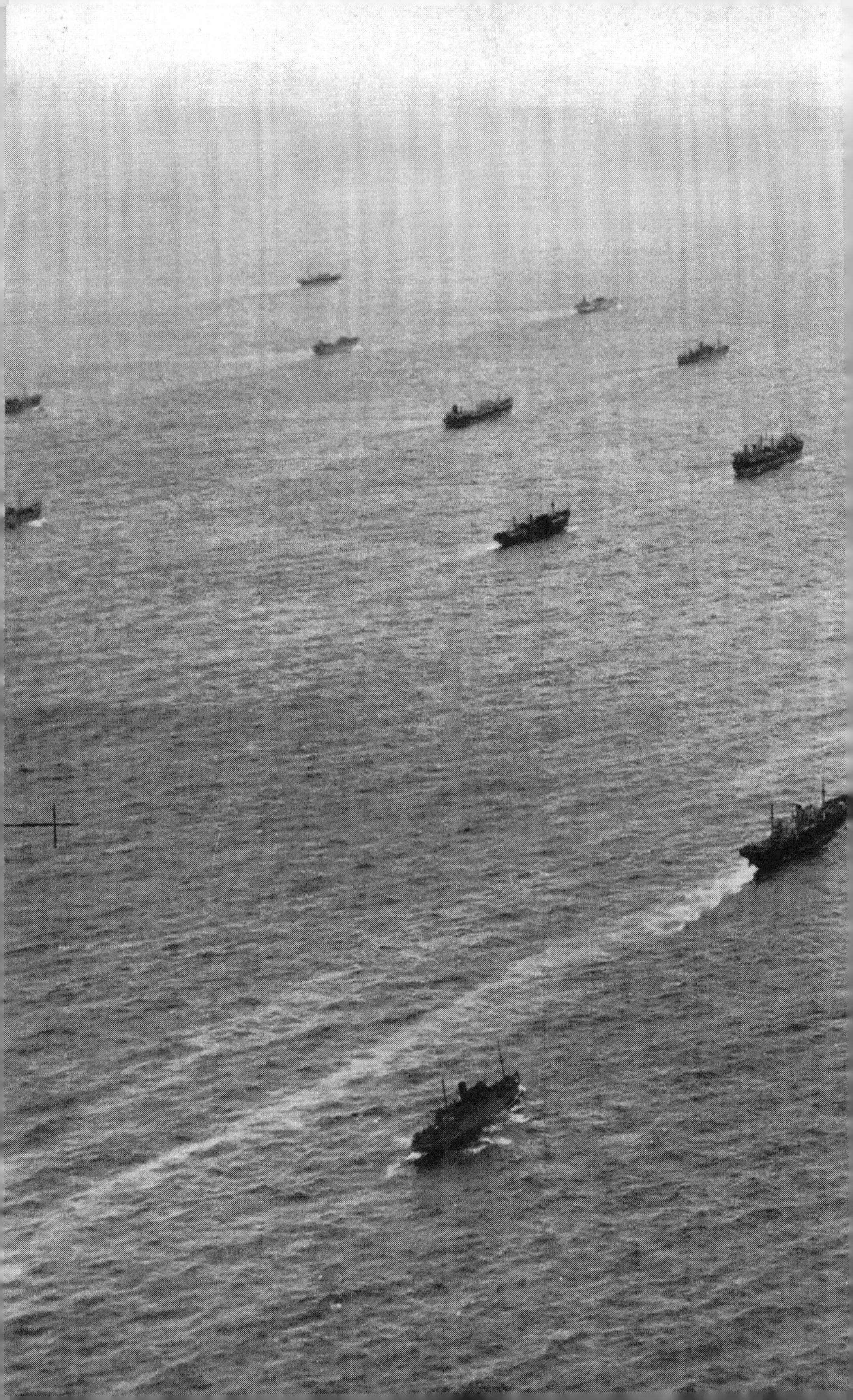

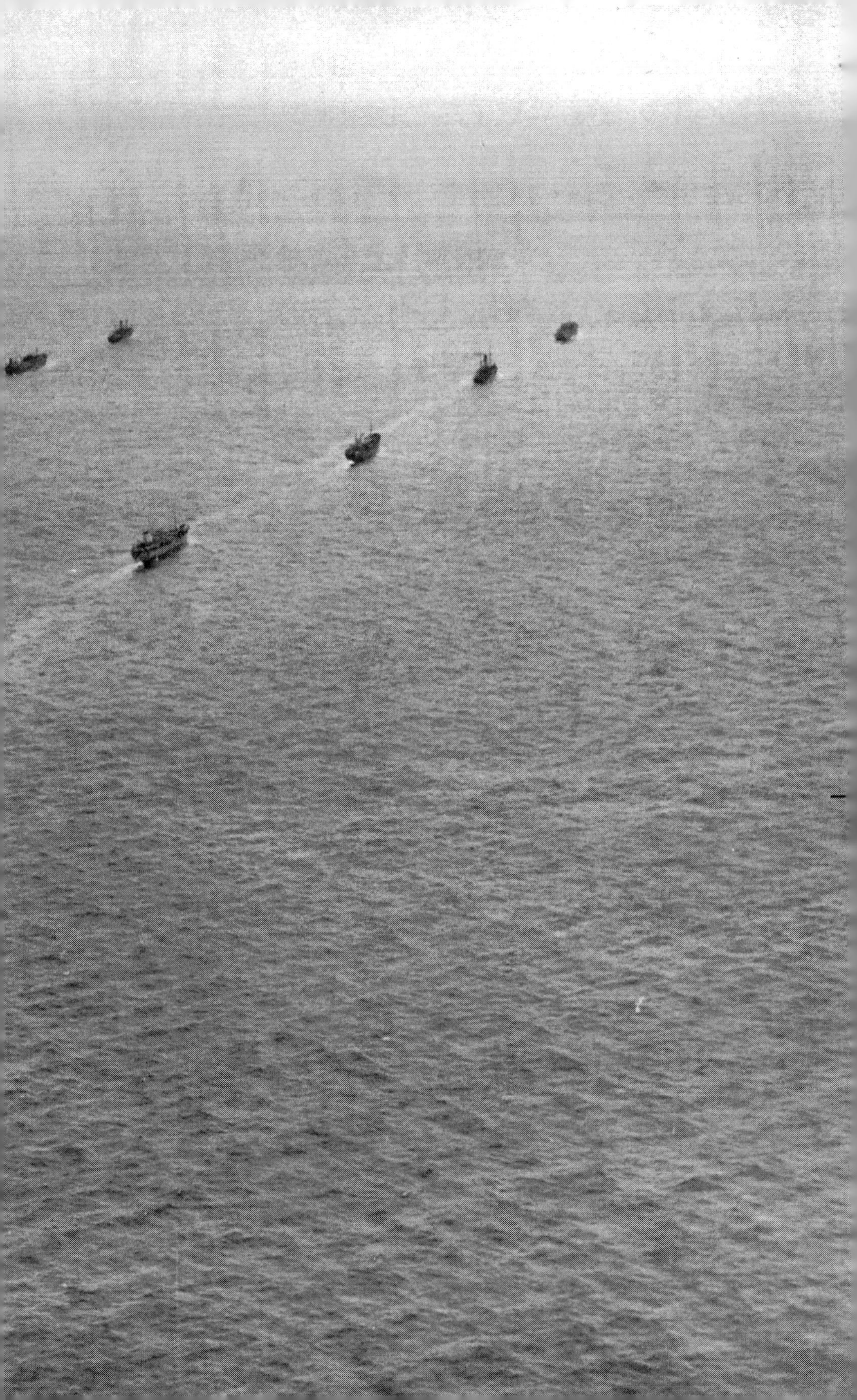

H.M.S. *Keppel* of the Western Approaches Command searching for Convoy H.X. 152, which had been scattered by heavy weather south of Iceland on 10th October 1941.

destroyers and corvettes slogged back and forth across the North Atlantic, protecting precious cargoes that enabled Britain to survive.'[1]

Almost simultaneously with the announcement of the changes recounted in the last paragraphs the Admiralty and Air Ministry jointly issued a new directive defining the duties of Coastal Command. As the contribution of the Royal Air Force to the maritime war was now increasing rapidly, the terms of this directive will be quoted in some detail. Under the operational control of the Admiralty Coastal Command was required to fulfil three functions. First was placed reconnaissance, both in the strategic sense, such as watching and identifying enemy ships in harbour, and in the tactical sense which included locating enemy ships at sea, break-out patrols, anti-U-boat sweeps, escort of shipping and so on. Second was placed the offensive against enemy ships, including U-boats, and, in specified areas, attacks on his merchant shipping and minelaying. The defensive function of protecting our own shipping from air attack when outside the range of Fighter Command's aircraft was placed third. It was in accordance with this policy that Coastal Command worked for the remainder of the war, and the extent to which each of its three functions came to be fulfilled will form no small part of the story of our later volumes.

After these digressions we must return to the convoy routes. In October U-boat sinkings fell to thirty-two ships of 156,554 tons, and analysis of the attacks showed that no ships were sunk within 400 miles of a Coastal Command base. Between 400 and 600 miles from such bases, to which distance the Catalinas could only occasionally reach, twelve ships were sunk, and beyond 600 miles, where no air cover could be afforded, fourteen ships were sunk. These figures showed clearly the reluctance of the U-boats to enter the zones covered by the long-range reconnaissance and bomber aircraft. But the drop in sinkings in October was also attributable in large measure to the detachment of U-boats to the Mediterranean. The German High Command were becoming increasingly anxious about their army in North Africa, and had become convinced of the inability of their Italian allies to safeguard the sea communications on which it depended. Accordingly a first group of six U-boats left their Biscay bases during the latter part of September and passed successfully through the Straits of Gibraltar. On the 4th of November a second group was ordered to follow them, and four made the passage of the Straits, though one, U.433, was sunk by the corvette *Marigold* soon

---

[1] S. E. Morison. *The History of United States Naval Operations in World War II*, Vol. I: (1948) *The Battle of the Atlantic*, p. 72.

afterwards. It was two of this group which, as will be told in a later chapter, sank the *Ark Royal* on the 13th of November. The Admiralty was not long in gaining knowledge of the enemy's intentions; air and surface patrolling from Gibraltar was intensified, and a reinforcement of six Hudsons of No. 233 Squadron was sent out. These aircraft were, however, not fitted for, or trained in, night anti-submarine work, and as the U-boats always forced the Straits in darkness it was that type of work which was particularly needed. The loss of the *Ark Royal* had, however, released a number of her Swordfish and their crews, which were better fitted and trained for this specialised work than the Hudsons. They soon began to make the passage highly hazardous to the enemy. The remarkable versatility of the Fairey Swordfish, the same slow, vulnerable and often maligned aircraft which had sunk the Italian battleships in Taranto, which had finally enabled the fleet to bring the *Bismarck* to action, and which had performed any number of other varied but important exploits, was thus again demonstrated. Besides reinforcing the Gibraltar patrols the Admiralty also suspended the sailing of convoys from that base for a time.

But the passage of the first two groups of U-boats into the Mediterranean did not complete the enemy's redispositions; he decided not only to send in a third group but also to divert boats from the North Atlantic to the approaches to Gibraltar from the west, in an attempt to deny the Straits to the reinforcements which, with the start of General Auchinleck's Libyan offensive on the 18th of November, he expected us to pass eastwards. The third group passed through the Straits at the end of November, but U.95 was almost at once sunk by the Dutch submarine O.21; and the boats diverted from the Atlantic also fared ill. U.206 was sunk by a patrolling Whitley in the Bay on the 30th, three others received damage from air attacks and turned back, while one developed defects.

At the end of November the German Naval Staff decided to keep ten U-boats in the eastern Mediterranean and fifteen to the east of the Gibraltar Straits. Three more passed Gibraltar on the 7th–8th of December and another three were sailed from the Biscay ports. The corvette *Bluebell* sank one of the latter, U.208, on the 11th of December.

By this time there were eighteen U-boats inside the Mediterranean and another ten were under orders to proceed there. Of the last reinforcements, U.451 was sunk by a naval Swordfish and three were damaged by air attacks and forced to return. The proportion of successful passages declined sharply after the middle of November.

The effect of the arrival of the German U-boats on the African campaigns will be told in a later chapter. Here we need only remark that the enemy at once realised that he could not relieve or replace

A LULL IN THE ATLANTIC BATTLE 475

the Mediterranean U-boats at will. Once past the Straits of Gibraltar they were, as Dönitz himself noted, 'caught in a trap'.

It thus came about that during the last two months of the year U-boat activity in the North Atlantic was at a low ebb. Furthermore, the increasing number of escort vessels had enabled the Western Approaches Command to augment the strength allocated to escort duty between British ports and the Mid-Ocean Meeting Point to eight groups, each of three destroyers and about six corvettes, while eleven homogeneous groups, each of five destroyers, were retained to reinforce the escort of any convoy which might be in trouble, or to deal with concentrations of U-boats. These were the origin of the 'Convoy Support Groups' which, much later, were to perform such valuable service. A simultaneous, though temporarily unsuccessful, endeavour was made to strengthen the Newfoundland Escort Force to eight groups.

As regards sinkings by U-boats and also merchant ship losses from all causes combined, November was the best month of the year.[1] The U-boats sank, in all, thirteen ships of 62,196 tons and our total losses amounted to only thirty-five ships of 104,640 tons. By the 8th of December there were only twenty-seven U-boats covering the entire Atlantic, and twelve of them were concentrated off Gibraltar. In that month sinkings in the North Atlantic were again small—nine ships of 45,931 tons—but other theatres swelled the total successes obtained by U-boats to twenty-six ships of 124,070 tons; and the heavy losses in the Far East caused by the sudden Japanese attack brought our total losses from all causes to 282 ships of nearly 600,000 tons. It will thus be seen how, just at the time when, in the Atlantic, a lull had been gained and a degree of mastery achieved, the onslaught of a new enemy denied us all the relief and benefit of the improvement.

We have so far dealt mainly with the U-boats' campaign against our merchant shipping during the present phase; the activities of the German long-range bombers have appeared incidentally in the story only where they affected particular actions between the convoys and U-boats. But the long-range bombers themselves added no small toll to the monthly sinkings, and even before the beginning of this period it had become clear that emergency measures must be taken to deal with them. The convoy routes to and from Gibraltar were specially vulnerable because their flank was exposed to the enemy's bomber bases in south-west France. In July attacks became serious. Our convoys were routed still further to the west to try to escape the Focke-Wulf's attentions; but this inevitably widened the gap between the

---

[1] See Appendix R.

cover which shore-based aircraft from Gibraltar and those of No. 19 Group from home bases could give to the convoys. The problem of bridging that gap became an important issue during the latter part of 1941. The Admiralty also pressed for the Focke-Wulf bases to be bombed, and this was occasionally done by Bomber Command, though with little effect. The sinkings went on, and among North Atlantic convoys as well as among those coming home from the south. In June, July and August enemy aircraft destroyed, in all waters, a total of forty-four ships of 94,551 tons and damaged a good many more. Furthermore, the co-operation between the long-range bombers and the U-boats was so good that the convoy escorts came to know only too well that the presence of one of the former, hovering out of gun range on the horizon, was the almost certain prelude to attack by the latter. The problem facing the Admiralty and the Air Ministry was, therefore, to give the convoys the means to drive off or, better still, destroy the shadower, and the means to defend themselves against low-level bombing attacks.

The shore defences at home surrendered some automatic guns to the merchantmen, and arrangements were also made to hasten the production and fitting of a variety of substitutes for guns, such as rocket projectors. But ship-mounted weapons, though essential to defence, could not by themselves be enough. What was needed was fighter aircraft. Coastal Command's strength in Northern Ireland was accordingly increased from fifty-six to ninety-six aircraft, some of Bomber Command's Blenheims were transferred, and it was also decided to add the new long-range Beaufighter to Coastal Command's establishment. These measures certainly improved matters, especially in the approach waters which could be reached fairly quickly by the shore-based fighters. But it soon became apparent that there were not nearly enough fighters, nor were they fast enough to reach threatened ships in time to prevent an attack. There could only be one solution—the ships must carry their fighter aircraft with them. This was not by any means a new idea, since the Navy had for a long time had carrier-borne fighters, but of them also there were very few and, compared with R.A.F. Hurricanes, they were of low performance. Again something better was needed, and the Chief of the Air Staff expressed the need pungently when he told his colleagues on the Chiefs of Staff Committee that he was 'convinced that neither shore-based aircraft . . . nor gun armament can secure our shipping . . . against the scale and type of attack that we must now expect. . . . The only method of protection likely to be effective is the shipborne high-performance fighter operating from specially converted ships which must accompany every convoy'.

The Admiralty was, in fact, a step ahead, for they were already converting the old seaplane carrier *Pegasus* and three merchant ships for this very purpose. These new naval auxiliaries were called fighter catapult ships. An ex-German prize (the *Hannover*) was also being fitted with a flight deck to become the first of the long line of auxiliary or escort aircraft carriers.[1] She was renamed H.M.S. *Audacity* and entered service in June 1941. We shall meet her again shortly. The fighter catapult ships *Maplin, Springbank, Ariguani* and *Pegasus* were ready in April. Two were sent to the Gibraltar route straight away, while the other two were kept in the North Atlantic until July, when they too went to guard the southern route. Early in August a Hurricane from the *Maplin* scored the first success by shooting down a Focke-Wulf 400 miles out to sea; but the *Springbank* was sunk in the heavy U-boat attack on convoy H.G. 73 in September, and the *Ariguani* seriously damaged in October.

But the Admiralty and the Air Ministry were not relying on these five ships only. Early in April 1941 the Battle of the Atlantic Committee was told that catapult equipment had been ordered for fifty merchantmen, and a start had been made on choosing the ships to be fitted. They were to be called catapult aircraft merchantmen (C.A.M.s) and, unlike the fighter catapult ships, which wore the White Ensign, would continue to ply their normal trade as merchant ships under the Red Ensign. Fighter Command provided sixty Hurricanes and the pilots; experiments and training went on apace and the first catapult launch took place on the last day of May. The *Empire Rainbow* was the first C.A.M. ship to be ready; and the first action between a C.A.M. ship's fighter and a Focke-Wulf took place on the 1st of November. The pilots of the R.A.F.'s merchant ship fighter unit and of the naval fighter catapult ships merit a special word. They knew that, once they had been catapulted, their patrol would probably end by a parachute descent into the sea, hoping to be picked up by a surface escort vessel. Their sorties demanded a cold-blooded gallantry.

While the stop-gap methods of dealing with the German long-range bombers were thus serving a purpose, better but more long-term plans were being made. The Naval and Air Staffs had no doubt that the case for the escort carrier was fully proven. In May the Battle of the Atlantic Committee was 'deeply impressed' with the value of ships of that class to afford protection against bombers and 'to provide a convoy with its own anti-submarine air patrols'. The conversion of five more ships was accordingly put in hand in Britain, and the first six escort carriers were requested from the United States under Lend-Lease. But none of these could be ready until the following year. The United States Navy will be the first to agree that it was these early British trials and experiments, and the measures which

---

[1] See p. 276.

arose out of them, that gave their own service such a flying start in escort carrier construction and operation. Indeed the United States Navy at once profited by our experience by ordering the conversion of four tankers for their own use. In due time the 'C.V.E.', as the Americans called the auxiliary or escort carrier, was to become a familiar sight with almost every convoy on all the oceans. But their birth dates to the spring and summer of 1941 and to our own efforts to combat the U-boat and the Focke-Wulf.

The *Audacity* (Commander D. W. Mackendrick) was sent to join the Gibraltar convoy escorts in September, and there she did such good work that the enemy soon regarded her presence as the greatest danger to his U-boats. Dönitz accordingly made her destruction their primary object. She carried six American 'Martlet' fighters and scored her first success by shooting down a Focke-Wulf while convoy O.G. 74 was being heavily attacked by U-boats and aircraft on the 20th and 21st of September.

Owing to the fierce attacks on the preceding Gibraltar convoys by the concentration of U-boats stationed off the Straits, the Admiralty held back convoy H.G. 76 until a strong enough escort could be collected to fight it through. By the 14th of December two sloops, three destroyers, seven corvettes and the *Audacity* had assembled at Gibraltar, and the convoy of thirty-two ships was ordered to sail. The escort was led by Commander F. J. Walker in the sloop *Stork*. He, by his thorough knowledge and understanding of U-boat tactics, by his experience with anti-submarine vessels and their weapons, and by his ability to weld a group of ships into a team, each of whose captains knew instinctively what was expected of him and carried it out unhesitatingly, became perhaps the most famous and successful escort group commander of the whole war. His sudden death in July 1944 from overstrain while still in command of his group was a great loss; but by that time he had shown what could be accomplished by carefully thought out tactics applied with unrelenting vigour, and the torch he had lit was carried on by the men he had trained.[1] With such a man in charge of a convoy it was certain that the powerful force of U-boats which Dönitz had assembled for its destruction would have no easy task.

The battle opened on the night of the 14th–15th of December as the convoy steamed west from Gibraltar. From that time onwards the convoy had, as its Commodore wrote in his report, 'few dull moments'. The first air attacks were made on two U-boats attempting the passage of the Straits. On the 15th the Australian destroyer *Nestor* sank U.127 off Cape St Vincent. Next day a Focke-Wulf

---

[1] See 'Walker's Groups in the Western Approaches', by Commander D. E. G. Wemyss. (Liverpool Daily Post and Echo, 1949.)

THE BATTLE OF CONVOY H.G. 76

sighted and reported the convoy and nine U-boats started to close in. On the 17th the convoy was out of air range from Gibraltar and thenceforth had to depend on the *Audacity's* Martlets, until it should come within reach of No. 19 Group's aircraft sent out from home bases. For the succeeding four days a continuous day-and-night battle was fought between the U-boats and the escort. U.131 was sunk by the surface escort aided by the carrier's aircraft on the 17th, U.434 by the surface escort next day, U.574 by Commander Walker himself on the 19th and U.567 by the surface escort on the 21st. Two Focke-Wulfs were also shot down. But neither the convoy nor its escort escaped unscathed. The destroyer *Stanley* which had aided in the sinking of U.131 and U.434 was herself torpedoed and sunk on the 19th; Walker's *Stork* was damaged in ramming U.574 and the *Audacity* fell victim to a U-boat some 500 miles west of Finisterre on the 21st. To her, however, will always belong the distinction of having first closed the air gap on the Gibraltar convoy route.

On the morning of the 22nd the convoy was met by a Liberator aircraft 750 miles from its base. Though Dönitz had reinforced the original attackers with three more U-boats, and it was one of them which sank the *Audacity*, he had realised by the 23rd that the battle was lost and then called off the attack. The escorts had indeed won a resounding victory, since five U-boats had been destroyed and only two merchant ships were lost.

After recounting the story of the ebb and flow of the struggle on the North Atlantic, Sierra Leone and Gibraltar routes it remains to tell of U-boat attacks on such of our shipping as had to cross the southern half of the North Atlantic, generally without escort. The first U-boat had appeared in those waters in July 1940, and a second had been sent out in the following winter. Though the sinkings had been fairly numerous the passage to and from the zone of operations was long, and to enable U-boats to work there effectively an ocean supply system was essential. When, in the winter of 1940–41, his successes on the northern routes showed a decline, the enemy had struck again further south. At first his U-boats were victualled and supplied by ships lying in the Canary Islands, an infringement of neutrality at which the Spanish Government had connived; but in July 1941 this was stopped by diplomatic action. The enemy then organised a system of supplying his U-boats at sea from ships specially sent out to meet them at secret rendezvous. The *Egerland* was the first U-boat supply ship, but she was soon intercepted and sunk in the South Atlantic.[1] He then tried to base his supply ships at Dakar, but

---

[1] See pp. 543–544 and Appendix N.

negotiations to that end with the French Vichy Government came to nothing. A second attempt to use ocean supply ships was frustrated as rapidly as the first by the interception of the *Python* and *Kota Penang*, and the sinking of the raider *Atlantis*.[1] The enemy thereupon abandoned the use of surface vessels for such purposes, and relied instead on the supply U-boats which he had meanwhile been developing. The first of this new type was U.469 which was commissioned in December 1941. Not until the following spring and summer did the first six boats of this class leave for the Atlantic; their activities will therefore be considered in a later volume. Here it is only necessary to remark how our success in making the broad oceans dangerous to the enemy's surface supply ships destroyed his hope of building up a far-reaching replenishment system for his U-boats, and severely restricted their capacity for extended long-range operations.

It remains only to discuss certain technical developments which were taking place at this time and which were to have important and unpleasant consequences for the U-boats. In attack from the air the need for shallower detonation of depth charges had been recognised by July, and they were thenceforth set to detonate at fifty feet and were invariably released in 'sticks'. But it was found that even this setting was too deep and did not produce lethal results. By the end of the year, therefore, a twenty-five-foot setting had become the aim, and development of a suitable pistol was started. It did not, however, enter service until the next phase. The depth charge 'patterns' which could be fired from surface ships had been increased from the five charges of the early days to ten or fourteen with favourable results. But reduction of the inevitable time lag in carrying out an asdic-directed attack had been the subject of close investigation by the Admiralty, and the need for an ahead-throwing weapon which would enable a rapid attack to be made during the run-in was realised. An earlier idea for a mortar which would throw a salvo of projectiles some 250 yards ahead of the attacker was therefore resurrected, and by the end of the current phase this weapon—called the 'Hedgehog'—was being manufactured. Though the best tactical method of using it was not at once achieved, it played an important part in the later phases of the campaign; but it never superseded the depth charge.

Meanwhile the development both of radar and of illuminants to bring the attacking ships—and, even more, attacking aircraft—rapidly and unseen to lethal distances by night or in low visibility was proceeding. If the nights and periods of fog could be made as dangerous to the U-boats as the daylight hours, their discomfiture would be greatly enhanced. Though the use of illuminants in conjunction with

---

[1] See pp. 542 and 544.

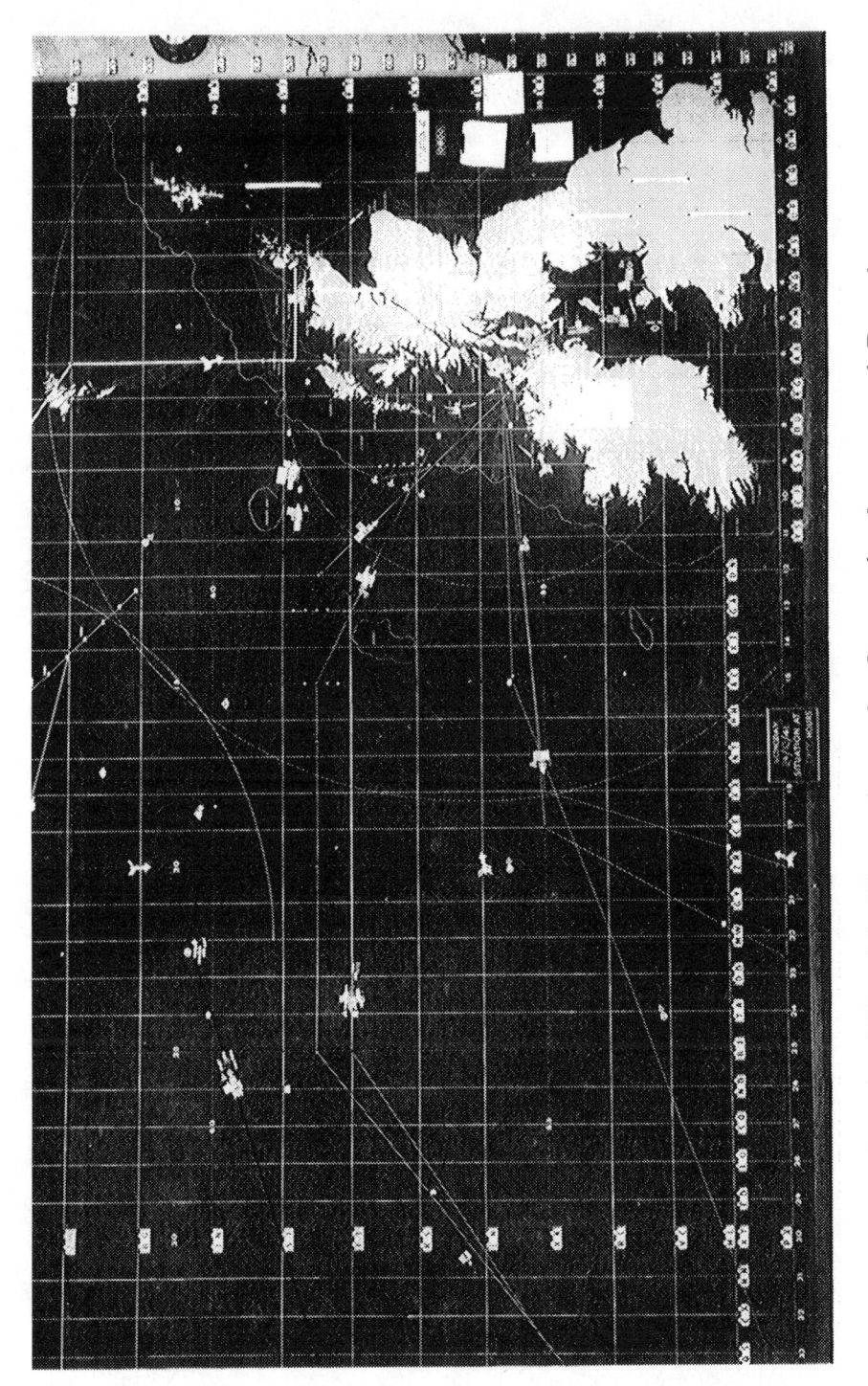

The Operational Plot of the Western Approaches Command at 8 a.m. on 24th December 1941.

H.M.S. *Audacity*, the first Auxiliary Aircraft Carrier, escorting a convoy in 58° 15′ North, 12° 46′ West on 15th September 1941. (See page 478.)

H.M.S. *Ariguani*, Fighter Catapult Ship, at sea in 55° 50′ North, 8° 00′ West on 8th July 1941. (See page 477.)

A SUMMARY OF THE CAMPAIGN

radar was now being intensively developed, it was not to become an accomplished fact until later. The shore organisation for locating and tracking the U-boats, the Admiralty's Submarine Tracking Room, working in close harmony with the Headquarters of Coastal Command, had now developed its art to a high pitch and it was unusual for the presence and approximate position of any U-boat to remain long concealed.

Long before the end of the present phase the Admiralty had started to look ahead to the campaign of the next winter in the Atlantic and had appointed a committee to study the problem in all its aspects, strategical, tactical and technical. That committee rendered its report on the 6th of May 1941 and the developments outlined above were in no small measure based on its recommendations. Though American participation in convoy escort duty, which could hardly have been foreseen in May, altered many of the strategic and organisational aspects of the Atlantic struggle, the principles which this committee laid down for dealing with the U-boat and the long-range bomber were soon proved well founded. On the long-disputed question whether the destruction of U-boats would be more effectively accomplished by hunting for them or by escorting convoys as strongly as possible, the Committee expressed its conviction that 'we cannot afford to weaken our convoy escorts to provide the ships required for searching forces until far greater strength is available than is at present in prospect'. Though the final vindication of the convoy system was not to take place until the next phase of the struggle, it is interesting to remark that on this subject the view of the 1941 committee corresponded exactly with that of the Committee on the Investigation of War Problems which had reported in September 1939.[1] Yet between the dates of the two reports much effort had been expended in endeavouring to catch and sink U-boats with hunting groups, and convoy escorts had undoubtedly been weakened by these misguided endeavours.

To summarise the results of the current phase of the Battle of the Atlantic, German and Italian U-boats had sunk, between the 1st of April and the 31st of December, 328 ships of over 1,576,000 tons, but no less than 206 of the sunken ships (over one million tons) were not sailing in convoy. They had lost twenty-eight U-boats in doing so, and twenty of them were destroyed by convoy escorts. In the north our evasive routing and escorts had wrested the initiative from the U-boats, and in the south the closing weeks of the period had produced the same result. It was only the lack of escort carriers and of long-range shore-based aircraft which prevented this trend being immediately exploited, and another year was to elapse before both

---

[1] See pp. 134–135.

became plentifully available. But the latter half of 1941 was, none the less, an important period in the Battle of the Atlantic, for it had made clear beyond doubt that not only was shipping best protected while in convoy, but that powerful surface and air escorts constituted by far the most effective means of destroying the U-boats themselves.

At the close of the year eighty-six operational U-boats were in commission and about 150 more were training or running trials. Fifteen of the former were in the Mediterranean, and thirty-five were allocated either to that theatre or to the waters off Gibraltar. This left only thirty-six U-boats for all the other areas and, of these, twelve were preparing for the assault on the east coast of America which was to bring them their second period of great success. For on the 7th of December the Japanese had attacked the Americans, and by noon of that fateful day a great part of the United States Pacific Fleet had been reduced to a wrecked and flaming shambles within the confines of Pearl Harbour.

CHAPTER XXII

HOME WATERS AND THE ARCTIC

1st June–31st December, 1941

> We shall do everything to help you that time, geography and our growing resources allow.
> *Mr Churchill to Stalin.* 7th July 1941.

AFTER the sinking of the *Bismarck* the Admiralty and Admiral Tovey reviewed the maritime war in the light of the surface ships still possessed by the Germans and their condition. Apart from the *Tirpitz*, now structurally complete and undergoing trials, the pocket-battleships *Admiral Scheer* and *Lützow*, the 8-inch cruiser *Admiral Hipper*, four 6-inch cruisers and about a dozen destroyers were believed to be in the Baltic and ready for action. The battle cruisers *Scharnhorst* and *Gneisenau* were in Brest, both believed to be damaged, and the *Prinz Eugen* reached that port on the 1st of June after her brief and fruitless Atlantic cruise.[1] The British authorities could not know that, in fact, the state of most of the German major warships was not such as to enable another raid in strength to be carried out against our Atlantic routes in the near future, and they had, therefore, to be prepared for such an eventuality. As refits and detachments on distant services had reduced the strength of the Home Fleet at this time, the Commander-in-Chief was anxious about his ability to deal with another break-out in force. The *Prince of Wales* was repairing the damage she had received from the *Bismarck*, the *Rodney* was about to refit in the United States, the *Repulse* was covering convoys off Newfoundland and the *Victorious* had sailed for Gibraltar on the last day of May, accompanied by two cruisers, with a cargo of Hurricanes for the Middle East. As for cruisers, the *Suffolk*, *Kenya* and *Aurora* were scouring the oceans for the enemy's supply ships—about which more will be said later—four others were on patrol off Iceland and the *Birmingham* was about to leave for the south with a W.S. convoy. Admiral Tovey had, therefore, only the *King George V*, two cruisers and about seven destroyers at Scapa at the beginning of June. Though he expected to be reinforced by the *Nelson*, two more cruisers and some fourteen destroyers within the next fortnight, he could not meanwhile feel that his strength was adequate for the tasks which he might be called on to perform. This

---
[1] See pp. 417–418.

made early warning of enemy movements more important than ever, and he therefore pressed for intensive air reconnaissance of the Skagerrak and its approaches. Coastal Command was able to meet this request and the speed with which accurate warning of enemy movements was now received greatly mitigated Admiral Tovey's anxiety regarding his meagre strength. It was soon shown that there was good cause for believing that the enemy would not keep idle those of his major warships which were fit for sea. On the 10th of June the Admiralty gave warning that an important ship—possibly the *Tirpitz*—was on her way out from the Baltic. It was, however, not the *Tirpitz* but the *Lützow*, and she was bound for Trondheim as a first step towards breaking out into the Atlantic. She was accompanied by the light cruisers *Emden* and *Leipzig* and five destroyers on the first part of her journey. Admiral Tovey took up his intercepting position south of Iceland and strengthened his patrols in the northern passages. By the evening of the 11th the Admiralty had correctly identified the principal warship involved in the movement. Coastal Command patrols and searches were reinforced and striking forces prepared. Next day the *Emden* and *Leipzig* were detached to Oslofiord while the pocket-battleship turned west with her destroyer screen to pass out of the Skagerrak. But she had not been sighted by 10 p.m. on the evening of the 12th.

The Commander-in-Chief, Coastal Command, now decided to send out his striking forces to search for the enemy themselves, and between 11 and 11.15 p.m. fourteen aircraft of Nos. 22 and 42 Squadrons (Beaufort torpedo-bombers) took off from their bases in Scotland. Just before midnight a patrolling Blenheim briefly sighted the German squadron off the Naze, and about two hours later No. 42 Squadron's striking force made contact.[1] At 2.18 a.m. on the 13th, an aircraft of this squadron piloted by Flight Sergeant R. H. Loveitt hit the *Lützow* with a torpedo and damaged her so severely that she took a heavy list and was for a time stopped. Two more of the same squadron's Beauforts attacked a few minutes later, but missed. By 3.20 the pocket-battleship was able to steam slowly towards the Norwegian coast. Meanwhile No. 22 Squadron was still seeking the target and, at 4.20, one of its aircraft got in an attack; but the torpedo missed and the aircraft was shot down by the German fighter escort which had now arrived. A bombing attack made by Blenheims soon after 5 a.m. also failed to inflict further damage and, powerfully escorted, the *Lützow* succeeded in reaching Kiel on the afternoon of the 14th of June. Not until January 1942 was she taken out of dock. The German account of this incident not only shows concern at the speed and accuracy with which British intelligence had again worked but mentions that the successful torpedo attack was carried out with

---

[1] See Map 5 (*facing p. 71*) and p. 331, footnote (1).

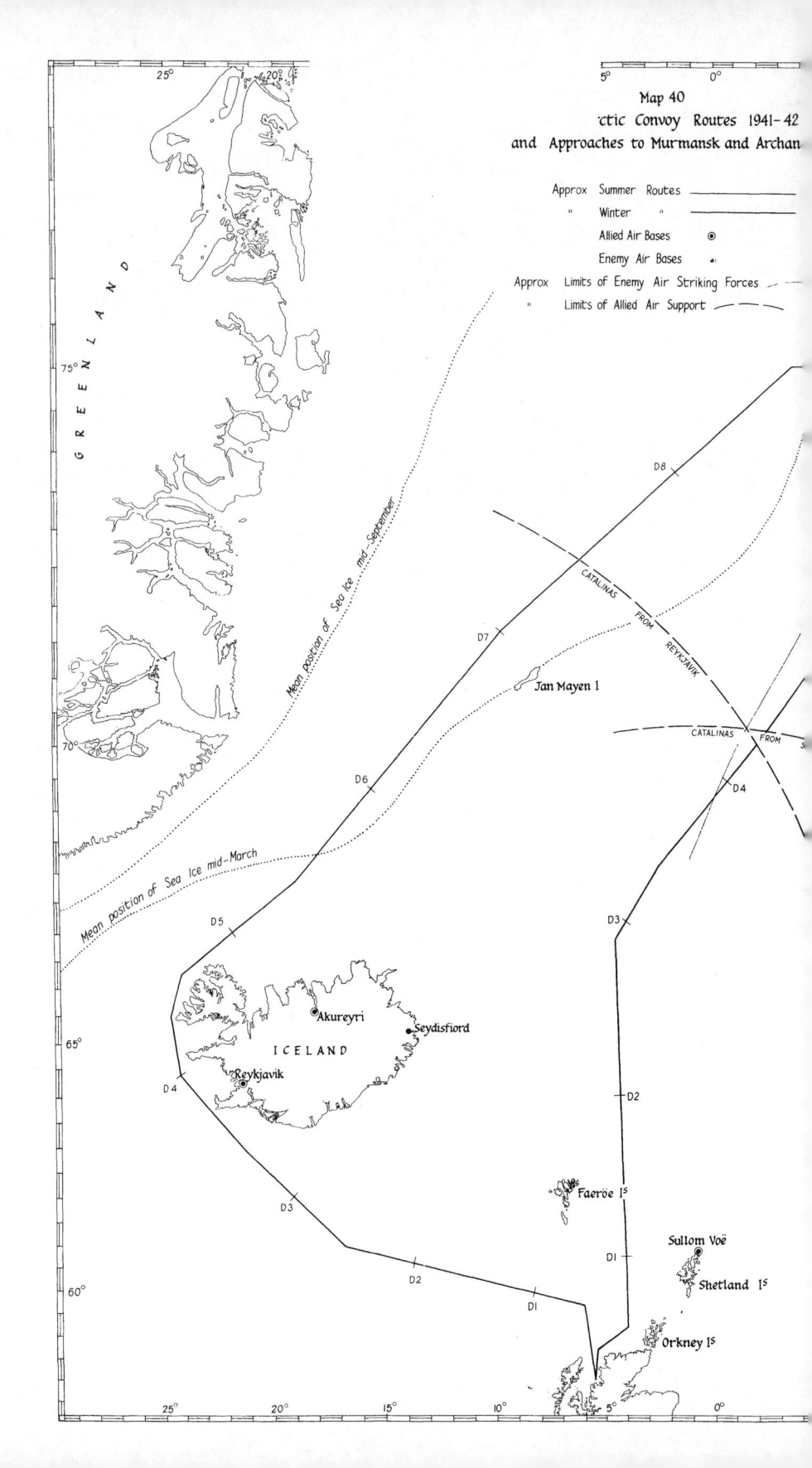

Map 40
 ctic Convoy Routes 1941-42
and Approaches to Murmansk and Archan

Approx Summer Routes ————
  "   Winter   "   ————
       Allied Air Bases   ⊙
       Enemy Air Bases   •
Approx Limits of Enemy Air Striking Forces ----
  "   Limits of Allied Air Support — — —

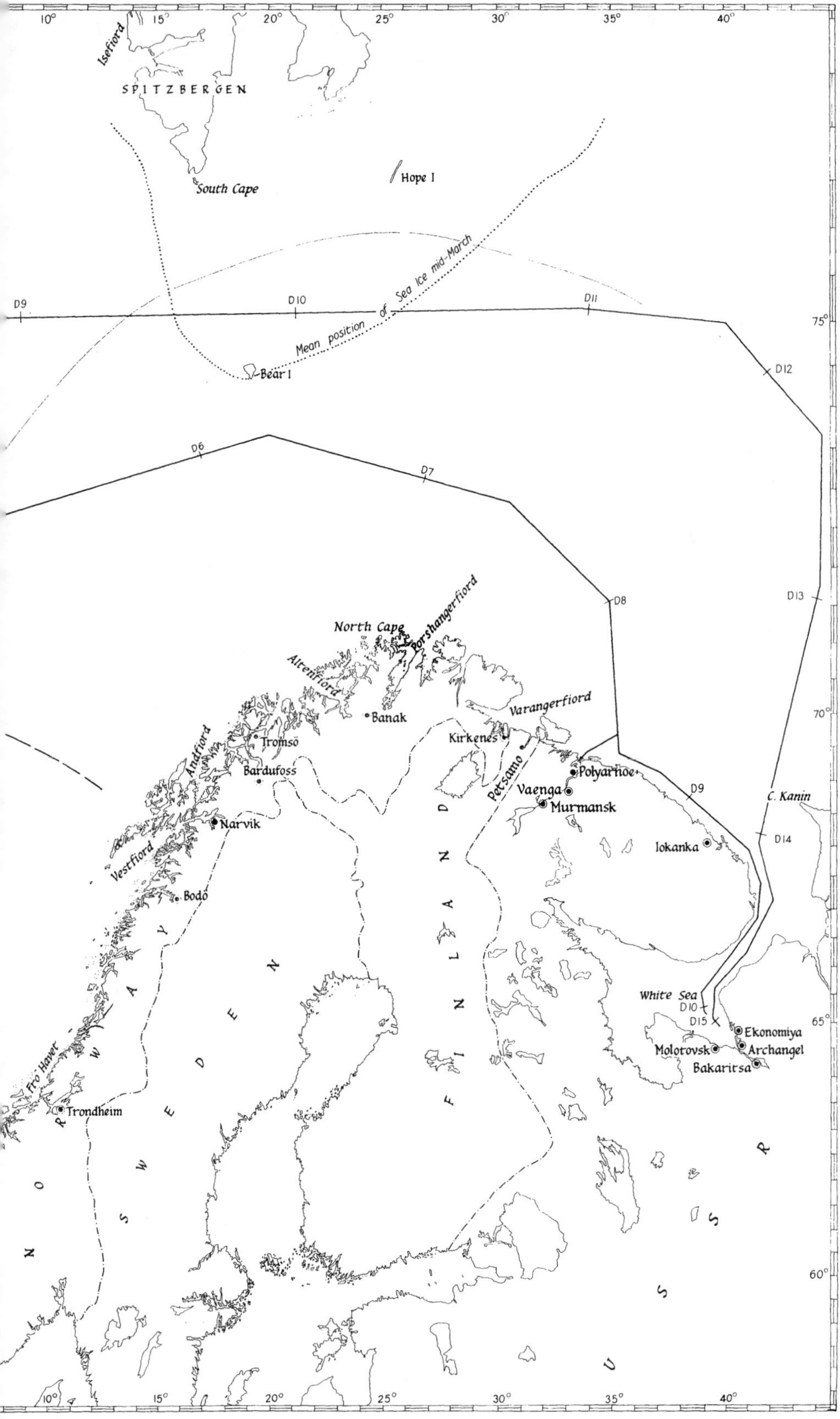

Isefiord
SPITZBERGEN
South Cape
Hope I
Mean position of Sea Ice mid-March
Bear I
D9
D10
D11
D12
D6
D7
D8
D13
North Cape
Porshangerfiord
Altenfiord
Banak
Varangerfiord
Kirkenes
Tromsö
Andfiord
Bardufoss
Polyarnoe
Vaenga
Murmansk
Petsamo
Narvik
Vestfiord
Bodö
Iokanka
C. Kanin
D14
White Sea
D15
Ekonomiya
Molotovsk
Archangel
Bakaritsa
Frö Havet
Trondheim
NORWAY
SWEDEN
FINLAND
USSR
10°
15°
20°
25°
30°
35°
40°
75°
70°
65°
60°

'superb dash' and took the pocket-battleship completely by surprise.

With the start of Hitler's onslaught on Russia a number of German warships was required in the Baltic to co-operate with the advancing armies and to harass the Russian communications in that sea. This reduced the probability of further Atlantic forays, though the possibility of their renewal at short notice could not, of course, be ignored. In addition it weakened the enemy's defence of his coastal traffic in the North Sea. The diversion to the east of the main strength of the Luftwaffe also made it possible for the Home Fleet to renew surface ship activity in waters previously commanded by the enemy's air power. Admiral Tovey had for some time wanted to strike against the Norwegian coastal shipping routes, but had been prevented from doing so by the many detachments made from his fleet.

But the opening of the Russian campaign had other and, in the long run, still more far-reaching consequences on our maritime strategy, for it gradually shifted the focus of the Home Fleet's responsibilities from the passages between Scotland and Greenland to the north-east, and in particular to the waters between northern Norway and the varying limits imposed by the Arctic ice. The first signs of this change came in July, when the Russians began to press for attacks to be made on the enemy's traffic moving between such ports as Kirkenes in north Norway and the formerly Finnish port of Petsamo, now in German hands.[1] This traffic was considered by the Russians to be of great importance to the enemy, and post-war evidence lends considerable support to their view. We now know that, well before the start of Hitler's attack on Russia, Raeder had stressed the need to occupy both Murmansk and Polyarnoe, and that later he several times renewed his pressure to achieve that object. Other records show the importance which the enemy attached to the nickel-producing area around Petsamo and to the severance of the Murman railway, both of which seem to have been regarded as more vital than the capture of Murmansk itself. Land operations aiming to capture Murmansk were, however, soon begun in the far north. Very difficult conditions and stubborn Russian resistance were at once encountered, so that little progress was made. The Russians seem to have had no illusions regarding the importance of their only ice-free northern port and of its slender communications to the south. On the enemy's side, only Raeder seems to have realised the full significance of that Russian link with the west. In London and Washington the need to pass British and American stores and equipment to the new ally through that entry was at once apparent, and both Governments soon promised to supply them on a very large scale. It was plain that the responsibility for the safe passage of the supply ships would fall on Admiral Tovey's fleet.

---
[1] See Map 40.

The Cabinet was anxious to meet the Russian requests, and the Admiralty therefore suggested to Admiral Tovey that the Home Fleet's aircraft carriers *Furious* and *Victorious* should strike at the enemy's coastal traffic in the far north. This, however, was a very different matter from the raids on the more southerly sections of the enemy-held coastline which were at the time in the mind of the Commander-in-Chief, and he pointed out that the risk to his carriers would be serious because of the closeness of enemy airfields and the continuous daylight. In view of what is now known it seems that the extent to which the Luftwaffe's bombers had been diverted to the eastern front was not, at the time, fully realised. However that may be, the Admiralty ordered the operation to be carried out, and Rear-Admiral W. F. Wake-Walker, flying his flag in the *Devonshire*, accordingly sailed from Scapa on the 23rd of July with the two aircraft carriers, the *Suffolk* and six destroyers in company.

Arrangements were made for the force to fuel in Iceland and again from a tanker sent to a rendezvous in the far north. If no transports were found on the coastal route enemy installations at Kirkenes and Petsamo were to be attacked. Unfortunately the element of surprise was lost when the force was sighted by reconnaissance aircraft on the 30th. No shipping was found at sea, and in the attacks on the two ports heavy fighter and anti-aircraft opposition was encountered. The results achieved were small and the aircraft losses heavy. More than half of the *Victorious*' striking force of twenty torpedo-bombers was shot down over Kirkenes. The *Furious*' aircraft met less opposition over Petsamo, but found the harbour empty. After making a smaller attack on Tromsö the force returned to Scapa. Perhaps the most valuable result of the operation was that the opportunity was taken to pass the minelayer *Adventure* through to Archangel with a cargo of mines for our new allies—a gesture of which, said Admiral Tovey, 'the Russians were most appreciative'.

While these unprofitable attacks were taking place in the far north, the watch on the enemy battle cruisers in Brest was never relaxed and on the 21st of July our aircraft reported that a move by the *Scharnhorst* appeared to be imminent. Next day it was confirmed that she had sailed. Admiral Tovey considered that three alternative intentions were possible. She might merely go to a more southerly French port to continue training her crew under easier conditions than prevailed in Brest; she might be bound for St Nazaire, or even Cadiz, to dock; or she might be about to attempt a return passage to Germany either by the northern route or up the English Channel. The Home Fleet at once came to short notice but was not this time needed, for on the 23rd our reconnaissance aircraft found the *Scharnhorst* in La Pallice. Heavy attacks were at once organised by Bomber and Coastal Commands. The first, by forty aircraft, was unsuccessful, but early in the afternoon of the 24th a daylight attack by fifteen Halifax bombers achieved no less than five direct hits. Although two bombs which penetrated the armoured deck failed to explode, the damage and flooding caused by the other three were serious. Late that evening she sailed again for Brest with 3,000 tons of flood water inside her. Though she was sighted on passage next morning in foggy weather and again attacked from the air, she succeeded in reaching harbour without receiving further damage, and on the 25th she was moved into dock. A survey revealed that at least eight months would be required to effect permanent repairs. Though the Admiralty was for some time unaware of it, the *Prinz Eugen* had also been damaged by a bomb hit on the night of the 1st–2nd July when forty-one heavy bombers had attacked Brest. It thus came to pass that, by the end of that month, the *Scharnhorst*, *Gneisenau* and *Prinz Eugen* were all immobilised inside the French port, and the enemy had been made to pay a heavy price for his attempt to use it as an advanced base for raids into the Atlantic.

As a lull in the bombing of Brest now followed and no further heavy attack was made until September, it will be appropriate to summarise the effort so far expended on immobilising the three ships. Between the 27th of March, when the first attack was made, and the end of July 1,962 tons of high explosive bombs and about 19 tons of incendiaries were dropped by 1,875 aircraft of which 1,723 came from Bomber Command. The chief brunt therefore fell, as was natural, on the command which possessed the lion's share of our air striking power. The actual hits obtained on the enemy ships were:

> One torpedo hit by Coastal Command on the *Gneisenau* on the 6th of April.
> Four bomb hits by Bomber Command on the *Gneisenau* on the 10th–11th of April.
> One bomb hit by Bomber Command on the *Prinz Eugen* on the 1st–2nd of July.
> Five bomb hits by Bomber Command on the *Scharnhorst* on the 24th of July.

In addition to the bombing attacks Bomber Command sent out 205 and Coastal Command 159 aircraft on minelaying missions and the two Commands together laid, during this period, a total of 275 mines off Brest. In all these sorties only thirty-four aircraft, three of them minelayers, were lost. The price paid cannot therefore be regarded as excessive. The damage to the ships was certainly the cause of extreme disappointment to the German Naval Staff, whose plans were thereby entirely upset.

None the less the chance not only to frustrate further raids by these powerful enemy warships against our trade routes but to destroy the ships themselves by air attack was at this time regarded by Bomber Command and by the Cabinet as an unfortunate, if necessary, diversion from bombing Germany, rather than as a heaven-sent opportunity to win a major success in the maritime war. As early as mid-April Bomber Command had protested against the continuation of the attacks on the grounds that the ships were 'sewn in by mines'. This had led to the Cabinet approving, on the 8th of May, the transfer of the main bombing effort back to Germany, on condition that regular reconnaissance of Brest harbour and frequent small attacks on the port were maintained. But it was agreed that if the Brest squadron showed any sign of movement it would once more become the primary target for the heavy bombers.

With the start of the enemy's campaign against Russia bombing policy was reconsidered, and on the 9th of July it was decided that naval targets, and the ships in Brest in particular, were to be regarded as diversions from the primary object of bombing north-west Germany. The enemy ships will therefore now be left in the French port doing their best to carry out repairs. They were certainly not left in peace, for the conditions laid down by the Cabinet were fully carried out by the Royal Air Force; not only was a constant watch kept on them but many light attacks were made. But for the next two months they were not again made the primary target of Bomber Command.

We must now return to the Home Fleet which, on the 12th of July, was told by the Admiralty to prepare a squadron to be based in the far north to work with the Russians. Admiral Tovey again expressed a strong preference for operations further south, where more important targets would be found and better air cover could be given to his ships. His views were reinforced when Rear-Admiral P. Vian, the commander designate of the force, returned from a flying visit to Murmansk and reported that the fighter defences were quite inadequate to allow a force to use it as a base with safety, and that attacks on enemy shipping off that coast were hardly practicable. But the Admiralty insisted on the importance of giving visible support to the Russians, and on the 27th of April Admiral Vian sailed from Iceland in the cruiser *Nigeria* with the *Aurora* and two destroyers. He made a reconnaissance of Spitzbergen, which the Admiralty had suggested as an alternative base to Murmansk, and reported that his objects could not be accomplished by using it as an advanced base, while operations close off the enemy-held coastline would probably prove suicidal. He twice attempted to approach the coast and was each time sighted at long range by enemy aircraft. After the second attempt the squadron returned to Scapa.

The Admiralty now abandoned the idea of basing such a force on Spitzbergen and decided instead to send an expedition there to destroy the coal installations, to evacuate the Russian and Norwegian inhabitants and to capture any shipping which might fall into its hands. On the 19th of August Admiral Vian sailed again to carry out those objects. The occupation of the island went smoothly; by a clever ruse the Norwegian naval lieutenant who had been appointed Military Governor kept the wireless station working and called for more colliers to be sent from Norway. The three ships which obediently arrived were duly seized and sent to England. By the 3rd of September the objects of the expedition had been successfully accomplished and Admiral Vian sailed for home. On the way back he took his two cruisers in towards the Norwegian coast to search for enemy shipping and, in the early hours of the 7th, while off Porshangerfiord, just to the east of North Cape, he met a German convoy in heavy weather and low visibility.[1] In the ensuing mêlée the training warship *Bremse* was sunk, but the two troop transports which she was escorting escaped. The *Nigeria* was damaged by ramming a wreck, but on the 10th of September Admiral Vian's force returned safely to Scapa.

Another call on the Home Fleet to help our ally at this time was one to carry forty-eight Hurricanes to Russia in the old aircraft carrier *Argus*, which had already several times done similar service for Malta, and a merchant ship.[2] The convoy assembled at Reykjavik and sailed north on the 21st of August with an escort of six flotilla vessels and covered by the *Devonshire*, *Suffolk* and *Victorious* under Rear-Admiral Wake-Walker. The merchantman with the crated fighters reached Archangel safely and the *Argus* successfully flew hers to Murmansk. An abortive attempt was made to strike at coastal shipping north of Tromsö with the *Victorious*' aircraft on the 3rd of September and, after fuelling at Spitzbergen, a second attempt was made further south. This time one ship was sunk, but such slight results could hardly justify the effort expended.

This series of operations in the far north produced many new and difficult problems for the Home Fleet, some of which would be aggravated if, as seemed likely, they had to be continued throughout the winter. It was true that when the perpetual daylight of summer gave place to the almost unbroken darkness of the winter the likelihood of air attack would be lessened. But other grave handicaps would remain or be aggravated. The lack of an advanced base on the route from Iceland to the Arctic ports of Russia and the undeveloped state of the Russian bases at the journey's end meant that the fleet had to carry along with it the fuel supply for the round trip; the severity of the weather called for special steps to keep the ships habitable, their crews warm and their weapons in order at temperatures at which they had not been designed to work. And constant anxiety was caused

---
[1] See Map 40 (*facing p. 485*).
[2] See p. 298.

by the knowledge that, for a great part of the journey, the enemy possessed excellent bases for surface ships, submarines and aircraft close on the southern flank of a route from which little deviation was possible. We now know that the enemy's absorption in the great land battles being fought further south had, in fact, so reduced his bomber strength in the north that Admiral Tovey's misgivings about sending ships to work without air cover close inshore were temporarily groundless; but it was not to be long before every one of the new anxieties was fully realised.

An inevitable consequence of the importance attached by the Cabinet to carrying help to Russia and affording her visible support, and of the simultaneous need to reinforce the Mediterranean and carry fighter aircraft to Malta, was that the Home Fleet's watch on the northern exits to the Atlantic had to be relaxed, in spite of the fact that the *Tirpitz*, *Scheer* and all four 6-inch cruisers were now believed to be ready for sea. The departure of a large convoy for the Middle East on the 11th of September further reduced Admiral Tovey's strength. On the other hand, the American occupation of Iceland in August and the President's more forward policy regarding the defence of the Atlantic routes eased the Commander-in-Chief's anxiety regarding a new break-out into the Atlantic, since, as soon as warning of such a movement was received by the Admiralty, the American naval and air forces based on Iceland would now join in the watch on the northern passages; they would, moreover, attack any enemy ship which might enter the United States' defence zone.[1] The significance of President Roosevelt's moves was not lost on the German Naval Staff; they realised that their surface ships would now find it much harder, if not impossible, to break out through the northern passages undetected and that, even if they managed to reach the Atlantic, the days when they could make prolonged cruises in those waters with impunity were over. But Hitler was insistent that the Navy should avoid incidents which might further provoke the United States, at any rate until his campaign against Russia had ended victoriously, and refused to allow any retaliatory steps. His eyes were still firmly fixed on the land battles in the east, and all Admiral Raeder's powerful reasoning could not convince him of the decisive nature of the struggle at sea.

It was a combination of the damage inflicted by the Royal Air Force on the enemy's Brest squadron, his present preoccupation in the Baltic—where Leningrad was now closely invested—and the more active American participation in the Battle of the Atlantic that enabled reinforcements at this time to be allocated to the Far East. The planning which led to such movements will be considered in a later chapter. Here it is only necessary to say that in August 1941, as part

---
[1] See pp. 470–471.

of a long-term project to build up a powerful Eastern Fleet by the following spring, the four *Royal Sovereign* class battleships, the *Prince of Wales*, the *Repulse* and the new aircraft carrier *Indomitable* were all earmarked for that service.

Towards the end of August the condition of the enemy ships in Brest was again reviewed, and the need to prevent them from completing their repairs led to a request that a heavy attack should be made during the period of the September moon. Accordingly fifty-six Bomber Command aircraft were sent over on the night of the 3rd–4th and a still heavier force of 120 aircraft was despatched on a similar mission ten days later. Though neither raid inflicted further damage on the ships themselves, our intelligence, confirmed by photographs which showed all three ships to have been continuously in dry dock since the end of July, made it virtually certain that they had all been seriously damaged in one or more of the earlier attacks. Accordingly the policy of frequent light raids was resumed in October and November; not until early in December was a heavy weight again directed at them. It will be convenient now to carry the story of the Brest squadron to the end of the year.

Early in December, partly as a result of the lessons drawn from the successful Japanese air attack on the American fleet in Pearl Harbour and partly because our intelligence now indicated that the ships' repairs were nearly completed, Bomber Command was instructed again to make the Brest squadron a primary target. Plans for daylight attacks were also to be prepared. From the 11th of December bombing and minelaying took place every night, and on the 15th the plan for a heavy night attack followed quickly by a daylight raid was approved. Next day the *Prinz Eugen* was seen to have undocked and the new proposal was therefore put into action forthwith. On the night of the 17th–18th 101 heavy bombers attacked, and early in the following afternoon forty-one more, covered by ten squadrons of fighters, carried out the first daylight operation. No direct hits were obtained, but the *Gneisenau* suffered minor damage to her hull and the lock gates of the dock in which the *Scharnhorst* was lying were hit, which prevented her from being undocked for four weeks. A heavy scale of attack was kept up until the end of the year and a second daylight raid took place on the 30th of December. But no more damage was inflicted on any of the ships.

From 1st of August to the end of the year 851 aircraft dropped 1,175 tons of high explosive and 10 tons of incendiary bombs on the Brest squadron. Eleven heavy bombers were lost and although considerable damage and dislocation was caused to the dockyard the ships themselves were never hit. All the damage caused to them had been inflicted in the raids of the previous April and July.[1]

---

[1] See pp. 393–394 and pp. 486–487.

To return now to the Home Fleet, at the end of September Admiral Tovey went to Iceland to meet the representatives of the American Commander-in-Chief, Atlantic, Admiral E. J. King. A series of conferences took place between the Commanders-in-Chief, Home Fleet and Western Approaches, and the Americans on inter-service communications, convoy routing and other matters on which close co-ordination was now essential. Meanwhile the first Q.P. convoy (North Russia—homeward), with the ship which had carried the Hurricanes to Archangel, had sailed on the 28th of September and, on the following day, the first outward-bound (P.Q.) convoy to North Russia left Hvalfiord in Iceland escorted by the *Suffolk*, two destroyers and an anti-submarine group. The great distance which the convoy and its escort had to traverse—between 1,400 and 2,000 miles, depending on the departure and terminal ports and on ice conditions—and the lack of any fuelling base on the route necessitated an oiler accompanying the convoy. She would fuel the escort of the eastbound convoy in the far north and then return with the westbound ships. An arrangement of this nature became a regular feature of all Russian convoys, and the problem of keeping the escorts supplied with fuel added to the intricacies of the double movements from the east and west which they involved. The escort of Q.P. 1 included the cruiser *London*, which had carried the British and American supply missions led by Lord Beaverbrook and Mr Harriman to Russia and now brought them home again.[1]

The first intention had been to run the P.Q. convoys on a forty-day cycle throughout the winter, but early in October the Admiralty expressed a desire to shorten this to a ten-day cycle.[2] As it took three weeks for the escorts to complete the round trip to Murmansk—or longer if Archangel was the destination—and at least one cruiser and two destroyers had to accompany each convoy, the resources of the Home Fleet were greatly strained to meet the requirements of the shorter cycle. Local escorts of anti-submarine trawlers were supplied for the first part of the eastward journey, and British minesweepers based on Archangel met and took in the convoys at its end. The beginning of this famous series of convoys was quiet enough, but, as the enemy came to realise the scale on which British and American ships were carrying aid to their hard-pressed ally through the Arctic ports, his reaction was to attack in a rising crescendo of fury with all the weapons in his armoury. The epic story of the struggle to fight the later convoys through the most arduous physical conditions that nature could produce and against the most relentless onslaughts that man could devise belongs to the succeeding years; but an indication

---

[1] For the purpose of this mission see W. S. Churchill. *The Second World War*, Vol. III pp. 402–403.

[2] See p. 92 for definition of convoy cycle.

of what lay ahead was given when, in the last month of 1941, the Germans reinforced their destroyer strength in northern Norway and decided to keep more U-boats constantly at sea in the far north.

It has been seen how the Russian request for attacks on German coastal shipping passing around the North Cape to Petsamo could not be met by the regular use of surface ships, and that attempts to strike at it with carrier-borne aircraft were not at all successful. Where other arms failed, however, our submarines were able to achieve a good deal. In the early days of August the first two (the *Tigris* and *Trident*) were sent to Polyarnoe to harass the enemy's coastal traffic, and in the following month the Russians had eleven submarines similarly employed. The Germans could not find enough anti-submarine escorts adequately to protect the shipping on which their army in the north greatly depended, and traffic was soon brought to a standstill. The German account states that this forced them to send military supplies and reinforcements up the Baltic and thence by the long overland route through Finland; it adds that the 'British Navy [thus] greatly relieved the strain on the Russian armies in the north'.

Apart from the patrols in the far north the Home Fleet submarines worked in the Bay of Biscay to intercept U-boats and surface ships making for French ports, on the northern U-boat transit route to the Atlantic and off the Norwegian coast. Though several attacks on U-boats took place in the Bay of Biscay, none was successful during the present phase. The submarines' dispositions and patrols were still at this time designed to deal with the enemy's warships rather than with his mercantile traffic; but in spite of this the home-based flotillas sank twenty merchant ships of 52,498 tons in 1941 and damaged five more of 13,700 tons.

Just as the *Lützow's* northward movement had caused considerable anxiety and had brought about a period of intense air activity in June, so did a brief movement by the *Scheer* in September, but this time without the happy result of sending her back to base crippled. Photographic reconnaissance on the 4th showed that she had left Kiel; she was sighted shortly afterwards by our aircraft passing north through the Great Belt and, later, at the entrance to Oslofiord. She was seen in Oslo the same day and on the 5th and 8th unsuccessful bombing attacks were made by a small number of No. 2 Group's American Fortress aircraft. On the 10th, air patrols were organised to deal with a possible break-out. Five days later the *Scheer* could not be found in Oslo; nor did a search of all likely ports succeed in finding her at once. But on the 18th of September photographs of Swinemunde showed that she was back in her original base and tension thereupon relaxed. Next month the movement of the same ship to Hamburg caused similar anxieties, this time aggravated by extremely bad weather, which made air reconnaissance difficult and increased the likelihood of the enemy choosing such a time for a break-out to the Atlantic. Not until the 28th of November was she again found back in Swinemunde. The stresses caused by these, actually insignificant, movements show that, although regular photographic reconnaissance of the enemy's bases conferred inestimable advantages, it was liable to lead to exaggeration of the importance of any movement by a major warship. Photographic reconnaissance cannot therefore eliminate the need for intelligence about the enemy's intentions derived from other sources.

Early in October the Home Fleet sailed in support of the *Victorious*, whose aircraft were this time to attack coastal traffic further south, in the approaches to Vestfiord. Two air striking forces swept that section of the coast on the morning of the 8th of October, several ships were found and attacked and all the aircraft returned safely. The Luftwaffe again made no attempt to attack the fleet.

Late that month a final decision was taken to send the *Prince of Wales* to Singapore as flagship of Admiral Sir T. Phillips, Commander-in-Chief designate, Eastern Fleet. Admiral Tovey protested strongly and pointed out that this left him only one ship, the *King George V*, capable of catching and fighting the *Tirpitz*; but the Admiralty held to its decision and on the 23rd of October the *Prince of Wales* sailed from the Clyde on her long journey to the east. No sooner had this happened than the air reconnaissance reports already mentioned indicated the possibility of a new break-out being attempted by the *Scheer* and, perhaps, the *Tirpitz*. Early in November Admiral Tovey therefore moved the main body of his fleet to Hvalfiord, and co-ordinated with Admiral Giffen, U.S.N., the dispositions which the British and American ships would take up. Two American battleships and two cruisers sailed on the 5th of November, at the same time as Admiral Tovey's ships, to patrol the exits. Apart from his flagship, the *King George V*, Admiral Tovey had at this time only the *Victorious*, three 8-inch and three 6-inch cruisers. The *Malaya* had joined Force H at Gibraltar, the light cruisers *Aurora* and *Penelope* had recently gone to Malta to harass the enemy's supply traffic to North Africa, and other ships were detached on ocean escort duty.[1] The American help was, therefore, all the more valuable, even though on this occasion the expectation of a break-out proved unfounded. The fleet returned to Scapa before the end of the month and the third Russian convoy, which had been stopped while the threat existed, then sailed.

The second P.Q. convoy sailed on the 18th of October and the third on the 9th of November. By the time that the fourth left on the 17th of November the port of Archangel was starting to freeze.

---
[1] See p. 532.

Although the Russians hoped to keep the port open all the winter and believed it to be possible, the danger of damaging valuable ships in the ice, or of having them frozen in, led to the decision to divert some of the merchant ships to Murmansk and to fuel the escorting destroyers there. The Admiralty's intelligence regarding the disposition of the German surface ships and the knowledge that five enemy destroyers had moved to northern Norway now made Admiral Tovey anxious to strengthen the Russian convoys' escorts; but the shortness of the convoy cycle made this impossible. Nor were the Russians able to help towards remedying the escorts' weakness. Early in December it was decided that the long hours of darkness and prevailing bad weather were a sufficient shield to the convoys after passing Bear Island, and that they should therefore disperse in those longitudes and proceed to their destinations unescorted. This reduced the strain on the Home Fleet as it enabled the escorts to fuel in Kola Inlet, instead of at Archangel, and then to return westward. The Russian convoys thus ran steadily and without loss until the end of the year, but after Q.P. 4 had been caught in the ice in the White Sea all convoys were diverted to Kola Inlet. The German endeavours to capture Murmansk had by this time been defeated, in no small measure because of their failure adequately to protect their coastal shipping on the route around North Cape to Kirkenes and Petsamo. As Hitler noted on the 22nd of September, 'enemy interference with our shipping lanes along the coast of the Arctic Ocean had decreased even more the prospect [of capturing Murmansk] this year'. But he decided that the nickel-producing area was so important that the campaign in the north must be continued; which meant that the attempt to control the sea routes off the Arctic coast must go on. Though the struggle in the Arctic Ocean had hardly yet begun, the importance of the enemy's failure to deprive the Russians of their ice-free port and so strangle the northern supply route is now clear.

Before taking leave of Admiral Tovey's command it may be useful to summarise the state of affairs in home waters at the end of 1941. In Norway in 1940 the German Navy suffered losses and damage, especially of destroyers, which crippled it not only during the crisis of the following summer but for many months thereafter. Then it had managed to re-enter on the scene in force, to make the successful Atlantic sorties of February and March, 1941, and had planned even more powerful forays for the early summer. Those hopes, however, were dashed by the damage inflicted on the Brest squadron by the Royal Air Force and by the sinking of the *Bismarck*. The attempt was next renewed on a smaller scale, but led only to the *Lützow* creeping back to her base much damaged. Clearly, therefore, the outlook had changed greatly in the Home Fleet's favour since the early months of the year.

Many factors had contributed to this important result. The air and sea watch on the northern passages had been much improved and was now reinforced by the Americans' presence in Iceland; the Admiralty's Intelligence Centre, fed by the Photographic Reconnaissance Unit and the visual reconnaissance patrols of Coastal Command, by study of the enemy's wireless traffic and by reports from many other sources, was now working with a speed and accuracy far removed from the uncertainties and failures of 1940. It was unlikely that any enemy warship could now, as a year earlier, reach our northern patrols before being reported, or even pass to and from the Atlantic undetected. But the *Tirpitz* was still a source of anxiety and compelled us to retain strong forces at Scapa; while the Brest squadron, though damaged, might manage to effect repairs and make further mischief at any time. And the vulnerability of the long, outflanked route to North Russia was ever-present in the minds of the Admiralty and the Commander-in-Chief. Though much had been accomplished, there was, therefore, no justification for relaxing our watchfulness.

It is an old lesson of maritime war that until an enemy ship is totally destroyed it will continue to have at least a deterrent effect on our strategy, and that one ship sunk is worth a good many damaged. Both the enemy battle cruisers, for example, had been torpedoed in the Norwegian campaign of 1940, yet re-emerged in the Atlantic early in 1941. They were damaged again while in French ports and yet, at the end of the year, they were still exerting a considerable influence on our naval dispositions and on the allocation of our air effort. Nor had the end of their story by any means yet been reached. Speculation on what might have occurred if events had taken a different course is not a function of history, but it is interesting to reflect on how great a relief would have been achieved if the *Scharnhorst* and *Gneisenau* had been sunk in any of the numerous engagements described in this volume instead of being merely damaged. That the Admiralty would then have been able to build-up the Eastern Fleet earlier and with more powerful forces is certainly one possibility.

'Convoy to Russia.' By Charles Pears.

(National Maritime Museum)

'Convoy entering Murmansk.' By Sir Norman Wilkinson.

(National Maritime Museum)

H.M.S. *Prince of Wales* with the Prime Minister on board passing through the columns of an Atlantic convoy on 15th August 1941.

CHAPTER XXIII

COASTAL WARFARE

1st April–31st December, 1941

> . . . Where, my dear Lord, is our Invasion to come from? The time is gone; owing to the precautions of Government, it cannot happen at this moment, and I hope that we shall always be as much on the alert as our enemies. . . .
>
> *Nelson to Lord St Vincent.* 13th August 1801.

It will be remembered that in the last three weeks of March the enemy was still succeeding by bombing, by mines and by torpedo attacks in causing considerable damage to our east coast traffic. The small coasters which had to carry a large and essential tonnage from the ports serving the industrial areas of the north-east to London and the south coast were not the only ships to suffer. A proportion of the ocean-going traffic which had been shepherded through all the Atlantic perils was detached from the ocean convoys to make for Oban or Loch Ewe on the west coast of Scotland; there it joined the convoys which passed north about the British Isles (W.N. convoys), and finally combined with the normal flow of east coast shipping in the F.S. and F.N. convoys between the Firth of Forth and the Thames. These large ships, with their cargoes of food or war materials from North America or the distant parts of the Empire, could not all be discharged on the west coast; the continued need to bring some of them to the east coast ports further enhanced the importance of the coastal convoy system and presented the enemy with good opportunities to use all his varied offensive weapons.

The Admiralty's problem was, as always, not only to protect our shipping throughout every stage of its journey from port of departure to destination, but to ensure that no avoidable delays were incurred. The unceasing search for means whereby the 'turn round' of shipping could be speeded thus led to the introduction, early in April, of fast convoys from Southend to the ports on the west coast of Scotland (E.C. convoys), and to accelerating the Channel convoys' timetables. The whole complex problem of achieving the smoothest and most rapid flow of shipping in and out of our ports was not only constantly discussed between the Admiralty's Trade Division and the

Ministry of War Transport but was at this time considered at almost every meeting of the Battle of the Atlantic Committee.

Of the weapons used by the enemy to attack our coastal traffic minelaying and aircraft bombing were still the greatest menaces. The minelaying campaign will be considered first.

At the start of this period moored minefields were being laid by enemy E-boats on the south coast while his aircraft repeatedly obstructed the east coast river estuaries with mines of the influence type. But the diversion of the main strength of the Luftwaffe to the Russian campaign and the lack of an effective air arm in the German Navy soon brought about a decrease in minelaying from the air, and our losses fell proportionately. Whereas for the first half of the year monthly sinkings caused by mines of all types had averaged over ten ships and some 12,000 tons, from July to November they fell to half that number of ships and an appreciably smaller tonnage. The last month of the year was, however, the worst month, and losses from mines then rose suddenly to a total of nineteen ships of 63,853 tons. Part of this rise was caused by events in the Far East with which we are not concerned in this chapter; but much of it came about through the German Navy taking over the work from which the Luftwaffe had been diverted, and also sending its E-boats, of which about a dozen could now be kept in service, to lay groups of mines in the swept channels used by our east coast shipping. Moreover a new phase in the unceasing war between the German designers of mine-firing mechanisms and the British scientists and technicians concerned with minesweeping devices opened in December, with the use by the enemy of a mine which was 'cocked' by a passing ship's magnetic influence and then fired by the ship's acoustic effects. This new mine could, in fact, be swept by the equipment already supplied to many of our minesweepers, but it had the not unimportant effect of making the 'degaussing' of our ships much less effective.

It will be appropriate now to survey the growth and development of our own minesweeping forces. Although the demand for minesweeping was, when this phase began, still increasing, the plans made by the Admiralty in the early days of war to fill the many deficiencies in minesweepers were now bearing fruit, and the new demands could therefore generally be met as they arose. Fast minesweepers, primarily designed to work with the fleet, were now building in Canada, Australia and India; minesweeping trawlers in Canada, Australia, New Zealand and Portugal; motor minesweepers in small yards all over the Empire, while in the United States work had started on the new wooden all-purpose minesweepers known as Yard Minesweepers (Y.M.S.). In the second year of the war (September 1940 to September 1941) our minesweeping forces increased from 698 to 971 ships and over 42 per cent of the new total was fitted to deal with mines of the influence type. Though the entry of Japan into the conflict lost us forty-nine ships building in the Far East, this did not materially affect the problem, as a steady stream of minesweepers was now coming forward from other sources.

During the whole of 1941 the minesweepers of the Nore Command swept no less than 1,285 ground mines—magnetics, acoustics and the combination of the two types already mentioned—and no less than 725 of these were dealt with by the little ships stationed in the Humber. On Christmas Eve the trawler *Rolls Royce* achieved the sweeping of her hundredth mine—'the first minesweeping trawler in history', said the Flag Officer, Humber, 'to score a century'. Her remarkable achievement epitomises the unceasing toil of the whole minesweeping service to keep the coastal channels clear. Losses among them were, as was to be expected, heavy, for no ship can seek out such hidden dangers without constantly imperilling herself. No less than sixty-nine vessels of the Nore Command were sunk by one or other cause in 1941, but over 36 million tons of shipping passed in and out of the Thames during the year for the loss of less than one-half per cent of that figure. Nearly all of it had been in convoy, and minesweeping was now synchronised with the convoy movements. Such figures show how successful was the Nore Command, where Admiral Sir G. H. D'Oyly Lyon had now relieved Admiral Drax as Commander-in-Chief, in carrying out the heavy responsibilities laid upon it.

If we turn now to the enemy's air assault, in May and June many bombing attacks were made on our coastal convoys and considerable losses suffered. The enemy was able to strike as he chose along the whole length of the route, wherever he might deem our defences weakest. In May the bombers sank, in all, sixty-five ships of 146,302 tons, and a substantial proportion of the losses occurred on the coastal routes. In June many attacks took place off north-east Scotland, between Cape Wrath and the Firth of Forth, and our coastal convoys were attacked no less than thirty-eight times. But losses fell to twenty-five ships of 61,414 tons. In the next month many night attacks took place, and these presented particularly difficult problems to the defence. But the enemy's bombing, like his air minelaying, now decreased substantially, and losses fell correspondingly until the end of the year. Hitler had, however, ordered that the offensive against our merchant shipping must continue in spite of the new land campaign on which he had embarked, and our coastal convoys were therefore by no means exempt from attack between August and the end of the year. Though the steady and unremitting assault of the previous months now became more sporadic, our defensive measures could not in any way be relaxed. The co-ordination of fighter protection for the coastal convoys had now improved and the number of sorties flown for that purpose increased steeply in April, May and June.[1] But fighter defence could still only be provided by day, and when the enemy switched to night attacks the whole onus rested on the escort vessels and on the crews of the merchant ships themselves. Though the shortage of anti-aircraft escorts remained serious—many such ships had to be sent to the Mediterranean at this time—the supply of new guns, balloons and protective devices was improving and priority for fitting them was given to ships sailing along the east coast. The combined effect of all these measures was to make a low approach to bomb-release position—so essential to success in attacks on shipping—increasingly hazardous to the enemy.

It thus happened that, although actions with enemy aircraft continued to be a regular occurrence for our coastal convoys, the losses suffered in the last six months of the year showed a generally favourable trend. Between January and May the average monthly rate of sinkings by aircraft had been fifty-two ships of about 150,000 tons. From June to December it decreased to fifteen ships of some 38,000 tons. Of all the factors which helped to bring this about there is no doubt that the Russian campaign was the greatest.

The enemy's employment of E-boats for minelaying has already been mentioned, but they continued also, on occasions, to use their torpedoes as well. Hence the need for the light craft of our Coastal Forces to escort convoys, to patrol the channels and to strike hard whenever these elusive targets could be located remained important. E-boats sank fourteen ships of 31,215 tons during the present phase, and although this was far smaller than the losses caused by either mines or bombing they continued to cause trouble on the east coast routes. Fortunately the same period saw a steady increase in the strength of our Coastal Forces, and also a long-awaited improvement in the type of boat available and in our boats' armaments. The Fairmile motor launches (M.L.s) were now plentiful.[2] Although they were too slow and too lightly armed to catch and sink E-boats they were valuable for local and short-sea escort work and to patrol the approach routes believed to be used by the enemy. They were also used offensively to lay mines in the enemy's shipping channels along the Dutch coast. But to deal with the E-boat the faster and more heavily armed motor gun-boat (M.G.B.) was far better than the motor launch. M.G.B.s were now entering service in some numbers and were being organised into flotillas on the east coast. On the 19th of November two of the 6th M.G.B. Flotilla led by Lieutenant-Commander R. P. Hichens, whose prowess at this type of warfare has already been mentioned, had a running fight with E-boats which had

---

[1] See p. 332 (Table 9).
[2] See p. 23.

MARITIME HAZARDS

been sent out to attack an east coast convoy.[1] Two of the Germans collided and were attacked while in tow by their consorts. One of them got safely back to Holland but the other was abandoned; she was boarded by our M.G.B.s, but sank later. Though German records reveal that their E-boat commanders chiefly feared our destroyer or aircraft convoy escorts, the work of the M.G.B. flotillas certainly contributed to the gradual gain of ascendancy over the E-boats.

Little mention has been made in this volume of shipping losses other than those caused by the enemy. But it will easily be understood that in time of war, when ships are darkened and steam without showing the normal lights, when navigation marks are either extinguished or only shown for brief and essential intervals and when large numbers of ships are often in close company, maritime risks are greatly enhanced. In fact such risks produced a steady toll of ships damaged or even lost from causes often connected with the war but not directly attributable to the enemy. In 1941 no less than 268 ships totalling 418,164 tons were sunk or destroyed by causes other than the U-boat, the mine, enemy aircraft and E-boats or surface raiders. It would be outside the scope of this story to give any detailed account of how and why such heavy losses occurred, but one example of the risks introduced by war-time measures will be mentioned. On the 6th of August the southbound convoy F.S. 69 was steaming in two columns down the Norfolk coast in very heavy weather. A change of course by the leading ship of one column was missed by those following and no less than six ships of that column and one of the escorting trawlers ran on to the Haisborough Sands.[2] At great peril to themselves, for the wrecks were disintegrating rapidly and big seas were sweeping over them and breaking on the sands, the other ships present and the lifeboats rescued all but thirty-seven of the 171 men comprising the crews of the stranded ships. The seamanship and gallantry of the two Cromer lifeboats, and the name of Coxswain H. G. Blogg, G.C., should be remembered as examples of the constant devotion of a service whose efforts saved many hundreds of lives and did much to minimise the risks our seamen accepted throughout the war.

Since we shall now for a time take leave of the story of the defence of our coastal shipping, it will be convenient to summarise the situation as it was at the end of 1941. Though there was no cause for belief that this part of the struggle at sea had been won, there were none the less solid grounds for satisfaction over the results accomplished

---

[1] See p. 330.
[2] See Map 13 (*facing p. 127*).

in the preceding two years and more. The extremely serious problems posed by the enemy's initial use of the magnetic mine had not only been overcome but had been followed by the successive and rapid defeat of each of his new under-water devices. Though he might have more surprises in store it seemed unlikely that the defence would again be caught napping. As to air attacks, we had progressed far since the days when Coastal Command had no suitable aircraft to protect the Coastal traffic and Fighter Command could only provide occasional cover within a few miles of the coast, when the shortage of weapons was such that ships were given fireworks instead of guns, and when the enemy's bombers were able to sweep our shipping lanes almost unhindered. Though much distance still had to be travelled along the road towards achieving a fully integrated system of off-shore defence by all arms, there was no doubt that the escort vessels and the merchantmen now sailed with something approaching confidence both in the protection which they could afford themselves and in that which others would, in need, provide for them. It was clear that we could build the right ships to deal with the E-boats and that our country had, in the R.N.V.R., plenty of young men well suited to that type of warfare. The defeat of the E-boat could only be a matter of time.

Yet, looking back from the present day to the period of the war with which this chapter deals, we are conscious that, even when full account is taken of all the favourable trends mentioned above, a big, unanswerable question still hangs in the mind. If Hitler, instead of attacking Russia, had concentrated the full weight of his air power against our commercial ports, our docks and dockyards, our unloading and storage facilities, our coastal shipping and river estuaries, and had he kept the might of the Luftwaffe so directed for months on end if need were, could this country have survived?

We will now turn from the defence of our own coastal shipping to the assault on the enemy's. By the middle of 1941 the severe restrictions on attacking merchant ships which the Government had imposed in the early days of the war had virtually all been removed, and our aircraft were free to attack such ships at sight in the North Sea and the Bay of Biscay.[1] Up to the start of the present phase the air offensive against the enemy's coastal shipping had produced small results. It had, in fact, been little more than a nuisance to him. Nor did the first six months of 1941 bring better results, since only fourteen ships of 25,587 tons were sunk in that period. The chief causes of the slow development of what was now recognised to be an import-

---

[1] See pp. 337, 338.

ant offensive campaign were the lack of a suitable striking force in Coastal Command, whose Beaufort torpedo-bomber had been much delayed; the concentration of Bomber Command on the offensive against Germany and, at times, against maritime targets such as the enemy's Brest squadron; the priority given to the Battle of the Atlantic; and the lack of tactical training in attacking shipping from the air. But by June 1941 the offensive was becoming better planned and co-ordinated, more and more suitable aircraft were ready to take part, and the low-level attacks developed by Bomber Command were producing better results, though at a heavy cost in aircraft losses. The real start of the offensive can be dated to this time.

Substantial claims to have sunk or damaged enemy shipping had for some months been made by the aircrews employed on this work, but it gradually became clear that to make correct estimates was extremely difficult and that the claims bore little relation to the true results obtained. Such a state of affairs is dangerous, for it may mislead those responsible for the strategic direction of the war, and so cause plans to be prepared on false premises. In July, therefore, the Air Ministry set up an Anti-Shipping Operations Assessment Committee analogous to the Admiralty's U-boat Attack Assessment Committee, which had, since the start of the war, been studying and pronouncing on all attacks on U-boats.[1] The Air Ministry Committee at once scaled down drastically, by more than a half, the claims made for the first months of the offensive; but post-war analysis has revealed that even the reduced figure was still far too high.

The division of responsibility for anti-shipping operations in various waters was not arrived at without much discussion between the three Royal Air Force Commands concerned; but in July it was agreed that Fighter Command, whose Hurricane bombers were soon to start work, would apply the air blockade of the Channel route, that No. 2 Group of Bomber Command (Blenheims) would strike against coastal shipping sailing between Wilhelmshaven and Cherbourg; No. 16 Group of Coastal Command would be responsible for the southern part of the North Sea and the Norwegian coast, and No. 18 Group for the northern part of the same area. The Bay of Biscay fell naturally to Coastal Command's No. 19 Group.

To compare the relative importance of the enemy traffic in the different areas, in the Bay of Biscay there was, at this time, little commercial traffic except for a flow of iron ore ships, mostly of small tonnage, between Bilbao and Bayonne and some blockade-running from Portuguese ports; in the Channel the traffic was irregular and entirely composed of military shipping; but from the northern Norwegian ports southward to Germany and Holland commercial traffic,

---

[1] See p. 23.

especially in iron ore, was of great importance; and the ships which supplied the German armies in the far north used the same routes. It was, therefore, off the Norwegian coast that the most plentiful and valuable targets were to be found. It will be convenient to consider the course of events in each area in turn.

No. 19 Group's effort was, when this phase opened, still chiefly concentrated on watching the enemy's Brest squadron, and it was not until July that it could turn its attention to the attack on enemy shipping, including U-boats making for their French bases and blockade-runners trying to reach western France from the outer oceans. In August the Group's sorties were extended, for the first time, as far south as the Spanish coast but, apart from sighting a ship which was later proved to be the *Komet* (Raider B) approaching Cherbourg homeward-bound, no success was achieved until December. On the 23rd of that month a successful blow was struck. A Sunderland of No. 10 Squadron (Royal Australian Air Force) and a Beaufort of No. 22 Squadron sighted a large tanker outward-bound. She was first of all damaged by the flying-boat's depth charges, then pursued by a destroyer and fresh air striking forces and finally, in spite of air and U-boat escort, torpedoed and sunk by a Beaufort off the north coast of Spain. She proved to be the ex-Norwegian ship *Ole Jacob* which had been captured in the Indian Ocean in November 1940 by the *Atlantis* and had since, in enemy hands, had an adventurous career.[1]

In the English Channel we had not, at the start of this period, yet found means to stop a substantial tonnage of military shipping and a number of destroyers and smaller warships passing through under cover of the enemy's air power and coastal guns. Moreover his minesweepers had been working in these narrow seas with considerable freedom. From April to the middle of June no less than twenty-nine merchant ships over 1,000 tons and eleven destroyers were known to have made the passage. This could not be tolerated and plans for a new offensive were therefore framed. But the Blenheims and Beauforts allocated to the duty, though they made many attacks in July, achieved no successes; and the Blenheims suffered heavy losses. Fighter Command took over the responsibility in that month, but the Hurricane bombers, from which better results were expected, were not yet ready. The daylight attacks in the Channel, though they sank no ships at this time, did force the enemy to move his traffic by night, and in September this became his normal practice. The change brought a long-awaited chance to the motor torpedo-boats stationed at Dover and, on the 8th, they made a successful attack on a convoy and sank one large ship and one escort vessel. On the 8th of October

---

[2] See p. 282.

the long-awaited 'Hurribombers' of No. 607 Squadron took over the air operations and, in December, No. 217 Squadron, which had been specially trained in the interception of shipping by control from ground stations equipped with Radar, joined in the offensive. But still success eluded the air strikes.

By the end of the year the enemy's daylight traffic had practically ceased, but post-war information makes it clear that this was not because of the losses inflicted. In fact the enemy had found that by making short coastwise passages at night he could achieve all that he needed. Admiral Ramsay's contemporary statement that 'the main factor in regaining control in the Straits of Dover has been the action of the Royal Air Force' is not borne out by what we now know, and, indeed, that such control had not been regained—especially by night or in low visibility—was very soon to be demonstrated.

The sighting of the returning raider *Komet* in the Bay of Biscay on the 23rd of November has been mentioned. She was met by escorting U-boats and reached Cherbourg on the 26th. Two days later, in very bad weather, she was reported off Cap Gris Nez under strong escort. The Dover Coastal Forces were sent out and fought a fierce action with the escort off Boulogne and Dunkirk on the night of the 27th–28th. But the raider escaped unharmed. Then air attacks started and were continued at intervals during the next two days as she progressed eastwards sheltered by low visibility. A Beaufort scored a hit with a bomb on the afternoon of the 29th, but it did not explode. The raider reached Hamburg the next day and so passes out of our story for nearly a year. While attention was concentrated on the *Komet* our intelligence indicated that another raider—actually the *Thor* (Raider E)—was about to attempt the westward passage of the Channel before starting her second cruise.[1] She actually left Kiel on the 30th and thus enjoyed the advantage of the same bad weather which had shielded the eastbound *Komet*. Air strikes failed to find her off the Dutch coast, and between the 7th and 16th of December she crept down-Channel, generally moving by night. The weather continued to favour the raider, and although searches and patrols were shifted to the south-west on succeeding days she finally reached the Gironde safely on the 17th and there made final preparations for her second cruise. The planning and execution of these two enemy movements had indeed been skilful. To the Admiralty and to the naval and air commands concerned it was made clear that, if the enemy chose his opportunity carefully, it would be extremely difficult to prevent the passage of the Straits by reasonably fast ships under powerful escort. The significance of this in relation to the Brest squadron was not lost on the Admiralty.

---

[1] See p. 384 for the return of the *Thor* from her first cruise.

To continue the account of the air offensive against shipping, in Bomber Command's sector extending from Wilhelmshaven to Cherbourg a big effort was made from July to September by daylight strikes against the important route between Emden and Rotterdam. The Blenheims bore the chief brunt and made many low-level attacks. September was their best month, when six small ships (5,726 tons) were sunk. But the losses suffered by No. 2 Group could not be sustained and in November the Blenheims were withdrawn. While these not very fruitful day operations were in progress, night patrols were carried out against E-boats working from Dutch bases to molest our east coast convoys, and vigorous night attacks were made on enemy shipping off the Dutch coast. But they accomplished little. In consequence of the heavy losses suffered by Bomber Command's Blenheims, No. 16 Group of Coastal Command resumed responsibility for anti-shipping work, by day and night, in these waters at the end of November. On the 9th of December its aircraft made repeated attacks on a convoy off the Dutch coast and sank an important ship of nearly 9,000 tons, the *Madrid*.

The Home Fleet's attempts to disrupt the coastal traffic by which the enemy was supplying his land forces in the far north have already been described, and it will be remembered that carrier-borne aircraft, light surface forces and submarines were all used and that they helped to defeat the German attempt to capture Murmansk.[1] The carrier aircraft also several times swept the coastal shipping routes further south. By the end of June Coastal Command's No. 18 Group, which now comprised two Hudson squadrons, two of Blenheim bombers, one of Beaufort torpedo-bombers and one of Blenheim fighters, was also able to devote more attention to the traffic off the Norwegian coast. Many attacks were made but the successes were only moderate and the losses suffered were heavy, for the enemy's fighter defences were well organised and effective. In September our policy was reconsidered but, apart from reorganising the patrols sent out to locate shipping, no changes were made and low-level bombing attacks were continued in the last three months of the year.

The actual results achieved during this phase of the air offensive against enemy shipping are best presented in tabular form (Table 15).

It is interesting to compare this table with that which covered the preceding twelve months.[2] Such a comparison reveals not only the growth of the air offensive against shipping but the substantially greater results achieved during the second phase, though at a heavy cost in aircraft losses. It is also instructive to compare the losses inflicted on the enemy with those suffered by ourselves from his air

---

[1] See pp. 486, 489 and 493.
[2] See pp. 339–340 (Table 11).

Table 15. The Air Offensive against Enemy Shipping, April–December 1941

I. Attacks at Sea by R.A.F. Aircraft

Month	Aircraft sorties against shipping	Number of ships sunk and tonnage	Number of ships damaged and tonnage	Aircraft losses	Remarks
1941 April	1,116	Nil	4— 42,005A	41	A. Includes *Gneisenau* (32,000) damaged by Coastal Command
May	897	6— 4,846	4— 4,351	16	
June	705	3— 6,931	1— 10,000C	31	C. *Lützow* damaged by Coastal Command
July	660	7— 5,421	1— 3,845	27	
August	619	4— 1,443	4— 5,922	27	
September	483	9—11,195	3— 10,515	16	
October*	668	8— 7,730	4— 9,082	26	
November†	484	7— 4,053	5— 10,085	11	
December	547	6—23,733	1— 287	20	
Totals	6,179	50—65,352	27—96,092	215	

* Fighter Command anti-shipping operations in the English Channel using Hurricane bombers started in October 1941.

† Bomber Command's No. 2 Group (Blenheims) was withdrawn from anti-shipping operations in November 1941.

II. Attacks by Naval Aircraft

(The number of sorties made and the aircraft losses suffered are not known)

Month	Number of ships sunk and tonnage	Number of ships damaged and tonnage	Remarks
1941 April	1—3,703	Nil	
May	1— 200	2—42,445B	B. Includes *Bismarck* (42,345 tons)
June	Nil	Nil	
July	1— 74	1— 1,460	
August	Nil	Nil	
September	3—4,400	1— 1,500	
October	Nil	3— 1,804	
November	Nil	5— 9,669	
December	Nil	2— 5,583	
Total	6—8,377	14—62,461	

attacks on our own coastal shipping during this and also the preceding phase.[1] It will be seen that the present phase saw a great decline in the enemy's offensive, the principal cause of which was the transfer

---

[1] See p. 332 (Table 9).

of his bombers to the Russian front, and that our own offensive had overtaken that of the enemy by the last month of the year. But even if due allowance is made for the fact that we were bound to present the Luftwaffe with a larger number of merchant ship targets than the Royal Air Force could find in enemy-controlled waters, and also for the greater number of sorties made by the Luftwaffe, the amount by which our own shipping losses still exceeded those inflicted on the enemy in this type of warfare is to be remarked.

Table 16. German Air Attacks on Shipping and Losses within 40 miles of the coast or of an R.A.F. Airfield, April–December 1941

Month	Estimated German air force sorties against shipping Day	Estimated German air force sorties against shipping Night	No. of merchant ships sunk Day	No. of merchant ships sunk Night	No. of merchant ships sunk but not known whether day or night	No. of fishing vessels sunk day and night	No. of British naval vessels sunk day and night	British fighter sorties in defence of shipping Day	British fighter sorties in defence of shipping Night
1941									
April.	1,706	590	4	10	1	3	6	7,876	—
May .	1,223	570	1	9	—	4	7	8,287	—
June .	789	435	2	14	—	2	7	7,331	—
July .	495	425	—	5	1	4	2	6,475	2,794
Aug. .	380	450	—	2	—	1	1	5,685	2,483
Sept. .	390	500	2	5	—	—	—	4,416	1,555
Oct. .	280	320	1	5	—	—	—	4,072	684
Nov. .	334	216	—	5	—	3	1	3,952	614
Dec. .	244	230	—	1	—	1	2	3,591	537
Totals	5,841	3,736	10	56	2	18	26	51,685	8,667

Thus in spite of the big effort made during these early months of the air offensive against enemy shipping, the successes achieved were only moderate. This result, combined with the heavy aircraft losses suffered, makes the picture drawn in this chapter somewhat sombre. Among the reasons why this was so there stands, firstly, the fact that attacks on shipping had not been included in the duties required of Coastal Command before the war.[1] Hence aircraft and their weapons were not designed to fulfil such a purpose, nor were crews trained in its execution. Then there was the reluctance of the British Government to permit warfare of this nature, even after the enemy's methods had abundantly justified reprisals. This again deferred the making of the necessary preparations for the offensive. Partly in consequence of

---

[1] See p. 35.

these influences the best weapon for attack against ships, the torpedo, was for a long time, and contrary to well-founded naval opinion, given second place to the bomb. The result was that when, in mid-1941, the offensive opened in earnest there was an acute shortage of torpedoes, and bombs had to be used against all except the most important targets. Another factor was that at the outbreak of war the belief had prevailed that a good percentage of hits would be obtained on ship targets in medium- or even high-level bombing attacks. Disillusion came quickly, but the mistake resulted in neglect of the dive-bomber and in our fighting the first two years of the war with no aircraft of that type except for a handful of naval Skuas. The change from medium- to low-level attacks was slow and, even when accepted, did not produce results comparable to those regularly obtained by German dive- and low-level bombers. There was also the persistent denial of a properly equipped striking force to Coastal Command and the claim of Bomber Command to be responsible for all bombing operations, which brought about a period of divided responsibility for attacks on shipping. Such were the main causes of the slow success of the air offensive against shipping. The men who flew the hundreds of sorties against ship targets were required to make do with aircraft of unsuitable types, which were ill-defended and ill-equipped. It is their unflinching acceptance of the new duty required of them, in full knowledge of the deficiencies from which their aircraft and weapons suffered, which is the brightest feature in the scene here depicted.

We will now turn to the offensive minelaying campaign in enemy-controlled waters. During the first three months of the year the lack of long-range bombers in Coastal Command and the preoccupation of Bomber Command with land targets in Germany had left the more distant, and more fruitful, waters practically free from air minelaying.[1] The Admiralty, which was responsible for deciding where mines should be laid and what types should be used, gave its requirements to Coastal Command, whose function it was to execute the work. As Coastal Command possessed no long-range minelaying aircraft of its own it could only meet the Admiralty's requirements, if they lay outside the range of its own aircraft, by asking Bomber Command to do the job. And since, by the decision taken in March, Bomber Command's minelaying was regarded as incidental to the training of its aircrews and secondary to the bombing of Germany, there could be no assurance that the distant lays planned by the Admiralty would be carried out. This difficulty, one which was in-

---

[1] See pp. 336–337 (Table 10).

herent in the organisation of our minelaying offensive, led to a division of responsibility between Coastal and Bomber Commands by areas. On the 1st of September it was decided that Coastal Command's sphere lay between Terschelling and St Nazaire, while that of Bomber Command would include all waters to the east and south of those places.[1] Though this decision, analogous to the division of anti-shipping operations to which reference was made earlier, did not solve all difficulties, it did release Coastal Command from the somewhat unfair position of being responsible for all operations but unable itself to carry out the more distant ones. As Bomber Command now devoted a rising effort to minelaying, the partition by areas was, on the whole, successful.

The middle of the year also saw an interesting change of minelaying technique. Up to that time the policy had been to strain the enemy's minesweeping forces, which we knew to be inadequate, by continually laying fresh fields while realising that they would be sparsely sown. The policy had, in fact, been highly successful. For a small effort and at a low cost in aircraft casualties considerable loss had been inflicted on the enemy. Now, however, that the enemy was known to be better supplied with sweepers and to be using mine destructor ships comparable to our own ships like the *Borde*, a change of policy was indicated.[2] Instead of constantly laying new fields it was decided to vary the composition of existing minefields by laying different types of mine, and mines with various delay devices or different anti-sweeping qualities. Thus the minelaying campaign moved one step further in the battle of wits between designers of mines and designers of counter-measures. Several new devices, embarrassing to the enemy, were first used at this time.

As regards operations, Coastal Command was, during this phase, almost exclusively concerned with mining the approaches to Brest, to hamper the movements of the enemy's squadron, and the waters off Lorient and St Nazaire which were the most important U-boat bases on the Biscay coast. In September one of its squadrons was detached to the Mediterranean, and many of the remaining aircraft had to be diverted to prepare for the expected sortie by the German battle cruisers from Brest. In consequence the Command's minelaying effort declined steadily and reached vanishing point in December. Bomber Command, however, not only helped in the mining of the Biscay ports but reached out to the western Baltic and Kattegat. Its aircraft laid 528 mines during the last six months of the year, and by far the best results were obtained in the more distant waters. The great majority of the enemy's mine casualties must therefore be attri-

---

[1] See Maps 5 (*facing p. 71*) and 22 (*facing p. 233*).
[2] See p. 101.

buted to Bomber Command's work. The results achieved during this phase are shown in the table below.

Table 17. The R.A.F.'s Air Minelaying Campaign, April-December 1941

Month	No. of sorties	Mines laid	No. of enemy vessels sunk and tonnage	No. of enemy vessels damaged and tonnage	Aircraft losses
1941					
April	209	174	2— 2,100	3— 5,982	11
May	230	174	1— 5,088	Nil	3
June	144	125	1— 60	Nil	5
July	238	193	7— 9,705	1— 1,432	6
Aug.	134	97	5— 715	Nil	7
Sept.	150	126	6— 1,254	2— 2,299	6
Oct.	92	73	5— 1,945	Nil	2
Nov.	153	122	8—12,213	Nil	11
Dec.	76	66	8— 4,511	3— 7,894	4
Totals	1,426	1,150	43—37,591	9—17,607	55

It is instructive to compare this table with that reproduced earlier to show the direct attacks made on shipping at sea. Though the latter inflicted, in this phase, the heavier losses on the enemy the difference is not very great, especially if the large warships which were damaged are excluded; and the number of sorties made in direct attacks and our aircraft losses both greatly exceed the totals of the minelaying offensive.[1] When the same figures are tabulated to cover the whole period of the two offensives up to the end of 1941, as is done in the table overleaf, and account is also taken of the great minesweeping effort which our minelaying imposed on the enemy, the superior return obtained from minelaying becomes more marked.

Minelaying by aircraft, submarines or coastal force craft and the bombing attacks on shipping were by no means the only measures employed at this time to disrupt the flow of the enemy's coastal traffic. The knowledge, experience and courage of our allies was frequently put to good use in the same cause. Though each operation was, taken by itself, a small affair, even pin-pricks, if applied often enough, become an open wound. One example will show what favourable results could, in this way, be obtained for a small effort. The Norwegian destroyer *Draug* left Scapa on the 1st of October with M.T.B. 56 (Lieutenant P. Danielsen, R.N.N.) in tow. The torpedo boat slipped her tow when thirty miles from the coast and quietly entered the Inner Leads south of Bergen.[2] Soon there came along a

---

[1] See p. 507 (Table 15, I).

[2] See Map 5 (*facing p. 71*).

Table 18. *Comparative results obtained by the Royal Air Force from Minelaying and from Direct Attack on Shipping at Sea, April 1940–December 1941*

3-month period	Air minelaying				Direct air attack at sea			
	Aircraft sorties	Enemy vessels sunk and tonnage	Enemy vessels damaged and tonnage	Aircraft losses	Aircraft sorties	Enemy vessels sunk and tonnage	Enemy vessels damaged and tonnage	Aircraft losses
April–June 1940	584	32— 36,927	2— 4,114	15	2,199	4— 8,720	2— 3,232	53
July–Sept. 1940	611	40— 35,735	5— 7,611	9	1,807	2— 1,655	8— 26,254	31
Oct.–Dec. 1940	312	14— 10,321	3— 5,345	7	1,034	3— 3,156	4— 18,176	37
Jan.–Mar. 1941	293	13— 16,356	3— 2,369	8	1,134	3— 9,907	2— 1,680	37
April–June 1941	583	4— 7,248	3— 5,982	19	2,718	9— 11,777	9— 56,356	88
July–Sept. 1941	522	18— 11,674	3— 3,731	19	1,762	20— 18,059	8— 20,282	70
Oct.–Dec. 1941	321	21— 18,669	3— 7,894	17	1,672	21— 35,516	10— 19,454	57
Totals	3,226	142—136,930	22— 37,046	94	12,326	62— 88,790	43—145,434	373

THE VAAGSO RAID

fully-laden escorted tanker, northward bound. Lieutenant Danielsen sank the tanker and also one of her escorts. He then withdrew at high speed to pick up the parent destroyer and both reached home waters safely without suffering a casualty. The irritation which such a success would cause to the enemy can easily be imagined.

The use of our maritime power suddenly to descend on widely separated parts of the enemy-held coastline with small bodies of specially-trained troops was a favourite project of the Prime Minister. The first raid in strength had been made in the previous March on the Lofoten Islands, and several small raids had been made on the French Channel coast during the summer.[1] With the steady growth of the Commandos, the provision of the special ships and craft which they required and the improvement of their training and equipment, it was natural that raids of this type should be continued and increased. Accordingly plans for a raid in some force were made during the autumn in the headquarters of the Combined Operations Command, the training of the landing parties was pressed ahead and the necessary special ships and craft assembled and prepared. The original intention was that the main assault should again take place in the Vestfiord area, but a powerful secondary operation against Vaagsö Island, just south of Stadtlandet, was planned to take place simultaneously, in order to divert attention from the more northerly assault and to accomplish certain other important objects.[2] In actual fact, for reasons to be described shortly, the Vaagsö operation became the main assault.

The force allocated to the northern attack was commanded by Rear-Admiral L. H. K. Hamilton in the cruiser *Arethusa* and consisted of eight destroyers, two Norwegian-manned corvettes and the necessary minesweepers, oilers and auxiliaries; the assault troops were carried in two converted cross-channel steamers, *Princess J. Charlotte* and *Prince Albert*. They all sailed from Scapa on the 21st and 22nd of December, but the *Princess J. Charlotte* soon had to return because of defects and this reduced the scope of the operation. A number of landings were made, however, in the approaches to Vestfiord and two coasters were captured. But on receiving intelligence of the movement of enemy air reinforcements northwards Admiral Hamilton, whose force had no fighter cover, decided to withdraw. On the 1st of January they were all back at Scapa with their prisoners. Though the Prime Minister was disappointed over the results and critical of the decision to withdraw, the Commander-in-Chief and the Admiralty fully supported Admiral Hamilton's decision to break off the raid.

While Admiral Hamilton was achieving this partial success Rear-

---
[1] See pp. 340, 341.
[2] See Map 14 (*facing p. 159*).

Admiral H. M. Burrough in the *Kenya* with four destroyers and the assault ships *Prince Charles* and *Prince Leopold* attacked Vaagsö Island. This raid, supported by skilfully executed bombing by home-based Hampdens, was entirely successful. The coastal batteries were silenced by bombardment and bombing, and the landing parties attained all their objectives with little loss to themselves, while the warships sank five merchant ships, two trawlers and a tug, totalling some 16,000 tons. The enemy's air attacks were beaten off by Coastal Command's long-range fighters, which came across from their bases in northern Scotland and the Shetlands. As one of the destroyers' seamen remarked, doubtless with memories of earlier experiences when there had been no fighter cover, 'it was nice to feel you hadn't got to be looking up all the time'. By the 28th all forces had returned to Scapa.

This success was, in Admiral Tovey's opinion, achieved by sound planning and excellent inter-service co-operation, and by the assault forces being well trained and equipped. But the operation actually had more far-reaching results than were perhaps realised at the time. It is now known that it convinced Hitler of our intention to invade Norway and that this 'intuition' became so fixed in his mind, to the exclusion of other alternatives, that it proved an important factor in the disposition of German naval and air forces, and also caused a large number of troops to be uselessly locked up in coastal defences and garrisons in that country.

To summarise the progress made in the offensive against the enemy's coastal shipping during the latter half of 1941, our various interferences off the Norwegian coast had not yet succeeded in inflicting decisive losses. The great majority of the ships which the enemy sailed in convoy on that route still arrived safely. Difficulties in supplying the German armies in the north during the winter of 1941–42 were chiefly caused by cold weather and the ice which, particularly in Oslo Fiord, obstructed the loading and sailing of his supply ships. But the traffic through the Kattegat, the Great Belt and in the western Baltic was seriously inconvenienced by our minelaying, and a great number of minesweepers was employed on the endeavour to keep the channels clear. Along the German North Sea and Dutch coasts the tempo of our offensive was rising and sailings were becoming more hazardous. In the Channel shipping only moved by night or in very bad weather. And the enemy was forced to try to defend a vast new front from North Cape to the Spanish frontier.

CHAPTER XXIV

THE AFRICAN CAMPAIGNS

1st June–31st December, 1941

> The Mediterranean is of necessity the vital point of a naval war, and you can no more change this than you can change the position of Mount Vesuvius.
> *Admiral Sir J. A. Fisher to Lord Selborne.*
> 1st December 1900.

THE last chapter which dealt with the control of the sea routes for the African campaigns ended with the fall of Crete and the return of the survivors of Admiral Cunningham's hard-driven fleet to Alexandria. Not only had the losses of ships been very severe, indeed almost crippling, but the strategic situation in the eastern Mediterranean was now changed greatly in the enemy's favour, since German bombers could range from their newly-won bases southwards to Africa in far greater strength and with dangerous freedom, while their fighters could protect their bombers over a wide zone in the same direction. Gone were the days when Admiral Cunningham could sweep the central Mediterranean to pass convoys into or out from Malta, or cover an occasional through convoy to Alexandria, hoping all the time that the Italian fleet would stand and meet him and fearing little from the Italian air force. His ships were now confined to the south-eastern corner of the sea which they had so long and successfully commanded, their main base at Alexandria was within easy range for air bombardment and the Suez Canal, on which so much depended, was exposed to heavy bombing and minelaying. While enemy bombers could work from Crete and Cyrenaica the replenishment of Malta from the east was plainly impracticable without strong fighter escorts; and the supply of Tobruk and its long-beleaguered garrison and of the Army's advanced bases on the Libyan frontier was also bound to be more difficult. Such were the immediate consequences of the defeat of the Army in Libya in April 1941 and of the fall of Greece and Crete in the following May and June. But the enemy had gained yet other advantages, for he could now use Benghazi as well as Tripoli as a main supply base for his African armies; and the routes from the Straits of Messina to Benghazi were shorter than those to the west of Sicily and thence down the African coast on which he had previously had to rely. The new traffic lane afforded better opportunities for evasive routing and passed through waters which, because of their greater depth, could less easily be mined. Our submarines, which had done such good work from Gibraltar, Malta and Alexandria in the preceding phase and on which the interruption of the enemy's supply traffic now depended to an even greater extent, were more exposed to the enemy's counter-measures, since they were forced to seek their prey at one or other end of the Benghazi route, and the enemy could concentrate his anti-submarine vessels and aircraft in those waters. On the other hand Benghazi was closer than Tripoli to the Alexandria base and, by reinforcing our submarine strength and patrolling in widely separated areas, we might compel the enemy to disperse his defences. It was also probable that valuable targets would now be found in the Aegean, through which sea the enemy was bound to try to pass supplies, and especially Roumanian oil, to Greece, Crete and Italy. A new emphasis thus came to be placed on submarine warfare, and measures to reinforce the Mediterranean flotillas were soon put in hand. As a start, the 8th Flotilla at Gibraltar was released from convoy escort duties of doubtful utility to work in the Tyrrhenian Sea, and this soon had the desired effect of drawing the enemy's defences away from the Benghazi route.[1] Other reinforcements followed, and thus began a period during which our submarines became the chief hindrance to the enemy's attempt to build up a land strength in North Africa sufficient to accomplish his intention of driving the Army of the Nile out of Egypt. But before telling the story of the struggle to control the short sea routes across the Mediterranean to Africa it is necessary to recount the measures taken to deal with two serious difficulties which arose immediately after the end of the battle for Crete—the threat to Syria and the increased danger in which Malta now stood.

By the middle of May the Cabinet had decided that action must be taken as quickly as possible, and in spite of the Army's many other pressing commitments, to prevent German infiltration into Syria. The campaign opened on the 8th of June.[2] To the Navy fell the usual duty of supporting the advance of the Army along the coast; the task was given to Vice-Admiral E. L. S. King, commanding the 15th Cruiser Squadron, with the cruisers *Phoebe*, *Ajax* and *Coventry* (anti-aircraft), the infantry landing ship *Glengyle* and eight destroyers. To begin with, adequate fighter protection was lacking because the R.A.F. had none to spare, and the naval aircraft sent to protect the ships proved no match for the French shore-based fighters. The German bombers flown from Crete to help the Vichy

---

[1] See p. 375.
[2] See W. S. Churchill. *The Second World War*, Vol. III, pp. 288–97, regarding the decision to occupy Syria.

THE SYRIAN CAMPAIGN

French air force consequently caused some trouble, as did the resistance offered by the large and fast French destroyers based on Beirut. On the 9th of June the *Janus* was disabled by two of the latter and had to be towed to Haifa and, on the 15th, the *Isis* and *Ilex* were both damaged by air attack. But the French flotilla-leader *Chevalier Paul* was sunk on the same day by naval torpedo-bombers from Cyprus; this exploit was particularly welcome because several engagements had shown that our own destroyers were neither fast enough nor heavily enough armed to catch and sink the French ships. Admiral Cunningham's strength, however, was at so low an ebb that he was reluctant to incur any avoidable loss and, on the 16th, he ordered that ships should not be used in daylight offshore operations until fighter protection could be provided. On the 21st of June Damascus was occupied and, two days later, another indecisive engagement was fought with the Vichy destroyers. This was their last attempt to intervene in the campaign. On the 25th the submarine *Parthian* sank the French submarine *Souffleur*, and offshore support of the Army by bombardments was now resumed by the surface ships, generally under fighter protection. On the 11th of July the Vichy High Commissioner accepted the Allied terms, and the campaign ended that night. Potentially dangerous developments, affecting not only the Army's whole position in the Middle East but also Iraq and beyond, were thus forestalled. The enemy made no attempt to reinforce the Vichy elements in Syria from the sea.[1]

While this brief campaign was in progress our hold on the Red Sea route was made yet firmer by the surprise seizure, on the 11th of June, of the port of Assab, in Eritrea, by a force of British and Indian troops from Aden, covered by ships of the Royal Navy and Royal Indian Navy. There were now no enemy bases or forces on the flank of the Red Sea route from which our convoys to Suez could be attacked. Thanks to the declaration which the President of the United States had made on the previous 11th of April, that the Red Sea was no longer a 'combat zone', American shipping was now allowed to sail right through to Suez. This eased the strain on our own resources, but produced the anomalous state of affairs that the American ships, which were unarmed and unconvoyed and sailed with lights burning, were very vulnerable to air attack at the end of their journeys; the British authorities naturally felt responsible for their safety and defence. Since the enemy was, for reasons already stated, now able to step up the tempo of his air raids on the Suez Canal and its terminal ports and, in July and August, frequently dropped both bombs and mines in those waters, the danger to shipping, our own as well as American, was real. Though interruptions to traffic through the

---

[1] See the forthcoming volume of this series by I. S. O. Playfair, *The Mediterranean and Middle East*, Vol. II, for a full account of the campaign in Syria.

Canal were fairly frequent the actual damage caused by the enemy's attacks, including those made on our bases at Alexandria and Haifa, was not at this time as severe as it might have been. But Admiral Cunningham took the precaution of sending the anti-aircraft cruiser *Carlisle* through to Suez in August. The most serious loss was that of the liner *Georgic* (27,751 tons) which was set on fire at Suez on the 14th of July and at first given up as a total loss.

The safety of the Red Sea routes and of the ports of discharge south of the Canal continued to be an anxiety to Admiral Cunningham though the responsibility lay with the Commander-in-Chief, East Indies. After discussion with Admiral Arbuthnot, Admiral Cunningham proposed to the Admiralty that the Red Sea should return to the Mediterranean Command and, in October, this was approved. The new arrangement had the advantage that the Army and Air Force Commanders in the Middle East would now have to deal with only one naval authority.

While these events were taking place in the eastern basin and Egyptian waters, far away to the west air reinforcements were again being ferried to Malta in yet another operation of the type now become almost traditional. The new aircraft carrier *Victorious* (Captain H. C. Bovell) had replaced the *Furious* for the final stage eastwards from Gibraltar, and the *Furious* was now used to carry the fighters from Britain to Gibraltar. On the 15th of June forty-seven Hurricanes were flown to Malta from the *Victorious* and *Ark Royal*, which were covered and escorted by the rest of Admiral Somerville's Force H. All but four of the fighters arrived safely. Ten days later the *Furious* had brought sixty-four more fighters to Gibraltar and they were flown to Malta on the 27th and 30th of June. No less than 142 aircraft were delivered safely to the island in this month, and some of them went on from there to Egypt. Although the end of air reinforcement by this means was not yet in sight, and Malta was not in fact to face its greatest trial for many months to come, its immediate problems were thus greatly eased. Moreover, the first of the enemy's offensives against Malta, which had started with the arrival there of the damaged *Illustrious* in January, ended in May, when much of the 10th German '*Fliegerkorps*' was transferred from Sicily to the Balkans.[1] A lull thus occurred, and the second big offensive did not start until December, when the Germans wished to neutralise the island in order that Rommel's army might be reinforced by sea. But the need to carry fuel, ammunition and stores to Malta by sea still continued and, for a time, submarines were used for that purpose. The minelayers *Rorqual* and *Cachalot*, which had comparatively large carrying capacity, were the first, but several other submarines also made storing trips from one or other end of the Mediterranean between

---
[1] See pp. 420–421.

this time and the end of the year. The *Cachalot*, however, was surprised on the surface and sunk by an Italian destroyer at the end of July, while engaged on what should have been her last trip to Malta before returning home to refit. It will be told shortly how the condition of the island was greatly improved by successful convoy operations from the west in July and again in September. The use of supply submarines declined thereafter, particularly from the west.

Second only to Malta as a source of anxiety and a difficult supply problem at this time was the besieged garrison of Tobruk. Though the Luftwaffe did not succeed in inflicting important damage on the survivors of Admiral Cunningham's fleet or on its bases, it did succeed in stopping the use of merchant ships to carry supplies to Tobruk. The task of replacing them fell, as was to be expected, chiefly on the hard-run destroyers, and the Australian Navy's *Stuart*, *Waterhen* and *Vendetta* now worked a regular night service thither from Alexandria. They were soon supplemented by the fast minelayers *Abdiel* and *Latona*, ships of a class for which many and varied services were found and whose employment in their designed rôle became, indeed, a rare occurrence. The *Latona* had left England on the 16th of May and arrived at Alexandria, by the Cape, on the 21st of June. But ships of no matter what class could not be expected long to survive the hazards which now beset the Tobruk route, and the sloop *Auckland* and the *Waterhen* were both lost in June. The failure of the land offensive (Operation 'Battleaxe'), launched on the 15th of May, to relieve the garrison and so to take this long-borne burden off the fleet, was a great disappointment.

It will be convenient now to carry on the story of Tobruk until, just before the end of the year, the relief was at last effected. The ships employed on the Tobruk run developed the special technique required for this work to such a pitch of efficiency that they were able to berth in complete darkness, discharge their cargoes and sail again within the hour. The usual practice was for two of Admiral Cunningham's destroyers to run in supplies every night, and for the fast minelayers to make a weekly trip to take men in and out. In August, for example, twenty-nine trips were made by destroyers and seven by the fast minelayers. It was natural that losses should be suffered by the ships which thus ran the gauntlet of the enemy's air power. The destroyer *Defender* was sunk by air attack on the 11th of July and many of the smaller ships suffered a similar fate; but the work none the less continued. To the normal problems of supplying the garrison was now added the need to withdraw the Australian brigade and to replace them with Polish and British troops. The exchange was carried out in several phases and was not finally completed until October. In all 19,568 men were taken to Tobruk and 18,865 carried back to Egypt during August, September and October.

In the autumn German U-boats arrived to help the Luftwaffe, pressure against the supply route increased and losses became more serious. The *Latona* was bombed and sunk off Bardia on the 25th of October, and the Australian sloop *Parramatta* was torpedoed by a U-boat in November. The small petrol and water carriers, which had done such excellent work and were almost irreplaceable, also suffered heavily. But the German U-boats did not get it all their own way; U.79 and U.75 were both sunk off the North African coast in December. We shall return to their activities shortly.

For all that the enemy could do, the process of building up the Tobruk garrison to play its part in the renewed offensive by the Army (Operation 'Crusader') continued. In particular tanks and artillery were carried there in 'A Lighters', later called Tank Landing Craft. When the land offensive started on the 18th of November, the reward for all this hazardous work by the Inshore Squadron was abundantly reaped; supplies for the advancing Army then poured in through Tobruk and the garrison itself played a big part in the Army's rapid advance westward.

A few figures may be quoted here to illustrate the size and scope of the Mediterranean Fleet's effort to keep the Tobruk garrison supplied. During the 242 days of the siege (12th of April to 8th of December, 1941) the following stores and men were transported:

Table 19. Stores and Men transported to and from Tobruk, April 1940-December 1941

72 tanks
92 guns
34,000 tons of stores
32,667 men replaced by 34,113 fresh troops
7,516 wounded and 7,097 prisoners withdrawn

The cost to the Navy was twenty-five ships sunk—including one fast minelayer, two destroyers and three sloops—and nine seriously damaged. Five merchant ships (11,000 tons) were sunk and four more seriously damaged, as were two hospital ships.

While preparations to resume the offensive in Libya were in train the possibility of striking elsewhere at the Axis position in the Mediterranean was being considered in London. In mid-October the Defence Committee considered launching a combined operation to capture Sicily and ordered a plan to be prepared. The draft plan expressed the intention to land at six points; thirty-five transports were to be sent from the west and fifteen from the east for the initial landings, and they were quickly to be followed by nearly a hundred more. Apart from these large requirements for troop transports the naval commitments were so vast that, to meet them, the Home Fleet would have to be stripped of all its capital ships except one, and of all its 6-inch cruisers; half the Atlantic escorts would have had to be taken away and the W.S. convoys stopped. The Naval Staff was not consulted until the planning was far advanced but, as soon as the realities of the proposal became apparent, expressed its strong opposition to any such undertaking. It appears that the Combined Operations Command had not related the requirements of the expedition to our other world-wide, inescapable commitments. The Prime Minister, however, whose eye was always seeking a possibility to strike offensive blows, was strongly in favour of the plan. He wanted to synchronise the attack on Sicily (Operation 'Whipcord') with the new desert offensive ('Crusader'), and on the 25th of October told the Commanders-in-Chief, Middle East, that 'for Whipcord it is probably a case of "Now or never" '.[1] Meanwhile the Chiefs of Staff were deliberating on the whole question and the impracticability of the undertaking became plain. Their view prevailed, and the proposal lapsed or was overtaken by other events. Another eighteen months were to pass and the whole strategic situation in Africa had to be transformed before such an undertaking became practicable.

But if 'Whipcord' was, in the autumn of 1941, an impossibility 'Crusader' achieved immediate success. Though it was, unhappily, to prove ephemeral, the Army's rapid recapture of the whole of Cyrenaica had the effect of restoring to the Mediterranean Fleet a reasonable freedom of movement in the eastern basin, since Royal Air Force fighters could now work from airfields much further to the west. The danger to Alexandria and the Suez Canal was reduced, and the enemy was forced once more to rely on the Tripoli route to supply his army.

We must now return to the western end of the Mediterranean and retrace our steps to the month of July. As no surface convoy could, for reasons already stated, be passed to Malta from the east it became essential that the attempt should be made from the west; and it was clear that great strength would be essential if a convoy was to be fought through successfully. A plan was therefore made to escort six storeships and one troop transport to Malta, and at the same time to bring out the fast auxiliary *Breconshire* and six empty merchantmen which had long been detained in the island. It was appropriately called Operation 'Substance' and the Admiralty ordered the detachment of the battleship *Nelson* and the cruisers *Edinburgh*, *Manchester* and *Arethusa* from the Home Fleet to reinforce Force H temporarily. The convoy left the Clyde on the 11th of July and reached Gibraltar eight days later. The operation started on the 21st and a mishap at

---
[1] W. S. Churchill. *The Second World War*, Vol. III, pp. 479–80, 486 and 488–89.

once occurred, when the troopship *Leinster* ran aground and had to be docked at Gibraltar. About one-fifth of the 5,000 troops embarked in the ships was thus left behind, including, by ill chance, the maintenance crews for the Royal Air Force aircraft in Malta.

Concurrently with Admiral Somerville's departure from Gibraltar Admiral Cunningham made a diversion in the eastern basin to deter the Italian fleet, which had ample, even overwhelming, strength based on Taranto, Messina and Palermo, from attacking the convoy; and eight of our submarines, by patrolling actively off the enemy bases and on his probable sortie routes, acted as an additional deterrent. The plan provided for the escort of the convoy as far as the Narrows between Sicily and Tunisia by the strengthened Force H. From that point Rear-Admiral E. N. Syfret in the *Edinburgh*, with the cruisers *Manchester* and *Arethusa*, the fast minelayer *Manxman* (serving as a cruiser) and ten destroyers, would take the convoy through to Malta. The empty merchant ships were to be sailed independently to the west during the movement.

Early on the 23rd all forces were concentrated to cover and escort the convoy through the dangerous stretch to the south of Sardinia, and the expected air attacks soon began. The *Manchester* was hit by a torpedo and so severely damaged that she had to be sent back to Gibraltar; the destroyer *Fearless* was crippled and, later, sunk by our own forces. But, thanks chiefly to the *Ark Royal's* fighters which beat off many attacks, the convoy and its escort reached the entrance to the Skerki Channel at 5 p.m. that day without having suffered further loss.

There Admiral Somerville hauled round to the westward with the heavy ships, while Admiral Syfret's cruisers and destroyers carried on towards Malta with the convoy. Air attacks continued until dusk and another destroyer, the *Firedrake*, was disabled and sent back to Gibraltar. Admiral Syfret took the bold action of steering north-eastwards for a time—directly towards Sicily—in the same way as had been done in Operation 'Excess' in the previous January.[1] Though the journey was thereby lengthened the danger from mines was reduced, and enemy aircraft sent out to make night attacks were thrown off the scent. The ruse was again successful and no mishap occurred until, after the convoy had turned south again in the early hours of the 24th and was passing Pantellaria, E-boats based on that island succeeded in torpedoing one storeship without, however, preventing her from reaching Malta. After daylight, since there was now no danger of the Italian fleet interfering, the cruisers went ahead to Malta, where they disembarked their troops and stores; the cruisers returned westward that same evening. The destroyers stayed with the convoy and they, too, all reached their destination safely on the 24th.

---

[1] See pp. 421–422.

Meanwhile the seven empty ships from Malta were running the gauntlet to the west, practically unescorted. Though not unmolested, all finally got through safely.

Admiral Somerville had steered to the west after leaving the convoy on the evening of the 23rd but, next afternoon, he altered again to the east to meet and escort Admiral Syfret's returning cruisers and destroyers. The *Ark Royal's* fighters again protected the fleet from high-level and torpedo-bombing attacks and, on the 27th of July, all ships were safely back at Gibraltar.

The complete success of the operation exceeded the most sanguine hopes. Losses were bound to be suffered on so hazardous an enterprise, but only one destroyer was actually sunk, while almost all the stores destined for Malta and all the reinforcements, except those left behind in the *Leinster,* had been safely delivered. The plan was cleverly designed and brilliantly executed. All the deceptive and diversionary measures were successful and, although the enemy certainly knew that a big movement was in train, he was kept guessing regarding our precise intentions until it was too late to intervene decisively. The incident showed that, even though supplies for Malta could not now be passed through from the east, a powerful and resolute force, skilfully directed, could still reinforce and revictual the island from the other direction. Much was owed to the skill of the veteran fighter pilots of the *Ark Royal*, much to the determination and experience of the cruiser and destroyers, but without, in Admiral Somerville's words, the 'steadfast and resolute behaviour' of the merchant ships themselves the success could not have been accomplished. Because of the mishap to the *Leinster* and the return of damaged ships to Gibraltar there were still some 1,800 troops and airmen to be carried to Malta before the job could be said to be completed. Early on the 31st of July the *Hermione, Arethusa, Manxman* and two destroyers sailed from Gibraltar with the last of the reinforcements and stores. They arrived safely on the 2nd of August, left again the same afternoon and were back at Gibraltar on the 4th. On the outward journey the *Hermione* rammed and sank the Italian U-boat *Tembien* off Tunis.

On the 26th of July, just after the arrival of the 'Substance' convoy, the Italians made a heavy attack on Malta with midget submarines, E-boats and aircraft. The defences were, however, very alert and virtually the whole attacking force was destroyed without having accomplished anything.

Because of its boldness and originality mention may be made of a minor operation carried out off the Italians' important northern bases at this time. The fertile imagination of Admiral Somerville had conceived the idea of using the fast minelayer *Manxman* to lay mines in the Gulf of Genoa, off Leghorn. She was accordingly disguised as a

French light cruiser, and left England on the 17th of August. After passing Gibraltar she hoisted the Tricolour and put her crew into French uniforms during the approach to the enemy coast, but cast off her disguise before laying her mines during the night of the 25th. She then used her high speed to get clear of the coast, redisguised herself for the return passage to Gibraltar and was back in England on the 30th. It was one of the rare occasions when a fast minelayer was used in her designed rôle.

In September air reinforcements were flown to Malta in two more of the familiar ferry operations from the *Ark Royal* and *Furious*. Forty-nine Hurricanes arrived safely, and concurrently with their flight the opportunity was taken to send a number of Blenheim bombers direct from Gibraltar to the island. The decision to build up an air striking force on the island fortress formed part of the Cabinet's plan to harass the enemy's North African supply route by every possible means. The measure of success achieved will be recounted shortly. Here it is only necessary to mention that the air element in the offensive consisted of Bomber Command Blenheims and, later, of Wellingtons sent out from England and of naval Swordfish and Albacore torpedo-bombers. Half a dozen Swordfish were flown in from the *Ark Royal* during the second phase of Operation 'Substance'. As that operation had ensured that there was a good supply of bombs and torpedoes in Malta, all types of aircraft were able to start work immediately.

Having seen how Malta was kept supplied at this critical juncture, it will be appropriate to turn to the offensive which, to a considerable extent, was waged from that island against the enemy's supply route to North Africa. Our submarines, which had recently been reinforced by a number of the new U class (630 tons), had begun to take toll of this traffic in the early summer.[1] Until the middle of the year our aircraft had not been used offensively to any great extent, because few bombers or torpedo-bombers could be spared and conditions on the island were not favourable to the long surival of a striking force stationed there. The present phase saw not only an increase in the strength of the Malta, Alexandria and Gibraltar submarine flotillas, with a corresponding rise in their activities, but also the start of a real air offensive against the enemy's supply traffic to North Africa and the stationing, once more, of surface ships at Malta for the same purpose. Thus was born a three-pronged campaign. Both sides realised that on this issue depended the ultimate fate of the armies in North Africa. Given a reasonable degree of control of those waters, the enemy could build up his forces far faster than we could by the long Cape route, and would probably drive us out of Egypt. Denied that control, the whole enemy force was caught in a trap from which there could be no escape. Though the German liaison

---
[1] See pp. 425 and 438–439.

staff in Rome realised the full implications, and did its best to make the Berlin authorities understand that to leave the struggle for control of the short sea routes to the Italians would be to court defeat in North Africa, the attention of Hitler, his advisers and of the Supreme Command was now directed eastward, to Russia, and their response to appeals from Rome was slow.

From the British angle a point of particular interest is that the submarine service came into its own during this phase. It was freed from all the early restrictions regarding attacks on merchant shipping (except in certain not very significant areas), and it was no longer required to devote its attention primarily to enemy warships. In British naval circles the submarine has generally been regarded as the weapon of the weaker naval power and, since we had usually possessed a substantial superiority in surface ship strength, the submarine service had been regarded as a subsidiary arm, which might, from time to time, achieve an important success but which was not likely to stand as the arbiter between victory and defeat. It is interesting to remark how the surface forces' weakness became the submarines' opportunity in the Mediterranean. Though their chance had been long in arriving, the young men who commanded the boats were not slow to seize it.

In June the 8th Flotilla, based on Gibraltar, had a very successful month. The *Clyde* and *Severn* and the Dutch submarines O.23 and O.24 obtained many successes off Genoa, Naples and the Sardinian coasts. At Malta there were now seven of the U class, but they found few targets between their base and Tunis, though the *Unbeaten* damaged the liner *Oceania* (19,500 tons) on the 16th. The *Triumph*, one of the Alexandria flotilla, sank the Italian U-boat *Salpa* off the Egyptian coast on the 27th. Next month the submarines' successes increased; the Admiralty sent congratulations to the three flotillas concerned, and Admiral Cunningham asked for more reinforcements, since 'each boat was worth its weight in gold' to him. Not only were both ends of the Italian supply routes to North Africa heavily attacked by the Malta and Alexandria flotillas but successful patrols were carried out in the Aegean against the enemy's traffic between Crete or Greece and the Dardanelles. The *Torbay* particularly distinguished herself in those waters and, among other successes, sank the Italian U-boat *Jantina* on the 5th. The *Union*, one of the Malta flotilla, was, however, sunk on the 20th by an Italian torpedo-boat.

In August the patrols followed the same general plan as in the preceding month. The Malta-based boats exerted a steady pressure off the Straits of Messina and the coast of Tunis. The *Unique* sank the *Esperia* (11,700 tons) from a convoy of four large liners on the 20th; on the 26th the heavy cruiser *Bolzano* was damaged by the *Triumph* and, three days later, the *Urge* attacked another convoy of large liners and damaged the *Duilio* (23,600 tons). But in the narrow and often shallow waters where these boats had to seek their targets losses were certain to be incurred, and P.32 and P.33, both newly arrived reinforcements for Malta, were lost off Tripoli during the month, probably on mines.

At the beginning of September the Malta boats were officially organised into the 10th Submarine Flotilla, under Captain G. W. G. Simpson, but operational control remained vested in the commander of the 1st Flotilla at Alexandria (Captain S. M. Raw) under the Commander-in-Chief, Mediterranean. This month marked a further increase in the successes obtained and over 65,000 tons of Axis shipping was sunk. The outstanding exploit was a combined attack by the *Upholder, Upright, Unbeaten* and *Ursula* against another of the fast Italian liner convoys. The targets were sighted early on the 18th by the *Unbeaten*, who, unable herself to attack, called up her nearest comrades by wireless. A brilliant attack by the *Upholder* (Lieutenant-Commander M. D. Wanklyn) resulted in the sinking of the liners *Neptunia* and *Oceania*, both of some 19,500 tons. The third ship of the convoy, the *Vulcania*, was also attacked but escaped damage. The boats of the 1st Flotilla also did well in September, when they patrolled off Benghazi and in the Aegean, while the *Triumph* was sent into the Adriatic. In addition to their offensive against shipping, our submarines were frequently used to land small raiding parties to destroy bridges and coastal railway lines, to land agents in enemy territory and to seek for survivors of the British services in Crete. A number of the latter were safely taken off. Though the submarines used their gun armaments to attack the small craft employed by the enemy in supplying his island garrisons and, occasionally, to finish off a damaged supply ship, the great majority of their successes was obtained in submerged attacks with the torpedo.

While the largest share of the losses suffered by the enemy on the supply route to North Africa was, during the present phase, still inflicted by our submarines, the air striking forces based on Malta were being built up and the R.A.F. bombers and naval torpedo-bombers had begun to exact a steady toll. The first six Blenheims (of No. 21 Squadron) had arrived in Malta at the end of April and immediately started, under the new Air Officer Commanding, Mediterranean (Air Vice-Marshal H. P. Lloyd), to carry out the Chief of the Air Staff's order that 'Malta's main task was to prevent Axis shipping running to Africa'.

The enemy convoys usually sailed from Naples and might be routed to the west of Sicily and through the Narrows, hugging the African shore to Tripoli, or through the Straits of Messina and thence eastward towards the Greek coast before turning south. If they took the easterly route they were more difficult to find and attack because

AIR ATTACKS ON ITALIAN CONVOYS

the few reconnaissance aircraft available at Malta could not cover the whole Ionian Sea.[1] Our tactics were based on regular air reconnaissance of all the main enemy ports, from which his probable movements were forecast; but the enemy proved clever at disguising his intentions, so that it was never easy to find his convoys or to keep in touch once they had been found. The policy was that when a convoy had been located the Blenheims would attack by day and the naval Swordfish by night, and in June and July both types scored successes against convoys passing through the Narrows. By the end of August a second Blenheim Squadron (No. 107) had arrived and Malta then had seven Marylands, thirty-two Blenheims, fifteen Wellingtons and a dozen naval Swordfish—all mainly employed in finding and attacking the enemy's African convoys. The Blenheims made many very gallant low-level attacks and, as in home waters, soon began to suffer heavy losses.[2] Though they obtained some successes it was the night torpedo attacks by the Swordfish which proved the more deadly. By the autumn the needs were plain; they were more torpedo-bombers of longer range, and radar to guide the attackers to their targets by night. Accordingly two squadrons of naval Albacores (Nos. 828 and 830) and some radar-fitted Wellingtons were sent to Malta. In September these new arrivals enabled the offensive to be increased. The enemy reacted, as was expected, by strengthening his convoy escorts. Though the Blenheims were suffering heavily it was decided that, with the approach of the new land offensive ('Crusader'), the importance of stopping the enemy's seaborne traffic was greater than ever and that their low-level attacks must go on. Our night air tactics were meanwhile being improved. After the Marylands had made a day contact with a convoy the radar-fitted Wellingtons would try to re-establish it the same night. If they were successful the torpedo-bombers would be called to the target by the radar aircraft and would attack at once, while other Wellingtons dropped flares to light the scene. Next day the Blenheims would strike at the ships which had survived the night attack. Often complete surprise was achieved and the convoys were thrown into utter confusion. Losses were again and again inflicted on ammunition ships and tankers, and the enemy's records leave no doubt of the seriousness with which he regarded them. The high proportion of torpedo hits obtained by the Swordfish and Albacores was particularly remarkable.

Besides making the many attacks briefly outlined above, the Malta-based aircraft worked in the closest co-operation with the surface ships (when they arrived) and with our submarines. Often all three arms had a share in the destruction of a convoy. The Italian

---

[1] See Map 26 (*facing p. 293*).

[2] See pp. 504 and 506.

Admiralty's statistics regarding their losses from all causes during this period are given below.

Table 20. Enemy Merchant Shipping Losses, June–September 1941

(1) Italian (includes losses outside the Mediterranean)

[Number of ships—tonnage]

Month	By surface ship	By submarine	By air attack	By mine	By other causes	Total
June	Nil	14— 30,501	3—12,278	2— 809	7—10,754	26— 54,342
July	Nil	9— 19,909	6—19,838	1— 7,970	1— 37	17— 47,854
Aug.	Nil	9— 17,252	11—35,195	2— 5,275	5— 222	27— 57,944
Sept.	Nil	11— 62,275	7—23,692	2— 498	6— 8,351	26— 94,816
Total	Nil	43—129,937	27—91,103	7—14,552	19—19,364	96—254,956

German documents reveal that, in addition to the Italian losses, the Germans themselves suffered the following shipping losses in the Mediterranean during this four-month period:—

(2) German (Mediterranean only)

Month	By surface ship	By submarine	By air attack	By mine	By other causes	Total
June to Sept.	Nil	1—1,829	3—11,294	1—2,373	Nil	5—15,496

It will be interesting to glance briefly at the view taken by the enemy of this offensive against his supply ships. In August the German authorities in Rome noted that 'losses [occurred] every other day' and that 'the situation cannot be endured'. Mussolini ordered air transport to be provided from Sicily for 15,000 men a month— a figure which was never achieved and, even had it been achieved, would have accentuated rather than solved the problem, because the corresponding heavy supplies could not be sent by air. In fact the German liaison staff in Rome noted at this time that 'air transport could never wholly replace sea transport'. In September the state of affairs had plainly worsened and was now described as 'catastrophic'. The German Staff in Italy demanded the return of the Luftwaffe in strength to Sicily. They stated that between the beginning of July and the end of September eighty-one Axis ships of 312,000 tons had been attacked in the Mediterranean and forty-four of 163,800 tons sunk, eighteen of them by air attack. In addition, 113 small ships, of unknown tonnage, were reported to have been attacked and sixty-

H.M.S. *Ark Royal* under bombing attack during Malta convoy operation, 15th–17th November, 1940. Taken from H.M.S. *Sheffield*.

Planet News L

Planet News

The sinking of H.M.S. *Ark Royal*, 14th November 1941. (See page 533.)

EVENTS IN THE PERSIAN GULF

four of them sunk. The tables above show that these contemporary figures were by no means exaggerated.

While these events were taking place inside the Mediterranean the enemy's eyes had turned towards Iran; he was preparing to create in that country a political situation which would give him control of its oilfields, and facilitate his progress towards India and the East. An influx of 'tourists' was the initial move organised from Berlin. The British Cabinet, in spite of its many anxieties and far-flung commitments, acted as rapidly and effectively as it had done in the case of the Iraq revolt of the preceding May.[1] On the 20th of August approval was given to disembark troops at the head of the Persian Gulf, and, if resistance was offered, to use force. The Iranian Navy was to be put out of action and the enemy merchant ships, which had long been sheltering in Bandur-Shahpur captured.[2] A very mixed force was sent. Under the Commander-in-Chief, East Indies (Vice-Admiral G. S. Arbuthnot), ships of the Indian and Australian Navies joined with those of the Royal Navy, and men from the Dominions and India were included in the ground forces. Five days after the order had been given from London the operation ('Countenance') started. Complete surprise was achieved and success was immediate. By the afternoon of the 25th, Abadan with its great oil refinery, the naval base at Korramshar and also Bandur-Shahpur had been captured. Of the five German and three Italian merchant ships in the latter port, one was wrecked by her crew but the rest were captured reasonably intact. Simultaneously with the combined operation in the Gulf the Army advanced from Iraq, occupied the oilfields in the north and dealt with the Persian land forces. On the 27th of August the Iranian Government resigned and, in the middle of September, the Shah abdicated. Thus did maritime power, promptly employed in decisive force, cut off the tentacle which the Berlin octopus had extended towards the oilfields and the even greater prizes beyond. And the southern flank of our Russian Allies was thereby safeguarded —a fact of which Moscow did not, perhaps, then or later appreciate the significance. With Syria now secured and Iraq and Iran in the hands of friendly governments the whole structure of Allied power in the Near and Middle East was greatly strengthened.[3]

It was natural that the success of the July convoy operation to revictual Malta should, after an interval, lead to the execution of a

---
[1] See p. 427.
[2] See Map 34 (*facing p. 426*).
[3] See the forthcoming volume of this series by I. S. O. Playfair, *The Mediterranean and Middle East*, Vol. II, for a full account of these events.

similar plan. Admiral Somerville again received substantial reinforcements from England, including the *Prince of Wales* which had been detached from the Home Fleet. He sailed for this operation ('Halberd') on the 24th of September with three battleships—the *Nelson*, in which his flag was now flying, *Rodney*, and *Prince of Wales*—the *Ark Royal*, five cruisers and eighteen destroyers. The convoy consisted of nine fifteen-knot ships, totalling some 81,000 tons, and about 2,600 troops were divided between the transports and the warships which, under Rear-Admiral H. M. Burrough in the *Kenya*, were to go through to Malta with the convoy. In essentials the plan was the same as in July. Elaborate precautions to mislead the enemy regarding our intentions were again taken, Admiral Cunningham again made a diversion in the eastern basin, while our submarines and aircraft patrolled and reconnoitred vigilantly off the enemy's bases. The first days followed a familiar pattern and, when air attacks started on the 27th, the *Ark Royal's* fighters again bore the chief brunt of the defence of the fleet and of the large convoy. The first air attacks were, however, conducted with more resolution and skill than before, and scored one success, when the *Nelson* was hit by a torpedo and had her speed considerably reduced. Later attacks generally failed to penetrate the gunfire of the powerful destroyer screen.

While the air battle was still in progress above and around the convoy, scouting aircraft reported that the Italian fleet was at sea and steering towards the convoy's course. As the *Nelson's* injury prevented her from playing the flagship's part in driving off the enemy, Admiral Somerville sent Rear-Admiral A. T. B. Curteis ahead with the other two battleships, two cruisers and a few destroyers while the *Ark Royal* prepared to launch her striking force. But the Italians soon turned for home, the torpedo-bombers failed to find them and Admiral Curteis' force was recalled. By 7 p.m. that evening, the 27th, the entrance to the Narrows was reached and Admiral Burrough went ahead with his five cruisers and nine destroyers, while the rest of the fleet turned westwards. Again the device of steering initially towards the Sicilian coast was adopted, and the enemy's records note that 'by choosing this course [the British force] avoided the minefields which had been laid to complete the barrage of the channel only a few days previously'. But, if the mines were successfully avoided, enemy aircraft were not this time wholly shaken off; night attacks followed under conditions made very difficult for the defence by the bright moon. One transport, the *Imperial Star*, was hit by a torpedo, and, after an effort had been made to tow her to Malta, her troops were taken off and she was sunk. But that was all. Early next day fighters from Malta took the convoy under their protecting shield. Admiral Burrough then went ahead with four of the cruisers and entered the

Grand Harbour at 11.30 a.m. on the 28th. The whole population of Malta appeared to be lined up in serried, cheering masses along the shore as the cruisers, with guards paraded and bands playing as though returning from a peace-time cruise, passed through the breakwater and up the stretch of sheltered water with which the Mediterranean Fleet had been so long and so intimately acquainted. Two hours later the convoy followed in. Meanwhile three empty merchant ships had left Malta and were steaming westwards practically unescorted. Their journey was not without incident, but they all reached Gibraltar safely.

Admiral Burrough's ships sailed again the same evening and took the southerly route, along the African shore, for the return journey. They were met by Admiral Curteis' force to the west of the Narrows next morning, the 29th, and they all proceeded in company towards Gibraltar, whither Admiral Somerville had already gone with the damaged *Nelson*. Though several U-boat attacks took place on the return journey, no damage was done and one Italian, the *Adua*, was sunk by the screening destroyers on the 30th.

This was the last Malta convoy of 1941 and the last of those operations to be dealt with in the present volume. It will therefore be appropriate to summarise the result of the three carried out in 1941 —Operation 'Excess' in January, 'Substance' in July and 'Halberd' in September.[1] Of the thirty-nine transports and storeships convoyed to and from Malta only one was lost. But strong forces were required to fight these convoys through and the escorting ships lost, in all, one cruiser and one destroyer sunk and one battleship, two cruisers and two destroyers damaged. The losses were, therefore, by no means disproportionate to the results achieved. The following table illustrates the scope and accomplishment of the three operations in fuller detail.

Table 21. Malta Convoys, 1941

Naval forces employed	Operation 'Excess' No.	Sunk	Dmgd.	Operation 'Substance' No.	Sunk	Dmgd.	Operation 'Halberd' No.	Sunk	Dmgd.
Capital ships	4	—	—	2	—	—	3	—	1
Aircraft carriers	2	—	—	1	—	—	1	—	—
Cruisers	8	1	1	5	—	1	5	—	—
A.A. ships	1	—	—	—	—	—	—	—	—
Destroyers	23	—	1	18	1	1	18	—	—
Corvettes	4	—	—	—	—	—	1	—	—
Submarines	3	—	—	8	—	—	9	—	—
Transports and merchant ships	14	—	—	13	—	2	12	1	—

[1] See pp. 421–422 and 521–23.

As we look back to-day on the strength possessed by the enemy, on the length of the route traversed and the 'many and great dangers' which beset that route, the measure of success achieved appears remarkable. That these three convoy operations and the frequent aircraft ferrying trips made by Force H saved Malta in 1941 cannot be doubted.

The last three months of 1941 brought what the First Lord of the Admiralty later described as 'the crisis in our fortunes'. Tremendous events, altering the whole course of the war, then took place and their repercussions were felt in every theatre, including the Mediterranean. The diversion of the enemy's Atlantic U-boats to the Gibraltar area and into the Mediterranean has been dealt with in an earlier chapter.[1] Here we are concerned only with their influence on the struggle for control of the Mediterranean sea routes.

The period opened well for the British cause. The substantial successes achieved by our submarines and aircraft against the North African supply routes, and the improved condition of Malta, made feasible a long-cherished project to station light surface forces there once again. Accordingly, on the 12th of October, Captain W. G. Agnew sailed from Scapa in the light cruiser *Aurora* with the *Penelope* (Captain A. D. Nicholl). His small squadron was called Force K. At Gibraltar he was joined by two destroyers of Force H, and they all arrived at Malta on the 21st. Though Force K formed a part of Admiral Cunningham's fleet and was, when necessary, used in conjunction with his other forces, its blows against the North African supply routes were directed by the Vice-Admiral, Malta, Vice-Admiral W. T. R. Ford. It was not long before Force K had its first opportunity. On the afternoon of the 8th of November an R.A.F. aircraft reported a convoy some forty miles east of Cape Spartivento. It is now known that it consisted of seven merchant ships with a close escort of six destroyers and a support force of two heavy cruisers and four more destroyers, in all greatly superior to Force K. Captain Agnew left harbour before dark, gained contact in the very early hours of the next morning and in a brief, crushing, night action sank all the merchant ships (some 39,000 tons) and one destroyer of the escort. The submarine *Upholder*, which was patrolling in the same area, sank another destroyer later. The powerful Italian forces present wholly failed to protect their charges. By 1 p.m. on the 9th Force K was back in Malta harbour, completely unscathed. Its action had, in the Commander-in-Chief's words, been 'a brilliant example of leadership and forethought', and the Italian Navy was, we now know,

---

[1] See pp. 473-75.

badly shaken by such a disaster overtaking a convoy under the very noses of its powerful escort. Next day General Rommel reported that transport to North Africa was completely stopped and that, of 60,000 troops promised to arrive at Benghazi, only 8,093 had so far got through.

Little more than a week after its first success Force K sailed again, this time to co-operate with a cruiser force from Alexandria in finding an important convoy of two ships carrying fuel from Greece to Benghazi. Captain Agnew left Malta early on the 24th with the *Aurora*, *Penelope* and the destroyers *Lance* and *Lively*. They sighted the convoy that afternoon when about 100 miles west of Crete, and again destroyed it completely. The Italian escort of two torpedo boats did its best to protect the merchant ships and escaped when they were clearly doomed. The German Staff reported that the sinking of these ships, the *Maritza* and *Procida*, made the fuel supply of the Luftwaffe in Africa critical.

Meanwhile other measures to strengthen the striking power of Malta were in train. On the 16th of October Admiral Somerville, now flying his flag in the *Rodney*, since the *Nelson* had been damaged in Operation 'Halberd', left Gibraltar to fly in a squadron of naval torpedo-bombers from the *Ark Royal*. This was successfully carried out. Then, on the 10th of November, he sailed again, this time with his flag in the *Malaya*, with the *Ark Royal*, *Argus* and *Hermione* and seven destroyers to launch thirty-seven Hurricanes and seven Blenheim bombers. At 3.41 p.m. on the 13th, when returning to Gibraltar from this successful operation, the *Ark Royal* was attacked by U.81 and U.205 and torpedoed amidships. The carrier took a heavy list and temporarily lost all power and light. By 9 p.m. that night she was in tow by two tugs, and the measures to control and correct the list appeared to have been successful. At midnight steam was raised in one boiler but, unhappily, fire broke out in the port boiler room two hours later. By 4.30 a.m. the list had increased to thirty-five degrees, and the ship was abandoned. She sank at 6.13 a.m. on the 14th of November, only twenty-five miles from Gibraltar. Only one man of her company perished.

The loss of this splendid ship, so often attacked and so repeatedly claimed sunk by the enemy, to only one torpedo hit was, of course, the cause of great disappointment and the subject of searching inquiry. The general conclusions were that the list taken by a damaged ship may appear more dangerous than it is, and that correction of a list by admitting sea water to compartments on the other side should be undertaken as quickly as possible. But for a fire in the port boiler room, which was caused by flooding of the funnel uptake resulting from the list on the ship, the *Ark Royal* would probably have been saved. But her loss, whether avoidable or not, was a grievous blow, especially as it came at a time when Admiral Cunningham was without an aircraft carrier. For the *Illustrious* and *Formidable* were both repairing battle damage in the United States, and the new aircraft carrier *Indomitable* had been damaged by accidental grounding off Kingston, Jamaica, on the 3rd of November while still working up her ship's company.

To exploit Force K's rapid success and in anticipation of the enemy strengthening his convoy escorts, Rear-Admiral H. B. Rawlings was now sent to Malta with the cruisers *Ajax* (Captain E. D. B. McCarthy) and *Neptune* (Captain R. C. O'Conor) and two more large destroyers. The reinforcements, which were called Force B, arrived on the 29th of November. On the 1st of December Force K obtained a third success by sinking, firstly, a supply ship and, secondly, a tanker loaded with fuel and troops for Libya and also its destroyer escort. The Germans now realised that, if the army in North Africa was to be saved, immediate counter-measures must be taken since 'hardly any regular transports have reached their destinations in the last few days'. On the 5th of December Hitler ordered the return of one *'Fliegerkorps'* of the Luftwaffe from Russia to Sicily.

But before this measure could make itself felt the Italian Navy suffered yet another reverse in a brilliant action fought by the destroyers *Sikh* (Commander G. H. Stokes), *Legion*, *Maori* and the Dutch *Isaac Sweers*. They had left Gibraltar on the 11th of December and were on their way to Alexandria to reinforce Admiral Cunningham's flotillas. At 2.30 a.m. on the 13th an enemy cruiser force, which had previously been reported by an R.A.F. Wellington from Malta, was sighted off Cape Bon in eastern Tunisia. Commander Stokes led his ships very close inshore and attacked with torpedoes from the enemy's blind side. The Italian account says that, because our destroyers had the land behind them, they could not be seen. The 6-inch cruisers *Alberto di Giussano* and *Alberico da Barbiano* (5,069 tons), which were carrying a deck cargo of petrol from Palermo to Tripoli, were sunk without loss to the Allied force.

Unhappily this success was more than offset by German U-boat attacks on our warships. On the afternoon of the 24th of November Admiral Cunningham sailed from Alexandria with his main forces to support the cruisers which were seeking the Italian fuel convoy already mentioned. Twenty-four hours later, at 4.29 p.m. on the 25th, the *Barham*, flagship of Vice-Admiral Pridham-Wippell, commanding the 1st Battle Squadron, was struck by torpedoes fired by U.331, which had successfully passed through the destroyer screen. She blew up with heavy loss of life within a few minutes. Her Commanding Officer (Captain G. C. Cooke) and 861 officers and men perished. Though the loss of this fine ship, the first British battleship to be sunk at sea, was kept secret for several months, the blow was a heavy one. Worse was to follow. Just before midnight on the 14th–15th of December the cruiser *Galatea*, sister ship to the *Aurora* and *Penelope* of Force K, was torpedoed and sunk by U.557 thirty miles west of Alexandria. Five days later disaster overtook Force K itself.

The *Neptune* and two destroyers left Malta on the 17th of December to join Force K and a squadron of three cruisers and fourteen destroyers from Alexandria, under Rear-Admiral Vian, which was escorting and covering the fast auxiliary *Breconshire* on one of her many trips to Malta. All that day Admiral Vian's force was attacked by bombers and torpedo-bombers. But it suffered no loss. It was known from our air reconnaissance that enemy heavy warships were at sea to the north, but the lack of an aircraft carrier in the fleet and the shortage of shore-based reconnaissance aircraft prevented them being shadowed continuously. The Alexandria force, in consequence, steamed to the west partially blindfolded and, at 5.45 p.m. on the 17th, suddenly ran into two Italian battleships and numerous light forces to the north-west of Benghazi. The enemy, who was actually covering a convoy of his own and was not seeking the British force, opened fire, but when, undaunted by the disparity in strength, the British cruisers and destroyers moved in to attack, he soon drew off to the north. An hour later the two forces were out of touch. This brief engagement was later given the name of the First Battle of Sirte.

Early on the 18th the *Neptune* and her destroyers met the *Aurora* and her consorts; they escorted the *Breconshire* safely to Malta. The whole force immediately left harbour again to search for a convoy which had been reported on the Tripoli route. Naval torpedo-bombers were also despatched, but the convoy made its destination on the 19th. At 1 a.m. that morning, when about twenty miles east of Tripoli, the *Neptune* struck two mines, one of which wrecked her propellers and steering gear. The other ships, following in her wake, sheered off immediately; but the *Aurora* and *Penelope* also struck mines, and the former was badly damaged. The *Aurora* was finally escorted back to Malta by two destroyers while the *Penelope*, which had suffered little injury, stayed to help the stricken *Neptune*, which, unfortunately, now drifted on to a third mine and took a heavy list to port. The destroyer *Kandahar* gallantly went to the rescue, but she too was mined and her stern was blown off. At about 4 a.m. the *Neptune* struck a fourth mine and capsized. All but one of her company were lost. Thirty-six hours later the *Jaguar*, which had been sent from Malta by Admiral Ford to search for the damaged *Kandahar*, succeeded in finding her. By a fine piece of seamanship she rescued most of the *Kandahar's* company; but the ship had to be sunk. Thus, in a matter of a few hours, was the Malta striking force's brief but brilliant career ended, and we had, once again, to rely on submarines and aircraft to interrupt the supply traffic to Africa. The enemy at once took advantage of this swing of the pendulum to run two convoys through to Tripoli and Benghazi and, by the end of the year, was able to report that the peril in which his armies had stood was considerably eased. A combination of good fortune and successful counter-action had, in fact, saved them for the time being.

We will now return to the unrelenting campaign waged by our submarines and Malta-based aircraft against the African supply traffic, since on them more than ever now depended. In September the German Staff in Italy assessed the submarine as 'the most dangerous weapon . . . especially those operating from Malta', and warned that 'a very severe supply crisis must occur relatively soon'. Admiral Raeder agreed and recommended 'the utmost acceleration of relief measures . . . if the loss of the entire German-Italian position in North Africa is to be prevented'. The effective strength of the three submarine flotillas engaged in this offensive varied a good deal from month to month. In October four more boats arrived in the Mediterranean but the *Tetrarch* was lost when homeward-bound from Alexandria. In mid-November the 1st Flotilla (Alexandria) had about ten boats and one minelayer; the 10th Flotilla (Malta) comprised a similar number of the U class, but the 8th Flotilla (Gibraltar) was at a low strength owing to defects among its five or six boats and diversions to special duties. Occasional storing trips to Malta from both ends of the Mediterranean were still necessary, but when, on the 18th of November, the Army's new offensive (Operation 'Crusader') started, Admiral Cunningham redisposed his submarines to intercept the supplies and reinforcements which the enemy was likely to try to pass to North Africa. The actual losses inflicted by the submarines declined at this time, partly because Force K and the Malta-based aircraft themselves took a heavy toll; but the aggregate sinkings by all arms remained high. In mid-November, by which time the Italian oil stocks were very low indeed, Hitler approved the transfer to the Mediterranean of anti-submarine material and devices, including asdics, and German technicians were sent to instruct the Italians in their use. In December these measures began to take effect; Malta was subjected to increased bombing once more, aircraft patrolled more actively over the waters where our submarines usually worked, and increasing numbers of E-boats, which because of their small silhouettes and high speeds were dangerous adversaries to a submarine, became available for patrols, minelaying and escort duties.

None the less, successes continued on a satisfactory scale. On the 21st of November the *Utmost* torpedoed and severely damaged the cruiser *Duca Degli Abruzzi* (7,874 tons); the *Upright* sank two large and important supply ships of some 13,000 tons from a convoy on the 13th of December and, next day, the *Urge* hit the battleship *Vittorio Veneto* (35,000 tons) and put her out of action for several months. But the *Perseus*, one of the 1st Flotilla, was mined and sunk off the western coast of Greece early in the month. One of her crew, a stoker, survived. Among all the stories of narrow escapes from death during the war his adventure must be unparalleled. When the *Perseus* sank in 170 feet of water with her back broken, he alone managed to get to the surface, using the submarine escape apparatus. He then swam some ten miles to the coast, where he was sheltered and befriended by the Greeks until, eighteen months later, he was rescued by a boat expedition and taken back to Egypt.

The Italian Admiralty's post-war statistics regarding their losses are shown in the table below.

Table 22. Enemy Merchant Shipping Losses, Oct.–Dec. 1941

(1) Italian (includes losses outside the Mediterranean)
[Number of ships—tonnage]

Month	By surface ship	By submarine	By air attack	By mines	By other causes	Total
Oct.	Nil	6—15,801	12—29,471	3—5,412	Nil	21— 50,684
Nov.	9—44,529	7—17,808	8—11,549	Nil	6—1,704	30— 75,590
Dec.	1— 1,976	7—31,624	5—11,992	2— 261	12—1,394	27— 47,247
Total	10—46,505	20—65,233	25—53,012	5—5,673	18—3,098	78—173,521

The German shipping losses in the Mediterranean during the same period were as follows:—

(2) German (Mediterranean only)

Month	By surface ship	By submarine	By air attack	By mines	By other causes	Total
October to December	2—10,502	1— 1,773	Nil	Nil	Nil	3— 12,275

It may be of interest to quote the Italian Admiralty's statistics comparing their merchant navy's position at the end of 1941 with that at the beginning of the year. On the 1st January they had 608 ships over 500 tons, totalling 2,205,980 tons, in the Mediterranean. They lost from all causes during the year 191 ships of 820,775 tons—nearly forty per cent. of their initial fleet—but gained from various sources, including new construction and repair, seventy-seven ships of 241,435 tons. On the last day of the year their merchant fleet must therefore have fallen to under 500 ships of 1,626,640 tons—a decline of nearly thirty per cent. It must have been plain to them that, if such a rate of decline was not arrested, the supply of their African armies could not be maintained.

It has been told how great a share of this achievement was accomplished by the British submarines, though at the cost of heavy losses. It is right to mention that, in contrast to our own submarines' successes, the Italian submarines which had been working in the same dangerous and difficult waters since Italy's entry into the war, and of which there had originally been no less than eighty ready for service, accomplished very little. Up to the arrival of the German U-boats in September they had only sunk eleven Allied supply ships, all of which were in the eastern basin and all unescorted. In addition they had two cruisers and a destroyer to their credit; but twenty-one of their own number had been sunk inside the Mediterranean.

The sinking of the *Barham* and *Ark Royal* by German U-boats and the crippling of Force K was not the end of the disasters which struck us in the Mediterranean at this time. On the very day that the *Neptune* and *Kandahar* were lost a clever and determined 'attack at source' was made on the fleet in Alexandria harbour. Three Italian 'human torpedoes' were launched from a submarine off the harbour entrance and penetrated the boom defences when they were open to admit our own ships. Their crews fixed delay-action mines to the hulls of the *Queen Elizabeth* and *Valiant* and, when the mines detonated at about 6 a.m. on the 19th of December, both battleships were seriously flooded and incapacitated for many months. Fortunately it was possible to keep them on even keels and the enemy's intelligence and air reconnaissance therefore failed to reveal the full measure of success achieved. But the Mediterranean Fleet's battle squadron had now been completely eliminated.

The tale of British naval losses recounted in the foregoing paragraphs was further swollen in other theatres and, in particular, by the disaster which, as will be explained in a later chapter, overtook the Eastern Fleet on the 10th of December. And, after the Japanese onslaught had started, the ships which the Dominions had for so long lent to Admiral Cunningham's command were required by their own governments for service nearer home. At the end of October Admiral Cunningham drew the Admiralty's attention to the effect of the transfer of six destroyers (four of them Australian) to the Eastern Fleet, which left him with 'only ten reliable destroyers to meet increasing commitments'. A few days later he protested strongly against being left without an aircraft carrier and pointed out that, if the Army's offensive succeeded, the maintenance of its momentum would depend on the ability of his fleet to work in the central Mediterranean—which it could not do in safety without carrier-borne fighters. The Commander-in-Chief's prophecy was to prove all too true but, unhappily, no aircraft carrier could be found to send him.

Never since the evacuation of the Mediterranean in 1796 had the Royal Navy been so hard pressed; it even seemed possible that a similar withdrawal might now have to be carried out. On the 10th of December the First Sea Lord asked Admirals Cunningham and Somerville what, in their opinion, would be the consequences of withdrawing all heavy ships from either or both of their commands. Admiral Cunningham, in his reply, stressed his anxiety to assist in overcoming the crisis which had arisen and said that, provided the Army obtained a firm hold in Cyrenaica and that really adequate air forces were based there and at Malta the withdrawal of further ships could be accepted as a gamble. If we were driven to such a resort 'our salvation', he considered, 'will lie in the air'.

While these momentous decisions were being weighed, the circumstances envisaged were, in fact, produced by the damage to the *Queen Elizabeth* and *Valiant* and, on Christmas Eve, the Admiralty told Admiral Cunningham that events had forced their acceptance. The two battleships, when repaired, and the three modern aircraft carriers *Illustrious*, *Formidable* and *Indomitable*, when ready, were all likely to be sent to the Far East. Air reinforcements for the Mediterranean, to replace the heavy ships of the fleet, were being considered. Though this programme was not actually carried out, it is of interest in showing the straits to which we were reduced by the naval losses suffered at this time. In his reply to this last message Admiral Cunningham urged that, in the endeavour to correct matters in the East, we should beware of losing our position in the Mediterranean. The latter, he said, must now rest on adequate and suitable air striking power.

The combined effect of the naval losses and diversions to other theatres was, as Admiral Cunningham had foreseen, that the success of the Army's offensive—for Benghazi was again occupied on Christmas Eve—could not be exploited. Its momentum was lost and a further advance westwards was made impossible, largely because the fleet could not guard its flank and guarantee its supply. Thus was the possibility of a final decision in Africa deferred for another year and more.

Of all the events which contributed to this shattering of our hopes the attack by Japan, which, in the First Sea Lord's words, 'added two great oceans . . . to the area in which our shipping was menaced' was certainly the greatest. But the German counter-measures to our offensive against the Libyan supply routes, including the diversion of U-boats from the Atlantic and the return of the Luftwaffe to Sicily, also played a part. None the less not only did the German U-boats suffer considerable losses in their new theatre—no less than seven were sunk there in November and December—but their transfer from the Atlantic brought us a most welcome easement in that vital theatre. The German Staff, when it ordered the U-boats to the Mediterranean, did not know of the Japanese intention to attack on the 7th of December, and could not therefore have foretold that a new ally would assist greatly towards propping up Italy and saving the Axis armies in Africa. But, in the long view, it may be doubted whether the redistribution of the enemy's U-boat strength brought him any advantage, because of the decline in his Atlantic offensive which it made inevitable.

CHAPTER XXV

OCEAN WARFARE
1st June–31st December, 1941

> Others may use the ocean as their road,
> Only the English make it their abode.
> Edmund Waller. *Of a War with Spain.*
> 1659.

THE second half of 1941, which produced such tremendous events in other theatres, was, until the 7th of December, remarkably quiet in the great expanses of the outer oceans, and our shipping flowed steadily homeward and outward with little interference and few losses, until it reached the U-boat-infested waters of the Atlantic. Until the intervention of Japan in December no enemy major warship appeared on the ocean trade routes, and German attempts to renew such forays were quickly frustrated, as, for example, in the torpedoing of the *Lützow*.[1]

On the 1st of June there were still four armed merchant raiders at large—the *Atlantis*, *Orion*, *Komet* and *Kormoran*—but they were having more difficulty in finding victims and in keeping themselves supplied with fuel and essential stores. Two of the four raiders mentioned above succeeded in returning to French ports during this phase, but the other two were sunk in the outer oceans. As only one raider was sent out from Germany in this period and she, the *Thor*, though she succeeded in passing down the Channel to the Gironde, did not start her second cruise until early in 1942, there were no German armed raiders at large at the end of the year.[2] There were solid grounds for satisfaction over the success of the Admiralty's counter-measures. The decline in the activities of the enemy warships and merchant raiders at this time is best illustrated by the following figures:—

Table 23. Allied Shipping Sunk or Captured by Enemy Warships and Armed Merchant Raiders, 1940–41

	Allied shipping sunk by warship raiders	Allied shipping sunk by armed merchant raiders
	Tons	Tons
Last 6 months of 1940 .	14 ships— 69,719	48 ships—326,013
First 6 months of 1941 .	37 ships—187,662	38 ships—190,623
Last 6 months of 1941 .	3 ships— 14,161	6 ships— 35,904

[1] See p. 484.
[2] See p. 505.

The greatest factor in bringing about this favourable trend was, without doubt, the ever-expanding use of convoy. No disguised raider ever attacked an escorted convoy; they always concentrated on ships sailing independently. As more and more ships sailed in convoy the enemy's chances of success dwindled. Apart from this the Admiralty's world-wide control of all Allied merchant shipping had improved greatly. Ships were now more easily routed away from dangers, and the patrolling of such waters by our cruisers and aircraft had been extended. Another factor was the succession of blows struck at the enemy's supply organisation at this time. Though we never discovered the exact positions of the fuelling rendezvous used by raiders in the South Atlantic and Indian Oceans, evidence regarding the movements of the supply ships was slowly and patiently accumulated in the Admiralty, and when it had become sufficiently strong to justify sending a search force—often to a considerable distance out in the remoter parts of the oceans—the Navy struck. By the beginning of June it was clear that the frustrated Atlantic sortie by the *Bismarck* and *Prinz Eugen* must have been preceded by the despatch of a number of supply ships; and it was considered likely that the movements of the armed merchant raiders and, possibly, those of U-boats ordered to the South Atlantic would be co-ordinated with the main foray on to the northern routes. It was a favourable moment to sweep the waters which the enemy was likely to use as ocean rendezvous, and British warships were quietly ordered to leave their several bases and proceed towards them. The results achieved were remarkable. Within a few weeks no less than nine of the enemy's widely scattered and well disguised supply ships were intercepted, and a blockade runner from Japan also fell into the well-cast net. The details of the successes achieved in the month of June are tabulated below; their ocean-wide distribution is shown on the accompanying chart (Map 41).

Conclusive evidence of the effect of these losses on the armed merchant raiders' operations is to be found in the War Diaries of their captains. Rarely can a better example of skilfully exercised central control in time of war have been provided. Nor did the June successes mark the end of the Admiralty's action against the supply ships. Early in October the cruisers *Kenya* and *Sheffield*, after taking part in Operation 'Halberd', were ordered to leave Gibraltar and search for a tanker which was believed to have left Bordeaux.[1] On the evening of the 3rd of October the *Kenya* sighted the ship to the north of the Azores, some 750 miles from the coast of Spain, and sank her. It was the *Kota Penang* on her way to supply U-boats and raiders in the South Atlantic and Indian Oceans.

---

[1] See pp. 480 and 530.

Map 41

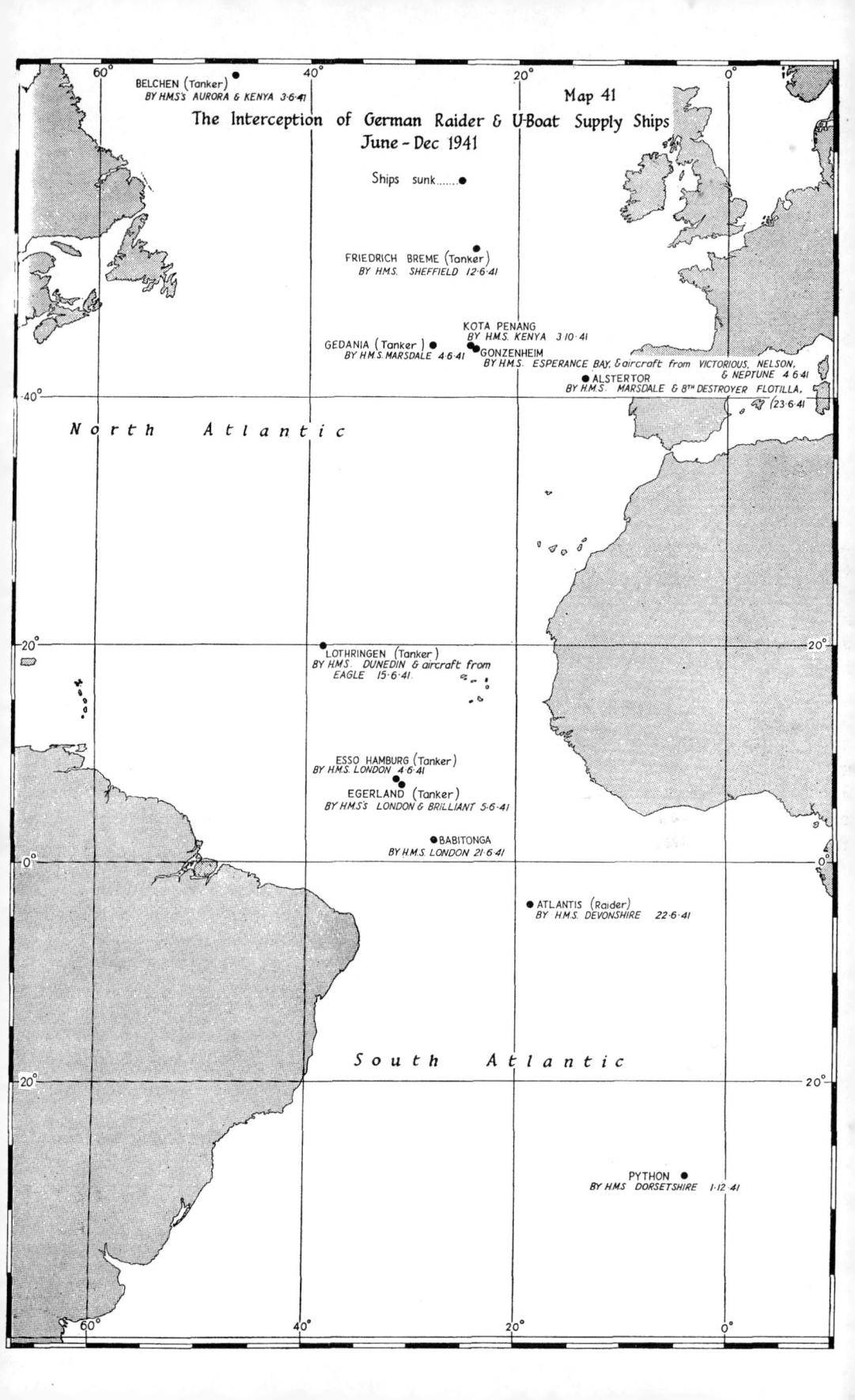

The Interception of German Raider & U-Boat Supply Ships
June – Dec 1941

Ships sunk......●

BELCHEN (Tanker)
BY HMS'S AURORA & KENYA 3·6·41

FRIEDRICH BREME (Tanker)
BY H.M.S. SHEFFIELD 12·6·41

KOTA PENANG
BY H.M.S. KENYA 3·10·41

GEDANIA (Tanker)
BY H.M.S. MARSDALE 4·6·41

GONZENHEIM
BY H.M.S. ESPERANCE BAY, & aircraft from VICTORIOUS, NELSON, & NEPTUNE 4·6·41

ALSTERTOR
BY H.M.S. MARSDALE & 8TH DESTROYER FLOTILLA. (23·6·41)

North Atlantic

LOTHRINGEN (Tanker)
BY H.M.S. DUNEDIN & aircraft from EAGLE 15·6·41

ESSO HAMBURG (Tanker)
BY H.M.S. LONDON 4·6·41

EGERLAND (Tanker)
BY H.M.S'S LONDON & BRILLIANT 5·6·41

BABITONGA
BY H.M.S. LONDON 21·6·41

ATLANTIS (Raider)
BY H.M.S. DEVONSHIRE 22·6·41

South Atlantic

PYTHON
BY H.M.S. DORSETSHIRE 1·12·41

Table 24. The Interception of German Supply Ships, June 1941

Name of supply ship	Supply duty	Date and position of interception	Result	Intercepting ships
Belchen (tanker)	*Bismarck*, *Prinz Eugen* and U-boats	3rd June 59° N. 47° W.	Sunk	*Aurora* and *Kenya*
Gedania (tanker)	*Bismarck*, *Prinz Eugen* and U-boats	4th June 43° 38' N. 28° 15' W.	Captured	*Marsdale*
Gonzenheim	*Bismarck* and *Prinz Eugen*	4th June 43° 29' N. 24° 04' W.	Scuttled	*Esperance Bay*, aircraft from *Victorious*, *Nelson* and *Neptune*
Esso Hamburg (tanker)	*Bismarck* and *Prinz Eugen*	4th June 7° 35' N. 31° 25' W.	Scuttled	*London*
Egerland (tanker)	U-boats and armed merchant raiders in South Atlantic	5th June 7° N. 31° W.	Sunk	*London* and *Brilliant*
Friedrich Breme (tanker)	*Bismarck* and *Prinz Eugen*	12th June 49° 48' N. 24° W.	Sunk	*Sheffield*
Lothringen (tanker)	*Bismarck*, *Prinz Eugen* and U-boats	15th June 19° 49' N. 30° 30' W.	Captured	*Dunedin* and aircraft from *Eagle*
Babitonga	Armed merchant raiders in South Atlantic	21st June 2° 05' N. 27° 42' W.	Scuttled	*London*
Alstertor	Armed merchant raiders and warships in Indian Ocean	23rd June 41° 20' N. 13° 32' W.	Scuttled	*Marsdale* and destroyers of 8th Flotilla

The Admiralty had for some time been concerned about the possibility of Vichy French ships being used to break our blockade and carry home supplies which would ultimately pass into enemy hands. When, in October, it was learned that a convoy was on passage from Indo-China to France by the Cape of Good Hope, it was decided to intercept it and to seize the ships regardless of the presence of a French warship escort. Accordingly a mixed force of cruisers and armed merchant cruisers from the South Atlantic and East Indies Stations, under the orders of the *Devonshire*, was sent to find the convoy. It was sighted on the 2nd of November to the east of the Cape of Good Hope and, although somewhat half-hearted attempts were made to scuttle the ships, all were finally seized in prize and taken into South African ports. The French escort made no attempt to intervene.

To turn now to the armed merchant raiders themselves, the *Atlantis* (Raider C) was in the South Atlantic at the beginning of the

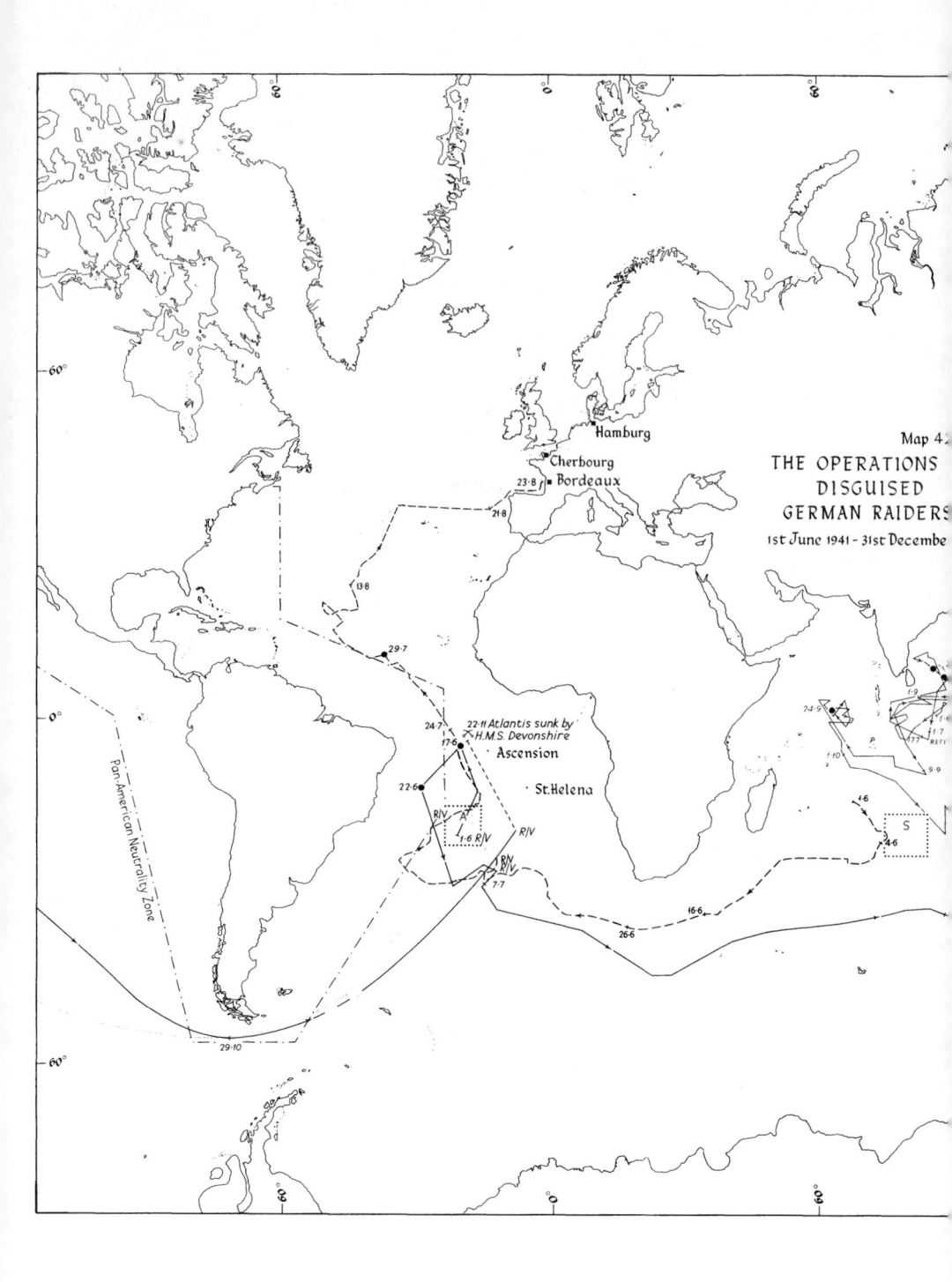

Map 4
THE OPERATIONS
DISGUISED
GERMAN RAIDERS
1st June 1941 - 31st December

120°
180°
120°
60°
60
Emirau Is.
Galapagos Is.
Tuamotu Arch.
Henderson Is.
Pitcairn Is.
Pan-American Neutrality Zone
1·8
Shark Bay
Courses Unknown
19·11
Kormoran
H.M.A.S. Sydney
sunk
Kermadec Is.
1·9
10·9
R/V
1·10
Auckland Is
29·10
Orion
Kormoran
Komet
Atlantis
Ships sunk with date 17·6
German rendezvous areas: A S
60
120°
180°
120°
60°

period and she sank two British ships there in June.[1] Both sent out raider reports before being overwhelmed by the enemy's gunfire. The *Atlantis* now moved south, met the *Orion* on the 1st of July and then rounded the Cape of Good Hope and passed into the Indian Ocean. There she found no victims; so she moved to the south of Australia and into the Pacific in the middle of August. After spending eighty days at sea without sighting a ship she secured, on the 10th of September, what was to prove her last prize, the Norwegian *Silvaplana* on passage from Java to New York with a valuable cargo. She surprised this ship at night, captured her and subsequently sent her back to France in prize. The *Atlantis* next made a rendezvous with the *Komet* and her supply ship, from whom she replenished with fuel and stores; she then steamed right across the Pacific to round Cape Horn at the end of October, and so re-entered the South Atlantic after steaming almost round the world—and accomplishing very little in the process.

On returning to her old theatre of operations she was ordered to act as a U-boat supply ship before continuing her homeward journey. It was while fuelling U.126 at a rendezvous just south of the equator that, on the morning of the 22nd of November, she was sighted by the cruiser *Devonshire* (Captain R. D. Oliver), whose catapult aircraft had first reported a suspicious ship's presence. Captain Oliver took no chances but manœuvred at long range while he asked the Commander-in-Chief, South Atlantic, at Freetown to confirm or deny the ship's identity. The instant that Admiral Willis reported that she could not be the ship she claimed to be, the *Devonshire* opened fire, and the raider soon blew up and sank in 4° 12′ South, 18° 42′ West.[2] Since his aircraft had reported that U-boats were almost certainly present Captain Oliver did not stop to recover survivors. The *Atlantis*' cruise had started on the last day of March 1940 and in the course of over twenty months' cruising she sank or captured twenty-two ships totalling 145,697 tons. Her captain and about 100 of her crew were picked up by U.126 and later transferred to the *Python*, which had been sent out to supply U-boats in the South Atlantic.[3]

To illustrate the many problems and difficulties encountered in searching for and identifying enemy raiders it may be told how, when an Admiralty oiler made a raider report on the 4th of November from a position in mid-Atlantic just north of the equator, no less than ten British and American warships searched the area for two days. The oiler's report had, however, been sent when an unseen

---

[1] See p. 382 and Map 42.
[2] See Maps 41 (*p. 543*) and 42.
[3] See p. 470.

enemy—probably a surfaced U-boat—had fired on her in the vague light of dawn, and no enemy raider was, in fact, present. But the search was not entirely fruitless, since the American cruiser *Omaha* and a destroyer met and captured the blockade runner *Odenwald* on the 6th of November and sent her to Trinidad. She was carrying a cargo of raw rubber from Japan, and her capture was the first tangible result of the more active and extensive patrolling in the Atlantic now carried out by United States warships.

Little more than a week after the *Devonshire*'s success her sister ship the *Dorsetshire* (Captain A. W. S. Agar, V.C.) was searching for supply ships in the relatively calm waters south and west of St. Helena.[1] On the afternoon of the 1st of December she sighted a suspicious ship and closed at high speed. The enemy, which proved to be the U-boat supply ship *Python*, abandoned ship and scuttled herself. She had on board, as already mentioned, many survivors from the *Atlantis*. U-boats which had been near by when she was sunk started to tow the *Python*'s lifeboats northwards, and the survivors were finally transferred to other German and Italian U-boats. They all eventually reached Biscay ports after covering a distance of more than 5,000 miles—a rescue for which the enemy must be given full credit.

The sinking of the *Atlantis* and *Python* was, unhappily, offset by the loss of the light cruiser *Dunedin*, which was torpedoed and sunk by U.124, with heavy loss of life, on the 24th of November whilst on a solitary patrol in the South Atlantic. The U-boat was making for the position in which the *Atlantis* had been sunk in order to rescue her crew, and it was by an unlucky chance that her course led her directly to the patrol area off St. Paul's Rocks given to the *Dunedin*.

The successes obtained by the *Devonshire* and *Dorsetshire* were the result of unremitting search and patrol work carried out mainly by the cruisers of the South Atlantic Command. They led directly to the withdrawal of U-boats from those waters and to the cancellation of the thrust which Admiral Dönitz had intended to make to the Cape of Good Hope. In view of the very important troop convoys which were moving through those waters at this time, the change of plan forced on the enemy must be assessed as an achievement of some importance.

To continue the story of the enemy raiders, the *Orion* (Raider A) was in the Indian Ocean at the start of this phase, but she had accomplished nothing in the preceding six months. Her last successes had been in the raid on Nauru Island in December 1940.[2] Early in June she fuelled from the ex-Norwegian prize *Ole Jacob*, which was

---

[1] See Map 41 (*p. 543*).
[2] See p. 283.

then sent back to Bordeaux but was intercepted by British ships and aircraft off the north coast of Spain.[1]

The loss of the supply ships now prevented the *Orion* from protracting her cruise, so she returned to the Atlantic by the Cape of Good Hope to meet the *Atlantis* near Tristan da Cunha on the 1st of July. Four weeks later, after seven and a half months of fruitless cruising, she obtained her final success when she sank the British ship *Chaucer*. Her victim, however, resisted gallantly and sent out a raider report. In mid-August the *Orion* was met by two U-boats and, later, by destroyers and minesweepers which escorted her to the Gironde on the 23rd. Her cruise had lasted 510 days and she had steamed over 112,000 miles. She shared seven victims of some 43,000 tons with the *Komet* but her personal score was only nine and a half ships of 57,744 tons, excluding the mining of the *Niagara*.[2] She was an old ship and, although not a very successful raider, had performed a remarkable feat in maintaining herself in seagoing condition for so long a period away from any proper base. She was never used again as a raider.

In August the *Komet* (Raider B), after steaming right across the Pacific from Australian waters, arrived in the vicinity of the Galapagos Islands. On the 14th she there sank a British ship—her first victim since the joint attack with the *Orion* against the island of Nauru in December 1940. Three days later she captured the Dutch ship *Kota Nopan* with a valuable cargo of rubber and manganese, and then sank the large British ship *Devon*, which had intercepted the *Kota Nopan's* raider report, but continued to steam straight ahead into the enemy's arms. Having thus profited from her sudden appearance in waters not previously visited by a raider, the *Komet* steamed south-west to a rendezvous with the *Atlantis* and a supply ship, from whom she fuelled. On the 10th of October she and her prize, the *Kota Nopan*, rounded Cape Horn and set course for France. The prize reached Bordeaux safely on the 17th of November, while the raider was met by U-boats and escorted to Cherbourg on the 26th. The story of her subsequent passage up the English Channel to Germany has already been told.[3] She herself, in a cruise lasting fifteen and a half months, only sank the three ships, totalling 21,378 tons, recently mentioned. But she shared a further seven ships of 43,162 tons with the *Orion*, so that her total accomplishment may be assessed as six and a half ships of 42,959 tons.

The last raider with whom we are here concerned is the *Kormoran* (Raider G). She entered the Bay of Bengal in June with the intention of mining the approaches to Madras; but the operation was never

---
[1] See p. 504.
[2] See p. 283.
[3] See pp. 504–505.

carried out. She did, however, sink a Jugoslav and a British ship in those waters on the 26th and then moved to a rendezvous in 6° South, 86° East, where she refitted herself in July before visiting the neighbourhood of Java and Sumatra. She obtained no successes, so her captain decided next to try the waters east of Madagascar which the *Pinguin* had found profitable three months previously; after a week's search she there sank a Greek ship. In five months' cruising in the Indian Ocean she sank only three ships of 11,566 tons. At the end of September she made for an ocean rendezvous in 32° 30′ South, 97° East, where, in mid-October, she met the supply ship *Kulmerland* bringing provisions and fuel from Japan. After replenishing herself, the raider decided to visit the waters off Shark's Bay in Western Australia. On the 19th of November she met the Australian cruiser *Sydney* in 26° 34′ South, 111° 00′ East. The story of the encounter was not pieced together until much later, for there were no survivors from the *Sydney*. But we now know that the two ships met at about 4 p.m., and that the cruiser closed and challenged the raider, who identified herself as a Dutch ship and made a wireless report purporting to come from her. The *Sydney*, with all her guns trained on the raider and apparently ready for instant action, then approached within 2,000 yards, on a parallel course, while endeavouring to establish the truth or falsity of her claimed identity. But, unlike the *Devonshire*, she never asked her shore authorities whether such a ship could be in the area at the present time.[1] At 5.25 p.m. she told the raider to hoist her secret call sign. The raider then knew that the game was up, for she lacked the means to bluff through that demand. She therefore cast off her disguise and opened fire with all her concealed weapons. The *Sydney* replied, but the few seconds' advantage gained by the enemy's possession of the initiative proved decisive; the cruiser was heavily hit around the bridge and struck by a torpedo as well, while her return fire did not cause immediate lethal damage to her adversary. The *Sydney*'s forward turrets were put out of action, but the after pair continued the fight and the *Kormoran* was soon heavily on fire. At about 5.45 the raider's engines broke down, but the action continued until nearly 6.30 p.m., by which time it was dark. The *Sydney* gradually disappeared over the horizon, burning fiercely, and a final glare seen at 10 p.m. may have been caused by her blowing up. Meanwhile the *Kormoran* herself was in great danger, for she still had many mines on board and was herself on fire. Her captain ordered the ship to be abandoned and scuttled and, shortly after midnight, she blew up. Of her crew of 400 no less than 315 were picked up later, or reached the Australian coast. Of the *Sydney* hardly a trace was ever found.

---

[1] See p. 545.

The story of the *Sydney's* last fight has been told in some detail because, as has been mentioned earlier, the situation in which her captain found himself was liable to occur in every contact with a suspicious ship, until a firm system of checkmating a raider's bluff by calling the shore authorities had been established. And, of course, the ability of the shore authorities confidently to tell a patrolling warship that the ship she had intercepted must be an enemy was absolutely dependent on having accurate knowledge of every true Allied merchant ship's position, all over the world, at any given time. Such knowledge was not easily amassed and kept ready for instant use in time of war, and the system was, in fact, not perfected until later. Yet, granted the difficulties of piercing raiders' disguises, the very close approach made by the *Sydney* during the exchange of signals was certainly injudicious.

As early as January 1940 one of our own 'Q ships' whose gun and torpedo armaments were about the same as the *Kormoran's* was intercepted off Sierra Leone by the *Neptune*, a sister ship of the *Sydney*, which was unaware of her true identity. The cruiser approached, and remained for some time steaming at slow speed, within a few hundred yards of the 'Q ship', whose captain later reported to the Admiralty that, had he been a German, he 'could have disabled [the *Neptune*] with two torpedoes and swept her upper deck'. But such complete secrecy enveloped the work of the 'Q ships' that the report was never circulated to the Naval Staff, and the fate from which the *Neptune* escaped actually overtook the *Sydney* more than eighteen months later. The unheeded warning of the 'Q ship' had not been the only pointer to the danger of making a close approach to a suspicious ship. The engagements between the raider *Thor* and the armed merchant cruisers *Carnarvon Castle* and *Alcantara* in July and December 1940, and the loss of the *Voltaire* in April 1941, had amply demonstrated the capacity of the enemy to hit back hard and suddenly; the Admiralty had issued several warnings to that effect.[1] Yet, in February 1941, the *Leander* also made a close approach to a suspicious ship which, had she been a German instead of an Italian raider, might well have brought on her the *Sydney's* fate.[2] The truth is clear. Though a comprehensive system of plotting the positions of all friendly merchant ships and the issue to them all of secret call signs are essential to success in anti-raider operations, it will always take time to establish such measures on a world-wide basis. Meanwhile the difficulty of identifying an intercepted ship will inevitably remain. But to make a close approach to a suspicious ship, on a favourable bearing for gun and torpedo fire, is to court disaster.

---

[1] See p. 285 and pp. 383–384.
[2] See p. 387.

THE LOSSES CAUSED BY RAIDERS 1939-41

Since there were, as already stated, no German surface raiders at large at the end of the present phase the moment is opportune to summarise their achievements from the beginning of the war until the end of 1941. They are best presented in tabular form.

Table 25. German Warship and Armed Merchant Raiders, 1939-41[1]

Ship	Period of cruise	Merchant ships sunk or captured	Remarks
Admiral Graf Spee	26/9/39 to 13/12/39	9— 50,089 tons	Destroyed in River Plate 17/12/39
Deutschland (renamed *Lützow* later)	26/9/39 to 15/11/39	2— 6,962 tons	Returned to Germany 15/11/39
Admiral Scheer	27/10/40 to 1/4/41	16— 99,059 tons	Returned to Germany 28/3/41
Admiral Hipper	30/11/40 to 27/12/40 1/2/41 to 14/2/41 15/3/41 to 28/3/41	10— 59,960 tons	Stationed at Brest 27/12/40 to 15/3/41 Returned to Germany 28/3/41
Scharnhorst *Gneisenau*	25/1/41 to 22/3/41	22—115,622 tons	Returned to Brest 22/3/41. Both damaged by air attack later
Bismarck	21/5/41 to 27/5/41	Nil	Sunk 27/5/41
Prinz Eugen	21/5/41 to 1/6/41	Nil	Returned to Brest. Damaged by air attack later
Total sinkings by warship raiders		59—331,692 tons	
Orion (A)	6/4/40 to 23/8/41	9½—57,774 tons	Returned to Germany 23/8/41
Komet (B)	9/8/40 to 30/11/41	6½—42,959 tons	Returned to Germany 30/11/41
Atlantis (C)	31/3/40 to 22/11/41	22—145,697 tons	Sunk 22/11/41
Widder (D)	14/5/40 to 31/10/40	10— 58,645 tons	Returned to Germany 31/10/40
Thor (E)	11/6/40 to 24/4/41	11— 83,301 tons	Returned to Germany 24/4/41
Pinguin (F)	22/6/40 to 8/5/41	28—136,551 tons	Sunk 8/5/41
Kormoran (G)	9/12/40 to 19/11/41	11— 68,274 tons	Sunk 19/11/41
Total sinkings by armed merchant raiders		98—593,201 tons	

[1] See Appendix M for full details of the German raiders and the losses they inflicted.

In reviewing the foregoing figures—the results of nearly twenty-eight months of unremitting struggle for the control of the broad oceans—it cannot but be remarked, firstly, how small were the losses inflicted by the enemy raiders in relation to the total traffic carried to and from this country and, secondly, how little was accomplished by the warship raiders. That the enemy caused considerable dislocation and delays to the flow of our shipping and made us disperse our naval strength, and in particular our slender resources of cruisers,

INTERCEPTION OF BLOCKADE RUNNERS

cannot be denied. Yet it is undoubtedly true that only once did the worst that his surface ships could do—in the North Atlantic in February and March 1941—produce a sufficiently serious state of affairs to threaten the whole structure of our maritime control.[1] Compared with the U-boat, the mine and air attacks on shipping, the surface raiders were a relatively small threat. Losses inflicted by U-boats in certain single months such as October 1940 or May 1941, and by aircraft in April 1941, approximately equalled the total losses caused by warship raiders in the entire twenty-eight months of war now under review. In the twelve months of 1940 mines alone sank a tonnage of shipping little less than all that the armed merchant raiders sank from the beginning of the war until the end of 1941.[2] That it was, to a great extent, the enemy's lack of overseas bases and the possession of such bases by ourselves, the Commonwealth nations and our Allies that prevented him from developing the surface ship threat is certain. The value of these bases, even if ill-equipped and ill-defended, to a nation dependent for its continued existence on maritime power should never be forgotten.

The enemy's attempts to break through the British blockade and to bring home from abroad cargoes of particular value to his war economy have appeared from time to time in our story, but no complete account of them has been given since the early days when the patrolling ships and aircraft of the Home Fleet sealed the northern passages to the Atlantic so effectively that, after the first weeks of the war, few enemy vessels succeeded in reaching home. With the fall of France and the opening to the enemy of all the ports on her Biscay coast, the chances of running the blockade successfully were greatly improved, and the enemy was not slow to exploit the opportunity. During 1941 fifteen German and seventeen Italian ships attempted to reach Axis-controlled ports in Europe. The majority started from South American ports, but ten came from the Canary Islands and four from Japan. Of the thirty-two ships which made the attempt fourteen of some 83,700 tons were intercepted; four of them were captured and the remainder scuttled themselves. Fourteen ships of 79,100 tons reached their destinations during the year and the remaining four of the total of thirty-two were still on passage. Four German ships sailed outward-bound from Europe for South America, but only one made the return journey successfully. The other three were among the fourteen ships intercepted. Apart from these attempts to run the blockade from the outer oceans there was, after the middle of 1940, a steady trickle of

---
[1] See pp. 371–377 and Appendix M.
[2] See Appendix R for full comparison of losses suffered from various causes.

contraband goods, carried in small ships, from Spain and Portugal to the French Biscay ports and a small amount of traffic in Spanish ships from eastern Spain to Italy. It was difficult to stop this traffic, but our aircraft were, by the end of the year, patrolling the north coast of Spain, and submarines had been sent to watch off Barcelona. There was good reason to expect that our hold on both routes would soon be tightened. A maritime blockade can never be made wholly impenetrable. The remarkable fact is that, even after the enemy had won the entire European seaboard from North Cape to the Spanish frontier, and with full allowance made for the benevolence (to the enemy) of the neutrality of Spain and Japan, so few ships actually succeeded in penetrating the blockade.

While comparative quiet prevailed on the broad oceans as 1941 drew to a close, the steady reinforcement of the Middle East theatre proceeded all the time, chiefly by means of the W.S. convoys of large liners which left England at about monthly intervals. Their progress was never seriously impeded by the enemy. The Prime Minister, however, was mindful of the possibility of new requirements arising, and conscious that the shipping which we possessed was inadequate to achieve his object of having two more British divisions well on the road to the Middle or Far East by the end of the year. Mr. Churchill has told of his efforts to procure American assistance to that end and of his ultimate success in obtaining the loan of ships to carry some 20,000 men.[1] The movement involved intricate and world-wide co-ordination. British troopships first carried the reinforcements across the North Atlantic to Halifax, which they reached on the 8th of November. There the soldiers transferred to the American transports, which sailed for Trinidad on the 10th escorted by the United States Navy. They arrived at Capetown—8,132 miles from Halifax—on the 9th of December, the day that Germany and Italy declared war on the United States. The American naval escort returned home when the convoy was nearing Durban and the Admiralty thereafter took over the responsibility. The main convoy reached Bombay, escorted by the cruiser *Dorsetshire*, on the 27th of December and the troopships were routed from there to Singapore.

---

[1] See W. S. Churchill. *The Second World War*, Vol. III, pp. 435-439.

CHAPTER XXVI

DISASTER IN THE PACIFIC
December 1941

> First there will be . . . fortitude—the power of enduring when hope is gone. . . . There must be patience, supreme patience. . . . There must be resilience under defeat . . . a manly optimism, which looks at the facts in all their bleakness and yet dares to be confident.
>
> John Buchan. '*The Great Captains*', *Homilies and Recreations* (1926), p. 88.

THE last chapters have described the unceasing struggle waged during the second half of 1941 in the Atlantic, in our home and coastal waters, in the Mediterranean and on the broad oceans. Throughout this period the Royal Navy had borne a tremendous burden and worked continuously to the limit of its resources. Each and every one of the ever-changing demands had been met and, at one period, it had seemed that reward might soon be reaped. Then, in the last month of the year, just when the dawn of a more hopeful day seemed to be breaking on the horizon, it was blotted out by the gloom of our heaviest disasters.

The reversal of the favourable trend in maritime affairs had first been felt in the Mediterranean theatre, as has already been told, but worse was to follow.

The possibility of war with Japan had, since pre-war days, never been far from the minds of the Chiefs of Staff and of the Admiralty. The pre-war naval plans had stated that British maritime strength was inadequate to ensure the control of our home waters, to contribute to the war against Italy in the Mediterranean and to fight Japan in the Far East as well.[1] If Japan actively joined the Axis powers the Mediterranean would have to be left to the French Navy. By no other means could an adequate fleet be sent to the East. Little was it foreseen that, when the occasion actually arose, there would be no French fleet to hold the Mediterranean. But the total loss of French maritime power did not alter the need to send substantial British naval strength to the East as soon as it could be done without undue risk to the vital home theatre, and plans to do so were repeatedly considered during 1941. The Admiralty was under no illusion

---
[1] See pp. 41–42.

regarding the great proportion of our total strength which would have to be sent out if the Eastern Fleet was to be able to fight the Japanese Navy on anything like equal terms, though the Prime Minister was inclined to consider its estimates of Japanese naval strength exaggerated. However, the Naval Staff adhered firmly to the view that the real requirement was to send out a powerful and balanced fleet, composed of all types of ship, including battleships and at least one aircraft carrier.

For the history of the gradual development of the Japanese plans to exploit the opportunity for further southward expansion, which the defeat of France and the tremendous preoccupations of Britain offered to her, the reader must refer to other volumes of this series. Here we need only remark that at the end of July 1941, when the German attack on Russia had reduced the danger of Soviet action in the north, the Japanese sent troops to Saigon in Indo-China and, shortly afterwards, made an agreement with Vichy France for the 'joint defence' of that country. Thus were the real designs of the Japanese leaders made clear, for it had always been realised in London that the nation which held in strength the coast of Indo-China, with its excellent base at Kamranh Bay, would control the whole South China Sea.[1] The validity of this opinion was soon demonstrated, since, once the necessary land, sea and air bases in Indo-China had been securely occupied, the Japanese increased pressure on Thailand (Siam) and finally, in December, invaded that country. Their forces had now reached the threshold of Malaya and the East Indian archipelago, and it was not to be expected that a challenge could long be deferred.

But while these important moves were in progress the attention of the Admiralty and Chiefs of Staff, for all their many cares and anxieties at this time, was constantly turning to the need to reinforce the Eastern Fleet. In particular, when, in August, the Prime Minister had telegraphed from the Atlantic Conference that the President of the United States was shortly to present the Japanese with a note making it plain that any further southward advance would probably mean war, the Chiefs of Staff considered what active steps should be taken. At the beginning of August the only effective capital ships in the Home Fleet were the *King George V* and *Prince of Wales*; of the Mediterranean Fleet's battle squadron the *Warspite* had been seriously damaged off Crete and was to be repaired in America. This left Admiral Cunningham the *Queen Elizabeth*, *Valiant* and *Barham*. Force H, at Gibraltar, had the *Nelson* and *Renown*. The *Malaya*, lately in Force H, the *Repulse* and *Royal Sovereign* were refitting in home dockyards, while the *Rodney* and *Resolution* were refitting in

---

[1] See Map 43 (*facing p. 565*).

America. Lastly the *Ramillies* and *Revenge* belonged to the North Atlantic Escort Force. Bearing in mind that the *Tirpitz* was known to be ready, or nearly ready, for operations and that the Italians were certainly superior to Admiral Cunningham's strength, it was plain that little, if any, margin of safety existed. The Chiefs of Staff recommended that, by mid-September, one battleship from the Mediterranean should be sent east—either the *Barham* or *Valiant*—and that four more battleships of the R class (all un-modernised ships) should follow by the end of the year. The first part of this proposal had not been carried out when the *Barham* was sunk on the 25th November. The possibility of substituting the *Valiant* was eliminated when, three weeks later, she and the *Queen Elizabeth* were damaged and immobilised in Alexandria harbour.[1] No additional cruisers were to be sent, nor could any fleet destroyers be spared until American assistance in the Atlantic had taken fuller effect. An aircraft carrier, probably the old *Eagle*, was, however, to go. Such a force had no possible chance of fighting the Japanese Navy but, if based on Ceylon, should, in the Chiefs of Staff's opinion, be able to prevent the disruption of our traffic in the Indian Ocean, at any rate for a time. It was intended that this should be the first stage of a long-term plan, which could not materialise before March 1942, to build up in the Indian Ocean, prior to sending it to Singapore, a fleet which would finally be composed of seven capital ships, one aircraft carrier, ten cruisers and some two dozen destroyers. The Prime Minister did not like the Admiralty's proposals for sending out the first reinforcements and has stated his reasons.[2] He wished instead to build up in the Simonstown–Aden–Singapore triangle a small but powerful force of fast modern battleships which, he considered, would have a deterrent effect on further Japanese aggression; and he drew an analogy between the influence of the *Tirpitz* on the Home Fleet and the suggested influence of a small but powerful eastern squadron on Japanese naval dispositions. The First Sea Lord had wished, in the first place, to use the four R-class battleships to protect the Indian Ocean routes and later, probably in December and January, to reinforce them with the *Nelson*, *Rodney* and *Renown* which he desired to base on Ceylon, not on Singapore. None of the new *King George V* class battleships could, in Admiral Pound's view, be spared from home waters 'unless the U.S.A. [could] provide a sufficiently strong striking force of modern battleships capable of engaging [the] *Tirpitz* and be prepared to allow one of their ships to replace one of our own *King George V* class if damaged'. On the 28th of August the First Sea Lord replied to the Prime Minister's note pressing for one of the modern battleships to be sent east, and stated

---

[1] See pp. 534 and 538.
[2] See W. S. Churchill. *The Second World War*, Vol. III, pp. 523–525.

the full and considered reasons why he could not recommend it. The basic difference in the two points of view was that the Admiralty's force would be defensive, but would be well placed strategically in the centre of a most important theatre, whereas the Prime Minister's force was potentially offensive and was to be based far forward, but in an area which the enemy was threatening to dominate. It proved impossible to reconcile the two points of view and the matter was not discussed again until mid-October, when the Foreign Office drew attention to certain ominous signs of Japanese intentions and asked for the question of capital ship reinforcement to be discussed by the Defence Committee.

At the meeting on the 17th of October the Prime Minister repeated his previous arguments; the First Lord demurred at his proposal to send out the *Prince of Wales*, while the Foreign Office considered that her arrival would, from the point of view of deterring Japan from entering the war, have a far greater effect politically than the presence in those waters of a number of the last war's battleships. This was a rather different argument from the Prime Minister's but lent general support to his view. The discussion ended by the Prime Minister inviting the First Lord to send as quickly as possible one modern capital ship, together with an aircraft carrier, to join up with the *Repulse* at Singapore. He added that he would not come to a decision on this point without consulting the First Sea Lord, but in view of the strong feeling of the Committee in favour of the proposal, he hoped that the Admiralty would not oppose this suggestion. The First Lord agreed to discuss the matter with Admiral Pound and to make recommendations in a few days' time.

On the 20th of October the proposal was again discussed by the Chiefs of Staff with the Prime Minister in the chair, and the First Sea Lord then developed the Admiralty's case more fully. He said that the deterrent which would prevent the Japanese moving south would not be the presence of one fast battleship, because they could easily afford to detach four modern ships to protect any southward-bound invasion force. But if the two *Nelsons* and four *Royal Sovereigns* were at Singapore they would have to detach the greater part of their fleet 'and thus uncover Japan' to the American Navy, on whose active co-operation in the event of a Japanese attack the First Sea Lord relied. It will be noted that this was somewhat different from the Admiralty's first proposal that the four old battleships should be based in the Indian Ocean. The Prime Minister said that he did not foresee an attack in force on Malaya, but chiefly feared raids from fast and powerful warships against our trade—to counter which the *Royal Sovereigns* would be useless—and the earlier argument of the Foreign Office about the political effect of sending out the *Prince of Wales* was restated.

THE 'PRINCE OF WALES' SENT EAST

The views of the First Sea Lord were plainly irreconcilable with those of the Prime Minister and of the Foreign Office. He therefore yielded so far as to suggest that the *Prince of Wales* should be sent to Capetown at once, and that her final destination should be decided after she had arrived there. This proposal was accepted by the Defence Committee, but next day, the 21st of October, the Admiralty told all British naval authorities that the *Prince of Wales* would leave shortly *for Singapore*. Though the Admiralty thus appears to have gone beyond the decision of the Defence Committee, it is likely that their signal, in spite of its categorical wording, was intended merely to give the authorities advance information of a probable redisposition of our forces. It is certain that such movements would never have been ordered by the Admiralty without higher approval. As recently as the 10th of October, when the Admiralty had told Admiral Cunningham about the intended despatch of reinforcements to the Indian Ocean, the Prime Minister minuted to the First Sea Lord that no such fleet movement was to be carried out until approved by him or the Defence Committee. Furthermore on the 31st of October and the 5th of November Mr Churchill told the Dominion Prime Ministers that, in order further to deter Japan, we were sending the *Prince of Wales* to join the *Repulse* in the Indian Ocean, and she would be noticed at Capetown quite soon. But, added the Prime Minister, her movements would be reviewed when she had reached Capetown, because of the danger of the *Tirpitz* breaking out into the Atlantic. It is, however, plain that the Prime Minister considered that the battleship's onward voyage to Singapore was very probable. On the last day of October he told the Chiefs of Staff so; and on the 1st of November he asked the First Sea Lord what his plans were if it was decided that she should go on to Singapore. When Admiral Pound replied that he intended 'to review the situation generally just before the *Prince of Wales* reaches Capetown', Mr Churchill assented.

Meanwhile the battleship had left home waters on the 25th of October flying the flag of Rear-Admiral Sir T. Phillips, who had been given the rank of Acting Admiral. Though we cannot be sure regarding what Admiral Phillips himself thought about the future movements of his flagship, there seems little doubt that he considered his destination to be Singapore, and never expected the decision to be reviewed, let alone altered, after he had reached Capetown. The *Prince of Wales* reached Capetown on the 16th of November, and if a review of her future movements then took place no record of it has been found in the Admiralty's or the Prime Minister's papers; the Chiefs of Staff and Defence Committees certainly did not consider the matter again.

Before Phillips had reached Freetown the Prime Minister telegraphed to Field Marshal Smuts introducing the Admiral and suggesting that they should meet. The South African Prime Minister readily agreed, and Phillips therefore left his flagship at Capetown to fly to Pretoria. We have no record of the conversations which took place there, but on rejoining his flagship Admiral Phillips told his Chief of Staff (Rear-Admiral A. F. E. Palliser) that Smuts agreed with the policy of sending the two capital ships to Singapore as a deterrent against further Japanese aggression, and that in order to accomplish such a purpose he considered it essential to give publicity to the movement. This was the actual intention of the British Cabinet. None the less on the 18th of November, Smuts telegraphed to the Prime Minister expressing his serious concern over the division of Allied strength between Hawaii and Singapore into 'two fleets . . . each separately inferior to the Japanese Navy . . .'. 'If the Japanese are really nippy', added the Field Marshal, 'there is here [an] opening for a first-class disaster'.

On the 11th of November, before Admiral Phillips had reached Capetown, the Admiralty ordered the *Prince of Wales* and *Repulse* to meet in Ceylon and proceed in company to Singapore. This message may have resulted from the review of the battleship's movements which the Prime Minister and First Sea Lord intended to make but, if that is the case, we have no record of the decision nor of who was present when it was taken. On the 23rd the Prime Minister mentioned to the Foreign Secretary that the most important current naval movements were those of the *Prince of Wales* and *Repulse*, which would soon be at Singapore.

The *Repulse* (Captain W. G. Tennant) had arrived at Durban on the 3rd of October with a W.S. Convoy, and had thereupon been detached to the East Indies Station. The new aircraft carrier *Indomitable*, which had also been earmarked for the Far East, had, as we have already told, been put out of action by accidental grounding.[1] The *Prince of Wales* reached Colombo on the 28th of November and there met the *Repulse* for the first time. The Admiralty now ordered Admiral Phillips to fly to Singapore ahead of his flagship, and thence on to Manila in order to co-ordinate plans with the Dominion, Allied and American Navies. Phillips replied that he considered it of great importance to make contact with the Commander of the United States Asiatic Fleet, and that he intended to make a two- or three-day visit to Manila early in December.

From the foregoing brief account of the discussions which led to the despatch of the two capital ships to Singapore it will be seen that the main purpose of the move pressed on the Admiralty by the Defence Committee was the political one of deterring Japan from further aggression. Bearing in mind that it was not known in London that Japan was, in fact, on the brink of war such a purpose was

---
[1] See p. 534.

ANXIETY DEEPENS

certainly reasonable; for it was still by no means certain that, in the event of a Japanese attack on ourselves, America would enter the war. It may therefore be felt that an attempt to deter a third powerful nation from joining our enemies, at any rate for a time, had to be made—even at the price of accepting great risks. None the less it seems that, had we possessed clearer knowledge of Japan's imminent intentions, the Admiralty's view would probably have prevailed. As the prospect darkened, the Admiralty's anxiety regarding the exposed position of Admiral Phillips' force deepened, and on the 1st of December they suggested to him that the two capital ships should leave Singapore. The Admiral was, in fact, considering a similar move at the time, and his staff was investigating the possibility of using Port Darwin in North Australia temporarily. Two days later the Admiralty suggested that Admiral Phillips should try to get some destroyers of the American Asiatic Fleet sent to Singapore and take the two big ships away from the threatened base to the eastwards. On reading this message the Prime Minister remarked that the ships' whereabouts should become unknown as soon as possible. On the same day, the 3rd of December, Admiral Phillips reported his intention to send the *Repulse* and two destroyers on a short visit to Port Darwin. They sailed on the 5th but were recalled next day when intelligence reached Singapore that a Japanese troop convoy had been sighted off the south coast of Indo-China steering west.

Mr. Churchill has recorded that by the evening of the 9th of December, when we were now at war with Japan, there was general agreement in London that the ships 'must go to sea and vanish among the innumerable islands'.[1] But it was by then too late to implement this strategy, for the squadron was already at sea seeking the Japanese landing forces.

It will be appropriate next to consider the strength and disposition of the other Allied forces in the Pacific. The Commander-in-Chief, China (Vice-Admiral Sir Geoffrey Layton), had three of the old light cruisers of the D class and two old destroyers at or near Singapore. Two Australian destroyers were also in the area. There were three more old destroyers and eight motor torpedo-boats at Hong Kong, and Admiral Phillips had with him four fairly modern destroyers, which was all that could be spared to him for anti-submarine screening. The light forces allocated to Admiral Phillips, who succeeded to Admiral Layton's command on the 8th of December, were therefore of mixed classes and performance and very weak in numbers. In Australian waters there were three cruisers, two

---

[1] W. S. Churchill. *The Second World War*, Vol. III, p. 547.

destroyers and one Free French light cruiser, while the two New Zealand cruisers were at Auckland. The Dutch naval forces in the East Indies were, on paper, considerable. Three light cruisers, six destroyers and thirteen submarines were based on Java. Admiral Layton was already controlling some of the Dutch submarines, but little progress had been made towards welding all these widely scattered ships into a single fleet under unified command.

The Americans had an advanced force known as the Asiatic Fleet (Admiral Thomas C. Hart, U.S.N.) comprising three cruisers, thirteen destroyers and twenty-nine submarines based on Manila, but their main strength, the Pacific Fleet, was at Pearl Harbour, nearly 6,000 miles from Singapore, under Admiral Husband Kimmel. It consisted of nine battleships, three aircraft carriers, twelve heavy and nine light cruisers, sixty-seven destroyers and twenty-seven submarines. The relative strengths of the combined Allied naval forces and those of Japan in the Pacific do not, therefore, show a great disparity on paper, except in aircraft carriers. They are tabulated below.

Table 26. Allied and Enemy Naval Forces in the Pacific, December 1941

	Capital ships	Aircraft carriers	Seaplane carriers	Heavy cruisers	Light cruisers	Destroyers	Submarines
British Empire	2	—	—	1	7	13	—
American	9	3	—	13	11	80	56
Dutch	—	—	—	—	3	7	13
Free French	—	—	—	—	1	—	—
Total	11	3	—	14	22	100	69
Japan	10	10*	6	18	18	113	63

* 6 fleet carriers, 4 light fleet carriers

But whereas the Japanese fleet was fully trained, with all its different arms closely integrated, and could be rapidly concentrated at any desired point, the Allied forces were widely dispersed and were not trained to work and fight together; each had its own commander, and rapid concentration was out of the question. The eyes of each nation had been focused more on the defence of its own territories than on creating a unified strategy to protect the whole theatre and, in marked contrast to the great share now taken by the United States in the Atlantic battle, no corresponding policy had been agreed for joint defence in the Pacific. Nor could such a policy, if approved by the respective governments, have led immediately to creating a unified fleet. In the Pacific the problem of supply over the vast distances involved will always be the controlling factor and, at this time, there were no properly developed bases between Pearl Harbour and Singapore which Allied ships, squadrons and aircraft could use.

Admiral Phillips now carried out his intention to visit his American colleague at Manila, and left Singapore by air for the Philippines on the 4th. We have no detailed record of the conversations which took place, though the memory of the staff officer who accompanied Admiral Phillips tells us that Admiral Hart revealed his main anxiety to be the safety of the sea supply line from the east to the Philippines and that General MacArthur, on the other hand, wanted the British squadron to come to Manila at once and expressed high hopes of repelling a Japanese landing. The two Flag Officers reached agreement on certain matters of policy though much was, probably inevitably, left nebulous. The agreement was signalled by Admiral Hart to Washington, whence the Navy Office passed it to the Admiralty on the 7th. It may be of interest to summarise that message.

The two Commanders-in-Chief accepted that in the early stages of war with Japan the initiative was bound to rest with the enemy. 'Definite plans cannot be drawn up', they said; 'the most we can do is to decide [the] initial dispositions that appear best.' The importance of preventing the Japanese penetrating the 'Malay barrier' was stressed. The dispositions decided on were, firstly, that 'the British battle fleet would be based on Singapore and act as a striking force against Japanese movements in the China Sea, the Dutch East Indies or through the Malay barrier'. Secondly, a cruiser striking force was to be based on eastern Borneo, Soerabaya and Port Darwin in order to cover and escort convoys in those waters. 'Minimum cruiser forces' for escort work were to be retained in Australian and New Zealand waters and in the Indian Ocean. The importance of co-ordinating their own actions with those of the American Pacific Fleet was next urged, and they asked to be told of the time-table for the movement of the Pacific Fleet westward against the main Japanese strongholds in the Pacific Islands.

To set up a joint headquarters was considered 'impracticable at this time', and strategic control was to remain 'with the respective Commanders-in-Chief', who would work together 'under the principle of mutual co-operation'. Tactical command was to be exercised on the same principles as in the Atlantic. Finally it was hoped to obtain the agreement of the Dutch, Australian and New Zealand authorities to these arrangements 'next week', after which details would be worked out by the two staffs. Admiral Phillips told the First Sea Lord that, in addition to the matter contained in the formal agreement, he and Hart had also decided that Singapore was unsuitable as the main base for future offensive operations, that Manila was the only possible alternative and that measures were in hand to enable the British battle fleet to move there by the following 1st of April. The tentative dispositions of the warships controlled by the two Commanders-in-Chief (or which they hoped to control) were as follows:—

SINGAPORE
Battleships: *Prince of Wales, Repulse, Revenge, Royal Sovereign.*
Cruisers: *Mauritius, Achilles* (N.Z.), *Hobart* (Australian), *Tromp* or *de Ruyter* (Dutch) and possibly *Australia* (Australian).
Destroyers: Ten British, six Dutch, four American.

SOERABAYA–BORNEO–PORT DARWIN
Cruisers: *Houston* (U.S.), *Marblehead* (U.S.), *Cornwall, Java* (Dutch).
Destroyers: Four American.

AUSTRALASIA
Cruisers: *Australia* or *Canberra* (Australian), *Perth* (Australian), *Leander* (N.Z.) and three armed merchant cruisers.

INDIAN OCEAN
Cruisers: *Exeter, Glasgow,* nine of the older 'C', 'D' and 'E' classes and five armed merchant cruisers.

On the particular issue of the U.S. Navy helping to fill the serious destroyer shortage in his fleet, which the Admiralty had raised, Admiral Phillips said that Admiral Hart's understanding was that we would build up our destroyer strength as the battle fleet was reinforced. Of the destroyers at present controlled by Hart 'one Division is at Balik-Papan (in East Borneo) and will proceed to Singapore on the declaration of war'.

But before this message had reached the Admiralty the whole of the intentions of the two Commanders-in-Chief had been frustrated, and their first steps towards building an integrated command system in the Pacific rendered obsolete.

At 8 a.m. on Sunday, the 7th of December, six Japanese aircraft carriers struck deadly blows, without warning, on the United States Pacific Fleet in Pearl Harbour.[1] Their aircraft attacked in two waves, the first consisting of forty torpedo-bombers, fifty high-level bombers and a like number of dive-bombers while the second comprised fifty high-level and eighty dive-bombers. About eighty fighters escorted the striking forces, whose strength and skill were indeed formidable.

---

[1] For a graphic account of the Pearl Harbour attack see S. E. Morison, *History of United States Naval Operations in World War II*, Vol. III (Oxford U.P., 1948), pp. 80–146.

ADMIRAL PHILLIPS GOES TO SEA

Within half an hour the Japanese had accomplished almost the whole of their object—the annihilation of the American battle fleet. The battleship *Arizona* was wrecked, the *Oklahoma* had capsized, the *West Virginia* was sunk and the *California* was sinking. The *Tennessee* and *Nevada* were seriously damaged. Only the *Pennsylvania*, which was in dock, and the *Maryland* escaped major injuries. Shore airfields had suffered badly but, fortunately, the great dockyard and the fuel storages were not heavily attacked. And, by good chance, an important part of the Pacific Fleet, including the aircraft carriers *Lexington* and *Enterprise*, thirteen cruisers and about two dozen destroyers, were at sea at the time of the attack, while the carrier *Saratoga* was on the west coast of America.

But American maritime power in the Pacific was temporarily extinguished, and all hope of successfully disputing control of the South China Sea and South-West Pacific was extinguished with it. The remaining forces of all the nations involved had either to be withdrawn at once or left to fight impossible odds to the finish. The latter course was chosen and, though their last fights made little or no difference to the enemy's progress, the gallantry of the ships and of their crews in tackling vastly superior numbers in one hopeless fight after another will always be a glorious episode in the annals of their services.

It would be easy to suggest, after the event, that the succession of defeats and disasters which now impended could have been avoided if only the governments of the countries concerned had concentrated all their forces in good time at one selected base—presumably Singapore. But, for political as well as strategic reasons, it was impossible for the American Government to move the Pacific Fleet there before the outbreak of war, and without that powerful fleet the enemy's control of the adjacent seas could not be disputed. It would be equally easy to suggest that, once it was obvious that the enemy's maritime control could not be disputed, all naval forces should have been withdrawn. But it was unthinkable for the navies to abandon the land and air forces to carry on the unequal fight alone, or to make no attempt to save the big civilian populations. In fact, once there, the ships had to fight as best they could with what they had, for they were committed to playing their part in the hopeless struggle. It was that requirement which, in the end, dictated the movements of Admiral Phillips' ships.

Attacks on Hong Kong, the Philippines and various Pacific islands, and the invasion of Siam and Malaya started simultaneously with the raid on Pearl Harbour; but here we can only consider the invasion of Malaya. On the 6th of December a large number of Japanese transports, under powerful escort, was sighted off the south-west point of Indo-China steering for the Gulf of Siam. The first landings directed against Malaya took place on the night of the 7th–8th at Singora on the 'neck' of the peninsula, in Siam, and at Kota Bahru, just inside the Malayan frontier.[1] All our airfields in the north of the Federation were heavily attacked at the same time.

Admiral Phillips decided that, given good fighter support and provided that he could achieve surprise, the chance of destroying enemy reinforcements and of cutting their line of supply, so that those on land might be thrown back, was not unfavourable, since none of the modern Japanese major warships had so far appeared in the area. The prospects were discussed on board the flagship on the morning of the 8th and the Admiral's views were supported by all the officers present at the meeting. Air reconnaissance to the northward of his course and fighter cover over the scene of his intended raid—for such it was—were requested. At 5.35 p.m. on the evening of the 8th, the *Prince of Wales, Repulse,* and four destroyers left Singapore and steered to the north-east. Admiral Phillips left his Chief of Staff at Singapore to act as his representative and to co-ordinate the naval requirements with those of the other services.

In the early hours of the next morning, the 9th, a message was received in the *Prince of Wales* from Admiral Palliser reporting that the fighter protection requested off Singora on the 10th could not be provided. A warning that strong Japanese bomber forces were believed to be stationed in southern Indo-China was also passed. The first of the two essential conditions laid down by Admiral Phillips had vanished; but he decided, none the less, to carry on, provided that he was not sighted by enemy aircraft during the 9th. He intended to make a lunge, with the heavy ships only, at the enemy landing forces at Singora early on the 10th. On the afternoon of the 9th Japanese naval aircraft were sighted by the flagship and the second condition, that of surprise, went the way of the first. Admiral Phillips thereupon decided that the risks involved had become unacceptable and at 8.15 p.m. he reversed course for Singapore, whence disturbing reports about Japanese air strength in the north and the disintegration setting in on shore were now being received. Shortly before midnight an 'Immediate' signal was received in the flagship from Admiral Palliser. It said: 'Enemy reported landing Kuantan, latitude 3° 50′ North', but gave no indication of the reliability of the report. Kuantan was much further south than the point at which Admiral Phillips had originally intended to attack and, moreover, was not far off the squadron's return course.[2] It was

---

[1] See Map 43 (*facing p. 565*).
[2] See Map 43.

Map 43
The Sinking of H.M.S.'s Prince of Wales and Repulse
10th December 1941

British in Red
Japanese in Blue
Air Bases ⊙ ⊙

FRENCH INDO CHINA

Camranh Bay

GULF OF SIAM

BANGKOK

Air striking force leaves
6 am Dec 10th
SAIGON

Approx track of Japanese striking force

Cape Cambodia

Intended position
6 am Dec 10th

Singora
Ar Star
Kota Baru
Gong Kedah
Sungei Patani
Butterworth

MALAYA

Kuala Lumpur

Kuantan

Kluang

SINGAPORE

8·15 pm Dec 9th
6·35 pm Dec 9th Destroyer Tenedos detached to Singapore
3 Japanese aircraft sighted

12·50 am Dec 10th
2 pm Dec 9th Reported by Japanese submarine

6 am Dec 10th
6·30 am Dec 10th Enemy aircraft sighted
8 am Dec 10th
11 am Dec 10th Enemy air attacks
Repulse sunk 12·33 pm
Prince of Wales sunk 1·20 pm
(positions approx)

Anamba Is
Natuna Is

Destroyer Tenedos bombed
9·50–10·20 am Dec 10th
12·56 am Dec 9th

Prince of Wales, Repulse and 4 Destroyers
sailed 5·35 pm Dec 8th

BORNEO

Scale
0 20 40 60 80 100 120
NAUTICAL MILES

over 400 miles from the airfields of Indo-China. The report made it necessary for Admiral Phillips to reconsider his decision to return to Singapore for two reasons. In the first place the possibility of surprising an enemy landing force during the critical period of disembarkation was attractive, and it was natural that he should wish to exploit it. Secondly, a road running inland from Kuantan made it possible for the enemy to cut the Army's line of communications up the centre of the Malay Peninsula by landing there. It was an important, even critical point, as Admiral Phillips understood perfectly well.

We have the memory of one of the Admiral's staff officers, who was with him throughout the greater part of this troubled night, to give us a clear idea of the Commander-in-Chief's reaction to the Kuantan report and of the reasons why he acted as he did. According to that witness Admiral Phillips considered that his Chief of Staff at Singapore would realise the effect that the Kuantan report would have on his movements, would expect him to go straight to the threatened point and would arrange fighter cover for his force when it arrived there. To signal his intentions and requirements might reveal his presence and so throw away his chance of surprising the enemy.

At about 1 a.m. on the 10th Admiral Phillips altered course to close the scene of the reported landings. No signal was sent to Singapore telling of his new intention. Actually the report of the Kuantan landing was false, and Singapore took no action to anticipate the squadron arriving there at dawn on the 10th. The difficulty which so commonly faces a flag officer in deciding whether to break wireless silence to keep his subordinates and his colleagues in the other services adequately informed of his intentions was mentioned earlier in another context.[1] In the present instance, after every reason for not informing Singapore of his change of plan has been reviewed, one cannot but feel that Admiral Phillips' belief that air cover would meet him off Kuantan, when he had given Singapore no hint that he was proceeding there, demanded too high a degree of insight from the officers at the base.

We now know that the first sighting report of the British force received by the enemy came from one of his submarines on the afternoon of the 9th, and that his 22nd Air Flotilla, a highly efficient formation which specialised in attacks on ships and comprised some ninety-eight aircraft, thereupon abandoned its intended raid on Singapore and prepared to strike at Admiral Phillips' squadron instead. Two battleships were also ordered to make contact. The Air Flotilla was not ready until about 6 p.m., but the threat to the troop transports was considered so great that it was decided to attempt a

---

[1] See p. 405.

night attack. The search was, however, unsuccessful and the aircraft returned to their base at about midnight. In the early hours of the 10th another Japanese submarine sighted Admiral Phillips' force and fired a salvo of torpedoes at it, all of which missed. She then surfaced and reported the British squadron to be on a southerly course. A new air search was promptly organised by the enemy. It was quickly followed by a striking force of some thirty bombers and fifty torpedo-bombers.

As Admiral Phillips closed towards the coast at dawn, it was obvious that no enemy forces were in the vicinity where the new landings had been reported. While he was investigating some small craft sighted offshore, the first enemy air activity developed. The Japanese striking force had missed the British squadron on its southward run almost to the latitude of Singapore but now, by ill luck, found its quarry on the return journey. Soon after 11 a.m. attacks started, firstly by high-level bombers and then by torpedo-bombers.[1] They were of the very nature which Admiral Phillips had decided he could not risk incurring while he lacked fighter protection. The *Repulse* was hit by a bomb in the first attack but was not very seriously injured. Then the first flight of torpedo-bombers came in and obtained two hits on the flagship, which damaged her grievously. A few minutes later another flight attacked the *Repulse*, almost simultaneously with a second bombing attack. Both were successfully avoided. Soon after noon Captain Tennant closed the flagship, now not under control, to try to help her. A third torpedo attack was now developing and, in spite of skilful manœuvring, the *Repulse* received one hit. Almost simultaneously, the *Prince of Wales*, now apparently incapable of taking avoiding action, was again attacked and received four more torpedo hits in quick succession. It was now 12.23, and fresh waves of torpedo-bombers were still coming in. Three minutes later another hit jammed the *Repulse's* steering gear and placed her at the mercy of the blows now relentlessly pouring on her. Three more torpedo hits in rapid succession sealed her fate and Captain Tennant, realising that the end was near, ordered all his men on deck. His report of the last moments of the *Repulse* must be quoted verbatim. 'When the ship had a list of 30 degrees to port I looked over the side of the bridge and saw the Commander and two or three hundred men collecting on the starboard side. I never saw the slightest sign of panic or ill-discipline. I told them from the bridge how well they had fought the ship, and wished them good luck. The ship hung [for several minutes] with a list of about 60 or 70 degrees to port and then rolled over at 12.33.' The destroyers picked up 796 officers and men of her company of 1,309, including Captain Tennant.

---

[1] See Map 43 (*facing p. 565*).

Meanwhile the *Prince of Wales* was in sorry state, steaming north at slow speed. At 12.44 she received a bomb hit which, however, did not greatly aggravate her damage. But she was settling rapidly in the water and listing heavily to port and was clearly doomed. At 1.20 p.m. she heeled over sharply, turned turtle and sank. The destroyer *Express* had previously gone alongside to take off her wounded and men not required to fight the ship. She, the *Electra* and *Vampire* rescued 1,285 of her complement of 1,612. Neither Admiral Phillips nor Captain Leach was among the survivors.

Thus was the first act in the tragedy of the South Pacific played out to the end. Any previous doubts regarding the efficiency of the Japanese air force had been dispelled in no uncertain manner, for the attacks had been most skilfully carried out. At trifling cost to themselves they had, by sinking two capital ships at sea, accomplished what no other air force had yet achieved—and they had accomplished the feat at a distance of some 400 miles from their bases. From the British point of view the blow, coming so soon after the heavy losses suffered in other theatres, was very severe. Mr Churchill has told how he received the news from the First Sea Lord, and his later account of the disaster to a silent House of Commons is also on record.[1] Though chance may have played a part in guiding the homeward-bound enemy striking force to the squadron's position, it had several times been reported by submarines and aircraft. It therefore seems unlikely that, even had Admiral Phillips not gone to Kuantan in search of a non-existent landing force, it would have escaped attack.

The divergent views expressed in the Chiefs of Staff and Defence Committees regarding the maritime strategy to be adopted in eastern waters have already been discussed; and it has been told how the Admiralty's representatives at the crucial meetings accepted the eastward movement of the capital ships, albeit reluctantly. Had a modern aircraft carrier been able to accompany the force, as had originally been intended, such a squadron might well have exerted a cramping influence on the enemy's strategy, even though it would still have been quite inadequate to fight the Japanese fleet. Whether it was wise to persist with the deterrent plan after the *Indomitable* had been put out of action is open to argument.

As to the conduct of his operations after Admiral Phillips had arrived on his station and Japan had launched her attack, the attempt to destroy the enemy landing forces is surely not open to criticism; for the Admiral could not possibly ignore such a threat to the base on which our whole position in his theatre depended. The only

---

[1] See W. S. Churchill. *The Second World War*, Vol. III, p. 551.

conclusion that can reasonably be drawn is that, after the tremendous events of the 7th of December had transformed the whole war and rendered all previous strategic considerations obsolete, it was inevitable that his ships should in the end, if not immediately share the fate of all the other Allied forces in the area.

After it was all over, the Chiefs of Staff asked the Commander-in-Chief, Far East, whether Admiral Phillips had asked for fighter cover while at sea, after he had abandoned his original plan, and whether Singapore had been kept informed of his position and revised intentions. Air Chief Marshal Sir Robert Brooke-Popham replied that no such request had been made while the squadron was at sea, and that Singapore had not been told of the change of plan or kept informed of the ships' position. The first information of the enemy air attacks which he had received came when the *Repulse* reported that she was being bombed, and fighters were then immediately despatched. They arrived in time to witness the rescue operations.

The loss of Admiral Phillips and of Captain Leach accentuated the tragedy. The former had been Deputy (and later Vice) Chief of Naval Staff for the first two gruelling years of the war. He had been the right hand of the First Sea Lord, had borne an immense burden with unshakable resolution and had won the complete confidence of the Prime Minister. At the age of only fifty-three and while still a Rear-Admiral, he had been selected to command a fleet which it was planned to build up to great strength as soon as possible. All these plans, hopes and intentions were now in ruins.

In justice to Captain Leach and the *Prince of Wales'* company it must be mentioned that, throughout her brief life, she never had a proper chance to reach full efficiency as a fighting unit. Only a few weeks after she first joined the Home Fleet, and while still suffering from serious technical troubles, she was hurried out to fight the *Bismarck*. As soon as she had repaired the damage then received she was sent to Newfoundland for the Atlantic Charter meeting—a mission which was bound to dislocate her internal economy and delay progress towards fighting efficiency. Then the long and hurried journey to the east began, and throughout that passage she lacked most of the aids, such as targets, necessary to improve her state. Admiral Phillips was well aware of this and his understanding of the condition of his flagship played a part in making him decide to turn back on the 9th of December. Even a fully efficient ship, however, could hardly have warded off the fate which overtook the battleship, and though her unsatisfactory condition is a minor issue compared with the strategic policy which placed her where she met her end, it is right that her exceptional difficulties should be left on record. With regard to the

Repulse it should be remembered that she was a very old ship, completed in 1916, and built for speed rather than strength. She had not even been modernised and re-equipped to the same extent as her sister ship the *Renown*. It was hardly to be expected that such a ship could successfully withstand blows of a far more lethal power, and of a totally different type from those which she had been designed a quarter of a century earlier to resist. The lessons driven home by the tragedy of the *Hood* are partly applicable to this second disaster to a British battle cruiser.[1] Parsimony towards the services in peace time will always bring such nemesis in war.

The only redeeming feature of the tragedy was the splendid conduct of the officers and men involved in it. The Royal Navy always seems to rise to its highest peaks of devotion and self-sacrifice in adversity. A young airman who flew over the scene while the destroyers were performing their work of rescue wrote to Admiral Layton these words: 'During that hour I had seen many men in dire danger waving, cheering and joking as if they were holiday-makers at Brighton. . . . It shook me, for here was something above human nature. I take my hat off to them, for in them I saw the spirit which wins wars'. The last, prophetic, sentence was indeed true, as all our enemies were to learn in due time, but the events of the 10th of December 1941 made it certain that the road to victory must still be long and arduous.

The epilogue can be briefly told. On the 11th of December Admiral Layton rehoisted his flag as Commander-in-Chief of an Eastern Fleet now almost non-existent. Since the survivors of the American Pacific Fleet had withdrawn to their west coast bases, the way to complete domination of the seas washing the East Indian archipelago, beyond which lay Australia and New Zealand, was now wide open to the enemy.

As soon as he had reassumed command Admiral Layton told the Admiralty that, if Singapore was to be held, reinforcements must be sent, and at once. But the truth was that such reinforcements did not exist and, even if the Mediterranean had been evacuated, we could not have sent out adequate strength in time to reverse the trend of the land campaign. On the 13th Admiral Layton, foreseeing that Singapore would soon be a beleaguered fortress and the naval base unusable, proposed to send everything he could, except his submarines, to Colombo, which, plainly, was the strategic centre round which our strength must be rebuilt. Next day the Admiralty approved his proposal and thus, under the impact of disaster, we reverted to the policy which the Admiralty had originally wished to adopt.

---

[1] See p. 417.

The problems of strategic control in the threatened area, however, had still not been solved. The survivors of the American Asiatic Fleet were controlled from Washington, and British, Dutch, Australian and New Zealand authorities still controlled the strategic dispositions of their own naval forces. But the Prime Minister arrived in Washington on the 22nd of December, having crossed the Atlantic in the *Duke of York*. Plans, necessarily of a long-term nature, to rebuild Allied maritime power in the Pacific were there formulated, and unified command of the A.B.D.A. (American-British-Dutch-Australian) area was agreed during his visit.[1]

Meanwhile Hong Kong, attacked on the 8th of December, fell on Christmas Day and the slender naval forces left there were all destroyed. On the 16th Borneo was invaded, and by the capture of its airfields and harbours the enemy was able to outflank Malaya and to facilitate his further penetration southwards. The Dutch submarines mentioned earlier obtained some successes against troopships and supply vessels and, before the end of the year, two British submarines were ordered to Singapore from the Mediterranean. But submarines alone could not hope to check the enemy's progress, let alone stop it, and the year closed with unbroken storm clouds hanging on the eastern horizon.

---

[1] See the forthcoming volume of this series by J. M. A. Gwyer, *Grand Strategy*, Vol. III.

Appendices

APPENDIX A

The Board of Admiralty
Sept. 1939–Dec. 1941

Date of appointment

First Lord: Rt. Hon. Winston L. Spencer Churchill   3.9.39
Rt. Hon. Albert V. Alexander   12.5.40

First Sea Lord and Chief of Naval Staff:
Admiral of the Fleet Sir A. Dudley P. R. Pound   12.6.39

Second Sea Lord and Chief of Naval Personnel:
Admiral Sir Charles J. C. Little   30.9.38
Vice-Admiral W. J. Whitworth   1.6.41

Third Sea Lord and Controller:
Rear-Admiral B. A. Fraser   1.3.39

Fourth Sea Lord and Chief of Supplies and Transport:
Rear-Admiral G. S. Arbuthnot   1.10.37
Vice-Admiral J. H. D. Cunningham   1.4.41

Fifth Sea Lord and Chief of Naval Air Services:
Vice-Admiral the Hon. Sir Alexander R. M. Ramsay   19.7.38
Vice-Admiral G. C. C. Royle   21.11.39
Rear-Admiral A. L. St. G. Lyster   14.4.41

Deputy Chief of Naval Staff (Vice-Chief of Naval Staff from 22.4.40):
Rear-Admiral T. S. V. Phillips   1.6.39
Vice-Admiral H. R. Moore   21.10.41

Assistant Chief of Naval Staff (Assistant Chief of Naval Staff (Trade) from 27.5.40):
Rear-Admiral H. M. Burrough   10.1.39
Rear-Admiral H. R. Moore   25.7.40
Vice-Admiral E. L. S. King   21.10.41

Assistant Chief of Naval Staff (Foreign):
Vice-Admiral Sir Geoffrey Blake (ret.)   8.4.40
Rear-Admiral Sir Henry H. Harwood   2.12.40

Assistant Chief of Naval Staff (Home):
Captain A. J. Power   27.5.40

Parliamentary and Financial Secretary:
Geoffrey Shakespeare, Esq.   28.5.37
Sir Victor A. G. A. Warrender, Bart.   4.4.40

Civil Lord: Captain A. U. M. Hudson   15.7.39

Controller of Merchant Shipbuilding and Repairs:
Sir James Lithgow, Bart.   1.2.40

Permanent Secretary:
Sir R. H. Archibald Carter   23.7.36
H. V. Markham, Esq.   5.12.40

APPENDIX B

The Defensive Arming of Merchant Ships

The position on 1st March 1941 was as follows:

1. Ships armed with anti-submarine guns:

	British	2,943
	Allied	491
	Total	3,434

2. Ships armed with heavy anti-aircraft guns (3-inch and 12-pounder): 1,693

3. Ships armed with one or more close-range anti-aircraft weapons:

	British	3,434
	Allied	997
	Total	4,431

4. Particulars of close-range anti-aircraft weapons supplied to ships:
    - Lewis guns 1,400
    - Savage Lewis guns . . . 1,250
    - Hotchkiss guns 4,589
    - Holman projectors . . . 1,051[1]
    - Parachute and cable equipments . 605[2]
    - Kite equipments 2,289

5. Heavy anti-aircraft machine guns (40-mm Bofors). The War Office was providing 200 of these to British ships.

6. Weapons supplied for 'shuttle services'. In addition to the anti-aircraft equipments tabulated under 4 above the following were supplied to ships sailing on certain routes and were manned on the principle of the 'shuttle service'.
    - (a) Naval: Channel convoys—150 Lewis guns.
      Gibraltar convoys—200 Savage Lewis guns.
    - (b) Army: Coastal convoys—1,000 various weapons.
      Personnel and M.T. ships—4 to 6 per ship.

7. Fishing vessels (total about 800) were supplied with machine guns before they went to sea on each occasion.

NOTES: (1) The Holman Projector was an extemporised weapon which used steam or compressed air to throw a Mills hand grenade.
(2) The Parachute and Cable (P.A.C.) equipment was a small rocket projector which carried up a wire on a parachute.

APPENDIX C

The Royal Navy and Royal Marines
Active and Reserve Strength, 1939–45

I. *Royal Navy Active Service Strength on 1st January 1939:*

Officers	9,762
Ratings	109,170
Total	118,932

II. *Royal Marines Active Strength before mobilisation:*

Officers and men	12,390

III. *Royal Navy and Royal Marine Reserve Strength (1st January 1939):*

R.N. Officers on Retired and Emergency Lists	8,545
R.N. Pensioners under 55 years of age	29,256
Royal Marine Pensioners under 55 years of age	2,406 (by 12.9.39)
Royal Fleet Reserve	13,684
Royal Fleet Reserve (Royal Marines)	1,082 (by 12.9.39)
Royal Naval Reserve Officers	1,641
Ratings	8,397
Royal Naval Volunteer Reserve. Officers	809
Ratings	5,371
Royal Naval Auxiliary Sick Berth Reserve	1,450
Royal Naval Wireless Auxiliary Reserve Officers	20
Ratings	579
Total	73,240

APPENDIX C, continued

IV. *Royal Navy and Royal Marines Increase in Strength, 1939–45:*

Date	R.N. and R.M. officers and men	W.R.N.S.	Merchant Navy personnel serving in R.N. under special agreements	Total strength
30.6.39	129,000	—	—	129,000
30.6.40	265,000	5,600	11,000	281,600
30.6.41	391,000	15,100	14,000	420,100
30.6.42	496,000	28,600	11,000	535,600
30.6.43	660,000	53,300	11,000	724,300
30.6.44	778,000	73,500	12,000	863,500
30.6.45	776,000	72,000	13,000	861,000

APPENDIX D

Particulars of principal British and Dominion warships in commission, preparing to commission or building in September 1939

(Dates in brackets are completion dates.
HA = High Angle, LA = Low Angle).

I. BATTLESHIPS

KING GEORGE V CLASS (all building):
King George V, Prince of Wales, Duke of York, Jellicoe (later *Anson*), *Beatty* (later *Howe*)
  Displacement: 35,000 tons
  Armament: 10 14-inch, 16 5·25-inch HA/LA
  Maximum speed: 28½ knots

NELSON CLASS: *Nelson, Rodney* (1927)
  Displacement: 33,900 tons
  Armament: 9 16-inch, 12 6-inch, 6 4·7-inch AA
  Maximum speed: 23 knots

ROYAL SOVEREIGN CLASS: *Royal Sovereign, Royal Oak, Resolution,*
Ramillies, Revenge (1916–17)
  Displacement: 29,150 tons
  Armament: 8 15-inch, 12 6-inch, 8 4-inch HA
  Maximum speed: 21 knots

QUEEN ELIZABETH CLASS: *Queen Elizabeth, Warspite, Valiant, Malaya, Barham* (1915–16). (*Warspite, Valiant* and *Queen Elizabeth* extensively modernised 1937–40)
  Displacement: 31,000 tons
  Armament: 8 15-inch, 8 to 12 6-inch, 8 4-inch HA or 8 4·5-inch HA/LA
  Maximum speed: 24 knots

II. BATTLE CRUISERS

Hood (1920)
  Displacement: 42,100 tons
  Armament: 8 15-inch, 12 5·5-inch, 8 4-inch HA
  Maximum speed: 31 knots

Renown (1916—extensively modernised 1936–39)
  Displacement: 32,000 tons
  Armament: 6 15-inch, 10 4·5-inch HA/LA
  Maximum speed: 29 knots

Repulse (1916)—As for *Renown* except secondary armaments 12 4-inch, 8 4-inch HA

III. AIRCRAFT CARRIERS

ILLUSTRIOUS CLASS: *Illustrious, Victorious, Formidable, Indomitable, Implacable, Indefatigable* (all building)
  Displacement: 23,000 tons
  Aircraft carried: 70
  Armament: 16 4·5-inch HA/LA
  Maximum speed: 30 knots

Ark Royal (1938)
  Displacement: 22,000 tons
  Aircraft carried: 60
  Armament: 16 4·5-inch HA/LA
  Maximum speed: 31 knots

III. AIRCRAFT CARRIERS (continued)

COURAGEOUS CLASS: *Courageous, Glorious* (1916, converted to aircraft carriers 1928–30)
  Displacement: 22,500 tons
  Aircraft carried: 48
  Armament: 16 4·7-inch HA/LA
  Maximum speed: 30 knots

Furious (1917, converted to aircraft carrier 1921–25)
  Displacement: 22,450 tons
  Aircraft carried: 33
  Armament: 10 5·5-inch, 8 4-inch HA
  Maximum speed: 30 knots

Eagle (1924—converted from battleship during construction)
  Displacement: 22,600 tons
  Aircraft carried: 21
  Armament: 9 6-inch, 4 4-inch HA
  Maximum speed: 24 knots

Hermes (1924)
  Displacement: 10,850 tons
  Aircraft carried: 15
  Armament: 6 5·5-inch, 3 4-inch HA
  Maximum speed: 25 knots

IV. HEAVY CRUISERS

Exeter, York (1931 and 1930 respectively)
  Displacement: 8,300 tons
  Armament: 6 8-inch, 4 4-inch HA
  Maximum speed: 32 knots

Dorsetshire, Norfolk (1930)
  Displacement: 9,950 tons
  Armament: 8 8-inch, 8 4-inch HA
  Maximum speed: 32 knots

Devonshire, London, Shropshire, Sussex (1929)
  Displacement: 9,850 tons
  Armament: 8 8-inch, 8 4-inch HA
  Maximum speed: 32 knots

Berwick, Cornwall, Cumberland, Kent, Suffolk, Australia (R.A.N.), *Canberra* (R.A.N.) (1928)
  Displacement: 10,000 tons
  Armament: 8 8-inch, 6 or 8 4-inch HA
  Maximum speed: 31½ knots

Edinburgh, Belfast (1939)
  Displacement: 10,000 tons
  Armament: 12 6-inch, 12 4-inch HA
  Maximum speed: 32½ knots

Southampton, Newcastle, Sheffield, Birmingham, Glasgow, Gloucester, Liverpool, Manchester (1937–39)
  Displacement: 9,100–9,400 tons
  Armament: 12 6-inch, 8 4-inch HA
  Maximum speed: 32 knots

Fiji, Kenya, Mauritius, Nigeria, Trinidad, Ceylon, Gambia, Jamaica, Uganda (all building)
  Displacement: 8,000 tons
  Armament: 12 6-inch, 8 4-inch HA
  Maximum speed: 31½ knots

V. LIGHT CRUISERS

Arethusa, Galatea, Penelope, Aurora (1935–37)
  Displacement: 5,220 tons
  Armament: 6 6-inch, 4 or 8 4-inch HA
  Maximum speed: 32 knots

Leander, Achilles, Perth (R.A.N.), *Sydney* (R.A.N.), *Hobart* (R.A.N.) (1933–36)
  Displacement: 6,830 to 7,270 tons
  Armament: 8 6-inch, 4 4-inch HA
  Maximum speed: 32½ knots

Ajax, Neptune, Orion (1934–35)
  Displacement: 6,985 to 7,215 tons
  Armament: 8 6-inch, 8 4-inch HA
  Maximum speed: 32½ knots

APPENDIX D, continued

V. LIGHT CRUISERS (continued)

Emerald, Enterprise (1926)
  Displacement: 7,550 tons
  Armament: 7 6-inch, 3 4-inch HA
  Maximum speed: 32 knots

Effingham, Frobisher, Hawkins (1919-25)
  Displacement: 9,500-9,850 tons
  Armament: 9 6-inch, 4 4-inch HA
  Maximum speed: 30½ knots

Despatch, Diomede, Delhi, Dunedin, Durban, Danae, Dauntless, Dragon (1918-22)
  Displacement: 4,850 tons
  Armament: 6 6-inch, 3 4-inch HA
  Maximum speed, 29 knots

Capetown, Colombo, Cardiff, Ceres (1917-19) (First two rearming as A.A. Cruisers)
  Displacement: 4,290 tons
  Armament: 5 6-inch, 2 3-inch HA
  Maximum speed: 29 knots

Caledon, Calypso, Caradoc
  Displacement: 4,180 tons
  Armament: 5 6-inch, 2 3-inch HA
  Maximum speed: 29 knots

Dido, Euryalus, Naiad, Phoebe, Sirius, Bonaventure, Hermione, Cleopatra, Scylla, Charybdis (all building)
  Displacement: 5,450 tons
  Armament: 10 5·25-inch HA/LA
  Maximum speed: 33 knots

VI. ANTI-AIRCRAFT CRUISERS

Coventry, Curlew, Cairo, Calcutta, Carlisle, Curacoa (1917-18, converted 1937-39)

Displacement: 4,200 tons
Armament: 8 4-inch HA
Maximum speed: 29 knots

VII. MINELAYERS

Adventure (1927)
  Displacement: 6,740 tons
  Armament: 4 4·7-inch HA, 340 mines
  Maximum speed: 28 knots

Abdiel, Latona, Manxman, Welshman (all building)
  Displacement: 2,650 tons
  Armament: 6 4-inch HA, 156 mines
  Maximum speed: 39¾ knots

VIII. DESTROYERS

	No.	Displacement	Armament (T.T. = Torpedo Tubes)	Max. Speed
LAFOREY CLASS (building):	1 leader 7 destroyers	1,935 tons 1,920 tons	6 4·7-inch 8 T.T.	36 knots
JAVELIN CLASS (1939):	2 leaders 14 destroyers	1,695 tons 1,690 tons	6 4·7-inch 10 T.T.	36 knots
KELLY CLASS (1939):				
TRIBAL CLASS (1938-39):	2 leaders 14 destroyers	1,870 tons	8 4·7-inch 4 T.T.	36½ knots
INTREPID CLASS (1937-38):	1 leader 8 destroyers	1,530 tons 1,370 tons	4 4·7-inch 10 T.T.	36½ knots
HERO CLASS (1936-37):	1 leader	1,505 tons	5 4·7-inch 8 T.T.	36½ knots
	8 destroyers	1,340 tons	4 4·7-inch 8 T.T.	36½ knots

VIII. DESTROYERS (continued)

	No.	Displacement	Armament (T.T. = Torpedo Tubes)	Max. Speed
GREYHOUND CLASS (1936):	1 leader	1,485 tons	5 4·7-inch 8 T.T.	36½ knots
	8 destroyers	1,335 tons	4 4·7-inch 8 T.T.	36½ knots
FEARLESS CLASS (1935):	1 leader	1,460 tons	5 4·7-inch 8 T.T.	36½ knots
	8 destroyers	1,375 tons	4 4·7-inch 8 T.T.	36 knots
ECLIPSE CLASS (1934):	1 leader	1,475 tons	5 4·7-inch 8 T.T.	36½ knots
	8 destroyers	1,375 tons	4 4·7-inch 8 T.T.	36 knots
DEFENDER CLASS (1932–33):	1 leader 8 destroyers	1,400 tons 1,375 tons	4 4·7-inch 8 T.T.	36 knots
CRUSADER CLASS (1932):	1 leader 4 destroyers (*Fraser* Class, R.C.N.)	1,390 tons 1,375 tons	4 4·7-inch 8 T.T.	36 knots
BEAGLE CLASS (1931):	1 leader 8 destroyers	1,400 tons 1,360 tons	4 4·7-inch 8 T.T.	35 knots
ACASTA CLASS (1930–31):	1 leader	1,540 tons	5 4·7-inch 8 T.T.	35 knots
	8 destroyers	1,350 tons	4 4·7-inch 8 T.T.	35 knots
AMAZON CLASS (1927–31):	4 destroyers (2 R.C.N.)	1,170– 1,350 tons	4 4·7-inch 6–8 T.T.	35–37 knots
ADMIRALTY-DESIGN LEADERS (1918–19):	6 (includes 1 R.A.N.)	1,530 tons	5 4·7-inch 6 T.T.	36½ knots
THORNYCROFT-DESIGN LEADERS (1919–25):	3	1,480 tons	5 4·7-inch 6 T.T.	36 knots
V AND W CLASSES (Admiralty and Thornycroft designs) (1917–24)	1 leader 42 destroyers (includes 4 R.A.N.)	1,090 tons 1,120 tons	4 4-inch 5–6 T.T.	34–35 knots
R AND S CLASSES (1917–24):	11	905 tons	3 4-inch 3 T.T.	34½–36 knots

IX. SUBMARINES

TRITON CLASS (1936–39)
Number: 15
Displacement: 1,100–1,600 tons
Armament: 1 4-inch, 10 torpedo tubes
Maximum speed: 9–15 knots

PORPOISE CLASS (Minelayers 1934–39)
Number: 6
Displacement: 1,500–2,157 tons
Armament: 1 4-inch, 6 torpedo tubes
Maximum speed: 9–15 knots

THAMES CLASS (1932–35)
Number: 3
Displacement: 1,850–2,700 tons
Armament: 1 4-inch, 6 torpedo tubes
Maximum speed: 10–22 knots

RAINBOW CLASS (1930–32)
Number: 4
Displacement: 1,475–2,030 tons
Armament: 1 4-inch, 8 torpedo tubes
Maximum speed: 9–17 knots

APPENDIX D, continued

IX. SUBMARINES (continued)

PARTHIAN CLASS (1930–31)
Number: 5
Displacement: 1,475–2,030 tons
Armament: 1 4-inch, 8 torpedo tubes
Maximum speed: 9–17 knots

ODIN AND OBERON CLASSES (1927–31)
Number: 9
Displacement: 1,475–2,030 tons
Armament: 1 4-inch, 8 torpedo tubes
Maximum speed: 9–16 knots

L CLASS (1918–19)
Number: 3
Displacement: 760–1,080 tons
Armament: 1 4-inch, 4 torpedo tubes
Maximum speed: $10\frac{1}{2}$–$17\frac{1}{2}$ knots

SHARK AND SWORDFISH CLASSES (1932–38)
Number: 12
Displacement: 670–960 tons
Armament: 1 3-inch, 6 torpedo tubes
Maximum speed: 10–15 knots

UNITY CLASS (1937–38)
Number: 3
Displacement: 540–730 tons
Armament: 6 torpedo tubes
Maximum speed: 10–11 knots

H CLASS (1918–19)
Number: 9
Displacement: 410–500 tons
Armament: 4 torpedo tubes
Maximum speed: $10\frac{1}{2}$–13 knots

X. ESCORT VESSELS

HUNT CLASS (all building—reclassified as destroyers on entering service in 1940)
Number: 20
Displacement: 900 tons
Armament: 4 4-inch HA
Maximum speed: 32 knots

EX V AND W DESTROYERS
Number: 15
Displacement: 1,090–1,100 tons
Armament: 4 4-inch HA
Maximum speed: 35 knots

EGRET CLASS (1938–39)
Number: 3
Displacement: 1,200 tons
Armament: 8 4-inch HA
Maximum speed: 19 knots

BLACK SWAN CLASS (1939–40)
Number: 4 (building)
Displacement: 1,250 tons
Armament: 6 4-inch HA
Maximum speed: 19 knots

BITTERN CLASS (1935–38)
Number: 3
Displacement: 1,190 tons
Armament: 6 4-inch HA or 4 4·7-inch HA
Maximum speed: 19 knots

GRIMSBY CLASS (1934–36)
Number: 8
Displacement: 990 tons
Armament: 4 4-inch HA
Maximum speed: $16\frac{1}{2}$ knots

GRIMSBY CLASS (R.A.N.) (1935–39)
Number: 4
Displacement: 1,060 tons
Armament: 3 4-inch HA/LA
Maximum speed: $16\frac{1}{2}$ knots

BRIDGEWATER, HASTINGS, SHOREHAM AND REPEAT SHOREHAM CLASSES (1929–33)
Number: 14
Displacement: 1,025 to 1,105 tons
Armament: 2 4-inch HA or 1 4-inch HA and 1 4-inch LA
Maximum speed: $16\frac{1}{2}$ knots

Indus and *Hindustan* (R.I.N.) (1930–35)
Number: 2
Displacement: 1,190 tons
Armament: 2 4-inch or 4·7-inch
Maximum speed: $16\frac{1}{2}$ knots

APPENDIX D, continued

XI. PATROL VESSELS

KINGFISHER CLASS (1935–38)
  Number: 6
  Displacement: 510–530 tons
  Armament: 1 4-inch HA
  Maximum speed: 20 knots

GUILLEMOT CLASS (building)
  Number: 3
  Displacement: 580 tons
  Armament: 1 4-inch HA
  Maximum speed: 20 knots

XII. MINESWEEPERS

BANGOR CLASS (building)
  Number: 10
  Displacement: 500 tons
  Armament: 1 4-inch HA
  Maximum speed: 16½ knots

HALCYON CLASS (1934–39)
  Number: 19
  Displacement: 815–875 tons
  Armament: 2 4-inch HA
  Maximum speed: 16½ knots

ABERDARE CLASS (1917–19)
  Number: 23
  Displacement: 675–710 tons
  Armament: 1 4-inch
  Maximum speed: 16 knots

XIII. MONITORS

Erebus, Terror (1916)
  Displacement: 7,200 tons
  Armament: 2 15-inch, 8 4-inch
  Maximum speed: 12 knots

XIV. NETLAYERS

Guardian, Protector (1932–36)
  Displacement: 2,900 tons
  Armament: 2 4-inch HA
  Maximum speed: 18–20 knots

APPENDIX E

The Distribution of British and Dominion Naval Strength, September 1939

I. HOME FLEET

   Battleships: 2nd Battle Squadron: *Nelson, Rodney, Royal Oak, Royal Sovereign, Ramillies.*
   Battle Cruiser Squadron: *Hood, Repulse.*
   Aircraft carriers: *Ark Royal, Furious* (training aircraft carrier).
   Cruisers: 18th Cruiser Squadron: *Sheffield, Edinburgh, Belfast, Newcastle.*
   12th Cruiser Squadron: *Effingham, Emerald, Enterprise, Dunedin, Cardiff, Delhi.*
   7th Cruiser Squadron: *Diomede, Dragon, Caledon, Calypso.*
   Destroyer Command: Cruiser *Aurora.*
   6th Destroyer Flotilla (8 destroyers).
   8th Destroyer Flotilla (9 destroyers).
   Depot Ship *Greenwich*
   Submarines: 2nd Submarine Flotilla: Depot Ship *Forth* and 14 submarines.
   6th Submarine Flotilla: Depot Ship *Titania* and 7 submarines.
   Minesweepers: 1st Minesweeping Flotilla: 7 Fleet minesweepers.
   A.A. Cruiser: *Calcutta.*
   Netlayer: *Guardian.*

II. CHANNEL FORCE

   Battleships: *Resolution, Revenge.*
   Cruisers: *Ceres, Caradoc.*
   A.A. Cruiser: *Cairo.*
   Aircraft carriers: *Courageous, Hermes.*
   18th Destroyer Flotilla (5 destroyers).

III. HUMBER FORCE

   Cruisers: *Southampton, Glasgow.*
   7th Destroyer Flotilla (9 destroyers).
   Minesweepers: 2.

IV. HOME WAR ORGANISATION OF DESTROYERS OTHER THAN THOSE SHOWN ABOVE

   11th Destroyer Flotilla (10 destroyers), Plymouth.
   12th Destroyer Flotilla (6 destroyers), Portland.
   15th Destroyer Flotilla (8 destroyers), Rosyth and Milford Haven.
   16th Destroyer Flotilla (6 destroyers), Portsmouth.
   17th Destroyer Flotilla (8 destroyers), Plymouth.
   19th Destroyer Flotilla (9 destroyers), Dover.
   Attached destroyers: Portsmouth, 4.

APPENDIX E, continued

V. Home Command Escort, Minesweeping and A/S Forces

Nore Command } Dover: 3 minesweepers.
Thames Estuary: 3 minesweepers, 9 minesweeping trawlers.
Portsmouth Command: 4 minesweepers, 4 minesweeping trawlers.
5 A/S trawlers.

Western Approaches Command } Plymouth Command: 3 minesweeping trawlers.
3 A/S trawlers.
6 escort vessels.

Rosyth Command: 8 escort vessels.

VI. Mediterranean Fleet

Battleships: 1st Battle Squadron: *Warspite, Barham, Malaya.*
Aircraft carrier: *Glorious.*
Cruisers: 1st Cruiser Squadron: *Devonshire, Shropshire, Sussex.*
      3rd Cruiser Squadron: *Arethusa, Penelope.* A.A. cruiser *Coventry.*
Destroyer Command: Cruiser *Galatea.* Depot Ship *Woolwich.*
      1st Destroyer Flotilla (9 destroyers).
      2nd Destroyer Flotilla (5 destroyers). (Ordered home.)
      3rd Destroyer Flotilla (9 destroyers).
      4th Destroyer Flotilla (8 destroyers).
Escort vessels: 4.
Submarines: Depot Ship *Maidstone*
      1st Submarine Flotilla (10 submarines).
Motor torpedo-boats: 1st M.T.B. Flotilla: Depot Ship *Vulcan* and 12 M.T.B.s.
Netlayer: *Protector.*
Minelayer: *Medusa.*
Minesweepers: 3rd Minesweeping Flotilla (5 Minesweepers).
Repair ship: *Resource.*

VII. North Atlantic Command

Cruisers: *Colombo, Capetown.*
Destroyers: 13th Destroyer Flotilla (9 destroyers).
Submarines: 2.
Minesweepers: 2.

VIII. China Station

Cruisers: 5th Cruiser Squadron: *Kent, Cornwall, Birmingham, Dorsetshire.*
Aircraft carrier: *Eagle.*
Destroyers: 21st Destroyer Flotilla (9 destroyers). (Ordered to Mediterranean.)
Escort vessels: 5.
Submarines: 4th Submarine Flotilla: Depot Ship *Medway*, 1 destroyer and 15 submarines.
Destroyers for local defence of Hong Kong: 5.
Minelayer: *Redstart.*
Motor torpedo-boats: 2nd M.T.B. Flotilla (6 boats).
River gunboats: 20.
Monitor: *Terror.*

APPENDIX E, continued

IX. SOUTH ATLANTIC COMMAND
   Cruisers: 6th Cruiser Squadron. *Neptune.*
   9th Cruiser Squadron. *Despatch, Dauntless, Danae, Durban.*
   South American Division: *Exeter, Ajax, Cumberland.*
   Destroyers: 4th Division of 2nd Flotilla (4 destroyers).
   Seaplane carrier: *Albatross.* Escort vessels: 4. Submarines: 2.

X. AMERICA AND WEST INDIES STATION
   Cruisers: 8th Cruiser Squadron: *Berwick, Orion, York, Perth* (R.A.N.)
   Escort vessels: 2.

XI. EAST INDIES STATION
   Cruisers: 4th Cruiser Squadron: *Gloucester, Liverpool, Manchester.*
   Escort vessels: 7 (including 5 R.I.N.).

XII. ROYAL AUSTRALIAN NAVY
   Cruisers: *Canberra, Australia, Sydney, Hobart, Adelaide.*
   Destroyers: 3.
   Escort vessels: 2.

XIII. ROYAL CANADIAN NAVY
   Destroyers: 6.

XIV. NEW ZEALAND DIVISION OF R.N. (Royal New Zealand Navy from 1.10.41)
   Cruisers: *Leander, Achilles.*
   Escort vessels: 2.

XV. MISCELLANEOUS SERVICES
   5th Submarine Flotilla (Training): Depot Ship *Alecto* and 8 submarines.
   Cadet's training cruiser: *Vindictive.*
   Surveying ships: 8.
   Motor A/S boats: 1st Flotilla, 5 boats.

XVI. SHIPS IN RESERVE
   Cruisers: *Hawkins, Frobisher.*
   Aircraft carrier: *Argus.*
   Minelaying cruiser: *Adventure.*
   Destroyers: 5.
   Minesweepers: 10.
   Seaplane carrier: *Pegasus.*

XVII. SHIPS UNDERGOING MAJOR REFITS AND REPAIRS

	Approx. completion date:
Battleships: *Queen Elizabeth*	Autumn 1940
Valiant	Under review.
Battle cruiser: *Renown*	September 1939.
Cruisers: *Suffolk*	September 1939.
London	August 1940.
Norfolk	September 1939.

   Escort vessel: 1.
   Destroyers: 14.
   A.A. cruisers: *Curlew, Curacoa, Carlisle.*

XVIII. SHIPS BUILDING (dates are dates of Naval Building Programmes)
   Battleships:
      1936 *King George V, Prince of Wales.*
      1937 *Duke of York, Jellicoe* (renamed *Anson* later), *Beatty* (renamed *Howe* later).
   Aircraft Carriers:
      1936 *Illustrious, Victorious.*
      1937 *Formidable, Indomitable.*
      1938 *Implacable.*
      1939 *Indefatigable.*
   Cruisers:
      1936 *Dido, Euryalus, Naiad, Phoebe, Sirius.*
      1937 *Bonaventure, Fiji, Hermione, Kenya, Mauritius, Trinidad.*
      1938 *Nigeria, Charybdis, Cleopatra, Gambia, Scylla, Jamaica, Ceylon, Uganda.*
   Flotilla Leaders and Destroyers:
      1936 1 (remainder of J Class already completed).
      1937 15. K and L Classes.
      1939 16. M and N Classes.
   Submarines:
      1936 2.
      1937 6.
      1938 3.
   Escort Vessels:
      1937 2.
      1939 2.
   Escort Destroyers (*Hunt* Class):
      1939 20.
   Fast Minelayers:
      1938 *Abdiel, Latona, Manxman.*
      1939 *Welshman.*
   Minesweepers:
      1939 20 *Bangor* Class.
            20 minesweeping trawlers.

XIX. SUMMARY of the distribution of British Empire naval strength by classes
   Battleships and Battle Cruisers:
Home Commands	9
Mediterranean	3
Total	12

   Aircraft Carriers:
Home Commands	5	(1 seaplane carrier)
Mediterranean	1	
South Atlantic	1	(seaplane carrier)
China	1	
Total	8	

APPENDIX E, continued

Fleet Cruisers:
- Home Commands 8
- Mediterranean 6
- East Indies 3
- China 4
- South Atlantic 4
- America and West Indies 4 (1 R.A.N.)
- Australia 4 (R.A.N.)
- New Zealand 2 (N.Z. Division)
- Total 35

Trade Route or Convoy Cruisers (including Anti-Aircraft Cruisers):
- Home Commands 15
- Mediterrranean 1
- South Atlantic 4
- North Atlantic 2
- Australia 1 (R.A.N.)
- Total 23

Fleet Destroyers:
- Home Fleet 33
- Nore 8
- Portsmouth 10
- Western Approaches 1
- North Atlantic 1
- South Atlantic 4
- Mediterranean 29
- China 8
- Canada 6 (R.C.N.)
- Total 100

Escort Destroyers, Sloops and Corvettes:
- Rosyth 18
- Portsmouth 10
- Western Approaches 26
- North Atlantic 8
- South Atlantic 4
- America and West Indies 2
- Mediterranean 4
- East Indies 7
- China 8
- Australia 7 (R.A.N.)
- New Zealand 2 (N.Z. Division)
- India 5 (R.I.N.)
- Total 101

Submarines:
- Home Fleet 16
- Mediterranean 9
- China 13
- Total 38

APPENDIX F

Summary of principal warships built for the Royal Navy under the 1939, War Emergency, 1940 and 1941 Naval Building Programmes, including Supplementary and Additional Programmes.

Note: Only ships which were actually completed and accepted into service are shown in this table. Ships converted from merchantmen are *not* included.

1939 Programme	War Emergency Programme	1940 Programme	1941 Programme
Aircraft carrier—*Indefatigable* Cruisers—*Bermuda, Newfoundland*	Cruisers—*Argonaut, Spartan, Royalist, Bellona, Black Prince, Diadem*		Cruisers—*Swiftsure, Ontario* (for R.C.N.)
Fast minelayer—*Welshman*		Monitor—*Roberts*	Monitor—*Abercrombie*
			Fast Minelayers—*Ariadne, Apollo*
			Escort carriers—*Archer, Avenger, Biter, Dasher, Attacker, Battler, Stalker, Hunter, Tracker, Fencer, Searcher, Chaser, Ravager, Striker, Pursuer* (all under Lend-Lease)
Flotilla leaders and Destroyers— Milne Class—8 Napier Class—8	Flotilla leaders and destroyers— Havant Class—6 (originally for Brazil) Onslow Class—8 Pakenham Class—8	Flotilla leaders and destroyers— Quilliam Class—8 Rotherham Class—8 Saumarez Class—8 Troubridge Class—8	Flotilla leaders and destroyers— Ulster Class—8 Valentine Class—8 (2 for R.C.N.) Wager Class—8 Zambesi Class—8 Caesar Class—8
Escort destroyers— Hunt Class—20	Escort destroyers— Hunt Class—36	Escort destroyers— Hunt Class—30	

APPENDIX F, continued

1939 Programme	War Emergency Programme	1940 Programme	1941 Programme
Escort vessels— Black Swan Class—2	—	Sloops— Modified Black Swan Class—18	Sloops— Modified Black Swan Class—9
—	—	Frigates— River Class—27	Frigates— River Class—27 Captain Class—64 (all under Lend-Lease)
Corvettes— Flower Class—56	Corvettes— Flower Class—60	Corvettes— Flower Class—25	Corvettes— Flower Class—10 (7 under Lend-Lease) Kil Class—15 (all under Lend-Lease)
—	Submarines— Triton Class—7 Unity Class—12 1940 'S' Class—5	Submarines— Triton Class—9 Unity Class—22 1940 'S' Class—13	Submarines— Triton Class—17 Unity Class—20 1940 'S' Class—15
Minesweepers— Bangor Class—20	Minesweepers— Bangor Class—16	Minesweepers— Bangor Class—12 Bathurst Class—20 Algerine Class—19	Minesweepers— 'A.M. 100' Class—22 (all under Lend-Lease) Algerine Class—30 (15 under Lend-Lease)
Trawlers— Tree Class—20	Trawlers— Lake Class—6 Shakespearian Class—12 Dance Class—20	Trawlers— Isles Class—67 Portadown Class—12 Hill Class—8 Round Table Class—8 Fish Class—4	Trawlers— Isles Class—22 Military Class—3

APPENDIX G

The German Navy at the Outbreak of War

Key to dispositions on 1/9/39: (W) Wilhelmshaven; (B) Brunsbüttel; (K) Kiel; (H) Hamburg; (S) Swinemünde; (St) Stettin; (P) Pillau; (D) Danzig; (Sea) At Sea

COMMANDER-IN-CHIEF WESTERN AREA (Wilhelmshaven)

Fleet tenders	*Gazelle* (C.-in-C. Fleet)
	Jagd (Flag Officer Commanding Pocket-battleships)
Pocket-battleships	*Admiral Scheer* (W) 6 11-inch, 8 5·9-inch, 6 4·1-inch H.A.
Battle cruisers	*Scharnhorst* (B) ⎫ 9 11-inch, 12 5·9-inch, 14 4·1-inch H.A.
	Gneisenau (B) ⎭
Light cruisers	*Nürnberg* (W) 9 5·9-inch, 8 3·5-inch H.A.
	Leipzig (W) 9 5·9-inch, 6 3·5-inch H.A.
	Köln (K) 9 5·9-inch, 6 3·5-inch H.A.
	Königsberg (W) 9 5·9-inch, 6 3·5-inch H.A.
	Emden (W) 8 5·9-inch, 3 3·5-inch H.A.
Heavy cruiser	*Admiral Hipper* (K) 8 8-inch, 12 4·1-inch H.A.

Destroyers—
  2nd Flotilla
    Paul Jacobi (W)
    Theodor Riedel (W)
    Hermann Schoemann (W)
    Karl Galster (W)
    Wilhelm Heidkamp (K)
  4th Flotilla
    Hans Lody (W)
    Erich Giese (H)
    Dieter v. Roeder (W)
    Hermann Künne (K)
    Hans Lüdemann (W)

⎫ 5 5-inch, 8 torpedo tubes

Torpedo boats—
  5th Flotilla   5 boats (K) ⎫ 1 4·1-inch, 6 torpedo tubes
  6th Flotilla   5 boats (W) ⎭

Motor torpedo-boats   Depot Ship *Tange*
  2nd Flotilla   6 boats (H)

Minelayers
  Tannenberg
  Cobra
  Roland
  Irben

U-boats—
  1st Flotilla   7 boats
  5th Flotilla   3 boats
  6th Flotilla   1 boat
  Training Flotilla   4 boats

APPENDIX G, continued

COMMANDER-IN-CHIEF EASTERN AREA

Old battleships	*Schleswig-Holstein* (S) *Schlesien* (K)	4 11-inch, 10 5·9-inch, 4 3·5-inch H.A.
Destroyers	*Max Schultz* (P) *Richard Beitzen* (Sea) *Georg Thiele* (Sea)	5 5-inch, 8 torpedo tubes
6th Division	*Friedrich Eckoldt* (P) *Bruno Heinemann* (S) *Bernd v. Arnim* (D) *Wolfgang Zenker* (D)	5 5-inch, 8 torpedo tubes
Torpedo boats—		
(Training)	4 boats 1 4·1-inch, 6 torpedo tubes	
3rd Division	*Leberecht Maass* (P) *Friedrich Ihn* (S) *Erich Steinbrinck* (Sea)	5 5-inch, 8 torpedo tubes
Motor torpedo-boats—		
1st Flotilla	Depot Ship *Tsingtau* and 6 boats	
Escort Flotilla	4 boats	
Minesweepers	T196 (Leader) and 8 boats	
Motor minesweepers	Depot Ship *van der Groeben* and 8 boats	
U-boats	8 boats	
Minelayers	*Preussen* *Otter* *Rhein* *Valencia* (netlayer)	

FORCES UNDER DIRECT OPERATIONAL CONTROL OF NAVAL WAR STAFF

Pocket-battleships	*Deutschland* (Sea) *Admiral Graf Spee* (Sea)	6 11-inch, 8 5·9-inch, 6 4·1-inch H.A.
U-boats	11 boats (Sea)	

Note on U-boat types in service or approaching completion in 1939

Type	'U' numbers	Displacement and armament T.T. = Torpedo Tubes	Year commissioned	Number
IA Pre-war Atlantic	25–26	850 tons 1 4·1-inch, 6 T.T.	1936	2
IIA Coastal	1–6	250–300 tons 3 T.T.	1935	6
IIB Coastal	7–24 120–121	250–300 tons 3 T.T.	1935 1940	20
IIC Coastal	56–63 137	250–300 tons 3 T.T.	1938–40 1940	9
IID Coastal	138–152	250–300 tons 3 T.T.	1940–41	15
VII Atlantic	27–36	625 tons 1 3·5-inch, 5 T.T.	1938–39	10
VIIB Atlantic	45–55 73–76 83–87 99–102	750 tons 1 3·5-inch, 5 T.T.	1938–39 1940 1941–42 1940	24
VIIC Atlantic	69–72	770 tons 1 3·5-inch, 5 T.T.	1940–41	4
IA Pre-war Atlantic	25–	(A total of 567 boats of this type was completed 1940–44)		
IX Atlantic	37–44	1,030 tons 1 4·1-inch, 6 T.T.	1938–39	8
IXB Atlantic	64–65 103–111 122–124	1,100 tons 1 4·1-inch, 6 T.T.	1939–40 1940 1940	14

APPENDIX G, continued

Note on Ships under construction or refitting

Name	Class	Armament	Laid down
Bismarck, Tirpitz	Battleships	8 15-inch, 12 5·9-inch	1939
Graf Zeppelin	Aircraft carrier	16 5·9-inch, 10 4·1-inch H.A. 40 aircraft	1938
Blücher, Prinz Eugen, Seydlitz, Lützow	Heavy cruisers	8 8-inch, 12 4·1-inch H.A. 12 torpedo tubes	1937–39
Karlsruhe	Light cruiser	9 5·9-inch, 6 3·5-inch H.A.	1927 Recommissioned [W] Nov. 1939

APPENDIX H

The Italian Navy. Strength and Disposition June 1940

I. TARANTO

    Battleships (3)   *Cavour* ⎫ 23,622 tons, 27 knots
                            Cesare ⎬ 10 12·6-inch, 12 4·7-inch, 8 3·9-inch H.A.

                          Vittorio Veneto   35,000 tons, 30 knots
            (not ready till August)   9 15-inch, 12 6-inch, 12 3·5-inch H.A.

    Heavy cruisers (3)
        1st Division   *Zara* ⎫
                            Fiume ⎬ 10,000 tons, 32 knots
                            Gorizia ⎭ 8 8-inch, 12 3·9-inch H.A.

    Light cruisers (5)
        8th Division   *Abruzzi* ⎫ 7,874 tons, 35 knots
                            Garibaldi ⎬ 10 6-inch, 8 3·9-inch H.A., 6 torpedo tubes

        4th Division   *Diaz* ⎫ 5,008–5,069 tons, 37 knots (*Savoia* 7,283 tons)
                            Di Giussano ⎬
                            Savoia ⎭ 8 6-inch, 6 3·9-inch H.A., 4 torpedo tubes (*Savoia* 6)

    Fleet destroyers (20)
        7th Division   *Freccia* ⎫
                            Dardo ⎬ 1,206 tons, 38 knots
                            Saetta ⎭ 4 4·7-inch, 6 torpedo tubes
                            Strale

        8th Division   *Folgore* ⎫
                            Fulmine ⎬ 1,220 tons, 38 knots
                            Baleno ⎭ 4 4·7-inch, 6 torpedo tubes
                            Lampo

        14th Division   *Vivaldi*
                            Da Noli ⎱ 1,628 tons, 38 knots
                            Pancaldo ⎰ 6 4·7-inch, 4 torpedo tubes
                            Malocello

        16th Division   *Da Mosto*
                            Da Verazzano ⎱ 1,628 tons, 38 knots
                            Pessagno ⎰ 6 4·7-inch, 4 torpedo tubes
                            Tarigo

    Escort and local defence destroyers (8)
        3rd T-B Division   *Stocco*
                                  Carini ⎱ 635–669 tons, 30–32 knots
                                  La Masa ⎰ 3 or 4 4-inch, 4 torpedo tubes
                                  Prestinari

        6th T-B Division   *Pilo*
                                  Mosto ⎱ 615 tons, 31–33 knots
                                  Missori ⎰ 5 4-inch, 4 torpedo tubes
                                  Sirtori

APPENDIX H, continued

Submarines (22) — *Gemma, Diamante, Malachite, Topazio, Marconi, Smeraldo, Salpa, Settimo, Settembrini, Sirena, Galatea, Naiade, Fisalia, Argonauta, Atropo, Zoea, Corridoni, Bragadino, Brin, Argo, Velella, Otaria*

Escort vessels (4) — *Otranto, Gallipoli, Galante, Cirene* (gunboats)

Minelayers (2) — *Vieste, Azio*

M.T.B.s (8)

II. NAPLES

Battleship (1) — *Littorio* — 35,000 tons, 30 knots
(not ready till August) — 9 15-inch, 12 6-inch, 12 3·5-inch H.A.

Light cruisers (4)
  7th Division — *D'Aosta, Attendolo* — 6,941–7,283 tons, 36–37 knots; 8 6-inch, 6 3·9-inch H.A.
  2nd Division — *Montecuccoli, Colleoni* — 5,069–6,941 tons, 37 knots; 8 6-inch, 6 3·9-inch H.A.

Fleet destroyers (4)
  13th Division — *Granatiere, Fuciliere, Bersagliere, Alpino* — 1,620 tons, 39 knots; 4 4·7-inch, 6 torpedo tubes

Escort and local defence destroyers (14)
  Unarmoured — *La Farina, Cantore* — 635 tons, 30 knots; 3 or 4 4-inch, 4 torpedo tubes
  5th T-B Division — *Cairoli, Schiafino, Abba, Dezza* — 615 tons, 30–32 knots; 5 4-inch, 4 torpedo tubes
  10th T-B Division — *Vega, Sagittario, Perseo, Sirio* — 642 tons, 34 knots; 3 3·9-inch, 4 torpedo tubes
  8th T-B Division — *Lupo, Lira, Lince, Libra* — 679 tons, 34 knots; 3 3·9-inch, 4 torpedo tubes

Submarines (11) — *Millelire, Mocenigo, Veniero, Glauco, Nani, Provana, Barbarigo, Emo, Morosini, Adua, Da Vinci.*

Minelayers (3) — *Buffoluto, Panigaglia, Vallelunga*

M.T.B.s (6)

III. SICILY (Messina and Augusta)

Heavy cruisers (4)
  3rd Division — *Pola, Bolzano, Trieste, Trento* — 10,000 tons, 32–35 knots; 8 8-inch, 12 3·9-inch H.A., 8 torpedo tubes (except *Pola*)

Light cruisers (3)
  6th Division — *Da Barbiano, Bande Nere, Cadorna* — 5,008–5,069 tons, 37 knots; 8 6-inch, 6 3·9-inch H.A., 4 torpedo tubes

APPENDIX H, continued

Fleet destroyers (16)
  9th Division   *Alfieri*
                     Oriani   1,729 tons, 39 knots
                     Carducci   4 4·7-inch, 6 torpedo tubes
                     Gioberti
  11th Division   *Artigliere*
                     Camicia Nera   1,620 tons, 39 knots
                     Aviere   4 4·7-inch, 6 torpedo tubes
                     Geniere
  12th Division   *Lanciere*
                     Carabinieri   1,620 tons, 39 knots
                     Corazziere   4 4·7-inch, 6 torpedo tubes
                     Ascari
  10th Division   *Maestrale*
                     Libeccio   1,449 tons, 38 knots
                     Gregale   4 4·7-inch, 6 torpedo tubes
                     Scirocco
M.T.B.s (8)

IV. Syracuse—Palermo—Tripoli

Submarines (17)   Medusa, Mameli, Capponi, Speri, Da Procida, Desgenys, Colonna, Pisani, Bausan, Tricheco, Squalo, Narvalo, Delfino, Bandiera, Menotti, Manara, Santarosa.

Escort and local defence destroyers (12)
  11th T-B Division   *Cigno*
                     Centauro   652 tons, 34 knots
                     Castore   3 3·9-inch, 4 torpedo tubes
                     Climene
  13th Division   *Circe*
                     Clio   679 tons, 34 knots
                     Calliope   3 3·9-inch, 4 torpedo tubes
                     Calipso
  14th Division   *Partenope*
                     Pallade   679 tons, 34 knots
                     Polluce   3 3·9-inch, 4 torpedo tubes
                     Pleiadi
Minelayers (2)   Durazzo, Pelagosa
M.T.B.s (12)

V. Sardinia (Cagliari)

Escort and local defence destroyers (8)
  4th T-B Division   *Orsa*
                     Pegaso   855 tons, 28 knots
                     Procione   2 3·9-inch, 4 torpedo tubes
                     Orione
  9th T-B Division   *Cassiopea*
                     Canopo   638–652 tons, 34 knots
                     Spica   3 3·9-inch, 4 torpedo tubes
                     Astore
Submarines (18)   Fieramosca, Marcello, Dandolo, Alagi, Aradam, Axum, Torelli, Diaspro, Corallo, Finzi, Tazzoli, Calvi, Bianchi, Iride, Onice, Bagnolini, Tarantini, Giuliani.
Minelayer (1)   *Buccari*   531 tons, 10 knots, 54 mines
M.T.B.s (6)

APPENDIX H, continued

VI. DODECANESE (Leros)

   Fleet destroyers (4)
      4th Division   *Crispi*
                          Ricasoli   } 935 tons, 35 knots
                          Sella   { 4 4·7-inch, 4 torpedo tubes
                          Nicotera

   Escort and local defence destroyers (2)
      15th T-B Division *Solferino*   } 862 tons, 32 knots
                          San Martino { 4 4-inch, 4 torpedo tubes

   Submarines (8)   *Gondar, Scire, Neghelli, Aschianghi, Durbo, Tembien, Beilul, Lafole.*

   Minelayer (1)   *Legnano*   615 tons, 15 knots
                                           2 4-inch, 80 mines

   M.T.B.s (20)

VII. LIBYA (Tobruk)

   Fleet destroyers (8)
      1st Division   *Zeffiro*
                          Borea   } 1,073–1,092 tons, 36 knots
                          Espero   { 4 4·7-inch, 6 torpedo tubes
                          Ostro
      2nd Division   *Euro*
                          Nembo   } 1,073–1,092 tons, 36 knots
                          Aquilone   { 4 4·7-inch, 6 torpedo tubes
                          Turbine

   Submarines (9)   *Ondina, Nereide, Anfitrite, Serpente, Dessie, Dagabur, Uarsciek, Uebi Scebeli, Turchese.*

   Escort vessels (3) *Valoroso, Palmaiolo, Alula* (gunboats)
   Depot ship (1)   *San Giorgio* (old cruiser)

VIII. TRIPOLI

   Escort and local defence destroyers (4)
      1st T-B Division *Airone*
                           Alcione   } 679 tons, 34 knots
                           Ariel   { 3 3·9-inch, 4 torpedo tubes
                           Aretusa

IX. ADRIATIC

   Battleship (1)   *Andrea Doria* 23,632 tons, 27 knots
                                                  10 12·6-inch, 12 5·3-inch, 10 3·5-inch H.A.

   Escort and local defence destroyers (6)
      15th T-B Division *Confienza*   } 862 tons, 32 knots
                          Palestro   { 4 4-inch, 4 torpedo tubes
      7th T-B Division *Cosenz*
                          Medici   } 635 tons, 30 knots
                          Bassini   { 4 4-inch, 4 torpedo tubes
                          Fabrizi

   Submarines (4)   *Ambra, Rubino, X2, X3*
   Escort vessel (1)   *Giovannini* (gunboat)
   M.T.B.s (8)

APPENDIX H, *continued*

X. Brindisi—Bari

Fleet destroyers (2) *Mirabello* } 1,383 tons, 35 knots
                     Riboty   } 8 4-inch, 4 torpedo tubes

M.T.B.s (8)

XI. Spezia

Battleship (1)   *Caio Duilio*   23,622 tons, 27 knots
                                      10 12·6-inch, 12 5·3-inch, 10 3·5-inch H.A.

Escort and local defence destroyers (13)
   12th T-B Division *Altair*
                       Antares   642 tons, 34 knots
                       Aldebaran   3 3·9-inch, 4 torpedo tubes
                       Andromeda
   16th T-B Division *Monzambano*
                       Curtatone   966 tons, 32 knots
                       Castelfidardo   4 4-inch, 6 torpedo tubes
                       Caltafimi
   2nd T-B Division *Papa*
                       Cascino   635 tons, 30 knots
                       Chinotto   3 4-inch, 4 torpedo tubes
                       Montanari
   Unattached   *Audace*

Submarines (18)   *Balilla, Toti, Sciesa, Jalea, Jantina, Console Generale Liuzzi, Ametista, Berillo, Zaffiro, Micca, Foca, Cappellini, Faa Di Bruno, H1, H2, H4, H6, H8*

Escort vessels (2)   *Rimini, Matteuci* (gunboats)

Submarine chaser (1)   *Albatros*

M.T.B.s (20)

XII. Red Sea

Fleet destroyers (7)
   5th Division   *Pantera*
                      Leone   1,526 tons, 34 knots
                      Tigre   8 4·7-inch, 4 torpedo tubes
   3rd Division   *Battisti*
                      Nullo   1,058 tons, 35 knots
                      Sauro   4 4·7-inch, 4 torpedo tubes
                      Manin

Escort and local defence destroyers (2)
                      Orsini   } 669 tons, 30 knots
                      Acerbi   } 6 4-inch, 4 torpedo tubes

Escort vessels (4)   *Eritrea, Ostia* (sloops)
                         Biglieri, Porto Corsini (gunboats)

M.T.B.s (5)

Submarines (8)   *Archimede, Ferraris, Galilei, Torricelli, Galvani, Gugliel-motto, Macalle, Perla*

APPENDIX J
The Principal British Mercantile Convoy Routes, 1939–41

Type	Code letters	Route	Dates of starting and ending
Coastal	E.N.	Methil–Clyde*	Started 2 Aug. 1940 Ended 6 April 1941 Restarted 3 Nov. 1941
	W.N.	*Clyde–Methil Oban–Methil	Started 16 July 1940 Started 3 Sept. 1941
	E.C. (replaced E.N.)	Southend–Loch Ewe, Oban and Clyde	Started 31 Mar. 1941 Ended 28 Oct. 1941
* Ocean-going ships called at Oban.			
Coastal	F.N.	Thames–Methil	Started 6 Sept. 1939
	F.S.	Methil–Thames	Started 7 Sept. 1939
Coastal	C.W.	Southend–Falmouth	Started 6 July 1940
		Southend–St Helen's (I. of W.)	Started 1 Sept. 1940
	C.E.	Falmouth–Southend	Started † July 1940
		St Helen's–Southend	Started 1 Sept. 1940 † No record of exact date.
North Sea	H.N.	Bergen–Methil	Started 7 Nov. 1939 Ended 9 April 1940
	O.N.	Methil–Bergen	Started 4 Nov. 1939 Ended 5 April 1940
Ocean Homeward	H.G.	Gibraltar–U.K.	Started 26 Sept. 1939
Ocean Homeward	H.X.	Halifax–U.K.	Started 16 Sept. 1939
Ocean Homeward	K.J.	Kingston (Jamaica)–U.K.	Started 15 Sept. 1939 Ended 8 Oct. 1939
Ocean Outward	O.A.	‡Thames outward by English Channel	Started 7 Sept. 1939 Ended 24 Oct. 1940
‡ After 3rd July 1940 ships in these convoys joined F.N. convoys, then outward through N.W. Approaches			
Ocean Outward	O.B.	§Liverpool outwards	Started 7 Sept. 1939 Ended 21 Oct. 1941 being subsequently renamed O.N.
§ These convoys used N.W. Approaches from 11th July 1940.			
Ocean Outward	O.N.S.	U.K.–Halifax (former O.B. Slow Convoy)	Started 26 July 1941
Ocean Outward	O.G.	U.K.–Gibraltar	Started 1 Oct. 1939
Ocean Outward	O.L.	Liverpool outwards (These were fast convoys. There were only 8 of them.)	Started 14 Sept. 1940 Ended 25 Oct. 1940
Ocean Homeward	S.C.	Halifax–U.K.	Started 15 Aug. 1940
Ocean Homeward	S.L.	Freetown, Sierra Leone–U.K.	Started 14 Sept. 1939
Ocean Outward	O.N.	U.K.–Halifax	Started 27 July 1941 (former O.B. convoy)
Ocean Outward	O.S.	U.K.–Freetown, Sierra Leone	Started 24 July 1941

598

APPENDIX K

German and Italian U-Boats Sunk, 1939–41, and Analysis of Cause of Sinking

TABLE I. GERMAN U-BOATS

Number	Date	Name and task of killer	Area
U.39	14 Sept. 1939	*Faulknor, Foxhound, Firedrake*—Sea Escorts	Off Hebrides
U.27	20 Sept. 1939	*Fortune, Forester*—Sea Patrol	Off Hebrides
U.12	8 Oct. 1939	Mine	Straits of Dover
U.40	13 Oct. 1939	Mine	Straits of Dover
U.42	13 Oct. 1939	*Imogen, Ilex*—Sea Escorts	S.W. of Ireland
U.45	14 Oct. 1939	*Inglefield, Ivanhoe, Intrepid, Icarus*—Sea Patrol	Off S. Ireland
U.16	24 Oct. 1939	Mine	Straits of Dover
U.35	29 Nov. 1939	*Kingston, Kashmir, Icarus*—Sea Escorts	East of Shetlands
U.36	4 Dec. 1939	*Salmon*—S/M Patrol	North Sea
U.55	30 Jan. 1940	*Fowey, Whitshed*, aircraft of No. 228 Squadron—Sea Escort/Air Support	West of Channel
U.15	30 Jan. 1940	Accidentally rammed by German warship	North Sea
U.41	5 Feb. 1940	*Antelope*—Sea Escort	South of Ireland
U.33	12 Feb. 1940	*Gleaner*—Sea Patrol	Firth of Clyde
U.53	23 Feb. 1940	*Gurkha*—On passage	South of Faeröes
U.63	25 Feb. 1940	*Escort, Narwhal, Inglefield, Imogen*—Sea Escorts	North Sea
U.31 (salved)	11 Mar. 1940	Bomber Command aircraft	Heligoland Bight
U.44	20 Mar. 1940	*Fortune*—Sea Escort	North of Shetlands
U.54	? Mar. 1940	? Mine	North Sea
U.50	10 April 1940	*Hero*—Sea Escort	N.N.E. of Shetlands
U.64	13 April 1940	*Warspite*'s aircraft—Air Escort	Vestfiord, Norway
U.49	15 April 1940	*Fearless*—Sea Escort	Norway
U.1	15 April 1940	*Porpoise*—S/M Patrol	Norway
U.22	? April 1940	Unknown	North Sea
U.13	31 May 1940	*Weston*—Sea Escort	North Sea
U.26	1 July 1940	*Gladiolus* and aircraft of No. 10 Squadron—Sea Escort/Air Support	S.S.W. Ireland
U.122	? July 1940	Unknown	North Sea
U.25	3 Aug. 1940	Mine	North Sea
U.51	20 Aug. 1940	*Cachalot*—S/M Patrol	Bay of Biscay
U.102	21 Aug. 1940	Unknown	North Sea
U.32	30 Oct. 1940	*Harvester* and *Highlander*—Sea Escorts	North Atlantic
U.31	2 Nov. 1940	*Antelope*—Sea Escort	North Atlantic
U.104	21 Nov. 1940	*Rhododendron*—Sea Escort	North Atlantic
U.70	7 Mar. 1941	*Camellia* and *Arbutus*—Sea Escorts	North Atlantic
U.47	8 Mar. 1941	*Wolverine*—Sea Escort	North Atlantic
U.99	17 Mar. 1941	*Walker*—Sea Escort	North Atlantic
U.100	17 Mar. 1941	*Walker, Vanoc*—Sea Escorts	North Atlantic
U.551	23 Mar. 1941	*Visenda*—Sea Escort	North Atlantic
U.76	5 April 1941	*Wolverine* and *Scarborough*—Sea Escorts	North Atlantic
U.65	28 April 1941	*Gladiolus*—Sea Escort	North Atlantic

APPENDIX K, continued

TABLE I. GERMAN U-BOATS—continued

Number	Date	Name and task of killer	Area
U.110	9 May 1941	*Aubrietia, Bulldog, Broadway*—Sea Escorts	North Atlantic
U.147	2 June 1941	*Wanderer* and *Periwinkle*—Sea Escorts	North Atlantic
U.138	18 June 1941	*Faulkner, Fearless, Forester, Foresight* and *Foxhound*—Sea Patrol	Straits of Gibraltar
U.556	27 June 1941	*Nasturtium, Celandine* and *Gladiolus*—Sea Escorts	North Atlantic
U.651	29 June 1941	*Malcolm, Violet, Scimitar, Arabis* and *Speedwell*—Sea Escorts	North Atlantic
U.144	? July 1941	Mined	Gulf of Finland
U.401	3 Aug. 1941	*Wanderer, St Albans, Hydrangea*—Sea Escorts	North Atlantic
U.452	25 Aug. 1941	*Vascama* and aircraft of No. 209 Squadron—Sea Escort/Air Support	South of Iceland
U.570 (Captured)	27 Aug. 1941	Aircraft of No. 269 Squadron—Air Support	South of Iceland
U.501	10 Sept. 1941	*Chambly* and *Moosejaw* (R.C.N.)—Sea Escorts	North Atlantic
U.207	11 Sept. 1941	*Leamington* and *Veteran*—Sea Escorts	North Atlantic
U.111	4 Oct. 1941	*Lady Shirley*—Sea Escort	Off Canary Islands
U.204	19 Oct. 1941	*Mallow* and *Rochester*—Sea Patrol	West of Gibraltar
U.580	11 Nov. 1941	Accident, collision	Baltic
U.583	15 Nov. 1941	Accident, collision	Baltic
U.433	16 Nov. 1941	*Marigold*—On passage	East of Gibraltar
U.95	28 Nov. 1941	S/M 021 (Dutch)—On passage	East of Gibraltar
U.206	30 Nov. 1941	Aircraft of No. 502 Squadron—Air Patrol	Bay of Biscay
U.208	11 Dec. 1941	*Bluebell*—Sea Escort	West of Gibraltar
U.127	15 Dec. 1941	*Nestor*—Sea Patrol	West of Gibraltar
U.557	16 Dec. 1941	Accident, Rammed by Italian torpedo-boat	Eastern Mediterranean
U.131	17 Dec. 1941	*Exmoor, Blankney, Stanley, Stork, Pentstemon* and aircraft from *Audacity*—Air/Sea Escorts	North Atlantic
U.434	18 Dec. 1941	*Stanley, Blankney*—Sea Escorts	North Atlantic
U.574	19 Dec. 1941	*Stork*—Sea Escort	North Atlantic
U.451	21 Dec. 1941	Aircraft of No. 812 Squadron—Air Patrol	Straits of Gibraltar
U.567	21 Dec. 1941	*Deptford, Samphire*—Sea Escorts	North Atlantic
U.79	23 Dec. 1941	*Hasty* and *Hotspur*—Sea Escorts	Eastern Mediterranean
U.75	28 Dec. 1941	*Kipling*—Sea Escort	Eastern Mediterranean

TABLE II. ITALIAN U-BOATS SUNK OR CAPTURED
11th JUNE 1940–31st DECEMBER 1941

Name	Date	Name and task of killer	Area
Macalle	14 June 1940	Accident	Red Sea
Provana	17 June 1940	*La Curieuse* (French)	Off Oran
Galileo Galilei (Captured)	19 June 1940	*Moonstone*—Sea Patrol	Red Sea
Diamante	20 June 1940	*Parthian*—S/M Patrol	Off Tobruk
Evangelista Torricelli	22 June 1940	*Kandahar, Kingston* and *Shoreham*—Sea Patrol	Red Sea
Luigi Galvani	23 June 1940	*Falmouth*—Sea Patrol	Persian Gulf
Liuzzi	27 June 1940	*Dainty* and *Ilex*—Sea Patrol	Off Crete
Argonauta	28 June 1940	Aircraft of No. 230 Squadron—Air Patrol	Central Mediterranean
Uebi Scebeli	29 June 1940	*Dainty* and *Ilex*—Sea Escorts	West of Crete
Rubino	29 June 1940	Aircraft of No. 230 Squadron—Air Patrol	Ionian Sea
Iride	22 Aug. 1940	Aircraft from *Eagle*—Air Patrol	Gulf of Bomba
Gondar	30 Sept. 1940	*Stuart* and aircraft of No. 230 Squadron—On passage	Off Alexandria
Berillo	2 Oct. 1940	*Havock* and *Hasty*—Sea Escorts	Off North Coast of Egypt
Gemma	6 Oct. 1940	Accident, Italian M.T.B.s	Aegean
Durbo	18 Oct. 1940	*Firedrake, Wrestler* and aircraft of No. 202 Squadron—Air/Sea Patrol	East of Gibraltar
Lafole	20 Oct. 1940	*Hotspur, Gallant* and *Griffin*—Sea Patrol	East of Gibraltar
Faa di Bruno	8 Nov. 1940	*Havelock*—Sea Escort	North Atlantic
Naiade	14 Dec. 1940	*Hyperion* and *Hereward*—Sea Escorts	Off Bardia
Tarantini	15 Dec. 1940	*Thunderbolt*—S/M Patrol	Bay of Biscay
Foca	? Dec. 1940	Unknown	Mediterranean
Marcello	6 Jan. 1941	Aircraft of No. 210 Squadron—Air Support	West of Hebrides
Nani	7 Jan. 1941	*Anemone*—Sea Escort	North Atlantic
Neghelli	19 Jan. 1941	*Greyhound*—Sea Escort	Eastern Mediterranean
Anfitrite	6 Mar. 1941	*Greyhound*—Sea Escort	Off Crete
Pier Capponi	31 Mar. 1941	*Rorqual*—S/M Patrol	Off Sicily
Glauco	27 June 1941	*Wishart*—Sea Escort	West of Gibraltar
Salpa	27 June 1941	*Triumph*—S/M Patrol	Off North Coast of Egypt
Jantina	5 July 1941	*Torbay*—S/M Patrol	Aegean
Tembien	2 Aug. 1941	*Hermione*—On passage	Off Tunis
Michele Bianchi	7 Aug. 1941	*Severn*—S/M Patrol	West of Gibraltar
Maggiori Baracca	8 Sept. 1941	*Groome*—Sea Escort	N.E. of Azores
Smeraldo	16 Sept. 1941	Unknown	Mediterranean
Alessandro Malaspina	21 Sept. 1941	*Vimy*—Sea Escort	North Atlantic
Fisalia	28 Sept. 1941	*Hyacinth*—Sea Patrol	Off Jaffa
Adua	30 Sept. 1941	*Gurkha* and *Legion*—Sea Escorts	Western Mediterranean
Galileo Ferraris	25 Oct. 1941	*Lamerton* and aircraft of No. 202 Squadron—Air/Sea Escorts	North Atlantic
Guglielmo Marconi	? Nov. 1941	Unknown	Atlantic
Amiraglio Caracciolo	11 Dec. 1941	*Farndale*—On passage	Off Bardia

TABLE III. ANALYSIS OF SINKINGS OF GERMAN AND ITALIAN U-BOATS BY CAUSE 1939–41

Cause	1939 German	1939 Italian	1940 German	1940 Italian	1941 German	1941 Italian
Surface ships	5	—	11	10	25	10
Shore-based aircraft	Nil	—	1 [salved]	2	3	1
Ship-borne aircraft	Nil	—	1	1	Nil	Nil
Ships and shore-based aircraft	Nil	—	2	2	1	1
Ships and ship-borne aircraft	Nil	—	Nil	Nil	1	Nil
Submarines	1	—	2	2	1	4
Bombing raids	Nil	—	Nil	Nil	Nil	Nil
Mines laid by shore-based aircraft	Nil	—	Nil	Nil	Nil	Nil
Mines laid by ships	3	—	2	Nil	Nil	Nil
Other causes	Nil	—	1	2	4	Nil
Cause unknown	Nil	—	3	1	Nil	2
Total	9	—	22	20	35	18

APPENDIX L

Operation 'Dynamo'—Summary of British and Allied ships employed, troops lifted, British ships lost or damaged

Class of ship	Number employed	Troops lifted	Lost by enemy action	Lost by other causes	Damaged (British only)
A.A. cruiser . . .	1	1,856	—	—	1
Destroyers and torpedo boats	56	102,843	9	—	19
Sloops and despatch vessels	6	1,436	—	—	1
Patrol vessels . . .	7	2,504	—	—	—
Gunboats . . .	2	3,512	1	—	—
Corvettes and chasseurs .	11	1,303	—	—	—
Minesweepers (large) .	38	48,472	5	1	7
Trawlers and drifters .	230	28,709	23	6	2
Special service vessels .	3	4,408	—	—	—
Armed boarding vessels .	3	4,848	1	—	2
Motor torpedo and anti-submarine boats . .	15	99	—	—	—
Schuyts . . .	40	22,698	1	3	—
Yachts	27	4,895	1	2	—
Personnel vessels . .	45	87,810	9	—	8
Hospital carriers . .	8	3,006	1	—	5
Cargo ships . . .	13	5,790	3	—	—
Tugs	40	3,164	6	1	—
Landing craft . . .	13	118	1	7	—
Lighters, hoppers and barges . . .	48	4,726	4	8	—
Small craft*—					
Naval motor boats .	12	96 ⎫			Not known
War Dept. launches .	8	579 ⎬ 7	7	135	
Private motor boats .	203	5,031 ⎪			
R.N.L.I. lifeboats .	19	323 ⎭			
Totals . . .	848	338,226	72	163	45

* The numbers of small craft taking part were probably greater than these figures, and the losses of small craft as well. The names of many small craft which took part were never reported or discovered.

APPENDIX M

Enemy Surface Commerce Raiders, 1939–41.

Performance Data and Particulars of Losses Caused

Name	Description	German operational number	British designation	Armament excluding light A.A. guns	Aircraft carried	Mines carried M: moored G: ground	Duration of sortie Sailing/termination date	Shipping sunk or captured No.	Shipping sunk or captured G.R. tons	Operating areas	Type of engines and radius of action	Max. speed (knots)	Remarks
Deutschland	Pocket-battleship	—	—	6 11-inch 8 5·9-inch 6 4·1 HA. 8 T. tubes	2	—	Aug. 1939 15th Nov. 1939	2	7,000	N.W. Atlantic	—	—	Undetected for 2 months. Renamed *Lützow* early in 1940.
Admiral Graf Spee	Pocket-battleship	—	—	6 11-inch 8 5·9-inch 6 4·1 HA. 8 T. tubes	2	—	Aug. 1939 17th Dec. 1939	9	50,000	S. Atlantic and Indian Ocean	—	—	River Plate action. Scuttled.
Atlantis	Auxiliary	Schiff 16	Raider C	6 5·9-inch 4 T. tubes	2	93M	31st Mar. 1940 22nd Nov. 1941	22	145,697	Atlantic, Pacific and Indian Oceans	Diesel 60,000 m. at 10 knots	18	Sunk by H.M.S. *Devonshire*, 22nd Nov. 1941.
Orion	Auxiliary	Schiff 36	Raider A	6 5·9-inch 6 T. tubes	2	228M	6th April 1940 23rd Aug. 1941	9½ (3½ shared)	57,744	Atlantic, Pacific and Indian Oceans	Turbine 35,000 m. at 10 knots	14⅞	Returned to home base.
Widder	Auxiliary	Schiff 21	Raider D	6 5·9-inch 4 T. tubes	1	60M	6th May 1940 31st Oct. 1940	10	58,645	Central Atlantic	Turbine 34,000 m. at 10 knots	18	Returned to home base.
Thor	Auxiliary	Schiff 10	Raider E	6 5·9-inch 4 T. tubes	1	90M	6th June 1940 30th April 1941	11	83,000	South and Central Atlantic	Turbine 40,000 m. at 10 knots	18	Engaged H.M.S.s *Alcantara* and *Carnarvon Castle*. Sank H.M.S. *Voltaire*. Returned to home base.
Pinguin	Auxiliary	Schiff 33	Raider F	6 5·9-inch 4 T. tubes	2	300M	22nd June 1940 8th May 1941	17 plus 11 whalers	136,551	Atlantic, Indian and Antarctic Oceans	Diesel 60,000 m. at 12 knots	18	Sunk by H.M.S. *Cornwall*, 8th May 1941.
Komet	Auxiliary	Schiff 45	Raider B	6 5·9-inch 4 T. tubes	1	25G	9th July 1940 30th Nov. 1941	6½ (3½ shared)	42,959	Pacific	Diesel 51,000 m. at 10 knots	19	Sailed by north-east passage and Bering Sea. Returned to home base.

APPENDIX M—continued

Name	Description	German operational number	British designation	Armament excluding light A.A. guns	Aircraft carried	Mines carried M: moored G: ground	Duration of sortie Sailing/termination date	Shipping sunk or captured No.	Shipping sunk or captured G.R. tons	Operating areas	Armed merchant raiders Type of engines and radius of action	Armed merchant raiders Max. speed (knots)	Remarks
Admiral Scheer	Pocket battleship	—	—	6 11-inch 8 5·9-inch 8 4·1 HA. 8 T. tubes	2	—	23rd Oct. 1940 1st April 1941	16	99,059	N. Atlantic, S. Atlantic and Indian Oceans	—	—	Sank H.M.S. *Jervis Bay* and 5 ships in convoy, 5th Nov. 1940. Returned to home base 1st April 1941.
Admiral Hipper	Heavy cruiser	—	—	8 8-inch 12 4·1 HA. 12 T. tubes	3	—	30th Nov. 1940 27th Dec. 1940	1	6,078	N. Atlantic	—	—	Returned to Brest to await second sortie.
Kormoran	Auxiliary	Schiff 41	Raider G	6 5·9-inch 4 T. tubes	2	280M 40G	3rd Dec. 1940 19th Nov. 1941	11	68,274	Central and S. Atlantic, Indian Ocean, Pacific	Diesel electric 70,000 m. at 10 knots	18	Sunk by and sank H.M.A.S. *Sydney*, 19th Nov. 1941.
Scharnhorst Gneisenau	Battle cruisers	—	—	9 11-inch 12 5·9-inch 14 4·1-inch HA.	4 (each)	—	22nd Jan. 1941 22nd Mar. 1941	22	115,622	N. and Central Atlantic	—	—	Returned to Brest and eventually to Germany in Feb. 1942.
Admiral Hipper	See above	—	—	See above	See above	—	1st Feb. 1941 13th Feb. 1941	8	34,000	West of Biscay	—	—	Sortie from and back to Brest. Eventually returned to Germany.
Ramb I (Italian)	Auxiliary	—	—	4 4·7-inch	?	?	Feb. 1941	Nil	Nil	Indian Ocean	—	?	Left Massawa 20th Feb. 1941. Sunk by H.M.S. *Leander* 27th Feb. 1941.
Bismarck	Battleship	—	—	8 15-inch 12 5·9-inch 16 4·1 HA.	4	—	21st May 1941 27th May 1941	Nil	Nil	N. Atlantic	—	—	Sunk by Home Fleet and Force H 27th May 1941.
Prinz Eugen	Heavy cruiser	—	—	8 8-inch 12 4·1-inch HA. 12 T. tubes	3	—	21st May 1941 1st June 1941	Nil	Nil	N. Atlantic	—	—	Escaped to Brest and eventually returned to Germany in Feb. 1942.

APPENDIX N

Table I. German Supply Ships working with Raiders and U-boats, 1939–41.

Ship (T) indicates Tanker	Working with or planned to work with	Remarks
Adria (T)	*Admiral Hipper Gneisenau Scharnhorst*	
Alstertor	*Pinguin, Komet, Orion, Kormoran*	23.6.41. Scuttled in 41° 12′ N.—13° 10′ W. after attack by aircraft and 8th Destroyer Flotilla.
Alsterufer	*Thor, Atlantis, Kormoran, Admiral Scheer*	27.12.43. Sunk by aircraft in 46° 32′ N.—18° 35′ W.
Altmark (T)	*Admiral Graf Spee*	Renamed *Uckermark* (q.v.).
Anneliese Essberger	*Komet*	Scuttled in Atlantic, 21.11.42.
Babitonga	*Atlantis*	21.6.41. Scuttled when intercepted by *London* in 02° 05′ S.—27° 42′ W.
Belchen (T)	*Bismarck, Prinz Eugen,* U-boats	3.6.41. Sunk by British naval forces in the Greenland area.
Coburg		4.3.41. Sunk by *Canberra* and *Leander* in 08° 40′ S.—61° 25′ E.
Dithmarschen (T)	*Admiral Hipper*	
Dresden	*Admiral Graf Spee, Atlantis*	Scuttled R. Gironde, August 1944
Egerland (T)	U-boats	5.6.41. Scuttled when intercepted by *London* and *Brilliant* in 07° N.—31° W.
Elsa Essberger	*Orion*	Scuttled in R. Gironde, August 1944.
Emmy Friederich	*Admiral Graf Spee*	Scuttled when intercepted by *Caradoc* in Caribbean, October 1939.
Ermland (T)	*Admiral Scheer, Gneisenau, Scharnhorst, Orion*	Scuttled in Nantes in August 1944.
Esso Hamburg (T)	*Gneisenau, Scharnhorst, Prinz Eugen*	4.6.41. Scuttled when intercepted by *London* and *Brilliant* in 07° 35′ N.—31° 25′ W.
Eurofeld	*Admiral Scheer, Thor, Widder*	Scuttled in St Nazaire in September 1944.
Friedrich Breme	*Admiral Hipper, Gneisenau, Scharnhorst*	12.6.41. Scuttled when intercepted by *Sheffield* in 44° 48′ N.—24° 00′ W.
Gedania (T)	U-boats	4.6.41. Captured in North Atlantic.

Table I—continued

Ship (T) indicates Tanker	Working with or planned to work with	Remarks
Gonzenheim	Bismarck, Prinz Eugen	4.6.41. Intercepted by *Renown*, scuttled and finally sunk by *Neptune*.
Ill (T)	Thor	
Kulmerland	Orion, Komet, Kormoran	Total loss after air raid on Nantes on 23.9.43.
Königsberg	Widder	Scuttled when intercepted by French warship on 16.6.40 in 41° 36' N.—10° 37' W.
Lothringen (T) (ex-Dutch *Papendrecht*)	Bismarck, Prinz Eugen, U-boats	15.6.41. Surrendered after interception by *Dunedin* and aircraft from *Eagle* in 19° 49' N.—25° 31' W.
Munsterland	Orion, Atlantis, Komet	Sunk by British coastal batteries off Cap Gris Nez on 20.1.44.
Nordmark (ex-*Westerwald*) (T)	Admiral Scheer, Thor, Kormoran, Widder, Atlantis, Pinguin, U-boats	
Portland	Admiral Scheer	13.4.43. Sunk by French cruiser *Georges Leygues* in 06° 12' N.—21° 45' W.
Regensburg	Orion, Thor, Komet	30.3.43. Scuttled when intercepted by *Glasgow* in 66° 41' N.—25° 31' W.
Rekum	Thor, Widder	21.3.44. Sunk in Channel by British long-range coastal batteries.
Rio Grande	Thor	4.1.44. Scuttled off Ascension Is.
Rudolf Albrecht (T)	Kormoran	
Samland (T)		16.6.40. Sunk by submarine 5 miles W. of Lister.
Schlettstadt (T)	Gneisenau, Scharnhorst	
Spichern (T)	Admiral Hipper, Prinz Eugen, Thor	Scuttled at Brest in August 1944.
Tannenfels	Thor, Atlantis	Scuttled in R. Gironde, August 1944.
Thorn (T)	Admiral Hipper	2.4.41. Sunk by submarine *Tigris* 100 miles S.W. of St Nazaire.
Uckermark (T) (ex-*Altmark*)	Gneisenau, Scharnhorst, Michel	30.12.42. Blew up and sank at Yokohama.
Weser	Orion	26.9.40. Captured by *Prince Robert* on leaving Manzanillo. (Never joined the raider.)
Westerwald (T) (renamed *Nordmark*)	Deutschland	See *Nordmark*.
Winnetou (T)	Orion	Sunk by enemy action in the Far East.

Table II. Captured ships used as Supply Ships to Raiders

Name	Captured	Subsequently
Tropic Sea (Nor.)	18 May 1940	Scuttled, 3.9.40.
Krossfonn (Nor.) (T) (renamed *Spichern*)	26 May 1940	See *Spichern* (Table I).
Tirranna (Nor.)	10 June 1940	Sunk 22.9.40.
Kertosono (Du.)	1 July 1940	Scuttled at Nantes, August 1944.
Nordvard (Nor.)	15 Sept. 1940	29.12.44. Sunk by aircraft in Oslo-fiord.
Storstad (Nor.) (T) (renamed *Passat*)	7 Oct. 1940	
Durmitor (Y-S)	21 Oct. 1940	Recaptured.
Teddy (Nor.) (T)	8 Nov. 1940	Sunk 14.11.40.
Ole Jacob (Nor.) (T) (renamed *Benno*)	10 Nov. 1940	Sunk by aircraft 24.12.41 in Puerto Carino, N.W. Spain.
Duquesa (Br.)	18 Dec. 1940	Sunk 20.2.41.
Ole Wegger (Nor.)	14 Jan. 1941	26.8.44. Scuttled at Rouen.
Solglimt (Nor.)	14 Jan. 1941	29.6.44. Scuttled at Cherbourg.
Pol IX (Nor.) (renamed *Adjutant*)	14 Jan. 1941	Minelayer. Sunk 1.7.41 by *Komet*.
Pelagos (Nor.) (OR)	15 Jan. 1941	
Sandefjord (Nor.) (T) (renamed *Monsun*)	18 Jan. 1941	11.8.44. Scuttled at Nantes.
Speybank (Br.) (renamed *Doggerbank*)	31 Jan. 1941	Fitted as armed minelayer. Sunk by U-boat on 3.3.43 in 31° N.—37° W.
Ketty Brovig (Nor.) (T)	2 Feb. 1941	Scuttled when met by *Canberra* and *Leander* 4.3.41.
British Advocate (Br.) (T) (renamed *Nordstern*)	20 Feb. 1941	24.7.44. Sunk by aircraft in R. Loire.
San Casimiro (Br.) (T)	15 Mar. 1941	Scuttled 20.3.41.
Bianca (Nor.) (T)	15 Mar. 1941	Scuttled 20.3.41.
Polykarp (Nor.) (T) (renamed *Taifun*)	15 Mar. 1941	3.5.45. Sunk by aircraft in Great Belt.
Canadolite (T) (renamed *Sudetenland*)	27 Mar. 1941	13.8.44. Sunk by aircraft in Brest.

Br. = British   Nor. = Norwegian   Du. = Dutch   Y-S = Yugo-Slav

APPENDIX O

The Battle of the Atlantic

Directive by the Minister of Defence

March 6, 1941.

In view of various German statements, we must assume that the Battle of the Atlantic has begun.

The next four months should enable us to defeat the attempt to strangle our food supplies and our connection with the United States. For this purpose—

1. We must take the offensive against the U-boat and the Focke-Wulf wherever we can and whenever we can. The U-boat at sea must be hunted, the U-boat in the building yard or in dock must be bombed. The Focke-Wulf and other bombers employed against our shipping must be attacked in the air and in their nests.

2. Extreme priority will be given to fitting out ships to catapult or otherwise launch fighter aircraft against bombers attacking our shipping. Proposals should be made within a week.

3. All the measures approved and now in train for the concentration of the main strength of the Coastal Command upon the North-Western Approaches, and their assistance on the East Coast by Fighter and Bomber Commands, will be pressed forward. It may be hoped that, with the growing daylight and the new routes to be followed, the U-boat menace will soon be reduced. All the more important is it that the Focke-Wulf, and, if it comes, the Junkers 88, should be effectively grappled with.

4. In view of the great need for larger numbers of escorting destroyers, it is for consideration whether the American destroyers now in service should go into dock for their second scale of improvements until the critical period of this new battle has been passed.

5. The Admiralty will re-examine, in conjunction with the Ministry of Shipping, the question of liberating from convoys ships between 13 and 12 knots, and also whether this might not be tried experimentally for a while.

6. The Admiralty will have the first claim on all the short-range A.A. guns and other weapons that they can mount upon suitable merchant ships plying in the danger zone. Already 200 Bofors or their equivalents have been ordered to be made available by Air Defence Great Britain and the factories. But these should be followed by a constant flow of guns, together with crews or nucleus crews, as and when they can be taken over by the Admiralty. A programme for three months should be made.

APPENDIX O, continued

7. We must be ready to meet concentrated air attacks on the ports on which we specially rely (Mersey, Clyde and Bristol Channel). They must therefore be provided with a maximum defence. A report of what is being done should be made in a week.

8. A concerted attack by all departments involved must be made upon the immense mass of damaged shipping now accumulated in our ports. By the end of June this mass must be reduced by not less than 400,000 tons net. For this purpose a short view may for the time being be taken both on merchant and naval shipbuilding. Labour should be transferred from new merchant shipbuilding which cannot finish before September 1941 to repairs. The Admiralty have undertaken to provide from long-distance projects of warship building or warship repairs up to 5,000 men at the earliest moment, and another 5,000 should be transferred from long-distance merchant shipbuilding.

9. Every form of simplification and acceleration of repairs and degaussing, even at some risk, must be applied in order to reduce the terrible slowness of the turn-round of ships in British ports. A saving of fifteen days in this process would in itself be equivalent to 5 million tons of imports, or a tonnage [equal to] $1\frac{1}{4}$ millions of the importing fleet saved. The Admiralty have already instructed their officers in all ports to aid this process, in which is involved the process of repairs, to the utmost. Further injunctions should be given from time to time, and the port officers should be asked to report what they have done and whether they have any recommendations to make. It might be desirable to have a conference of port officers, where all difficulties could be exposed and ideas interchanged.

10. The Minister of Labour has achieved agreement in his conference with employers and employed about the interchangeability of labour at the ports. This should result in a substantially effective addition to the total labour force. In one way or another, at least another 40,000 men must be drawn into ship-repairing, shipbuilding, and dock labour at the earliest moment. Strong propaganda should be run locally at the ports and yards, in order that all engaged may realise the vital consequences in their work. At the same time, it is not desirable that the Press or the broadcast should be used unduly, since this would only encourage the enemy to further exertions.

11. The Ministry of Transport will ensure that there is no congestion at the quays, and that all goods landed are immediately removed. For this purpose the Minister will ask the Chairman of the Import Executive for any further assistance required. He should also report weekly to the Import Executive upon the progress made in improving the ports on which we specially rely by transference of cranes, etc., from other ports. He should also report on the progress made in preparing new facilities at minor ports, and whether further use can be made of lighterage to have more rapid loading or unloading.

12. A Standing Committee has been set up of representatives from the Admiralty Transport Department, the Ministry of Shipping, and the Ministry of Transport, which will meet daily and report all hitches

APPENDIX O, *continued*

or difficulties encountered to the Chairman of the Imports Executive. The Imports Executive will concert the whole of these measures and report upon them to me every week, in order that I may seek Cabinet authority for any further steps.

13. In addition to what is being done at home, every effort must be made to ensure a rapid turn-round at ports abroad. All concerned should receive special instructions on this point, and should be asked to report on the measures which they are taking to implement these instructions, and on any difficulties that may be encountered.

APPENDIX P

Chronological Summary of Moves by the United States Government affecting the War at Sea, 1939–41.

5th September 1939	President orders organisation of Neutrality Patrol.
November 1939	Neutrality Act repealed. War material supply on 'cash and carry' basis starts.
July 1940	President declares policy to be 'all aid [to Britain] short of war'. U.S. Naval Mission under Rear-Admiral R. L. Ghormley arrives in London to study British experience and methods.
24th July 1940	Exchange of lease of British bases in Western Hemisphere for fifty old U.S. destroyers agreed in principle. The exchange agreement was not formally ratified until 2nd September.
29th January to 27th March 1941	British–U.S. Staff discussions in Washington. Combined strategy framed.
1st February 1941	United States Atlantic Fleet formed under command of Admiral E. J. King.
11th March 1941	Presidential assent given to Lend-Lease Bill.
March 1941	U.S. mission under Captain L. Denfeld arrives to choose naval and air bases in British Isles.
3rd April 1941	President orders transfer of ten coastguard cutters to Britain.
4th April 1941	Arrangements made to refit British warships in U.S. dockyards.
7th April 1941	U.S. naval and air bases opened in Bermuda. Air bases on east coast of Greenland opened.
11th April 1941	American Defence Zone extended to all waters west of 26° West (announced 18th April). Red Sea declared no longer to be a 'combat zone'.
15th May 1941	U.S. naval forces take over the base at Argentia, Newfoundland.
27th May 1941	President Roosevelt announces Unlimited National Emergency.
7th July 1941	U.S. forces relieve British garrison in Iceland.
19th July 1941	U.S. Navy ordered to escort shipping of any nationality to and from Iceland.
10th August 1941	Atlantic Charter meeting off Argentia between President Roosevelt and Mr Churchill.

APPENDIX P, *continued*

1st September 1941	U.S. Navy allowed to escort convoys comprising ships of any nation in Atlantic.
4th September 1941	C.-in-C., U.S. Atlantic Fleet, ordered to implement Western Hemisphere Defence Plan No. 4. Incident between U.S.S. *Greer* and U.652 south of Iceland..
11th September 1941	President Roosevelt announces, 'From now on if German or Italian vessels of war enter these waters they do so at their own peril'.
16th September 1941	Convoy H.X. 150 sails with U.S.N. escort.
17th October 1941	U.S.S. *Kearney* torpedoed while escorting Convoy S.C. 48.
31st October 1941	U.S.S. *Reuben James* sunk while escorting Convoy H.X. 156. These were the first casualties to the U.S. Navy.
7th and 11th November 1941	U.S. merchant ships allowed to be armed and to enter war zones.

APPENDIX Q

German U-boat Strength, 1939-41.

Date	Operational	Training and trials	Total	New boats commissioned in previous quarter
September 1939	49	8	57	7
January 1940	32	24	56	4
April 1940	46	6	52	9
July 1940	28	23	51	15
October 1940	27	37	64	22
January 1941	22	67	89	30
April 1941	32	81	113	47
July 1941	65	93	158	53
October 1941	80	118	198	69
January 1942	91	158	249	49

APPENDIX R

TABLE I

British, Allied and Neutral Merchant Ship Losses and Causes

(Tonnage—Number of ships)

1939

Month	Submarines	Aircraft	Mine	Warship raider	Merchant raider	E-boat	Unknown and other causes	Total
September	153,879 (41)	—	29,537 (8)	5,051 (1)	—	—	6,378 (3)	194,845 (53)
October	134,807 (27)	—	29,490 (11)	32,058 (8)	—	—	—	196,355 (46)
November	51,589 (21)	—	120,958 (27)	1,722 (2)	—	—	—	174,269 (50)
December	80,881 (25)	2,949 (10)	82,712 (33)	22,506 (4)	—	—	875 (1)	189,923 (73)
Total	421,156 (114)	2,949 (10)	262,697 (79)	61,337 (15)	—	—	7,253 (4)	755,392 (222)

1940

Month	Submarines	Aircraft	Mine	Warship raider	Merchant raider	E-boat	Unknown and other causes	Total
January	111,263 (40)	23,693 (11)	77,116 (21)	—	—	—	2,434 (1)	214,506 (73)
February	169,566 (45)	853 (2)	54,740 (15)	1,761 (1)	—	—	—	226,920 (63)
March	62,781 (23)	8,694 (7)	35,501 (14)	—	—	—	33 (1)	107,009 (45)
April	32,467 (7)	13,409 (7)	19,799 (11)	—	5,207 (1)	151 (1)	87,185 (31)	158,218 (58)
May	55,580 (13)	158,348 (48)	47,716 (20)	—	6,199 (1)	694 (1)	19,924 (18)	288,461 (101)
June	284,113 (58)	105,193 (22)	86,076 (22)	25,506 (2)	29,225 (4)	6,856 (3)	48,527 (29)	585,496 (140)

TABLE I (continued)

1940 (continued)

Month	Submarines	Aircraft	Mine	Warship raider	Merchant raider	E-boat	Unknown and other causes	Total
July	195,825 (38)	70,193 (33)	35,598 (14)	—	67,494 (11)	13,302 (6)	4,501 (3)	386,913 (105)
August	267,618 (56)	53,283 (15)	11,433 (5)	—	61,767 (11)	1,583 (2)	1,545 (3)	397,229 (92)
September	295,335 (59)	56,328 (15)	8,269 (7)	—	65,386 (8)	14,951 (7)	8,352 (4)	448,621 (100)
October	352,407 (63)	8,752 (6)	32,548 (24)	—	30,539 (4)	1,595 (1)	17,144 (5)	442,985 (103)
November	146,613 (32)	66,438 (18)	46,762 (24)	48,748 (11)	74,923 (9)	—	2,231 (3)	385,715 (97)
December	212,590 (37)	14,890 (8)	54,331 (24)	20,971 (3)	25,904 (5)	8,853 (2)	12,029 (3)	349,568 (82)
Total	2,186,158 (471)	580,074 (192)	509,889 (201)	96,986 (17)	366,644 (54)	47,985 (23)	203,905 (101)	3,991,641 (1,059)

1941

Month	Submarines	Aircraft	Mine	Warship raider	Merchant raider	E-boat	Unknown and other causes	Total
January	126,782 (21)	78,597 (20)	17,107 (10)	18,738 (3)	78,484 (20)	—	532 (2)	320,240 (76)
February	196,783 (39)	89,305 (27)	16,507 (10)	79,086 (17)	7,031 (1)	—	11,702 (5)	403,393 (102)
March	243,020 (41)	113,314 (41)	23,585 (19)	89,838 (17)	28,707 (4)	—	10,881 (8)	529,706 (139)
April	249,375 (43)	323,454 (116)	24,888 (6)	—	43,640 (6)	2,979 (3)	42,245 (21)	687,901 (195)
May	325,492 (58)	146,302 (65)	23,194 (9)	—	15,002 (3)	20,361 (9)	1,052 (4)	511,042 (139)
June	310,143 (61)	61,414 (25)	15,326 (10)	—	17,759 (4)	4,999 (3)	27,383 (9)	432,025 (109)
July	94,209 (22)	9,275 (11)	8,583 (7)	—	5,792 (1)	—	3,116 (2)	120,975 (43)
August	80,310 (23)	23,862 (9)	1,400 (3)	—	21,378 (3)	3,519 (2)	230 (1)	130,699 (41)
September	202,820 (53)	40,812 (12)	14,948 (9)	7,500 (1)	8,734 (2)	6,676 (3)	4,452 (4)	285,942 (84)
October	156,554 (32)	35,222 (10)	19,737 (4)	—	—	3,305 (2)	3,471 (3)	218,289 (51)
November	62,196 (13)	23,015 (10)	1,714 (5)	—	—	17,715 (7)	—	104,640 (35)
December	124,070 (26)	72,850 (25)	63,853 (19)	6,661 (2)	—	—	316,272 (213)	583,706 (285)
Total	2,171,754 (432)	1,017,422 (371)	230,842 (111)	201,823 (40)	226,527 (44)	58,854 (29)	421,336 (272)	4,328,558 (1,299)

TABLE II

British, Allied and Neutral Merchant Ship Losses according to theatres

(Tonnage—Number of ships)

1939

Month	North Atlantic	United Kingdom	South Atlantic	Mediterranean	Indian Ocean	Pacific	Total
September	104,829 (19)	84,965 (33)	5,051 (1)	—	—	—	194,845 (53)
October	110,619 (18)	63,368 (24)	22,368 (4)	—	—	—	196,355 (46)
November	17,895 (6)	155,668 (43)	—	—	706 (1)	—	174,269 (50)
December	15,852 (4)	152,107 (66)	21,964 (3)	—	—	—	189,923 (73)
Total	249,195 (47)	456,108 (166)	49,383 (8)	—	706 (1)	—	755,392 (222)

1940

Month	North Atlantic	United Kingdom	South Atlantic	Mediterranean	Indian Ocean	Pacific	Total
January	35,970 (9)	178,536 (64)	—	—	—	—	214,506 (73)
February	74,759 (17)	152,161 (46)	—	—	—	—	226,920 (63)
March	11,215 (2)	95,794 (43)	—	—	—	—	107,009 (45)
April	24,570 (4)	133,648 (54)	—	—	—	—	158,218 (58)
May	49,087 (9)	230,607 (90)	6,199 (1)	2,568 (1)	—	—	288,461 (101)
June	296,529 (53)	208,924 (77)	—	45,402 (6)	15,445 (2)	19,196 (2)	585,496 (140)
July	141,474 (28)	192,331 (67)	31,269 (6)	6,564 (2)	15,275 (2)	—	386,913 (105)
August	190,048 (39)	162,956 (45)	—	1,044 (1)	31,001 (5)	12,180 (2)	397,229 (92)
September	254,553 (52)	131,150 (39)	17,801 (1)	5,708 (2)	39,409 (6)	—	448,621 (100)
October	286,644 (56)	131,620 (43)	—	2,897 (1)	14,621 (2)	7,203 (1)	442,985 (103)
November	201,341 (38)	92,713 (48)	—	—	57,665 (7)	33,996 (4)	385,715 (97)
December	239,304 (42)	83,308 (34)	—	—	—	26,956 (6)	349,568 (82)
Total	1,805,494 (349)	1,793,748 (650)	55,269 (8)	64,183 (13)	173,416 (24)	99,531 (15)	3,991,641 (1,059)

APPENDIX R, continued

TABLE II (continued)

1941

Month	North Atlantic	United Kingdom	South Atlantic	Mediterranean	Indian Ocean	Pacific	Total
January	214,382 (42)	36,975 (15)	58,585 (17)	—	10,298 (2)	—	320,240 (76)
February	317,378 (69)	51,381 (26)	—	8,343 (2)	26,291 (5)	—	403,393 (102)
March	364,689 (63)	152,862 (73)	—	11,868 (2)	—	287 (1)	529,706 (139)
April	260,451 (45)	99,031 (40)	21,807 (3)	292,518 (105)	14,094 (2)	—	687,901 (195)
May	324,551 (58)	100,655 (99)	11,339 (2)	70,835 (19)	3,663 (1)	—	511,042 (139)
June	318,740 (68)	86,381 (34)	10,134 (2)	9,145 (3)	7,625 (2)	—	432,025 (109)
July	97,813 (23)	15,265 (18)	—	7,897 (2)	—	—	120,975 (43)
August	83,661 (25)	19,791 (11)	—	5,869 (2)	—	21,378 (3)	130,699 (41)
September	184,546 (51)	54,779 (13)	15,526 (2)	15,951 (4)	10,347 (3)	4,793 (1)	285,942 (84)
October	154,593 (32)	35,996 (12)	5,297 (1)	22,403 (6)	—	—	218,289 (51)
November	50,215 (10)	30,332 (20)	4,953 (1)	19,140 (4)	—	—	104,640 (35)
December	50,682 (10)	56,845 (19)	6,275 (1)	37,394 (9)	837 (5)	431,673 (241)	583,706 (285)
Total	2,421,700 (496)	740,293 (350)	133,916 (29)	501,363 (158)	73,155 (20)	458,131 (246)	4,328,558 (1,299)

Index

INDEX

(The suffix letter 'n' denotes a footnote)

Aalesund: proposed occupation of, 183
Aandalsnes: naval party lands at, 183; air attacks on, 183-4; reinforcements for, 185, 187; decision to evacuate, 188; evacuation, 189
Abdiel, H.M.S.: mines Brest approaches, 393; joins Mediterranean Fleet, 434; runs stores into Crete, 443; supplies for Tobruk, 519
Aberdeen: anti-submarine trawlers at, 130; trawlers bombed off, 142
Abrial, Vice-Admiral: responsible for Belgian coast operations, 207, 211; Dunkirk evacuation, 226
Abyssinia: assault on Italian positions, 307; surrender, 426
Acasta, H.M.S.: sunk by *Scharnhorst* and *Gneisenau* after torpedoing former, 195-6, 199, 259
Achilles, H.M.S.: 49; in raider hunting group, 114, 116; off Rio de Janeiro, 117; River Plate battle, 118-121; search for raider *Orion*, 283
Acoustic mine: *see* Minelaying, Enemy
Adelaide, H.M.A.S.: 49
Aden: contraband control base at, 43; expedition from to capture Assab, 517
Admiral Graf Spee, German pocket battleship: controlled by Naval Staff, 57; leaves for Atlantic, 58; reported in South Atlantic, 70; objective in Atlantic, 112; escapes detection by aircraft warning, 113; hunting groups for, 114; victims of, 115; fuels from *Altmark* and rounds Cape of Good Hope, 115-7; Battle of River Plate, 118-20; scuttled, 121; details of, 604
Admiral Hipper, German cruiser: under C.-in-C., West, 56; attack on Norway shipping frustrated, 153; in force for Trondheim, 160, 163; leaves Trondheim, joins Admiral Lütjens, 176; sortie off Norway, Operation 'Juno', 194, 259; sortie off Bear Island and Spitzbergen, 260; attacks Middle East convoy W.S. 5A, 263, 291, 369; Atlantic sortie, 287, 290, 391; unsuited to commerce raiding, 292; at Brest, 368; leaves Brest on second sortie, 364, 371; attacks convoy S.L.S. 64, 372, 391; returns to Brest and Kiel, 372, 376, 379; attacked from the air, 390-1; believed in Baltic, 483; details of, 605
Admiral Scheer, German pocket battleship: under C.-in-C., West, 56; bombed in Schillig Roads, 66; wrongly reported in Atlantic, 113, 116; refitting during Norway campaign, 163; at Wilhelmshaven, 261; commerce raiding in Atlantic, 263, 280, 285, 287, 351; attacks convoy H.X. 84, 287-9; moves to South Atlantic, 290; captures *Duquesa*, 290-1; refits in South Atlantic, 367; searches for W.S. 5A, 369;

Admiral Scheer—cont.
in Indian Ocean, 368, 370, 381-3; returns to Kiel, tonnage sunk, 371-2, 376, 379; exchanges stores and prisoners with *Kormoran*, 386; believed returning home via Denmark Strait, 392; believed in Baltic, 483; believed ready for sea, 490; moves to Oslo, 493; returns to Swinemunde, 494; details of, 605
Admiralty: outline of organisation, 1941, 14; organisation described, 15-27; intervention in conduct of operations, 26-7; naval air organisation, 32; control of merchant shipping, 45; control of Humber Force, 45; joint staff with Air Ministry, 72; Home Fleet base policy, 77-9; failure to defend Scapa, 80; dispositions after attack on *Rawalpindi*, 85; protection against magnetic mines, 99; asks for more aircraft for minelaying, 125; anti-submarine warfare plans, 134-5; Department for A.A. Weapons, 140; agreement with Air Ministry regarding convoy patrols, 142-3; intervenes in operation against *Altmark*, 152; orders for Narvik operations, 173-5, 178; intervention in Norway campaign discussed, 201; plans for Dunkirk evacuation, 212, 216, 218, 221; destroyers withdrawn from Dunkirk, 223; action to neutralise French Fleet, 240-5; plans against invasion of U.K., 248-54, 257; difference with C.-in-C., Home Fleet, 250, 252, 259; request for Trondheim air reconnaissance, 260; request for aerial minelaying, 261; cancels Home Fleet plans because of invasion threat, 262; defensive minefields, Orkneys-Iceland, 263; retains A.M.C.'s in Northern Patrol, 265, 271; orders regarding French traffic, Gibraltar Straits, 272; danger to Atlantic islands from Biscay ports, 273, 380; orders concerning Vichy French ships, 275-6; problem of armed merchant raiders, 280; orders to Force K, search for *Scheer*, 290; on proposed evacuation of Eastern Mediterranean, 297; enquiry into Spartivento action, 303-4; ships to fire on unidentified aircraft, 322; responsibility for aerial minelaying, discussions with Air Ministry, 335-6; passage of French force for Dakar, Gibraltar Straits, 309-14; attitude towards Dakar expedition, 315; Trade Plot established, weekly meeting on Trade Protection, 350; warns Admiral Tovey of Atlantic break-out, 373-4; co-operation with Coastal Command, 358, 481; opposes formation of escort groups, anti-submarine training transferred to West Coast, 359; proposal to transfer Coastal Command to, 360-1; use of wireless intercepts in tracking submarines, 362, 469; measures to eliminate straggling from

621

622　INDEX

Admiralty—*cont.*
convoys, 363; orders minelaying, Iceland-Faeröes, 390; comment on raider action with *Cornwall*, 385; orders during *Bismarck* operations, 407; strategic control during *Bismarck* operations, 416; proposal to block Tripoli, 431-2; doubts about 'Tiger' convoy for Egypt, 437; control of R.C.N. ships on convoy duty, 453; Tracking Room information for Western Approaches, 456; agreement on air policy in U-boat warfare, 459; views on convoy escorts, June, 1941, 464, 466; resists Cabinet proposal to transfer bombers from Battle of Atlantic, 467; responsible for Atlantic convoy routes after Plan 4, 471; new directive (with Air Ministry) to Coastal Command, 473; presses for Focke-Wulf bases to be bombed, 476; problem of coastal convoy protection, 497; escapes by fast ships, Dover Straits, 505; on Vestfiord raid by Admiral Hamilton, 513; opposes plan to capture Sicily, 521; detaches Home Fleet ships for Malta convoy, 521; congratulates Mediterranean submarines, 525; action against raider supply ships, 542; plans for war with Japan, 553; reinforcement of Eastern Fleet, 554-5; despatch of *Prince of Wales*, 556-8; anxiety on exposed position of Admiral Phillips, 559; members of Board of; Appendix A, 573

Adolf Leonhardt, German s.s.: intercepted by *Shropshire*, 117

Adolph Woermann, German s.s.: intercepted by *Neptune*, 116

Adriatic: Italian plans for closing, 294; submarine patrol in, 526

Adua, Italian U-boat: sunk in Malta convoy 'Halberd', 531

Adventure, H.M.S.: Dover Straits mine barrage, 96; damaged by mine, 100; conveys mines for Russians to Archangel, 486

Aegean Sea: control passes to enemy, 436; enemy targets in, 516; submarine patrols in, 525

'Aerial', Operation (evacuation from N.W. France), 230, 232, 237, 239

Afric Star, s.s.: sunk by *Kormoran*, 386

Afridi, H.M.S.: sunk in evacuation of Namsos, 189

Afrika Korps: arrives in Libya under Rommel, 423; supplies to, 431; submarine check to success of, 439. *See also* Libya, etc.

Agar, Captain A. W. S., V.C.: intercepts supply ship *Python*, 546

Agnew, Captain W. G.: commands Force K, Malta, 532; convoy actions, 532-3

Agulhas, Cape: mining by German raider off, 280, 281

Air Defence of Great Britain (A.D.G.B.): fighter cover for East Coast convoys, 108; concentration against Luftwaffe during pre-invasion period, 322

Air Ministry: Admiralty agreements with, 1924, 1937, 29-31; policy to attack German industry, 65; investigates North Sea reconnaissance and attacks on shipping, 72; proposes bomber patrols over enemy bases,

Air Ministry—*cont.*
102; trade defence squadrons formed, 107; allocation of mines to, 123; provision for aircraft minelaying, 124-5; attitude to trials of depth charges, 135; expects unrestricted air war on shipping, 137; standing fighter patrols for East Coast convoys, 142; successful defence of Norwegian convoys, 143; cancels proposed strike at Stavanger, 171; on R.A.F. service at Dunkirk, 218; ferrying of aircraft into Malta, 298; strengthens fighter patrols for convoys, 324; responsibility for aerial minelaying, 335-6; proposed transfer of Coastal Command to Admiralty, 360-1; agreement with Admiralty on Coastal Command expansion, 361; agreement with Admiralty on air policy in U-boat warfare, 459; resists Cabinet proposal to transfer bombers from Battle of Atlantic, 467; directive to Coastal Command, 473; Anti-Shipping Assessment Committee set up, 503

Air power and air cover: influence on maritime strategy, 3, 5; decisive factor in U-boat defeat, 6; watching of enemy ports simplified, 9; lack of sea/air co-operation before 1937, 39; threat to mercantile ports and shipping, 45, 137; possibilities of close blockade, 54; conditions maritime control off Norway, 171; effects of, under-estimated in Norway, 179, 199; complaints of inadequacy of at Dunkirk, 217; German attempt to conquer by, 255; importance in Dover Straits, 256; strengthens defence against invasion, 258; in Battle for Crete, enemy control disputed, 440, 447-8; importance in Mediterranean after loss of heavy ships, 539

Air/Sea Rescue: Directorate established, Jan., 1941, 332-3

Aircraft, Naval: *see* Fleet Air Arm

Aircraft carriers: use in anti-submarine operations, 6; ships in service, 1939, 31, 577; Home Fleet deprived of, 76, 87; withdrawal from submarine hunting, 106; Mediterranean Fleet without, 538; needed in Far East, 554-5; auxiliary carriers introduced, 476-7; case for escort carriers proved, 477

Ajax, H.M.S.: in raider hunting group, 114, 116-7; intercepts *Ussukuma*, 117; River Plate battle, 118-21; battle off Cape Matapan, 428; evacuation of Greece, 436; in Battle for Crete, 441, 445; campaign in Syria, 516; sent to Malta, 534

Ajax, French submarine: sunk by *Fortune* at Dakar, 317

Albacore aircraft: offensive against North African supply route, 524, 527

Albatross, H.M.S.: 48; in South Atlantic, 274

Alberico da Barbiano, Italian cruiser: sunk by destroyers, 534

Alberto di Giussano, Italian cruiser: sunk by destroyers, 534

Alcantara, H.M.S.: in South American Division, 274; action with *Thor*, 277, 285

Alexander, Rt. Hon. A. V., First Lord: meeting with Admiral Darlan, 237; on 'crisis in

Alexander, Rt. Hon. A. V., First Lord—*cont.*
our fortunes', 532; resists despatch of *Prince of Wales*, 556
Alexandria: Mediterranean Fleet at, 48-9; lack of facilities, 77; French Squadron at, 241-2, 296; U-boat patrols off, 292; reinforcements arrive at, 295; Fleet to remain at, 297; supplies for Malta, 300; small convoy passed through Mediterranean to, 301; *Illustrious* arrives at, 422; supplies to Greece from, 424; Greek warships arrive at, 434 and *n*; limitations as a base, 435; distance from Crete, 440; within easy range for air bombardment, 515; effect of recapture of Cyrenaica on, 521; submarines increased, 524, 536; attacked by human torpedoes, 538, 555
Alster, German s.s.: captured by *Icarus*, 178
Alstertor, German supply ship: scuttled, 606
Alsterufer, German supply ship: sunk, 606
Altmark, German supply ship: sails for Atlantic, 58, 113; missed by *Ark Royal*, fuels *Graf Spee*, 115-7; reported off Bergen, 151; intercepted, 152; British prisoners recovered from, 153; pretext for Operation 'Wilfred', 157; renamed *Uckermark*, 606-7
Ambuscade, H.M.S.: damaged off St. Valéry, 231, 232
America and West Indies Station: force on, 1939, 48, 585; protection against raiders, 43; force on, 1940, 276
Ammunition: 40 per cent. expenditure off Norway, 171; of A.A. ships, Norway, 184; shortage of A.A., 186
Amphibious expeditions, merits of, 11; planning of, 199
Amsterdam: oil reserves fired at, 208
Andania, H.M.S.: sunk by U-boat, 265
Anglo-German Naval Agreement; signed, 52; abrogated by Germany, 52
Anneliese Essberger, German supply ship: scuttled, 606
Anson aircraft: low performance of, 36-8; replaced by Hudsons, 66
Antelope, H.M.S.: sinks U.41, 131; re-sinks U.31, 353
Anthony, H.M.S.: in Dunkirk evacuation, 221
Anti-aircraft defence: protection of convoys, 34; ineffective in Home Fleet, 69; lack of at Scapa, 79; increased at Scapa, 81; pre-war reliance on for convoy escorts, 106-7; provision of in merchant ships, 109-10, 139, 363, 364; Admiralty Department formed for, 140; insufficient to protect Fleet, Norway, 171; limitations of A.A. ships, Norway, 184; special 'Channel Guard' formed, 324-5; new weapons for merchant ships, 476; importance in night defence of coastal convoys, 500
Anti-Submarine Warfare Division: work of, 23
Anton Schmidt, German destroyer: sunk at Narvik, 174
Antwerp: German sea traffic with, 144; demolition at, 207-8; evacuation of, 210
Aquitania, s.s.: first Canadian troop convoy, in collision, 89; transport of Australian troops, 270

Arabis, H.M.S.: attacks U.101, 133
Arandora Star, s.s.: evacuation of Biscay ports, 233, 238
Arawa, H.M.S.: raider *Kormoran* escapes from, 386
Arbuthnot, Vice-Admiral G. S.: commands expedition to Persian Gulf, 529
Arbutus, H.M.S.: in sinking of U.47 and U.70, 364
Archangel: *Adventure* carries mines to, 486; Hurricane aircraft sent to, 489, 492; British minesweepers based on, 492; ice conditions, ships diverted to Murmansk, 494-5
Ardent, H.M.S.: sunk by *Scharnhorst* and *Gneisenau*, 195-6
Area Combined Headquarters (A.C.H.Q.): establishment of, 19, 36
Arendal: German landing at, 164-5
Arethusa, H.M.S.: joins Home Fleet, 151; sights *Altmark*, 152; operations off Norway, 159; landings at Molde and Aandalsnes, 185; evacuation from Aandalsnes, 188; joins Nore Command, 205; escorts bullion ships from Holland, 208; at Le Verdon for evacuations, 237; joins Force H, 242; action against French at Oran, 242-4; escort duty from Gibraltar, 392; raid in Vestfiord area, 513; in Malta convoy 'Substance', 521, 522; conveys troops to Malta, 523
'Arethusa' class cruisers: patrol of Iceland-Faeröes gap, 394
Argus, H.M.S.: 31; ferries aircraft—to Malta, 298, 533; to Takoradi, 298; to Gibraltar, 434; to Russia, 489
Ariguani, H.M.S.: fighter catapult ship, seriously damaged, 477
Arizona, U.S. battleship: wrecked at Pearl Harbour, 562
Ark Royal, H.M.S.: 31, 47, 106; Home Fleet patrol, 65; attacked by U.39, 68; aircraft lost in attacking U.30, 68, 105; enemy aircraft shot down by Skua, 69; in Atlantic hunting group, 70, 114; misses *Altmark*, 115; intercepts *Uhenfels*, 116; returns from Freetown, 131; interception of German shipping from Vigo, 150; covers landing at Bjerkvik, Norway, 191; covers Narvik evacuation, 193, 194, 198; attack on Trondheim, 198; joins Force H, 242; action against French at Oran, 242-4; covers through convoy for Alexandria, 301; action off Cape Spartivento, 301-3; expedition to Dakar, 309, 314-7; aircraft sights enemy battle cruisers, Atlantic, 377-9; covers convoy 'Excess', Mediterranean, 421; air attacks on Genoa, Leghorn and Spezia, 425; takes part in *Bismarck* operations, 410-16, 438; *Sheffield* attacked in error, 412; accuracy of air reconnaissance, 416; flies Hurricanes to Malta, 434, 437-8, 518, 524; in Malta convoys—'Substance', 522-3, and 'Halberd', 530; sunk by U-boat near Gibraltar, 533, 474
Arliss, Captain S. H. T.: in evacuation from Crete, 445
Armando Diaz, Italian cruiser: sunk by *Upright*, 425

624   INDEX

Armanistan, s.s.: sunk by U.25, 132
Armed Merchant Cruisers: allocated to Northern Patrol, 46; work in Northern Patrol, 67; temporary withdrawal after *Rawalpindi* loss, 85; return to Northern Patrol, 89; heavy losses from U-boats, 265, 270; Northern Patrol ships to work from Halifax, 265, 270; 46 available Feb. 1940, 270-1; no match for German raiders, 271, 384; improvement of fighting power, 285; withdrawn from convoy routes and used as troopships, 454
Army: troops for Iceland and Faeröes, 345; faith in the Navy, Crete evacuation, 447. *See also* British Expeditionary Force, Convoys (Troop), War Office, etc.
Army of the Nile: offensive begun, December 1940, 420; supply of by Inshore Squadron, 422; difficulties of, 423; driven back to Egypt, 425, 433; special tank convoy for, 437; consequences of defeat, 515; retains hold on Egypt, 516; Operation 'Battleaxe', 519; Operation 'Crusader', 520-1, 527, 536; success not able to be exploited, 539
Aruba: defence of oil installations at, 276
Arucas, German s.s.: intercepted by *York*, 150
'Asdic' detecting device: pre-war estimate of, 34 & *n*, 106; performance unknown to Germans, 56; success of, 68, 90; ineffective against surface U-boats, 130, 355; Germans instruct Italians in, 536
Assab: captured by British and Indian troops, 517
Assiniboine, H.M.C.S.: capture of *Hannover*, 276
Athelking, m.v.: sunk by *Atlantis*, 281
Athenia, s.s.: sunk by U.30 on first day of war, 103
Atlantic: disputed control of, 3; exits to, watched by Northern Patrol, 45; German naval policy in, 55; first Atlantic U-boat base (Lorient), 346; Italian U-boats start work in, 347; American co-operation in, 348; ease of German access to, 1941, 368; German air group formed for reconnaissance in, 362; 'Security Zone' extended to 26° W., 455; meeting between Churchill and Roosevelt, 470; collaboration of Canadian, U.S. and Royal Navies in, 471; Atlantic Charter, 569
Atlantic, Battle of: 91, 93; higher loss among independent ships, 94-5; U-boats available for, 1939, 103; convoy routes diverted further north, 266, 451-3; Prime Minister's directive on, 339, 364, 459, 609 (text); new cycle of slow convoys from Sydney, C.B., 344; peak period of U-boat success, 1940, 348-9; developments in American policy, 456; gap of 300 miles not covered by air escort, 459, 460; tactical use of aircraft in, 461; sinkings by U-boat in, 463-75; Battle of Atlantic Committee formed, 364, 481, 498; Iceland's part in, 452-3; more active American participation, 490; escort strength, 464; proposal to divert Coastal Command bombers from, 467; Western Hemisphere Defence Plan No. 4, 470; first incidents with American escorts,

Atlantic, Battle of—*cont*.
472, 613; Battle of Atlantic Committee and C.A.M. ships, 477
Atlantis, hospital ship: with *Orama* when sunk, 194, 196
Atlantis, German raider: cruise of, 279-82; mining off Cape Agulhas, 280; leaves Australian routes, 282; in northern Indian Ocean, 367; meets *Admiral Scheer*, 369; further operations of, 381-3; meets *Kormoran*, 386; in South Atlantic, 470, 544; sunk by *Devonshire*, 480, 545; survivors in *Python*, 546; details of, 604
Auchinleck, General C. J. E.: succeeds General Mackesy, Narvik area, 192; evacuation from Narvik, 193; offensive in Libya, 474
Auckland: raider minelaying off, 283; New Zealand cruisers at, 559
Auckland, H.M.S.: lands naval party at Aandalsnes, 183; evacuation from Aandalsnes, 189; sunk in carrying supplies to Tobruk, 519
Audacity, H.M.S.: captured as m.v. *Hannover*, 276, 477; with convoy H.G. 76, 478-9; sunk by U-boat, 479
Aurora, H.M.S.: 47; Home Fleet patrol, 65; assists disabled *Spearfish*, 68; sortie to intercept *Gneisenau*, 71; escorts Narvik convoy, 82; operations after attack on *Rawalpindi*, 84-7; flagship of Admiral Evans for Plan R.4, 157, 162; conveys Lord Cork to Narvik area, 180; in operations against *Bismarck*, 396, 408; search for enemy supply ships, 483; reconnaissance of Spitzbergen, 488; sent to Malta, 494; in Force K, Malta, 532; convoy actions, 532-3; damaged by mines off Tripoli, 535
Australia: places cruiser at Admiralty's disposal, 261; minesweepers built in, 498; troops withdrawn from Tobruk, 519; Japanese threat to, 570
Australia, H.M.A.S.: 49; attack on *Richelieu* at Dakar, 245; expedition to Dakar, 261, 309, 315, 317; escorts troop convoy W.S. 5B, 370, 391-2
Autocarrier, s.s.: in Dunkirk evacuation, 227
Automedon, s.s.: sunk by *Atlantis*, 282
Auxiliary Patrol: origin of, 249; trawlers and drifters for, 251, 253; conflicting views on value of, 258
Avonmouth: first B.E.F. convoys from, 63
Azores: immunity from German attack, 2; limit of U-boat operations, 1939, 59; German threat to, from Biscay ports, 272, 273, 379; Italian U-boats off, 347; German U-boat patrol off, 462

Babitonga, German supply ship: intercepted by *London*, 382, 606
Backhouse, Admiral Sir Roger: First Sea Lord, illness and death, 15-6, 79; doubts about air patrols, North Sea, 37; examines Home Fleet base policy, 77
Baghdad: revolt against Regent of Iraq suppressed, 427
Balloon Barrage: Mobile Flotilla formed, 324
Baltic: German forces released by Russian

INDEX

Baltic—*cont.*
   pact, 53, 54; minefields in, 55; R.A.F. minelaying in, 337, 510, 514; German warships in, 1.6.41, 483; Leningrad closely invested, 490
Balzac, s.s.: sunk by *Atlantis*, 382
Barham, Lord: quoted, 8
Barham, H.M.S.: 48; to join Home Fleet, 89; covers first Canadian troop convoy, 89; torpedoed by U.30, 90; leaves Gibraltar for Dakar, 261; joins Mediterranean Fleet, 300; expedition to Dakar, 309, 314, 317; battle off Cape Matapan, 428-30; proposed use to block Tripoli, 431-2; in Battle for Crete, damaged, 444; sunk by U.331, 534, 555
Barker, Lieutenant-Commander J. F.: lost in *Ardent*, 195-6
Barneveld, s.s.: captured by *Admiral Scheer*, 369
Barry: first B.E.F. convoys from, 63
Bartolomeo Colleoni, Italian cruiser: sunk by *Sydney*, 299
Bases: essential element of sea power, 6; defence of, 23; air threat to exaggerated, 68, 75; for Home Fleet, policy, 76-8; problems of in Norway, 184, 199
Basilisk, H.M.S.: sunk in Dunkirk evacuation, 225
Basra: Indian troops sent to, 427
Bass Straits: enemy minelaying in, 286
Bathurst, Gambia: refuelling base for convoy escorts, 454; air reinforcement for, 460; West African Air Command set up, 460; heavy losses off, 470
Batory, Polish m.v.: evacuations from St. Nazaire and Bayonne, 234-5, 238
'Battleaxe', Operation: Army offensive in Libya, 519
Battles: River Plate, 118-21; first Narvik, 172-5; second Narvik, 177-8; of Britain, begins, 256, assessment of, 448; off Calabria, 298-9; off Cape Spartivento, 302-4; off Cape Matapan, 427-31; sinking of *Bismarck*, 395-418; for Crete, 440-9; first Battle of Sirte, 535; sinking of *Prince of Wales* and *Repulse*, 566-9
Battleships: changed uses for, 6, 74; as convoy escorts, 391; disposition of, August, 1941, 554; eliminated from Mediterranean, 538; list in commission, etc., Appendix D, 577
Bayonne: evacuation from, 237-8; enemy ore traffic to, 503
Beachy Head: enemy air attacks off, 142; German invasion plans, 255
Beagle, H.M.S.: evacuation from St. Nazaire, 234; demolition party for Bordeaux, 237
Bear Island: sortie of *Hipper* to, 260; Russian convoys to disperse off, 495
Béarn, French aircraft carrier: in raider hunting group, Atlantic, 114; at Martinique, 276
Beaufort aircraft: 260; use for minelaying, 124; considered for Malta, 438; torpedo hit on *Lützow*, 484; delay in production, 503; sinking of *Ole Jacob*, 504; attack on enemy shipping, English Channel, 504; hit on *Komet*, 505
Beirut: French destroyers in Syria campaign, 517

Belchen, German supply ship: sunk, 606
Belfast: value as a base, 46
Belfast, H.M.S.: 47; damaged by mine in Forth, 78, 100
Belgium: German invasion of, 192, 205-6; responsibility for naval operations off, 207; opposition to demolitions at Zeebrugge, 211; collapse of Army of, 216; seeks an armistice, 218
Bell, Captain F. S.: H.M.S. *Exeter*, 116
Benarty, s.s.: sunk by *Atlantis*, 281
Benghazi: enemy route to, 306; captured by Allies, 420; Inshore Squadron at, 423; recaptured by enemy, 431; bombarded by light force, 437; enemy use of, 515-6; stoppage of enemy transport to, 533; enemy convoys resumed, 536; reoccupied by Allies, 539
Bergen: convoys to Methil from, 93, 130; *Altmark* examined at, 152; plan 'R.4' to occupy, 157, 162; German landing at, 148, 163-5, 180; British naval attack on cancelled, 170, 187, 201-2; R.A.F. attack on, 171-2; *Königsberg* sunk at, 172
Bering Sea: passage of raider *Komet*, 280
Berkeley, H.M.S.: at Bordeaux, wireless link in evacuations, 237
Bermuda: convoy assembly point, 270, 343; bases in leased to Americans, 347-8; U.S. take over air and naval bases, 455, 612
Bernd Von Arnim, German destroyer: sunk at Narvik, 177 *n*
Berwick, H.M.S.: joins Home Fleet, 70; in raider hunting group, 114; intercepts German *Uruguay*, 150; embarks troops for plan 'R.4', 157; troops disembarked, 161; in Norway campaign, 172; for South Atlantic hunting group, 290; convoy W.S.5A, slight damage in action with *Hipper*, 291; joins Mediterranean Fleet, 300; action off Cape Spartivento, 302; lands Royal Marines in Iceland, 345
Bethouart, General: commands French forces, Narvik area, 191
Bevan, Captain R. H.: in *Leander*, sinks raider *Ramb I*, 387
Bickford, Lieutenant-Commander E. O. B.: success in H.M.S. *Salmon*, 102
Bickford, Captain J. G.: in Operation 'Wilfred', 157; patrols minefield, 173
Bideford, H.M.S.: damaged in Dunkirk evacuation, 222
Bilbao: enemy ore traffic from, 503
Binney, Vice-Admiral Sir T. H.: Anti-Submarine Committee, 134
Birmingham, H.M.S.: 49; off Norway, 156, 159; escorts first Norwegian convoy, 180; conveys final reinforcement, Aandalsnes, 185; joins Humber Force, 188; evacuation from Aandalsnes, 189; ordered to Harwich, 205; on patrol during *Bismarck* operations, 396; escort of W.S. convoy, 483
Biscay, Bay of: plans for U-boat war in, 56; submarines to intercept U-boats in, 266, 267; German use of ports, 272; submarine patrols started in, 333-4; 'sink at sight' zone extended to, 338, 502; search for enemy

626 INDEX

Biscay, Bay of—*cont.*
    battle cruisers, 377; attacks on U-boats in, 461-2
Bismarck, German battleship: believed ready in 1940, 257; fitting out at Hamburg, 261; completes first trials, 368; prepares for Atlantic sortie, 376; passes the Skaw, 378; false report, 392-3; to be joined by *Gneisenau*, 393-4; British battleships tied down by her, 395; leaves Gdynia, 395; sighted by *Suffolk*, 397; Home Fleet loses touch, 400; in action with Home Fleet, 401-18; sinking of *Hood*, 405-6; sunk by *Dorsetshire*, 11, 415; Force H assistance in operations, 438; effect of sinking on enemy plans, 495; supply ships rounded up, 542; details of, 57, 592, 605
Bison, French destroyer: sunk in Namsos evacuation, 189
Bittern, H.M.S.: lands naval party at Aandalsnes, 183
Bjerkvik: landing at, 191
Black Sea: blockade leakage from, 44
Black Swan, H.M.S.: lands naval party at Aandalsnes, 183
Blackburn, Captain J. A. P.: commands *Voltaire* in action with *Thor*, 383-4
Blanche, H.M.S.: sunk by mine, 100
Blenheim aircraft: protection of East Coast shipping, 39, 107; in Battle of Cape Matapan, 429; bombing attack on *Lützow* fails, 484; attack on enemy shipping, English Channel, 504; ditto, Emden-Rotterdam, 506; sent to Mediterranean, 524; arrival in Malta, 526, 527, 533; enemy convoys attacked by day, 527
Blockade, British: enforcement of, 9, 43, 65; leaks in, 44; enforcement by Northern Patrol, 46; German anticipation of, 54-5; proclaimed, 64; evasion of by Norwegian coast route, 156; not relaxed in spite of Atlantic challenge, 394; attempts to break summarised, 551-2. *See also* Contraband Control
Blockade, Enemy: Hitler declares total blockade of U.K., 349
Blücher, German cruiser: to complete in 1940, 57; in Oslo landing, 164; sunk, 165
Bluebell, H.M.S.: sinks U.208, 474
Blyskawica, Polish destroyer: escape to England, 69
Blyth: submarines at, 47; submarine patrols from, 64; enemy mining off, 126
Boadicea, H.M.S.: damaged in Operation 'Cycle', 232
Bodö: detachment landed at, 191; reinforced, 192; evacuated, 192
Bolzano, Italian cruiser: damaged by *Triumph*, 525
Bomba, Gulf of: attacked by *Eagle's* aircraft, 307
Bombay: transport of troops from, 274; transport of troops to, 552
Bomber Command: *See* Royal Air Force: Bomber Command
Bombs, anti-submarine: ineffective, 135; lack of trial under action conditions, 136

Bonaventure, H.M.S.: escorts convoy W.S.5 A, 291; escorts 'Excess' convoy, Mediterranean, 421
Bonham-Carter, Rear-Admiral S. S.: commands Halifax Force, 270
Borde, H.M.S.: first mine destructor ship, 101; damaged, 127
Bordeaux: evacuations from, 237; meeting of First Lord and Darlan, 237; demolition at cancelled, 238; bombing by Coastal Command, 352; convoys routed out of aerial range of, 362; German aircraft at, for attacks on Gibraltar convoys, 468
Borneo: invaded by Japanese, 570
Botha aircraft: type unsuccessful, 124
Boulogne: transport of B.E.F. stores to, 64; isolated by German advance, 212; Guards Brigade conveyed to, 212-3; evacuation of, 213-4
Bovell, Captain H. C.: in *Argus*, ferries aircraft into Malta, 298; commands *Victorious* in *Bismarck* operations, 396; ferries aircraft to Malta in *Victorious*, 518
Bowhill, Air Marshal Sir F. W.: Commander-in-Chief, Coastal Command, 36; introduces use of depth charges, 135; succeeded by Air Marshal Joubert, 459
Boyd, Captain D. W.: attack on Italian Fleet, Taranto, 300; convoys for Piraeus and Malta, 421
Brazen, H.M.S.: sinks U.49, 190
Breconshire, H.M.S.: passed into Malta, 432-3; withdrawn from Malta, 521; returns to Malta, 535
Bremen, German s.s.: Home Fleet search for, 65, 84
Bremse, German cruiser: in landing at Bergen, 163, 170; damaged, 165; sunk off North Cape, 489
Brest: French 'Force de Raid' at, 51; transport of B.E.F. to, 63; threatened by German advance, 229; evacuation from, 232-3, 236; demolition at, 234; R.A.F. patrol and bombing of, 292, 393; minelaying off, 335; U-boat base, 349; German battle cruisers at, 9, 371, 376, 378; Home Fleet and Force H disposed off, 392; approaches to mined, 393; *Prinz Eugen* damaged at, 487; summary of R.A.F. effort against, 487; main bombing effort transferred to Germany, 488; R.A.F. attack on resumed, 491; details of air effort against, 1941, 491, 495; effort of No. 19 Group against, 504; use of English Channel for passage to, 506; mining by Coastal Command, 510
Bretagne, French battleship: at Oran, 241; blown up, 244
Bridge, Captain A. R. M.: commands *Eagle*, 300
Briggs, Flying Officer D. A.: sights *Bismarck*, 411
Brighton Queen, s.s.: sunk in Dunkirk evacuation, 225
Brilliant, H.M.S.: demolitions and evacuation, Antwerp, 210; intercepts German supply ships, 606
Bristol Channel: troop convoys from, 63;

INDEX

Bristol Channel—*cont.*
U-boat minelaying, 127; convoys from Thames start, 323; Fighter Command and defence of, 331
British Emperor, s.s.: sunk by *Pinguin*, 384
British Expeditionary Force: transport of, Portsmouth responsibility, 44; cover by Channel Force, 45, 63; numbers transported, 63-4; leave traffic, 64; mine barrage protection to, 96; advance into Belgium, 206; retreat to Channel ports, 211-2; plans for withdrawal, 212, 215; evacuation from Dunkirk, 216-228; evacuation from other Channel and Atlantic ports, 229-240; numbers evacuated, 239, numbers lifted from Dunkirk, 603
British Union, m.v.: sunk by *Kormoran*, 386
Broke, H.M.S.: evacuation from Brest, 234
Bromet, Air Vice-Marshal G. R.: Commands 19 Group, Coastal Command, 360
Brooke-Popham, Air Marshal Sir R.: Commander-in-Chief, Far East, on lack of fighter cover for Admiral Phillips, 568
Brownrigg, Admiral Sir H.: 47
Bruges, s.s.: sunk at Havre, 231
Brunsbüttel: *Hipper* detected at, 291
Bulgaria joins the Axis, 424
Bulldog, H.M.S.: damaged in Operation 'Cycle', 232
Burges-Watson, Rear-Admiral F.: demolition party, Bordeaux, 237
Burrough, Rear-Admiral H. M.: raid on Vaagsö, 513; Malta convoy 'Substance', 530, 531
Burza, Polish destroyer: escape to England, 69; damaged at Calais, 215

C.V.E.: Escort Carriers, *see* under United States Navy
Cabinet, British: ten-year rule on war risk, 39; delay over Scapa defences, 78; on mining Norwegian waters, 97, 156; forbids bombing of enemy bases, 102; diversion of shipping to West Coast, 143; measures to prevent enemy scuttling, 150; postpones Operation 'Wilfred', 157; relaxes restrictions on attacks on enemy merchant ships, 172; bases intended in Norway, 178; decision to abandon central Norway, 185; first priority for Narvik, 186; anxiety for Narvik expedition, 191-2; decision to retire from Norway, 192, 205; threat to Low Countries anticipated, 206; evacuation from Dunkirk authorised, 216; policy for B.E.F. after Dunkirk, 229; orders evacuation from Biscay ports, 233; cancels demolition at Bordeaux, 238; action to neutralise French Fleet, 240-5; plans against invasion of U.K., 250-1, 257, 259; policy towards French warships, West Indies, 276; expedition to Dakar—approved, 308, considered impracticable, 315; plans to capture Atlantic islands, 380; hopes in Middle East deferred, 420; priority for reinforcements to Greece, 423-4; anxiety over enemy supplies to Afrika Korps, 431; approves withdrawal

Cabinet, British—*cont.*
from Greece, 434; removes restrictions on submarines, Mediterranean, 439; anxious to meet Russian requests in Arctic, 486, 490; transfers main bombing effort back to Germany, 488; intervention in Syria, 516; build-up of Malta aircraft, 524; expedition to Iran, 529; publicity for move of *Prince of Wales* to East, 558
Cachalot, H.M.S.: sinks U.51, 266; supplies to Malta, 518; sunk by Italian destroyer, 519
Cadart, Rear-Admiral: evacuation of Namsos, 190
Caen: transport of petrol to, 63; demolition of fuel reserves, 233
Cairo, H.M.S.: escorts Dover minelayers, 96; defence of Norwegian convoys, 143; escorts French troops to Namsos, 183; reinforcements for Bodö, 192; damaged at Narvik, 193
Calabria: action with Italian Fleet off, 298-9
Calais: use by train ferries, 63, 64; demolition party sent to, 212; no general evacuation from, 214; captured by Germans, 215; rescues from, 215-6
Calcutta, H.M.S.: defence of Norwegian convoys, 143; evacuation of Aandalsnes, 189; in Dunkirk evacuation, 219; collision with H.M.C.S. *Fraser*, 238; joins Mediterranean Fleet, 299; evacuation from Crete, 445; sunk, 446.
Caledon, H.M.S.: 47
California, U.S. battleship: disabled at Pearl Harbour, 562
Calypso, H.M.S.: 47
Cambridgeshire, H.M.S.: at loss of *Lancastria*, 235
Camellia, H.M.S.: sinking of U.47 and U.70, 364
Campbell, Flying Officer K.: torpedoes *Gneisenau*, 393; awarded V.C., 393*n*
Campbell, Sir R.: evacuated in *Galatea* from St Jean de Luz, 237
Campbeltown: Anti-Submarine School established, 359
Campioni, Admiral: action off Cape Spartivento, 302-3
Canada: first troop convoys arrive from, 89; third troop convoy, 151; later convoys, 274; reinforcements for Iceland, 345; slow cycle of convoys from Cape Breton, 344-5; minesweepers built in, 498
Canadian Cruiser, s.s.: sunk by *Admiral Scheer*, 369
Canadolite, m.v.: captured by *Kormoran*, 386, 608
Canary Islands: German threat to, 272-3, 379; use by German supply ships, 283, 479; plans to capture, 380; enemy blockade runners from, 551
Canberra, H.M.A.S.: 49; intercepts *Ketty Brövig* and *Coburg*, 381, 606, 608
Canterbury: damaged in Dunkirk evacuation, 222, 227
Cap Gris Nez: long-range shelling of convoys from, 325
Cap Norte, s.s.: captured by Northern Patrol, 67
Cape Breton Island: slow cycle of convoys starts from, 344-5
Cape of Good Hope: diversion of Mediterranean traffic to, 42, 271; *Graf Spee* rounds

Cape of Good Hope—*cont.*
  116-7; *Admiral Scheer* rounds, 369-70; protection of route to, 380; *Orion* rounds, 383; threatened U-boat offensive off, 470
Cape St. Vincent: Convoy H.G. 73 attacked off, 468
Cape Verde Islands: first U-boat arrives off, 275; *Admiral Scheer* off, 290; *Scharnhorst* and *Gneisenau* off, 375; German threat to, 379
Capetown: transport of South African troops from, 274; transport of troops from Halifax to, 552; *Prince of Wales* arrives at, 557
Capetown, H.M.S.: 48; supports East African campaign, 426
Caradoc, H.M.S.: 47; intercepts *Emmy Friederich*, 116, 606
Cardiff, H.M.S.: 47
Caribbean: responsibility for shipping in, 348
Carinthia, H.M.S.: sunk by U-boat, 265
Carlisle, H.M.S.: lands parties at Molde and Aandalsnes, 183; heavy air attacks on, 184; sent to Mediterranean, 188; arrives Alexandria, 295; for Red Sea convoys, 296; in Battle for Crete, Captain killed, 442; sent to Suez, 518
Carnarvon Castle, H.M.S.: action with raider *Thor*, 285
Caroline Islands: use by German supply ships, 278
Carton de Wiart, Major-General A., V.C.: arrives at Namsos, 182; first reinforcements, 183; evacuation from Namsos, 190
Casablanca: French Fleet arrives from Brest, 234; *Jean Bart* arrives from St. Nazaire, 236, 240; suggested operation against, 272; loss of French naval base at, 273; no further action to be taken against, 309-10; French squadron arrives from Toulon, 312, and leaves for Dakar, 314-5
Caslon, Captain C.: commands naval forces, Lofoten raid, 341
'Catapult', Operation: action against French Fleet, Oran, 242-5
Catapult Aircraft Merchant (C.A.M.) Ships: to sail under Red Ensign, 477
Cavagnari, Admiral: on Italian naval war plans, 294
Cedarbank, s.s.: sunk off Norway, 185
Ceres, H.M.S.: 47; supports East Africa campaign, 426
Cesare: see Giulio Cesare
Ceylon: plans for Eastern Fleet at, 555
Chad Territory: declares for General de Gaulle, 311, 319
Channel Force: based at Portland, 45; covers transport of B.E.F., 63, 64; Dover mine barrage, 96
Channel Guard: formed to stiffen A/A defence of convoys, 324-5
Channel Islands: evacuations from, 239
Chaucer, s.s.: sunk by raider *Orion*, 547
Cherbourg: transport of B.E.F. to, 63; threatened by German advance, 229; troops moved to from Havre, 231; evacuation from, 232; invasion forces bombarded at, 255

Chevalier Paul, French destroyer: campaign in Syria, damaged, 517
Chiefs of Staff: work of, 16-20; inquiry into trade protection, 1936, 33-4, 355; proposals for Scapa defences, 78; diversion of shipping to West Coast, 143; attack on Trondheim cancelled, 186; plans against invasion, 259; on Red Sea convoys, 296; on proposed withdrawal from Eastern Mediterranean, 297; on reinforcement of Malta, 298; on proposed capture of Pantellaria, 304; postponement of expedition to Atlantic Islands, 380; Battle of Atlantic recommendations, 364; on sending of Beauforts to Malta, 438; request appreciation on Crete, 443; on plan to capture Sicily, 521; plans for war with Japan, 553; reinforcement of Eastern Fleet, 554-5; despatch of *Prince of Wales*, 557
China Station: *see* Far East
Chrobry, Polish transport: arrives at Namsos, 182; sunk in Narvik area, 191-2
Churchill, Right Hon. Winston, First Lord: returns to Admiralty, 15; on loss of *Royal Oak*, 80; visits to Home Fleet, 80-2, 88, 155; on mining Norwegian coast route, 97, 156; on hunting groups for U-boats, 134; interception of *Altmark*, 152; disembarkation of troops for Plan 'R.4' 161; on Hitler's strategic blunder in Norway, 179; urges attack on Trondheim, 186; influence on conduct of Norway operations, 202; question on invasion, 1914, 248; on armed merchant cruisers, 271
Churchill, Right Hon. Winston, Prime Minister: on invasion threat to U.K., 251-4, 257-9; on merchant shipping losses, 253; suggested operation at Casablanca, 272; on proposed evacuation of Eastern Mediterranean, 296-7; suggested supply of Egypt through Mediterranean, 300; on proposed capture of Pantellaria, 304; supports expedition to Dakar, 308; directive on Battle of Atlantic, 339, 364, 459, 609 (text); directive on stopping enemy traffic to Libya, 432; on bombardment of Tripoli, 433; faith in 'Tiger' convoy for Egypt, 437; offer of U.S. Coastguard cutters, 454; Atlantic meeting with President, 470; favours Commando raids on enemy coastline, 513; critical of Vestfiord raid, 513; favours plan to capture Sicily, 521; procures American shipping assistance, 552; on plans for an Eastern Fleet, 555; favours sending *Prince of Wales*, 556-8; loss of *Prince of Wales* and *Repulse*, 567; arrives in Washington, 570
City of Bagdad, s.s.: sunk by *Atlantis*, 281
City of Flint, American s.s.: intercepted by *Deutschland*, 70, 113
City of Paris, s.s.: damaged by magnetic mine, 99
Civil Population: avoidance of air attacks on, 65, 75
Clan Campbell, s.s.: 'Tiger' convoy, tanks for Egypt, 437

INDEX

Clan Chattan, s.s.: 'Tiger' convoy, tanks for Egypt, 437
Clan Forbes, s.s.: convoy for Malta, 301
Clan Fraser, s.s.: convoy for Malta, 301; blown up at Piraeus, 434
Clan Lamont, s.s.: 'Tiger' convoy, tanks for Egypt, 437
Clan Macalister, s.s.: sunk in Dunkirk evacuation, 222
'Claymore', Operation: raid on Lofoten Islands, 341-2
Clement, s.s.: sunk off Brazil by *Graf Spee*, 113-5
Climatic conditions: severe cold, East Coast, 1940, 141, 147; German Fleet encounters ice difficulties, 153; air operations frustrated by ice and snow, 154; influence on German invasion plans, 250, 258; influence on aircraft reconnaissance, 288; poor visibility, Dakar expedition, 316-7; ice conditions, Murmansk, 494-5; ice conditions, Oslo Fiord, 514
Clyde: temporary Home Fleet base, 78, 80; disadvantages as base, 81; visits of First Lord, 80-2, 88; use by Home Fleet until magnetic sweeps produced, 88; first Canadian troop convoy arrives, 89; first troop convoy from, 92; unrestricted U-boat war extended to, 129; U.33 sunk in, 131; Home Fleet cruisers at, invasion threat, 252; minefield in St. George's Channel approach route, 263; Fighter Command takes over defence of, 331; Home Fleet ships at, 378; anti-submarine instruction at, 359; escort groups working from, 452; bases chosen by U.S. Mission, 455
Clyde, H.M.S.: patrolling in South Atlantic, 117; torpedoes *Gneisenau*, 199, 259-260; success in Mediterranean, 525
Coastal Batteries: use in Dover Straits, 256
Coastal Command: *see* Royal Air Force: Coastal Command
Coastal Craft and Coastal Forces: MA/SBs or MLs for, 325; details of, 329; first motor gun boats for, 330; attacks on enemy convoys by, 333; at Suda Bay, Battle for Crete, 440; work of, in home waters, 1941, 500; Dover Straits action with *Komet* and escort, 505; M.T.B. 56 sinks tanker off Bergen, 511
Coburg, German supply ship: intercepted by *Leander* and *Canberra*, 381, 606
Codes and Cyphers, British: misplaced confidence in, 267; enemy capture of, in merchant ships, 283
Codrington, H.M.S.: quick passage from Scapa to Dover, 207-8; conveys Dutch Crown Princess to England, 208; off-shore patrols, Holland, 210; in Dunkirk evacuation, 225; in Havre evacuation, 231
Colombo, H.M.S.: 48
Combined Operations Command: proposed capture of Mediterranean islands, 304; formation and training of, 340-2; first raid in strength against Lofoten Is., 341, 513; plans to capture Atlantic islands, 380; 'Glen' ships sent to Mediterranean for,

Combined Operations Command—*cont.*
435; raid on Vaagso, 513-4; plan to capture Sicily, 520-1
Commissaire Ramel, French s.s.: sunk by *Atlantis*, 282
Communications, Sea: disputed control of, more common, 3, 305
Conder, Commander E. R.: at evacuation of Boulogne, 213
Conidaw, trawler: evacuations from Calais, 215
Conte Rosso, Italian s.s.: sunk by *Upholder*, 439
Contraband Control: bases for, 43; neutral objection to, 44; start of, 64, 67; ships intercepted, numbers, 67; control of enemy exports introduced, 102; sweeps off Dutch coast, 142; evasion of on Norwegian coast route, 156. *See also* Blockade
Convoys mentioned: A.P. 1, A.P. 2, 274; C.W. 8, C.W. 9, 323-5; F.S. 9, F.S. 10, 142; F.S. 69, 501; H.G. 1, 93; H.G. 73, 468, 477; H.G. 76, 478; H.N. 5, 90; H.N. 14, 131; H.N. 20, 143; H.N. 24, 159; H.N. 25, 148, 172; H.X. 1, 93, 343, 345; H.X. 79, H.X. 79A, 350; H.X. 84, 287-9, 351; H.X. 89, 289; H.X. 90, 353; H.X. 106, 374; H.X. 112, 365; H.X. 121, 463; H.X. 126, 459, 463; H.X. 129, 453; H.X. 133, 466-7; H.X. 150, 471, 613; H.X. 156, 472, 613; K.J.F. 1, 93; M.T. 20, 142; N.P. 1, 180, 182, 190; O.A. 80, 129, 344, O.A. 203, 326; O.B. 84, 131; O.B. 293, 365; O.B. 318, 463; O.G. 18, 132, 344; O.G. 74, 478; O.N. 25, 148, 159; P.Q. 1, 492; Q.P.1, 492; S.C. 1, 344; S.C. 3, 344; S.C. 7, 350; S.C. 26, 463; S.C. 42, 468-9; S.C. 44, 468; S.C. 48, 613; S.L. 67, 376; S.L. 81, 453; S.L. 87, 468; S.L.S. 64, 372; T.C. 3, 151; T.C. 9, 392; W.S. 5A, 163, 291, 369; W.S. 5B, 370, 391; W.S. 6, 392
Convoys, Trade: change in escort types, 6, 391; escorts weakened by hunting groups, 10, 134-5; organisation, Trade Division responsible, 21; conflicting views on, 1936, 33-4; plans for introduction of, 44, 92; from Norway, Home Fleet cover, 82, 84; 'unescorted convoy' a misnomer, 92; first Gibraltar-Capetown convoy, 92; Thames-Firth of Forth (F.N. and F.S.), 93 & *n*; ships above 15 and under 9 knots excluded, 93-4; 4 sinkings in 5,756 sailings, 94; temporary use of Tyne vice Forth, 94, 130; more economical of tonnage, 95; first co-ordinated attacks by U-boats, 104; escort by corvettes, 133; exposure of waiting shipping, Southend, 137; problem of passing through narrow swept channels, 139; increase on East Coast, 142; Low Country ships joining O.A. convoys, 142; four-day cycle for Norwegian convoys, 147; escorts diverted to invasion duties, 250, 253, 346-7; fast Halifax convoys discontinued, 269; increased size of, and use of Bermuda, 270; from Gibraltar, 1940, 272, 344; from Sierra Leone, 1940, 274-5; 344-5; numbers leaving Freetown, 275; immunity from raider attack, 286-7; dis-

Convoys, Trade—*cont.*
organisation by H.X. 84 attack, 289; dive-bombing of Channel convoys, 322; coastal convoys (C.W., C.E.), Thames to Bristol Channel, 323; temporary stoppage of Channel convoys, 324; long-range shelling of, from Cap Gris Nez, 325; losses reduced by sailing in, 328; slow convoys from Sydney, C.B., 344; extension of escorts westward, 345, 451, 463; losses by U-boat, July-October, 1940, 348-9; increased escorts for, 352, 452-3; fresh methods of protection for, 352-3, 358-60; night surface attacks by U-boat packs, 354-60; evasive routing, 356, 362-3; vindication of convoy system, 357, 481; value of battleship escort 379, 391, 452; sinkings, January-February, 1941, 362-3; sinking of stragglers, 363; sinkings by raiders, January-February, 1941, 364; escorted right across Atlantic, 451-3, 463; through escorts to Freetown (O.S.), 454; ditto, Gibraltar, 454; complexity of escort problem, 456; O.N.F. and O.N.S. convoys instituted, 457; speed limits reconsidered, 457-8; comparison of independents and convoyed ships, 458; re-organisation of air protection, 458-9; first Russian convoys, 492; later Russian convoys, 494; coastal convoy system, F.N., F.S., W.N., 497; escort vessel strength (table), 464; sinkings by U-boat, April-June, 1941, 463-4; ditto, July-September, 1941, 466-7, 468; air attacks on Gibraltar convoys, 468, 475-6; U.S. naval escorts for, 471; difficulties of refuelling at sea, 471; sinkings by U-boat, October, 1941, 473, and November, 1941, 475; no attack by armed merchant raiders, 542; principal convoy routes, Appendix J, 598

Convoys (Troop): support after landing, 11; B.E.F., no enemy reaction, 63; first Canadian convoys, 89; first Clyde-Gibraltar convoy, 92; strong escorts for, 95; third Canadian convoy arrives, 151; for plan 'R.4', Norway, 157; first Norway convoy, 180; last convoys from Narvik, 194, 196-8; from St. Nazaire on evacuation, 235; from Brest, 236; from La Pallice, 236; for Middle East, Home Fleet escort, 262; troop convoys not seriously interfered with, 274; numbers calling at Freetown, 275; protection against raiders, 280; immunity from raider attack, 286-7; for Malta and Alexandria, action off Spartivento, 301-3; for Dakar, 308, 314-5; for Duala, 320; loss of *Mohamed Ali el Kebir*, 349; strong escorts for Mideast (W.S.) convoys, 391; 'Excess', Piraeus and Malta, 421; 'Lustre', Greece, 424; numbers conveyed to East Africa, 427; 'Tiger' special tank convoy, Egypt, 437; to and from Tobruk, 519; for Malta, 'Substance', 521-3, and 'Halberd', 530-2; W.S. convoys maintained, 552.

Coode, Lieutenant-Commander T. P.: leads air attack on *Bismarck*, 413

Cooke, Captain G. C.: lost in *Barham*, 534

Copenhagen: German occupation of, 164
Cork and Orrery, Admiral of the Fleet Lord: Flag Officer, Narvik, 180; plan for immediate attack abandoned, 190; in supreme command, Narvik, 191; to retire from Narvik after capture, 192; Narvik evacuation, 193-4; relations with Home Fleet Command, 200; enquires into Spartivento action, 303
Cornwall, H.M.S.: 48; in raider hunting group, 274; expedition to Dakar, 314-5; search for raiders, Indian Ocean, 383; sinks *Pinguin*, 383-5
Corvettes: valuable service of, 133; first in South Atlantic, 275; four passed through Mediterranean, 301; use in escort groups, 359; rate of completion, 464.
Cossack, H.M.S.: intercepts *Altmark* and rescues prisoners, 151-3; damaged in second Battle of Narvik, 177; attacks enemy convoy off Egersund, 262; in *Bismarck* operations, 414
Costa Rica, s.s.: sunk in evacuation from Greece, 436
Côte d'Argent, s.s.: in Dunkirk evacuation, 227
'Countenance', Operation (expedition to Iran): 529
Courage, Lieutenant-Commander R. E.: in first Battle of Narvik, 173
Courageous, H.M.S.: 31, 47; sunk by U.29, 105-6
Courbet, French battleship: arrives in Britain, 240
Coventry, H.M.S.: evacuation from Narvik, 193-4; joins Mediterranean Fleet, 299; through convoy from Gibraltar, 301; evacuation from Crete, 446; campaign in Syria, 516
Creasy, Captain G. E.: in charge of off-shore patrols, Holland, 210
Crested Eagle, special service vessel: sunk in Dunkirk evacuation, 222
Crete: occupation of, 300, 419; occasional fighter protection from, 424; aircraft from in Matapan battle, 428-9; threatened by enemy control of Aegean, 436; Battle for, 440-9; decision to evacuate, 444; numbers withdrawn from, 446; evacuation by submarine, 526
Cromarty Firth: enemy mining in, 126
Cromer: enemy mining off, 126-7; enemy air attacks off, 142; lifeboat service off, 501
Cruisers: use for convoy escort, 6, 391-2; total reduced from 70 to 58, 43; inadequate for ocean convoys, 45; 'C' and 'D' classes removed from Northern Patrol, 68; disposed to counter invasion threat, 252; number in Home Fleet, December, 1940, 268; few available for overseas, 270, 275-6; Azores patrol by, 273; list in commission, 578. *See also* Armed Merchant Cruisers
'Crusader', Operation: offensive in Libya, 520-1, 527, 536
Cumberland, H.M.S.: 48; misses *Graf Spee*, 113, 115; in raider hunting group, 114, 117; intercepts *Ussukuma*, 117; ordered to River Plate, 120; enters Montevideo, 121;

Cumberland, H.M.S.—*cont.*
  escorts first W.S. troop convoy, 274; search for raider *Thor*, 277, 285; in South American Division, 290; expedition to Dakar, 314-5; damaged by shore battery, 316
Cunningham, Admiral Sir A. B.: D.C.N.S., on Scapa defences, 78; C.-in-C., Mediterranean, 48-9; *Warspite* returns as flagship, 188, 295; situation after French collapse, 241; negotiates with French at Alexandria, 242; attitude towards Oran operation, 244; reinforcements for, 262, 295; on proposed evacuation of Eastern Mediterranean, 296-7; first encounter with Italian Navy, 298-9; supply of Malta, 300; meets through convoy from Gibraltar, 301; criticises enquiry into Spartivento action, 303; revictuals and visits Malta, 304; on proposed Commando operations, 304; action against Italian routes to North Africa, 305-6; ascendancy within Mediterranean, 419; convoys for Piraeus and Malta, 421-2; defeat of Luftwaffe essential, 422; small convoy for Malta, 423; Battle off Cape Matapan, 427-31; action against supplies to Libya, 431-2, 438; on bombardment of Tripoli, 433; on enemy bombing of Piraeus, 434; withdrawal from Greece, 435-6; 'Tiger' reinforcements for, 437; on Malta situation, 438; Battle for Crete, 440-9; on Crete evacuation, 446; situation after Crete, 515; reluctant to incur loss in Syria, 517; Red Sea returns to Mediterranean Command, 518; supply of Tobruk, 519; diversion for Malta convoy 'Substance', 522; on value of submarines, 525; diversion for Malta convoy 'Halberd', 530; on action by Force K, 532; flotilla reinforcements, and loss of *Barham*, 534; submarines redisposed, 536; transfer of ships from, 538; on withdrawal of heavy ships, 539; capital ships with, August, 1941, 554
Cunningham, General Sir A. G.: on East Africa campaign, 426
Cunningham, Vice-Admiral J. H. D.: 70; leaves for Norway, 161; joins Admiral Forbes, 170; evacuation of Namsos, 189-90; evacuation of King of Norway, 197; expedition to Dakar, 308-19; expedition to Duala, 320
Curaçao: defence of oil installations at, 276
Curacoa, H.M.S.: lands parties at Molde and Aandalsnes, 183; damaged by air attack, 184
Curlew, H.M.S.: sunk in Narvik area, 191
Curteis, Rear-Admiral A. T. B.: Commands 2nd Cruiser Squadron, 237; in *Calcutta* off Gironde, 238; in *Bismarck* operations, 408; in Malta convoy 'Halberd', 530-1
Custance, Rear-Admiral W. N.: 49
'Cycle', Operation: evacuation of Havre, 231; numbers, 'Cycle' and 'Aerial', 239
Cyclops, H.M.S.: attached to Home Fleet, 69
Cyprus: threatened by enemy control of Aegean, 436; naval aircraft in Syria campaign, 517

Dakar: raider patrols from, 117; French ships arrive from Brest, 234, 240; action against *Richelieu* at, 245; movement to intercept *Richelieu*, 273; watch on French ships at, 275; no further action to be taken against warships at, 309-10; expedition against, Operation 'Menace', 261, 300, 308-19; attempts to base U-boat supply ships at, 479-80
Dalrymple-Hamilton, Captain F. H. G.: commanding *Rodney* during *Bismarck* operations, 412
Damascus: occupied in Syria campaign, 517
Danae, H.M.S.: 48
Danielsen, Lieutenant R., R.N.N.: raid off Bergen, 511
Dardanelles: enemy control of approaches to, 436; submarine patrols off, 525
Daring, H.M.S.: sunk by U-boat, 131
Darlan, Admiral: meeting with Admiralty chiefs at Bordeaux, 237; German use of his name, 241; supports resistance at Oran, 243
Darwin, Port: possibility of use by Eastern Fleet, 559; cruiser striking force proposed for, 561
Dauntless, H.M.S.: 48
Davisian, s.s.: sunk by *Widder*, 284
de Gaulle, General: expedition to Dakar, 308-20
Decoy ships ('freighters'): use of, 136-7, 197, 363; meeting with H.M.S. *Neptune*, lesson not circulated, 549
Defence Committee: ruling by, for new measures to protect shipping, 350-1; proposal to transfer Coastal Command to Admiralty, 360-1
Deal: in German invasion plans, 255
Defender, H.M.S.: sunk in carrying supplies to Tobruk, 519
Defensively Equipped Merchant Ships (D.E.M.S.): organisation of, 21-2, 46; delay in opening fire on U-boat, 133; armament against aircraft, 139; lack of A.A. gunners, War Office help, 140-1; marines or seamen for, 363; numbers and armament, Appendix B, 574
De-gaussing of ships: plans for, 99 & *n*; department formed for, 101
Delfzijl: German invasion assembly port, 255
Delhi, H.M.S.: Operations after attack on *Rawalpindi*, 84-6; in South Atlantic, 274; expedition to Dakar, 315
Demolitions: in Low Countries, plans, 207, executed 208-10; in France, 212-3, 266, 233-4, 238
'Demon', Operation: withdrawal from Greece, 434-5; losses in 'Demon' and 'Lustre', 446
Den Helder: *see* Helder
Denmark: ships not allowed to join Allied convoys, 133; German invasion of, 162, 164, 169; minelaying by Bomber Command off, 337
Denmark Strait: watched by Northern Patrol, 45, 265-6; *Atlantis* breaks through, 281; *Widder* breaks through, 284; *Thor*, *Pinguin* and *Komet* break through, 286; *Admiral Scheer* breaks through, 287; lack of cruisers for patrol, 287; *Admiral Hipper* and

INDEX

Denmark Strait—*cont.*
  Kormoran break through, 291, 367; weakness of air reconnaissance in, 292; *Admiral Scheer* returns through, 371, 392; battle cruisers break through, 373; air reconnaissance in, 376; minelaying in, 390; patrolled by 8-inch cruisers, 394
Depth charges: trials for use from aircraft, 135; most effective anti-submarine weapon, 136; used by German aircraft, 266; shallower detonation of, 480
Derna: captured by Allies, 420
Derrien, French Admiral: joins Admiral Forbes, Norway, 170; evacuation of Namsos, 189
Despatch, H.M.S.: 48; covers through convoy for Alexandria, 301
Destroyers: disposition in Home Waters, 1939, 47; oversea, 48-9; numbers effective, 1939, 50; German lack of, 53; minelaying by, 97-8, 123; strain on, May, 1940, 210; losses at Dunkirk, 228; force for anti-invasion duties, 249-50; shortage in Home Fleet, 197, 253, 268; 16 from Home Fleet arrive Alexandria, 295; 'Hunt' class to replace older ships in convoy work, 395; transfer of American to R.N., 347-8, 612; use of in Escort Groups, 359; 4th Flotilla in *Bismarck* operations, 412, 414; ex-American on Atlantic convoy route, 452; numbers in commission, etc., 1939, Appendix D, 579
Deutschland, German pocket battleship: renamed *Lützow*, controlled by Naval staff, 57; sails for Atlantic, 58, 112; presence in Atlantic known, 70, 113-6; wrongly reported to have attacked *Rawalpindi*, 82-3, 115; recalled from Atlantic, 121; Appendix M, 604
'*Deutschland*' class, pocket battleships: 51; expected use for commerce raiding, 45
Devon, s.s.: sunk by raider *Komet*, 547
Devonshire, H.M.S.: 48; joins Home Fleet, 70; operations after attack on *Rawalpindi*, 84-7; embarks troops for plan 'R.4', 157; troops disembarked, 161; in Norway campaign, 172; evacuation of Namsos, 189; evacuation of King of Norway, 197; expedition to Dakar, 261, 308-9, 314, 317; search for raider *Kormoran*, 386; strikes on enemy coastal traffic, far north, 486; covers convoy with aircraft for Russia, 489; Vichy French convoy intercepted, Cape of Good Hope, 544; sinks raider *Atlantis*, 545
Diamond, H.M.S.: rescues survivors from *Slamat*, 436
Dido, H.M.S.: joins Home Fleet, 262; joins Mediterranean Fleet, 434; in Battle for Crete, damaged, 441, 445
Dieppe: Use by hospital ships, 63; blocking of, 230
Diether Von Röder, German destroyer: sunk at Narvik, 177*n*
Diomede, H.M.S.: 47
Displacement of warships: method of computing, 57*n*
Distribution of British and Dominion Naval strength, 1939, Appendix E, 583

Dodecanese: Italian defence of communications, 294; proposed Commando operations against, 304; air attacks from, 424
Dogger Bank: air protection for fishing fleet, 139
Doggerbank (ex-*Speybank*): German minelayer and supply ship, 381
Domala, m.v.: bombed off Isle of Wight, 142
Dönitz, Admiral: in command of U-boat fleet, 54; plans for 300 U-boats, 59, 356 & *n*; plans attack on Scapa, 74; attitude to unrestricted war on shipping, 104; first trials of 'wolf-pack' tactics, 131; views of, on Italian U-boats, 347; orders night surface attacks, 356; lack of G.A.F. co-operation with, 362; decides U-boats to continue normal patrols during cruiser foray, 395; orders suspension of U-boat operations (*Bismarck*), 408-9; stands by his long-term policy, 462
Doric Star, s.s.: sunk by *Graf Spee*, 117
Dorsetshire, H.M.S.: 49; in raider hunting group, 114; ordered to River Plate, 120; attack on *Richelieu* at Dakar, 245; in South Atlantic, 274; search for armed merchant raider, 277; search for *Admiral Scheer*, 290; takes part in *Bismarck* operations, 410, 415; fires final torpedoes into *Bismarck*, 415; sinks supply ship *Python*, 546; escorts troop convoy to Bombay, 552
Douglas, H.M.S.: attacks U-boat, 131
Dover: mine barrage in Straits of, 45, 47, 96, 104, 130; enemy mines off, 63, 127; ships for Belgian and Dutch coast, 207, 210; withdrawal of B.E.F. controlled from, 212; reinforcements for Dunkirk evacuation, 221; striking force base against invasion, 249-50; enemy guns mounted in Straits, 256; M.T.B.'s attack enemy convoy, 504-5
Dover Command: independence of, 48; offensive sweeps from (by coastal craft), 330
Downs: contraband control in, 43, 142; enemy air minelaying in, 128; artificial focal area for shipping, 130; exposure of shipping awaiting convoy, 138; O.A. convoys in, 142
D'Oyly-Hughes, Captain G.: in *Glorious*, conveys fighter aircraft to Norway, 185; sinking of *Glorious*, 195-6
Dragon, H.M.S.: 47; in South Altantic, 274; search for *Admiral Scheer*, 290
Draug, Norwegian destroyer: raid off Bergen, 511
Drax, Admiral Sir R.: Nore Command reinforced, 205; command of ships off Low Countries, 207, 210; request for cruisers, 208; on defence against invasion, 258; relieved by Admiral D'Oyly Lyon, 499
Dresden, German supply ship: in South Atlantic, 382, 606
Dreyer, Admiral Sir Frederick: Inspector of Merchant Navy Gunnery, 140
Duala, Cameroons: expedition to, 320
Duca Degli Abruzzi, Italian cruiser: torpedoed by *Utmost*, 536
Duchess of York, s.s.: evacuation from St Nazaire, 234-5

INDEX

Duilio, Italian s.s.: damaged by *Urge*, 525-6
Duke of York, H.M.S.: conveys Prime Minister to America, 570
Dummy battleships: at Scapa, 155
Dunbar-Nasmith, Admiral Sir M., V.C.: 47; evacuation from St. Nazaire, La Pallice, and Gironde ports, 232-8; Commander-in-Chief, Plymouth Command, 360
Dundee, H.M.S.: sunk while escorting S.C. 3, 344
Dundee: Submarines at, 47; submarine patrols from, 64
Dunedin, H.M.S.: 47; capture of *Hannover*, 276; escorts convoy W.S. 5A, 291; intercepts *Lothringen*, 607; sunk by U.124, 546
Dunkerque, French battle cruiser: 52; movement after attack on *Rawalpindi*, 85; in raider hunting group, 114; at Oran, 240-1; damaged at Oran, 244
Dunkirk: headquarters of French 'Amiral Nord', 207; use by train ferries, 63-4; evacuation from: reduces Home Fleet, 197; Belgian coast operations conducted from, 211; armies supplied through, 212; evacuation from: begun, 216; air cover complaints, 217; air attacks, troops diverted to beaches, 219; daily totals of men, 221 & *n*, 222, 224-7; all ships diverted to beaches, 223; routes used by ships, 219, 223; demolitions, 226; harbour blocking, 227; statistical summary, 603
Dunoon: Portland anti-submarine school moved to, 359
Dupleix, French cruiser: patrolling from Dakar, 117
Duquesa, s.s.: captured by *Admiral Scheer*, 290-1, 608
Durban, H.M.S.: 48
'Dynamo', Operation: withdrawal from Dunkirk, 216-228, 239; statistical summary, Appendix L, 603

E-boats, Enemy: start of operations by, *Kelly* damaged, 145; attacks on Channel convoys, 324; attacks on East Coast convoys, 329; first one destroyed in Nore Command, 330; losses caused by, 330; minefields laid by, 498; torpedo attacks by, 500; ships to deal with, 502; night patrols against, Dutch coast, 506; from Pantellaria, attack on Malta convoy, 522; attack on Malta, 523; increased use in Mediterranean, 536
Eagle, H.M.S.: 31; in raider hunting group, 114; in Mediterranean, 295; action off Calabria, 298-9; misses attack at Taranto, 300; Swordfish success in Gulf of Bomba, 307; sighted by raider *Atlantis*, 382; aircraft operations in Red Sea, 426; intercepts *Lothringen*, 607
East Africa: Italian bases in, 49; build-up of Allied forces in, 271, 274; control of coastal routes, 308, 426;
East Coast, Great Britain: air protection for shipping, 39, 108; Tyne to Thames convoys, 45; enemy mining off, 99-102, 128; mine barrier begun, 125-6; gap between East Coast and Dover barrages, 127; doubtful merit of defensive minefield, 130;

East Coast, Great Britain—*cont.*
 convoy terminal moved to Tyne, 130; start of air attacks on shipping, 138; shipping diverted north-about, 263, mine barrier completed, 263; tonnage of shipping using, 1941, 333
East Indies Station: force on, September, 1939, 49, 585; protection against raiders, 49; position after French collapse, 241; escort of W.S. troop convoys, 274; raider countermeasures, 370; troop transport in, to April, 1941, 427; Red Sea transferred to Mediterranean Command, 518; expedition to Iran, 529; Dutch naval forces in, 559
Eastern Fleet: plan to build up, 491, 494; transfer of Mediterranean ships to, 538; plans for, 554-5; Admiral Layton succeeds Admiral Phillips, 569
Eclipse, H.M.S.: damaged off Norway, 176
Economic Warfare, Ministry of: action on enemy cargoes, 43-4
Edinburgh, H.M.S.: 47; transferred to Humber Force, 69; operations after sinking of *Rawalpindi*, 84-7; support in Lofoten raid, 341; escorts Canadian troop convoy T.C. 9, 392; in *Bismarck* operations, 408, 410; in Malta convoy 'Substance', 521-2
Edward-Collins, Vice-Admiral Sir G. F. B.: in 2nd Cruiser Squadron, 159; joins Admiral Forbes, Norway, 172; lands parties at Molde and Aandalsnes, 183, 185; ordered to Sheerness, 188; evacuation from Aandalsnes, 188-9, 447; recovers gold and shipping from Ijmuiden, 208
Effingham, H.M.S.: 47; in Atlantic hunting group, 70; lost by grounding, Narvik area, 192
Egerland, German supply ship: scuttled, 479, 606
Egersund: German occupation of cable station, 164; enemy convoy attacked off, 262
Egypt (*see also* Middle East): risk of loss of, 297; troops sent to Greece, 300; suggested supply through Mediterranean, 300; enemy threat to, 524
Eidsvold, Norwegian coast defence ship: disabled at Narvik, 165
Eire, Republic of: denies use of bases, 46; possibility of German invasion, 251; shipping diverted to N.W. approaches, 263; route round southern Ireland abandoned, 349; need for bases is emphasised, 351-2
Elbe Estuary: aircraft minelaying in, 124, 335; ice difficulties in, 153
Elizabeth Bakke, s.s.: escapes from Gothenburg, 391
Ellis, Captain R. M.: commands *Suffolk* in *Bismarck* operations, 395
Elsa Essberger, German supply ship: scuttled (1944), 606
Emden, German cruiser: 51; bombed off Wilhelmshaven, 66; in landing at Oslo, 164; wrongly identified in Narvik, 393; presumed ready for service, 394; leaves for Trondheim, 484
Emerald, H.M.S.: 47; in Atlantic hunting group, 70; escorts Halifax convoys, 114, 270; escorts Middle East troop convoy, 370

634 INDEX

Emile Bertin, French cruiser: at Scapa, 158; leaves for Norway, 159; conveys French troops to Namsos, 183; at Martinique with bullion, 276
Emirau Island: raider prisoners landed at, 283
Emmy Friederich, German s.s.: intercepted by *Caradoc*, 116, 606
Empire Rainbow, s.s.: first C.A.M. ship in service, 477
Empire Song, s.s.: sunk in 'Tiger' convoy to Egypt, 437
Empress of Britain, s.s.: bombed off Donegal, sunk two days later by U.32, 351
Ems Estuary: aircraft minelaying in, 124
Endras: 'ace' U-boat commander, 348
English Channel: disputed control after June, 1940, 4; Channel Force based on Portland, 45; Germans anticipate closing of, 54, 56; first trade convoys through, 93; Dover Straits mine barrage, 96; first enemy attack on shipping in, *Domala*, 142; necessity to maintain shipping flow in, 321; Mobile Balloon Barrage Flotilla for, 324; defeat of enemy attempts to close, 325-6; bombing of ships in, 331; shipping tonnage in, 1941, 333; extension of 'sink at sight' zone, 338; all but coastal convoys re-routed, 349; convoy time-tables accelerated, 497; enemy use by night, 505, 514
Enterprise, H.M.S.: in Atlantic hunting group, 70; escort of Halifax convoys, 114, 270; action against French at Oran, 242; search for raider *Thor*, 285; search for *Admiral Scheer*, 370
Enterprise, U.S. aircraft carrier: escapes attack on Pearl Harbour, 563
Erich Giese and *Erich Koellner*, German destroyers: sunk at Narvik, 177*n*
Eritrea: assault on, 307; surrender of, 426
Ermland, German supply ship: at work in Pacific, 277-8, 606
Escort carriers: *see* Aircraft carriers
Escort Groups: formation and training of, 358-60; tactics and strength of, 464, 466; main U-boat target, 470; Newfoundland Escort Force, 453, 475
Escort Vessels: numbers in commission, etc., 1939, Appendix D, 581
Esk, H.M.S.: converted for minelaying, 97; lays in German mined area, 123; in Dunkirk evacuation, 221; sunk by mine off Texel, 334
Eskimo, H.M.S.: in second Battle of Narvik, damaged, 177
Esmonde, Lieutenant-Commander E.: special air reconnaissance, *Bismarck* operations, 408
Esperia, Italian s.s.: sunk by *Unique*, 525
Esso Hamburg, German supply ship: scuttled, 606
Ettrick, m.v.: evacuation from Bayonne, 238
Eurofeld, German supply ship: scuttled (1944), 606
Eurylochus, s.s.: sunk by *Kormoran*, 386
Evans, Admiral Sir E. R. G. R.: plan 'R.4', Norway, 157
'Excess', Operation (convoys for Piraeus and Malta): 421, 423

Exeter, H.M.S.: 48; in raider hunting group, 114, 116-7; River Plate battle, 118-21
Exmouth, H.M.S.: sunk by U-boat, 130
Express, H.M.S.: converted for minelaying, 97; lays in German mined area, 123; in Dunkirk evacuation, 221, 227; damaged by mine off Texel, 334

Faeröe Islands: watch on Iceland-Faeröes passage, 45, 65, 67, 265; covering force at Scapa, 252, 263; minefield off, 264; need for radar station in, 266; lack of cruisers for patrol, 287; anxiety for security of, 345; troops landed in, 345; defence measures for, 346; minelaying, Iceland-Faeröes, 390; cruiser patrol, Iceland-Faeröes, 394; patrol during *Bismarck* operations, 396
Fairlie: Anti-Submarine Experimental Station at, 359
Falkland Islands: cruisers at, 1939, 116-7
Falmouth: enemy mining off, 126, 328
Far East: recall of warships from, and provision for, 1939, 42; protection against raiders, 43; British forces in, 1939, 49, 584; French forces in, 1939, 51; reinforcements allocated to, 490; ships building in, lost after entry of Japan, 499; warships transferred to, 528-9; plans for war with Japan, 553
Fearless, H.M.S.: sinks U.49, 190; sunk in Malta convoy 'Substance', 522
Fécamp: transport of B.E.F. stores to, 64
Fegen, Captain E. S. F.: in *Jervis Bay*, action with *Admiral Scheer*, 288; awarded V.C., 289
Fenella, s.s.: sunk in Dunkirk evacuation, 222
Fifth Sea Lord: appointed, 32; responsibilities, 26
Fighter Command: *see* Royal Air Force, Fighter Command
Fighter Direction: *see* Radar
Fiji, H.M.S.: expedition to Dakar, torpedoed by U-boat, 261, 308-9; watch on northern passages, 371; patrols Atlantic convoy route, 378; in Battle for Crete, 441-2; sunk by aircraft, 442
Finland: German U-boats ordered in, 51; German supplies sent overland through, 493
Firedrake, H.M.S.: damaged in Malta convoy 'Substance', 522
Firth of Forth: air attack on Fleet in, 75; enemy mining in, 78; trade convoys to and from, 93, 497; temporary use of Tyne for convoys, 94
Fiume, Italian cruiser: sunk in Battle of Matapan, 429-30
Flamborough Head: Convoy F.S. 9 attacked off, 142; Auxiliary Patrol positions off, 251; tonnage of shipping off, 1941, 333
Flamingo, H.M.S.: lands naval party at Aandalsnes, 183
Fleet Air Arm: Admiralty control restored, 1937, 26, 29-31; aircraft types in service, 1939, 31; numbers, 32; minelaying by, 123, 125; defence of Norwegian convoys, 143;

INDEX

Fleet Air Arm—*cont.*
  Königsberg sunk at Bergen, 165, 172; in Norway, tribute by Captain Troubridge, 196; attack on Trondheim, 198; attack on Italian Fleet, Taranto, 300-1; action off Spartivento, 302-3; success in Gulf of Bomba, 307; *Malaya* aircraft sights enemy battle cruisers, 375; ditto, *Ark Royal* aircraft, 377; pre-war conception of use of, 355; in Battle off Cape Matapan, 428-30; in *Bismarck* operations, 396, 407-13; Malta Swordfish bomb Tripoli, 433; attacks on enemy shipping, April-December, 1941 (table), 507; no dive-bomber except Skua, 509; campaign in Syria, 516-7; build-up of Malta striking force, 526; fighter catapult ships, 476-7
Flushing: demolition party sent to, 207; demolition opposed, 208; evacuation of, 209
Foch, French cruiser: patrolling from Dakar, 117
Folkestone: deep minefield to Gris Nez, 96; plans for German landing, 255
Forbes, Admiral Sir C.: C.-in-C., Home Fleet, on Admiralty intervention in conduct of operations, 27, 202; dispositions, 31.8.1939, 47; first operational patrol, 64-5; scarcity of Northern Patrol cruisers, 67; selects Loch Ewe as base, 68; on A/A fire of Fleet, 69; sortie to intercept *Gneisenau*, 71; on air threat to naval bases, 75; examines Fleet base policy, 77-9; mining danger in Forth, 78; opposes move of base to Clyde, 80-1; covers Norwegian convoys, 82, 93; operations after attack on *Rawalpindi*, 82-7; transfers flag to *Warspite*, 88; covers first Canadian troop convoy, 89; defence of Norwegian convoys, 143, 147; Fleet maintenance in severe weather, 147; reorganises cruiser squadrons, 151; operations against *Altmark*, 152; German attack on Norway shipping frustrated, 153; covers Operation 'Wilfred' and Plan 'R.4', 157-8; German occupation of Norwegian ports, 159-67; dispositions, 8.4.1940, 169-70; campaign in Norway, 171-202; on degree of enemy air attack, 179; on plan for Trondheim, 'Hammer', 186-7; assistance in Narvik evacuation, 193, 197; relations with Narvik Command, 200; assistance to Nore Command, 207-8; differs from Admiralty on invasion plans, 250-2, 259; concern at merchant shipping losses, 253; on defeat of Luftwaffe, 256; on invasion possibility, 257-9; attacks shipping off Norway, 262; forces lent for convoy protection, 263; sceptical of defensive minefields, 264; proposes withdrawal of Northern Patrol A.M.C.'s, 265; movement to intercept *Hipper*, 287, and *Scheer*, 289; on weakness of air reconnaissance, 292; relieved by Admiral Tovey, 267
Force H: constituted at Gibraltar, 8, 241, 252, 296; composition and status, 242; Home Fleet ships for, 262; operations after Oran, 272-3; not available to search for *Scheer*, 289; covers Mediterranean reinforcements, 299-300; covers through convoy for Alexandria, 301; action off Spartivento, 302-4; French movements, and relations with North Atlantic Command, 310-4; bombardment of Genoa, 372, 425; search for enemy battle cruisers, Atlantic, 377-8; escorts troop convoy W.S. 6, 392; watch on German battle cruisers in Brest, 392; air threat to from Sardinia, 420; passage of 'Excess' convoy, 421-2; in *Bismarck* operations, 307, 410-15, 438; 'Tiger' convoy, tanks for Egypt, 437; aircraft ferrying to Malta, 518, 533; reinforced for Malta convoys 'Substance', 521-3, and 'Halberd', 530-2; destroyers join Force K, Malta, 532
Force K.: *see under* Malta
Ford, Vice-Admiral W. T. R.: Vice-Admiral, Malta, 532; sends help to *Kandahar*, 535
Foreign Office: on Norway and Northern Barrage, 97; notice of mining German waters, 124; opposes mining of Norwegian coastal route, 156; delay in deciphering Tangier report, 312; favours sending *Prince of Wales* to Singapore, 556-7.
Foresight, H.M.S.: damaged by shore battery, Dakar, 316
Forfar, H.M.S.: sunk by U-boat, 353
Formidable, H.M.S.: arrives Scapa on completion, 262; in hunting group, Freetown, 263, 290; for Mediterranean, delayed by Suez Canal mines, 423; aircraft from mine Mogadishu, 426; Battle off Cape Matapan, 428-30; at bombardment of Tripoli, 433; in Battle for Crete, 440, 444; repairing in United States, 534; likely to be sent to Far East, 539
Forth, H.M.S.: depot ship, 47; transferred to Halifax, 334, 375
Fortress aircraft: attack on *Scheer* at Oslo, 493
Fortune, H.M.S.: sinks U.44, 132, 155; sinks French submarine *Ajax*, Dakar, 317
Foudroyant, French destroyer: sunk in Dunkirk evacuation, 225
Fowey, H.M.S.: sinks U.55, 129
France: enemy control in, 8; restricts use of Channel ports, 64; sends troops to Narvik, 191; troops evacuated from Dunkirk, 222; signs surrender, 229; armistice terms for Fleet, 241; first major German warships to use a port in, 291; risk of war with, 309; prior knowledge of Dakar expedition, 315; use of bases by German Air Force, 322, 349; use of ports by U-boats, 346; attempts to base U-boat supply ships on Dakar, 479-80; convoy from Indo-China intercepted, 544. *See also* French Fleet
Franco, General: possibility of joining Axis, 380
Franconia, s.s.: damaged in St. Nazaire evacuation, 235
Fraser, H.M.C.S.: sunk in collision, 238
Frauenheim: 'ace' U-boat commander, 348
Freetown, Sierra Leone: base of South Atlantic Command, 43, 48, 115; first trade convoy from, 93-4; cover to convoy route, 241; 10 armed merchant cruisers at, 271; importance after fall of France, 273; forces at, 274;

Freetown, Sierra Leone—*cont.*
convoy traffic, 275, 344-5; Dakar expedition sails for, 308, and arrives, 315; Dakar expedition leaves, 316, and returns, 319; U-boat sinkings off, 351, 353; enemy battle cruisers in area, 375; Sunderland flying boats for, 354; raider cover off, 386; responsibility for convoys to, 453; first continuous escort to, 453-4; ex-U.S. Coastguard cutters on convoy route, 455; U-boat sinkings off, 463, 470; reinforcements for convoy escorts, 471
'Freighters': *see* Decoy ships
French, Admiral Sir W.: 48
French Air Force: in Syria campaign, 516-7
French Fleet: responsible for Western Mediterranean, 42, 50; general disposition, 1939, 51; cooperation in raider hunting, 114; submarine flotilla for North Sea, 149; interception of enemy shipping from Vigo, 150; conveys troops to Namsos, 183; evacuates Brest, 234; proposal to Darlan to move, 237; withdrawal from France after surrender, 240; disposition, end June, 1940, 240-1; armistice terms for, 241; British action to neutralise, 242-5; traffic through Gibraltar Straits after Oran, 272; not to proceed south of Dakar, 275; watch on West Indies ships, 276; squadron in Eastern Mediterranean, 295; effect of loss of in Western Mediterranean, 297; Dakar expedition, move of ships from Toulon, 309-14; in Dakar operation, 315-9; resistance in Syria, 517; loss of, effect on Far East plans, 553
Friedrich Breme, German supply ship: scuttled, 606
Fuelling: difficulties in South American Division, 116; difficulties in Atlantic, 471
Furious, H.M.S.: 31, 47; only carrier with Home Fleet, 70; sortie to intercept *Gneisenau*, 71; cover for Halifax convoy, 75; at Halifax, 85; rejoins Home Fleet, 88; first Canadian troop convoy, 89; escort of Halifax convoys, 114; leaves Clyde for Norway without fighters, 170-1; air attack on Trondheim, 172, 175; air attack on Narvik, 177; abortive result, 177, under Lord Cork in Narvik area, 180; conveys fighters to Narvik area, 191; tribute to airmen by Captain Troubridge, 196; attack on Norway shipping and Tromso, 262; transport of aircraft to Takoradi, 262, 268; escorts convoy W.S. 5A, 291; ferries aircraft to Malta, 437; strike at enemy coastal traffic, far north, 486; ferries aircraft for Malta to Gibraltar, 518, 524
Fylingdale, s.s.: in last convoy from Norway, April, 1940, 148

Galatea, H.M.S.: 48; interception of German shipping from Vigo, 150; in operations off Norway, 158-9; lands parties at Molde and Aandalsnes, 183, 185; ordered to Sheerness, 188; evacuation from Aandalsnes, 188-9; joins Nore Command, 205; evacuates Ambassador from St Jean de Luz, 237; in

Galatea, H.M.S.—*cont.*
Bismarck operations, 396, 408; sunk by U.557, Mediterranean, 535
Gallant, H.M.S.: damaged in Dunkirk evacuation, 222; damaged by mine, Mediterranean, 421
Garnons-Williams, Captain G. A.: blockships for Ostend and Zeebrugge, 211; blocking of Dieppe, 230
Gedania, German supply ship: captured, 606
Genoa: bombarded by Force H, 425
Genoa, Gulf of: U-boat patrols in, 293; minelaying by *Manxman*, 523-4
Gensoul, Admiral: French Fleet at Oran, 242-5
Georg Thiele, German destroyer: sunk at Narvik, 177*n*
Georges Leygues, French cruiser: Dakar expedition, passes Gibraltar, 309; arrives Dakar, 315; sinks supply ship *Portland*, 607
Georgic, m.v.: evacuation from St Nazaire, 234-5; set on fire at Suez, 518
German Air Force: better prepared than Navy, 53; plans to attack British shipping, 53; to attack ports and bases, 55; numbers allotted to maritime operations, 60; bomber threat to Home Fleet exaggerated, 80; minelaying by, 100; attacks on seaborne trade by, 106-10; unwilling to meet Navy's requests, 137, 143; attacks on East Coast shipping and lights, 138; sinks own destroyers off Terschelling, 142; superiority off Norway, 171; small scale interference with B.E.F. evacuation, 239; table of losses to Allied shipping by, 332; need to defeat R.A.F. before invasion, 251, 254; attempt to conquer by air power alone, 255; defeated in Battle of Britain, 256; use of depth charges, 266; use of bases on French and Dutch coasts for attacks against Allied shipping, 322, 349; concentration over Southern England as prelude to invasion, 322; offensive against ports and docks, 330-1; use of bases in Norway, 349; first Focke-Wulf 'Kondors', 349; tactics against convoy evasive routeing, 356; new reconnaissance group formed in Atlantic, 362; to co-operate with U-boat Command, 362; part of, transferred to German Navy by Hitler, 362; sinkings by Jan./Feb., 1941, 362-3; move to Sicilian airfields, 420; first encounter with Mediterranean Fleet, 421-2; onslaught on Malta begun, 423, 425; absent during bombardment of Tripoli, 433; interference with Greek evacuation, 436; diverted to Russian campaign, 463, 486, 498, 500, 508; attacks on coastal convoys, 499; merchant ship losses inflicted by, 1941, 500, 508; ascendancy in central Mediterranean, 515; in Syrian campaign, 516-7; stops use of merchant ships to supply Tobruk, 519; return in force to Sicily demanded from Rome, 528; fuel supply in Africa critical, 533; aircraft returned from Russia to Sicily, 534; attacks on Gibraltar convoys, 468; 475-6

INDEX 637

German Army: confidence in invasion plans, 254-5

German Naval Staff: plans for war on British shipping, 53, 104; attitude to international law, 56; anxiety over Norway plan, 164; criticism of Admiral Marschall, 200; plans for invasion, Operation 'Sealion', 254-9; unwilling to occupy Atlantic islands, 275; commerce raiding in Atlantic, 291, 368; diversion to cover return of *Admiral Scheer*, 371, 376; low endurance of 'Hipper' class, 372; ambitions for Atlantic sortie, 376, 379; concern over *Hipper*, 390; plans for *Bismarck* and *Prinz Eugen*, 394; deterred by Roosevelt policy in Atlantic, 490; reports North Africa fuel supply critical, 533; assessment of Malta submarine threat, 536; U-boat dispositions, 474

German Navy: battle cruisers at Brest, 9; growth of, 1920-39, 51-2; Battle Instructions, 1939, 53-56; composed of modern ships, 58; dispositions, August, 1939, 58; aircraft allotted to, 60; first R.A.F. attacks on, 65-6; similarity in heavy ship silhouettes, 83; lack of search radar, 86; illegality of minelaying by, 98, 102; ordered to observe Hague Conventions, 103; hampered by German air attacks on light vessels, 138; organisation for Norway campaign, 163; defects of torpedoes, 164; main strength risked in Norway, 180; tested by Norway campaign, 201; unable to dispute Home Fleet control, June 1940, 230; force available for invasion of U.K., 249; inadequate to protect invasion fleet, 254-5; arrangements with Italian Navy, 295; shortage of aircraft for, 326; part of G.A.F. transferred to, by Hitler, 362; press for stronger air defences for Brest, 393; reinforced to attack Russian convoys, 493; lack of effective air arm in, 498; disputes with other services, 20, 39, 361-2; use of mine destructor ships, 510; details of, outbreak of war, Appendix G, 590; supply ships, list of, Appendix N, 606

Gibraltar: base for North Atlantic operations, 8, 43; defence of Straits of, 42; contraband control, 43; light forces at, 48; limit of U-boat operations, 1939, 59; poorly protected base, 77; first convoys, 92-4; evacuations from Southern France, 238-9; Force H constituted at, 241-2, 296; French traffic through Straits, 272; proposed move of Mediterranean Fleet to, 297; convoy passed through Mediterranean, 301; 8th Submarine Flotilla formed at, 306; French force passes (Dakar expedition), 309; O.G. convoys (direct to Gibraltar) started, 344; air forces in, 353-4; possible German attack on, plans for alternative base, 380; escorts for convoys to and from, 392; responsibility for convoys to, taken over by Western Approaches, 453-4; reinforcements for convoy escorts, 471; through convoys to, 460; reorganisation of Air command, 454; air attacks on convoys from, 468, 475-6; 8th Submarine

Gibraltar—*cont.*
Flotilla redisposed, 516; submarines increased, 524; submarine successes, 525; U-boats pass successfully through Straits, 473-4; air reinforcements for, 474; U-boats moved to the Western Approaches to, 474; *Audacity* sent to join Gibraltar convoy escorts, 478; submarines at, November 1941, 536; *see also* Force H

Giffen, Admiral, U.S.N.: assists to patrol northern exits, 494

Giorgios Averoff, Greek cruiser: arrives at Alexandria, 434*n*

Gironde River: evacuation from, 237; *Tarantini* sunk off, 267; *Thor* arrives on second cruise, 505

Giulio Cesare, Italian battleship: action off Calabria, 298; action off Cape Spartivento, 302

Gladiolus, H.M.S.: sinks U.65, 463

Gladiator aircraft: attempted use from frozen lake, Norway, 185

Glasfurd, Comdr. C. E.: lost in *Acasta*, 195-6

Glasgow, H.M.S.: in Humber Force, 47, 64; assists disabled *Spearfish*, 68; covers West Indies tanker convoy, 76; operations after attack on *Rawalpindi*, 84-7; embarks troops for plan 'R.4', 157; troops disembarked, 161; joins force off Norway, 170; lands naval party at Namsos, 181-2; lands reinforcements, Molde and Aandalsnes, 185; evacuates King and Government of Norway from Molde, 188; joins Mediterranean Fleet, 300; lands Royal Marines in Iceland, 345; searches for *Admiral Scheer*, Indian Ocean, 370, 383; intercepts *Regensburg*, 607

Gleaner, H.M.S.: sinks U.33, 131

Glenearn, H.M.S.: evacuation from Greece, 435

Glengyle, H.M.S.: evacuation from Greece, 435; evacuation from Crete, 445; campaign in Syria, 516

Glennie, Rear-Admiral I. G.: in Battle for Crete, 441

Glenroy, H.M.S.: evacuation from Greece, 435

Gloire, French cruiser: Dakar expedition, passes Gibraltar, 309; intercepted, proceeds to Casablanca, 315

Glorious, H.M.S.: 31, 48; raider hunting in Indian Ocean, 114; conveys fighters for frozen lake, Norway, 185; conveys fighters to Narvik area, 191; embarks R.A.F. fighters from Narvik, 193; sunk by *Scharnhorst*, 195-6; *Devonshire* near when attacked, 197; weak intelligence of enemy moves, 198; German luck in finding, 200

Gloucester, H.M.S.: 49; arrives at Alexandria from East Indies, 295; hit in action off Calabria, 299; carries troops to Malta, 421; damaged by air attack, 422; Battle off Cape Matapan, 428; supports light forces at Malta, 434; in Battle for Crete, 441-2; sunk by aircraft, 442

Glowworm, H.M.S.: in Operation 'Wilfred', 157; sunk by *Hipper*, 158, 160

Gneisenau, German battle cruiser: design, 52, 58; referred to by Germans as battleship,

Gneisenau, German battle cruiser—*cont.*
52*n*; under C.-in-C., West, 56; sortie of, October 8-10, 70; sortie of, November, and sinking of *Rawalpindi*, 83-7; attack on Norway shipping frustrated, 153; in Norwegian campaign, 163; action with *Renown*, damaged, 165-6, 169; escapes south, 176; sortie off Norway, Operation 'Juno', 194; sinking of *Glorious*, *Acasta* and *Ardent*, 195-6; torpedoed by *Clyde*, damaged, 259-60, 266; leaves Trondheim for Kiel, movement to intercept, 259-60; under repair at Kiel, 261; abortive sortie, December 1940, 292; at Kiel, 368; in North Atlantic, 371; sortie, January-March 1941, 373-9, 364, 389, 391; to join *Bismarck* and *Prinz Eugen*, 393; torpedoed by Coastal Command, 393; three times hit in bomber raid while in dry dock, 393; in Brest, 483, 487; minor damage in further Brest raids, 491; considerable influence until sunk, 496; Appendix M, 605

Godfroy, Admiral: French Squadron at Alexandria, 241, 296; squadron immobilised, 242

Göring, Marshal: bombers not allowed to attack convoys, March 1940, 143; confidence in ability to protect invasion force, 254; disputes with Raeder over G.A.F. control in Atlantic, 362

Goldenfels, German m.v.: converted to raider *Atlantis*, 278*n*

Gonzenheim, German supply ship: scuttled, 607

Gort, Field-Marshal Lord: withdrawal of B.E.F., 212; evacuation begun, 216; emergency defences of perimeter, 221; returns to England, 224

Graf Spee; see *Admiral Graf Spee*

Graf Zeppelin, German aircraft carrier: expected to complete in 1940, 57; work suspended, 368

Grafton, H.M.S.: at Calais, 215; sunk in Dunkirk evacuation, 222

Grand Fleet, 1914-1918: policy in regard to invasion, 248, 252

Graph, H.M.S.: ex-U.570, 467

Greece: U-boat patrols off, 293; Italian invasion, 300; Allied assistance to, 420; priority for reinforcements to, 423; German invasion, 424, 431; 'Lustre' convoys to, 424-5, 431; Blenheims from join in Matapan battle, 429; Piræus bombing, Navy deprived of main base, 434; withdrawal from approved by Cabinet, 434; withdrawal effected, 435-6; King of, evacuated from Crete, 443

Greenland: minefield from Orkneys to, 264; need for radar station in, 266; German battle cruisers off, 374; U.S. air bases in, 455; S.C.42 attacked off, 468; U-boats ordered to work off Cape Race, 472

Greenock: *see* Clyde

Greer, U.S. destroyer: attacked by U.652, 472

Grenade, H.M.S.: sunk in Dunkirk evacuation, 222

Greyhound, H.M.S.: in Operation 'Wilfred', 157; at Calais, 215; damaged in Dunkirk evacuation, 222; sunk by aircraft, Battle for Crete, 442

Grimsby: fishing fleet attacked, 322

Grom, Polish destroyer: escape to England, 69

Guadeloupe: watch on French warships at, 276

Guardian, H.M.S.: lays nets at Loch Ewe, 68

Guiana, British: bases in, leased to the Americans, 347-8

Gulzar, yacht: last to enter Calais, 215

Gurkha, H.M.S.: sinks U.53, 131; sunk by air attack off Norway, 171

Hague Conventions: see International Law

Haifa: contraband control, 43; minesweepers at, 49; *Janus* towed to, 517; enemy air attacks on, 518

'Halberd', Operation (convoy for Malta), 530-3, 542

Hale, Lt.-Cdr. J. W.: attack on Italian Fleet, Taranto, 300

Halifax, Nova Scotia: naval base at, 8; first trade convoy from, 93; escort of trade convoys, 114; Northern Patrol A.M.C.s to work from, 265; fast convoys from discontinued, 269; escort force at, 270-1; convoys disorganised by attack on H.X. 84, 289; *Forth* and submarines transferred to, 334, 375; convoy four-day cycle, 343; relief of congestion in, 344; enemy battle cruisers on convoy route, 374, 376

Halifax, Lord: sails for U.S.A. in *King George V*, 391

Halifax aircraft: direct hits on *Scharnhorst*, 487

Hallett, Commodore T. J.: Dunkirk evacuation, in charge of Bray, 223; assists *Jean Bart* to leave St Nazaire, 236

Halsey, Captain T. E.: evacuation from the Hook, 209

Hamburg, s.s.: fish factory ship, sunk in Lofoten raid, 341

Hamilton, Rear-Admiral L. H. K.: raid in Vestfiord area, 513

'Hammer', Operation: attack on Trondheim (cancelled), 186

Hampden aircraft: use for minelaying, 124; raids on Kiel and Wilhelmshaven, 261; raid on Vaagsö, 514

Hampton, H.M.S., minelayer: lays in East Coast barrier, 126

Hannover, m.v.: captured, towed to Jamaica, 276; becomes auxiliary carrier, H.M.S. *Audacity*, 477

Hans Ludemann, German destroyer: sunk at Narvik, 177*n*

Harbours and Ports: defence and immobilisation against invasion, 256

Hardy, H.M.S.: in Operation 'Wilfred', 157; in first Battle of Narvik, 173-4; disabled, 175

Harstad: Convoy N.P. 1 disembarks at, 190; evacuation from, 193-4, 198; German operation against, 'Juno', 194, 200

Hart, Admiral T. C., U.S.N.: C.-in-C., Asiatic Fleet, 558; force at Manila, 560; visited by Admiral Phillips, 561; agreement on use of forces, 561-2

INDEX

Harvester, H.M.S.: in Dunkirk evacuation, 221; sinks U.32 with *Highlander*, 353
Harwich: light forces at, 47; French submarines at, 149; destroyers for, threat to Low Countries, 188; *Birmingham* ordered to, 205; evacuations from Holland to, 209; striking force base against invasion, 249, 253
Harwood, Rear-Admiral Sir H.: fuelling anxieties, 116; concentrates South American Division off River Plate, 117; Battle of River Plate, 118-21; promoted to Rear-Admiral, 120*n*; force under, 274; succeeded by Commodore Pegram, 285
Hasty, H.M.S.: captures German *Morea* off Portugal, 150
Havant, H.M.S.: sunk in Dunkirk evacuation, 225
Havelock, H.M.S.: evacuation from St Nazaire, 234
Havock, H.M.S.: in Operation 'Wilfred', 157; in first Battle of Narvik, 173-5; sinks *Rauenfels*, 175; in Battle off Cape Matapan, 430
Havre: transport of B.E.F. vehicles to, 63; base opened at, 64; enemy air attacks off, 142; evacuation of, 231, 233; German invasion assembly port, 255
Hawkins, H.M.S.: in South American Division, 274; escorts troop convoy W.S. 5 B, 370
Haxby, s.s.: sunk by *Orion*, 282; prisoners in *Tropic Sea*, 283
Haydon, Brigadier J. C.: commands land force in Lofoten raid, 341
Hebe, H.M.S.: in Dunkirk evacuation, 223
'Hedgehog': new anti-submarine device, 480
Helder, Den: enemy use as a base, 322
Heligoland: mining of approaches to, 55, 97-8; air attack on anticipated, 56; first air reconnaissance of, 66; enemy A.A. ships off, 144; submarine patrols off abandoned after loss, 148; submarine sightings off, 149; enemy activity, April 1940, 158
Henderson, Vice-Admiral Sir R. G.: first Rear-Admiral, Aircraft Carriers, 30; Controller of the Navy, and death, 79
Hereward, H.M.S.: conveys Queen Wilhelmina to Harwich, 209; lost in evacuation from Crete, 445
Hermann Künne, German destroyer: sunk at Narvik, 117*n*
Hermes, H.M.S.: 31, 47; in raider hunting group, 114; patrolling from Dakar, 117; attack on *Richelieu* at Dakar, 245; in South Atlantic, 274; in hunting group, St Helena, search for *Scheer*, 290; supports East Africa campaign, 426
Hermione, H.M.S.: operations against *Bismarck*, 396, 408; conveys Malta reinforcements, and sinks submarine *Tembien*, 523; aircraft ferrying to Malta, 533
Hero, H.M.S.: in Operation 'Wilfred', 157
Hichens, Lt-Cdr. R. P.: Coastal Force operations by, 330, 500-1
Highlander, H.M.S.: evacuation from St Nazaire, 235; sinks U.32 with *Harvester*, 353
Hipper, German cruiser: *see Admiral Hipper*

Hitler, Adolf: plans to invade England, 10, 254-6; appeasement policy towards, 25, 78; policy of, 1933-39, 52; miscalculations of, 53; refuses transfer of warships to Russia, 57*n*; approves increase of U-boats, 59-60; departs from Hague Conventions, 103-4; asks Japan for use of bases, 111; avoids incidents with U.S.A., 112; orders start of commerce raiding, 112-3; on River Plate battle, 121; restrictions on bombing, 137; invasion of Denmark and Norway, 162-3, 179; curbed by maritime power, 240; on occupation of Atlantic islands, 273, 380; concentrates against British overseas supplies, 338-9; declares total blockade of British Isles, 349; neutral shipping to be sunk at sight, 349; approves completion of *Graf Zeppelin*, 368; transfers part of Air Force to Navy, 362; moves aircraft to Sicily, 420; timetable for Russia upset by Crete, 449; orders attack on Russia, 463; anxious not to provoke U.S.A., 490; failure to capture Murmansk, 495; offensive against merchant shipping to continue, 499; mistake in attacking Russia, 502; believes Allies will invade Norway, 514; ignores appeals for North Africa force, 525; orders return of aircraft from Russia to Sicily, 534; transfers anti-submarine material to Mediterranean, 536
Hobart, H.M.A.S.: 49
Holland: invasion of anticipated, Nov. 1939, 69; German invasion of, 192, 205; overwhelmed by air superiority, surrenders, 206; evacuation of Queen and Government, 209; Navy withdrawn to England, 210; troops for Curaçao and Aruba, 276; use of bases in by Air Force for attacks on shipping, 322; naval forces in East Indies, 559
Holland, Captain C. S.: negotiates with French at Oran, 243-4
Holland, Vice-Admiral L. E.: Joint Admiralty-Air Ministry staff, 73; plan for Trondheim attack, 'Hammer', 186; conveys reinforcements to Alexandria, 301; action off Spartivento, 302-3; in operations against *Bismarck*, 396, 398-406; lost in H.M.S. *Hood*, 405-6
Home Fleet: Admiralty intervention in conduct of operations, 27; tactical offensive by, 44; detachment for Humber, 45; disposition on 31.8.1939, 47; Orkneys and Shetlands Command under, 48; first operational patrol, 64-5; temporary base at Loch Ewe, 68 *et seq.*; ineffective A.A. fire of, 69; reinforcements for, 69-70; sortie to intercept *Gneisenau*, 71; raider hunting groups detached, 70, 72; air attacks on, Firth of Forth and Scapa, 75, 155; deprived of aircraft carrier, 76; main bases, policy, 76-8; handicap of undefended base, 80; two squadrons to be based on Clyde, 81; operations after attack on *Rawalpindi*, 82-7; covers Canadian troop convoys, 89, 392; summary of operations, first phase, 90; cover and escort for Norwegian con-

INDEX

Home Fleet—*cont.*
voys, 93, 143, 147-8; cover and escort for troop convoys, 95, 392; destroyer-minelayers attached, 97; U-boats in wait for, March 1940, 132; maintenance in severe cold, 147; interception of German shipping from Vigo, 150; escort of third Canadian troop convoy, 151; operations against *Altmark*, 151-3; German attack on Norway shipping frustrated, 153-4; returns to Scapa, March 1940, 155; covers Operation 'Wilfred', 156-8; campaign in Norway, 169-200; reduced by threat from Italy, 188, 295; covers Narvik evacuation, 193-4; strength reduced by Dunkirk evacuation, 197; reinforcements sent to Nore, 205; influence of control over Coastal Command, 230; destroyers reach Dover in a day, 250; effect of anti-invasion plans, 251; main forces for Rosyth in event of invasion, 252; cruisers dispersed around coasts, 252; operational capacity restricted, 253; influence of German invasion threat, 257, 262; reverts to normal functions, 259; plans for Norway operations cancelled, 262; forces lent for convoy protection, 263, 452; cover for minelaying operations, 264; move to intercept *Scheer*, 289; covers northern passages against *Hipper*, 292; ships lent for Dakar operation, 308-9, 314; cover for Lofoten Islands raid, 341; difficulty of watching northern passages, 368, 371; movements to intercept battle cruisers, 373-4, 376, 378; measure of control over Coastal Command, 361; attacks on *Scharnhorst* and *Gneisenau*, 389; operations against *Bismarck*, 390, 395-418; protection for minelaying squadrons, 390; break-out of merchant ships from Sweden, 391; small margin of forces, 392; strength of, 1.6.1941, 483; effect of Russian campaign, 485; operations, June-Dec. 1941, 486-496; ships lent for Malta convoy 'Substance', 521; *Prince of Wales* lent for Malta convoy 'Halberd', 530; only two effective capital ships, August 1941, 554

Hong Kong: destroyers and M.T.B.s at, 559; attacked by Japanese, 563; surrenders, 570

Hood, H.M.S.: compared with *Scharnhorst*, 58; Home Fleet patrol, 65; bombed by enemy aircraft, 69; sortie to intercept *Gneisenau*, 71; covers Narvik convoy, 82; movement after attack on *Rawalpindi*, 85; in need of refit, 88; covers first Canadian troop convoy, 89; returns to Scapa, 155; joins Force H, 242, 272; action against French at Oran, 242-244; again based at Scapa, 268; search for *Scheer*, 289; search for battle cruisers, Iceland, 377 & *n*; patrols Atlantic convoy route, 378; diverted to hunt *Bismarck* (false report), 393; convoy cover from Iceland, 394; *Bismarck* operations, 396, 398-406; sunk in action, 405-6, 416-7, 569

Hook of Holland: demolition party sent to, 207-8; opposition to demolition, 208-9; evacuation from, 209; enemy base, 322; E-boat encounters off, 330

Horton, Vice-Admiral Sir Max: appointed Vice-Admiral (Submarines), 68

Hospital Ships: to use Dieppe, 63; enemy disregards Hague Conventions at Dunkirk, 218

Hostile, H.M.S.: in first Battle of Narvik, 173-5

Hotspur, H.M.S.: in Operation 'Wilfred', 157; in first Battle of Narvik, 173-4; damaged, 175; sights French force, Gibraltar Straits, 312; in evacuation from Crete, 445

Hudson aircraft: replacement of Ansons by, 38, 66; sighting of *Altmark*, 152; sighting of German battle cruisers, 378

Human torpedoes: Italian attack on Fleet at Alexandria, 538

Humber: British minefield to Tyne, 96; traffic suspended by ice, 141; minelaying in, 328; minesweeping by trawlers from, 499

Humber Force: 45, 47, 64; under direct Admiralty control, 69; sortie to intercept *Gneisenau*, 71; covers Dover minelaying, 96; reinforced, threat to Low Countries, 188; German threat of invasion, 249, 252

Hunter, H.M.S.: in Operation 'Wilfred', 157; in first Battle of Narvik, 173-4; sunk, 175

Hunting Groups: for submarines, unsuccessful, 10, 130, 132, 134; for raiders, formed, 70, 113-4; movements of, 116-8, 263; not available in South Atlantic, July 1940, 275, 280; formed in South Atlantic, Nov. 1940, 290

Hurricane aircraft: defence of Norwegian convoys, 143; defence of Scapa, 155; loss in ferrying operation to Malta, 298; further ferrying to Malta, 434, 437, 518, 524, 533; sent to Egypt in 'Tiger' convoy, 437; fivefold increase at Malta, 437; in *Victorious* for Middle East, 483; in *Argus* for Russia, 489; Hurricane bombers introduced, 503-5

'Hurry', Operation (ferrying aircraft to Malta), 298

Hutchinson, Lt.-Cdr. C. H.: in *Truant* sinks *Karlsruhe*, 172

Hyperion, H.M.S.: in Operation 'Wilfred', 157

Icarus, H.M.S.: mining in German mined area, 123; captures *Alster*, 178; in Dunkirk evacuation, 225

Iceland: immunity from German attack, 2; Iceland-Faeröes passage watched, 45, 65, 67, 265; covered by force at Scapa, 252, 263; minefield north of, 264; need for radar station in, 266; lack of cruisers for patrol, 287; air squadron to cover Denmark Strait, 288; troops despatched to, 345; Canadian reinforcements for, 345; Air Force formed in, part of Coastal Command, 347, 452; advance refuelling base in, 352, 451; minelaying off, 390; *Hood* and destroyers based on, 394; 'Arethusa' class in Iceland-Faeröes gap, 394; patrol of Iceland-Faeröes passage during *Bismarck* operations, 396; air reinforcements, 452; vital part in Battle of Atlantic, 453; U.S. Marines land in, 455, 490, 496, 612; air strength in, 459-60; progress on bases hastened, 463; U-boat concentration off,

INDEX 641

Iceland—*cont.*
467; American forces to be supplied by U.S. ships, 472; U.S. air forces come under British command, 472

Ijmuiden: minefield off, demolition party sent, 207-8; Crown Princess evacuated from, 208; blocking of, 210; enemy base at, 322; encounters with E-boats off, 330

Ilex, H.M.S.: damaged in Syria campaign, 517

Illustrious, H.M.S.: joins Mediterranean Fleet, 299; attack on Italian Fleet, Taranto, 300-1; 'Excess' convoy, Malta, 421; severely damaged by air attacks, 421-3, 518; repairing in U.S.A., 534; considered for Far East, 539

'*Illustrious*' class carriers: two to complete in 1940, 50

Imperial, H.M.S.: sunk in Crete evacuation, 445

Imperial Defence, Committee of: pre-war statement on trade protection, 107

Imperial Star, m.v.: sunk in Malta convoy 'Halberd', 530

Impulsive, H.M.S.: mining in German mined area, 123

India: troops sent to Iraq, 427; minesweepers built in, 498. *See also* Royal Indian Navy

Indian Ocean: armed merchant raiders in, 111; hunting group in, 114; *Graf Spee* in, 116; *Atlantis* in, 281,381-2; *Admiral Scheer* in, 367, 369; *Komet* moves into, 368; *Orion* moves into, 383; raider fuelling position never discovered, 542; *Kormoran* in, 548; plans against Japanese in, 555; capital ships sent to, 557

Indicator loops: to be provided at Scapa, 81 & n; in Dover mine barrage, 96

Indo-China: Japan occupies bases in, 554; enemy bombers reported in, 564

Indomitable, H.M.S.: allocated to Eastern Fleet, 491; damaged by grounding, Jamaica, 534, 558; likely to be sent to Far East, 539

Inglefield, H.M.S.: damaged by shore battery, Dakar, 316

Inshore Squadron, Mediterranean: formed to supply Army of the Nile, 422; assistance to Tobruk, 520

Intelligence, British: quality of, 1940, 19; faulty, 1939, 71, 90, 98, 392-3; weakness in *Rawalpindi* operations, 87, 116; of enemy movement against Norway, 158-60; from Norway, ignored or misinterpreted, 179; weakness of North Sea air reconnaissance, 197-8; faulty at Brest, 234, and St Nazaire, 236; of German invasion plans, 249, 250, 259; lack of confidence in, 253; of German ships, Trondheim, faulty air reports, 260-1; value of in attack on Taranto, 301; first of raider *Orion*, four months after start of cruise, 283; from Dakar, delayed, 308; of northern passages, lack of, 372; of enemy Atlantic sorties, accuracy of, 373-4, 379, 484; limitations of photographic reconnaissance, 494; improved speed and accuracy, 496; interception of U-boat wireless signals, 469

Intelligence, German: speed and accuracy of, 87-8; success in locating submarines, 266-7; obtained from captured merchant ships, 281-2, 381; use of wireless intercepts from Western Approaches, 469

Intelligence, Vichy French: of expedition to Dakar, 315, 319

Intelligence Division, Admiralty: work of, 18-20, 24

International Law: attitude of German Naval Staff, 56; minelaying operations and, 98, 102; Hitler breaks away from, 103-4; Hague Conventions disregarded by Germans at Dunkirk, 218; conduct of raider captain, 279

Intrepid, H.M.S.: converted for minelaying, 98; in *Altmark* operations, 152; damaged in Dunkirk evacuation, 222

Invasion: defence against, British policy, 9, 247-51; forces to deal with, 252-3; convoy escorts weakened for, 253-4; conflicting German views on, 254-5; Operation 'Sealion' abandoned, 256; Admiral Forbes on risk of, 256-8; forces concentrated to detect, 287; threat recedes in autumn, 1940, 288

Invergordon: air patrol from, 36

Ionian Sea: Malta aircraft unable to cover, 527

Iran: combined operation in, 'Countenance', 529

Iraq: revolt against Regent suppressed, 427; enemy threat forestalled by Syria campaign, 517; Army advances into Iran, 529

Iron Duke, H.M.S.: base ship, Scapa, beached after bombing, 75

Irwin, Major-General M. N. S.: expedition to Dakar, 308

Isaac Sweers, Dutch destroyer: sinking of Italian cruisers, 534

Isis, H.M.S.: campaign in Syria, damaged, 517

Isle of Wight: *Domala* bombed off, 142; in German invasion plans, 254

Isle of Sheppey: mined from the air, 328

Italian Air Force (Regia Aeronautica): non-interference with Red Sea convoys, 296; in action off Calabria, 299; threat from less than expected, 419; strength in Sicily, 420

Italian Fleet: summary of, 1939, 61; armed merchant raider, 279, 386; submarine strength considerable, 293; war plans, 294; influence on British strategy, 295; action off Calabria, 298-9; sighted by Force H, 299; threat to Mediterranean route less effective, 300; attacked by naval aircraft at Taranto, 5, 300-1; action off Cape Spartivento, 302-3; sea routes to North Africa disputed, 305-6; German spur to use of, 424; losses in East Africa, 426; Battle off Cape Matapan, 427-31; deterred from attacking convoy 'Substance', 522; ditto, convoy 'Halberd', 530; shaken by loss of Africa convoy, 532-3; loses two cruisers off Cape Bon, 534; first Battle of Sirte, 535; German instruction in anti-submarine devices, 536; small success of submarines, 538; strength and disposition, June 1940, Appendix H, 593

2S

Italy: Admiralty war plans against, 41, 44, 49, 60, 294; Home Fleet reduced by threat from, 188; invades Greece, 300; surrender in East Africa, 426; merchant shipping losses, 1941, 537-8
Ivanhoe, H.M.S.: converted for minelaying, 98; in *Altmark* operations, 152; sunk by mine off Texel, 334

Jacob van Heemskerck, Dutch cruiser: leaves for England, 210
Jade-Weser estuaries: aircraft minelaying in, 124; ice difficulties in, 153
Jaguar, H.M.S.: damaged in Dunkirk evacuation, 222; rescues crew of *Kandahar* off Tripoli, 535
Jamaica: trade convoys from 93-4; exchange A.A. merchant ship gunners in, 141; German *Hannover* towed to, 276; *Indomitable* grounds off, 534
James, Admiral Sir William: evacuation of Havre, 231, St Valery, 232, Cherbourg and St Malo, 232-3, and Channel Islands, 239
Jantina, Italian U-boat: sunk by *Torbay*, 525
Janus, H.M.S.: disabled in Syria campaign, 517
Japan: uncertain attitude after 1936, 41; provision for defence against, 42; facilities for German raiders, 111; German merchant ships escape to, 276; German supply ships work from, 278, 367; entry into war, effect of, 538-9; blockade breakers from, 551; plans for war with, 553; sends troops to Indo-China, 554; hopes of deterring by a battle force in Far East, 556-8; attacks Pearl Harbour, 482, 562; invades Malaya, 563
Japanese Navy: attack on Pearl Harbour, 5, 562-3; final destruction of, 11; armed merchant raiders, 279; British plans against, 555-8; relative strength of (table), 560
Java: Dutch naval forces at, 559
Jean Bart, French battleship: leaves St Nazaire for Casablanca, 234, 236, 240; suggested operation against, 272, 309
Jeanne d'Arc, French cruiser: at Guadeloupe, 276
Jervis, H.M.S.: in Battle off Cape Matapan, 430
Jervis Bay, H.M.S.: action with *Admiral Scheer*, 288-90; 371
John Bakke, Norwegian s.s.: escapes from Gothenburg, 391
Joubert de la Ferté, Air Marshal Sir P.: Joint Admiralty-Air Ministry staff, 72; C.-in-C., Coastal Command, 459; proposes bombing of Biscay U-boat bases, 459
Juniper, H.M.S.: sunk in Narvik evacuation, 194
Juno, H.M.S.: sunk in Battle for Crete, 441
'Juno', Operation (German sortie off Norway), 194-5, 200

Kandahar, H.M.S.: sunk by mines off Tripoli, 535
Karl Peters, German depot-ship: in landing at Bergen, 163
Karlsruhe, German cruiser: in landings in Norway, 163-4; sunk by *Truant*, 172

Kashmir, H.M.S.: sunk in Battle for Crete, 443
Kattegat: aircraft minelaying in, 125, 510, 514; submarine patrols in, 187
Kearney, U.S. destroyer: torpedoed off Greenland, 472, 613
Keith, H.M.S.: sent to Boulogne, Commanding Officer killed, 213; sunk in Dunkirk evacuation, 225
Kelly, H.M.S.: damaged by E-boat, towed to Tyne, 145; sunk in Battle for Crete, 443
Kennedy, Captain E. C.: lost in *Rawalpindi*, 82-7
Kennedy-Purvis, Admiral Sir C.; C.-in-C., America and West Indies, 276
Kent, H.M.S.: 49
Kenya, H.M.S.: joins Home Fleet, 262; sent to meet Sierra Leone Convoys, 292; in *Bismarck* operations, 396, 408; search for enemy supply ships, 483; raid on Vaagsö, 513; 'Halberd' convoy for Malta, 530; sinks enemy tanker, Atlantic, 542
Kerguelen: used by German supply ships, 278, 282, 284, 367
Kerr, Captain R.: commanding *Hood* in operations against *Bismarck*, 396
Ketty Brövig, Norwegian tanker: captured by *Atlantis*, later intercepted by *Leander*, 381, 608
Keyes, Admiral of the Fleet Sir Roger: proposed capture of Mediterranean islands, 304
Kiel: base of Naval Group Commander, East, 54; warships under repair at, July 1940, 260; R.A.F. raids on, 1940, 261; minelaying off by R.A.F., 335
Kiel Canal: submarine patrols off, 64; aircraft minelaying in, 124
Kimberley, H.M.S.: captures German *Wahehe*, 150; in evacuation from Crete, 445
Kimmel, Admiral H., U.S.N.: C.-in-C., Pacific Fleet, Pearl Harbour, 560
King, Admiral E. J.: in command of U.S. Atlantic Fleet, 454, 612; Staff meets Admiral Tovey, Iceland, 492
King, Vice-Admiral E. L. S.: in Battle for Crete, 440-2, 445-8; in campaign in Syria, 516
King George V, H.M.S.: leaves Tyne for Rosyth and Scapa, 262, 268; moves to intercept *Admiral Scheer*, 371; covers Halifax convoys, 376; sails from Scapa with Lord Halifax on board, 391; at Scapa, May 1941, 394; flagship of Home Fleet during operations against *Bismarck*, 396, 406-17; failure of 14-inch armament of, 417; at Scapa June 1st, 1941, 483; only ship capable of catching and fighting *Tirpitz*, 494; in Home Fleet, 554
'*King George V*' class, battleships: under construction, 50; outclassed by *Bismarck*, 57; not to be spared from Home Fleet without U.S. assistance, 555
King George V., s.s.: in Dunkirk evacuation, 226
King John, m.v.: sunk by *Widder*, 284
King Orry, armed boarding vessel: sunk in Dunkirk evacuation, 222
Kinnaird Head: U-boat attacks off, 130

INDEX

Kipling, H.M.S.: rescues survivors from *Kelly* and *Kashmir*, 443
Kirkenes: enemy traffic from, Russian request for attack, 485; attack on, 486
Kirkwall, Orkneys: contraband control base at, 67
Kismayu: captured by British, 426
Kjell, Norwegian torpedo boat: at interception of *Altmark*, 152
Kola Inlet: Russian convoy escorts to fuel in, 495
Köln, German cruiser: under C.-in-C., East, 57; sortie of, 70; minelaying off Tyne, 102; in landing at Bergen, 163, 170; leaves Bergen, 172; wrongly identified at Narvik, 393; presumed ready for service, 394
Komet, German armed merchant raider: cruise of, 278; passage to Bering Sea, 279-80; in company with *Orion*, 283; attacks Nauru, 284, 286, 367; meets *Pinguin* at Kerguelen, 385; sighted by Coastal Command, 504; attacked in Dover Straits but escapes, 505; meets *Atlantis*, 545; returns to Bordeaux, total sinkings, 547; sunk in English Channel, 279; Appendix M, 604
Königsberg, German cruiser: to join C.-in-C., East, 57; in landing at Bergen, 163, 170; sunk by naval aircraft, 165, 172
Königsberg, German supply ship: scuttled, 607
Kormoran, German raider: 279; break-out, 286; passes Denmark Strait, 291, 367, 386; meets *Admiral Scheer*, South Atlantic, 370; operations by, 386-7; in Bay of Bengal, 547; sunk after action with *Sydney*, 548; Appendix M, 605
Kota Bahru: Japanese land at, 563
Kota Nopan, Dutch m.v.: captured by raider *Komet*, 547
Kota Pinang, enemy supply ship: sunk by *Kenya*, 470, 480, 542
Kretschmer, U-boat Commander: 'Ace' U-boat commander in Battle of the Atlantic, 348; sinks *Laurentic* and *Patroclus* in Atlantic, 351; attacks convoy H.X. 90, *Forfar* sunk, 353; commands U.99, 365; captured when U-boat sunk, 365
Kristiansand (South): 150n; German landing at, 163-5, 180; *Karlsruhe* sunk off, 172
Kristiansund: 150n
Kuantan: report of Japanese landing, 564; Admiral Phillips proceeds to, 565; lack of fighter cover at, 568
Kulmerland, German supply ship: fuels *Kormoran*, 548; lost (1943), 607

L.23, H.M. submarine: sightings off Heligoland, 149
La Coruña, German s.s.: intercepted by *Maloja*, 150
La Pallice: evacuation from, 232, 236; numbers, 237; used as U-boat base, 349; *Scharnhorst* damaged at, 487
La Rochelle: minelaying off, 335
Lady of Mann, s.s.: in Dunkirk evacuation, 227
Lagos: transport of troops from, 274
Lancastria, s.s.: sunk in evacuation from St Nazaire, 235

Lance, H.M.S.: in Force K convoy action, 533
Langsdorff, Captain, *Admiral Graf Spee*: at Montevideo, 120; suicide, 121
Larcom, Captain C. A. A.: commands *Sheffield* in *Bismarck* operations, 410
Latona, H.M.S.: supplies for Tobruk, 519; sunk off Bardia, 520
Laurentic, H.M.S.: sunk by U-boat, 265, 351
Layman, Comdr. H. F. H.: in first Battle of Narvik, 173
Layton, Vice-Admiral Sir G.: in 18th Cruiser Sqdn., 159; joins Admiral Forbes, Norway, 170; detached to attack Bergen, 170; sweep off Norway, 172; escorts Convoy N.P. 1, 180; diverted to Lillesjona, 182; sent to Humber on threat from Low Countries, 188; evacuation from Aandalsnes, 189, 447; C.-in-C., China, force with, 559; airman's letter to, 569; proposals after loss of Admiral Phillips, 570
Le Havre: *see* Havre
Le Triomphant, French destroyer: arrives in Britain, 240
Le Verdon: evacuation from, 237-8
Leach, Captain J. C.: commands *Prince of Wales* in action with *Bismarck*, 396, 406-7; lost in *Prince of Wales*, 567-8
Leamington, H.M.S.: sinks U.207 with *Veteran*, 469
Leander, H.M.S.: 49; intercepts *Ketty Brövig* and *Coburg*, 381, 606, 608; sinks raider *Ramb I*, 387, 549, 605
Leatham, Vice-Admiral R.: 49; importance of Red Sea, 296; raider counter-measures, 370; support of East Africa campaign, 426; suppression of revolt in Iraq, 427
Leathers, F. J.: Minister of War Transport, 21n
Leche, s.s.: German blockade runner, intercepted, 394
Leghorn: bombarded by Force H, 425; minelaying by *Manxman*, 523
Legion, H.M.S.: sinking of Italian cruisers, 534
Leigh light: invented by Sq./Ldr. H. de V. Leigh for use against surface U-boats, 358, 461
Leinster, m.v., troopship: runs aground off Gibraltar, 521, 523
Leipzig, German cruiser: under C.-in-C., West, 56; minelaying off Tyne, and torpedoed by *Salmon*, 102; repairing during Norway campaign, 163; leaves for Trondheim, 484
Leopard, French destroyer: arrives in Britain, 240
Leros: proposed Commando attack on, 304
Lexington, U.S. aircraft carrier: escapes attack on Pearl Harbour, 563
Libreville: French squadron intended for, 315; de Gaulle plans to attack, 320
Libya: Malta threat to communications with, 49; Italian defence of communications, 294; Italian tonnage passed to, 1940, 307; effect of German Air Force on campaign in, 420; consequences of Allied defeat in, 515; offensive resumed in, 520; air offensive against enemy supplies, 524; enemy fuel supply critical, 533-4; enemy convoys resumed after loss of Force K, 536

Light vessels: attacked by German aircraft, 138
Lights: extinguished in Thames Estuary, 100
Lillesjona: transports arrive at, 182
Littorio, Italian battleship: to complete in 1940, 61; sunk at Taranto, 300
Lively, H.M.S.: in Force K convoy action, 533
Liverpool: convoy routing from, 89; *Barham* docked at after torpedoing, 90; first O.B. convoys from, 93; enemy mining off, 126-7, 328; unrestricted U-boat zones extended to Mersey, 129; minefield in St George's Channel approach route, 263; Fighter Command and defence of, 331; anti-submarine instruction at, 359; heavy air raids on, 463
Liverpool, H.M.S.: 49; arrives at Alexandria from China, 295
Lloyd, Air Vice-Marshal H. P.: A.O.C., Mediterranean, 526
Local Defence Division, Admiralty: work of, 24; lack of, before May 1939, 79
Loch Ewe: use as temporary base, 68, 71, 74, 75; *Nelson* mined off, 78, 87; peril to Fleet at, 80-1; use known to Germans, 87; enemy mining continues, 126; convoy assembly base, 497
Lofoten Islands: Home Fleet cruise to, 1939, 82; Home Fleet off, Norway campaign, 177; raid on, 341-2, 513
London, Port of: all channels but one closed by enemy mines, 128; to be kept working to full capacity, 322
London, H.M.S.: conveys Beaverbrook Mission to Russia, 492; intercepts *Babitonga*, *Egerland* and *Esso Hamburg*, 606
London Protocol: signed, 1936, 52
Londonderry: value as a base, 46; anti-submarine instruction at, 359; escort groups based at, 452, 454; bases chosen by U.S. Mission, 455
Longmore, Air Marshal Sir A.: in Coastal Command, 1936, 33; organisation of No. 201 Group, Mediterranean, 422
Lorentz W. Hansen, Norwegian s.s.: sunk by *Deutschland*, 70, 113
Lorient: U.51 sunk off, 266; minelaying off, 335; first Atlantic U-boat base, 346, 349; U-boat from goes to Freetown, 351; bombing by R.A.F., 352; U-boat Command established at, 354; mining by Coastal Command, 510; attacked by Bomber Command, 468
Lorina, s.s.: sunk in Dunkirk evacuation, 222
Lorraine, French battleship: in Eastern Mediterranean, 295
Lothringen, German supply ship: surrenders, 607
Loveitt, Flt. Sgt. R. H., torpedoes *Lützow*: 484
Lübeck: aircraft minelaying off, 124
Lucy, Lieut. W. P.: sinking of *Königsberg*, 172
'Lustre', Operation (reinforcements to Greece) 424-5; 80 per cent of numbers evacuated, 436; losses in 'Lustre' and 'Demon', 446
Lütjens, Vice-Admiral: in Norway campaign, 163; engages *Renown*, 165-6; escapes south, 176; commands battle cruiser sortie, 373-9; disagreement with Raeder on *Bismarck* plans, 393; agrees with Dönitz on U-boat

Lütjens, Vice-Admiral—*cont*.
policy, 395; operations of *Bismarck* and *Prinz Eugen*, 395-418; goes down in *Bismarck*, 415
Lützow (ex-*Deutschland*), German pocket battleship: controlled by Naval Staff, 57; in landing at Oslo, 164-5; torpedoed by *Spearfish*, 177; under repair at Kiel, bombed, 261; wrongly identified at Narvik, 393; presumed ready for service, 394; believed in Baltic, 483; moves north, 484, 493; hit by Beaufort aircraft torpedo, 484, 495; 541
Lützow, German cruiser: transferred to Russia, 1940, 57*n*, 58
Lyon, Admiral Sir G. H. D'O.: 48; raider hunting groups under, 114, 117; on Freetown as naval base, 273; succeeded by Vice-Admiral Raikes, 275; C.-in-C., Nore Command, 499

MacArthur, General D., U.S. Army: suggests British squadron for Manila, 561
Mack, Captain P. J.: commands destroyers at Malta, 431; success against enemy convoy to Libya, 432
Mackay, H.M.S.: in Dunkirk evacuation, 221; damaged, 222
Mackendrick, Comdr. D. W.: commands *Audacity* on Gibraltar convoys, 478
Mackesy, Major-General P. J.: leaves Scapa for Narvik, 180; succeeded by General Auchinleck, 192
Madagascar: raider *Atlantis* off, 381; raider *Kormoran* off, 548
Madras: *Kormoran* abandons minelaying off, 386
Madrid: French warship movements reported from, 311-2, 314
Madrid, German s.s.: sunk by Coastal Command aircraft, 506
Magnetic mine: *see* Minelaying, Enemy
Mahan, Captain A. T.: on maritime concentration, quoted, 7
Maid of Orleans, s.s.: in Dunkirk evacuation, 225
Maidstone, H.M.S.: 48
Makeig-Jones, Captain W. T.: lost in *Courageous*, 105-6
Malaya: transport of troops to, 274; Japanese advance towards, 554, 561; Japanese invasion, 563
Malaya, H.M.S.: 48; raider hunting in Indian Ocean, 114; escorts third Canadian troop convoy, 151; in Halifax escort force, 270; arrives at Alexandria, 295; action off Calabria, 298; sights enemy battle cruisers, Atlantic, 375; covers convoy 'Excess', Mediterranean, 421; bombardment of Genoa, etc., 425; refits in America, 455; joins Force H, 494; aircraft ferrying to Malta, 533; refits at home, 554
Malcolm, H.M.S.: evacuation from the Hook, 209; Dunkirk evacuation, 221, 227
Maloja, H.M.S.: intercepts *La Coruña*, 150
Malta: contraband control, 43; insecurity of, 48; forces at, 49; considered indefensible, 77; importance as air base, 293; Italian

INDEX

Malta—*cont.*
attitude towards, 295; risk of loss of, 297; ferrying of aircraft into, 298; reinforcements for, 299-300; supply of, and visit of Admiral Cunningham, 300, 304; importance as base against North Africa routes, 305; submarines at, 306; situation, end 1940, 419; air strength in, Jan. 1941, 420; military convoy for, 'Excess', 421; onslaught by Luftwaffe begun, 423, 425; destroyer force to attack Libya convoys, 431; *Breconshire* passed to, and empty ships from, 432-3; supply of aircraft to, 433-4, 437; relief to, 'Tiger' convoy, 437; enemy aircraft destroyed, Jan.-May 1941, 437; situation in May 1941, 438; first priority for fighters after home, 449; situation after Crete, 515-6; further air reinforcements, 518, 524; end of first enemy offensive, May 1941, 518; supply by submarine, 518-9; 'Substance' convoy for, 521-3; attacked by midgets, E-boats and aircraft, 523; surface force returns to, 524; submarine successes, 525-6; 10th Submarine Flotilla formed at, 526; build-up of air striking forces, 526; numbers of aircraft types, 527; 'Halberd' convoy for, 530-2; 1941 convoys to (table), 531; Force K based at, 532-3; Force B sent to, 534; *Breconshire* escorted to, loss in Force K, 535; submarines at, Nov. 1941, 536
Manchester, H.M.S.: 49; captures German *Wahehe*, 150; covers convoy O.N. 25, 159; joins force off Norway, 170; escorts first Norwegian troop convoy, 180; conveys final reinforcement, Aandalsnes, 185; joins Humber Force, 188; evacuation from Aandalsnes, 189; lent to Nore Command, 208; conveys troops to Alexandria, 301; on patrol during *Bismarck* operations, 396; in Malta convoy 'Substance', damaged, 521-2
Mandasor, s.s.: sunk by *Atlantis*, 381
Manela, H.M.S.: depot-ship at Reykjavik, 452
Manila: U.S. Asiatic Fleet at, visit of Admiral Phillips, 558, 560-1
Manwaring, Captain P. C. W.: commands *Cornwall* in action with *Pinguin*, 384-5
Manxman, H.M.S.: escorts Malta convoy 'Substance', 522; conveys troops to Malta, 523
Maori, H.M.S.: in *Bismarck* operations, 414, 416; sinking of Italian cruisers, 534
Maplin, H.M.S.: fighter catapult ship, 477
Marianas Group: used by German supply ships, 278, 284; *Orion* refits in, 367
Marigold, H.M.S.: sinks U.433, 473-4
Maritime Regiment, Royal Artillery: formation, 141; soldiers from sent to merchant ships, 363
Maritza, s.s.: sunk by Force K, 533
Marschall, Vice-Admiral: Atlantic sortie and sinking of *Rawalpindi*, 83-8; attack on Norway shipping frustrated, 153-4; sortie off Norway, 'Juno', 194; criticised by German Naval Staff, 200
Marshall Islands: used by German supply ships, 278, 284

Martin, Captain B. C. S.: commands *Dorsetshire* in *Bismarck* operations, 415
Martinique: watch on French warships at, 276
Maryland, U.S. battleship: escapes major injury at Pearl Harbour, 562
Maryland aircraft: value of reconnaissance at Taranto, 301; seven at Malta, August 1941, 527
Mashona, H.M.S.: sunk off Galway, 416
Massawa: Italian force at, 296; raider *Ramb I* leaves, 387; attacked by *Formidable* aircraft, 426
Matapan, Cape, Battle of: instigated by Germans, 424; details of the action, 427-31
Maund, Captain L. E. H.: commands *Ark Royal* in *Bismarck* operations, 410
'Maurice', Operation (pincer attack on Trondheim), 182-3; force evacuated from Namsos, 190
Mauritius: raider searches from, 383
Mauritius, H.M.S.: escorts convoy W.S. 6 to Gibraltar, 392
McCarthy, Captain E. D. B.: commands *Ajax* at Malta, 534
McGrigor, Captain R. R.: commands *Renown* in *Bismarck* operations, 410
Mediterranean: enemy zone of control in, 3; provision for in 1939 war plan, 41; diversion of mercantile traffic via Cape, 42; Western basin a French responsibility, 42, 50; tactical offensive in, 44; forces reduced in 1939, 48-9; French forces in, 1939, 51; British, French and Italian forces compared, 61; lack of properly defended base, 76-7; failure of U-boat thrust into, 104; reinforced on threat from Italy, 188; evacuations from Southern France, 238; serious situation after French collapse, 241; Home Fleet ships sent to, 262, 295; shipping diverted via Cape, 271, 273-4; Italian U-boat threat in, 293; air power dominant factor in, 293; proposed evacuation of Eastern basin, 297; additional reinforcements for, 299; convoy passed through to Alexandria, 301; sea route closed except for occasional military convoys, 305; situation at end of 1940, 419; first encounter with Luftwaffe, 420-2; restrictions on submarine warfare removed, 439; German fears for their communications in, 473; U-boats transferred to, 473-4; Coastal Command squadron detached to, 510; situation in June, 1941, 515; submarines reinforced, 516; Red Sea returns to Med. Command, 518; stores and men taken to Tobruk (table), 520; attacks on enemy convoys, 524-7; enemy shipping losses (tables), 528, 537; submarine strength, mid-November 1941, 536; battle squadron eliminated, 538; possibility of withdrawal from, 539; capital ships in, August 1941, 554
Medway, H.M.S.: 49
'Menace', Operation (expedition to Dakar), 261, 300, 308-20

2S*

Merchant Shipping, Allied: essential element of sea power, 7; Admiralty assumes control of, 21, 45; numbers of ships armed, 22, 46; numbers and tonnage of, 1939, 42 & *n*; air threat to ports, 45; routing of, and lack of Eire bases, 46; U-boat war on denounced by Germany, 1936, 52; German instructions for war on, 55; unrestricted war on, 56, 103-4; suspension during *Rawalpindi* operations, 87; ships above 15 and under 9 knots excluded from convoy, 93-4; co-operation of owners and masters, 94; higher loss among unescorted ships, 94-5; degaussing of ships, 101; losses to Dec. 1939, 106; over-reliance on A.A. defence, 106, 109; provision of A.A. gunners, 110; evasive routing, 113; losses from mining, 126-8; losses from U-boats, Jan.-May 1940, 131-3; Danish ships not allowed in convoys, 133; unrestricted air war on, 137; air attacks off East Coast, 138; lack of A.A. guns for, 139; Inspector of Merchant Navy Gunnery appointed, 140; plastic armour and other devices, 140; losses from air attack, Jan.-June 1940, 138, 142-4; loss increased by diversion of escorts, 253; diverted to North-West approaches, 263; steady stream of independent sailings, 270; protection in South Atlantic, 273; resistance to armed merchant raiders, 279; losses from raiders, 1940, 280; diversion to West Coast ports, 322; Grimsby fishing fleet attacked, 322; firing on unidentified aircraft, 322-3; losses from minelaying, 1940, 328; losses from air attack, 1940-41, 322; tonnage in East Coast and Channel convoys, Jan.-June 1941, 333; losses from U-boats, July-Oct. 1940, 348-9; 350-1; weekly Trade Protection Meeting, Admiralty, 350; new measures of protection, 350-1, 353; sinkings by U-boat, Nov.-Dec. 1940, 353-4; losses in battle cruiser sortie, Jan.-March 1941, 379; sinkings by U-boat and aircraft, Jan.-Feb. 1941, 362-3; new A.A. protection, 363-4; sinkings among stragglers, 363; sinkings by raider, Jan.-Feb. 1941, 364; prisoners released at Mogadishu, 426; speed limits for convoys reconsidered, 457; independent and convoyed ships compared, 458; tonnage using Thames, and losses, 1941, 499; supply of balloons and protective devices, 500; losses from air attack, 1941, 500; losses by marine casualties, 1941, 501; losses by German air attacks, April-Dec. 1941 (table), 508; sinkings by U-boat, April-June, 1941, 463-4, July-Sept., 466-8, Oct., 473, and Nov., 475; losses raised by entry of Japan, 475; C.A.M. ships to sail under Red Ensign, 477; gallant behaviour in Malta convoy 'Substance', 523; losses by warship and merchant raiders (table), 541; captured ships used as supply ships to raiders, Appendix N, 608; abstract of losses and causes, Appendix R, 615. *See also* Defensively Equipped Merchant Ships.

Merchant Shipping, Enemy: attempts to reach home, Dec. 1939, 89; ordered to neutral ports, 121; losses by aircraft minelaying, April-May 1940, 125; losses by air attack, 1940, 144, 323; interceptions en route to Germany, 149-50; scuttling policy when intercepted, 150; losses by capture or scuttling to 5.4.1940, 151; restrictions on attacks on relaxed, 172, 337; watch on in neutral American ports, and interceptions, 276; attack on, in Mediterranean, restricted, 305; attacks on German coastal traffic, 333; Italian losses, 1940, 307; extension of 'sink at sight' zones, 338, 502; tables of attacks by aircraft, 1940-41, 339-40; captures at Mogadishu, 426; losses in Mediterranean, Jan.-May 1941, 439; tonnage sunk, Jan.-June 1941, 502; areas of, relative importance, 503-4; use by night of English Channel, 505; air attacks on, April-Dec. 1941, (table), 507; causes of slow success of air offensive on, 509; comparative results of minelaying and direct attack, (table), 512; Mediterranean losses, June-Sept. 1941 (table), 528; ditto, Oct.-Dec. 1941, 537; captures at Bandur-Shahpur, 529

Merchant Shipping, Neutral: Hitler extends 'sink at sight' to, 349; U.S. ships allowed in Red Sea, 426, 517; losses and causes, Appendix R, 615

Merignac, near Bordeaux: enemy air base for attacks on shipping, 349

Mers-el-Kebir: *see* Oran

Mersey: *see* Liverpool

Methil: convoys from Bergen, 93; terminal moved to Tyne, 130

Meyrick, Vice-Admiral Sir S.: 48; succeeded by Admiral Kennedy-Purvis, 276

Michel, German raider: conduct of captain, 279; fitting out, 368

Mid-Ocean Meeting Points (MOMPS): introduced, 471; escorts strengthened up to, 475

Middle East: build-up of Allied forces in via Cape, 271, 274, 448; air power reinforced from Takoradi, 320; monthly convoys to, 391; need for increased air forces, 422; second priority for fighters after home, 449; one naval authority in, Red Sea Command transferred, 518: steady reinforcement of, 552

Midget submarines: attack on Malta, 523. *See also* Human torpedoes

Mimi Horn, German m.v.: intercepted by *Transylvania*, 150

Minelaying, British, by aircraft: development of, 123; search for suitable type, 124; numbers laid, April-May 1940, 125; Admiralty requests for, 261, 335; main effort for anti-invasion targets, 335; table of R.A.F. campaign, 1940-41, 336; from *Formidable* at Mogadishu, 426; summary of effort against enemy ships, Brest, 487; policy between Admiralty, Coastal and Bomber Commands, 509-10; R.A.F. minelaying, April-Dec. 1941 (table), 511; comparative results, minelaying and direct attack (table), 512

INDEX

Minelaying, British, by warships: on East Coast, 45, 90, 96-7, 125-6; Northern Barrage anticipated by Germans, 55; conversion of train ferries for, 64, 96; Scapa controlled minefields, 81 & *n*; Dover Straits barrage, 95-6, 104; Northern Barrage plans, 97, failure, 264; in Heligoland Bight, 97-8; British magnetic mines, 99; in German mined area, 123; deep fields off Moray Firth, 126, 130; doubtful merit of defensive fields, creating focal areas, 130, 263; Operation 'Wilfred', Norway, 156-8; off Ijmuiden, 207-8; at Oran to prevent French Fleet escape, 243; south of St George's Channel, 263; East Coast barrier completed, 263, 334; interrupted by lack of escorts, 264; Orkneys-Faeröes-Iceland-Greenland, 264, 266, 334, 390; in track of enemy coastal convoys, 333; anti-invasion lays by destroyers, 334-5; by submarines, Mediterranean, 425; off Italian ports, Battle for Crete, 440; by Coastal Forces, home waters, 500; by *Manxman* off Leghorn, 523-4; list of minelayers, Appendix D, 579
Minelaying, Enemy: German illegal use, British retaliation, 44; threat to estuaries and ports, 45, 100; in Baltic and Heligoland approaches, 55, 66; by U-boats off British bases, 56, 104; off Loch Ewe, *Nelson* damaged, 78, 87-8; effect of magnetic mine threat, 88; sortie in central North Sea, 89; North Sea declared area, 98; magnetic mine not new, British counter-measures, 99; magnetic mine recovered, 100; losses due to, 100-2; field laid off Tyne, 102; mine stocks when war began, 102; principal cause of shipping losses, 1939, 106; armed merchant raiders equipped for, 111; extension of in 1940, 126; by U-boats, S.W. Approaches, 132; by aircraft, April-May, 1940, 143, 322; at Brest during evacuation, 234; to protect invasion forces for U.K., 255; by raider off Cape Agulhas, 280-1; by raider off Auckland, 183; by raider off Australia, 286; magnetic mine threat overcome, 326-7, 502; acoustic mine in use, 326-7, 328, 498; losses from, 1940, 328; off Texel, 334; by raider off New Zealand, 385; by aircraft in Suez Canal, 423; in Malta harbours, 438; against coastal traffic, home waters, 498; barrage in Sicilian Channel, 530
Minesweeping, British: Staff Division formed for, 22-3, 99; need for magnetic sweeps, 88; magnetic sweeps developed, 99-101; sweeps by aircraft, 101, 127; enemy use of explosive sweep destructors, 127; first LL trawlers, 127; LL sweepers sent to Holland, 206; off Ostend, 211; acoustic sweeps in Thames Estuary, 327; night sweeping started, 327; building programme increased, 329; Scapa minesweepers for escort groups, 452; development in second year of war, 498; Nore Command, numbers of mines swept, 499; mine-

Minesweeping, British—*cont.*
sweepers in commission, etc., 1939, Appendix D, 582
Minesweeping, Enemy: in Norway invasion, 164; improvement in technique, 510; in western Baltic, 514
Mistral, French destroyer: arrives in Britain, 240
Mo: detachment landed at, 191-2
Mobile Balloon Barrage Flotilla: *see* Balloon Barrage
Mobile Naval Base Defence Organisation (M.N.B.D.O.): manned by Royal Marines, 25; intended for Suda Bay, Crete, 424
Mobilisation: rapidity of, 24-5
Mogadishu: mined by *Formidable* aircraft, Merchant Navy prisoners released, 426
Mohamed Ali el-Kebir, s.s.: sunk off Ireland, 349
Mohawk, H.M.S.: lost in attacking Libya convoy, 432
Molde: naval party lands at, 183; reinforcements for, 185; evacuation, 188-9
Mombasa: transport of troops to, 274
Mona's Queen, s.s.: sunk in Dunkirk evacuation, 222
Montcalm, French cruiser: evacuation of Namsos, 189; passes Gibraltar, 309; arrives Dakar, 315
Montevideo: *Graf Spee* takes refuge at, 119-21
Montrose: air patrol from, 36
Montrose, H.M.S.: in Dunkirk evacuation, 221; damaged, 222
Mopan, s.s.: sunk by *Admiral Scheer*, 288
Moray Firth: deep minefield off, 126, 130; U-boats active off, 130, 132, 263; convoy attacked by aircraft in, 326
Morea, German s.s.: captured by *Hasty* off Portugal, 150
Mosjöen: detachment landed at, 191
Motor Anti-Submarine Boats, Motor Launches: *see* Coastal Craft
Mountbatten, Captain Lord Louis: in Battle for Crete, 441, 443
Mozambique Channel: *Graf Spee* in, 116; *Admiral Scheer* in, 369
Munsterland, German supply ship; sunk (1944), 607
Murmansk: *Bremen* arrives at, 65; *City of Flint* arrives at, 70, 113; German raider fitted out at, 111; German tanker reaches Narvik from, 180; German plan to occupy fails, 485, 506; first convoys to and from, 492; Archangel ships diverted to, 495
Murray, Commodore L. W.: takes over Newfoundland Command, 453
Mussolini: directive on naval war plans, 294-5; air transport for Africa from Sicily, 528

Naiad, H.M.S.: escorts convoy W.S. 5A, 292
Namsos: troops sent to, 180; naval party landed at, 181-2; heavy air attack on, 183; naval support at, 187; decision to evacuate, 188; evacuation successful, 189-90
Nantes: transport of B.E.F. to, 63; threatened by German advance, 229; evacuation from, 234, 236
Naples: enemy convoys from, 526

Narvik: iron ore convoy from, 82; enemy iron ore traffic from, 97, 144, 149, 156; plan 'R.4' to occupy, 157; German ships bound for, 160-1; German landing at, 2,000 troops in destroyers, 163-5, 170; first Battle of, 10th April 1940, 172; naval air attack unsuccessful, 177; second Battle of, 13th April, 177-8; setback to initial enemy landing, 180; first Allied troops for, 180; slender German hold on, 185; Cabinet gives first priority to, 186; close blockade of, 187; convoy N.P. 1 arrives, plan for immediate attack abandoned, 190; Lord Cork in supreme command, 191; difficulties at, 192; final assault on 192-3,; evacuated, 193-4; German invasion threat and, 249; new offensive against iron-ore traffic from, 338; ships in harbour wrongly identified as *Lützow*, etc., 393

Narwhal, H.M.S.: at sinking of U.63, 131; sunk, 266

Nauru: attacked by raiders, 283-4, 367, 546

Naval Air Division, Admiralty: work of, 26

Naval Control Service: work of, at the ports, 21, 45; value of, 94

Naval Construction, British, 1939: 50; 1939-1941 naval building programmes, Appendix F, 588

Naval Construction, German: 52, 57, 59

Naval Strength, British, 1939: 50

Naze, The (Essex coast): sinkings off, 331

Nelson, H.M.S.: 47; Home Fleet patrol, 65; sortie to intercept *Gneisenau*, 71; damaged by mine off Loch Ewe, 78, 87-8; covers Narvik convoy, 82; operations after attack on *Rawalpindi*, 84-7; again based at Scapa, 268; search for *Admiral Scheer*, 289; search for battle cruisers, 373-4, 376-7; sighted by raider *Atlantis*, 382; to reinforce Home Fleet, 483; in Malta convoy 'Halberd', damaged, 530; suggested for Eastern Fleet, 555

Neptune, H.M.S.: 48; intercepts *Adolph Woermann*, 116; patrolling in South Atlantic, 117; search for *Admiral Scheer*, 290; arrives at Alexandria, 295; expedition to Duala, 320; in Scapa at beginning of *Bismarck* operations, 396; meeting with 'Q'-ship off Sierra Leone, 549; sinks *Gonzenheim*, 607; sent to Malta, 534; sunk by mines off Tripoli, 535

Neptunia, Italian m.v.: sunk by *Upholder*, 526

Nestor, H.M.A.S.: sinks U.127, 478

Neutrals: delay to shipping by blockade, 43; German use of for supply ships, 55; use of Allied convoys, 95; warned by Germans from war zone, 104; U.S. Neutrality Patrol order, 112, 612; Scandinavian, advantage to Germany, 162; reaction to attack on French Fleet, Oran, 244; 'sink at sight' extended to neutral shipping, 349

Nevada, U.S. battleship: seriously damaged at Pearl Harbour, 562

New York, German s.s.: returns to Germany, 70

New Zealand: ports mined by raider auxiliary, 385; minesweeping trawlers built in, 498

New Zealand Division, Royal Navy: 49, 585; cruisers at Auckland, 559; tentative dis-

New Zealand Division, Royal Navy—*cont.*
positions in Pacific, 561-2

New Zealand Star, m.v.: convoy for Alexandria, 301; 'Tiger' convoy, tanks, for Egypt, 437

Newcastle, H.M.S.: joins Home Fleet, 69; sortie to intercept *Gneisenau*, 71; covers West Indies tanker convoy, 76; operations after sinking of *Rawalpindi*, 84-7; joins Admiral Vivian, Harstad evacuation, 198; joins South American Division, 285, 290; meets through convoy from Gibraltar, 301

Newfoundland: bases in, leased to the Americans, 347-8; Newfoundland Escort Force constituted, 453, 475; separate naval command established, 453; U.S. Navy take over base at Argentia in, 455; R.C.A.F. air escorts from, 460; U.S. planes fly 'Neutrality Patrols' from, 460, 472

Newhaven: German invasion plans, 249

Newport, Mon.: first B.E.F. convoys, 63

Newton Beech, s.s.: sunk by *Graf Spee*, 115

Niagara, s.s.: sunk by raider mine, salvage of bullion, 283, 547

Nicholl, Captain A. D.: commands *Penelope* in Force K, Malta, 532

Nicholson, Brigadier C.: defence of Calais, 215

Nigeria, H.M.S.: cover for Atlantic convoys, 292; gives close support to Lofoten Is. raid, 341; watch on northern passages, 371; search for enemy battle cruisers, 376; patrols Atlantic convoy route, 378; reconnaissance of Spitzbergen, 488; action with enemy convoy off North Cape, 489

Noble, Admiral Sir P.: 49; C.-in-C., Western Approaches (Liverpool), 360

Nordmark, German tanker: meets *Admiral Scheer*, 290, 369, 370; fuels *Kormoran*, 386; Appendix N, 607

Nore Command: responsibility of, 44; local defence forces, 47; menace of enemy mining, 100-1; shortage of destroyers, 127; magnetic minesweeping in, 128; sweeps against U-boats ineffective, 130; exposed state of shipping off Southend, 137; fighter aircraft protection for shipping, 138; French submarine flotilla in, 149; reinforced on threat to Low Countries, 205; operations off Holland, 207, 210; ships for Dunkirk evacuation, 216; Auxiliary Patrol developed in, 251; reinforced for invasion threat, 252-3, 258; acoustic and magnetic minesweeping by, 327; losses from enemy minelaying in, 328; offensive sweeps by coastal craft from, 330; mines swept by, 1941, 499

Norfolk, H.M.S.: joins Home Fleet, 69-70; in Atlantic hunting group, 70; operations after attack on *Rawalpindi*, 84-7; damaged by air raid on Scapa, 155; in hunting group, Freetown, 263, 290; covers Sierra Leone route, 386; escorts two North Atlantic convoys, 392; takes part in action with *Bismarck* and *Prinz Eugen*, 396-8, 410

Norge, Norwegian coast defence ship: disabled at Narvik, 165

Norman, Lieut. E. D.: in *Upright*, sinks *Armando Diaz*, 425

INDEX

Normandy: Allied landing in, 12
Normannia, s.s. sunk in Dunkirk evacuation, 222
North, Admiral Sir Dudley: 48; Force H not under orders of, 242; attitude towards Oran operation, 244; French movements, Admiralty instructions, 309-10; passage of French force, Toulon to Dakar, 311-4; relieved in North Atlantic Command, 314
North Africa: Allied landing in, 4, 12; French naval bases in 42; campaign against Italian routes to, 305; Auchinleck's Libyan offensive, 474
North Atlantic Station (Gibraltar): protection against raiders, 43; light forces of, 48; loss of *Armanistan*, 132; position of Force H in, 242; French movements, Admiralty instructions, 309; convoy escorts from, 344
North Channel: Italian U-boats in, 347
North Foreland: enemy mining by disguised merchant ship, 127; tonnage of shipping off, 1941, 333
North Sea: difficulties of continuous air patrol, 37; directive to Home Fleet, 44; German naval policy in, 54-5; weakness of air reconnaissance, 72, 90, 197; enemy mined area, 98; southern area and and invasion threat, 248-9; submarine patrols against U-boats in, 333; 'sink at sight' zone extended to, 338; Coastal Command principal duty to watch exits of, 355; aircraft transferred from to Western Approaches, 364
Northern Barrage: *See* Minelaying, British
Northern Ireland: use of bases in, 46, 352; shipping diverted to, 349; *Empress of Britain* bombed off Donegal Bay, 351; long-range fighters sent to, 362-3; establishment of advance fuelling base in, 451; air strength in, 460, 476; German U-boats stationed off, 462, 467
Northern Patrol: Coastal Command co-operation with, 35, watch on northern exits to Atlantic, 46; work of, 1939-40, 67; cruisers withdrawn from, 68, 70; use of Sullom Voe, Shetlands, 74; Home Fleet cover to, 75; loss of *Rawalpindi*, 82-7; reduced by magnetic mine danger, 88-9; ships intercepted, Jan.-April 1940, 149-51; vulnerability, 249; cover against invasion of Eire, 251; efficiency reduced by removal of trawlers, 264; heavy losses from U-boats, 265; A.M.C.s to work from Halifax, 265, 271
Northwood: Coastal Command Headquarters at, 36
Norway: enemy control in, 8; air patrol to, 36; attitude towards Northern Barrage, 97; convoys from, started November 1939, 93, 130; first air attacks on convoy from, March 1940, 143; German campaign in, 143, 145, 162-202; last trade convoy from, 148; submarine patrols off, March 1940, 149; attitude towards *Altmark*, 152; escape of Royal Family and Government, 165; decision to evacuate central Norway, 185; King and Government evacuated from Molde, 188; decision to retire from, 192;

Norway—*cont.*
205; lessons of campaign, 199-201; German gains from campaign, 201; Greece and Crete campaigns compared, 447; Government give aid and intelligence for Lofoten Island raid, 341; whale-oil factory ships sunk, 384; five Norwegian ships escape from Gothenburg, 391
Norwegian waters: German violation of, 70, 97; British minelaying in, 123, 156-8, 337; sea and air strikes in, 262; British submarine patrols temporarily abandoned, 333, restarted, 334; 'sink at sight' zone extended to, 338; enemy shipping traffic in, 504, 514; small raids in by Norwegian forces, 511-2; Vestfiord and Vaagsö raids, 513-4
Nubian, H.M.S.: evacuation of Namsos, 189; in battle off Cape Matapan, 430
Nürnberg, German cruiser: under C.-in-C., East, 57; minelaying off Tyne, torpedoed by *Salmon*, 102; repairing during Norway campaign, 163; arrives at Trondheim, 260; returns to Kiel, 260

O.13, Dutch submarine: sunk in North Sea, 266
O.21, Dutch submarine: sinks U.95 in Mediterranean, 474
O.22, Dutch submarine: sunk in North Sea, 267
O.23, Dutch submarine: success in Mediterranean, 525
O.24, Dutch submarine: success in Mediterranean, 525
Oban: convoy assembly base, 497
Ocean Boarding Vessels: replace A.M.C.s in Western Patrol, 265
Oceania, Italian m.v.: damaged by *Unbeaten*, 525; sunk by *Upholder*, 526
O'Conor, Captain R. C.: commands *Neptune* at Malta, 534
Odenwald, German m.v.: captured by U.S. cruiser *Omaha*, 546
Oerlikon gun: ordered for merchant ship defence, 139-40
Oil Pioneer, tanker: sunk in Narvik evacuation, 194
Oklahoma, U.S. battleship: capsized at Pearl Harbour, 562
Ole Jacob, Norwegian tanker: captured by *Atlantis*, 282; fuels raider *Orion*, 546; sunk by aircraft off Spain, 504, 608
Oliver, Captain R. D.: in *Devonshire*, sinks raider *Atlantis*, 545
Omaha, U.S. cruiser: captures blockade runner *Odenwald*, 546
Onslow, Captain R. F. J.: attack on *Richelieu* at Dakar, 245
Operational Intelligence Centre, Admiralty: work of, 18-22
Operations: *see under* respective code names, 'Aerial', 'Dynamo', etc.
Operations Division, Admiralty: work of, 20-21
Orama, s.s.: sunk in Narvik evacuation, 194, 196
Oran: French Fleet at, 241; action against French ships, 242-5, 314; Admiralty instructions after action, 309

Orfordness: enemy mining off, 126; ships sunk off, 331
Orion, H.M.S.: 48; arrives Alexandria from West Indies, 295; Battle off Cape Matapan, 427; evacuation from Greece, 435; in Battle for Crete, damaged, 441, 445
Orion, German armed merchant raider: first cruise, 278-9, 282-4; refits in Marianas, 367; resumes cruise, 382, 386; meets *Atlantis*, 545; fuels from *Ole Jacob*, 546; returns to Gironde, summary of cruise, 547; Appendix M, 604
Orizaba, German s.s.: wrecked off Norway, 150
Orkneys: air patrols off, 37; contraband control in, 43-4; shortage of labour in, 78-9; defensive minefield creates focal area for shipping, 130, 263; defence of convoys by naval fighters, 143; naval bombers from sink *Königsberg*, 172; naval air strikes from, 262; convoy protection from, 263; minefield to Faeröes, 264. *See also* Scapa
Orkneys and Shetlands Command: established, 48
Orzel, Polish submarine: escapes to Rosyth, 69; sinks transport off Norway, 164; sinks tanker off Norway, 179*n*
Oslo: German landing at, 163-4; *Blücher* sunk at, 165; main point of German invasion, 176, 180; *Admiral Scheer* attacked at, 493; ice conditions at, 514
Ostend: plans for blocking, 208; evacuations from 211; blocking abandoned, 211; R.A.F. attack invasion barges, 255
Otranto, s.s.: evacuation of Biscay ports, 233
Otranto Straits: action with enemy convoy in, 301
Ouragan, French destroyer: arrives in Britain, 240
Ouvry, Lt-Comdr J. G. D.: dissects enemy magnetic mine, 100
Oxley, H.M.S.: accidentally sunk by *Triton*, 66

P.32, H.M.S.: lost off Tripoli, 526
P.33, H.M.S.: lost off Tripoli, 526
Pacific Fleet, U.S. Navy: strength of, 560; agreement between Admirals Hart and Phillips, 561; attacked at Pearl Harbour, 562-3; survivors withdrawn to West Coast bases, 569-70
Palliser, Rear-Admiral A. F. E.: Chief of Staff to Admiral Phillips, 558; reports landing at Kuantan, 564-5
Panama: German raider off, 283
Pantellaria: proposal to capture, 304; E-boats attack Malta convoy 'Substance', 522
Paris: fall of, 229
Paris, French battleship: arrives in Britain, 240
Parramatta, H.M.A.S.: sunk by U-boat, 520
Parry, Captain W. E.: H.M.S. *Achilles*, 116
Parthian, H.M.S.: sinks French submarine in Syria campaign, 517
Partridge, Captain R. T., R.M.: sinking of *Königsberg*, 172
Passat (ex-Norwegian *Storstad*): German minelaying by, 286, 608
Patroclus, H.M.S.: sunk by U-boat, 265, 351

Patrol Service, Royal Naval: minesweeping by, 23. *See also* Auxiliary Patrol
Patterson, Captain W. R.: commands *King George V* in *Bismarck* operations, 396
Pearl Harbour: U.S. Pacific Fleet at, 560; Japanese attack on, probably inspired by Taranto, 5; lesson of, and Brest attacks, 491; U-boat preparations after, 482; summary of attack, 562-3
Pegasus, H.M.S.: at Scapa when *Royal Oak* was sunk, 73; on convoy duties, 363; converted to carry fighters, 476-7
Pegram, Captain F. H.: lands naval party at Namsos, 181-2; Commodore, South American Division, 285
Peirse, Air Vice-Marshal R. E. C.: visits Home Fleet, 80
Penelope, H.M.S.: 48; joins Home Fleet, 151; at Scapa, 158; leaves for Norway, 159; to assist *Glowworm*, 160; in Norwegian campaign, 161, 174; runs ashore, 175; sent to Malta, 494; in Force K, Malta, 532; convoy actions, 532-3; damaged by mines off Tripoli, 535
Pennland, s.s.: sunk in evacuation from Greece, 436
Pennsylvania, U.S. battleship: escaped injury at Pearl Harbour, 562
Penzance, H.M.S.: sunk by U-boat, 344
Perseus, H.M.S.: sunk by mine off Greece, stoker's remarkable escape, 537
Persia: *see* Iran
Persian Gulf: transport of troops to, 274; Operation 'Countenance' in, 529
Personnel, Naval: numbers, 1939 and 1944, 24
Perth, H.M.A.S.: 48-9; Battle off Cape Matapan, 428; evacuation from Greece, 436; Battle for Crete, 440; evacuation from Crete, 445
Pétain, Marshal: asks for an armistice, 229
Petsamo: *Hipper* sortie for shipping from, 260; enemy traffic from, Russian request for attack, 485, 495; attack on, 486
Phillips, Captain A. J. L.: commands *Norfolk* in *Bismarck* operations, 396
Phillips, Admiral Sir T. S. V.: dispositions on threat to Norway, 158; appointed C.-in-C., Eastern Fleet, 494; arrives Capetown in *Prince of Wales*, 557; meets Field Marshal Smuts and arrives Colombo, 558; visit to Manila, 560-1; agreement with Admiral Hart, 561; effect of Pearl Harbour on movements of, 563; leaves Singapore, 564; alters course for Kuantan; force attacked by aircraft, 566; lost in *Prince of Wales*, 567-8
Phoebe, H.M.S.: joins Home Fleet, 262; escorts Convoy W.S.5 B, 391-2; evacuation from Greece, 436; escorts 'Tiger' convoy for Egypt, 437; evacuation from Crete, 445; campaign in Syria, 516
Pinguin, German raider: leaves Germany, 279; in South Atlantic, 282; supplies at Kerguelen, 284; sinkings by, 286; meets *Admiral Scheer* and attacks whaling fleet, 367, 370, 384, 386; sunk by *Cornwall*, 383-5; Appendix M, 604

INDEX

Piorun, Polish destroyer; in *Bismarck* operations, 414
Piræus: military convoy for, 421; 'Lustre' convoys for, 424; Italian sortie against leads to Matapan action, 427; convoys to resumed, 430; heavy German air attacks, 434; evacuated, 436
Plans Division, Admiralty: work of, 17-20
Plate, River: Allied control off, 4; cruisers concentrate off, 117; Battle of, 118-21, 153; cover for trade from, 274; cruiser concentration off, 1940, 285
Plover, H.M.S.: Dover Straits mine barrage, 96
Plymouth: suggested base for Home Fleet battleships, 251; Home Fleet cruiser at, 252. *See also* Western Approaches Command
Plymouth Command: separated from Western Approaches, 360; No. 19 Group, Coastal Command, formed for, 360
Pola, Italian cruiser, sunk in Battle of Matapan, 429-30
Poland: German plans to attack, 53-4; escape of warships to England, 69; German hopes after campaign ends, 103, 112; President returns from France, 237; troops conveyed to Tobruk, 519
Polyarnoe: German plan to occupy, 485; British submarines sent to, 493
Poole: evacuation from Cherbourg and St Malo, 233; possible limit of German invasion, 258
Port Hobart, m.v.: sunk by *Admiral Scheer*, 290
Port Said: minesweepers at, 49
Port Stanley: auxiliary war vessels at, 274
Portland: force at, 31.8.1939, 47; Anti-Submarine School moved to Dunoon, 359
Portland, German supply ship: sunk (1943), 607
Portsmouth: transport of B.E.F., 44, 63-4; local defence forces, 47; U-boat minelaying off, 127; striking force base against invasion, 249, 252
Portsmouth Command: assists Nore Command, 207; ships for Dunkirk evacuation, 216; evacuation of Havre, 231; evacuation of Cherbourg and St Malo, 232-3; evacuation of Channel Islands, 239
Portugal: plans to occupy Atlantic islands of, 273; ships sunk by U-boats off, 353; minesweeping trawlers built in, 498; blockade running from, 503, 552
Pound, Admiral Sir Dudley: First Sea Lord, service of, 15-17; intervention in conduct of operations, 27, 202; visits to Home Fleet, 80, 88; dispositions on threat to Norway, 158, 161; meets Admiral Darlan at Bordeaux, 237; on position in Eastern Mediterranean, 296-7; on ferrying aircraft to Malta, 298; on proposal to capture Pantellaria, 304; movement of French squadron from Toulon, and relief of Admiral North, 312, 314; on stopping supplies to Libya, 431-2; proposed withdrawal of heavy ships, Mediterranean, 539; on plans for Eastern Fleet, 555; opposes despatch of *Prince of Wales*, 555-6; agrees to her going to Capetown, 557; loss of capital ships off Malaya, 567

Prague, s.s.: damaged in Dunkirk evacuation, 225
Pretoria Castle, H.M.S.: search for *Admiral Scheer*, 290
Pridham-Wippell, Vice-Admiral H. D.: raid into Otranto Straits, 301; Battle off Cape Matapan, 427-431; evacuation from Greece, 435-6; Battle for Crete, 444, 448; loss of flagship *Barham*, 534
Prien, U-boat Commander: sinks *Royal Oak* at Scapa, 73-4; U-boat 'ace' in Battle of Atlantic, 348-9; commands U.47, and lost in her, 365
Primauguet, French cruiser: arrives Casablanca from Dakar, 315
Prince Albert, special service vessel: raid on Vaagsö, 513
Prince Charles, special service vessel: raid on Vaagsö, 514
Prince David, H.M.C.S.: search for raider *Thor*, 383
Prince of Wales, H.M.S.: at Scapa, May 1941, 394; *Bismarck* operations, 396, 398-417; damaged in action, 406; failure of 14-in. armament, 417; under repair, 483; allocated to Eastern Fleet, 491; Atlantic Charter meeting in, 569, 470; leaves Clyde for Singapore, 494; in Force H for 'Halberd' convoy to Malta, 530; needed in Home Fleet, 554-5; Admiralty object to Far East move, 556; arrives Capetown, 557, and Colombo, 558; leaves Singapore, attacked by aircraft, 566; sunk, 567-9
Prince Leopold, special service vessel: raid on Vaagsö, 514
Prince Robert, H.M.C.S.: intercepts supply ship *Weser*, 277, 607
Princess J. Charlotte, special service vessel: defective, withdrawn from Vaagsö raid, 513
Princess Maud, s.s.: in Dunkirk evacuation, 227
Princess Victoria, H.M.S.: minelaying in East Coast barrier, 125-6; defensive field off Dutch coast, 208
Prinz Eugen, German cruiser: to complete in 1940, 57n; absent from Norway campaign; completed at Kiel, damaged by aircraft, 261; trials completed, 368; preparations for Atlantic sortie, 376; to be joined by *Gneisenau*, 393; ready for service, 394; damaged by mine, 395; leaves Gdynia for Atlantic with *Bismarck*, 395; sighted by *Suffolk*, 397; Home Fleet loses touch with, 400; in action with Home Fleet, 401-9; escapes to Brest, 409, 417, 483; damaged at Brest, 487; undocked at Brest, 491; details of, Appendix M, 605
Procida, s.s.: sunk by Force K, 533
Protector, H.M.S.: arrives at Alexandria from Home Fleet, 295
Provence, French battleship: at Oran, 241; damaged at Oran, 244
'Puma', Operation (plans to capture Atlantic islands), 380
Python, German supply ship: crew of *Atlantis* transferred to, 545; intercepted on way to refuel U-boats, 480, 470, 546

652   INDEX

Q ships: *see* Decoy ships
Queen *of the Channel*, s.s.: sunk in Dunkirk evacuation, 221
Queen *Elizabeth*, H.M.S.: search for enemy battle cruisers off Iceland, 377 & *n*; with Force H, escorts 'Tiger' convoy, Mediterranean, 437; in Battle for Crete, 444; damaged by human torpedoes, Alexandria, 538-9, 555
Queen *Elizabeth*, s.s.: maiden voyage, 270

'R.4' Plan, Norway: 157, 161; abandoned, 162, 166, 178
Rabaul, m.v.: sunk by *Atlantis*, 382
Radar: introduction of airborne, 5; lack of in *Newcastle* during *Rawalpindi* operations, 86; origin of fighter direction, 109; in *Admiral Graf Spee*, 118; nullified by high cliffs, Norway, 184; need for in Iceland, Greenland, and Faeröes, 266; need for in escort vessels, 331-2; in aircraft, of little use, 350; in German battle cruisers, efficiency, 373; use of in anti-U-boat warfare, 357-8, 480-1; need for in Mediterranean ships, 422; use of during operations against *Bismarck*, 397, 401, 404-5, 409; in Battle off Cape Matapan, 430; delay in fitting longrange sets in aircraft, 451; interception of shipping by aircraft control from ground stations, 505; in Wellington aircraft sent to Malta, 527
Raeder, Admiral: 51-4; favours unrestricted war on shipping, 56, 103-4; 'Z' Plan of, 57, 59; plans for increased U-boat production, 60; first Atlantic sortie by heavy ships, 83; report on sinking of *Rawalpindi*, 87-8; plans for armed merchant raiders, 111-2, 116; submarine minelaying in Clyde too dangerous, 131; urges bomber attacks on convoys, 143; plans to invade Norway, value of bases, 162-3; invasion of Belgium and Holland, 206; unable to dispute Home Fleet control, June 1940, 230; on reduction of British convoy escorts, 253; plans for invasion, Operation 'Sealion', 254-5; on occupation of Atlantic islands, 273, 380; suspends work on *Graf Zeppelin*, 368; congratulates Lütjens on battle cruiser sortie, 374, 379; congratulates *Atlantis* on a year's raiding, 382; disputes with Göring over control of aircraft, 362; plans for *Bismarck* and *Prinz Eugen*, 394; plan to occupy Murmansk and Polyarnoe, 485; failure to convince Hitler on struggle at sea, 490; on position in North Africa, 536
Raiders, enemy, surface: use of heavy ships as, 6; menace to seaborne trade, 35; air patrols to locate, 37; anticipated use of, 45; conversions delayed, 53; action with naval forces not to be sought, 55; plans for 26 German merchant raiders, 111; start of attacks approved by Hitler, 112-3; hunting groups for, 113 *et seq.*; air attack on merchant raiders limited by Hague Rules, 144; A.M.C.s no match for, 265; threat to Atlantic convoys, 266; action with *Alcantara*, 277; details and supply plans,

Raiders, enemy surface—*cont.*
277-9; operations of, 279-87, 364, 368-87; use of aircraft by, 383; difficulty of piercing disguise of, 385, 387, 549; none at large at end of 1941, 541; fuelling rendezvous never discovered, 542; supply ships intercepted (table), 544; abstract of achievements, 1939-41 (table), 550; threat from relatively small, 551; performance data and losses caused, Appendix M, 604
Raikes, Vice-Admiral R. H. T.: commands Northern Patrol, 68; C.-in-C., South Atlantic, 275; diverts shipping east of Cape Verde, 290
Ramb I, Italian raider: 279, 426; sunk by *Leander*, 387; Appendix M, 605
Ramillies, H.M.S.: 47; escorts troop convoy for Gibraltar, 92; in Mediterranean, 295; meets through convoy from Gibraltar, 301; action off Cape Spartivento, 302; escorts convoy H.X. 106, 374; escorts W.S. 5B, 391-2; in *Bismarck* operations, 407-8; 410; in North Atlantic Escort Force, 555
Ramsay, Vice-Admiral B. H.: 48; responsible for Belgian coast operations, 207; plans port demolitions, Low Countries, 208; directs demolitions and blocking, 210; to control withdrawal of B.E.F., 212; evacuation from Boulogne, 213-4; assistance to Calais garrison, 215; evacuation from Dunkirk, 216-28
Ramsey, Vice-Admiral C. G.: 48
Ramsgate: in German invasion plans, 254; ships sunk off, 331
Rangitane, m.v.: sunk by *Orion*, 283
Ranja, Norwegian s.s.: escapes from Gothenburg, 391
Rauenfels, German s.s.: sunk by *Havock*, 175, 178
Raw, Captain S. M.: commands 1st Submarine Flotilla, Alexandria, 526
Rawalpindi, H.M.S.: sunk in action with *Scharnhorst*, 82-8, 115
Rawlings, Rear-Admiral H. B.: in Battle for Crete, 440-3, 445, 448; commands Force B, Malta, 534
Reconnaissance: *see* Intelligence
Red Sea: defence of, forces strengthened, 42, 49; position in, after French collapse, 241; closed to shipping until formation of convoys, 296; convoy protection, 307; Italian threat illusory, 419; U.S. declares no longer a 'combat zone', 426, 517, 612; Italian naval losses in, 426; shipping protection in, 427, 518; capture of Assab, 517; returns to Mediterranean Command, 518
Regensburg, German supply ship: at work in Pacific, 277-8; scuttled (1943), 607
Rekum, German supply ship: sunk (1944), 607
Renouf, Rear-Admiral E. de F.: troops conveyed to Malta, 421
Renown, H.M.S.: compared with *Scharnhorst*, 58; Home Fleet patrol, 63; in hunting group, Atlantic, 70, 114; sinks s.s. *Watussi*, 117; returns from Freetown, 131; interception of German shipping from Vigo, 150; returns to Scapa, 155; in Operation 'Wilfred', Norway, 159; in Norwegian

INDEX 653

Renown, H.M.S.—*cont.*
campaign, 160; action with *Gneisenau*, 165-6, 169, 176; returns to Scapa, 180; cover for returning Norwegian convoys, 197; movement to intercept *Gneisenau*, 259; flagship of Force H, 272; covers through convoy for Alexandria, 301; action off Cape Spartivento, 302-3; movement to intercept French squadron, Gibraltar, 312-3; search for enemy battle cruisers, Atlantic, 377; covers convoy 'Excess', 421; bombardment of Genoa, etc., 425; in *Bismarck* operations, 410-2; suggested for Eastern Fleet, 555; intercepts *Gonzenheim*, 607

Repulse, H.M.S.: 47; compared with *Scharnhorst*, 58; Home Fleet patrol, 65; sortie to intercept *Gneisenau*, 71; cover for Halifax convoy, 75; at Halifax during attack on *Rawalpindi*, 85; rejoins Home Fleet, 88; escorts first Canadian troop convoy, 89; with *Barham* when torpedoed, 90; escort of Halifax convoys, 114; returns to Scapa, 155, 158; leaves for Norway, 159; to assist *Glowworm*, 160; in Norwegian campaign, 161; unmodernised, 166; ordered to Vestfiord, 167, 169; joins Admiral Whitworth, 174; investigates enemy report, Iceland, 197; joins Admiral Vivian, 198; movement to intercept *Gneisenau*, 259; again based at Scapa, 268; search for *Admiral Scheer*, 289; cover for Atlantic convoys, 292; search for battle cruisers, 373-4; in *Bismarck* operations, 396, 407, 411; covers convoys off Newfoundland, 483; allocated to Eastern Fleet, 491; refitting at home, 554; proposed for Singapore, 556; at Colombo, 558; proposed visit to Port Darwin, 559; leaves Singapore, 564; sunk by aircraft, 566, 568-9

Reserves, Naval: strength and mobilisation of, 25; Appendix C, 575

Resolution, H.M.S.: 47; escorts first Canadian troop convoy, 89; escort of Halifax convoys, 114; joins Force H, 242; action against French Fleet, Oran, 242-4; in Halifax escort force, 270; expedition to Dakar, 309, 314; hit by shore batteries, Dakar, 317; hit by submarine torpedo, 318; refitting in America, 455, 554

Resource, H.M.S.: 48

Reuben James, U.S. destroyer: sunk while escorting British convoy, 472, 613

Revenge, H.M.S.: 47; escorts second Canadian troop convoy, 89; escort of Halifax convoys, 114, 270; ordered to stand by for *Bismarck* operations, 408; in North Atlantic Escort Force, 555

Reykjavik: landings at, 345; naval base established at, 345; control of Iceland Air Force from Combined Headquarters, 347, 452

Rhodes: proposed Commando attack on, 304; air attacks from, 424

Rhododendron, H.M.S.: sinks U.104, 353

Richelieu, French battleship: removal from Brest, 233; arrives Dakar, 240; action against at Dakar, 245, 473, 309, 317

Rio de Janeiro: cover for trade from, 274; cruiser concentration off, 285

Rio de Janeiro, German s.s.: sunk by *Orzel*, 164

Rio Grande, German supply ship: scuttled (1944), 607

Robb, Air Vice Marshal J. M.: O.C. No. 15 Group Coastal Command and responsible for Western Approaches, 360

Rockall: diversion of convoy routes off, 266

Rodney, H.M.S.: 47; Home Fleet patrol, 65; sortie to intercept *Gneisenau*, 71; covers Narvik convoy, 82; operations after attack on *Rawalpindi*, 84-7; defects in, 88; flag of C.-in-C., Home Fleet, 90; returns to Scapa, 155, 158; leaves for Norway, 159; in Norwegian campaign, 161, 166, 169, 172; slight damage by air attack, 171; returns to Scapa, 180, 186; cover for last Norwegian convoys, 197; again based at Scapa, 268; search for *Admiral Scheer*, 289; search for battle cruisers, 373-4; covers Halifax convoys, 376; sights enemy battle cruisers, 376; at Scapa, May 1941, 394; takes part in *Bismarck* operations, 407, 410, 412, 415; to refit in United States, 483, 554; in Malta convoy 'Halberd', 530; in Force H, aircraft for Malta, 533; suggested for Eastern Fleet, 555

Rolls Royce, H.M. trawler: 100 mines swept by, 499

Rommel, General: arrival with Afrika Korps, 423; supplies to, 431; submarine check to success of, 439; reports transport to North Africa stopped, 533

Rona, North; defensive minefield off, 263

Roope, Lt.-Comdr G. B.: H.M.S. *Glowworm*; engages *Hipper*, awarded posthumous V.C., 158, 196

Roosevelt, President: Neutrality Patrol order, 112; reaction to B.E.F. evacuation, 240; announces Red Sea no longer a combat zone, 426, 517; Atlantic meeting with Churchill, 470; policy on defence of Atlantic routes, 490; summary of moves by U.S. Government, Appendix P, 612

Rorqual, H.M.S.: sinks Italian U-boat, 425; carries supplies to Malta, 518

Rostock, German s.s.: captured off Spain, 150

Rosyth: Home Fleet base at, policy, 77-8; preferred to Clyde as temporary base, 80-1; Home Fleet main forces to use on invasion, 252; Home Fleet moves to, 257

Rosyth Command: responsibility of, 44; light forces of, 48; U-boat hunting group in, 132; assistance to Nore Command, 207, 250; contributes ships to Dunkirk evacuation, 221

Rosyth Escort Force: responsibility for East Coast convoys, 93; convoy difficulties in swept channels, 139

Rotherham, Comdr G. A.: carries out special reconnaissance during search for *Bismarck* and *Prinz Eugen*, 396

Rotterdam: German sea traffic with, 144; opposition to demolition of oil stocks, 208

Rouen: transport of B.E.F. stores to, 64; captured, 231

Rouen, s.s.: in Dunkirk evacuation, 226

Roumania: passage of oil from, 516

Rowley, Captain H. A.: in *Gloucester*, Battle for Crete, 441

Royal Air Force: absorption of R.N.A.S., 1918, 29; assistance to R.N., 33, 39; aircraft available for naval service, 35; weakness of North Sea reconnaissance, 72, 90; Home Fleet base policy and, 77; attacks limited by Hague Rules, 144; unrestricted attacks on shipping permitted after invasion of Norway, 145; harassment of enemy airfields, Norway, 187; in Norway campaign, tribute to, 196; in Dunkirk evacuation, complaints analysed, 217-8; evacuation of, from Brest, 234; German threat of invasion, 250-1, 253; German plan to neutralise before invasion, 254-5; Battle of Britain begins, 256; searches over South Atlantic, 276; weakness of reconnaissance, North Sea, 292; opposed to naval order re opening fire on unidentified aircraft, 323; extension of 'sink at sight' zones, 338; tables showing attacks at sea by R.A.F., 1940-1941, 339; tactical use of aircraft in Atlantic battle, 461; damage to enemy squadron at Brest, 487, 490; responsibility for anti-shipping operations, 503; attacks on enemy shipping, April-December 1941 (table), 507; air minelaying campaign, April-December 1941 (table), 511; supply Hurricanes for C.A.M.s, 477

Royal Air Force: Advanced Air Striking Force: transport to France, 63

Royal Air Force, Bomber Command: use of against German industrial targets, 1, 65; sinking of *Tirpitz* by, 5; attacks on naval targets, 33; forbidden to attack submarines, 38; first attacks on German Fleet, 65-6; failure to attack German forces, 71-2, 102; squadrons lent to Coastal Command, 72-3; Wellington converted for mine disposal, 101, 127; forbidden to bomb enemy bases, 102; minelaying by, 123, 125, 335-7; first success in U-boat war, 132; reports German Fleet move, North Sea, 153; revision of rules for attacking enemy warships, 154; percentages of loss in attacking naval targets, 154; attacks German squadron, 7th April 1940, 159; attacks Bergen, 9th April, 172; fails to find enemy squadron, 12th April, 176; attacks invasion barges, Ostend, 255; asked to attack Kiel and Wilhelmshaven, 261; bombs *Admiral Hipper* at Brest, 292, 393; attacks on enemy 'coastal' convoys by, 33; restriction on bombing merchant ships relaxed, 337; plans to attack enemy battle cruisers, 378; increased attack on French naval bases, 379; scores three hits on *Gneisenau*, 393; mines approaches to Brest, 393; main strength for Germany and Atlantic, 448; proposal to bomb Biscay U-boat bases turned down, 459; summary of hits on enemy ships at Brest, 487; protest at continued bombing of Brest, 488; heavy attacks on Brest resumed, 491; concentra-

Royal Air Force, Bomber Command—*cont*.
tion on offensive on Germany, 503; low level attacks on enemy shipping, 503; No. 2 Group to attack shipping between Wilhelmshaven and Cherbourg, 503, 506; claim to be responsible for all bombing operations, 509; area for minelaying by, 510; proposal to bomb Biscay U-boat bases, 468, 476; Lorient bombed, 468

Royal Air Force: Coastal Command: development of in the War, 5; links with Admiralty and Naval Commands, 19; primary role, and transfer of control to Admiralty, 30, 33; proposed use as striking force, 1937, 34; war organisation incomplete, 1939, 36; aircraft type limitations, 37-8; Ansons replaced by Hudsons, 66; reports German naval force off Norway, 70-1; bomber squadrons lent to, 72-3; sights enemy forces, North Sea, 89; action directive against U-boats, North Sea, 104-5; protection of merchant shipping, 107-8, 347; minelaying by, 123, 335; search for minelaying aircraft type, 124; harrying U-boats on passage, 129; ineffective bombs, and trials with depth charges, 135-6; unprepared for attacks on shipping off Norway, 145; interception of enemy shipping from Vigo, 150; interception of *Altmark*, 152; search of Heligoland Bight, 158-9; plan to attack Stavanger airfield cancelled, 171; fails to find enemy squadron, 12th April 1940, 176; not informed of Narvik evacuation, 198; air reconnaissance of Trondheim, June-July, 260; difficulties of reconnaissance, Autumn 1940, 288; patrols Brest approaches, 292; protection for Channel convoys, 324; minelaying campaign, 1940-41, 335-6; responsibility for new offensive, 338; new torpedo-bombers for, 338; put on anti-invasion patrols, 347; inadequacy of strength, 347, 351; formation of Iceland Air Force, 347, 452; attacks on U-boat bases stepped up, 353; reports *Hipper* back at Brest, 372; reconnaissance of northern passages, 376; pre-war conception of use of, 355; cover for Biscay approaches, 377; sights German battle cruisers, 378, 395-7; primary duty to watch North Sea exits, 355; watch on Brest intensified, 378; Radar fitted for surface U-boat detection, 358; use of Leigh Light, 358; co-operation with Submarine Tracking Room, 358, 481; No. 15 Group, Western Approaches (Liverpool), 360, 452; No. 19 Group, south west area (Plymouth), 360; proposal to transfer to Admiralty, 361; control of, when Home Fleet at sea, 361; programme for expansion of agreed to, 361; attack and torpedo *Gneisenau*, 393; mines the approaches to Brest, 393; intense reconnaissance during search for *Bismarck*, 396, 411, 416; Beaufort aircraft torpedoes *Lützow*, 484; improvement in methods of convoy-escorting by, 458-9; air cover for westbound convoys extended to 35° W.,

INDEX

Royal Air Force: Coastal Command—*cont.*
458; strength of No. 15 Group, 459-60; summary of effort against enemy ships, Brest, 487; No. 200 Group transferred to, 460, disbanded, 460; tactical use of aircraft against U-boats, 451, 467; lack of success against U-boats, 461; No. 19 Group covers S.W. Britain and Biscay area, 461; No. 18 Group covers waters north of Shetlands, 462; U.570 surrendered to, 467; proposal to divert long-range bombers from Battle of Atlantic, 467; Air Ministry-Admiralty directive, 473; reconnaissance patrols, value, 496; improvement in shipping protection, Dec. 1941, 502; lack of suitable striking force, 503, 509; reinforcement for in Northern Ireland, 476; division of responsibility for shipping attacks, 503; No. 19 Group extends activity, Bay of Biscay, 504; resumes responsibility for anti-shipping work, Wilhelmshaven-Cherbourg, 506; not designed to attack shipping, 508; no long-range minelaying aircraft, 509; in raid on Vaagsö, 514

Royal Air Force: Far East: all airfields attacked, 563; air reconnaissance and fighter cover requested by Admiral Phillips, 564-5, 568

Royal Air Force: Fighter Command: maritime use, 6, 33; links with Admiralty and Naval Commands, 19; untrained in sea/air co-operation, 39; squadron sent to Wick, 75; no fighters at Scapa, 79; squadrons for North Scotland, 81; trade defence squadrons formed, 107-6; cover for East coast shipping against air attack, 138-9; successful defence of Norwegian convoys, 143; extemporised station on frozen lake, Norway, 185; squadrons landed in Narvik area, 191; covers Narvik evacuation, 193; loss of aircraft and crews in *Glorious*, 195; aircraft sent to Holland, 209; service at Dunkirk 218, 224; cover for Havre evacuation, 231; defeats German attempt to destroy R.A.F., 256; difficulties of protecting little ships by, 322, 324; curbing of dive bombing of Channel convoys by, 325; losses of, while protecting Channel convoys, 326; takes over responsibility for defence of Clyde, Mersey and Bristol Channel, 331; long-range fighters transferred to N. Ireland, 362-3; to protect inshore convoys, 363; margin of strength for, 448-9; protection for coastal convoys improved, 499; to apply air blockade of Channel route, 503; takes over attack on shipping, English Channel, 504; supplies 60 Hurricanes to C.A.Ms. 477

Royal Air Force: Gibraltar Command: Air Combined Headquarters set up in Gibraltar, 460

Royal Air Force: Mediterranean: difficulties of, 306; organisation and control of 201 Group, 422; co-operation in battle off Cape Matapan, 428; bombing of Tripoli, 433; casualties at Malta, 437; in evacuation from Crete, 444; need to strengthen, 447;

Royal Air Force: Mediterranean—*cont.*
benefit by recapture of Cyrenaica, 521; build-up of Malta striking force, 526

Royal Air Force: West Africa Command: headquarters set up at Bathurst, 460.

Royal Australian Air Force: search for raider *Orion*, 283; attacks *Ole Jacob* off Spain, 504

Royal Australian Navy: strength, 1939, 49, 578, 580-1, 585; in expedition to Iran, 529; destroyers join Eastern Fleet, 538; tentative dispositions in Pacific, 561-2

Royal Canadian Air Force: co-operation of, with Coastal Command, 458-9; in Newfoundland, 460, 472

Royal Canadian Navy: 50, 580, 585; escorts first Halifax convoy, 93; convoy escort, 343; size at beginning of war, 451-2; co-operation in Atlantic convoy escorts, 451-3; ships available for Newfoundland Escort Force, 453; ships of to be controlled by Admiralty, 453; accepts responsibility for convoy routes to south of Iceland, 453; collaboration with British and U.S. Navies in Atlantic, 471.

Royal Indian Navy, 49, 581, 585; in capture of Assab, 517; in expedition to Iran, 529

Royal Marines: strength, 1939 and 1944, 251, Appendix C, 575; guard for demolition parties, Rotterdam, 209; party sent to Boulogne, 213; evacuation from Boulogne, 273-4; guard for port of Calais, 215; landings by, in Iceland and Faeroes, 345; units at Suda Bay, Crete, 424.

Royal Naval Volunteer Reserve: Air Branch formed, 1938, 32; service in Coastal Forces, 502.

Royal Navy: personnel strength, 1939 and 1944, 24; out-of-date ships in, 58; difference with Royal Air Force over order to open fire on unidentified aircraft, 323; table showing attacks on enemy shipping by naval aircraft, 340; pre-war concepts of anti-U-boat warfare, 355-6; shortage of flotilla vessels for U-boat warfare, 356; anti-submarine training, 359; transfer to, of U.S. Coastguard cutters, 454; table of Escort Vessel strength, June 1941, 464; collaboration with Canadian and U.S. Navies in the Atlantic, 471; active and reserve strength, 1939-45, Appendix C, 575; warships in commission, or building, 1939, Appendix D, 577; principal ships built for, 1939-41 programmes, Appendix F, 588

Royal Oak, H.M.S.: 47, sortie to intercept *Gneisenau*, 71; sunk at Scapa, 73-4, 78-9; causes of loss, 80.

Royal Sovereign, H.M.S.: 47; in Halifax escort force, 270; arrives at Alexandria, 295; action off Calabria, 298; escorts Canadian troop convoy T.C.9, 392; refitting at home, 554.

'*Royal Sovereign*' class: allocated to Eastern Fleet, 491, 555

Royal Sovereign, s.s.: in Dunkirk evacuation, 226-7.

Russia: pact with Germany, 53-4; German use of Murmansk, 111; German campaign

Russia: pact with Germany—*cont.*
against, 256; time-table upset, 449; assists raider *Komet*, 279; convoys to, submarine escort, 375; German campaign opens, 463, 485; Home Fleet assistance to, 488; undeveloped state of bases in, 489; first convoys to and from, 492; British-American Supply Missions, 492 & *n*; submarines at Polyarnoe, 493; protection of convoys to, 495; southern flank safeguarded in Iran, 529

Sabre, H.M.S.: in Dunkirk evacuation, 221, 225, 227
St George's Channel: defensive minefield in, 263
St Helena: hunting group for raiders off, 290
St Helier, s.s.: in Dunkirk evacuation, 226
St Jean de Luz: evacuation from, 237-8
St Malo: transport of B.E.F. stores to, 64; evacuation, 232-3; demolition, 233
St Nazaire: transport of B.E.F. to, 63; evacuation from, 232-7; numbers evacuated, 236; minelaying off, 335, 510
St Valéry-en-Caux: evacuation from fails, 231-2
Saladin, H.M.S.: damaged in Dunkirk evacuation, 222
Salmon, H.M.S.: sights enemy forces, 89; sinks U.36 and torpedoes enemy cruisers, 102; sightings off Heligoland, 149; sunk, 266
Salpa, Italian U-boat: sunk by *Triumph*, 525
Samaria, s.s.: collision with *Aquitania* and *Furious*, 89
Samland, German supply ship: sunk, 607
Samois, launch: rescues casualties at Calais, 215
San Demetrio, m.v.: attacked by *Admiral Scheer*, 289
San Domingo: German merchant ships caught off, 276
Saratoga, U.S. aircraft carrier: escapes attack on Pearl Harbour, 563
Sardinia: convoy for Alexandria met off, 301; Italian air strength in, 420; submarine patrols off, 425
Scapa: Home Fleet base, 8; first patrol from, 64; air threat to exaggerated, 68, 75; *Royal Oak* sunk at, 73, 78, 80; defence works hastened, 74, 79; air attack on Fleet at, 1939, 75; poilcy, as main base, 76-81, 88; anti-submarine trawlers at, 130; air attack on Fleet at, March 1940, 155; enemy air reconnaissance of, 198; covering force against invasion of Eire, 251; Home Fleet at, Dec. 1940, 268, March 1941, 378, and May 1941, 394; minesweeping flotillas based on, 452; Home Fleet strength, 1.6.1941, 483
Scarborough, H.M.S.: sinks U.76 with *Wolverine*, 463
Scarpanto Island; enemy air base attacked, 444
Scharnhorst, German battle cruiser: design, 52, 58; referred to by Germans as battleship, 52*n*; sinking of (1943), 11; under C.-in-C., West, 56; sinking of *Rawalpindi*, 82-7; attack on Norway shipping frustrated, 153; in Norwegian campaign, 163;

Scharnhorst, German battle cruisers—*cont.*
action with *Renown*, 165-6, 169; escapes south, 176; sortie off Norway, Operation 'Juno', 194; sinks *Glorious* and destroyers, damaged by torpedo, 195-6, 259; bombed from *Ark Royal* at Trondheim, 198; returns to Germany, 199; at Trondheim, 259; leaves Trondheim, attacked by aircraft, 260; under repair at Kiel, 260-1; abortive sortie, December, 1940, 292; at Keil, 368; in North Atlantic, 371; sortie, January-March 1941, 373-9, 364, 389, 391; refitting, 393; in Brest, 483; damaged by bombs at La Pallice, 486-7; dock at Brest hit, 491; considerable influence until sunk, 496; details of, Appendix M, 605.
Scheer, German pocket battleship: see *Admiral Scheer*
Schepke, U-boat Commander: lost in U-100, 365
Schillig Roads: German Fleet in, 65-6; U.31 sunk in, 132
Schleswig-Holstein, German battleship: in occupation of Denmark, 164
Schuhart, Lieut.: commands U.29 and sinks *Courageous*, 106
Schultz, U-boat Commander: attacks Convoy H.X.90, *Forfar* sunk, 353
'Schuyts', Dutch: in Dunkirk evacuation, 216, 221.
Scientist, s.s.: sunk by *Atlantis*, 281
Scimitar, H.M.S.: in Dunkirk evacuation, 221
Scotia, s.s.: sunk in Dunkirk evacuation, 225
Scotstoun, H.M.S.: sunk by U-boat, 265
Scott, Rear-Admiral R. J. R.: command in Iceland, 453
Seahorse, H.M.S.: lost in Heligoland Bight, 148
Sealion, H.M.S.: chases minelayer *Ulm*, 128; work off Norway, 179*n*
'Sealion', Operation: German invasion of U.K., planned, 254, abandoned, 256
Security: excessive precautions, troop convoy, 89; ditto, Narvik evacuation, 198
Selsey Bill: plan for German landing at, 255
Severn, H.M.S.: success in Mediterranean, 525
Seychelles: raider *Atlantis* works off, 381
Seydlitz, German cruiser: to complete in 1940, 57*n*, 58
Shark, H.M.S.: sunk off Norway, 266
Sheerness: striking force base against invasion, 249, 252, 258
Sheffield, H.M.S.: 47; Home Fleet patrol, 65; assists disabled *Spearfish*, 68; sortie to intercept *Gneisenau*, 71; operations after attack on *Rawalpindi*, 84-7; at Scapa, 158; leaves for Norway, 159; in Norwegian campaign, 161, 169-70; lands reinforcements, Molde and Aandalsnes, 185; joins Humber Force, 188; evacuation from Aandalsnes, 188-9; lent to Nore Command, 208; covers through convoy for Alexandria, 301; covers convoy 'Excess', 421; bombardment of Genoa, etc., 425; in *Bismarck* operations, 410-13; attacked in error by Swordfish aircraft, 413; search for enemy tanker, Atlantic, 542; intercepts *Friedrich Breme*, 606

INDEX

Shetlands: separate command with Orkneys, 48; defence measures for, 346; attacks on U-boats from, 462.
Shikari, H.M.S.: in Dunkirk evacuation, 221; last ship to leave Dunkirk, 227
Shipbuilding: industry an essential element of sea power, 6
Shipping, Ministry of: *see* Transport, Ministry of
Shropshire, H.M.S.: 48; in raider hunting group, 114; intercepts *Adolf Leonhardt*, 117; ordered to River Plate, 120; supports East Africa campaign, 426
Sicilian Narrows: passage of through Mediterranean convoy, 301-2, of 'Excess' convoy, 421, of 'Substance' convoy, 522, and 'Halberd' convoy, 530; proposed capture of Pantellaria, 304; route of enemy convoys through, 526, and attacks on them, 527
Sicily: Allied landing in (1943), 12; threat to Malta from, 49; enemy aircraft strength in, Jan. 1941, 420; need to attack airfields in, 422; German aircraft transferred to Balkans, 518; plan to capture, Oct. 1941, 520; German aircraft return from Russia, 534
'Sickle', Operation (landings at Molde and Aandalsnes), 183-5
Sierra Leone: *see* Freetown
Signal Division, Admiralty: work of, 24
Sikh, H.M.S.: operations against *Bismarck*, 414; sinking of Italian cruisers, 534
Silvaplana, Norwegian m.v.: captured by *Atlantis*, 545
Simeon, Captain C. E. B.: in *Renown*, Operation 'Wilfred', 157
Simonstown: auxiliary war vessels at, 274
Simpson, Captain G. W. G.: commands 10th Submarine Flotilla, Malta, 526
Simson, Captain D. J. R.: killed in action at Boulogne, 213
Singapore: tragic history as naval base, 76: *Prince of Wales* leaves for, 494; plans for battle fleet at, 555-7; capital ships at, 558-9; agreement with U.S. C.-in-C. concerning, 561; Admiral Phillips leaves, 564
Singora: Japanese land at, 563-4
Sirte, first Battle of, 535
Skagerrak: projected raid into, 68; unrestricted air attacks permitted in, 145; submarine patrols in, 187, 267; request for air reconnaissance of, 484
Skagerrak, German tanker: in Norway invasion, 148
Skeena, H.M.C.S.: escorts S.C.42, attacks U-boat, 469
Skipjack, H.M.S.: sunk in Dunkirk evacuation, 225
Skjel Fiord: *Aurora* arrives with Lord Cork, 180
Skua naval aircraft; sink *Königsberg* at Bergen, 172; only dive-bombers in use up to 1941, 509
Slamat, s.s.: sunk in evacuation from Greece, 436
Smuts, Field Marshal: meets Admiral Phillips, concern over division of Allied strength, 558

Snapper, H.M.S.: work off Norway, 179*n*; lost on Biscay patrol, 334
'Snow flake': illuminant in anti-submarine warfare, 357
Sobieski, Polish m.v.: evacuation from St. Nazaire, 234-5, and Bayonne, 238
Somali, H.M.S.: escorts troops on Lofoten Islands raid, 341
Somaliland, British: evacuated, 307; recaptured, 426
Somaliland, Italian: blockaded, 307; surrendered, 426
Somerville, Vice-Admiral Sir J.: appointed to command Force H, 242, 296; attack on French Fleet, Oran, 242-4; transfers flag to *Renown*, 272; to watch Atlantic islands, 273; not able to search for *Scheer*, 289; covers Mediterranean reinforcements, 298; covers through convoy for Alexandria, 301; action off Cape Spartivento, 302-4; expedition to Dakar, 299, 308-14; relations with North Atlantic Command, 310-2; search for enemy battle cruisers, Atlantic, 377; blockading force off Brest, 392; ascendancy within Mediterranean, 419; 'Excess' convoy for Piraeus and Malta, 421; bombardments of Genoa, Leghorn and Spezia, 425; in *Bismarck* operations, 407, 438; ferrying aircraft to Malta, 518; 'Substance' convoy for Malta, 522-3; minelaying in Gulf of Genoa, 523; 'Halberd' convoy for Malta, 530-2; further aircraft ferrying to Malta, 533; proposed withdrawal of heavy ships from, 539
Souffleur, French submarine: sunk off Syria, 517
South Africa: aircraft from sights *Watussi*, 117
South America: U.S. Neutrality Patrol off, 112
South American Division: forces of, 48; fuelling difficulties, 116
South Atlantic Command (Freetown): force in, 1939, 584; protection against raiders, 43; cruisers of, 48; raider report, October 1939, 70, 113; raider hunting groups in, 114; increased problems after fall of France, 273; forces in, July 1940, 274; raider and U-boat arrive in, 275, 277; mines laid by raider, 280; disturbance to shipping, 281; ships for Dakar expedition, 315; raiders in, 1.1.1941, 367; *Atlantis* in, 382; air reinforcements for, 460; losses from U-boats in, 470; supplies for U-boats in, 479-80; raider fuelling position never discovered, 542
Southampton: first B.E.F. convoy, 63; reinforcements for Calais, 214; evacuation from Cherbourg and St. Malo, 233
Southampton, H.M.S.: in Humber Force, 46, 64; assists disabled *Spearfish*, 68; bombed in Firth of Forth, 75; operations after attack on *Rawalpindi*, 84-7; covers convoy O.N. 25, 159; joins force off Norway, 170; conveys Major-Gen. Mackesy from Scapa, 180; evacuation from Aandalsnes, 188-9; evacuation from Narvik, flag of Lord Cork, 193-4; conveys troops to Alexandria, 301, and to Malta, 421; sunk by air attack, 422

Southend: first Channel convoys from, 93; exposure of shipping awaiting convoy from, 137; Home Fleet cruisers at during invasion threat, 252, 258; convoys to be maintained from, 322; Channel Guard at, 325; mined from the air, 328

Spain: German U-boats ordered in, 51; plans to occupy Atlantic islands of, 273; possibility of entry into war, 297; Italian U-boats in Spanish waters, 347; possible German invasion of, 380; passage of enemy troops to attack Gibraltar refused, 380; U-boats supplied in Canary Islands, breach of neutrality, 479; blockade breaking from, 552

Spartivento, Cape, Calabria: action by Force K off, 532

Spartivento, Cape, Sardinia: Admiral Somerville's action off, 302-4

Spearfish, H.M.S.: disabled off Horn Reef, escorted home, 68; torpedoes *Lützow*, 177; sunk, 266

Speybank, m.v.: captured by *Atlantis*, renamed *Doggerbank*, 381, 608

Spezia: bombarded by Force H, 425

Sphinx, H.M.S.: sunk by aircraft, 142

Spichern, German supply ship: scuttled (1944), 607, 608

Spitfire aircraft: sent to Wick, 75: success on convoy patrol, 142

Spitzbergen: sortie of *Hipper* to, 260; reconnoitred by Admiral Vian, 488; demolition and evacuation mission, 489

Springbank, H.M.S.: fighter catapult ship, sunk by U-boat, 477

Starfish, H.M.S.: lost in Heligoland Bight, 148

Stavanger: plan 'R.4' to occupy, 157, 162; R.A.F. attack on airfield cancelled, 171, 179-80; bombarded by *Suffolk*, 186; enemy air base at, 350; convoys routed out of aerial range of, 362

Stephenson, Commodore G. O.: Dunkirk evacuation, in charge off La Panne, 223; commands *Western Isles*, anti-submarine training, 359

Sterlet, H.M.S.: sunk off Norway, 179*n*

Stevens, Captain E. B. K.: evacuation from St Nazaire, 235

Stier, German raider: fitting out, 368

Stokes, Commander G. H.: sinks two Italian cruisers, 534

Stonegate, s.s.: sunk by *Deutschland*, 115-6

Stork, H.M.S.: in convoy battle with H.G. 76, 478; sinks U.574, 479

Storstad, Norwegian tanker: captured, converted for enemy minelaying, 286, 608

Strasbourg, French battle cruiser, 52; in raider hunting group, 114; at Oran, 240-1; escapes to Toulon, 244

Strathaird, s.s.: evacuation of Biscay ports, 233; possibly sighted by *Atlantis*, Indian Ocean, 381*n*

Streonshalh, s.s.: sunk by *Graf Spee*, 118

Stuart, H.M.S.: in Battle off Cape Matapan, 430; supplies to Tobruk, 519

Sturgeon, H.M.S.: accidentally attacks *Swordfish*, 66; sinks enemy tanker off Obrestadt, 334

Submarines, Allied: patrols off Norway beyond aircraft limit, 37, 64, 66; off Horn Reef, etc., 64, 66; difficulties of maintaining position, 66; attached to Home Fleet, 69; dispositions after attack on *Rawalpindi*, 84; Heligoland Bight patrols abandoned, 148; patrols off Norway, March, 1940, 149; southern area, Norway, left to, 171; difficult work of, Norway, 179; in Skagerrak and Kattegat, 187; dispositions for expected invasion, 266; severe losses in North Sea, 266; 10 arrive Alexandria from the East, 295; strength in Mediterranean, 305, and heavy loss, 306; 8th Flotilla formed at Gibraltar, 306; attacks on enemy coastal convoys, and Biscay patrols, 333; primary task to attack enemy warships, 334; 'T' class moved to Halifax, 334, 375; minelaying by, 335; escort of trade convoys by, 375; pre-war conception of use of, 355; Brest and Biscay patrols, 378, 493; work in Mediterranean, 425, 438; removal of restrictions in Mediterranean, 439; operations in North Russia, 493; tonnage sunk by, home waters, 1941, 493; greater risk to, in Mediterranean, 516; Mediterranean reinforcements, 516, 524; carriage of supplies to Malta, 518-9; cover for Malta convoy 'Substance', 522; campaign against enemy shipping, Mediterranean, 525-6; 10th Flotilla formed at Malta, 526; enemy assessment of, Mediterranean, 536; in Far East, 560, 570; number in commission, etc., 1939, Appendix D, 580

Submarines, Enemy: *see* U-boats

'Substance', Operation (convoy for Malta), 521-3, 524

Suda Bay, Crete: advanced base established at, 300, 305; development of base, 424; Mediterranean Fleet fuels at, 433; limitations as a base, 435; Battle for Crete, 440-9

Suez: distance from Clyde for troop transports, 271; A.P. convoys arrive from home in five weeks, 274; control of southern approaches to, 308; U.S. ships allowed to sail to, 426, 517

Suez Canal: mine dispersal by aircraft, 101; first magnetic mines in, 423; exposed to bombing and minelaying, 515, 517; relief by recapture of Cyrenaica, 521

Suffolk, H.M.S.: 50; joins Home Fleet, 69-70; in Atlantic hunting group, 70; operations after attack on *Rawalpindi*, 84-7; bombards Stavanger, damaged, 186; in *Bismarck* operations 395-8, 401, 404, 407, 409-11; search for enemy supply ships, 483; strike on enemy coastal traffic, far north, 486; covers convoy with aircraft for Russia, 489; escorts first P.Q. (Russian) convoy, 492

Sunderland aircraft: sinking of U.55, 129; action off Cape Spartivento, 302-3; sighting of *Ole Jacob*, 504

Sunfish, H.M.S.: sightings off Heligoland, 149; sinkings by off Norway, 179*n*

Supply ships, German: secret organisation to support, 55, 112; use of Mariana Islands,

INDEX 659

Supply Ships, German—*cont.*
278, 284, 367; efficiency of, 369; in Atlantic battle cruiser sortie, 373, 376, 379; with *Atlantis*, 382; fuelling position never discovered, 542; nine intercepted in June, 1941, 542, 544 (table); list of, Appendix N, 606
Surcouf, French submarine: arrives in Britain, 240; transferred to Halifax, 375
Sussex, H.M.S.: 48; in raider hunting group, 114; joins Admiral Vivian, Harstad evacuation, 198
Swansea: first B.E.F. convoys, 63
Sweden: iron ore traffic from, 156; Norwegian ships escape from Gothenburg, 391
Swinemünde: base of Naval Group Commander, East, 54
Swordfish, H.M.S.: accidentally attacked by *Sturgeon*, 66; sunk, 267
Swordfish aircraft: minelaying by, 125; attack on Italian Fleet, Taranto, 301; success in Gulf of Bomba, 307; success in Red Sea, 426; in battle off Cape Matapan, 429; bombing of Tripoli, 433; crippling of *Bismarck*, 438; offensive against North Africa supply route, 524; night attacks on enemy convoys, 527; 12 at Malta, August, 1941, 527
Sydney, C.B.: see Cape Breton Island.
Sydney, H.M.A.S.: 49; arrives at Alexandria from Australia, 295; sinks *Bartolomeo Colleoni*, 299; sunk after action with raider *Kormoran*, 548-9
Syfret, Rear-Admiral E. N.: 'Substance' convoy for Malta, 522-3
Sylt: bomber attack on enemy seaplane base, 154-5
Syria: threatened by enemy control of Aegean, 436; campaign in, 516-7, 529

Tacoma, German s.s.: at scuttling of *Graf Spee*, 121
Tai Shan, s.s.: Norwegian, escapes from Gothenburg, 391
Tairoa, s.s.: sunk by *Graf Spee*, 117
Takoradi: transport of aircraft to, 262, 268, 291, 298; transport of troops from, 274; African air route from, 320, 419; *Eurylochus* sunk with aircraft for, 386
Tangier: French warship movements reported from, 311-12
Tannenfels, German supply ship: scuttled (1944), 607
Tarantini, Italian U-boat: sunk by *Thunderbolt*, 267
Taranto: naval air attack on Italian Fleet, 5, 300-1
Tarpon, H.M.S.: sunk off Norway, 179n
Task Forces: development of, 6
Tasman Sea: raider *Orion* in, 283
Taurus, s.s.: Norwegian, escapes from Gothenburg, 391
Teddy, Norwegian tanker: captured by *Atlantis*, 282, 608
Tembien, Italian U-boat: sunk by *Hermoine* off Tunis, 523
Tennant, Captain W. G.: S.N.O., Dunkirk, during evacuation, 216; berths ships

Tennant, Captain W. G.—*cont.*
alongside east mole, 219; embarkations from outer harbour, 221; communication difficulties, 223; hazardous conditions in port, 224; directs final evacuation, 226; commands *Repulse* in *Bismarck* operations, 396; arrives Colombo in *Repulse*, 558; saved from wreck of *Repulse*, 566
Tennessee, U.S. battleship: seriously damaged at Pearl Harbour, 562
Terror, H.M.S.: damaged at Benghazi, sank later, 423
Terschelling: submarine patrols off, 64; German destroyers sunk by own aircraft off, 142; minelaying by Coastal Command, 510
Tetrarch, H.M.S.: lost in Mediterranean, 536
Teviot Bank, H.M.S.: lays mines in East Coast barrier, 126; in Operation 'Wilfred', 157-8
Texel: 20th Flotilla runs into minefield off, 334
Thailand (Siam): invaded by Japan, 554, 563
Thames, H.M.S.: sunk, 266
Thames Estuary: aircraft for anti-submarine duty, 38; convoys from, 45, 93; light forces in, 47; enemy minelaying in, 100-1, 126-8; first LL sweepers at work in, 127; convoys from Bristol Channel start, 323; minesweeping by night in, 327; mined from the air, 328; shipping bombed in, 331; shipping tonnage using East Coast route, Jan.-June 1941, 333; development of coastal convoy system 497; tonnage using, 1941, 499
Thistle, H.M.S.: sunk by U.4, 164, 179n
Thor, German raider: first cruise, 279; sinkings by, 284-6, 383-4; actions with *Alcantara* and *Carnarvon Castle*, 285; meets Admiral *Sheer*, 291, 367, 369; sinks H.M.S. *Voltaire*, 383; escapes down Channel on second cruise, 505, 541; details, Appendix M, 604
Thorn, German supply ship: sunk by *Tigris*, 607
Thorshavn: see Faeröes
Thunderbolt, H.M.S.: sinks Italian *Tarantini*, 267
'Tiger', Operation (special tank convoy through Mediterranean), 437, 440
Tigris, H.M.S.: sent to Polyarnoe, 493; sinks *Thorn*, 607
Tirpitz, German battleship: details of, 57; under construction at Wilhelmshaven, 261; necessary to destroy battleship convoy escorts, 395; under trials, 483-4; believed ready for sea, 490; influence on Home Fleet, 555; threat of Atlantic break-out, 557
Tirrana, Norwegian tanker: captured by *Atlantis*, sunk by *Tuna*, 281, 608
Titania, H.M.S.: 47
Tobermory: see *Western Isles*, H.M.S.
Tobruk: captured by Allies, 420; reopened in five days, 422-3; invested by enemy, 433; difficulty of supply, 515; supplied by destroyers and fast minelayers, 519; supplied by 'A' lighters, 520; stores and men conveyed to (table), 520
Togo, German raider: fitting out, 368; damaged on first cruise, 279

INDEX

Torbay, H.M.S.: sinks Italian *Jantina*, 525
Torpedoes: lack of in Mediterranean, 306; neglect of in aircraft attack on shipping, 509
Tottenham, s.s.: sunk by *Atlantis*, 382
Toulon: French Fleet at, 241; ships from Oran arrive at, 244; move of ships to West Africa, 311, 315, 319
Tovey, Admiral Sir J. C.: C.-in-C., Home Fleet, 267; raid on Lofoten Islands, 341; search for *Scharnhorst* and *Gneisenau*, 371-9, 392; cover for Middle East troop convoys, 378; meets escaping Norwegian ships, 391; watch on German ships in Brest, 392; operations against *Bismarck* and *Prinz Eugen*, 395-418; situation after sinking of *Bismarck*, 483; requests air reconnaissance of Skagerrak, 484; plans for Norwegian and Arctic operations, 485-90; meets U.S.N. officers in Iceland, 492; protests at departure of *Prince of Wales*, 494; on Vestfiord and Vaagsö raids, 513-4
Trade Division, Admiralty: work of, 21-2, 94, 141, 497; weekly Trade Protection meeting, 350
Trafalgar, m.v.: sunk by *Atlantis*, 382
Transport, Ministry of: responsible for tonnage procurement, 21 & *n*; chartering of neutral ships, 95; withdrawal of B.E.F., 212; heavy call on for troop transport, 271; armed merchant cruisers revert to, 454
Transports: tactical loading of, 190 & *n*
Transylvania, H.M.S.: intercepts German *Mimi Horn*, 150; sunk by U-boat, 265
Trawlers: taken up for Auxiliary Patrol, 251; needed for convoy escort, 253; removed from A.P. for anti-invasion duties, 264; at Freetown, 274; use of in escort groups, 359
Trevanion, s.s.: sunk by *Graf Spee*, 115-6
Triad, H.M.S.: work off Norway, 179*n*
Tribesman, s.s.: sunk by *Admiral Scheer*, 290
Trident, H.M.S.: sent to Polyarnoe, 493
Trinity House: light vessels not used for war purposes, 138
Tripoli: enemy route to, 306; Allied advance towards stopped, 420; route to disputed by submarines and aircraft, 425; proposal to block the port, 431; proposal to bombard, 432; enemy forced to rely on for army supplies, 521; *P.32* and *P.33* lost off, 526; Italian cruisers with petrol for, sunk, 534; Force K loss by mines off, 535; enemy convoys resumed, 536
Triton, H.M.S.: sinks *Oxley* by accident, 66; intercepts *Wangoni*, 150
Triumph, H.M.S.: sinks Italian *Salpa*, 525; damages Italian *Bolzano*, 525; Adriatic patrol, 526
Troilus, s.s.: escapes from raider *Atlantis*, 381
Tromsö: King and Government of Norway conveyed to, 188; sortie of *Hipper* to, 260; attacked by *Furious* aircraft, 262, 486
Trondheim: German warships in, 148: plan 'R.4' to occupy, 157; German ships bound for, 160-1; German landing, 163-5, 170; proposed naval air attack on, 171-2, 175; attack unsuccessful, 176; setback to initial enemy landing, 180; Allied pincer

Trondheim—*cont.*
movement against, 182-3, 185; plan for frontal attack 'Hammer' cancelled, 186-7; *Hipper* arrives at, 194; attacked by Fleet Air Arm, 198; German warships leave, 259; air reconnaissance unreliable, 260; convoy for attacked by *Cossack*, etc., 262; submarine patrols off withdrawn, 266
Tropic Sea, Norwegian m.v.: captured by *Orion*, 283, 608
Troubridge, Captain T. H.: tribute to airmen of *Furious*, 196
Truant, H.M.S.: sinks German ship off Norway, 149; sinks *Karlsruhe* off Norway, 172
Tsingtau, German depot-ship: in landings in Norway, 164
Tuna, H.M.S.: sinks *Tirrana* off Gironde, 281
Tunis: Italian attack on not considered possible, 294
Turakina, s.s.: sunk by *Orion*, 283
Tyne: convoys from, 45, 94; British Humber-Tyne minefield, 96; German minefield off, 102; convoy terminal moved to from Methil, 130; Convoy F.S. 10 attacked off, 142; *King George V* completed in, 262
Tynwald, s.s.: in Dunkirk evacuation, 227
Tyrrhenian Sea: Italian plans for closing, 294; 8th Submarine Flotilla works in, 516

U-boat war: 45; denounced by Germany, 1936, 52; aircraft factor in, 6; hunting groups unsuccessful, 10, 130, 132, 134; tracking room in O.I.C., 18, 362; assessment of attacks, 23, 134, 503; conflicting views on convoy, 34; Coastal Command contribution, 35; Bomber Command and, 38; Dover Straits mine barrage, 45, 96; sea/air hunting units, 46; Coastal Command action directive, 105; first joint air/sea success, 129; origin of 'wolf-pack' tactics, 131, 354-60; lack of German sea/air co-operation, 362; directive by Prime Minister on, 364, 459, 609
U-boats (German): ordered in Spain and Finland, 51; Dönitz in command, 54; to attack coastal shipping, 55; to mine British bases, 56; sent to operational areas, August 1939, 56; numbers and dispositions on outbreak of war, 59, 103; plans for increased production, 60; easy targets in unescorted ships, 94; loss in Dover barrage, 96; numbers available in Atlantic, 103; to attack without warning, 104, 128; minefields a limited deterrent, 126-7; zones of unrestricted attack widened, 130; surface attacks by night, 130; success against independent ships, 131-2; first attack on a Norwegian convoy, 131; main strength deployed against Norway, 143; Norway dispositions discovered, 164, 190; unsuccessful in disputing evacuation from France, 230, 234; to intercept anti-invasion forces, 255; only one destroyed by mine in northern fields, 264; Allied submarines to intercept, 266; in South Atlantic, sinkings off Freetown, 275; supply ships for, 278; renewed attacks off Free-

INDEX

U-boats (German)—*cont.*
town, 291; heavy attacks in N.W. Approaches, 339; use of French ports, 346; peak period of success, 1940, 348-51, 354; sinkings by, Nov.-Dec. 1940, 353-4; night surface attacks by, 354-60; Command established at Lorient, 346, 354; Asdics ineffective against night surface attacks, 355; weakness of 'pack' tactics, 356; Air Force group to co-operate with, 362; sinkings by, Jan.-Feb. 1941, 362-3; wireless from intercepted and used for tracking, 362; attacks on 'stragglers', 363; to continue normal patrols during cruiser foray, 395; operations suspended during chase of *Bismarck*, 408-9, 412; construction not delayed by Allied bombing, 459; concrete shelters in Biscay ports, 459; tactical use of aircraft against, 461; numbers destroyed up to Sept. 1941, 461; arrival in Eastern Mediterranean, 519; numbers operating, 1941, 462, 467; sinkings by, April-June 1941, 463-4; new evasive tactics of, 466; sinkings by, July-Sept. 1941, 466-8; attacks on convoys S.C. 42 and 44, 468-9; escort vessels to be primary targets, 470; attacks on convoy H.G. 76, 478-9; supply ships in South Atlantic, 479-80; sinkings, by Oct. 1941, 473; transferred to Mediterranean, 473-4; decline in numbers in North Atlantic, 475; sinkings by, Nov. 1941, 475; to work off southern Greenland, 472; sinkings by, and losses, April-Dec. 1941, 481; strength and disposition, 31.12.41, 482; withdrawn from South Atlantic after supply ship sinkings, 480, 546; types in service, 1939, Appendix G, 591; list of those sunk, 1939-41, and causes, Appendix K, 599-602; strength of, 1939-41, Appendix Q, 614

U-boats (Italian): numbers available, 1940, 293; to operate in Atlantic, 295, 347; in Red Sea, fate of, 296; numbers destroyed to Sept. 1941, 461; sinkings by, and losses, April-Dec. 1941, 481; small success of, 538; list sunk or captured, 1940-41, Appendix K, 601-2

U-boats (Japanese): sighting reports of Admiral Phillips's force, 565, 566

U.13: sunk by *Weston*, 133
U.22: lost, probably mined, 133
U.25: sinks *Armanistan*, 132
U.27: sinking of, 68
U.29: sinks H.M.S. *Courageous*, 105-6
U.30: sinks *Athenia*, 103; captures pilots from *Ark Royal*, 68; torpedoes *Barham*, 90
U.31: sunk by Bomber Command (first success) but salved, 132; sunk again by *Antelope*, 353
U.32: sinks *Empress of Britain*, 351; sunk by destroyers, 351, 353
U.33: sunk by *Gleaner*, 131
U.36: sunk by *Salmon*, 102
U.39: sinking of, 68, 105
U.41: sunk by *Antelope*, 131
U.44: sunk by *Fortune*, 132, 155
U.47: sinks *Royal Oak* at Scapa, 73-4; sunk, 364; commanded by Prien, 365

U.49: sunk by *Fearless* and *Brazen*, 190
U.51: damaged by airborne depth charge, 350; sunk by *Cachalot*, 266
U.53: sunk by *Gurkha*, 131
U.55: sinking of, first joint air/sea success, 129
U.63: sinking of, 131
U.64: sunk by *Warspite's* aircraft, 177
U.65: sunk by *Gladiolus*, 463
U.70: sunk by corvettes and destroyer, 364
U.75: sunk off North Africa, 520
U.76: sunk by *Wolverine* and *Scarborough*, 463
U.79: sunk off North Africa, 520
U.81: attacks *Ark Royal*, 533
U.95: sunk by Dutch submarine O.21, 474
U.99: sunk by *Walker* and *Vanoc*, commanded by Kretschmer, 365
U.100: sunk by *Walker* and *Vanoc*, commanded by Schepke, 365
U.101: attacked by *Arabis*, 133
U.104: sunk by *Rhododendron*, 353
U.110: sunk in attack on convoy O.B. 318, 463
U.124: sinks cruiser *Dunedin*, 546
U.126: rescues survivors of raider *Atlantis*, 545
U.127: sunk by H.M.A.S. *Nestor*, 478
U.131: sunk in attack on Convoy H.G. 76, 479
U.205: attacks *Ark Royal*, 533
U.206: sunk by Coastal Command, 462, 474
U.207: sunk by *Veteran* and *Leamington*, 469
U.208: sunk by *Bluebell*, 474
U.331: sinks H.M.S. *Barham*, 534
U.433: sunk by *Marigold*, 473-4
U.434: sunk in attack on Convoy H.G. 76, 479
U.451: sunk by Swordfish aircraft, 474
U.452: sunk by Catalina aircraft and *Vascama*, 467
U.469: first of supply U-boats, 480
U.501: sunk in attack on Convoy S.C. 42, 469
U.551: sunk by *Visenda*, 365
U.556: near *Ark Royal* and *Renown* during *Bismarck* operations, 412; sunk in attack on Convoy H.X. 133, 466
U.557: sinks *Galatea*, 535
U.567: sunk in attack on Convoy H.G. 76, 479
U.570: surrenders to Coastal Command aircraft, refitted as H.M.S. *Graph*, 467
U.574: sunk by *Stork*, Convoy H.G. 76, 479
U.651: sunk in attack on Convoy H.X. 133, 466
U.652: attacks U.S. destroyer *Greer*, 472, 613

Uhenfels, German s.s.: intercepted by *Ark Royal* group, 116
Ulm, German minelayer: lays field off Smith's Knoll, 128
Ulster Prince, m.v.: lands troops in Faeröes, 345; sunk in evacuation from Greece, 436
Unbeaten, H.M.S.: damages liner *Oceania*, 525; combined attack on Italian convoy, 526
Undaunted, H.M.S.: lost in Mediterranean, 439
Undine, H.M.S.: lost in Heligoland Bight, 148
Union, H.M.S.: sunk by Italian torpedo-boat, 525
Unique, H.M.S.: sinks Italian *Esperia*, 525
United States: arming of merchant ships, 22; objection to ships diverted to Orkneys, 43; German desire to avoid friction with, 56; neutrality legislation of, 104, 454, 612; reaction to evacuation of B.E.F., 240;

United States—*cont.*
attitude towards French warships, West Indies, 276; bases for destroyers agreement, 347-8, 612; aircraft for Western Approaches, 364; Lord Halifax sails for in *King George V*, 391; Red Sea no longer a 'combat zone', 426, 517; transfer of Coastguard cutters to R.N., 454; increasing help in Battle of Atlantic, 454-6; 'Security Zone' extended to 26° West, 455; refit of British ships in American yards, 455; air bases in Greenland, and Bermuda, 455; naval base in Newfoundland, 455; landing of Marines in Iceland, 455-6, 490; choice of British bases in case of war, 455; 'Neutrality Patrols' flown from Newfoundland, 460; Hitler anxious not to provoke, 490; 'Yard' minesweepers built in, 498; Defence Plan No. 4 implemented, 470; supplies to Iceland in U.S. ships, 472; mixed British and U.S. convoy escorts to be avoided, 472; destroyer *Greer* in action with U.652, 472, 613; air escorts from Argentia, 472; escort carriers requested under Lease-Lend, 477; Germany and Italy declare on, 552; note to Japan, 554; summary of moves by affecting the war at sea, Appendix P, 612

United States Navy: development of carrier-borne aircraft, 5; 477-8; Atlantic Fleet created, 454; Atlantic Fleet Support Group formed, 455; conferences with British in Iceland, 492; assists to patrol northern exits, 494; cruiser *Omaha* captures blockade runner, 546; escort of troop transports, Halifax to Durban, 552; assistance in Atlantic, 555; Asiatic Fleet at Manila, visit of Admiral Phillips, 558-61; Pacific Fleet at Pearl Harbour, 560; Japanese attack on Pearl Harbour, 5, 482, 562-3; first casualties, October 1941, 613

Upholder, H.M.S.: success of, Captain awarded V.C., 439; in combined attack on Italian convoy, 526; sinks Italian destroyer, 532

Upright, H.M.S.: sinks cruiser *Armando Diaz*, 425; in combined attack on Italian convoy, 526; sinks two supply ships, 536-7

Urge, H.M.S.: damages *Duilio*, 525-6; damages *Vittorio Veneto*, 537

Ursula, H.M.S.: attacks enemy warships, 102; sinks German ship off Norway, 149; in combined attack on Italian convoy, 526

Uruguay, German m.v.: intercepted by *Berwick*, 173

Usk, H.M.S.: lost in Mediterranean, 439

Ussukuma, German s.s.: intercepted by *Ajax* and *Cumberland*, 117

Utmost, H.M.S.: torpedoes Italian cruiser, 536

Vaagsö Island: Combined Operations raid on, 513-4

Valentine, H.M.S.: lost off Dutch coast, 209-10

Valiant, H.M.S.: 50; escorts third Canadian troop convoy, 151; returns to Scapa, 155, 158; leaves for Norway, 159; in Norwegian campaign, 161, 166, 169, 172; escorts Convoy N.P.1 to Narvik, 190; covers

Valiant, H.M.S.—*cont.*
Narvik evacuation, 194, 198; news of loss of *Glorious*, 196-7; joins Force H, 242; action against French at Oran, 242-4; joins Mediterranean Fleet, 299; 'Excess' convoys for Piraeus and Malta, 421; Battle off Cape Matapan, 428-30; Battle for Crete, 440; damaged by human torpedoes, Alexandria, 538-9, 555

Vanoc, H.M.S.: evacuation from St Nazaire, 235; sinking of U.99 and U.100, 365

Vanquisher, H.M.S.: in Dunkirk evacuation, 225, 227; in St Nazaire evacuation, 236

Vascama, H.M.S.: with Catalina aircraft sinks U.452, 467

Vega, H.M.S.: blocking operations, Ostend and Zeebrugge, 211; ditto, Dieppe, 230

Vendetta, H.M.A.S.: supplies for Tobruk, 519

Venetia, H.M.S.: evacuation of Boulogne, C.O. wounded, 213-4

Venezuela: defence of oil ports, 276

Venomous, H.M.S.: demolition party for Calais, 212; evacuation of Boulogne, 213-4; in Dunkirk evacuation, 226-7

Verity, H.M.S.: ammunition for Calais, 215; in Dunkirk evacuation, 221

Vernon, H.M.S., torpedo school: countermeasures for magnetic mines, 99-100

Versailles Treaty: repudiated by Germany, 52

Veteran, H.M.S.: with *Leamington* sinks U.207, 469

Veules: evacuation from, 232

Vian, Rear-Admiral P. L.: in *Cossack*, operations against *Altmark*, 151-3; evacuation of Namsos, 189; commands 4th Flotilla in *Bismarck* operations, 412-4; visits Murmansk and reconnoitres Spitzbergen, 488; expedition to Spitzbergen, 489; commands squadron in first Battle of Sirte, 535

Victoria Cross, awards of: Lt-Comdr Roope, 158; Captain Warburton-Lee, 175; Captain Fegen, 289; F./O. Campbell, 393; Lt-Comdr Wanklyn, 439

Victorious, H.M.S.: operations against *Bismarck*, 396, 407-13; leaves for Gibraltar with Hurricanes, 483; strike at enemy traffic, Kirkenes, 486; covers convoy with aircraft for Russia, 489; shipping strike off Norway, 494; flies aircraft to Malta, 518

Vigo: interception of German shipping from, 150

Villiers, Lt-Comdr L. de L.: in first Battle of Narvik, 173

Vimiera, H.M.S.: escorts Guards Brigade to Boulogne, 213; evacuation of Boulogne, 213-4; damaged off Calais, 215

Vimy, H.M.S.: demolition party for Boulogne, 212; port party for Boulogne, C.O. mortally wounded, 213; in Dunkirk evacuation, 221

Vindictive, H.M.S.: evacuation from Narvik, 193-4

Visenda, H.M.S.: sinks U.551, 365

Vittorio Veneto, Italian battleship: action off Cape Spartivento, 302; action off Cape Matapan, 429-30; torpedoed by submarine *Urge*, 537

INDEX

Vivian, Rear-Admiral J. G. P.: evacuation of Narvik, 193
Voltaire, H.M.S.: sunk by raider *Thor*, 383-4, 549
Vulcania, Italian m.v.: attacked by *Upholder*, 526

Wahehe, German s.s.: captured in Northern Patrol, 150
Wake-Walker, Rear-Admiral W. F.: countermeasures for magnetic mines, 99; Dunkirk evacuation, command off Belgium, 223; reports beach embarkation practically impossible, 224; flagship *Keith* sunk, 225; control from motor-boat in Dunkirk harbour, 226; commands 1st Minelaying Squadron, 263; commands 18th Cruiser Squadron in *Bismarck* operations, 396-8, 400-1; carries on engagement after death of Admiral Holland, 406-7; strike on enemy coastal traffic in far north, 486
Wakeful, H.M.S.: sunk in Dunkirk evacuation, 222
Walcheren: Dutch resistance continued in, 209
Walker, Commander F. J.: commands escort group, Convoy H.G. 76, 478-9
Walker, H.M.S.: helps to sink U.99 and U.100, 365
Wangoni, German s.s.: intercepted by *Triton*, escapes, 150
Wanklyn, Lt-Comdr M. D.: in *Upholder*, awarded V.C., 439; sinks two Italian liners, 526
War Cabinet: *see* Cabinet, British
War Office: defence of Home Fleet base, Scapa, 78; machine-gunners in merchant ships, 141; withdrawal of B.E.F., 212, 221*n*
War Plans, British: approved in January 1939, 17, 41
War Registry, Admiralty: work of, 24
Warburton-Lee, Captain B. A. W.: in Operation 'Wilfred', 157; ordered to Narvik by Admiralty, 173, 201; question of reinforcement for, 174; killed in action, awarded posthumous V.C., 175, 196
Warspite, H.M.S.: 48; disposition after attack on *Rawalpindi*, 85; joins Home Fleet, 88; covers first Canadian troop convoy, 89; escort of Halifax convoys, 114; leaves Clyde for Norway, 170; joins flag of C.-in-C., 172; in second Battle of Narvik, sinks U.64, 177; under Lord Cork in Narvik area, 180; leaves Narvik for Mediterranean, 188; flag of C.-in-C., Mediterranean, 295; in action off Calabria, 299; convoys for Piraeus and Malta, 'Excess', 421; Battle off Cape Matapan, 428-30; in Battle for Crete, 440; hit by bomb, seriously damaged, 442; repaired in America, 554
Wash, The: northern limit of possible German invasion, 249, 257
Waterhen, H.M.A.S.: sunk in carrying supplies to Tobruk, 519
Watussi, German s.s.: sunk by *Renown*, 117
Wavell, General Sir A.: success in Western Desert, 419

Wellington aircraft: raids on Kiel and Wilhelmshaven, 261; sent to Mediterranean, 524; 15 at Malta, August 1941, 527; sighting by leads to Italian cruiser loss, 534
Wells, Vice-Admiral L. V.: raider hunting, South Atlantic, 115; arrives Gibraltar in *Ark Royal*, 242
Weser, German supply ship: leaves Mexico for Pacific, 277; captured by *Prince Robert*, 607
Weser Estuary: aircraft minelaying in, 124; ice difficulties in, 153
Wessex, H.M.S.: ordered to Boulogne, 214; sunk off Calais, 215-6
West Africa: independent Air Command for, 460; sinkings off decline, 461; German U-boats stationed off, 462; strengthening of forces in, 463; sinkings off, 470
West Indies: plans for U-boat war in, 56; cover for tanker convoy, 76; patrol against French warships in, 245; armed merchant raider in, 277, 284; bases in leased to United States, 347-8
West Virginia, U.S. battleship: sunk at Pearl Harbour, 562
Western Approaches: defined, 91
Western Approaches Command: at Plymouth, responsibility of, 44; destroyer flotillas in, 47-8; cover for B.E.F. transport, 63; favours hunting groups for U-boats, 134-5; interception of enemy shipping from Vigo, 150; assistance to Nore Command, 207; evacuation from Biscay ports, 232-3; convoys escorted to 17° West, 250, 344, 451; weakened to provide anti-invasion force, 253; more escort vessels for, 351, 364; formation of escort groups in, 358; H.Q. moved to Liverpool, 360; Admiral Sir P. Noble appointed C.-in-C., 360; extension of convoy cover to 35° West, 451-2; escorts based at Greenock and Londonderry, 452; takes over convoy routes to Gibraltar and Sierra Leone, 453-4; responsible for whole Atlantic convoy system, 456-7; wireless messages from intercepted by Germans, 469; economy of force after Plan 4, 471; reinforcements for Gibraltar and Sierra Leone escorts, 471; escort forces in North Atlantic, 475
Western Isles, H.M.S.: anti-submarine training establishment, Tobermory, Vice-Admiral G. O. Stephenson to command, 359
Western Patrol: established, A.M.C.'s replaced by O.B.V.'s, 265
Westerwald, German supply ship: sails for Atlantic, 58, 607
Westminster, H.M.S.: damaged off Dutch coast, 210
Weston, H.M.S.: sinks U.13, 133
Weymouth: enemy mines off, 64; evacuation from Cherbourg and St Malo, 233
Whaling fleets, Allied: attacked by raider *Pinguin*, 367
'Whipcord', Operation (attack on Sicily), 521
Whippingham, s.s.: conveys 2,700 men in one passage from Dunkirk, 225
Whitley, H.M.S.: sunk off Belgian coast, 211

Whitley aircraft: raids on Kiel and Wilhelmshaven, 261

Whitshed, H.M.S.: escorts Guards Brigade to Boulogne, 213; evacuation of Boulogne, 213-4; in Dunkirk evacuation, 225, 227

Whitworth, Vice-Admiral W. J.: covers minelaying off Norway, 157-8; action with *Scharnhorst* and *Gneisenau*, 165-6; off Vestfiord, 167, 172; orders to, 173; decides against reinforcing 2nd Flotilla, Narvik, 174; protest at conflicting orders, 175; second Battle of Narvik, 177; decides against occupation of Narvik, 178

Widder, German raider: first cruise, conduct of captain, 279; sinkings by, 284-5; returns to Brest, 288, 368; Appendix M, 604

Wild Swan, H.M.S.: demolition party for Dunkirk, 212; evacuation of Boulogne, 213-4

'Wilfred', Operation (minelaying off Norway), 156-8, 164, 166, 282

Wilhelm Heidkamp, German destroyer: sunk at Narvik, 174

Wilhelmina, H.M. Queen: brought to Harwich in *Hereward*, 209

Wilhelmshaven: base of Naval Group Commander, West, 54; submarine patrols off, 64; *Emden* attacked off, 66; R.A.F. raids on, 1940, 261

Wilk, Polish submarine: escape to England, 69

Williamson, Lt-Cdr K.: attack on Italian Fleet, Taranto, 300

Winchelsea, H.M.S.: in Dunkirk evacuation, 225-6

Winchester, H.M.S.: damaged off Dutch coast, 209-10

Windsor, H.M.S.: evacuation of Dutch Government, 209; evacuation of Boulogne, 214; in Dunkirk evacuation, 225-6

Winnetou, German supply ship: leaves Las Palmas, 277, 607

Wireless Telegraphy: Admiralty control of stations, 24; raider reports by merchant ships, 114-5; Western Approaches messages intercepted by Germans, 469; silence of Admiral Phillips, 565

Wodehouse, Rear-Admiral N. A.: 48

Wolfgang Zenker, German destroyer: sunk at Narvik, 177n

Wolfhound, H.M.S.: ammunition for Calais, 215; in Dunkirk evacuation, 224

Wolfsburg, German s.s.: intercepted in Northern Patrol, 150

Wolsey, H.M.S.: wireless link in Dunkirk evacuation, 224

Wolverine, H.M.S.: evacuation from St Nazaire, 234; helps to sink U.47 and U.70, 364; with *Scarborough* sinks U.76, 463

Women's Royal Naval Service: revival of, and strength in 1944, 26

Woodhouse, Captain C. H. L.: in H.M.S. *Ajax*, 116

Woolwich, H.M.S.: 48

Worcester, H.M.S.: in Dunkirk evacuation, 221

'Workshop' (code name for Pantellaria), q.v.

Would Channel: closed Dec. 1939, reopened Sept. 1940, 327

Wright, Comdr J. P.: in first Battle of Narvik, 173

Wryneck, H.M.S.: rescues survivors from *Slamat*, 436

York, H.M.S.: 48; in raider hunting group, 114; intercepts German *Arucas*, 150; embarks troops for Plan 'R.4', 157; troops disembarked, 161; in Norway campaign, 172; conveys final reinforcement to Aandalsnes, 185; evacuation of Namsos, 189; lent to Nore Command, 208; torpedoed at Suda Bay, Crete, 424

Yugoslavia: German invasion of, 431

Zamzam, Egyptian s.s.: sunk by *Atlantis*, 382

Zara, Italian cruiser: sunk in Matapan battle, 429-30

Zeebrugge: plans for blocking of, 208, executed, 211; opposition to demolition, 211

Zenker, German Admiral: 51

Zulu, H.M.S.: in *Bismarck* operations, 414

S.O. Code No. 63-111-21-4*.